THE ENCYCLOPEDIA OF

20TH CENTURY
AIR WARFARE

THE ENCYCLOPEDIA OF
20TH CENTURY
AIR WARFARE

EDITED BY
CHRIS BISHOP

amber
BOOKS

Published in 2004 by Amber Books Ltd
Bradley's Close
74-77 White Lion Street
London N1 9PF
United Kingdom
www.amberbooks.co.uk

ISBN 1-904687-26-1

This material was previously published in 1997 in
The Aerospace Encyclopedia of Air Warfare Vols. I and II

Contributors: David K. Donald, Robert F. Dorr, John Heathcott,
                 Jon Lake, Daniel March and Soph Moeng

Illustrators: Chris Davey, Keith Fretwell, Mark Rolfe, John Weal,
                 Keith Woodcock and Iain Wyllie

The publishers would like to thank the following organizations for their
help in providing photographs for this volume:
Aerospace Collection, Aérospatiale, Associated Press, Bundesarchiv, Dassault Aviation, Robert F. Dorr,
Peter Foster, Gamma Liaison, Imperial War Museum, MacClancy Collection, Peter March,
Herman Potgeiter, Tim Ripley, Royal Air Force, Royal Air Force Museum, Royal Navy,
Frank Spooner Pictures, UK Ministry of Defence, US Air Force, US Customs Service,
US Department of Defense, US Navy, US Marine Corps.

Printed in Italy

CONTENTS

Section One: 1911–1945

Section Two: 1945 to the Gulf War

Introduction

The years that followed the Wright Brothers' historic flight in December 1903 saw amazing advances in the development of heavier-than-air flying machines, and also some significant steps forward in techniques that would play a major part in the development of air combat. It was the Italians who were the first to demonstrate the usefulness of the aircraft in their war with Turkey in 1911.

Warfare breeds new technology; and the single most important technological development in the air war of 1914–18 was the synchronized machine gun, enabling the weapon to fire forwards through the propeller disc. With this new-found ability to use the whole aircraft as an aiming platform came a scientific approach to aerial fighting; experienced pilots began to formulate tactics and combat manoeuvres that formed the sound base on which future air combat manuals would be built. By the early 1930s, air power was again proving its worth in localised conflicts around the world: particularly in China, the target of Imperial Japan's aggressively expansionist policies. Then came the Spanish Civil War, which saw the biggest use of air power in Europe since 1918.

BLITZKRIEG

Poland was quickly overwhelmed by the combined might of air power and fast-moving armour, and a new word – Blitzkrieg – entered the lexicon of warfare. The same tactics, employed in the early summer of 1940, brought about the rapid collapse of France and the Low Countries, leaving Britain to face the might of Nazi Germany alone. Now, for the first time in history, during that fierce summer of 1940, a nation tried to bring another to its knees by the use of air bombardment on an unprecedented scale, and failed in the attempt. The Battle of Britain was Germany's first defeat of World War II, and with it Hitler's interest in invading the British Isles evaporated.

For a time, the well-tested Blitzkrieg tactics worked well; but the vast distances, combined with dogged resistance and the fearsome extremes of the Russian winter, finally brought the German offensives to a halt. From then on, the

air campaign in Russia became the preserve of the ground-attack aircraft, and as the Russians began their relentless drive westward in the wake of the German defeat at Stalingrad they developed close support tactics that formed the basis of the Soviet Air Force's future offensive doctrine.

Meanwhile, in December 1941, Japanese naval aircraft crippled the US Pacific Fleet at Pearl Harbor and opened a new theatre of war. One after the other, the Allied bastions in the Pacific and South-East Asia crumbled and fell. Here was air power exercised to its fullest and most effective potential, with the destruction of the enemy's main offensive assets followed by the rapid establishment of local air superiority throughout the operational area. The wholesale loss of land bases in the Pacific and Indian Ocean left the Allies with the aircraft carrier as the only means at their disposal for striking back at the Japanese empire, at least for the time being. The result was that the major naval engagements of the Pacific war were fought by carrier aircraft, acting in the role of long-range artillery, without the vessels that launched them ever sighting one another.

The decision by the Allies to deal with Germany first, then

Japan, led to the rapid establishment of a USAAF heavy bomber force in England. After preliminary attacks on targets in German-occupied Europe, this force – the Eighth Army Air Force – began daylight attacks on targets in Germany, beginning with the northern ports, in January 1943. In the months to come the Americans would learn a bitter lesson, which was that unescorted bombers could not penetrate into a hostile fighter environment in daylight, without suffering unacceptable losses. RAF Bomber Command had learned that lesson very early in the war, and as a consequence had switched to night operations, with all their attendant problems of navigation and target identification. The quest for a solution to these problems accelerated the development of sophisticated electronic aids to navigation and bombing, which in turn precipitated a drive to develop countermeasures against them. The electronic war that unfolded in the night sky over Germany formed the pattern for what is today a vital aspect of air warfare.

Meanwhile, in the Atlantic, the application of naval air power proved critical in the defeat of the German U-boats. The mere presence of an aircraft escorting an

Rocket projectile Typhoon aircraft, which destroyed German radio locations prior to D-Day.

Allied convoy was enough to force a U-boat to dive, and thus lose its ability to keep pace with its target. Gradually, as the so-called 'Mid-Atlantic gap' was closed by VLR (Very Long Range) aircraft such as the Sunderlands, Catalinas and Liberators, U-boat successes had dwindled by mid-1943, and the vital Allied convoys got through with their supplies for the Allied war effort in Europe.

TOWARDS VICTORY

The weeks that followed the Allied landings in Normandy in June 1944 witnessed the application of tactical air power on an unprecedented scale, as the weight of the tactical air forces was turned towards the goal of isolating the battlefield and proceeding with the systematic destruction of all enemy forces in the combat zone. It was during this phase of the war in northwest Europe that jet aircraft appeared in combat for the first time, the operational debut of the German Arado Ar 234 bomber/reconnaissance aircraft being followed by that of the Messerschmitt Me 262 fighter and Britain's Gloster Meteor, which saw limited action against the German V-1 flying bomb – the world's first cruise missile. For a time, the Me 262 presented a serious threat to Allied air superiority, but attacks on its air bases, coupled with a shortage of fuel created by strategic air attack, meant that it was never available in sufficient numbers to have the desired impact. Even more revolutionary was the Messerschmitt Me 163 rocket fighter, which registered a few successes against the American daylight bombers.

As the war in Europe drew to a close, a new phase of the war in the Pacific began with the capture of island bases which brought the Japanese home islands within striking distance of a new American strategic bomber, the Boeing B-29. One after another, Japan's cities were razed by incendiary attack, as what remained of her offensive air and naval capability was destroyed by roving carrier aircraft or by long-range Mustang fighters. Japan's final weapon was suicide attack, which was used to maximum effect in the battle for Okinawa; but even that could not prevent her ultimate defeat, her industries shattered by the American strategic bombing offensive. Japan was finished long before the most awesome weapon of all, the atomic bomb, fell on Hiroshima and Nagasaki.

The war that erupted in Korea in June 1950 required the use of tactical air power on a scale not seen since the Battle of Normandy, for it was the United Nations' only means of blunting the North Korean offensive during the crucial early weeks of the conflict. The brunt of the ground attack work, initially, was borne by piston-engined types that had excelled themselves in World War II, the Mustang and Corsair, but the real workhorse of the campaign was the Lockheed F-80 Shooting Star, America'a first operational jet fighter-bomber. More than adequate for ground attack, the F-80 was however no match in air combat for the swept-wing MiG-15, which appeared in Korean skies in November 1950. It was countered by the North American F-86 Sabre, the two types battling for supremacy over northwest Korea in history's first jet-versus-jet battles. For the most part, the MiGs were flown by Russians, whole fighter divisions and regiments being assigned to bases in Manchuria for combat duty.

LESSONS FROM KOREA
The Korean War had a dramatic effect on the organisation and equipment of both the USAF and the Soviet Air Force. Strategic Air Command, which had already begun re-equipping some of its B-29 medium bomber wings with the improved B-50 when hostilities broke out, now quickly phased out the rest of its B-29 bombers, converting some to the flight refuelling tanker role, and by the end of 1954 they had been entirely replaced by the Boeing B-47 Stratojet. In 1955 the heavy bomber wings, then equipped with the huge Convair B-36, began to re-equip with the Boeing B-52 Stratofortress. To facilitate

The F-117A Stealth Attack Aircraft, which proved its worth in Operation 'Desert Storm', in the Gulf War of 1991.

rapid deployment, and to extend the range of the SAC bomber force, the SAC tanker fleet was also greatly expanded, with orders placed for KC-135 jet tankers to replace the Command's existing KB-50s and KC-97s, both of which had superseded the KB-29s. The Russians, meanwhile, had viewed the losses sustained by the USAF's B-29s over Korea with concern; their sole strategic bomber, the Tupolev Tu-4 Bull, had been copied from B-29s that had come down on Soviet territory after raids on Japan in World War II. Late in 1952 the Tupolev design bureau began work on a strategic jet bomber that was to emerge as the Tu-16 Badger, which was roughly the equivalent of the B-47, and during the next two years two strategic heavy bombers, the Myasischchev Mya-4 Bison and the Tupolev Tu-95 Bear, also made their appearance.

Great changes also swept through the USAF Tactical Air Command as a result of the Korean War. Before the end of 1953 TAC's remaining F-51 and F-80 units had equipped with F-86F fighterbombers, followed by the nuclear-capable F-86H. By the middle of 1954 TAC's light bomber units had begun to receive the Martin B-57 Canberra, which in turn gave way to the F-100 Super Sabre from 1957. Also in 1954, TAC began to receive swept-wing F-84F Thunderstreaks to replace its Thunderjets, many of which were assigned to European NATO air forces. Later, from the same Republic Aviation stable, came the F-105 Thunderchief, TAC's first true weapons system.

The Russians, always tactically-minded, fielded the Sukhoi Su7 Fitter, which replaced ground-attack versions of the MiG-15 and MiG-17 — neither of which was suited to the role — from 1956. The Fitter, which was also widely exported, became the standard Soviet tactical support fighter-bomber, and remained so for two decades in a number of developed versions. On both sides of the Iron Curtain, three years of jet combat experience over the Yalu was woven into the designs of new air interceptors. In the United States, the agile brain of Lockheed's Clarence Johnson and his design team gave birth to the revolutionary F-104 Starfighter, while Russia's answer was the MiG-21.

All-weather fighters, too, assumed high priority; in 1955 the USAF received the first examples of the Convair F-102 Delta Dagger, the outcome of a USAF requirement dating back to 1950, and in the following year Soviet air defence squadrons received the Yakovlev Yak-25 Flashlight. The lessons of Korea were also absorbed by the British, who accelerated deployment of their nuclear deterrent force (the V-force) and ordered fighter types like the Hawker Hunter and Gloster Javelin into 'super-priority' production. Both, eventually, would be replaced by the Mach 2 English Electric Lightning interceptor. The French, too, continued the development of their Dassault Mirage family of advanced combat aircraft.

Korea had shown the need for a transport aircraft with a large load-carrying capacity that could

operate from rough airstrips, and again it was Lockheed that came up with the answer in the C-130 Hercules, the most versatile transport aircraft ever designed. The second involved the multi-role combat aircraft, and here it was the US Navy that provided the lead. The Korean War had proved beyond all doubt that the fast attack carrier was still the most vital unit in modern naval warfare; at the same time, the deficiencies of the Navy's standard jet types — the F9F Panther and the F2H Banshee — over Korea had aroused serious misgivings, and propeller-driven attack types could no longer hope to survive in a hostile fighter environment. These shortcomings lead to the development of the Douglas A-4 Skyhawk, which was rolled out of Douglas's El Segundo factory only 19 months after its inception and which flew for the first time in June 1954. At the same time, work went ahead on what was to become the world's first multi-role supersonic combat aircraft — the McDonnell F-4 Phantom. Both types were to play a dominant part in Vietnam over a decade later.

MODERN REQUIREMENTS
The air war over Vietnam, in its turn produced two requirements, one for a close support aircraft that could operate from primitive sites close to the front line, and the other for an agile combat aircraft. The first was met by the British Harrier V/STOL aircraft, while the second produced the USAF's McDonnell Douglas F-15 and the Navy's Grumman F-14 Tomcat. In 1991, the F-15 proved its value as an air superiority fighter over Iraq, where its principal adversary was its Russian-built equivalent, the MiG-29.

The principal object of air warfare — to establish air superiority in support of ground operations — has not changed since World War I. Today, elements of the air forces of one or other of the former major power blocs may be called upon to operate anywhere in the world. Aircrews may find themselves locked in combat with aircraft and weapon systems built in their own countries and sold to Third World powers, flown by opponents trained by the same system as themselves.

Section One:
1911–1945

WORLD WAR I AND THE INTERWAR YEARS

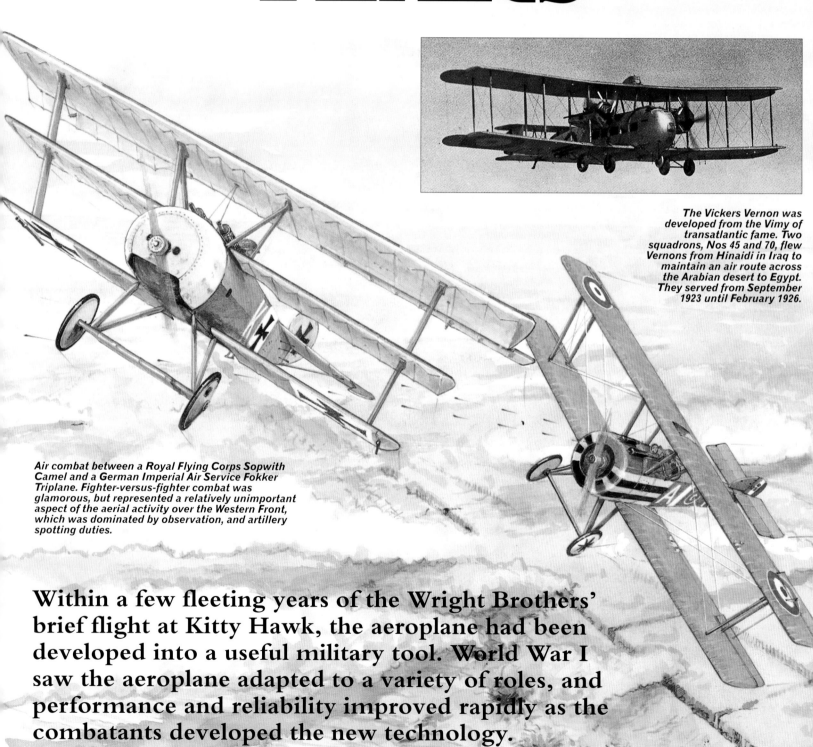

The Vickers Vernon was developed from the Vimy of transatlantic fame. Two squadrons, Nos 45 and 70, flew Vernons from Hinaidi in Iraq to maintain an air route across the Arabian desert to Egypt. They served from September 1923 until February 1926.

Air combat between a Royal Flying Corps Sopwith Camel and a German Imperial Air Service Fokker Triplane. Fighter-versus-fighter combat was glamorous, but represented a relatively unimportant aspect of the aerial activity over the Western Front, which was dominated by observation, and artillery spotting duties.

Within a few fleeting years of the Wright Brothers' brief flight at Kitty Hawk, the aeroplane had been developed into a useful military tool. World War I saw the aeroplane adapted to a variety of roles, and performance and reliability improved rapidly as the combatants developed the new technology.

The Italo - Turkish War

SEPTEMBER 1911 - SEPTEMBER 1912

Long before World War I the aeroplane was being considered as potential military equipment, the US Army calling for demonstration by Orville Wright of his aircraft as far back as 1908. It was during such a flight at Fort Myer that he crashed on 17 September that year, killing Lieutenant Thomas E. Selfridge, US Signal Corps, and injuring himself. Thus died the first military man in an aeroplane.

It was just three years later, on 25 September 1911, that Italy mobilised a special expeditionary Army Corps with an Air Flotilla for despatch to Libya to counter Arab-Turkish occupation of the town of Tripoli. Under the command of Captain Carlos Piazza, the Air Flotilla comprised five operational pilots, six reserve pilots and 30 ground crew; their aircraft were three Nieuports, two Blériots, two Farmans and two Etrich Taubes.

AIR RECCE

Tripoli was stormed on 5 October, and 10 days later work started to unload the crated aircraft from ships anchored offshore, the first being air tested a week later. In the meantime, the Turks had counterattacked and the Italian beachhead was becoming precarious. On 23 October, Piazza took off on a dawn flight in his Blériot with orders to discover the exact whereabouts of the enemy's main forces, a mission successfully accomplished when he discovered a number of Turkish encampments and reported his findings on landing after a 59-minute flight. Six reconnaissance flights were carried out during 23-25 October, a flight by Captain Ricardo Moizo in a Nieuport on the third day being met by rifle fire, three shots passing through his wings. The location of some 8,000 enemy troops opposing the Italian forces was vital in re-arranging the Italian line. Before the end of the month Lieutenant Guilio Gavotti and naval Lieutenant Ugo de Rossi had also

made ready their aircraft.

The next role undertaken by the Air Flotilla was artillery observation when Piazza and Moizo performed spotting duties for the Italian warship *Sardegna* bombarding the Zanzur Oasis, but this was handicapped by the pilots' inability to signal the effects of the gunnery until Piazza hit on the idea of dropping small tins containing messages to the gunnery officer. By the end of November successful artillery spotting was being carried out as a matter of routine.

On 1 November the first bombs ever dropped by an aeroplane on operations were released by Lieutenant Gavotti in his Etrich Taube. On that occasion he dropped three 4.4-lb (2-kg) Cipelli grenades over the Taguira Oasis and another at Ain Zara. Refinements in weapons followed when an engineer, Lieutenant Bontempelli, produced a cylindrical bomb containing explosive and shrapnel, of which 10 could be carried aloft in a box container which, after operation of a lever in the cockpit, would drop them singly or in a 'stick'.

Atrocious weather at the turn of the year did not prevent the Italian pilots from supporting the Italian advance towards Ain Zara, working out a system of flying manoeuvres to indicate the presence of threatening enemy forces. Occasional instances in which the ground forces would not believe the pilots' reports prompted Piazza to have a camera fitted to his Bleriot, the only

difficulty being that the aircraft had to land after taking each photograph as it was impossible to change plates in the air. The Italian aircraft were also used to drop propaganda leaflets among tribal groups in successful efforts to win their support for the Italian cause.

During the winter two replacement Farmans were received at Tripoli to allow maintenance on other aircraft which were beginning to show signs of considerable wear and tear. With them came Lieutenant Oreste Salomone, newly trained in Italy, who was to gain fame in World War I with the award of Italy's highest gallantry decoration, the Gold Medal for Valour.

At the end of 1911, as the campaign moved east and north into Cyrenaica, a new flotilla came into being at Homs, near Benghazi under the command of Captain Montu. It was in this theatre that the Turks began using anti-aircraft artillery, and it was in one of the

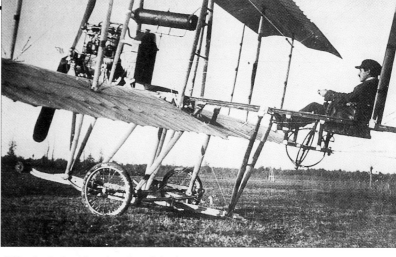

Gianni Caproni with his Ca-5 biplane at Malpensa, Italy in 1911. Several widely differing types of biplanes had been evolved during 1910 and 1911. The last, with variable tail-incidence and cambered wings, was not an effective machine.

first Bristol two-seaters to reach Africa that naval Lieutenant Roberti was flying a reconnaissance sortie when his aircraft was hit and his propeller struck by shrapnel; in a congratulatory gesture typical of the time, Roberti dived low over the enemy battery scattering his personal visiting cards (some of which he found on display in a Turkish museum 14 years later).

The first operational night flights were made by the Cyrenaica Flotilla, Captain Marengo making five night reconnaissance sorties between May and July 1912, and on 11 June he dropped several bombs on a Turkish camp in moonlight shortly before dawn, the first night bombing attack in history. Tragedy struck on 12 August, when the first Italian pilot was killed during an operational flight, although the accident was caused by loss of control (probably due to a severe thermal near the ground).

ITALIAN LEAD

As the Libyan campaign drew to an end the achievements of the Italian air flotillas were hailed by the international press as a new chapter in warfare, and certainly gained military attention throughout Europe. Though no evidence can be found to confirm the presence of any British observer with the Italians, one cannot be blind to the coincidence that it was in April 1912 that the formation of the Royal Flying Corps was announced, followed almost immediately by the opening of the Central Flying School; at this, reconnaissance, artillery spotting and night flying were the main constituents of the military flying training course, all of which were being practically demonstrated by the Italians in Libya with their tiny air flotillas.

Above: When flying first became a recognised military sideline, the heavier-than-air 'specialists' grew into the Aviation Battalion during the Tripoli campaign with some Bleriot XIs in 1912, the floatplane being called 'Hydro-avion'. The lettering on the tail stands for 'Società Italiana Transaerea'.

Left: An Italian Caproni biplane of 1910 powered by an 18.63-kW (25-hp) Millen engine driving a pusher propeller. Aerodynamic experiments of all kinds were tried, including the effects of flexible surfaces.

The Opening Rounds

APRIL 1914 – APRIL 1915

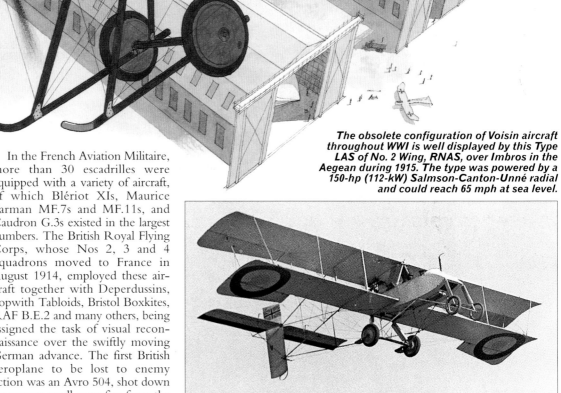

The first successful strategic air raid on Germany, on 8 October 1914, resulted in the destruction of the new German Army Zeppelin LZ25, which had been fully inflated inside its shed. Flt Lt 'Reggie' Manx, flying a Sopwith Tabloid, surveys the damage caused by his bombs.

The obsolete configuration of Voisin aircraft throughout WWI is well displayed by this Type LAS of No. 2 Wing, RNAS, over Imbros in the Aegean during 1915. The type was powered by a 150-hp (112-kW) Salmson-Canton-Unné radial and could reach 65 mph at sea level.

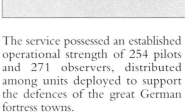

T o many of the pioneer air enthusiasts, the very concept of using aeroplanes as weapons of war was not only distasteful but a prostitution of a sporting machine. Such a perception ignored the fact that the Italo-Turkish War had ever been fought, and that soldiers and sailors of a score of nations had already become proficient in the skills of flying. In America five Curtiss A-1s had been employed for reconnaissance during the Vera Cruz incident in April 1914, and the French had employed aeroplanes during a colonial campaign in Morocco early that year.

In Europe alone, France, Germany, Russia, the UK, Turkey, Belgium, Italy and Bavaria already had military air arms, the purpose of which was almost exclusively reconnaissance, the two first-named nations being measurably the most advanced both in equipment and tactical concept. Even so, no aeroplane at the outbreak of war was equipped with a gun of any sort, it being generally thought unlikely that a rifle or pistol shot from one moving aircraft would prove fatal against another.

In the French Aviation Militaire, more than 30 escadrilles were equipped with a variety of aircraft, of which Blériot XIs, Maurice Farman MF.7s and MF.11s, and Caudron G.3s existed in the largest numbers. The British Royal Flying Corps, whose Nos 2, 3 and 4 Squadrons moved to France in August 1914, employed these aircraft together with Deperdussins, Sopwith Tabloids, Bristol Boxkites, RAF B.E.2 and many others, being assigned the task of visual reconnaissance over the swiftly moving German advance. The first British aeroplane to be lost to enemy action was an Avro 504, shot down by enemy small arms fire from the ground on 19 August.

FIRST BOMBS

The Germans, whose Military Aviation Service had formally existed since October 1912, went to war with 246 first-line aeroplanes of numerous types, of which the Taube monoplane, and Albatros and Aviatik biplanes predominated.

The service possessed an established operational strength of 254 pilots and 271 observers, distributed among units deployed to support the defences of the great German fortress towns.

There was no specific organisation or plan in being to commit any of these air services to armed combat duties, so ,no attempt was made by either side in the early weeks of

The Blériot XI was one of history's significant aircraft. Before the beginning of WWI, the RFC and RNAS had taken delivery of a number of Blériots. At the outbreak of hostilities, five squadrons were equipped with the type.

the war to interfere with the enemy's use of the skies over the Western Front, other than the instinctive use of the infantryman's rifle. The employment of the aeroplane as a bomber had not been overlooked, however, and it was not long before individual pilots started out on what can only be regarded as courageous, if foolhardy ecapades: one Leutnant Franz von Hiddeson dropped (by hand) two light bombs from his Taube over Paris on 13 August. The first bomb to fall from an aeroplane on English soil was another such light bomb which dropped into a Dover garden on Christmas Eve, 1914. By

Modelled closely on the Aviatik B.I of 1914, the more efficient Aviatik B.II appeared in 1915. It had a lightened but stronger structure and a more powerful engine, though still no provision for the fitting of any armament.

then a number of planned bombing attacks had been executed, notably the attack on 8 October by two pilots of the British RNAS based at Antwerp who, in Sopwith Tabloids, bombed Cologne railway station and the airship shed at Dusseldorf; in the latter attack Flight Lieutenant R.L.G. Marix destroyed the brand-new German airship Z IX.

Inevitably, airmen of the opposing air services encountered each other in the air, and it soon became customary for the observers, if not the pilots themselves, to carry rifles and pistols with which to persuade their opponents to vacate that particular part of the sky. The first aeroplane to be shot down (as distinct from being forced down by 'aggressive manoeuvres') was a German Aviatik, shot down by the French pilot Sergeant Joseph Franz in a Voisin over Reims using a free-mounted Hotchkiss gun on 5 October. (A British pilot, Lieutenant L.A. Strange, had fitted his Farman biplane with a Lewis gun in the very first days of the war, but had been ordered to remove it as it severely restricted the aircraft's performance.)

AIR COMBAT

Elsewhere, drastic means were being adopted to destroy enemy aircraft. Staff Captain Nesterov of the Imperial Russian Air Service, flying an unarmed Morane-Saulnier, rammed an Austrian two-seater over Galicia flown by Leutnant Baron von Rosenthal; both pilots were killed. An even more unorthodox method was employed by another Russian, Staff Captain Kazakov, who trailed a grapnel below his Morane-Saulnier MS 5; with this he engaged the wing of an Albatross two-seater near Gusov and then struck the enemy aircraft with his landing gear.

Notwithstanding these primitive forms of combat, efforts were being made to fit guns in aeroplanes early in the war, rifles and machine-guns at first being mounted on makeshift pylons for use by the observer. In France, Roland Garros became the world's first pilot to destroy an opponent using a fixed, forward-firing machine-gun in his Morane Type L parasol monoplane. With steel deflector wedges bolted to the propeller blades to deflect bullets that would otherwise damage them, Garros shot down an Aviatik over the Western Front on 1 April 1915. The era of true air combat had opened.

The Bristol Boxkite was a refined copy of the Henri Farman biplane, with a 50-hp (37-kW) Gnôme rotary piston engine. Here Lt Eric Harrison receives congratulations from an Army official after a flight in a Boxkite on 1 March 1914.

Early warplanes

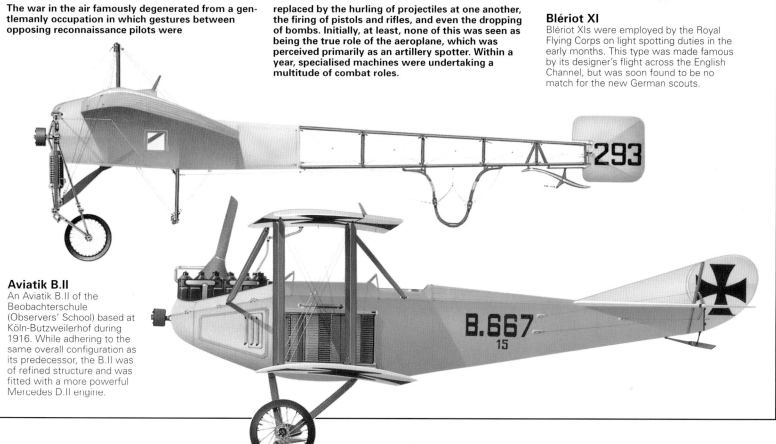

The war in the air famously degenerated from a gentlemanly occupation in which gestures between opposing reconnaissance pilots were replaced by the hurling of projectiles at one another, the firing of pistols and rifles, and even the dropping of bombs. Initially, at least, none of this was seen as being the true role of the aeroplane, which was perceived primarily as an artillery spotter. Within a year, specialised machines were undertaking a multitude of combat roles.

Blériot XI
Blériot XIs were employed by the Royal Flying Corps on light spotting duties in the early months. This type was made famous by its designer's flight across the English Channel, but was soon found to be no match for the new German scouts.

Aviatik B.II
An Aviatik B.II of the Beobachterschule (Observers' School) based at Köln-Butzweilerhof during 1916. While adhering to the same overall configuration as its predecessor, the B.II was of refined structure and was fitted with a more powerful Mercedes D.II engine.

Battle of the Front Gun

APRIL 1915 - APRIL 1916

Left: The RFC's first dedicated fighting scout was the Airco D.H.2, this example being one of the first to be delivered to No. 24 Squadron at Hounslow, commanded by Major Lanoe Hawker VC, late in 1915.

Above: The Fokker E III monoplane was a compact and agile fighting machine. With a single synchronised machine-gun, it dominated the Western Front during the latter half of 1915, despite lack of numbers.

Although the idea of mounting a machine-gun in the nose of an aeroplane to fire forward through the propeller had been conceived before World War I, only the French had ordered such an aircraft (the Morane Type I) for service. This had proved unreliable and it was not until the Frenchman Roland Garros, flying a Morane Type L with Escadrille MS 23, shot down three German aircraft in April 1915, that the era of dedicated air combat opened. His aircraft was equipped with a machine-gun on the nose and steel deflector plates on the propeller blades to prevent the bullets shooting off the blades,

a device evolved by Saulnier. Garros was forced down behind the German lines on 19 April and taken prisoner, his Morane being closely examined by the enemy.

In the meantime, the German engineer Schneider had already developed an interrupter gear which mechanically prevented the gun from firing at the instant a propeller blade passed the gun muzzle, and this was being incorporated in a small monoplane fighting scout

Below: A B.E.2c on the Western Front. These aircraft gave good service in the reconnaissance role during early 1915, but they were extremely vulnerable in any form of air combat.

then being produced by Anthony Fokker for the Germans.

ALLIED LOSSES

When originally conceived, the Fokker E-type monoplane was not intended for offensive air combat but simply as an escort for reconnaissance aircraft which were becoming ever more widely used over the Western Front, and was initially issued in small numbers to the Fliegerabteilungen. It was when such men as Boelcke, Immelmann and Kastner came to fly the new scout that they appreciated the supreme advantage of the synchronised gun as an offensive weapon and quickly mastered the basic skills necessary to stalk and shoot down unsuspecting enemy pilots.

As more German pilots learned

Above: The Germans recognised the need to fire a gun directly forward along the aircraft's axis, through the propeller. Fokker produced his E-type monoplanes with suitable interruptor gear.

these rudimentary tactics with the Fokker E I, losses among British and French observation aircraft increased rapidly, with little in the way of immediate remedy in sight. The first French aircraft fell to the new German 'fighting scout' in June, and the following month two British B.E.2c aircraft were forced down. By November the depredations of the Fokker monoplanes had given rise to the 'Fokker Scourge', though in fact at that time there were probably fewer than 80 Fokkers in service over both Eastern and Western Fronts. Already the first Allied pilots were becoming known to the public for their prowess in air combat, the legendary Georges Guynemer having shot down his first victim while flying a Morane-Saulnier Type N on 19 July. He had survived being shot down once and, on his l9th birthday on Christmas Eve 1915, he was awarded the Cross of the Legion d'Honeur for having destroyed two enemy aircraft. During the next three months he shot down six more.

None of the Allied pilots attracted the adulation commanded by the German Max Immelmann, dubbed by his colleagues 'the Eagle of Lille'. Taught to fly the Fokker monoplane by Oswalde Boelcke, Immelmann was regarded with almost spectral awe by his enemies, and shot down 15 Allied aircraft before finally being killed near Lens on 18 June 1916. His mentor, Boelcke, was, however, the true originator of air combat tactics and, with his extraordinary gifts of patience and meticulous instruction, brought a new level of flying discipline to the pilots whom he personally coached. He, like

Unequal opponents

The Fokker E series monoplanes were introduced to counter Allied observation aircraft, which proved extremely vulnerable to the German scouts, with their forward-firing armament. The

Fokker's dominance was short-lived, however, with the introduction of British pusher scouts which had forward-firing guns manned by a dedicated gunner.

Fokker E III
Though reminiscent of the pre-war Blériot Type XI, the Fokker monoplane (an E III shown here) was a compact and highly manoeuvrable aircraft. The final 'Eindecker' variant was the E IV, which featured a more powerful engine.

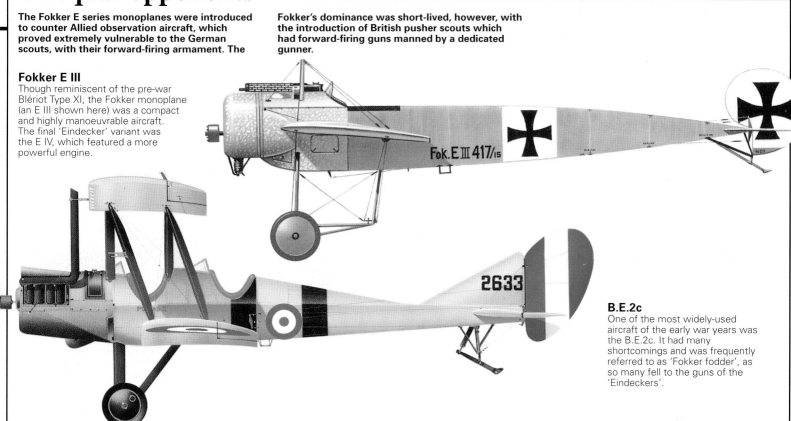

B.E.2c
One of the most widely-used aircraft of the early war years was the B.E.2c. It had many shortcomings and was frequently referred to as 'Fokker fodder', as so many fell to the guns of the 'Eindeckers'.

Although initially delivered in 1915 to reconnaissance units, it was soon realised that the Fokker E-types possessed real combat potential. Thus began the 'Fokker Scourge' phase of the war in the air.

Immelmann, was awarded the coveted Pour le Merite, before he met his death on 28 October 1916 with a score of no fewer than 40 victories. He has remained the father figure of German fighter aviation.

The British were slow to introduce the sychronised front gun and, unlike the French and Germans, cointinued to produce biplane designs. The merits of the biplane (maximising lifting area while retaining excellent agility, and structural integrity) should not be overlooked. The pusher layout was adopted so that a front gun could be mounted without the need for any interrupter gear. Thus it was that the Airco D.H.2 pusher biplane

The Morane-Saulnier Type N had a fixed 0.315-in (8-mm) Hotchkiss or 0.303-in (7.7-mm) Vickers or Lewis machine-gun. The RFC received 24 of the type, the principal operator being No. 6 Squadron.

equipped the Royal Flying Corps' first true fighter squadron, No. 24, commanded by Major Lanoe G. Hawker VC; it did not reach the Western Front from England until February 1916. The F.B.5 and F.E.2 pusher biplanes predated the D.H.2, but neither was as successul as a fighter.

Losses among B.E.2c aircraft of the RFC over the Western Front had reached alarming proportions during the latter half of 1915, for this type of aircraft (a veritable forest of struts and wires) retained no more than a modest performance provided it was not encumbered by a defensive gun; when such a gun was fitted, perforce unable to fire through the propeller, the aircraft was so slow and cumbersome as to invite swift destruction should a German scout appear. Both this and the F.E.2b were in truth two years out of date when they reached the front, and it speaks volumes that Lanoe Hawker's pilots in their ungainly D.H.2s were able partly to redress the balance of superiority, first during the early stages of the

Battle of Verdun and, more important, during the great Battle of the Somme in 1916.

PUP APPEARS

In the fact that such aircraft as the B.E.2c and F.E.2b had taken so long to appear lay the reasons for the prolonged success of the Fokker E-types. Petty squabbling was rife in the British aircraft industry, and where the Royal Aircraft Factory at Farnborough should have provided guidance and leadership there was little but acrimony and jealousy, compounded by inter-service rivalry for aircraft contracts. It fell to the commercial firm of Sopwith Aviation to provide a remedy, but it was not until February 1916 that the first Pup appeared with its single front gun and Sopwith-Kauper interrupter gear, and even this had been ordered by the Admiralty. Moreover, not until September of that year did the Pups of RNAS squadrons finally put paid to the Fokkers' superiority.

The Year Of The Somme

FEBRUARY 1916 - OCTOBER 1916

The first true British fighter Squadron was No. 24. Its commanding officer, Major Lanoe Hawker, had won the Victoria Cross on 25 July 1915 when, flying a Bristol Scout armed with a single-shot cavalry carbine, he forced down three machine gun-armed enemy two-seaters. The Bristol Scout was not a fighter in the true sense but had been supplied in small numbers for the protection of observation aircraft. In February 1916 Hawker took No. 24 Squadron to France equipped with the D.H.2, a single-seat pusher biplane armed with a free-firing front gun. The aircraft was manoeuvrable and sensitive on the controls. Although fitted with a movable gun in the nose, its pilots soon adopted the practice of fixing the gun to fire along the line of flight and aiming the aircraft directly at the target. Lieutenant Tidmarsh was the first to open the squadron's score with a victory near Bapaume on 2 April.

German ace Günther stands in front of his Albatross C I. The type was in service on the Western Front by the late summer of 1915, and was well liked by its crews as a reliable aircraft.

Above: There was little to distinguish the Fokker D IV from the D I, apart from slightly larger dimensions, a twin-gun armament and a 160-hp (119-kW) Mercedes D.III engine. Its performance was inadequate.

Thereafter No. 24 achieved a fast-growing reputation for determination and skill in countering the 'Fokker Scourge', being joined shortly after by two more D.H.2 squadrons, Nos 29 and 32.

FIGHTER REAPPRAISAL

The Germans, meanwhile, recognising that the superiority of the Fokker E-type monoplanes must soon be disputed by the Allies, were already early in 1916 introducing the Fokker D I and Halberstadt D II biplanes with single synchronised 'Spandau' (LMG 08/15) machine-guns. These were aircraft of neat but conventional appearance, and with better handling characteristics than the monoplanes. The whole concept of air fighting was undergoing reappraisal in the German air force, largely as a result of representations by Oswald Boelcke. He had demonstrated (with Immelmann) the superiority of the E-types in 1915, on return from a tour of the front early in 1916 was given command of a new fighting unit, Jasta 2 equipped with Fokker D Is and D IVs. This represented the beginning of the creation of a large number of dedicated air combat units (after the formation of the first RFC fighter squadrons, it should be noted). Notwithstanding the success of the relatively small number of D.H.2s, the French were the first among the Allies to introduce a truly successful fighting scout, the Nieuport 17, which arrived at the front late in March. It was faster by 10 mph (16 km/h) than any British aircraft and was

armed with a single synchronised front gun. It also served in large numbers with the RFC, and among the British pilots who gained their first victories in this excellent little aeroplane was Captain Albert Ball (later VC, DSO and MC), who destroyed an Albatros D I in May and a Roland C II on 2 July.

The prolonged Battle of Verdun had started late in February 1916, and was to drag on for many months. Inevitably, the increasing dependence on aircraft for artillery observation by both sides led to frequent air combats between opposing Fokkers, Halberstadts, Nieuports and D.H.2s, not to mention the widespread destruction of poorly-armed reconnaissance aircraft. By the start of the bloody Battle of the Somme in July there were dozens of dedicated fighter squadrons in action over the Western Front.

BEWARE THE STALKER

Operations by both sides took much the same form, with single observation aircraft sent to cover closely defined sections of the front line, their pilots seldom being instructed to penetrate more than a mile or so into enemy airspace. They would occasionally be escorted by a flight of fighting scouts, but more often a flight or even a squadron would patrol within sight of the reconnaissance aircraft, the pilots keeping watch for enemy

The Nieuport enjoyed high speed and superb manoeuvrability, making it an excellent biplane de chasse or 'destroyer'. These are French Nieuport 17s. Note the gun housing above the upper wing.

scouts. Some use was made of decoy aircraft, which it was hoped would lure the defending scouts away from their charges, after which the lumbering B.E., F.E., Voisin or Aviatik would be easy prey for prowling scouts.

This was the era of the lone 'stalker', of whom Ball in his Nieuport was one of the most deadly, while McCudden of No. 29 Squadron in a D.H.2 scored the first of his 57 victories on 6 September. The Frenchman Charles Nungesser had been flying Nieuports of various types since late 1915, and by the end of 1916 had destroyed 20 enemy aircraft, despite constant pain from unhealed wounds. In the German air service, Immelmann had been killed on 18 June, followed by Boelcke on 28 October, but a new star was in the ascendant. Rittmeister Manfred Freiherr von Richthofen, the greatest German flying name to emerge from the War, had joined Jasta 2 under Boelcke in September, and scored the first of 80 air victories on 17 September while flying an Albatros D II. It has been estimated that by the end of that year more than a dozen German scout pilots had gained at least a dozen victories.

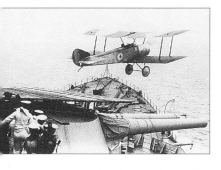

Left: The Sopwith Pup entered service with both the RFC and RNAS in 1916. Here a Pup takes off from an improvised platform over the guns of a British warship off the Belgian coast.

Right: The American-manned Lafayette Escadrille received some examples of the Nieuport 21, powered by an 80-hp (60-kW) Le Rhône engine. This example is seen at Cachy on the Somme in 1916.

It was in September that German air superiority over the Western Front was first challenged, with the arrival in France of such excellent Allied fighting scouts as the Sopwith Pup which, though in no way radical, proved such a delightfully manoeuvrable aircraft that in even only moderately skilled pilots' hands it could outfly and outfight almost any German aircraft extant. Pups of the RNAS were in action over the Belgian and French coast in September, and the following month No. 8 (Naval) Squadron was formed in the Somme area; within 50 days 'Naval Eight' had destroyed 20 German aircraft.

Right: A Halberstadt D II of Kampfeinsitzer Staffel II, the type which began to replace the Fokker Eindecker in 1916. It was robust and popular but never achieved the success or status of the Albatros.

Fighters of 1916

1916 was a year of great change for Britain's Royal Flying Corps. Following his appointment as RFC commander in France, Trenchard reduced the reliance on inefficient Royal Aircraft Factory products by purchasing D.H.2s and Nieuport scouts, and introduced separate, specialised scout, reconnaissance and bombing squadrons. He also decentralised his force, assigning individual wings (one observation and reconnaissance, one fighting) to different armies on the ground. The resulting British air superiority over the Somme was briefly challenged by Germany's new fighter circuses.

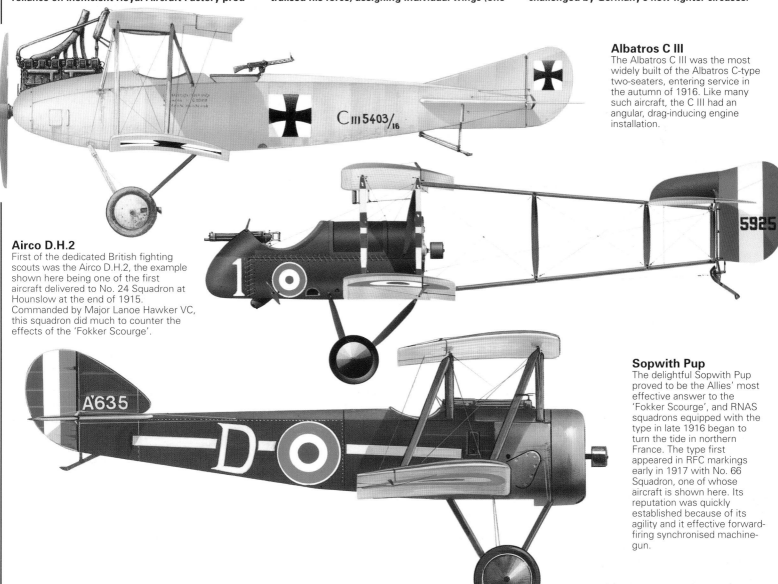

Albatros C III
The Albatros C III was the most widely built of the Albatros C-type two-seaters, entering service in the autumn of 1916. Like many such aircraft, the C III had an angular, drag-inducing engine installation.

Airco D.H.2
First of the dedicated British fighting scouts was the Airco D.H.2, the example shown here being one of the first aircraft delivered to No. 24 Squadron at Hounslow at the end of 1915. Commanded by Major Lanoe Hawker VC, this squadron did much to counter the effects of the 'Fokker Scourge'.

Sopwith Pup
The delightful Sopwith Pup proved to be the Allies' most effective answer to the 'Fokker Scourge', and RNAS squadrons equipped with the type in late 1916 began to turn the tide in northern France. The type first appeared in RFC markings early in 1917 with No. 66 Squadron, one of whose aircraft is shown here. Its reputation was quickly established because of its agility and it effective forward-firing synchronised machine-gun.

Hunters And Aces

DECEMBER 1916 – DECEMBER 1917

Above: No. 22 Squadron became a fighter squadron when it received its Bristol Fighters. These were used primarily for long offensive patrols into enemy territory. This F.2B is pictured at Agincourt in 1917.

The highly agile Sopwith Triplane proved deadly in the hands of the RNAS squadrons. These aircraft served with No. 201 Squadron, RNAS, at Bailleul in France.

The year 1917 brought home to the Western nations all the horrors of modern warfare, with the start of unrestricted submarine operations, the first major aeroplane raids against civilian targets and the first use of tanks on the Western Front. On that dismal front trench warfare ensured a continuation of bloody stalemate, while overhead the Allied air forces began the year with a tenuous possession of air superiority.

Both the British and the French were slow to exploit the limited tactical successes they had achieved in the air during the autumn of 1916, and persisted in using slow and vulnerable bombing and reconnaissance machines in the mistaken assumption that small numbers of fighting scouts, patrolling nearby, would be adequate to defend them. Air fighting tactics were not developed, other than by individual example, with the result that the Germans were able to gain the measure of such aircraft as the Sopwith Pup and Nieuport 17, and in so doing quickly evolved improved combat tactics which were embraced in the flying training programmes.

OBSOLETE FIGHTERS

The Royal Aircraft Factory R.E.8 was introduced before the end of 1916 and, despite shortcomings that immediately became apparent, was delivered in fast-growing numbers in the new year to the RFC. Other patently outdated aircraft, such as the B.E.2e, F.E.2b and F.E.8, continued in service, while promising aircraft like the S.E.5a, Sopwith Camel and Sopwith Triplane suffered persistent delays before delivery got under way to the RFC, a situation that resulted in searching questions in the British parliament.

In the meantime, the German air force had set its sights on creating an impressive force of Jagdstaffeln (Jastas, or 'hunting squadrons'), aiming to establish 37 such units by April 1917, each with 14 aircraft of which the new Albatros D III was to provide the principal equipment. When this formidable force started concerted operations over the Western Front it achieved absolute

mastery and took the Allies totally unawares. The R.E.8 was to suffer terrible casualties for, having apparently learned from previous experience, its designers had so increased the aircraft's stability that its manoeuvrability suffered disastrously. Good fighters were too few in number to afford protection, with the result that April 1917 became known in RFC annals as 'Bloody April'. Squadron after squadron was decimated, and within the space of one month no fewer than 316 pilots and observers were lost. By the same token, an increasing number of German pilots achieved fame on account of their mounting victory

Fokker Dr Is of Jasta (abbreviation of Jagdstaffel, or fighter squadron) 12 at Marle in 1917. These bear the old-style Croix Pattée (so-called Maltese Cross) insignia on the tail and fuselage.

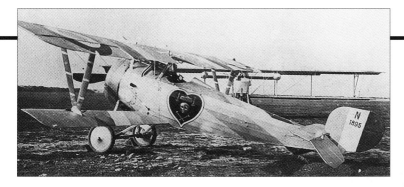

The Nieuport 17 from France was the personal mount of many World War I aces, this one belonging to French ace Charles Nungesser. It was in a Nieuport 17 that 'Billy' Bishop won his VC on 2 June 1917.

Below: The first successful landing on a ship underway was made on 2 August 1917, when Sqn Ldr E.M. Dunning touched down on HMS Furious. The straps helped the deck crew to bring the aircraft to rest.

tallies; there is no doubt that this period marked a summit of German achievement in the air that was not to be matched again until the advent of the Fokker D VII in 1918.

Forced by the events of April to take drastic action, the RFC now introduced the new scouts and, with commendable speed, the Sopwith F1 Camel, with 130-hp (97-kW) Clerget rotary, appeared over the Western Front. It was in time to join combat in July over the great 3rd Battle of Ypres which lasted until November, a battle which cost the Allies almost half a million

casualties, and gained little more than the capture of a ridge between Armentières and Dixmude. It did nevertheless serve to reduce the German pressure on the French after the collapse of their spring offensive.

This was the period of swiftly improving combat training in the RFC and, with such aircraft as the improved S.E.5a, the Camel and the Bristol F.2B Fighter, the balance began to swing back in the Allies' favour. Men like Mannock, Bishop, McCudden, Fullard and Collishaw became household names in the UK, no less than those of von

Opposing armed scouts

Trenchard had begun to replace his general purpose squadrons with dedicated bomber, observation and scout squadrons in 1916, and was

responsible for the introduction of a range of new fighters with which the RFC could take on the new German Pfalz, Fokker and Albatros scouts.

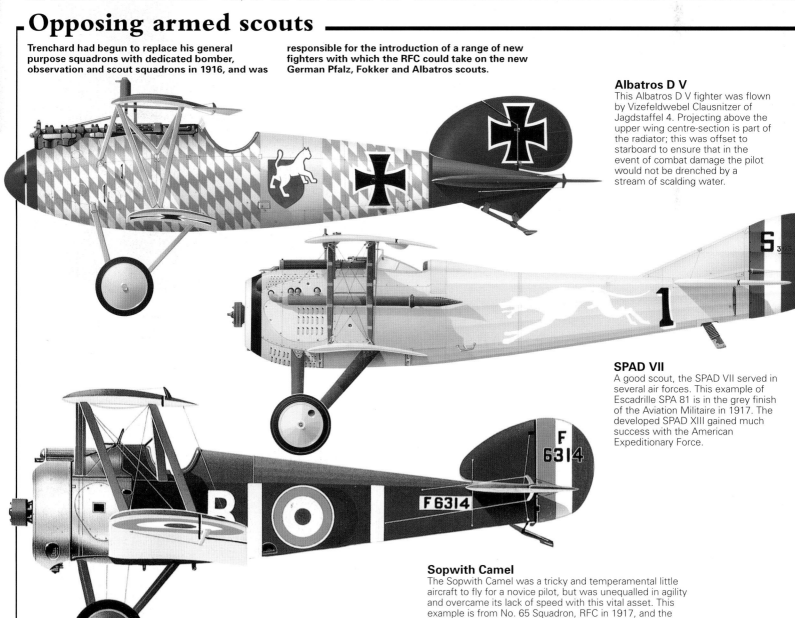

Albatros D V
This Albatros D V fighter was flown by Vizefeldwebel Clausnitzer of Jagdstaffel 4. Projecting above the upper wing centre-section is part of the radiator; this was offset to starboard to ensure that in the event of combat damage the pilot would not be drenched by a stream of scalding water.

SPAD VII
A good scout, the SPAD VII served in several air forces. This example of Escadrille SPA 81 is in the grey finish of the Aviation Militaire in 1917. The developed SPAD XIII gained much success with the American Expeditionary Force.

Sopwith Camel
The Sopwith Camel was a tricky and temperamental little aircraft to fly for a novice pilot, but was unequalled in agility and overcame its lack of speed with this vital asset. This example is from No. 65 Squadron, RFC in 1917, and the colours and markings are typical of the period.

Above: The Sopwith Triplanes of Black Flight, No. 10 Squadron, RNAS, were led by the Canadian Flt Sub-Lt Raymond Collishaw, who eventually destroyed a total of 68 enemy aircraft.

Major Edward 'Mick' Mannock scored 73 victories, the highest tally of any RFC pilot. Awarded the DSO and two bars, and MC and one bar, he was posthumously awarded the VC post-war for his actions.

Below: Major J. T. B. McCudden, DSO and bar, MC and bar, MM and Croix de Guerre, who flew (in particular) with No. 56 Squadron RFC was credited with 57 victories. He received the VC on 2 April 1918.

Above: Lt Col (later Air Marshal) W. A. Bishop DSO and bar, MC, DFC, Ld'H, C de G, of No. 60 Squadron, here with Nieuport Scout B1566, was credited with destroying 72 aircraft, gaining the VC on 2 June 1917.

British Aces

From 1917 Britain's Royal Flying Corps was well-equipped and well-led, and several of its pilots (and those of the RNAS) amassed large victory tallies. Several came within a whisker of matching Richthofen's record-breaking 80 victories.

USA Aces

The first American combat pilots in action entered the fray before their country joined the war, flying with the French Lafayette Escadrille. American aces included the legendary Rickenbacker and Frank Luke, most famous for the black art of balloon-busting.

Initially (and unhappily) equipped with Nieuports early in 1918, American squadrons changed to the SPAD XIII, one of the greatest exponents of which was Lt Frank Luke Jr, who achieved 21 victories.

Cpt Eddie Rickenbacker (the top American ace of WWI with 26 victories) became Commander of the 94th Aero Squadron, American Expeditionary Force. He is pictured with a SPAD XIII.

German Aces

Of all the fighting powers, Germany did most to encourage a 'cult' of aces, showering its most successful pilots with decorations, promoting them to lead their own units, and encouraging public interest in their exploits.

Below: The death of Hauptmann Oswald Boelcke on 28 October 1916 was a great loss to the Germans. It was primarily Boelcke's suggestion that specialist fighter units were established.

Above: 'The Eagle of Lille', Lt Max Immelmann, was one of the early German aces of WWI and his exploits captured the imagination of the German public. One of the first exponents of the Fokker E-type, he was killed in 1916.

French Aces

The French aircraft industry produced some of the finest scouts of the war, most notably in the Nieuport and SPAD families of fighters. Fittingly enough, it also produced some high-scoring individual pilots.

By mid-1916, famed French aerial fighter Georges Guynemer was a top scorer. He gained his first victory on 19 July 1915 and eventually achieved 54 victories, the second highest tally of all French aces. He was killed in September 1917.

Charles Nungesser was one of the legendary trio of French aces who scored heavily in 1917, achieving a total score of 45 in his Nieuport 17bis C1. An upward-firing Lewis gun enabled attacks to be made from below enemy aircraft.

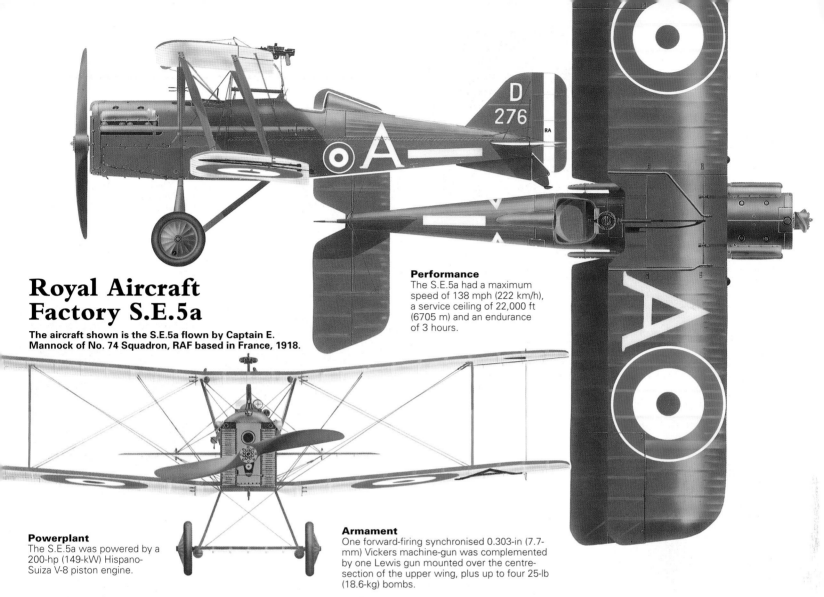

Royal Aircraft Factory S.E.5a

The aircraft shown is the S.E.5a flown by Captain E. Mannock of No. 74 Squadron, RAF based in France, 1918.

Performance
The S.E.5a had a maximum speed of 138 mph (222 km/h), a service ceiling of 22,000 ft (6705 m) and an endurance of 3 hours.

Powerplant
The S.E.5a was powered by a 200-hp (149-kW) Hispano-Suiza V-8 piston engine.

Armament
One forward-firing synchronised 0.303-in (7.7-mm) Vickers machine-gun was complemented by one Lewis gun mounted over the centre-section of the upper wing, plus up to four 25-lb (18.6-kg) bombs.

The Albatros scout introduced twin front guns, and was one of the aircraft with which the Germans sought to wrest air superiority from the Allies in late 1916. Here a trio of Albatros D Is of Jagdstaffel 2 are takes off on 28 October 1916.

Schleich, Manfred von Richthofen and Berthold in Germany. Against the new British scouts, and the French SPADs and Nieuports, were flown the new Albatros D Vs and Fokker Dr I triplanes (the latter flown by von Richthofen himself, and its most dashing exponent, Werner Voss). In the French air force, the legendary Georges Guynemer failed to return from combat in his SPAD on 11 September when his score stood at 54 victories, but the superb marksman René Fonck and the indomitable Charles Nungesser were already far along the road to stardom among fighter pilots. Yet for all these supreme individual

achievements, usually the product of the pilots' preference for lone patrol and single-handed combat, the pattern of air fighting was undergoing change, and the era of combat between formations of fighters had already dawned. The Germans in July had created a menacing new tactic with the formation of their first 'flying circus', in effect a wing of Jastas, commanded by Manfred von Richthofen. The purpose of this large fighting formation was to switch quickly from sector to sector of the front to achieve local air superiority. As much as anything else, this tactic convinced the RFC (and RNAS) of the importance of training for squadron combat. It was significant that many of the British high-scoring pilots were posted home to training units, where they could put their experience to good effect in the combat training of new squadrons.

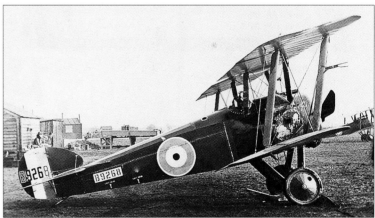

Above: The Sopwith Camel replaced the Pup in service on the Western Front and was arguably the finest British fighter of WWI, although it was tricky to fly. This is an early 1F.1 version.

Below: Known as the 'Harry Tate', the Royal Aircraft Factory R.E.8 entered RFC service at the end of 1916. The type suffered catastrophic losses during 'Bloody April' in 1917 under attack by German scouts.

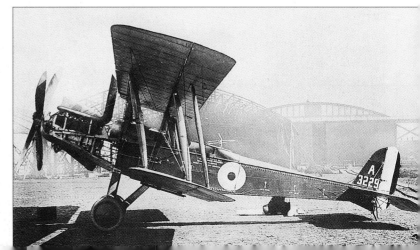

The Bloody Red Baron

The most successful fighter pilot of the Great War was Baron Rittmeister (Cavalry Captain) Manfred von Richthofen. An excellent shot, Richthofen was only an average pilot, but a good writer!

"Your opponent often slips downwards over one wing, or lets himself fall like a dead leaf in order to shake off an attack. In order to stick to him, one must on no account follow his tactics, since one has no control over a machine while falling like a dead leaf. Should one's opponent try to evade attack by such tricks, one must dive with him without losing sight of him....

"Looping the loop is worse than worthless in air fighting. Each loop is a great mistake. If one has approached one's adversary too close, a loop only offers him a big advantage. Change of speed should

be relied upon to maintain the desired position, and this is best effected by adjusting the throttle.

"The best method of flying against the enemy is as follows. The officer commanding the group, no matter how large, should fly lowest, and should keep all machines under observation by turning and banking. No machine should be allowed either to advance or to hold back. The whole squadron should advance on a curved course: flying straight on above the front is dangerous, as even planes of the same type develop different speeds. Surprise can be avoided only when flying in close order.

Known as 'The Red Baron', Manfred von Richthofen was World War I's most successful aerial fighter, shooting down 80 enemy aircraft in less than 15 months at the Western Front.

"Many English airmen try to win advantages by flying tricks while engaged in fighting, but as a rule it is just these reckless and foolish stunts that lead them to their deaths.

"The second of April was a particularly warm day for my Jasta..... I was still in my bed when my orderly ran in exclaiming, 'Herr Leutnant, the English are here!' Half asleep, I looked out of the window and saw, circling over the airfield, my 'dear friends'.

"In spite of everything, I was the last to be airborne, and my comrades were already close to the enemy. Suddenly, however, one of the impertinent fellows dropped on me from above, hoping to force me down. Calmly I let him come at me, and then we began a merry dance. My opponent flew on his back, he did this, he did that. He was flying a two-seater, but I was superior to him, and he soon realised that he could not get away from me.

"It didn't take long. I squeezed below him and fired a burst, but without doing serious damage. We were some two kilometres behind the Front and I expected him to land, but I had misjudged my opponent: when he was only a few

This line-up of Albatros D IIIs is from von Richthofen's Jasta 11. The second aircraft in the line is the all-red machine flown by the Rittmeister himself, known to the RFC as le petit rouge *(the little red).*

metres from the ground he suddenly levelled up, flying straight ahead in an attempt to shake me off. Too bad for him! I attacked him again, flying so low that I was afraid I would hit the houses in the village below. The Englishman kept fighting back, and near the end I felt my machine being hit. I must not let up now: he must fall. He flew at full speed into a block of houses, and there wasn't much left. Once more, an example of splendid daring: he defended himself right to the end.

"By the end of April the English

Von Richthofen's Dreidecker

Conceived as a counter to the Sopwith Triplane, the Fokker Dr I was one of the most agile combat aircraft in history. Flown by such accomplished airmen as Manfred von Richthofen, the small number built shot down many times their own number of enemy aircraft on the Western Front.

Fokker Dr I
One of the most famous aircraft of all time, this is the Fokker Dr I flown by Rittmeister Freiherr von Richthofen at the time of his death. The Dr I was designed to emulate the success of the Sopwith Triplane but, apart from those flown by Richthofen and Voss, was never to achieve this, its performance being overshadowed by other German scouts.

Despite all that has been written about it, the Fokker Triplane was difficult to fly and was not as successful in service as is generally believed. Here von Richthofen is depicted downing an RFC S.E.5.

Production Fokker Dr Is reached JG 1 from 12 October 1917. The fame of the agile machine had spread and von Richthofen's pilots eagerly awaited their new aircraft. Here the 'Red Baron' lands after a raid.

had devised a fine scheme either to capture me or to shoot me down, and to this end they had set up a special squadron to patrol our sector. . . . [On 29 April] we flew up to the Front, hoping to find the enemy. After some 20 minutes the first arrived and really pounced on us.

"There were three Englishmen in SPAD single-seaters, who thought themselves superior to us because of the excellence of their

machines. Wolff, my brother and I were flying together: three against three, just as it should be.

"My opponent was the first to fall, his engine shot to pieces, I believe. He decided to try to land nearby but, as I gave no quarter, I attacked him a second time and his whole plane fell to bits. The wings dropped off like pieces of paper, and the fuselage fell like a stone, burning fiercely. It plunged into a marsh. It was impossible to dig out, and I never learnt my adversary's name.

"Wolff and my brother had attacked the opponents at the same time, and forced them to the ground not far from my victim."

Richthofen had now scored 52 kills. But on 1 May he went on leave to celebrate his 25th birthday – and Bloody April was over.

The simple black wooden coffin bearing Richthofen's body was carried with dignity, and he was buried with full military honours by No. 3 Squadron, Australian Flying Corps at Bertangles on 22 April 1918.

Below: Manfred von Richthofen, who flew this Triplane when he shot down his 60th victim on 1 September 1917, is seen on the right behind General von Lossberg, who is talking to the pilot.

The German Spring Offensive

NOVEMBER 1917 - JUNE 1918

After the end of the 3rd Battle of Ypres in November 1917 there followed a relative lull in the air fighting over the Western Front. The British, French and Germans set about strengthening their air forces, the Germans for their part preparing for a final great offensive to defeat the Allies before the arrival in France of the Americans who were expected to be ready to enter the fighting early the following summer.

As already mentioned, the German air force had created the first of its Jagdgeschwader (popularly known as the 'flying circuses', literally hunting wings) in July 1917

under Manfred von Richthofen, and such had been the success gained by this formidable fighting formation that two more (JG 2, initially comprising Jastas 12, 13, 15 and 19, and JG 3 with Jastas 2, 26, 27 and 36) were formed on 1 February 1918 under Rudolf Berthold and Bruno Loerzer respectively. Simultaneously another type of formation came into being: this was the Jagdgruppe, usually of no more than two or three Jastas. This unit was of a more transient nature and was created simply for convenience during a specific operation or offensive; a total of 12 such Jagdgruppen (Nos 1 to 12) being formed from time to time during 1918.

Elsewhere in Germany, trials were held in January 1918 to decide on new fighter equipment for the Jastas, and the choice fell on the Fokker D VII, one of the best German fighting scouts to achieve major production during the last year of the war. Unfortunately, it did not achieve significant deliveries in time for the beginning of the great German offensive in March.

The L.V.G C II was the first aircraft to drop bombs on London, when six light bombs were dropped near Victoria Station on 28 November 1915. It continued in a variety of roles throughout 1917.

Between July 1917 and November 1918, the Sopwith Camel destroyed 1,294 enemy aircraft, achieving more victories than any other type of aircraft in the war. Only the Fokker Dr I could match its agility.

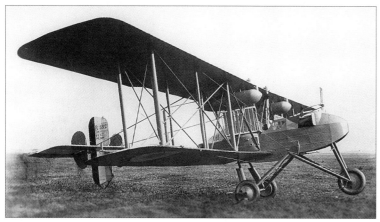

The Bréguet Biplane Type M.5 bomber was the winner of the competition for high-powered Avions in October 1915 and was much used for night-bombing in 1916-17. It was developed from the earlier Br M.4.

Right: In combat, the S.E.5a soon proved a formidable fighter and it quickly became associated with the foremost British pilots of the day. These are No. 1 Squadron S.E.5s at Clairmarais on 3 July 1918.

German scouts

The German Imperial Air Service used a bewildering array of fighters, with several different types often flying together within the same unit. Often streamlined, and usually powered by inline engines, the best German scouts were a match for the best machines operated by the Allies for long periods of the war. The best was the Fokker D VII, but it came too late to turn the tide.

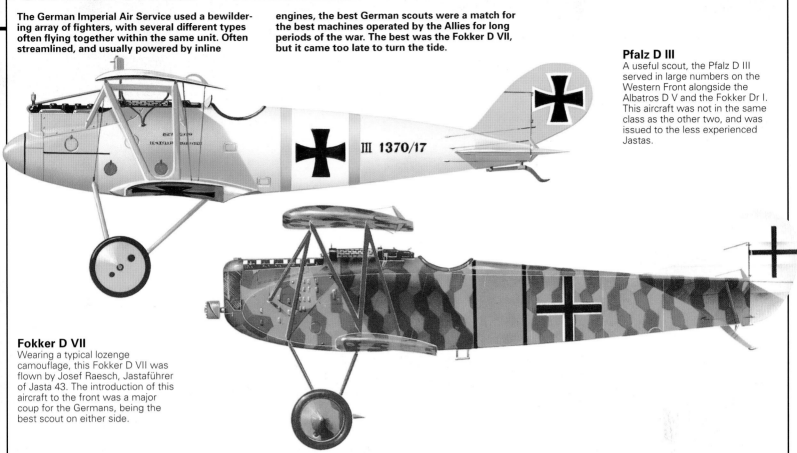

Pfalz D III
A useful scout, the Pfalz D III served in large numbers on the Western Front alongside the Albatros D V and the Fokker Dr I. This aircraft was not in the same class as the other two, and was issued to the less experienced Jastas.

III 1370/17

Fokker D VII
Wearing a typical lozenge camouflage, this Fokker D VII was flown by Josef Raesch, Jastaführer of Jasta 43. The introduction of this aircraft to the front was a major coup for the Germans, being the best scout on either side.

Instead, the majority of the 80 Jastas were equipped with Albatros D Vs and D Vas, Pfalz D IIIs and D IIIas, and Fokker Dr I triplanes.

At the time of the German offensive there were 2,047 aircraft facing the Allies, of which 1,680 were deployed on the British Front; of the latter, 475 were single-seat fighting scouts flying with 51 Jastas.

The RFC and RNAS, on the other hand, contented themselves with building up their strength of Camel, S.E.5a and Bristol Fighter squadrons, and by March there were in France nine squadrons with the Camel (151 aircraft), 10 with the S.E.5a (163 aircraft), six with the Bristol Fighter (79 aircraft) and nine with other miscellaneous fighting scouts (130 aircraft, including the excellent SPAD S.XIII, Nieuport 17 and Nieuport 27). These squadrons bore the brunt of the air combat over the British front, but were also assisted by a

A British S.E.5a (probably flown by Mannock or McCudden) on 21 June 1918, advertising the fact that 39 'Huns' had been shot down by his squadron within a two-week period.

number of French escadrilles on a short-term basis.

HEAVY FIGHTING

The German offensive opened on 21 March, by which time the establishment of RFC scout squadrons had been increased by 50 per cent to 24 aircraft each. Already heavy air fighting had broken out as the Germans sought to prevent Allied reconnaissance aircraft of V Corps from exposing the massive assembly of troops and artillery. As the enemy barrage opened on 21 March, Camels of No. 46 Squadron attacked the German gun batteries north of Bourlon Wood as No. 3 Squadron strafed enemy infantry. No. 54 Squadron was tasked with

escort of the corps reconnaissance machines. The following day Camels of Nos 73 and 80 Squadrons shot down six German scouts, and on 24 March Captain

J.L. Trollope of No. 43 Squadron set a new record by alone shooting down six aircraft in one day, a feat equalled by Captain H.W. Woollett of the same squadron on 12 April.

The French Nieuport 28 was the ultimate member of this famous line. It was initially intended to equip American scout units in France in 1918, but it was replaced in favour of the SPAD S.XIII.

Below: The Fokker D VII, ordered into immediate production in January 1918, was operational within three months. More effective than the D V series, it was only matched by the Sopwith Snipe and SPAD XIII.

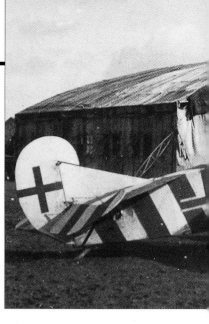

Above: The best German single-seat fighter of World War I, the Fokker D VII was just too late to take part in the opening phase of the Kaiserschlacht (Emperor's Battle) on the Somme.

Left: Ground and aircrew sort out their gear at a hastily improvised airfield in France on 25 March 1918. The aircraft are R.E.8s of No. 15 Squadron RFC, one of the most widely used observation types.

The Pfalz D III was an unequal-span biplane fitted with a 160-hp (119-kW) Mercedes D.III inline engine. It first entered service on the Western Front in late 1917, and was much underrated by both of the opposing forces.

reconnaissance over the battlefield, and it was now that the French pilot René Fonck began his extraordinary spell of multiple victories, and on 9 May alone destroyed six of the enemy (dispatching three in 45 seconds). By the end of the German offensive Fonck's score was approaching 50, and he was to continue up to 75 to become the leading Allied ace by the end of the war.

TOP GUNS

By now air combats frequently involved more than 100 aircraft. These huge fights certainly accounted for the large individual victory scores being achieved by British, French and German pilots for the days were ending when

Nine days later fell the greatest of the war's legendary scout pilots when a Canadian Camel pilot, Captain A.R. Brown of No. 209 Squadron, shot down a Fokker Dr I triplane near Corbie; in it died Manfred von Richthofen, victor of 80 air combats.

Now fully aware of the serious nature of the German offensive, the RAF (which had formally come into being on 1 April) rushed eight more scout squadrons to France. The American squadrons, which had already started arriving in France, were not yet considered battle-ready.

On the French front the Aéronautique Militaire, facing 367 German aircraft (of which 168 were scouts in 18 Jastas), successfully denied the enemy unrestricted

Above: A wide arc of parked Albatros D III and D V aircraft of Jasta 12, with an A.E.G two-seat biplane Type C IV behind – a type used for observation and reconnaissance.

The Breguet 14, powered by a Renault 12F engine, was issued to a number of well-known reconnaissance Escadrilles and served with great distinction during a number of battles in 1917 and 1918.

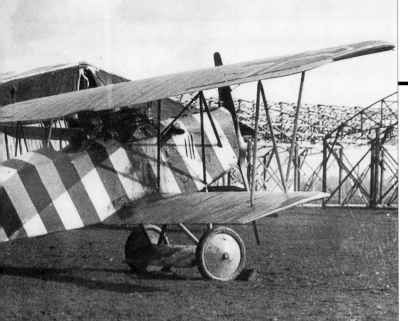

Left: The Fokker Dr I triplane (103/17) in which the German ace Leutnant Werner Voss (with a total of 48 victories credited) was killed during combat on 23 September 1917.

Above: Pilots, now in their RAF uniforms, surrender the contents of their pockets before embarking on a patrol on 17 June 1918. The long leather coats were essential for operations in open cockpits.

pilots would be ordered off on lone patrols. The large formations could be sighted at long range and accordingly engaged by equally large formations of defending scouts. As the German offensive ground to a halt on 14 June it became clear that the enemy ground forces had run out of steam, possibly for good, and that, with the Americans now streaming into France in large numbers, it might require no more than one great 'push' eastwards to end the war.

Fighters for a new force

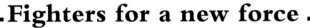

On 1 April 1918, the RFC and RNAS were amalgamated to form a new independent air arm, the Royal Air Force. Its new commander placed great faith in strategic bombing operations, but upon its formation the RAF was very much a tactical air force, with huge numbers of scouts whose primary purpose was to shoot down other aircraft. When the German offensive ran out of steam, these types carried the war to the enemy, undertaking fighter sweeps and strafing missions.

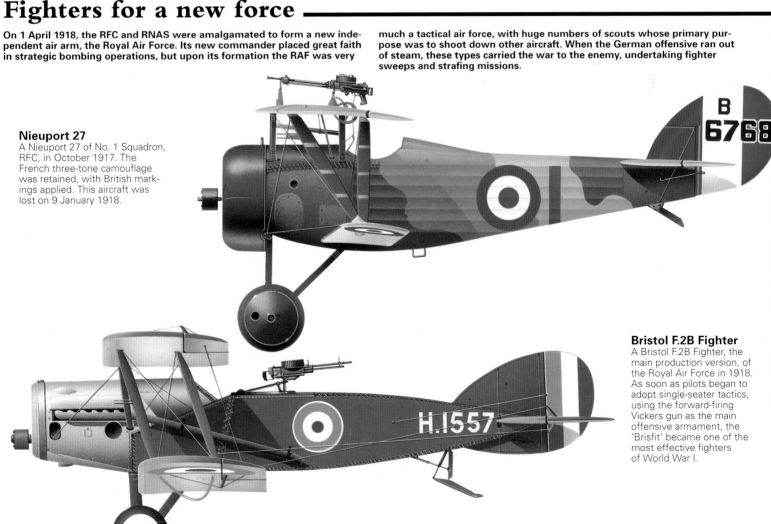

Nieuport 27
A Nieuport 27 of No. 1 Squadron, RFC, in October 1917. The French three-tone camouflage was retained, with British markings applied. This aircraft was lost on 9 January 1918.

Bristol F.2B Fighter
A Bristol F.2B Fighter, the main production version, of the Royal Air Force in 1918. As soon as pilots began to adopt single-seater tactics, using the forward-firing Vickers gun as the main offensive armament, the 'Brisfit' became one of the most effective fighters of World War I.

The Final Curtain

JUNE 1918 - NOVEMBER 1918

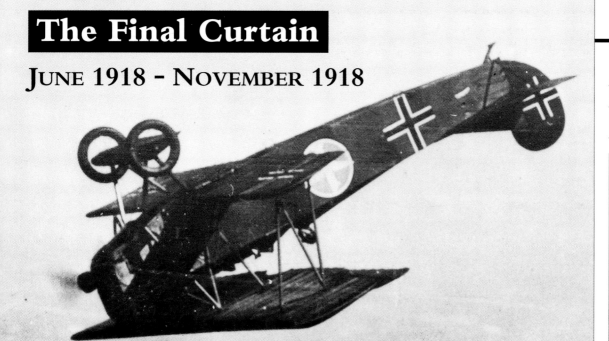

A Fokker D VII executes a loop. The D VII became operational from April 1918 and was soon in combat with the latest Allied aircraft. Faster than the Sopwith Camel, only the Snipe and SPAD XIII could match it.

If the defeat of the German offensive of March-June 1918 suggested that the energy of the enemy army had been catastrophically sapped, such was by no means evident in the air. A number of Jastas were certainly withdrawn from the front to re-man and re-equip for, by June, deliveries of the superb new Fokker D VII were well under way; by the end of that month no fewer than 270 had been received by the fighting units. Indeed, at the moment that Manfred von Richthofen was killed on 21 April, JG 1 was already scheduled to

receive the new aircraft, and did so during the remainder of that month.

It was now that the first American scout squadrons took their place in the line. In fact, the 94th and 95th Squadrons (of the 1st Pursuit Group) had arrived at Villeneuve in February and March, and had carried out their first combat sortie on 15 March when Major Raoul Lufbery led an unarmed patrol over the lines in Nieuport 28s. The Americans disliked this aircraft (as they did the Camel), however, and opted to change to the SPAD S.XIII. During the summer and autumn of 1918 they began to accumulate an impressive score of victories. Their leading aces, Captain Eddie Rickenbacker and Lieutenant Frank Luke, gained scores of 26 and 21 respectively;

third in the list was Lufbery himself, with 17, but this pilot was killed on 19 May.

On 18 August the great British offensive ('the Big Push') opened in Flanders. In support, either directly or at longer range, were 13 squadrons with the S.E.5a, 17 with the Camel, six with the Bristol Fighter, four with the new Sopwith Dolphin, 14 with the R.E.8, four with the F.K.8, five with the D.H.4, 14 with the D.H.9/9A, seven with the F.E.2b/d and seven with the O/400 heavy bomber, for a total of 91 squadrons fielding almost 1,700 aircraft.

AIR SUPERIORITY

On the French front, where an initial counter-offensive had opened on 18 July, the Aéronautique Militaire had undergone continuous strengthening with almost complete standardisation among the scout escadrilles with the SPAD S.XIII, there being 49 subordinate escadrilles and 10 independent escadrilles thus equipped. In addition there were 23 bomber escadrilles flying Breguet 14s, Caproni 10s and Voisin 10s, the Breguets being used in the 'ground attack' role; there were also almost 140 artillery and army cooperation escadrilles, the majority of which flew Breguet 14s and Salmson 2s. By the beginning of August the Aéronautique Militaire possessed a front-line strength of over 2,800 aircraft, a total that would grow to 3,222 within four months.

From the beginning of this final phase of the air war, the Allies pos-

Just before the Armistice, No. 201 Squadron's second VC was awarded to Canadian Major William Barker DSO, MC, for shooting down four Fokker D VIIs on 27 October, while wounded and heavily outnumbered.

sessed air superiority, as much on account of excellent fighting aircraft as of the much improved standard of combat training, following the rotation of experienced pilots to training units in the rear. For their part the Germans formed a fourth Jagdgeschwader, this time under the command of Ritter Eduard von Schleich, the veteran Bavarian who had won the Pour le Merite a year earlier and gained a score of 35 victories. During those last months of the war the 'flying circuses' inflicted very heavy casualties among the

S.E.5as of No. 85 Squadron lined up at St Omer on 21 June 1918. The upper wing-mounted Lewis gun was in addition to the Vickers machine-gun fixed to the top of the fuselage, and fired through the propeller arc.

Airco DH.4s of 'A' Flight, No. 27 Squadron RFC at Serny, Pas de Calais on 17 February 1918. No. 27 played an important role in the development of reconnaissance techniques and bad weather flying.

The Sopwith Snipe was designed around the new Bentley rotary engine, and was intended as the ultimate successor to the Camel. However, only around 100 Snipes reached France before the Armistice.

Final fighters

There was little to choose between the various fighter types in service at the end of the war, when newer aircraft were beginning to replace even the Fokker DVII, S.E.5 and Sopwith Camel.

Unfortunately for Germany, the war had already been lost on the ground, and, it must be said, on the home front as well as on the battlefield.

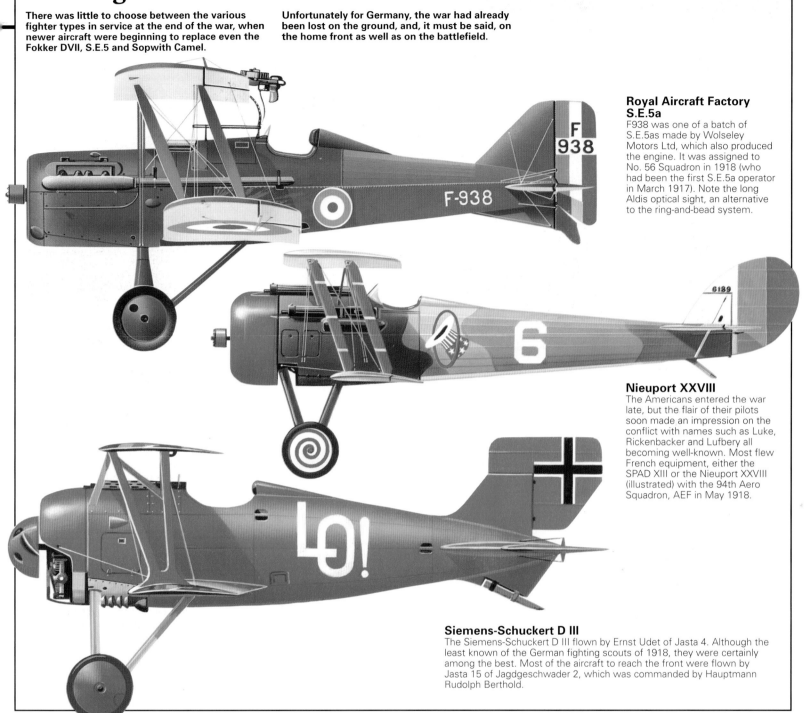

Royal Aircraft Factory S.E.5a
F938 was one of a batch of S.E.5as made by Wolseley Motors Ltd, which also produced the engine. It was assigned to No. 56 Squadron in 1918 (who had been the first S.E.5a operator in March 1917). Note the long Aldis optical sight, an alternative to the ring-and-bead system.

Nieuport XXVIII
The Americans entered the war late, but the flair of their pilots soon made an impression on the conflict with names such as Luke, Rickenbacker and Lufbery all becoming well-known. Most flew French equipment, either the SPAD XIII or the Nieuport XXVIII (illustrated) with the 94th Aero Squadron, AEF in May 1918.

Siemens-Schuckert D III
The Siemens-Schuckert D III flown by Ernst Udet of Jasta 4. Although the least known of the German fighting scouts of 1918, they were certainly among the best. Most of the aircraft to reach the front were flown by Jasta 15 of Jagdgeschwader 2, which was commanded by Hauptmann Rudolph Berthold.

Allied air forces, not least among the relatively inexperienced Americans. When the American land forces launched an attack west of Metz on 20 September, JG 2 alone destroyed 89 American aircraft in two days.

It was in September that the RAF began to receive the first examples of the new Sopwith Snipe fighting scout, a derivative of the successful Camel and one which was to survive in service for some years after the war. In the event, very few reached operational squadrons in France, and its place in the history of the war is almost entirely filled by the epic fight by a lone pilot. Major W.G. Barker, who was attached to No. 201 Squadron to gain experience in the new aircraft, was on patrol high above the Forêt de Mormal on 27

October when he became involved in a prolonged fight with more than 15 enemy aircraft. Despite being severely wounded, he shot down at least four of the enemy (including three Fokker D VIIs) before crash-landing behind the British lines; he survived to be awarded the Victoria Cross.

Like the Snipe, the German Fokker D VIII parasol monoplane scout also failed to reach operational squadrons in significant numbers but, with a speed some 10 mph (16 km/h) higher than that of the Snipe, and much lighter on the controls, there is little doubt but

Originally known as the Fokker E V, the D VIII did not arrive at the front in any great numbers. It was the fastest scout to see service and possessed good agility, but suffered from structural problems.

that this aircraft would have otherwise given the Allied pilots a great deal of trouble. Be that as it may, it was the D VII that came to be most respected by the Allies, so much so that the terms of the Armistice specifically named this aircraft (*in erster Linie alle apparate D VII*, or 'particularly first-line aircraft known as D VII') to be handed over.

The fighting on the Western Front was the key to the war's outcome. With internal strife inside Germany, shortages of food and the loss of the Hindenburg Line in October, the strength and power of the German air force had become superfluous. On 11 November the war ended when armistice terms were negotiated in France.

The Russian Front

AUGUST 1914 – SEPTEMBER 1918

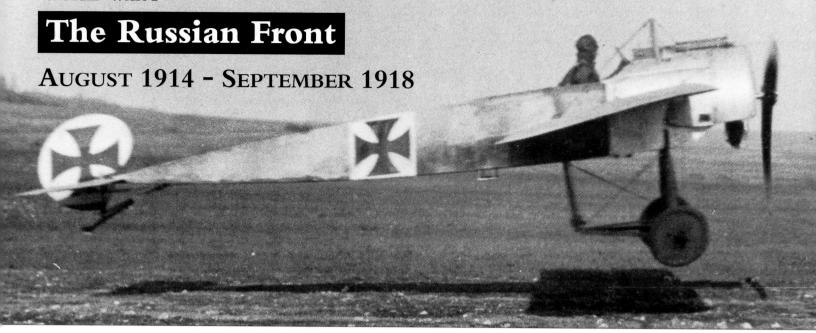

Left: One of the four-engined Sikorsky Ilya Mourometz heavy bombers that served so well from 1915. Type B used four Salmson-Canton-Unne radials of 200 hp and 135 hp (two of each). It could carry 1,102 lb of bombs.

Though not an exceptional aircraft in terms of performance or agility, the Fokker E III achieved results by means of its unique synchronised machine-gun, offset to starboard and firing straight forward through the propeller, making aiming easy.

The war between Germany and Austria-Hungary on the one hand and Tsarist Russia on the other lasted for three years before dying out with the onset of the Russian Revolution in October 1917. At the outbreak of war the frontier dividing the two empires stretched from midway between Riga and Danzig on the Baltic coast, running west of Warsaw south through Galicia (now southern Poland) and finally southeast to the mouth of the Danube on the Black Sea coast. Early air fighting predominated in Galicia and the north, the Germans at first deploying little air strength in the east, and the Russians possessing even less of an air force in any case. When the war opened

An Ilya Mourometz G-9 heavy bomber used by the Imperial Russian Army during WWI. Few were identical, a result of continual improvement. Shortages led to a mix of powerplants on some aircraft.

the Imperial Russian Air Service had a total of 244 aeroplanes, 12 airships and 46 kite balloons, of which 145 aeroplanes were in the field; most were of French design, produced under licence by such companies as Duks, Russo-Baltic and Lebedev. Notable exceptions were the four-engined Sikorsky bombers which started bombing operations over the Eastern Front on 15 February 1915; no fewer than 73 of these huge aeroplanes were produced by the Russo-Baltic Wagon Works during the war.

Early combat was no less primitive in its tactics than in the West. The first Russian pilot to achieve fame was Piotr Nesterov (a pre-war pilot of renown), who was killed while gaining his only air victory near his airfield at Sholkiv by ramming a German aircraft in his Nieuport; Sholkiv was later renamed in his honour. Relentless pressure by the Central Powers

forced the Russian armies back in the Ukraine where constant operations were flown in the Lutsk and Kovel regions, with frequent attacks being made to destroy the railway centre at Kovel. One of the great Russian pilots, Aleksandr Kazakov, spent most of his combat career in this area and became the top-scoring pilot on the front, some of his early victims being Fokker monoplanes when they arrived in the east late in 1915. In 1917 he commanded the newly-formed No. 1 Fighter Group, but this broke up at the time of the revolution and Kazakov made his way north to Archangelsk to join the British who landed there in 1918; he died needlessly while practising aerobatics in a Camel the following year. His decorations included the British DSO, MC and DFC.

RUSSIAN EX-PATS

The bomber designer Igor Sikorsky was later to make his home in the USA. Another to do so was Alexander de Seversky, who had an outstanding combat record on the Eastern Front, much of it spent in the Riga region with the Imperial

Naval Air Service. During his first night bombing flight he was shot down into the sea and his bomb exploded, blowing off his right leg; despite this, he returned to command fighter aviation in the Baltic area and went on to destroy 13 German aircraft. He was in the USA at the time of the revolution and so decided to apply for American citizenship, later creating the Seversky Aero Corporation in 1922.

There is no doubt that the Russian air forces possessed many fine pilots, no less courageous and skilled than their opponents in the German and Austro-Hungarian air services. And their aircraft, though generally lagging about six months behind those in the West (as was the German equipment), were adequate and well serviced. The weakness lay in the command structure, a failing that permeated all the forces of Tsarist Russia. The officer corps was treated with elitism far

Although the Anatra D had serious design faults, it was widely operated by the Russians. It became operational in mid-1916 and was powered by a 130-hp (97-kW) Clerget rotary engine.

Powered by a 110-hp (82-kW) Le Rhone rotary engine, the Nieuport 17 was fast-climbing and highly manoeuvrable. It was flown by the Imperial Russian Air Service, and some survived in Bolshevik use.

beyond that of other nations, so that when setbacks and ultimate disaster faced the Russian forces, disintegration followed in numerous units, although the air force was probably less affected than the army.

Collapse of discipline, particularly in the Ukraine, immediately before the October Revolution literally cut the ground from under the air force. Despite orders forbidding the continuation of hostilities against the Germans, many Russians fought on. One such incident involved Lieutenant Commander Viktor Utgov of the Black Sea Fleet who, flying a Grigorovich M-9 seaplane from the

carrier *Imperator Nicolai Pervyi*, attacked a German U-boat with bombs, only to be summoned before the sailors' revolutionary executive to explain his conduct. (He also emigrated to the USA and joined Sikorsky, only to be killed in a flying accident with the US Marine Corps.)

Many Russian airmen served on the Western Front, and others learned to fly with the RFC in the UK. Likewise, a number of individual French pilots (as well as some French squadrons) served in Russia. The Imperial Russian air forces also numbered a few women among their pilots, the most famous (or

The Zeppelin-Staaken R IV – the first of the series to carry the 'R' (Riesenfugzeug, or giant aircraft) designation – had five 240-hp (179-kW) Maybach Mb.IV engines giving a top speed of 78 mph (125 km/h).

infamous) being Princess Eugine Shakhovskaya; one of the first women to learn to fly in Russia before the war, she became a reconnaissance pilot on the Riga front. After the revolution it is said that she was chief executioner in the Tcheka at Kiev.

OCCUPATION COMPLETE

By the summer of 1918 German forces occupied a gigantic area of Russia, including the entire Ukraine and almost all the territory to the west of the River Don.

The main fighter of the Austro-Hungarian air arm was the Aviatik (Berg) D I, seen here in modified form. The fighting on the Russian front was not as compeititive as on the Western front.

However, if Germany had 'killed herself by victories' (*Wir siegen uns zum Tod*), the skills and courage of the Imperial Russian air forces may have unwittingly contributed to the widespread popular appeal of revolutionary opportunism in the armed forces simply on account of the adulation the officer corps attracted.

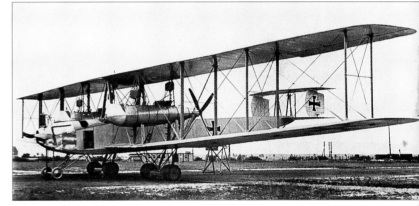

Opposing Fighters

The Imperial Russian Air Service fought with courage, but was not well led, and operated in support of an army that was no match for the German

army. When Revolution came, the Air Service disintegrated, with some factions going over to the Bolsheviks, and others to the White Russians.

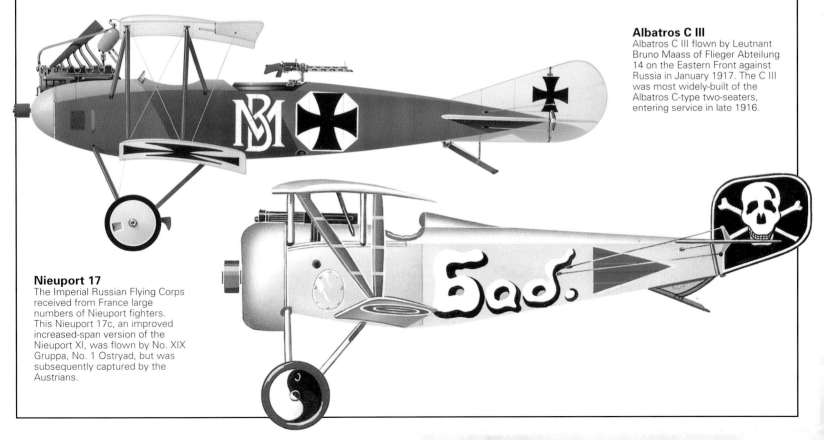

Albatros C III
Albatros C III flown by Leutnant Bruno Maass of Flieger Abteilung 14 on the Eastern Front against Russia in January 1917. The C III was most widely-built of the Albatros C-type two-seaters, entering service in late 1916.

Nieuport 17
The Imperial Russian Flying Corps received from France large numbers of Nieuport fighters. This Nieuport 17c, an improved increased-span version of the Nieuport XI, was flown by No. XIX Gruppa, No. 1 Ostryad, but was subsequently captured by the Austrians.

The Italian Front

MAY 1915 - NOVEMBER 1918

Originally known as the Caproni 600HP (the total horsepower of its three engines), the Ca 5 first flew in 1917. Although unpopular with its crews, 669 examples were built. Maximum bombload was 900 kg.

The outbreak of war in the south in May 1915 found the Italian army poorly prepared for action, despite fielding a total of 35 divisions against 25 Austrian. The frontier was largely Alpine, the four Italian armies being deployed in the Trentino, Cadore, Carnia and Isonzo sectors, of which the last-named absorbed 14 divisions, with seven in reserve. The Austrians, however, possessed a considerable superiority in artillery.

In the air, the Italian Aeronautica del Regio Esercito (Royal Army Air Service) was better prepared, with 14 squadriglie of Nieuports, Maurice Farmans and Blériots in the field. Faced with ineffective opposition by the Austro-Hungarian air force these squadriglie gave a good account of themselves, particularly in recon-

naissance duties, during the first general offensive which involved a combined advance by all four armies. Gradually the fighting concentrated on the eastern flank where the Isonzo plain provided the best opportunities for greatest gain, and it was in this sector that the Italians made their biggest gains in the early months. By the autumn, however, following Russian defeats in Galicia, Austrian forces had been freed for service on the Isonzo, incorprating increasing numbers of German aircraft including Rumpler and Aviatik C Is, which now provided the Austrian artillery with fairly effective spotting services. In this, the 2nd Battle of the Isonzo, the Italians had greatly reorganised their air force, greater emphasis being placed on bombing and reconnaissance. Capronis and Farmans were employed in the former tasks, and

Macchis, Farmans and Caudrons in the latter.

The Italians progressively reduced their fighting scout strength early in 1916, retaining two squadrons of Nieuport 11s for the defence of Santa Caterina and Aquileia. Successive battles were fought on the Isonzo front, as gradually the Austro-Hungarians built up their ground and air forces. As the Italian Capronis flew daylight bombing raids over the Alps a small

number of Fokker E I monoplanes became available to mount token opposition; increasing numbers of Lohner and Lloyd reconnaissance aircraft were introduced into service, together with Fokker B IIs and D IIs. The first aircraft to make its mark on the front was the Brandenburg D I, the famous 'Star-Strutter'. This was flown by the top-scoring Austrian, Godwin Brumowski, who led Fliegerkompanie (Flik) 12 and whose aim it was to create an elite fighting unit on the same lines as those beginning to appear on the Western Front. Opposite him the great Italian ace, Francesco Baracca (whose personal emblem, the Cavallino Rampante, or prancing horse, is to this day adopted in the Italian air force) had by November 1916 destroyed five enemy aircraft; before the end of the war, while flying Nieuports and SPADs, he was to top the Italian scout fighters with a score of 34 victories.

After the desperate battles of the winter of 1916-17, in which appalling weather conditions and hardships sapped the morale of Italian fighting personnel from the warmer south, the fortunes of Italy continued to deteriorate. However, the failure of the Austrian Bainsizza offensive also took its toll and Austria was forced to seek assistance from Germany, a massive build-up

Above: The Rumpler C I was one of the best German two-seaters in 1916, providing the Austrian forces with an effective spotting platform. Armament comprised one rear-mounted Parabellum machine-gun.

Left: Designed by Ernst Heinkel for Hansa und Brandenburgishe, the C I was built under licence in Austria and saw widespread use by the Austrian forces. Here pilots of Flik 7 have returned from a raid on Milan on 16 February 1916.

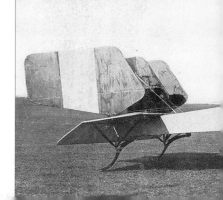

Air war over Italy

The Austro-Hungarian air forces primarily used German-designed aircraft, while the Italians used a mixture of French, British and indigenously-built machines. The Italian Aeronautica del Regia Esercito began the war enjoying a significant advantage over the smaller, less well-equipped Austro-Hungarians. By the end of the war, the combatants were more evenly matched in the air, although the Italians retained a slight edge.

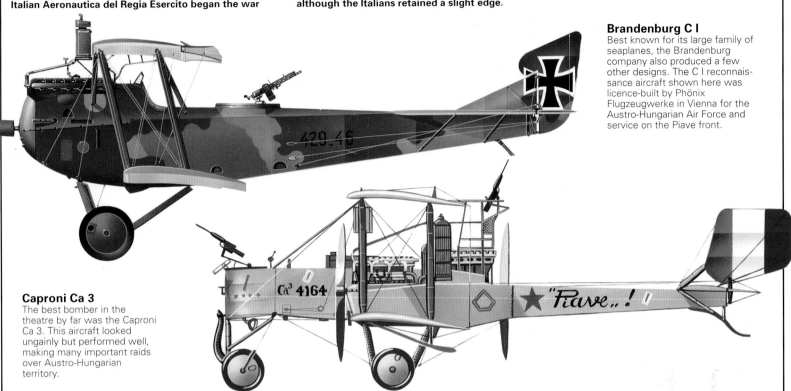

Brandenburg C I
Best known for its large family of seaplanes, the Brandenburg company also produced a few other designs. The C I reconnaissance aircraft shown here was licence-built by Phönix Flugzeugwerke in Vienna for the Austro-Hungarian Air Force and service on the Piave front.

Caproni Ca 3
The best bomber in the theatre by far was the Caproni Ca 3. This aircraft looked ungainly but performed well, making many important raids over Austro-Hungarian territory.

Among the top-scoring Italian pilots were Francesco Baracca (with 34 kills) and Silvio Scaroni (with 26 kills). The leading Italian pilots flew SPAD and Nieuport scouts.

that was to result in the crushing defeat at Caporetto in October 1917 of the Italians, who were utterly unprepared for the use against them of gas shells. As the entire front threatened to collapse under the weight of attack by five armies, the Allies rushed reinforcements to Italy, particularly from

France; these included 11 British and French divisions, and four RFC squadrons (of Camels and Bristol Fighters) and three French escadrilles.

FIERCE BATTLES
By a supreme effort of bravery and sacrifice the Italians eventually mended the front and held the Austro-Hungarian assault on the Piave. Fighting in the air continued to rage furiously, the Italians having resurrected their fighting scout squadriglie such that by the time of

Caporetto they possessed eight Hanriot HD 1 squadriglie, four of SPAD S.VIIs and three of Nieuports. Caproni bombers equipped 14 squadriglie, and the excellent Ansaldo light reconnaissance bomber entered service in January 1918, later performing a number of epic missions. Air combat in the theatre brought to the fore numerous great pilots, Baracca continuing to score heavily until his death on the Piave front on 19 June. Teniente Silvio Scaroni, who only opened his air fighting score in November 1917 and flew Nieuports and Hanriots, survived the war with 26 victories, and reached the rank of general.

In the Austro-Hungarian air force Brumowski had progressed

from the Brandenburg D I to the two-gun Albatros D III, leading a 'flying circus' of these aircraft during the Caporetto campaign. Julius Arigi, whose victory score reached 32, also flew Albatros D IIIs, and survived beyond World War II having numbered among his flying students the Luftwaffe's Walter Nowotny and Hans-Joachim Marseille. Third highest-scoring pilot was the Polish-born Frank Linke-Crawford, commander of Flik 60, whose combat score increased rapidly over Caporetto but who was killed on 31 July 1918.

Following the great Italian victory at Vittorio Veneto on 30 October an armistice was signed between Austria and Italy on 4 November.

Left: A Caproni Ca 3, of which 299 were built. Powered by three 150-hp (112-kW) Isolta Fraschini V.4B engines, the Ca 3 proved to be the most successful Allied bomber of World War I.

Below: The Albatros C III began operations during the latter half of 1916. Its single rear-mounted defensive Parabellum machine-gun was supplemented by a Spandau machine-gun for forward attack.

Zeppelins At War

SEPTEMBER 1914 - AUGUST 1918

Paradoxically, it was not the Germans but the French (or rather a Brazilian who lived in France) who first produced a practical airship: Alberto Santos-Dumont built some 15 non-rigid dirigibles by 1904 before being diverted to heavier-than-air craft. In Germany Count Ferdinand von Zeppelin, pursuing earlier theories of the Austrian engineer David Schwartz, began trials with a compartmented, rigid airship in 1900, the LZ 1, but it was not for several years that success attended his trials.

By the beginning of World War I, however, more than a score of very large airships had been produced in Germany, seven of them by Luftschifflbau Zeppelin for its associated airship-operating company Deutsche Luftschiffahrts AG (Delag), an airline that made 1,588 flights totalling 107,205 miles (172525 km) in the five years before the war and carried 32,722 passengers. As early as 1909 the German war ministry took over

two airships, the LZ 3 and LZ 5, for crew training, and it was Kapitan Kahlenberg of the 1st Prussian Airship Battalion who was in fact in command of LZ 7 *Deutschland* when it crashed in June 1910, though without loss of life.

The outbreak of war put an end to anything resembling commercial airship operation in Germany, although as late as 1917 a naval craft, the L 59, was called on to carry supplies to German forces in East Africa; it was recalled, when near Khartoum, having flown 4,200 miles (6760 km). Among the seven airships on army charge in August 1914 were the LZ 11 *Viktoria Luise*, taken over by the XVIII Corps, LZ 13 *Hansa* by the VII Corps (and used for training) and the LZ 17 *Sachsen* by the XIX Corps; in addition the LZ 25 (IX) was being completed to an army order. The Imperial navy had suffered catastrophe in 1913 when LZ 14 was lost at sea and LZ 18 exploded near Berlin, killing most of the service's trained crews. During the war Luftschiffbau Zeppelin built a total of 95 rigid airships, production of their giant craft (most of which were about 492 ft/150 m long) continuing at the

rate of about one every fortnight. German army and navy airship stations had been established before the war (some of which were taken over from Delag) at Baden-Baden, Berlin, Bremen, Brunswick, Dresden, Dusseldorf, Emden, Hamburg, Cologne, Leipzig, Mannheim, Nordholz, Potsdam and Stuttgart.

BOMBERS

Most of the early wartime operations by the German airships were navigation exercises, but on the night of 2/3 September 1914 LZ 17, flying from Cologne, dropped three bombs of about 200 lb (91 kg) on Antwerp before returning safely to base. Three months later this airship was transferred to the Eastern Front where it is said to have made half a dozen bombing raids before being handed over to the navy for training duties.

Of the two airships LZ 25 (IX) and LZ 26 (XII), the former was destroyed in its shed at Dusseldorf on 8 October in the epic bombing attack by Flight Lieutenant R.L.G. Marix, RNAS, in a Sopwith Tabloid. The latter, a 500-ft (153-m) airship, delivered to the army in December, was one of the

The Zeppelin airships were the most successful lighter-than-air aircraft of the war, performing patrol and bombing missions with equal facility. Their success led to civil versions after the war.

first to fly a sortie over the British Isles.

The first authenticated raids over the UK were by the naval Schutte-Lanz L 3 and L 4, flying from Hamburg and Nordholz on 19 January 1915; their bombs fell in the area of Great Yarmouth, Norfolk, causing numerous casualties. A third airship turned back following engine trouble. L 3 and L 4 were later wrecked on the coast of

Peter Strasser was the head of the airship detachment. Following the loss of the L 2 with the loss of all on board, Strasser chartered the privately-owned **Hansa** *and got his key personnel back in the air to help to restore confidence.*

The last Zeppelin raid on England took place on 5 August 1918. In the later raids, the Zeppelins tried to reach safety above 21,400 ft and for a while were able to evade the British fighters.

Above: On 11 August 1918, Lt S.D. Culley in a Camel spotted Zeppelin L 53 at 19,000 ft over Heligoland. Although at his aircraft's ceiling, he was able to fire at the airship which burst into flames and broke in two.

Cpt W. Leefe Robinson of No. 39 Squadron flying BE.2C 2092 shot down the German airship SL 11 at Cuffley on the night of 2/3 September 1916, for which action he was awarded the VC.

Jutland during a second raid attempt.

As explained elsewhere, all German air raiding policies at the beginning of the war were under tight political control, the Kaiser himself withholding sanction for indiscriminate bombing. Nevertheless, despite an almost total lack of black-out precautions in the UK, the German naval airships (soon followed by those of the army) began flights over East Anglia, southern England and northern France. The first bombs to fall on London were dropped by a German army airship on 31 May 1915.

A week later the first German airship, LZ 37 (captained by Oberleutnant Otto van de Haegen, and flying in company with LZ 38 and LZ 39), was destroyed in 'air combat' over Ghent, Belgium, on the night of 6/7 May when Flight

Bomb release switches on a Zeppelin. They had caused much alarm and a deflection of resources to defence, but the physical damage inflicted by the Zeppelins was in no way commensurate with the effort.

Sub-Lieutenant R.A.J. Warneford RNAS, flying a Morane-Saulnier parasol monoplane from Dunkirk, struck the craft's hull with a small bomb, an action fraught with hazard and one for which the British pilot was recommended for the Victoria Cross. Warneford, who had to force land after his successful exploit, lost his life in a flying accident a fortnight later, before his award was gazetted.

Further German airships were lost in action at an increasing rate as the frequency of attacks was stepped up, but it was not until the night of 2/3 September 1916 that one was shot down over British soil

German Naval Zeppelin LZ 53 leaving its hangar for a night attack on England during WWI. The biggest airship raid of the war was on the night of 2/3 September 1916, when 14 crossed the coast, although none reached London.

when Lieutenant William Leefe Robinson of No. 39 (Home Defence) Squadron, RFC, shot down SL XI at Cuffley, Hertfordshire; Leefe Robinson was also awarded the Victoria Cross.

LONDON HIT

By the end of 1916 the German airships, of which about 50 were in service, were carrying bombs of up to 600-lb (272-kg) weight, roughly twice the size of those capable of being carried by the early twin-engined bombing aeroplanes. On 27/28 November that year two German naval airships were destroyed in a single night over the English East Coast, the same night that six tiny bombs fell for the first time on London from an aeroplane. The airship raids continued throughout 1917, being launched wholly independently of the Gotha raids which started on 25 May. On 21 August the German naval airship L 23 was shot down off the Danish coast by a Sopwith Pup launched from a platform on the light cruiser HMS *Yarmouth* and flown by Flight Sub-Lieutenant B.A. Smart, RNAS.

It was perhaps ironic that it was the build-up of the UK's home defences against the aeroplane raids that eventually led to the discontinuation of the airship raids on the UK, the last to cause casualties being on 12 April 1918.

German Long-Range Bombing

MID 1915 – APRIL 1918

Although the origins of strategic bombing probably lie in the Russian use of the Sikorsky four-engined bombers early in 1915, the Germans sought to extend the operations by their growing fleet of airships with development of the large aeroplane, of whose manufacturers the Siemens-Schuckert, Gothaer-Waggonfabrik and Zeppelin-Staaken companies were actively engaged in producing experimental examples at that time. Origins of the German use of bombers lay in the so-called battle-planes which equipped the first Kampfstaffeln (battle squadrons) of mid-1915, and although such large aircraft were generically referred to as K-types, such as the AEG K I, the first operational bombing units

were codenamed Carrier Pigeon Units (Brieftauben Abteilungen), one of which was based at Ostend, ostensibly for attacks against south east England and the busy Channel ports. Because of delays in bringing the larger aircraft up to reliable service standard, these units continued to fly relatively small aircraft of the B- and C-type and were therefore capable of no more than nuisance raids with very small bombs.

On the Eastern Front the large multi-engined battleplanes, such as the Siemens Forssman (obviously inspired by the Sikorsky bombers), Siemens-Schuckert Steffen R I and Zeppelin-Staaken VGO (Versuchs Gotha Ost) had undergone operational trials over the front with both the army and navy, and although most were either found to be alto-

Above: The one-off DFW R I flew only a single mission (on the Eastern Front), crashing on landing when it aborted its second mission.

Top: The VGO II was the first successful R-plane, and the first in a long line of Staaken giant bombers.

gether unsatisfactory or in need of further development, establishment of front-line Kampfgeschwader (battle wings) went ahead in 1916 for the purpose of launching worthwhile bombing raids on strategic targets well behind the Russian and French fronts. Such a policy of carrying the war to the rear areas, and the consequent endangering of civilian lives by premeditated acts of war, was the outcome of persistent pressure by the German military and naval staffs upon the Kaiser to permit military targets within cities remote from the battle theatres to be attacked from the air. Such a policy ignored the absence of any workable bomb-aiming equipment, so that any damage of a military value would be quite fortuitous.

The Brieftauben Abteilung Ostende was withdrawn to Bulgaria in mid-1916 and redesigned Kampfgeschwader Nr 1 (KG 1), three of its Staffeln (squadrons) being detached to form the basis of KG 3 (known as Kagohl 3). This

was in turn moved to Ghent with the stated purpose of starting raids on the UK with Gotha and Friedrichshafen bombers under the command of Hauptmann Ernst Brandenburg, the first of which was launched on 25 May 1917. On that day 23 Gotha G IVs set out for London but, on finding the British capital obscured by cloud and haze, turned for home and dropped their bombs on Folkestone, killing 95 and injuring 260 – higher casualties than in any previous raid by airship or aeroplane.

OUTCRY IN BRITAIN

As an outcry erupted in the British Parliament at the defences' inability to counter this daylight raid, Brandenburg launched an attack on

Above: The best known of the R-planes was the Zeppelin-Staaken R VI, of which 18 were built. They formed the backbone of the heavy bomber squadrons on the Western Front, and at least two were shot down, one by anti-aircraft fire and one by a night-fighter.

Right: The SSW R VIII was the largest aircraft built during World War I. Too late to see operational service, the aircraft was examined as a possible carrier for wire- or radio-guided glide bombs of between 300 and 1000 kg. It taxied but never flew.

The German Giants

The Germans built only some 65 long-range Riesenflugzeug (giant aircraft or R-planes), and of these only about 30 reached the front, augmenting larger numbers of Gothas and Friedrichshafens. The R-planes saw service on the Eastern Front, where air supremacy could often be assumed. Following the withdrawal of the Zeppelin from bombing raids over England, Gothas and the later Staaken R-planes took over. None of the Staakens were lost to enemy action.

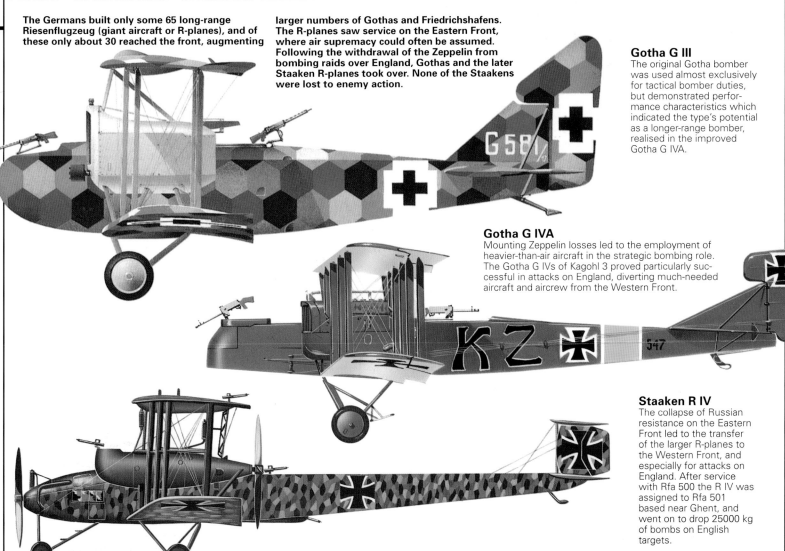

Gotha G III
The original Gotha bomber was used almost exclusively for tactical bomber duties, but demonstrated performance characteristics which indicated the type's potential as a longer-range bomber, realised in the improved Gotha G IVA.

Gotha G IVA
Mounting Zeppelin losses led to the employment of heavier-than-air aircraft in the strategic bombing role. The Gotha G IVs of Kagohl 3 proved particularly successful in attacks on England, diverting much-needed aircraft and aircrew from the Western Front.

Staaken R IV
The collapse of Russian resistance on the Eastern Front led to the transfer of the larger R-planes to the Western Front, and especially for attacks on England. After service with Rfa 500 the R IV was assigned to Rfa 501 based near Ghent, and went on to drop 25000 kg of bombs on English targets.

the naval town of Sheerness on 5 June by 22 Gothas; little damage was done, but 45 people were killed. One of the raiders was shot down by the ground defences. The next raid, flown on 13 June, marked the climax of Kagohl 3's fortunes: 20 Gothas set out for London, where the majority of bombs fell on the dock area and East End. One bomb fell on an infants' school at Poplar, killing 16 young children. Other bombs fell in the City, causing damage and casualties near St Paul's cathedral and Liverpool Street station. As Brandenburg brought his bombers home without loss, London counted 162 dead and 432 injured.

The clamour in the UK caused the defences to be strengthened by withdrawal of fighters from France and the establishment of gun and balloon belts around London and other Home County targets. The result in turn was to encourage the

The Gotha G IV mounted a daylight bombing campaign against England from 25 May 1917, and London from 13 June. Some 401 civilians were killed, two fighters were shot down, and six RFC aircrew were killed. The Gothas also forced new Sopwith Camels to be witheld from the front.

Germans to attack by night, and on the evening of 3 September 1917 four Gothas attacked Chatham, one bomb falling on a naval barracks, killing 131 ratings and injuring 90 others in the worst single bomb incident of the war. During the following 30 nights the Gothas flew 64 sorties over England, reaching London on six occasions.

Meanwhile, the Germans had been making ready a new weapon, the R-type bomber (Riesenflugzeug, or giant aeroplane). These truly colossal aircraft, most of which were built by Zeppelin-Staaken, originated in the VGO 1 that had flown in 1915, and in various forms were powered by four (and sometimes five) Maybach or Mercedes engines. They formed the equipment of two units, Riesenflugzeug-abteilungen 500 and 501, and operated from the Ghent area both over France and south east England. With a wing span of over 138 ft (42 m) and a crew of at least seven, Rfa

501's R VIs carried out a total of 11 raids on the UK between 18 December 1917 and 20 May 1918. On 28 January an R VI, with the unit commander Hauptmann Richard von Bentivegni aboard (he was not himself a pilot), dropped a 661-lb (300-kg) bomb on a printing works in London, killing 38 and injuring 85. On the night of 16/17 February an R VI dropped a 2,205-lb (1000-kg) bomb on the Royal Hospital, Chelsea, the heaviest bomb to fall on the UK during the war.

The Gothas did not have it all their own way, and eight were shot down by fighters and AAA. Nine more were lost in an abortive raid which ran into severe headwinds, and 10 were written off after landing, most badly shot up by RFC fighters.

Allied Bombing

AUGUST 1915 – NOVEMBER 1918

It was not until 1915, when in August that year Colonel Hugh Trenchard assumed command of the RFC in France, that a single British squadron was specifically assigned the task of supporting the army by bombing operations. And with nothing better than the Royal Aircraft Factory B.E.2 available, such long-distance raids that could be undertaken fell to the French to launch. The only aircraft that existed in any numbers were Voisin IIIs which could carry a bomb load of 132 lb (60 kg); this archaic single-pusher biplane, of which no fewer than 2,162 were ultimately built in France alone, served on the Western Front as well as in Russia and Italy.

In December 1915 the first purpose-built heavy bomber made its maiden flight in the UK. This design had been ordered by the Admiralty, yet it was not until November of the following year that the first example reached an operational unit. In the meantime, little more than sporadic short-range bombing operations by B.E.2c and R.E.7 aircraft could be carried out by the RFC. The majority of bombs dropped were the 20-lb (9-kg) Hales weapon, but from early in 1916 an increasing number of 112-lb (50.8-kg) bombs became available and, on 30 June, six R.E.7s of No. 21 Squadron each dropped one of the new 336-lb (152.4-kg) RAF heavy-cased bombs over Lille railway station.

NAVAL BOMBERS

Meanwhile, the RNAS's 3rd Wing had assembled under Captain W.L. Elder, RN, with the intention that from bases in the Vosges its 35 Sopwith 1½-Strutters and Short bombers would be able to reach the Saar industrial area. However, demands for aircraft to support ground operations on the Western Front resulted in most RNAS 1½-Strutters being transferred to the RFC, and it was not until October 1916 that the 3rd Wing was strong enough to launch a powerful bombing raid, nine 1½-Strutters and six French Breguet bombers attacking the Mauser factory at Obendorf on 12 October.

It was the RNAS 5th Wing at Dunkirk that received the first Handley Page O/100 heavy bomber in November 1916, followed shortly afterwards by the 3rd Wing, then based at Luxeuil. It was the latter that carried out the first British night raid by a heavy bomber when a single O/100 bombed Moulin-les-Metz railway station on 16/17 March 1917. Four days later the RFC's first squadron (No. 100) formed and trained specifically for night bombing arrived in France, albeit without aircraft.

In October 1917 there was formed the RFC's 41st Wing under Lieutenant Colonel (later Marshal of the RAF Lord) C.L.N. Newall with the expressed purpose of mounting

Above: Designed and developed to make it possible for the RAF to mount attacks on German targets from the UK, the Handley Page V/1500 was the first practical strategic bomber, although too late to see service during WWI.

Over 400 Handley Page O/400 heavy bombers were built during 1917/18. In August 1918, Nos 97, 115 and 215 went to France equipped with O/400s and carried the brunt of the bombing offensive.

a strategic bombing campaign against German industrial targets. It was intended ultimately that this wing would operate independently of the tactical elements of the RFC so as to avoid its strength being squandered by local military commanders. The initial components of this wing were No. 55 Squadron (Airco/de Havilland DH.4 day bombers), No. 100 (Royal Aircraft

Above: Members of the 11th Squadron, American Expeditionary Force, pose by their Airco DH.4s at Maulan, France in 1918. The DH.4 was built in America with the Liberty engine, and by the time of the Armistice 3,227 had been built – 1,885 of which were shipped to France.

Right: One of France's best-known warplanes, the Breguet 14 was built in the A.2 class for reconnaissance, and B.2 class for bombing. It was widely used in the latter role, and was also supplied to the American Expeditionary Force.

RFC bombers

Under the leadership of Major General Trenchard, the RFC, and then the autonomous RAF, built up a powerful bomber arm, and developed the theory and practice of independent strategic bombing as a means of actually winning a war. Trenchard's legacy shaped the inter-war and World War II RAF, and found its natural conclusion in the Bomber Command night offensive of World War II.

Airco DH.4

The Airco DH.4 bomber, known in the RFC as the 'Flaming Coffin' because the fuel tank was located between the two crew members, first went to France with No. 55 Squadron, RFC in March 1917. This Westland-built example is seen in the markings of No. 2 Squadron, RNAS at Bergues in 1918.

Handley Page O/400

At the time that the RAF was formed on 1 April 1918, the RFC's standard day bomber was the O/400, An aircraft from No. 207 Squadron at Ligescourt, France is shown here. This was the first British squadron used solely for long-range night bombing, and the first to operate Handley Page bombers.

Concerns about the effectiveness of night bombing were dispelled by the exploits of the Handley Page O/400 squadrons during 1918. Up to 40 O/400s could be airborne on good nights attacking German targets.

Factory F.E.2b night bombers) and No. 16 (Naval) (O/100 night bombers); in February 1918 the wing was reorganised as VIII Brigade and three months later Nos 99 and 104 Squadrons (both with DH.9s) were added.

During the period between October 1917 and May 1918 this force carried out 142 raids, of which 57 were over German territory and included such cities as Koblenz, Cologne, Mainz, Mannheim and Stuttgart.

With the creation on 1 April 1918 of the Royal Air Force by the amalgamation of RFC and RNAS, the way was clear to extend further the independence of VIII Brigade and, on 6 June, under the command of Major General Sir Hugh (later Marshal of the RAF Lord) Trenchard, was formed the

Structurally similar to its predecessor, the DH.9 used identical mainplanes and tail surfaces. It was not a successful aircraft in its intended role as a long-range bomber and was rapidly replaced by the DH.9A

Independent Force. This comprised Nos 55, 99, 100, 104 and 216 Squadrons (the last-named was previously No. 16 (Naval) Squadron), to which were added in August and September Nos 97, 115 and 215 Squadrons with Handley Page O/400 bombers and No. 110 Squadron with D.H.9a aircraft. No. 100 Squadron also converted to O/400s.

This force continued the bombing task, begun by the 41st Wing, right up to the Armistice. In the last five months of the war it dropped a total of 550 tons of bombs, of which 390 tons were delivered at night. Among the targets were Bonn, Darmstadt, Frankfurt, Kaiserslautern, Karlsruhe, Rombas, Saarburg, Wiesbaden and Zweibrucken, as well as further visits to the cities attacked by the 41st Wing.

That these bombing raids began to have a serious effect on the German morale, already severely strained by civil unrest, was evidenced by a rapid increase in the enemy fighter defences. To counter this it was proposed to add a squadron of Sopwith Camels as escort to the force. Casualties were high, with a total of 109 aircraft lost (of which 69 were the big Handley Pages).

During the last five months of the war the weight of RAF bombs increased dramatically, the most notable being the 1,600-lb (726-kg) (later increased to 1,800-lb/816-kg) bomb capable of being carried by

the O/400. Shortly before the Armistice, deliveries began of a new, much larger bomber, the Handley Page V/1500, capable of lifting the 3,360-lb (1524-kg) bomb, and it was intended that No. 166 Squadron with V/1500s would bomb Berlin. On the day the war ended three of these huge aircraft were bombed-up and ready for take-off from Bircham Newton.

The Short Bomber was produced only as a stop-gap until Handley Page aircraft became available. Basically a Short 184 seaplane conversion, it went into action on 15 November 1916 with the RNAS.

Colonial Operations

1918 – 1939

The UK's Royal Air Force emerged from World War I the most powerful air force in the world, having taken a major part in the air campaigns in the West. Within a couple of years of the Armistice the RAF was faced with a far more sinister fight for survival, as the generals and admirals squabbled to acquire for their own services the slender defence funds allowed by the British Treasury. Sir Eric Geddes, wartime First Lord of the Admiralty and for long an opponent of an autonomous RAF, achieved almost total emasculation of the RAF, reducing its squadrons

Above: Over a five-year period, 435 Bristol Fighters were issued to the overseas squadrons of the RAF, to help maintain law and order in Iraq, Baluchistan and the North-West Frontier of India.

from 188 to 25, and its personnel from 291,000 to 28,300, inclusive of overseas deployment.

It was indeed overseas that Sir Hugh Trenchard saw his opportunity to foster the survival of his service, first during the Chanak Crisis of 1920 in Turkey, when a small force of RAF personnel lent stability in a flashpoint situation, and then in the age-old trouble spots in the Middle East. Ever since the end of

hostilities with the Turks the British Army had waged a costly and exhausting campaign against warring factions in Iraq in efforts to stabilise the area. Trenchard's policy was to concentrate a major part of the surviving RAF in the Middle East (there was only a single fighter squadron left in the UK in 1920) and use his resources sparingly but firmly in a wide-ranging campaign of air policing. For this he deployed the Snipes of No. 1 Squadron, Bristol F.2Bs of No. 6

In 1928 the RAF evacuated over 500 British citizens caught up in a civil war in Afghanistan. Here Lord Irwin inspects No. 70 Squadron at Hinaidi on completion of the evacuation of Kabul on 2 February 1929.

Squadron and D.H.9As of Nos 8, 30 and 55 Squadrons in Iraq, all World War I aircraft but representative of the RAF's equipment until the mid-1920s. Faced initially with little more than inter-tribal strife, the RAF squadrons quickly evolved a pattern of 'benevolent policing',

Above: The Vickers Vimy served from late 1918 until 1931. This example flew with No. 216 Squadron at Heliopolis from June 1922 to January 1926.

Right: At the end of September 1922, No. 25 Squadron was sent to Turkey with Sopwith Snipes for a period, returning in October 1923. Here two Snipes are at a field location at San Stefano during the Chanak crisis in 1923.

seldom firing a gun in anger and more often than not simply staging a demonstration. Frequently, however, the wear of sand and dust caused engine failures far out over the desert, and a burst of Lewis gun from a downed F.2B was sometimes needed to keep inquisitive tribesmen at a respectful distance until help arrived from the nearest British army post. Very soon relative peace reigned in the area, an achievement that had previously cost the army much time and money. The RAF proved itself a

The Vickers Vincent replaced the Wapitis and Fairey IIIFs that had served overseas for so long. This No. 47 Squadron Vincent near Khartoum in 1936 carries a varied array of wing-mounted bombs.

A formation of Fairey Flycatchers of No. 405 Flight from HMS Glorious flies over Malta in the late 1920s. This much-admired fighter served with every aircraft-carrier of the period during its 10 years' service.

highly cost-effective force and gained a fine reputation, on which Trenchard played heavily to acquire new aircraft. The big Vernons of No. 70 Squadron gave excellent service, moving units around the Middle East, and in 1926 these were replaced by Victorias at Hinaidi; two years later they evacuated 500 British nationals caught up in the Afghan civil war. Also in 1928 the old DH.9A began giving place to the Westland Wapiti, a process that continued until 1932.

In Egypt and India the pattern

had been much the same. To provide defence for the Suez Canal a total of eight squadrons served in Egypt during the 1920s, while No. 14 Squadron was based in Palestine until the outbreak of World War II, latterly co-operating with the Palestine Police in maintaining some semblance of peace between Jew and Arab and re-equipping with Fairey Gordons in 1932.

NORTH-WEST FRONTIER

Deployment of the RAF in India was more extensive throughout the inter-war period, most squadrons

serving some time on the North West Frontier; stations such as Risalpur, Peshawar and Kohat became familiar postings for RAF flying personnel. The majority of squadrons in India were on permanent deployment, Nos 5, 20, 28 and 31 taking out Bristol F.2Bs in 1919-20, and keeping them until 1929-30 when they received Wapitis. No.5 continued to fly

1933 saw the widespread adoption of the Hawker Osprey by ships of the Royal Navy. This Mk III is from No. 447 Catapult Flight with the 1st Cruiser Squadron, Mediterranean Fleet.

Desert patrollers

The RAF's light bombers were able to reinforce British control of its more troublesome colonies very cheaply, proving adaptable, versatile, and capable of quickly reacting to any crisis, uprising or

banditry. Rebel villages were occasionally bombed to provide an example, but seldom until the inhabitants had been warned. The use of aircraft proved much more economical than using Army units.

Airco DH.9A
The Royal Air Force in the Middle East was mainly concerned with policing operations and used army co-operation types such as the Bristol Fighter and the Airco DH.9A ('Nine-ack') for this role. Guns were seldom fired in anger, as the RAF was mostly up against tribesmen, and the sight of an aircraft was enough to deter any hostile actions.

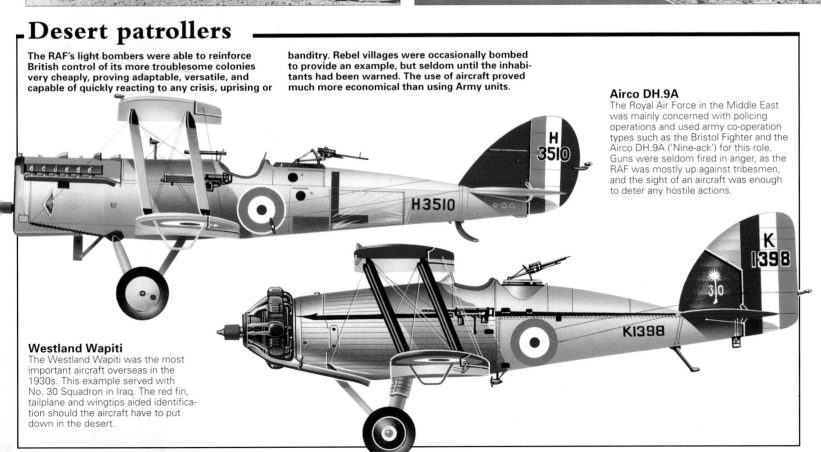

Westland Wapiti
The Westland Wapiti was the most important aircraft overseas in the 1930s. This example served with No. 30 Squadron in Iraq. The red fin, tailplane and wingtips aided identification should the aircraft have to put down in the desert.

Vickers Vimy

The Vickers FB.Mk 27 Vimy bomber arrived in RAF service just too late to see action in World War I. It continued in production, however, and became the standard heavy bomber for the beginning of the 1920s. Several aircraft were sold for civilian use and were used for trail-blazing long-distance flights – across the Atlantic and from England to Australia were just two such feats. Those in RAF service were used mainly in the Middle East, with Nos 45, 58, 70 and 216 Sqns and No. 4 Flying Training School, while Nos 7 and 9 Sqns in the UK together with 'D' Flight of No. 100 Sqn also flew them until re-equipped with Virginias. The aircraft shown, F3184, served in Egypt with No. 70 Squadron.

Dimensions
The Vimy spanned 68 ft 1 in (20.75 m) and had a length of 43 ft 6.5 in (13.27 m). Its height was 15 ft 7.5 in (4.76 m) and its wing area totalled 1,330 sq ft (123.56 m²).

Armament
The Vimy defended itself with two or four 0.303-in (7.7-mm) Lewis Mk III machine-guns (with up to 12 97-round ammunition drums) in nose, dorsal and ventral positions, and carried a normal bombload of up to 2,476 lb (1123 kg).

Performance
Maximum speed of the Vimy Mk IV was 103 mph (166 km/h) at sea level. It could climb to 5,000 ft (1525 m) in 22 minutes and had a service ceiling of 7,000 ft (2135 m). At 81 mph (130 km/h), the Vimy had a range of 910 miles (1464 km).

Powerplant
The Vimy Mk IV was powered by two 360-hp (269-kW) Rolls-Royce Eagle VIII V-12 water-cooled engines.

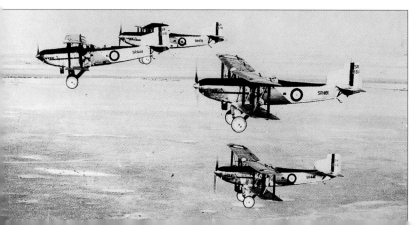

Below: Four Fairey IIIFs of No. 47 Squadron made the 11,000-mile Cairo-Cape-Cairo flight. The aircraft left Heliopolis near Cairo on 30 March 1927, reached Cape Town on 21 April and returned on 22 May.

Right: The Hawker Hardy was produced as a replacement for the Westland Wapitis of No. 30 Squadron engaged in policing duties in Iraq. The first aircraft that went to Iraq joined No. 30 Squadron at Mosul.

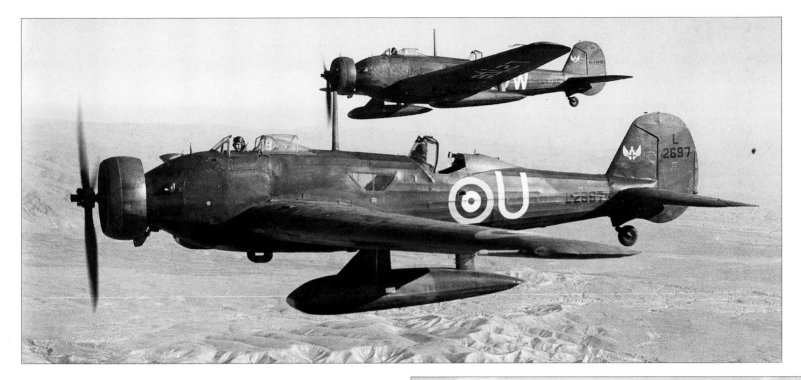

these until the beginning of World War II, but Nos 20 and 28 changed to Audaxes in the mid-1930s, and No. 31 became a transport squadron with Valentias in 1939. No. 60 Squadron was equipped in turn with DH.10s, DH.9As and Wapitis. As the strength of the RAF increased perceptibly during the late 1920s, Nos 11 and 39 Squadrons, both with Wapitis, were sent out to India so that by the mid-1930s there were 13 RAF squadrons serving on the sub-continent.

DEPLOYMENTS

A minor crisis in China threatened the safety of the international settlement at Shanghai and prompted the despatch of No. 2 Squadron with Bristol Fighters from Manston in April of 1927, but it was returned later that year to re-equip with Atlases.

The continued presence of the RAF in Iraq (on aerodromes at Mosul, Baghdad, Hinaidi, and elsewhere) prompted the construction of a single large, centralised base at Habbaniyah in 1934. This became

Entering service in 1937, the single-engined Vickers Wellesley bomber served mainly in the Middle East. These aircraft, flying over an area of Transjordan in 1938, are from No. 14 Squadron.

Right: The RAF in the Middle East was on the alert during the invasion of Abyssinia by Italy in 1935. This Fairey Gordon Mk I of No. 47 (General purpose) Squadron is flying over Kassala in Sudan.

in effect the focal point of the British military presence in the country, not only providing maintenance and training facilities but also becoming the base of No. 30 Squadron equipped with Hardy aircraft, developed specifically for the air policing role.

The last major Imperial deployment of the RAF overseas before World War II was undertaken when the Italian adventure in Abyssinia threatened the security of the sea route through the Red Sea. Accordingly, so as to reinforce the British presence in the Canal Zone and at Aden, Nos 12 (Harts) and 41 (Demons) Squadrons were sent to

Aden, No. 45 (Harts) to Kenya, No. 35 (Gordons) to the Sudan, and Nos 29 (Demons) and 33 (Harts) to Egypt; No. 22 Squadron with Vildebeests was based on Malta to cover any hostile movement by the Italian fleet. The following year, with the subjugation of Abyssinia, the crisis passed and these squadrons returned home where preparations for possible world war were now under way.

Left: Fairey IIIF Mk IVMs of No. 47 Squadron moored on the Nile at Khartoum. The IIIFs were operated on floats for three months of the year. Note the original squadron badge on the tail fin.

Above: No. 33 at RAF Eastchurch became the first Hawker Hart day bomber squadron in February 1930. A wing of Hart squadrons was sent to reinforce the RAF in the Middle East after Italy invaded Abbysinia.

American Flashpoints

1922 – 1935

Aviation had come early to South America. One of the early pioneers of flight was the Brazilian Alberto Santos-Dumont, who had contributed so much to European flying in the first decade of the 20th century. Military air forces had, before World War I, been created in Argentina, Brazil, Chile and Peru, to which Uruguay was added in 1916. It was not long before the age-old abrasive politics arising from contentious border demarcation, arbitrary ethnic divisions and external industrial exploitation involved the Central and South American states in self-imposed strife, though relatively few of the coups and revolutions were staged by more than a few troops. Military aircraft were scarcely in

Above: Upon the outbreak of war in Leticia, the Colombian air force was ordered to purchase a single warplane. This Curtiss Falcon, 'Ricaurte', transported Benjamin Mendez Rey on a sensational flight from New York to Bogota in 1928.

Below: The Breda Ba 44 was a six-passenger cabin biplane powered by two 200-hp de Havilland Gipsy engines, and a small number were acquired by the Paraguayan air force from Italy in 1934 for use as transport aircraft.

Above: A Curtiss Wright Osprey general-purpose biplane, of which Bolivia received 20. With the aircraft is General R. Martinez Pitar of the Commission de Neutrality at Villa Montes in June 1935.

evidence during the continuous internal strife that existed in Mexico between 1922 and 1926, or during the bloodless coup in Guatemala of 1924, or the Cuban revolution of 1930.

In 1932, however, conflict between Peru and its neighbour, Colombia, broke out when the border territory of Leticia (previously awarded to Colombia in a

1922 treaty) became a source of disputed sovereignty. Peruvian forces entered Leticia in 1932 and ejected Colombian officials, installing their own provincial administration. Colombia at that time possessed a small air force comprising a handful of Curtiss Hawk biplane fighters, Curtiss O-1 Falcon reconnaissance biplanes and a small number of other American and European air-

craft. Peru, on the other hand, had been strengthening its air force, the Cuerpo de Aeronautica del Peru (CAP), since 1929, and already possessed Curtiss Hawk and Nieuport 121 fighters, Vought 02U-1E Corsair observation aircraft, Douglas M-4 bombers and Boeing 40B-4 transports; orders had also been placed in the UK for Fairey Fox II bombers and some Fairey Gordon general-purpose aircraft.

Flying proficiency was generally lacking on both sides, though there were a number of incidents involving air combat. While the Colombian air force was handicapped by the lack of established aerodromes within 200 miles (320 km) of the disputed border territory, the CAP contrived to use its fighters and observation aircraft in support of the ground forces to some effect; its bombers, being sea-

One of the two Dornier C29s of the Colombian air force. This particular aircraft is believed to be the one flown by Von Karl Maringer.

planes and based on the coast some 600 miles (960 km) from the war zone, were not used. When in April 1933 the Peruvian president Luis Sanchez Cerro was murdered, Peru became more conciliatory and hostilities died down; a year later Leticia was formally returned to Colombia.

While the Peruvian-Colombian conflict was at its height a major war was raging between Bolivia and Paraguay. Both nations had for many years been disputing sovereignty of the Chaco Boreal, a dispute fuelled by the belief by foreign interests that large oil deposits lay undeveloped in the territory. In 1928 Paraguayan forces had seized a Bolivian fort, and immediately a series of isolated but bloody clashes followed. A truce had been negotiated by the Pan American Conference and League of Nations, but this failed to hold and in 1932 all-out warfare between the two states erupted.

MERCENARIES

The small Paraguayan air force possessed a number of Italian Fiat CR.30 biplane fighters, Bergamaschi AP.1 monoplane fighters, Caproni Ca 101 three-engine bombers and Breda Ba 44 transports, while the larger Bolivian Cuerpo de Aviacion flew about 60 Curtiss Wright Osprey general-purpose aircraft, Curtiss Hawk IA fighters and Junkers W.34s converted as bombers. From 1933 onwards both sides made considerable use of their air forces. A high proportion of the aircrews were foreign mercenaries although, with the assistance of an Italian military aviation mission, the standard of training among Paraguayan flying personnel quickly improved. Numerous air combats took place, particularly when both sides began flying bombing raids, and it has been suggested that each air force lost about 30 aircraft. Best known pilot of the war was undoubtedly Major Rafael Pavon

War over the Chaco Boreal

From 1932 Paraguay and Bolivia were at war over the sovereignty of the undeveloped territory of the Chaco Boreal, believed to include significant oil and mineral deposits. The war raged until 1935, and some 88,000 men lost their lives.

The fighting on the ground was accompanied by fierce fighting in the air, with intensive bombing raids and sporadic fighter engagements accounting for some 60 aircraft losses.

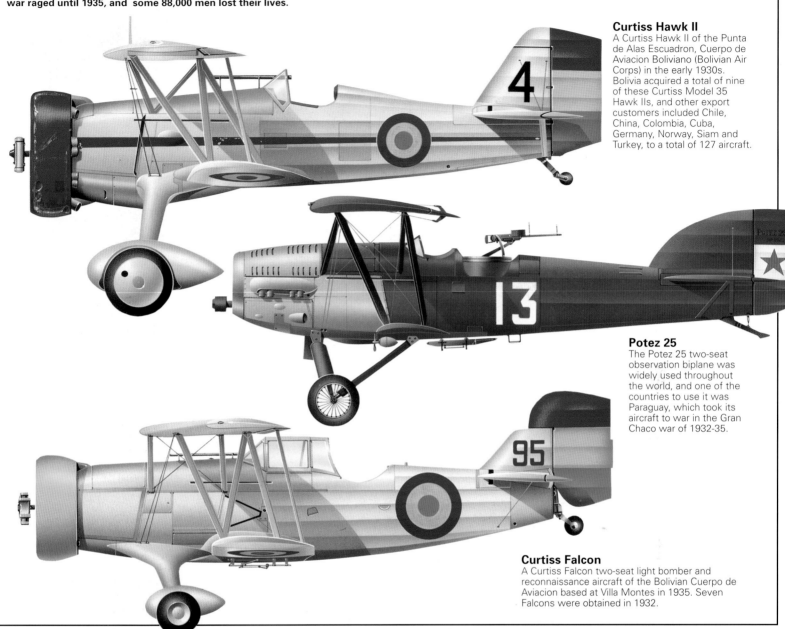

Curtiss Hawk II
A Curtiss Hawk II of the Punta de Alas Escuadron, Cuerpo de Aviacion Boliviano (Bolivian Air Corps) in the early 1930s. Bolivia acquired a total of nine of these Curtiss Model 35 Hawk IIs, and other export customers included Chile, China, Colombia, Cuba, Germany, Norway, Siam and Turkey, to a total of 127 aircraft.

Potez 25
The Potez 25 two-seat observation biplane was widely used throughout the world, and one of the countries to use it was Paraguay, which took its aircraft to war in the Gran Chaco war of 1932-35.

Curtiss Falcon
A Curtiss Falcon two-seat light bomber and reconnaissance aircraft of the Bolivian Cuerpo de Aviacion based at Villa Montes in 1935. Seven Falcons were obtained in 1932.

Left: During the conflict there was a sudden need to acquire further Curtiss Falcons that could serve as light bombers and reconnaissance aircraft. These new Falcons for export had better engines and a different fuselage.

Below: A Curtiss Triplane Type 18T, powered by a 400-hp Curtiss 12-cylinder water-cooled Vee engine with a maximum speed of 163 mph. Designed for the US Navy, one was imported into Bolivia in 1919, and was known as the Wasp.

who, in Curtiss Hawks, was credited with three combat victories and came to be dubbed the Bolivian 'ace of aces'.

A further truce was arranged in 1935 and the Chaco Treaty was signed at Buenos Aires dividing the Chaco Boreal between the two belligerents, Paraguay gaining by far the greater area. Both sides had suffered heavy casualties (Paraguay 36,000 men and Bolivia 52,000), and both were rendered economically exhausted by the Chaco War which achieved precious little, as the oil interests that had led to such bitter jealousies were not to be realised for many years to come.

The Nomonhan Incident

MAY – SEPTEMBER 1939

A formation of Nakajima Ki-27s on patrol. This type held air superiority for the Japanese throughout the conflict, largely on account of the superior training of the Japanese pilots, many of whom had previously fought Polikarpov aircraft over China.

Fought over the remote steppelands of Mongolia, the conflict now usually known as the Nomonhan Incident occupied 129 days just as World War II was breaking out in Europe in 1939. Despite the involvement of tens of thousands of troops and hundreds of aircraft, the incident is scarcely recorded in the history books of the West. Moreover, like the Spanish Civil War, it provided practical experience for combatant nations that were to be involved in World War II.

At a point where the Khalkha river formed the border between the Soviet-Mongolian province of Doronod and Japanese-administered Manchukuo, a band of nomadic tribesmen strayed into Soviet territory on 10 May 1939 and were pursued back by Mongolian border guards. *Ad hoc*

The Mitsubishi A5M was the forerunner of the 'Zeke'. The model shown here has an enclosed cockpit but was succeeded by an open cockpit version, which in turn gave place to the A5M4 (known to the Allies as 'Claude'). It featured a fixed spatted undercarriage.

Japanese air reconnaissance disclosed an unexpected build-up of military forces on the west bank of the Khalkha river and, smarting from previous humiliations by the Soviet Union, the Kanto-gun (the Japanese defence command in China) forthwith created a local detachment comprising about 50 aircraft in the area, with its headquarters at Hailar, some 100 miles (160 km) behind the border; the majority of these aircraft were Type 97 (Nakajima Ki-27) fighters.

AIR BATTLES

The Soviet forces comprised a cavalry division, a rifle corps and an armoured brigade, supported by three air regiments, also of about 50 aircraft, of which about 40 were Polikarpov I-15 biplane and Polikarpov I-16 monoplane fighters. Following the shooting down

The Mitsubishi Ki-30 Army Type 97 Light Bomber was introduced into active service in China in 1938. The Ki-30 was the first Japanese light bomber to possess such modern features as an internal bomb-bay and a variable-pitch propeller.

of a V-VS reconnaissance aircraft by the Japanese, a number of isolated air combats took place during May, in which the Type 97 fighters confirmed their superiority by shooting down a score of Soviet aircraft without loss to themselves.

The Soviets replied by sending a further fighter regiment of I-16s to the war zone, and at the same time established a group of airfields (little more than strips cleared on the steppeland) around the township of Tamsag Bulag. On 22 June the V-VS staged a number of sweeps and raids on the Japanese ground positions lining the Khalkha river, and fierce air battles developed. The Soviet attacks stung the Kanto-gun into retaliation, and on 27 June 30 Japanese bombers with an escort of 74 fighters twice raided the V-VS airfields around Tamsag Bulag.

Opposing fighters

Air battles over the battlefront provided invaluable combat experience for the participants. While the Japanese returned to their units to pass on the lessons they had learned, many of the Russians fell victim to Stalin's purges. Both air staffs learned valuable lessons. The Japanese continued development of new fighters, which were ever more agile, and also continued the development of close support tactics, using air power to support ground forces. The Russians realised that the era of the biplane fighter was over, and pressed on with monoplane fighters.

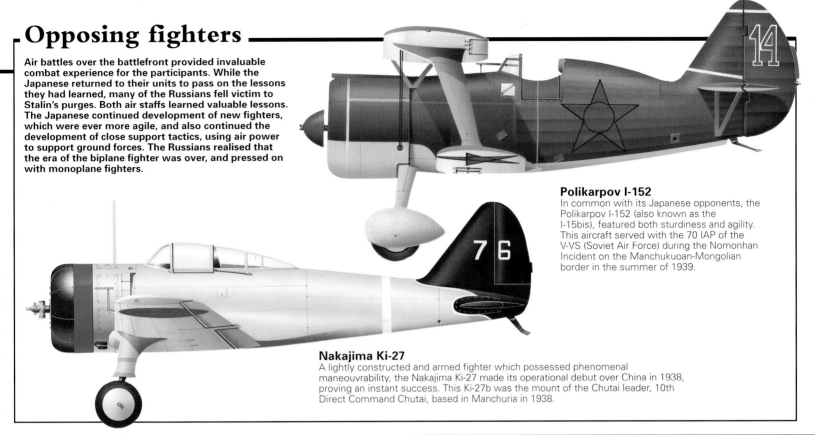

Polikarpov I-152
In common with its Japanese opponents, the Polikarpov I-152 (also known as the I-15bis), featured both sturdiness and agility. This aircraft served with the 70 IAP of the V-VS (Soviet Air Force) during the Nomonhan Incident on the Manchukuoan-Mongolian border in the summer of 1939.

Nakajima Ki-27
A lightly constructed and armed fighter which possessed phenomenal maneouvrability, the Nakajima Ki-27 made its operational debut over China in 1938, proving an instant success. This Ki-27b was the mount of the Chutai leader, 10th Direct Command Chutai, based in Manchuria in 1938.

On 2 July two Japanese divisions attacked across the Khalkha and came under heavy air attack by up to 60 Tupolev SB-2 bombers. Air combats between the opposing air forces were now frequently involving up to 100 fighters on each side, but still the Japanese proved superior, their fighters taking heavy toll of the I-15 biplane fighters opposing them. At the end of July the V-VS introduced 20-mm cannon-armed I-16 Type 17 monoplane fighters, and these to a large extent redressed the balance.

As Japanese losses in the air began to mount during August (particularly among their more experienced pilots), the Soviets, now commanded by Komkor Georgi Zhukov, mounted a large-scale attack by 100,000 troops and 800 tanks across the Khalkha, aiming to trap the Japanese forces in a giant pincer movement. Supporting this offensive were more than 500 aircraft, including a

The Polikarpov I-16 was the main fighter employed by the Soviets over Nomonhan, and the best. It was a good match performance-wise for the Nakajima Ki-27 (Type 97) but its pilots were not as well trained as the Japanese.

half regiment of Tupolev TB-3 four-engined heavy bombers which began night raids on Japanese supply lines in the rear. Through sheer tenacity and skill the Japanese managed to cling to a slender air superiority, although the SB-2s and TB-3s started making raids from 19,685 ft (6000 m) which gave them some immunity. When the Soviet fighters began strafing attacks on the forward Japanese airfields, losses among the Type 97 fighters increased rapidly.

HEAVY LOSSES

Just as it seemed that the Soviet forces were poised to destroy the two Japanese divisions on the eastern side of the Khalkha, the first heavy snow of the winter began falling on 11 September, effectively halting all activity on the ground. Air combat continued until 16 September, when peace negotiations between Tokyo and Moscow brought the conflict to an end.

The small war had been extraordinarily vicious, involving 120,000 Soviets and 80,000 Japanese on the ground, while each side lost upwards of 200 aircraft. The fighting had demonstrated unequivocally to the Soviets that the age of the

Above: The Tupolev SB-2bis was the bomber version produced during 1938. It had a crew of three and had a maximum speed of 450 km/h. Armament consisted of four machine-guns, and normal bombload was 600-kg. Some 60 were in service during this period.

Below: Japan acquired a number of Fiat BR.20 Cicognas from Italy and used them along the Manchurian border on bombing raids. The BR.20s also fought with the Nationalist forces in the Spanish Civil War.

biplane fighter was at an end (although the I-15 continued in service for almost two more years), and it also confirmed the SB-2 as an efficient light bomber by the standards of the day. The Japanese could take comfort in the excellence of their pilots, while the Type 97 fighter had continued to dominate the skies in the absence of really modern fighters.

The real lesson was missed. Foreign correspondents and

observers were forbidden access to the war front, with the result that Western staffs remained blissfully ignorant of the high standard of training and equipment in the Imperial Japanese Army Air Force. This standard was to enjoy further progressive improvement, so that when the Pacific war broke out two years later the Japanese proved immeasurably superior to the Allied forces ranged against them.

Spanish Civil War JULY 1936 – MARCH 1939

Left: By far the most capable fighter in the Spanish Civil War was the Messerschmitt Bf 109. Most were Jumo-powered Bf 109Bs, Cs and Ds, although a few DB 601-powered Bf 109Es arrived at the end.

Below: The Dornier Do 17 was one of the modern types evaluated in combat by the Legion Condor. The Do 17E-1 bomber served with 2.K/88 while the Do 17F-1 camera-carrying reconnaissance platform flew with 1.A/88. Both proved able to evade Republican fighters with some ease.

Years of international antagonism between extremist socialism and fascism throughout continental Europe sparked into bloody civil war in Spain on 18 July 1936, when right-wing army officers rose against an ineffective and corrupt socialist administration. The government (Republican) air force was poorly equipped with a hotch-potch of obsolete Nieuport-Delage NiD.52 fighters, Breguet 19 reconnaissance bombers, some Vickers Vildebeest torpedo-bombers and a handful of other old foreign aircraft.

Sensing that the Nationalist forces were even more badly equipped, Nazi Germany quickly assembled a force of modern aircraft and volunteers for support of General Francisco Franco, and within a week the first Junkers Ju 52/3m bomber-transports were on their way to Morocco to airlift large numbers of troops from Africa to bolster the Nationalists. Some of the

Nationalist fighters

The Spanish Civil War provided Luftwaffe and Italian fighter pilots with invaluable combat experience. Initially they flew biplane fighters against Russian-flown Polikarpov I-15s operating in support of the Republican cause. Later, monoplane fighters were introduced, combatting Republican Polikarpov I-16s.

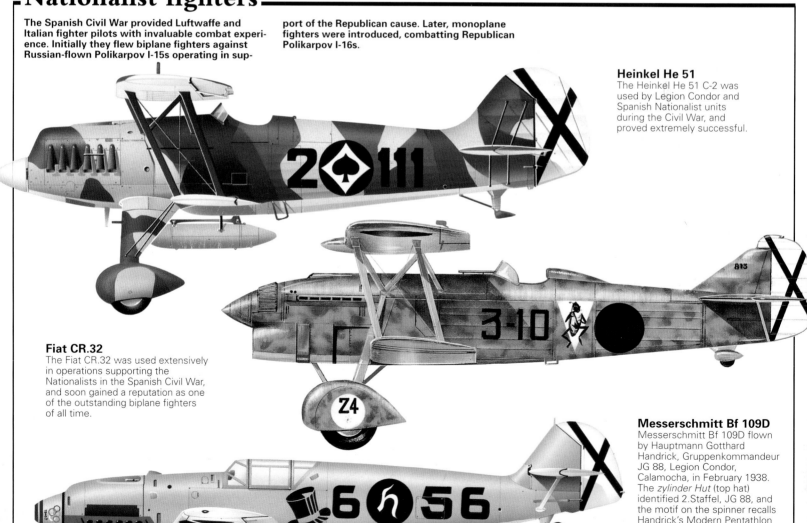

Heinkel He 51
The Heinkel He 51 C-2 was used by Legion Condor and Spanish Nationalist units during the Civil War, and proved extremely successful.

Fiat CR.32
The Fiat CR.32 was used extensively in operations supporting the Nationalists in the Spanish Civil War, and soon gained a reputation as one of the outstanding biplane fighters of all time.

Messerschmitt Bf 109D
Messerschmitt Bf 109D flown by Hauptmann Gotthard Handrick, Gruppenkommandeur JG 88, Legion Condor, Calamocha, in February 1938. The *zylinder Hut* (top hat) identified 2.Staffel, JG 88, and the motif on the spinner recalls Handrick's Modern Pentathlon Gold Medal at the 1936 Olympic Games in Berlin.

Fighters for the Republic

Republican air forces inherited aircraft from the pre-Civil War air force, and augmented these with aircraft supplied (and often manned) by the USSR. The Republicans also took into service aircraft captured from the Nationalists. The Republican pilots were from a similarly diverse range of backgrounds, and included International Brigade volunteers, front-line Soviet pilots and loyal Spaniards.

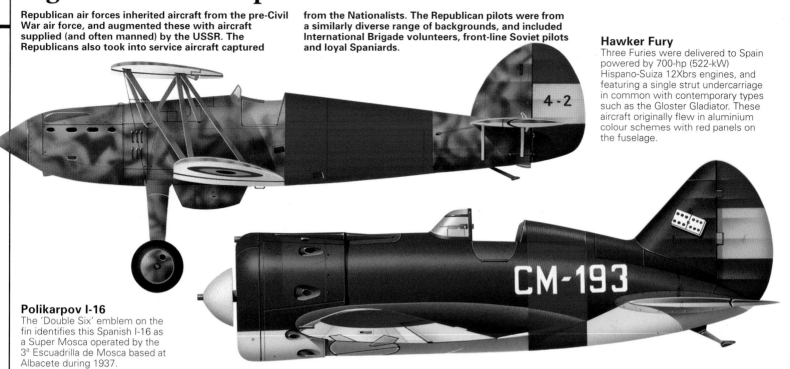

Hawker Fury
Three Furies were delivered to Spain powered by 700-hp (522-kW) Hispano-Suiza 12Xbrs engines, and featuring a single strut undercarriage in common with contemporary types such as the Gloster Gladiator. These aircraft originally flew in aluminium colour schemes with red panels on the fuselage.

Polikarpov I-16
The 'Double Six' emblem on the fin identifies this Spanish I-16 as a Super Mosca operated by the 3ª Escuadrilla de Mosca based at Albacete during 1937.

Left: A dozen Savoia-Marchetti S.M.81 bombers, together with a similar number of Fiat CR.32 fighters from Fascist Italy, took part in the Civil War. As in the early Heinkel He 111s, the S.M.81 carried its bombs vertically stowed, resulting in an untidy trajectory which did not help the aiming accuracy.

Below: One of the first of the new types to see operational service with Legion Condor was the Heinkel He 111B-1, in action with 3./K 88 (3rd Staffel of Kampfgruppe 88). They carried a variety of individual markings including this Scottie dog on the fin of one aircraft.

NiD.52 pilots had also joined the Nationalists and one of these, Teniente Miguel Guerro Garcia, shot down half a dozen Republican aircraft in the first fortnight of the war. In August the nationalist air force quickly gained strength with six Heinkel He 51 fighters and further Ju 52/3m bomber transports from Germany, and a dozen Savoia-Marchetti S.81s and a similar number of Fiat CR.32s from Fascist Italy. The S.81s went into action on 5 August, bombing a Republican warship; soon after, their initial trooping completed, the Ju 52/3m aircraft started bombing raids in support of Franco's northward advance.

The Republicans had also appealed for foreign assistance, and during August about 60 French aircraft (Dewoitine D.371s, D.372s, D.501s and D.510s, Potez 54s, Loire–Nieuport LN.46s and Blériot-Spad S.510s) arrived.

By the end of the year the flow of foreign aircraft to both sides was well established, the German con-

In the autumn of 1936, Polikarpov I-16 Type 5 fighters were delivered to the Spanish government at the start of the Civil War. A total of 278 were delivered, including this Type 10, known as the 'Super Rata'.

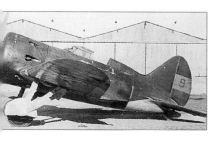

Below: A crashed Nieuport-Delage NiD.52 C1 of the Republican Forces. A French-designed aircraft, 91 were licence-built by Hispano Aviation at Guadalajana. At the outbreak of the war, six squadrons were still equipped with NiD.52 C1s and these were flown by both Republican and Nationalist pilots.

tingent having been organised into the Legion Condor, under General Hugo Sperrle, with Ju 52/3ms, He 51s, He 45s, He 46s, He 59s, He 70s and Henschel Hs 123s. The Italians, now formed into an autonomous Aviazione Legionaria, had added Meridionali Ro 37bis reconnaissance bombers to further CR.32s and S.M.81s. The Soviet Union, demanding full payment in gold, had supplied the first of a large number of Polikarpov I-15 biplane and I-16 monoplane fighters and some Tupolev SB-2 twin-engined bombers.

ENTER THE Bf 109

Most of these aircraft were deployed on the Madrid front in October where the Nationalists threatened the capital. It was the superiority of the I-15 and I-16 fighters that frustrated Nationalist air operations around Madrid, and it was the failure by such aircraft as the He 51 and CR.32 to secure air superiority that prompted the despatch of 45 Messerschmitt Bf 109B monoplane fighters early in 1937, as well as 30 Heinkel He 111B and 15 Dornier Do 17F bombers, from Germany.

Stalemate around Madrid in 1937 was followed by a Nationalist offensive in the north. Many of the He 51s and CR 32s were handed over to the Spaniards upon the arrival of the Bf 109Bs, and delivery of the new SM.79 allowed the more vulnerable Ju 52/3m aircraft to confine their operations to night bombing, while a shipload of Czech Aero

A.101 bombers, intended for the Republicans, was captured and put into service with Franco's forces. It was during the Nationalist drive in the north that an air attack on the small fortified town of Guernica was seized on by the socialist propagandists to point to the supposedly indiscriminate bombing by the fascists, yet neither side was innocent of such lapses.

Three main Republican counter-offensives in 1937 gained only limited success and did not succeed in diverting Nationalist air strength from the northern front, which crumbled in August. However, licence-production of the excellent I-16 fighter had contributed to a numerical superiority in Republican aircraft during the summer and led to yet further acceleration of German aircraft deliveries to the Legion Condor, including Junkers Ju 87 dive bombers and further Bf 109s, and Fiat BR.20 bombers to the Aviazione Legionaria.

During the spring of 1938, heartened by their victory in the north, the Nationalists succeeded in reaching the Mediterranean coast between Barcelona and Valencia, thereby cutting Republican-held

MAIN OFFENSIVES

Santander
Bilbao
Guernica
Victoria
Nationalist Offensive March-June 1937
Leon
Santiago
FRANCE
Logrono
Zaragossa
Republican Offensive July 1938
Barcelona (falls to Nationalists 25th January 1939)
PORTUGAL
Republican Offensive penetrates Nationalists Front, May1937
Salamanca
Madrid falls to Nationalists, 27th March 1939
Madrid
Getafe
MAJORCA
Toledo
Nationalists reach coast, April 1938
Italian raids by S.79 bombers
Republican Offensives, July 1938
Nationalist Checked, October1936
Nationalist Offence, February 1937
Valencia
Merida
IBIZA
Badajoz
NATIONALIST SWEEP AUGUST 1936
Cordoba
Murcia
Seville
NATIONALIST SWEEP AUGUST 1936
Principal airfields
Granada
MEDITERRANEAN SEA
Jerez
Malaga
Rota

This map of Spain during the Civil War shows the key offensive moves of both Nationalist and Republican forces from July 1936 to March 1939. The Nationalists cut through from south to north, enabling east and west points to be taken.

Airlift of Nationalist forces

Tetuan

territory in two. That April the first Bf 109Cs replaced the last of the German-flown He 51s and, led by the great German pilot Werner Mölders, succeeded at last in mastering the I-16. As the Republican forces desperately fought to avoid defeat, the majority of Soviet volunteer pilots melted away and returned home. All the while, the Nationalist air force grew in strength, taking over German equipment as newer aircraft arrived in the country. On the central front in particular the Legion Condor proved almost invincible, and in November Franco crossed the Ebro and soon after was driving toward

Below: Three modified DH.89Ms were delivered to the Spanish government in December 1935 for police duties in Morocco. When the Civil War began they were formed into Grupo 40 and operated on the Nationalist side.

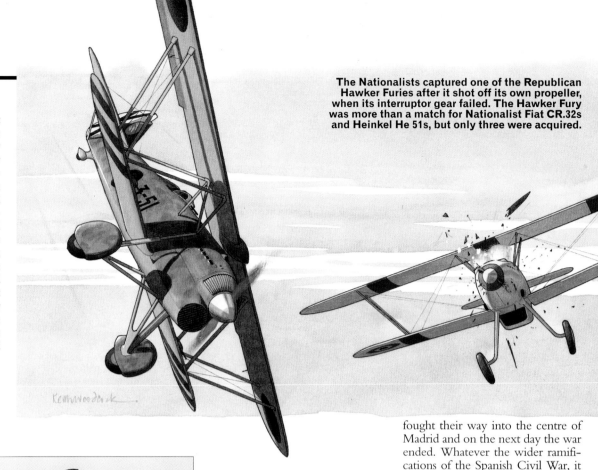

The Nationalists captured one of the Republican Hawker Furies after it shot off its own propeller, when its interruptor gear failed. The Hawker Fury was more than a match for Nationalist Fiat CR.32s and Heinkel He 51s, but only three were acquired.

Barcelona. Early in 1939 the Germans introduced the first cannon-armed Bf 109Es and the Italians delivered a few Fiat G.50s, and these (together with the earlier Bf 109Bs and Bf 109Cs) effectively dominated the air, Mölders himself becoming the highest-scoring German with 14 victories.

On 27 March the Nationalists fought their way into the centre of Madrid and on the next day the war ended. Whatever the wider ramifications of the Spanish Civil War, it had proved the ideal testing ground for the infant German Luftwaffe, conceived as it was as an aerial support arm for the German army, and the success of close-support aircraft was classically demonstrated. German propagandists were quick to point to the devastating power of the dreaded Ju 87 dive-bomber, soon to terrorise half of Europe.

Bombers at War

Both sides made extensive use of bombers during the Spanish Civil War, ushering in a terrible new era of air warfare. If the much-hyped attack on Guernica was created as much by propaganda and deliberate demolition by the Republicans as by the Nationalist's bombers, there were plenty of less well-known examples of the awesome destructive potential of the modern bomber.

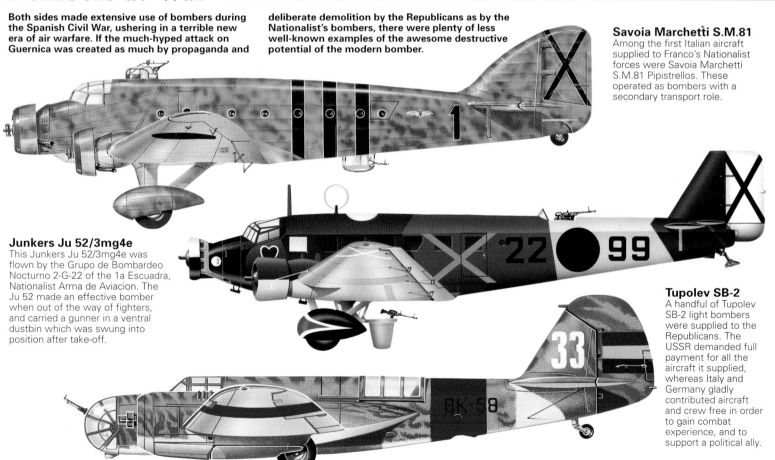

Savoia Marchetti S.M.81
Among the first Italian aircraft supplied to Franco's Nationalist forces were Savoia Marchetti S.M.81 Pipistrellos. These operated as bombers with a secondary transport role.

Junkers Ju 52/3mg4e
This Junkers Ju 52/3mg4e was flown by the Grupo de Bombardeo Nocturno 2-G-22 of the 1a Escuadra, Nationalist Arma de Aviacion. The Ju 52 made an effective bomber when out of the way of fighters, and carried a gunner in a ventral dustbin which was swung into position after take-off.

Tupolev SB-2
A handful of Tupolev SB-2 light bombers were supplied to the Republicans. The USSR demanded full payment for all the aircraft it supplied, whereas Italy and Germany gladly contributed aircraft and crew free in order to gain combat experience, and to support a political ally.

WORLD WAR II IN EUROPE

The Blitzkrieg on Poland opened on 1 September 1939 with raids by fleets of Ju 87 dive-bombers and He 111 and Do 17 medium bombers. They smashed the essential war factories, airfields and vital lines of communications. The flames of Warsaw and the whine of the Stukas were to be the harbingers of a hell that was to last for nearly six years. World War II had begun.

A Junkers Ju 87B Stuka in a classic pose, with its load of one 250-kg (551-lb) SC250 and four 50-kg (110-lb) SC50 bombs dropping away, just before the aircraft pulls out of its steep dive. The terrifying wail of the 'Jericho trumpet' sirens, mounted at the top of their main undercarriage legs, was to become a trademark of the Blitzkrieg.

On 1 September 1939, Poland's capital, Warsaw, was heavily bombed by Luftwaffe Heinkel He 111s. Their principal target was the PZL aircraft factory, but as this photograph shows, a considerable amount of damage was inflicted on civilian property.

Blitzkrieg on Poland

SEPTEMBER 1939

At 04.15 on 1 September 1939, World War II shattered an uneasy European peace as the German 3rd, 4th, 8th, 10th and 14th Armies burst across Poland's western frontiers as the components of two army groups embarking on a huge pincer movement designed to close successively at Kutna, Warsaw and Brest Litovsk, thereby encircling the ill-prepared Polish armies under General Smigly-Rydz. From the first moments of the crushing attack, the young Luftwaffe hurled some 2,000 modern aircraft into the battle with scant worry from the opposing Lotnictwo Wojskowe (Polish air force), which was quickly seen to be not only poorly equipped but badly organised and deployed; the Poles could field fewer than 200 obsolete PZL P.7 and P.11 fighters and a similar number of light bombers.

Over the battlefields themselves roared nine Gruppen of Junkers Ju 87 dive-bombers (some 366 aircraft), spearheading and supporting the devastating Blitzkrieg tactic whose theory had been proved in the Spanish Civil War. As aircraft and armour blasted its way through the Polish defences, the German bomber force ranged far afield against vital lines of communication, against the Polish war factories and against airfields in the rear. Three Kampfgeschwader of Heinkel He 111 heavy bombers (about 300 aircraft) and four of Dornier Do 17s (400 aircraft) were active on the first

Left: Polish air force PZL P.37 Los bombers of the 1st Air Regiment based near Warsaw. Many were lost in September 1939 as they attacked the German troops and armour without any effective fighter escorts.

Above: Henschel Hs 123As carrying four 50-kg (110-lb) SC50 bombs on racks under their wings. These retain the sling under the fuselage for a single 250-kg (551-lb) SC250 bomb.

day: 60 He 111s of I and III/KG 4 bombed Krakow airfield as 30 similar aircraft of II/KG 4 dropped 22 tons of bombs on Lemburg airfield, destroying six Polish fighters on the ground. The Putzig/Rahmel naval base was heavily hit from the air by I/KG 1, and the all-important PZL fighter factory was badly damaged in

a raid by II/LG 1 on Warsaw/Okecie airport.

The main fault in the Polish air force deployment lay in the rigid affiliation of fighter and bomber squadrons, bound tightly into autonomous regiments, to specific armies themselves regionally deployed. There was thus no

Opposing fighters

The greatly superior Messerschmitt Bf 109E 'Emil' equipped the Jagdverband in September 1939. It was faster, more manoeuvrable, had better armament and was generally more versatile than the best the Polish air force had available.

PZL's P.11 first flown in 1931, was powered by a Bristol Mercury VI engine, giving it a top speed of 390 km/h (243 mph) compared to the Bf 109E's 578 km/h (359 mph). Most P.11s only had two 7.7-mm machine-guns; a few had four guns.

Messerschmitt Bf 109E
The Luftwaffe had 850 Bf 109E-1 fighters and Bf 109E-1B fighter-bombers equipping 12 Gruppen on the eve of the invasion of Poland. This 'Emil' is painted in the 1939 markings of III/Jagdgeschwader 27, with dark-green upper surfaces and light-blue/grey undersides. Five of the Gruppen of Bf 109Es with 200 aircraft, actually took part in the invasion, of which 67 were lost, mainly to Polish ground fire.

PZL P.11c
The Polish air force received 175 examples of the all-metal P.11c fighter in 1935/36. These equipped 12 squadrons when the German army invaded Poland in 1939. They faced overwhelming odds, but still managed to claim 126 Luftwaffe aircraft in early air battles. This P.11c carries the markings of 121 Eskadra, 111 Dyon of the 2nd Air Regiment, based at Krakow.

Left: The Luftwaffe had 400 He 111Hs in September 1939. Heinkels of KG 2, KG 4, KG 26, KG 27 and II/LG 1 were in daily action. At first, raids went far beyond the front line, but as the Poles fell back towards Warsaw, bombing concentrated on the beleaguered capital.

Above: A triumphant Messerschmitt Bf 110 crew is seen during the short Polish campaign. Having learned at an early stage not to engage the nimble PZL P.11 fighters in close-in combat, the Bf 110s were highly successful when using dive and climb tactics. Most of the missions were flown as top cover for He 111 bombers.

flexibility in air defence, more than half the air force being withheld from battle until imminently threatened by the German advance. The Poles' trouble was that the Luftwaffe recognised no such parochial niceties and was frequently free to attack its targets with scarcely any opposition. Quickly realising the fatal flaw in their organisation, some of the Polish fighter squadrons abandoned their assigned bases and sought to attack the German bomber formations wherever they were reported.

Unfortunately the aged P.7 and P.11 fighters on which Poland's air defence rested almost exclusively, were no match for the German Messerschmitt Bf 109Es, whose

pilots were given free rein to hunt the Polish skies. Nevertheless, there were numerous instances of reckless courage by the defending pilots who, with scant heed of appalling odds, waded into the big German formations.

POLAND CRUSHED

By the end of the third day the Luftwaffe had a total of 55 aircraft destroyed, 71 aircrew killed, 39 wounded and 94 missing. Polish casualties, on the other hand, had reached the loss of 46 fighters and about 60 light bombers; roughly a quarter of the entire air force in just three days. The light bomber force (the only arm of the Polish air force to be tightly reined within its

regional deployment) had carried out several setpiece raids against German armour assembly areas with some success, but with crippling losses to flak and fighters. In one memorable attack by 28 P.23 light bombers in the Radomski–Piotrków area more than half the aircraft failed to return.

After 10 days the invading armies had virtually isolated a dozen Polish divisions in the Kutno area, and the Poles attempted to mount a concerted counter-attack against the German forces, now nearing Warsaw itself. This proved to be the last fully sustained resistance by the

Polish army in the field, now desperately handicapped by the surging masses of civilian refugees seeking escape from the ravaged towns and villages. No more than about 100 Polish fighters and bombers remained airworthy, and these were flown into battle piecemeal, their pilots seldom briefed as to the strength or presence of the enemy's air force. By 13 September German aircraft losses had risen to 150 aircraft destroyed, but as the German army closed its ring of steel around the capital, resistance by the Polish air force dwindled to nothing. Those pilots who could, made good

Below: Eleven Polish air force squadrons operated PZL P.23b Karas tactical bombers in 1939. They suffered heavy losses. The remains of this crashed example are being examined by the crew of a Luftwaffe Fieseler Fi 156C Storch.

Right: The Luftwaffe's Ju 87 Stuka received a formidable reputation in the Blitzkrieg. This was on the basis of its tactical rather than general bombing success. Here armourers are priming 250-kg (551-lb) bombs before another attack.

Tactical bombers

A total of 210 three-seat PZL P.23b army support bombers were built for the Polish air force, equipping 11 squadrons. By September 1939 the slow, inadequately-armed aircraft was nearing obsolescence and was an easy target for German gunners.

Specifically designed as a 'Sturzkampfflugzeug' (dive-bomber) the Junkers Ju 87 was very successful against Polish forces, destroying all but two of the Polish surface warships and virtually wiping out an entire infantry division at Piotrków station.

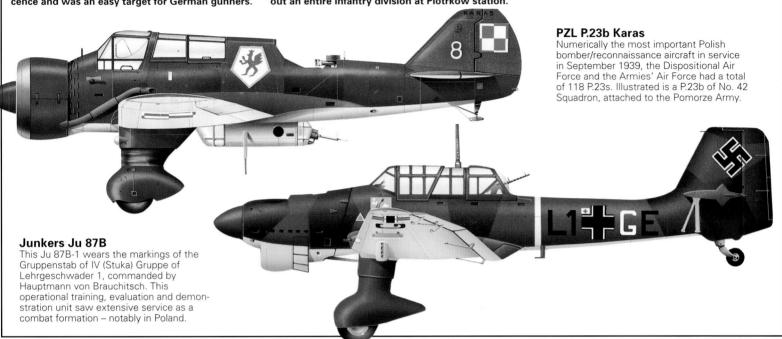

PZL P.23b Karas
Numerically the most important Polish bomber/reconnaissance aircraft in service in September 1939, the Dispositional Air Force and the Armies' Air Force had a total of 118 P.23s. Illustrated is a P.23b of No. 42 Squadron, attached to the Pomorze Army.

Junkers Ju 87B
This Ju 87B-1 wears the markings of the Gruppenstab of IV (Stuka) Gruppe of Lehrgeschwader 1, commanded by Hauptmann von Brauchitsch. This operational training, evaluation and demonstration unit saw extensive service as a combat formation – notably in Poland.

Left: A PZL P.11c fighter, riddled with bullets, after a crash landing. The Polish air force had 12 squadrons flying this mid-1930s fighter against the overwhelming might of the Luftwaffe.

Above: Every effort was made by the Polish army and air force to prepare for the threat of invasion by Germany and Russia. Here a pair of balloon barrage/observation blimps are being prepared.

their escape to neighbouring countries, and thence to the West, later joining the French and British air forces to continue their fight.

With tacit agreement on partitioning rights with Germany, the Soviet Union invaded Poland from the east on 17 September and, although Warsaw continued to resist until 27 September, the last concentration of Polish forces in the Modlin fortress was defeated on the following day and the campaign ended.

TOTAL WAR
The short Polish campaign sparked World War II, with the UK and France siding with Poland against Germany on 3 September, though neither country was in any position,

militarily or geographically, to offer any assistance during the four short weeks needed by Germany to crush all opposition. Those weeks witnessed a demonstration of total war. If the world had thus far been indifferent to the portents of Spain, the flames of Warsaw and the whine of Stukas were to be the harbingers of hell that would not be quenched or quelled for six long years to come.

Right: A Messerschmitt Bf 109E-1 with the markings of 1/JG 20 (later redesignated 8/JG 51). This was the first version powered by the 821-kW (1,100-hp) DB 601A and had four MG 17 machine-guns (two in the nose and one in each wing). This enabled it to eclipse its opponents for the first eight months of the war.

The Winter War

SEPTEMBER 1939 – MARCH 1940

Left: During the early part of the war, the Fokker D.XXI represented the Finnish fighter force (in addition to a handful of obsolete Bristol Bulldogs). They performed admirably, scoring many victories until the odds became too great. The Finnish air force shot down more than 50 Russian aircraft, almost all falling to the D.XXIs.

Below: Despite its biplane configuration, the Gloster Gladiator proved a handful for the Russian fighters. Thirty Gladiator Mk IIs, all of them ex-RAF aircraft, were supplied for use by the Finnish air force between December 1939 and February 1940. Most were fitted with a ski landing gear.

Opportunist intervention by the Soviet Union in the latter stages of Poland's rape by Germany was to be expected following the Ribbentrop-Molotov Pact of August 1939. The Winter War between Finland and the USSR, which broke out on 30 November that year, was the outcome of the Soviet Union's failure to steamroll Finland into giving her the use of land and bases to safeguard her approaches to Leningrad through the Gulf of Finland in the event of an attack by Germany.

The conflict, which lasted for 14 weeks, was fought largely on the shores of the huge Lake Ladoga and on the vital Karelian Isthmus in the south. The Finns, conscious of the hazards implicit in resistance to Soviet demands, had built a formidable line of defence, the Mannerheim Line, across the

Karelian Isthmus, this neck of land constituting the direct line of approach to Viipuri and the capital itself, Helsinki. In the air the Finns possessed a small but well-trained air force of some 145 aircraft, of which 114 were operational when war broke out. These comprised three squadrons of Fokker C.X reconnaissance biplanes and two squadrons of Bristol Blenheim Mk Is which constituted the bombing force. Two fighter squadrons were equipped with Fokker D.XXIs, although one squadron still had a flight of aged Bristol Bulldogs. Obsolete Blackburn Ripons and Junkers K.43s were employed for coastal duties.

SOVIET FORCES

Against Finland was ranged a total of 696 Soviet aircraft in support of ground forces, plus some 20 aircraft operating from Estonian bases. Main

equipment consisted of Tupolev SB-2 and Ilyushin DB-3 medium bombers, Tupolev TB-3 heavy bombers and about 230 Polikarpov I-15bis biplane fighters, deployed along virtually the length of frontier from north to south.

Air attacks against targets in

southern Finland by Estonia-based bombers on the first day found the defences unprepared but when repeated on the following day, met a spirited defence by the D.XXIs, whose pilots destroyed 10 of the raiders; a Bulldog was lost and a D.XXI was shot down by Finnish

Fighters in winter

With a strong family resemblance to the earlier I-15 biplanes, the I-16 flew in prototype form in December 1933. Its fuselage, of monocoque construction, was skinned with plywood. The

Gladiator represented the pinnacle of more conventional biplane design of the 1930s. Although it featured such advances as an enclosed cockpit, it was soon outclassed by the new monoplanes.

Gloster Gladiator

Halfway through the battle, help arrived from Britain in the shape of Bristol Blenheim Mk IVs, Gloster Gauntlets and Gloster Gladiators. One of the latter is illustrated, equipped with skis for operation from snow during the winter conditions and appropriately camouflaged.

Polikarpov I-16

Polikarpov fighters equipped all the fighter regiments facing Finland. Most were I-15s, but some I-16 monoplanes were employed. In winter camouflage, this aircraft served with the 4 IAP in the Lake Ladoga region.

Opposing bombers

Eleven 'long-nosed', Mercury XV-powered Blenheim Mk IVs were made available from Britain in late-1939, along with a number of Gauntlet and Gladiator fighters. Tupolev's SB-2 was produced in large numbers and was to remain operational throughout World War II, armed with four machine-guns and able to carry up to 600 kg (1,323 lb) of bombs. The first Finnish kill of the Winter War was an SB-2.

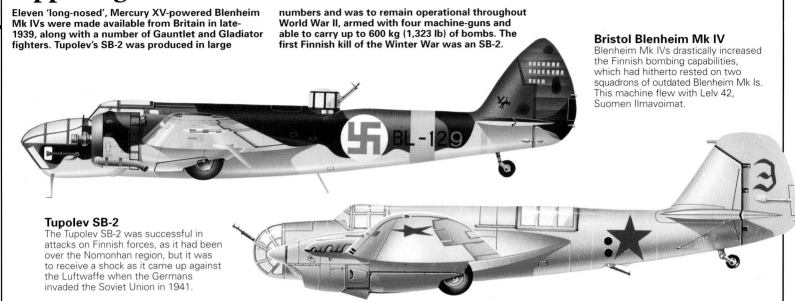

Bristol Blenheim Mk IV
Blenheim Mk IVs drastically increased the Finnish bombing capabilities, which had hitherto rested on two squadrons of outdated Blenheim Mk Is. This machine flew with Lelv 42, Suomen Ilmavoimat.

Tupolev SB-2
The Tupolev SB-2 was successful in attacks on Finnish forces, as it had been over the Nomonhan region, but it was to receive a shock as it came up against the Luftwaffe when the Germans invaded the Soviet Union in 1941.

ground defences in error. Atrocious weather now set in, preventing any further air action for three weeks, a period spent by both sides in building up their strength. On the ground the Finnish army, better-equipped to fight in the fierce snowstorms, held the Soviet attacks almost everywhere, small infiltrating forces inflicting enormous losses on Soviet convoys moving up to the Karelian Front. In the Soviet air force, Polikarpov I-16 monoplane fighters started arriving at the front, and early in the New Year the total number of Soviet aircraft in the Finnish theatre grew to around 1,500.

By the end of 1939 the Finnish air force had been credited with destroying more than 50 enemy aircraft, almost all falling to the D.XXIs, but also two or three to the ancient Bulldogs. On 6 January, as the Finns counter-attacked fiercely in Karelia and to the north of Lake Ladoga, eight DB-3s raided the Utti area; all were shot down by D.XXIs, six of them by one pilot.

It was at this point in the war that help arrived from Finland's Allies. Eleven Blenheim Mk IV bombers. 24 Gloster Gauntlets and 30 Gloster Gladiators were sent from the UK; 30 Morane-Saulnier MS.406 fighters arrived from France and, from Sweden, a volunteer force of four Hawker Harts and a dozen Gladiators arrived to fight in the north. Some Italian Fiat G.50s had also arrived in December.

FACING DEFEAT

As the Finnish counter-attack stabilised the front line, the Soviets stepped up the air attacks to cover a big build-up on the ground. On 17 January D.XXIs destroyed nine SB-2s, on 19 January five and on 20 January 13. Despite these significant successes, there were signs that the Soviets were beginning to avoid combat with the Finnish fighters, preferring to attack the bombers; in three weeks during January about half the Blenheims were lost.

In the first week of February the Soviet army launched a massive and ultimately decisive offensive towards Viipuri. As the Finnish fighters, now including Gladiators and G.50s, which first entered combat service on 2 and 26 February respectively fought desperately to prevent the large Soviet bomber formations from interfering in the ground battle, air combat became perceptibly less one-sided than hitherto. There were still

outstanding successes for the Finnish pilots, but their losses were mounting rapidly as when on 29 February, a large formation of I-16s attacked one of the Gladiator bases, destroying five Gladiators and a D.XXI while they were taking off.

Despite defending Viipuri successfully right up to the end, the Finns recognised the war situation as hopeless. By the end of the first week in March the strength of the opposing Soviet air force was estimated at 2,000 aircraft, whereas that of the Finns was dwindling rapidly. Some 44 Brewster Buffalo fighters were on their way from the United States, but arrived too late. On 13 March the Finns agreed to an armistice, being forced to cede a large part of Karelia and other tracts in the north to the Soviet Union. It was perhaps strange, however, that Finland was permitted to retain her air force in which the tardy Buffaloes were to form an important element.

Below: The Polikarpov I-15bis (or I-152) biplane was a later version of the I-15 with a conventional strut-braced upper wing centre-section, to remedy Soviet air force complaints of poor pilot visibility. Power was provided by a 559-kW (750-hp) M-25V radial engine.

Above: Lt Jorma Sarvanto of the Finnish air force in his Fokker D XXI. He became the first fighter airman to shoot down six enemy aircraft during a single combat in World War II when he attacked a force of seven DB-3 bombers on 6 January 1940.

Right: The Ilyushin DB-3F was widely used on the Finnish front by the Soviets. It featured a lengthened glazed nose, with a machine-gun at the front. This captured example force-landed behind Finnish lines.

The Scandinavian Conquest

APRIL 1940

Motivated as much by concern for the continuing supply of Swedish iron ore along the Norwegian coast to the furnaces of the Ruhr as for the security of his left flank in his planned attack on the Soviet Union, Hitler decided to eliminate Norway as a potential enemy foothold in the north. Because of the long distances involved, the Junkers Ju 87 dive-bomber was scarcely to be used, ground support being provided by some 70 Messerschmitt Bf 110C heavy fighters and only 40 Ju 87Rs. A bomber force of 290 Heinkel He 111Hs and Junkers Ju 88As possessed the range to reach central

Norway, and to the extreme north once Norwegian bases had been captured. In the likely absence of serious fighter opposition, no more than a single Gruppe (30 aircraft) of Bf 109Es was deployed.

By far the largest element of the air arm was to comprise about 500 Junkers Ju 52/3m transports, and these aircraft were to be employed to deliver waves of assault forces during the first 10 days of the campaign.

NORWAY INVADED

The UK for her part had been planning an occupation of northern Norway with the very object of denying German use of the port of Narvik and when, on 9 April, the German blow fell on Denmark and southern Norway, the Royal Navy was already at sea and an RAF

squadron of Gloster Gladiators (No. 263) in the process of preparation for service in Scandinavia.

RAF aircraft were also already active in the German Bight as German naval forces were approaching the Norwegian coast but, as no troop transports were sighted, the sailing of British convoys was delayed. Such was the extent to which the Germans were able to conceal their preparations that Denmark was effectively overrun in a single day, paratroops being dropped on the airfields of Aalborg-Ost and Aalborg-West, followed by the arrival of further airborne infantry brought in by the swarms of Ju 52/3m transports. Denmark's handful of Gloster Gauntlets, Hawker Nimrods and Fokker D.XXIs had no chance to oppose

Above: German Fallschirmjäger (paratroopers) come down in Norway. This campaign marked the first use of such troops, whose shock value proved to be high, but at the cost of significant casualties.

the lightning attack.

Meanwhile, as German warships steamed up Oslo Fjord and seaborne landings were carried out along the south Norwegian coast, the Bf 110s strafed the airfields of Oslo-Förnebu and Stavanger-Sola, easily disposing of the small number of Norwegian Gladiators which rose in defence. The following day the airfield at Trondheim-Vaernes fell and with the constant arrival of men, guns, fuel and ammunition, brought in by the transport aircraft, it seemed that the whole of Norway would be quickly

Left: One of a small number of sturdy Heinkel He 115 floatplanes flown by the Royal Norwegian Air Force. Together with three others, it made bombing attacks on the invading German forces, before being flown to Scotland.

Obsolete fighters

The Danish Hawker Nimrod Mk II stood little chance against the invader's modern fighters. It had a top speed of just 315 km/h (196 mph) and was armed with two Vickers Mk III machine-guns.

Similarly the Norwegian Gladiator Mk IIs were little better with four Colt 7.7-mm (0.303-in) machine-guns and a top speed of 414 km/h (257 mph). All 12 aircraft were lost in the defence of Oslo.

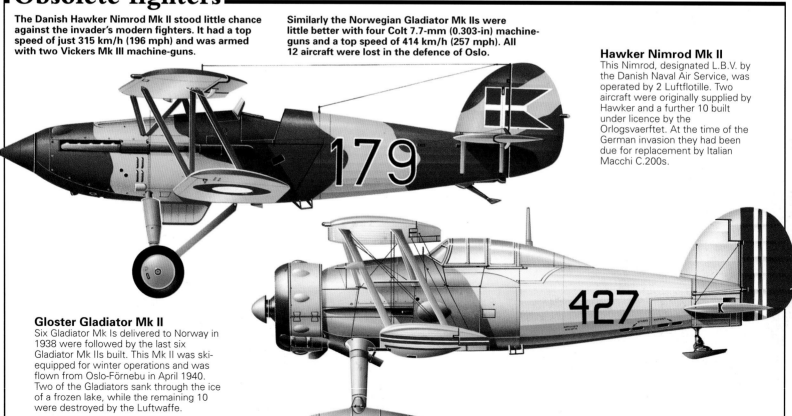

Hawker Nimrod Mk II
This Nimrod, designated L.B.V. by the Danish Naval Air Service, was operated by 2 Luftflotille. Two aircraft were originally supplied by Hawker and a further 10 built under licence by the Orlogsvaerftet. At the time of the German invasion they had been due for replacement by Italian Macchi C.200s.

Gloster Gladiator Mk II
Six Gladiator Mk Is delivered to Norway in 1938 were followed by the last six Gladiator Mk IIs built. This Mk II was ski-equipped for winter operations and was flown from Oslo-Förnebu in April 1940. Two of the Gladiators sank through the ice of a frozen lake, while the remaining 10 were destroyed by the Luftwaffe.

Luftwaffe supreme

The latest Messerschmitt Bf 109E-3s had two MG 17s in the nose and two in the wings, plus an MG FF/M firing through the propeller shaft, ensuring the Luftwaffe's air supremacy over Scandinavia.

Although soon replaced by the superior three-engined Do 24, the Dornier Do 18 served well in the air-sea rescue role, proving particularly useful during the invasion of Denmark and Norway.

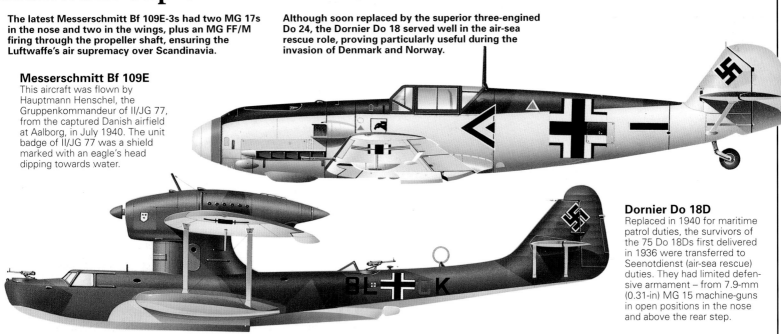

Messerschmitt Bf 109E
This aircraft was flown by Hauptmann Henschel, the Gruppenkommandeur of II/JG 77, from the captured Danish airfield at Aalborg, in July 1940. The unit badge of II/JG 77 was a shield marked with an eagle's head dipping towards water.

Dornier Do 18D
Replaced in 1940 for maritime patrol duties, the survivors of the 75 Do 18Ds first delivered in 1936 were transferred to Seenotdienst (air-sea rescue) duties. They had limited defensive armament – from 7.9-mm (0.31-in) MG 15 machine-guns in open positions in the nose and above the rear step.

over-run within the next few days.

After the initial delay, however, British forces were quickly on the scene. A German advance force which had sailed to Narvik in the far north was isolated by the destruction of its supporting naval force.

Fleet Air Arm Blackburn Skuas of No. 803 Squadron dive-bombed and sank the *Königsberg* at Bergen, and the similar *Karlsruhe* was torpedoed by a British submarine. British land forces were put ashore at Narvik on 15 April, at Namsos on 16 April and at Andalsnes on 18 April. At once the Luftwaffe retaliated with its Ju 87s, bombing the ports so heavily as to render them virtually unuseable.

Five days later 18 RAF Gladiators of No. 263 Squadron landed on the

Left: The view through the glazed nose of a Heinkel He 111 sweeping in towards a small Norwegian port. Operating against minimal fighter opposition, the German Kampfgruppen provided ground forces with essential tactical support as the invasion proceeded.

frozen Lake Lesjaskog near Andalsnes, having flown off the carrier HMS *Glorious*. The Luftwaffe was again ready for them and, as a result of the extreme cold, difficulty was experienced in getting the Gladiators into the air, most of them being destroyed on the ice in raids which started the next day. Although about half a dozen raiders were claimed shot down in 36 hours, the frozen lake was unuseable by 25 April. The surviving aircraft were destroyed where they stood, and the wrecked ports of Andalsnes and Namsos were evacuated on 30 April and 2 May respectively. The members of No. 263 Squadron returned to the UK to re-equip with a fresh complement of Gladiators.

COUNTER ATTACK
The British now decided to concentrate an attack on the port of Narvik, despite the rapid and relatively simple build up of German forces in the south. No. 263 Squadron with its new Gladiators embarked on HMS

Furious, this time accompanied by No. 46 Squadron with Hawker Hurricanes, arriving at Bödo and Bardufoss on 26 May. An assault by British, Norwegian, French and Polish forces on 28 May succeeded in eliminating the German forces at Narvik, but such were the distances involved that it became all too obvious that to sustain what could be little more than an isolated garrison was out of the question. German air attacks were increasing daily, despite the RAF pilots' success in downing some 20 of the enemy raiders. In an effort to bring their aircraft home, the pilots volunteered to land aboard HMS *Glorious* for passage home but within 48 hours the ship, the aircraft and all but two of the pilots were at the bottom of the ocean, sent there by salvoes from the German warships *Scharnhorst* and *Gneisenau*.

On 7 June King Haakon of Norway left his shores aboard HMS *Devonshire* and on the following day Allied forces were extricated from Narvik. The campaign was over. Once more the overwhelming superiority of the Luftwaffe had contributed a vital weapon, this time the use of massive delivery of airborne infantry proving decisive. It was moreover but a dress rehearsal for worse to come.

Left: The German Fallschirmjäger, here preparing to board a Junkers Ju 52/3m three-engined transport aircraft, were fully air-mobile Luftwaffe paratroops. They could be delivered into the battlefield by parachute, glider or tactical transport aircraft.

Right: A formation of Luftwaffe Junkers Ju 88A-4s heading for a bombing raid over northern Norway in April 1940. This, the first longer wing-span version, had more powerful Jumo 211J engines and greater range than earlier versions of the bomber.

Blitzkrieg in the West

10 MAY 1940 – 22 JUNE 1940

Following a massive and not wholly unobserved build-up of land and air forces along her frontiers with France and the neutral Low Countries, Germany on 10 May 1940 launched an overwhelming offensive westwards. Recognising the futility of a frontal assault on the established Maginot Line, Hitler chose to attack through the Netherlands and Belgium, and strike directly at the Channel ports, thereby isolating the British army in the north, before striking south at Paris, so outflanking the French army concentrated on the border facing Germany.

Supporting the attack by some 75 divisions were Luftflotten II and III, comprising 4,000 front-line aircraft, of which more than 400 were Junkers Ju 52/3m transports, recently redeployed from the Norwegian campaign, as well as the full panoply of Blitzkrieg, the Ju 87s, Ju 88s, Dornier Do 17s, Heinkel He 111s, Messerschmitt Bf 109s and Bf 110s. Opposing this array of might were some 130 Dutch, 150 Belgian, 1,600 French and 450 British aircraft based in northern France; however, not only were the Allied airmen outnumbered by odds of about two to one, but two-thirds of their aircraft were at best obsolescent.

DUTCH COLLAPSE

Moreover, the element of surprise enabled the Luftwaffe to concentrate its strength where needed, so that within a matter of four days, during which Rotterdam suffered a catastrophic raid by Heinkel He 111s, the Netherlands had

Above: Although they only carried a small bombload, these Dornier Do 17Zs of the Kampfgruppen performed with credit when the German Blitzkrieg was launched in May 1940. However, they were easy prey when intercepted by Spitfires.

Right: A German fallschirmjäger (paratrooper) leaving a Junkers Ju 52/3m three-engined transport at low-level, during the invasion of the Low Countries. He is using a static line for quick parachute deployment. Some 400 of these aircraft were transferred to the region after the Scandinavian conquest.

Above: Crew walking out to a Fairey Battle of No. 218 Squadron, somewhere in France, where it was part of the Advanced Air Striking Force. This unit, along with most of the RAF's Battle squadrons, was wiped out within a few days of the start of the German Blitzkrieg at the beginning of May 1940.

Right: On 10 May 1940, nine Fokker D.XXIs of the Dutch air force, including '241' seen here, took part in a battle with a similar number of Messerschmitt Bf 109s. '241' was the only Dutch aircraft lost, the German formation losing half their number. This was an unrepresentative victory, however, as the Bf 109 was a superior machine.

Left: Invasion of the Netherlands on 10 May 1940. German paratroops being dropped from a trio of Junkers Ju 52/3ms during the opening offensive. Operation 'Fall Gelb' was the swift assertion of German air superiority, the support of ground forces and the launch of a series of parachute operations.

Below: The Belgian air force acquired 22 Gloster Gladiators, five of which are seen here on delivery. The Belgian Aéronautique Militaire could muster just 15 surviving Gladiators to fight against the invading German forces in May 1940. They were quickly overwhelmed.

Below: An aerodynamically refined and structurally robust fighter, this French air force Dewoitine D.520 could not match the Luftwaffe's Messerschmitt 109s for level speed, but had a marked edge in manoeuvrability.

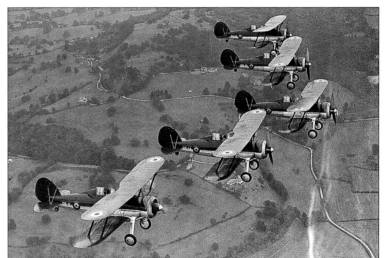

capitulated. Belgium, now the scene of powerful German armoured thrusts, quickly lost the key defence positions vital to its survival, the great Fort Eben-Emael falling to a dawn attack by glider-borne troops on the first day. Key crossing points on the Albert Canal were captured intact by the Germans and, despite frantic efforts by RAF Fairey Battle and Bristol Blenheim bombers to destroy them, this enabled the German columns to continue their swift advance, reaching Abbeville long before the end of the month.

Within 10 days the Belgian air force had virtually ceased to exist, while losses among the RAF Battle squadrons had reached about 70 per cent. In the RAF only the Hawker Hurricane succeeded in matching the modern German aircraft, and it was estimated that around 200 of the enemy fell to their guns in the first fortnight.

BELGIUM FALLS

In the French Armée de l'Air the Dewoitine D.520 fighter was of roughly equal quality to the British Hurricane, but only some 150 of

Lowly defenders

The Dutch air force had a total of just 132 aircraft, including 28 Fokker D.XXI and 23 Fokker G.1a fighters to face more than 1,000 Luftwaffe fighters. Likewise the Belgian air force only had a handful of fighters and light bombers, including Hurricanes, Gladiators and Fairey Battles. The strongest air force was the French Armée de l'Air, with 278 MS. 406s, 98 Curtiss Hawks and 36 Dewoitine D.520s.

Fokker G.1a
This Dutch heavy fighter and ground-attack aircraft had twin booms and a central nacelle for a crew of three. A total of 36 G.1as were delivered to the Netherlands Army Air Service from 1938 and about two-dozen were serviceable at the time of the German invasion.

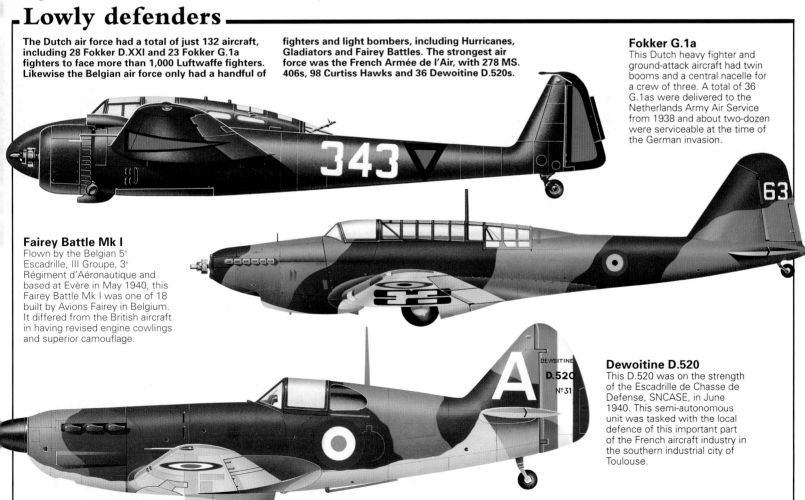

Fairey Battle Mk I
Flown by the Belgian 5e Escadrille, III Groupe, 3e Régiment d'Aéronautique and based at Evère in May 1940, this Fairey Battle Mk I was one of 18 built by Avions Fairey in Belgium. It differed from the British aircraft in having revised engine cowlings and superior camouflage.

Dewoitine D.520
This D.520 was on the strength of the Escadrille de Chasse de Defense, SNCASE, in June 1940. This semi-autonomous unit was tasked with the local defence of this important part of the French aircraft industry in the southern industrial city of Toulouse.

Above: The Junkers Ju 52/3m was the workhorse of the Blitzkrieg, dropping paratroops in Norway, Greece and the Low Countries, towing gliders and keeping the armies re-supplied as they scythed their way through Europe.

Below: Spitfires were in action day after day over the Dunkirk beaches, trying to establish air superiority and so enable the troops to escape across the Channel. This Spitfire Mk I was shot down on 6 June 1940.

these aircraft were available during the Battle of France. However, until the RAF's Supermarine Spitfire was committed to battle in the later stages, the German Bf 109 was the supreme fighter in French skies and this, together with highly effective mobile flak which accompanied the advancing German columns, took tremendous toll of British and French light bombers.

Above: A formation of Bristol Blenheim Mk IVs of No. 139 Squadron over France in 1940. This unit deployed in September 1939 and flying from Plivot lost the bulk of its aircraft attacking German columns as the invasion advanced westward towards the Channel ports.

The latter, when not being clawed out of the smoke-filled skies over the land battle, were pulverized on their bases.

By 26 May the Belgian front had collapsed and almost 400,000 British and French soldiers were falling back on the port of Dunkirk. At this point Hermann Goering prevailed on Hitler to allow his air force to annihilate the Allied armies trapped with their backs to the sea. As orders were issued in the UK to evacuate these forces by sailing an armada of small vessels to Dunkirk, Spitfires, Hurricanes, Boulton Paul Defiants and Blenheim fighters,

hitherto reserved for defence of the British Isles, were ordered to protect the great evacuation. Numerous heavy attacks by German He 111s, Ju 87s, Ju 88s and Do 17s were launched against the port and beaches during the following week, some of which inevitably penetrated the fighter defence.

Mighty invaders

Carrying forward its successes in Poland and Scandinavia, the Ju 87 began to lose its edge as it faced better Allied defences. The He 111 successfully provided the main bomber force for the Blitzkrieg. Supreme fighter over Europe, the Bf 109 took a high toll of the Allies' fighters and bombers.

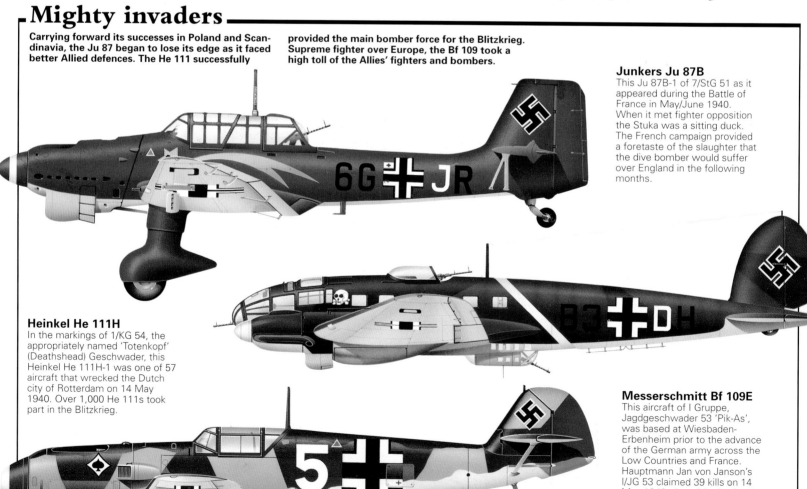

Junkers Ju 87B
This Ju 87B-1 of 7/StG 51 as it appeared during the Battle of France in May/June 1940. When it met fighter opposition the Stuka was a sitting duck. The French campaign provided a foretaste of the slaughter that the dive bomber would suffer over England in the following months.

Heinkel He 111H
In the markings of 1/KG 54, the appropriately named 'Totenkopf' (Deathshead) Geschwader, this Heinkel He 111H-1 was one of 57 aircraft that wrecked the Dutch city of Rotterdam on 14 May 1940. Over 1,000 He 111s took part in the Blitzkrieg.

Messerschmitt Bf 109E
This aircraft of I Gruppe, Jagdgeschwader 53 'Pik-As', was based at Wiesbaden-Erbenheim prior to the advance of the German army across the Low Countries and France. Hauptmann Jan von Janson's I/JG 53 claimed 39 kills on 14 May 1940, the crisis day for the Allied air forces.

Casualties were very high on both sides, but by 3 June some 336,000 men of the British and French armies, though with scarcely any of their equipment, had been evacuated to safety.

RETREAT

As the German army closed swiftly on the Channel ports, which fell in rapid succession despite all possible support by RAF aircraft based in England, the remaining elements of the British air forces that had been deployed across the Channel fell back westwards through France, giving what cover they could to the ragged remains of the BEF and French force until eventually evacuated from Cherbourg, Brest, St Nazaire and other ports. The German army now swung south towards Paris, the first massive air raids on the capital being launched on 3 June; French fighter pilots claimed the destruction of 26 aircraft in the first attack, but lost almost as heavily. Despite great

gallantry by the men of the Armée de l'Air, however, German air superiority was never threatened, and the final land assault opened on 5 June. On 14 June Paris fell, and eight days later an armistice was signed.

The campaign that had lasted just six weeks had cost the Luftwaffe the loss of 1,254 aircraft, but most of those aircrew who survived being shot down were now released by the French to return to their units. Much of the surviving French air force escaped to the unoccupied zone in France under a

Above: A formation of six Hurricanes from No. 73 Squadron, that flew with No. 1 Squadron in the AASF over France. As their outline resembled the French Dewoitine D.520 and they were operating with the Armée de l'Air, the Hurricanes were painted with distinctive rudder stripes.

Left: Two Junkers Ju 87B-2 dive bombers returning to their temporary bases in France after a successful attack. The VIII Kliegerkorps, the main tactical strike force, had some 380 Stukas for the Low Countries' Blitzkrieg.

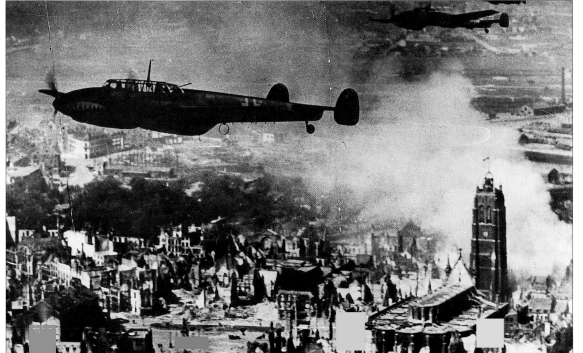

puppet government in Vichy, or to French territory in North Africa; some pilots made their way to the UK, where they joined the RAF.

The RAF itself had lost a total of 944 aircraft, of which 386 were Hurricanes and 67 Spitfires, fighters whose loss was to be sorely felt in the summer months to come. More important were the many professional pilots lost, whose peacetime training could never be matched by that of the men now rapidly filling the depleted ranks of RAF Fighter Command.

Left: Messerschmitt Bf 110C-2 'Zerstörer' over Dunkirk in June 1940. The heavy, twin-engined fighter met its match when it came up against RAF Hurricanes and Spitfires by day. It later had a much more distinguished career as a night fighter.

Battle of Britain: The Assault

JULY – OCTOBER 1940

BRITAIN ON ITS KNEES
A pair of Junkers Ju 88A-5s; the first of the improved version with increased wingspan. These aircraft shown approaching the English coast are from I/KG 54. In 1940 Ju 88s made up a large proportion of the 2,800 aircraft that bombarded Britain.

Following the invasion of Norway and the fall of France and the Low Countries in May and June 1940, and as the RAF set about dressing its wounds, the Luftwaffe moved up to bases lining the coasts facing the British Isles. For the all-out air attack, intended to eliminate RAF Fighter Command in preparation for an invasion of the islands, the Luftwaffe disposed its forces in three air fleets, Luftflotte III based in north-west France, Luftflotte II in north-east France and the Low Countries, and Luftflotte V in Norway and Denmark.

By early July the German air forces facing the UK fielded about 2,800 aircraft comprising 1,300 Heinkel He 111, Junkers Ju 88 and Dornier Do 17 bombers, 280 Junkers Ju 87 dive-bombers, 790 Messerschmitt Bf 109 single-seat fighters, 260 Messerschmitt Bf 110 and Junkers Ju 88C heavy fighters and 170 reconnaissance aircraft of various types, of these totals roughly half were immediately combat-ready. Facing them, RAF Fighter Command possessed 640 fighters, the great majority of them Hawker Hurricanes and Supermarine Spitfires.

THE BATTLE BEGINS

The daylight Battle of Britain opened at the beginning of July with relatively scattered raids by small formations of German bombers against coastal targets in southern England and against

Above: A Messerschmitt Bf 110C-4 operated by Zerstörergeschwader 52, provides a fighter escort for Heinkel and Dornier bombers on their raids over Britain. Bf 110s received a severe mauling by the RAF during the Battle of Britain.

Below: Palls of smoke fill the sky over London, silhouetting Tower Bridge and the Tower of London, after massive Luftwaffe bombing raids on the East London docks area on 7 September 1940. This was a month of heavy German losses.

...denn wir fahren gegen Engeland!

Heute wollen wir ein Liedlein singen;
trinken wollen wir den kühlen Wein
und die Gläser sollen dazu klingen,
denn es muß, es muß geschieden sein.

Kommt die Kunde, daß ich bin gefallen,
daß ich schlafe in der Meeresflut;
weine nicht um mich, mein Schatz, und denke
für das Vaterland, da floß sein Blut.

Unsre Flagge, und die wehet auf dem Mast,
sie verkündet unsres Reiches Macht;
denn wir wollen es nicht länger leiden,
daß der Engelsmann darüber lacht.

Gib mir deine Hand, deine weiße Hand,
leb wohl, mein Schatz;
leb wohl, mein Schatz, leb wohl.
Lebe wohl, denn wir fahren, denn wir fahren
denn wir fahren gegen Engeland, Engeland!
H. LÖNS

Above: During the early days of the Battle of Britain German morale was extremely high due to their successful conquest of France. This postcard depicts three Ju 87 Stuka bombers accompanied by a comical song predicting an easy conquest of the British Isles. Three months later the mood of the Luftwaffe had dramatically changed.

Right: A flight of Luftwaffe Messerschmitt Bf 109Es flying along the French coast early in 1940. With their superior performance and more experienced pilots, the 16 Gruppen of Bf 109s wreaked havoc on the RAF's Spitfires and Hurricanes during the long summer of 1940.

shipping in the English Channel, the initial object being to test the defences and to discover the extent to which they relied upon the coastal radar chain, known to have existed since before the war. As the month wore on the anti-shipping attacks increased in ferocity, as did German losses, and it became clear that the British radar was not only highly efficient but gave substantial warning of approaching raids.

LUFTWAFFE LOSSES

German losses in July amounted to some 220 aircraft and, as the Germans finalised plans for the all-out assault, scheduled for mid-August, there followed a lull in the fighting. The first heavy raids, against shipping in the Channel, were launched on 8 August by large formations of Ju 87s escorted by Bf 110s but, as was to be confirmed during the next few days, both these aircraft were found to be extremely vulnerable in the face of attacks by the Hurricanes and Spitfires, and losses were exceptionally heavy. Further shipping attacks were carried out on 11 August, but now the raiders were more adequately protected by Bf 109 single-seaters. This phase continued until 18 August, particularly severe fighting taking place on 12, 13, 15, 16 and 18 August. As a result of heavy losses suffered, the Ju 87 was

largely withdrawn from the battle after 18 August.

By now raids were penetrating further inland, and on 15 August aircraft of Luftflotte V attempted to attack targets in northern England,

but suffered so badly that such raids were not repeated during the Battle.

A reappraisal of the tactics being employed led to a marked shift during the next phase of the attack which began at the end of August.

Left: A Luftwaffe Messerschmitt Bf 109E after crash landing with battle damage in a cornfield at Berwick near Eastbourne. It is painted in the standard 1940 colour scheme, with only the upper surfaces of its wings and fuselage camouflaged.

Below: The remains of a Junkers Ju 88A-1 of KG 30, the first Luftwaffe unit to operate the bomber, after it had been shot down while on a raid over the Home Counties in 1940.

Fighters of the Reich

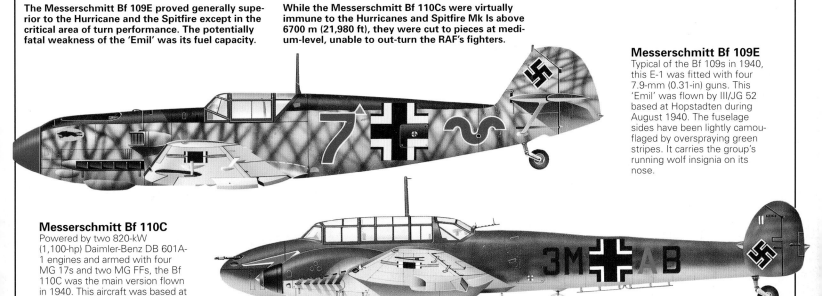

The Messerschmitt Bf 109E proved generally superior to the Hurricane and the Spitfire except in the critical area of turn performance. The potentially fatal weakness of the 'Emil' was its fuel capacity.

While the Messerschmitt Bf 110Cs were virtually immune to the Hurricanes and Spitfire Mk Is above 6700 m (21,980 ft), they were cut to pieces at medium-level, unable to out-turn the RAF's fighters.

Messerschmitt Bf 109E
Typical of the Bf 109s in 1940, this E-1 was fitted with four 7.9-mm (0.31-in) guns. This 'Emil' was flown by III/JG 52 based at Hopstadten during August 1940. The fuselage sides have been lightly camouflaged by overspraying green stripes. It carries the group's running wolf insignia on its nose.

Messerschmitt Bf 110C
Powered by two 820-kW (1,100-hp) Daimler-Benz DB 601A-1 engines and armed with four MG 17s and two MG FFs, the Bf 110C was the main version flown in 1940. This aircraft was based at Amiens during July 1940 with I/Zerstörergeschwader 2.

Following complaints by the Bf 109 pilots that they were badly handicapped when employed in the bomber-escort role, the Jagdgeschwader were allowed to resume the 'free chase' tactics over southern England, frequently catching the RAF fighters either during take-off or landing, or as they returned short of fuel and ammunition after combat.

This was unquestionably the most successful phase from the Luftwaffe's viewpoint and would have quickly brought the defences to their knees had the Germans persisted. However, exasperated at continuing losses, Göering ordered the attack to switch from the RAF to the British civilian population with a sudden massive attack on East London in the late afternoon of 7 September.

Below: A camera gun photograph from a Bf 109E showing an RAF Hurricane Mk I on fire after a dog-fight. The Luftwaffe fighter was particularly successful against the slower, British fighters flown by less experienced pilots in 1940.

SCREAM OF THE STUKA
A Stuka releases its load of bombs – a single 250-kg (551-lb) SC250 and four smaller 50-kg (110-lb) SC50s during its vertical dive. Entry into the dive and the 6*g* pullout were fully automatic, leaving the pilot with the task of steering the aircraft to put his bombsight reticule over the target.

This marked the turning point of the whole battle, and the easing of pressure on the fighters allowed them a much-needed respite. In the course of further heavy daylight attacks on London, particularly on 15 September and on south-east England at the end of the month, the Germans took a heavy beating; the British fighter pilots no longer

Below: Armourers with a 500-kg (1,102-lb) SC500 bomb that was carried externally on the Heinkel He 111H is shown here. These bombs began to feature prominently during the latter part of the Luftwaffe's assault on Britain.

had to fight over their airfields and could concentrate on the great armadas making their way ponderously towards some unfortunate town or city.

The very heavy losses of September constituted the Luftwaffe's first major setback of the war; survival of the British fighter defences led to postponement of the invasion (and its eventual abandonment), and the final phase, which occupied most of October,

consisted of no more than nuisance raids by high-flying aircraft (usually Bf 109s) carrying single bombs, which were dropped with little hope of causing significant damage.

The daylight Battle of Britain cost the Luftwaffe a total of 2,020

Right: The legendary Oberstleutnant Adolf Galland flying his Messerschmitt Bf 109E-3 with Jagdgeschwader 26 in France during the autumn of 1940. His personal 'Mickey Mouse' emblem is carried below the cockpit and the unit Schlageter badge behind the engine's supercharger intake.

aircraft destroyed, and more than 200 aircrew killed or missing. As with the RAF's losses in France, a high proportion of these men were the most experienced in the German air force and had been responsible for evolving and proving the battle tactics employed. Nevertheless, whereas the British could regard the final outcome of the Battle of Britain as a resounding victory, it was by no means the end of the air assault, which now continued (with very different results) under cover of darkness.

Above: A mass formation of Heinkel He 111Hs forms up over France before climbing to cross the English Channel and another heavy raid, in July 1940. The He 111H, with its 435 km/h (270 mph) top speed, proved a difficult aircraft for the RAF to shoot down, compared with the Dornier Do 17.

Right: A high-flying Heinkel He 111H-2 photographed as it headed across London on 7 September, to drop its eight 250-kg (551-lb) bombs onto the Surrey and West India Docks. The better-armed H-2 version carried its weapons in the fuselage either side of a central gangway.

Bombers over Britain

The Junkers Ju 87 dive-bomber's almost legendary reputation from the first year of the war was shattered during the Battle of Britain, with severe losses. The Luftwaffe's most successful bomber, the Heinkel He 111H, was relatively fast and often survived heavy battle damage. The Dornier Do 17's defensive armament was inadequate, but it could outrun RAF fighters in a shallow dive.

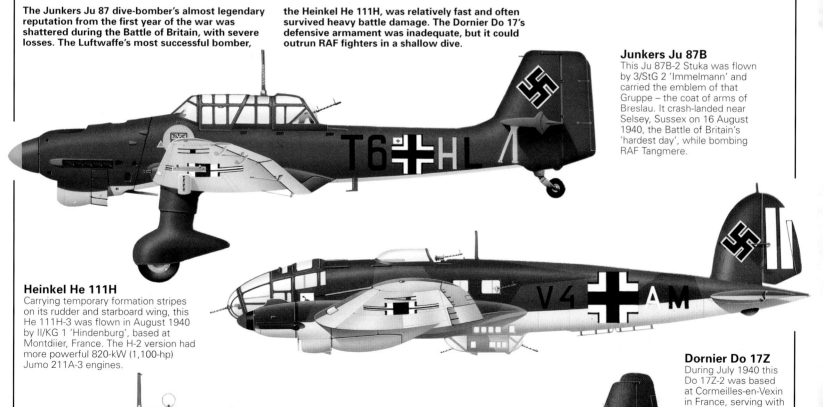

Junkers Ju 87B
This Ju 87B-2 Stuka was flown by 3/StG 2 'Immelmann' and carried the emblem of that Gruppe – the coat of arms of Breslau. It crash-landed near Selsey, Sussex on 16 August 1940, the Battle of Britain's 'hardest day', while bombing RAF Tangmere.

Heinkel He 111H
Carrying temporary formation stripes on its rudder and starboard wing, this He 111H-3 was flown in August 1940 by II/KG 1 'Hindenburg', based at Montdiier, France. The H-2 version had more powerful 820-kW (1,100-hp) Jumo 211A-3 engines.

Dornier Do 17Z
During July 1940 this Do 17Z-2 was based at Cormeilles-en-Vexin in France, serving with 9/KG 76. This unit was heavily involved in attacking RAF airfields in Kent during the Battle of Britain.

Battle of Britain: The Defence

JULY – OCTOBER 1940

A Spitfire I breaks to starboard during a head-on attack on a Messerschmitt Bf 109E. The Spitfire's superior agility made it more than a match for the Bf 109, although the more experienced Luftwaffe pilots tended to use better tactics. Many downed Spitfire pilots were able to return to the battle, bailing out over friendly territory. Britain's aircraft industry also proved better at replacing the aircraft which were lost in action.

The unexpected month-long respite after the Dunkirk evacuation allowed RAF Fighter Command time to rest and re-equip most of its weary squadrons, and to some extent broadcast among its pilots vital information regarding German fighting tactics.

At the head of Fighter Command, Air Chief Marshal Dowding divided his air defences into three groups: No. 11 in the south under Keith Park, No. 12 in the Midlands under Trafford Leigh-Mallory and No. 13 in the north under Richard Saul. A fourth group, No. 10 under Quintin Brand, would shortly be added to cover the southwest.

Dowding disposed a total of 640 fighters at the beginning of July 1940, including 347 Hawker Hurricanes, 199 Supermarine Spitfires, 69 Bristol Blenheim night-fighters and 25 Boulton Paul Defiants; slightly over half his strength was deployed in the south. The key airfields of Biggin Hill, Kenley, Croydon, Hornchurch, Manston and Tangmere constituted a defensive ring round London and the Thames estuary. To provide early warning and a degree of fighter control, the south and east coasts were covered by a network of radar stations which could detect approaching raids at a distance of about 100 miles (160 km).

RAF STRETCHED

The German attacks of July, aimed principally at shipping and coastal targets in the south, proved something of a strain on the British pilots. They were obliged to fly standing patrols over the convoys until the German tactics were recognised for what they were, and orders given

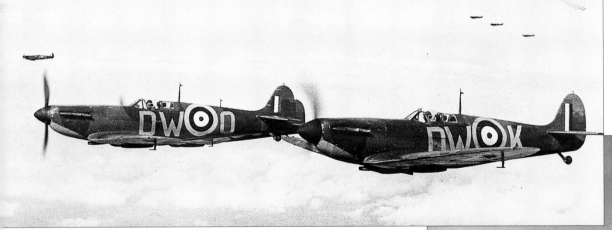

Above: Supermarine Spitfire Mk IAs of No. 610 (County of Chester) Squadron, Royal Auxiliary Air Force, on patrol over Kent in the summer of 1940. During August No. 610 played a vital role in the defence of Biggin Hill, before being withdrawn to Acklington at the end of the month for the defence of Newcastle.

Right: High above the clouds, Hurricanes of No. 1 Squadron. After fighting previously with the AASF in France, the squadron returned to the UK and re-equipped with factory-fresh Hurricane Is. During the Battle of Britain, the squadron flew from Northolt, Hawkinge, Tangmere, Manston, North Weald and Heathrow before returning to Wittering on 9 September 1940.

Above: A Spitfire I returns to base over the Kent coast during the Battle of Britain. Though it played a smaller role in the Battle of Britain compared to the less glamorous Hurricane, the Spitfire was arguably the most important Allied aircraft of WWII.

Below: Taken at Gravesend in August 1940, this group photograph shows Hurricane pilots of No. 85 Squadron. The CO is Sqn Ldr Peter Townsend, seen leaning on a stick, necessitated by the loss of a toe during combat over Croydon.

In 1940, Fighter Command had a mix of RAF regular, auxiliary and reserve pilots, borrowed Bomber and Coastal Command, test and Fleet Air Arm pilots – with British, Commonwealth and foreign nationalities, all of whom fought in the Battle of Britain. As with so many of the Few, not all could be aces; pen-portraits of six of them are illustrated below. The Battle of Britain instilled a brand of camaraderie that will forever be associated with the wearing of air force blue.

Sqn Ldr Douglas Bader

This tin-legged hero shot down 22 aircraft – a remarkable score considering that he became a POW less than a year after the Battle of Britain. A crash in a Bristol Bulldog in 1931 cost him both his legs. A key figure in No. 12 Group, Bader was perhaps the leading supporter of the theoretically superior but tactically inferior 'Big Wing' formation advocated by the commander of No.12 Group, Sir Trafford Leigh Mallory.

Sqn Ldr Peter Townsend

Peter Townsend was commanding officer of No. 85 Sqn at Martlesham and Debden during the battle. He was shot down by the gunner of Do 17 on 11 July and baled out into the sea, where he spent some time before rescued. Later wounded near Croydon, Townsend evened the score by destroying six German aircraft. He achieved further success as a night-fighter pilot. He retired from the RAF as Group Captain Peter Townsend DSO,CVO,DFC in 1956.

Sgt James Lacey

Having learned to fly in the RAFVR in 1937, at the outbreak of war 'Ginger' Lacey joined No. 501 Squadron flying Hurricanes. In the Battle of France he shot down five enemy aircraft and was awarded the Croix de Guerre. Shot down or forced to land nine times, he achieved a score of 23, most of them during the Battle, including on 13 September an He 111 which had just bombed Buckingham Palace.

Flt Lt 'Sailor' Malan

Adolph 'Sailor' Malan, a South African, was commissioned into the RAF in 1935 from the Merchant Navy. He flew with No. 74 Squadron, one of the first to receive the Spitfire in January 1939. An outstanding shot, he ordered his guns harmonised at only 250 yards, from the usual 400 yards. Appointed CO of No. 74 Sqn at the height of the Battle, his final tally probably exceeded 35 but many kills he gave to inexperienced wingmen.

Flt Lt Bob Stanford Tuck

Bob Stanford Tuck was another Battle of Britain pilot whose career was cut short over France when he was shot down in January 1942 with an accredited tally of 29 victories. Commissioned in 1935, by 1940 he was a squadron leader in command of No. 257 Squadron, flying Hurricanes. One of the Battle's best practitioners of deflection shooting, he owed much to his pre-war skills as a shot. Stanford Tuck was a superb fighter leader, and an inspiration to those he led.

Sqn Ldr 'Paddy' Finucane

Brendan Finucane (with 32 victories credited) commanded No. 452 Squadron RAAF, with Spitfires, operating from RAF Kenley and Redhill. An outstanding pilot, and leader of the Hornchurch Wing, he was forced to ditch his Spitfire on 15 July 1942 when a flak hit drained the coolant from his engine. Finucane died when he hit the water near Le Touquet.

---

not to engage enemy fighters unnecessarily. British losses in the July combats amounted to 77 fighters, of whose pilots roughly half survived. A particularly savage combat on 19 July had shown the two-seat Defiant to be unsuitable for day fighting, and it was temporarily withdrawn out of harm's way.

HEAVY LOSSES

The onset of the main assault on 8 August was competently countered by Park's squadrons, whose pilots quickly spotted the weaknesses of the Junkers Ju 87 and Messerschmitt Bf 110, and set about developing effective tactics to deal with them. The appearance of large formations of Messerschmitt Bf 109s, which were superior in most respects to the Hurricane, caused the British controllers, where possible, to order their Spitfires against the enemy fighters, while the Hurricanes fought the slower, lower-flying bombers.

The resumption of 'free chase' sorties by the Bf 109s at the end of

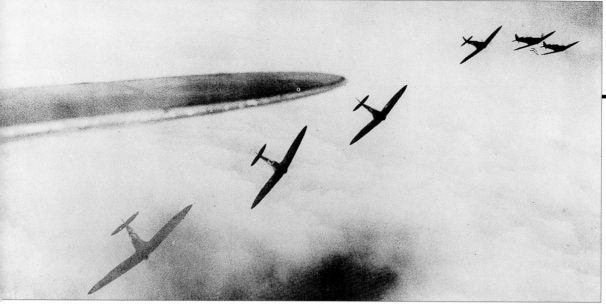

Left: Spitfire Is peel off for the camera. In the Battle of Britain the RAF inevitably had to climb to meet the enemy, and seldom had the height advantage. Experience over France led to a revision of tactics, which intensified during the Battle of Britain.

RAF FIGHTER COMMAND GROUPS & FIGHTER STATIONS

The size, nature and disposition of Fighter Command in 1940 was entirely the result of Hugh Dowding's efforts in building it up before the war, in the face of considerable opposition, and a prevailing doctrine which placed the emphasis on offensive operations by bombers. Dowding argued the case for the importance of fighter defences, and the necessity of defending the home base. During the belated rush to expand the RAF in the late 1930s he pressed for a minimum of 45 fighter squadrons and took a close interest in the development of new aircraft, weapons and tactics, as well as in new equipment and technologies, including radar. He oversaw the formation of Fighter Command's groups and ensured that its assets were well distributed to meet all potential threats.

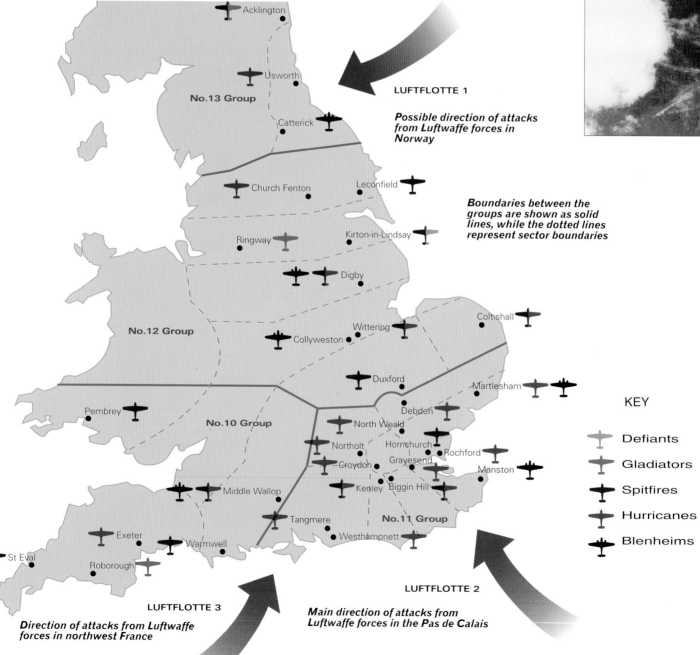

Acklington

Usworth

No.13 Group

Catterick

LUFTFLOTTE 1

Possible direction of attacks from Luftwaffe forces in Norway

Church Fenton

Leconfield

Boundaries between the groups are shown as solid lines, while the dotted lines represent sector boundaries

Ringway

Kirton-in-Lindsey

Digby

Coltishall

No.12 Group

Wittering

Collyweston

Duxford

Martlesham

Pembrey

Debden

No.10 Group

North Weald

Northolt

Hornchurch

Rochford

Croydon

Gravesend

Manston

Kenley

Biggin Hill

Middle Wallop

Tangmere

No.11 Group

Exeter

Westhampnett

St Eval

Warmwell

Roborough

LUFTFLOTTE 3

Direction of attacks from Luftwaffe forces in northwest France

LUFTFLOTTE 2

Main direction of attacks from Luftwaffe forces in the Pas de Calais

KEY

Defiants

Gladiators

Spitfires

Hurricanes

Blenheims

Below: For Londoners and residents of Southeast England, the Battle of Britain was an unforgettable sight – a display of aerial strategy marked out in white condensation trails against the deep blue sky of the summer of 1940.

Right: With the onset of the Battle, controllers in the operations rooms at Fighter Command, groups and sectors were able to follow the progress of operations visually with the help of plotters who moved pieces representing all friendly and hostile forces.

August certainly posed a serious threat to Dowding's defences, so much so that by 5 September Fighter Command's losses were running at the rate of an equivalent of two whole squadrons every day. Moreover, there was little the RAF pilots could do to combat them.

Losses during the past four weeks had deprived many squadrons of their most experienced members, and very young men with no more than two or three months' squadron service were being promoted to command; the aircraft themselves were now showing severe wear and

tear, despite frantic efforts by their manufacturers and repair organisations. Bowing to the inevitable, Dowding was forced to withdraw some of his finest squadrons to the relative quiet of the north to rest and re-equip, bringing to the south newly-formed and inexperienced squadrons, among them the first Canadian, Polish and Czech squadrons of the RAF.

NEW APPROACH
It was at this time that the differing tactics favoured by Park and Leigh-

Mallory came into sharp focus, the former advocating use of single squadrons (because of the short time available in the south to assemble larger forces) and the latter favouring the committing of whole fighter wings to battle. Both men were probably justified in their own combat environments, and it must be said that, given adequate warning, Park himself tried to employ two or three squadrons simultaneously. There were, however, occasions when Leigh-Mallor's wing tactic failed to operate efficiently as

RAF Fighters

Merlin-engined fighters formed the bulk of RAF Fighter Command. Great things were expected of the Defiant, but it proved slow and cumbersome, and vulnerable to belly and head-on attacks. The

Hurricane was altogether more successful and destroyed more enemy aircraft than all the rest of the defences put together.

Defiant Mk 1
This aircraft, of No. 264 Squadron, entered service with the squadron in June 1940 and was used for the disastrous day combat role. The Germans thought the aircraft were Hurricanes and attacked from behind, but once the Defiant formation was broken the RAF aircraft – with no forward-firing guns – was easy prey. N1535 was lost in action on 24 August 1940 on a day operation.

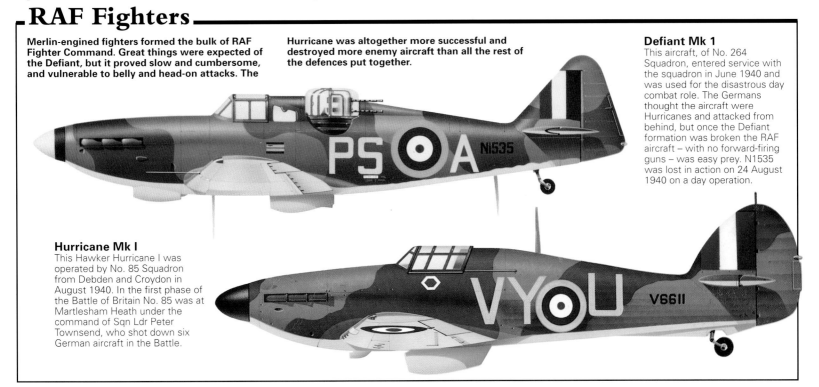

Hurricane Mk I
This Hawker Hurricane I was operated by No. 85 Squadron from Debden and Croydon in August 1940. In the first phase of the Battle of Britain No. 85 was at Martlesham Heath under the command of Sqn Ldr Peter Townsend, who shot down six German aircraft in the Battle.

Supermarine Spitfire Mk I

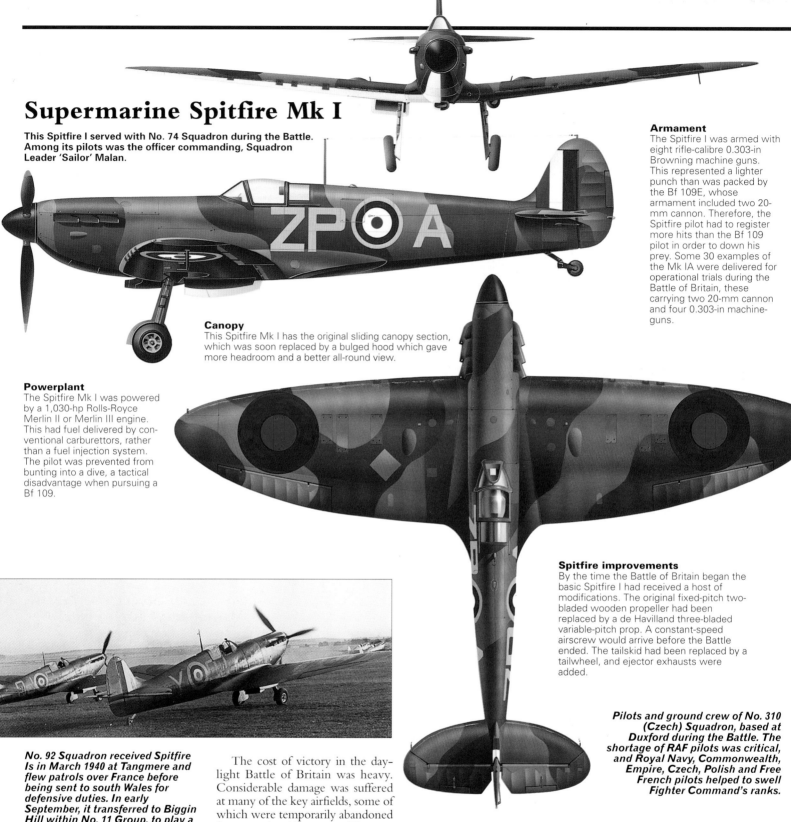

This Spitfire I served with No. 74 Squadron during the Battle.
Among its pilots was the officer commanding, Squadron
Leader 'Sailor' Malan.

Armament
The Spitfire I was armed with
eight rifle-calibre 0.303-in
Browning machine guns.
This represented a lighter
punch than was packed by
the Bf 109E, whose
armament included two 20-
mm cannon. Therefore, the
Spitfire pilot had to register
more hits than the Bf 109
pilot in order to down his
prey. Some 30 examples of
the Mk IA were delivered for
operational trials during the
Battle of Britain, these
carrying two 20-mm cannon
and four 0.303-in machine-
guns.

Canopy
This Spitfire Mk I has the original sliding canopy section,
which was soon replaced by a bulged hood which gave
more headroom and a better all-round view.

Powerplant
The Spitfire Mk I was powered
by a 1,030-hp Rolls-Royce
Merlin II or Merlin III engine.
This had fuel delivered by conventional carburettors, rather
than a fuel injection system.
The pilot was prevented from
bunting into a dive, a tactical
disadvantage when pursuing a
Bf 109.

Spitfire improvements
By the time the Battle of Britain began the
basic Spitfire I had received a host of
modifications. The original fixed-pitch two-
bladed wooden propeller had been
replaced by a de Havilland three-bladed
variable-pitch prop. A constant-speed
airscrew would arrive before the Battle
ended. The tailskid had been replaced by a
tailwheel, and ejector exhausts were
added.

*Pilots and ground crew of No. 310
(Czech) Squadron, based at
Duxford during the Battle. The
shortage of RAF pilots was critical,
and Royal Navy, Commonwealth,
Empire, Czech, Polish and Free
French pilots helped to swell
Fighter Command's ranks.*

*No. 92 Squadron received Spitfire
Is in March 1940 at Tangmere and
flew patrols over France before
being sent to south Wales for
defensive duties. In early
September, it transferred to Biggin
Hill within No. 11 Group, to play a
part in the Battle raging over Kent.*

a result of the time taken to assemble.

Be that as it may, the victory
gained by RAF Fighter Command
was achieved as much by the
courage, resilience and skill of the
RAF pilots and their ground crews
as by the extraordinarily close-knit
organisation that existed within the
command, and there is no doubt
that the extent to which the radar
chain had been integrated into the
fighting processes came as an
unpleasant surprise to the enemy.

The cost of victory in the daylight Battle of Britain was heavy.
Considerable damage was suffered
at many of the key airfields, some of
which were temporarily abandoned
for operational purposes. The cost
in aircrew lives was heavy, more
than 500 men being posted killed
or missing, yet on the last day of the
Battle (31 October) Fighter Command possessed eight more squadrons in the front line than on the
first day, and replacement pilots
were arriving from the training
schools twice as quickly as they had
in July, to continue a tradition that
would for ever be remembered by a
grateful nation: survival had been
achieved through the prowess in
combat of just 3,030 airmen, forever remembered as The Few.

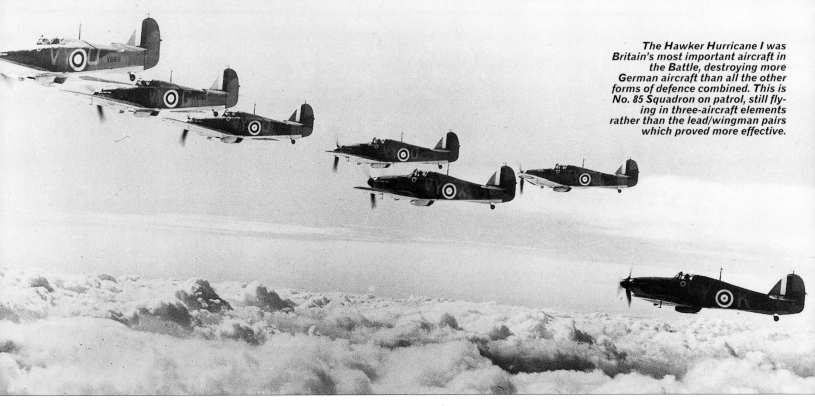

A view from one of the Few

Flight Lieutenant D.M.Crooke flew Spitfire Is with No.609 'West Riding' Squadron, an Auxiliary unit which flew from Northolt, Middle Wallop and Warmwell during the Battle of Britain. Here he describes his first kill.

During the month of July the two air forces tested one another out, examining each others' tactical weaknesses and strengths. The RAF, for instance, gradually learnt to give up its tactics of attacking in fixed V formation, and evolved the use of pairs of aircraft or 'finger four' detached sections.

THE SECRET OF SUCCESS

As Flight Lieutenant D. M. Crook of No. 609 Squadron later wrote of those July days: "We had not yet learnt that it did not pay to go out to sea to meet the enemy, but to let them come to us. Also we did not realise the importance that height meant. Afterwards we used to get as high as possible before going into action. This is the whole secret of success in air fighting."

The chief test pilot of Supermarine was (then) Flying Officer Jeffrey Quill, who fought for a time with No. 65 Squadron from Hornchurch: "When the battle heated up, the job of the Spitfire squadron was to climb up, engage the German fighter escort, and let the bombers go by . . . We'd see a bloody great formation of Dorniers coming in at 12,000 ft. We'd be told to ignore them. Up above were their fighter escorts.

"Our job was to get up and engage those fighters, get a good old dogfight going, get everything milling around, during which time the bombers would be groaning inexorably along. With any luck,

by the time they got anywhere near their target, we'd have forced all their fighter escorts out of position and down would come our Hurricanes to get at the bombers. These two aircraft together – plus the radar – those were the things that won the Battle of Britain."

The Germans began by attacking convoys in the Channel. Meanwhile, bombing attacks were also mounted on naval installations at Portland, on 4 and 9 July. In the first raid, defending British fighters arrived too late, but on the second occasion long-distance radar gave sufficient warning, and Spitfires from No. 609 Squadron were ordered into the air.

Crook and two companions were patrolling over Weymouth. "I saw one or two Huns appear, and recognised them as Junkers 87 divebombers. I immediately turned on my reflector sights, put my gun button on to 'fire' and settled down to enjoy a little slaughter of a few Ju 87s, as they are rather helpless machines. . . when I happened to look round behind. To my

intense surprise and dismay, I saw at least nine Messerschmitt 110s about 2,000 ft above us.

"This completely altered the situation. We were now hopelessly outnumbered, and in a very dangerous position. I immediately called up Peter and Michael and shouted desperately, 'Look out behind!' I have never felt so desperate or so helpless in my life as when, in spite of my warnings, these two flew steadily on, apparently quite oblivious of the fact that they were going to be struck down from the rear in a few seconds.

"At that moment the leading Messerschmitt opened fire at me and I saw his shells and tracer bullets going past just above my head. They were jolly close too. I immediately did a very violent turn to the left and dived through a layer of cloud just below.

"I saw dimly a machine moving in the cloud on my left and flying parallel to me. I stalked him through the cloud, and when he emerged into a patch of clear sky I saw that it was a Ju 87.

"I was in an ideal position to attack, so I opened fire and put the remainder of my ammunition – about 2,000 rounds – into him at very close range. Even in the heat of the moment I well remember my amazement at the shattering

effect of my fire. Pieces flew off his fuselage and cockpit covering, a stream of smoke appeared from the engine, and a moment later a great sheet of flame licked out from the engine cowling and he dived down vertically. The flames enveloped the whole machine and he went straight down, apparently quite slowly, for about 5,000 ft, until he was just a shapeless burning mass of wreckage . . . I followed him down, and saw him hit the sea with a great burst of white foam."

FIRST KILL

The victim of Crook's first kill was Hauptmann Freiherr von Dalwigk, holder of the Knight's Cross. Sai Crook: "I had often wondered what would be my feelings when killing somebody like this, and especially when seeing them go down in flames.

"I was rather surprised to reflect afterwards that my only feeling had been one of considerable elation – and a sort of bewildered surprise because it had all been so easy."

Early British Bombing

SEPTEMBER 1939 – DECEMBER 1940

Left: The Air Component of the British Expeditionary Force in France had two squadrons of Bristol Blenheim Mk IVs (Nos 53 and 59). Both squadrons were based at Poix for long-range tactical reconnaissance and bombing.

Left: The Air Component of the British Expeditionary Force in France had two squadrons of Bristol Blenheim Mk IVs (Nos 53 and 59). Both squadrons were based at Poix for long-range tactical reconnaissance and bombing.

Above: A rare photograph of No. 50 Squadron aircrew lined up in front of one of their Handley Page Hampdens at RAF Waddington. The squadron participated in the RAF's first raid on enemy land targets on the night of 19/20 March 1940.

Below: A Blenheim Mk IV of No. 226 Squadron from RAF Wattisham en route to its target over France in 1940. No. 2 Group Blenheims took heavy losses in their low-level attacks on enemy targets in France and the Low Countries.

The Royal Air Force went to war against Germany steeped in the Trenchard tradition that the heavy bomber was its principal weapon, yet the aircraft with which it was equipped (the Vickers Wellington, Armstrong Whitworth Whitley and Handley Page Hampden) proved to be wholly inadequate to impose any significant pressure upon the enemy. It was not only poorly equipped to navigate and bomb accurately at night but disastrously vulnerable by day. Nor was the British Air Staff single-minded as how best to employ its so-called heavy bombers.

In September 1939 the RAF possessed 10 squadrons of Wellingtons, 10 of Hampdens and nine of Whitleys, of which the Wellington was undoubtedly the best. It was in the mistaken belief that it could defend itself in the presence of enemy fighters, however, that the Wellington was first committed to daylight attacks during the first four months of the war. In deference to government restrictions on endangering the enemy's civilian population, the targets were German naval forces in or near their home ports. From the outset, German radar gave notice of the bombers'

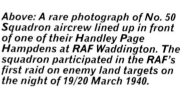

approach so that flak and fighters were able to take a heavy toll. The last such raid, on 18 December, cost the loss of 12 out of 24 Wellingtons of Nos 9, 37 and 149 Squadrons. Scarcely any damage was inflicted on German ships, and thereafter the Wellingtons were confined to bombing at night.

If the efforts of the Wellington crews were disappointing, those of the RAF light bombers, the Bristol Blenheim Mk IVs, were more promising and from the first day of the war the type performed a

Left: The crew of a Wellington Mk IC of No. 149 Squadron take a last minute look at the map before boarding their aircraft. By the end of 1940 Wellingtons equipped no fewer than 19 squadrons of RAF Bomber Command.

Early twin-engined types

Without a power-operated gun turret the twin-engined Hampden had inadequate defence against enemy fighters. Although slower than the Hampden, the Whitley could carry a useful load over a good range and was used to drop leaflets during the propaganda war. Both took part in the first bombing raid in March 1940. Blenheims were far more successful as low-level coastal attackers.

Handley Page Hampden Mk I
A No. 5 Group Hampden Mk I (P1320) flown by No. 106 Squadron based at RAF Finningley in April 1940. The Mk I carried a crew of four, was armed with three 7.7-mm (0.303-in) Vickers machine-guns and had a bombload of 1814-kg (4,000 lb).

Armstrong Whitworth Whitley Mk V
This all-black painted Armstrong Whitworth Whitley Mk V was flown by No. 78 Squadron for night operations from RAF Dishforth and RAF Linton-on-Ouse between September 1939 and April 1941.

Bristol Blenheim Mk IV
Built by the Rootes shadow factory at Speke, Liverpool, this Blenheim Mk IV had rear defence guns fitted under the nose in December 1940 while serving with No. 40 Squadron at RAF Wyton.

Left: The rear gunner emerging from the tail turret of an Armstrong Whitworth Whitley. This aircraft (K8942) served with Nos 51 and 166 Squadrons before being relegated to training duties with 10 OTU, 7 BGS and finally 7 AGS in 1943.

Above: Packets of propaganda leaflets are loaded onto a Whitley for a night-time 'Nickelling' raid over Germany in the autumn of 1939. Whitley squadrons were given this thankless task, starting on the night of 3/4 September 1939.

over German towns at night, the bombing restrictions preventing the delivery of high explosive. Night after night these lumbering, angular aeroplanes set course from the UK to discharge their paper bundles with scarcely any interference from German defences, their worst enemy being bad weather. Early in 1940 Whitleys of No. 77 Squadron, flying from Villeneuve in France, dropped leaflets over Prague, Vienna and cities in Poland.

BOMBING STARTS
The third of the heavy trio was the Hampden – nicknamed the 'flying suitcase' on account of its deep, narrow fuselage. This was the only British bomber not to be armed with a power-operated gun turret, and was indeed appallingly vulnerable to enemy fighter attack. Fortunately the Germans possessed scarcely any night-fighter defence during the first eight months of the war.

Following the dropping of German bombs on British soil on 16 March 1940, which killed a civilian in the Orkneys, the RAF attacked an enemy land target four nights later when 26 Whitleys and 15 Hampdens attacked the seaplane base at Hörnum-on-Sylt. In the following month Wellingtons joined the attack with a raid on Stavanger airfield in Norway.

It was not until after the German offensive had opened in the West on 10 May that Bomber Command aircraft were permitted to attack the German mainland, although their targets were still strictly confined to military objectives. Moreover, because of inadequate navigation equipment and outdated bombsights, few bomber crews attacked their briefed targets.

number of outstanding raids, although the small number and size of their bombs (the largest of which was the 227-kg [500-lb] weapon), severely limited the damage caused. Yet the numerous attacks against targets off the north German coast, carried out with great gallantry and often in poor weather, probably achieved more than all the raids by the heavy bombers combined.

The Whitley was the slowest of all the British bombers – though a rugged weight-lifter – and was assigned the nebulous task of dropping loads of propaganda leaflets

Right: A Whitley Mk V of No. 58 Squadron taking off from RAF Linton-on-Ouse at sunset for a night bombing raid over Germany in May 1940. The Whitley had a good range that enabled it to reach Poland, but at the expense of a significant bombload.

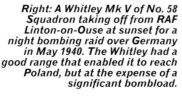

Vickers Wellington Mk IC

Vickers' Type 415 Wellington Mk IC, had a redesigned hydraulic system, a 24-volt electrical system and the substitution of beam guns in the midship position for the unsatisfactory ventral turret. The Pegasus XVIII-powered bomber set the standard for subsequent marks in the early war years.

Construction

With its unique geodetic 'basket weave' method of construction, the first prototype was flown on 15 June 1936, with the first production Mk I following on 23 December 1937. Aircraft were built at Chester and Blackpool, as well as Weybridge.

Powerplant

The Wellington Mk IC was equipped with two 783-kW (1,050-hp) Bristol Pegasus XVIII nine-cylinder radial engines, giving a maximum speed of 378 km/h (235 mph) at 4724 m (15,500 ft).

Armament

Two 7.7-mm (0.303-in) Browning machine-guns in each of the power-operated nose and tail turrets; two manually operated 7.7-mm (0.303-in) beam guns (replacing a single-gun ventral turret). The normal maximum internal bombload was 2041 kg (4,500 lb).

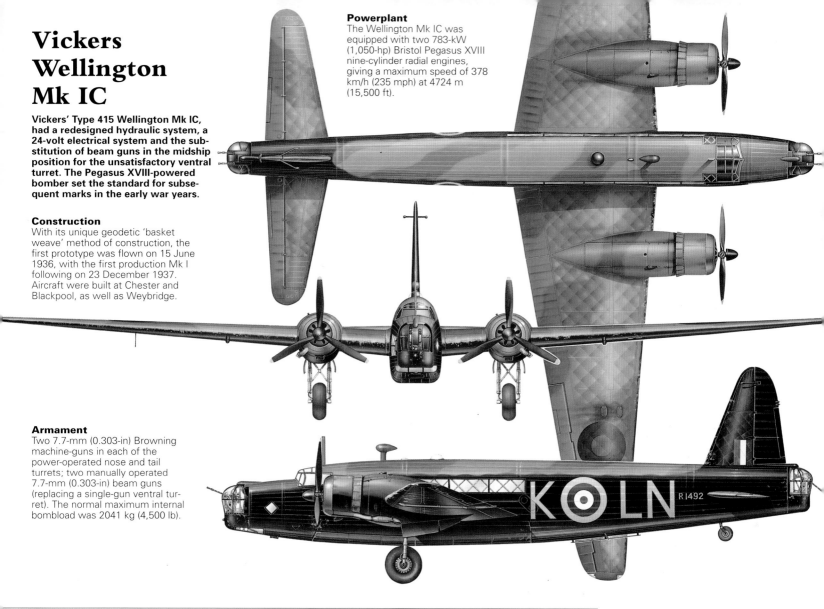

When eventually the War Cabinet lifted the restrictions on British bombing over Germany on 15 May and 99 Wellingtons, Whitleys and Hampdens opened Bomber Command's strategic bombing offensive with attacks on oil and steel targets in the Ruhr, fewer than

30 crews claimed even to have identified their target. Bomber Command was further restricted in its attacks on Italian targets (when that nation entered the war on 10 June), and although Wellingtons deployed to the south of France the French government curtailed their attacks for fear of reprisal raids on their territory.

During the Battle of Britain a number of RAF bomber bases were attacked by the Luftwaffe and some

Left: Sgt John Hannah (left) who, at 18, was awarded the Victoria Cross for putting out a serious fire on Hampden Mk I P1355 while over Antwerp. With him is P/O C.A.H. Connor who received the DFC for bringing the aircraft back to base.

bombers (mostly Whitleys) were destroyed. However, three achievements marked the climax (if such it can be called) of this stage of British bombing. On 11/12 June 36 Whitleys flew from the UK, refuelling in the Channel Islands, to attack targets in northern Italy and, although only 12 crews claimed to have bombed Turin or Milan, the long flight over the Alps in poor weather represented something of an epic of endurance. On 1 July a Hampden, flown by Flying Officer Guy Gibson (later Wing Commander, VC) dropped Bomber Command's first 907-kg (2,000-lb) bomb over Kiel, the heaviest bomb thus far carried by the RAF in World War II. Additionally, on

Left: The Handley Page Hampden Mk I equipped 10 squadrons in September 1939. By the end of the year, following heavy losses, they had been switched from day to night operations. The last of 500 aircraft was delivered in July 1940.

25/26 August 81 Wellingtons, Whitleys and Hampdens set out for the first time for Berlin, and 29 of their crews claimed to have bombed the German capital.

Despite these very modest beginnings, Bomber Command was aware of its own shortcomings and before the end of 1940 the first true heavy bombers, the Avro Manchester, Short Stirling and Handley Page Halifax, were arriving in the RAF. The new year would see a significant strengthening of bombing muscle, though its aim would still be suspect.

A Battle Lost

On that fateful day, 18 December 1940, a daylight raid on enemy warships by Wellington Mk IAs of No. 9 Squadron resulted in a massacre at the hands of Luftwaffe Messerschmitt Bf 109 and Bf 110 fighters. Five of the squadron's aircraft were lost.

"The first thing I knew was that I felt cold around my feet and legs. I looked down, and saw only water beneath me! The guns refused to fire, too, and when I looked up I saw both barrels had been blown off. Then a hail of cannon shells passed in front of me and blew the Perspex out of the turret."

On 18 December 1940, 24 Wellington Mk IA bombers left England for a major daylight bombing raid on German warships at Wilhelmshaven. Only 12 of the aircraft survived as the formation was mauled by German fighters. One of the lucky ones amongst them – for surely luck it was – was WS-G, No. 9 Squadron's 'G for George', piloted by Sergeant John Ramshaw and with Charlie Driver, an 18-year-old fitter/rigger in the front turret.

Driver's position was precarious,

Below: In June 1939 a New Zealand Flight was formed to train with these Wellington Mk IAs. In April 1940 it was redesignated No. 75 Squadron at RAF Feltwell and began night bombing operations, moving soon afterwards to RAF Mildenhall.

to say the least. The turret had been demolished around him, and as he turned to make his way back into the body of the fuselage he found his way blocked by smoke and flame. He tore off one of his big leather outer gauntlets and used that to beat out the flames. When he got back and up to the cockpit, he found Ramshaw sitting calmly at the controls, whistling a popular tune, apparently unconcerned that the entire Luftwaffe seemed intent on shooting them out of the sky.

"You okay, Charlie?" he asked, and Driver stuck up both thumbs in acknowledgement. Sergeant Hewitt, the second pilot, couldn't believe that Driver had emerged alive from the wreckage of the turret.

FIGHT TO SURVIVE

G-George's rear turret had fallen silent too, its guns jammed, and the surrounding Messerschmitts knew it. One turned in for the kill, cannon shells smashing into the tail of the aircraft. Rear-gunner Walter Lilley was struggling in silence to clear his weapons when he was hit, and died there, far from help or comfort.

Lilley had downed one and perhaps two of the attacking aircraft and now, as if his life were sufficient restitution, the fighters fell away, ammunition and fuel running low. Somehow G-George was still in the air but Driver, looking out of the astrodome, couldn't imagine how.

"As I looked out, I saw all the fabric flapping on the wings. The

insides were all exposed and it was as though someone had taken a great knife and carved all along the leading edge of the wings. The nose of the aircraft was sheared away, but I'd closed the bulkhead doors behind the front turret when I'd got out, to keep the air blast from the rest of the fuselage. The engines looked like someone had used a sledgehammer and a great chisel on them."

Worse was still to come – the fuel tanks had been perforated. Driver was told to work the hand pump that sucked petrol from the reserve fuel tank. For 30 long minutes he pumped as hard as he

could and then, inevitably, felt the pump sucking air. First one engine died, and then the other.

They all knew that they would not make land but, instead, would have to ditch their stricken aircraft in the cold December sea. Then, in the distance, Ramshaw made out an alien shape – a Grimsby trawler! "I can see a ship!" he shouted excitedly over the intercom. "I'm going to try and make for it." The rest of the crew braced themselves as best they could.

The Wellington hit hard, within a quarter of a mile from the fishing boat, the impact tearing away more

of its torn fabric. Ramshaw smashed his head into the windscreen and, only half-conscious, could barely help himself. It was young Charlie Driver who released the rubber dinghy from its stowage in the aft part of the port engine nacelle, and then he and the wireless operator, Leading Aircraftman Conolly, made their way out onto the wing. Ramshaw, too, had struggled out through the cockpit top and fell into the sea. Driver and Conolly grabbed him as best they could and bundled him into the dingy. Then they and Hewitt clambered in too, just as G-George put her nose down and took Lilley

Above: Crews of Wellington Mk IAs of No. 149 Squadron walking out to their aircraft. Although the Wellington's geodetic construction made it very strong, its inadequate defensive guns left it vulnerable to critical damage by Luftwaffe fighters.

to a watery grave.

Quarter of an hour later they were picked up by the trawler and taken on the 16-hour journey back to Grimsby.

It took the sacrifice of the aircraft and crew on missions like this to wake up Bomber Command to the suicide of unescorted daylight bombing.

The Night Blitz

SEPTEMBER 1940 – MAY 1941

German defeat in the daylight Battle of Britain frustrated plans to invade the British Isles in the early autumn of 1940. Instead, Goering believed that his bomber force could impose a military solution to the war by repeated heavy attacks on London and other cities by night. The first such major attack was launched against the dock area of East London on the night of 7/8 September just as the Battle of Britain was reaching its decisive phase. Moreover, German bombers continued to visit London for more than 50 consecutive nights, creating infinitely greater damage and casualties than in the whole of the daylight assault.

LIMITED DEFENCE

Seldom more than 100 Heinkel He 111s, Dornier Do 17s and Junkers Ju 88s operated on any single night in this savage attack on the British capital yet, despite being without any form of fighter protection, they were able to escape any significant loss, such was the poor state of the British night-fighter defences. Up to this stage the obsolescent Bristol Blenheim, flying with extremely rudimentary airborne radar, backed up by a few single-seat Hawker Hurricanes had constituted the

Above: Junkers Ju 88A-4s are seen en route to their targets. Main force Luftwaffe bombers were all able to find their targets using Knickebein radio beams, while the elite and expert pathfinders of Kampfgruppe 100 used the more accurate X-Gerät to mark targets with incendiaries.

Right: The Heinkel He 111 was the mainstay of the Luftwaffe's night bombing force. This one shows a typical over-painted night camouflage colour scheme, with toned-down national insignia.

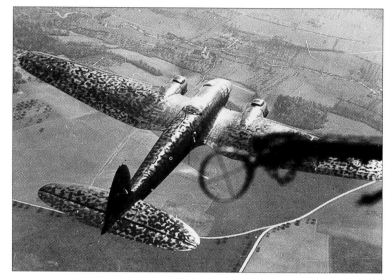

fighter defence at night. In September the first purpose-designed night-fighter, the heavily armed Bristol Beaufighter, started arriving in service with more effective radar, together with some Boulton Paul Defiant turret-equipped two-seaters (discarded as day fighters), but it would be many months before these aircraft would achieve noticeable results against the night raiders.

INDUSTRY TARGETED

Although the Nazi leadership espoused no pretence at achieving military damage in the night assault on London, the Luftwaffe itself recognised that worthwhile results from the night assaults could be gained only by striking at British industrial centres much farther afield, and had thus been developing navigation aids to enable its bombers to reach into the heart of the nation. Employing narrow radio beams transmitted from continental stations across the British Isles, the Germans started flying pathfinder He 111s of Kampfgruppe 100 specially equipped with radio receivers that enabled them to fly accurately towards distant targets, which they would mark with incendiary bombs to guide the crews of the main bombing force.

Above: A market trader in the East End of London continues his fruit-selling among the ruins of the Blitz. The Luftwaffe deliberately targeted London's East End, hoping that attacks on the densely packed population might lead Britain to sue for peace.

Right: Although devoid of any interception aids, the Hawker Hurricane was widely used as a night-fighter throughout the winter of 1940-41. This No. 85 Squadron Hurricane was used in the battle against night raiders over southern England.

Despite the existence of this equipment being discovered by the British, the defences were caught unawares when, on 14/15 November, KGr 100 led 437 bombers against Coventry, causing enormous damage, killing 380 civilians and seriously injuring 800 others. In the final week of November further heavy raids were launched against London, Southampton, Bristol, Plymouth and Liverpool. In December, Manchester and Sheffield were added to the list of stricken cities. Much in line with the growth of British bombs at this stage of the war, German weapons were in the main the 1,102-lb (500-kg) high explosive bomb, although huge numbers of 4.4-lb (2-kg) incendiary bombs were showered over British towns and cities during the Blitz. However, growing numbers of 2,205-lb (1000-kg) bombs were carried by the He 111s to short-range targets, as well as highly-destructive parachute 'mines', the latter being adaptations of the German sea mine fitted with a barostatic fuse to give maximum blast effect.

FIRE BOMBS

The year ended with a particularly vicious incendiary raid on the City

An early Ju 88A-1 runs up its engines at night. As a bomber, the type could carry a useful load at a reasonable speed. The Ju 88 owed much of its success to its high speed and concentrated defensive armament, and it survived far longer than its contemporaries.

of London which, carried out when the Thames was at low tide and during a weekend when few fire watchers were in their offices, caused grievous damage among centuries-old churches and other treasured buildings.

The second half of the Blitz brought about marked improvements in the British defences. Gradually the RAF night-fighters began to take a noticeable toll of the bombers: three in January, four in February, 22 in March, 48 in April and 96 in May. During the same five months the guns and balloons claimed a total of about 120 enemy aircraft. Meanwhile, Nottingham, Avonmouth, Merseyside, Swansea, Belfast, Clydeside, Hull, Sunderland and Newcastle were all heavily raided, in addition to still further attacks on the previous victims. Not only were the night-fighter crews becoming proficient in operating their airborne radar in collaboration with the new ground-control radar stations, but the gun

defences were also being steadily strengthened throughout the country. In February the first massed batteries of ground-to-air rockets went into action for the first time.

By May Hitler was completing his plans for the great assault on the Soviet Union, which the Luftwaffe

Left: Flying above the cloud tops, this Do 17Z-2 of 9./KG 76 is approaching the English coast. Previously criticised for being underpowered with a full bombload, the Do 17Z-2 had the 746-kW (1,000-hp) Bramo 323P engines that featured two-speed superchargers, which restored the bombload to 1000 kg (2,205 lb).

Right: A Luftwaffe Ju 88 bomber crew adjusts their parachute harnesses before departing on a night raid over England.

Luftwaffe night bombers

Attacks on Britain's centres of population were in part a reaction to the RAF's night raids against German cities. Although targets like docks, rail centres and factories were attacked where **possible, the primary aim of the campaign was to dislocate industry by exhausting and sapping the morale of the workers, to terrorise the civilian population and bring England to the negotiating table.**

Junkers Ju 88A-1
Losses by day forced the RAF and the Luftwaffe to turn to nocturnal bombing. This Junkers Ju 88A-1 served with II/KG 52 'Edelweiss' from Melun-Villaroche in the winter of 1940 during the night Blitz against Britain. National markings were obscured and lamp-black distemper applied to the undersurfaces.

Heinkel He 111H
This Heinkel He 111H-3 flew with 2./KGr 100 from Vannes in Britanny. It is equipped with *X-Gerät* pathfinder gear which allowed the Gruppe to mark targets with extraordinary accuracy for other 'main force' bombers. It was widely used during the night Blitz.

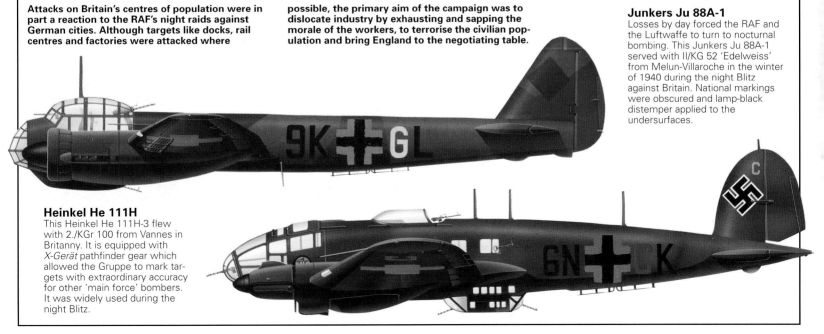

would be called on to support. With no appearance of a crack in British morale, the bulk of German bomber forces was moved from Western Europe eastwards, and the night Blitz on the UK petered out.

CIVILIANS KILLED

The bombing had indeed done little lasting damage to the UK's ability to wage war. Most serious was that caused in the aircraft industry, the output of which was reduced by about 20 per cent for almost six months (at the Supermarine, Short, Bristol, Avro and Vickers factories). In addition, 70,000 tons of food stocks had been destroyed. However, no more than 0.5 per cent of the nation's oil stocks were destroyed and most of the damage caused to the railways was quickly repaired. On the other hand, no fewer than 52,000 civilians had been killed and almost 80,000 severely injured, not to mention well over 120,000 rendered temporarily homeless.

Above left: The Bristol Blenheim Mk IF was the RAF's only practical night-fighter at the beginning of WWII, when it was already operational with Nos 25 and 29 Squadrons.

Above: A Boulton-Paul Defiant Mk II night-fighter of No. 256 Squadron at RAF Squires Gate, responsible for the night defence of Liverpool. The Defiant was relegated to the night-fighter role following its disastrous showing in daylight.

Left: As the battle continued, the RAF was fortunate to be able to call on increasing numbers of skilled aircrew of foreign origins, mostly refugees from occupied Europe, such as this group of Polish airmen.

Above: The view from the nose of a Dornier Do 17, dubbed 'The Flying Pencil', in daylight formation over southern England. The extensively glazed nose offered no armour protection to the machine-gunner/bomb-aimer.

Night defenders

In late 1940 and early 1941, night-fighter technology was in its infancy, and little more than a token effort could be made to combat the Luftwaffe's night bombers. One of the reasons for the replacement of Dowding as C-in-C Fighter Command was the perception that he had failed to make even this token effort, and had not assigned single-seat fighters to night defence.

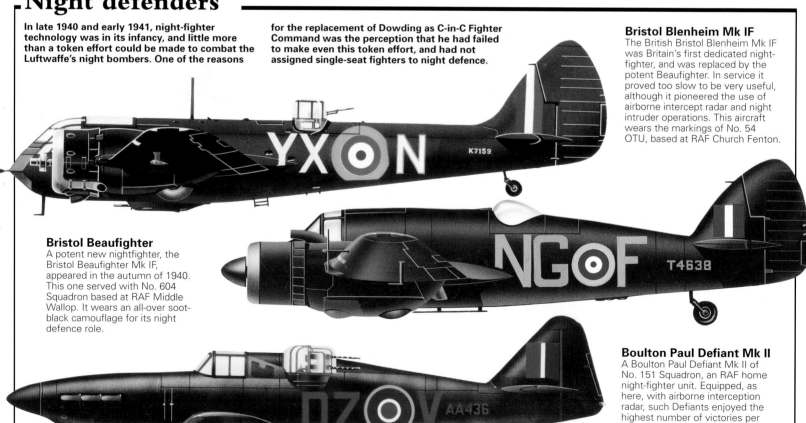

Bristol Blenheim Mk IF
The British Bristol Blenheim Mk IF was Britain's first dedicated night-fighter, and was replaced by the potent Beaufighter. In service it proved too slow to be very useful, although it pioneered the use of airborne intercept radar and night intruder operations. This aircraft wears the markings of No. 54 OTU, based at RAF Church Fenton.

Bristol Beaufighter
A potent new nightfighter, the Bristol Beaufighter Mk IF, appeared in the autumn of 1940. This one served with No. 604 Squadron based at RAF Middle Wallop. It wears an all-over soot-black camouflage for its night defence role.

Boulton Paul Defiant Mk II
A Boulton Paul Defiant Mk II of No. 151 Squadron, an RAF home night-fighter unit. Equipped, as here, with airborne interception radar, such Defiants enjoyed the highest number of victories per interception of any British night-fighter type deployed during the winter of 1940-41.

With overpainted **Hakenkreuz** *and with the white sections of the* **Balkenkreuz** *obscured, this Ju 88A-1 from 1./***KG** *51 was used in the night Blitz against British cities.*

Night Attacker

Peter Stahl flew the Ju 88 on night bombing missions over England, and here describes a typical mission.

"The sudden howling of the port engine shocks me awake. Next to me, Hans, my navigator, hangs in his harness, his head resting against the cabin glazing. I call Theo and Hein over the intercom. Asleep! Our Ju 88 has climbed from take-off to 4200 m. The engine temperatures are much too low because the engine flaps are still open; the fuel service tanks are nearly empty. None of us is wearing oxygen masks – had we continued in our sleep we would have passed cleanly and quietly into the next world.

"Fly, sleep, eat, and fly again – that is how it has been for weeks. Ahead are the outlines of the coast. The searchlights grope for us but there is no AA fire. The enemy gunners are not asleep, so that means night-fighters. Some of the lights have been grouped in fives. As a result our path is accurately marked by a pyramid of lights that wanders along with us.

"Frequently our aircraft is hit full-on by a beam that temporarily blinds me. The beam wanders with us for endlessly long moments before slipping away again, which shows that, when flying at high altitude, our matt-painted bombers can no longer be optically traced from the ground.

"I glimpse one twin-engined night fighter as it crosses my path 100 m ahead, but he is up-moon and misses us. Then, as if reporting nothing more unusual than a shooting star, of which we see hundreds every night, my gunner reports calmly over the intercom, 'Night-fighters to port behind.'

"I pull the Ju 88 into a steep half-roll to port and let it fall upside down into the night. I have just levelled off when Hein repeats his warning. The Devil! Once more we shoot like a stone into the pitch blackness below. Then a third time! By now we are just 800 m high, dragging our 2000 kg of explosives and with a long climb ahead of us to reach a decent altitude for attack. That we have escaped the night-fighter is due to the excellence of our aircraft, and I find myself stroking the control column in gratitude.

"As I climb back to our attack altitude we meet cloud and the aircraft develops slight icing-up. At 6000 m the temperature has dropped to -30°C, but the icing-up has stopped.

"The cloud clears and almost immediately the anti-aircraft guns pick us up. The shells burst ahead of and behind us and any attempt at evasion seems pointless. Nevertheless, I force myself to try every trick in my book, every anti-aircraft evasion manoeuvre I know, but in vain. Things are so bad that I catch myself several times wanting to drop my weapons blind into the night.

"Suddenly, a red reflection is visible beyond the horizon. There is no need for navigation now and I vary my approach route in an attempt to avoid areas with particularly massed anti-aircraft fire.

"As we get nearer, the anti-aircraft fire becomes thicker and it seems as if thousands of searchlights are in action. The approach flight through this blazing inferno, punctuated by the explosions of

anti-aircraft shells, seems endlessly long and I am forced to fly evasive manoeuvres time and again.

"But what we experience over the target surpasses anything one could possibly imagine. The whole city seems to be ablaze. In addition the target is lit up by flare-bombs that flash at irregular intervals.

"With throttled-back engines I begin a glide towards my allocated target. Suddenly my Ju 88 is met by accurate anti-aircraft fire that forces me to turn away. I mark time until the exploding shells concentrate around another aircraft, and then use that moment to go into a steep incline at high speed towards my release point.

"Our targets are locks in the dock area. Hans has an easy task aiming our mines. I fly over the burning port in accordance with his instructions. We can recognise every detail shown to us on aerial reconnaissance photographs as if it were daytime. My stopwatch is running, and exactly on the second we see two fiery explosions in our area – our mines.

FRIENDLY COAST AHEAD

"Suddenly a string of parachute flares burst into blinding light just to the left of us and exactly at our altitude. I immediately bank away to starboard. Continually and at irregular intervals I vary my flight direction and my engine revs, changing their sound. The minutes drag endlessly until we finally see the coast. My nerves are ready to give up. Without further ado I throttle back to 'noiseless' running and nose down into high speed flight knowing that this will bring me into range of the light AA coastal batteries. I don't care any more, and rely on luck to avoid areas of massed anti-aircraft fire.

"Then it happens! A blinding

flash. We are hit. I pull up our Ju 88 and cast a quick glance over the instruments. Everything seems normal and there are no injuries among the crew.

"I pull back on the throttle levers but the port engine continues to run at full revs. A shell splinter must have severed the throttle controls. I switch it off and the Ju 88 flies slanting in the dark night.

"Ahead of us the searchlights that finger the sky are our own, and we are glad to see them. We fire the identification flares but the searchlights continue beaming in our faces. Suddenly light AA guns open up on us. I am forced to fly a series of dangerous evasive turns over my stopped engine.

"This deadly game of searchlight and light AA guns follows us along the coast. Already exhausted with fear and lack of sleep, my crew give way to fury, firing back with their machine-guns at our own men.

"As we approach our base I prepare my crew for the peculiarities of a one-engined landing. Visibility is excellent, so, contrary to accepted practice, I let down my undercarriage rather than make a belly landing. This takes time as I have only half the normal hydraulic pressure. Aboard the aircraft nobody says a word.

"I estimate my height as we glide in for touch-down on the flare path. Too low! We hit with the port wing and crash onto the ground in complete darkness. The scraping slide along the ground seems endless. The starboard engine howls up and can not be stopped. Terrified of fire, we are desperate to get out and away from the aircraft but the cabin roof has jammed. Soldiers smash at the cabin and we tumble clear.

"The fire-fighters and doctors are quickly on the scene. The soldiers tell the doctor, a young one fresh to the front, that none of us is badly hurt. We watch him crawl into the Ju 88. He reappears with the aircraft clock as a souvenir.

"For Hans, the doctor's conduct is the straw that finally breaks the camel's back. Calmly he walks up to the doctor, takes the clock and hits him in the face with such force that the medicine man slithers over the wing and falls flat on the grass below.

"So ends another flight over London."

The Balkans and Crete

OCTOBER 1940 – MAY 1941

Left: Hs 126s served widely in the east on army co-operation duties. Their service in Greece was notable, this aircraft being seen over Athens. The yellow theatre bands were worn as the campaign was in mainland Europe. Aircraft on operations outside Europe wore white bands.

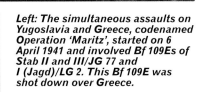

Left: The simultaneous assaults on Yugoslavia and Greece, codenamed Operation 'Maritz', started on 6 April 1941 and involved Bf 109Es of Stab II and III/JG 77 and I (Jagd)/LG 2. This Bf 109E was shot down over Greece.

Above: Luftwaffe attack on Greece on 10 April 1941. The Greek army surrendered on 20 April and one week later the fall of Athens brought the campaign to a conclusion. Within less than a year, the British and Commonwealth armies had been forced to evacuate the continent in extremis.

Despite the eventual voluntary alignment by the other Balkan powers with the Axis, Hitler was aware that both Yugoslavia and Greece represented weak spots in his southern flank for his forthcoming attack on the Soviet Union. After weeks of little progress by the Italians in their own attack on Greece through Albania, Hitler accordingly decided to eliminate these potential Allied footholds in the Balkans.

Italy had struck at Greece on 28 October 1940, and in answer to appeals by the Greek government an RAF squadron of Blenheims was immediately sent from North Africa for the defence of Athens, and by the end of November two more Blenheim squadrons and two of Gladiators followed. Before the year was out the Gladiators were operating patrols over the Albanian frontier, though contact was seldom made with the Régia Aéronautica. Wellingtons, flying from Egypt, carried out occasional raids against Italian supply ports, but in general bad weather hampered air operations. Nevertheless the Gladiator pilots were credited with the destruction of around 30 Italian aircraft by the end of December, for the loss of 10 aircraft.

BALKANS INVADED

Fearing that the RAF might use Greek airfields from which to bomb the Romanian oil fields, Hitler began his move into the Balkans on 1 March 1941, with German troops entering Bulgaria. Within seven days three more RAF squadrons, including one of Hurricanes, were sent to Greece,

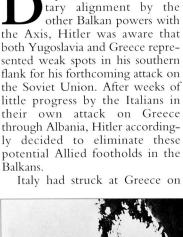

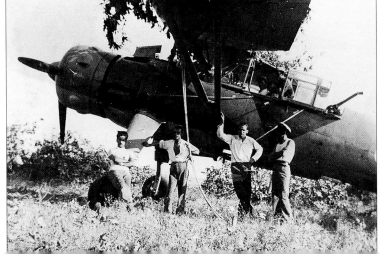

Left: In addition to its traditional role of army co-operation, the Henschel Hs 126B-1 was also used for battlefield reconnaissance and artillery spotting in 1940-41. Following the introduction of the Fw 189, the Hs 126 was relegated to second-line duties.

Above: Junkers Ju 87B Stukas and their lethal bomb-loads on a Greek airfield. As with other invasions, Stukas played a major role in the Wehrmacht's campaign in Greece and the Balkans.

Below: The Savoia-Marchetti SM.79 Sparviero (Sparrowhawk) medium bomber of the Régia Aéronautica was well respected by its antagonists and lauded by its crews for its handling qualities and sturdiness. This formation of five SM.79s is seen over typical Balkan terrain.

which were opposed by fewer than 500 Yugoslav, British and Greek aircraft, all but a few of them (the Hurricanes and Blenheims) being hopelessly outdated.

Despite all that these few aircraft could do, assisted by the long-range Wellingtons, the Germans had gained their first objectives (the occupation of Yugoslavia and the capture of Salonika) by 14 April. The previous day an entire formation of Blenheims had been shot down north of Monastir, and on 15 April enemy aircraft virtually wiped out a Blenheim squadron (No. 113) on the ground at Niamata.

EVACUATION

Development of the German two-prong advance southwards decided the fate of Greece, and with overwhelming enemy air superiority quickly eroding the RAF's resources capable of supporting the British and Greek armies, the only question remaining was how much of the air forces could be evacuated? In the event the three fighter squadrons, Nos 33, 80 and 208, now equipped with Hurricanes, remained until the last moment. In

one of the final air combats over the Piraeus the South African Squadron Leader M.T.St J. Pattle, the war's highest-scoring RAF pilot, was shot down and killed on 20 April. Four days later the last British fighters left Greek soil for the last time.

Some of the surviving aircraft from the Greek campaign landed on the island of Crete, and this soon became the next subject of German attention. On 20 May Luftwaffe Ju 52/3ms started dropping paratroops

Above: An early Macchi MC.200 Saetta, with the relatively low-powered Fiat A.74 RC.38 engine. The Régia Aéronautica first used the MC.200 in action against Malta and then Greece, but it was no match for later fighter types.

Below: The camouflage of this Dornier Do 17Z-2 does little to conceal it against the blue of the Mediterranean. A participant in the spring 1941 offensive against Greece, this particular aircraft belonged to Kampfgeschwader 2.

followed by two more shortly after this. Before the end of the month a military coup in Yugoslavia threatened that country's ties with the Tripartite Pact and on 6 April the German army and air force attacked both Greece and Yugoslavia, launching a devastating and ruthless air attack on Belgrade. Supporting the Balkan campaign, Luftflotte IV fielded some 1,200 modern aircraft,

Bombers over the Adriatic

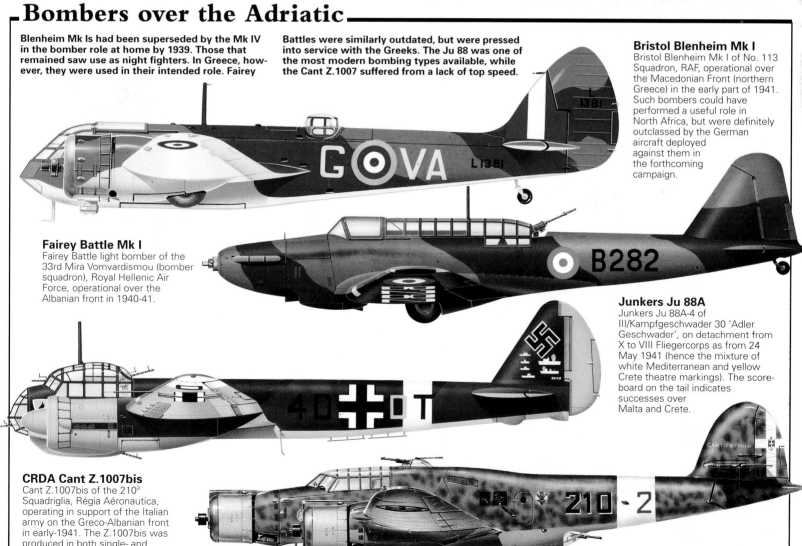

Blenheim Mk Is had been superseded by the Mk IV in the bomber role at home by 1939. Those that remained saw use as night fighters. In Greece, however, they were used in their intended role. Fairey

Battles were similarly outdated, but were pressed into service with the Greeks. The Ju 88 was one of the most modern bombing types available, while the Cant Z.1007 suffered from a lack of top speed.

Bristol Blenheim Mk I
Bristol Blenheim Mk I of No. 113 Squadron, RAF, operational over the Macedonian Front (northern Greece) in the early part of 1941. Such bombers could have performed a useful role in North Africa, but were definitely outclassed by the German aircraft deployed against them in the forthcoming campaign.

Fairey Battle Mk I
Fairey Battle light bomber of the 33rd Mira Vomvardismou (bomber squadron), Royal Hellenic Air Force, operational over the Albanian front in 1940-41.

Junkers Ju 88A
Junkers Ju 88A-4 of III/Kampfgeschwader 30 'Adler Geschwader', on detachment from X to VIII Fliegercorps as from 24 May 1941 (hence the mixture of white Mediterranean and yellow Crete theatre markings). The scoreboard on the tail indicates successes over Malta and Crete.

CRDA Cant Z.1007bis
Cant Z.1007bis of the 210ª Squadriglia, Régia Aéronautica, operating in support of the Italian army on the Greco-Albanian front in early-1941. The Z.1007bis was produced in both single- and twin-finned versions.

Left: Hawker Hurricane Mk Is were supplied abroad in small quantities in 1939, with 25 delivered to Yugoslavia. They were the best fighters available to the Yugoslavs, but could do little more than dent the Axis effort.

as gliders delivered infantry with the object of securing the island's landing grounds. To support the invasion the German air force mustered 650 first-line aircraft, 700 transports and 80 gliders. Opposing them were no more than a dozen Hurricanes, a handful of Fleet Air Arm Fulmars and some Gladiators dispersed on the two airfields and single rudimentary landing strip, although further limited support could be summoned from far-off Egypt. Since 14 May the Germans

had made clear their intention to invade Crete, with constant air attacks on the airfields, which the Hurricane pilots did their utmost to counter. By the eve of the invasion only seven fighters remained airworthy, and these were reluctantly evacuated to Egypt.

Despite the elimination of the island's fighter defence, the invasion certainly did not go according to plan, and the paratroops dropped initially at the two airfields were either wiped out or beaten off, and the glider landings were effectively contained. It was only after repeated waves of paratroops had been dropped that the airfields were eventually captured, after which the hosts of Ju 52/3ms started landing.

Fighters over the Adriatic

While aircraft like the Hawker Hurricane were available to Allied forces in the Balkans and Mediterranean, their limited numbers meant that they made little impression on the Luftwaffe.

Aircraft like PZL P.24s were out-classed and presented a negligible threat to Bf 110s and MC.200s that in other circumstances would have been at a severe disadvantage.

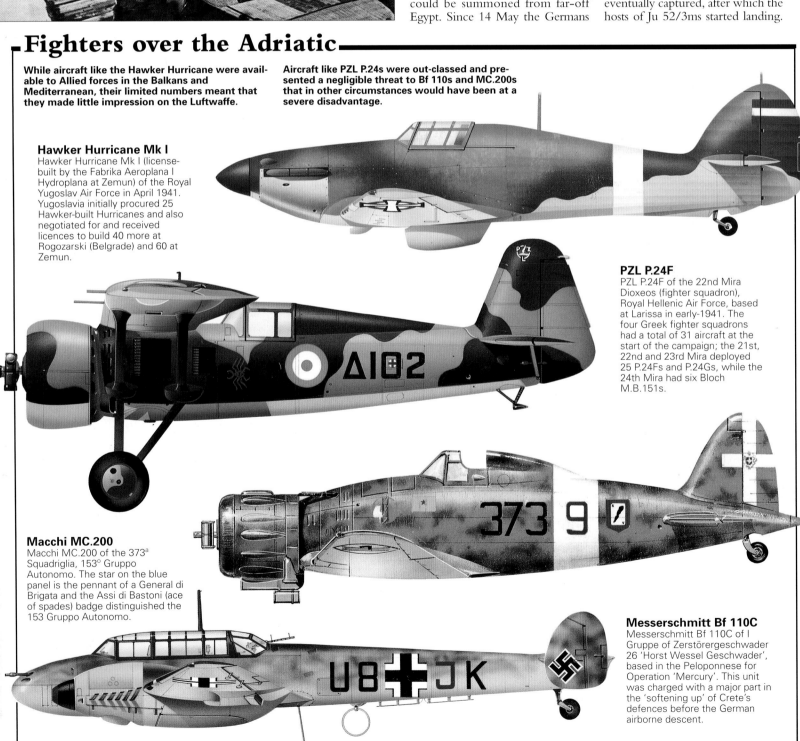

Hawker Hurricane Mk I
Hawker Hurricane Mk I (license-built by the Fabrika Aeroplana I Hydroplana at Zemun) of the Royal Yugoslav Air Force in April 1941. Yugoslavia initially procured 25 Hawker-built Hurricanes and also negotiated for and received licences to build 40 more at Rogozarski (Belgrade) and 60 at Zemun.

PZL P.24F
PZL P.24F of the 22nd Mira Dioxeos (fighter squadron), Royal Hellenic Air Force, based at Larissa in early-1941. The four Greek fighter squadrons had a total of 31 aircraft at the start of the campaign; the 21st, 22nd and 23rd Mira deployed 25 P.24Fs and P.24Gs, while the 24th Mira had six Bloch M.B.151s.

Macchi MC.200
Macchi MC.200 of the 373ª Squadriglia, 153º Gruppo Autonomo. The star on the blue panel is the pennant of a General di Brigata and the Assi di Bastoni (ace of spades) badge distinguished the 153 Gruppo Autonomo.

Messerschmitt Bf 110C
Messerschmitt Bf 110C of I Gruppe of Zerstörergeschwader 26 'Horst Wessel Geschwader', based in the Peloponnese for Operation 'Mercury'. This unit was charged with a major part in the 'softening up' of Crete's defences before the German airborne descent.

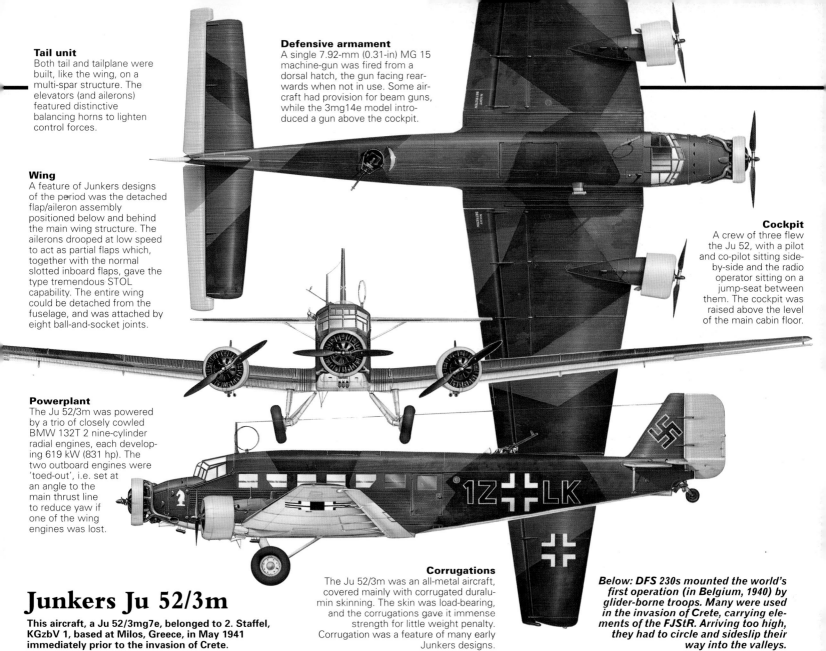

Tail unit
Both tail and tailplane were built, like the wing, on a multi-spar structure. The elevators (and ailerons) featured distinctive balancing horns to lighten control forces.

Defensive armament
A single 7.92-mm (0.31-in) MG 15 machine-gun was fired from a dorsal hatch, the gun facing rearwards when not in use. Some aircraft had provision for beam guns, while the 3mg14e model introduced a gun above the cockpit.

Wing
A feature of Junkers designs of the period was the detached flap/aileron assembly positioned below and behind the main wing structure. The ailerons drooped at low speed to act as partial flaps which, together with the normal slotted inboard flaps, gave the type tremendous STOL capability. The entire wing could be detached from the fuselage, and was attached by eight ball-and-socket joints.

Cockpit
A crew of three flew the Ju 52, with a pilot and co-pilot sitting side-by-side and the radio operator sitting on a jump-seat between them. The cockpit was raised above the level of the main cabin floor.

Powerplant
The Ju 52/3m was powered by a trio of closely cowled BMW 132T 2 nine-cylinder radial engines, each developing 619 kW (831 hp). The two outboard engines were 'toed-out', i.e. set at an angle to the main thrust line to reduce yaw if one of the wing engines was lost.

Junkers Ju 52/3m

This aircraft, a Ju 52/3mg7e, belonged to 2. Staffel, KGzbV 1, based at Milos, Greece, in May 1941 immediately prior to the invasion of Crete.

Corrugations
The Ju 52/3m was an all-metal aircraft, covered mainly with corrugated duralumin skinning. The skin was load-bearing, and the corrugations gave it immense strength for little weight penalty. Corrugation was a feature of many early Junkers designs.

Below: DFS 230s mounted the world's first operation (in Belgium, 1940) by glider-borne troops. Many were used in the invasion of Crete, carrying elements of the FJStR. Arriving too high, they had to circle and sideslip their way into the valleys.

Left: The three-engined Junkers Ju 52/3m 'Tante Ju' or 'Iron Annie' was by far the most common transport on all German fronts; an Axis equivalent to the C-47. Here one is dropping paratroops during the invasion of Crete.

Below: While Messerschmitt fighters hound the defences with strafing runs, Ju 52/3m transports, one on fire after being hit by AA guns, unload the men of 1 Fallschirmjäggeregiment over Heraklion, Crete.

In spite of some fighter cover, provided at long range from Egypt, the Germans landed almost 30,000 troops and by the end of the month Crete was in enemy hands.

HEAVY LOSSES

The campaign had cost the British forces dear. Apart from the loss of 38 RAF aircraft, the Royal Navy lost three cruisers and six destroyers sunk, and a battleship, carrier, six cruisers and eight destroyers damaged. About 15,000 Imperial troops were either killed or taken prisoner.

On the other hand the Luftwaffe suffered the loss of more than 200 aircraft, of which about half were Ju 52/3m transports. Of far greater significance, however, was the fact that the Balkan campaign had taken six weeks longer than planned and effectively delayed the opening of the great assault on the USSR. Apart from the severe losses among the vital transport aircraft, those six weeks may have been decisive in the conduct of Operation 'Barbarossa' before the onset of the dreaded Russian winter.

Into North Africa

JUNE 1940

Left: Two Bf 109E-4 Trops of JG 27 patrol over the Western Desert. White codes identify the aircraft as belonging to the 1st Gruppe. The Bf 109E enjoyed great success in North Africa, although it was rapidly replaced by later versions.

Below: On return from an operational sortie, the pilot of a Gladiator is rushed to debriefing at a desert location. Gladiators continued to serve in the Western Desert throughout 1941.

Believing that he would be deprived of the spoils of war when German forces burst into northern France, Benito Mussolini entered the war alongside Hitler on 10 June 1940. At a stroke the balance of naval power in the Mediterranean swung in favour of the Axis, even more heavily after the French fleet refused to continue operations on the Allied side and was accordingly attacked by the Royal Navy in its North African ports.

Three immediate threats to British strategic interests were posed by Italy's entry into the war: the naval base at Malta would be threatened by Italian air forces in Sicily; Italian forces in Cyrenaica were uncomfortably close to the vital Suez Canal and the British naval base at Alexandria; and a large Italian colonial army (and air force) threatened British bases in East Africa and the Arabian peninsula at the southern end of the Red Sea.

Little could be done to strengthen Malta's defences immediately and the island was left much to its own devices, recourse being found in a handful of obsolete Gloster Sea Gladiators and some Hawker Hurricanes with which to provide a measure of air defence. Fortunately, the Italians underestimated the strategic value of Malta and did little to attack the naval base from the air, at least for a month or so.

GLADIATORS

In the Western Desert, however, the position was more critical and in the face of considerable Italian numerical air superiority the RAF possessed an extraordinary mix of obsolescent aircraft with which to defend an enormous expanse of territory. Nevertheless, by dint of ingenious deployment and careful use of the resources available, the two Gladiator squadrons managed to exact a considerable toll of Italian aircraft during the early months of the desert war, while General Wavell was able to set about his brilliant campaign which took his army far into Cyrenaica. Gradually, the RAF was able to send a trickle of reinforcements to the Middle East, at first by convoy through the Mediterranean and later to Takoradi in the Gold Coast for overland flight to the Canal Zone.

Left: L5857 was the last of 50 Bristol Bombay Mk Is built and flew out to join No. 216 Squadron in the summer of 1940. It served its entire career with the squadron as a transport aircraft, being finally destroyed in an air raid on Kufra on 25 September 1942.

Left: The RAF created havoc with the Italian Air Force during the Battle of the Western Desert and Libya. This Fiat CR.42 crashed and burned out near Bandia in January 1941 after attempting a landing with one of its wheels shot away.

Above: Italian Air Force Savoia-Marchetti SM.79s. A total of four Stormi with 125 SM.79s was available in support of Marshal Graziani's land forces, based at Castel Benito, Bin el Bhera, Benina and El Adem.

Above: Frustrated by the Italians' inability to gain a decisive victory in North Africa, the Germans moved a major force of aircraft to the Mediterranean including Ju 87s such as this Ju 87D-1 Trop belonging to the 1st Staffel of I/StG 3 in late 1941.

Right: Bombing up a Blenheim Mk I for a sortie over the Western Desert in 1940 is this crew of No. 113 Squadron at a desert strip in Egypt. The Blenheim Mk I was almost entirely replaced by the Blenheim Mk IV in the desert campaign during 1941-42.

Vickers Wellingtons and Lockheed Hudsons were flown out directly from the UK, and Hurricanes and Bristol Blenheims arrived by the Takoradi route; other aircraft were crated and shipped out by the sea route round the Cape of Good Hope.

In East Africa the Italians gained early successes by invading and overrunning British Somaliland, and by doing so posed a threat to Aden.

However, in support of another brilliant counteroffensive by Commonwealth forces, RAF Vickers Wellesleys and Gladiators operating alongside aircraft of the South African Air Force succeeded in defeating elements of the Italian air force in East Africa. In due course the Italian presence in the horn of Africa was eliminated.

It was at the moment of triumph for Wavell's forces, which reached

Bombers in the Desert

Most of the bombing missions in the early desert air war were performed by light and medium bombers. This was primarily due to the fluid nature of the war, and to the fact that the targets were small and scattered. Most of the 'heavies' were desperately needed in the European theatre.

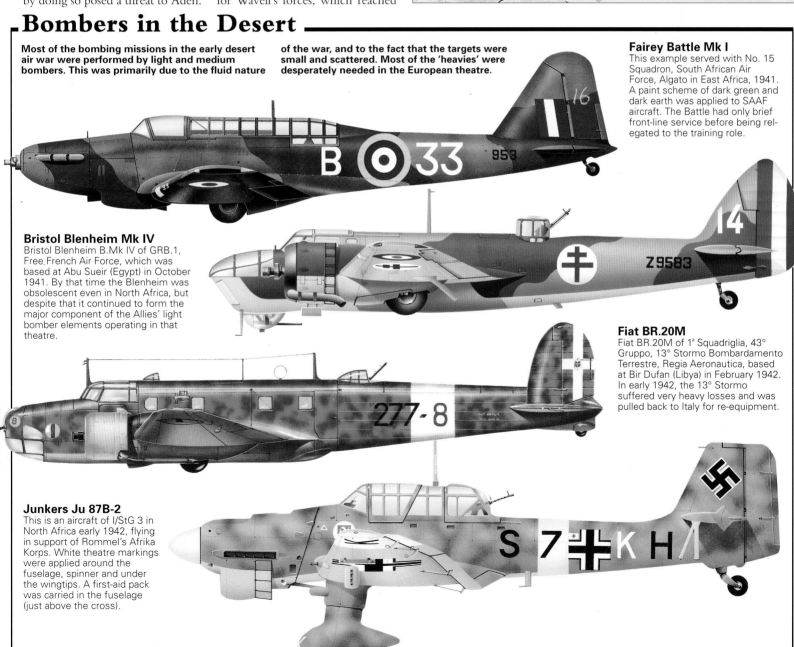

Fairey Battle Mk I
This example served with No. 15 Squadron, South African Air Force, Algato in East Africa, 1941. A paint scheme of dark green and dark earth was applied to SAAF aircraft. The Battle had only brief front-line service before being relegated to the training role.

Bristol Blenheim Mk IV
Bristol Blenheim B.Mk IV of GRB.1, Free French Air Force, which was based at Abu Sueir (Egypt) in October 1941. By that time the Blenheim was obsolescent even in North Africa, but despite that it continued to form the major component of the Allies' light bomber elements operating in that theatre.

Fiat BR.20M
Fiat BR.20M of 1ª Squadriglia, 43° Gruppo, 13° Stormo Bombardamento Terrestre, Regia Aeronautica, based at Bir Dufan (Libya) in February 1942. In early 1942, the 13° Stormo suffered very heavy losses and was pulled back to Italy for re-equipment.

Junkers Ju 87B-2
This is an aircraft of I/StG 3 in North Africa early 1942, flying in support of Rommel's Afrika Korps. White theatre markings were applied around the fuselage, spinner and under the wingtips. A first-aid pack was carried in the fuselage (just above the cross).

RAF Middle East had to make do with early Hurricanes, but managed to notch up some notable successes. The first fully-equipped unit was No. 274 Squadron. Here a quartet of newly arrived aircraft is air tested.

Benghazi in the first North African desert offensive, that RAF units were called on to go to the assistance of Greece (a campaign described elsewhere), a critical weakening that was to be compounded by events in Iraq in 1941.

Following a rebellion in support of the pro-Axis Rashid Ali, the large RAF base at Habbaniyah in Iraq came under attack supported by German and Italian aircraft, a threat only countered (and eventually overcome) by the deployment of ill-afforded Wellingtons, Blen-

Fighters of the Desert War

With the air conflict in Europe at full swing during 1940/41, the state-of-the-art fighters such as the Spitfire could not be spared for the North African campaign during the early phase of the desert action.

Nevertheless, the Tomahawks and Hurricanes were sufficiently capable to gain ascendancy over the Italian opposition. All this changed in the spring of 1941 with the arrival of the Messerschmitt Bf 109E.

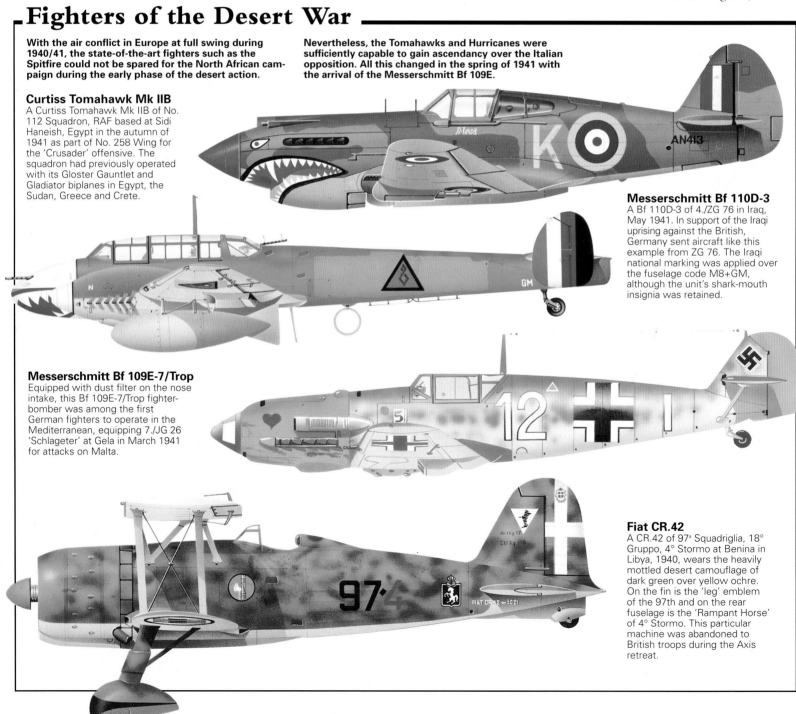

Curtiss Tomahawk Mk IIB
A Curtiss Tomahawk Mk IIB of No. 112 Squadron, RAF based at Sidi Haneish, Egypt in the autumn of 1941 as part of No. 258 Wing for the 'Crusader' offensive. The squadron had previously operated with its Gloster Gauntlet and Gladiator biplanes in Egypt, the Sudan, Greece and Crete.

Messerschmitt Bf 110D-3
A Bf 110D-3 of 4./ZG 76 in Iraq, May 1941. In support of the Iraqi uprising against the British, Germany sent aircraft like this example from ZG 76. The Iraqi national marking was applied over the fuselage code M8+GM, although the unit's shark-mouth insignia was retained.

Messerschmitt Bf 109E-7/Trop
Equipped with dust filter on the nose intake, this Bf 109E-7/Trop fighter-bomber was among the first German fighters to operate in the Mediterranean, equipping 7./JG 26 'Schlageter' at Gela in March 1941 for attacks on Malta.

Fiat CR.42
A CR.42 of 97ª Squadriglia, 18° Gruppo, 4° Stormo at Benina in Libya, 1940, wears the heavily mottled desert camouflage of dark green over yellow ochre. On the fin is the 'leg' emblem of the 97th and on the rear fuselage is the 'Rampant Horse' of 4° Stormo. This particular machine was abandoned to British troops during the Axis retreat.

Right: The establishment of Fliegerführer Afrika in Cyrenaica for the support of General Feld-Marshall Rommel's Afrika Korps in early February 1941 resulted in the recapture of El Agheila, and the subsequent advance to Sollum on the Egyptian frontier in April 1941. Here Ju 52/3m transports, with Bf 110 fighter escorts, are on a resupply operation to a forward area.

Below: This is a Bf 109E-7/Trop of 7.Staffel of Jagdgeschwader 26 operating from Aia El Gazala in June 1941 under Fligerführer Afrika.

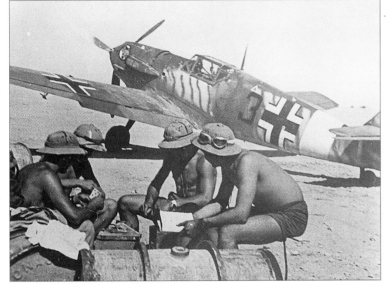

One of the most successful American bombers to enter the fight with the RAF was the Martin Baltimore, used exclusively in the Middle East, serving as a medium day-bomber and on anti-shipping reconnaissance. This is a Mk II version over the Western Desert.

heims, Gladiators and Hurricanes for defence of the base.

No sooner had the danger in Iraq been eliminated in the spring of 1941 than the Vichy French presence in Syria posed a threat to the Suez Canal (by possible defection to the Axis) as well as to important oil pipe lines, and it was decided to invade the country. This campaign, successfully completed in mid-July, involved the use of some 60 Hurricanes, Curtiss Tomahawks, Gladiators, Blenheims and Fairey Fulmars of the RAF, RAAF and the Fleet Air Arm.

Frustrated by the Italians' inability to gain a decisive victory in North Africa, the Germans moved the advance elements of a major force of aircraft to the Mediterranean (notably a Geschwader, JG 27 of Messerschmitt Bf 109Es) early in 1941, and these were quickly followed by Junkers Ju 87 and Junkers Ju 88 bombers. It was the arrival of this Fliegerkorps in the theatre that first posed a major threat to Malta; for a period its use as a naval base was severely restricted, and it was only sustained by sailing aircraft-carriers into the Mediterranean and flying off fairly large numbers of Hurricanes to land on the island's airfields.

GAINING STRENGTH

Meanwhile, RAF strength in the Middle East was growing steadily. By November 1941, on the eve of the British 8th Army's second offensive into Cyrenaica against Erwin Rommel's Afrika Korps (Operation Crusader), RAF, Middle East Command comprised 29 squadrons of Hurricanes, Tomahawks, Curtiss Mohawks, Morane-Saulniers, Blenheim fighters and Fulmars, and 11 squadrons of Wellingtons, Blenheim bombers, Wellesleys, Douglas Bostons and Martin Marylands, as well as a dozen second-line squadrons, a total of almost 1,000 aircraft.

Ranged against them were some 600 German and 1,200 Italian first-line aircraft.

At sea both the Royal Air Force and Fleet Air Arm were at work seeking out and attacking enemy supply vessels bringing troops and equipment from Europe to North Africa, a task carried out with increasing success, particularly between the Italian ports and Tripolitania. The theatre had assumed the status of a major war theatre.

Above: The Macchi MC.200 Saetta (lightning) proved adequate over Yugoslavia and Greece, but was soon outclassed in North Africa. This example is in the colours of 371ª Squadriglia, 22º Gruppo in 1940.

Right: The Curtiss Tomahawk served the RAF well in the desert, these shark-mouthed examples operating with No. 112 Squadron at Sidi Hanneish in late 1941. The type could master the Italian fighters with ease, but was outclassed by the Bf 109E.

Taranto

11/12 NOVEMBER 1940

O n the night of 11/12 November 1940, 21 British Fairey Swordfish torpedo-bomber biplanes struck at the Italian fleet in Taranto harbour and in the first major and successful strike by naval aircraft, effectively redressed in British favour the balance of sea power in the Mediterranean.

Italy's entry into the war in June 1940 and the subsequent elimination of the French fleet had given the Axis superiority at sea in the Mediterranean; a situation that seriously threatened British convoys sailing to the UK with vital food, forces and munitions from the dominions east of Suez. Moreover, following Italy's attack on Greece in October that year, undisputed use of the Aegean and Adriatic by the Axis powers posed considerable difficulties in the support of any British foothold in the Balkans that might be considered.

Below: The Swordfish was designed to be flown at the very slow speeds required in carrier operations. With a single 45.7-cm (18-in) 730.3-kg (1,610-lb) torpedo under the fuselage it had a range of 879 kilometres (546 miles) and proved ideal for the Taranto attack.

Below: HMS Illustrious, the carrier that launched the Swordfish aircraft that carried out the devastating attack on the Italian ships at Taranto on 11 November 1940. She is seen here in the Mediterranean with full war paint and Swordfish on the flight deck.

Key to any operations in the central Mediterranean by the Royal Navy lay in the continued use of Malta, both as a naval and air base and it was with a fine sense of history that it had been intended to bring the Italian fleet to battle on 21 October (Trafalgar Day) with a British fleet of four battleships and battle-cruisers, two carriers (*Eagle* and *Illustrious*), 10 cruisers and four destroyer flotillas. Despite the

Right: Martin Marylands were used for aerial reconnaissance of enemy ports and to report on shipping movements in the Mediterranean. A Maryland flown from Malta by P/O Adrian Warburton spotted the Italian fleet at Taranto in November 1940.

sailing of two convoys through the Mediterranean, the Italian fleet (comprising five battleships, 14 cruisers and 27 destroyers) declined to leave its base at Taranto; moreover, following a number of near misses from Italian bombers, the carrier *Eagle* was suffering mechanical troubles, necessitating the transfer of her Swordfish aircraft to the *Illustrious*.

FLEET LOCATED

The action was accordingly postponed and as a preliminary step a reconnaissance of Taranto was ordered on 10 November. A Maryland of No. 431 Flight, RAF, flown by Pilot Officer Adrian Warburton, was despatched from Malta that day and following an epic wave-top tour of the enemy port carried out in the face of intense flak, full details

Above: Shore-based, carrier-based and even catapulted from naval ships, the Fairey Swordfish was a very effective torpedo-bomber, although it was already obsolete and ready for replacement at the outbreak of World War II.

of the Italian fleet's dispositions were brought back and reported to Rear Admiral Lumley Lyster, the flag officer aboard *Illustrious*. The same evening the crew of an RAF flying-boat reported that a sixth Italian battleship had also entered Taranto.

Encouraged by the survival of the Maryland, Lyster decided to launch a strike against the Italian ships where they lay. On the evening of 11 November two waves of Swordfish flew off *Illustrious* at a position 274 kilometres (170 miles) south-east of

Anti-shipping aircraft

The Martin Maryland, designed as a light bomber, had its greatest success as a Fleet Air Arm reconnaissance aircraft, locating the Italian fleet at Taranto in November 1940.

The Swordfish, affectionately nicknamed the 'Stringbag', was able to use its slow speed and manoeuvrability to advantage, weaving in through the balloon barrage to attack the Italian ships.

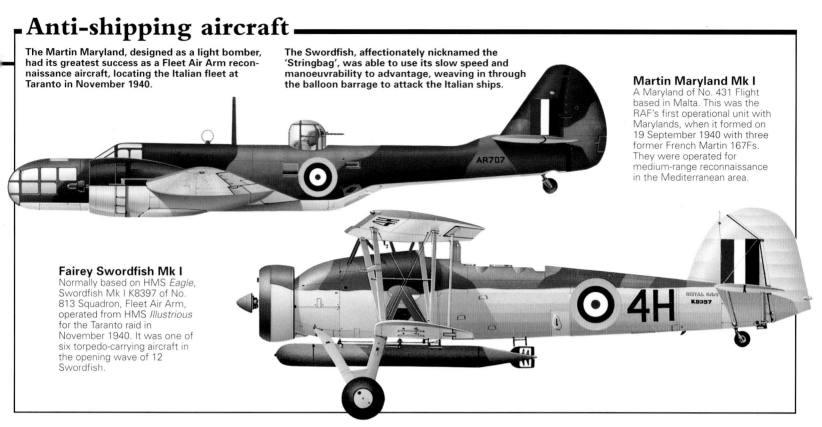

Martin Maryland Mk I
A Maryland of No. 431 Flight based in Malta. This was the RAF's first operational unit with Marylands, when it formed on 19 September 1940 with three former French Martin 167Fs. They were operated for medium-range reconnaissance in the Mediterranean area.

Fairey Swordfish Mk I
Normally based on HMS *Eagle*, Swordfish Mk I K8397 of No. 813 Squadron, Fleet Air Arm, operated from HMS *Illustrious* for the Taranto raid in November 1940. It was one of six torpedo-carrying aircraft in the opening wave of 12 Swordfish.

Taranto. The first formation, led by Lieutenant Commander Kenneth Williamson, comprised 12 aircraft (six with torpedoes, four with bombs and two with bombs and flares), the second wave of nine aircraft (five with torpedoes, two with bombs and two with bombs and flares) followed 40 minutes later, led by Lieutenant Commander John Hale.

Despite the obvious significance of the Maryland's appearance over the naval base on the previous day, the Italians were evidently caught completely unaware when Williamson's aircraft swept into Taranto harbour; added to this was the fact that the balloon barrage, which had been expected to cause some embarrassment during the attack, had been almost wholly destroyed by storms the day before. Moreover, the Italians had decided against the use of anti-torpedo nets on the pretext that they restricted the movement of their ships.

Two flares quickly disclosed the position of the new battleship *Littorio* (35562 tonnes/35,000 tons) and this was promptly sunk at her moorings by three torpedoes. Two older battleships, *Conte di Cavour* and *Caio Duilio* (both of 23979 tonnes/23,600 tons) were also hit, the former never to sail again and the latter, beached to prevent her sinking, severely crippled. In the inner harbour a heavy cruiser and a destroyer were also hit.

SWORDFISH LOSS

In due course the gun defences came into action and two Swordfish were shot down, including that flown by Williamson himself although he and his crewman survived to be taken prisoner. Another Swordfish failed to release its torpedo.

At a single blow half of Italy's battle fleet had been put out of action, a blow from which the Italians never fully recovered. On numerous occasions during the following three years their fleet declined battle with the Royal Navy, having been deprived of capital ship superiority. In the naval Battle of Cape Matapan on 28 March 1941, when a powerful force of Italian battleships might otherwise have crippled Admiral Cunningham's Mediterranean Fleet, the two enemy capital ships (albeit one of them damaged) sought safety by flight, leaving three cruisers and two destroyers to be sunk by Royal Navy. In the subsequent evacuation of Greece and Crete by British forces, losses among ships of the Royal Navy were grievous, being in the main inflicted from the air. Had the bulk of the Italian battlefleet been intact at that time, they would have been immeasurably worse.

TARANTO STRIKE
On the night of 11 November 1940 two waves of Swordfish flew 274 km (170 miles) from the new aircraft carrier **HMS *Illustrious*** and descended on the unsuspecting Italian battle fleet, causing so much damage that it changed the course of the whole war in the Mediterranean. For the first time a naval battle fleet had been destroyed by aircraft alone, without the fire-power of warships.

Malta

JUNE 1940 – JULY 1943

Left: HMS Indomitable en route to Malta in 1942 with its mast head pennants flying. Hawker Hurricanes and Fairey Albacores are arranged on the flight deck. Photo taken from HMS Victorious with Hurricanes and Fairey Fulmars in the foreground.

Right: An Italian Air Force three-engined Cant Z.1007bis 'Alcione' (Kingfisher) heavy bomber, releasing its bombload during a raid on Grand Harbour, Valetta in mid-1941.

O f all the British strategic bases overseas during World War II, the tiny rocky island of Malta, athwart the central Mediterranean, was probably the most important and accordingly, the most savagely assaulted from the air. At the time of Italy's entry into the war on 10 June 1940 Malta served two purposes: a British naval replenishment base on the maritime route through the Mediterranean to and from the Suez Canal and the Far East, and as a limited staging point for long-range flights from the UK to the Middle East.

Despite the completion of four air bases (at Hal Far, Luqa, Takali and a flying-boat station at Kalafrana), there was no organised fighter defence and only a naval gunnery flight in June 1940. When the Italians began somewhat desultory air attacks in that month, however, four Sea Gladiators were hurriedly uncrated and used to fly patrols against the raids (three of them ultimately being dubbed 'Faith', 'Hope' and 'Charity', though more with one eye on legend than with historical accuracy); before a fortnight was out four Hurricanes on their way out to North Africa were commandeered by the island for its defence.

These slender forces proved adequate to discourage the Italians from increasing their pressure on the island for several weeks, but it soon became obvious that, with major land operations imminent in North Africa, the need to reinforce both sides in Egypt and Cyrenaica

Left: The first 'Hurribombers' – Hurricane Mk IIBs fitted with bomb racks – went into action from Malta on 20 October 1941. This aircraft, about to scramble at Hal Far airfield, carries a 113-kg (250-lb) bomb under each wing.

would impose on Malta a vital role, lying as it did directly across the Italian supply route to Tripoli.

HURRICANES ARRIVE

On 2 August 12 Hurricanes were flown off the carrier *Argus* to the island, where they formed No. 261 Squadron and with adequate fighter defence now established, three reconnaissance Marylands of No. 431 Flight arrived from the UK. A second instalment of 12 Hurricanes, flown off the *Argus* on 17 November, was overtaken by tragedy, eight of them being lost at sea after running out of fuel. Meanwhile, Wellingtons – which had been staging at Malta on their raids from North Africa against targets in Italy – were now allowed to remain on the island to form No. 148 Squadron. It was also a Maryland of No. 431 Flight that carried out the superb reconnaissance of Taranto harbour before the epic raid by Fleet Air Arm Swordfish on the night of 11/12 November.

Throughout General Wavell's brilliant offensive in Egypt and Cyrenaica during the winter of

---

Carrier fighters

The Fairey Fulmar was the Fleet Air Arm's first carrier-borne monoplane fighter with the same level of fire-power as the Hurricane and Spitfire, when it was introduced in June 1940.

About 100 Gloster Sea Gladiators, the last of the Fleet Air Arm's biplane fighters, saw service from 1938. Four aircraft were borrowed from the RAF in June 1940 and fought in the defence of Malta.

Fairey Fulmar Mk I
Powered by a 805-kW (1,080-hp) Rolls-Royce Merlin II engine, the Fulmar had a top speed of 458 km/h (284 mph). It first saw action with the Fleet Air Arm defending the Malta convoys against the Italian Air Force. A good match for the Italian fighters, they were, however, outclassed by the Luftwaffe and were replaced by Seafires during 1943.

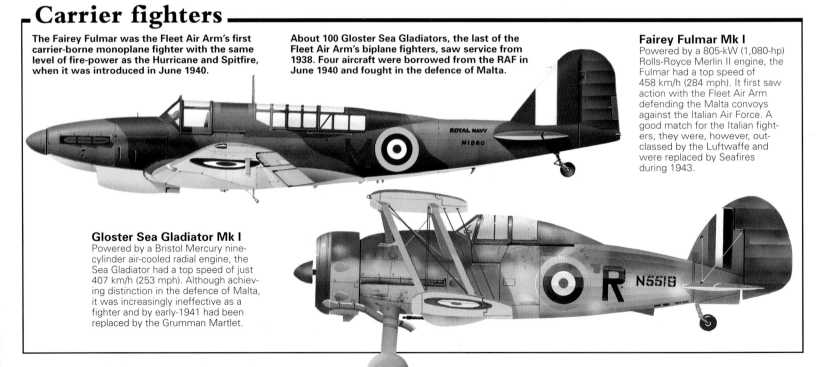

Gloster Sea Gladiator Mk I
Powered by a Bristol Mercury nine-cylinder air-cooled radial engine, the Sea Gladiator had a top speed of just 407 km/h (253 mph). Although achieving distinction in the defence of Malta, it was increasingly ineffective as a fighter and by early-1941 had been replaced by the Grumman Martlet.

Malta bombers

The Italian Régia Aéronautica flew German-built Junkers Ju 87B-2s carrying up to 1000 kg (2,205 lb) of bombs for attacks on Malta. Flown by inexperienced pilots, many were lost to defending fighters.

Junkers Ju 88A-5s were flown from Sicily by the Luftwaffe on very effective day and night raids against strategic targets in Malta and shipping convoys in the Mediterranean on a daily basis.

Junkers Ju 87B

This Italian Air Force Ju 87B-2 Stuka was based at Gars el Arid in September 1941, with the 209 Squadriglia, 101 Gruppo Autonomo (independent group) for precision dive-bombing attacks against Allied shipping in the Mediterranean and important targets in Malta.

Junkers Ju 88A

This Ju 88A-5 was used by the III Gruppe of Lehrgeschwader 1 for operations against Malta during early-1941, when the unit was based at Catania, Sicily, as part of Fliegerkorps X. The strengthened undercarriage of the A-5 made it more suitable for operations from the poorly prepared Sicilian airstrips.

Above: One of the three famous Sea Gladiators, named 'Faith', 'Hope' and 'Charity'. The three were in crates on the island en route to Egypt, when they were hurriedly assembled and flown by RAF pilots in the initial fighter defence of Malta, until the arrival of the first Hurricanes.

1940/41, the Wellingtons from Malta constantly raided Tripoli and Castel Benito, operations that brought swift reaction by the Axis with the arrival in Sicily late in December of the advance units of the German Fliegerkorps X; a force that within a month had grown to some 250 modern aircraft. On 10 January, 60 Ju 87s and He 111s attacked a British convoy in the Sicilian narrows, severely damaging the carrier *Illustrious* and the cruisers *Southampton* and *Gloucester*. The carrier limped into harbour at Malta where she became the target of heavy and repeated attacks by the Luftwaffe and Régia Aéronautica for more than a week. With losses increasing among the Hurricanes, the Wellingtons now had to be withdrawn to North Africa and, with Malta thus largely disarmed, the Germans were able to send about

half of Fliegerkorps X to Cyrenaica to support Rommel's counter-offensive in the Western Desert.

CONVOYS GET THROUGH

The relief of pressure on Malta now allowed the British to sail a large convoy almost unscathed through the Mediterranean to Alexandria in May, by which time a second Hurricane squadron (No. 185 with Mk IIs) had been formed on the island. In June Fliegerkorps X was moved to Greece, Crete and the Dodecanese, a move that coincided with the arrival of Air Chief Marshal Sir Arthur Tedder to take over Middle East Command. At once the Wellingtons returned to Malta, together with Blenheims and further Marylands, and these aircraft renewed the attacks on the Italian ports and convoys, sinking over 71100 tonnes (70,000 tons) of enemy shipping in the last two months of 1941.

When two convoys reached Malta without loss Hitler resolved to eliminate the island once and for all, ordering Luftflotte II from the USSR to Italy before the end of the year under Albert Kesselring. There now started a four-month

nightmare for Malta. Throughout January and February 1942 attacks by several dozen bombers were commonplace with never a day without raids, the targets in the main being the airfields. On 7 March 15 Spitfires reached the island from a carrier, but within a week the number of Hurricanes was down to 30, and at this point Kesselring started raids using 150 aircraft or more. The Wellingtons were withdrawn once more and April found the island seriously short of food, fuel and fighters, three out of four supply ships having been sunk. At the height of the assault, on 20 April, 47 more Spitfires arrived, followed by 62 on 9 May (having flown off the American carrier *Wasp*). Amidst rumours that the Germans were preparing to invade the island, Malta was awarded the George Cross for its sustained resistance.

It was now that Hitler stepped in with changed priorities (the first being the recapture of Cyrenaica) and Kesselring moved a large proportion of his aircraft to North Africa to support Rommel. The following month two convoys were

sailed to Malta from east and west, of which one from Alexandria was forced to turn back. Two supply ships managed to reach the beleaguered island and the German offensive ran out of steam at El Alamein.

Following Montgomery's famous victory in November 1942, the aircraft on Malta, which had been preying on the supply convoys to North Africa, were further reinforced. For the next six months they took an increasing toll of Axis shipping in the central Mediterranean which was at first seeking to sustain the hard-pressed Axis forces and later desperately trying to extricate the beaten German and Italian forces from North Africa. The final irony of Malta's monumental achievement was reached when her fighter squadrons, numbering 12, provided air cover for the invasion of Sicily that was launched in July 1943.

Below: Spitfire Mk Vc being loaded on to the carrier USS Wasp at Glasgow in April 1942, to reinforce Malta. Fitted with four 20-mm cannon, tropical filters and 90-gallon slipper tanks, the Spitfires were flown north of Algiers.

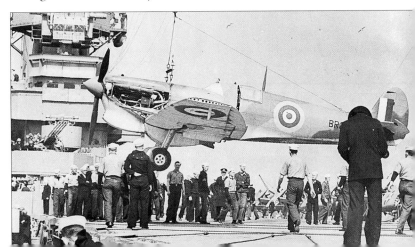

Operation 'Barbarossa'

JUNE 1941 – JANUARY 1942

Eclipsing all other German strategic planning during the first two years of the war was Hitler's determination to attack and defeat the Soviet Union. To do so it was necessary to eliminate any potential threat from the West to avoid the age-old German nightmare of war on two fronts. Following Italy's inability to impose a decisive solution in the Mediterranean and Balkans, Germany eventually launched her massive offensive in the East with the enemy still undefeated in the West and South and, as it transpired, with inadequate time to reach Moscow before the onset of the first Russian winter.

INVASION

The assault on the Soviet Union was launched before dawn on 22 June 1941 along a front that stretched from the Baltic to the Black Sea, the three army groups (under Leeb, Bock and Rundstedt) advancing 80 km (50 miles) in the

Above: A pair of Polikarpovs, armed with two synchronised machine-guns over the top of a powerful M-25V engine, operating on the Eastern Front in the summer of 1941. Initial losses in Operation 'Barbarossa' decimated the I-16 inventory, but it was still the most common V-VS fighter to oppose the Luftwaffe until October 1942.

Left: Ju 87D-1 Stuka of II/JG 77, Luftflotte 4 on a sortie over the Eastern Front near Kuban/ Krymskaja. The revival in the fortunes of the Stuka was evident in the battles of 1941-42. This rugged aircraft gave invaluable support to German ground forces.

Below: During a break between sorties, Soviet pilots have a nerve-steadying cigarette and play dominoes. The Polikarpov I-16 is on an airfield in the region of the Khalkhin-Gol river in Barga province in July 1941.

first 24 hours. Supporting the huge offensive were four Luftflotten (air fleets) which between them deployed 19 Jagdgruppen of Bf 109Es and Bf 109Fs (600 aircraft), seven Stukagruppen of Ju 87 dive-bombers (more than 200 aircraft) and 24 Kampfgruppen of He 111s, Do 17s and Ju 88s (about 850 aircraft), as well as more than 1,000 other transport and reconnaissance aircraft.

Despite warnings from the West and the impossibility of concealing the German preparations for the attack, the Soviet Union was taken by surprise and when, on the first day, the Luftwaffe set out to destroy

Luftwaffe in the East

Hs 123s were originally intended as dive-bombers, though their careers were short-lived as the Stuka became available from 1937. The last examples were withdrawn in 1944. The STOL (short take-off and landing) Storch saw service on several fronts as an army co-operation and reconnaissance aircraft. The Do 17Z was the major production version of this medium bomber.

Henschel Hs 123A
On the Eastern Front the Hs 123 proved its worth in the close support role. During bad weather, when airfields were turned into mudbaths, the Hs 123s continued to operate by the simple expedient of removing the wheel fairings. This example wears the markings of 4. Staffel/Schlachtgeschwader 2, on the southern sector of the Russian Front in the winter of 1942-43.

Fieseler Fi 156C Storch
This Fi 156C Storch carries the codes of the Geschwaderstab of Lehrgeschwader 2, and was used on the Don sector of the Eastern Front during August 1942, operating as part of the Kurierstaffel Oberkommando der Luftwaffe.

Dornier Do 17Z
Dornier Do 17Z-2 of the Croatian-manned 10. Staffel of Kampfgeschwader 3 on the Central Sector of the front in December 1941: the Croatian Ustachi emblem is carried below the flight deck. The whole of KG 3 was committed to Operation 'Barbarossa' in June 1941, under II Fliegerkorps.

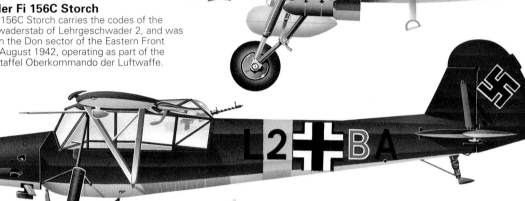

Above: As the position in the East worsened for the Soviets, production of the LaGG-3 fighter was stepped up, and although underpowered, it was available in quantity. Its design eventually led to the excellent La-5 and La-7 fighters.

the Soviet air force the German pilots found the enemy still on the ground. So widely dispersed were the Soviet airfields that the Luftwaffe was only able to send three or four aircraft against each, yet, by use of large numbers of 2-kg and 10-kg (4.4-lb and 22-lb) fragmentation bombs, they were able to devastate the grounded aircraft.

The relatively small numbers of outdated I-16 fighters which rose to defend their bases were swatted like flies by the experienced Luftwaffe pilots in their superb Bf 109s. During that first day the Soviets admitted the loss of more than 1,200 aircraft.

MOSCOW HIT
The airfield strikes were quickly followed by an attack by 127 He 111s and Ju 88s on Moscow, 104 tons of HE and 46,000 incendiary bombs being dropped; this was followed within 48 hours by two further raids by 115 and 100 aircraft. The massacre of Soviet aircraft

continued to occupy the Luftwaffe throughout July and August, and not unnaturally huge personal victory tallies were amassed by individual pilots; by mid-August four of the Jagdgeschwader (JG 3, JG 51, JG 53 and JG 54) had each passed a score of 1,000 enemy aircraft destroyed. On the ground it

Below: Widespread aerial reconnaissance during the preceding months had pinpointed every forward V-VS base and these came under sustained attack by Luftwaffe Ju 88s.

МАЛЫЙ ТЕАТР
ФРОНТУ

МАЛЫЙ ТЕАТР
ФРОНТУ

Tyrkowo attacked the Soviet fleet at Kronstadt, and a single bomb dropped by Oberleutnant Hans Rudel sank the Soviet battleship *Marat*. By the end of that month the front stretched from the Crimea in an almost straight line north to Leningrad.

Despite the weather the German armies managed to struggle forward and by early December reached Rostov, Voronezh and the outskirts of Moscow itself just as the first snows fell. This effectively brought air operations to a halt, as well as catching the Germans hopelessly ill-prepared for the rigours of the

seemed likely that the German army would be in Moscow before Christmas. The Soviet capital had not been Hitler's primary objective, however, and his orders to first secure the grain-rich Ukraine (which resulted in the capture of 650,000 Soviet troops) placed the entire campaign in jeopardy. In September the Finns advanced down the Karelian isthmus thereby helping to complete the investment of Leningrad. Not until October did Hitler renew the advance towards the Soviet capital, but by then it was too late.

Despite the widespread use of

the incisive Blitzkreig tactics, which had hitherto overwhelmed so many armies in the previous two years, the German offensive slowed as autumn rains clogged the lengthening supply roads and organised partisan operations took their toll behind the German front. Increasing use was made of Ju 52/3m transports to bring up

supplies, but serviceable landing grounds were few and far between.

On 23 September Ju 87s of Stukageschwader 2 based at

Allies on the Eastern Front

Intended as a high-speed bomber, Tupolov SB-2s had been used during the Spanish Civil War. Around 6,500 were built, most during 1941-42. The only RAF fighters to fly with the Russians on the

Eastern Front were the Hurricane Mk IIs of No. 151 Wing. Though poorly-armed and difficult to fly, MiG-3s were produced from 1941 and had a better top speed than earlier Russian fighters.

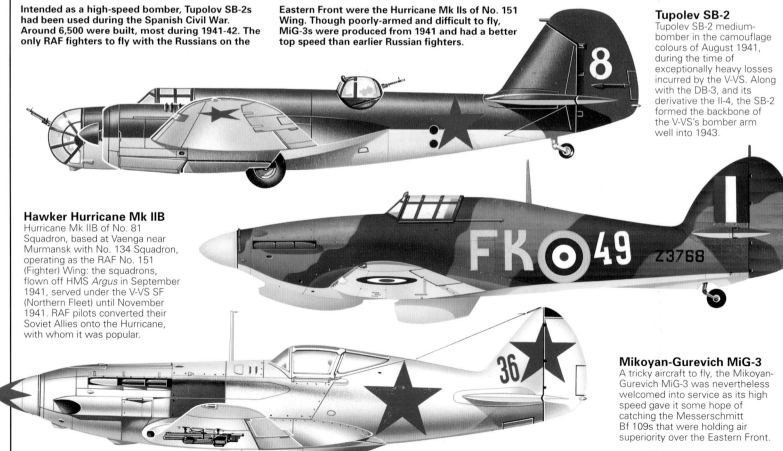

Tupolev SB-2
Tupolev SB-2 medium-bomber in the camouflage colours of August 1941, during the time of exceptionally heavy losses incurred by the V-VS. Along with the DB-3, and its derivative the Il-4, the SB-2 formed the backbone of the V-VS's bomber arm well into 1943.

Hawker Hurricane Mk IIB
Hurricane Mk IIB of No. 81 Squadron, based at Vaenga near Murmansk with No. 134 Squadron, operating as the RAF No. 151 (Fighter) Wing: the squadrons, flown off HMS *Argus* in September 1941, served under the V-VS SF (Northern Fleet) until November 1941. RAF pilots converted their Soviet Allies onto the Hurricane, with whom it was popular.

Mikoyan-Gurevich MiG-3
A tricky aircraft to fly, the Mikoyan-Gurevich MiG-3 was nevertheless welcomed into service as its high speed gave it some hope of catching the Messerschmitt Bf 109s that were holding air superiority over the Eastern Front.

Above: The first British convoys with Hawker Hurricanes for the Soviet air force arrived at Murmansk in September 1941, originally serving with No. 151 Wing, RAF. This example in Russian markings takes off on a sortie over the Karelian front.

cruel winter. Loathe to waste Luftwaffe resources where they would be useless, the Germans started moving some of their fighters and dive-bombers to the Mediterranean in December to support operations against Malta and the British forces in North Africa.

COUNTER ATTACK

Then on 6 December the Soviet commander Georgi Zhukov (of Nomonhan fame) launched a counter-attack with a fresh, well-equipped army in the Moscow area and, without the means to provide adequate air support for the ground forces, the Germans were forced to pull back. The bid to capture the Soviet capital was at an end.

At this time, however, both the Luftwaffe and V-VS were hurriedly introducing improved aircraft. The Bf 109E was now finally being replaced on all units by the Bf 109F; the Do 17 had almost disappeared from front-line service, being replaced by the Do 217, while new versions of the He 111, Ju 88 and

Ju 52/3m were starting to arrive at the front. Among the Soviet aircraft the I-15 and I-16 were being withdrawn at last as deliveries of modern LaGG-3s, MiG-3s and Yak-1s were frantically stepped up. Production of the Il-4 bomber (which had first raided Berlin on 8 August 1941) and Il-2 close-support aircraft was accelerating, and the first British convoys bringing Hurricane fighters had been arriving at Murmansk

Above: A pair of winter-camouflaged Heinkel He 111H-16s of KG 1/27 on a sortie over the Eastern Front in 1943. These aircraft have external bomb racks, indicating that the inner bomb bays were used to house auxiliary fuel tanks.

since September. Hitler's dream of a speedy victory in the East was being shattered as his fighting men struggled to survive the frosts and snows of their first Russian winter.

Above: Primitive means were adopted for dealing with weaponry on the Eastern Front during the winter of 1941-42. Here, bombs are off-loaded into the snow before being mounted underneath appropriately-camouflaged Ju 87s. All servicing had to be done in the open.

Left: Serving under Colonel-General N. N. Voronov's IA P-VO command in the defence of Moscow, winter-camouflaged MiG-3 fighters of the 12th IAP stand ready for action. The MiG-3 was exceptionally fast, being capable of 640 km/h (398 mph). Two of the aircraft in this line-up retain the dark-green/dark-brown summer camouflage.

Channel Dash

FEBRUARY 1942

Left: Seen over choppy Channel waters is a Bristol Beaufort of No. 22 Squadron. F/O Campbell from No. 22 was awarded the Victoria Cross for damaging the Gneisenau during a daring raid on Brest harbour from which he did not return.

In February 1942 there occurred what was for the Royal Navy and the Royal Air Force one of the most humiliating events of the entire war. Three German warships, *Scharnhorst*, *Gneisenau* and *Prinz Eugen*, escaped an elaborate blockade in Brest harbour, sailed through the Dover Straits in daylight and reached their German ports despite all the British could do to prevent them.

Since early-1941 the powerful battle-cruisers *Scharnhorst* and *Gneisenau* had lain in Brest, where they had put in after destructive forays in the Atlantic and where they were joined by the heavy cruiser *Prinz Eugen* on 1 June. Thereafter this trio posed a considerable threat to British convoys not only crossing the North Atlantic but sailing to and from Gibraltar and further afield. Accordingly, at the insistence of the British Admiralty, they had attracted the constant attention of RAF Bomber and Coastal Commands; however, in the first two months of attacks on Brest with over 1,100 sorties flown

against the port, only four bombs damaged the ships, and it was decided to 'sew them in' using sea mines. On 6 April a single Beaufort, flown by Flying Officer Kenneth Campbell of No. 22 Squadron, managed to torpedo the *Gneisenau*, causing damage that took six months to repair. Throughout the remainder of 1941 an enormous tonnage of British bombs fell on Brest but caused little more than superficial damage to the warships, and in February 1942 the Germans decided on a bold bid to sail them back to Germany through the English Channel (Hitler being convinced that the UK was about to launch an invasion of Norway). The maritime operation was to be codenamed 'Cerberus', while 'Thunderbolt' covered the elaborate plans to provide air cover

Right: Six Swordfish of No. 825 Squadron, led by Lt Cdr Eugene Esmonde (who was awarded a posthumous Victoria Cross for his leadership and supreme gallantry), attacked the German ships, but all six were shot down.

during the voyage. The breakout from Brest was scheduled for the late-evening of 11 February.

NIGHT ESCAPE

To counter the threat of such an escape a British submarine lay off Ushant and the RAF covered the port with reconnaissance by day and operated radar watches ('Stopper') with Hudsons at night.

Delayed by a Bomber Command raid on the port itself that night, the German ships slipped their moorings shortly before midnight and sailed out unseen by the submarine and set course north-east up the Channel. Unfortunately at that critical moment the radar in the patrolling Hudson had become unserviceable and the German ships escaped undetected. By first light the following morning they had passed the Cherbourg peninsula. A further routine Coastal Command precaution, a patrol between Boulogne and Le Havre ('Habo'), had been recalled owing to the forecast of fog.

It was at this point that the first German day fighters arrived over the German ships to provide cover against the expected RAF attacks,

and these were spotted on British coastal radar at 08.30 but were dismissed by Fighter Command (under Air Vice-Marshal Leigh-Mallory) as being some sort of German air-sea rescue exercise. Two hours later the pilots of two Spitfires on an *ad hoc* sweep over the Channel spotted the German fleet and, under orders not to break radio silence, sped back to their base at Kenley to report, landing at 11.10. Thus it was not until 11.25 that the British air and naval authorities were fully aware that the enemy ships were at large in the Channel. By then they were entering the Dover Straits under the protection of numerous destroyers and E-boats, as well as swarms of Fw 190As and Bf 109Fs of Adolf Galland's JG 2 and JG 26.

BREAK-OUT SUCCEEDS

To counter such a break-out from Brest, the RAF (as part of Operation 'Fuller') had earmarked 100 Bomber Command aircraft and three squadrons of Beaufort torpedo-bombers, while the Fleet Air Arm had stationed a squadron (No. 825) of Swordfish at Manston. None of the Bomber Command aircraft were in the south of England and were only at four hours' standby; only seven of the Beauforts and the Swordfish were ready and loaded up with torpedoes.

As the German ships passed through the Dover straits the heavy guns on the Kent coast opened up, but their shells all fell wide of the mark. Three fighter squadrons were ordered off to escort the Manston Swordfish which, at 12.20, took off

and made for the enemy. Only one of the Spitfire squadrons, No. 72, arrived on time and was heavily engaged by the German fighters. Beset all around by Focke-Wulf Fw 190s and Messerschmitt Bf 109s and faced by a veritable wall of flak, Lieutenant Commander Eugene Esmonde led his old torpedo biplanes into the attack. All were shot down and none of their torpedoes found their mark. Esmonde himself was awarded a posthumous Victoria Cross.

As the German ships passed out of British coastal radar cover a few Beauforts attacked with torpedoes, but again without success, as did a group of British destroyers. Between then and darkness on the evening of 12 February 242 RAF bombers set out to attack but fewer than 40 crews claimed even to have seen their targets. The enemy ships did not escape unscathed, however, the *Scharnhorst* exploding a mine off Walcheren in the early afternoon

and another off Terschelling late that evening before limping into Wilhelmshaven; the *Gneisenau* also struck a mine but made Cuxhaven safely.

The bold Operations 'Cerberus' and 'Thunderbolt' had succeeded beyond all expectations, while 'Fuller', 'Stopper' and 'Habo' failed dismally. Ironically Bomber Command alone reaped an ill-earned reward: it no longer had the tiresome task of raiding Brest.

Above: The escape of the Scharnhorst, Gneisenau and Prinz Eugen was a tragic episode for the Swordfish. All six of the attacking aircraft were shot down, losing 13 crew. The Swordfish was subsequently used mainly on anti-submarine duties.

Below: The German warships Gneisenau, Scharnhorst and Prinz Eugen during the Channel dash. Torpedo attacks failed to inflict any damage, although in the event the Scharnhorst was partially crippled by mines previously dropped by the RAF.

Adversaries over the Channel

Only in service since mid-1941, Focke-Wulf Fw 190s of JG 26 were called upon to provide air cover for the break-out. Their first clashes with RAF Spitfire Mk Vs in 1941 had demonstrated its superiority; something that was not addressed until the

Spitfire Mk IX appeared in July 1942. Bristol's Beaufort was Coastal Command's standard torpedo-bomber from 1940 to 1943, until superseded by the Beaufighter. Early examples had Bristol Taurus engines; Mk IIs used Twin Wasps.

Focke-Wulf Fw 190A
One of the earliest Fw 190s to get into action was this A-2 flown by the Kommandeur of 1/JG 26 in early-1942 from St Omer in France. This was the year that the formidable nature of the Fw 190 could no longer be doubted by the RAF's senior officers.

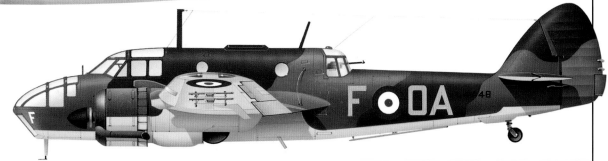

Bristol Beaufort Mk I
The Bristol Beaufort was used for a number of torpedo attacks on the German ships. This No. 22 Squadron aircraft had managed to score a single hit on the *Gneisenau* in April 1941.

Dieppe

19 AUGUST 1942

Since the moment of French capitulation in June 1940 and the loss of the UK's last foothold in continental Europe, the cornerstone of possible eventual victory against Germany was assumed to be a return in force by British forces across the English Channel. Such a major amphibious landing on a hostile coast was an unknown venture, particularly in the age of the military aeroplane.

It was therefore decided in 1942 to mount a major operation across the Channel as something of a rehearsal for the eventual invasion, then believed to be a practical possibility in 1943; the objective chosen was the French port of Dieppe. The opportunity was to be taken to test the enemy's reaction to such a landing in force particularly in the air, and a major object was to attract the Luftwaffe in France into the air where it was hoped it could be decisively beaten. By mid-1942 it was hoped to be able to deploy as many as 60 fighter and fighter-bomber squadrons plus 10 reconnaissance and light bomber squadrons in the area of the landings, to counter the estimated German force of 250 fighters and 220 bombers based in France and the Low Countries. More important, it was hoped to field a dozen squadrons of the new 644-km/h

(400-mph) Typhoons and Spitfire Mk IXs which were calculated to be more than a match for the new German Fw 190A. Command of the air operations was in the hands of Air Vice-Marshal Leigh-Mallory.

DOOMED

From the outset matters went wrong with the British plans. After a couple of postponements (which are thought to have given the Germans an inkling of a pending attack), the operation was finally launched at first light on 19 August. The large number of Spitfire Mk V fighter squadrons took off before dawn to cover the landing areas and indeed provided powerful cover for the troops on the beaches as the Blenheims and Bostons attacked targets in and around Dieppe itself, and laid smokescreens over the beaches. Further afield Defiants with jamming equipment attempted to blind enemy radar as American B-17s carried out a raid on the important German fighter base at Abbeville.

At first the Luftwaffe reacted with only single Staffeln of Bf 109Fs and Fw 190As, and these were heavily engaged by the patrolling Spitfires. By mid-morning, however, enemy air activity was quickly increasing with the appearance of formations of Do 217 bombers and

a number of low-level bombing attacks by Fw 190A-4s which managed to penetrate beneath the RAF fighter cover and escape unscathed.

On the ground the Canadian and commando forces proved unable to capture vital enemy positions overlooking Dieppe, while the Churchill tanks were inadequately armed to knock out enemy strongpoints as they floundered up and down the shingle beaches. Garbled communications suggested that the Canadians were well established in the town so that support by the Hurricane fighter-bombers was called off at a critical point in the battle, resulting in heavy casualties among these troops.

There is no doubt that the huge armada of covering fighters prevented the German bombers from carrying out their attacks accurately on the ships and only two vessels were hit by enemy bombs. However, while the Spitfire Mk V pilots had been briefed not to continue combat too far from Dieppe, the Spitfire Mk IXs and Typhoons were allowed free rein. Unfortunately

persistent development trouble with the latter had limited its entry into service and only a single wing was available for action at the time of the Dieppe operation and even then only with a number of flying restrictions. The only occasion on which Typhoons were in action was when they were accidentally attacked by a squadron of Canadian-flown Spitfire Mk IXs. Two Typhoons were lost when their tail units broke off as their pilots attempted to escape by diving away.

By late afternoon the assault ships were withdrawing across the Channel, still covered by the Spitfire Mk V squadrons. At first it was thought, by examination of the RAF pilots' combat reports, that the RAF had indeed won a signal victory. Early estimates suggested that more than 100 German aircraft had been shot down, compared with the loss in combat of 106 RAF aircraft in addition to 32 others written-off at base. German records later revealed that the Luftwaffe aircraft losses totalled no more than 48.

LESSONS LEARNT

The tactical lessons learned at Dieppe were indeed sobering. Ground support by the fighter-bombers and light bombers had been wholly inadequate, and there had been little or no effective communication between the landing forces and the supporting pilots.

Overall the ratio of fighters to support aircraft had been far too great, and the supposed superiority of the latest RAF aircraft proved illusory, while control of the fighters had been conducted at land-based radar stations too remote from the actual battle.

Ironically the value of the Dieppe landing lay in one vital piece of information: that the Allied forces, their tactics, equipment and training in 1942 fell far short of the standard obviously required for a successful invasion of Europe. There was, alas, no means of persuading the Soviet Union (which had been pressing the UK to open a 'second front' without delay) of this unpalatable fact.

Below: A German soldier surveys the tragic sight of Allied troops killed in battle and their abandoned equipment on the beach at Dieppe. It was to be almost two more years before the Allies succeeded in landing and holding the Channel coast of Europe. Then, ground support by Allied aircraft was properly planned and much more effective.

Combat fighters

The Spitfire Mk V, of which some 6,500 were built, proved to be underpowered when it came face-to-face with the Fw 190. The supercharged Merlin 60 engine with a four-blade propeller and other refinements was introduced as the improved Mk IX. The Fw 190 first appeared over northern France in mid-1941 and immediately won the respect of Allied aircrew who quickly suffered at its hands. Superior to the Bf 109 in almost every respect, the Fw 190 had a major impact over Dieppe.

Focke-Wulf Fw 190A

In 1942, the Focke-Wulf Fw 190 factories switched to the A-4 model, with methanol/water boost for the engine and a better radio (with small aerial mast on the fin). The A-4 was flown by the adjutant of Stab III/JG 2 'Richthofen', one of the top-scoring fighter wings of all time. Its base in September 1942 was Poix.

Spitfire Mk VB

This Spitfire VB is in the colours of No. 340 Squadron, a Free French fighter unit. At the time of Dieppe it was operating from RAF Hornchurch and involved in fighter sweeps over northern France. The Cross of Lorraine emblem is carried under the cockpit.

Cross-Channel Operations

OCTOBER 1941 - JUNE 1943

W hen viewed against events elsewhere, the scale and objectives of operations conducted by the Luftwaffe and RAF across the English Channel after the end of the Battle of Britain were minor. The principal difference lay in the fact that the British (and later the American) attacks were continuous and increasing in tempo, whereas those of the Germans were sporadic and, in general, of strictly limited effort.

The RAF's aims were threefold: to deny access by enemy coastal shipping to ports along the French

coast; to disrupt all military (but particularly air) operations in northern France; and to defeat the relatively small German air force in France and the Low Countries in the air. To do this Fighter Command set about increasing its strength in 1941 by introducing the excellent Supermarine Spitfire Mk V, a version that eventually equipped no fewer than 71 squadrons. The Spitfire Mk VC variant was capable of carrying up to 500 lb (227 kg) of bombs. Hawker Hurricane Mk IIs, of which the four-cannon Hurricane

Above: Early Hawker Typhoon IBs of No. 56 Squadron based at RAF Manston on an operational sortie across the Channel in early 1943. At this time, No. 56 was using the Typhoon for small-scale fighter or fighter-bomber attacks on ground targets of opportunity.

Mk IIC fighter-bomber was the outstanding version, equipped a further 42 squadrons; they eventually carried up to 1,000 lb (454 kg) of bombs.

From the beginning, the light bombers of No. 2 Group (Bristol Blenheims and Douglas Bostons) were tasked with Operation

Above: This Bf 109G-6/R6 was serving in the summer of 1943 with II/JG 26, one of the crack fighter units in northern France.

Below: A Westland Whirlwind I of No. 263 (Fighter) Squadron before modification to carry bombs under the wings. Operating from Warmwell in Dorset, No. 263 was involved in offensive sweeps over France.

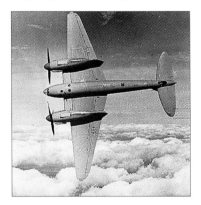

Above: In the mid-war years, the de Havilland Mosquito joined the Spitfire for longer-range photo-reconnaissance missions. This Mosquito PR.Mk IV was based at RAF Benson in early 1943 with a detachment of No. 540 Squadron, and used for photographic flights over occupied France.

Taking the war to the enemy

Offensive sweeps over occupied France began soon after the Battle of Britain (initially with Spitfires). These differed from the Luftwaffe's post-Battle of Britain nuisance raids in having ambitious and extensive aims: the disruption of all military operations in France, the denial of French Channel ports to coastal shipping, and the defeat of the Luftwaffe in the air, winning local temporary air superiority.

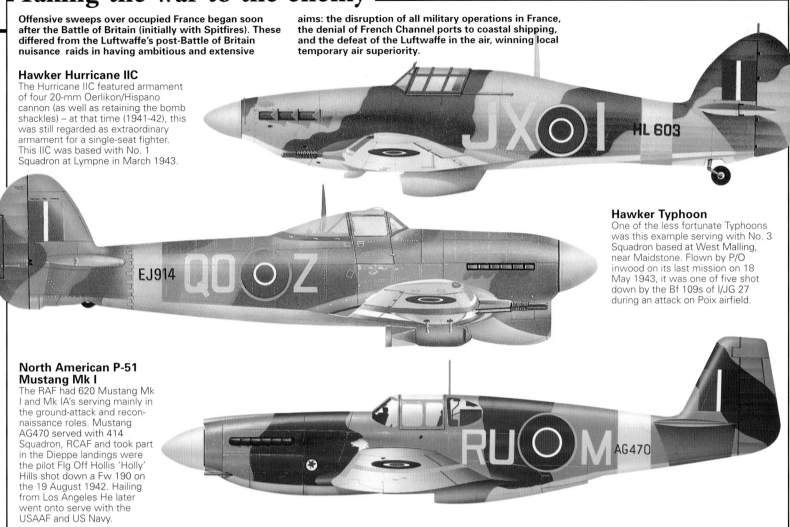

Hawker Hurricane IIC
The Hurricane IIC featured armament of four 20-mm Oerlikon/Hispano cannon (as well as retaining the bomb shackles) – at that time (1941-42), this was still regarded as extraordinary armament for a single-seat fighter. This IIC was based with No. 1 Squadron at Lympne in March 1943.

Hawker Typhoon
One of the less fortunate Typhoons was this example serving with No. 3 Squadron based at West Malling, near Maidstone. Flown by P/O inwood on its last mission on 18 May 1943, it was one of five shot down by the Bf 109s of I/JG 27 during an attack on Poix airfield.

North American P-51 Mustang Mk I
The RAF had 620 Mustang Mk I and Mk IA's serving mainly in the ground-attack and recon-naissance roles. Mustang AG470 served with 414 Squadron, RCAF and took part in the Dieppe landings were the pilot Flg Off Hollis 'Holly' Hills shot down a Fw 190 on the 19 August 1942. Hailing from Los Angeles He later went onto serve with the USAAF and US Navy.

Channel Stop', a constant offensive against enemy coastal shipping in the Channel. Upon the arrival of the fighter-bomber Hurricanes this task was taken over by Fighter Command on 30 October 1941, while the light bombers concentrat-ed on land targets under heavy Spitfire protection. The Spitfires

The Focke-Wulf Fw 190, which first appeared over France in October 1941, dominated the skies for many months. RAF intelligence could not believe that this squat, angular fighter had the measure of the sleek and slender Spitfire V.

An unusual view of an RAF Boston Mk III, over Charleroi in France. The bulged twin-gun packs can be seen on each side of the nose, with the open bomb doors beyond. Normal bombload of the Boston was four 500-lb (227-kg) bombs.

themselves had initiated the first of the offensive sweeps, known as Rhubarbs, as early as 20 December 1940, and these continued to grow in scope until by 1942 as many as 500 aircraft would sweep along the French coast, trailing their coat in an effort to lure the Luftwaffe into the sky. Occasionally (and particu-

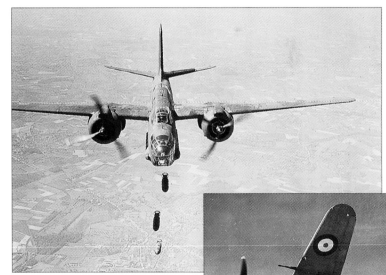

larly when German radar reported British light bombers approaching key fighter airfields), the Messer-schmitt Bf 109Fs of JG 2 and JG 26 would come up to intercept, and heavy air fighting would ensue; by and large, however, air combats tended to involve only the smaller formations.

SUPERIOR FOCKE-WULF
This pattern changed dramatically with the introduction of the Focke-Wulf Fw 190A, an excellent fighter that quickly proved superior

Early in 1941, the Hurricane IIC entered service with the RAF, and many were used on Channel sweeps and bomber escorts over France. Attrition was comparative-ly high and combat with Bf 109s was viewed with some apprehen-sion by Hurricane pilots.

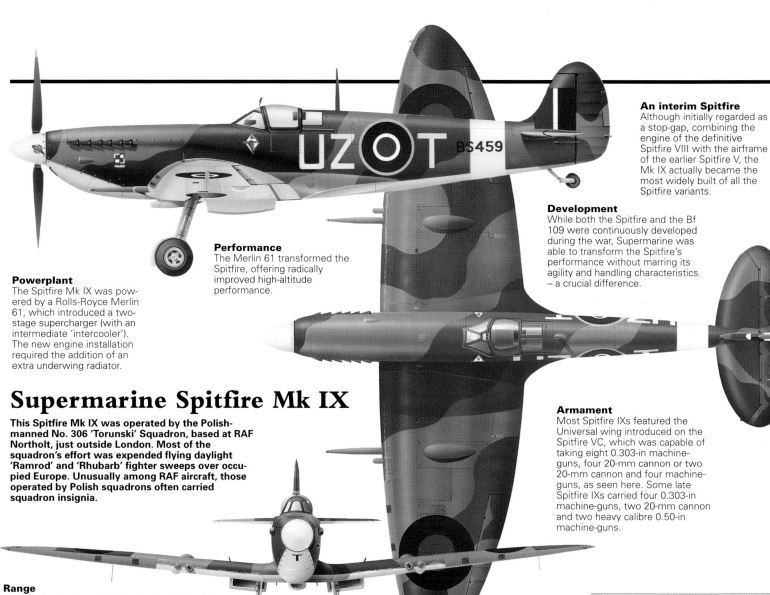

An interim Spitfire
Although initially regarded as a stop-gap, combining the engine of the definitive Spitfire VIII with the airframe of the earlier Spitfire V, the Mk IX actually became the most widely built of all the Spitfire variants.

Development
While both the Spitfire and the Bf 109 were continuously developed during the war, Supermarine was able to transform the Spitfire's performance without marring its agility and handling characteristics – a crucial difference.

Performance
The Merlin 61 transformed the Spitfire, offering radically improved high-altitude performance.

Powerplant
The Spitfire Mk IX was powered by a Rolls-Royce Merlin 61, which introduced a two-stage supercharger (with an intermediate 'intercooler'). The new engine installation required the addition of an extra underwing radiator.

Supermarine Spitfire Mk IX

This Spitfire Mk IX was operated by the Polish-manned No. 306 'Torunski' Squadron, based at RAF Northolt, just outside London. Most of the squadron's effort was expended flying daylight 'Ramrod' and 'Rhubarb' fighter sweeps over occupied Europe. Unusually among RAF aircraft, those operated by Polish squadrons often carried squadron insignia.

Armament
Most Spitfire IXs featured the Universal wing introduced on the Spitfire VC, which was capable of taking eight 0.303-in machine-guns, four 20-mm cannon or two 20-mm cannon and four machine-guns, as seen here. Some late Spitfire IXs carried four 0.303-in machine-guns, two 20-mm cannon and two heavy calibre 0.50-in machine-guns.

Range
Even without external fuel tanks, the Spitfire Mk IX carried sufficient fuel to range over a large part of occupied Europe. The Spitfire IX pilots could create as much mayhem as they liked and still have fuel to get home.

Spitfire vs Bf 109

Despite the arrival on both sides of more modern fighters designed in the light of combat experience, the Spitfire and Messerschmitt Bf 109 met in combat over Europe from the first months of the war to the last days. The late-mark Spitfires and 109s that battled over Berlin, however, were far different beasts than those that first encountered each other at Dunkirk in May 1940. The Bf 109 was a slightly older design, having first flown in

September 1935, six months before the Spitfire, and had undergone considerable development, not to mention a combat blooding in Spain, by the outbreak of war in September 1939. In comparison with the Spitfire Mk I, the Bf 109E was higher-powered, faster-climbing (at lower altitudes) and better-armed. Conversely, the Spitfire was more manoeuvrable at all speeds and altitudes. Weights, range and maximum speed were all very similar. After

After its return from the USSR, No. 81 Squadron became part of the Hornchurch wing, equipped with Spitfire Mk VBs.

the Battle of Britain the Luftwaffe and RAF introduced new fighters, specifically the Fw 190 and Typhoon, but recognised the soundness of the Bf 109 and Spitfire design and developed them almost beyond recognition. In early 1942, the two main versions in

service were the Spitfire Mk V and Bf 109F. The 'Friedrich' introduced the more powerful DB 601E engine and the Spitfire Mk V, the similarly-uprated Merlin 45, boosting the maximum speeds and climb rates. The increase in weight affected the manoeuvrability and handling of both types – more detrimentally in the case of the Messerschmitt.

The next developments were the Spitfire Mk IX and Bf 109G, both of

No. 222 Squadron moved to RAF Coltishall in November 1940, from where it began to fly offensive operations early in 1941. The Spitfire Mk VB, seen here, equipped the squadron from August 1941.

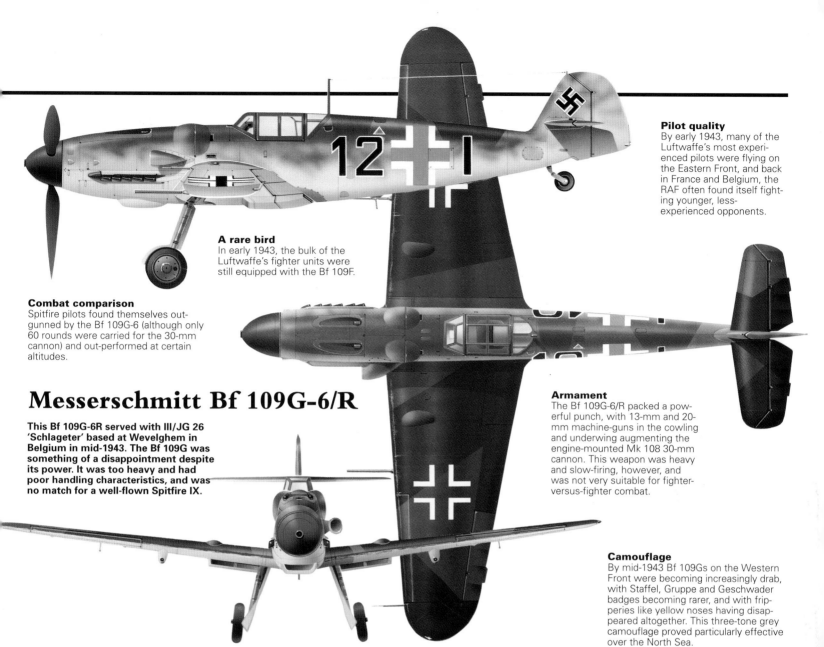

Pilot quality
By early 1943, many of the Luftwaffe's most experienced pilots were flying on the Eastern Front, and back in France and Belgium, the RAF often found itself fighting younger, less-experienced opponents.

A rare bird
In early 1943, the bulk of the Luftwaffe's fighter units were still equipped with the Bf 109F.

Combat comparison
Spitfire pilots found themselves outgunned by the Bf 109G-6 (although only 60 rounds were carried for the 30-mm cannon) and out-performed at certain altitudes.

Messerschmitt Bf 109G-6/R

This Bf 109G-6R served with III/JG 26 'Schlageter' based at Wevelghem in Belgium in mid-1943. The Bf 109G was something of a disappointment despite its power. It was too heavy and had poor handling characteristics, and was no match for a well-flown Spitfire IX.

Armament
The Bf 109G-6/R packed a powerful punch, with 13-mm and 20-mm machine-guns in the cowling and underwing augmenting the engine-mounted Mk 108 30-mm cannon. This weapon was heavy and slow-firing, however, and was not very suitable for fighter-versus-fighter combat.

Camouflage
By mid-1943 Bf 109Gs on the Western Front were becoming increasingly drab, with Staffel, Gruppe and Geschwader badges becoming rarer, and with fripperies like yellow noses having disappeared altogether. This three-tone grey camouflage proved particularly effective over the North Sea.

Right: A Polish pilot with No. 303 Squadron looks at his tally of 'kills' on the side of his Spitfire VB at RAF Kirton-in-Lindsey, Lincolnshire on 15 August 1942.

Below: The availability of the DB 601E engine at the beginning of 1942 resulted in the Bf 109F-3.

Below: A Spitfire VB in service with No. 92 Squadron at RAF Biggin Hill in late 1941. A total of 6,479 Spitfire Vs was built.

which entered service in 1942 to general acclaim. The Spitfire Mk IX was a hasty lash-up, a means of getting the new two-stage Merlin 60 series engine into a Spitfire as soon as possible to counter the threat of the Focke-Wulf Fw 190A. The airframe was that of the Mk V, but the result became the most numerous of all Spitfire variants, and in widespread use right to the end

of the war. Messerschmitt responded with the Bf 109G, driven by a DB 605 engine to give increased speed. This, too, became the most numerous variant, although it was built in a plethora of sub-variants.

One of the triumphs of Supermarine's design team was maintaining the excellent flying qualities of the Spitfire while constantly improving

the performance, a philosophy not adopted by Messerschmitt, who took the path of improving outright performance and adaptability at the expense of handling. Even so, the later Spitfires were less pleasant to fly than the earlier marks and had trickier ground handling characteristics than the lower-powered early models. From a pilot's point of view, the mid-series Spitfire Mk IX and Bf 109F models were generally regarded as the best of their respective breeds. The ultimate marks of the two great fighters to see combat in this war were the Griffon-engined Spitfire F. Mk 21 and the DB-605 (with water-methanol injection)-powered Bf 109K

The Spitfire Mk 21 had nearly double the engine power of the Mk I and 25 per cent greater maximum speed as did the Bf 109K compared to the E. Whereas the Spitfire's loaded weight increased by 75 percent between the Mk I and the much larger F. Mk 21, the Bf 109 grew little and a loaded K was 27 per cent heavier than an E.

Defending Fortress Europe

Although the introduction of the Fw 190 and Bf 109G gave the Luftwaffe an aircraft superior to the RAF's Spitfire V, the RAF maintained the initiative, accepting heavier casualties but remaining on the offensive. The introduction of the Spitfire IX helped, but later Fw 190s (like the A-4 illustrated below) proved a match for the best of the Merlin Spitfires. At the end of the day, there were too few Luftwaffe fighters in France to stop the RAF's offensive.

Focke-Wulf Fw 190A-4
Far more heavily armed than the Messerschmitt Bf 109F and early Bf 109G, the Focke-Wulf Fw 190A-4 and close relatives multiplied in 1942. In the hands of the outstandingly skilled and experienced pilots in JG 2 and JG 26, the aircraft scored on average 5:1 against the RAF. This A-4 served with 2./JG 2 at Abbeville in May 1943.

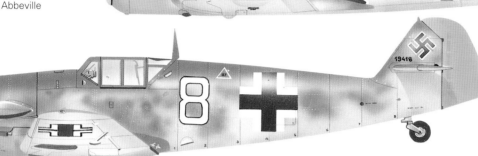

Messerschmitt Bf 109G
From early 1942 the Messerschmitt Bf 109G became the standard production variant of the Luftwaffe's most numerous fighter, production building up to over 14,000 in 1944 alone. One of the early versions with light armament (one cannon and two machine-guns) was the G-4; this example operated from Poix with I/JG 27.

In February 1941, No. 601 Squadron based at RAF Northolt began taking part in offensive sweeps over northern France and flew the early sorties with Hurricane IIBs, before Spitfires began to dominate day offensive operations.

to the RAF's Spitfire Mk V. Fortunately for Fighter Command not more than about 60 of these aircraft were operational by February 1942 and, although losses among British aircraft began to increase, there was a breathing space in which to find a remedy.

FIGHTER-BOMBERS

As told elsewhere, the Hawker Typhoon was introduced into service before all its problems had been solved and, together with the Spitfire Mk IX, was entering service by the time of the Dieppe operation of August 1942. By then, though, the Fw 190A-3 fighter-

A Mustang I of No. II(AC) Squadron. Army Co-operation Command's Allison Mustangs were superb at low level and were used for the longest range cross-channel missions, even flying over Germany itself from October 1942.

bomber, capable of carrying a 1,102-lb (500-kg) bomb, was serving with JG 2 in France. Thirty of these aircraft launched a vicious attack on Canterbury, Kent, on 30 October. Moreover, misled into believing that the Fw 190A-3 was the latest variant in service when an example landed intact in south

Wales on 23 June 1942, the British received an unpleasant surprise when confronted by the more powerful Fw 190A-4 which could outrun both the Spitfire Mk IX and Typhoon (the latter initially beset by restrictions).

When, during the winter of 1942-43, the newly-formed Schnell-kampfgeschwader 10 (SKG 10) fighter-bomber wing began a series of daylight hit-and-run attacks with Fw 190A-4s, the RAF was forced to deploy disproportionately large forces of fighters to counter the

Below: In the European Theatre the first P-47 Thunderbolts and P-51 Mustangs in action were given white bands across the tail and around the nose to stop them being mistaken for 190s and 109s.

The Westland Whirlwind was the first single-seat twin-engined fighter to see RAF service. Its existence was a closely guarded secret in the early days of the war, and problems with the Rolls-Royce Peregrine engines meant that only two RAF squadrons – Nos 263 and 137 – received Whirlwinds.

threat. Heavy damage was inflicted in a raid on London on 20 January 1943; in March SKG 10 struck Ashford, Eastbourne and Hastings, and the following month returned to Eastbourne and destroyed a ball-bearing factory at Chelmsford in Essex.

New Spitfire

Excellent though the stop-gap Spitfire Mk IX was, its performance at low altitude was inadequate to match that of the Fw 190A-3 and Fw 190A-4 fighter-bombers, and a new variant was hurriedly introduced: the Spitfire Mk XII with Griffon engine and clipped wings. (At low levels the Spitfire Mk VB with its single-stage low-blown Merlin 45, 46 or 50 was the equal of a Mk IX, especially in LF.Mk VB form with clipped wings which provided for a greater rate of roll.) Together with the Typhoon, whose snags had been largely cured and which was fast and adequately reliable at low level, the Spitfires grad-

Right: No. 601 Squadron, an Auxiliary Air Force Squadron, operated the Hurricane I from RAF Northolt, seen here in January 1941. The following month it received the later Hurricane IIB and made offensive sweeps over northern France until August, when it re-equipped with Bell Airacobras.

ually got the measure of the snap raids and, by late spring 1943, these had tailed off. In any case, with pressure mounting on other fronts, most Fw 190 fighter-bombers were being moved elsewhere.

By mid-1943 the Americans had arrived in the UK in sufficient numbers for the fighters and fighter-bombers of the US Army Air Force to make a significant contribution to the cross-Channel air

Right: No. 310 Squadron was formed at RAF Duxford in July 1940 as a fighter unit with Czechoslovak personnel. It received Spitfire VBs in November 1941 and flew them on operations from RAF Perranporth in Cornwall until May 1942.

offensive. On 13 April the Republic P-47s of the 56th Fighter Group entered combat for the first time with a sweep in the St Omer area, being followed into action in

later months by the 55th, 78th, 353rd 358th, 359th and 361st Fighter Groups of the 66th Fighter Wing, VIII Fighter Command. By the end of the year the Allies had at their disposal more than 2,200 Spitfires, Hurricanes, Typhoons, P-47 Thunderbolts, Lockheed P-38 Lightnings and North American P-51 Mustangs based in the UK. Their operations were divided between cross-Channel sweeps and escort missions with the British and American medium and heavy bombers which were by then mounting a devastating offensive against German-occupied Europe.

Showing the distinctive white identification bands, these P-47D-I-RE Thunderbolts are from the 62nd Fighter Squadron, 56th Fighter Group. At altitudes below 15,000 ft, the new Fw 190 proved to be more than a handful for the big American fighter, although above that height the P-47 could out-run and out-turn the Fw 190.

British Night Bombing

1941-1942

Left: Handley Page Halifax B.Mk II of No. 35 (Madras Presidency) Squadron, operating from RAF Linton-on-Ouse, North Yorkshire in May 1942. The bulbous Boulton Paul Mk III turret, with its raised fairing on top of the fuselage, created a great deal of drag.

Below: A morale boosting newspaper photograph that showed "the crew of the bomber 'MacRobert's Reply' all ready to take off for a raid over enemy territory". The Short Stirling Mk I of No. 15 Squadron at RAF Wyton, carried the coat of arms of the MacRobert family, the cost of the aircraft being donated by the family.

"We'll do our job - -if you'll do yours"

A s the German night blitz reached its climax at the beginning of 1941, RAF Bomber Command was beginning the long process of building a force of truly heavy bombers with which to carry the war back to the German people. The first land-marks in this process were reached when four-engined Short Stirlings of No. 7 Squadron bombed Rotterdam in the Netherlands on 10/11 February, Avro Manchesters of No. 207 Squadron attacked Brest on 24/25 February, and Handley Page Halifaxes of No. 35

Below: An Avro Manchester Mk IA, that flew with No. 207 Squadron from RAF Waddington in 1941. Incessant problems with the two Vulture engines made operations difficult and it was replaced by the Lancaster in 1942.

Squadron raided Le Havre on the French coast on 10/11 March; two nights later Manchesters and Halifaxes made their first attack on German soil with a raid on Hamburg. It was, however, the twin-engined Vickers Wellington that dropped the RAF's first 1814-kg (4,000-lb) bombs when

aircraft of Nos 9 and 149 Squadrons attacked Emden on the last night of March. Emden was again attacked on 27 April, this time in daylight by the Stirlings of No. 7 Squadron. On the night of 8/9 May Bomber Command assembled the largest force to date for raids on Germany when 360 aircraft of all types attacked Bremen and Hamburg.

By the end of 1941 Bomber Command possessed three

operational squadrons of Stirlings, three of Manchesters and three of Halifaxes, in addition to 21 Wellington squadrons, seven of Handley Page Hampdens and five of Armstrong Whitworth Whitleys, a total of about 420 aircraft (excluding Bristol Blenheim and Douglas Boston light bombers), of which fewer than 60 were four-engined bombers. However, the first examples of a new bomber had been delivered to No. 44 Squadron, this

Left: One of the first RAF squadrons to convert to the Lancaster Mk I in 1942 was No. 50 Squadron based at RAF Swinderby, Lincolnshire. No. 50 soon had its much improved bombers in action on heavy night-bombing raids.

Below: Against a backdrop of swirling clouds and fading evening light, a Lancaster Mk I of No. 83 Squadron, runs up its four Rolls-Royce Merlin engines before taxi-ing out for take-off and another night attack on Germany in 1942.

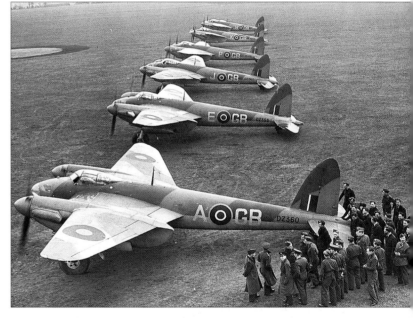

Above: The more than adequate upper field of fire from the mid-upper and rear turrets was offset by the Halifax's undefended ventral area. This weakness was readily exploited by German night-fighters.

Below: A line-up of Mosquito B.Mk IVs at RAF Marham in 1942. These light bombers of No. 105 Squadron, that had been on strength since December 1941, were used for high-speed, long-range bombing raids. Their speed allowed them to fly without fighter escort.

at the continuing inaccuracy of bombing attacks, not to mention the slow delivery of four-engined bombers, Harris at once ordered maximum priority for the introduction of new navigation and bombing aids (the rudimentary 'Gee' had been in limited service for about six months, and a short-range bombing aid, 'Trinity', had proved disappointing). He also gave orders for new tactics to be employed in an effort to increase bombing accuracy

Above: The RAF's first four-engined bomber, the Short Stirling Mk I was flown mainly by No. 3 Group, Bomber Command during 1941-42. Although agile for its size, the Stirling suffered from being underpowered when fully laden.

Below: Hampdens of No. 44 Squadron in formation. This unit began bombing operations with the Hampden after the German invasion of Norway, but at the end of 1941 became the first squadron to convert to the Lancaster.

Avro Lancaster being a four-engined development of the Manchester which, because of persistent engine problems, was soon discontinued and withdrawn.

1942 thus became the single most formative year for Bomber Command during the war. On 22 February Air Marshal Arthur Harris assumed the leadership of the command, a position he was to occupy with spectacular achievement for the remainder of the war. Disturbed

Early bombing twins

Limited by its bombload and service ceiling, the twin-engined Whitley's main impact was not in the bomber-offensive but was in 'nickelling' raids dropping propagandist leaflets over occupied Europe.

The Vickers Wellington Mk IC was the mainstay of Bomber Command through to late-1941, when it was progressively replaced by the bigger, four-engined Stirlings, Halifaxes and Lancasters.

Armstrong Whitworth Whitley Mk V

Whitleys helped carry the offensive into the heart of Germany, although nearly half of their bombs fell on open country. This Mk V flew with No. 77 Squadron in 1941.

Vickers Wellington Mk IC

The Wellington Mk IC with Pegasus XVIII engines and fitted with additional beam guns was the most successful bombing version built. This aircraft of No. 301 (Polish) Squadron flew from Swinderby and survived until 26 June 1942, when it was shot down on a raid over Bremen.

Right: A Boston Mk III of No. 226 Squadron returning to RAF Swanton Morley, on 7 May 1942. The first Boston Mk IIIs arrived during the summer of 1941, replacing Blenheims on daylight coastal raids and anti-shipping strikes.

Left: A formation of Short Stirling Mk Is of Mildenhall-based No. 149 Squadron. Stirling Mk Is flew long-range missions into Germany and Italy until replaced by the improved Mk III in 1943.

was awarded the Victoria Cross.

On the night of 30/31 May Harris launched his first '1,000-bomber' raid, undertaken as much as a propaganda coup as an attempt to swamp the German defences and thereby reduce the loss rate. A total of 1,046 bombers, culled from every Bomber Command squadron, as well as the operational training units, set out to attack Cologne in Operation 'Millennium'; 40

aircraft were lost out of the 898 that were believed to have bombed their target. At dawn the following day Bomber Command de Havilland Mosquito photo reconnaissance and bomber aircraft of No. 105 Squadron were over the city to observe the results of the raid in their first operational mission. Two nights later, on 1/2 June, 956 bombers attacked Essen for the loss of 31 aircraft, and on 25/26 June

Above: A de Havilland Mosquito Mk IV of No. 139 Squadron operating from RAF Marham. The Mk IV was the first light-bomber version to go into service and could carry four 227-kg (500-lb) bombs and was powered by Merlin XXI engines.

Right: Crews from No. 106 Squadron at Coningsby celebrate with their CO, Wg Cdr Guy Gibson, the morning after the first 1,000-bomber raid on Cologne on 31 May 1942. Behind them is a Manchester IA (left) and a Mk I (right).

and effect, and the first of these (the concentration of bombers in space and time over the target) was used with good results in a raid by 223 aircraft against the Renault factory near Paris on the night of 3/4 March.

ENTER THE LANCASTER

On the same night that the Renault works were being bombed, the great Lancaster bomber was making its operational debut, a mining sortie; its first bombing mission, a raid

by No. 44 Squadron on Essen, was flown on 10/11 March. Exactly one month later the RAF's first 3629-kg (8,000-lb) bomb was dropped by a No. 76 Squadron Halifax on the same target.

April saw the first of the Lancaster's spectacular 'set piece' attacks with a daylight low-level raid by 20 aircraft of Nos 44 and 97 Squadrons against the MAN plant at Augsburg on 17 April; seven aircraft were lost, but the leader, Squadron Leader John Nettleton,

Light bombers

Replacing Blenheims from May 1942, Mosquito Mk IVs of No. 2 Group proved very difficult for the Luftwaffe fighters to catch and enjoyed the lowest loss rate of any Bomber Command aircraft.

Also replacing Blenheims, the improved Boston Mk IIIs entered service in February 1942 and were used for low-level strikes against enemy shipping and coastal airfields and power stations.

de Havilland Mosquito Mk IV

Delivered in RAF Fighter Command markings (sky tailbands and yellow leading edges) this late Mosquito Mk IV light bomber was flown by No. 105 Squadron from RAF Marham in the summer of 1942. No. 105 made an epic Mosquito raid on the Gestapo HQ in Oslo on 25 September 1942.

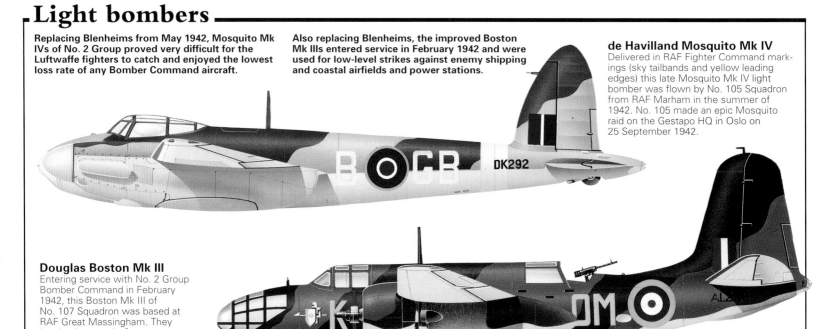

Douglas Boston Mk III

Entering service with No. 2 Group Bomber Command in February 1942, this Boston Mk III of No. 107 Squadron was based at RAF Great Massingham. They bombed targets in German-occupied northern Europe for the next two years.

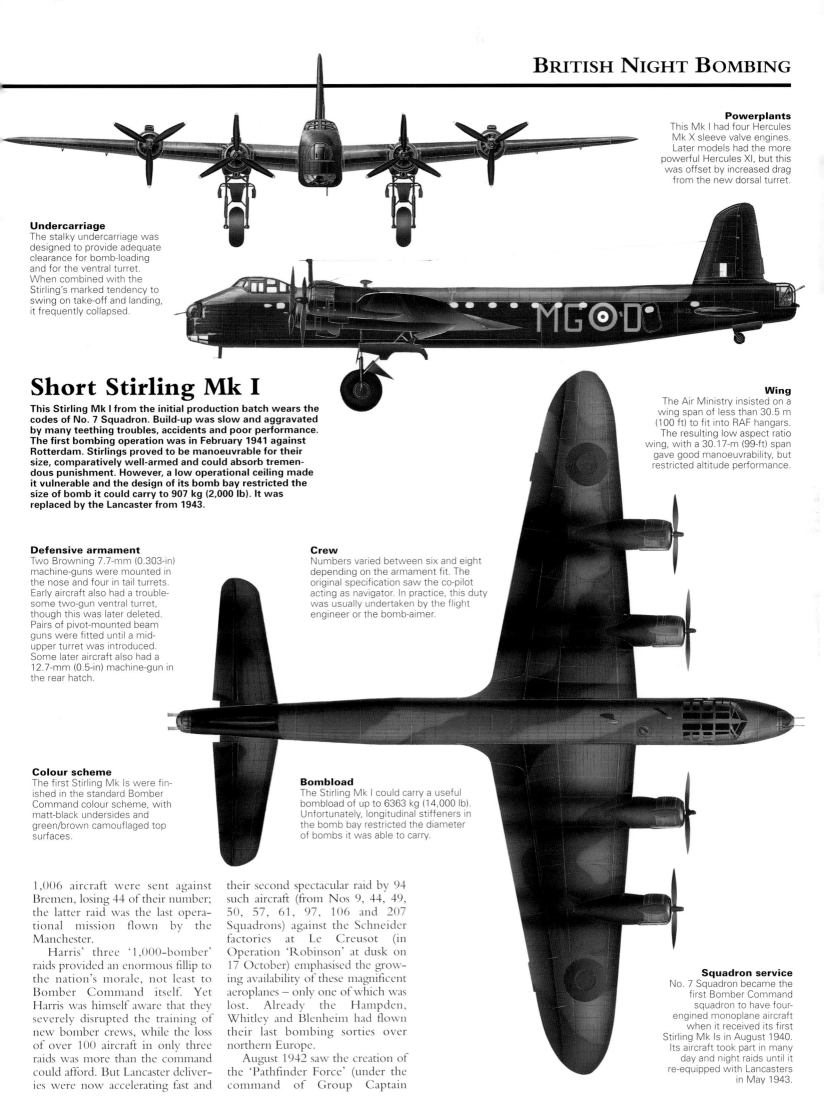

Powerplants
This Mk I had four Hercules Mk X sleeve valve engines. Later models had the more powerful Hercules XI, but this was offset by increased drag from the new dorsal turret.

Undercarriage
The stalky undercarriage was designed to provide adequate clearance for bomb-loading and for the ventral turret. When combined with the Stirling's marked tendency to swing on take-off and landing, it frequently collapsed.

Short Stirling Mk I

This Stirling Mk I from the initial production batch wears the codes of No. 7 Squadron. Build-up was slow and aggravated by many teething troubles, accidents and poor performance. The first bombing operation was in February 1941 against Rotterdam. Stirlings proved to be manoeuvrable for their size, comparatively well-armed and could absorb tremendous punishment. However, a low operational ceiling made it vulnerable and the design of its bomb bay restricted the size of bomb it could carry to 907 kg (2,000 lb). It was replaced by the Lancaster from 1943.

Wing
The Air Ministry insisted on a wing span of less than 30.5 m (100 ft) to fit into RAF hangars. The resulting low aspect ratio wing, with a 30.17-m (99-ft) span gave good manoeuvrability, but restricted altitude performance.

Defensive armament
Two Browning 7.7-mm (0.303-in) machine-guns were mounted in the nose and four in tail turrets. Early aircraft also had a troublesome two-gun ventral turret, though this was later deleted. Pairs of pivot-mounted beam guns were fitted until a mid-upper turret was introduced. Some later aircraft also had a 12.7-mm (0.5-in) machine-gun in the rear hatch.

Crew
Numbers varied between six and eight depending on the armament fit. The original specification saw the co-pilot acting as navigator. In practice, this duty was usually undertaken by the flight engineer or the bomb-aimer.

Colour scheme
The first Stirling Mk Is were finished in the standard Bomber Command colour scheme, with matt-black undersides and green/brown camouflaged top surfaces.

Bombload
The Stirling Mk I could carry a useful bombload of up to 6363 kg (14,000 lb). Unfortunately, longitudinal stiffeners in the bomb bay restricted the diameter of bombs it was able to carry.

Squadron service
No. 7 Squadron became the first Bomber Command squadron to have four-engined monoplane aircraft when it received its first Stirling Mk Is in August 1940. Its aircraft took part in many day and night raids until it re-equipped with Lancasters in May 1943.

1,006 aircraft were sent against Bremen, losing 44 of their number; the latter raid was the last operational mission flown by the Manchester.

Harris' three '1,000-bomber' raids provided an enormous fillip to the nation's morale, not least to Bomber Command itself. Yet Harris was himself aware that they severely disrupted the training of new bomber crews, while the loss of over 100 aircraft in only three raids was more than the command could afford. But Lancaster deliveries were now accelerating fast and

their second spectacular raid by 94 such aircraft (from Nos 9, 44, 49, 50, 57, 61, 97, 106 and 207 Squadrons) against the Schneider factories at Le Creusot (in Operation 'Robinson' at dusk on 17 October) emphasised the growing availability of these magnificent aeroplanes – only one of which was lost. Already the Hampden, Whitley and Blenheim had flown their last bombing sorties over northern Europe.

August 1942 saw the creation of the 'Pathfinder Force' (under the command of Group Captain

Left: The nose blister on the Lancaster gave the bomb aimer the best view of any wartime bomber. Here a bomb aimer presses the button on a Mark IX bomb sight to release his load over the target.

Below: Armourers attend to a 907-kg (2,000-lb) bomb about to be loaded aboard a Whitley Mk V in May 1941. The Armstrong Whitworth bomber continued to carry the night offensive to Germany until the end of April 1942.

D.C.T. Bennett), a number of squadrons tasked with leading major raids and marking the target with easily identifiable coloured bomb bursts. The PFF flew its first mission against Flensburg on the night of 18/19 August. Before the year was out a new navigation and bombing aid, 'Oboe', was first used in a raid by specially-equipped Mosquitoes of No. 109 Squadron on Lutterade on the night of 20/21 December. In the first 10 months of Harris' command the UK's bomber force had more than trebled its striking power, and could now begin to deliver its punches where they were intended to land.

Heavy bombers

The Avro Manchester was an operational failure, largely because of its unreliable Rolls-Royce Vulture engines. The more successful Handley Page Halifax was the first RAF four-engined bomber to drop bombs on Germany, on the night of 12/13 March 1941. The Avro Lancaster, powered by Rolls-Royce Merlin engines was the RAF's most famous and successful bomber of World War II.

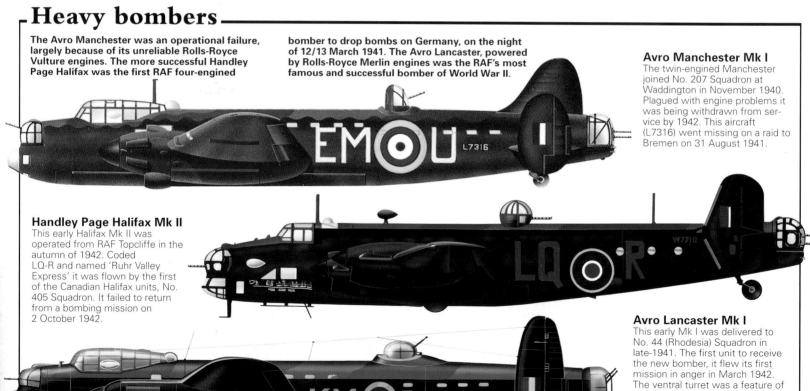

Avro Manchester Mk I
The twin-engined Manchester joined No. 207 Squadron at Waddington in November 1940. Plagued with engine problems it was being withdrawn from service by 1942. This aircraft (L7316) went missing on a raid to Bremen on 31 August 1941.

Handley Page Halifax Mk II
This early Halifax Mk II was operated from RAF Topcliffe in the autumn of 1942. Coded LQ-R and named 'Ruhr Valley Express' it was flown by the first of the Canadian Halifax units, No. 405 Squadron. It failed to return from a bombing mission on 2 October 1942.

Avro Lancaster Mk I
This early Mk I was delivered to No. 44 (Rhodesia) Squadron in late-1941. The first unit to receive the new bomber, it flew its first mission in anger in March 1942. The ventral turret was a feature of early Lancasters. In R5508 Sqn Ldr J. D. Nettleton led a low-level daylight attack on the MAN factory at Augsburg and was subsequently awarded the Victoria Cross.

Left: Another night, another sortie. Wellingtons bore the brunt of RAF Bomber Command's night campaign until the arrival of the four-engined 'heavies'. They then served with Operational Training Units, seeing further action on the 1,000-bomber raids over Germany.

Against the Odds

Bomber Command's operations in 1941 were marked by examples of human strength, mechanical weakness and by the courage of the young aircrew like 22-year-old New Zealander Sergeant James Ward of No. 75 (NZ) Squadron, whose battle against a fire in the air earned him the highest award for bravery.

"All of a sudden, over the middle of the Zuider Zee, I saw an enemy machine coming in from port," said a young New Zealand sergeant-pilot in an anonymous account broadcast by the BBC describing his adventures over Europe on the night of 7 July 1941. His name was James Ward, he came from Wanganui and he was 22. He would never see 23.

"There was a slamming alongside, and then chunks of red-hot shrapnel were flying all over the place. The squadron leader (R.P. Widdowson, though the listening public weren't allowed to know that) put the nose down, to try to dive clear.

"We'd been pretty badly damaged in the attack. The starboard engine was hit, and the hydraulics were out, which meant the landing gear was hanging half down and useless, and the bomb doors were open. The wireless was out, too, and the front gunner had been shot in the foot. Worst of all, fire was burning up through the upper surface of the starboard wing, where a fuel feed pipe had been split. We burst a hole in the side of the fuselage (for once the Wellington's fabric covering worked in its crew's favour) and some of us got going with the fire extinguisher, but the fire was too far out, and we couldn't reach it. Then we tried

throwing coffee from our flasks at it, but that didn't work either.

"I had a good look at the fire and I thought there was a sporting chance of reaching it by getting out through the astrodome, sliding down the fuselage, and out onto the wing. There was a short length of rope there, attached to the dinghy (stowed in a compartment at the rear of the starboard engine nacelle). We tied that around my chest and I climbed out. I still had my parachute on, and it was getting in the way. I wanted to take it off, but they wouldn't let me.

"I punched and kicked holes in the fabric so that I could get a hold of the structure members. Joe the navigator was holding on to the rope so that I wouldn't sort of drop straight off.

"I went out three or four feet along the wing. The fire was burning up through the wing like a big gas jet, and it was blowing back past my shoulder. I had the cockpit cover in one hand – I didn't realise how big and bulky it was – and the wind kept catching it and trying to blow it, and me, away. I kept bunching it under my arm, and

Right: Crews of Wellington Mk ICs of No. 149 Squadron at RAF Mildenhall walk to their aircraft prior to departure for a night mission. No. 149 Squadron started night operations in May 1940 and converted to Stirlings in November 1941.

then it would blow out again.

"I was lying flat on the wing, but I couldn't get very close because of the parachute on my chest. The wind kept lifting me, and once it slapped me right back against the fuselage, but I managed to hang on. I stuffed the cover down through the hole in the wing onto the pipe where the fire was, and it went out, but as soon as I took my hand away the terrific draught blew the cover out and away. I just couldn't hold on to it any longer.

"There was nothing to do then but to get back in. I pulled myself back along the wing, and up the side of the fuselage. Joe kept the rope taut, and that helped. I got back partly in to the astrohatch, but by that time I was completely done in. Joe pulled me in, and I just lay where I fell.

"Just when we were in reach of the English coast, the fire flared up again – some petrol had formed a pool inside, and that caught. I remember thinking to myself, 'This is pretty hard after having got as far as this', but after an initial flare-up it died right out,

much to our relief.

"The trouble was the undercart now. We pumped it down with the emergency gear, and then the pilot landed at another aerodrome, not our own, one that had a lot more space. He put it down beautifully, and though we ended up in a barbed wire entanglement, no-one was hurt."

For his heroism, Sergeant Ward was awarded the Victoria Cross, though he was to go missing later, on another sortie over Germany.

1941 can be characterised by human strength, mechanical weakness and by courage like Sergeant Ward showed on that July night. But to RAF Bomber Command, especially, that courage could never be enough. Britain, entirely alone apart from far-flung remnants of her Empire, was fighting a 'war of production' as much as a shooting war. When war depends on technology, he who can produce the most will win and Bomber Command was at the spearhead of technology.

Below: A German anti-aircraft defence battery opens up during an RAF night raid in November 1941. The British bombers needed cloud breaks to 'see' their targets, but this allowed the German searchlights to illuminate them for the waiting guns.

The Night Fighter War

1939–1945

Left: Despite official preference for Spitfire development, the Hurricane had a major advantage – its thicker wing sections could accommodate a variety of weapons including 20-mm cannon, as shown by this all-black Hurricane Mk IIC night-fighter.

Below: Designed from the outset as a night-fighter, the Heinkel He 219 was the best of this specialised breed of aircraft to see service during the war. Only small numbers reached the front line, but they were devastating against Allied bombers.

In 1939 neither the RAF nor the Luftwaffe possessed in service a force of night-fighters capable of countering significantly the threat of the night bomber, both air forces depending almost exclusively upon *ad hoc* use of day fighters working in collaboration with searchlights and broadcast instructions from ground controllers. True, RAF Fighter Command was experimenting with a handful of Bristol Blenheims of No. 25 Squadron equipped with rudimentary airborne radar (AI.Mk III), but it was not until the night of 21/22 July 1940 that the first German bomber fell to the guns of a radar-equipped Blenheim.

In September 1940 the RAF began receiving its first purpose-designed night-fighter, the Bristol Beaufighter with AI.Mk IV and by early 1941 (during the latter stages of the German Blitz) the British night fighters were beginning to take a substantial toll of the night raiders. The Luftwaffe had recognised the threat posed by the RAF's night-bomber force in 1940 and had created the first of its

Below: A Boulton Paul Defiant Mk II night fighter, equipped with airborne interception radar and flown by No. 151 Squadron from RAF Wittering. These Defiants achieved the highest number of victories per interception of any British night fighter deployed during the winter of 1940-41. Defiants were the first RAF fighters in squadron service with a four-gun turret.

Left: The Ju 88G-6b was the first production night-fighter version of the Ju 88 with radial engines, all previous service variants having in-line engines with annular radiators. G-6bs also adopted the enlarged tail surfaces of the Ju 188.

night-fighter wings, Nacht-jagdgeschwader 1 (NJG 1), with Messerschmitt Bf 110s, in July of that year. For most of 1940 the German night-fighter crews attacked visually with the aid of searchlights, but by early the following year, under Oberst Josef Kammhuber, a chain of radar stations ('Giant Würzburg' sets) had been established from Denmark to the Swiss border to form the Himmelbett system. By June 1941 five night-fighter Gruppen were operational with Bf 110, Dornier Do 17 and Junkers Ju 88 night-fighters. After early trials with an infra-red-sensing device (Spanner Anlage) had been abandoned, early German airborne radar gave promising results and late in 1941 the Telefunken company was producing the Lichtenstein BC radar which had a range of about 4 kilometres (2.5 miles); by the following

Left: Home-based Mosquito night fighters first entered service in January 1942 and defended Britain for over three years. This NF. Mk II flew with No. 23 Squadron, the first to take the Mosquito to the Mediterranean when it moved to Malta in late-1942.

Luftwaffe night birds

The first German night fighter was the twin-engined Messerschmitt Bf 110 in July 1940. It had no aids other than a searchlight. It was not until 1942 that a successful airborne radar was adopted. The heavily-armed Fw 190A-6/R11 with its additional radar was effective in 1944. Fortunately for the Allies the He 219A Uhu did not enter mass production; it would have had a devastating effect on the bomber formations.

Messerschmitt Bf 110G
Messerschmitt Bf 110G-4b/R3 of 7.Staffel III/NJG 4, Luftflotte Reich based in north-west Germany in 1943-44. Equipped with FuG 220b Lichtenstein SN-2 radar, FuG 16zY fighter director and flame dampers, this was the final G-series production model. Night-fighter colour schemes varied at this stage of the war.

Focke-Wulf Fw 190A
This pale-grey Fw 190A-6/R11 of I/NJG 10 was flown by Oberleutnant Hans Krause from Werneuchen in August 1944. The pilot's insignia comprised his nickname 'Illo' beneath the 'Wilde Sau' emblem. Krause was awarded the Knight's Cross. Note Neptun radar arrays and two-shade grey on upper wing surface.

Heinkel He 219A
An He 219A-2/R1 of I/NJG 1 operating from Westerland (Sylt) in the spring of 1945. The night-fighter camouflage included black undersurfaces applied during night ground-attack sorties against Allied ground forces crossing the North German Plain.

summer most Luftwaffe night-fighters were equipped with this or the simplified Lichtenstein C-1 version.

RADAR EQUIPPED
Meanwhile the RAF had standardised with the Beaufighter Mks IF and IIF, equipped with metric AI.Mk IV (with a range of about 6.4 kilometres/4 miles under ideal conditions) and by May 1941 some 200 aircraft were in service. At this time British ground control of night fighters was far superior to the German introduction in January 1941 of the plan position

Below: Unarmed Douglas Havoc 'Turbinlite' fighters carried AI radar and a large searchlight in the nose to illuminate a target for accompanying Hurricane fighters. The scheme achieved only limited success.

indicator (PPI) enabling a single controller to distinguish fighter and target on a single display, whereas the Germans employed two operators (one for each aircraft) at separate sets.

Early in 1942 the centimetric AI.Mk VII was introduced in the Beaufighter Mk VIF with Nos 68 and 604 Squadrons, followed by AI.Mk VIII, the new equipment providing better definition, although the pilot-display radar

Above: It was as a night fighter that the early Blenheims proved particularly successful. Some 200 Blenheim Mk IFs were converted with four under-fuselage machine-guns and airborne interception (AI) radar.

proved unpopular. Another night-fighting tactic, the use of airborne searchlights (Turbinlites) in Douglas Havoc aircraft to illuminate enemy bombers so that accompanying Hawker Hurricanes could close for the kill, was tried by 10 RAF

Black (k)nights

The Hurricane Mk IIC introduced four 20-mm Oerlikon/Hispano cannon. In mid-1941 it was the mainstay of Fighter Command's night intruder and home-defence squadrons. Beaufighter Mk IIFs entered service with eight night-fighter squadrons from April 1941. Undoubtedly the most successful of the RAF's black-painted night fighters was the fast, well-armed Mosquito.

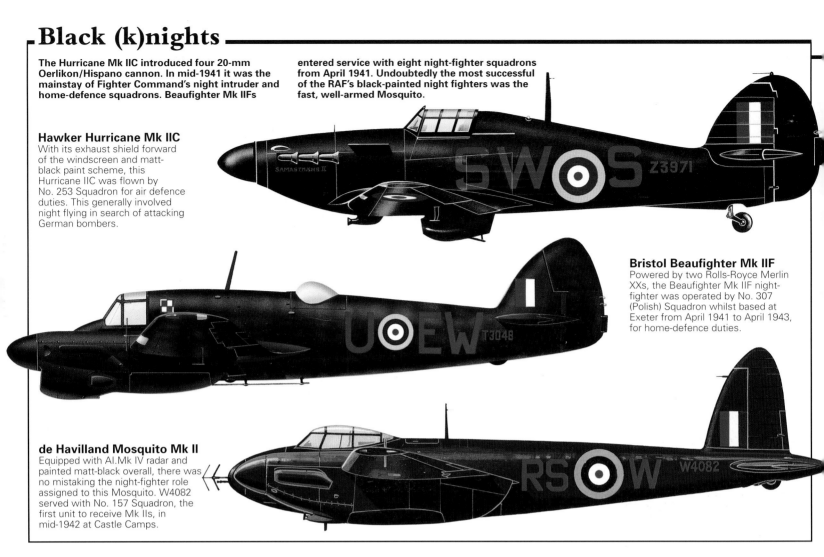

Hawker Hurricane Mk IIC
With its exhaust shield forward of the windscreen and matt-black paint scheme, this Hurricane IIC was flown by No. 253 Squadron for air defence duties. This generally involved night flying in search of attacking German bombers.

Bristol Beaufighter Mk IIF
Powered by two Rolls-Royce Merlin XXs, the Beaufighter Mk IIF night-fighter was operated by No. 307 (Polish) Squadron whilst based at Exeter from April 1941 to April 1943, for home-defence duties.

de Havilland Mosquito Mk II
Equipped with AI.Mk IV radar and painted matt-black overall, there was no mistaking the night-fighter role assigned to this Mosquito. W4082 served with No. 157 Squadron, the first unit to receive Mk IIs, in mid-1942 at Castle Camps.

squadrons during 1942-43, but met with little success and was abandoned. Havocs were also fitted with AI radar.

MOSQUITO

The finest of all British night fighters was unquestionably the de Havilland Mosquito, of which the Mosquito Mk II version entered service in May 1942. Fitted successively with AI.Mks IV, V, VIII, IX and the American Mk X, the Mosquito continued in service until the end of the war, gradually replacing the Beaufighter and ultimately serving with 24 squadrons of the RAF, performing night defence intruder and bomber support operations.

In the Luftwaffe, relatively little effort could be spared for offensive night-fighter operations, the pressing need being for night defence against the increasing attacks by RAF Bomber Command which, by 1943, were assuming a devastating scale. At the end of 1942 the German night-fighter force comprised a total of 389 operational aircraft, of which 300 were Bf 110s; Kammhuber's defences had destroyed a total of 1,291 British bombers during the year, about

Below: A pair of Messerschmitt Bf 110E-1/U1 night fighters of VII/NJG 4 over France. E-1/U1s carried the Spanner Anlage infra-red sighting sensor. As night fighters, Bf 110s were increasingly effective, serving in the role for nearly five years.

Left: The Heinkel He 219A-7/R1 carried SN-2 radar and armament of six 30-mm and two 20-mm cannon. The 'Roman' VI indicated fitment of FuG 220d with Streuwelle (dispersal waveband) No. VI.

Below: The last wartime night-fighter version of the Mosquito was the NF.Mk 30, introduced in 1944. From the summer, these aircraft provided protection for RAF bomber streams over Germany.

GERMANY'S NIGHT DEFENCE

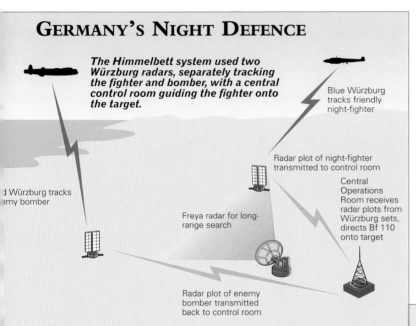

The Himmelbett system used two Würzburg radars, separately tracking the fighter and bomber, with a central control room guiding the fighter onto the target.

Blue Würzburg tracks friendly night-fighter

Radar plot of night-fighter transmitted to control room

Central Operations Room receives radar plots from Würzburg sets, directs Bf 110 onto target

d Würzburg tracks emy bomber

Freya radar for long-range search

Radar plot of enemy bomber transmitted back to control room

Above: The Junkers Ju 88G-6b carried an SN-2 radar array in the nose (often referred to as a 'toasting fork'), with a rear-warning aerial at the tail, though the latter was not always fitted. Schräge Musik (Jazz) upward-firing MG151 cannon were mounted amidships, allowing attacks on Allied bombers to be made from below.

Germany's night-fighter defences swiftly evolved from a system based on searchlights and visual reports of incoming enemy aircraft to a highly efficient layered defence, with a belt of coastal radar stations, a searchlight zone along the German border and with integrated defence zones around the most important targets.

By 1941 enemy bombers attacking the German heartland had to penetrate the Himmelbett zones on the Dutch coast, the illuminated night-fighter zones further inland, and then the combined night-fighter zones over the targets themselves. Fortunately for the Allied bomber crews each Himmelbett station could only deal with one aircraft at a time, so while one Lancaster was being dealt with, his comrades could usually slip through. British countermeasures, notably 'Window' (strips of aluminium foil deliberately dropped by aircraft in the formation to deceive the enemy radar), eventually rendered the system virtually unuseable.

This, combined with the limitations of the Himmelbett zones saw the new 'Wilde Sau' and 'Zamhe Sau' tactics introduced in mid-1943. 'Wilde Sau' met with early success and there was a rapid build-up of single-seat night-fighter units, but by October, RAF countermeasures began to bite. These included changes in tactics, the use of 'spoof' raids to confuse ground controllers and further radar jamming.

By the autumn of 1943 Himmelbett had been abandoned altogether. The new, more flexible system of night-fighter control now employed by the Luftwaffe was to be combined with new airborne equipment the following year. SN-2 radar, operating on frequencies as yet unjammed by the RAF, was used in concert with passive Naxos and Flensburg emissions detectors (which homed on Allied Monica tail-warning and H₂S radar emissions) and Schräge Musik cannon to put the Bf 110s and Ju 88s of the Nachtjagdgeschwaders in the ascendancy until the summer of 1944.

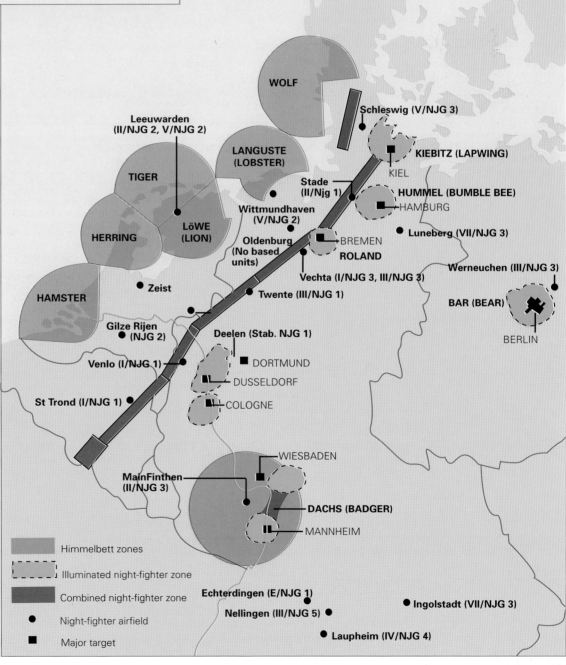

WOLF

Schleswig (V/NJG 3)

KIEBITZ (LAPWING)

KIEL

Leeuwarden (II/NJG 2, V/NJG 2)

LANGUSTE (LOBSTER)

Stade (II/Njg 1)

HUMMEL (BUMBLE BEE)

HAMBURG

TIGER

Wittmundhaven (V/NJG 2)

Luneberg (VII/NJG 3)

LöWE (LION)

Oldenburg (No based units)

BREMEN

ROLAND

HERRING

Werneuchen (III/NJG 3)

Vechta (I/NJG 3, III/NJG 3)

Zeist

Twente (III/NJG 1)

BAR (BEAR)

HAMSTER

BERLIN

Gilze Rijen (NJG 2)

Deelen (Stab. NJG 1)

Venlo (I/NJG 1)

DORTMUND

DUSSELDORF

St Trond (I/NJG 1)

COLOGNE

WIESBADEN

MainFinthen (II/NJG 3)

DACHS (BADGER)

MANNHEIM

Himmelbett zones

Illuminated night-fighter zone

Combined night-fighter zone

Echterdingen (E/NJG 1)

Night-fighter airfield

Nellingen (III/NJG 5)

Ingolstadt (VII/NJG 3)

Major target

Laupheim (IV/NJG 4)

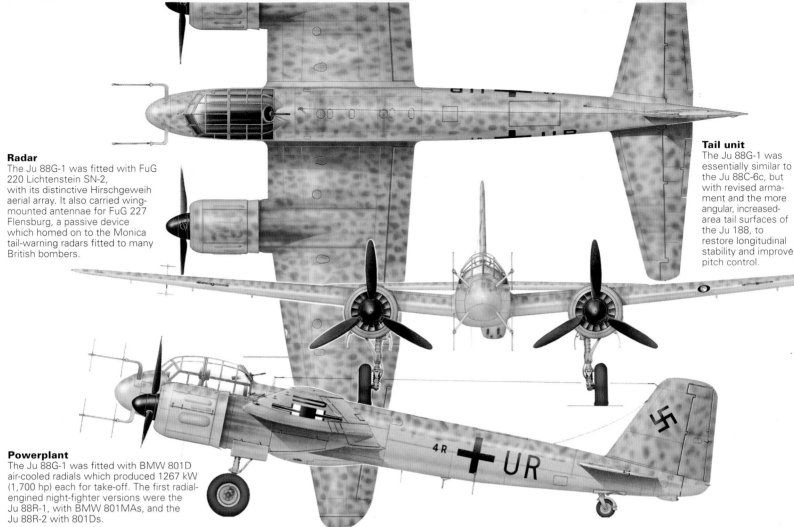

Radar
The Ju 88G-1 was fitted with FuG 220 Lichtenstein SN-2, with its distinctive Hirschgeweih aerial array. It also carried wing-mounted antennae for FuG 227 Flensburg, a passive device which homed on to the Monica tail-warning radars fitted to many British bombers.

Tail unit
The Ju 88G-1 was essentially similar to the Ju 88C-6c, but with revised armament and the more angular, increased-area tail surfaces of the Ju 188, to restore longitudinal stability and improve pitch control.

Powerplant
The Ju 88G-1 was fitted with BMW 801D air-cooled radials which produced 1267 kW (1,700 hp) each for take-off. The first radial-engined night-fighter versions were the Ju 88R-1, with BMW 801MAs, and the Ju 88R-2 with 801Ds.

Junkers Ju 88G-1

This most formidable night fighter was almost unknown until the crew of 4R+UR, a Ju 88G-1 of 7./NJG 2, became lost on the night of 12/13 July 1944 and landed in error at RAF Woodbridge, Suffolk, presenting the British with vital information about the SN-2 radar and FuG 227 Flensburg.

Crew
The crew of the Ju 88 was reduced to three in the night-fighter, by elimination of the bombardier/second pilot. A fourth crewman was later added to cope with the increased number of detection devices.

Fuel
Standard fuel tankage was provided in four wing tanks located either side of the engine nacelles, augmented by an auxiliary tank in the forward bomb bay.

Left: The only Luftwaffe unit to operate the Messerschmitt Me 262B-1a/U1 night fighter was Kommando Welten (later 10./NJG 11). This interim two-seat night fighter is fitted with FuG 218 Neptun V air interception radar and FuG 350 ZC (Naxos) passive homer.

commentary from the ground.

It was also during the second half of 1943 that the Germans introduced upward-firing cannon (Schräge Musik) into their night fighters; stalking the British heavy bombers from astern, the German pilots positioned themselves below their target and opened fire. Being thus attacked from a blind spot, the British remained unaware of this new tactic and literally hundreds of bombers were thus shot down. By mid-1944 the best of all German night-fighters, the Heinkel He 219, had re-equipped I/NJG 1; some versions of this superb aircraft were

armed with as many as eight cannon (including Schräge Musik), its most successful exponent being Major Hein-Wolfgang Schnauffer (121 victories); on one occasion he shot down seven Avro Lancasters in the space of 17 minutes.

The night-fighter war was a constant battle of measures and countermeasures, of jamming, feints and deception. Although the Allies sustained technical superiority throughout the war, German ingenuity produced expedients that enabled the Luftwaffe to take an enormous toll of the night bombers over the Reich.

Below: The Focke-Wulf Ta 154 night fighter, constructed of wood, was Germany's equivalent to the DH Mosquito. Fitted with Hirschgeweih (Stag's Antlers) antennas for Lichtenstein SN-2 radar, it saw service with I/NJG 3 from January 1945.

two-thirds of them having fallen to his fighters. A serious setback, however, occurred on the night of 24/25 July 1943 when Harris' bombers first dropped large quantities of 'Window' jamming strips during their great raid on Hamburg. At a stroke the Würzburg and Lichtenstein screens of the Himmelbett system were rendered useless and this immediately prompted the introduction of new night-fighting tactics, codenamed 'Wilde Sau' and 'Zahme Sau' (respectively Wild and Tame Sow). The former involved the use of

freelancing day fighters which, being without radar, were unaffected by the 'Window' jamming. The latter tactic employed a master

Night Fighter

Even with help from radar, the Luftwaffe's night fighters found intercepting Allied bombers at night a risky business. Apart from their own anti-aircraft guns they had to beware the bomber's own fire power. Top-scoring Bf 110 night-fighter ace Leutnant Wilhelm Johnen describes his first mission in the role on 11 July 1941.

"I was on my feet in a flash when the warning came," he says, "and through the door and halfway to the aircraft before I knew what was going on. The ground controller told us to make for the Westerland sector, and I took off and climbed up through the cloud, the variometer showing a steady climb rate of nine feet per second and the airspeed indicator about 210 mph. The rain was lashing against the fuselage and running down the cockpit canopy in torrents.

"Right on top of them.

"My controller was very faint by now, and the headwinds had almost doubled our flying time to the interception point. Not only that, but the British had the benefit of a tail wind, and were moving very fast indeed. It felt just hopeless. The controller had vectored us onto a course of 130 degrees, and I suddenly had the feeling that we were right on top of them.

"Suddenly the aircraft was flung wildly to one side. We'd been right behind the Tommis without knowing it, and had got caught in their slipstream. 'There's one!' shouted Risop, my radio operator, 'Right ahead and level with us.' I let off the safety catch of the six cannon, and the red lights flashed up 'Ready', but in that instant the bomber broke away to starboard. We didn't see another thing all night, and eventually got home very late after making some mistakes with our navigation."

Even with effective ground control radar, intercepting bombers at night was a hit and miss affair. Up until 26 March 1942, the German night fighters had stayed out of the Ruhr valley itself for fear of becoming targets for their own anti-aircraft guns, but on that night the tactics changed. Johnen was one of the first crews to mix it with the bombers over their targets, taking them at their most vulnerable, flying straight and level on their bomb runs.

"The nearer I approached the target, the brighter it got around me. A sea of light from the searchlight batteries blinded me whenever I looked down. The flak was exploding all around, and I felt like I was flying through Hell itself. A shell burst about 50 yards ahead, and in the next moment the Bf 110 was shaken in an invisible giant's fist. Risop was firing off identification flares as fast as he could. 'Are those bloody idiots trying to shoot us down?' he roared, reloading the flare pistol yet again. I put the aircraft into a steep left-hand turn, and then suddenly the searchlights caught a British bomber ahead and below me. I dived on him, the aircraft shaking wildly as the airspeed indicator shot up to 330 mph. I fired bursts into the fuselage, tearing off huge chunks of fabric, and then the Tommi burst into flames and turned over on his back. There

were three, four, five others on fire too, falling like comets to the ground.

"By now, many of the bombers had lost their nerve, and were dropping their bombs wildly. Suddenly Risop shouted 'There's one above us.' I could just recognise the outline of an enemy aircraft, flying to the north, away from the conflagration on the ground. I forced myself to stay calm and pointed the nose up, toward the belly of the enemy aircraft. 'It's a four-engine,' stammered Risop. 'We haven't seen this type before!'" It was, in fact, one of the new Short Stirlings, biggest and slowest of the new breed of British heavy bombers. But, slow though it was, the Stirling had one thing going for it – a gun turret in its belly. This was to be Johnen's downfall that night.

"I was close now, and took a breather, thinking us safe in the bomber's blind spot. But I had made a big mistake. I throttled back to let him get a little way ahead. 'It's time to fire,' said Risop, 'otherwise his rear gunner will spot us. Put your trust in God, and wade in!' Those were Risop's last words.

"As I opened fire, so did he. The tracer came at us like water from a garden hose. He lashed my

Above: Normally Leutnant Johnen would have had no difficulty in climbing out of the Bf 110's cockpit, but after the fighter had been ripped apart by the unexpected fire from the underside of an RAF Stirling it was a very different matter.

cockpit and fuselage, and in a fraction of a second my aircraft had turned into a flaming torch. Risop slumped over his radio, killed by the machine-gun bullets. All around me was a sea of flame. I tried to get one leg over the side of the cockpit, but the centrifugal force held me in I gave up all hope of getting out, and sat, my hands up over my face. We must have fallen about 9,000 feet when suddenly the aircraft exploded, throwing me out. I was on fire myself by this time, and thought of my parachute, but the stout canvas had saved it from the flames. I landed in a flooded meadow, up to my neck in mud. Saved! Then I passed out."

Right: Messerschmitt Bf 110-4b/R3 with FuG 220 Lichtenstein SN-2 radar and earlier FuG 212 for close-in work. Severely outclassed in the day-fighter role, the Bf 110 was well suited to attacking bombers at night. Heavily armed, the type had good endurance and enough capacity to carry radar and other specialised electronic equipment.

THE TURNING POINT

Despite being a failure as an RAF interceptor, Sydney Camm's Typhoon proved its worth in 1943 and 1944 in the new role of close-support aircraft. Along with the American P-47 Thunderbolt, it proved devastating against German armour and infra-structure, with its four 20-mm cannon and eight rockets or two 227-kg (500-lb) bombs.

The beginning of the end of the war in Europe came with the failed German invasion of Russia, thwarted by the harsh winter of 1942-43. By then the US 8th Air Force had arrived in Britain and planning of an all-out invasion of occupied Europe was proceeding. Operation 'Overlord' came in June 1944. The Reich was to survive less than 12 months.

The 8th Air Force's contribution to the war effort was crucial. Their first raid on Germany from bases in England came in January 1943 and after two years daylight raids had helped deprive Germany of its ability to wage war. The human cost was huge for both sides.

From Demyansk to Stalingrad

DECEMBER 1941 – FEBRUARY 1943

Left: The Dornier Do 17Z-2 was capable of carrying a 1000-kg (2,205-lb) bombload. This example, one of the last in front-line service, fought on the Eastern Front in Autumn 1942 with 15.(Croat)/KG 53 'Condor Legion' Croatian Volunteer Staffel.

Throughout the first five months of Hitler's invasion of the Soviet Union the Germans enjoyed almost unrelenting success in their drive eastwards, only just (but disastrously) failing in their bid to capture Moscow before the onset of that first Russian winter. Having halted the German advance in front of their capital, the Soviet armies, better prepared for warfare in the savage cold, opened their counter offensives early in December 1941 on the Leningrad, Moscow and Kharkov fronts. Almost entirely paralysed by the weather conditions, the Luftwaffe decided to remove much of its strength from the East, redeploying V Fliegerkorps to Belgium, and five Gruppen of its latest Messerschmitt Bf 109F fighters to the Mediterranean, thereby reducing its strength from about 2,400 aircraft to 1,700 on the 3200-km (2,000-mile) Eastern Front. And despite a desperate lack of modern aircraft (as well as the loss of some 5,000 sustained since 'Barbarossa' opened the previous summer), the Soviets were able to force the German armies back as much as 320 km (200 miles) in some areas.

COUNTER OFFENSIVE

In the course of this violent reversal of fortunes for the German army, the Soviets pierced the German front line between the Army Groups 'Centre' and 'North' and, early in February 1942, succeeded in isolating the whole of X Corps at Demyansk. Realising that the loss of some 100,000 men in a crumbling front could mean disaster for the entire German army in the north, the Luftwaffe collected every available transport aircraft (the Ju 52/3m alone was scarcely affected by the winter conditions, having air-cooled engines) and started a massive supply operation to the Demyansk pocket. Between mid-February and mid-May, when the Germans were able to open up a land corridor to the trapped army, about 400 aircraft airlifted 24,000 tonnes of supplies and 15,500 troops into the pocket, and evacuated 20,000 casualties. Losses amounted to 262 aircraft, and the increasing toll being taken by the Soviet 20-mm and 37-mm AA guns brought realisation to the Germans of the impossibility of sustaining major air operations in more

Above: 'Hero of the Soviet Union' – Russian fighter pilot I. Chubarev standing alongside a wrecked Luftwaffe aircraft that he had brought down by ramming it with his own fighter.

Left: Ilyushin Il-2s depart from a forward base on a combat mission in 1942. These are early single-seaters. More Il-2 'Stormoviks' were built than any other type of aircraft in aviation history.

Over the Russian Front

The Henschel Hs 129 was designed to back-up the Ju 87 dive bomber. It carried more armour, with the pilot protected by a 7.62-cm (3-in) thick windscreen. It was operated in the close-support and ground-attack role. Built as a glider tug, troop transport, freighter and air ambulance, the Ju 52/3m remained in production throughout the war serving on every front, not least in Russia where it provided essential air supply.

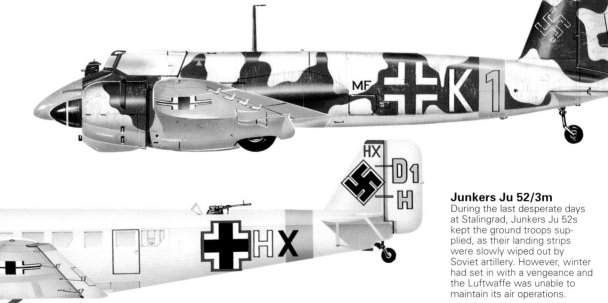

Henschel Hs 129B
The German version of the 'Stormovik' was the Henschel Hs 129. This was heavily-armed and could absorb much battle damage in its role of destroying enemy tanks. Later versions appeared with massive anti-armour cannon carried under the central fuselage.

Junkers Ju 52/3m
During the last desperate days at Stalingrad, Junkers Ju 52s kept the ground troops supplied, as their landing strips were slowly wiped out by Soviet artillery. However, winter had set in with a vengeance and the Luftwaffe was unable to maintain its air operations.

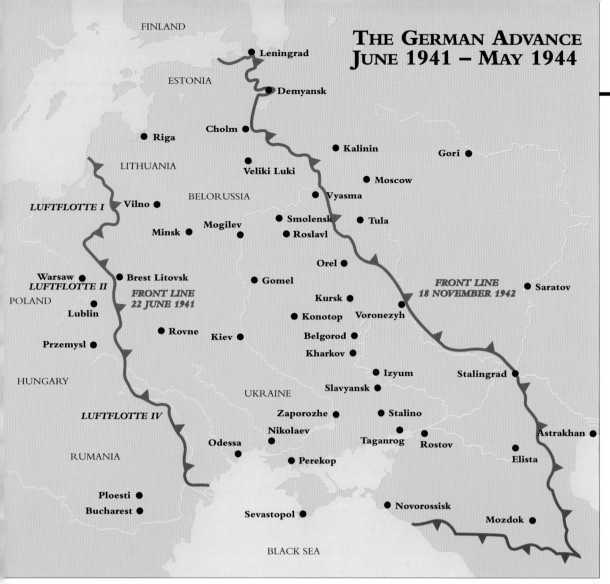

THE GERMAN ADVANCE
JUNE 1941 – MAY 1944

FINLAND

Leningrad

ESTONIA

Demyansk

Cholm

Riga

Kalinin

Gori

LITHUANIA

Veliki Luki

Moscow

BELORUSSIA

Vyasma

LUFTFLOTTE I Vilno

Smolensk

Tula

Mogilev

Minsk

Roslavl

Orel

Warsaw
LUFTFLOTTE II Brest Litovsk

Gomel

*FRONT LINE
18 NOVEMBER 1942* Saratov

POLAND

*FRONT LINE
22 JUNE 1941*

Kursk

Voronezyh

Lublin

Konotop

Przemysl

Rovne

Kiev

Belgorod

Kharkov

HUNGARY

UKRAINE

Izyum

Stalingrad

Slavyansk

LUFTFLOTTE IV

Zaporozhe

Stalino

Nikolaev

Astrakhan

Taganrog

Rostov

RUMANIA

Odessa

Perekop

Elista

Ploesti

Novorossisk

Bucharest

Sevastopol

Mozdok

BLACK SEA

Illustrating the areas of conflict between the Soviet and Wehrmacht forces, this map covers the period June 1941 to May 1944. The front-line as at 18 November 1942 was the extent of the German advance prior to the Stalingrad counter-offensive.

The extent of the front line in the USSR by December 1941 was awe-inspiring in its length: from Pechenga on the White Sea, the front stretched for some 2,380 km (1,480 miles) through tundra, forest, marshland, woods and steppes, via Lake Lagoda and the beseiged city of Leningrad, the salients in Belorussia at Bryansk and to the east of Smolensk and Vyasma and the grain fields of the Ukraine, to the Sea of Asov east of Rostov.

The Soviet winter counter-offensive started in the snows before Moscow on 5 December, with other offensives taking place in the north in an attempt to relieve Leningrad, and in the south against Kharkov. At several points the German armies, hamstrung by frozen guns and tanks in temperatures approaching minus 35 degrees Celsius, faced crisis: Germany's troops were at first totally unprepared for the severity of the Russian winter. In the savage fighting of the that winter, the Soviet armies made good ground.

two-seat Il-2m3 'Stormovik' close-support aircraft.

While ferocious fighting raged around Demyansk to the north, the Germans went over to the offensive in the south, and in April 1942 Army Group 'South' attacked in the southern Ukraine and the Crimean peninsula, supported by VIII Fliegerkorps and the newly-formed 1.Fliegerdivision. Sevastopol fell on 4 July after a prodigious air assault in which VIII Fliegerkorps had flown 23,750 sorties and its He 111s, Ju 87s and 88s

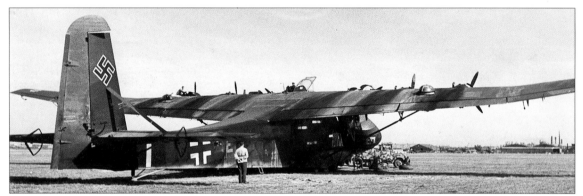

than one theatre simultaneously; indeed, the losses at Demyansk was never completely made good and many of the Luftwaffe's most experienced transport pilots were lost. Moreover, after a disastrous period of reduced Soviet aircraft production during the latter half of 1941, while aircraft plants had been moved out of danger east of the Urals, production began to make

Above: Messerschmitt Me 323E-2 Gigant heavy transport of I/TG 5 in the southern sector of the Eastern Front in the summer of 1943. The I-III Gruppe of Transportgeschwaden 5 was formed in May 1943 and served in the USSR and Mediterranean.

spectacular recovery in 1942, particularly with improved aircraft such as the Yak-1 and LaGG-3 fighters and, soon after, the

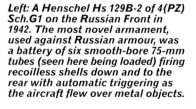

Left: A Henschel Hs 129B-2 of 4(PZ) Sch.G1 on the Russian Front in 1942. The most novel armament, used against Russian armour, was a battery of six smooth-bore 75-mm tubes (seen here being loaded) firing recoilless shells down and to the rear with automatic triggering as the aircraft flew over metal objects.

Above: A Junkers Ju 87D of 9/St.G.77, with temporary winter camouflage, on the Eastern Front in the winter of 1942. Soon, the vulnerability of the Ju 87 would see its wholesale replacement by the Focke Wulf Fw 190A, the Stukas being reassigned to Nachtschlacht (night attack) units.

Above: An eighth 'kill' on the Russian Front being painted on the tail of a Messerschmitt Bf 109F by its pilot during the initial phase of the conflict on the Eastern Front. Several German pilots racked up large scores against the Russians.

had dropped 20,530 tonnes of bombs on the fortress town. With the reduction of the Barvenko pocket, the Soviet armies lost half a million men killed and as prisoners in just over three weeks and the way was now clear for Hitler's major summer offensive eastwards towards Voronezh and into the Caucasus to capture the Maikop oilfields.

Considerable efforts had strengthened the Luftwaffe in the east to 2,750 aircraft, and new types (the Ju 87D-1 and Henschel Hs 129B1/R2 anti-tank aircraft and Fw 190A fighters) were now entering service. The advance stormed forward and achieved considerable success until, after intervention by Hitler who, in this moment of assumed victory, assumed personal command, the 11th Army was switched from the Caucasus to the Leningrad front, and the 6th Army, under General von Paulus, was ordered against Stalingrad.

To the Soviets the city of Stalingrad was a patriotic symbol and the Soviet armies were ordered to stand firm, if necessary defending it to the last man. As von Paulus split his 6th Army to create two fronts, the Soviets hastily assembled a new army group and set about the destruction of the Axis forces piecemeal. On 23 November the Soviets closed their pincers to the west of the city just as the dreaded winter set in.

WINTER DEFEAT

The Soviet air strength in the area was not particularly great, with no more than about 600 Pe-2s, Yak-1s, LaGG-3s, Il-4s and a few of the new

Right: Although rugged, the Lavochkin LaGG-3 was under-powered and lacked manoeuvrability, but it performed well as a fighter and fighter-bomber to the end of the war and was used as an escort fighter for Il-2 ground-attack aircraft.

La-5s. When ultimately the Luftwaffe attempted once more to sustain an encircled army from the air, by assembling transport aircraft from every corner of Europe, they failed to repeat their earlier successes, for the Soviet armies quickly dominated with artillery every available landing ground round Stalingrad. By the end of November heavy snow was falling and temperatures plummeting. One by one the landing grounds were over-run, until by mid-January 1943 only

Above: The Gotha 242 tactical transport was a simple steel-tubed machine with fabric-covered fuselage and wooden wings and tail. Towed behind He 111s and Ju 52s, they were easy prey for the Soviets and were relegated to duties behind the front.

Gumrak remained available. When that also fell, only the dropping of supplies by parachute was possible. The last supply sortie was flown on 3 February, but the German 6th Army was already finished, shot, frozen to death or captured.

Red air force resistance

The Ilyushin Il-4 was derived from the mid-1930s TsKB-26 low-wing transport and its range, speed and reasonable offensive capability ensured widespread service against the invading Germans.

The series of fighter aircraft developed from the Yak-1 design ranks alongside leading contemporary fighter aircraft of the Allies and Axis, like the P-51 Mustang, Spitfire and Bf 109.

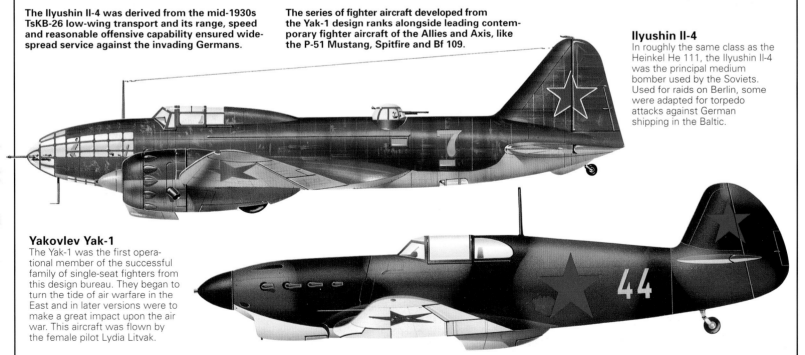

Ilyushin Il-4
In roughly the same class as the Heinkel He 111, the Ilyushin Il-4 was the principal medium bomber used by the Soviets. Used for raids on Berlin, some were adapted for torpedo attacks against German shipping in the Baltic.

Yakovlev Yak-1
The Yak-1 was the first operational member of the successful family of single-seat fighters from this design bureau. They began to turn the tide of air warfare in the East and in later versions were to make a great impact upon the air war. This aircraft was flown by the female pilot Lydia Litvak.

Alamein and 'Torch'

JANUARY 1942 – MAY 1943

Left: These four Spitfires Mk Vs, with under-nose Vokes air filters, are from No. 417 Squadron, RCAF that flew in the Middle East from April 1942. By the eve of the Battle of El Alamein on 24 October 1942, the Western Desert Air Force had increased to two full groups.

The redeployment of important elements of the RAF from North Africa to the Balkans in 1941 had left the British fatally exposed following Wavell's brilliant advance into Libya and with the arrival of the Afrika Korps, supported by Luftwaffe fighters and dive-bombers, the British army in the Western Desert was forced back almost to the Egyptian frontier once more. This was in turn followed by an offensive, Operation 'Crusader', commanded by General Auchinleck which relieved Tobruk and carried the 8th Army west once more to beyond Benghazi. Throughout this advance Hurricanes, Tomahawks and Blenheims of the RAF, RCAF, RAAF and SAAF were constantly in action, as were Wellingtons and Baltimores against enemy ports and

Left: Blenheims were replaced by Martin Baltimores with the Desert Air Force, entering service with No. 223 Squadron in January 1942. This Baltimore Mk III is leaving a trail of bombs across a line of vehicles.

airfields, maintaining a marginal but vital degree of air superiority over the less numerous aircraft of the Luftwaffe and Régia Aéronautica.

Auchinleck made a fatal error, however, preferring to concentrate on mopping up enemy resistance and strengthening his positions rather than striking forward at El Agheila before the enemy could counter-attack. It was Rommel who, with shorter supply lines, struck first and quickly forced the 8th Army back once more, this time beyond the Egyptian border. However, as a result of gallant delaying actions, notably by the South Africans at Tobruk and the Free French at Bir Hakim in May 1942, vital time was gained in which to establish a 'last defence line' before Cairo at El Alamein. It was at Bir Hakim on 6 June that the new Hurricane Mk IID 'tank

Right: Hawker Hurricane Mk IIDs of No. 6 Squadron over the Western Desert searching for Afrika Korps tanks. Known as 'Tank Busters' these Hurricanes carried two 40-mm Vickers S cannon, used effectively against tanks, armoured vehicles and transports. The squadron adopted the name 'Flying Can Openers' after their exploits.

Desert fighter support

Used extensively against the Afrika Korps the Hurricane Mk IIB 'Hurribomber' could carry 227 kg (500 lb) of bombs under its 12-gun wings. This reduced its speed and made it vulnerable to Luftwaffe Bf 109s. Even with reduced armour and less fuel, the P-39N Airacobra lacked the agility for air-to-air combat, but served the French well as a close-support fighter and fighter-bomber.

Hawker Hurricane Mk IIB

This tropicalised Hurricane Mk IIB was flown by No. 73 Squadron in the Western Desert in 1942. It carries its pre-war squadron flash on the fuselage sides. The Hurricane Mk IIB introduced the new 12 machine-gun wing and retained the bomb-tank shackles introduced on the Mk IIA series 2 'universal' wing.

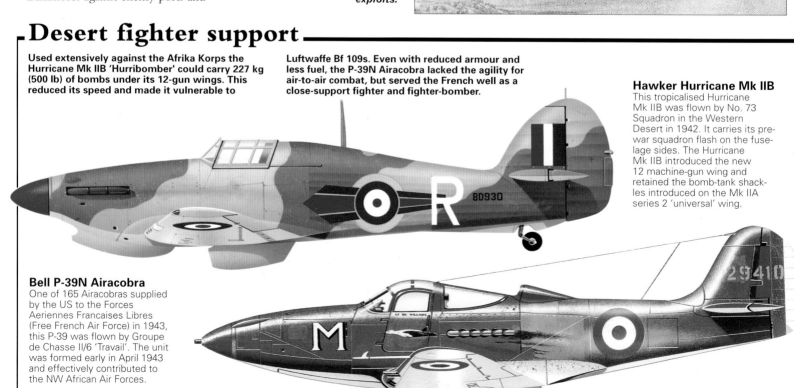

Bell P-39N Airacobra

One of 165 Airacobras supplied by the US to the Forces Aeriennes Francaises Libres (Free French Air Force) in 1943, this P-39 was flown by Groupe de Chasse II/6 'Travail'. The unit was formed early in April 1943 and effectively contributed to the NW African Air Forces.

Attack bombers

Although it had tricky low-speed handling qualities and high critical speed, the Beaufighter Mk I gave good service in the hot and dusty conditions of the desert, well suited to its robust airframe.

The B-25C, operated by the USAAF and the RAF as the Mitchell Mk II, had increased range and could carry up to 2359 kg (5,200 lb) of bombs, for its attack missions in the Western Desert.

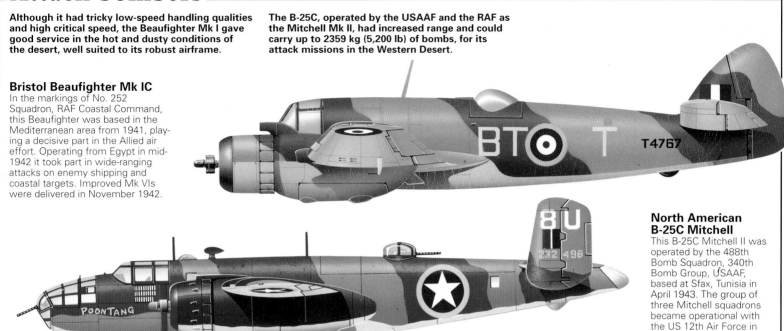

Bristol Beaufighter Mk IC
In the markings of No. 252 Squadron, RAF Coastal Command, this Beaufighter was based in the Mediterranean area from 1941, playing a decisive part in the Allied air effort. Operating from Egypt in mid-1942 it took part in wide-ranging attacks on enemy shipping and coastal targets. Improved Mk VIs were delivered in November 1942.

North American B-25C Mitchell
This B-25C Mitchell II was operated by the 488th Bomb Squadron, 340th Bomb Group, USAAF, based at Sfax, Tunisia in April 1943. The group of three Mitchell squadrons became operational with the US 12th Air Force in April 1943.

Left: Grumman F4F-4 Wildcats of the US Navy prepare to take-off from the USS Ranger in November 1942 as part of the Operation 'Torch' landings in North Africa. The Wildcats struck at French airfields in Morocco on this, their first mission in the Mediterranean.

Below: Halifax B.Mk Is of No. 462 Squadron were the only four-engined RAF bombers in the Middle East, arriving in July 1942. Though originally formed in Palestine from detachments of Nos 10 and 76 Squadrons, their sorties were flown against the Afrika Korps from Egypt.

buster' was first used to good effect against enemy armour. No. 6 Squadron, later known as the 'Flying Can-Openers', was the first to use the twin 40-mm Vickers 'S' gun-equipped Mk IID. This armament brought the Hurricane's top speed down to just 460 km/h (286 mph), but its anti-armour capability was devastating; during one day No. 6 Squadron destroyed 16 Axis tanks and their success continued into the following year.

LAST STAND
And so it was that after two years of advance and retreat in North Africa the famous 8th Army found itself with its back to the Suez Canal

while the victorious Afrika Korps seemed poised for the final thrust. However, by prodigious efforts the Allied forces had accomplished a massive build-up by the time the Axis forces were brought to a halt at Alamein. In the 18 months since Tedder had assumed command in the Middle East his air force had undergone transformation, now comprising 96 squadrons, of which 60 were British, 13 American, 13 South African, five Australian, two Greek, and one each of Rhodesian, French and Yugoslav, for a total of 1,500 first-line aircraft, of which 1,200 were deployed in the Western Desert. Among his modern aircraft were Spitfire Mk Vs,

Kittyhawks, Beaufighters, Beauforts, Marauders and Halifaxes, as well as 10 squadrons of Wellingtons and five Liberator squadrons. Against them were deployed some 3,000 Axis aircraft, of which only about 700 were based in North Africa, and only half of these were serviceable.

On the ground General Bernard Montgomery concentrated a vastly superior army, outnumbering the Axis forces by almost two to one in men, tanks and guns. On 23

October 1942 he was ready to strike at El Alamein, preparing his attack with a massive artillery bombardment of German and Italian positions as six squadrons of Wellingtons bombed them from the air. The next day the fighter-bombers joined in and the RAF and SAAF Hurricane Mk IID tank-busters went for the enemy armoured vehicles. For a week the great battle raged as German Ju 87s joined in attempts to halt the British armoured thrusts, but were almost

Left: A Messerschmitt Bf 110E of 8/ZG 26 based at Berca under Fliegerfuhrer Afrika in 1942. The support fighter saw action during the Alam Halfa and El Alamein conflicts. It continued to serve in North Africa in small numbers.

Above: A Junkers Ju 88D reconnaissance aircraft from 1(F)/121 that was shot down over North Africa after being intercepted by USAAF fighters. For desert operations it was fitted with engine sand filters, sun blinds and survival equipment.

Left: Good desert camouflage is provided by this Messerschmitt Bf 109E-4/Trop of 1 Gruppe Jagdgeschwader 27, as it flies over the Libyan desert in the summer of 1942. At first JG 27's Bf 109Es were superior to the Allied fighters.

Below: One of the 616 P-40M Kittyhawk Mk IIIs supplied for service in the Middle East. This aircraft from No. 112 Squadron has the famous shark-mouth paint scheme 'borrowed' from the Luftwaffe's II/ZG 76 'Shark' Gruppe Bf 110s.

invariably caught by covering British and American Kittyhawks. On 4 November the 1st Armoured Division broke through the enemy line and at once the Axis began a long westward retreat. At sea Axis supply ships, desperately trying to bring supplies to the Cyrenaican ports, were subjected to incessant air attack, no fewer than 18 vessels heavily laden with guns, fuel and

food being either sunk or forced to return to Italy or Greece on account of damage.

MARSEILLE: FIGHTER ACE

Almost symbolic of the Luftwaffe's misfortunes at this time was the loss in an accident of Hauptmann Hans-Joachim Marseille, the widely-respected fighter pilot and highest-scoring pilot in the West;

Left: Forced down by an air attack, a Junkers Ju 52/3m transport is finished off by a strafing run. Losses in North Africa followed heavy losses in Russia, and although the numerical strength was made up nothing could replace the skilled aircrews.

Below: Captain Roy E. Whittaker, USAAF in a P-40 Warhawk at a desert airfield in North Africa. On 18 April 1943 he shot down three Ju 52s and a Messerschmitt Bf 109 in "the great aerial battle over the Sicilian Straits".

'SWIFT IN DESTRUCTION'

This was the motto of No. 112 Squadron RAF, which flew Curtiss Tomahawks from July 1941, followed by Kittyhawks from December until mid-1944. Throughout the campaign in the Western Desert, No. 112 carried out support fighter-bomber missions for the 8th Army and after the rout of Axis forces at El Alamein, moved westwards into Tunisia.

Desert Hurricane

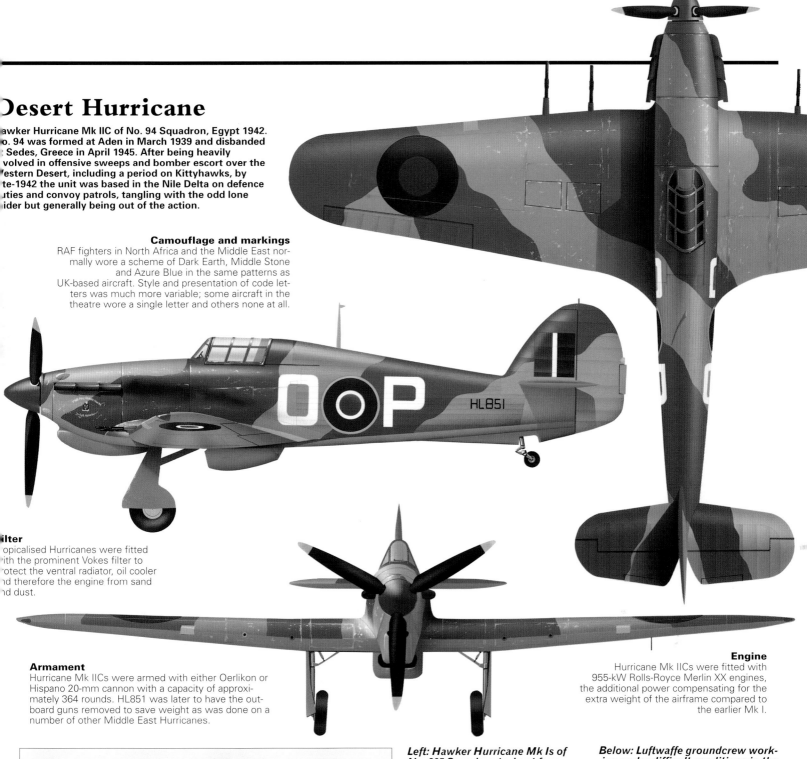

Hawker Hurricane Mk IIC of No. 94 Squadron, Egypt 1942. No. 94 was formed at Aden in March 1939 and disbanded at Sedes, Greece in April 1945. After being heavily involved in offensive sweeps and bomber escort over the Western Desert, including a period on Kittyhawks, by late-1942 the unit was based in the Nile Delta on defence duties and convoy patrols, tangling with the odd lone raider but generally being out of the action.

Camouflage and markings
RAF fighters in North Africa and the Middle East normally wore a scheme of Dark Earth, Middle Stone and Azure Blue in the same patterns as UK-based aircraft. Style and presentation of code letters was much more variable; some aircraft in the theatre wore a single letter and others none at all.

Filter
Tropicalised Hurricanes were fitted with the prominent Vokes filter to protect the ventral radiator, oil cooler and therefore the engine from sand and dust.

Armament
Hurricane Mk IICs were armed with either Oerlikon or Hispano 20-mm cannon with a capacity of approximately 364 rounds. HL851 was later to have the outboard guns removed to save weight as was done on a number of other Middle East Hurricanes.

Engine
Hurricane Mk IICs were fitted with 955-kW Rolls-Royce Merlin XX engines, the additional power compensating for the extra weight of the airframe compared to the earlier Mk I.

Left: Hawker Hurricane Mk Is of No. 237 Squadron taxi out for a mission in May 1942. Together with No. 208 Squadron, this unit was mainly responsible for tactical reconnaissance for the 8th Army.

Below: Luftwaffe groundcrew working under difficult conditions in the desert. Junkers Ju 87D-1/Trop aircraft like this one, suffered heavy losses in the air and on the ground, largely due to their lack of speed.

after attaining the extraordinary total of 158 victories he was killed while baling out of his Bf 109 after engine failure.

JG 27's Marseille was a 22-year-old Berliner who had already claimed seven Spitfires shot down while flying Bf 109Es over the English Channel. When Luftwaffe high command deployed two Gruppen of JG 27 to Libya from the Eastern Front, it had re-equipped with the 'F'-model and by the beginning of 1942 his score was around 50 and increasing rapidly. For example, on 3 June, while escorting Ju 87s, his Staffel was attacked by RAF P-40s: Marseille destroyed six in 11 minutes, using the bare minimum of ammunition. A fortnight later he downed six more aircraft, this time in six minutes. The following day his score stood at 101 and he was

Junkers bombers

The Ju 87D had a redesigned airframe with lower drag, increased bombload, armour and better, faster-firing defensive weapons and was used for army support rather than dive-bombing.

A tropicalised version of the lower-powered Ju 88A-5, the A-10 did not perform well in the high temperatures of North Africa and was withdrawn to bases north of the Mediterranean during 1942.

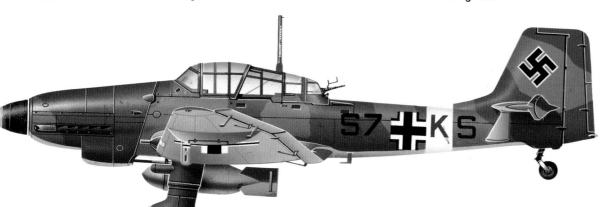

Junkers Ju 87D
Carrying a 1000-kg (2,205-lb) SC1000 bomb under its fuselage, this Ju 87D-1/Trop shows the much improved aerodynamic shape of the 'D' in comparison with the preceding 'B' model. 'S7+KS' was flown by 8 Stuka-geschwader 3 at Derna, Libya, in June 1942. It had an unusual brown/sand colour scheme.

Junkers Ju 88A
Flown by Lehrgeschwader 1 in support of Rommel's Afrika Korps, this Ju 88A-10 was withdrawn to Crete for anti-shipping strikes against the Royal Navy by October 1942. Here it was flown by II/LG 1 from Heraklion.

awarded Swords to his Knight's Cross.

The first day of September 1942 saw JG 27 at the zenith of their achievement. As Rommel advanced towards El Alamein, daily Ju 87 attacks on the Tobruk garrison were escorted by JG 27 fighters. Tedder's Middle East Command flew a total of 674 sorties to protect the British 8th Army; Marseille flew three times in the course of that day. By the late evening JG 27 had claimed 26 aircraft (20 Kittyhawks, four Hurricanes and two Spitfires) for the loss of one pilot killed, one taken prisoner and one posted missing. Marseille had destroyed no less than 17 himself.

SEVENTEEN IN A DAY

All 17 were identified in Allied records. Congratulations came at once from Generalfeldmarschall Kesselring and brought the award of the Diamonds to the Knight's Cross the following day. By 15

September Marseille had reached a score of 150 victories; that day he had shot down seven aircraft in 11 minutes. By dusk on the 30th, by which time he was flying a Bf 109G-2, he was dead – the victim of engine failure and bad luck as his parachute became entangled with his aircraft's tailplane.

As the victorious 8th Army swept eastwards for the last time, British fighters landed at Gazala, 160 kilometres (100 miles) inside Cyrenaica on 17 November; two days later they were at Matruba, 80 kilometres (50 miles) farther on. Two Hurricane squadrons even landed behind the enemy forces, so

Above: A Messerschmitt Bf 109F 'White 11' of 1/JG 27 behind Allied lines near to El Adem early in 1942. It had been hit in the radiator and the Luftwaffe pilot had made a successful crash landing in the desert, before being captured by British troops, here collecting souvenirs.

swiftly were the Allied fighters accompanying the advance.

It was at this moment that, as the Axis forces were desperately preparing to stand firm in Tripolitania, the Allies launched their master stroke when, on 8 November, American and British forces, sailed from the west, put ashore in considerable strength in

Above: A six-engined Messerschmitt Me 323D-2 transport landing at a desert airfield in North Africa, arriving from Trapani with ammunition and fuel. Serving with KGzbV 323 (later TG 5) the Me 323s suffered severely at the hands of Allied fighters and bombers.

Right: In the dust and sand of the Western Desert, that not only reduced visibility but caused severe wear to aircraft engines, these Hurricane Mk IID 'tank-busters' of No. 6 Squadron taxi out for take-off at Sidi bu Amid in January 1943, during the rout of the Afrika Korps.

Morocco and Algeria under cover
of carrier-borne aircraft and others
operating from Gibraltar.

These landings, Operation
'Torch', immediately threatened
the whole Axis position in North
Africa. Straightaway Tunisia was
occupied by the Germans as air
reinforcements from Italy and Sicily

landed at airfields in the north.
RAF and USAAF fighters and
bombers (Spitfires, Mosquitoes,
Beaufighters, P-38s, P-39s, P-40s,
B-17s, B-24s, B-25s and B-26s), as
well as troop-carrying C-47s,
poured ashore at Algerian airfields.

SURRENDER

The Luftwaffe made numerous
raids but Allied air superiority was
such that little vital damage was
suffered. In the south the 8th
Army, after being held at Mareth,
broke through the enemy lines in
March 1943 with constant air
support from RAF and USAAF

Below: A pair of N. American B-25C
Mitchells of the USAAF's 9th Air
Force come in to land at a desert
airfield captured from the Germans
early in 1943 as the Allied forces
moved relentlessly westwards. The
wrecked aircraft, a Messerschmitt
Me 210A, belonged to III/ZG 1.

fighters and fighter-bombers. By 1
May only a small perimeter in the
north-east of Tunisia held out and,
despite considerable efforts to sustain this by air from Sicily, the Axis
forces in North Africa finally surrendered to the Allies under
General Alexander on 12 May.

Below: On 8 November 1942,
Operation 'Torch', the Allied invasion of French North West Africa,
converted the El Alamein defeat
into a crisis for the Axis in the
whole Mediterranean theatre. Some
difficulties in Anglo-American
co-operation allowed some early
German countermeasures.

PRELUDE TO VICTORY

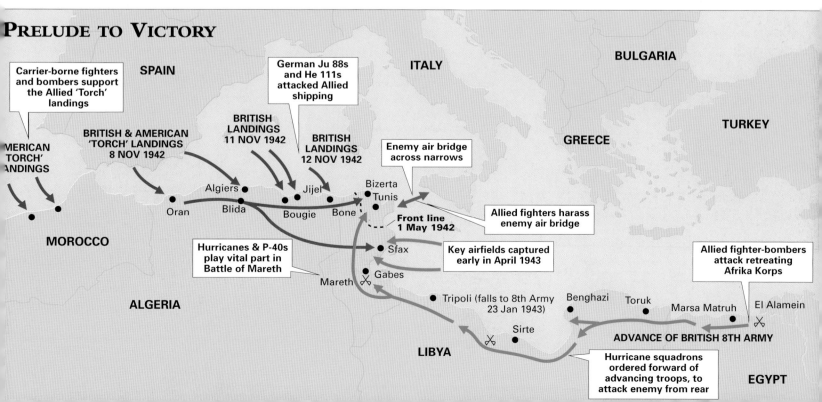

Carrier-borne fighters
and bombers support
the Allied 'Torch'
landings

SPAIN

German Ju 88s
and He 111s
attacked Allied
shipping

ITALY

BULGARIA

BRITISH & AMERICAN
'TORCH' LANDINGS
8 NOV 1942

BRITISH
LANDINGS
11 NOV 1942

BRITISH
LANDINGS
12 NOV 1942

Enemy air bridge
across narrows

GREECE

TURKEY

AMERICAN
'TORCH'
LANDINGS

Algiers

Blida

Jijel

Bougie

Bone

Oran

Bizerta
Tunis

Allied fighters harass
enemy air bridge

MOROCCO

Front line
1 May 1942

Hurricanes & P-40s
play vital part in
Battle of Mareth

Sfax

Gabes

Mareth

Key airfields captured
early in April 1943

Allied fighter-bombers
attack retreating
Afrika Korps

ALGERIA

Tripoli (falls to 8th Army
23 Jan 1943)

Benghazi

Toruk

Marsa Matruh

El Alamein

Sirte

ADVANCE OF BRITISH 8TH ARMY

LIBYA

Hurricane squadrons
ordered forward of
advancing troops, to
attack enemy from rear

EGYPT

The Condor Threat

WORLD WAR II IN EUROPE

1940-1943

From the moment German forces reached the Atlantic coast of France, the threat to the UK's vital lifelines in the Atlantic (from surface raiders, submarines and aircraft) took on an infinitely more menacing character. The Luftwaffe had not envisaged long-range maritime air operations to the same extent as the RAF, its flying-boats and seaplanes (the Dornier Do 18 and Heinkel He 59) were more suited to short-range coastal work in the

The Heinkel He 115 was an outstandingly tough aircraft. In 1941, Fl. Fü Atlanik had a complement of 24 He 115B-2 torpedo-bombers with KüFlGr 906 and the reconnaissance 3.(F)/123. This example is seen circling two German warships.

North Sea).

Instead, work was hurriedly undertaken to adapt the one proven long-range aircraft possessed by Germany, the commercial Focke-Wulf Fw 200 Condor, to embark on land-based maritime operations

over the Atlantic now that suitable bases existed in Norway and western France. The four-engined Fw 200 had originated in 1936 and in the two years immediately before the war had flown a number of spectacular long-distance flights. Stemming from a Japanese order for a maritime reconnaissance version

One of the first batch of American-built CVE escort carriers – HMS Biter – has six Hurricanes securely lashed down on the pitching deck in heavy Atlantic weather. Biter was launched on 18 December 1940 and undertook convoy escort duties for most of its service with the Royal Navy.

(which was not completed), the manufacturers continued the adaptation to meet Luftwaffe requirements, and six development aircraft were delivered to I/KG 40 in Denmark in April 1940. Two months later, equipped with Fw 200Cs, this unit moved to Bordeaux-Merignac to start opera-

From both ship and shore the Arado Ar 196 performed uncomplainingly on patrol duties. The type served in coastal waters around France, in the Aegean, the Baltic and Norwegian coasts.

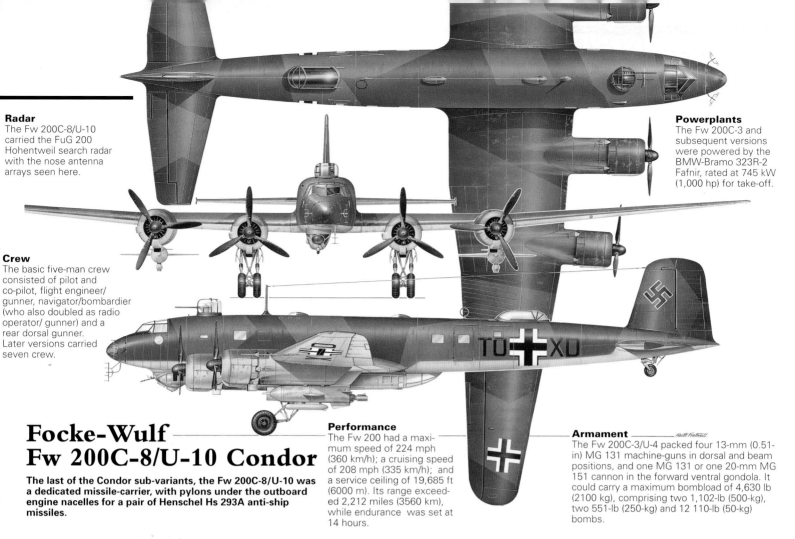

Radar
The Fw 200C-8/U-10 carried the FuG 200 Hohentweil search radar with the nose antenna arrays seen here.

Powerplants
The Fw 200C-3 and subsequent versions were powered by the BMW-Bramo 323R-2 Fafnir, rated at 745 kW (1,000 hp) for take-off.

Crew
The basic five-man crew consisted of pilot and co-pilot, flight engineer/ gunner, navigator/bombardier (who also doubled as radio operator/ gunner) and a rear dorsal gunner. Later versions carried seven crew.

Focke-Wulf Fw 200C-8/U-10 Condor

The last of the Condor sub-variants, the Fw 200C-8/U-10 was a dedicated missile-carrier, with pylons under the outboard engine nacelles for a pair of Henschel Hs 293A anti-ship missiles.

Performance
The Fw 200 had a maximum speed of 224 mph (360 km/h); a cruising speed of 208 mph (335 km/h); and a service ceiling of 19,685 ft (6000 m). Its range exceeded 2,212 miles (3560 km), while endurance was set at 14 hours.

Armament
Keith Fretwell

The Fw 200C-3/U-4 packed four 13-mm (0.51-in) MG 131 machine-guns in dorsal and beam positions, and one MG 131 or one 20-mm MG 151 cannon in the forward ventral gondola. It could carry a maximum bombload of 4,630 lb (2100 kg), comprising two 1,102-lb (500-kg), two 551-lb (250-kg) and 12 110-lb (50-kg) bombs.

Two Blohm und Voss BV 138s, widely known as 'Flying Clogs', and a Dornier Do 24 rest at their moorings, next to a slipway. Most BV 138s operated in the harsh environment of the northern oceans, seeing a lot of service around the Norwegian coast. They proved easy meat for Allied fighters.

Fw 200C-3 Condor F8+GH was photographed while serving with I/KG 40 in Greece in 1942. It does not carry the white Mediterranean theatre band and was probably on temporary detachment.

tions against British shipping, flying patrols from France over the Western Approaches and landing at Trondheim or Stavanger in Norway.

ALLIED SHIPPING SUNK

Under the command of Oberstleutnant Geisse, I/KG 40's 15 Fw 200Cs sank 90,000 tons of Allied shipping in August and September. On 26 October, an aircraft flown by Hauptmann Bernhard Jope attacked and crippled the 44,348-ton liner *Empress of Britain* off the Irish coast; the ship was later sunk by a U-boat while under tow.

By the end of 1940 a total of 26 Fw 200s had been completed, and such was the threat they posed to British convoys beyond the protection of land-based fighters that drastic steps were being taken by the British to protect their ships. The first of these involved the erection of catapults on merchant ships from which Sea Hurricane fighters could be launched on the appearance of a Condor. There was no possibility of providing aircraft-carriers for convoy escort at that stage of the war, so the Hurricane pilots, once launched against a raider, had either to ditch in the path of the convoy in the hope of being rescued or try to reach land. The first CAM-ship, SS *Michael E*,

Luftwaffe flying-boats and floatplanes

While the Condor won much of the glory as a result of its early successes and huge range, a variety of other aircraft played their part in the Luftwaffe's war against Allied shipping. Among the most important of these were the flying-boats and floatplanes, which performed patrol, minelaying and anti-shipping duties. They were augmented by land-based Ju 88s, He 111s and He 177s.

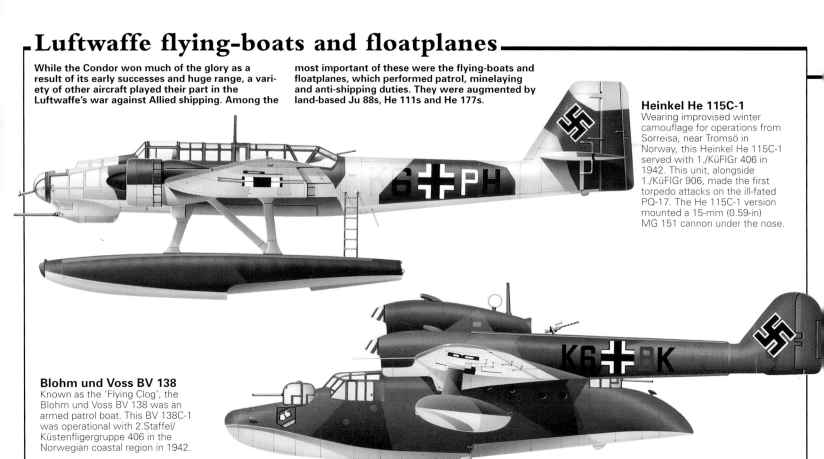

Heinkel He 115C-1
Wearing improvised winter camouflage for operations from Sorreisa, near Tromsö in Norway, this Heinkel He 115C-1 served with 1./KüFlGr 406 in 1942. This unit, alongside 1./KüFlGr 906, made the first torpedo attacks on the ill-fated PQ-17. The He 115C-1 version mounted a 15-mm (0.59-in) MG 151 cannon under the nose.

Blohm und Voss BV 138
Known as the 'Flying Clog', the Blohm und Voss BV 138 was an armed patrol boat. This BV 138C-1 was operational with 2.Staffel/Küstenfligergruppe 406 in the Norwegian coastal region in 1942.

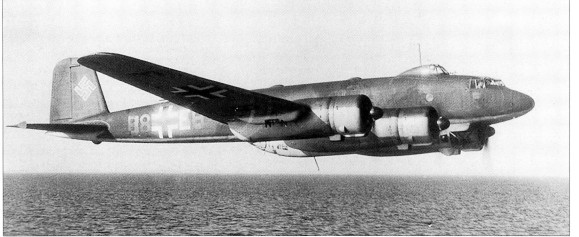

Above: The first military version of the Focke-Wulf Condor was the Fw 200C-1. This Condor served with 3 Staffel of Kampfgeschwader 40, which operated from Bordeaux-Merignac. The Condor was regarded by the Allies as a real danger to convoys.

Above: The kill tally on a successful Condor, with the estimated tonnages of each victim. As well as attacking ships, the Condors shadowed Allied convoys, reporting their position to the waiting U-boat Wolf Packs, which could inflict even greater carnage.

Left: A Sea Hurricane on the catapult of a CAM ship. Before escort carriers became available, they afforded one-shot protection to merchant ships and convoys, with only a minimal loss of cargo capacity. The cost was high, however.

set sail on 27 May 1941 but was torpedoed before launching her Hurricane. On 3 August, however, a Condor was shot down by a Sea Hurricane Mk IA flown by Lieutenant R.W.H. Everett, RNVR, after launching from the *Maplin*, a converted naval escort.

The next expedient was to provide merchantmen with flight decks (MAC-ships, or merchant aircraft carriers) and a substantial conversion programme began to prepare large numbers of Sea Hurricanes to enable them to operate from catapults and flight decks.

With the appearance of fighters over the Atlantic convoys the tactics of the Condors changed, the raiders preferring to retire, only returning once the Hurricane had ditched. Occasionally, the big aircraft stayed to fight it out. Their defensive armament underwent progressive increase until by the end of 1941 they carried three heavy machine-guns, two light machine-guns and a 20-mm cannon. Airframe strengthening and increased engine power allowed progressively heavier bombloads, but early in 1942 the employment of Fw 200s changed again, the aircraft being used to shadow and report the position of convoys to allow U-boats to close in for their

Left: The Fw 200C-3/U-2 featured a distinctive bulge in the gondola for the Lofte 7D bombsight. This necessitated a reorganisation of the ventral armament. The Condor proved vulnerable to Allied fighters, and even to prowling Sunderlands.

Above: The crew of an Fw 200 briefs prior to a mission. The Fw 200C-3/U-2 version of this maritime reconnaissance and anti-shipping aircraft had an increased crew of six, subsequently increased to seven in later versions.

attacks. Also in 1942 the Fw 200C-4 appeared with FuG 200 Hohentweil and Rostock shipping search radar.

The sailing of the first North Cape convoys to the USSR resulted in about half the in-service Condors being moved to Norway early in 1942, others later being transferred to southern Italy to operate against the Malta convoys. This dilution of the German raiders in the West was further exacerbated by the removal of 18 aircraft to assist in transport operations at Stalingrad at the beginning of 1943, and it was not until the middle of

that year that KG 40 was able to reassemble about 40 Fw 200Cs in western France.

By then a new weapon had appeared in the German anti-shipping arsenal; the radio-controlled, rocket-powered Hs 293A missile, two of which could be carried under the outboard engine nacelles of the Fw 200C-6 and Fw 200C-8 versions. On the first occasion the new weapons were flown operationally by III/KG 40, on 28 December 1943, the missile-carrying Condor was forced down by a patrolling Sunderland before the Hs 293s could be launched.

Any account of German maritime air operations should include mention of the Heinkel He 177 four-engined bomber. This aircraft also engaged in anti-shipping work, both as a carrier of the Hs 293A missiles, LT 50 torpedoes and FX 1400 Fritz X guided bomb and as a maritime reconnaissance aircraft serving with KG 40. In 1944, however, the relentless pressure by the Allies and loss by the Germans of their air bases in the Mediterranean and western France led to the with-

The weapon most associated with the Heinkel He 177A-5/R2 in the anti-shipping role was the Henschel Hs 293A missile. These were carried under the wings or, as here, on a special pylon fitted to the covered forward bomb bay.

drawal of the maritime units to Germany. There, they joined in the crucial work of transportation as the Allies closed the ring on the Reich, and maritime warfare by aircraft over the Atlantic drew to a conclusion.

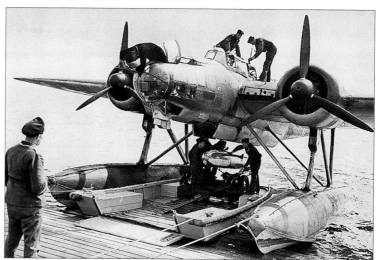

Left: The Heinkel He 115 was a hardy addition to the coastal fleet. It was used for all coastal duties, including patrol, anti-shipping and minelaying. This view shows the typical Heinkel planform, derived from the pre-war He 70 mailplane.

Above: A close-up of an He 115B shows the extensive glazing around the nose. There were flat-pane windows in the bottom of the nose for accurate aiming by the bombardier, whose duty it also was to fire the nose-mounted MG 15.

The Mighty Eighth Arrives

MAY 1942 – JUNE 1943

The Pearl Harbor debacle of December 1941 not only found the United States ill-prepared for war against Japan but ill-equipped to undertake participation in a war in Europe and it was to be many months before a sizeable air force could be assembled for an assault on Germany, an

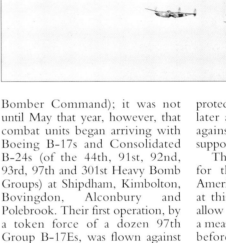

Above: In mid-1942 the newly arrived B-17s quickly went into action on daylight raids against targets in France and Holland. They flew from bases in East Anglia with fighter cover provided by RAF Spitfires and suffered no losses until September.

assembly that would be diluted by attempts to create an expeditionary air force to support the Allied landings in North Africa which would materialise in November 1942.

The first administration elements of the US VIII Bomber Command under Major General Carl A. Spaatz arrived in the UK on 22 February 1942 (the same day that Harris took over the leadership of RAF

Left: In the nose of a B-17 the bombardier sights his target through the telescopic eye-piece of the Norden bombsight. He takes over control of the aircraft using the Automatic Flight Control Equipment connected to the autopilot on the final bomb run.

Bomber Command); it was not until May that year, however, that combat units began arriving with Boeing B-17s and Consolidated B-24s (of the 44th, 91st, 92nd, 93rd, 97th and 301st Heavy Bomb Groups) at Shipdham, Kimbolton, Bovingdon, Alconbury and Polebrook. Their first operation, by a token force of a dozen 97th Group B-17Es, was flown against Rouen under heavy RAF Spitfire

protection on 17 August; two days later a similar raid by 24 aircraft against Abbeville was flown in support of the Dieppe landings.

The provision of fighter escorts for these raids ran counter to American bomber tactics advocated at this time and was intended to allow the bomber crews to achieve a measure of operational experience before being called on to fly unescorted raids. The whole

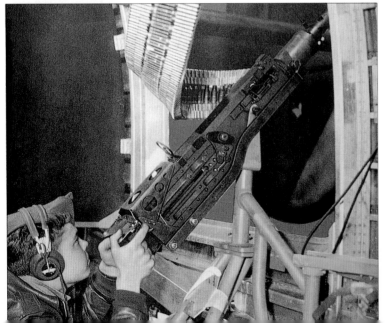

Left: The port waist gunner, with a 12.7-mm (0.5-in) machine-gun on a B-24 Liberator. The advantage of this gun position was that the gunner could move around and was not cramped up like the turret gunners, but he had to stand over the gun for hours in the freezing cold.

Above: The crew of B-24 Liberator 'Jenny' from the 93rd Bomb Group happily celebrate their safe return from a bombing raid on Wilhelmshaven. The aircraft was on the first USAAF daylight operation against mainland Germany on 29 January 1943.

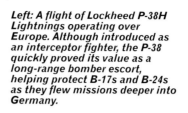

Left: A flight of Lockheed P-38H Lightnings operating over Europe. Although introduced as an interceptor fighter, the P-38 quickly proved its value as a long-range bomber escort, helping protect B-17s and B-24s as they flew missions deeper into Germany.

Below: B-24D Liberators lined up on the Consolidated Vultee Aircraft Corporation flight-line at San Diego, California ready for despatch to USAAF bomb wings in Europe. The B-24D was the first mass-produced version of the Liberator and featured turbocharged engines to improve performance at altitude.

Left: 'Lil', a B-17F of the 359th Bomb Squadron, 303rd Bomb Group, being bombed-up at Molesworth, Cambridgeshire, before setting off on a long-range mission against a German factory.

philosophy of the US Army Air Corps and US Army Air Force had, for a decade, centred on daylight bombing by formations of heavily-armed bombers capable of defending themselves by mutual gun protection. With the arrival in service of the high-flying B-17, altitude had added a further element to their supposed immunity from fighter interception.

DAYLIGHT RAIDS

Already a number of B-17Cs (without tail guns) had been supplied to the RAF in 1941, but British experience on operations with these aircraft in unescorted daylight raids had not been satisfactory, as a result principally of tactical misuse. Undeterred, the Americans continued to fly more and more B-17Es to the UK and for the remainder of 1942 contented themselves with relatively short-range operations against such targets as Amiens, Rotterdam and Wevelghem, all with heavy Spitfire escort and all without combat loss. The Luftwaffe drew first blood when, on 6 September during a raid by the 92nd, 97th and 301st Groups on St Omer, Messerschmitt Bf 109Gs of JG 2 and JG 26 shot down two B-17s. The following day a raid on Rotterdam escaped without loss

Bombers of the 8th

B-17 Flying Fortresses entered USAAC service in 1939, the first mission from England being flown on 17 August 1942 using B-17Es. The most common variant being the better-armed B-17G.

The first B-24 flew four years after the B-17 and boasted a better range than the Fortress, though at the expense of altitude performance. More B-24s were built than any other US wartime aircraft.

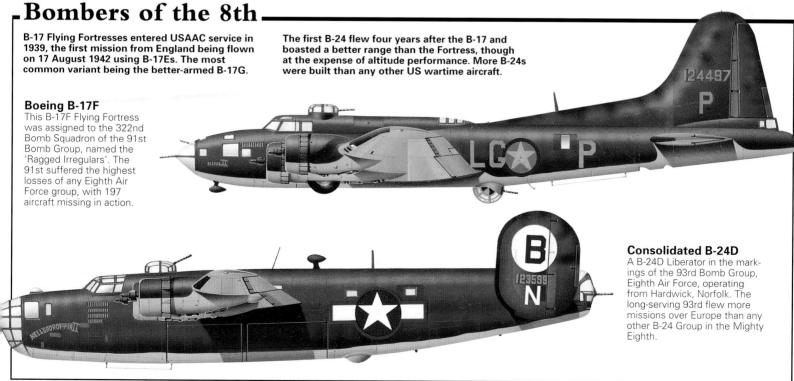

Boeing B-17F

This B-17F Flying Fortress was assigned to the 322nd Bomb Squadron of the 91st Bomb Group, named the 'Ragged Irregulars'. The 91st suffered the highest losses of any Eighth Air Force group, with 197 aircraft missing in action.

Consolidated B-24D

A B-24D Liberator in the markings of the 93rd Bomb Group, Eighth Air Force, operating from Hardwick, Norfolk. The long-serving 93rd flew more missions over Europe than any other B-24 Group in the Mighty Eighth.

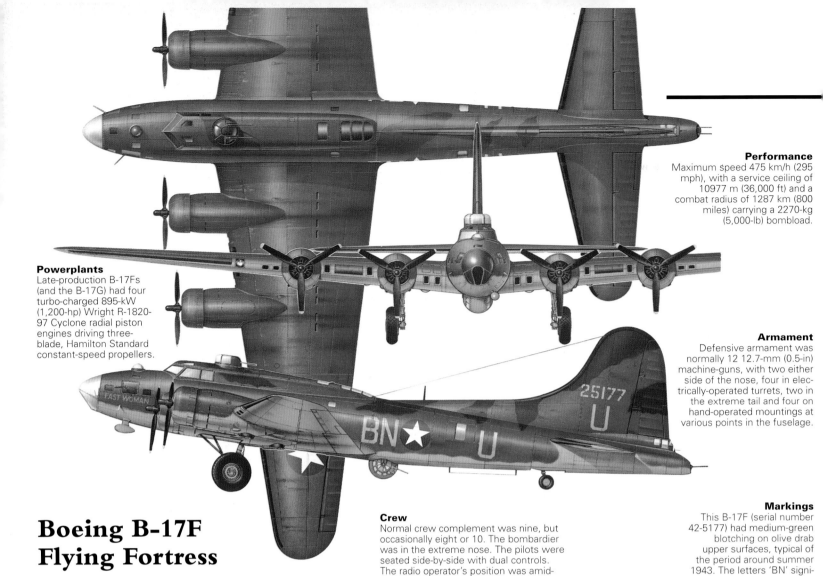

Performance
Maximum speed 475 km/h (295 mph), with a service ceiling of 10977 m (36,000 ft) and a combat radius of 1287 km (800 miles) carrying a 2270-kg (5,000-lb) bombload.

Powerplants
Late-production B-17Fs (and the B-17G) had four turbo-charged 895-kW (1,200-hp) Wright R-1820-97 Cyclone radial piston engines driving three-blade, Hamilton Standard constant-speed propellers.

Armament
Defensive armament was normally 12 12.7-mm (0.5-in) machine-guns, with two either side of the nose, four in electrically-operated turrets, two in the extreme tail and four on hand-operated mountings at various points in the fuselage.

Boeing B-17F Flying Fortress

42-5177 is an 8th Air Force aircraft in the colours of the 359th Bomb Squadron, 303rd Bomb Group, based at Molesworth from 1942/1945.

Crew
Normal crew complement was nine, but occasionally eight or 10. The bombardier was in the extreme nose. The pilots were seated side-by-side with dual controls. The radio operator's position was amidships. Gunners were located in the two turrets, in 'waist' positions either side of the fuselage and in the extreme tail.

Markings
This B-17F (serial number 42-5177) had medium-green blotching on olive drab upper surfaces, typical of the period around summer 1943. The letters 'BN' signify the 303rd Bomb Group, the individual aircraft's code letter being 'U' for 'Uncle'.

despite a vicious fight with Focke-Wulf Fw 190s of JG 1.

Gradually, as the B-17s began raiding further afield; the British fighters had to turn back part-way to the target leaving the bomber crews to prove their ability to defend themselves. On 9 October 108 B-17Es and B-24Ds raided Lille and on their return flight were attacked by the fighters of JG 2 and

JG 26. A measure of the savage battle that followed may be judged by the fact that the American gunners claimed to have destroyed 56 enemy fighters when in fact only

Left: Although rammed by a following B-17 when their aircraft slowed down with an engine failure, the crew managed to nurse this Fortress back to its base in England. The B-17's fin and rudder, together with the rear gunner's hatch were all smashed by the propellers of the second bomber.

one, an Fw 190A-4 of JG 26, was shot down.

Already the German fighter pilots were evolving tactics to combat the big American bombers; they had learned that closing from astern and abeam subjected them to withering and prolonged crossfire from the massed 12.7-mm (0.5-inch) heavy machine-guns of the bombers. They discovered that the frontal attack was the most deadly (as had been demonstrated by RAF

Left: B-26 Marauders served only briefly with the 8th Air Force, their first mission taking place on 14 May 1943. On 17 May this low-level raid on a power station near Ijmuiden, was repeated with 11 aircraft – none returned. The B-26 was more suited to a tactical role; the few Bomb Groups operating the type (like the 387th) transferred to the 9th Air Force in November.

Below: Flying in close formation for defensive protection also had its perils. The port tailplane of this B-17 has been struck by bombs dropped by another Fortress higher up in the formation. Though very strong, stricken bombers such as this seldom recovered. Miraculously this crew survived.

Right: B-17Fs of the 390th Bomb Group, 13th Bomb Wing taking advantage of the bombers' ability to climb to high altitude, with their faster escorts, P-47 Thunderbolts, weaving a defensive pattern and making condensation trails above.

Below: These P-47D Thunderbolts of the 62nd Fighter Squadron, 56th Fighter Group escorting a B-24 Liberator, have distinctive nose and tail bands to help Allied aircrew identify them. The P-47 looked similar to the Luftwaffe's Focke-Wulf Fw 190 when seen from a distance.

Below: An Eighth Air Force Flying Fortress departing the French coast after a daylight raid on the submarine pens at St Nazaire. The bombers remained vulnerable to attack from Luftwaffe fighters all the way back to their East Anglian bases.

Fighter Command during the Battle of Britain), both the B-17E and B-24D being armed with only single hand-held guns in the nose. The head-on attack demanded great skill and nerve, allowing no more than a snap burst; however, it usually required no more than one or two cannon shells in the pilots' cockpit of a B-17 to bring about the bomber's end. In a raid by five groups on St Nazaire ('Ramrod' No. 38) on 23 November, four B-17s were shot down in frontal attacks. The biggest air battle to date, on 20 December, involved 101 B-17s and B-24s and nearly 200 Fw 190s during a raid on an aircraft park near Paris, too far from British bases for the Spitfires to

Fighters of the 8th

Entering service in January 1943 with the 4th FG the P-47C was thought heavy and unresponsive. It proved to be tough, have enormous firepower and performed well in combat.

After early difficulties the improved P-38J entered combat service in Europe during August 1943. With shortcomings as an interceptor it was used mainly for long-range ground-attack missions.

Republic P-47C
In the markings of the 334th Fighter Squadron, that became part of the Eighth Air Force's 4th Fighter Group in September 1942, this new P-47C Thunderbolt entered service at Debden, Essex in March 1943.

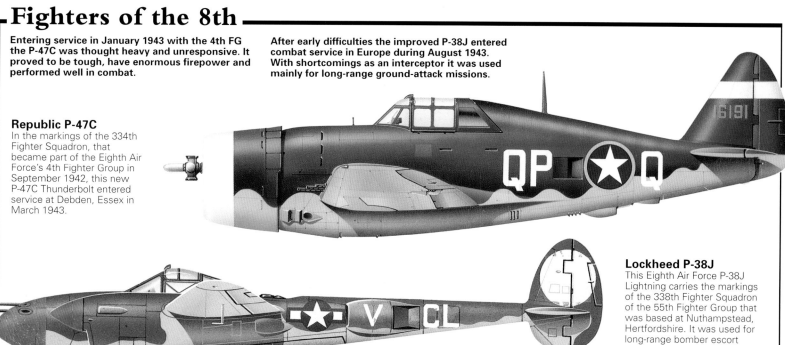

Lockheed P-38J
This Eighth Air Force P-38J Lightning carries the markings of the 338th Fighter Squadron of the 55th Fighter Group that was based at Nuthampstead, Hertfordshire. It was used for long-range bomber escort duties in the spring of 1944.

provide continuous escort. Six B-17s were lost (each with a 10-man crew), and six Fw 190s were shot down by the American gunners.

The New Year brought the Americans' first raid on German territory when 91 heavy bombers attacked Wilhelmshaven on 27 January 1943, the raiders now flying more compact box formations to give increased mutual gun protection. Poor weather then restricted the VIII Bomber Command's attacks to relatively short-range targets until the late spring that year, by which time its strength had risen to 10 groups (despite the move by some units to North Africa to bolster the creation

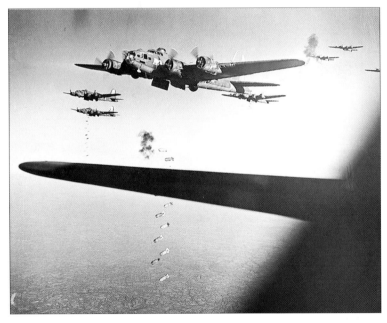

Above: Eighth Air Force B-17s release their sticks of bombs on a daylight raid over Germany. Bombers were at greatest risk from anti-aircraft fire as they maintained a straight and level bomb run over a target below.

Below: A pair of 4th Fighter Group P-47Cs on their dispersal at Debden, Essex in April 1943. This big fighter was able to escort high-flying B-17s into Germany and proved a match for the Luftwaffe's Fw 190s above 4572 m (15,000 ft).

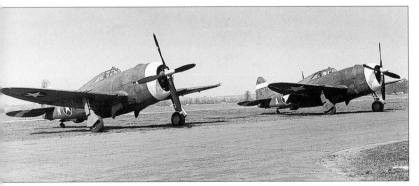

Above: The Scottish-born pilot of this Eighth Air Force B-17F, Lieutenant Bob McCallum, surveys the extensive damage to his bomber after its return from a mission over Germany in August 1943. On only his second mission the Fortress was hit by flak and caught fire. The ball-turret gunner, Sgt Maynard Smith climbed up into the aircraft and managed to extinguish the fuselage fire. He was awarded the Congressional Medal of Honor – America's highest award for bravery.

of the US 12th Air Force).

May 1943 marked a turning point for the American heavy bomber offensive. A raid on 1 May by 79 B-17s on St Nazaire found the bombers flying the last few miles to the target with their escorting Spitfires, losing seven of their num-ber to the fighters of III/JG 2. On 4 May a raid by the newly-introduced B-17Fs, some with increased nose armament, attacked Antwerp, their escort of RAF Spitfires being joined by US VIII Fighter Command Republic P-47Ds for the first time; despite interception by upwards of 70 enemy fighters no bombers were lost. The philosophy of unescorted daylight raids by the Americans (like those by the RAF three years earlier) had been shown to be fallacious.

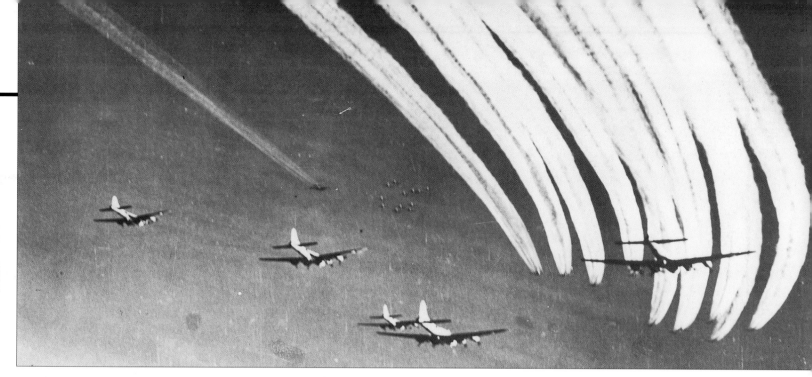

Left: North American P-51B-5-NA Mustang (43-6885) 'Texas Terrier III' of the 354th Fighter Squadron wearing battle claims on its nose. Four swastikas represent Luftwaffe 'kills' and eight bombs signify successful ground-attack missions. The P-51B, carrying two underwing fuel tanks and fitted with six 12.7-mm (0.5-in) guns in its wings, was the USAAF's first effective long-range escort fighter.

Above: One of the hallmarks of the Eighth Air Force daylight bombing raids over Europe were the vapour trail patterns produced by the bombers at high altitude. The crews did not like this signature across the skies as it pinpointed their position for the gunners below and the waiting Luftwaffe. The B-17s maintained close formation so as to offer maximum fire protection against the fighters.

IN ACTION

American bombers flew their first combat missions against occupied Europe in the summer of 1942, when a dozen bombers attacked railway yards at Rouen. At that time, the Eighth Air Force had just begun to establish its administrative echelons in England, and was in no position to play a major part in the air campaign against Germany – as yet. Though employed in small numbers at first, the US Army Air Force began to build its strength on the 'unsinkable aircraft carrier' which was the British Isles. By the spring of 1943, VIII Bomber Command of the Eighth Air Force was sending more than 100 bombers at a time on missions and numbers were climbing rapidly.

BUILDING BASES

The huge build-up of bombers, fighters and supporting aircraft required an equally large build-up of infrastructure and support facilities. Fortunately, the eastern counties of England are wide and flat. In some cases, the Americans simply took over older RAF stations, building and extending runways and putting in hangars, workshops, accommodation and all of the other facilities needed to keep bomber and fighter squadrons flying against the enemy. But there were only so many fields that could be taken over and a massive building programme saw the development of many new sites.

FLAT FIELDS

American bomber and fighter bases were concentrated in a broad strip of fertile flatlands stretching from the coast of East Anglia through the Fen country to the East Midlands. The RAF's night bombers were mostly based in Lincolnshire to the north.

EIGHTH AIR FORCE BASES IN 1943

- Heavy bombers
- Medium bombers
- Fighters
- Transports
- Photo reconnaissance

PETERBOROUGH

Horsham St Faith

Shipdham

NORWICH

Polebrook

Grafton Underwood

Alconbury

Hardwick

Molesworth

Snetterton Heath

Chelveston

Kimbolton

Horham

NORTHAMPTON

CAMBRIDGE

Thurleigh

Podington

Bury St Edmunds

Framlingham

Duxford

BEDFORD

Bassingbourn

Ridgewell

IPSWICH

Earls Colne

Debden

COLCHESTER

OXFORD

Andrews Field

Mount Farm

Bovingdon

Hendon

LONDON

Aldermaston

The U-boat War

1942 – 1943

Above: When war was declared, the Avro Anson formed the mainstay of RAF Coastal Command. This Anson I of No. 48 Squadron, based at Hooton Park, is seen over a convoy leaving Liverpool. A few Ansons remained until late 1942.

Below: A Sunderland Mk I of No 10 Squadron RAAF on patrol from Mount Batten, in 1942, shows the two dorsal gunners' cockpits provided early in the war. By February 1943, Coastal Command had nine squadrons of Sunderlands.

Above: The most important long-range type in RAF service was the Liberator, here exemplified by a Mk III. The Liberator allowed Coastal Command to considerably close the mid-Atlantic gap where convoys were unprotected by patrol aircraft.

The Battle of the Atlantic was essentially a campaign against the German U-boat, a struggle that lasted from the first day of the war to the last. There were other facets such as the German surface raiders, which could be and were dealt with by the Royal Navy on the high seas, and by RAF Bomber Command while in port; and the Luftwaffe's maritime aircraft which, by and large, were the eyes of the U-boats themselves. It was at the moment in 1940 when the German army occupied the French Atlantic ports (Brest, St Nazaire and Lorient) that the Battle of the Atlantic took an ominous turn for the UK. As soon as the U-boats could find haven in those western ports (and those in northern Norway), the Western Approaches to British ports became the hunting grounds for German submarines. RAF Coastal Command, with its limited numbers of long-range aircraft, the Sunderlands and Hudsons, had its work cut out to escort the inbound convoys, let alone perform long and systematic sea patrols.

By February 1941, after a winter which not only restricted flying by the British aircraft but also the activities of the U-boats, shipping losses began to rise alarmingly, and in March 530,000 tons of shipping went to the bottom, followed by 644,000 tons in April. Moreover, at this time the Germans began introducing ocean-going submarines whose depredations now extended far beyond the range of any British flying-boat.

RADAR-EQUIPPED

By mid-1941 more than half of Coastal Command's aircraft, which now included ex-Bomber Command aircraft such as the Whitley, had been equipped with ASV (air-to-surface vessel) radar which was capable of locating a surfaced U-boat in the dark or bad weather. Although this equipment had not yet produced many successful submarine 'kills', the threat of unheralded attack from the air certainly

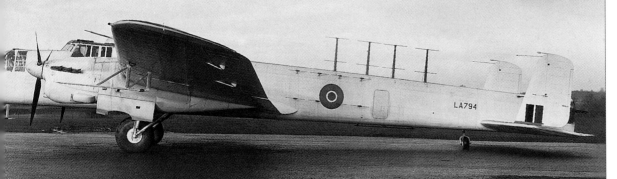

Above: A Whitley Mk VII, one of a number built for maritime reconnaissance duties that joined Coastal Command in 1942. It was the first operational aircraft to carry the new ASV Mk II air-to-surface radar, and the basic crew was increased to include a radar operator.

Right: A successful attack by a Whitley on a German U-boat 'somewhere' in the Bay of Biscay resulted in the destruction of the U-boat. The depth charges have exploded on their target, throwing up a column of water.

Left: Wellington GR.Mk XIII JA412/S of No. 221 Sqn surveys the seas off the North African coast while on a sortie from Gibraltar in 1943. The aircraft carries the white low-visibility colours for maritime work and ASV Mk II search radar.

Below: Boeing Fortress IIA FK186 was one of many B-17Es alloted to Coastal Command. Arriving in the UK in March 1942, it joined No. 220 Squadron. Together with the Liberator, the B-17s were able to close off part of the 'Atlantic Gap'.

Above: The majority of RAF B-17Fs went to Nos 206 and 220 Squadrons operating from the Azores. They filled the important role of covering the mid-Atlantic, until replaced by the more effective Liberator. Radar aerials can be seen on the nose and under the wings.

by Bomber Command on factories engaged in submarine production, but these were regarded by that command as superfluous to the bomber's main tasks, and in any case had little lasting effect on account of poor navigation and bombing efficiency. Another task, undertaken jointly by Bomber and Coastal Commands, was the widespread mining of waters outside German ports in the North Sea and Baltic in attempts to prevent U-boats from being sailed from the naval yards into the Atlantic.

Though all these efforts collectively produced some results, it soon became all too clear that

discouraged U-boat captains from passing through the Bay of Biscay on the surface, and thereby reduced by a small margin the submarine's cruising range. Other expedients were attempted to reduce the U-boat threat, in particular attacks

Admiral Karl Donitz was fast acquiring a very large fleet of submarines. When the United States entered the war against Germany he was able to order a sizable force of U-boats to operate off the American coast where, within six months, they sank an enormous number of unescorted ships.

By then, however, many improvements in tactics, weapons and aircraft were being introduced, not least the magnificent American Catalina flying-boat. Depth charges had been considerably improved, and the range of ASV (now fitted throughout Coastal Command) increased. And the Leigh Light, an

Early sub-hunters

The emphasis placed on Bomber Command operations meant that Coastal Command was initially limited to using the short-ranged aircraft with which it had begun the war, augmented by

Bomber Command's rejects. The Command never received Lancasters, and, apart from its relative handful of Sunderlands, had to rely on Lend-Lease for longer-range multi-engined types.

Lockheed Hudson Mk VI
An uncoded Lockheed Hudson Mk VI of No. 608 SquadronRAF Coastal Command, operating from Blida in Algeria in early 1943, carryies ASV Mk II search radar and eight rockets. The rockets were used successfully against U-boats in the Mediterranean.

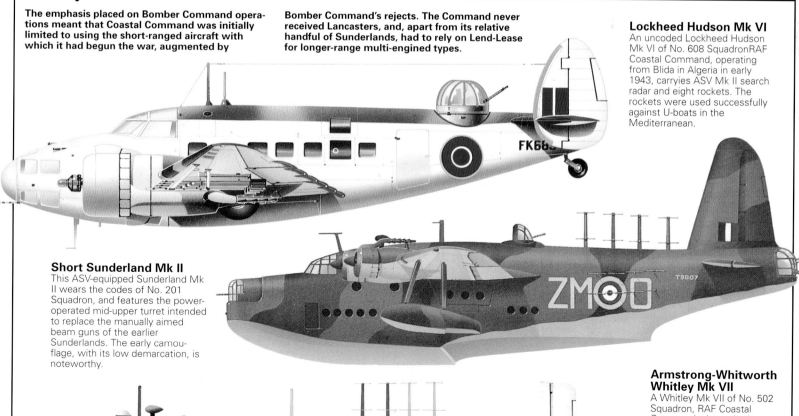

Short Sunderland Mk II
This ASV-equipped Sunderland Mk II wears the codes of No. 201 Squadron, and features the power-operated mid-upper turret intended to replace the manually aimed beam guns of the earlier Sunderlands. The early camouflage, with its low demarcation, is noteworthy.

Armstrong-Whitworth Whitley Mk VII
A Whitley Mk VII of No. 502 Squadron, RAF Coastal Command, shown in the colour scheme adopted in late 1942. Fitted with ASV radar, it gave valuable service on anti-submarine patrols over the Bay of Biscay.

The Consolidated Catalina was operated by Coastal Command on long-range, extended-endurance patrols in the Atlantic and Bay of Biscay. Here a Catalina releases a depth charge close to the diving U-boat.

airborne searchlight, was in use, causing submerged travel by U-boats in transit to be further increased. There remained, however, a large gap in mid-Atlantic which could be covered neither by Catalinas from the UK nor by those in the USA, Canada and Iceland, and only a handful of the very-long-range (VLR) Liberator Mk Is were in service. The answer therefore lay in the use of escort-carriers, small converted merchantmen capable of carrying half a dozen Swordfish aircraft equipped with ASV and depth charges.

To exploit the existence of the

Greenland Gap, Donitz introduced 'wolf pack' tactics in August 1942 which, until the creation of hunter-killer groups of corvettes and frigates, decimated the convoys. When Coastal Command made greater efforts to attack U-boats in transit through the Bay of Biscay, the Luftwaffe responded by operating increased patrols by Junkers Ju 88s and Focke-Wulf Fw 190 fighters, and the numbers of air combats with RAF Sunderlands, Wellingtons and Beaufighters increased sharply before the end of 1942.

Gradually the number of VLR Liberators increased, and with the securing of the West African seaboard following the Torch land-

Depth charges from a Sunderland straddle a U-boat, already partly disabled by another aircraft and unable to dive to escape further attack. The wake demonstrates the U-boat's attempts at evasion.

One of the most important jobs for Coastal Command was protecting the convoys sailing regularly to and from Britain. The transatlantic inbound convoys were the principal target for the U-boats.

Long range from Lend-Lease

The Catalina was actually evaluated by the RAF before the war, and was soon ordered in large numbers. The RAF's first Fortresses were delivered to Bomber Command, but proved unreliable, under-armed and lacking in payload. They were transferred to Coastal Command, which then received all of the later Fortress IIs. The very long range of the Liberator made it a natural for Coastal Command, which took the bulk of the 1,889 delivered.

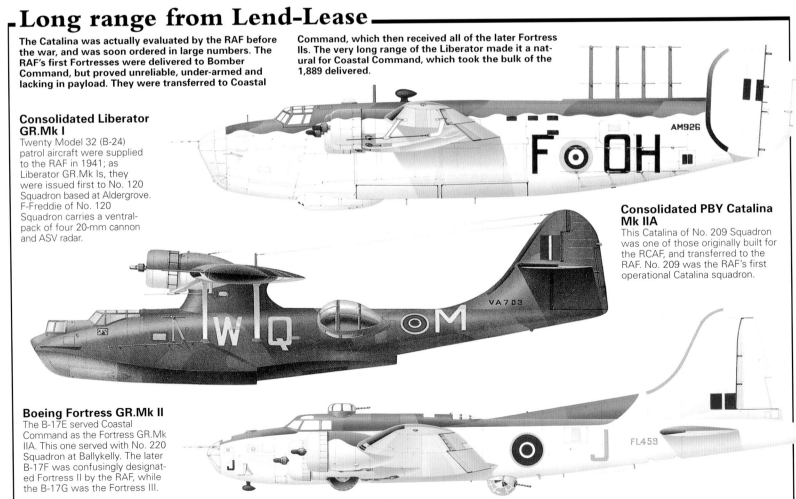

Consolidated Liberator GR.Mk I
Twenty Model 32 (B-24) patrol aircraft were supplied to the RAF in 1941; as Liberator GR.Mk Is, they were issued first to No. 120 Squadron based at Aldergrove. F-Freddie of No. 120 Squadron carries a ventral-pack of four 20-mm cannon and ASV radar.

Consolidated PBY Catalina Mk IIA
This Catalina of No. 209 Squadron was one of those originally built for the RCAF, and transferred to the RAF. No. 209 was the RAF's first operational Catalina squadron.

Boeing Fortress GR.Mk II
The B-17E served Coastal Command as the Fortress GR.Mk IIA. This one served with No. 220 Squadron at Ballykelly. The later B-17F was confusingly designated Fortress II by the RAF, while the B-17G was the Fortress III.

Guarding the Convoys

It was once calculated that a single four-engined aircraft operated by Coastal Command made a contribution to Britain's war effort 200 times greater than that of a similar aircraft serving with Bomber Command. Such a statement is highly controversial and Coastal Command's contribution is hard to quantify. Certainly it helped enforce the blockade which virtually cut off Germany's ports from merchant shipping, and played a crucial role in ensuring that Allied convoys 'got through' without suffering unacceptably high losses. The Command's aircraft also inflicted grievous losses on German shipping, and above all on the German navy's U-boat arm. But the war against the U-boat was never decisively won. As the war ended advanced new U-boats were entering service. They were capable of spending longer time submerged, and were pre-fabricated to escape the effects of bombing.

At first glance, the map opposite paints a reassuring picture, with convoy routes enjoying land-based air cover for much of their length. Even the gaps in the mid-Atlantic could be partly covered, using British and American aircraft-carriers. But in large areas of their radii of action, RAF VLR patrol aircraft were operating in enemy airspace, and outside the range of friendly fighters. Over the North Sea and off the Norwegian coast, for example, the RAF's lumbering Liberators, overloaded with fuel and weapons, had to contend with flak ships and enemy fighters. Many were shot down, and many simply disappeared, falling victim to weather, errors by exhausted crews, or even to the Liberator's fuel-burning heaters, blamed by many for unexplained losses. Even where they could operate unmolested, there were never enough patrol aircraft, and the wily U-boat skipper could often slip through the net.

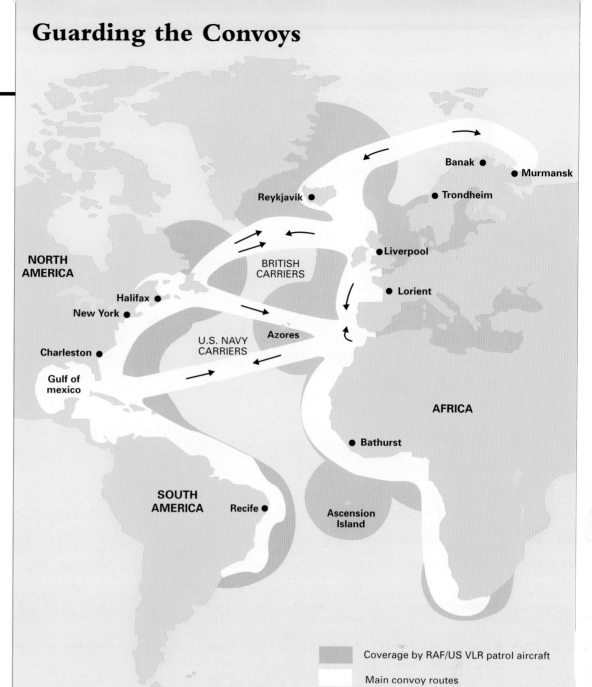

Banak • Murmansk
Reykjavik • • Trondheim
Liverpool
BRITISH CARRIERS
NORTH AMERICA
Halifax •
New York • • Lorient
Charleston • Azores
U.S. NAVY CARRIERS
Gulf of mexico
AFRICA
• Bathurst
SOUTH AMERICA Recife •
Ascension Island

Coverage by RAF/US VLR patrol aircraft

Main convoy routes

ings (which were themselves achieved with very little interference from U-boats), the sinkings by enemy submarines were slowly reduced from the peak monthly total of 814,000 tons in November 1942 to an average of 130,000 tons a month during the last six months of 1943. The greater figures had been largely accounted for by the Americans' reluctance to adopt the convoy system in the western areas

of the Atlantic, particularly off the Brazilian coast and in the Caribbean. This decision was reversed during the second half of 1943, by which time the Greenland Gap had been closed. With Catalinas, Sunderlands, Wellingtons and Liberators operating from Iceland in the north to Ascension Island in the south, the U-boat was reduced from a predatory wolf to a hunted dog.

Above: Consolidated Liberator FL927/G was delivered as a Liberator Mk III, but was subsequently converted to GR.Mk V standard (shown here) as a Very Long Range (VLR) aircraft with a Leigh Light under the starboard wing for night anti-submarine duties.

A Catalina Mk IB of No. 202 Squadron, based at Gibraltar from April 1941, was one of a batch of 225 Catalinas delivered to Scottish Aviation at Prestwick and Saunders-Roe at Beaumaris for processing before delivery. The Catalina had a longer endurance than the Sunderland, but could not carry such a heavy warload.

143

Sicily and Italy

10 July – 11 September 1943

Left: The A-36A Apache (as it was officially, though not commonly known) dive-bomber was armed with up to six 12.7-mm (0.5-in) guns and could carry two 227-kg (500-lb) bombs. A-36As created havoc in Sicily and southern Italy in 1943.

Throughout the final campaign which led to the destruction of Axis forces in northern Tunisia, the Allies had been assembling considerable strength at sea, on land and in the air with which to assault continental Europe from the south. It remained essential to keep the enemy guessing where that assault would be made: Sicily, Sardinia, the south of France or the Italian mainland.

In the event the blow fell on Sicily on 10 July 1943, by which date the Allied air forces in the Mediterranean (Mediterranean Air Command, commanded by Air Chief Marshal Sir Arthur Tedder) had grown to huge proportions, with 104 squadrons of fighters (Spitfires, Hurricanes, Beaufighters, Mosquitoes, P-38s, P-39s and P-51s), 95 squadrons of bombers (Mosquitoes, Bostons, Baltimores, Mitchells, Wellingtons, Marauders, Blenheims, Halifaxes, B-17s and B-24s) and 29 squadrons of transport aircraft (Halifaxes, Albemarles and Dakotas), as well as 43 other squadrons (reconnaissance, maritime patrol, torpedo bombers, meteorological, air-sea rescue and so on).

SICILY INVADED

Supported by fighters and bombers flying from Tunisia, Algeria and Malta, the main landings were carried out in southern Sicily the British 8th Army being put ashore from landing craft in the Gulf of Noto and the US 7th Army in the Gulf of Geta. A major feature of the operation was to be the landing of airborne forces near the Ponte Grande bridge in the British sector and at Gela in the American. Unfortunately owing to bad weather and inexperience among the American transport crews these airborne forces became widely scattered and 69 out of 137 Horsa and Hadrian gliders released fell in the sea. Nevertheless the scattering of the forces did serve to panic the Italian defenders, and by the 12th a bridgehead 32-km (20-miles) deep and about 80-km (50-miles) wide had been secured. Already a number of airfields had been over-run and airstrips constructed, and by the 15th more than a dozen fighter squadrons of the RAF, SAAF and USAAF were operating from Sicilian territory. From the outset the Allies possessed mastery of the air, although in the early stages of the invasion the Luftwaffe (notably Luftflotte II under Generalfeldmarschall Wolfram von Richthofen) and to a much lesser extent the Régia Aéronautica, attempted to mount air attacks against the invaders, using bombers based in Italy and Focke-Wulf Fw 190 fighter-bombers at makeshift airfields at Palermo, Castelvetrano and near Catania. Intruder Beaufighters and Mosquitoes operated with considerable success by night as British and American fighters sought out

Below: A Lockheed F-5E Lightning (unarmed, camera-equipped P-38J) of the 23rd Photo Squadron, 3rd Photo Group, taking off from an airfield in North Africa on a reconnaissance mission over Sicily in 1943.

Allied attackers

After the successful invasion of Italy efforts were made to change the name of the A-36 Apache to Invader. Both names were used, but it was Mustang that stuck. The A-36 differed principally from early P-51s in having dive brakes fitted above and below the wing. USAAF and RAF Marauders served over the skies of southern Italy, from bases in North Africa.

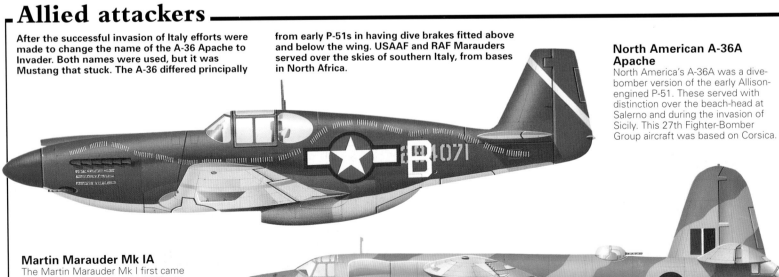

North American A-36A Apache
North America's A-36A was a dive-bomber version of the early Allison-engined P-51. These served with distinction over the beach-head at Salerno and during the invasion of Sicily. This 27th Fighter-Bomber Group aircraft was based on Corsica.

Martin Marauder Mk IA
The Martin Marauder Mk I first came into RAF service in August 1942 with No. 14 Squadron. Based in Egypt, this unit flew its Marauders on bombing and maritime strike missions off the coasts of Italy and Sicily.

Axis defenders

'Gustav', the Messerschmitt Bf 109G, was introduced in the late-summer of 1942 and was built in larger numbers than any other version. However, despite performance improvements, it was becoming Germany's second fighter, after the Fw 190. The three-engined Cant Z.1007 Alcione (kingfisher) first flew in 1937, the Z.1007bis variant having a 1000-kg (2,205-lb) internal bombload capacity.

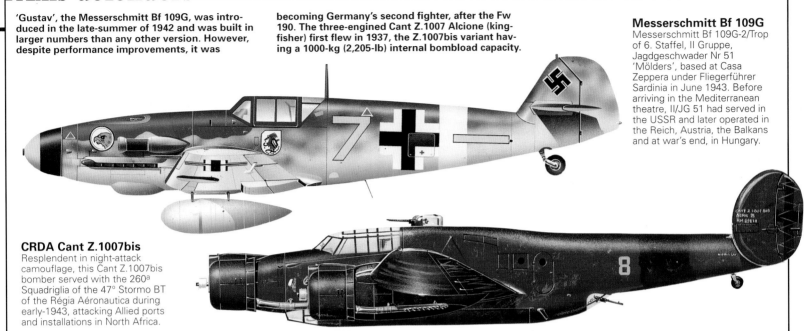

Messerschmitt Bf 109G
Messerschmitt Bf 109G-2/Trop of 6. Staffel, II Gruppe, Jagdgeschwader Nr 51 'Mölders', based at Casa Zeppera under Fliegerführer Sardinia in June 1943. Before arriving in the Mediterranean theatre, II/JG 51 had served in the USSR and later operated in the Reich, Austria, the Balkans and at war's end, in Hungary.

CRDA Cant Z.1007bis
Resplendent in night-attack camouflage, this Cant Z.1007bis bomber served with the 260ª Squadriglia of the 47° Stormo BT of the Régia Aéronautica during early-1943, attacking Allied ports and installations in North Africa.

Left: RAF groundcrew about to service a 'tropicalised' Spitfire Mk Vb of No. 43 Squadron at Pachino, Sicily in August 1943. The airfield was captured just days before the unit's arrival on 30 July. No. 43 spent the rest of the war in Italy.

Above: An unfortunate example of the Reggiane Re.2001s active in the defence of Italy in 1943.

and destroyed enemy aircraft in the air and on the ground by day. Within a week the German and Italian air forces were scarcely able to put up any worthwhile resistance in the air. When B-17s and B-24s appeared over the Strait of Messina such enemy fighters that attempted to intercept them had had to fly from Sardinia and central Italy.

By 5 August the entire western part of Sicily had been over-run and the Axis forces had been squeezed into an area in the north-east of the

Below: A Focke-Wulf Fw 190A Jabo (fighter-bomber) of I/SG 4 in central Italy in the summer of 1943.

island, with desperate efforts being made to protect the likely escape route through Messina. And all the time, as the Axis tried to send supplies and fresh forces south to bolster the defences in the 'toe' of Italy, RAF Wellingtons and Mitchells joined the American heavy bombers in attacks on communications centres at Battipaglia, Foggia and Salerno, as well as the airfields at Crotone, Grottaglie, Leverano and Vibo Valentia.

Yet for all the efforts by the Allied air forces the Axis commanders with great skill extricated the bulk of their land forces out of Sicily. But in the five weeks of fighting the German and Italian air forces had lost some 1,850 aircraft, compared with the loss of fewer than 400 British and American aircraft.

The stepping stone to Europe had been secured, yet the Allies paused less than three weeks before moving against the Italian mainland. Haste was essential as many of the enemy airfields in southern Italy had not been destroyed in recent attacks by Tedder's bombers, and delay would simply allow their repair. The Allied plan was to land the British 8th Army on the toe of

Italy, assault the Taranto naval base in the 'heel' with the 1st Airborne Division and then put ashore the US 5th Army in the Gulf of Salerno, some 320 km (200 miles) to the north.

ITALY SURRENDERS

The first landings across the Strait of Messina by the 8th Army were carried out on 3 September (Operation 'Baytown') and continued for five days, meeting relatively little resistance thanks to an unrelenting air offensive against the enemy supply route down the full length of Italy by medium and heavy bombers of the RAF and

USAAF. On 11 September the 8th Army reached a line from Belvedere to Crotone.

Two days earlier the US 5th Army had gone ashore at Salerno. On the eve of those landings, however, the Italian government had announced the nation's surrender.

Below: An Italian armourer adds some personal messages to bombs intended for Allied targets in southern Italy. The significance of the umbrella painted on the bomb in the foreground is unknown.

Adventures in Italy

SEPTEMBER 1943 – JUNE 1944

Left: A pair of Spitfire Mk IXs of No. 241 Squadron on patrol over the Naples area in 1943. The Mk IX was a stop-gap development to get the more powerful, two-speed, two-stage Rolls-Royce Merlin 60 engine into a basic Mk V airframe.

Below: B-17 Flying Fortresses of the USAAF's 15th Air Force flying over the Mediterranean en route from their bases in Italy in mid-1944, to military targets in France. Attacks were mounted on a shuttle basis from both England and Italy.

The surrender by the Italian government effectively deprived Germany of significant participation by the Regia Aéronautica in the defence of Italy against the Allies, and although some elements elected to fight on alongside the Luftwaffe, the majority either melted away to their homes or joined the Allies. The defection by their ally, as the Germans saw it, only served to stiffen their resolve to fight every yard of the way back through the Italian peninsula.

In attempts to leapfrog northwards and hasten their advance, the Allies planned two major seaborne landings behind the enemy lines, the first at Salerno on 9 September 1943 and another, rather later, at Anzio, which eventually took place in the following January.

As already stated, the landing by the US 5th Army at Salerno was in effect part of the planned invasion of Italy and, by diverting enemy forces from the 8th Army in the extreme south was intended to ease the establishment of a substantial beach-head. In this it was singularly successful, but resistance by the Germans at Salerno was unexpectedly stiff. Against the troops that landed on the beaches the Luftwaffe used about four Staffeln of Fw 190 fighter-bombers, whose pilots had to contend not only with patrolling Spitfires and Lightnings but also barrage balloons brought ashore by RAF parties. The Luftwaffe was, however, able to score one significant success when a Do 217-launched Hs 293 guided missile scored a direct hit on the British battleship *Warspite*, which had been supporting the landings, and put her out of commission for six months.

SUCCESS IN THE BALANCE

The success of the landings remained in the balance for three days as the Germans counterattacked strongly on the ground, and although the airfield at Monte Corvino had been captured at the outset it was unusable so long as it was dominated by German guns. By 15 September four landing strips constructed by Allied airfield engineers were in operation, one of them having been in use by Lightnings since 11 September. Within a week of the landings

Above: Attack on German transports in Italy by a P-47D Thunderbolt of the 79th Fighter Group, 15th Air Force. One of the three outstanding USAAF fighters of World War II, the big, radial-engined P-47 had eight 12.7-mm (0.50-in) guns in its wings, making it one of the heaviest-armed fighters.

Above: The Luftwaffe had some success with their advanced 'Fritz X' glide bomb, sinking the battleship Roma after Italy surrendered. 'Fritz X' and the equally sophisticated Hs 293 guided missile were launched from Dornier Do 217K-2s like this one. The latter was effectively used against the Warspite.

Right: A Messerschmitt Bf 109G-2/Trop on an airfield in Italy – an Italian Air Force three-engined Cant Z.1007bis heavy bomber is in the background. The Bf 109 was built in greater numbers (30,500) than any other fighter in World War II. It was flown by the Luftwaffe very effectively in all theatres.

Fighters over Italy

First flown on 19 April 1942, the Macchi MC.205V Veltro was a well-armed fighter-bomber powered by a licence-built Daimler-Benz DB.605 engine. It saw brief service before the Italian surrender.

Messerschmitt's Me 410 Hornisse was the last and most successful in the line of heavy fighters that commenced with the Me 210 in 1939. Over 1,000 Me 410s entered Luftwaffe service in 1943/44.

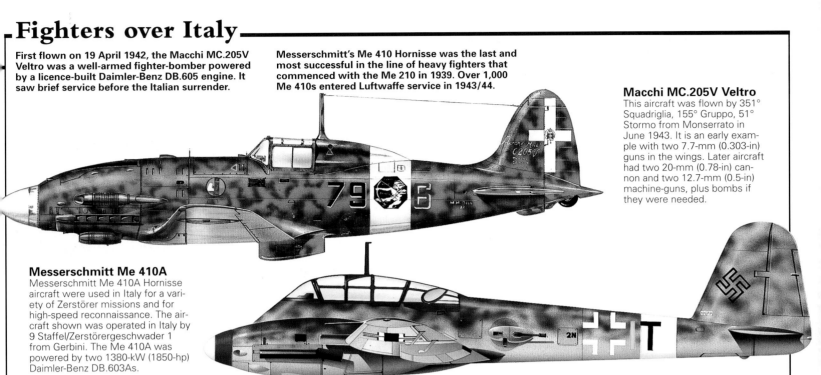

Macchi MC.205V Veltro
This aircraft was flown by 351° Squadriglia, 155° Gruppo, 51° Stormo from Monserrato in June 1943. It is an early example with two 7.7-mm (0.303-in) guns in the wings. Later aircraft had two 20-mm (0.78-in) cannon and two 12.7-mm (0.5-in) machine-guns, plus bombs if they were needed.

Messerschmitt Me 410A
Messerschmitt Me 410A Hornisse aircraft were used in Italy for a variety of Zerstörer missions and for high-speed reconnaissance. The aircraft shown was operated in Italy by 9 Staffel/Zerstörergeschwader 1 from Gerbini. The Me 410A was powered by two 1380-kW (1850-hp) Daimler-Benz DB.603As.

Left: De Havilland Mosquito NF.Mk IIs of No. 23 Squadron operating from RAF Luqa, Malta flew intruder missions over Southern Italy in the Autumn of 1943, the first 'Mossies' to serve in the Mediterranean. The squadron detached to Sigonella, Sicily later in the year and flew 'roving commissions' over enemy positions attacking trains, transport columns and airfields.

Below: Early autumn, 1943 was an eventful time for the Allied forces as they made slow progress northwards through Italy. Despite the Allied air forces superior numbers Generalfeldmarschall Kesselring displayed brilliant improvisatory skills and conducted his holding campaign as directed by Hitler to sap the Allies' strength and delay an invasion of NW Europe.

several squadrons of Seafires and Spitfires were ashore, and these joined the battle to blunt the enemy counter attacks; while the Royal Navy put ashore reinforcements of armour, the American 505th and 509th Airborne Regiments were dropped on 14 and 15 September in areas where the front line was most threatened. By the evening of 15 September enemy efforts to contain the beach-head were spent, thanks to the combined efforts of the British and American land, sea and air forces. On the following day units of the US VI Corps broke out

Above: This Italian-based Focke Wulf Fw 190 fighter-bomber operated from Viterbo with I/SG 4 in late-1943. It has been temporarily resprayed and has a partially obliterated balkenkreuz and swastika. The dorsal bulge houses MG 131s.

ADVANCES IN ITALY

ITALY

FRANCE

Turin • Milan • Brescia • Vicenza • Treviso • Llubljana • Zagreb
Verona • Padua
Parma • Farrara • Bihac
Genoa • Bologna • Ravenna
Nice • Rimini • YUGOSLAVIA
Cannes • Pesaro
St Tropez • Pisa • Ancona
22.8.44

6.6.44 • 1.1.44 • Adriatic Sea

CORSICA

Rome • Nettuno • Cassino
Anzio

Mediterranean Sea

Operation SHINGLE 21.1.44
The Allied air forces mustered over 2,600 aircraft to oppose over 450 Luftwaffe aircraft.

SARDINIA

Naples

Salerno • Brindisi
Taranto

Operation AVALANCHE 9.9.43
Air cover was provided by land-based Spitfires, P-38s and A-36s, the Royal Navy providing Seafires and Martlets.

Operation SLAPSTICK 9.9.43
• Little opposition here meant that several Allied air force units could become quickly established.

KEY TO MAP
• localities
• air bases
◄ Allied invasion forces
— Allied advance northward

Operation HUSKY 10.7.43
The Allied invasion of Sicily was opposed by Luftwaffe Bf 109G fighters, Fw 190A fighter-bombers and Ju 88A bombers from first light. Allied fighter cover initially came from Spitfire and P-40 units.

Messina • Reggio

SICILY

Operation BAYTOWN 3.9.43
RAF fighters encountering only light opposition, thanks to Allied bombing of German supply routes.

TUNISIA

Cockpit
From 1943 P-47Ds were given a cut-down rear fuselage and teardrop canopy to improve visibility from the cockpit. A small dorsal fillet was later introduced to restore directional stability.

Powerplan
The P-47 was constructed around th giant Pratt & Whitney R-2800-59V Double Wasp engine with super charging that developed 1891-kV (2,535 hp). In addition to the super charger the P-47 also had a 114-litr (30-US gal) water tank for boosting

Republic P-47D Thunderbolt

P-47Ds replaced the 527th Fighter Squadron's A-26 Invaders during 1944 in the fighter-bomber role.

Undercarriage
The wide-track undercarriage was very stable on semi-prepared surfaces, its length provid-ing clearance for the big four-blade propeller. To save space inside the wing, the struts were telescopic when retracted.

Armamen
Eight 12.7-mm (0.5-in) machine-guns were fitted, there also being provision for a maxi mum external load of 1134 kg (2,500 lb including bombs, napalm or eight rockets

from the perimeter in the south to link up with the advancing 8th Army at Vallo di Lucania.

ANZIO LANDING
Thereafter, the Allied advance northwards in Italy continued apace until by 1 January 1944 it was being held by the Germans on a line run-ning from the mouth of the River Garigliano in the south-west to Ortona on the Adriatic coast. When it became clear that the Germans were standing on a pre-pared line, and would be difficult to dislodge, the Allies once more launched a seaborne landing further north at Anzio, in the hope of turn-ing the German right flank; at the same time it was hoped to draw the enemy air force into the air to protect that flank where it could be destroyed by the vastly superior numbers of Allied aircraft. A pre-lude to the landing which took place on 22 January, was an all-out air attack on the Italian airfields in central Italy, carried out to such good effect that not one enemy reconnaissance sortie was successful in detecting the landing force, and 50,000 British and American troops arrived unscathed on the enemy beaches. Here the Allied comman-der, Major General Lucas, made an error of judgement, preferring to consolidate his beach-head rather than to strike hard inland, a move that would unquestionably have severed the enemy supply routes to the south. As it was, the Germans

Below: A flight of Junkers Ju 52/3mg5ᵉ seaplanes of 1 Seetransportstaffel, based at Skaramanga (Piraeus) under X Fliegerkorps, on a supply mission over the Aegean during German operations against Kos and Leros.

Above: With a total of 9,816 aircraft built, the North American B-25 Mitchell was by a short head the most important of the AAF's medi-um bombers, and certainly the most versatile and widely used. This aircraft is from the 414th BS.

Above: Bombs dropping over Rome in the first air-attack on the capital by B-17 Flying Fortresses of the North-west African Air Forces. The Allies entered Rome on 4 June 1944.

Above: A formation of Lockheed P-38s buzz their base in Italy as they return from escorting heavy bombers on a raid over Austria. These 15th Air Force fighters were dubbed 'fork-tailed devil' by the Luftwaffe.

Left: The Allied bombers met less resistance from German night fighters, as their number was reduced to just over 400 by September 1943. This Italian searchlight battery is trying to illuminate bombers for the defending anti-aircraft guns.

had time to mount heavy-armoured counter-attacks which, though only just failing to break through to the beaches, succeeded in containing the landing areas and forcing the invaders on to the defensive. In the air the Luftwaffe switched two Gruppen of Junkers Ju 88s to Italy from Greece and Crete, and one of Dornier Do 217s equipped with Hs 293 missiles to the south of France; these air reinforcements proved unsuitable for support of the land battle at Anzio and many of the Ju 88s were destroyed by air attacks on their airfields. In the event the enemy air force was unable to support the powerful German ground forces in the area; but equally the Allied ground forces were unable to break out of their beach-head, despite the overwhelming air superiority of the RAF and USAAF.

BREAKTHROUGH

On 15 March the Allied air forces attempted to breach the main line in the south by destroying the great monastery at Monte Cassino. In

Above: From 1943 Martin B-26 Marauders appeared in Italy with the 17th, 319th and 320th Bomb Groups of the USAAF. Here, Marauders attack an ammunition dump at La Spezia, 40 miles south-east of Genoa in 1944.

four hours wave after wave of medium bombers dropped over 1000 tonnes of bombs, pounding the ancient building to rubble. Yet still the line held, and it was not until May that the Allies were finally able to pierce the defences and resume their advance northwards. The Anzio pocket was reached and relieved, and on 4 June the Allies at last entered Rome.

US-built fighters in Italy

During April 1944 Merlin-engined P-51B/C Mustangs re-equipped the 31st and 52nd Fighter Groups, providing long-range escort for the bombers and ground-attack support for the armies.

The first major production version of the Airacobra, the P-39N was an effective ground-attack aircraft, being rugged and able to absorb and remain airborne with severe battle damage.

North American P-51C Mustang
This red-tailed P-51C was flown by the 332nd Fighter Group, the only black fighter unit in the USAAF. The 'razorback' Mustang did not have the good all-round visibility that the British-devised Malcolm hood gave to the RAF's aircraft.

Bell P-39N Airacobra
In Italian Co-Belligerent Air Force markings, this P-39N was based at Canne, Italy with 4° Stormo (Caccia Terrestre). This unit operated flew reconnaissance and air-support missions over the Adriatic Sea.

Hamburg, Ruhr and Berlin

1943–1945

Top: Rolls-Royce Merlin-engined Avro Lancaster – mainstay of the night bombing offensive.

Below: Mosquito B.Mk XVI with a pressurised cockpit could fly at 12200 m (40,000 ft). This aircraft was flown by No. 571 Squadron with No. 8 (Pathfinder) Group.

Shortly after the 'Torch' landings in North Africa, the British and American leaders conferred at Casablanca to determine the future course of the war. One result was a directive, put before Air Marshal Harris, setting out his bombing priorities, which were "The progressive destruction... of the German military, industrial and economic system, and the undermining of the morale of the German people to a point where their capacity for armed resistance is fatally weakened." To begin to achieve this objective RAF Bomber Command was now fairly well-equipped, possessing on 4 March 1943 a total of 18 Lancaster squadrons, 11 of Halifaxes, six of Stirlings and 15 of Wellingtons, all operational at night, for a total of 321 Lancasters, 220 Halifaxes, 141 Stirlings and 268 Wellingtons.

GREAT OFFENSIVE

The first manifestation of the great night bombing offensive that now broke over Germany, and lasted until the end of the war, was what came to be known as the Battle of the Ruhr. This started on the night of 5/6 March 1943 with a raid by 442 aircraft against Essen – the first full-scale operation in which the

Above: A Lancaster photographed at 5486 m (18,000 ft) over Hamburg on the night of 30/31 January 1943, the night that pathfinder Stirlings and Halifaxes used H_2S radar for the first time operationally over Germany.

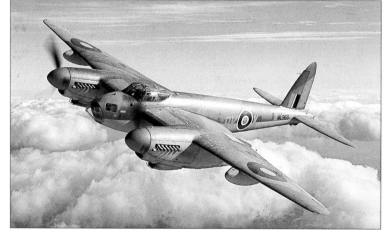

Below: A line-up of 12 Vickers Wellington Mk IIIs and Mk Xs. When the offensive began, RAF Bomber Command had 15 squadrons of Wellingtons with a total of 268 aircraft on strength.

Right: The seven-man crew boarding Lancaster Mk I ED810 (VN-Z) of No. 50 Squadron at RAF Skellingthorpe on 15 April 1943. They took part in a heavy night-bombing raid on the German city of Stuttgart. The crew are wearing Mae Wests and carrying their parachutes and soft leather helmets. Fur-lined boots are necessary to combat the low night-time temperatures.

navigation and bombing aid 'Oboe' was successfully used.

Six weeks later Bomber Command carried out one of its most famous raids of all time, the attack (Operation 'Chastise') on 16/17 May by 19 Lancasters of No. 617 Squadron, led by Wing Commander Guy Gibson, against the Möhne, Eder, Sorpe and Schwelme dams whose hydro-electric stations supplied power to the industrial Ruhr. Dropping special 4196-kg (9,250-lb) 'bouncing' mines, the Lancasters breached the Möhne and Eder dams for the loss of eight aircraft; Gibson survived to be awarded the Victoria Cross for

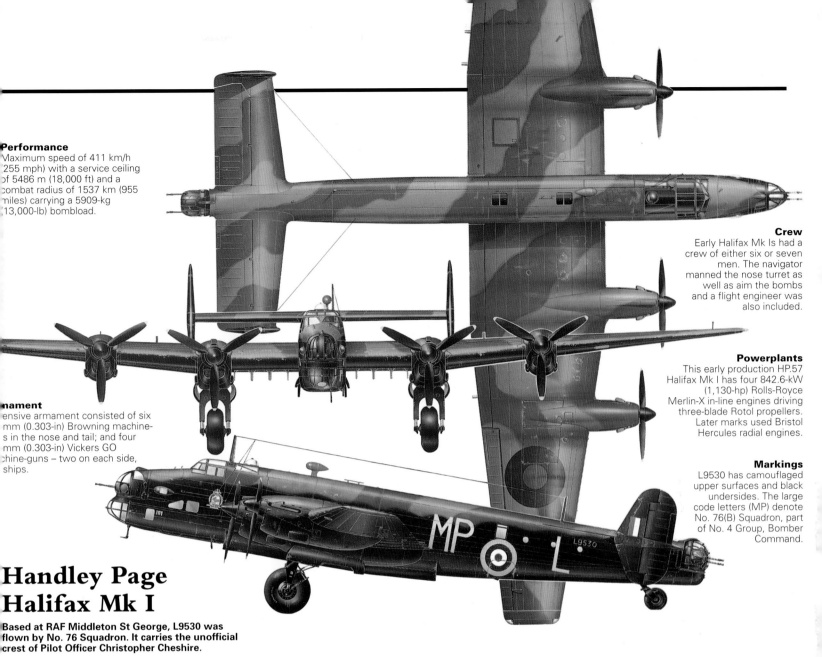

Performance
Maximum speed of 411 km/h
(255 mph) with a service ceiling
of 5486 m (18,000 ft) and a
combat radius of 1537 km (955
miles) carrying a 5909-kg
(13,000-lb) bombload.

Crew
Early Halifax Mk Is had a
crew of either six or seven
men. The navigator
manned the nose turret as
well as aim the bombs
and a flight engineer was
also included.

Armament
Defensive armament consisted of six
7.7-mm (0.303-in) Browning machine-
guns in the nose and tail; and four
7.7-mm (0.303-in) Vickers GO
machine-guns – two on each side,
amidships.

Powerplants
This early production HP.57
Halifax Mk I has four 842.6-kW
(1,130-hp) Rolls-Royce
Merlin-X in-line engines driving
three-blade Rotol propellers.
Later marks used Bristol
Hercules radial engines.

Markings
L9530 has camouflaged
upper surfaces and black
undersides. The large
code letters (MP) denote
No. 76(B) Squadron, part
of No. 4 Group, Bomber
Command.

Handley Page Halifax Mk I

Based at RAF Middleton St George, L9530 was
flown by No. 76 Squadron. It carries the unofficial
crest of Pilot Officer Christopher Cheshire.

his leadership on the raid.

The Battle of the Ruhr continued until June, and was considered
highly successful for the widespread
damage caused, being made possible principally on account of the
radio aids available which were efficient at the relatively short ranges
involved in flights to the Ruhr.

OPERATION 'GOMORRAH'

As new Lancaster and Halifax
squadrons continued to join
Bomber Command, Harris was
now determined on the destruction
of a single vital city in Germany,

and on the night of 24/25 July
launched 791 heavy bombers
against Hamburg, the first of four
massive raids on the city in 10 days
(Operation 'Gomorrah'), carried
out in concert with the heavy
bombers of the USAAF which
attacked the city during daylight
hours. Hamburg was chosen not
only on account of its importance as
an industrial city but for the manner
in which the great port could be
distinguished on H$_2$S radar, a blind
bombing and navigation aid that
had been in use by Bomber
Command for some six months.

*Above: Bombs about to be loaded
onto a Short Stirling Mk I of No. 218
Squadron at RAF Marham. A design
feature that limited the Stirling's
usefulness was its
divided bomb bay, which restricted
the heaviest bomb that could be
carried to 1814 kg (4,000 lb).*

*Right: Ground staff manoeuvre a
bomb trolley conveying a 1814-kg
(4000-lb) 'blockbuster' bomb under
the bomb bay of a Mosquito. From
February 1944 some B.Mk IVs and all
B.Mk IXs were modified to carry this
large bomb that had hitherto been
confined to the heavy bomber force.*

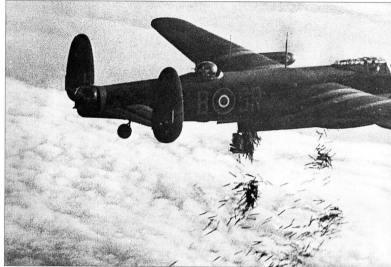

('Oboe' could not be used because of Hamburg's distance from the UK.) A vital ingredient in the raids on Hamburg was the first significant use of 'Window'; vast clouds of tin-foil strips dropped by the bombers to saturate enemy radar screens with spurious signals. In the four Bomber Command raids 2,630 bombers attacked Hamburg, dropping 8759 tonnes of bombs which destroyed more than 6,000 acres of the port, killed more than 41,800 inhabitants and injured over 37,000. The loss of 87 aircraft represented less than three per cent of the aircraft despatched and was well within sustainable limits.

The devastating Battle of Hamburg encouraged Harris to open his last great setpiece assault, this time on Berlin itself (although numerous other targets continued to be attacked before, during and after the attacks on the German capital). On the night of 18/19 November 1943, Bomber Command sent 444 bombers, of which 402 attacked the city, losing nine aircraft, while a simultaneous attack was carried out by 325 bombers on Mannheim, the first occasion on which two heavy raids were launched on a single night.

Top: A Halifax bomber silhouetted during an attack on a flying bomb site on the night of 5/6 July 1944.

Above: Flying from RAF Linton-on-Ouse, this Halifax was from No. 35 Squadron, a pathfinder unit.

Top right: A Lancaster of No. 101 Squadron drops a cloud of reflective 'Window' to jam German radar.

Right: The 5443-kg (12,000-lb) 'Tallboy' bomb could only be carried by modified Lancasters.

RAF bombers of 1942

The Short Stirling was the RAF's first four-engined monoplane heavy bomber. Entering service in August 1940, its load limitations saw it being replaced by the Halifax and Lancaster in 1943.

Entering service in May 1942, bomber versions of the Mosquito were Bomber Command's fastest aircraft, equipping 38 squadrons. Their greatest successes were as Pathfinders for the night offensive.

Short Stirling Mk I
This aircraft (W7455) is in the colours of No. 149 Squadron, based at RAF Mildenhall Suffolk, in the early part of 1942. Most Stirling Mk Is were operated by No. 3 Group, Bomber Command from 1940 to 1943.

de Havilland Mosquito B.Mk IX
As built, the B.Mk IX carried 'Oboe' Mk I, a 907-kg (2,000-lb) bombload and had an operational ceiling of about 10975 m (36,000 ft). Virtual immunity from Luftwaffe night fighters meant exhaust flame dampers were not fitted. LR508 was a pathfinder with No. 105 Squadron.

Illustrated above is Lancaster B.Mk I LM220 of No. 9 Squadron based at RAF Bardney in 1944, named 'Getting Younger Every Day'. Powered by Rolls-Royce Merlin 24s driving paddle-blade propellers, the bomber was equipped to carry the massive 5443-kg (12,000-lb) 'Tallboy' bomb.

Below: A 'vic' formation of No. 207 Squadron Lancaster Mk Is flying from RAF Bottesford in June 1942. The nearest aircraft (R5570, coded EM-F) was lost on the night of 8/9 December 1942, during a raid on Turin, Italy.

Left: The crew of Halifax HR837 from No. 158 Squadron based at RAF Lisset, amidst the damage caused by a 'friendly' bomb dropped by another Halifax flying above it while over Cologne on 28/29 June 1943. HR837 completed 11 more operations before being transferred to No. 1656 Heavy Conversion Unit on 12 April 1944.

The offensive against Berlin continued through the winter of 1943/44, almost invariably in bad weather but, despite the employment of Bomber Command's specialist Pathfinder Group, No. 8, commanded by Air Commodore D.C.T. Bennett, and the use of sophisticated marking and radio countermeasures techniques, the concentration of damage and accuracy of bombing fell far short of expectations. A total of 16 major raids was launched before the 'battle' ended on 24/25 March 1944, involving 9,111 bomber sorties. The raids cost the command a total of 587 aircraft and more than 3,500

aircrew killed or missing – an unsustainable loss rate of 6.4 per cent. The damage and casualties inflicted were considerably less than at Hamburg, and the Battle of Berlin failed in its purpose of breaking the spirit of the German people.

One other major raid was launched by Bomber Command at this time (before it was switched to attacks in support of the coming Normandy landings); 795 four-engine bombers being sent to Nuremberg on 30/31 March 1944. On account of inaccurate weather forecasting, inefficient pathfinding and poor raid planning, the bomber stream disintegrated and suffered

heavily from German night-fighter attacks; more than 100 bombers were lost. Worse, Nuremberg was scarcely hit by the bombers.

During the final eight months of the war, Bomber Command returned to Germany in greater strength than ever. It was to end the war with 56 Lancaster squadrons, 17 of Halifaxes and 18 of Mosquitoes,

for a total of 2,370 aircraft. New navigational and radar jamming equipment and new types of bomb were also available. The 5443-kg (12,000-lb) 'Tallboy' had proved its worth in the sinking of the battleship *Tirpitz* in 1944 and the even larger 9979-kg (22,000-lb) 'Grand Slam' was to be employed against strategically important bridges at Bielefeld and Arnsberg the following year.

The RAF's priority target, however, was the German oil industry, an industry that was so completely devastated that it was to be the chronic lack of aviation fuel that finally grounded the once-formidable Luftwaffe.

Left: Bomb trolleys carry their deadly load to the waiting aircraft at RAF Marham. The armourers are making final adjustments before loading four of the 227-kg (500-lb) bombs on to this de Havilland Mosquito B.Mk IV (DZ360) of No. 105 Squadron.

The Dambusters Raid

Known as Operation 'Chastise', the breaching of the Möhne and Eder dams in Germany's Ruhr Valley was one of World War II's most daring bomber raids. Carried out by the cream of the RAF, the 'Dambusting' mission took a heavy toll on the young pilots that flew them.

By the dead of night, a select group of RAF bombers mounts a precision attack on the Ruhr dams, spearheading one of World War II's most spectacular missions. The power stations served by the huge dams fed Germany's greatest industrial complex, but the dams were immensely strong structures. A bomb capable of breaching one would have been far too heavy for even the sturdy Avro Lancaster to carry. Barnes Wallis, one of Britain's greatest aircraft designers, proposed a less conventional weapon. He showed that, if an explosive could be detonated against the underwater portion of the dam, the shock waves would weaken and, eventually, collapse the structure. Wallis designed a spinning cylindrical mine which, when dropped from low level, would ricochet along the water surface

Right: One of No. 617 Squadron's Lancaster Mk IIIs specially modified for the 'Dams Raid' in May 1943. The dorsal durret was removed and the lower fuselage rebuilt to take the trapeze from which the bomb was released.

before sinking against the dam wall and detonating by means of hydrostatic fuses. Tests with half-size weapons proved that the idea could be successful. Britain's Air Ministry identified the most important targets as the Möhne, Eder, Sorpe, Lister, Schwelme and Ennepe dams. Wing Commander Guy Gibson was chosen to head an elite new unit, No. 617 Squadron. Gibson, a veteran of three tours of operations, was allowed to hand-pick his aircrews.

Over the next two months, Gibson trained his men in extreme

Above: Photographic reconnaissance of the Möhne Dam after the raid by Lancasters of No. 617 Squadron led by Wg Cdr Guy Gibson, reveals a breach in the top of the dam, the water from the lake having flooded the land below. The damage to the wall was not as extensive as had been hoped for.

precision flying skills, but he could not reveal their targets for security reasons. A night attack was planned for the 16 May 1943, to take advantage of both maximum moonlight and high water behind the dams. The crews were given no mission details until the day before the raid. By then, 20 modified Lancaster B.Mk IIIs had been delivered to RAF Scampton in Lincolnshire. The bomb had to be

Left: A modified Lancaster Mk III taxies in at RAF Scampton after a training flight by No. 617 Squadron. This unit was specially formed in great secrecy on 23 March 1943 as part of No. 5 Group with the early destruction of the Möhne and Eder Dams as its primary objective.

'DAMBUSTERS' MAY 1943
An Avro Lancaster Mk III of No. 617 Squadron runs in at high speed and very low level, trying to avoid the German flak. It had to precisely release its Barnes Wallis-designed 'bouncing bomb' for it to be effective against the wall of the dam.

Above: Wg Cdr Guy Gibson, Commanding Officer of No. 617 Squadron, with his crew about to board Lancaster Mk III ED932, in which he led the 'Dams Raid' from RAF Scampton on 16/17 May 1943. He was awarded the Victoria Cross for gallantry.

massive target in the moonlight. He flew a perfect attack as the gun defences burst into life. Flight Lieutenant J.V. Hopgood's Lancaster was hit by flak as it approached. As Squadron Leader H.B. Martin's Lancaster bored in, Gibson flew over the dam to draw off enemy fire. Martin's mine dropped accurately. 'Dinghy' Young, accompanied by Gibson and Martin to distract the enemy gunners, dropped a third mine on target. It was the next attack, by Flight Lieutenant D.J.H. Maltby, that caused the great concrete structure to collapse. The circling pilots watched in awe as a 100-m (110-yard) breach opened up, and 134 million tonnes of water burst into the valley below. Ordering Martin and Maltby to return home, Gibson set course for the Eder. Located in a deeper valley than the Möhne, the Eder dam proved a far more difficult target to attack. Flight Lieutenant D.J. Shannon had to make six abortive runs before successfully delivering his mine. Maudslay's mine struck the Parapet and blew up on impact, destroying the Lancaster. It was the last remaining weapon, dropped by Pilot Officer L.G. Knight, that finally breached the Eder, causing an even greater spectacle than at the Möhne, as 200 million tonnes of water burst down the narrow valley.

Farther afield, McCarthy made his way alone to the Sorpe, where he dropped his mine accurately, but only succeeded in crumbling a stretch of the dam's parapet. Gibson ordered three of the mobile

released at exactly 18.3 m (60 ft) above the water, at a speed of 402 km/h (250 mph), and at a distance of between 366 m (400 yards) and 411 m (450 yards) from the target. Precision was vital to avoid the bomb disintegrating on impact, or bouncing over the target. The height was measured by two spotlights under the nose and tail, whose beams formed a figure '8' on the surface of the water at precisely 18.3 m (60 ft).

Gibson led nine aircraft against the Möhne dam. A second group of five Lancasters, led by Flight Lieutenant Joseph C. McCarthy, an American, was to attack the Sorpe dam. The remaining five Lancasters, under Flight Lieutenant W.C. Townsend, were to serve as a 'mobile reserve'. The Sorpe formation took off just before 21.00, but ran into flak over the Netherlands. Two Lancasters were destroyed, and two forced to turn back. Only McCarthy himself was left, flying 100-km behind the others after a delayed take-off. Gibson's force, operating in three flights of three aircraft, flew further to the south. Gibson led the first flight, followed at 10-minute intervals by Squadron Leader Henry Maudslay and Squadron Leader 'Dinghy' Young. The reserve group took off at about midnight.

Skirting the main Ruhr defences, Gibson easily sighted his

reserve aircraft to back up this attack, but only one managed to do so, and the damaged dam survived. The last two reserve Lancasters were ordered to make for the Lister and Schwelme dams. The latter dam was attacked, but without success. The aircraft detailed for the Lister dam was apparently shot down – its crew failed to return to base. Wing Commander Guy Gibson was awarded the Victoria Cross for his unsurpassed bravery and determined leadership.

GALLANT HEROES

Gibson became synonymous with the generation of men who, night after night, braved enemy flak and fighters to take the war to the

German homeland. Although he was to lose his life over enemy territory a year later, his squadron – proudly adopting the nickname 'Dambusters' – survived as an elite unit. Charged with mounting especially hazardous attacks, No. 617 successfully accounted for a long list of vital targets, from helping to sink the German battleship *Tirpitz* to destroying the Bielefeld viaduct in western Germany.

Right: The full extent of the damage inflicted on the areas below the breached Möhne and Eder Dams only became apparent some days later as the flood water spread through the valleys downstream. The effect on German morale was at least as important as the actual interruption to the war effort.

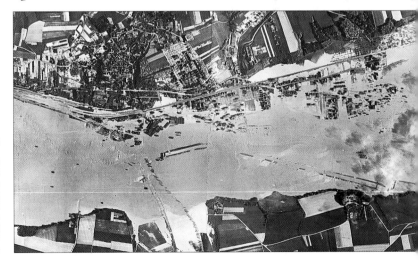

'Dams Raid' Lancaster

The bombers used in the raid were specially modified Lancaster B.Mk IIIs, powered by four American-built Packard Merlin engines. The bomb doors were removed and a pair of V-crutches added below the aircraft's centre of gravity from which the 4196-kg (9250-lb) weapon was suspended. Before launch, the bomb was spun in the reverse direction by a chain drive, so it would skip across the water.

Lancaster B.Mk III
Lancaster B.Mk III (Mod) ED912/G of No. 617 Squadron, based at RAF Scampton in May 1943. This was a specially modified aircraft to drop the oil drum-shaped 'Upkeep' dam-busting mine, shown on its special trapeze under the cutaway fuselage. The 'G' suffix to the serial number indicates a top secret aircraft for which an armed guard was to be provided.

Kursk and the Ukraine

JUNE 1943 – MAY 1944

Above: A Schwarm of Junkers Ju 87Ds breaks formation before landing after a mission in the winter of 1942-43. Winter conditions on frontline airfields were extremely harsh, with engine starting a recurrent problem.

Below: A winter-camouflaged Ju 88A-4 of AufKlGr. 122 over the Eastern Front in 1943. This view illustrates well the extensive glazing which afforded the Ju 88's crew excellent visibility.

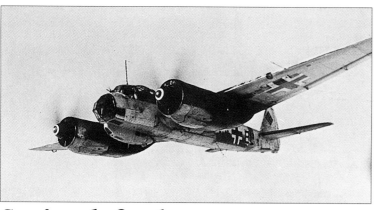

Above: German troops on the Eastern Front gather around the wreckage of a downed Soviet bomber to inspect the damage.

With the German army's surge eastwards thwarted at Stalingrad during the winter of 1942-43, the German high command decided on a major offensive on the central sector of the Eastern Front in June 1943 to eliminate the large Soviet salient around Kursk. Because of German fears of an Allied invasion of Europe in the Mediterranean, the great attack, Operation Zitadelle, was delayed until 5 July.

Both sides desperately needed a major victory, the Germans to break a deteriorating stalemate south of Moscow, and the Soviets to convince themselves that they were capable of defeating the German army in the summer, and not merely in the mud and snow of winter. Deployed on the central front were 4,600 aircraft of the 1st, 2nd, 15th and 16th Air Armies of

Soviet defenders

After its virtual destruction during the initial German invasion, the Red Air Force was rebuilt using aircraft produced in factories east of the Urals. By mid-1943 the Soviet air forces had large numbers of highly effective combat aircraft, most dedicated to support of the ground forces. The Lavochkin La-5FN was a superb tactical fighter, while the Ilyushin Il-2 was arguably the best ground attack aircraft of the war. Types like these allowed the USSR to challenge German air superiority.

Lavochkin La-5FN
This Lavochkin La-5FN was flown by the 1 Czechoslovak IAP in the Ukraine in 1944. Several Czech units were formed within the Red Air Force. The La-5FN was among the aircraft which turned the tables on the Luftwaffe, proving fast enough and manoeuvrable enough at low level to outfight the Bf 109 and Fw 190. The Soviets also managed to produce a steady flow of well-trained pilots, while the Luftwaffe suffered as the war progressed from a woeful lack of skill and experience in all but the few remaining *Experten*.

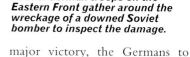

Ilyushin Il-2
The Il-2 was conceived as a specialised armoured ground-attack aircraft. The Russian national insignia assumed many forms, including stars with circles in the centre, with dark/light shades in each of the five arms or with a yellow (or white) border when on a dark background. This Il-2m3 on the Eastern Front in 1943 had stars with borders.

Above: By far the most important variant of the basic Il-2 design was the Type 3, which incorporated 15° of sweepback on the outer wings in an attempt to eradicate the stability problem of the Il-2M.

Below: Il-2s depart from a forward base on a combat mission, probably in 1943. These are quite early single-seaters, though the nearest aircraft has a VYa cannon whose barrels were longer than those of the ShVAK.

the Soviet air force, plus 2,750 of the 5th and 17th Air Armies held in reserve. They comprised huge numbers of Ilyushin Il-2 and Il-2m3 Sturmovik close-support aircraft armed with improved guns and other anti-tank weapons, together with like numbers of Lavochkin La-5FNs, Yakovlev Yak-9s and American-supplied Bell P-39Q Airacobras. Against them the Luftwaffe could muster some 2,100 first line aircraft, out of a total of about 2,500 deployed on the entire Eastern Front. Principal German aircraft included the Focke-Wulf Fw 190A, Junkers Ju 87D, Messerschmitt Bf 109G, Heinkel He 111, Junkers Ju 88 and Henschel Hs 129. The Luftwaffe, however, was to suffer acute fuel shortages during that desperate summer, largely as the result of the activities of Soviet partisans who

destroyed large numbers of supply trains and severely damaged the German communications network, particularly in the key Minsk-Smolensk sector.

BLITZKREIG

Operation Zitadelle opened during the afternoon of 5 July. Crack Panzer divisions equipped with the new Panther and Tiger tanks were hurled into a typical Blitzkreig wedge assault against superior numbers of Soviet tanks in the greatest, most ferocious armoured battle in history. In support, the German armies flew formations of Hs 129 anti-tank aircraft armed with 37-mm guns and hollow-charge armour-piercing bombs, as well as large numbers of Ju 87D bombers. The Luftwaffe's support aircraft did enormous damage among the massed Soviet tanks and, after a

Left: A Soviet armourer prepares a VYa 23-mm cannon on an Il-2M3. In 1942, the ShVAK guns were replaced by the much harder-hitting VYa. The rear gunner of this two-seater had a 12.7-mm (0.5-in) UB machine-gun with 150 rounds of ammunition.

Below: As the war in the east progressed, both VVS and Luftwaffe used night harassment techniques against opposing infantry, small aircraft dropping light bombs. Among the wide range of types used by the Luftwaffe was the Heinkel He 50.

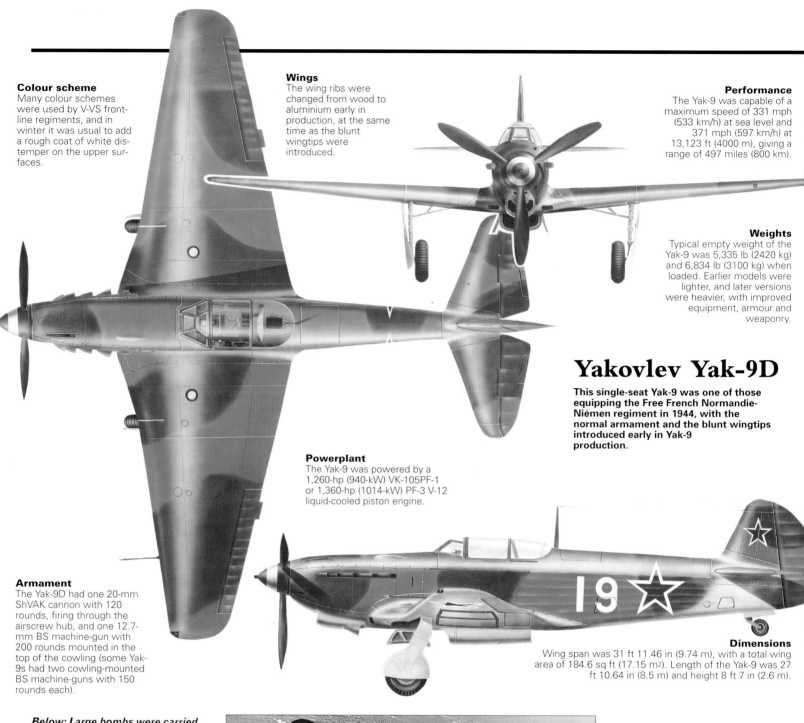

Colour scheme
Many colour schemes were used by V-VS front-line regiments, and in winter it was usual to add a rough coat of white distemper on the upper surfaces.

Wings
The wing ribs were changed from wood to aluminium early in production, at the same time as the blunt wingtips were introduced.

Performance
The Yak-9 was capable of a maximum speed of 331 mph (533 km/h) at sea level and 371 mph (597 km/h) at 13,123 ft (4000 m), giving a range of 497 miles (800 km).

Weights
Typical empty weight of the Yak-9 was 5,335 lb (2420 kg) and 6,834 lb (3100 kg) when loaded. Earlier models were lighter, and later versions were heavier, with improved equipment, armour and weaponry.

Yakovlev Yak-9D

This single-seat Yak-9 was one of those equipping the Free French Normandie-Niémen regiment in 1944, with the normal armament and the blunt wingtips introduced early in Yak-9 production.

Powerplant
The Yak-9 was powered by a 1,260-hp (940-kW) VK-105PF-1 or 1,360-hp (1014-kW) PF-3 V-12 liquid-cooled piston engine.

Armament
The Yak-9D had one 20-mm ShVAK cannon with 120 rounds, firing through the airscrew hub, and one 12.7-mm BS machine-gun with 200 rounds mounted in the top of the cowling (some Yak-9s had two cowling-mounted BS machine-guns with 150 rounds each).

Dimensions
Wing span was 31 ft 11.46 in (9.74 m), with a total wing area of 184.6 sq ft (17.15 m²). Length of the Yak-9 was 27 ft 10.64 in (8.5 m) and height 8 ft 7 in (2.6 m).

Below: Large bombs were carried externally, this being a 1000-kg (2204 lb) weapon. This He 111 is operating on the Eastern Front in January 1943 and has a washable white distemper applied over the standard camouflage for winter operations.

Above: A Ju 88A-4 of III LG.1 over the Russian Front in 1943. From 1940, all Ju 88s were based on the long-span A-4 version which had better handling, no structural limitations and the more powerful Jumo 211J engines.

week's desperate fighting on the flat grasslands, involving more than 3,000 tanks not to mention the Soviets' 20,000 artillery pieces, it seemed that the Germans were on the point of breakthrough.

Then, General Georgi K. Zhukov, the Soviet commander-in-chief, ordered into action a completely fresh tank army supported by swarms of Il–2s. Generalfeldmarschall von Manstein, the German commander, feared the annihilation of his exposed armoured thrust. He urged the supreme command to allow a withdrawal of German forces to the heavily defended line on the Dniepr river, but was peremptorily overruled by Hitler who ordered a fighting stand to be made, during which the Soviet air force took a heavy toll of the vital German transport vehicles. The Soviets went on to widen the Kursk salient, and then launched a sustained attack northwards toward Orel.

Much of the blame for the defeat at Kursk was laid at the door of the Luftwaffe. In spite of the policy of absolute priority of aircraft and

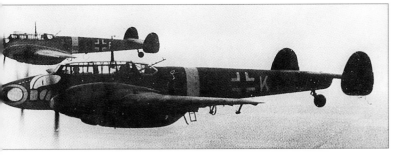

Left: Bf 110 C-4/Bs of Zerstörergeschwader Nr.1, reformed from SKG 210, operated in the USSR in 1942/43. They saw action in the Caucasus and at Stalingrad under VIII Fliegerkorps.

Above: Often dubbed the 'Russian Mosquito', the Petlyakov Pe-2 was nowhere near as versatile as its RAF counterpart, but it nevertheless proved highly valuable as a level and dive bomber on the Eastern Front.

resources on the Eastern Front, which were to be protected by the maintenance of fighter superiority, the Germans lost more than 900 aircraft during the week-long battle over Kursk compared with some 600 Soviet aircraft lost. German air superiority, unquestioned in the first two years of the war, now rapidly evaporated. The tide had indeed turned in the air war. Coming close on the heels of the destruction of the Luftwaffe in Sicily, the priority in the East was now abolished, many fighters and all Zerstörer units being withdrawn for 'defence of the Reich'. The ground attack (Schlacht) units of

the Luftwaffe underwent fundamental reorganisation, the Fw 190F and Fw 190G gradually replacing the aged Ju 87D; at the same time, the Nachtschlachtgruppen (night strike groups) were upgraded in importance, their largely nuisance operations being widened to embrace a concerted campaign against the Soviet railway network.

Right: Luftwaffe personnel examine a crashed Il-2 Sturmovik on the Russian Front. One of the most famous of the Soviet Union's wartime aircraft, total production of the Il-2 totalled 36,000, built between 1941 and 1944.

Luftwaffe Schlachtflieger

To take part in the huge land battles on the Eastern Front, the Luftwaffe developed its ground attack units enormously. The Ju 87D remained a stalwart of the campaign, as did the specialised Henschel

Hs 129. Perhaps the most capable aircraft were the Fw 190F and G, used in numbers by SchG 1 and 2. These could carry heavy bombloads and introduced dedicated anti-personnel weapons.

Focke-Wulf Fw 190F
This Fw 190F-2 was flown by Leutnant Fritz Seyffardt of 6./SchG 1, based in the Ukraine in May 1943. Seyffardt was one of several ground attack pilots to achieve respectable kill totals, ending the war with 30 kills, mostly over Ilyushin Il-2s. The speed and bomb-carrying ability of the Fw 190F made it a capable attacker, but there were never enough to radically affect the outcome of the fighting.

Henschel Hs 129B
Two units received the Hs 129B-3/Wa for operational use in the winter of 1944/45, these being 10.(Pz)/SchG 9 and 14.(Pz)/SchG 9 (illustrated). With the PaK-40 fitted, the two MG 17s were removed and the trough faired over.

Junkers Ju 87G
Even more cumbersome and vulnerable than previous variants, the anti-tank Ju 87G-1 nevertheless proved extremely effective in the hands of an expert. This early example is seen in the markings of the Versuchskommando (test commando for anti-armour warfare) in April 1943; note the Kommando tank emblem.

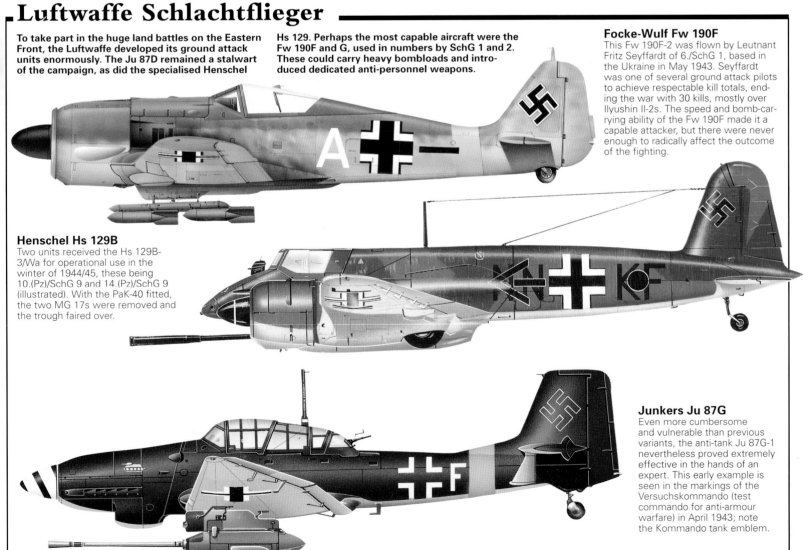

The widespread withdrawal of German fighters from the East gave the Soviets the opportunity to exploit their growing strength in the air. Their own fighters were now more of a match for the Germans, and thanks to numerical superiority could at least provide powerful protection for the Soviet bombers and Il-2s if they could not dominate the front.

SOVIETS FIGHT BACK

In January 1944, with the support of 1,200 aircraft including those of

Above: The Petlyakov Pe-2 first proved its versatility as a light bomber during the battles for the Kursk Salient in 1943. Although later overshadowed by the Tupolev Tu-2, the Pe-2 performed well until the end of the war.

the Red Banner Baltic Fleet, the 2nd Soviet Shock Army secured the relief of Leningrad. By that time the Yak-9 and La-5FN were able to overwhelm the German fighters, and many of the Luftwaffe's most experienced pilots, men like Heinz Schmidt with 173 victories and Max Stotz with 189, were killed.

Above: Indications that the Luftwaffe might not be invulnerable came early. Here smiling Soviet pilots celebrate with their leader Gussarov (centre), who shot down 15 German aircraft between 11-17 May 1942.

Meanwhile in the south, following a Soviet offensive at the end of 1943 in the Kiev region, the Soviets opened their crushing winter campaign in the Ukraine. In January 1944, as the 1st Guards Army and 1st Tank Army smashed their way west towards Zhitomir, supported by General Krasovsky's 2nd Air Army, they trapped some 60,000 Axis troops in the Cherkassy pocket. Roughly half of that number managed to escape during the following month, thanks to air supplies dropped to them by Luftwaffe transport aircraft. In May the last

German aircraft left the isolated Crimea, where 300 Luftwaffe machines were lost as 26,000 Germans fell into Soviet hands.

Nose detail of a crashed Soviet Il-2 Sturmovik in summer 1944. The engine is a large 1007-kW (1,350-hp) liquid-cooled AM-35. The cockpit seated the pilot and radio operator/rear gunner/observer in tandem.

Above: Leutnant Fritz Seyffardt jumps from his Schlacht Fw 190, coded green A. Seyffardt flew the type with 6./SchG 1 and then with 5./SG 2 'Immelmann', trying to stop the advance of the Red Army.

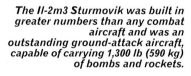

Shturmovik!

Many Soviet veterans remember the Il-2 as the aircraft which won the Great Patriotic War. Here a young Soviet pilot describes his first combat mission, flying as a gunner in the Il-2 Shturmovik of his new flight commander.

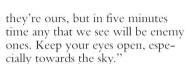

"The C.O. had ordered that I should fly in the aircraft of the flight (zveno) commander. This is Senior Lieutenant Leonid Yefremov, a young, thick-set, rectangular lad of about 23 years old. His snub-nosed face, a boyish aggressiveness on it, is comic.

"Have you ever flown in a Sturmovik? No! Well then, take as many newspapers as you can, you'll need them, for I expect you'll leave your dinner in the cabin." He said to his air gunner, "Vanya, show the battalion commissar how to play your instrument. I don't want to be vulnerable if I meet up with the Messerschmitts". I climb into the cabin and soon the engine is roaring.

Then suddenly...My body is dragged towards the tail. I have to brace myself against the sides of the cabin so as not to hit my forehead against the machine-gun. A few moments later the earth is dropping, falling away beneath us. I can just make out the voice of the pilot somewhere behind the crackling in the earphones, "Well, battalion, still alive?"

"Yes I am."

"Well then, as you're alive, keep both eyes skinned, for heaven's sake."

I report to the pilot, that our two companions are joining up.

"Thank you, they'll form up close to us now."

Suddenly we spot a column of tanks.

"Are you going to attack?" I ask.

"Don't be in such a hurry, they're ours, but in five minutes time any that we see will be enemy ones. Keep your eyes open, especially towards the sky."

Then we experience explosions of A.A. shells. The pilot weaves the aircraft from side to side as he starts evasive action. The no. 2 and no. 3 are doing the same. It's a most unpleasant sensation, but the AA fire at last breaks off.

"Well, battalion, have you still got your dinner or have you given it up to God?"

"I've still got it, still got it. All in order." I make my report as boldly as possible.

"Their firing was pretty poor. If they don't get me the first time, they've had it. I don't let the second salvo get near the aircraft."

"Battalion, attention, in a moment we'll be making our attack." At once his voice loses its boyish intonation and becomes very commanding.

"Prepare to attack" Almost at once, "Attack!" For a fraction of a second I am lifted up and feel weightlessness. The tail of the aircraft rises in the air. The others are diving with us. I see a flash and black cigars belching flames race towards the earth, overtaking our aircraft. These must be the rocket projectiles. Then my whole body shakes as the great aircraft shudders all over. I guess that the cannons are being fired. So this is what a Sturmovik attack means. The aircraft shuddering with the fever of the cannon fire.

"Look out, the swine have got their Oerlikons on to us." The earphones give this warning.

Oerlikons? What are Oerlikons?" The aircraft again goes into evasive action. In the very thick of the enemy equipment fires are raging and several bright red balls seem to hang over this crushed press of vehicles. They seem to hang for a moment and then apparently breaking their bonds they race up and flash past the cabin to rise up into the sky. Oerlikon. This unknown word is now clear to me.

At this moment out of the very bellies of our fellow Shturmoviks a stick of bombs falls away. Not looking away I follow their path down until the whole stick has dived into the melee of vehicles and tanks. The explosions throw out fiery sparks. Now the aircraft is again climbing up into the sky.

"Well battalion, are you still alive?"

"I'm alive."

"Why didn't you open fire?"

"I didn't manage to, I was so pressed down I would not have been able to swing the gun."

Fair enough. Don't try to fire when we're coming out of the dive or you'll hit our tail. But now we'll be making the second run, then you fire some bursts. I'll go lower. O.K.?"

"O.K. I'll try."

The aircraft makes a steep turn at height. The other two aircraft are close beside us. "Stand by, battalion, I'm going in again."

Once more the tail rises and I'm lifted out of my seat against the gun. The fuselage shudders and I already know that this means that the cannon are firing. The earth is now close. The vehicles, tanks,

The Il-2m3 Sturmovik was built in greater numbers than any combat aircraft and was an outstanding ground-attack aircraft, capable of carrying 1,300 lb (590 kg) of bombs and rockets.

Germans in green uniform race past us. Suddenly the heaviness leaves my shoulders.

"Battalion, it's now your turn to speak, fire!"

With a feeling of relief I put my eye to the sight. In the cross-wires there are the running soldiers, the rearing horses, the vehicles and trailers.

I press the trigger with my thumbs. A long line of tracer goes across the mass of enemy equipment. The gun almost jumps from my hands. I hold it tighter and again press on the trigger.

"That's the stuff, carve them up".

"I'm going in on the column again. Stand by, only short bursts or you'll melt the barrel," says the pilot. "Going right down to the deck," warn the earphones, "Fire, Fire! Look, they're running like spiders!" I hear a warrior's laugh of triumph.

The cross wires of the sight slip over the very centre of the enemy column. I press strongly on the trigger. The line of tracer draws a punctured line along the column. The tracer bullets pour out, stinging and I don't as much see this as feel it. I see how one of the lorries bursts into flames.

"Enough. You'll melt the gun." This said jokingly to me and then, in the commander's tone, "hunchbacks, join up, join up."

"We'll return to the chicken house," says the pilot and at once adds "congratulations on your first operational sortie, comrade battalion commissar."

The Il-2 was originally built as a single-seater, but combat experience rapidly showed the need for rear defensive armament. A second cockpit with rear-facing gunner was added in the Il-2M, reducing the numbers lost to Luftwaffe fighters. The greatest assets of the Il-2 were its simplicity and strength, which allowed it to operate in all conditions and with low-skilled and often brutal maintenance. The semi-retracting undercarriage allowed it to make wheels-up landings with only minor damage.

Daylight Heavies Triumph
1943–1945

During mid-1942, the USAAF's 8th Air Force arrived in England and embarked on a massive daylight 'precision' bombing campaign which lasted until the end of the war, complementing the RAF's night offensive. Boeing B-17s were augmented by Consolidated B-24 Liberators, seen here bombing a target near Tours in France.

been conceived as an escort fighter and, until long-range drop tanks could be produced for it, its radius of action remained much the same as that of the Spitfire Mks V and IX, at about 150 miles (240 km).

VULNERABLE BOMBERS

This was an uncomfortable period for Major General Ira C. Eaker, commanding the US 8th Air Force. The Americans were under political pressure to extend their bombing operations further afield, but their early Boeing B-17E, B-17Fs and Consolidated B-24Ds were demonstrably unable to fend for themselves in the face of fast-increasing fighter opposition over France and the Low Countries. VIII Fighter Command was transferred from British to American control in an effort to co-ordinate better escort tactics by the P-47s as the first efficient drop tanks were issued to the fighter groups; these still enabled the P-47s to fly only 50 miles (80 km) farther,

Below: Serving with the 379th Fighter Squadron, 362nd Fighter Group, 9th Air Force, this is a P-47D-II-RE equipped to carry a bomb on the fuselage centreline. Two 150-US gal (568-litre) wing drop tanks could be carried in place of the centreline tank when a bomb was carried.

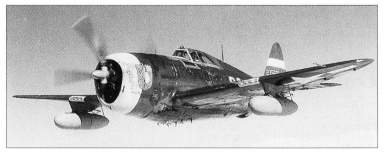

Just as the Casablanca Directive was issued by the Allied Chiefs of Staff on 21 January 1943, setting out the objectives of the British and American bomber offensive, the first American Republic P-47 unit (the 56th Fighter Group) was reaching operational status in England. Two months later the 4th Fighter Group (formed out of volunteer-manned squadrons of the RAF) converted from Supermarine Spitfires to P-47s. These groups, together with the 78th, joined the RAF's Spitfires in escorting the American daylight raids over Europe in May. Unfortunately, the P-47 had not

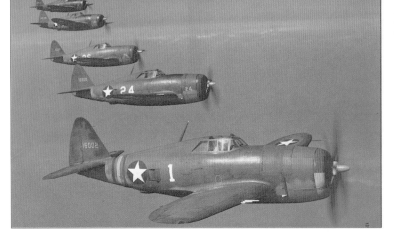

Left: P-47B Thunderbolts of the 56th Fighter Group in formation during training in the US. Aircraft '1' is flown by the CO, with pilots of the 61st Fighter Squadron flying the other aircraft. Using P-47Cs, this group was the first to fly Thunderbolts in the European theatre of operations.

Right: The North American P-51 Mustang was the most effective escort fighter of the war, with sufficient range to escort the bombers all the way to the target, and agile enough to be able to fight Bf 109s and Fw 190s on even terms when it got there. Here Don Gentile, one of the Mustang's greatest exponents, walks away from 'his' P-51B.

however. On 26 June some 250 B-17s attacked Villacoublay, and only the P-47s remained with the bombers all the way. As soon as the Spitfires turned back, the Americans were attacked by the Messerschmitt Bf 109Gs and Focke-Wulf Fw 190As of JG 2 which quickly shot down five B-17s, while JG 26 destroyed four P-47s.

Gradually, the American fighter pilots worked out their own tactics, mastered the tricky fuel handling of the P-47 and, by the late summer of 1943, were beginning to take an increasing toll of German fighters. Thus encouraged, the 8th Air Force launched its first long-distance raid against Schweinfurt and Regensburg deep inside Germany on 17 August, it being intended that fighters would cover the bombers as far as the

Above: The elimination of paint from the B-17 gave a measurable gain in speed on reduced fuel consumption (because cruising speed was pre-set at a figure all aircraft could easily maintain at full load). These B-17Gs, built by Douglas, served with the 711th Bomb Squadron, 447th Bomb Group, based at Rattlesden.

Right: Boeing B-17s bore the brunt of the American offensive, and gained the appreciation of many of its crews for its ability to withstand terrible punishment and still make it back to base. Here a tight formation release their bombloads over the target at Marienburg in Germany.

German border, return for fuel and then meet the raiders on their way home. Unfortunately, the presence of fog at some of the bomber bases caused the timing of the two raids to go wrong, thereby enabling the enemy fighters to make two interception attacks after the escort had turned for home. Of the 376 aircraft despatched, some 60 were shot down. A second mission to

Flames and debris spew backwards from an 8th Air Force B-17 hit moments before bomb release in April 1944. The USAAF suffered far greater losses than the RAF during bombing raids, mainly due to their insistence on daylight attacks.

the ball-bearing plant at Schweinfurt was flown by 291 B-17s on 14 October but, still without fighter protection for

Daylight heavies

The Boeing B-17 and Consolidated B-24 conducted the USAAF's strategic offensive against Germany. With its aircrafts' sophisticated Norden bombsights and daylight tactics, the USAAF presented itself as practitioners of pinpoint bombing of selective targets, aimed at devastating key industries, as compared to the RAF's crude bludgeoning of area targets by night, which aimed to disrupt German industry and morale as a whole. In fact, RAF night bombing (using Pathfinders and navaids like H2S) was more accurate than the USAAF's day bombing, taken as a whole.

Consolidated B-24D Liberator
The Little Gramper was a Consolidated B-24D flown by the 491st Bomb Group as a lead-ship. These war-weary aircraft were used to assemble the huge formations over England, ensure everyone was in position and then send them on their way. The colours were deliberately bright for high visibility.

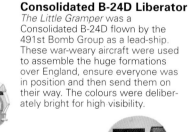

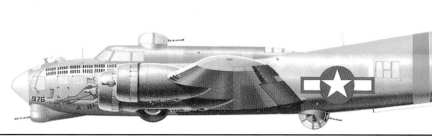

Boeing B-17G Flying Fortress
This famed B-17G *A Bit o' Lace* of the 711th BS, 447th BG based at Rattlesden, had nose art painted and signed by Milton Caniff (nose art, often featuring the female form, was invariably well executed). The 447th did not use squadron code letters but ended the war with this colourful yellow scheme.

more than half the flight, 60 more bombers were shot down; five others crashed in England and 133 were badly damaged.

FIGHTERS ARRIVE

The remedy for these catastrophic losses was already at hand, however, with the arrival in England during that autumn of the 354th Fighter Group, the first to fly the superb North American P-51 Mustang, a long-range fighter that was to remain unrivalled for the remainder of the war. When a third attack by 238 B-17s of the USAAF's 1st Bombardment Division returned to Schweinfurt on 24 February 1944, the fighter escort accompanied the

entire raid and bomber losses were held to 11 aircraft.

Throughout 1944 the Americans continued to build up their bomber strength, the B-17G, the B-24G and the B-24H being introduced with twin-gun nose turrets to counter the deadly head-on attacks by German fighters. In the latter half of February a concerted day and night assault by RAF and US bombers (Operation Argument, otherwise known as 'Big Week') was launched, in which a total of 16,500 tons of bombs was dropped in five days and nights, the Germans losing more than 150 fighters. On 4 March the Americans carried out their first daylight raid on Berlin

(complementing RAF Bomber Command's night Battle of Berlin, then at its height): 609 B-17s and B-24s with P-47, Lockheed P-38 and P-51 escort achieving considerable damage for the loss of 68 bombers and 13 fighters.

Like those of RAF Bomber

Command, the heavy bombers of the US 8th Air Force were largely withdrawn from strategic operations in preparation for the coming Normandy invasion, switching to attacks on German airfields and transportation targets in France and the Low Countries.

Above: Easter egg and pin-up girl. This special 'egg' has been prepared by members of the 8th Air Force Ordnance Unit to be dropped over Germany in Easter 1944. A hoist is being used to move the bomb.

Right: Colonel Tom Christian, Group Commander of the 361st Fighter Group, leads three aircraft of the 375th Fighter Squadron. The P-51D marked an improvement over the earlier P-51B in many respects.

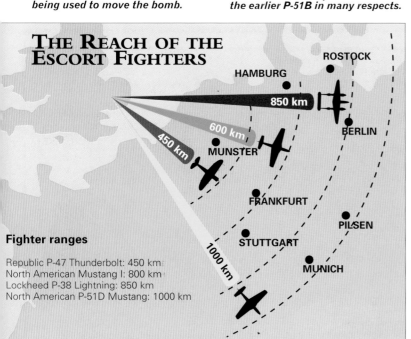

THE REACH OF THE ESCORT FIGHTERS

Fighter ranges

Republic P-47 Thunderbolt: 450 km
North American Mustang I: 800 km
Lockheed P-38 Lightning: 850 km
North American P-51D Mustang: 1000 km

ROSTOCK

HAMBURG

850 km

600 km

450 km

BERLIN

MUNSTER

FRANKFURT

PILSEN

STUTTGART

1000 km

MUNICH

Left: The Eighth Air Force always planned on operating with a fighter escort. This was originally provided by short-ranged RAF Spitfires, which could range little further than Paris. There were never enough P-38s to escort the 8th Air Force bombers, and the aircraft were, in any case, to prove unreliable and ineffective. The Republic P-47 entered 8th Air Force service in March 1943, and this proved more reliable, and more effective, though it could reach little further than the German border. In RAF service the Allison-engined Mustang I had proved capable of attacking targets in Germany, but the aircraft's performance was poor at high altitude, and it was not suitable for bomber escort duties. The Merlin-engined Mustang offered even greater range, with superior altitude performance, and promised to be able to escort the bombers all the way to any target, even Berlin. This was of crucial importance, promising to make the difference between success and failure of the daylight bomber offensive.

In August the American bombers began heavy attacks on the German oil industry, synthetic oil plants at Gelsenkirchen and Ludwigshafen being attacked by British-based bombers on 16, 24 and 26 August, and the Ploesti oil plants by Italian-based B-24s of the 15th Air Force on 17 and 18 August. In September the B-17s and B-24s raided Bremen, Koblenz, Frankfurt, Hamm, Karlsruhe, Kassel, Magdeburg, Mainz, Munster, Osnabruck and Stuttgart. The toll of German cities and industries devastated by bomb and fire continued to rise.

HITLER POUNDED

As the German army was forced back within the boundaries of the Reich, so the ferocity of air fighting increased as the German fighter pilots struggled to defend their homeland. The Messerschmitt Me

Liberators of the 458th Bombardment Group, based at RAF Horsham St Faith, en route to a target, with a P-51 escort. Bombers began to lose their drab camouflage soon after it was removed from the fighters of the Eighth Air Force. In clear, cloudless weather, towards the end of the war, USAAF bombers proved more accurate than the RAF's night bombers, but as soon as there was cloud, heavy flak or fighter opposition, accuracy figures declined dramatically.

163 rocket interceptor and Me 262 jet fighter appeared and began to take a serious toll of the bombers but – the perimeter contracted from the west, east and south, as Allied bombers 'shuttled' to bases in the Soviet Union, as the Allied long-range fighters maintained constant attacks on the German airfields, and as enemy oil stocks dwindled – the British and American heavy bombers continued to pound Hitler's Germany into rubble. By late April 1945 the 8th Air Force bombers had little left to attack but targets in southern German, Austria and Czechoslovakia. Their last major raid was on the Skoda works at Pilsen on 25 April 1945.

Above: Waist gunners inside a B-17. Two 0.5-in (12.7-mm) machine-guns on hand-operated mountings were fitted just aft of the trailing edge of the wing, firing through opening side ports.

Above: By mid-1944, most USAAF fighters operating in Europe had shed their camouflage in favour of natural metal, a step instigated primarily to gain extra speed in combat. This P-38L Lightning is escorting B-17Gs over Germany.

Right: Flight crew and ground crew discuss the successful 50th mission of B-17 Idiot's Delight on a base in East Anglia in March 1944. Mascot Flak Jr is being held by one of the crew. The pilot is signing the release for the aircraft.

'Little Friends'

Flying in daylight over the enemy homeland in a lumbering B-17 or B-24 was a dangerous business, even with the protection of escort fighters, which were soon referred to by the grateful bomber crews as 'Little Friends'. The P-51 and P-47 formed the backbone of the Eighth Air Force's escort fighter force, but also undertook independent fighter sweeps and ground attack missions.

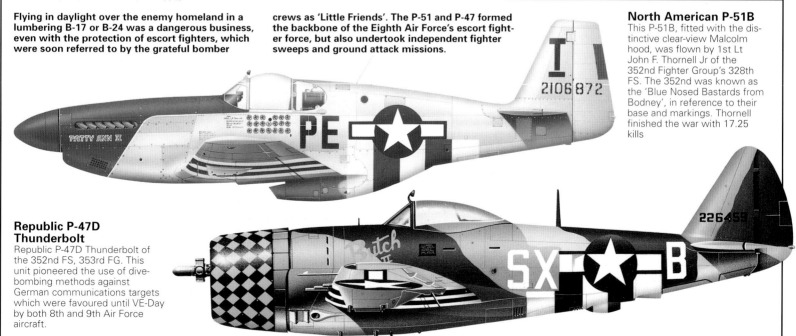

North American P-51B
This P-51B, fitted with the distinctive clear-view Malcolm hood, was flown by 1st Lt John F. Thornell Jr of the 352nd Fighter Group's 328th FS. The 352nd was known as the 'Blue Nosed Bastards from Bodney', in reference to their base and markings. Thornell finished the war with 17.25 kills

Republic P-47D Thunderbolt
Republic P-47D Thunderbolt of the 352nd FS, 353rd FG. This unit pioneered the use of dive-bombing methods against German communications targets which were favoured until VE-Day by both 8th and 9th Air Force aircraft.

Left: Seconds to live. A direct flak hit on the starboard wing has doomed this B-24 Liberator over Ploesti. The heavily laden bomber had not completed its bombing run when it received the fatal hit.

Ploesti stands without parallel in regard to Liberator operations. For US strategists, the destruction of Hitler's major oil source was worth the air strike gamble of high losses. This B-24D flies low enough to feel the heat from the burning oil tanks.

B-24 bombardier over Ploesti

Leroy Newby was the bombardier of a B-24 of the 460th Bombardment Group, and he flew on the nightmare mission to Ploesti, during which he and his crew had to face heavy flak and enemy fighters.

"There was a chorus of groans when the curtains were drawn back and the crews in the briefing room could see where the blue yarn stretched out to indicate our target for the day. Sherm and me, though, weren't surprised. We'd been to the special briefing

Left: B-24s fly over the burning refineries at Ploesti on 1 August 1943. Of the 177 Liberators (some borrowed from the 8th Air Force) that took off from bases in North Africa, 54 were destroyed and 532 aircrew were killed or captured.

for lead bombardiers and navigators half an hour earlier. We already knew the 460th was going to Ploesti."

Leroy Newby - Ted to friends - was a young lieutenant whose job was as simple and straightforward as could be: all he had to do was wait until he had the target located in his bombsight and then press the release toggle. Of course, the Germans and Bulgarians defending Ploesti would have other ideas, and something of the order of a thousand anti-aircraft guns to put them into practice....

"Our *Hangar Queen* was

assigned as deputy lead in the first attack unit. If the mission lead plane aborted or was forced out of formation en route, all the responsibility for navigation and target pick-up would fall on us. Gulp.

"They had passed out pictures taken by P-38s just a few days before. Our specific target was the Xenia refinery, complete with its 'tank farm' storage complex, on the northwest edge of the city.

"We departed base and were soon leaving a thick contrail along with 500 other bombers. Sherm was hard at it, updating his weather information.

"'Newb, the weather data looks okay to me," Sherm finally said. I

sighed with relief. No changes. All I had to do was find the target.

"'Lead bomb doors are opening,' called out Bob Kaiser. I immediately opened ours, and flipped the switch that armed the bombs. Then I looked around me.

"There wasn't a single cloud at our altitude, though it was cloudy higher up. Small, dense clouds that dispersed and reformed . . . not over the city itself, but forming a ring: black clouds below, white clouds above...."

The black clouds were Flak 37 guns, 88-mm pieces that fired shells weighing over 20 pounds. Above were the heavier Flak 39s that fired 34-lb 105-mm shells at

The big oil refineries at Ploesti in Romania were the source of the majority of oil supplies for the Nazi war machine. The target was considered so vital that the commander of the 9th Air Force (then based in North Africa) expected to lose 50 per cent of his force in an all-out attack, but considered it would be "well worth it" if the target was hard hit with total losses. For **Operation Tidal Wave**, the famous low-level attack on Ploesti, two Libyan-based B-24 groups were joined by three more from the 8th Air Force based in England. The 1 August 1943 raid is a legend in USAF history: the Liberators flew so low that their gunners fought duels with anti-aircraft gunners on the ground, at least one B-24 was set alight by flames from burning oil tanks, and a total of four Medals of Honor was won by aircrew participating in the raid. With the capture of bases in Italy in 1944, more frequent, high-level raids could be mounted on the Romanian oilfields. The raids on Ploesti finally halted production in August 1944, as the Russian armies approached. The attacks on German oil targets generally, more than any other factor, kept much of the Luftwaffe grounded in the last months of the war.

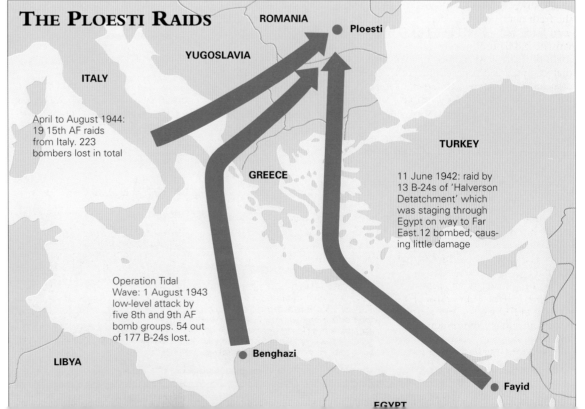

THE PLOESTI RAIDS

ROMANIA

Ploesti

YUGOSLAVIA

ITALY

April to August 1944: 19 15th AF raids from Italy. 223 bombers lost in total

GREECE

TURKEY

11 June 1942: raid by 13 B-24s of 'Halverson Detatchment' which was staging through Egypt on way to Far East.12 bombed, causing little damage

Operation Tidal Wave: 1 August 1943 low-level attack by five 8th and 9th AF bomb groups. 54 out of 177 B-24s lost.

LIBYA

Benghazi

Fayid

EGYPT

TARGET PLOESTI
B-24J Hangar Queen of the 460th BS was assigned as deputy lead in a later attack on Ploesti. Leroy Newby was the bombardier.

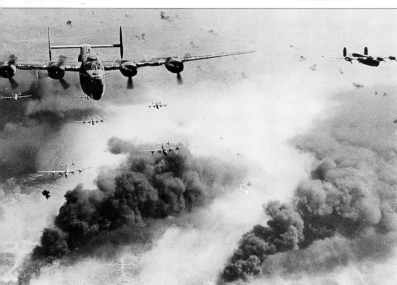

Left: Among the most memorable missions flown by Liberators during the course of the war was the attack on the Concordi Vega oil refinery at Ploesti, Romania, in June 1944. 15th Air Force B-24Js are seen under heavy anti-aircraft fire on a later Ploesti mission.

Right: On 23 June 1944, 761 heavy bombers hit the Ploesti refineries, the largest force to be sent against the Romanian target, followed by another 377 on 24 June. On 9 and 15 July, both raids were directed by pathfinder aircraft.

the B-17s, 4,000ft above.

"The black and white clouds came in different sizes and shapes. Small, sharp, jagged clouds were the fresh ones, and they were harmful if they were close. If you saw the red flash of the explosion itself, then there was a good chance that you were near enough for it to damage your aircraft. The larger, rounded puffs were old explosions.

"What they were doing was setting up a box barrage, bigger by far than the size of the bomber formation, and surrounding the bomb release point. The gunners, each firing a round every three or four seconds, tried to keep the box filled with exploding shells. They knew they couldn't stop the formation, but by hitting a 'plane or two, causing the formation to split open to avoid the careening aircraft, they could affect our accuracy.

"As for us, our instructions were very clear. Fly into, and through, the box of flak. No evasive action, just get in and get out. A straight line is the shortest distance....

"Being deputy lead, I had to

run checks of my own to compare with the computations going on in the lead aircraft. I worked away at it for a while, and then, before things got too serious, I tried to locate the actual aiming point. I got a shock. I'd been expecting a two-abreast tank farm that ran generally east-west in a rectangular strip. The picture in my bombsight was a square tank farm. Nothing like our target. I checked with the pictures: nothing like it.

"'Sherm,' I shouted, 'did we turn early?'

"'Yeah,' he answered, 'about a minute. Why?'

"'This is the wrong target!'

"'Right or wrong,' came the pilot's voice, 'this is the one we're going to bomb.' Because the target was such a different shape, all the data I'd entered about bomb drop

A 15th Air Force Liberator just after making a high-level bomb run over Ploesti. Note the vapour trails and open bomb bay. Almost 7,500 bomber sorties were flown against Ploesti, totalling some 13,469 tons of explosives and incendiaries.

intervals and such was meaningless, and there was no time to apply more than a hasty correction.

"Luckily, we were going to attack the tank farm on the diagonal, so there was still a chance that we'd get our stick of eight bombs inside it and do some real damage. Then I realised that the area over the target was actually blanketed by dense cloud, and I wasn't going to be able to see the aiming point for the last 20 or 30 seconds of my bomb run.

"I was now fully alert, I could see that we were about eight seconds away from bomb release. The cloud covered the aiming point itself, and all I could do was rely on offsets, guessing at where our target lay from things that I could see. I watched the sight tick off the last seconds of angle, then heard the bomb releases let go. 'Bombs away!' I tried to play it cool but I couldn't. I knew I'd done well

under difficult conditions.

"'Bomb doors closed,' I reported next, more matter-of-factly this time. Despite it being minus 60 outside, and not much warmer inside, I was soaked from the waist up. Even my feet felt warm, and that was really rare.

"As we banked away from the target, Major James's voice came over the intercom. 'We've been working for the government up to now,' he said, 'but from here on in, we're in business for ourselves.' He was right. Our sole job now was to get home in one piece.

"The return trip was fairly uneventful and the coffee and doughnuts served by the Salvation Army sure tasted good after that mission, and the shot of old Overholt whiskey that we were allowed after every mission hit the spot, too. And it was our turn to stand down tomorrow. The world didn't seem so bad a place after all."

Back into France

JUNE – SEPTEMBER 1944

Above: As the Allies advanced inland after D-Day, the fighter-bomber units of the US 9th Air Force moved from bases in southern England to semi-prepared strips near the front line. Here, examples of 'bubble-top' and 'razorback' P-47Ds await the take-off signal at a forward base.

Below: a Marauder crosses a Normandy beach scattered with landing craft as it returns from a mission over France. The medium-bombers of the 9th AF and the RAF were tasked with disrupting communications to prevent German forces massing for counter-attacks.

Above: Wearing partially-removed 'invasion stripes' and an impressive bomb tally, 'DeeFeater', a Martin B-26B Marauder of the 596th Bomb Squadron, 397th Bomb Group flies over England after the invasion. The 596th BS moved to Dreux in France during the campaign to keep close to the front line.

Left: A P-51D Mustang displays a full set of the 'invasion stripes' applied on the eve of D-Day to all aircraft directly involved in supporting the landings to distinguish them as friendly. Unusually here, the white stripes are edged in black. In July stripes began to be removed from upper surfaces to restore some camouflage effect.

Almost exactly four years after the British Expeditionary Force had staged its near-miraculous evacuation from Dunkirk, the Allies once more set foot in strength on French soil when on 6 June 1944, under the supreme command of General Eisenhower, British, American and Canadian forces landed in Normandy. They did so with complete mastery of the air.

For some months past the RAF and USAAF had been preparing the way for the invasion, British and American heavy bombers striking at key points in the French road and rail system to prevent the movement of reinforcements once the invading forces had landed. To this task was added the offensive against the flying-bomb sites in the Pas de Calais, while the fighter-bombers and light bombers of the 2nd

Tactical Air Force struck at coastal targets (the E-boat bases, radar stations, airfields and coastal gun batteries) along the French coast. On the eve of the landings themselves the Allied Expeditionary Air Force comprised 173 squadrons of fighters and fighter-bombers, 59 squadrons of light and medium bombers and 70 squadrons of transport aircraft; in addition to some 50 other support

Left: Airspeed Horsa and General Aircraft Hamilcar gliders line up on RAF Tarrant Rushton's runway, just prior to D-Day. The Halifax glider tugs belong to No. 298 Squadron. The Horsa carried 20-25 troops, while the latter could hold a seven-tonne light tank into battle.

squadrons, there was also the might of RAF Bomber Command and the US 8th Air Force. In all, the Allies could count on close to 12,000 aircraft with which to support the invasion.

6 JUNE 1944

The assault on the French coast was indeed a highly co-ordinated effort by the land, sea and air forces. As 145,000 men went ashore from the sea on the first day, considerable use was made of airborne forces, the US IX Troop Carrier Command's C-47s dropping large numbers of paratroops behind the American beachhead area, their task being to consolidate an area from which an advance could be made up the Cotentin peninsula to capture the port of Cherbourg. In the event the American airborne operations were not wholly successful, the 81st and 101st Airborne Divisions being scattered over too wide an area to be fully effective. In the eastern sector, behind the British and Canadian beaches, the Stirlings, Albemarles, Halifaxes and Dakotas of the RAF's Nos 38 and 46

Groups dropped 4,310 paratroops and towed about 100 gliders to secure vital objectives such as coastal batteries, river bridges and road junctions.

As part of the elaborate deception plans undertaken to conceal the true location of the assault area during the night of 5/6 June a squadron of Lancasters (No. 617)

had flooded the skies over the Channel far to the north-east with 'Window' in a slow-moving cloud designed to suggest on enemy radar an approaching invasion fleet; a similar operation was carried out by Halifaxes and Stirlings off Boulogne. These feints certainly played their part in discouraging the Germans from committing their reinforcements until the real landings had gained a powerful foothold in Normandy.

ALLIED AIR UMBRELLA

Throughout that first day, as more and more men and vehicles

Above: In a textbook example of a precision strike, Allied bombers sever a rail viaduct in France during the Normandy campaign. Just visible at the top of the picture (and on the shadow of the bridge) is a train, which reportedly managed to come to a stop before the breach.

Left: One of the better Allied tanks in Normandy was the British Sherman Firefly with the 17-pdr gun, though it was available only in limited numbers. Allied tactical air-power did much to reduce the threat of the generally-superior German tanks.

Allied support aircraft

Douglas Boston Mk IIIs entered service in late-1941 as an anti-shipping and daylight medium-bomber. Their primary role on D-Day was smoke-laying, to shield the invading flotilla.

de Havilland's 'Wooden Wonder', the Mosquito was unmatched by anything in the USAAF inventory in the high-speed reconnaissance role. Almost 200 were delivered to the Americans.

Douglas Boston Mk IIIA
The USAAF's Douglas A-20C became the Boston Mk IIIA in RAF service. No. 342 ('Lorraine') Squadron was employed on smoke-laying missions on D-Day. No. 2 Group, Bomber Command's medium-bombers were transferred to the AEAF in the lead-up to the landings.

de Havilland Mosquito PR.Mk XVI
Unlike 40 Canadian-built Mosquitoes, designated F-8s, the PR.Mk XVIs were used operationally. Over 100 were delivered to the 8th Air Force from early-1944; this example flew with the 653rd Bomb Squadron (Light), 25th Bomb Group in the weather-reconnaissance role.

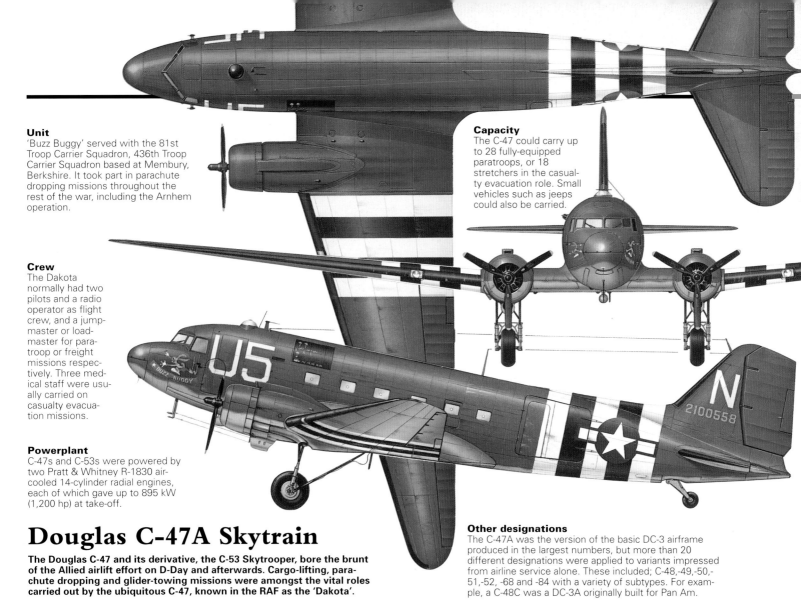

Unit
'Buzz Buggy' served with the 81st Troop Carrier Squadron, 436th Troop Carrier Squadron based at Membury, Berkshire. It took part in parachute dropping missions throughout the rest of the war, including the Arnhem operation.

Crew
The Dakota normally had two pilots and a radio operator as flight crew, and a jump-master or load-master for para-troop or freight missions respec-tively. Three med-ical staff were usu-ally carried on casualty evacua-tion missions.

Powerplant
C-47s and C-53s were powered by two Pratt & Whitney R-1830 air-cooled 14-cylinder radial engines, each of which gave up to 895 kW (1,200 hp) at take-off.

Capacity
The C-47 could carry up to 28 fully-equipped paratroops, or 18 stretchers in the casual-ty evacuation role. Small vehicles such as jeeps could also be carried.

Other designations
The C-47A was the version of the basic DC-3 airframe produced in the largest numbers, but more than 20 different designations were applied to variants impressed from airline service alone. These included; C-48,-49,-50,-51,-52, -68 and -84 with a variety of subtypes. For exam-ple, a C-48C was a DC-3A originally built for Pan Am.

Douglas C-47A Skytrain

The Douglas C-47 and its derivative, the C-53 Skytrooper, bore the brunt of the Allied airlift effort on D-Day and afterwards. Cargo-lifting, para-chute dropping and glider-towing missions were amongst the vital roles carried out by the ubiquitous C-47, known in the RAF as the 'Dakota'.

Above: The first tasks of the Allied engineers following the invasion were to build artificial harbours ('Mulberrys', one of which can be seen in the background) and to build emergency landing strips for aircraft out of fuel or too badly damaged to make it across the Channel. This P-38J Lightning has been saved by one such strip, built virtually on the water's edge within a week of D-Day.

Below: Coastal Command's strike forces were employed in keeping the German naval forces in France (by this time no longer comprising large surface warships) away from the invasion fleet. This is a Beaufighter TF.Mk X of No. 455 (RAAF) Squadron.

Left: With smoke-laying tubes visi-ble below the aircraft, these No. 88 Squadron Boston Mk IIIAs are seen during Operation 'Starkey'. During this September 1943 exercise tac-tics to be used in June 1944 were tested by tempting an enemy response to a Channel convoy.

stormed ashore, the Allied air forces put up an enormous umbrella of protective fighters to keep watch for the Luftwaffe. Indeed the German air force react-ed slowly and sluggishly with the relatively small number of aircraft available (a total of around 500 ser-viceable aircraft in the whole of Luftflotte III's assigned area). Only a small number of enemy air attacks developed and the damage caused by them was negligible. The Allies, on the other hand, recorded a total of 14,674 operational sorties on that first day, for the loss (mainly to flak) of 113 aircraft.

The initial assault phase ended with the delivery of 256 gliders to the inland dropping zones, carrying reinforcements to the men of the British 6th Airborne Division. Heavy tank-carrying Hamilcar gliders were now used for the first time to bring the Tetrarch tank into action.

For four days after D-Day the Allies were content to consolidate their beachhead as the tactical sup-port Typhoons, Spitfires, Mustangs, Lightnings and Thunderbolts ranged over northern France, attacking road convoys and trains struggling to deliver German rein-forcements to the battle area. Within 10 days more than half a million men had been landed on the Normandy beaches, scarcely troubled on their voyage from the

Above: A vital part was played by Allied photo-reconnaissance aircraft in plotting the movements of enemy supplies and reinforcements so that they could be targeted by the tactical air units. In addition to Spitfires, both the RAF and USAAF used Mosquitoes in this role. This is an RAF PR.Mk XVI – note the camera windows under the fuselage and the 'invasion stripes'.

Below: The Spitfire was widely used as a fighter-bomber in Normandy, a role for which the type was not entirely suited. Battle of Britain ace Squadron Leader Geoffrey Page is seen with fingers crossed in his 'bombed-up' No. 132 Squadron Spitfire Mk IX in France. He was severely wounded in September. No. 132 was back in Britain by September and in December had left for the Far East.

UK by the Luftwaffe, thanks to the continuing efforts of the 2nd Tactical Air Force to pin the German aircraft to their bases. By 10 June (after only three days' work by the airfield engineers) the first landing strip on French soil had been completed and thereafter RAF Spitfires and Typhoons were able to operate close-up behind the land battle, the Typhoons in particular proving deadly with their rocket armament.

BREAKOUT

The Americans were the first to break out of the beachhead, striking north towards Cherbourg before the end of June, and west and south during July. By the middle of August the British 2nd Army and the Canadian 1st Army had advanced south from Caen so that some 16 German divisions

Above: The British equivalent of the 9th Air Force was the 2nd TAF (Tactical Air Force). 2nd TAF struck at German communications, headquarters, supply depots and armour concentrations. The main bomber type used was the B-25, such as these Mitchell Mk IIs of No. 226 Squadron seen just after D-Day. Mosquitoes were also widely used.

faced encirclement and annihilation at Falaise. After a week of pounding from the air and ground the bulk of the German 7th Army was decimated and the remainder in flight across France, all the while harried by the rocket-firing Typhoons, the Thunderbolts and Lightnings by day, and the Mosquitoes of the RAF's No. 2 Group by night. On 25 August Paris was liberated by its own citizenry and on 3 September the Welsh Guards swept into Brussels.

AEAF fighter-bombers

It was during the Normandy campaign that Allied fighter-bombers came into their own as a close-support weapon against targets directed by commanders on the ground. For this role the RAF had the superb (if imperfect) Typhoon, designed as a fighter but more successful in ground attack. The Americans detailed quantities of their air superiority fighters, the P-47 Thunderbolt and P-51 Mustang, to close air support, the latter, with its liquid-cooled engine, proving vulnerable to ground fire.

Hawker Typhoon Mk IB
Built by Gloster Aircraft, this aircraft wears the markings carried by No. 198 Squadron between mid-1943 and D-Day. On 10 April 1943 No. 198 flew its first 'Rhubarb' fighter-bomber sortie against targets of opportunity across the Channel. It moved to France in July 1944.

North American P-51B Mustang
At least two pilots of the 353rd Fighter Squadron, 354th Fighter Group scored kills in the 'Beantown Banshee'. The 354th was the first Group in Europe (of either the 8th or 9th air forces) to receive Mustangs, and was still operating P-51Bs at D-Day, when many groups had converted to the P-51D.

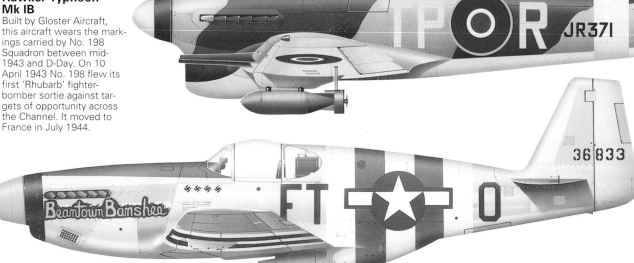

Typhoon Attack

The Typhoon proved a devastating weapon against enemy ground forces when called into action from an airborne 'cab rank' position. Forward air controllers were stationed with Allied armoured units and could call in enormous firepower at very short notice. Ground fire of all calibres could be murderous, however, and many pilots never pulled out of their attack runs.

"I was a little afraid of the brute as I stood in front of it. I felt it was something mysterious and dangerous and I longed to master the monster, to break it in, like a thoroughbred," writes Belgian ace Charles Demoulin of his first encounter with the Typhoon. Decorated with the Croix de Guerre and the DFC, Squadron Leader Demoulin was to fly over 500 sorties in the legendary 'Tiffy' during the last three years of World War II.

"The long-awaited Typhoon had been planned to replace the Spitfire but was in fact a cruel disappointment to the RAF. Far faster from ground level to 10,000 ft, the Typhoon lost most of its power at the altitude where much of the combat took place. This was an insurmountable setback, for even with its supercharger the huge 2,200-hp engine could not compensate for the seven tons it had to move through the sky – against a mere 3.5 tons for the Spitfire."

The early Typhoon also had a bad habit of losing its ailerons in a steep turn, and the tail rivets wouldn't stand the stress of a steep dive. And as if that weren't enough, the Napier 24-cylinder sleeve-valve engine had an average life of about five flying hours before it packed up without warning. The cylinder sleeves causing the trouble were changed more often, and even replaced with another kind of steel, but engine reliability was never up to the standard of the Rolls-Royce engine in the Spitfire.

"Added to these vices, the aircraft had to be held hard with full rudder on take-off to counteract the torque, and oxygen had to be on at all times because the cockpit filled with exhaust fumes!" No wonder young pilots were nervous

Below: With Allied air superiority over the battlefield, the German Panzer armies had little protection from air attack. If they remained in depots, they would be destroyed by medium and heavy bombers, if they moved into the open, they were easy meat for the rocket-armed Typhoons. This knocked-out Panther V shows the foolishness of breaking cover on a clear day.

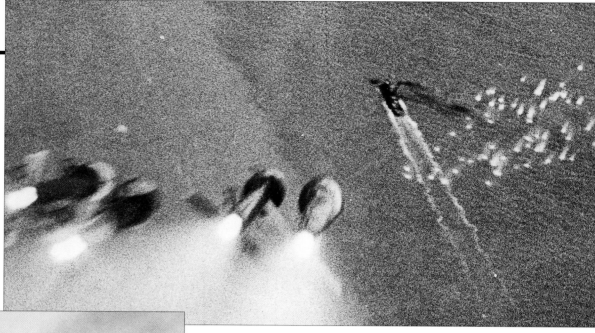

Right: A battery of rockets from a Typhoon streak towards a Dutch barge. Typhoons were also tasked with attacking targets of opportunity, and coastal shipping came under that ambit as well as motor transport and tanks. The splashes are caused by sighting rounds from the Typhoon's cannon.

Below: The standard 27.2-kg (60-lb) RP (rocket projectile) as fitted to the Typhoon was guaranteed to destroy soft-skinned and lightly-armoured vehicles with one hit, which was usually sufficient to disable a main battle tank. The Typhoon crews worked hard to support the frantic pace of operations in Normandy.

as they prepared for take-off on their first flights.

But many – and not just in the RAF – became great supporters of the Typhoon as a fighting machine, crediting the aircraft with playing a decisive role in the destruction of the German army.

"The Typhoon was a wonderful war machine, with its formidable armament of four 20-mm cannon firing more than 600 rounds per minute and its level top speed of about 410 mph. A new kind of warfare was found for this monster: low-level fighter sweeps, low-level attack, dive-bombing and, later, equipped with eight 60-lb rockets, as an assault aircraft specialising in ground attack. As such it was the most successful tank and armour buster ever produced.

"Working the 'Cab Rank' system, the Typhoons were able to respond in minutes to any call from the forward troops. 'Cab Rank' consisted of direct radio liaison between a controller pilot advancing with the attacking ground troops, and the airborne Typhoons, the ground-based controller calling down one or more aircraft from the 'Cab Rank'. The guidance became so accurate and the description so precise that a low-level aircraft could pinpoint targets as small as a sniper or a Panzer hidden in a thicket.

"Short of the atomic bomb, the war still had to be won by classic means – by beating the enemy on the ground and by occupation of his territory. It was by destroying most of the German armoured forces that the 2nd Allied Tactical Air Forces made the balance tip in our favour during and after the Normandy battle."

From June to September 1944, an average of 380 Typhoons made some 35,000 sorties, launching 265,000 rockets and firing 13,000,000 20-mm shells. This was at the cost of 243 Typhoons lost, 173 severely damaged and 75 less badly hit by flak. During the same period over 1,000 German tanks out of 3,000 (reinforcements included) were put out of action by Typhoons. They destroyed 12,000 to 15,000 vehicles, over 50 trains, about 30 barge-bridges and a great many gun positions. Thousands of German soldiers fell to their fire.

Left: From 11 July, No. 257 Squadron was fully engaged in the Normandy battles with its Typhoon Mk IBs. Apart from a brief interlude with rockets, the squadron operated in the bombing role until disbanded in March 1945. Ground-attack sorties were punishing on aircraft and pilots alike and the replacement rate for both was very high.

British Flat Tops

1940–1945

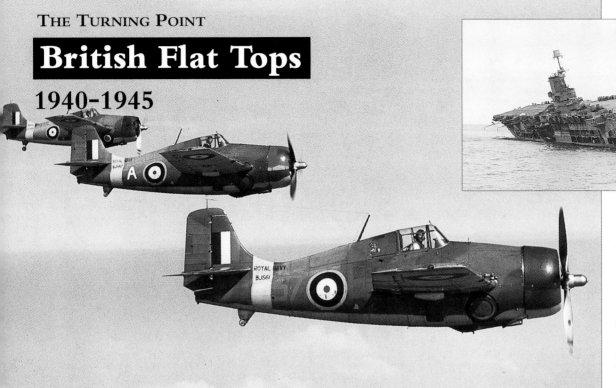

Above: German wartime radio claimed many times to have sunk the British carrier HMS Ark Royal. On 12 November 1941, while returning to Gibraltar after flying off aircraft reinforcements for Malta, she was torpedoed by U-boat U-81 and sank some 14 hours later.

Left: The Grumman Martlet Mk I first entered FAA service with No. 804 Squadron in July 1940, replacing Sea Gladiators. Originally ordered by the French, these aircraft had fixed wings, a Wright Cyclone engine and four guns.

The British, American and Japanese navies made considerable use of aircraft-carriers throughout World War II, indeed the survival of the three US fleet carriers of the Pacific Fleet at the time of the attack on Pearl Harbor was counted as of major importance in America's ability to countenance a successful war against Japan. And it was the US Navy and that of Japan which fought the great set-piece naval battles involving the aircraft-carrier in the role of capital ship.

The UK, on the other hand, after desultory and generally costly use of carriers in isolation on anti-submarine work and in support of land operations, lost both the old *Glorious* and *Courageous* in the first nine months of the war, neither as a direct result of air action. In due course the Royal Navy came to employ the much smaller escort carriers and the

Below: Equipping eight operational squadrons by mid-1941, the Fairey Fulmar was to play a vital and successful role in the shadowing of the German battleship Bismarck. Here a Fulmar lands on HMS Victorious after a patrol of the shipping lanes.

hybrid merchant aircraft carriers in the role of anti-submarine convoy escort, their complements of but a dozen or so aircraft being deemed adequate for the strictly limited-range patrols. By the end of 1940 the Royal Navy possessed a total of seven fleet carriers, comprising the veteran *Argus*, *Furious*, *Eagle* and *Hermes*, and the modern *Ark Royal*, *Illustrious* and *Formidable*; to these were to be added the *Victorious* and *Indomitable* in 1941, and the *Implacable* and *Indefatigable* (all of 23369 tonnes/23,000 tons) in 1944.

MALTA SUPPLIED

One of the first vital tasks undertaken by the British carriers was the reinforcement of Malta and the Middle East with the transporting of crated aircraft to Takoradi in West Africa after Italy's entry into the war in 1940; the frequent sailing of carriers with fighters for Malta involved no fewer than 25 operations before the end of 1942, the *Argus* making five voyages, the *Ark Royal* 12, the *Furious* seven, the *Victorious* one and the *Eagle* nine (as well as two by the American *Wasp*), delivering a total of 718 aircraft.

The first outstanding action by

Above: Fairey designed the Albacore as a replacement for the Swordfish, though the 'Stringbag' was to outlive its intended successor, FAA pilots preferring the older machine.

Right: Designed as a torpedo-bomber, the Grumman Avenger was, in FAA service, also used to drop mines and depth bombs.

Fighters of the Fleet

The first seaborne Sea Hurricanes were the CAM-ship-based 'Catafighters'. Arrester hook fitted Mk IBs for the carriers followed, though these were soon replaced by Seafires. The FAA formed its first Corsair squadron in 1943; eight units were so equipped by the end of the year. The first examples of the Grumman Wildcat in FAA service had been ordered by France and were known as Martlets.

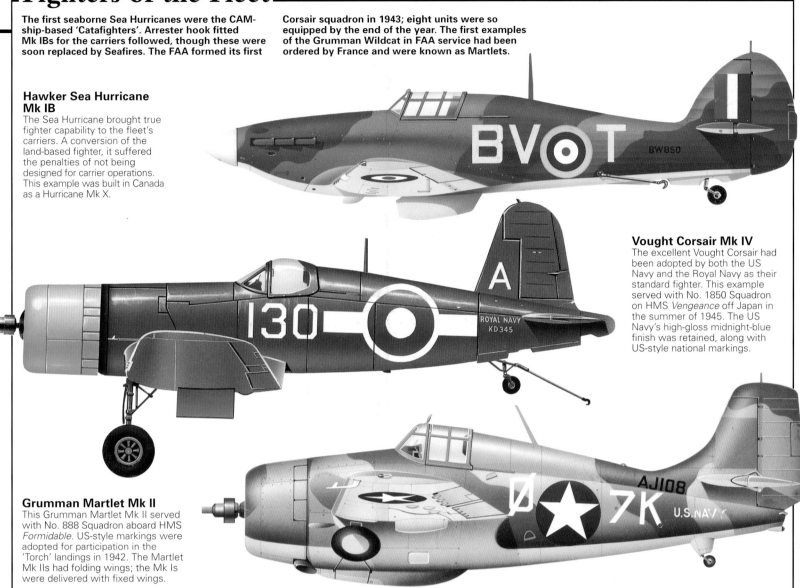

Hawker Sea Hurricane Mk IB
The Sea Hurricane brought true fighter capability to the fleet's carriers. A conversion of the land-based fighter, it suffered the penalties of not being designed for carrier operations. This example was built in Canada as a Hurricane Mk X.

Vought Corsair Mk IV
The excellent Vought Corsair had been adopted by both the US Navy and the Royal Navy as their standard fighter. This example served with No. 1850 Squadron on HMS *Vengeance* off Japan in the summer of 1945. The US Navy's high-gloss midnight-blue finish was retained, along with US-style national markings.

Grumman Martlet Mk II
This Grumman Martlet Mk II served with No. 888 Squadron aboard HMS *Formidable*. US-style markings were adopted for participation in the 'Torch' landings in 1942. The Martlet Mk IIs had folding wings; the Mk Is were delivered with fixed wings.

and destroying her steering, thereby allowing the British heavy ships to close their quarry. On 13 November that year *Ark Royal* was torpedoed by a U-boat in the Mediterranean and sank on the following day while under tow.

The air war in the Mediterranean involved British carriers in their most hazardous and spectacular fighting, particularly while protecting the Malta convoys. A total of 13 such convoys was sailed either from Gibraltar or Alexandria between

Left: A Fleet Air Arm Grumman Martlet II being 'waved down' on the deck of a Royal Navy carrier. The Martlet had a distinguished service record, gaining immense respect from pilots for its manoeuvrability, reliability and potent firepower.

Below: In the heat of the Mediterranean circa 1942, Martlets, Albacores and Sea Hurricane Mk IBs are seen aboard an unidentified RN carrier. Sea Hurricane Mk IBs were converted from Hurricane Mks I, IIA and IIB as well as a few Canadian-built Mk Xs and XIIs.

carrier-borne aircraft of the Royal Navy was the brilliantly executed night attack by 21 Swordfish led by Lieutenant Commander Kenneth Williamson from the *Illustrious* on 11/12 November 1940 against the Italian fleet at Taranto harbour. Three of Italy's six battleships were sunk or crippled for a cost of two aircraft, an action that restored the balance of naval power in the Mediterranean following the elimination of the French fleet at Dakar.

In the famous naval action in the North Atlantic which finally brought about destruction of the German battleship *Bismarck*, Swordfish from the *Ark Royal* on 26 May 1941 scored two vital torpedo hits on the enemy ship, slowing her

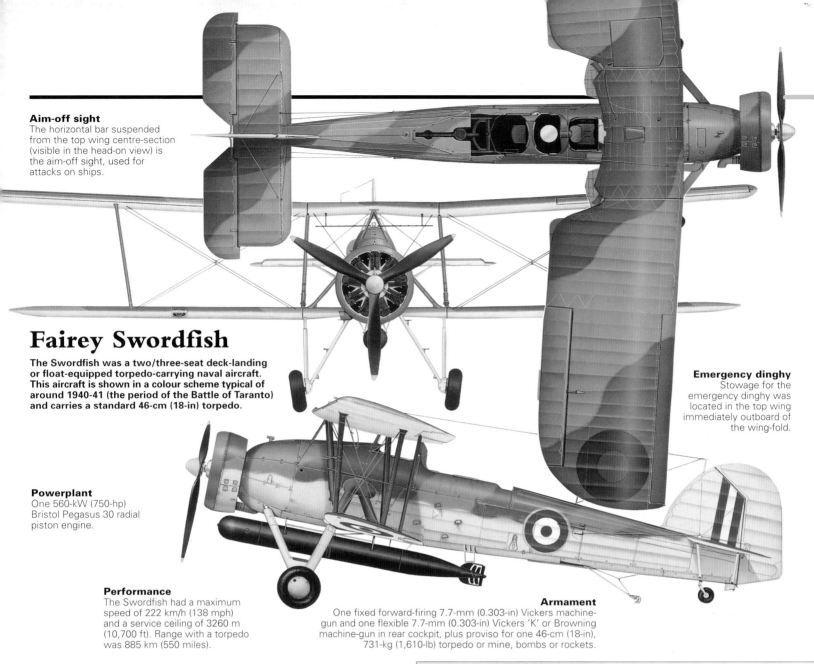

Fairey Swordfish

The Swordfish was a two/three-seat deck-landing or float-equipped torpedo-carrying naval aircraft. This aircraft is shown in a colour scheme typical of around 1940-41 (the period of the Battle of Taranto) and carries a standard 46-cm (18-in) torpedo.

Aim-off sight
The horizontal bar suspended from the top wing centre-section (visible in the head-on view) is the aim-off sight, used for attacks on ships.

Emergency dinghy
Stowage for the emergency dinghy was located in the top wing immediately outboard of the wing-fold.

Powerplant
One 560-kW (750-hp) Bristol Pegasus 30 radial piston engine.

Performance
The Swordfish had a maximum speed of 222 km/h (138 mph) and a service ceiling of 3260 m (10,700 ft). Range with a torpedo was 885 km (550 miles).

Armament
One fixed forward-firing 7.7-mm (0.303-in) Vickers machine-gun and one flexible 7.7-mm (0.303-in) Vickers 'K' or Browning machine-gun in rear cockpit, plus proviso for one 46-cm (18-in), 731-kg (1,610-lb) torpedo or mine, bombs or rockets.

August 1940 and January 1943, eight of them including carriers in their escort. Most of their sailings provoked enemy air action, and of the 80 merchant ships which set out 24 were sunk. The bitterest convoy action involving carriers was that of August 1942 when, in Operation 'Pedestal', 14 merchantmen were accompanied by no fewer than four carriers, two battleships, seven cruisers and 24 destroyers. The convoy had to run the gauntlet of mines, E-boats and U-boats, as well as more than 200 German and Italian bombers and torpedo bombers and, despite all the efforts of the pilots of the carrier-borne Sea Hurricanes and Wildcats (as well as up to 200 aircraft based on Malta itself), casualties were heavy, the carrier *Eagle* being sunk by a

Above: Seafire Mk IBs on the flight deck of a Royal Navy fleet carrier in 1943 – part of a batch of 48 conversions from Spitfire Mk VBs. Apart from the introduction of a retractable 'V' frame arrester hook, they were almost identical to their land-based counterparts.

Left: No less than 19 FAA squadrons received Corsairs, with a total of 1,977 being built for the Royal Navy. The long-range fuel tank on this Corsair Mk II has burst after coming adrift in a heavy landing, its contents catching fire.

U-boat and the *Indomitable* and *Victorious* being damaged; two cruisers, a destroyer and nine merchantmen were also sunk, and two cruisers and five merchantmen damaged.

For the most part the convoys that sailed to the Soviet Union past the North Cape from Iceland were protected by the small escort carriers, as were the merchant convoys which sailed into British ports from the Atlantic, their aircraft being mainly tasked with anti-submarine duties, although on some occasions they were launched to intercept shadowing enemy aircraft. Use of fleet carriers in the Atlantic was confined to covering the passage of important troop convoys, fleet carriers only occasionally being deployed against U-boats.

HERMES LOST

In the Far East the UK suffered an early loss when the *Hermes*, one of the oldest carriers afloat and the first to be designed as such from the outset, was sunk by Japanese carrier-borne dive bombers off Ceylon on 9 April 1942 without having taken any significant part in the war in the Far East. In the last year of the war the *Illustrious*, *Indefatigable*, *Indomitable* and *Victorious* formed the carrier element of Task Force 57,

Right: The Fairey Barracuda acquitted itself well in its exacting range of duties, more often used as a dive-bomber than a torpedo-bomber. The type saw service in the Atlantic and Pacific theatres.

Left: Prior to the raid of 3 April 1944 on the Tirpitz in Alten fjord, crews are briefed with the aid of a relief map of the area. Forty-two Barracudas were flown from Victorious and Furious in two groups with heavy fighter escort, and the battleship received 15 direct hits, killing 300 of the crew.

taking part in the operations off the Ryukus with strikes by Corsairs, Hellcats and Avengers. *Formidable* relieved *Illustrious*, and on 1 April 1945 *Indefatigable* was hit by a Japanese suicide aircraft, only her armoured deck preventing fatal damage. Both *Victorious* and *Formidable* were later hit by these weapons, and both were similarly saved from destruction.

Left: A No. 818 Squadron Fairey Swordfish Mk II, one of the main Blackburn-built production batch, aboard escort carrier HMS Tracker. Swordfish were widely used from the relatively small escort carriers, particularly in the North Atlantic.

Torpedo-bombers

An attempt to replace the venerable Swordfish, the Fairey Albacore was always overshadowed by its illustrious forebear. Despite its enclosed cockpit, it was never as popular with its crews.

Grumman's TBF, which served with distinction in US Navy service in the Pacific, was made available under Lend-Lease arrangements from 1943. Until January 1944 it was known as the 'Tarpon'.

Fairey Albacore
Though not as well-known as the Swordfish, Albacores performed usefully, especially in the Mediterranean. Mid-1942 saw the peak in Albacore operations, with no fewer than 15 squadrons equipped aboard carriers protecting convoys to Russia as well as in the Indian Ocean and Mediterranean.

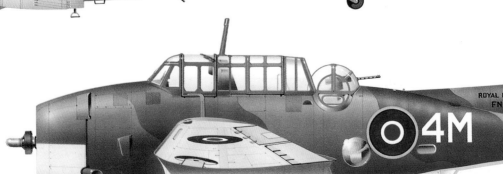

Grumman Avenger Mk I
A total of 402 Grumman TBF-1Bs (Avenger Mk Is) were acquired by the Royal Navy, with No. 832 Squadron being the first to equip in January 1943. They operated initially from escort carriers or shore bases on anti-submarine patrols. This aircraft served with No. 846 Squadron at Macrahanish in western Scotland.

Race to the Reich

AUGUST 1944 – MAY 1945

The destruction of German Forces south of Caen in mid-August 1944 was followed by the collapse of organised resistance throughout northern France as the Canadian 1st, British 2nd, and US 1st and 3rd Armies sped eastwards during the latter part of that month, Paris being liberated (from within) on 25 August. The British reached Brussels on 3 September and Antwerp on the following day. The US 3rd Army reached Verdun on 1 September, sweeping on to Metz and linking up with the US 7th Army as it advanced northwards having landed in the south of France on 15 August.

During this great onrush the Allied air forces were constantly in action, as their ground echelons strove to establish and re-establish fresh bases close-up behind the advancing armies. Before the crossing of the Seine, Mosquitoes, Mitchells, Mustangs, Bostons,

Above: The Thunderbolts of the 9th Air Force undertook the bulk of US fighter-bomber missions in Europe in the last months of the war, but the type was still a worthy dogfighter as the 18½ kill markings on this P-47D show. This was the mount of No. 353 Fighter Squadron's commanding officer Glenn Eagleston, who is receiving guidance from an airman as he taxies across his French base in late-1944.

Right: After the devastation wreaked on the French railway system in the build-up to D-Day, the Allied air force turned their attention to the German system. This marshalling yard near Limburg was flattened by 9th Air Force medium and light bombers. Some degree of service could often be resumed in a few days with emergency repairs.

Spitfires and Wellingtons of No. 2 Group attacked the ferries and barges at Rouen and elsewhere as German fighters attempted to interfere; these were engaged by No. 83 Group's Spitfires and the US 9th Air Force's P-47s and P-51s, which together claimed more than 100 of the enemy destroyed during the last week in August.

As RAF Bomber Command joined in attacks on German coastal garrisons from St Nazaire to Dunkirk, which had been bypassed by the advancing armies, the Dakotas, Stirlings and Halifaxes of RAF Transport Command were called on to mount the British airborne assault at Arnhem, while the C47s of the US IX Troop Carrier Command delivered the 82nd and 101st Airborne Division against targets on the Maas and Waal rivers. Unfortunately there were insufficient RAF aircraft available to carry the entire British 1st Airborne Division (and the Polish Parachute Brigade) in one journey and, while

Left: As with the other main US fighters, the P-51 and P-47, the Lockheed P-38 Lightning was employed as a fighter-bomber. In addition to conventional dive-bombing, the P-38 was used for formation level bombing guided by a modified aircraft with a bomb-aimer housed in the nose. There were several such variants, such as this P-38L with AN/APS-15 BTO (Bombing Through Overcast) radar.

Left: When Allied troops began to capture German airfields they made a number of surprising discoveries, including French Dewoitine D.520 fighters, used as operational trainers by the Luftwaffe. Captured US and British aircraft in airworthy condition were also found.

Below: The Messerschmitt 262 was potentially the best fighter of the war, but was not available in sufficient numbers when needed. By the time they entered service, even fuel for towing tractors was scarce.

the American forces duly secured their targets, the British attack at Arnhem failed despite the constant delivery by air of supplies. Unfortunately, as a result of recurring administrative problems, the 2nd Tactical Air Force was not brought fully into action to support the Arnhem action, and Nos 38 and 46 Groups lost 55 transport aircraft shot down and 320 others damaged by flak.

OVER THE RHINE

Elsewhere the Germans kept up attacks on the vital Nijmegen bridge over the Waal, now in British hands, sending among other aircraft the Mistel weapon; this comprised an unmanned Ju 88 bomber packed with explosives with a piloted fighter mounted on top, the pilot at the last minute releasing the bomber and guiding it towards its target. These attacks failed to hit the bridge and during the last week in September the Spitfires of No. 83 Group claimed the destruction of 46 German aircraft.

The airborne attacks in the north had been part of an Allied plan to cross the lower Rhine in force, liberate the Netherlands and outflank the Ruhr. Farther south, however,

the Americans were meeting with stiff resistance and by 18 November had reached a line running roughly along the German borders with Belgium, Luxembourg and France. Meanwhile the RAF had been engaged in supporting a major operation to clear the island of

Right: Although designed to replace the Bf 110 in the long-range fighter role, the high speed and heavy firepower of the Me 410B made it an effective interceptor. Unfortunately, it was not manoeuvrable enough to shake-off Allied escort fighters.

Walcheren at the entrance to the Scheldt, thereby opening up the great sea port of Antwerp. In attacks which lasted from 3 October to 8 November Bomber Command attacked gun batteries and dykes, dropping almost 9000 tonnes of bombs as the 2nd Tactical Air Force flew some 10,000 sorties, dropped 1500 tonnes of bombs and fired 11,600 rockets.

On 16 December the 5th and 6th Panzer Armies, assisted by bad weather and the element of surprise, attacked in the Ardennes between the US 9th and 7th Armies, and within a week had penetrated some 96 km (60 miles). The poor weather prevented large-scale air action and it was without significant air support that the Americans were eventually able to counter-attack and crush the German attack. Among the enemy

Reich defenders

As the war came to its inevitable conclusion in Europe, German aircraft designers came up with ever more outrageous fighter and interceptor designs, a few of which reached service. Most units, however, remained equipped with the old stalwarts – the Bf 109 and the Fw 190. By 1945 even the latest versions of both were outclassed in the hands of all but the few remaining expert pilots.

Messerschmitt Bf 109K
The last of all the many Messerschmitt 109 variants to see service in any numbers with the Luftwaffe was the pressurised K-4. This variant served with only a few units such as I/JG 27 based at Rheine in December 1944.

Focke-Wulf Fw 190A
The A-8 version of the famous Focke-Wulf fighter was optimised for the ground-attack role. By late-1944, fighter units had a mainly defensive role, as evidenced by this I/JG 1 machine based at Twenthe, the Netherlands in December 1944.

Engine
Unlike previous Fw 190 models which were powered by the BMW 801 radial, the D series were fitted with the liquid-cooled Jumo 213, giving 1670 kW (2,242 hp) at sea level. The unusual annular radiator allowed a low-drag airframe with the same frontal area as the Fw 190A-G series.

Focke Wulf Fw 190D-9

The last major variant of the successful Fw 190 series, the D-9 had many features of the later Ta 152s, such as the Jumo engine, but retained the short wing of earlier models. Regarded as an 'emergency solution' until the Ta 152 could enter service, the D-9 was in fact superior to most fighters of its time and built in reasonable quantity.

Armament
Originally, the D-9s were armed with a pair of 20-mm MG 151 cannon in the wings and a pair of 7.9-mm (0.31-in) MG 17 machine guns above the engine, all guns firing through the propeller arc. Later, the wing cannon were removed and the fuselage guns replaced with 13-mm (0.51-in) MG-131 machine guns.

Undercarriage
The Fw 190 featured an outboard-mounted, inward-retracting main undercarriage layout. This design corrected one of the main faults of the Messerschmitt 109 (and the Spitfire), namely tricky ground-handling characteristics of the narrow-track outward-retracting landing gear.

Unit
This particular unit served with the Third Gruppe of Jagdgeschwader 6 (III/JG 6) at Welzow in March 1945, one of a number of units to receive the type before the end of the war. The coloured fuselage bands signified aircraft assigned to home defence.

Left: The Hawker Tempest supplanted the Typhoon (from which it was developed) in many squadrons from the Spring of 1944. Tempests were utilised mainly as fighters over Europe and on air defence (anti-V-1) duties in England.

Below: British paratroops await take-off in a Dakota for the ill-fated Arnhem landings, 17 September 1944. Operation 'Market Garden' was nearly a success but suffered from poor co-ordination and a lack of air support.

aircraft that did appear were some of the new bomber versions of the Me 262 jets.

The bad weather that had dogged Allied air operations during the Ardennes attack improved gradually during the last few days of 1944, and Allied offensive action by the 2nd Tactical Air Force was resumed. However, unsuspected by

British and American intelligence, the Luftwaffe had for some weeks been planning a great setpiece operation against the RAF and USAAF bases in northern Europe, the OKL believing that sufficient destruction could be caused to severely disrupt Allied operations to buy time to reorganise the defence of Germany. After assembling some 800 fighters

Above: The introduction of the longer-ranged bubble-canopy P-51D spelled the end for the Luftwaffe fighter force as serious opposition. The pilot of this P-51, 2nd Lieutenant Urban Drew of the 361st Fighter Group shot down a pair of Me 262s on the same day in the last weeks of the war.

Left: The skies over Germany were no place for a lone Luftwaffe fighter in the Spring of 1945. This Fw 190 has been caught at low level by an American fighter, whose gun camera records the fatal hits (probably on the auxiliary fuel tank), and its destruction.

and 11 the bases at Asch, St Trond and Le Culot, and JG 53 the base at MetzFrescaty. Surprise was almost universal as the attacks came in soon after 09.00 hours. Considerable damage was caused and about 500 Allied aircraft were destroyed or later scrapped but, after the defences had recovered from the shock, about 300 German aircraft were shot down or crashed on the way home. But whereas the Allies were able to replace their losses within a few days (relatively few aircrew were killed), the German losses, which included some 230 airmen, were little short of disastrous. Indeed the folly of the operation was voiced by many senior German commanders, but they were confronting Nazi leaders fanatically blind to the realities of unquenchable Allied air supremacy and the inevitable grounding of the Luftwaffe through lack of fuel, just four months away.

and fighter-bombers of all types (including Me 262 and Ar 234 jets) from units all over the Reich into the attack, Operation 'Bodenplatte' (Baseplate), was launched soon after first light on New Year's Day 1945, JG 1, 3, 6, 26, 27 and 77 attacking bases at Volkel, GilzeRijen, Eindhoven, Brussels, Ursel, Antwerp and Woensdrecht, JG 2, 4

Right: During the 'Battle of the Bulge' poor weather hampered the Allied air forces and US troops in Bastonge were besieged. On 27 December the weather lifted enough for supply drops, as watched here by the crew of a US mobile AA gun.

High-speed Tempest

The Typhoon, which had originally been designed as a Spitfire replacement, proved a deadly ground attacker but a disappointment as a fighter. Its main faults were addressed in the Tempest, which introduced a new wing, improved engine and enlarged fin. The Tempest was one of the fastest aircraft of the war at low level and proved particularly suitable for intercepting 'Divers', or V-1 flying bombs.

Hawker Tempest Mk V

No. 486 (NZ) Squadron moved from Matlaske to the Continent in September 1944 after a successful period intercepting V-1 flying bombs. In addition to the two V-1 kills marked here, NV706 also shot down a Bf 109 in February 1945 in the hands of Squadron Leader K. G. Taylor-Cannon who scored four kills with the squadron.

HEAVY WEATHER OPERATIONS
In atrocious conditions A-20 Havocs of the 410th Bomb Group prepare to take-off from a 9th Air Force base in France on another mission against Axis positions.

Havoc Pilot into Battle

Of the three types of medium bomber in service with the USAAF in Europe at war's end, the least well-known was the Douglas A-20 Havoc, though it had carried out the first missions of the 8th Air Force in 1942. A single-pilot aircraft, it lacked the glamour of its contemporaries, but could take a lot of punishment and still brought crews home. Here, an A-20 pilot describes a particularly harrowing mission.

"**D**on't worry about the aircraft overhead," General Eisenhower told his troops in the outline briefing for Operation 'Overlord', the D-Day landings on the north coast of France, "they'll be ours." He was right. However, that did not necessarily mean that missions over France were a picnic for the crew involved.

"The instant we got within range of the guns, they started firing. We were getting light and heavy flak in intense and accurate doses. The only evasive action we could take was a constant weaving which at least made the ground gunners move their guns, if nothing else. McEvilly was talking to me all the time, pointing out the landmarks, so I'd know we were on course. The two gunners were pretty calm and cool, considering the amount of flak being sent up. Every few seconds I'd look the 'plane over, along with those of my wingmen, and even at this point, I could see quite a few holes in fuselages and wings.

"Suddenly McEvilly called out. 'Here's our IP' (Initial Point for the bomb run.) At the same instant I saw what I thought was our first box ahead of us, and also the target. At this point I was quite excited, as our navigation was working out perfectly despite poor visibility. The A-20s in front of us were catching hell and it was as bad to watch them as it

was to be in it ourselves. They had already settled down on their target run when the proverbial hell broke loose. A box barrage of 1,500 – 2,000 bursts of heavy flak came up just as they dropped their bombs and three ships burst into flames from direct hits. We couldn't watch them any longer, as we were near enough to begin our target run, and we had to settle down to straight and level flying.

"We were pretty silent now, as we had all seen what happened ahead of us, and were tightening ourselves up, expecting the worst. McEvilly was busy on his sight and took a quick look around. All aircraft were still there and flying OK, but my own aircraft had a lot of holes in it. Even as I watched I saw two four-inch holes appear in the left wing as if by magic. Mike was saying 'Steady – left – left –,' and then the long-awaited 'Bombs away'.

"With bombs gone, I made a steep diving turn left and had a chance to look around again. What I saw didn't please me. There were

Right: A formation of A-20s of the 647th Bomb Squadron, 410th Bomb Group with full 'invasion stripes' crosses the channel on its way to bomb yet another marshalling yard. All the Havocs are 'gun-nosed' except that at the top of the picture which carries a bomb-aimer, upon whose signal the rest of the formation would release their load.

at least 2,000 bursts of heavy flak filling the sky around us and light flak tracers were coming from every direction. I had decided to head for the deck and come out fast, but as we were diving down, the flak increased and McEvilly hollered down the intercom, 'I don't think we'll ever get down in one piece.'

"After taking a quick look around I decided he was right. Looking ahead I saw a low-lying bank of clouds so we headed for them, still weaving and bobbing like a broken field runner. We were at about 2,500 ft and Meldrum was shooting at the flak positions. I helped keep his morale up, and he swears he killed 'hundreds of them'.

Left: The main medium bomber used by the US air forces in the European theatre was the Martin B-26 Marauder. Despite a poor early reputation, the B-26 went on to have the lowest loss-rate of any US bomber. Medium-level operations exposed aircraft to the heaviest concentrations of flak, however, and many Marauders fell like this.

heavy and light flak the enemy bade us farewell for the afternoon.

"Out over the Channel we took stock. No-one was hit, though a piece of flak broke the glass in the nose where Mike had bent over his sight. Our A-20 was a sieve, but still flying with both engines still running. The left engine sounded rough and as all the engine instruments were shot out I couldn't tell much about it.

"As we neared the English coast, we had a conference to determine whether to make for the base or land at an emergency field and chose the latter as the most sensible answer.

"After making a wide circle of the field we came in on the approach. I didn't want to make any steep turns without a rudder, so it took us four minutes to circle the field. As we settled down into the field, we could see people watching. It was an emergency field and they figured something was likely to happen. There was a strong crosswind and I knew we would hit crooked as the 'plane couldn't be straightened up at the last instant. Suddenly we hit and started to bump along. I knew without looking that we had a flat tyre and warned the boys to hold on. We were moving left towards a steep embankment, but we stopped right on the edge of it. I breathed a sigh of relief, got out and wanted to kiss the ground."

"It was at about this point that I felt my rudder pedals swing free and informed the boys that my rudder pedals were out. The A-20 was flying pretty well though and we were just going into the cloud bank when Hyroad told me that one of our 'planes appeared to be going down or at least had dropped out of formation.

"An important point I forgot to mention is that we got a good look at the target as we turned away and we had hit it squarely. At this time, however, we were too busy to be elated over that.

"The cloud cover was working swell, as it was thick enough to screen us but thin enough for us to keep our formation. Suddenly, however, we ran smack through some heavy clouds and got separated from all but one A-20. As I checked my aircraft over I noticed oil pressure was dropping and at the same time my fuel pressure was low. This spelled single engine operation to me, which on instruments, is rather difficult, and with no rudder is next to impossible. I

checked my trim tab and found it OK. I warned McEvilly and the gunners to be ready to jump at an instant's notice. If the trim tab didn't compensate for the rudder I'd have to cut the good engine and abandon ship.

"As if we didn't have enough trouble, we started getting ice. In less than a minute, we had an inch of it on the wings and the ship was feeling heavy. But by this time I decided the engine would be OK for if it were going to stop it should have stopped already.

"Now we were emerging from the clouds and could see water ahead, but we were still over land.

Right: The Douglas A-26 Invader began to reach English-based combat units in September 1944, and equipped several bombardment groups by the end of hostilities. A number of nose configurations appeared on the A-26, including a glazed bombardiers nose, and four, six and eight-gun solid noses. This is a six-gun A-26B, also armed with dorsal and ventral twin-gun turrets and pairs of single-gun packs under each wing.

We had about 90 seconds to fly for the coast and they started shooting again. We were all mad by now so we flew right out in the open but did take the precaution of a little weaving. With a parting flurry of

Final Year in the East

MARCH 1944 - MAY 1945

Above: Colonel M.V. Avdyeyev leads a formation of 6th Guards Fighter Aviation Regiment Yak-9s on patrol over the Crimea in 1944. Some 16,000 Yak-9s were delivered, and these did more than any other aircraft to help turn the tide against the Germans.

Below: German assistance and a force of 350 modern combat aircraft, including this Bf 109G-6, were not enough to help Finland halt the Soviet steamroller, and the campaign in Finland ended in September 1944.

As the Soviet spring offensive of 1944 gained momentum in the Ukraine, the Luftwaffe faced an increasingly desperate task of attempting to cover the German army in its fighting withdrawals eastwards. To do so, the Jagdverband could field a daily average in March that year of about 330 serviceable fighters along the entire 1,800-mile (2897-km) front from northern Finland to the Black Sea. Opposing them were around 3,000 first-line Soviet aircraft, of which roughly half were modern fighters. The balance was to some extent redressed by the superlative quality and experience of many of the German pilots, but even among these the losses were very heavy. Nevertheless, on 23 March 1944 JG 54 was the second

Above: The Yak-3 established a tremendous reputation as the best dogfighter on the Eastern Front. Operating conditions were so appallingly harsh that only the toughest and simplest fighters could remain airworthy.

Right: The Focke-Wulf Fw 190A-5/U8 fighter-bomber, which appeared on the Eastern Front in 1943, could carry up to 2,205 lb (1000 kg) of bombs. Here one of the ground crew guides the pilot across the snow.

Luftwaffe fighter wing to destroy its 7,000th enemy aircraft (a milestone already reached by JG 51 'Mölders' in the previous September).

FINNS DEFEATED

By that month the Soviet armies had overrun all but the eastern quarter of the Ukraine and were attacking through a gap between the 1st and 4th Panzer Armies. In

the north on 10 June, the Soviets attacked the Finns and invaded the Karalian isthmus with the 21st and 23rd Armies, supported by 750 aircraft of the 13th Air Army. Bolstered by a tiny detachment of Luftwaffe pilots and aircraft, the

Ilmavoimat (Finnish air force) maintained a stout resistance with about 350 aircraft but, 10 days later, the key city-port of Viborg fell to the Soviets and on 4 September a ceasefire ended the campaign in Finland.

A measure of the scale of operations on the Eastern Front in mid-1944 may be gained by the fact that, compared with 54 divisions deployed against the Allies in France and Belgium, Germany had massed 164 divisions against the Soviets; yet compared with about 2,600 Luftwaffe aircraft in the East the Soviet air force now mustered a total of 13,000 first-line aircraft. Astonishingly, the Luftwaffe was able to display its traditional skill and when, in June 1944, the US 8th and 15th Air Forces began their shuttle bombing flights to Soviet bases, about 180 He 111s of KG 4,

Above: Luftwaffe pilot Captain Phillip achieved 213 victories on the Eastern Front. The emblems are II Group, I Group and III Group of JG 54 'Grunherz', Luftflotte 1.

Below: Supremely versatile and universally popular, the Focke-Wulf Fw 189 Uhu was essentially a low-altitude aircraft, befitting its tactical reconnaissance role.

Above: Taken in the latter part of 1944, this photo shows Il-2M3 two-seaters on the Eastern Front, which by this time had been pushed forward beyond the borders of the Soviet Union into Poland, Romania and other countries.

Below: Lavochkin's best wartime fighter was the La-7, distinguished by the smooth upper cowl lines. Like the Yak-3, the La-7 was exceptionally agile at low level, where most of the fighting on the Eastern Front took place.

Last of the Luftwaffe

By late 1944 the Luftwaffe was a shadow of its former self, facing superior aircraft, and even some better trained pilots on every front. The rapid introduction of new types and the assistance of new allies could do little to change the course of the war, and catastrophe followed calamity as the once-mighty Luftwaffe covered the Wehrmacht's retreat.

Messerschmitt Bf 109G-10
Messerschmitt Bf 109s were used throughout the entire Russian campaign. By 1944, the Bf 109G-10 was in action and these proved a challenge to Soviet pilots if flown well. Three years of war had taken their toll on the *experten* and the Jagdgruppen, and many Bf 109s were flown by less experienced pilots and units. This G-10 was flown by Kroat Jagdstaffel at Eichwalde, as denoted by the fuselage cross and fin shield.

Heinkel He 177A-5/R6
A Heinkel He 177A-5/R6 Greif operated by 1 Gruppe, KG 1 'Hindenburg' in May 1944. Led by Oberstleutnant Horst von Riesen, KG 1 assembled some 90 He 177s for attacks on Allied communications and military concentrations.

Arado Ar 232B-0
The ugly Arado Ar 232B-0 was a four-engined development of the twin-engined Ar 232A (of which only two prototypes were built). Nicknamed *Tausendfussler* (millipede), a small number served on the Eastern Front in 1944.

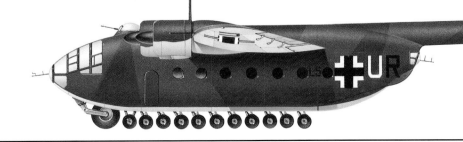

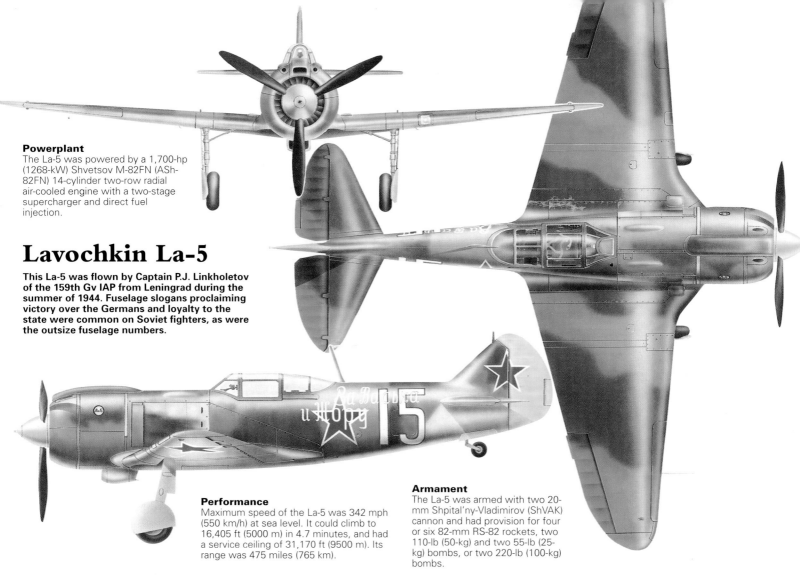

Powerplant
The La-5 was powered by a 1,700-hp (1268-kW) Shvetsov M-82FN (ASh-82FN) 14-cylinder two-row radial air-cooled engine with a two-stage supercharger and direct fuel injection.

Lavochkin La-5

This La-5 was flown by Captain P.J. Linkholetov of the 159th Gv IAP from Leningrad during the summer of 1944. Fuselage slogans proclaiming victory over the Germans and loyalty to the state were common on Soviet fighters, as were the outsize fuselage numbers.

Performance
Maximum speed of the La-5 was 342 mph (550 km/h) at sea level. It could climb to 16,405 ft (5000 m) in 4.7 minutes, and had a service ceiling of 31,170 ft (9500 m). Its range was 475 miles (765 km).

Armament
The La-5 was armed with two 20-mm Shpital'ny-Vladimirov (ShVAK) cannon and had provision for four or six 82-mm RS-82 rockets, two 110-lb (50-kg) and two 55-lb (25-kg) bombs, or two 220-lb (100-kg) bombs.

The long-nose Fw 190D-9 appeared on the Russian Front in early 1945 and restored some of the balance over the Yak-3 and La-7. Several were captured by the Soviet navy Baltic Fleet and used by them.

27 and 55 caught the American B-17s on the ground at Poltava on 22 June, destroying 47 of them as well as the base's fuel dump.

SOVIETS STORM THROUGH

The city of Vilna fell to the Soviet armies on 9 July, completing the recapture of Belorussia and opening the way for an advance into north-eastern Poland while, farther south, Marshal Konev's forces reached the Vistula 130 miles (210 km) south of Warsaw. At this point German resistance on the central front stiff-

ened and the swift advance by the Soviet armies temporarily over-extended their supply lines. The Soviets therefore switched the focus of their great offensive to the Balkans, and on 20 August two Soviet army groups, supported by more than 1,700 aircraft of the 5th and 17th Air Armies, launched an offensive on the Odessa front against Romania, where the puppet Axis government was overthrown three days later. Bulgaria capitulated on 8 September, but despite the loss of almost 20 German divisions and the capture of the Ploesti oilfields, the surviving Axis air forces in the Balkans (largely comprising the Luftwaffe's Luftflotten II and IV – the former redeployed from France in August – and the small

Hungarian air force) continued to fight desperately against the huge Soviet air forces.

HEAVY LOSSES

By December 1944 the Eastern Front extended from the mouth of the Niemen river on the Baltic coast to Warsaw and on to Budapest. During the previous six months the German army had suffered the loss of more than 800,000 men in the east and almost 400,000 in the west and south. The Soviets now fielded 55 armies and six tank armies, while their first-line aircraft strength had increased to more than 15,500, against which Germany could muster fewer than 2,000.

Following requests by the Americans, who had suffered some 40,000 casualties during the

Ardennes offensive late in December 1944 and sought relief from German pressure, the Soviets started their final winter offensive earlier than originally planned. On 13 January 1945 the drive opened in East Prussia but met with stubborn resistance at the fortress town of Konigsberg, efforts by the Soviet air force to assist being hampered by bad weather. On 17 January Warsaw was finally captured, and a fortnight later the 5th Shock Army and 2nd Guards Army crossed the frozen Oder river at Kustrin, only

Towards the end of 1943, the first Petlyakov Pe-2FTs left the assembly lines with new VK-105PF engines, the same as used for the Yak-3 and Yak-9. This gave the Pe-2FT a welcome increase in performance of 40 km/h.

RUSSIAN ACES

The great Soviet drive in the centre was held in two stages. The second offensive, known as the Lvov-Sandemii campaign, started on 13 July 1944. Mention should be made of the work of the 2nd VA. Ten units were given Gvdaya (Guards) titles, while 17 pilots became Heroes of the Soviet Union. From 1944, the standard of combat fighting of Soviet fighter pilots had steadily improved, and by the end of the war many had gained large scores.

Above: Alexander I. Pokryshkin was a leading ace in the Kuban campaign in 1943 flying P-39 Airacobras of N.V. Isayev's 16th GV IAP, then as a Captain. Promoted to Major, he became a full Colonel by 1945.

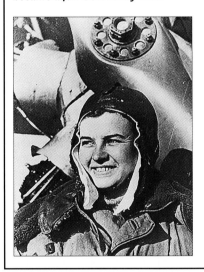

Below: Dimitri G. Glinka, seen here in 1943 and already an ace. By the end of the war he was credited with 50 'kills'.

Left: Pictured on the Second Belorussian Front in 1945, Lt Natasha Meklin of the Tamansky (Women's) Air Regiment made some 1,000 combat sorties during World War II.

Above: On the Second Belorussian Front in 1944, Soviet fighter pilot 1st Lt Kiselyov is pictured with the burnt out wreckage of his ninth downed enemy aircraft.

Right: Lt Colonel Ivan N. Kozhedub, the V-VS's leading ace, claimed the last of his 62 'kills' on 19 April 1945. Flying a Lavochkin La-7 with the 176 'Guards' IAP, Kozhedub destroyed 12 enemy aircraft, including an Me 262 jet fighter on 15 February 1945.

Below: Alexander Pokryshkin is congratulated after another successful aerial battle. By the end of the war he had been awarded the title 'Hero of the Soviet Union' three times.

Left: Production of the Il-4 long-range bomber lasted from 1936 until 1944. This line-up of new aircraft of the final version awaits delivery in 1944. Powered by 1,000-hp M-88B engines, the Il-4 achieved a maximum speed of 410 km/h.

about 50 miles (80 km) east of Berlin; to the southeast Soviet armies reached and invested Breslau.

The final three months of the war were characterised by increased savagery in the air as the shrinking perimeter of Hitler's Reich eased the problems of defence. The Luftwaffe even switched a large proportion of its surviving fighter forces (including JG 1, JG 3, JG 6,

Right: The best-known Red Air Force fighter unit (at least in the West) was the French-mannd 'Normandie' regiment, given the honour title 'Niemen' in 1944. After flying Yak-9s, the unit changed to the excellent Yak-3 (illustrated).

Victory in the Air

By 1945 the Luftwaffe had been beaten on all fronts. Yak-9s roamed at will, picking off young inexperienced German pilots (and some of the exhausted *experten*) while Il-2s supported Zhukhov's headlong rush on Berlin. Though crude and lightweight, Russia's combat aircraft were establishing a well-earned reputation for combat effectiveness.

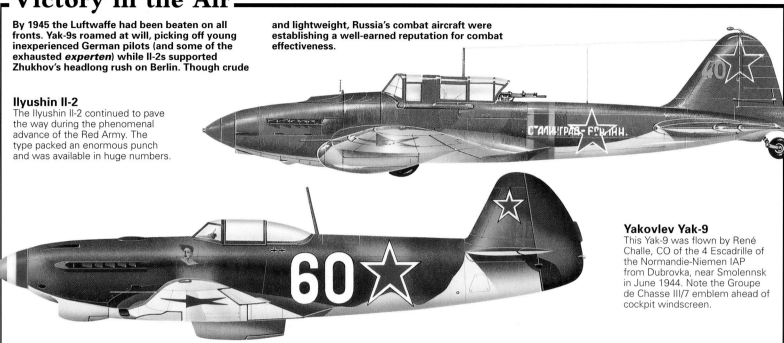

Ilyushin Il-2
The Ilyushin Il-2 continued to pave the way during the phenomenal advance of the Red Army. The type packed an enormous punch and was available in huge numbers.

Yakovlev Yak-9
This Yak-9 was flown by René Challe, CO of the 4 Escadrille of the Normandie-Niemen IAP from Dubrovka, near Smolennsk in June 1944. Note the Groupe de Chasse III/7 emblem ahead of cockpit windscreen.

JG 11 and JG 77) from the west and south to the east, believing that their pilots would stand a better chance of countering the Soviet air force despite the overwhelming odds. The German air force resorted to desperate measures to halt the advancing Soviets, employing the extraordinary Mistel composite aircraft in widespread attacks on the Soviet bridges and bridgeheads over the Oder and Vistula, and achieving a considerable measure of success.

As the Soviet armies fought their way through Berlin's streets early in May, the once-vaunted Luftwaffe lay scattered on its few remaining airfields, finally grounded without fuel and at the mercy of Allied bombers.

Above: Pilots of Schlachtgeschwader 2 'Immelmann' rest between missions. The Stab and II Gruppe used Fw 190As and Fs on the Russian Front. A few Fw 190D-9s were used right at the end.

Below: Throughout the war, the designation Tu-2S remained unchanged, despite modifications. Only 1,111 of this fast, popular aircraft were built – about one-tenth of Pe-2 production.

Above: A line-up of 1st Czechoslovak Fighter Regiment Lavochkin La-5FN fighters at Proskurov in the Ukraine on 11 September 1944. The regiment was formed with a nucleus of ex-RAF Czech pilots.

Below: The twin-engined Ar 232 V2. Because of the demands of Fw 190 production for BMW engines, most Ar 232s had lower-powered engines. Ar 232s of Transportflierstaffel 5 flew missions into Soviet territory.

Sporadic attacks were made against bridges on the Eastern Front, but heavy losses were suffered by the Mistels. Development continued with the combination of Ju 88G-10s (Mistel C) and H-4s (Mistel B) with the Fw 190A-8. Here an Fw 190 releases its Ju 88 missile, closely followed by a second combination.

Mistel attack

Using surplus Ju 88 night-fighters or bombers as makeshift guided missiles was just one of the desperate schemes attempted by the Luftwaffe during the final year of the war. A pilot tells his story.

"The Mistels were diving now, their airspeed indicators hovering around 600 km/h. The leading Oberfeldwebel turned into his final approach from the south and went into an even steeper dive, sending his speed up still further. He had to retrim the aircraft to counteract the increased forces acting on his controls, but the target, the railway bridge at Steinau, remained steady in his reflex sight.

"This was the most important part of the whole procedure, to keep the composite aircraft rock steady on the final target approach flight. Even the slightest movement on the controls affected the delicate mechanism of the gyroscopes controlling the automatic pilot. 'Flying on your nerves,' the pilots called it, discussing such missions to well-defended targets, but now, in action, there wasn't the time to think about it. Altitude, airspeed and target were the important things.

"The ideal release point was around a thousand metres from the target. At that distance the flying bomb was unlikely to miss. But at that range, neither were the light anti-aircraft gunners.

"The airspeed indicator was up to 650 km/h now, the Mistel in a steady high-speed dive, correctly trimmed and free of any acceleration. The autopilot was working perfectly, and the whole contraption could have been flown hands-off if necessary. But where was the AA fire we dreaded, and where were the other aircraft?

"I could see the bridge clearly now, make out its every detail. An iron girder structure, resting on pillars of solid masonry. To be sure of destroying it, the Mistel would have to hit one of these pillars, and that would need pinpoint precision and a fair bit of luck as well.

"In the sight I could see, framed, the bridge section on the left bank. A final slight correction, and the illuminated graticule and the pillar coincided exactly. Now! A slight pressure on the release button, the muffled sound of light detonations as the explosive bolts went, and then the controlling fighter was free again! A steep bank to the west, and then I could look around at the spot on the ground where I had aimed the flying bomb. An enormous fountain was climbing, climbing up into the sky. I couldn't decide whether it was water or mud, earth and more solid debris from the bridge structure itself.

"But there was little time for sightseeing, for now the Soviet anti-aircraft guns were firing like mad, and anyway a great cloud of smoke was billowing over the bridge, obscuring it from view. Suddenly, another Bf 109 appeared alongside. The initial cold shock, that it could have been an enemy fighter, gave way to joyous relief at having a comrade alongside for company and mutual protection. We both stuck up our thumbs. No problems!

"Neither of us cared exactly where we were. Out of habit we'd both pressed our stopwatches over the target, and now relied on spotting a railway line, a town or, better still, an Autobahn, to help us locate ourselves. We were both 'old foxes', and navigating in daylight, in good weather, over our own homeland was certainly no problem. And we'd both successfully flown our first live Mistel operation!"

The Einsatz-Staffel of IV Gruppe of KG 101 flew its first operation with the Mistel 1 pilotless missile on 24 June 1944, with the pilot of the Bf 109F-4 fighter aiming the Ju 88A-4 missile.

The Jet Goes to War

MAY 1944 – MAY 1945

Among the closely guarded secrets of the early part of the war was the work being done both in the UK and Germany on the gas turbine as a powerplant for aircraft. In particular, British intelligence was unaware that Germany had successfully flown a small research jet aeroplane, the Heinkel He 178, as

Left: The pilot climbs into a Messerschmitt Me 163B-1a at Bad Zwischenahn where it was flown by the trials and test unit Erprobungskommando 16 that accepted its first aircraft in May 1944 and pioneered the rocket plane's entry into service with the Luftwaffe.

early as 27 August 1939, five days before the outbreak of World War II. For years parallel work had been carried out by Frank Whittle in the UK but, because of lack of official interest, his work had been slow and underfinanced. It was not until May 1941 that the first British research jet, the Gloster E.28/39, powered by a Whittle

Above: A Rolls-Royce Welland-powered Gloster Meteor Mk I, the 11th production aircraft, that was delivered to No. 616 Squadron in July 1944. The Meteor was the only Allied jet to see action in the war.

engine, was first flown.

In the belief that the war would be short-lived, work on the development of an operational jet

Jet and rocket pioneers

German engineers made giant strides with turbojet and rocket propulsion. The Me 163 suffered many accidents resulting from its lethal fuel mixture but was mildly successful as an interceptor. The

He 162 was an abortive attempt to provide a mass-produced jet fighter and was too late for service. The Ar 234 was the world's first jet bomber. Its service entry was delayed by production problems.

Messerschmitt Me 163B
This Komet saw service with JG 400 at Brandis. It was one of 279 aircraft delivered to the Luftwaffe and had two 30-mm Rheinmetall MK 108 cannon fitted in the wing roots, each with 60 rounds of ammunition carried in the top of the fuselage.

Heinkel He 162A
Powered by the improved BMW 003E-1 turbojet, this He 162A-2 Salamander was flown by II/JG 1 at Leck in the spring of 1945. For operations, 50 aircraft were reorganised as part of the Einsatz Gruppe I/JG 1. No encounters with Allied aircraft were confirmed before the war ended.

Arado Ar 234B
Ar 234B Blitz reconnaissance bombers were powered by two Junkers Jumo 004B turbojets. This aircraft, carrying bombs under its engine nacelles, was flown by 9/KG 76 in February 1945. Ar 234s made high-level reconnaissance flights over England, beyond the reach of fighters.

Below: A Messerschmitt Me 262A-1a Schwalbe of EJG 2. In the interceptor role the twin-jet could carry 24 R4M rockets under its wings, in addition to the four built-in 30-mm MK 108 cannon. It had 100 rounds for the upper guns and 80 for the lower pair, giving formidable firepower.

METEOR VERSUS FLYING BOMB
Meteor Mk Is joined the battle against the 'Doodlebugs' on 27 July 1944, when an aircraft from No. 616 Squadron flew its first successful operational sortie from RAF Manston, Kent.

aircraft in Germany went ahead relatively slowly until 1940, the Heinkel company pushing on with development of its pioneer HeS 3b and HeS 6 turbojets. Discouraged by the problems with single-engine installation, however, the company ventured to produce a twin-jet fighter, the He 280, the first prototype of which, powered by two 500-kg (1,102-lb) thrust HeS 8 (109-006) turbojets, was flown on 2 April 1941. This design was not adopted by RLM for production and is of interest if only to illustrate

the weight of interest by the German aircraft industry in jet power, while the UK was still only taking its first faltering steps in the concept.

Meanwhile the Messerschmitt company had also opted for a twin-jet layout for a fighter. This turbojet fighter, the Me 262, was designed around a pair of Junkers 109-004A turbojets, of which the first example was bench-run in November 1940. Because flight engines were not available in time, the first Me 262 prototype was flown under piston

Below: For take-off the Arado Ar 234A, the first version of the Blitz, sat on a large trolley. This could be steered by the pilot using its nosewheel; brakes were fitted to the mainwheels. Once it reached flying speed the trolley was released. A retractable skid and outriggers were used for landing.

Right: A Messerschmitt Me 163B-1a receiving hydrogen peroxide (T-stoff) fuel for its Hellmuth Walter RII-211 rocket motor. It could carry only enough fuel for six minutes at full throttle after which it would have to glide back to its base – leaving no margin for error by the pilot.

Left: An Me 163B takes off, jettisoning its take-off dolly. If jettisoned too early this could bounce back up into the departing Komet; sometimes they refused to release at all. However, compared with the hazards of landing on the aircraft's retractable skid, take-offs were relatively safe.

Right: JG 400, based at Brandis in 1944, carried the famous badge depicting a 'rocket-powered flea' and the inscription 'Wie ein floh – aber Oho!' (Only a flea – but Oho!) on the noses of its Me 163B-1as. JG 400 recorded nine Allied bomber kills, including two probables.

engine power on 18 April 1941, and it was not until 15 March 1942 that a Messerschmitt Me 262 was flown under all-jet power, being fitted with a pair of 840-kg (1,852-lb) thrust Junkers 109-004A-0 turbojets. By October that year 60 Me 262s had been ordered for use as development aircraft. From the fifth aircraft onwards a nosewheel landing gear arrangement was adopted in place of the tailwheel type previously used.

It was not until November 1943 that any urgency was afforded to the Me 262 programme, and it was Hitler himself who, despite protests from the Luftwaffe, insisted that the aircraft should go ahead, but only as a bomber which he assumed to be

capable of carrying a 500-kg (1,102-lb) bomb to England. Nevertheless, Messerschmitt continued also to press ahead with a fighter version armed with four 30-mm cannon, and during the summer of 1944 the first pre-production Me 262A-0s were delivered to Erprobungsstelle Rechlin for service trials, the fighter version being named the Schwalbe (swallow) and the bomber the Sturmvogel (stormbird). The first operational fighter unit, Kommando Nowotny (led by the fighter ace Major Walter

Above: This Me 262A-1a was flown by III Gruppe of Ergänzungs-Jagdgeschwader 2. The conversion unit, formed on 2 November 1944 at Lechfeld, flew many sorties against Allied aircraft in the spring of 1945. Leutnant Bell downed a P-38 Lightning with this particular aircraft on 21 March 1945.

Nowotny), was formed at Achmer and Hesepe on 3 October 1944 with about 20 Me 262A fighters for defence against the American daylight heavy bombers. Although the appearance of the new jets caused consternation among the American crews, the early jets achieved poor

Above: Messerschmitt AG built no fewer than 70 pre-production Me 163Bs at Regensburg, all assigned to particular operational or mechanical problems. The most dangerous phase of flight was the landing, which had to be perfect every time. Here the 35th Me 163B, coded GH+IN, glides safely to a halt on its skid.

Right: Gloster Meteor F.Mk III EE274 operating with No. 616 Squadron at B.58 Melsbroek, Belgium early in 1945. Deliveries of these more reliable Welland-powered Meteors to the RAF commenced on 18 December 1944 and a No. 616 detachment joined the 2nd Tactical Air Force in Belgium in January.

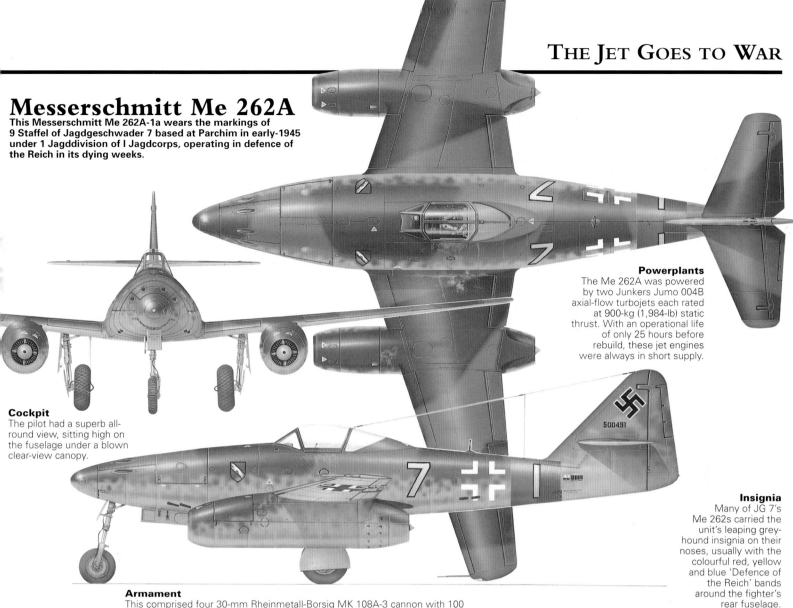

Messerschmitt Me 262A

This Messerschmitt Me 262A-1a wears the markings of 9 Staffel of Jagdgeschwader 7 based at Parchim in early-1945 under 1 Jagddivision of I Jagdcorps, operating in defence of the Reich in its dying weeks.

Powerplants
The Me 262A was powered by two Junkers Jumo 004B axial-flow turbojets each rated at 900-kg (1,984-lb) static thrust. With an operational life of only 25 hours before rebuild, these jet engines were always in short supply.

Cockpit
The pilot had a superb all-round view, sitting high on the fuselage under a blown clear-view canopy.

Insignia
Many of JG 7's Me 262s carried the unit's leaping grey-hound insignia on their noses, usually with the colourful red, yellow and blue 'Defence of the Reich' bands around the fighter's rear fuselage.

Armament
This comprised four 30-mm Rheinmetall-Borsig MK 108A-3 cannon with 100 rounds per gun for the upper pair and 80 rounds for the lower guns, aimed with a Revi 16B gunsight or Askania EZ42 gyro-stabilised sight. It also had provision for 12 R4M air-to-air rocket projectiles under each wing.

*Left: While an Me 262 gets close in behind a **USAAF P-51 Mustang**, another P-51 bears down on the less manoeuvrable jet fighter, in this gun-camera photograph. The Mustangs were escorting heavy bombers on a raid over **Germany**.*

Below: Operated by the German Aviation Experimental Establishment (DVL) in April 1944 for high-speed testing and engine trials, this Me 262 was in fact the first prototype to fly on turbojet power alone on 18 July 1942. It was written off on 12 September 1944 following an Allied air raid.

results because of their sluggish acceleration after pilots had been cruising slowly to increase patrol time. When Nowotny was killed on 8 November a new unit, JG 7, came into being, and early in 1945 another unit, Jagdverband 44 commanded by General Adolf Galland and crewed by some of the Luftwaffe's top fighter pilots (including Barkhorn, Steinhoff, Lützow and Späte) was formed. Although lack of fuel and poor serviceability reduced the average airworthy strength of this unit to no

Above: This Me 163B-1a, under tow from a 'Scheuschlepper' tug, carries the colour scheme adopted by JG 400 Erganzungsstaffel, the Komet training squadron based at Brandis. Operating the aircraft with its highly volatile fuel caused many problems for this training unit.

more than about six aircraft, JV 44 destroyed more than 40 Allied aircraft in about a month.

JET DEFENDERS

Before the end of the war Me 262 fighters equipped about half a

Above: A Heinkel He 162A at speed showing clearly the turned-down wingtips first introduced to overcome manoeuvrability problems. The aircraft had such difficult handling characteristics that even experienced fighter pilots found it an unforgiving handful to fly.

widespread use which could have threatened the continuation of the heavy American daylight bomber offensive in the last year of the war. They were not immune to attack from Allied fighters, particularly in the hands of experienced pilots, and there were occasions when Tempest and P-51 pilots succeeded in downing the enemy jets.

Despite its late start, the RAF introduced the Meteor Mk 1 twin-jet fighter into service (with No. 616 Squadron) in July 1944, before the first fully-operational Luftwaffe jet fighter unit was formed. Benefiting from British jet research, the Americans too had produced a jet fighter – the Lockheed P-80 Shooting Star. By VE-Day two examples were being readied for combat in Italy and two had reached England.

However, despite these developments there was no jet-versus-jet combat in World War II.

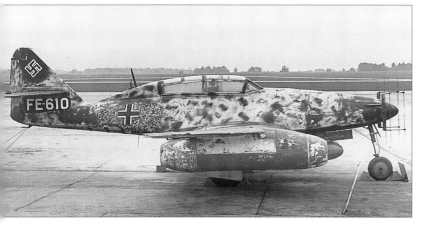

Below: This two-seat Me 262B-1a/U1 under test in the USA after the war. It had been captured after service with 10/NJG 11. Its armament was two 30-mm MK 108A-3s and two 20-mm MG 151/20 cannon. The air interception radar in the nose was a FuG 218 (Neptun V).

which had been equally protracted, but which also entered service on a limited scale) undoubtedly caused some concern to the Allies on account of their very high speed and heavy armament, Hitler's interference certainly prevented their

Below: An Me 262A 'Schwalbe' captured intact by advancing American troops on 18 April 1945. Except for a damaged undercarriage it was fairly intact. Partly hidden in a wood, it was fuelled and its guns were loaded. Over the period from March 1944 to 20 April 1945 the Luftwaffe received 1,433 Me 262s.

dozen Gruppen, including some night-fighter Staffeln whose two-seat radar-equipped Me 262B-1a/U1 aircraft were used in the night defence of Berlin in the last weeks of the war. Bomber versions of the Me 262 also entered service alongside another German jet bomber, the Arado Ar 234, an exceptionally 'clean' twin-jet aircraft which was also used to fly reconnaissance missions at up to 12250 m (40,200 ft) over the

UK and Italy without any fear of interception by Allied fighters.

Although the appearance of these German jet aircraft (as well as the rocket-powered Messerschmitt Me 163 Komet, development of

Right: The adoption of a tricycle undercarriage on the improved Arado Ar 234B enabled bombs to be carried under the fuselage centre-section. This aircraft has a 1000-kg (2,200-lb) SC1000 'Hermann' bomb used for the attacks on the Remagen bridges early in 1945.

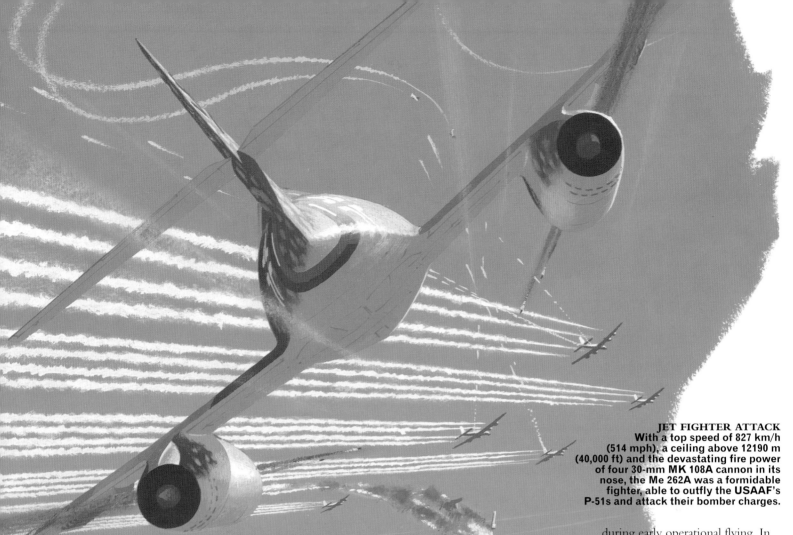

Into Combat

Had it not been for Hitler's demand that the Messerschmitt Me 262 be developed as a bomber, the Allies would have faced a much more devastating adversary in a high-performance air defence fighter. Erprobungskommando 262 evaluated the new aircraft operationally in the fighter role from mid-1944. Leutnant 'Quax' Schnoerrer of EKdo 262 recounts his early experiences.

"When I took off with my mob on 21 March, I thought it was to go against a large American force attacking the Leipzig/Dresden area. The radio jamming was particularly heavy that day and as a result communication was just about impossible. At 24,000 ft and still south of Dresden, I came upon a lone B-17 Flying Fortress flying east at the same altitude as the main force but 16 miles off to the side and four behind. It had four P-51 Mustangs as its escort and it seemed to me that it must be on some special mission. I decided to have a go at it.

"I made a pass close beneath the Mustangs, who followed my lads away, trailing black smoke. That meant they were flying at full throttle. I looked down at the airspeed indicator. Plenty in reserve and no need to worry about them.

"The Boeing was ahead of me now, making a left-hand turn. At about 3,000 ft the rear gunner opened up to try to harass me into making a mistake, but that was all over in seconds. At about a third of that range my wingman and I both opened up with our cannon, giving it a short burst, allowing our guns to lead the bomber. We saw a dozen rounds or more strike the fuselage and between the engines, and then our superior speed took us past him.

"We curved round in a wide circle, the Mustangs still behind us but just dwindling dots now, and observed the bomber's end. It spun down through 6,500 ft, pieces breaking off the whole time and then exploded."

A scene perhaps more reminiscent of 1943 than of 1945. By that time the Luftwaffe wasn't shooting down too many Allied bombers on the raids that were taking them

Right: The Me 262 was a remarkably responsive yet docile aircraft, with pleasantly harmonised controls and comfortable stick forces. A tendency to snake at high Mach numbers made it somewhat more difficult to get its guns onto a target at long range.

daily ever deeper into Germany, in ever-increasing strength. Just one thing stood between the Allies and total air supremacy – the world's first jet fighter.

However, Hitler's insistence that the Me 262 be employed in the bombing role, plus the daily devastation of German industry caused by the Allies bombing campaign, prevented the large-scale introduction of Me 262 fighters. Consequently, providing pilots with enough experience in the radical new fighter to allow successful combat operations hampered their effectiveness further.

Leutnant Schnoerrer also encountered 'teething' difficulties

during early operational flying. In fact, on one of his first jet missions he had a very lucky escape. After making an attack on American B-17s he entered a high-speed dive to escape pursuing fighters.

"I pulled back on the stick with all my strength, but the 262 just refused to come out of the dive. Finally, in desperation, I jettisoned my canopy to evacuate the aircraft: this caused a change of trim, and the aircraft came out of it by itself. When I landed I could see the ripples on the skin of the wings. The aircraft was a complete write-off."

Despite the brilliance of the design the Me 262 entered service too late to change the course of the war. By early-May 1945 the shortage of resources and pilots had rendered the Luftwaffe's jet aircraft force impotent.

WORLD WAR II IN THE PACIFIC

The Imperial Japanese Navy's principal torpedo-bomber was to be known to the Allies as 'Kate'. The Nakajima B5N was, despite its vulnerability, able to score notable successes at Pearl Harbor and later in the Pacific theatre.

Japan made its intentions clear with the attack on Pearl Harbor that began the Pacific war on 7 December 1941. They gambled all on a war of short duration, but for almost four years battles were to rage on land, sea and in the air.

Capital ships of the Pacific Fleet ablaze at their moorings. USS West Virginia (BB-48), in the foreground, was hit by six or seven torpedoes and two bombs and lost 105 crew, including its captain. Behind is the USS Tennessee (BB-43).

Pearl Harbor

7 DECEMBER 1941

The Japanese air attack on the American naval base at Pearl Harbor, Hawaii, was the manifestation of militarist expansionism that had gained expression in the Tokyo government as the result of a decade of successful adventures on the Chinese mainland, which had witnessed unremitting strengthening of Japan's army and navy. It was

acknowledged that such territorial expansion in the Pacific would inevitably provoke war with the United States, and to have any chance of defeating the industrial might of that nation it was essential to open hostilities sooner rather than later, so as to take advantage of the USA's unpreparedness. The Roosevelt administration, on the other hand, after years of

pre-occupation with events in Europe, began backing its traditional friends, the UK and France, against Germany, with the supply of war materials; it woke up to the Japanese threat in the Pacific during 1941, but could do little but make token efforts to strengthen American outposts on Wake and Midway islands.

DIPLOMACY FAILS

Even as Japanese and American diplomats met in Washington in attempts to reduce acrimony between the two nations and so to avert war, a large Japanese naval task force was at sea on course for Pearl Harbor. This force was not in fact

Above: On Ford Island, bewildered sailors look over the assembled PBY Catalina flying-boats and OS2U Kingfisher floatplanes, all with varying degrees of damage. A total of 188 American aircraft were destroyed. Only 30 of the 350 attacking aircraft were shot down.

the principal Japanese thrust, but was intended to prevent the US Pacific Fleet from interfering with their major assault in the south against the East Indies, whose oil and rubber resources were so vital to Japan's long-term strategic plans.

The strike force which made for Pearl Harbor comprised the six attack carriers, *Akagi, Hlryu, Kaga, Shokaku, Soryu* and *Zuikaku,* supported by two battleships, two

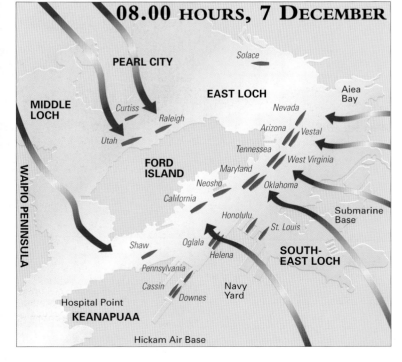

08.00 HOURS, 7 DECEMBER

PEARL CITY

Solace

MIDDLE LOCH

EAST LOCH

Aiea Bay

Curtiss

Raleigh

Nevada

Utah

Arizona

Vestal

WAIPIO PENINSULA

FORD ISLAND

Tennessee

West Virginia

Maryland

Neosho

Oklahoma

California

Honolulu

St. Louis

Submarine Base

Shaw

Oglala

Oglala

Helena

SOUTH-EAST LOCH

Pennsylvania

Cassin

Navy Yard

Hospital Point

Downes

KEANAPUAA

Hickam Air Base

Left: The first wave of more than 180 Japanese aircraft, led by Commander Fuchida, closed on Oahu from the north, with dive-bombers and fighters peeling off to deal with the various air bases while the torpedo bombers took Pearl Harbor from two sides.

Below: A still from a Japanese newsreel, this frame shows a Zero from the Hiryu departing on a sortie over Pearl. A6Ms provided fighter cover for the strike aircraft, but as their was little opposition to the attack, they resorted to strafing ground and waterborne targets.

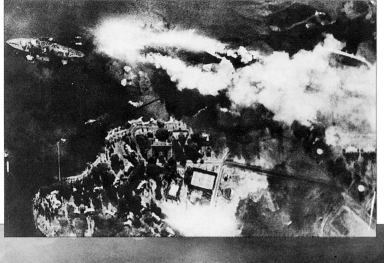

Left: A Japanese photograph showing Pearl Harbor ablaze after the devastating attack. The most vital targets of all, however, had been missed. By chance, the three Pacific fleet carriers, **Enterprise, Lexington** and **Saratoga** were at sea at the time of the attack.

Above: Dawn, 7 December 1941, north-east of Hawaii. Aboard the carrier **Shokaku,** a Mitsubishi A6M2 Zero fighter and several Nakajima B5N2 torpedo-bombers prepare to launch. In all, 94 of the latter took part in the Pearl raid; only six were lost.

heavy cruisers, one light cruiser, nine destroyers and three submarines. Anchored in Pearl Harbor were eight battleships, eight cruisers, 29 destroyers, five submarines and 44 other naval vessels. Fortunately for the Americans the Pacific Fleet's three aircraft-carriers, *Enterprise, Lexington* and *Saratoga,* whose survival was to be crucial in the subsequent Pacific war, were at sea or on the west coast of the USA.

Led by Commander Mitsuo Fuchida, the first wave of the Japanese air strike, comprising 51 Aichi D3A1 dive-bombers, 49 Nakajima B5N2 level bombers, 40 B5N2 torpedo-bombers and 43 Mitsubishi A6M2 Zero fighters,

Left: Ford Island, Pearl Harbor, as seen from a Japanese aircraft in the first wave of the air attack. The torpedo burst alongside 'battleship row', which marks a hit on either the **USS** West Virginia or **USS** Oklahoma, and places the time at about 08.00 hours.

Fighters at Pearl

Mitsubishi's A6M came as a revelation to the US Navy, with its exceptional range and manoeuvrability. It was destined to take part in almost every major action involving the Imperial Japanese Navy.

The Wildcat was one of a new breed of aircraft to enter service with the US Navy and Marine Corp. Only a handful of Squadrons had re-equipped with the F4F at the time of Pearl Harbor

Mitsubishi A6M2 Zero
One of the Zeros making up the fighter complement aboard the *Hiryu,* this machine took part in the attack of 7 December 1941. The navy had taken delivery of 328 A6Ms by then; these equipping most front-line fighter units. This total comprised the initial production A6M2 Model 11 and (from the 65th aircraft) Model 21 with folding wingtips for easier stowage aboard carriers.

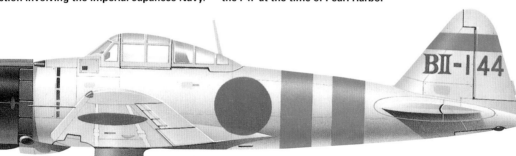

Grumman F4F-3A Wildcat
The Wildcat was one of the US Navy's state-off-the-art aircraft when they entered the war. This aircaft is from VF-6 aboard USS Enterprise and flown by Ensign James G Daniels on 7 December 1941. Enterprise was at Wake island when the Japanese attacked Pearl Harbour.

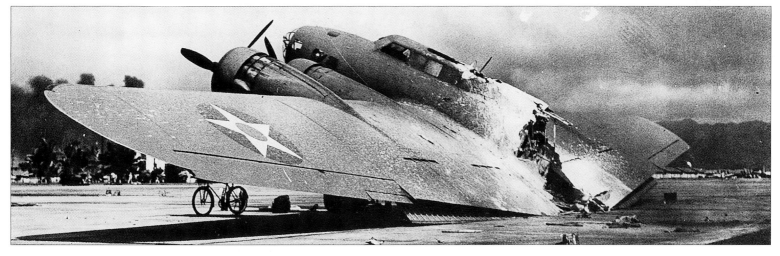

Above: An official Japanese photograph of B5N2s en route to Pearl Harbor. Only five of these torpedo bombers were shot down. Thirty aircraft were lost in total; a small number for the results gained.

Above: USAAF aircraft were lost at Hickham Field. This B-17C of the 19th Bombardment Group lies near Hangar No. 5 after the attack. Many Flying Fortresses were lost at Hickham; the following day more were destroyed at Clark Field in the Philippines.

Below: The destroyer USS Shaw was in Floating Dock No. 2 on 7 December. Bombs hitting the forward portion of the ship ruptured oil tanks and spread fire throughout the ship. Eventually the forward magazine exploded spectacularly, as seen here.

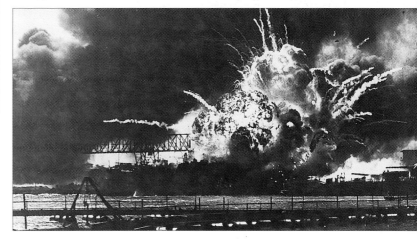

started launching from their carriers at 06.00 on 7 December 1941; 75 minutes later a second wave of 78 D3A1s, 54 B5N2s and 35 A6M2s, led by Lieutenant Commander Shigekazu Shimazaki, took off and set course for the American base.

The first bomb to strike home in the devastating attack fell at 07.55 on the naval air station on Ford Island, destroying six PBY flying-boats and putting out of action an entire patrol squadron. The attack achieved total surprise. Expecting to find five carriers anchored in Pearl Harbor, the Japanese pilots were quickly ordered to concentrate their attention on the battleships, neatly moored along Ford Island. The battleship *Nevada,* at the head of the row, was hit by a single torpedo

before her crew cast off and the ship took a couple of direct hits by bombs; as she made for the open sea she was again hit by bombs and had to be beached with 50 dead aboard. Next in line, the *Arizona* was hit by several torpedoes as well as eight bombs before her shattered hulk sank to the shallow bottom, taking 1,103 crewmen with her. The *West Virginia* received half a dozen torpedo hits and settled to the bottom with 105 dead. Next, the *Oklahoma* was hit by five torpedoes and capsized, trapping 415 men. The last ship in 'battleship row' was the *California*, struck by two torpedoes; with unsecured watertight compartments she eventually foundered three nights later having lost 98 of her crew.

AIRCRAFT DESTROYED
Elsewhere numerous other naval vessels were sunk or severely damaged as the Japanese pilots turned their attention to the airfields and naval air stations. At Kaneohe Field

27 of the 33 PBY flying-boats were destroyed and the remaining six damaged. At Ewa Field there were 49 US Marine Corps fighters and scout bombers; after the Japanese attacks 33 had been destroyed, and none of the remainder could be flown. The story was much the same at the US Army's Hickham Field, where the aircraft were lined up in neat rows; at Wheeler Field 42 US Army aircraft were also destroyed.

Total cost to the Japanese raiding formations amounted to nine A6M2 fighters, 15 D3A1 dive-bombers and five B5N2s, plus one of the latter which ditched near its carrier. Five midget submarines

were also lost without achieving any damage. The air attack had gained spectacular results, killing 2,335 American personnel, leaving four battleships sunk or sinking, damaging four others, sinking three destroyers and a minelayer, and severely damaging two cruisers and a repair ship. In all, 188 aircraft had been destroyed in the air and on the ground, and almost every other aircraft (including several which arrived over Pearl Harbor at the height of the raid having flown from *Enterprise* in ignorance of the attack) was damaged to some extent.

The last of the Japanese aircraft had been recovered aboard their carriers by 13.00 on 7 December. By then the United States was finally at war.

Left: The Japanese carrier Akagi, commissioned in 1927, led the task force of 7 December. Notable features included the small port side island, boiler gases exhausting via a massive downward-curved funnel on the starboard side. The ship was sunk in June 1942.

Malaya and Burma

DECEMBER 1941 – JUNE 1942

Left: A pair of Mitsubishi G3M2 Naval Type 96 attack-bombers (Allied codename 'Nell'). Some 200 G3M2s were serving with front-line Japanese units at the outbreak of war and 60 took part in the mission which led to the sinking of the Prince of Wales and Repulse.

Below: A formation of Brewster Buffaloes from No. 243 Squadron based at Kallang, Singapore. Rejected as a first-line fighter in Europe, Buffaloes diverted to the Far East for the defence of Singapore were hopelessly outclassed by the Japanese Zero.

I f the Japanese gained total tactical surprise in their attack on Pearl Harbor, strategic surprise was no less complete against the British in Southeast Asia. Token forces had been spared for the defence of the Malayan peninsula for some years, particularly for the British naval base at Singapore. By December 1941 the British air forces in the whole of the Far East fielded 362 aircraft, of which 233 were serviceable. In Malaya there were four RAF squadrons of Blenheims (Nos 27, 34, 60 and 62), two squadrons (Nos 36 and 100) of antiquated Vildebeest torpedo biplanes, two RAAF squadrons of Hudsons (Nos 1 and 8) and three Catalina flying-boats of No. 230 Squadron. Fighter defence rested upon 52 Buffaloes of No. 243 Squadron, RAF, No. 488 Squadron, RNZAF, and Nos 21 and 453 Squadrons, RAAF. Ranged against this force was the Imperial Japanese Army's 3rd Hikoshidan comprising 11 Sentais and four independent Chutais. Powerful elements of the Japanese fleet were also available, although in the early stages of the Malayan campaign most of its aircraft were shore based, including at least two Sentais of the excellent Mitsubishi A6M fighter.

On 7 December 1941 Japanese forces moved against northern Malaya and were soon ashore at Kota Bharu. The RAF's initial task was to locate and report the whereabouts of Japanese invasion convoys; the Blenheims, Hudsons and Vildebeests were soon in action but were able to do little to hinder the landings. On the following morning Singapore experienced the first of many air raids, and it soon became clear that the Buffaloes were quite inadequate to match the modern Japanese aircraft. Elsewhere at Alor Star a Japanese raid destroyed all but two of No. 62 Squadron's Blenheims. By the evening of 8 December only 50 RAF aircraft remained serviceable.

Meanwhile reinforcements had been ordered to Singapore, the battleship *Prince of Wales* and the battle cruiser *Repulse* having arrived on 2 December. On 8 December these ships set sail to find and attack the

Above: There had not been enough Hurricanes to defend Singapore in January 1942, but subsequently the type became the RAF's main fighter in action against the Japanese, remaining in Burma until the end of the war. Engine air filters were fitted for the tropical conditions.

Japanese invasion fleets in the north, but within 48 hours had been spotted by the Japanese who dispatched 60 Mitsubishi G3M2 and 26 G4M1 bombers to attack. Devoid of fighter protection, the British warships were quickly sunk, with heavy loss of life.

SINGAPORE FALLS

The other reinforcements (51 Hurricanes shipped by sea) took much longer to arrive and were not ready for action until 20 January 1942, by which time the Japanese army had advanced to within 160 km (100 miles) of Singapore. On that day 27 unescorted Japanese bombers were caught by the Hurricanes whose pilots destroyed eight of the raiders. The next day the bombers returned with an escort of A6M fighters which in turn shot down five Hurricanes without loss. Within a week only 21 Hurricanes were airworthy; by the time the Japanese opened their

direct assault on Singapore island only 10 Hurricanes and a handful of Buffaloes and Vildebeests were available at any one time, and these continued to fight as best they could throughout the two-week evacuation, despite their landing strip at Kallang being under constant Japanese fire. On 15 February the island fortress surrendered.

Long before the fall of Singapore the Japanese had embarked on the conquest of Burma to safeguard their right flank in Southeast Asia. Emulating the German pattern of terror raids, Japanese bombers attacked Rangoon on 23 December 1941, showering the densely-packed marketplaces with fragmentation bombs, killing 2,000 civilians

Below: When the A6M2 Zero was pitted against the Allies in December 1941, its speed, range and manoeuvrability took them by surprise. During the first six months of the war, Zeros of the Striking Force and the 11th Air Fleet proved more than a match for most Allied fighters.

Below: Unable to counter the threat from Japanese aircraft based in Thailand, the Buffaloes of No. 453 Squadron, RAAF fell back to Singapore on 24 December where they merged with No. 21 Squadron. However, the shortcomings of the Buffalo soon led to heavy losses.

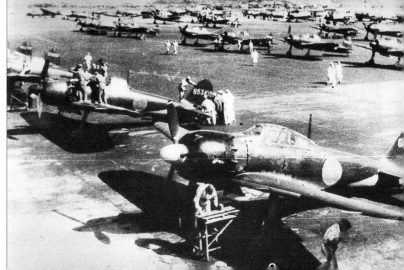

Opposing forces

In the opening period of conflict the RAF and its Allies were outclassed by the superior Japanese front-line fighters and bombers. Many of the Far East-based aircraft were obsolete or unserviceable.

Bombers like the Blenheim were decimated by the well-armed Japanese fighters, while there was little defence for the Fleet against the torpedo bombers like the Mitsubishi G3M 'Nell'.

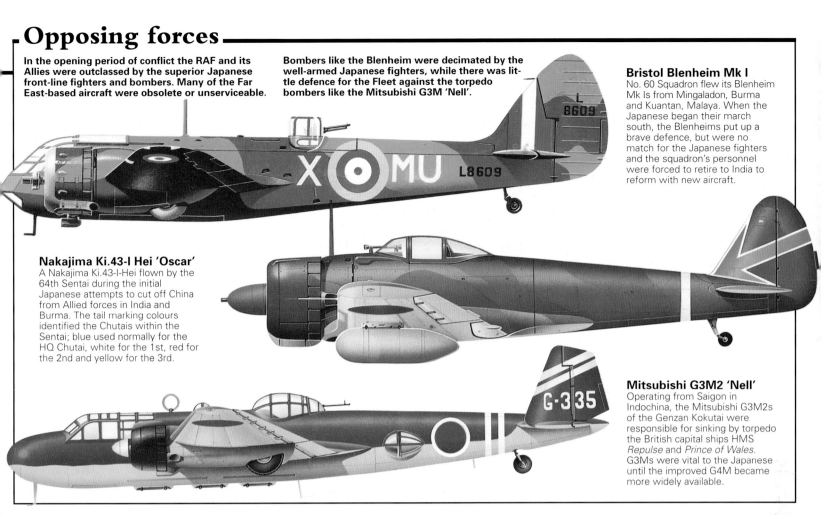

Bristol Blenheim Mk I
No. 60 Squadron flew its Blenheim Mk Is from Mingaladon, Burma and Kuantan, Malaya. When the Japanese began their march south, the Blenheims put up a brave defence, but were no match for the Japanese fighters and the squadron's personnel were forced to retire to India to reform with new aircraft.

Nakajima Ki.43-I Hei 'Oscar'
A Nakajima Ki.43-I-Hei flown by the 64th Sentai during the initial Japanese attempts to cut off China from Allied forces in India and Burma. The tail marking colours identified the Chutais within the Sentai; blue used normally for the HQ Chutai, white for the 1st, red for the 2nd and yellow for the 3rd.

Mitsubishi G3M2 'Nell'
Operating from Saigon in Indochina, the Mitsubishi G3M2s of the Genzan Kokutai were responsible for sinking by torpedo the British capital ships HMS *Repulse* and *Prince of Wales*. G3Ms were vital to the Japanese until the improved G4M became more widely available.

Above: The Mitsubishi Ki-21 'Sally' began to see major service during the autumn of 1938 over China. Initially successful against negligible Chinese air defences, the Ki-21 was terribly outclassed when faced with Allied fighter aircraft.

in this raid and 5,000 more in a Christmas Day attack. However, whereas most of the Far Eastern air force, such as it was, had been deployed for the defence of Singapore, Burma was of less obvious strategic value and accordingly merited much weaker air defences. In all, these comprised just 16 Buffaloes of No. 67 Squadron, RAF and 21 P-40s of the American Volunteer Group (AVG). For the attack on Burma

the Japanese brought up no fewer than 40 aircraft.

Despite the presence of Ki.27 and Ki.43 escort fighters, the Buffaloes and P-40s claimed the destruction of 36 of the Christmas Day raiders, and continued to dispute air superiority over Rangoon for more than a month; however, although reinforced by 30 Hurricanes and a squadron of Blenheims, they could not halt the Japanese advance in southern Burma and on 30 January 1941 the important British airfield at Moulmein was over-run. Threatened by an encircling thrust from the north-east, the great port of Rangoon was evacuated early in March and the surviving components of the RAF began the long retreat northwards. Using such makeshift airstrips that existed in the dense jungle, the squadrons of 'Burwing' (Blenheim Mk IVs of No. 45 Squadron, No. 67 Squadron with some aged Hurricanes and a few Hudsons of No. 139 Squadron) carried out sporadic attacks on the invaders; their last significant attack was made on Japanese aircraft at Mingaladon airfield on 21 March, the destruction of 27 enemy aircraft being claimed.

By mid-1941 the Japanese had

Left: Capable of over 563 km/h (350 mph), the Nakajima Ki-43 Hayabusa (Allied codename 'Oscar') was built in larger numbers than any other front-line aircraft used by the Japanese Army. Remaining in production throughout the war, a total of 5,900 of these fighters were built by war's end.

Below: Mitsubishi G3M 'Nell' bombers of the Japanese 22nd Air Flotilla, whose task was to supplement the support given by the 3rd Air Division to the 25th Army in Malaya and North Borneo. Its 90 G3M2s were augmented by 42 G4M1s from the 21st Air Flotilla.

over-run almost the whole of Burma. In the final stages of the campaign the Dakotas of No. 31 Squadron, RAF, and the C-47s of the 2nd Troop Carrier Squadron, USAAF, evacuated 8,616 men, women and children from Magwe, Myitkyina and Shwebo. It was only the onset of the monsoon season that brought the invaders to a halt at India's border, within bombing range of the vital port of Calcutta.

Loss of the East Indies

DECEMBER 1941 - APRIL 1942

Left: By the end of 1941, things were going so well for the Japanese in Malaya and the Philippines that a new offensive was begun early in 1942. By seizing Timor, the Japanese severed the air reinforcement route from Australia to the Netherlands East Indies.

Below: A Mitsubishi Ki-21 Army Type 97 Heavy Bomber (codename 'Sally') in flight. Much liked by Japanese airmen because of its good handling characteristics and easy maintenance, the Ki-21 gave good service during the early months of the war.

As if to emphasise the vital importance to Japan of concluding a swift and successful war in the Pacific, the capture of the Philippines, Marianas, Carolinas, East Indies and New Guinea was virtually completed within the space of four months.

Just three days after the attack on Pearl Harbor, the Japanese overran the garrison on Guam in the Marianas on 10 December 1941. Five hundred US Marines on Wake Island, attacked the following day, held out until 23 December, blasted from the air and sea despite all the handful of F4F Wildcats could do against the raiding Japanese bombers, flying from Kwajalein in the Marshall Islands. In all, 21 Japanese aircraft were shot down.

By the time Wake Island fell the Japanese were already making rapid progress in their Philippine invasion where heavy raids on the fateful 7 December had destroyed 12 of the

TARGET TOKYO: THE DOOLITTLE RAID

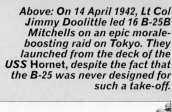

Above: On 14 April 1942, Lt Col Jimmy Doolittle led 16 B-25B Mitchells on an epic morale-boosting raid on Tokyo. They launched from the deck of the USS Hornet, despite the fact that the B-25 was never designed for such a take-off.

America's first strike against the Japanese homeland was one of the most daring raids of the Pacific war. On 16 April 1942, 16 B-25B Mitchells were launched against Tokyo from the carrier USS Hornet, 1000 km out in the Pacific. Led by Lt Col James H. Doolittle, the Mitchells bombed Tokyo, Kobe and Nagoya, before making for China. The first Mitchell, piloted by Doolittle, left the deck at 8.20 a.m., followed by the remaining aircraft at three-minute intervals. Although they reached their targets successfully, material damage was slight, and several aircraft were shot down or crashed. Combat damage meant that the surviving B-25s had to head for the nearest neutral territory rather than going on to the planned bases in China. Although little was gained in military terms, the raid demonstrated to the American public, and the Japanese, that the USA could hit back.

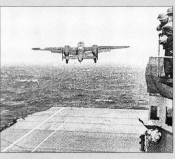

One of Doolittle's B-25s takes off from the Hornet. The aircraft were modified to carry 1,141 US gal of fuel, almost double the normal capacity. They were probably the heaviest aircraft that had ever taken off from an American aircraft-carrier.

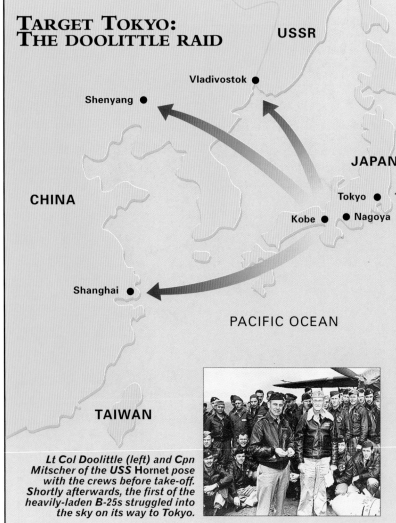

Lt Col Doolittle (left) and Cpn Mitscher of the USS Hornet pose with the crews before take-off. Shortly afterwards, the first of the heavily-laden B-25s struggled into the sky on its way to Tokyo.

The attackers

The Japanese Imperial Navy's D3A divebomber came as an unpleasant shock to the Allies – during the early part of 1942, it wiped out most of the Allied surface vessels in the southwest Pacific. The

Mitsubishi Ki-30 Army Type 97 Light Bomber (code-named 'Ann') was used by the Japanese 5th Air Division to support the East Indies campaign. The type was afterwards relegated to training duties.

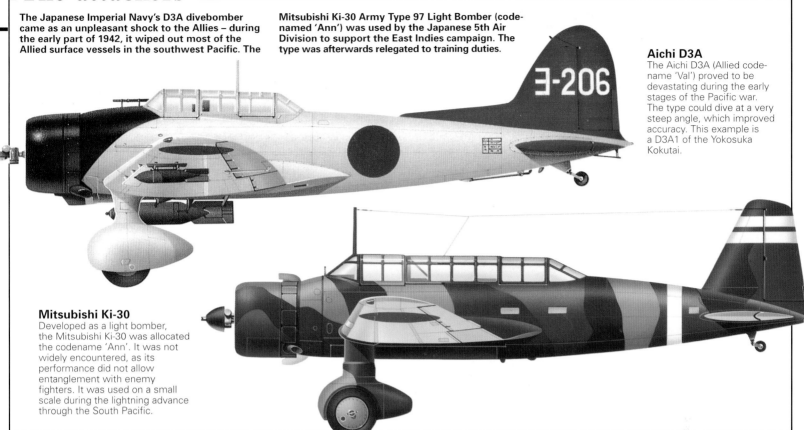

Aichi D3A
The Aichi D3A (Allied code-name 'Val') proved to be devastating during the early stages of the Pacific war. The type could dive at a very steep angle, which improved accuracy. This example is a D3A1 of the Yokosuka Kokutai.

Mitsubishi Ki-30
Developed as a light bomber, the Mitsubishi Ki-30 was allocated the codename 'Ann'. It was not widely encountered, as its performance did not allow entanglement with enemy fighters. It was used on a small scale during the lightning advance through the South Pacific.

Left: Nakajima B5N2 Naval Type 97 'Kate' carrier-borne torpedo bombers fly over Wake Island when the 2nd Carrier Division attacked the island on 21 December 1941. The B5N2 continued to be used in the offensive role until 1944.

Below: The Battle of the Java Sea, which settled the fate of the Netherlands East Indies, took place on 27 February 1942. A hastily assembled Allied land force was outfought and Java was occupied on 12 March. Here a B-17 burns after a raid on Bandung airfield.

Below: In the Pacific, the objective was to stop the Japanese drive and push it back to the home islands. Here Lt Edward H. 'Butch' O'Hare stands by his US Navy F4F-4 Wildcat, in which he downed five Japanese aircraft in combat.

Right: Douglas TBD Devastators were the main torpedo-bombers aboard US carriers for the first year of the war. Slow and vulnerable, they were savaged by Japanese fighters. Seen on deck is a mix of Devastators and SBD Dauntlesses.

35 B-17s in the theatre, and went on to knock out the others in the following days; this force had been regarded as second only in importance to the American Pacific Fleet. As the Americans retreated in Luzon towards the Bataan peninsula, General MacArthur attempted to save Manilla from needless damage and casualties by declaring it an 'open city'. He might have saved himself the trouble, for on 27 December the Japanese subjected it to a series of savage air attacks. As MacArthur prepared to make a stand on the Bataan peninsula following the Japanese capture of Cavite on 2 January 1942, other enemy forces were embarking in large convoys for landings in New Guinea and the Solomon Islands, where they duly arrived on 23 January.

Meanwhile, as the British and Commonwealth forces in Malaya failed to stem the Japanese advance towards Singapore, efforts were being made to rush RAF reinforce-

ments of fighters to the Far East, and although some Hurricanes did arrive during January to assist in the defence of the great port, it was the same story everywhere: too little, too late. A regrouping of Japanese carriers in mid-February allowed

four of them, the *Hiryu*, *Soryu*, *Akagi* and *Kaga*, to steam through the East Indies and launch nearly 200 aircraft for a very heavy raid on the Australian port of Darwin, sinking a dozen ships and causing immense damage in the town.

Nakajima B5N2 'Kate'

At the outbreak of the Pacific war, the 'Kate' was the most advanced carrier-borne torpedo bomber in the world. During the following 12 months, it delivered fatal blows to three separate US Navy carriers and supported Japanese amphibious attacks on the entire war front. By 1944, technical developments had rendered the aircraft obsolete and it ended its service in second-line units.

Crew
The 'Kate' had a crew of three in an enclosed cockpit, comprising a pilot and an observer/navigator who doubled as a bomb-aimer in the level-bombing role. Seated between the pilot and the radio operator, he could see the target by opening a pair of small folding doors in the floor of the fuselage. The radio operator also manned the machine-gun.

Markings
This aircraft was flown by a squadron leader of the Pearl Harbor attack force launched from the Flagship of Vice Admiral Nagumo's fleet, the 36,500-ton *Akagi*.

Protection
The 'Kate' suffered from a failing common to many Japanese aircraft of the early part of the war, in that range and performance had been achieved at the expense of defensive armour and self-sealing tanks.

Armament
The inadequate defensive armament consisted of one flexible rear-firing 7.7-mm Type 92 machine-gun. Offensive capability consisted of one 800-kg 18-in torpedo or three 551-lb bombs.

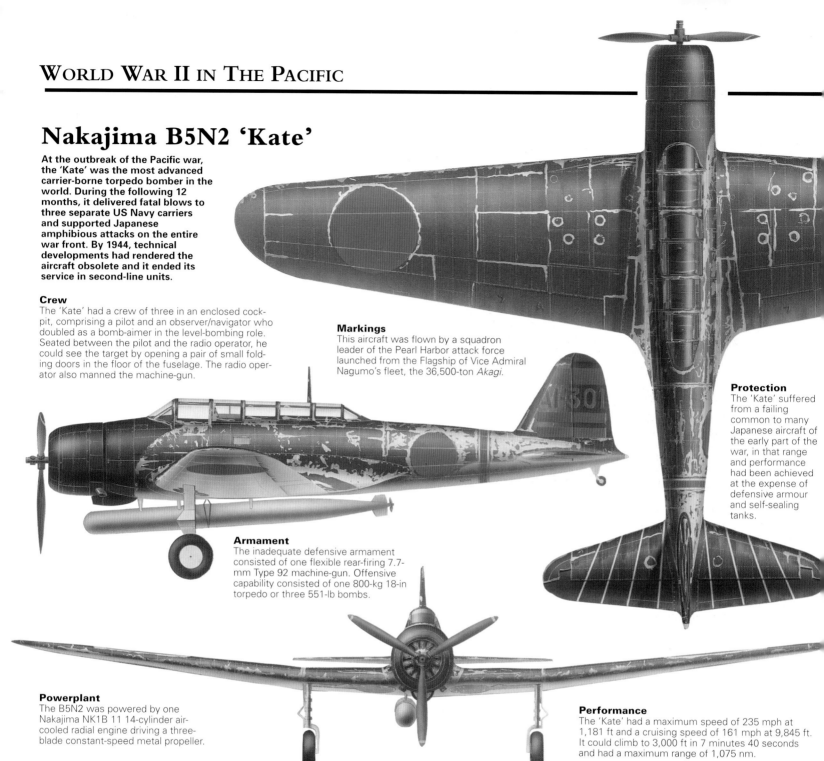

Powerplant
The B5N2 was powered by one Nakajima NK1B 11 14-cylinder air-cooled radial engine driving a three-blade constant-speed metal propeller.

Performance
The 'Kate' had a maximum speed of 235 mph at 1,181 ft and a cruising speed of 161 mph at 9,845 ft. It could climb to 3,000 ft in 7 minutes 40 seconds and had a maximum range of 1,075 nm.

February had begun with the first significant American offensive air action when, on 1 February, carrier aircraft attacked the Japanese base at Kwajalein. This was a minor triumph amid a chapter of disasters, and several ships (mostly troop transports) were either sunk or damaged. But nothing could deflect the Japanese from their next prize, the rich island of Java, defended by some 120,000 Allied troops with scarcely any air cover. Sumatra was effectively abandoned to the Japanese, for its few small airfields were capable only of supporting small numbers of fighters (some Hurricanes had arrived by sea, only

Left: The Aichi D3A1 'Val' was designed as a carrier-borne dive-bomber. It served with Admiral Nagumo's Strike Force and acquitted itself well, despite its approaching obsolescence and its vulnerability to even the least effective Allied fighters. With proper air cover, the Allies could have saved many of the ships which fell to the 'Val'. Over 470 of these aircraft were delivered to the Japanese navy.

Left: An Allied agreement in early 1942 defined the Indian Ocean west of the Malayan peninsula as a British zone of responsibility, but the Royal Navy could only muster a token force for its protection. Here, the heavy cruisers HMS Cornwall and HMS Dorsetshire are under air attack on 5 April 1942.

to be quickly overwhelmed). The Americans accordingly sailed the veteran carrier *Langley* from Freemantle in Australia, with 32 P-40Es aboard and orders to land them at Tjilatjap on the south coast of Java; also sailed at the same time

Below: An early production Douglas SBD-3 Dauntless, sporting an overall light grey colour scheme and small national insignia, flies over USS Enterprise (CV-6). The SBD was at the forefront of operations in the Pacific.

Right: The Curtiss P-36/Hawk 75 was an intermediate development between the Hawk biplane and the P-40 Warhawk. It was exported to the Netherlands – these aircraft are serving in the Netherlands East Indies in early 1942.

was the freighter *Seawitch* with 27 other fighters in crates. The carrier *Langley* was discovered by Japanese aircraft when only 70 miles (113 km) from its destination and sunk with the loss of all its aircraft; the *Seawitch* arrived a day or so later but was unable to unload its cargo, which was then dumped overboard. On that day, 28 February, a large Japanese fleet put ashore its invasion force on Java's north coast. Without any effective air cover the fate of the island and its defenders was sealed. With little cohesive action by ships of the British, Dutch, Australian and American

navies, the Japanese carrier aircraft were able to sink the Allied naval vessels piecemeal, while the Battle of the Java Sea cost them the loss of 14 out of 19 ships and delayed the invasion of Java by no more than a single day. On 9 March the defend-

ers of Java surrendered and 98,000 British, American and Dutch troops passed into captivity. Two days later General MacArthur was ordered to leave Corregidor island in Manila Bay to establish new headquarters in Australia, leaving an embattled garrison to slog it out until it was finally forced to surrender on 9 April. Of the 76,000 taken prisoner, 10,000 were to die in captivity.

CARRIERS SURVIVE

These shattering Allied losses had involved giving up virtually every island between continental Asia and Australia to the Japanese. The cost in men and materials had been prodigious, yet one factor alone perhaps saved American strategy in the Pacific: the survival of the three big carriers, *Enterprise, Saratoga* and *Lexington*. When a fourth carrier, the *Yorktown*, was transferred from the Atlantic to the Pacific, the effective number of carriers remained at three when *Saratoga* was damaged by a submarine's torpedo and put out of action for five months.

It was to be the *Yorktown* that staged a morale-boosting operation on 18 April 1941 when, accompanied by the *Enterprise*, it steamed to within 620 miles (1000 km) of Japan and launched 16 US Army B-25 Mitchells, led by Lieutenant Colonel James Doolittle, in a raid on Tokyo. Little material damage was caused, and all the aircraft were lost after force landing in China (their crews were repatriated later), but the raid's effect on the morale of the American nation was enormous, coming as it did after four months of unremitting defeat and disaster.

Undoubtedly the finest Japanese aircraft of the early years of the war, the Mitsubishi A6M 'Zero' seemed untouchable in a dogfight. It remained a major threat until the stronger, faster Grumman F6F Hellcat was introduced in 1943.

Valiant defenders

The Japanese assembled an armada of some 2,950 aircraft for their push through the Pacific. They set a 100-day timetable for the invasion of Malaysia and Singapore, Guam, Wake Island, Luzon and Java.

Allied aircraft were outnumbered, and many were obsolete, and despite a brave and desperate defence the Allies endured a succession of defeats. Java fell on 9 March, within the Japanese timetable.

Douglas SBD Dauntless
Neutrality stripes on the fin were soon deleted on US Navy aircraft, and national insignia were reduced in size. The Douglas SBD Dauntless was the aircraft which first allowed the US Navy carriers to carry the war back to the Japanese navy.

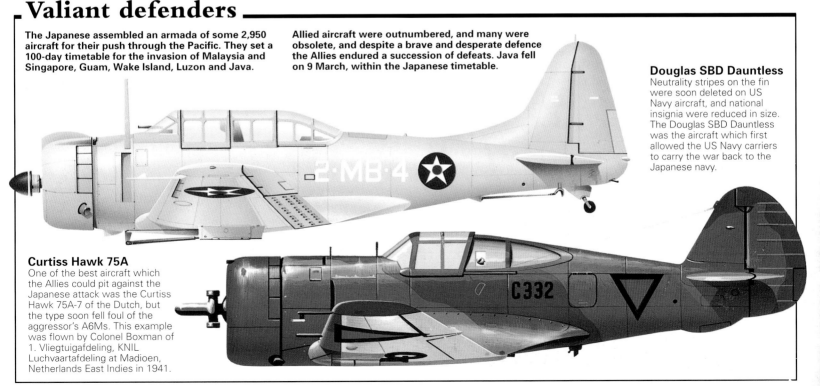

Curtiss Hawk 75A
One of the best aircraft which the Allies could pit against the Japanese attack was the Curtiss Hawk 75A-7 of the Dutch, but the type soon fell foul of the aggressor's A6Ms. This example was flown by Colonel Boxman of 1. Vliegtuigafdeling, KNIL Luchvaartafdeling at Madioen, Netherlands East Indies in 1941.

Chennault's Flying Tigers

DECEMBER 1941 – JUNE 1944

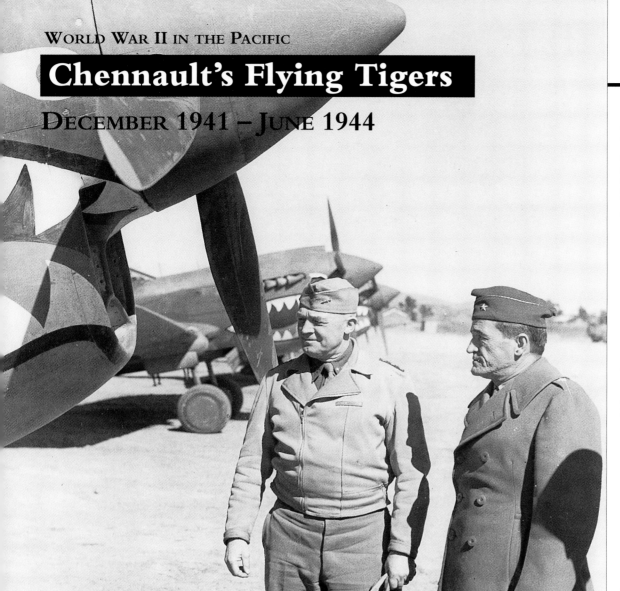

at Mingaladon to cover the Burmese port of Rangoon. This had all been achieved by the time the Japanese entered the war in December 1941.

The Americans were quickly in action against the Japanese, shooting down six of a formation of 10 enemy bombers which attacked Kunming on 20 December, but fared less well when the Japanese attacked Rangoon on 23 December, losing two pilots. Thereafter the American Volunteer Group (AVG), as it became known, contributed substantially to the defence of Burma but, despite extraordinary ingenuity to keep the

Below: The 23rd Fighter Group in China was originally the American Volunteer Group, famously known as the 'Flying Tigers'. This tiger wears Uncle Sam's hat to signify his entry into United States service in 1942 and grasps a shredded Japanese flag.

As the call 'Remember Pearl Harbor' reverberated throughout the United States in 1942, a force of American airmen and aircraft was carrying the war to the Japanese in China and, despite virtual isolation by distance and relative inaccessibility, did much to slow their advance in Southeast Asia.

As long ago as 1936 a retired USAAC major, Claire Lee Chennault, had been invited by the Chinese to create a fighter defence system against the Japanese by instructing young pilots in modern fighting tactics and improvising with the few aircraft available. In due course the Chinese government negotiated to obtain 100 P-40Bs from the USA under Lend-Lease terms (of these 90 arrived at Kyedaw in 1941), Chennault having in 1940 recruited 80 ex-USAAC, US Navy and US Marine Corps volunteer pilots and 150 groundcrew members. With scarcely any official backing from Washington, Chennault organised this force into two squadrons operating out of Kunming to protect the vital Burma Road (which carried supplies to the Chinese) and a third

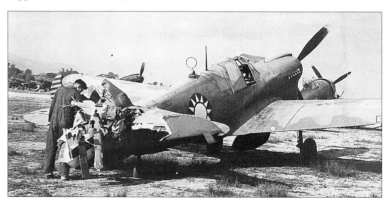

Left: The American Volunteer Group in China blossomed into the 23rd Fighter Group – this group of officers and enlisted men of one of the constituent squadrons, the 74th Fighter Squadron, pose on one of their P-40 aircraft at Kunming, China on 1 February 1943.

Above: During the last two years of the war 377 Curtiss P-40 Warhawks were supplied to China. Most were P-40Ns, as seen here. The damage to the fin and rudder of this example was possibly caused by a ground collision. Note the P-47 Thunderbolt in the background.

Adversaries over China

Though Curtiss lost a USAAC competition for a new fighter to Seversky, the company persevered and won export orders for their radial-engined Model 75 Hawk. The USAAC eventually placed an order, the type serving as the basis for the later inline-engined P-40. 'Dinah' was the Allied code-name for the Ki-46, originally built as a high-speed reconnaissance and destined to serve until 1945.

Curtiss 75 Hawk
The predecessor of the Curtiss P-40 was the P-36, known to Curtiss as the Hawk 75. Flown alongside the P-40 in the colours of the Chinese Nationalist Air Force from Kunming, these fighters were not as capable as the P-40 and gave the Japanese little trouble.

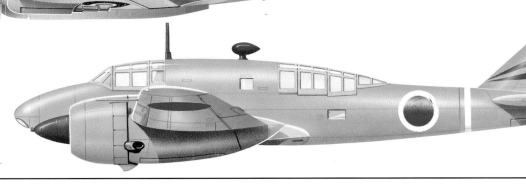

Curtiss 81-A2 Hawk
Flown by Charles Older of the 3rd Squadron 'Hell's Angels' of the American Volunteer Group commanded by Brig. General Claire L. Chennault, this Curtiss Hawk (P-8268) was based at Kunming, China, in the spring of 1942. Among its distinctive markings are 10 victory symbols below the windscreen.

Mitsubishi Ki-46-II
The Mitsubishi Ki-46-II 'Dinah' was allowed almost free reign over the skies of China in late-1941 and early-1942. The opposing Curtiss fighters did not have the performance to catch it at its operating height. This example served with the 51st Dokuritsu Dai Shijugo Chutai (Independent Squadron).

*Below: A P-40 undergoing maintenance under armed guard at the **C**hinese **A**ir **S**ervice **C**ommand facility at **K**unming, where both Chinese and American servicemen worked on the AVG's aircraft. 'Tiger's teeth' on the nose of the aircraft were an AVG trademark.*

Right: Curtiss Model 75Ms Hawk (export version of the P-36) were delivered to China from August 1938. This version was supplied with non-retractable undercarriage. Only 30 were built by Curtiss, with 82 reputedly built by the Central Aircraft Manufacturing Company.

aircraft serviceable (as spares were available only by cannibalisation) the American losses mounted rapidly. The American pilots were credited with 286 victories over Burma and southern China within four months (the true figure was probably nearer 150) and by March, when Rangoon fell to the Japanese, only six P-40s and six Hurricanes (which had been provided by the RAF as reinforcements) remained airworthy in the squadron in the south; 14 others were still flying from Kunming.

As the Japanese army advanced inexorably north through Burma the AVG continued to retain its identity under its indefatigable condottiere, fighting alongside the Buffaloes (and later Hurricanes) of No. 67 (Fighter) Squadron RAF, and striving to operate in appalling conditions from hastily prepared strips hacked out of the Burmese jungle. By May 1942 the beaten Allied army in Burma had retreated as far as Imphal, capital of the Indian state of Manipur, as the survivors of the AVG made their way back into China.

AVG RECOGNISED

Despite constant opposition to the existence of the AVG by the American ground commander in

THE 'FLYING TIGERS'

During only 30 weeks of combat, the American Volunteer Group (AVG) in China claimed 297 enemy aircraft confirmed destroyed, and 40 destroyed on the ground. Twenty-six aces emerged from the ranks of the 'Flying Tigers' – two later earned the Medal of Honor ('Pappy' Boyington and Jim Howard). Four pilots were lost in air combat, six died from ground fire whilst strafing, three died in accidents and three more were killed by enemy bombs. Three became POWs.

Major J.R. Alison

John Alison (left) was a frustrated instructor pilot in England and Russia until he managed to wrangle an assignment with the AVG. On 30 July 1942, he found three Japanese 'Betty' bombers at 4572 metres (15,000 ft) and proceeded to shoot them all down. He became one of the legendary aces in the theatre with 10 aerial victories. His decorations included the Distinguished Service Cross, Distinguished Flying Cross, Silver Star, Legion of Merit, Purple Heart – and a British Distinguished Service Order.

Capt. A. Baumler

Captain Albert 'Ajax' Baumler (right) was a top-notch pilot who emerged from the Stateside arrivals. His P-40 carries the insignia of the 23rd Fighter Group in China. The 23rd was, at first, the only fighter group to oppose the Japanese in China and followed what became a consistent course of air operations – bombing and strafing enemy airfields, troop and supply installations and preventing effective bombing by the Japanese Air Force.

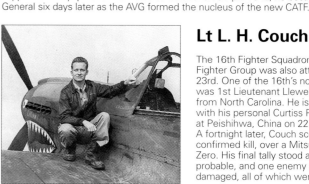

Brig. General C. L. Chennault

Retired USAAC Captain Claire Lee Chennault worked at building an air force for the Nationalist Chinese. He believed that a well-led force of fighters could stop a large force of bombers – not a popular school of thought in the Air Corps of the 1930s. He left in the spring of 1937 at the age of 47, suffering slight deafness. By early-1941, he was planning to obtain American aircraft to be flown by volunteers against Japan. On the AVG's absorption into the USAAF, he was promised higher priority in obtaining supplies and equipment. Promoted to Colonel on 9 April 1942, he became a Brig. General six days later as the AVG formed the nucleus of the new CATF.

Col R. L. Scott

The first commander of the 23rd Fighter Group was Colonel Robert L. Scott, an adventurer at heart. Arriving in China in April 1942, he managed to obtain a P-40 from Chennault and flew combat missions with the AVG. He is seen sitting in the cockpit of his P-40K-I with kills recorded on the fuselage. Before he left for the States, he assumed the leadership of Fighter Command, CATF in February 1943 and was able to pass on his experience of P-40 operations in China.

Lt L. H. Couch

The 16th Fighter Squadron of the 51st Fighter Group was also attached to the 23rd. One of the 16th's notable pilots was 1st Lieutenant Llewellyn H. Couch, from North Carolina. He is seen here with his personal Curtiss P-40E 'Lillian I' at Peishihwa, China on 22 October 1942. A fortnight later, Couch scored his only confirmed kill, over a Mitsubishi A6M Zero. His final tally stood at one kill, one probable, and one enemy aircraft damaged, all of which were Zeros.

China, Lieutenant General J.W. ('Vinegar Joe') Stilwell, who saw the 'Flying Tigers' only as a bunch of barely disciplined mercenaries intent on diverting supplies from his own troops (rather than a vital protection of his own supplies), the American government came to accept the importance of the AVG in China, and forthwith dispatched a number of the improved, six-gun P-40E, of which 30 reached Chennault's command. Chennault himself was reinstated in the active list of the USAAF and promoted to major general, while the AVG was renamed the China Air Task Force as President Roosevelt personally directed Stilwell to ensure it received all possible assistance and supplies.

KUNMING HELD

Largely through the continuing efforts of Chennault's pilots, the

Left: Sergeant Elmer J. Pence, with the help of his pet monkey, adds another Rising Sun symbol to a Curtiss P-40E of the 26th Fighter Squadron, 51st Fighter Group, which was operating in China in 1944 as part of the 14th Air Force. The 197-litre (43-US gallon) centreline drop tank was a standard fitting on many P-40s to improve range.

Above: The American Volunteer Group was divided into three squadrons of 18 aircraft each. The 1st Pursuit Squadron, whose emblem is shown, was the 'Adam and Eve' (commemorating the first pursuit in history), led by Robert Sandell. The 2nd was known as the 'Panda Bears' and the 3rd, the 'Hell's Angels'.

Madam Chiang Kai-shek, the National Secretary of Aviation (regarded by many as the real power in Nationalist China) had given Chennault nearly $9m via the China Defense Supplies Corporation to obtain the fighters he wanted. One hundred Hawk 81-A2s were assigned to China, these being replaced later with versions of the P-40 Warhawk, shown here. Note the 'Hold'n my own' tail art.

Above: An early P-40B (Hawk Model 75-A2) of the 23rd Fighter Group landing at Kunming, China, after a mission on 15 September 1942. Some of these aircraft had seen action with the RAF in the Western Desert, with others coming from Panama.

concentrations and railways; they also flew escort for American bombers attacking Canton, Shanghai and Hong Kong. They operated against the Japanese during the enemy offensives towards Changsha and Chungking, and in the Tungting Hu region. They remained at Kunming until September 1943 when they moved to Kweilin in the north to provide air defence of the Chinese terminus of the 'Hump' air route for supplies from India to China. In due course the Flying Tigers gave up their P-40s in favour of the P-51D, and it was with these aircraft that they were in action against the Japanese forces which advanced down the Hsiang Valley in June 1944, earning a Distinguished Unit Citation. The following spring they helped to rout the enemy and then harassed the Japanese during their final retreat in China. Chennault himself was appointed to command the US 14th Air Force from its inception until the end of the Pacific War.

Japanese failed to reach and capture Kunming, although the Burma Road ceased to be of use with the Japanese in possession of almost all Burma. On 4 July 1942 the China Air Task Force was formally integrated into the USAAF (later as a component of the 14th Air Force) as the 23rd Pursuit Group, its three component squadrons becoming the 74th, 75th and 76th Pursuit Squadrons.

During the following year these were in constant action against the Japanese, intercepting raids on Allied airfields and strafing enemy airfields, river craft, troop

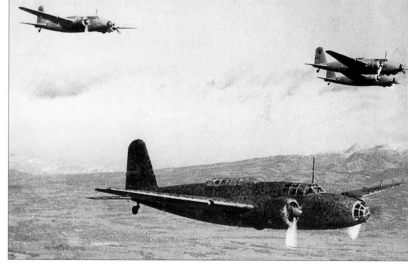

Above: A formation of Kawasaki Ki-48s (Allied codename 'Lily') over China. The Ki-48 was a fast bomber, broadly comparable to the Bristol Blenheim and the Russian Tupolev SB-2. Designed originally as a day bomber, being fast enough to escape interception, it was manufactured in large numbers from the summer of 1940 to the autumn of 1944. Those in China were among the first in service.

Left: Pilots run to their P-40s on a base in China after hearing the air-raid warning. Chennault was continually amazed that the Japanese did not try to destroy the 'Flying Tigers' on the ground, since there was no protection or dispersal system in operation. Lines of P-40s at Pearl Harbor had suffered terribly in similar circumstances.

The Battle of the Coral Sea

1942

On the same day that the British fortress of Singapore fell to the Japanese, Admiral Halsey took the Enterprise group out of Pearl Harbor to hit Wake Island.

Pursuing their drive south-wards towards Australia early in 1942, the Japanese mounted what they termed Operation MO to capture Port Moresby in New Guinea, thereby eliminating Allied air attacks on their bases at Kavieng and Rabaul in the Solomons, and laying open the coast of Australia for attacks by their own land-based bombers. To do this a number of naval groups and invasion fleets were assembled, totalling 70 ships of which two were large carriers (the *Shokaku* and *Zuikaku*), and one a small carrier (the *Shoho*); between them these ships embarked 51 B5N

The Grumman F4F Wildcat was the principal fighter available to the US Navy until 1943. At Coral Sea, in 1942, the F4Fs found it difficult to contain the superior Mitsubishi A6M Reisen. These Wildcats are lined-up on the deck of the Lexington *on 18 May 1942 during the ship's last days.*

'Kate' torpedo bombers, 42 D3A 'Val' dive-bombers and 54 A6M 'Zero' fighters. In addition, the Japanese could call on about 120 aircraft land-based at Rabaul. The US task force in the area (Task Force 17 under Rear Admiral Frank Fletcher) included the carriers *Lexington* and *Yorktown*, whose air strength comprised 25 TBD Devastator torpedo-bombers, 74 SBD Dauntless dive-bombers and 44 F4F Wildcat fighters.

As the result of code-breaking, American intelligence learned that a Japanese fleet would enter the Coral Sea early in May, so that Admiral Fletcher, guessing that Port Moresby was its destination, was able to scout the area around Guadalcanal. Finding a small Japanese force off Tulagi on 4 May, Fletcher launched three strikes from the *Yorktown*, dropping 76 bombs and 22 torpedoes and sinking a destroyer and three minesweepers

for the loss of one TBD and two F4Fs. The *Lexington* meanwhile was still far to the south.

FLAT-TOPS FOUND

On the night of 5/6 May the two large Japanese carriers entered the Coral Sea but, despite land- and carrier-based patrols by both sides, neither fleet was detected for many hours, although the Japanese aircraft found and sank the detached American destroyer *Sims* and the

Aichi D3A1 Naval Type 99 Carrier-Bomber Model 11 – Allied codename 'Val'. The 'Val' had a fixed spatted undercarriage, and in its heyday was a highly effective aircraft although it could carry only one 250-kg bomb under the fuselage and two 60-kg bombs underwing.

oiler *Neosho*. Early in the morning of 7 May a *Yorktown* aircraft apparently reported two Japanese carriers and four heavy cruisers 225 miles (360 km) northwest of the American task force (now joined

Airbrakes extended, this Dauntless is caught in classic dive-bomber pose. Early SBDs could carry a 1,200-lb (545-kg) bombload, but this increased with the later SBD-5 model. This SBD-3 was aboard USS Enterprise (CV-6) in March 1942.

up), and within two hours 93 aircraft had been launched to the attack; unfortunately, the sighting report had been decoded incorrectly and the force detected was of no importance and comprised no carriers. The American strike did, however, come up with the Japanese covering group consisting of the light carrier *Shoho* and its escorting ships. Despite the presence of a few enemy fighters, the 53 SBDs and 22 TBDs went into the attack, sinking the *Shoho* with 13 bombs and seven torpedoes; it was after this attack that Lieutenant Commander Robert Dixon radioed back to

Lexington his famous signal 'Scratch one flat-top'. That evening the Japanese commander, Admiral Takagi, launched a search/strike by 27 aircraft, these being intercepted by American Wildcats whose pilots claimed nine aircraft shot down. The survivors had a difficult flight back to the Japanese carriers and only seven succeeded in landing on.

LEXINGTON LOST

Early on 8 May Japanese air patrols found the American carriers and, just as a strike by 69 D3As and B5Ns was approaching the *Lexington* and *Yorktown*, a force of 82 American aircraft was making for the Japanese carriers, whose position had just been reported 175 miles (280 km) to the northwest. At 11.15 the Japanese attack started, and five minutes later two torpe-

does and five bombs struck the *Lexington*, and one bomb hit the *Yorktown*. The former was badly damaged but, as the Japanese aircraft made off, the crew of the big carrier appeared to be controlling the raging fires. An hour later, however, its aviation fuel tanks exploded and at about 20.00 in that evening the *Lexington* was abandoned to be sunk by American torpedoes, the first American carrier to be lost in World War II.

The American strike aircraft had meanwhile spotted the Japanese carriers, aircraft from the *Yorktown* attacking the *Shokaku* an hour before noon; all their torpedoes missed or failed to explode, and only two bombs found their mark. Although damaged and unable to launch or recover aircraft, the *Shokaku* remained afloat, while the *Zuikaku* recovered all the surviving strike aircraft.

Both sides now withdrew, the Japanese having one small carrier sunk and a large carrier badly damaged. Admiral Takagi had lost more

*The Japanese carrier **Shokaku** is seen ablaze and badly damaged, although still afloat, on 8 May 1942 following an attack by US Navy aircraft during the Battle of the Coral Sea.*

than 100 of his aircraft and, with no more than 39 survivors able to fly, decided to postpone the invasion of Port Moresby for two months. More important was the loss of many of the best and most experienced Japanese naval airmen, a loss that would be keenly felt in the great battles to come.

US VICTORY

The sinking of the *Lexington* was a considerable blow to the Americans who, now that the *Yorktown* was also damaged, had only the *Enterprise* and *Hornet* operational in the Pacific. Despite the adverse ship loss tally, and the fact that Japan could still count five large carriers operational in the Pacific, the Battle of the Coral Sea (the first in history to be fought by opposing warships that never saw nor fired on each other, and the first fought entirely by aircraft) was generally regarded as an American victory. Admiral Fletcher had succeeded in his purpose of frustrating a Japanese invasion of Port Moresby. It was the first sign that the lightning Japanese advance was slowing.

Coral Sea should have been a major Allied victory – Port Moresby had been saved, the Shoho sunk, the large carrier Shokaku damaged and most of its aircraft destroyed. However, while the damaged US carriers Yorktown and Lexington, with the Hornet and Enterprise on the way to relieve them, headed for Pearl Harbor for repairs, a series of internal explosions on the Lexington led to its abandonment and subsequent total loss.

The Tide Turns at Midway

3/5 JUNE 1942

The Japanese strategic plan in the Pacific was to establish by conquest an outer defence perimeter from Kiska in the Aleutians to Port Moresby, passing through Midway, Wake, the Marshalls and the Gilberts. Key bastion of this line of defence would lie at Midway, whose capture would extend the homeland warning network and serve as a base for the future capture of Pearl Harbor. Moreover the Japanese naval commander-in-chief, Admiral Yamamoto, believed that any battle to defeat the US Pacific Fleet must be fought and won in 1942 before the vast American naval building programme bore fruit, and correctly assumed that an attack on Midway would bring about such a battle.

For the assault on Midway Yamamoto assembled four fleets, of which one was an invasion force

and three were heavy support forces; in all, these forces included five large carriers (the *Akagi, Kaga, Hiryu, Soryu* and *Junyo*), three light carriers, 11 battleships and 100 other naval vessels. Of the large carriers, the first four embarked a force of 81 B5N 'Kate' torpedo bombers, 72 D3A 'Val' dive-bombers and 72 A6M Zero fighters. The American fleet covering Midway was divided between two task forces under Rear Admiral Fletcher and included the carriers *Enterprise, Hornet* and *Yorktown* (the latter having completed speedy repairs since sustaining damage in the Battle of Coral Sea a month earlier); the American ships carried 42 TBD Devastator torpedo-bombers, 82 SBD Dauntless dive-bombers and 79 F4F Wildcat fighters. There were also valuable American PBY patrol flying-boats and some of the new TBF Avenger torpedo aircraft based at Midway, as well as some older aircraft.

As yet the Japanese were not aware that any American task force was in the area of Midway, and only after a number of incomplete sighting reports had been received did suspicion dawn that American carriers were nearby. All through 3 June the American aircraft based on Midway carried out attacks on the Japanese fleet, inflicting little damage but forcing the carriers to keep launching their fighters for defence.

Above: Airbrakes extended, this Douglas SBD Dauntless is caught in classic dive-bomber pose at Midway. Early SBDs carried a 545-kg (1,200-lb) bombload, but by the end of the war this had increased with the introduction of the SBD-5.

This in turn prevented the Japanese from launching strikes against the American naval force, now known to include at least one carrier.

HEAVY LOSSES

Early on 4 June a PBY reported the positions of two Japanese carriers but, suspecting that at least two other carriers were also in the area, Admiral Fletcher launched only two limited strikes, one of which (from the *Hornet*) failed to locate its target, some of its aircraft running out of fuel and landing in the sea, the remainder having to land on Midway. The other strike, composed of 15 TBDs of Torpedo Squadron Eight (VT-8), found and attacked the *Kaga*; every one was shot down. This was followed by 14 TBDs of VT-6 from the

Above: PBY-5 Catalinas operated by the US Navy played a vital part leading up to the battle, providing warning of the approaching Japanese fleet. Their prodigious 4500-km (2796-mile) range was useful when flying from Midway.

Below: The shattered Japanese carrier force retreated westward from Midway, leaving the crippled 'Mogami'-class cruisers Mogami and Mikuma, part of the 7th Cruiser Squadron, to make for the safety of Wake Island.

Right: The USS Yorktown at Midway, turning hard to port in an attempt to avoid a torpedo attack by 'Kate' aircraft from the Japanese carrier Hiryu. The Hiryu was found some miles to the north-east and sunk by American aircraft that day.

Mighty Avenger

Grumman's TBF Avenger was a strongly-built, mid-wing monoplane with a weapons-bay large enough for a torpedo or 908 kg (2,000 lb) of other ordnance. Making its operational debut at Midway in June 1942, well over half the Avengers constructed were to be built by General Motors' Eastern Aircraft division, as the TBM.

Grumman TBF-1 Avenger
This TBF-1 was one of those that went into action with Navy Squadron VT-8 on 4 June 1942 and failed to return. The aircraft had only just arrived to replace the unit's TBDs. Fortunately the navy already had no doubt that in this aircraft they had the world's best carrier-based attack aircraft.

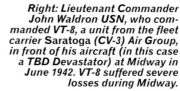

Above: When darkness fell on 4 June in mid-Pacific, the smoking hulls of four Japanese aircraft carriers signified the turning fortunes of war. Their aircraft also suffered. Here a 'Kate' from one of the carriers plummets towards the sea after a direct hit.

Enterprise; only four survived. Last came 12 TBDs of VT-3 from the *Yorktown*; all of which were shot down. And not a single torpedo found its mark.

By now the *Akagi*, *Kaga*, *Soryu* and *Hiryu* were fairly close together, and their position was known. At 09.55 the first SBDs came in to the attack and within 30 minutes the first three of these carriers had been heavily damaged by direct bomb hits. Thus far the American losses among the carrier aircraft amounted to 37 TBDs, 16 SBDs and 14 F4Fs. At 10.40 on 4 June the surviving Japanese carrier *Hiryu* launched a

strike by 18 dive-bombers whose pilots discreetly followed the departing SBDs back to their carrier, the *Yorktown*, and carried out a highly courageous attack. All but five of the Japanese aircraft were shot down, but the heavy damage inflicted caused the carrier to sink three days later. Ironically, just as the attack on the *Yorktown* started, 10 of her SBDs attacked the *Hiryu*, scoring four direct hits.

The final stages of the Battle of Midway involved isolated attacks by American shore-based aircraft against the Japanese fleet, but little further damage was done. The *Soryu* eventually sank during the evening of 4 June with 718 men; five minutes later the *Kaga* blew up and sank with 800 of her crew. The *Akagi* and *Hiryu* both remained afloat until 5 June, both being abandoned to be torpedoed by Japanese destroyers, the *Hiryu* taking 416 of

Right: Lieutenant Commander John Waldron USN, who commanded VT-8, a unit from the fleet carrier Saratoga (CV-3) Air Group, in front of his aircraft (in this case a TBD Devastator) at Midway in June 1942. VT-8 suffered severe losses during Midway.

her crew to the bottom. As the Japanese fleet withdrew, now without air cover, a strike by 57 SBDs from *Enterprise* and *Hornet* found the Japanese cruisers *Mikuma* and *Mogami*, sinking the former and badly damaging the latter.

Midway may be regarded as one of history's decisive battles. It ended Japan's carrier domination of the Pacific, without which the American fleet could at last begin to contain the forward momentum of the Japanese advance. That advance would continue for many months, but with the cumulative losses among her best naval airmen at Coral Sea and Midway the Imperial

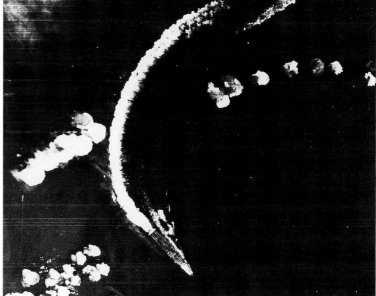

Japanese Navy would no longer operate in safety from the air. Midway confirmed the carrier as the major warship in the Pacific; within a month the USA would have a further 131 carriers in construction or on order.

Above: The Japanese carrier Hiryu under attack by Midway-based B-17 bombers early in the battle that was to mark the turning point against the Japanese sweep across the Pacific. No bombs found the target on this occasion, but the carrier was sunk later by navy SBD Dauntlesses.

After Midway: The Solomons

AUGUST 1942 – FEBRUARY 1943

Operation 'Cactus' was the Allied invasion of the island of Guadalcanal in the Solomons chain. Japanese forces had built up on the island with the intention of cutting communications between the US and its bases in Australia. On 7 August 1942, a massive assault was launched, with many strikes by carrier-based Douglas SBD Dauntless dive bombers.

Left: Grumman had built fighters for the US Navy since 1931, but their first monoplane was the F4F Wildcat, which entered USN service in late-1940. Generally inferior to the Zero in performance, the Wildcat was more durable and more heavily armed, and with better-trained pilots, achieved a kill ratio of nearly six-to-one in air combat during 1942.

The loss of four Japanese carriers at Midway gave the Americans the chance of seizing the initiative, if only for a short time, before the Japanese reorganised their fleets. It was therefore decided to mount a series of operations whose ultimate object was to recapture Rabaul in the north of New Britain. To do this it was necessary to secure the Solomon Islands which stretched away to the south east for 960 km (600 miles) and particularly the large jungle-clad island of Guadalcanal with its half-completed airfield (later named Henderson Field), as well as the island of Tulagi where the Japanese had established a seaplane base.

On 6 August 1942 Task Force 61, under Vice-Admiral Fletcher, with the carriers *Enterprise*, *Saratoga* and *Wasp*, a battleship, 14 cruisers, 31 destroyers and 23 transports, entered the Solomon Sea. Aboard these ships were 99 F4F Wildcat fighters, 103 SBD Dauntless dive-bombers and 41 TBF Avenger torpedo bombers, plus 19,000 US Marines. Early the following day the US Marines went ashore on Tulagi and Guadalcanal, and within 24 hours the Japanese local defences had been overwhelmed, prompting immediate reaction by the Japanese commander at Rabaul who sent a raid by 27 G4M bombers, escorted by 18 A6M Zero fighters against the invasion force. Among the Japanese fighter pilots was Saburo Sakae, a veteran who had already amassed a score of 57 victories; after claiming his 58th victim (an SBD) he was hit by crossfire from a formation of TBFs. His aircraft was badly damaged but, despite injuries to both eyes and being paralysed down his left side, he managed to fly his aircraft the 1030 km (640 miles) back to Rabaul after a flight of more than six hours. (He later rejoined combat operations to gain a total victory tally of 64, including an aircraft shot down on the last day of the war).

JAPANESE RETALIATION

After a second air strike, which cost the Japanese 15 aircraft, a night attack by enemy surface forces caught part of the American invasion force unawares between Tulagi and Guadalcanal, sinking four heavy cruisers with the loss of 1,000

Left: Ordnancemen aboard Enterprise *load a 227-kg (500-lb) bomb onto a Dauntless of Scouting Squadron 6 (VS-6). The date was 7 August 1942, the first day of air attacks on Guadalcanal. For the next five months, the Solomon Islands were the centre of furious naval and air activity, the Allies controlling the skies by day and the Japanese the sea at night.*

Right: All major powers made use of large flying-boats in the war. These are Kawanishi H6K2, Naval Type 97s – known to the Allies as 'Mavis'. A total of 176 of this parasol-winged boat was built. Designed for maritime reconnaissance, in 1942 they were also used as long-range bombers.

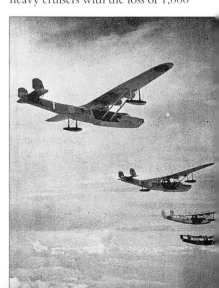

Defenders of Guadalcanal

In the Spring of 1942, the A6M Zero had met modern Wildcat fighters for the first time at the Battles of the Coral Sea and Midway, but it was another year before an example was captured, evaluated and weaknesses identified. The D4Y Suisei (Comet) was a high-speed light bomber first operated in the reconnaissance role. G4Ms were built in larger numbers than any Japanese bomber.

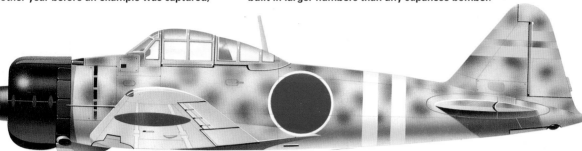

Mitsubishi A6M2 Zero
The A6M2 was the first version of the Navy Type 0 Naval Fighter to enter service and was the fighter that swept all before it from Pearl Harbor to the Dutch East Indies. This Zero ('Zeke' to the Allies) flew with the 6th Kokutai at Rabaul.

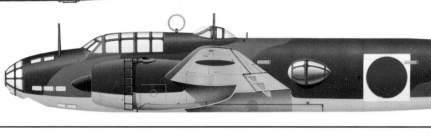

Yokosuka D4Y3 Suisei
'Judy', as it was known to the Allies, has been compared to the de Havilland Mosquito as a high-speed bomber, used for reconnaissance and as a night fighter. It was the fastest carrier-borne dive-bomber of World War II, the type seeing service in the Solomons. This is a late-production, radial-engined D4Y3 Model 33.

Mitsubishi G4M1
G4Ms served from Australia to the Aleutians in large numbers, despite having unprotected fuel tanks and a lack of armour that earned it the nickname 'Flying Lighter'. This aircraft of the 705th Kokutai was part of the large build-up of Japanese aircraft on Rabaul.

Below: Featuring in the Solomons, 'Judy' gained a reputation as one of the better dive-bombers of the war; it had a reasonable turn of speed, at least when compared to other aircraft of this type. However, the D4Y carried little protection against enemy gun fire – a problem not addressed by the Japanese – thus its full potential was never realised.

Right: The Consolidated PBY Catalina was the main US patrol aircraft of the war and the first US aircraft to carry sea-search radar. The 'Cat' was also used for anti-submarine, transport and air-sea rescue missions. In the Solomons, specially-camouflaged 'black cats' attacked Japanese surface ships at night with torpedoes.

lives in the Battle of Savo Island. Worried by the presence of a large land-based air force, and with his cruiser escort seriously depleted, Fletcher obtained sanction to withdraw his carriers from the area. Throughout the following week the US Marines toiled to complete the airstrip on Guadalcanal and, despite constant attacks by Japanese aircraft, 19 US Marine Wildcats and 12 SBDs landed on the new airfield from the escort carrier *Long Island*.

JAPANESE COUNTERATTACK
Events now followed rapidly. The Japanese dispatched a carrier-escorted invasion force with the carriers *Ryujo*, *Shokaku* and *Zuikaku* (with 168 aircraft) to land 1,500 troops for the recapture of Guadalcanal. On 24 August, after the Japanese force had been sighted by PBYs, the American carriers hastily returned, their SBDs and

Left: The Battle of Santa Cruz was the last major sea action of the Solomons campaign. The Japanese had two carriers badly damaged, but the loss of Hornet and damage to Enterprise reduced the available US carrier force to one. Here, a bomb misses Enterprise, the bomber itself crashed on the far side of the ship.

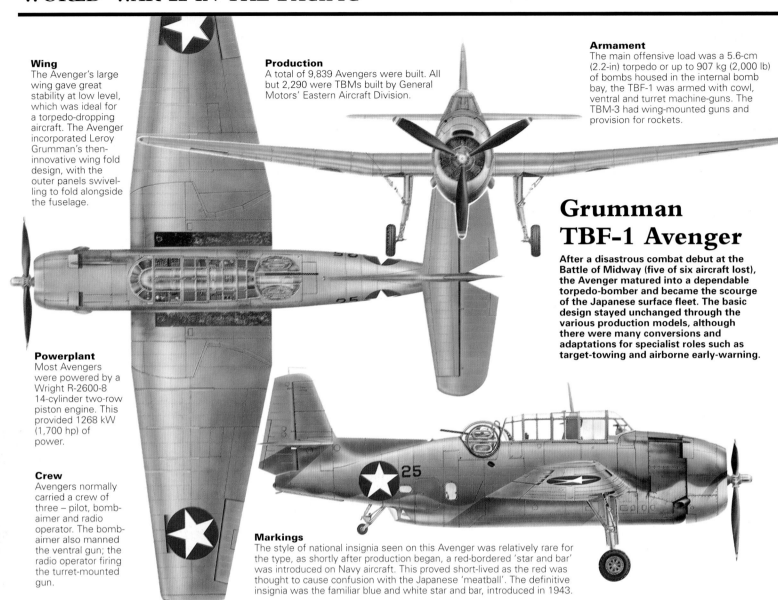

Wing
The Avenger's large wing gave great stability at low level, which was ideal for a torpedo-dropping aircraft. The Avenger incorporated Leroy Grumman's then-innovative wing fold design, with the outer panels swivelling to fold alongside the fuselage.

Production
A total of 9,839 Avengers were built. All but 2,290 were TBMs built by General Motors' Eastern Aircraft Division.

Armament
The main offensive load was a 5.6-cm (2.2-in) torpedo or up to 907 kg (2,000 lb) of bombs housed in the internal bomb bay, the TBF-1 was armed with cowl, ventral and turret machine-guns. The TBM-3 had wing-mounted guns and provision for rockets.

Grumman
TBF-1 Avenger

After a disastrous combat debut at the Battle of Midway (five of six aircraft lost), the Avenger matured into a dependable torpedo-bomber and became the scourge of the Japanese surface fleet. The basic design stayed unchanged through the various production models, although there were many conversions and adaptations for specialist roles such as target-towing and airborne early-warning.

Powerplant
Most Avengers were powered by a Wright R-2600-8 14-cylinder two-row piston engine. This provided 1268 kW (1,700 hp) of power.

Crew
Avengers normally carried a crew of three – pilot, bomb-aimer and radio operator. The bomb-aimer also manned the ventral gun; the radio operator firing the turret-mounted gun.

Markings
The style of national insignia seen on this Avenger was relatively rare for the type, as shortly after production began, a red-bordered 'star and bar' was introduced on Navy aircraft. This proved short-lived as the red was thought to cause confusion with the Japanese 'meatball'. The definitive insignia was the familiar blue and white star and bar, introduced in 1943.

Below: May 1942 saw the Japanese consolidating their hold on the Solomons, from which they could threaten Australia. On 7 August 1942 a Marine force went ashore on Tulagi and Guadalcanal. This photograph was taken from an SBD that day after a raid on Tenambogo.

Right: The A6M3 Navy Type 0 Model 32 reached the Solomons theatre before the US invasion. This latest model of the ubiquitous Zero featured folding wingtips for carrier operations and was known to the Allies at first as 'Hap', then 'Hamp', and later 'Zeke 32'.

Below: SBD Dauntlesses take-off from an airstrip on Russell Island in November 1942. The landings on Guadalcanal were to be the first of a long series of actions aimed at isolating Japan's key position in the south-west Pacific. The 'island-hopping' up the island chain was bitterly contested.

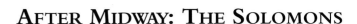

Above: The Mitsubishi Ki-46 'Dinah' was the principal Japanese reconnaissance aircraft of the war. With a top speed of 600 km/h (375 mph) and a ceiling of 10830 m (35,530 ft) the Dinah was almost immune from interception until the last part of the war.

Below: Following the capture of the Solomons, the islands became a major base for US and New Zealand aircraft. Land-based naval aircraft such as SBD Dauntlesses, F4F Wildcats and Marine Corps TBF Avengers like these carried out patrols and anti-shipping strikes.

Above: Most Japanese heavy bomber units operated the Mitsubishi Ki-21-II 'Sally'. Very successful in the early part of the war, and remaining in service until the surrender, it was outclassed by modern Allied fighters. This Ki-21 operated with the 14th Bomber Sentai, 3rd Chutai.

TBFs sinking the *Ryujo* that afternoon. But shortly afterwards, as both sides launched strikes against the opposing carriers, a big air battle developed. The *Enterprise* was hit by three bombs, but despite severe damage, remained in action. By the end of the day the Battle of the East Solomons had cost the Japanese the loss of a light carrier and 61 aircraft, and the Americans withdrew the *Enterprise* for repairs, her SBDs landing on Guadalcanal to help the US Marines. Following an attack by land-based B-17s which sank a Japanese destroyer and damaged another, the Japanese temporarily abandoned their attack on the island.

Japanese submarines then took up the hunt, torpedoing the *Saratoga* on 31 August (the carrier being withdrawn once more for repairs), and sinking the *Wasp* on 15 September.

One further major battle was fought in the Solomon Islands campaign, the Battle of Santa Cruz Islands, fought at the end of October. By then the Americans could deploy but two carriers, the *Enterprise* and *Hornet* with a total of 70 Wildcats, 72 SBDs and 29 TBFs. Against them Yamamoto sent a force which included the *Shokaku*

and *Zuikaku* once more, and the *Junyo* and *Zuiho* with a total of 222 aircraft. On 26 October the *Enterprise* launched a search/strike by 16 SBDs which found and scored two hits on the *Zuiho*. On the same day a 62-aircraft strike attacked the American carriers, hitting the *Hornet* (which sank later), while at the same moment American SBDs attacked the Japanese carriers, hitting the *Shokaku* with at least three bombs. The Japanese launched a further strike whose pilots were able to concentrate on the *Enterprise* which was hit by three more bombs but which, by skillful manoeuvring, avoided nine torpedoes.

TACTICAL VICTORY

The Battle of Santa Cruz Islands ended the Solomon campaign at sea; it was a tactical victory for the Japanese despite damage to two

carriers and the loss of 90 aircraft. The Americans, who lost 74 aircraft, were now down to one operational carrier in the Pacific, the *Enterprise* returning to sea after hasty repairs. Desperate fighting went on in Guadalcanal itself for seven months until in February 1943 the Japanese evacuated 11,000 survivors, leaving

21,000 dead on the island; by that time the battle had cost them 900 aircraft, two battleships and the *Ryujo* sunk, as well as 21 other naval vessels. Not until the Battle for the Marianas in June 1944 would major units of the Japanese navy again engage their counterparts in the US Pacific Fleet.

Right: USS Wasp had 29 serviceable Grumman F4F Wildcat fighters aboard on 7 August 1942. To protect slower attack aircraft increasing numbers of escort fighters were needed. A number of Marine Corps F4F units were committed to the front line during the fight for control of the Solomons.

Island Hopping

OCTOBER 1943 – JULY 1944

WORLD WAR II IN THE PACIFIC

Left: Sweeping across Karas harbour in Dutch New Guinea, one of these Douglas A-20Gs is caught by flak and plunges out of control. This scene was to be repeated many times throughout the rest of the Pacific war as American bombers pounded Japanese defences.

Below: By early-December 1943, the 45th Fighter Squadron, 15th Fighter Group, 7th Air Force, had moved to Nanumea Island, east of the Solomons. Here mechanics are servicing 'Geronimo', a Curtiss P-40 Warhawk.

Fortified and garrisoned by the Japanese during the 1930s, the Marshalls, Carolines and Marianas formed a defence perimeter across the Pacific which interrupted the direct routes from the USA and Pearl Harbor to Southeast Asia, the East Indies and Australia. Following Japan's attack on Pearl Harbor the British colonies in the area, the Gilbert and Ellice islands, were captured and incorporated into the Japanese defence perimeter. And it was the tiny atolls of Tarawa and Makin that were to be recaptured first by the Americans, their airfields providing the key bases from which further island-hopping operations would be covered.

Operation 'Galvanic', the assault on the Gilberts, involved the newly-organised Task Force 50 under Rear Admiral Charles A. Pownall, the largest assembly of

carriers hitherto concentrated: six fleet and five light carriers supported by six fast battleships, six cruisers and 21 destroyers. Split into four task groups, these carriers opened their attacks on 19 November 1943 with raids on Jaluit and Mili in the Marshalls to prevent Japanese aircraft based there from interfering

Right: The continuing need to differentiate between the US national insignia and those of the Axis powers brought major changes in 1943, with white rectangles added to the star, as here on a formation of Grumman F4F Wildcats.

over the Gilberts, keeping up their attacks for five days as the US Army went ashore on Makin on 20 November, supported by aircraft from the *Essex*, *Enterprise* and *Bunker Hill* fleet carriers and the *Belleau Wood*, *Monterey* and *Independence* light carriers. Meanwhile another carrier task group with the *Saratoga* and *Princeton* under Rear Admiral

Left: A B-24 Liberator being loaded with fragmentation bomb clusters prior to a raid on Tarawa on 18 November 1943. Each bomb bay could carry 1814 kg (4,000 lb) of bombs, and the bomb doors rolled up the outside of the fuselage in a similar way to a roll-top desk.

Frederick Sherman had been hitting airfields on Bougainville in the Solomons, where the carrier aircraft destroyed 33 Japanese aircraft and sank nine supply ships and 11 lesser vessels for the loss of three aircraft. And in a major air strike on Rabaul, American carrier aircraft damaged four Japanese cruisers, while the crews of 97 Hellcats, Dauntlesses and Avengers claimed the destruction of about 25 enemy aircraft.

US CARRIER LOST

In yet another task group of Task Force 50, the escort carrier *Liscome Bay*, which was about to launch a strike over the Gilberts on the

morning of 23 November, was struck by a torpedo from the Japanese submarine *I-175*. On board were almost 200 bombs of weights up to 907 kg (2,000 lb), and the torpedo evidently struck the bomb store. There was a colossal explosion which blasted the vessel apart and killed 643 crew members including Rear Admiral Henry M. Mullinnix, the task group commander. This was the only US warship lost during this phase of the American drive across the central Pacific.

The successful assault on Tarawa was accomplished in three days. It also marked a new air fighting tactic by naval aircraft, that of radar-guided night-fighting. A radar-equipped TBF Avenger, accompanied by a pair of F6F Hellcats, would be launched, and the TBF would vector the F6Fs into visual range of the target. In the first operational sortie, on 26/27 November, the F6Fs were slow in closing up to the TBF and it was left to the latter's pilot, Commander John Phillips, to shoot down the first target, a G4M 'Betty', with his two wing machine-guns; later in the same sortie, as the F6Fs closed up, the

Right: Douglas SBD-5 Dauntless aircraft returning from a bombing run on an airfield on Param Island in the Truk Atoll, with other SBDs bearing down to strafe the remains. The SBD-5 was powered by the improved R-1820-60 engine.

Left: The most widely employed Japanese land bomber was the Mitsubishi G4M, codenamed 'Betty'. This had paved the way for the lightning advance through the Pacific in 1942, although it proved no match for Allied fighters.

Below: Only the immense industrial capacity of the United States could have sustained the vast effort required to conduct a war on the scale of the Pacific campaign, with forces committed to huge strategic drives through the theatre.

The two main axes in the Pacific were from Australia and along the Solomon Islands, and a fleet-borne push from atoll to atoll through the central Pacific – island hopping.

In the central Pacific, Admiral C. Nimitz was the Allied forces commander; the south Pacific forces were under the command of Admiral W. Halsey, while the south-west Pacific forces were the responsibilty of General D. MacArthur.

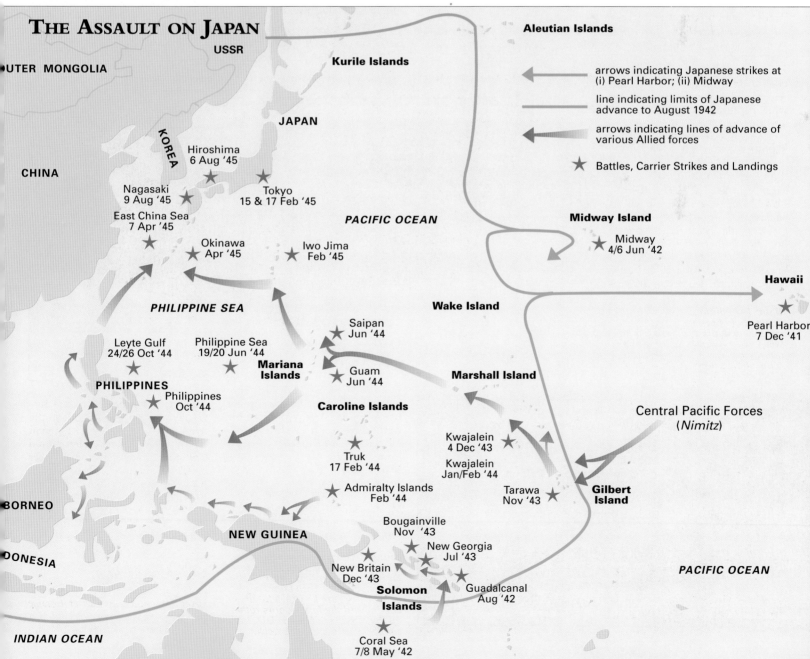

THE ASSAULT ON JAPAN

Aleutian Islands

USSR

OUTER MONGOLIA

Kurile Islands

JAPAN

KOREA

CHINA

Hiroshima 6 Aug '45

Nagasaki 9 Aug '45

Tokyo 15 & 17 Feb '45

East China Sea 7 Apr '45

Okinawa Apr '45

Iwo Jima Feb '45

PACIFIC OCEAN

Midway Island

Midway 4/6 Jun '42

Hawaii

PHILIPPINE SEA

Wake Island

Pearl Harbor 7 Dec '41

Leyte Gulf 24/26 Oct '44

Philippine Sea 19/20 Jun '44

Saipan Jun '44

Mariana Islands

Guam Jun '44

Marshall Island

PHILIPPINES

Philippines Oct '44

Central Pacific Forces (*Nimitz*)

Caroline Islands

Kwajalein 4 Dec '43

Kwajalein Jan/Feb '44

Truk 17 Feb '44

Admiralty Islands Feb '44

Tarawa Nov '43

Gilbert Island

BORNEO

Bougainville Nov '43

New Georgia Jul '43

PACIFIC OCEAN

NEW GUINEA

INDONESIA

New Britain Dec '43

Guadalcanal Aug '42

Solomon Islands

INDIAN OCEAN

Coral Sea 7/8 May '42

→ arrows indicating Japanese strikes at (i) Pearl Harbor; (ii) Midway

— line indicating limits of Japanese advance to August 1942

➤ arrows indicating lines of advance of various Allied forces

★ Battles, Carrier Strikes and Landings

Land-based air power

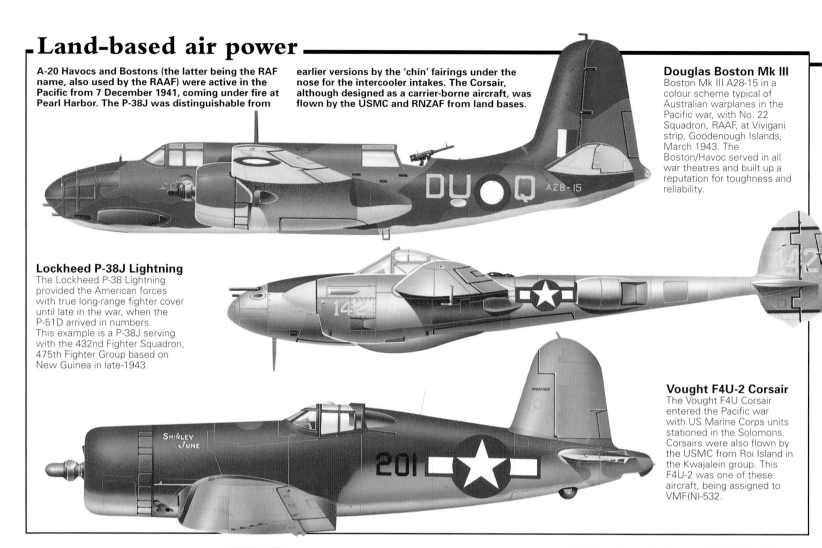

A-20 Havocs and Bostons (the latter being the RAF name, also used by the RAAF) were active in the Pacific from 7 December 1941, coming under fire at Pearl Harbor. The P-38J was distinguishable from earlier versions by the 'chin' fairings under the nose for the intercooler intakes. The Corsair, although designed as a carrier-borne aircraft, was flown by the USMC and RNZAF from land bases.

Douglas Boston Mk III
Boston Mk III A28-15 in a colour scheme typical of Australian warplanes in the Pacific war, with No. 22 Squadron, RAAF, at Vivigani strip, Goodenough Islands, March 1943. The Boston/Havoc served in all war theatres and built up a reputation for toughness and reliability.

Lockheed P-38J Lightning
The Lockheed P-38 Lightning provided the American forces with true long-range fighter cover until late in the war, when the P-51D arrived in numbers. This example is a P-38J serving with the 432nd Fighter Squadron, 475th Fighter Group based on New Guinea in late-1943.

Vought F4U-2 Corsair
The Vought F4U Corsair entered the Pacific war with US Marine Corps units stationed in the Solomons. Corsairs were also flown by the USMC from Roi Island in the Kwajalein group. This F4U-2 was one of these aircraft, being assigned to VMF(N)-532.

TBF's turret gunner opened fire at what he assumed to be a Japanese bomber but was in fact the fighter flown by Commander Butch O'Hare, the US Navy's first fighter ace and holder of the Medal of Honor. He was never seen again.

The next phase of the American offensive involved the assault of Kwajalein and Namur islands in the Marshalls; Operation 'Flintlock', on 31 January 1944. In support was Task Force 58, reconstituted under Rear Admiral Mark A. Mitscher from TF 50, now with six fleet and six light carriers. Among their aircraft were the first F4U-2 Corsair and F6F-3N Hellcat radar night-fighters. During the six-day operations to capture the key Marshall islands, American carrier aircraft destroyed some 150 Japanese aircraft (mostly on the ground), for the cost of 49 of their own number.

ON TO ENIWETOK
Following the capture of Kwajalein, Sherman's carrier task group descended upon Eniwetok atoll, 480 km (300 miles) to the west and almost mid-way between the Marshalls and the next archipelago, the Carolines. Eleven days after the fall of Kwajalein the amphibious forces of the US 5th Fleet went ashore and eliminated the Japanese garrison at Eniwetok.

The climax of the American destruction of Japan's central Pacific defence perimeter arrived with the

Left: The Mitsubishi A6M3 ('Zeke' 22) was the version without folding wingtips that was used in the south-west Pacific from the spring of 1942. These Zeros are with 204 Flying Group at Rabaul in New Britain in 1943.

Below: On 21 August 1943 a formation of Liberators on a bombing mission came across a Naval Type O Transport, Aircraft Model 11 or L2D (a Douglas DC-3 licence-built in Japan) which was promptly shot down by the dorsal gunner from one of the B-24s.

Left: Smoke plumes rise from installations on Dublon Island in September 1944 as B-24 Liberators of the 7th Air Force continue the neutralisation of the Japanese Truk bastion. Battered Eten Island lies to the right of Dublon.

assault on Truk atoll, capital of the Carolines, 1050 km (650 miles) north of Rabaul in New Britain. The first air strikes on Truk (apart from pre-emptive attacks launched during previous assaults elsewhere) were flown at dawn on D-Day, 17 February 1944. On the airstrips the US Navy pilots found 365 Japanese aircraft parked nose to tail, destroyed at least 125 of them and sank 30 merchant vessels, a cruiser, three destroyers and a sub-chaser.

Right: US paratroopers dropped from USAAF C-47 Skytrain transports float down on to the beachhead at Noemfoor in July 1944. This advance brought the Allies to New Guinea's western end.

Below: 'El Diablo IV', a B-25D-10-NC, flies over New Britain Island while operating with the 5th Air Force to attack Cape Gloucester. More than 2359 kg (5,200 lb) of bombs could be carried by the Mitchell; 2,290 B-25Ds were built.

Curtiss SB2C-3 Helldiver

Despite its great accomplishments in the Pacific theatre, the Helldiver was never popular with aircrew – the designation was said to mean 'Son of a Bitch, 2nd Class'. This aircraft flew with CV-19 aboard the USS *Hancock*, 1943-44.

Powerplant
The SB2C-3, which began to appear in 1944, had an uprated Wright Cyclone R-2600-20 14-cylinder, air-cooled radial piston engine.

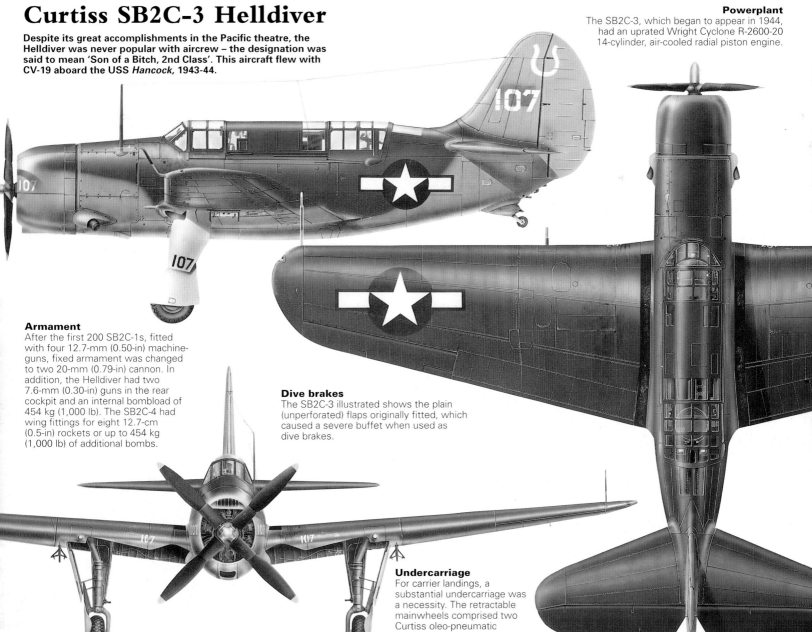

Armament
After the first 200 SB2C-1s, fitted with four 12.7-mm (0.50-in) machine-guns, fixed armament was changed to two 20-mm (0.79-in) cannon. In addition, the Helldiver had two 7.6-mm (0.30-in) guns in the rear cockpit and an internal bombload of 454 kg (1,000 lb). The SB2C-4 had wing fittings for eight 12.7-cm (0.5-in) rockets or up to 454 kg (1,000 lb) of additional bombs.

Dive brakes
The SB2C-3 illustrated shows the plain (unperforated) flaps originally fitted, which caused a severe buffet when used as dive brakes.

Undercarriage
For carrier landings, a substantial undercarriage was a necessity. The retractable mainwheels comprised two Curtiss oleo-pneumatic shock-absorber struts raised inwards into the undersides of the wings.

WORLD WAR II IN THE PACIFIC

The success of the devastating air strikes deprived the Japanese of effective air cover when the amphibious forces assaulted the islands, and in contrast to the 2,677 Japanese defenders who died the US casualties totalled 399.

Reduction of the Japanese garrisons in the large archipelagoes, successfully accomplished between November 1943 and February 1944, was followed by a temporary withdrawl of the American carrier forces to regroup for the next phase, the great thrust into the south-west Pacific.

Above: A B-24 Liberator makes an emergency landing on one mainwheel after an attack against the Marshall Islands. By the end of 1943, the B-24 was by far the most important long-range bomber in the Pacific area.

Left: A B-25 Mitchell of the 5th Air Force low over the harbour at Rabaul, New Britain, in an attack which sank or damaged 26 Japanese ships on 2 November 1943.

Below: On 16 June 1943, Lieutenant Murray J. Shubin (below with his P-38 Lightning named 'Oriole') of the 339th Fighter Squadron destroyed five enemy fighters and claimed a sixth as a probable during a 45-minute air battle.

Imperial Japanese warriors

The Imperial Japanese Navy had been operating flying-boats since the 1930s and the 'Mavis' (its Allied codename) gained a reputation as one of the best flying-boats of the war. 'Dinah' was the name given to the Ki-46, a high-speed reconnaissance type and bomber that was initially immune from fighter attack. The Ki-49 bomber first flew in 1939 and later filled transport and ASW roles.

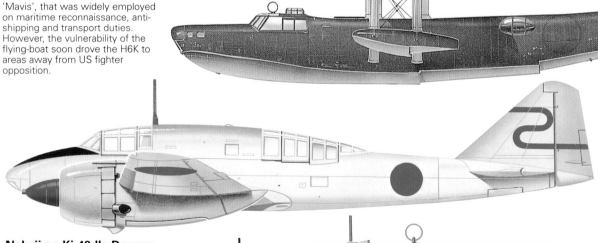

Kawanishi H6K
A fine flying-boat from the Kawanishi stable was the H6K 'Mavis', that was widely employed on maritime reconnaissance, anti-shipping and transport duties. However, the vulnerability of the flying-boat soon drove the H6K to areas away from US fighter opposition.

Mitsubishi Ki-46-II
The Mitsubishi Ki-46 was used originally as a fast reconnaissance aircraft, but this effective aircraft was soon employed in an offensive role. This Ki-46-II flew with the 76th Dokuritsu Hikochutai, East Indies in 1943.

Nakajima Ki-49-IIa Donryu
The 'Storm Dragon' ('Helen' to the Allies) was found to be underpowered, and more powerful engines came with the Ki-49-II. Shown here is a Ki-49-IIa of the 3rd Chutai, 61st Sentai. Its lack of speed was to remain a problem.

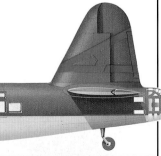
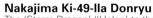

Corsair versus Zero

Captain R. Bruce Porter, USMC, recounts his experience flying Corsairs in the summer of 1943, as he downs a Zero during an early-morning patrol while flying from near Guadalcanal.

"We were at 18,000 ft and heading north-west... the remainder of the squadron, and three other alert squadrons, were dispersed nearby or right behind us. Thus we had 32 Corsairs and Wildcats flying as a leading wedge and nearly an identical number coming on as a follow-up force. The New Zealanders managed to launch another 30 P-40 fighters...

"I do not think I was ever so exhilarated as I was during that flight... I was just commenting to myself what a beautiful day it was when my earphones suddenly crackled with an incoming all-squadrons message: 'Tally ho! Zeros at 11 O'clock. Angels 25.' I charged my guns and turned on my reflector sight, which cast an image of a gunsight, complete with distance calibrations, on the windscreen in front of my face.

"Within seconds, I saw silvery glints against the bright-blue background of the sky. The enemy fighter formations were coming in from all directions... all the best training in the world could not abate the instant of surprise when my eyes locked on to a target of their own.

"I never consciously pressed my gun-button knob... I seemed to know enough to allow my instincts to prevail over my mind. My guns were bore-sighted to converge in a cone about 300-yards ahead. Anything within that cone would be hit by a stream of half-inch steel-jacketed bullets. My Corsair shuddered slightly as all the guns fired, and I saw my tracer passing just over the Zero's long birdcage canopy...

"My turn was easy. I did not pull too many Gs, so my head was absolutely clear. I came up with a far deflection shot and decided to go for it. It gave the Zero a good lead and fired all my guns again. As planned, my tracers went ahead of him, but at just the right level. I kicked my left rudder to pull my round in towards his nose.

"If that Japanese pilot had flown straight ahead, he would have been a dead man. Instead, that superb pilot presented me with a demonstration of the Zero's best flight characteristic... as soon as my quarry saw my tracer pass in front, he simply pulled straight up and literally disappeared from within my reflector sight... I was so in awe of the manoeuvre that I was literally shaking with envy... then I pulled my joystick into my belly and banked as hard to the left as I dared.

"There he was! He was just beyond my reach. If I were to get a clear shot, I would have to pull up in an even steeper climb... I held my breath and sucked in my gut to counteract the pressure, but I felt the forces of gravity steadily mount up and press me into my seat...

He had me in a tight loop by then. All the alarm bells went off in my head at the same time, but I hung on despite the grey pall that was simultaneously passing over my eyes and my mind.

"I finally reached the top of the loop, a point where all the forces were in equilibrium. Suddenly, the G forces relaxed. I was not quite weightless, but neither was I my full body weight. There was a moment of grogginess, then the grey pall totally cleared. I noticed that the horizon was upside down and that the Zero was in my sights!

"It was now or never. I squeezed the gun-button beneath my right index finger. The eerie silence in my cockpit was broken by the steady roar of my machine-guns. The Zero never had a chance. It flew directly into the cone of deadly half-inch bullets. I was easily able to stay on it as the stream of tracer first sawed into the leading edge of the left wing. I saw little pieces of metal fly away from the impact area and clearly thought I should nudge my gunsight – which is to say, my entire Corsair – a hair to the right. The stream of tracer worked its way to the cockpit. I clearly saw the glass canopy shatter, but there was so much glinting, broken glass and debris that I could not see the pilot. The Zero wobbled, and my tracer fell into first one wing root, then the other, striking the enemy's unprotected fuel tanks. The Zero blew up, evaporated."

Left: Pictured in the cockpit of his A6M2 Zero in 1943, this cheerful pilot is believed to be WO Yoshira Hashiguchi of the 3rd Flying Group in 1943. The Zero's gun sighting system is visible behind the windscreen.

Left: Perhaps the greatest piston-engined naval fighter of all, the F4U (and Goodyear-built FG) Corsair took some time to develop, some of the first going to VF-71. Here early F4U-1s are returning to the USS Yorktown in 1943.

Saipan and Guam

FEBRUARY – JULY 1944

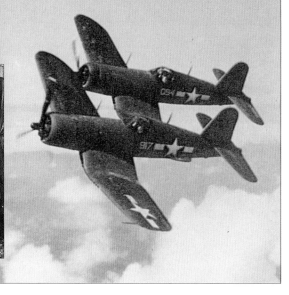

A combat formation of Vought F4U-1 Corsair fighters of the celebrated US Marine Corps 'Black Sheep' squadron (VMF-124) banks over the island of Bougainville in the Solomons. Corsairs were found to be highly effective at ground attack and were widely used in this role.

Inset: Nearly all of the American Corsairs in the Pacific theatre were flown by the US Marine Corps, accounting for 2,140 enemy aircraft. The 'Black Sheep' squadron was based in the Marianas, where 'Pappy' Boyington leads his men out to their aircraft.

Key to the US Navy's success in the Gilberts, Marshalls and Carolines had been the inability of the Japanese to bring into action any significant numbers of naval aircraft to contest air superiority over the landings. Indeed, following earlier heavy losses, the Japanese had been hard at work reorganising their depleted carrier forces. By mid-May the Japanese fleet at Tawi Tawi off the coast of Borneo included the surviving veterans *Zuiho*, *Shokaku* and *Zuikaku*, the new *Taiho*, the *Hiyo* and *Junyo*, and the light carriers *Chitose*, *Chiyoda* and *Ryuho*. These nine vessels constituted the largest force of carriers ever assembled under a Japanese task force commander. Although a new generation of aircraft, such as the improved A6M5 'Zeke' fighter-bomber, the D4Y3 'Judy' and the B6N1 'Jill' torpedo/attack bombers, were joining the fleet in growing numbers in 1944, the real weakness lay in a chronic shortage of experienced fliers. Two years of heavy fighting had taken a huge toll of Japan's naval airmen, and the replacements would now be pitted against vastly improved US aircraft, notably the F6F Hellcat and F4U Corsair.

Furthermore, following the assault on Truk in February 1944, the American carriers withdrew to reorganise, re-equip and re-crew. By June Task Force 58 had grown to five task groups with 15 carriers, the fleet carriers *Bunker Hill*, *Enterprise*, *Essex*, *Hornet*, *Lexington*, *Wasp* and *Yorktown*, and the light carriers *Bataan*, *Belleau Wood*, *Cabot*,

The Mitsubishi J2M-5 Thunderbolt (Allied codename 'Jack') naval interceptor fighter had a supercharged engine and could reach 20,000 ft in less than six minutes from take-off. It was used to intercept high-flying USAAF B-29s.

Cowpens, *Langley*, *Monterey*, *Princeton* and *San Jacinto*; between them they embarked no fewer than 480 Hellcat day and night fighters, 199 Avengers, 222 Helldiver and Dauntless dive-bombers and three Corsair night-fighters.

In Marianas skies

The Mitsubishi Ki-46 'Dinah' was one of the best reconnaissance aircraft of the war and was active until the end of hostilities over the Marianas' B-29 bases. About five times as many Curtiss SB2C

Helldiver carrier-based dive-bombers were produced as were 'Dinahs', but the type's development was protracted and it was never very popular with its air or ground crews, unlike the sleek Mitsubishi.

Mitsubishi Ki-46-III

With the capture or destruction of air bases in the Marianas, the long-ranged Ki-46s based elsewhere came into their own for tracking Allied movements. In 1944, the main service version was the improved Ki-46-III.

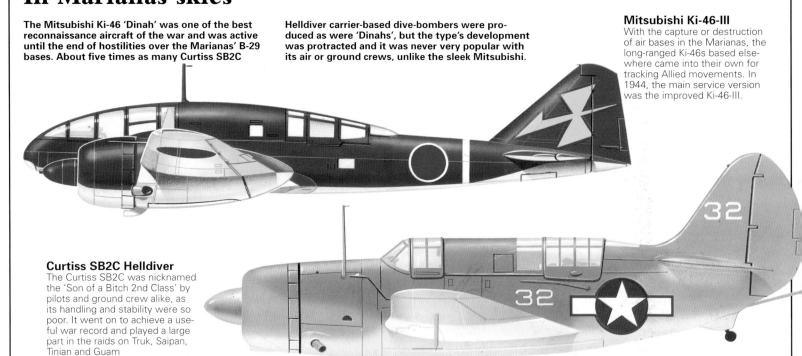

Curtiss SB2C Helldiver

The Curtiss SB2C was nicknamed the 'Son of a Bitch 2nd Class' by pilots and ground crew alike, as its handling and stability were so poor. It went on to achieve a useful war record and played a large part in the raids on Truk, Saipan, Tinian and Guam

Fighting 'boats

The Japanese Kawanishi H8K 'Emily' is generally acknowledged as the best four-engined flying-boat to see service in World War II. The H8K2 variant had sea search radar and armament of five 20-mm cannon and one machine-gun. The closest US equivalent was the twin-engined Martin PBM Mariner, which was comparitvely lightly-armed (eight machine-guns), faster but shorter-ranged.

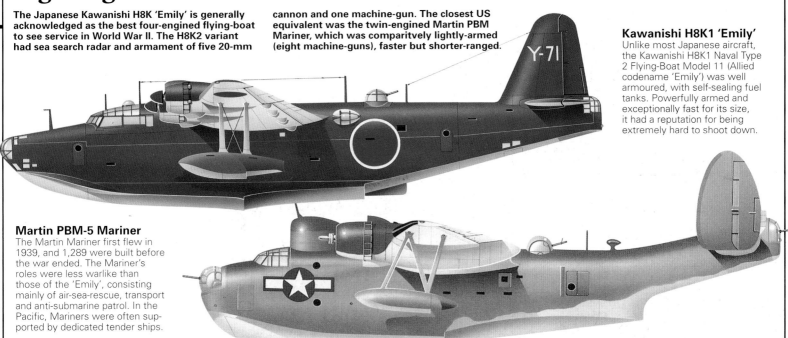

Kawanishi H8K1 'Emily'
Unlike most Japanese aircraft, the Kawanishi H8K1 Naval Type 2 Flying-Boat Model 11 (Allied codename 'Emily') was well armoured, with self-sealing fuel tanks. Powerfully armed and exceptionally fast for its size, it had a reputation for being extremely hard to shoot down.

Martin PBM-5 Mariner
The Martin Mariner first flew in 1939, and 1,289 were built before the war ended. The Mariner's roles were less warlike than those of the 'Emily', consisting mainly of air-sea-rescue, transport and anti-submarine patrol. In the Pacific, Mariners were often supported by dedicated tender ships.

Left: A formation of 18 Grumman TBF Avengers returns to the carrier USS Enterprise after a mission. Due to its range, the Avenger was the most widely used type for air patrols to counter the constant threat of submarines to vital Allied convoys.

Below: Throughout the war in the Pacific, the Nakajima B5N 'Kate' took its toll of Allied shipping. This excellent torpedo-bomber figured in all the naval engagements after Pearl Harbor until superseded by the same company's B6N.

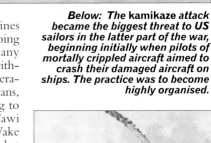

BUILD-UP IN THE MARIANAS

The newly appointed Japanese commander-in-chief, Admiral Soemu Toyoda, recognised that the American operations in the Central Pacific were but a prelude to a major and sustained thrust either westwards or southwestwards, and that such a thrust would pose a serious threat to their forces in New Guinea and the East Indies. He decided on a plan, Operation A-Go, to seek a decisive battle with the US 5th Fleet, his own forces being spearheaded by his carriers. In order to be close to the fuel source of the Borneo oil fields, Toyoda chose to base his fleet at Tawi Tawi (accepting the risk of using their characteristically highly volatile fuel in his ships).

As soon as US reconnaissance aircraft exposed the Japanese naval concentration at Tawi Tawi, US Navy submarines flocked to the area and by mid-June had torpedoed four oilers and five destroyers.

The presence of these submarines prevented the Japanese from going to sea for training, so that many new aircrews had to remain without adequate experience of operations with the fleet. The Americans, on the other hand, while failing to entice the Japanese out of Tawi Tawi, sailed for Marcus and Wake in order to gain 'controlled' combat experience for their new airmen, flying strikes during the last 10 days of May with relatively light losses.

The US plans now included the capture of Saipan and Guam, respectively at the north and south

Below: The kamikaze attack became the biggest threat to US sailors in the latter part of the war, beginning initially when pilots of mortally crippled aircraft aimed to crash their damaged aircraft on ships. The practice was to become highly organised.

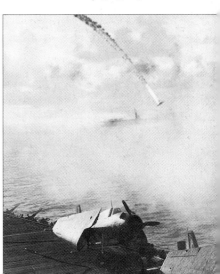

Left: A P-47D-20-RA Thunderbolt of the 19th Fighter Squadron, 318th Fighter Group in the Marianas prepares for a dive bombing mission to Pagan Island, Saipan. Airfields were quickly established once an island was captured.

Northrop P-61 Black Widow

Illustrated here is one of the most famous P-61s operated in the Pacific Theatre. P-61B-1-NO 42-39403 was almost unique in having the dorsal gun barbette fitted. Other features of the B model included a slightly longer nose and four external pylons.

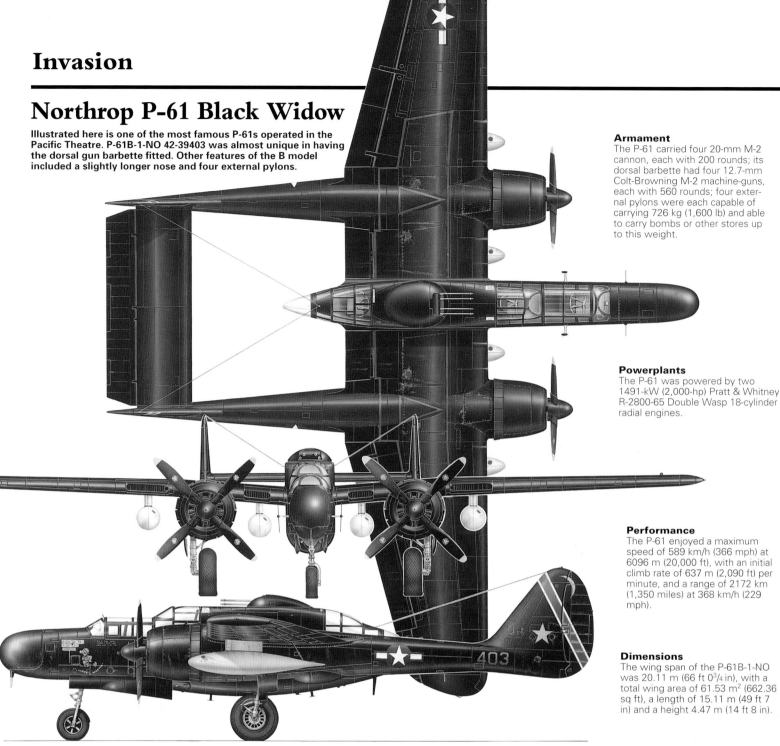

Armament
The P-61 carried four 20-mm M-2 cannon, each with 200 rounds; its dorsal barbette had four 12.7-mm Colt-Browning M-2 machine-guns, each with 560 rounds; four external pylons were each capable of carrying 726 kg (1,600 lb) and able to carry bombs or other stores up to this weight.

Powerplants
The P-61 was powered by two 1491-kW (2,000-hp) Pratt & Whitney R-2800-65 Double Wasp 18-cylinder radial engines.

Performance
The P-61 enjoyed a maximum speed of 589 km/h (366 mph) at 6096 m (20,000 ft), with an initial climb rate of 637 m (2,090 ft) per minute, and a range of 2172 km (1,350 miles) at 368 km/h (229 mph).

Dimensions
The wing span of the P-61B-1-NO was 20.11 m (66 ft 0¾ in), with a total wing area of 61.53 m² (662.36 sq ft), a length of 15.11 m (49 ft 7 in) and a height 4.47 m (14 ft 8 in).

---

ends of the Mariana chain, and the stage was now being set for what was to be the greatest-ever carrier battle, the Battle of the Philippine Sea, in which the once-vaunted Japanese carrier force would be crushingly defeated and suffer huge losses in aircraft.

The preliminary actions of Operation Forager against Saipan and Guam opened on 11 June as the American carriers launched strikes against Saipan and Tinian with 208 Hellcats and eight Avengers, destroying about 36 enemy aircraft on the ground. On the following day a small Japanese convoy was attacked from the air as it sailed from Saipan, losing 10 merchant ships, a torpedo boat and three sub-chasers. On 15 June US Marines landed on Saipan.

TACTICAL ERROR

Two days earlier, however, now warned of the presence of the American 5th Fleet, the Japanese navy sortied from Tawi Tawi, a sailing immediately reported by the submarine *Redfin* to Admiral

Left: US Marine Corps pilots on a Pacific island before embarking for a mission. Although a standard pilots uniform was issued, few pilots wore it as only the inflatable Mae West, helmet and goggles were deemed essential.

The Mitsubishi A6M5 Naval Type 0 Carrier-borne Fighter Model 52 was an advanced version of the A6M with strengthened wings, and could be dived at speeds in excess of 400 mph. The A6M5a (above) was fitted with a long-barrel, belt-fed cannon.

Left: A large group of 7th US Air Force personnel watch a B-24J take-off from an airstrip in the Marianas. Following in the wake of the liberation forces, the USAAF was eager to get bases nearer to the Japanese mainland.

Above: By 1944, security measures resulted in unit insignia no longer being painted on aircraft, only individual aircraft numbers within the unit. These SBD-3s are described as 'returning to their carrier after a dive-bombing mission'.

Spruance. This admiral then made one of the few major controversial decisions of the American naval campaign in the Pacific. He cancelled the imminent invasion of Guam and ordered most of the assault and supply ships off Saipan to disperse; he also ordered all five

task groups of TF 58 to concentrate to meet the Japanese threat. It has been argued that he should have allowed the fast battleships of Task Group 58.7 under Vice Admiral Willis Lee to remain independent. With the subsequent decimation of the Japanese carrier forces, in which

the battleships would take little or no part during the Battle of the Philippine Sea, such a powerful force of ships could have been deployed in readiness to destroy the remaining Japanese fleet without fear of air attackr. While the gruesome naval battle was being fought, the island of Saipan eventually fell on 9 July after 14,000 Americans had fallen dead or wounded; Japanese dead totalled 30,000.

Right: Perched on the wings of P-47Ds of the 19th Fighter Squadron, 218th Fighter Group, Saipan, crew chiefs guide pilots along a taxiway to the runway. Without this guidance, the pilot would be forced to zig-zag to keep the route ahead in view.

A Mitsubishi G4M Betty naval attack bomber in a semi-derelict state on an island in the Marianas. Probably the best known Japanese bomber, the G4M had considerable range capability, achieved by light-weight structure and a total lack of armour protection.

Right: The guns are manned and ready as an F6F Hellcat lands on the deck of the USS Lexington (CV-16, part of CVAG-16) during a Japanese air attack in the Battle of Saipan. On 19 June, Dauntless dive-bombers flew their last major combat operation from the carrier.

The Marianas Turkey Shoot

JUNE – AUGUST 1944

Left: Outbound Republic P-47 Thunderbolts on island patrol have the right of way as they flash across the end of the runway at a strategic base in the Marianas in August 1944.

Below: Despite its unpopularity in service, resulting in the re-interpretation of its designation as 'Son of a Bitch, 2nd Class', some 7,000 Curtiss SB2C Helldivers were built. These aircraft are returning to a carrier of Task Force 58.1 following a bombing mission over Chici-Jima on 7 June 1944.

The June of 1944 found the American forces heavily committed in their 'island-hopping' advance through the central Pacific, and the US forces were by that time far inside the original empire defence perimeter declared by the Japanese some two years previously. The success that attended this bloody advance was rendered possible by the steady build-up of powerful American naval forces, not least in carriers, in the Pacific. On 15 June 20,000 US Marines supported by US carrier aircraft and a heavy naval bombardment, went ashore on Saipan.

BATTLE FLEETS PREPARE

As soon as the Japanese supreme command learned of this landing, it ordered the 'destruction' of the US Pacific Fleet by the Japanese Mobile Fleet. In effect the American force then located in the Philippine Sea comprised Task Force 58, commanded by Vice-Admiral Marc A. Mitscher, with seven fleet carriers (the *Bunker Hill*, *Enterprise*, *Essex*, *Hornet*, *Lexington*, *Wasp* and *Yorktown*), eight light carriers, seven fast battleships, eight heavy cruisers, 12 other cruisers and 66 destroyers. Embarked in the carriers were 199

TBF/TBM Avenger torpedo bombers, 222 SB2C Helldiver and SBD Dauntless divebombers and 483 F6F Hellcat fighters. Against them the Japanese Mobile Fleet under Vice-Admiral Jisaburo Ozawa, consisted of five fleet carri-

ers (the *Hiyo*, *Junyo*, *Shokaku*, *Taiho* and *Zuikaku*), four light carriers, five battleships, seven heavy cruisers, two light cruisers and 23 destroyers; embarked were 99 B5N and B6N torpedo bombers, 206 dive-bombers and 145 A6M Zero

Left: P-38L-1 Lightning 'Little Red Head II' of the 318th Lightning Provisionals, being fitted with large drop tanks for a long-range mission from Isley Field, Saipan, Marianas in mid-1944. With two 1136-litre (300-gallon) drop tanks the 'L' had a range of 4184 km (2,600 miles).

Above: No aircraft was to have greater impact on the Japanese than the Grumman F6F Hellcat. The type formed the backbone of the US Navy's fighter defences throughout the offensive stages of the war. This aircraft awaits its next mission on board CV-10 USS Yorktown in June 1944.

Day and night fighters

Immensely powerful and heavily-built, P-47's served the USAAF in Europe and the Pacific and the RAF in the Far East. The primary production variant was the P-47D, later examples of which had a bubble canopy, which greatly improved visibility. The first purpose-built night fighter in the USAAF was the radar-equipped P-61. In service from 1944, these aircraft filled a secondary ground-attack role.

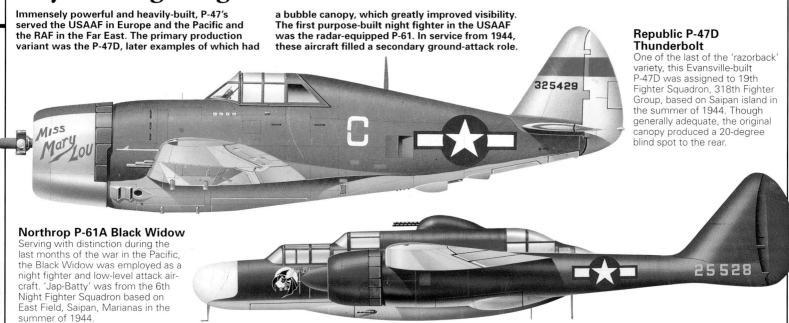

Republic P-47D Thunderbolt
One of the last of the 'razorback' variety, this Evansville-built P-47D was assigned to 19th Fighter Squadron, 318th Fighter Group, based on Saipan island in the summer of 1944. Though generally adequate, the original canopy produced a 20-degree blind spot to the rear.

Northrop P-61A Black Widow
Serving with distinction during the last months of the war in the Pacific, the Black Widow was employed as a night fighter and low-level attack aircraft. 'Jap-Batty' was from the 6th Night Fighter Squadron based on East Field, Saipan, Marianas in the summer of 1944.

Right: The Vought OS2U Kingfisher was to prove the most useful of the observation and scout aircraft available to the US Navy at this time. Easily recognised by its large centreline and smaller underwing floats, deliveries totalled 1,006 when production ceased in 1944.

Below: A Nakajima Ki-49 Donryu (Storm Dragon) – Allied codename 'Helen' – being strafed on an airfield in the Marianas. The Ki-49 was intended to replace the Mitsubishi Ki-21 'Sally', but units equipped with them suffered heavy losses during the Allied advance from the Philippines.

fighters.

After sightings of the units of the Japanese fleet by US submarines, Admiral Spruance, commanding the American 5th Fleet, ordered Task Force 58 to assemble on 18 June, when it was located by a Japanese carrier search aircraft. That night the Mobile Fleet also assembled for battle and was spotted on radar by a PBM Mariner patrol flying-boat. By early on 19 June Task Force 58 was some 160-km (100-miles) west of Guam in the Marianas, the Japanese Mobile Fleet about 320 km (200 miles) farther west. Sporadic air fighting occurred around dawn as Hellcats were launched to investigate radar reports of enemy aircraft; these proved to be search aircraft from the Japanese battleships and cruisers. Soon afterwards the first powerful strikes were launched by the Japanese carriers, and just after the *Taiho* had flown off 42 aircraft the carrier was struck by a torpedo from the US submarine *Albacore* (a second torpedo would have hit had its track not been spotted by a Japanese pilot who dived his aircraft on to the missile and exploded it).

Warned by radar of the

Above: Lt Cdr Kiyokuma Ikajima (seated) in front of his Mitsubishi A6M5 of the 203 Flying Group in the Marianas. The A6M was known to the Japanese airmen as the 'Rei Sentoki', or Zero fighter, a term commonly abbreviated to 'Reisen'.

Left: A somewhat later design than the Catalina, the Martin PBM Mariner was a larger aircraft and superior in performance, although it served in smaller numbers. Here a Mariner is operating from a mobile seaplane tender on patrol bombing missions and protective cover flights for the Pacific Fleet.

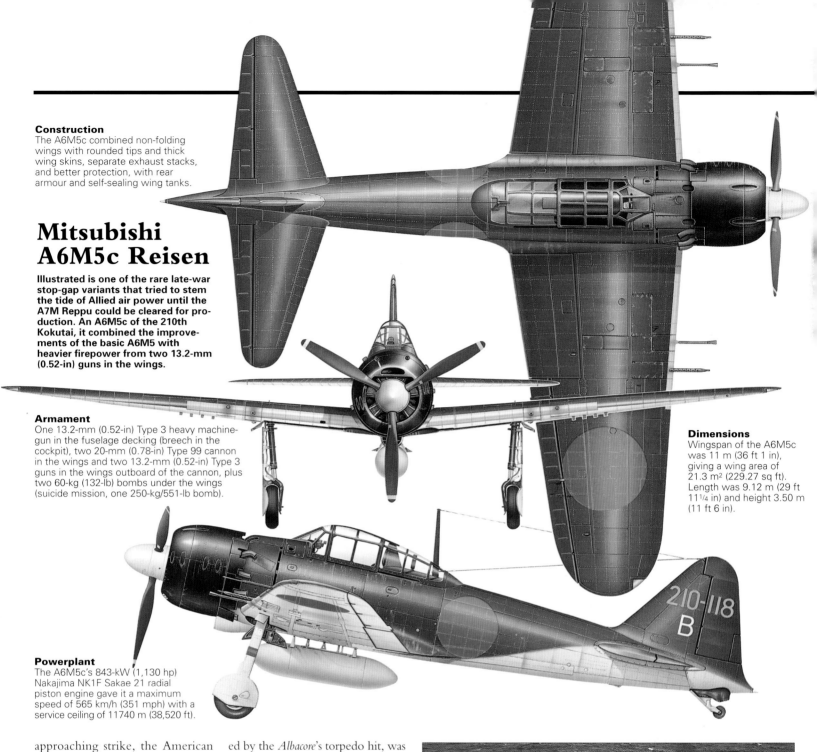

Mitsubishi A6M5c Reisen

Illustrated is one of the rare late-war stop-gap variants that tried to stem the tide of Allied air power until the A7M Reppu could be cleared for production. An A6M5c of the 210th Kokutai, it combined the improvements of the basic A6M5 with heavier firepower from two 13.2-mm (0.52-in) guns in the wings.

Construction
The A6M5c combined non-folding wings with rounded tips and thick wing skins, separate exhaust stacks, and better protection, with rear armour and self-sealing wing tanks.

Armament
One 13.2-mm (0.52-in) Type 3 heavy machine-gun in the fuselage decking (breech in the cockpit), two 20-mm (0.78-in) Type 99 cannon in the wings and two 13.2-mm (0.52-in) Type 3 guns in the wings outboard of the cannon, plus two 60-kg (132-lb) bombs under the wings (suicide mission, one 250-kg/551-lb bomb).

Dimensions
Wingspan of the A6M5c was 11 m (36 ft 1 in), giving a wing area of 21.3 m² (229.27 sq ft). Length was 9.12 m (29 ft 11¼ in) and height 3.50 m (11 ft 6 in).

Powerplant
The A6M5c's 843-kW (1,130 hp) Nakajima NK1F Sakae 21 radial piston engine gave it a maximum speed of 565 km/h (351 mph) with a service ceiling of 11740 m (38,520 ft).

approaching strike, the American carriers launched every available fighter. The US Navy and US Marine pilots destroying 42 of the 69 attacking aircraft. Apart from a single bomb hit on the battleship *South Dakota*, little damage was done and the raiders failed to reach the carriers. Shortly after 11.00 a second strike by 109 aircraft was spotted on radar. Again the Hellcats were launched and this time only about 15 of the raiders returned to their carriers. A third strike by 47 aircraft followed, and this time about half of them failed to find the American ships; of the others, seven were shot down. Yet one more strike, by 82 aircraft, was launched before midday on 19 June, no fewer than 73 of them being destroyed, many of them by the ships' guns as well as some caught by Hellcats as they tried to land on Guam.

Meanwhile the *Taiho*, whose seaworthiness had been little affect-

ed by the *Albacore*'s torpedo hit, was in trouble as her crew fought to get the fires under control; these efforts were succeeding when the ship's ventilating system was opened to dissipate the fumes of leaking fuel; suddenly in mid-afternoon a tremendous explosion occurred in

Above: An F6F Hellcat landing on the new USS Hornet (CV-11), after a raid over the Marianas in June 1944. During what became known as 'The Great Marianas Turkey Shoot', the Japanese lost 346 aircraft, while the US lost 130.

Left: Seen on 26 June 1944, this Thunderbolt 'Hed up 'N locked' fell victim to a Japanese sniper's bullet on Saipan. Some usable parts have been salvaged, including the four 12.7-mm (0.5-in) machine-guns from the starboard wing.

Left: One of the last of the 'razor-back' P-47D Thunderbolts 'Lady Ruth' was serving with the 19th Fighter Squadron, 318th Fighter Group, based on Saipan, Marianas islands in July 1944. Armourers are using an improvised rig to test the alignment of the P-47's 12.7-mm (0.5-in) machine-guns.

back on their carriers in the darkness and short of fuel. A total of 130 American aircraft were lost during the day, compared with three Japanese carriers, two oilers and 346 aircraft.

Little wonder the Battle of the Philippine Sea earned the gruesome nickname among the US Navy of 'The Great Marianas Turkey Shoot'. By 10 August Saipan had

the big carrier and she eventually capsized, Ozawa and his staff having been transferred to a destroyer; 13 aircraft went down with her.

Disaster had overtaken another Japanese carrier, this time the Pearl Harbor and Coral Sea veteran *Shokaku* being hit by three torpedoes from the American submarine *Cavallo* soon after midday. Once more volatile gases spread through the ship from ruptured fuel tanks and three hours later she blew up and sank, taking with her 1,263 men and nine more aircraft.

THE 'TURKEY SHOOT'

It was now the turn of the Americans to launch strikes against the Japanese fleet. Starting at 18.40 a total of 216 aircraft were flown off, split into half a dozen groups, one of which sank two Japanese fleet oilers. Another attacked the Japanese 2nd Carrier Division, two torpedo hits being made on the *Hiyo*, which later sank; the *Junyo*

was hit by two bombs but escaped. Elsewhere the *Zuikaku* was struck by one bomb, as was the light carrier *Chiyoda*. Although the Japanese fighters reacted strongly and shot down about 20 of the American aircraft, far more were destroyed in accidents as their pilots tried to land

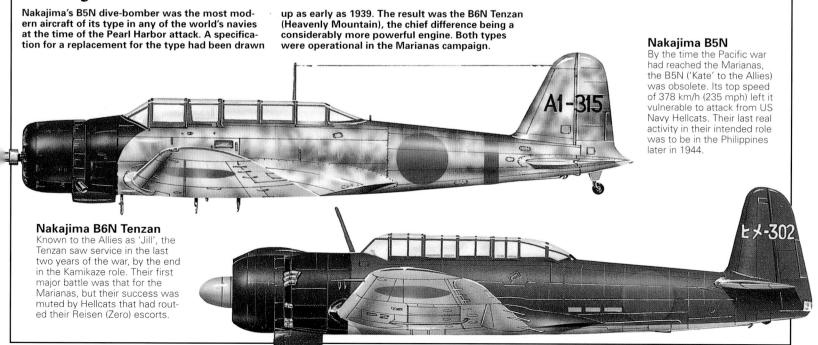

Left: A Japanese Navy B6N 'Jill' succumbs to anti-aircraft fire while attacking the USS Yorktown (CV-10). Air-to-air attack was another hazard, especially when escorting A6M Reisen fighters fell to American Hellcats.

Above: The islands of the Pacific were littered with crashed aircraft. This wrecked Mitsubishi A6M is symbolic of the devastating firepower brought to bear upon Japan's air forces, mainly by the US Navy's F6F Hellcats.

Nakajima's dive-bombers

Nakajima's B5N dive-bomber was the most modern aircraft of its type in any of the world's navies at the time of the Pearl Harbor attack. A specification for a replacement for the type had been drawn up as early as 1939. The result was the B6N Tenzan (Heavenly Mountain), the chief difference being a considerably more powerful engine. Both types were operational in the Marianas campaign.

Nakajima B5N

By the time the Pacific war had reached the Marianas, the B5N ('Kate' to the Allies) was obsolete. Its top speed of 378 km/h (235 mph) left it vulnerable to attack from US Navy Hellcats. Their last real activity in their intended role was to be in the Philippines later in 1944.

A1-315

ヒ×-302

Nakajima B6N Tenzan

Known to the Allies as 'Jill', the Tenzan saw service in the last two years of the war, by the end in the Kamikaze role. Their first major battle was that for the Marianas, but their success was muted by Hellcats that had routed their Reisen (Zero) escorts.

Philippine Landings

NOVEMBER 1944 – MARCH 1945

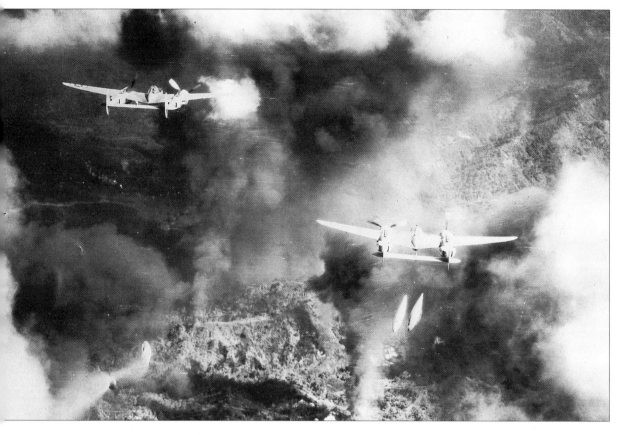

Above: The invasion of Luzon began with a fiercely opposed landing at Lingayen Gulf. Here a Kamikaze is diving on the USS Columbia on 6 January 1945. The aircraft hit the main deck of the ship, causing extensive damage.

Left: The 5th and 13th Air Forces were placed in the new Far East Air Forces (FEAF) under General Kenney, putting around 500 P-38s at his disposal. Here P-38Js drop napalm bombs near Ipo Dam, Luzon.

After the great carrier battle of the Marianas, American forces went on to complete the capture of Saipan, thereby providing an important base for subsequent B-29 attacks on Japan. They landed on Guam on 21 July, and on Tinian four days later. The final capture of Guam on 10 August marked the end of the American campaign in the Central Pacific and the end of organised Japanese carrier warfare. The *Hiyo* had been sunk by air action, and the *Taiho* and *Shokaku* had been sunk by US submarines, while no fewer than 1,223 Japanese naval aircraft had been destroyed in the two-month campaign.

Four further Japanese carriers, the *Zuikaku*, *Chitose*, *Chiyoda* and *Zuiho*, went to the bottom during the battles of Leyte Gulf. On 30 November, only 11 days after her commissioning, the huge ex-battleship aircraft-carrier *Shinano* (69152 tonnes/68,060 tons) was sunk by the submarine USS *Archerfish* in Tokyo Bay. Before the end of the year the carriers *Unryu*, *Shinyo*, *Taiyo*, *Chuyo* and *Unyo* had been sunk and the *Junyo* was permanently crippled. During the same period the US Navy lost but one carrier, the light-carrier *Princeton*.

UNEXPECTED ENEMY

Although the initial landings on Leyte marked the start of the Philippines campaign, the invasion of the main island, Luzon, did not take place until 9 January 1945, four divisions being put ashore in Lingayen Gulf. Already Task Force 38 had to contend with a powerful new enemy: atrocious weather. On 18 December a fully-fledged typhoon struck the fleet; three destroyers capsized with the loss of more than 800 men; aircraft tore loose in the carriers, starting fires as they ripped up electric cabling; the *Cowpens*, *Monterey* and *San Jacinto* between them lost 33 aircraft, 19 others were swept off the battleships and cruisers, and the smaller escort carriers lost a further 94. Such losses and the search for survivors in the mountainous seas delayed the ultimate assault on Luzon.

As pre-emptive strikes against Japanese air bases on Formosa were being flown by the carriers of TF 38 in the first week of 1945, the Lingayen Gulf assault force, carried by the US 7th Fleet under Vice-Admiral Thomas C. Kinkaid. came under heavy Japanese suicide attacks as it approached the landing area. The escort carrier *Ommaney Bay* was hit and sunk on 4 January,

Above: A Curtiss SB2C Helldiver is flagged off on a mission from USS Hancock (CV-19) on 25 November 1944. On the same day, a Kamikaze exploded directly over the ship, and burning debris started several fires.

Right: B-24M Liberators, including examples from the 494th Bomb Group nearest the camera, at an airstrip on Angaur Island in the Carolines. From here raids were made against the Philippines.

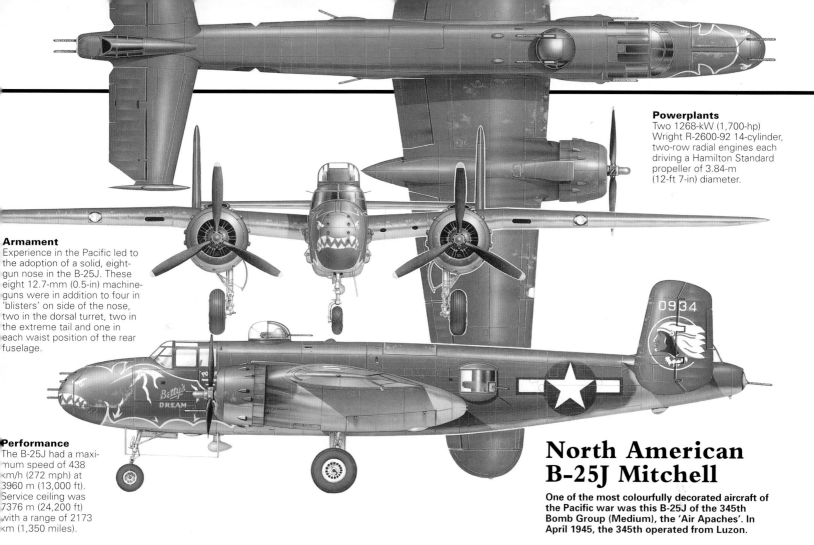

Powerplants
Two 1268-kW (1,700-hp) Wright R-2600-92 14-cylinder, two-row radial engines each driving a Hamilton Standard propeller of 3.84-m (12-ft 7-in) diameter.

Armament
Experience in the Pacific led to the adoption of a solid, eight-gun nose in the B-25J. These eight 12.7-mm (0.5-in) machine-guns were in addition to four in 'blisters' on side of the nose, two in the dorsal turret, two in the extreme tail and one in each waist position of the rear fuselage.

Performance
The B-25J had a maximum speed of 438 km/h (272 mph) at 3960 m (13,000 ft). Service ceiling was 7376 m (24,200 ft) with a range of 2173 km (1,350 miles).

North American B-25J Mitchell

One of the most colourfully decorated aircraft of the Pacific war was this B-25J of the 345th Bomb Group (Medium), the 'Air Apaches'. In April 1945, the 345th operated from Luzon.

Above: View from the USS Essex *on 25 November 1944 as a 'Banzai' suicide bomber heads towards the carrier after being hit by flak. It landed on the edge of the port side of the deck forward of the No. 2 elevator.*

Above: TF 38 returned to Ulithi Atoll without hitting Luzon again in December 1944 because of a typhoon. Taken from the USS Essex *(CV-9), this picture shows the Task Group as it enters Ulithi.*

and the following day the *Manila Bay* was damaged and suffered more than 70 casualties; on 8 January both the *Kitkun Bay* and the *Kadashan Bay* were badly damaged and had to retire from the battle.

On 9 January, as the American forces went ashore in Lingayen Gulf, Admiral William F. Halsey's 3rd Fleet (including TF 38), with eight fleet carriers, five light carriers, two escort carriers, six battleships,11 cruisers and 61 destroyers,

entered the South China Sea, its main task being to locate and destroy the two battleship carriers, *Hyuga* and *Ise*, and also to prevent the Japanese from sending reinforcements to Luzon. Although the giant carriers were not found, the American carrier aircraft flew wide-ranging strikes over French Indochina, China proper and Formosa; few targets were found.

BLOODY ADVANCE

Suicide attacks around Luzon continued to increase, the Australian cruiser *Australia* being hit five times. Fighting on the ground grew fiercer and, despite an order from General Yamashita to evacuate Manila, a Japanese admiral organised resistance by 20,000 men in the naval base. Bataan fell on 16 February, and Corregidor (in Manila Bay) on 28 February. By then, however, the bulk of the American carrier forces had moved

on to prepare for the invasion of Iwo Jima. Indeed, with the steady but bloody advance through Luzon, and the over-running or building of airstrips on the island, it now fell to the fighter and fighter-bomber squadrons of the USAAF and US Marine Corps to provide cover over the battlefield, and to the guns of the fleet to create a curtain of fire

against the suicide attacks.

On 4 March 1945, after 173 days ashore on Luzon, American forces finally captured the shattered city of Manila, having lost more than 40,000 in dead and wounded, and more than 360 aircraft. Ten days later Iwo Jima also fell to the Americans. The US 10th Army, and the 16 carriers of Task Force 58 in support, were poised for assault on the last stepping stone to Japan: Okinawa.

Below: The Philippines played host to the Vought F4U-1 Corsairs of the US Marine Corps. These excellent aircraft were soon found to be highly capable at ground attack and were widely employed in this role.

The Battle of Leyte Gulf

SEPTEMBER – OCTOBER 1944

Mid-1944 found the US forces in the Pacific engaged in two main offensives towards the Philippines, one under the direction of Admiral William F. Halsey north-west from Guadalcanal along the northern coast of New Guinea, the other through the Gilberts, Marshalls and Marianas led by Admiral Raymond A. Spruance's 5th Fleet. Between the two thrusts Task Force 38 with 16 carriers struck the major Japanese bases in the Palaus and at Yap early in September, expecting to

Above: Hellcats, Avengers and Dauntlesses on Lexington's deck before the massive three-day series of air strikes was launched against Japanese air power on Formosa from 12/14 October 1944.

encounter heavy Japanese resistance in the air. In the event opposition was very light and the American ships and aircraft went on the rampage, destroying 58 aircraft and sinking 15 supply ships.

Surprised by the relatively weak defences, Halsey changed his plans and initiated air attacks on the central Philippines, the islands of Bohol, Cebu, Leyte, Negros, Panay and Samar. In two days the American carrier aircraft destroyed 478 aircraft and sank some 60 small ships, all for the loss of nine aircraft. Moving his sights up, Halsey now attacked the main island of Luzon and on 22 September his carrier aircraft destroyed 300 more Japanese aircraft. He went further, putting forward a proposal for the invasion of Leyte two months earlier than planned. As General MacArthur was at sea and observing radio silence the proposal went before Roosevelt and Churchill, who were in conference at Quebec, and approval for the plan was given without any delay. By the time

Left: Leyte marked the end of the Imperial Japanese Navy as an effective force. This destroyer in Ormol Bay is being attacked by a gunship version of the B-25, 'skip-bombing' two 454-kg (1,000-lb) bombs.

Halsey had been forced by bad weather to leave Luzon waters on 24 September his pilots had destroyed more than 1,000 aircraft and about 150 ocean-going ships for the loss of 72 aircraft.

COMBINED FLEET

At the time of these preliminaries to the invasion of the Philippines, the Japanese still possessed eight completed carriers with a total theoretical complement of 400 aircraft; however, neither the pilots nor aircraft existed to equip them fully. Recognising that the naval and air forces remaining in the Philippines stood no chance of withstanding the combined strength of Task Force 38 and Task Group 77.4

Above: Curtiss SB2C Helldivers return to USS Hornet (CV-12) following strikes over the Philippines. Admiral Halsey's intention was to destroy any potential opposition prior to the invasion of the islands.

under Rear Admiral Thomas L. Sprague with 18 escort carriers and 500 aircraft, the Japanese decided to assemble the Combined Fleet with four of their carriers and two battleship carriers (the *Ise* and *Hyuga*).

On 17 October US Army Rangers began going ashore on the islands in the mouth of Leyte Gulf, covered by Task Group 77.4. Meanwhile, uncertain of the ultimate invasion point, the Japanese Combined Fleet had split into three groups, two diversion attack forces

Once mighty 'Zeke'

First flying in 1939, the Mitsubishi A6M Reisen (Zero Fighter) became the symbol of Japanese air power; more were produced than any other Japanese type. When it entered service in 1942 it matched the speed, armament and protection of Allied fighters and despite being judged obsolete in 1943, continued in production. Allied types like the Hellcat ultimately challenged its superiority.

Mitsubishi A6M2 Reisen
The Mitsubishi A6M was still providing the main fighter assets of the Japanese navy at the time of Leyte Gulf. This A6M2 of the 402nd Chutai, 341st Kokutai was land-based at Clark Field, Manila in the Philippines, for many years an American air base. 'Zeke' was the Allied codename.

Right: Aircraft on the USS Intrepid prepare to launch strikes against the Philippines after spending a quiet Thanksgiving Day at sea. Those closest to the camera are Hellcats, with Helldivers beyond.

being despatched to the Lingga Roads and the Ryukyu Islands, 640 km (400 miles) and 480 km (300 miles) respectively to the west of Leyte. As reports came in of the American landings the main Japanese naval force sailed from Formosa.

INTO BATTLE

The first battle involved Task Force 38, whose northern-most carrier group, with the carriers *Essex*, *Lexington*, *Langley* and *Princeton*, was attacked by about 160 land-based aircraft (hurriedly moved from Formosa to the Philippines) on 23 October. When seven F6F Hellcats intercepted the attackers one American pilot, Commander David McCampbell, shot down at least nine within one hour. The *Princeton* was hit by two bombs and after internal explosions had reduced her to a hulk she was sent to the bottom by American torpedoes. Following the location of the first Japanese diversion attack force, 259 American carrier aircraft took off to attack the enemy ships which now included the 46-cm (18.1-in) gunned battleships *Musashi* and *Yamato*. The former was hit by no fewer than 19 torpedoes and about 10 bombs before the 65027-tonne (64,000-ton) ship sank, taking with her more than 1,000 of her crew. In another battle, this time involving Vice-Admiral Nishimura's force of two battleships, a heavy cruiser and four destroyers, Vice-Admiral

Right: Almost all the major air combats in the Pacific theatre from August 1943 onwards were dominated by the F6F-5 Hellcat. Here a Hellcat gets the take-off flag aboard USS Randolph.

Kinkaid's force sank both the Japanese capital ships and two destroyers in history's last battleship-versus-battleship engagement, in Surigao Strait.

The next phase opened when carrier aircraft from TF 38 spotted the Japanese carriers approaching on 25 October. Strikes were sent off, hitting and sinking the *Chitose*, and damaging the *Zuiho* and *Zuikaku*; later that day another strike sank the *Zuiho*. In another action involving the American escort carriers 320 km (200 miles) to the south-west, the US ships

were less fortunate when four Japanese heavy cruisers engaged them, damaging the *Kalinin Bay*, *Fanshaw Bay* and *White Plains*, and sinking the *Gambier Bay*.

It was at this point that the Japanese first introduced their Kamikaze (suicide) aircraft, the first to achieve success being a Zero pilot who struck and damaged the escort carrier USS *Santee*, another

Left: The Yokosuka D4Y 'Judy' was a naval carrier-borne reconnaissance aircraft to replace the Aichi D3A2 'Val'. About 140 D4Y1s and 35 D4Y1-Cs took part in the Battle of the Philippine Sea. Nearly all were lost.

damaged the *Suwannee*, and then the *St Lo* was hit and sunk, the first American warship to be sunk by suicide aircraft.

The Battles of Leyte Gulf marked the end of the Imperial Japanese Fleet as a powerful and balanced fighting force, its losses of four carriers, three battleships, nine cruisers and eight destroyers comparing with the American loss of three carriers and two destroyers. The fighting on Leyte continued until the spring of 1945 but, with Japanese naval power virtually eliminated, the final outcome was never in any doubt.

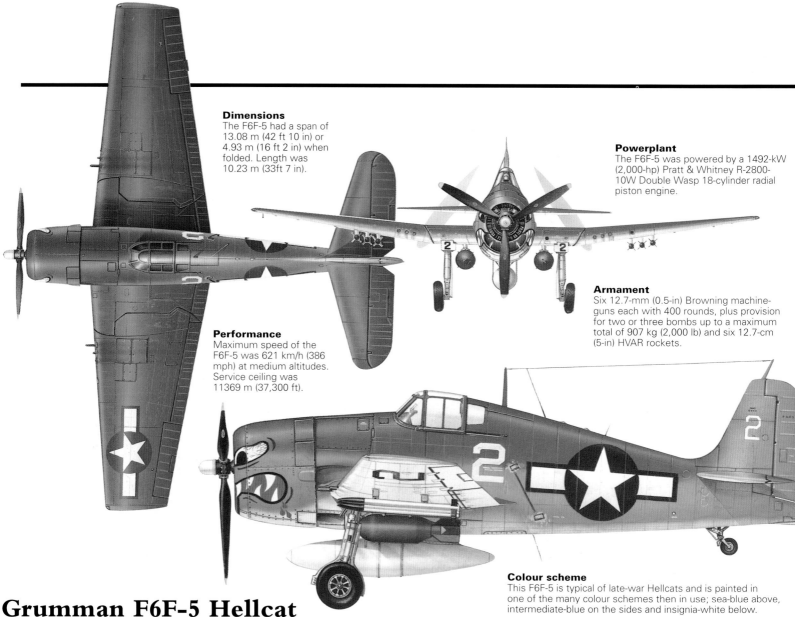

Dimensions
The F6F-5 had a span of 13.08 m (42 ft 10 in) or 4.93 m (16 ft 2 in) when folded. Length was 10.23 m (33ft 7 in).

Powerplant
The F6F-5 was powered by a 1492-kW (2,000-hp) Pratt & Whitney R-2800-10W Double Wasp 18-cylinder radial piston engine.

Performance
Maximum speed of the F6F-5 was 621 km/h (386 mph) at medium altitudes. Service ceiling was 11369 m (37,300 ft).

Armament
Six 12.7-mm (0.5-in) Browning machine-guns each with 400 rounds, plus provision for two or three bombs up to a maximum total of 907 kg (2,000 lb) and six 12.7-cm (5-in) HVAR rockets.

Colour scheme
This F6F-5 is typical of late-war Hellcats and is painted in one of the many colour schemes then in use; sea-blue above, intermediate-blue on the sides and insignia-white below.

Grumman F6F-5 Hellcat

The F6F-5 was the major production version of the Hellcat with over 6,300 built. This example flew with VF-27 aboard USS *Princeton* in 1944.

Above: The Wildcat was in the twilight of its career by the end of 1944. Some remained in use aboard escort carriers (CVEs), specifically FM-2s. The FM-2 was an F4F-8 built by the Eastern Aircraft division of General Motors and was distinguished by its taller tailfin.

Left: Japanese battleship carrier Ise or Hyuga in action off Engano on 25 October. Smoke from anti-aircraft guns is evident as the vessel comes under air attack. As 'decoy' carriers at Leyte Gulf, neither ship operated aircraft in action.

Above: Intrepid opened the aerial part of the battle just after 08.00 on 24 October 1944 when one of its Helldivers spotted the Japanese Force in the Sibuyan Sea. This Helldiver just made it back to the Intrepid as it ran out of fuel.

The Kamikaze threat

Above: A comrade tightens the 'Hachimaki' for a Japanese Kamikaze pilot ready for a mission in late-1944. The 'Hachimaki' was a Samurai symbol of courage and composure before the battle and was worn by all Kamikaze pilots. A number of different aircraft types were used in the role, including fighters and dive-bombers.

Right: The Japanese Southern Force was routed during the night of 25 October 1944 in Surigao Strait, but TF-38 was decoyed to attack the Northern Force off Cape Engano. This gave the Center Force a golden opportunity to disrupt the Leyte landings, a chance that was lost when they attacked escort carriers off Samar. Here an explosion on USS St Lo (VC-65) of Carrier Unit One following a Kamikaze hit, sinking within the hour.

Left top: The Battle of Leyte Gulf saw the first widescale use of Kamikaze aircraft. Here a pilot is cheered off by groundcrew as he sets off in his bomb-laden Mitsubishi A6M. These attacks caused major problems for the Allied fleets.

Left: Dramatic picture of a Kamikaze manoeuvring his Zero to crash on the deck of the USS Missouri. Fortunately on this occasion the aircraft went into the sea. Many of the Kamikazes ended their mission by being shot down.

Above: A damaged Japanese dive-bomber plunges towards the escort carrier USS Kitkun Bay (CVE-71) off Leyte, October 1944. After the failure of the Sho operation, flights of up to five suicide aircraft with one or two escorting fighters became the principal weapon of the Imperial Navy whose ships were no longer able to operate as a fleet. In the foreground are Grumman Avengers aboard another of the carriers of Task Force 38.

Burma and China

MARCH 1944 – AUGUST 1945

After months of limited advance and counter-offensive in northern Burma, the Japanese embarked on their last major offensive in March 1944, thrusting towards Assam in the northwest. Now reformed as Long-Range Penetration Groups (LRPs), the Chindits were parachuted into the jungle behind enemy lines at Indaw on 5 March and, after overland reinforcement, began construction of a number of landing strips (of which 'Broadway' was the most important); within a week 9,000 Allied troops had been flown deep into enemy-held territory. However, when the Japanese launched an attack against the airfields being used to fly supplies over 'the Hump' into China, they also destroyed 'Broadway', together with most of the RAF fighters based there.

Above: A Short Sunderland Mk III with full ASV Mk III radar seen serving with No. 230 Squadron when it returned to the Far East and operated in the Burma campaign in 1944. The Sunderland is in Pacific theatre markings, and is pictured after landing on a jungle river for the first time.

Below: The flight crew of C-46 Commando Polly the Queen turns the propellers prior to start-up at Chenyi in China on 6 January 1945. The two engines are 2,100-hp (1566-kW) Pratt & Whitney Double Wasp 18-cylinder radials, driving four-bladed Hamilton Standard propellers.

RAF Hurri-bombers make a low-level attack on a Japanese-held bridge on the Tiddim Road in Burma in October 1944. Hurricane Mk IIs and Mk IVs remained in front-line service in the Far East until 1945.

In May 1944, No. 42 Squadron moved into the Imphal fighting, where its Hurricanes were highly active on army close-support bombing and strafing. In addition, they flew a large number of Rhubarb sorties in search of targets of opportunity.

In the course of the Japanese advance the defended towns of Kohima and Imphal were surrounded and besieged. By June it seemed that Imphal would be forced into surrender but, in the nick of time, General Slim's 14th Army managed to reach and break through the Japanese perimeter. Within days the withdrawal of the enemy had turned to rout, as RAF, SAAF and USAAF fighters and fighter-bombers began a year-long operation to destroy the Japanese forces in Burma.

By that time (July 1944), Air Command, Southeast Asia, commanded by Air Chief Marshal Sir Richard Peirse, had grown to a total of 90 squadrons, of which 26 were American (flying P-38s, P-40s, P-51s, B-24s, B-25s and C-47s), four were Indian (flying Hurricanes), one a Canadian squadron with Catalinas and one a South African squadron with Venturas. The remaining 58 were of the RAF, flying Thunderbolts, Spitfires, Hurricanes, Beaufighters, Mosquitos, Wellingtons, Liberators, Sunderlands and Catalinas.

As the new advance (somewhat cautious at first) began, and the Allied forces found abundant evidence that the Japanese army was

Below: This is a Mitsubishi Ki-51, Allied codename 'Sonia'. With over 1,500 built, it was used as a ground-attack and tactical reconnaissance aircraft and was so successful that it remained in production for most of the war.

Japanese attackers

Although the best Allied aircraft enjoyed a small qualitative edge by 1944, the gap was slight, and the Japanese forces based in China included some highly effective aircraft types. However, the biggest change since the start of the war in the Far East lay in the fact that the Allies no longer regarded the Japanese as being invincible, and morale was much higher.

Nakajima Ki-44
Lacking the agility of other Japanese fighters, the Nakajima Ki-44 followed a more Western approach and proved fast and stable, with excellent climb and dive capabilities. This is a Ki-44-IIb, flown by the commanding officer of the 85th Sentai from Canton, China, during 1944.

Mitsubishi Ki-46
Illustrating one of the many colour schemes applied to Japanese aircraft in World War II, this Mitsubishi Ki-46-II 'Dinah' displays the leaping tiger motif of the 18th Chutai, 82nd Sentai operating in China in 1944. The Ki-46 proved particularly effective in the recce role.

Nakajima Ki-49
The Nakajima Ki-49-I 'Helen', Army Type 100 Heavy Bomber, was underpowered, and more powerful engines were introduced on the Ki-49-II. Its performance was little improved and the type was easy prey for Allied fighters over Burma and China. This is a Ki-49-IIa of the 3rd Chutai, 95th Sentai.

Right: An Australian-built Bristol Beaufighter Mk 21 of No. 22 Squadron, with whom it served during the final year of the war in the Far East. The Beaufighter's arsenal of bombs, rockets and guns wrought widespread havoc among river and jungle targets throughout the Burma campaign until the final liberation of Rangoon.

Below: Often confused with the similarly shark-mouthed 23rd FG, the 51st Fighter Group painted all its Mustangs with the aggressive decoration, while within the 23rd FG only the 76th Squadron aircraft were so adorned. The P-51B was a mainstay of the USAAF in the Far East.

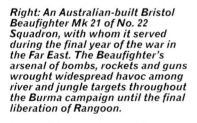

far from invincible, a heightened morale gripped the Allied aircrews. Combat procedures and weapons, hitherto confined to the European war, were adopted. The dreadful napalm weapon, found so effective in the jungle, came into use, as did Air Support Signals Units for the control of 'cab ranks', the patrols by fighters over the battlefield.

ADVANCE SOUTH

When the 1944 monsoon season arrived in July all effective operations by the Japanese air force in Burma ceased. By then the Allies were closing up to the Irrawaddy, and their air forces, particularly the long-range Liberators, concentrated on the enemy supply lines to prevent a build-up of reinforcements. By the end of the rains in November, when the advance southwards resumed, the Japanese

Below: A Waco CG-4A Hadrian glider on tow behind a C-47. In March 1944, the second Wingate Chindit operation in Burma involved Hadrians landing in a jungle clearing by night, 150 miles behind the main Japanese lines. The CG-4A could carry 15 equipped troops, including two acting as pilots.

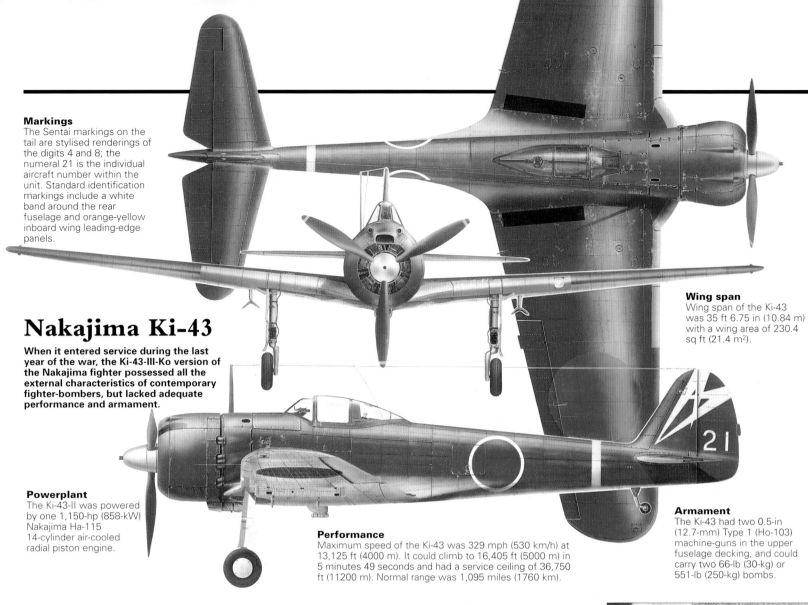

Markings
The Sentai markings on the tail are stylised renderings of the digits 4 and 8; the numeral 21 is the individual aircraft number within the unit. Standard identification markings include a white band around the rear fuselage and orange-yellow inboard wing leading-edge panels.

Nakajima Ki-43

When it entered service during the last year of the war, the Ki-43-III-Ko version of the Nakajima fighter possessed all the external characteristics of contemporary fighter-bombers, but lacked adequate performance and armament.

Wing span
Wing span of the Ki-43 was 35 ft 6.75 in (10.84 m) with a wing area of 230.4 sq ft (21.4 m²).

Powerplant
The Ki-43-II was powered by one 1,150-hp (858-kW) Nakajima Ha-115 14-cylinder air-cooled radial piston engine.

Performance
Maximum speed of the Ki-43 was 329 mph (530 km/h) at 13,125 ft (4000 m). It could climb to 16,405 ft (5000 m) in 5 minutes 49 seconds and had a service ceiling of 36,750 ft (11200 m). Normal range was 1,095 miles (1760 km).

Armament
The Ki-43 had two 0.5-in (12.7-mm) Type 1 (Ho-103) machine-guns in the upper fuselage decking, and could carry two 66-lb (30-kg) or 551-lb (250-kg) bombs.

could muster no more than 125 aircraft in the entire theatre. In the North Shan States efforts were made to open the Burma Road from Mandalay to China as a Chinese Expeditionary Force fell on and captured Wangting on 21 January 1945, supported by aircraft of the USAAF in China. Exactly two months later the northern capital of Mandalay fell to the 14th Army as the Chinese fought their way southwards through Lashio and Hsipaw. Throughout this campaign the needs of more than 350,000 fighting men were supplied by the Dakotas of the Combat Cargo Task Force, an achievement which, having regard to the harsh weather conditions, hazardous terrain and a desperate enemy, was acknowledged by Slim as the vital component of the 14th Army's victory. Even when a sudden Japanese thrust menaced Kunming in distant China, the Dakotas were quickly switched to fly 25,000 Chinese troops, their guns and pack animals across the 'Hump' to meet the threat.

The advance southwards from Mandalay was double-pronged along the great rivers, the Irrawaddy and the Sittang, while XV Corps advanced down the

Right: The B-24 Liberator was much sought after due to its endurance. Range was often of paramount importance in air attacks on Japanese targets. This B-24 is attacking positions at Armapura in Burma in January 1945.

Left: Thunderbolt Is of No. 134 Squadron transferred from India to Burma in December 1944. One of the leading American fighters of WWII, the Thunderbolt did not enter operational service with the RAF until August 1944, and it was then used exclusively by SE Asia Command against the Japanese.

coast, leapfrogging islands until Taungup was reached and captured on 28 April. Occasionally Ki-43 fighters tried to interfere, but these were always quickly overwhelmed by the ever-present Spitfires, Hurricanes and Thunderbolts. Soon there was no remaining usable base or airstrip available to the Japanese aircraft, and all air opposition evaporated.

TRAPPED

The great seaport of Rangoon was itself captured after a landing by XV Corps from the sea on 2 May, and four days later a link-up was

Known by the Japanese as 'Whispering Death', the Bristol Beaufighter Mk X was supremely effective in the low-level strike role, especially against jungle river traffic. Here a 'Beau' lands between others of the type.

achieved with IV Corps advancing down the Sittang. Trapped in the Burmese hinterland lay some 20,000 Japanese troops, sick and hungry yet fanatically determined to break eastwards across the Sittang into the mountains of Indo-China. In 10 days' concerted action by Allied tactical aircraft, the RAF

alone flew more than 3,000 sorties and dropped 1,500,000 lb (680400 kg) of bombs and napalm, killing 10,000 of the enemy. By the end of July the Japanese had been defeated throughout Burma. Plans were already in hand to mount Operation Zipper, the invasion of Malaya and the capture of Singapore. It was never put into action. On 9 August the second atomic bomb, which fell on the city of Nagasaki, persuaded the Japanese to acknowledge final defeat.

A P-40K of the 23rd Fighter Group at Kweilin, China early in 1944. A C-46 Commando of the 14th Air Force can be seen on finals behind. Note the five victory emblems below the canopy and the pilot's personal emblem next to the fuselage star.

Above: Sqn Ldr G. Kerr DFC, CO of No. 152 Squadron, is seen with his strikingly decorated Spitfire Mk VIII. In July 1944, the squadron moved forward to landing strips around Imphal, from where it provided escorts for supply-dropping C-47s.

Allied fighter-bombers

The Allied air forces in Burma and China were primarily engaged in supporting the army. Tactical operations were more common than strategic, and air transport and close air support duties assumed a huge importance. The P-51 Mustang, the Hawker Hurricane and the P-47 Thunderbolt were among the most important types.

Hawker Hurricane Mk IIC
The ubiquitous RAF operational aircraft throughout the last three years of the war was the Hawker Hurricane. The most common version was the Mk IIC, which featured four 20-mm cannon and long-range tanks.

North American P-51A Mustang
The P-51A was the original USAAF version of the Mustang, with an Allison engine and only four 0.5-in (12.7-mm) wing guns. This example, with a direction-finding loop antenna on the rear fuselage, was flown by the 1st Air Commando's CO, Colonel Philip Cochran, in Burma in 1944.

Republic Thunderbolt Mk II
At least 830 P-47s were supplied to the RAF, most of them late-block P-47Ds known to the Commonwealth air forces as Thunderbolt Mk IIs. This P-47D-30 served with No. 79 Squadron, RAF on the Burmese central front in late 1944, based at Wangjing. The P-47 was nicknamed the 'Jug', a contraction of 'Thunderjug' (a toilet) and not of the word juggernaut, as has so often been claimed.

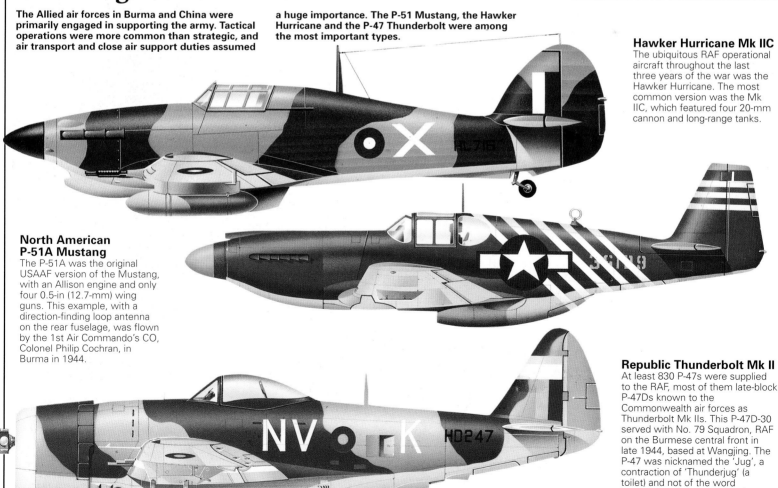

The Aleutians and Kuriles

A CATALINA, NAVY 'DUMBO', PATROLS ALONG ALEUTIAN COAST.

DECEMBER 1941 – AUGUST 1945

Above: A US Navy PBY-5A pictured over the Aleutians in 1944. In areas such as this, with consistently bad weather, the range of these reliable amphibians brought many crews to safe landings on land or water.

Below: The P-40K Warhawk had a dorsal fin which made it the ugliest of the type. Here one with a long-range fuel tank attached is preparing to taxy across a pierced steel planking (PSP) surface.

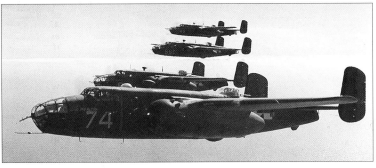

Above: North American B-25B or C Mitchells of the 77th Bomb Squadron, 28th Bomb Group, flying in close formation over waters south-east of Attu, Aleutian Islands in September 1943.

Among the lesser-known war theatres in the war against Japan was the North Pacific, an ill-defined geographical area that embraced the chain of Aleutian Islands which extend westwards from Alaska, and the Kurile Islands that run north-east from Japan towards the Kamchatka peninsula.

At the time of Pearl Harbor the air defence of Alaska and the northern Pacific was vested in the USAAC's 28th Composite Group which had recently been trained to operate in Arctic conditions and had its headquarters at Elmendorf, Alaska. It possessed two pursuit squadrons, the 18th and 34th with P-40Bs, plus the 36th, 37th and 73rd Squadrons with a miscellany of aircraft, including a small number of bombers. However, it was beyond the scope of this group to perform long-range reconnaissance, and although the Japanese task force which attacked Pearl Harbor from the north had sailed from Hittokappu Bay in the Kuriles it was not detected by the American air force.

ALEUTIANS VULNERABLE

It was part of the Japanese overall war strategy to create an outer defence perimeter stretching from Kiska in the Aleutians southwards through Midway, and the capture of the islands of Attu, Adak and Kiska were intended to divert American attention from the major attack on Midway. This part of the plan did not succeed and the American commander, Rear Admiral Frank Fletcher, concentrated his naval forces (including all his available carriers) to win the great Battle of Midway; by so doing he was forced to leave the Aleutians exposed to attack from the air and sea. By June 1942 American air forces in the immediate area of the Aleutians comprised some 100 USAAF P-40s, 12 B-17s, 24 B-26s and 20 US Navy PBY flying-boats.

The Japanese launched a strike/invasion force which included the carrier *Junyo* and *Ryujo* with 30 Mitsubishi A6M fighters, 24 dive-bombers and 20 torpedo-bombers.

American aircraft in the north

Over 2,300 P-40E Warhawks were built, the most numerous variant until the P-40N. Powered by the ubiquitous Allison V-1710, the Curtiss designation was Model 87-A3 Hawk. As the Lockheed Hudson was a development of the Model 14 Super Electra passenger transport, the Ventura was derived from the larger Model 18 Lodestar. Venturas introduced better armament and performance.

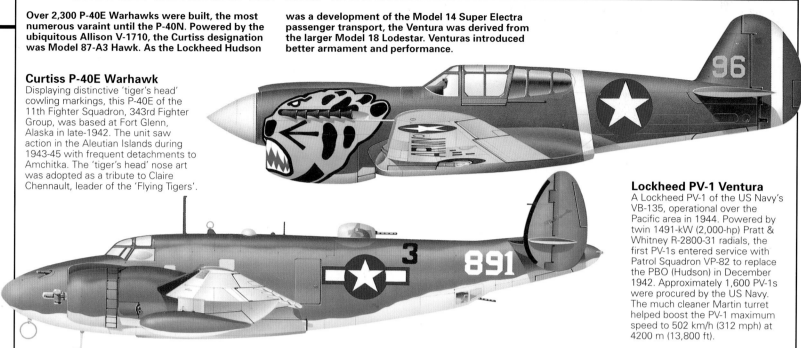

Curtiss P-40E Warhawk
Displaying distinctive 'tiger's head' cowling markings, this P-40E of the 11th Fighter Squadron, 343rd Fighter Group, was based at Fort Glenn, Alaska in late-1942. The unit saw action in the Aleutian Islands during 1943-45 with frequent detachments to Amchitka. The 'tiger's head' nose art was adopted as a tribute to Claire Chennault, leader of the 'Flying Tigers'.

Lockheed PV-1 Ventura
A Lockheed PV-1 of the US Navy's VB-135, operational over the Pacific area in 1944. Powered by twin 1491-kW (2,000-hp) Pratt & Whitney R-2800-31 radials, the first PV-1s entered service with Patrol Squadron VP-82 to replace the PBO (Hudson) in December 1942. Approximately 1,600 PV-1s were procured by the US Navy. The much cleaner Martin turret helped boost the PV-1 maximum speed to 502 km/h (312 mph) at 4200 m (13,800 ft).

As carrier strikes were launched against Dutch Harbor in the eastern island of Unalaska, 2,500 troops would land and seize the three western islands. The air strike on Dutch Harbor was duly carried out on 3 June and achieved the destruction of three PBY flying-boats for the loss of four aircraft. One of these was an A6M which force-landed on Akutan Island, the first such aircraft to fall into American hands in a repairable state; its recovery and subsequent testing by the USAAF was to prove of inestimable value to the Allies.

The following day the Japanese launched a further strike against Dutch Harbor, causing considerable damage to shore installations, losing five further aircraft. The B-17s located and attacked the Japanese carriers but failed to hit them and lost one of their own number. Meanwhile the invasion of the western islands was postponed while Admiral Yamamoto sent the carrier *Zuiho* (and later the *Zuikaku*) north as reinforcements lest the Americans should now attempt to

reinforce the Aleutians by diverting carriers. No such carriers could be spared and the Japanese duly went ashore on Kiska and Attu, to find them occupied by just 10 unarmed men. To have attempted to defend and sustain these islands at that stage of the Pacific war would have over-taxed the USA's air and naval forces beyond their strength. As it was the Japanese retained their toehold on a tiny part of the American continent (sic) for just one year.

DIVERSIONARY TACTICS
Meanwhile the 28th Composite Group was joined in Alaska by the newly constituted 343rd Fighter Group whose 11th, 18th, 54th and 344th Fighter Squadrons were equipped with P-38s and P-40s, initially at Elmendorf and Fort Glenn in Alaska, and later at Adak. It was largely this move forward by these squadrons that prompted the Japanese to withdraw hurriedly from Kiska, only just before a joint US-Canadian assault force landed. Both this island and Attu were reoccupied by the Americans in

July and August 1943, aircraft of the 28th and 343rd Groups moving into bases there almost immediately.

In particular the 28th Group's B-24s flew long-range reconnaissance and bombing missions over the Kuriles, latterly 'trailing their coat' to attract Japanese fighters and thereby weaken their forces in the south, a strategy that earned the Group a Distinguished Unit Citation. The 343rd Group, which had been heavily engaged in strafing attacks on Kiska prior to the American re-occupation, flew no further combat missions after October 1943.

The presence of some 50 B-24

Above: Kawasaki's Ki-45 KAI Toryu (Dragon Killer) or Army Type 2 two-seat fighter had the Allied code-name 'Nick'. This is a KAId cannon fighter version introduced before the end of the war for anti-shipping strikes.

Liberators, which flew sporadic raids over the Kuriles during the last 16 months of the war, caused the Japanese to divert two Sentais of Ki-45 'Nick' heavy-fighters to the north of the Japanese homeland, a force of some 40 aircraft that would otherwise have been a useful element in the defence against the disastrous raids by the American B-29 Superfortresses.

Below: A group of P-38Gs between missions in the Aleutians in 1943. The first P-38 victory over a Japanese aircraft came as early as 4 August 1942 when two Lightnings shot down a pair of 'Mavis' flying-boats.

Right: US Navy PV-1s operated in all weathers on anti-shipping strikes and attacks on the Japanese bases at Paramushiro and Shimushu, and fought off attacks by defending Mitsubishi A6M3 Reisens.

Iwo Jima

JANUARY – FEBRUARY 1945

By January 1945 US fleet dispositions were being made for an assault on and capture of the island of Iwo Jima, just 1223-km (760-miles) south of Tokyo itself, and roughly the same distance north of Saipan. Principal covering naval force under Vice-Admiral Mitscher was Task Force 58 (the Fast Carrier Force) comprising five task groups sailing a total of 11 fleet carriers and five light carriers plus 100 battleships, cruisers and destroyers. The assault force destined for Iwo Jima itself, a force of more than 1,000 ships, included Rear Admiral Durgin's Task Group 52.2 with 12 escort carriers, embarking a total of 226 F4F Wildcats and 138 TBM Avengers, some of whose pilots were trained in gunnery spotting.

The importance of Iwo Jima lay in its location almost directly in the path of B-29 Superfortress heavy bombers flying from Saipan on raids over Japan, enabling the Japanese observation posts to alert interceptor fighters both on Iwo Jima and in the

homeland. Once captured the island could be used by the USAAF as a base for fighters to escort the B-29s.

To cover the approach by Task Group 52.2, Task Force 58 sailed to within 97 km (60 miles) of Tokyo and launched a number of strikes in the area of the Japanese capital, attracting some 100 enemy aircraft into the air and shooting down about 40. On the following day, 17 February, Mitscher carried out searches for Japanese shipping and failing to find any, turned the great fleet south for Iwo Jima.

THE END IN SIGHT

On 19 February the Fast Carrier Force struck the island with both big-gun bombardment from two of the eight battleships and strikes by Helldivers, Avengers and Corsairs. Meanwhile, evidently believing the US fleet still to be close to Tokyo, the home-based Japanese aircraft did not interfere with the invasion force off Iwo Jima until the evening of 19 February, by which time no fewer than 40,000 US Marines had

gone ashore under cover of fighters from the carriers *Enterprise* and *Saratoga*. When the Japanese aircraft did arrive they failed to get through to the invasion transports and were heavily engaged by the naval fighters which, with gunfire from the fleet joining in, shot down a dozen of the attackers. On 21 February the *Saratoga* was detached from

Above: A USAAF Consolidated B-24M Liberator of the 7th Air Force over the flaming beachhead of Iwo Jima, with Suribachi Mountain in the background. The last B-24 model to be built in large quantities, the 'M' variant was distinguished by a lightweight tail turret. By the beginning of 1945, over 6,000 Liberators were in operational strength with the USAAF, equipping 45 Groups.

Above: A group of young Japanese Kamikaze pilots are briefed the night before a mission, early in 1945. The Americans experienced Kamikaze attacks for the first time during the Battle of Leyte Gulf in October 1944, when five carriers off Saman were attacked by Japanese suicide pilots.

Left: In the closing months of the war, Allied air power was overwhelming. Here a US Marine Corps TBM-3E from the USS Essex, with a 227-kg (500-lb) bomb under each wing, accompanies a formation of Curtiss SB2Cs over the Japanese mainland, with Mount Fujiyama beyond.

Pacific bombers

Over 4,000 of the well-defended B-25J Mitchell were built. It differed from the B-25H in having a glazed nose housing one fixed and two movable 12.7-mm (0.5-in) guns and R-2600-29 engines.

The carrier-based SB2C-3 Helldiver first appeared in 1944. It had an uprated R-2600-20 engine that developed 1417 kW (1,900 hp) with the aid of a supercharger. Bombload was 907 kg (2,000 lb).

North American B-25J Mitchell
Flamboyant artwork characterised the B-25s operated by 'The Falcons', the 498th Bomb Squadron, 345th Bomb Group. The Group's 'Air Apache' marking appeared on the tail. This B-25J was at Luzon in April 1945.

Curtiss SB2C-3 Helldiver
This SB2C-3 is seen in mid-war camouflage. It was on the strength of VB-3, operating in support of the Iwo Jima landings with Task Force 58 from the carrier USS *Yorktown* (CV-10) in February 1945. Underwing APG-4 radar is fitted.

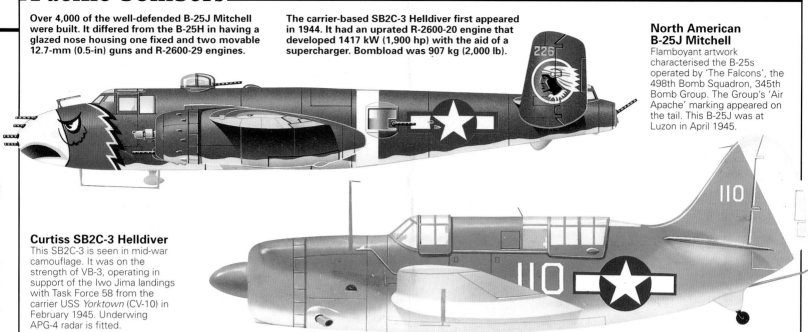

Above: The capture of Iwo Jima's airfield allowed these USAAF P-51D Mustangs of the 21st FG to operate on long-range escort missions with B-29 Superfortresses of the 20th Air Force to bomb mainland Japan. The following month, they penetrated to Tokyo for the first time.

Task Force 58 with three destroyers to cover the amphibious forces, and at about 17.00 hours that afternoon was attacked by six Japanese aircraft manned, as it transpired, by suicide pilots. Two were hit by the carrier's guns but struck the ship's side where their bombs exploded; the bomb from a third aircraft struck the forward end of the flight deck, a fourth also struck the flight deck and a fifth hit the starboard side of the ship; the sixth aircraft was shot down. Two hours later the *Saratoga* was again attacked, this time by five suicide aircraft, one of which struck the flight deck but bounced overboard, its bomb causing further damage. Yet the old carrier survived; with 123 dead or missing and 192 injured, and 42 of her aircraft destroyed or jettisoned, she was ordered to retire from the area, returning to active duty after only two months under repair.

Later on that same evening the

February, but poor weather curtailed the carrier strikes and few combats ensued; instead Mitscher turned his attention against Okinawa to the west but, apart from securing useful reconnaissance of the island, found little in the way of targets. Within a fortnight the capture of Iwo Jima had been completed, no further significant air attacks having troubled the land or naval forces, while aircraft from the escort-carrier *Anzio* had sunk two Japanese submarines on

escort-carrier *Bismarck Sea* was hit by two suicide aircraft, and soon afterwards became a raging inferno; her captain ordered her to be abandoned and just as the survivors got clear a torpedo hit blew the carrier apart. She went down with 218 of her crew, 19 Wildcats and 15 Avengers.

In an effort to prevent further attacks by suicide aircraft, the Fast Carrier Force was detached north towards Japan once more on 23

26 and 27 February.

During the Iwo Jima operations the guns and pilots of the Fast Carrier Force and Task Group 52.2 were estimated to have destroyed 393 enemy aircraft in the air and a further 200 on the ground. Task Force 58 had, however, lost 95 aircrew and 143 aircraft. Far more significant, a key base had been secured within fighter range of Japanese airspace and without any irreplaceable losses among the vital American carrier task forces.

Left: Task Force TF-58, consisting of 166 ships, sailed on 12 February 1945 and was the first carrier strike to hit the Japanese mainland since Doolittle's raid three years earlier. With Japan itself under attack, the assault on Iwo Jima began. US troops are seen raising the Stars and Stripes on the island.

Below: The aftermath of a direct hit by a Kamikaze aircraft on the USS Saratoga *on 21 February 1945. A total of 123 men were killed and 192 injured; 42 aircraft were either destroyed or had to ditch as they were left with nowhere to land.*

Okinawa

MARCH – JULY 1945

Left: USS Randolph (CV-15) was hit by a Japanese suicide attack on 11 March with the loss of 27 men, but by the first week of April it had been repaired and returned to operations off Okinawa. F6F-5 Hellcats of Fighter Squadron 12 (VF-12) leave Randolph's deck on a ground-attack sortie.

their home waters, causing some damage, particularly to the light carrier *Ryuho*. Pre-occupation with these attacks on the Japanese naval vessels allowed a number of Japanese bombing raids to take off, the aircraft making for Task Group 52.2, whose *Wasp* was hit and badly damaged; 102 men were killed and 269 injured, but her crew managed to extinguish the fires and within an hour she was recovering her aircraft. Almost simultaneously the fleet carrier *Franklin* suffered two bomb hits which started massive fires in her hangar and set off explosions that continued to rock the ship for hours. In an epic of a sea rescue only 90 kilometres (55 miles) from Japan, the carrier was saved, although 832 of her crew perished. In attacks over Japan the Task Force pilots claimed the destruction of 432 enemy aircraft during

The invasion of Okinawa, an island which lies almost midway between Formosa and the southernmost point in the Japanese homeland, involved an assault and support force second only in size to that thrown against the Normandy coast in Europe 10 months previously, but far exceeded that great operation in the distances and logistics involved. If the American naval forces had been fortunate to escape serious losses in the Iwo Jima assault, the Japanese were about to react with the utmost force and ferocity at Okinawa. Once more the 5th Fleet Task Force 58 would provide the naval muscle in the assault and its protection.

thought to be based; warned of the Americans' approach many of the Japanese aircraft were withdrawn out of range of the carrier aircraft. Fifty aircraft did take-off to attack the Task Force, however, but only caused superficial damage. Meanwhile the carrier aircraft had found and attacked Japanese warships in

JAPAN ATTACKED

Before the fleet sailed from Ulithi to the south-west of the Marianas, the fleet carrier *Randolph* was hit by a suicide aircraft flying from Minami Iwo, and put out of action with 27 men killed. On 14 March 1945 Task Force 58 sailed north to attack airfields in Japan where the majority of suicide units were

Above: P-38L Lightnings routinely carried drop tanks for long-range missions. This P-38L of the 475th Fighter Group at Lingayen Airstrip, Luzon, is equipped with two auxiliary tanks; one of 1173-litres (310 US gallons) capacity and the other 625 litres (165 US gallons).

Left: Two Nakajima B5N2 carrier-borne attack-bombers (Allied code-name 'Kate') flying over the Yamato. This Naval Type 97 was one of the most successful torpedo-bombers ever built and had the ability to remain airborne for over four hours. Production of the 'Kate' totalled some 1,150.

Below: The TF 58 strike against mainland Japan came under very heavy air attack. The most serious raid on 19 March damaged the Wasp and Intrepid and nearly sank the Franklin, whose entire complement of aircraft was lost, along with 832 men killed and 270 wounded.

the opening of Operation 'Ten-Go', a concerted suicide assault by surface and air forces. No fewer than 4,500 aircraft would be involved in suicide and conventional attacks on the Americans. Of all the extraordinary elements of this operation was the sailing of the super-battleship *Yamato* (65027 tonnes/64,000 tons) from Japan on 6 April, it being intended to penetrate right to the Okinawa invasion beaches and destroy as many transport ships as possible before being overwhelmed by American bombs and guns. Fortunately the huge ship was detected on her departure from

18/19 March, and the following day the American ships withdrew as further attacks, now by suicide pilots, were aimed at the carriers, causing some damage to the *Enterprise*. Two days later the *Franklin*, *Enterprise* and *Wasp* left the combat area for repairs.

On 23 March the assault on Okinawa opened with air strikes by TF 58's carrier aircraft and a bombardment by 10 battleships, which lasted a week. The invasion was to be supported by the 13 remaining fast carriers, by six light carriers and by no fewer than 18 escort carriers, between them embarking more than 1,000 aircraft. A further 10 escort carriers were loaded with replacement aircraft and the US Marine fighters which would be based on Okinawa.

MASS SUICIDE ATTACKS

When the landing assault on Okinawa was launched on 1 April the Japanese responded by ordering

Left: Two B-25J Mitchells of the 345th Bomb Group (Medium) of the 5th Air Force attack a Japanese warship on 29 March 1945. The Group adopted the name 'Air Apaches' and carried a Red Indian head on the fins of their aircraft and at war's end was based off Okinawa.

Right: A Japanese Kawasaki Ki-61 Swallow (Allied codename 'Tony') makes a suicide dive on the escort carrier USS Sanganon (CVE-26) at Kerama Retto in the Okinawa Group on 4 May 1945, missing the carrier by less than 7.6 m (25 ft).

From Okinawa to Japan

The last stepping stone on the way to Japan was the island of Okinawa. Once established there, bombing raids on the mainland could begin. B-24s had served in many theatres and took on this role from spring 1945. While the most important operators of the type were the Marines (in a fighter-bomber role), the F4U was conceived as a carrier-based fighter for the US Navy.

Consolidated B-24J Liberator

One of the last B-24s to see action, this B-24J-CO was given a particularly flamboyant paint scheme by the 43rd Bomb Group operating against the Japanese mainland from Ie Shima in the Spring of 1945.

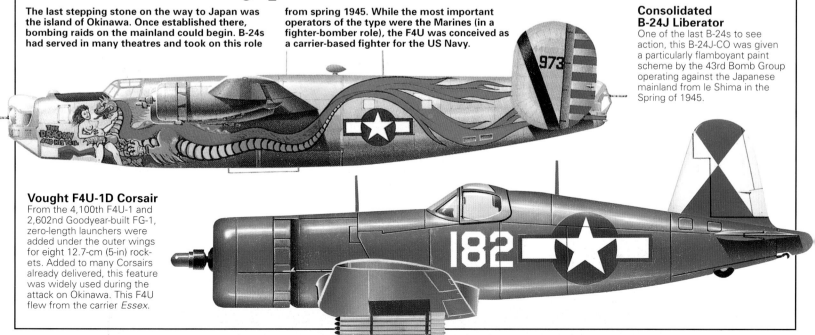

Vought F4U-1D Corsair

From the 4,100th F4U-1 and 2,602nd Goodyear-built FG-1, zero-length launchers were added under the outer wings for eight 12.7-cm (5-in) rockets. Added to many Corsairs already delivered, this feature was widely used during the attack on Okinawa. This F4U flew from the carrier *Essex*.

home waters, shadowed by Mariner flying-boats and ultimately attacked by a strike of 280 carrier aircraft from Task Force 58, including 98 Avenger torpedo aircraft. Inevitably the *Yamato* succumbed, but only after being hit by 10 torpedoes and five bombs, taking to the bottom 2,498 of her crew; with her went an accompanying light cruiser with almost 450 men, hit by seven torpedoes and 12 bombs.

A HARD BATTLE

The reduction of Okinawa itself occupied three months and involved one of the greatest naval/air campaigns ever fought. The early part of April was marked by sustained conventional and suicide attack. On the same day that the *Yamato* was sunk the American carrier *Hancock* was badly damaged by a suicide aircraft; on 11 April the *Enterprise* (recently rejoined after repairs) was again hit, as was the carrier *Essex*. On 11 May the fast carrier *Bunker Hill* (Mitscher's flagship) was hit by bombs and suicide aircraft, but was saved after losing 389 of her crew.

When the Okinawa campaign was officially declared ended on 2 July 1945, it was calculated that the Japanese had launched some 34,000 sorties by 6,000 aircraft, many of them suicide attacks. US pilots and gunners claimed 2,336 shot down, losing a total of 790 aircraft. American naval losses amounted to 33 ships sunk (including 13 destroyers) and 119 severely damaged, including nine fleet carriers, one

Unique Swallow

Known to the Allies as 'Tony', the Hien (Swallow) was unique in the Japanese air forces in having a liquid-cooled engine, long tapered nose and high aspect-ratio wings. It was initially thought to be a licence-built Messerschmitt Bf 109 or an unknown Italian design. Its service was not extensive, but during the mid-war years it was the only Japanese aircraft able to engage fast Allied fighters.

Kawasaki Ki-61 Hien
Crudely applied green paint was an attempt to tone down the natural metal finish on this Ki-61-I KAI of the 3rd Chutai, 19th Sentai. This group fought over Leyte Gulf in the Philippines as well as Okinawa and Formosa.

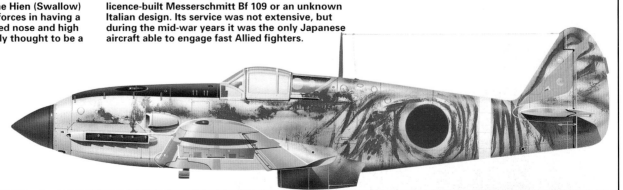

Following the early Pacific carrier battles, when the myth of the supremacy of the Japanese Zero had been shattered, and with the introduction of new US fighters such as the Hellcat and Mustang, the victory tallies of Allied pilots began to mount. There was intense competition to see who would become the top ace of the theatre. As it was, the two top scorers flew P-38 Lightnings, a type that had a checkered career elsewhere, but which was ideal for the long-range overwater missions common in the Pacific.

Major Gregory 'Pappy' Boyington

Leader of the most famous of all USMC squadrons, VMF-214 'Black Sheep', 'Pappy' Boyington (left) had scored six victories over Burma while serving with the American Volunteer Group before returning to the Marine Corps as commander of the 'Black Sheep' over the Solomon Islands. Boyington had scored 25 victories by the time he was shot down in January 1944 (after scoring three more times) and was captured by a Japanese submarine. With 28 kills, he was the top pilot in the Marine Corps.

Major Richard I. Bong

With 40 kills confirmed, Richard Bong (right) was the top-scoring US pilot of the war, and remains to this day the highest ranking American ace of all time. Dick Bong flew P-38 Lightnings with the 5th Air Force in New Guinea. By April 1944, he had surpassed Eddie Rickenbacker's World War I score of 28 (the first US pilot to do so) and was sent home on leave. Continuing to increase his score on his return, Bong was awarded the Medal of Honor later in 1944 and scored his 40th and final victory on 17 December.

Lt Col Robert E. Westbrook

Leading ace of the 13th Air Force, USAAF, Westbrook (left), shot down his 17th Japanese aircraft on 30 September 1944 over Japanese-held Kendari Field in the southern Celebes. His eventual total was 20 kills, of which 13 were accomplished while flying a P-38. Westbrook was killed on 22 November 1944 while with the 18th Fighter Group, in a strafing attack on enemy shipping, the first mission of his eighth combat tour.

Lt Cdr David McCampbell

David McCampbell (above) was the commander of Air Group 15 on USS *Essex* (CV-9) in 1944. On 19 July 1944, he shot down seven Japanese aircraft in two sorties and on 24 October a further nine (a record for a US pilot). In addition, McCampbell was credited with 21 aircraft destroyed on the ground. All McCampbell's kills were scored in F6F Hellcats, which were usually named 'Minsi' after a ladyfriend. With 34 victories, McCampbell was the leading Navy ace.

Major John C. Herbst

Major Herbst (also known as 'Pappy') flew the A-36A Apache version of the P-51 Mustang (right) with the 23rd Fighter Group in China. Prior to his arrival in the China Burma India (CBI) theatre in late-1944 he had scored one kill over Europe. At war's end John Herbst had taken his total to 19, and was by then the relatively advanced age (for a fighter pilot) of 35 years. Like Richard Bong, 'Pappy' Herbst was killed in the crash of a P-80 Shooting Star in 1946.

Major Robert W. Moore

With a total of 12 victories, Robert W. Moore (left) was not one of the top-ranking Pacific aces, but was the top scorer of the 7th Air Force. In the last few months of the war, Moore, aged 23, commanded the 45th Fighter Squadron of the 15th Fighter Group. All his kills were scored against fighters over the Japanese home islands while flying P-51s from Okinawa on gruelling round-trip missions of 2575 km (1,600 miles).

light carrier and three escort carriers, nine battleships and 37 destroyers. Obviously the Japanese suicide attacks posed a serious threat in all the operations of 1945, but such were the enormous reserves and resources now available to the Americans that the losses, grievous though they were, could be shrugged aside, and never in fact endangered the success of the campaign.

Left: P-47D 'Little Rock Ette' is seen being used by pilots and ground-crew of the 19th Fighter Squadron, 318th Fighter Group at Ie Shima on 11 July 1945 to hang a scoreboard showing the number of Japanese aircraft shot down.

Above: The Hellcat was developed to counter the Japanese Zero, the dominant fighter during early Pacific actions. It proved so effective that recorded a 9:1 kill ratio. Here a Hellcat waits a mission from USS Randolph in March 1945.

The Bombers finish Japan

JANUARY – AUGUST 1945

Boeing B-29s drop incendiaries high over Japan. Although the atomic bomb raids caused greater emotional and political fallout, the firestorms at Yokohama caused far greater casualties. Seven square miles of the city were completely razed by the B-29s.

If controversy still rages about the effect of bombing on Germany in World War II, there is no questioning the effect of the American Superfortress campaign in the Far East. The USAAF's B-29s literally burned and blasted the heart out of Japan. The cost in dollars was prodigious, yet without the big bombers the cost in American lives, in an invasion of the Japanese homeland, would have been horrifying.

Plans to produce a 'super bomber' had been laid in January 1940, long before the USA entered the war, calling for a 400-mph (644-km/h) aircraft capable of delivering 2,000 lb (907 kg) of bombs over a range of 5,300 miles (8530 km). Initial development was leisurely by later standards, and only after Pearl Harbor was the utmost priority afforded to the new aircraft,

and on 21 September 1942 the first XB-29 was flown. By that time orders for 1,664 production examples had been placed.

THE B-29 GOES TO WAR

On 1 June 1943 the 58th (Very Heavy) Bombardment Wing was activated in the USA for initial service trials and B-29 crew training. The future pattern of the war in the Pacific had been decided and, with fortunes running in the Allies' favour in Europe, the big bomber was henceforth only considered in the context of the war against Japan. With four 2,200-hp (1641-kW) engines, the service version, with a span of 141 ft 3 in (43.05 m), had a speed of 358 mph (576 km/h) at 25,000 ft (7620 m), a maximum range of 4,100 miles

Faced with an increasing air threat against the home islands, the Japanese were forced to develop new interceptor fighters. One such design was the Nakajima Ki-44 Army Type 2 Shoki (Demon), known to the Allies as 'Tojo'.

(6600 km) and a maximum bombload of 20,000 lb (9072 kg). In every respect it eclipsed all other in-service aeroplanes anywhere in the world; in an unparalleled feat of engineering a total of 3,970 of these very large bombers was built by Boeing, Bell and Martin in just three years.

The first B-29s to arrive in the Far East were those of the US 20th Air Force which landed at Kwanghan in China on 24 April 1944. No fewer than nine huge bases had been constructed by 700,000 Chinese labourers in India and China to accommodate the new bomber force. It flew its first raid on 5 June, attacking Bangkok in Thailand, and on 15 June 50 aircraft were sent against Yawata in Japan, the first American raid on the

Ground crews of the 500th BG ready a B-29 for action. This posed scene compresses the activity involved to launch a mission, but gives an idea of the effort required for each of hundreds of bombers.

Last ditch defence

The Japanese fighters of the early war period were tailored to long-range escort and designed for manoeuvrability at the expense of armour protection and armament. The arrival of modern US fighters and bombers made the 'Zero' and 'Oscar' obsolete, although these types remained in production until late in the war. New types were introduced, but too late to make a difference.

Kawasaki Ki-61-I KAIc
The Ki-61 was a departure from all previous Japanese fighters in having an inline engine (a Kawasaki-built Daimler-Benz DB 601A), and significant armour protection. This aircraft belonged to the 244th Sentai, one of four assigned to the defence of Tokyo. Unable to reach the B-29s, the Ki-61 was more successful against US Navy fighters.

Mitsubishi J2M3 Raiden
The Mitsubishi Raiden (Thunderbolt) was originally designed as a Naval interceptor. Dogged by technical problems, service test pilots complained about poor visibility. Production progressed at a very slow rate from 1943. The J2M3, fitted with six cannon, was the most important model and once in service was extremely popular with pilots in the bomber-destroyer role.

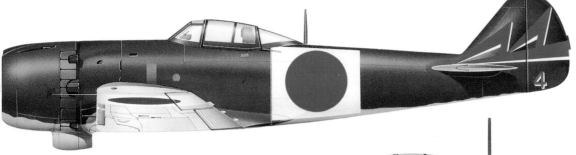

Nakajima Ki-84-Ia Hayate
Designed by Nakajima as a replacement for its own Hayabusa ('Oscar'), the Ki-84 Hayate (Gale), with the Allied reporting name 'Frank', was the best fighter produced in quantity in 1944-45. The white around the national insignia on this 7th Sentai Ki-84 indicates its home defence assignment.

Kawasaki Ki-100-Ib
When the supply of Ha-140 engines for the Ki-61-II KAI dried up due to teething and production troubles, Kawasaki fitted the 14-cylinder Mitsubishi Ha-112-II radial to spare Ki-61-II KAI airframes. The resulting Ki-100 was a superb interceptor, much feared by the B-29 crews.

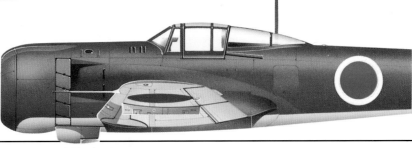

The nose of this B-29 of the 881 BS, 500 BG sheared off in a crash landing on Saipan. All the crew survived, shocked but uninjured, despite the runaway bomber demolishing another B-29 and a tractor before stopping. Captain James Pearson had flown over 2400 km (1,500 miles) from Musashino with only two good engines following a fighter attack.

Left: Another mission over, a B-29 of the 40th Bomb Group slips in to Kadena in the last few days of the war. The 40th BG was part of the 58th BW and flew missions over the 'Hump' from India before moving to West Field on Tinian in February 1945 for the final assault on Japan.

There have been few aerial campaigns as intense as that flown against Japan at the end of the Pacific war. The super base at Tinian had seven parallel runways. Isley Field on Saipan had only two, and there are 145 B-29s lined up on one of them in this August 1945 photo.

Below: The Kawasaki Ki-61 Hein (Swallow) was the only Japanese fighter with an inline engine to see service. Despite many engine and production difficulties, the 'Tony' was the only Army fighter able to fight at the B-29's altitude.

The Superfortress was the most sophisticated and most powerful bomber of the war. Four Wright R-3350 engines provided enough power for a B-29 to reach most of Japan's industrial centres and return, sometimes on only three.

Japanese mainland since Doolittle's B-25 raid back in April 1942.

The great distances from the Indian and Chinese bases to Japan severely limited the bombloads of the B-29s, while bad weather rendered such raids of only limited effect. However, the capture of the Marianas in mid-1944 was followed by another marathon feat as American service engineers built five vast new bases (two on Guam, two on Tinian and one on Saipan), each capable of handling 180 B-29s. On 24 November 111 B-29s, led

by General Emmett O'Donnell, took off to raid the Nakajima engine works at Musashi; however, only 24 bombers found their target.

NIGHT ATTACKS

On 20 January 1945 Major General Curtis E. LeMay assumed command of XXI Bomber Command, USAAF, and at once announced a radical change of bombing policy and tactics by the B-29s. Henceforth the bombers would attack with incendiary bombs by night, individually and from below 10,000 ft (3050 m), and with reduced defensive armament in the

B-29s of the 497th and 498th Bomb Groups form up on the way to Japan. Formations were not as tight as those flown by the 8th Air Force over Europe, but the flak and fighter defences were not as tough at B-29 altitudes, either.

interests of increased bombloads.

The first such attack was made on 9/10 March by 302 aircraft against Yawata and Tokyo; for the loss of 14 aircraft, over 16 sq miles (41.4 km²) of the Japanese capital were reduced to ashes. In 10 days, five raids on Tokyo, Yawata, Nagoya, Osaka and Kobe – 29 sq miles (75.1 km²) of Japan's main industrial centres – were destroyed

Decorated B-29s

Nose art was a feature of both Allied and Axis aircraft, especially bombers. Masters of this form of expression were the Americans, and the 'Superfort' provided the biggest canvas of all for the cartoon characters and pinups close to the hearts of men far from home. In March 1945, an order came down to remove the paintings, whether suggestive or not, although examples remained until war's end.

B-29 Superfortress

Crew
The B-29 had an 11-man crew for most missions. The forward compartment housed pilot, bombardier, engineer, navigator and radar/radio operators. The gunners were seated in the aft compartment.

Weapons load
The B-29 had capacity for up to 9075 kg (20,000 lb) of bombs in two huge bays, each of which had its own bomb-loading winch. Bomb release was sequenced to maintain centre of gravity.

Bombs
The main weapon used aginst Japanese cities was the incendiary bomb, such as the M-47, filled with napalm and loaded in clusters tied together with cord.

Markings
Dina Might belonged to the 421st BS, 504th BG. The rear fuselage bands denoted a bombing formation lead aircraft.

Fire control
The four rotating turrets were controlled by three gunners and the bombardier, and sighted through the various glass domes. A simple computer control system allowed one gunner to direct any or all of the guns depending on the threat.

by 10,100 tons of bombs. On 25/26 May the hardest-hitting raid was flown when 464 B-29s, led by pathfinders, attacked Tokyo, destroying 18.9 sq miles (48.95 km²) of the city for the loss of 26 aircraft. In these great fire raids (and others, including a raid on Yokohama where 85 per cent of the city was gutted) well over half a million Japanese civilians were killed and 13 million others rendered homeless.

Many historians have averred that continuation of the B-29 fire raids could by themselves have smashed the Japanese nation into surrender. It fell, however, to the delivery of two atomic bombs against Hiroshima and Nagasaki by the B-29s *Enola Gay* and *Bock's Car* of the USAAF's 509th Composite Group on 6 and 9 August 1945 respectively to convince the Japanese of the futility of continuing the war. Apart from special

Compared to the bases in India and China, the facilities in the Marianas were all that could be desired. Much of the islands' area was consumed by massive parking areas to disperse hundreds of B-29s from the threat of air attack.

training and the strictest security, the delivery of these awesome weapons posed no major operational problems and the bombs duly detonated above the doomed Japanese cities, killing more than 100,000 persons instantly; thousands were to die the next day, and the next.

ABRUPT ENDING

The B-29s' atomic bombs ended the war, quickly and surgically. As already suggested they may well have been superfluous having regard to the systematic destruction being achieved by the 'conventional' fire raids on Japanese cities and industry. Apart from almost certainly avoiding even greater carnage and destruction that would have accompanied such raids, the demonstration of those diabolical weapons was the convincing prelude to the post-war policy of 'peace by deterrent', and the deterrent to world war was to be the threat of nuclear weapons. Had Hiroshima and Nagasaki not been sacrificed someone, somewhere, would have attempted a more horrifying demonstration.

Above: No. 356 Squadron, RAF, Liberator ground crews celebrate the Japanese surrender, which was formally signed on 2 September 1945. RAF and USAAF B-24s played a pivotal role in the war against Japan.

Below: Phosphorous bombs dropped by a fighter explode above 7th Air Force B-24s over Okinawa. Despite its fearsome appearance, this weapon was mostly ineffective, as was the Japanese secret weapons programme in general.

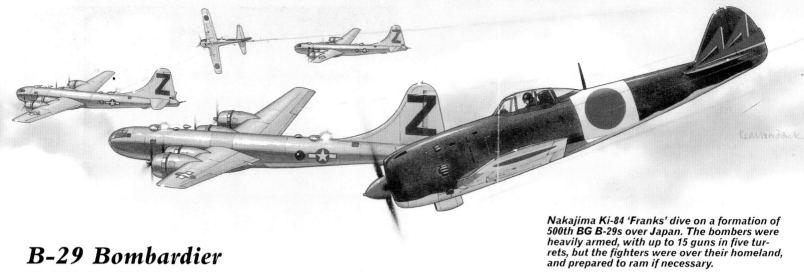

B-29 Bombardier

The B-29 ushered in a new era, operating at extreme ranges and vast heights. Pressurised, carrying a huge ordnance load, and with their supercharged engines, the B-29s were the first of a new generation.

"I inspected the 28 500-lb bombs in the Superfortress. This was the heaviest bomb load we had ever carried. The bombs were wired together, two to a shackle. I had never seen bombs loaded that way and I didn't feel comfortable with it. My job was to aim and drop the bombs.

"I walked back from our Superfortress to join Major Tom Vaucher and the rest of the crew.

"This was my first operation as lead bombardier of the formation. We expected heavy flak and Japanese interceptors. I would have been nervous without the extra weight.

"I had been selected for special training as lead bombardier. That I had passed the course didn't make me any more confident than I had been when I had first been told of the new tactic.

"As we approached the coast, I spotted two innocent-looking ships lying offshore. Next moment the sky around us filled with bursts. The bursts were so close I could see the red flashes as the shells exploded. The sides of the plane

Whereas high explosives were needed to level the cities of Europe, incendiaries were more effective against the paper houses of Japan. This photograph was used in a leaflet, itself dropped to warn a city of an impending fire raid.

echoed with the explosions. Flak ships! And we were flying straight on in.

"'The target's clear,' I called to Vaucher.

"'You take the turn,' Vaucher responded. I grabbed the turn knob on the stabiliser and slowly turned the aeroplane. The effort of concentration temporarily blotted out my awareness of the continuing flak.

"I looked over the sight to check we were on line for the target, then switched to the telescope and used the turn knob to bank the plane until the vertical hair in the telescope split the target. I felt the drama of the moment, knowing that 14 B-29s depended on my work.

"We were drifting off. I made a slight course correction. It looked good. My hands trembled slightly as I adjusted the rate knobs until the crosshairs stayed steady on the aiming point

"Ten more seconds and I could do nothing more. I glanced anxiously back at the sight.

"'Bombs away!' I yelled, and salvoed quickly.

"'Rear bomb bay clear,' the tail gunner reported.

"I waited for Carmona to announce the front bomb bay clear so I could close the doors.

"'Eight bombs hung up and the

arming wires pulled out,' came Carmona's nervous report. 'They are hanging nose-down with the arming vanes backwards and forwards.

"If the arming vanes spun off and the bombs dropped, they would explode when they collided with each other. The Superfortress, with us in it, would be blown to pieces. In desperation I pressed the salvo switch several times but nothing happened.

"Vaucher said, 'How dangerous is it leaving them that way?'

"I said, 'Dangerous. Once we're back over the sea I'll try kicking them free.'

"For the last 10 minutes I had been oblivious to the flak. Now I could feel it again, bursting close. I looked over the bomb sight to spot the bombs. Twenty-three thousand feet below us the Japanese aircraft plant stood out in stark relief. Then tiny puffs of smoke spotted the buildings. The smoke spread and the plant seemed to rise up, then disintegrate. After so many misgivings now, finally, I could relax, sure of myself.

"'How are the bombs holding?' I called back to Mike Egan. 'The arming vanes still on?'

"'Same position, Captain Morrison.'

"'Fighter at nine o'clock!'

"I put the bombs out of my mind and searched the sky. Two fighters, one on each side of the formation, circled waiting for an opening. Suddenly the fighter to our right dived at us. I tracked him and when he was in range let go a long burst, but still he came on.

"As he passed right over the top of us, a huge, blossoming, yellowish-white mass descended in a shower of streamers.

"'What's that?' yelled Todd from the top turret.

"'Phosphorus bomb,' Vaucher told him.

"'I'm going back in the bomb bay to see if I can pry the bombs loose,' I told Vaucher.

"I edged my way out of the cabin and into the navigator's compartment. My Mae West and parachute made movement difficult. And I had to carry a portable cylin-

der of oxygen for my mask.

"'I waited a minute or two for my breathing to steady before crawling out along the narrow catwalk on the left side of the bay. I didn't want to look down but couldn't avoid doing so – 23,000 feet of nothing, then the white caps of the ocean. I shuddered and looked away quickly.

"I pulled some cotter pins out of my pocket, leaned far over into the bomb bay, left hand clutching the rack, and felt for the nose fuse of the first bomb. Fingers stiffening with the cold, I fumbled the cotter pin into the fuse.

"Fourteen to go. The longer I took the colder I'd get, and the more clumsy. My arms were shaking both with fear and from the extreme exertion of reaching down into the bay from the 10-inch-wide catwalk while gripping desperately to the rack.

"At last it was done. I was so exhausted I had to stand on my narrow perch for a minute or two to get my breathing steady and my nerves back under control before trying to push the bombs free.

"I struggled with a screwdriver to pry loose the wires that were holding the bomb in place. It was no use. Finally I gave up and edged my way back into the forward cockpit.

"We all felt as if we were riding a keg of dynamite as we approached the field.

"'Land her like a case of eggs,' the co-pilot told Vaucher. 'This is no time to go bouncing 10 feet in the air.'

"The wheels hit and ran. Egan yelled, 'They're still in place.'

"I wiped the sweat off my face and grinned back at Vaucher. He taxied over to the parking area, cut the engines, and shouted down to the ground crew to stand clear. 'We've got bombs hung up in the front bay.'

"'I'm going to open the bomb bay doors,' I said.

"The bomb doors snapped open. Eight 500-lb bombs smashed onto the crushed-stone parkway. Time stood still for a second.

"'I told you I didn't think they'd go off,' I told Vaucher."

The final act

Above: **Enola Gay** *was a B-29-45-MO built by Martin at Omaha. On 6 August 1945 it was to become the single most famous aircraft of the war, and change the face of warfare forever. This is pilot Paul Tibbets (with pipe) with his crew.*

Below: By mid-1944, Japan's empire had shrunk enough for B-29s to attack the homeland from bases in China. With the construction of five huge bases on the Marianas at the end of the year, all the major centres came under threat of bombing.

Above: 'Little Boy' was the code-name of the atomic bomb that exploded over Hiroshima at 9.30 a.m. on 6 August 1945. Made with uranium 235 and developed in great secrecy, the bomb exploded with the force of 20,000 tons of TNT.

Below: Hiroshima after the bomb: it was not just the scale of destruction or number of casualties that was so shocking, as worse had been caused by the firebomb raids, but the sheer power of a single weapon and the lingering effects of fallout.

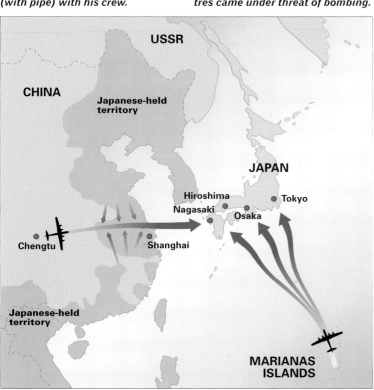

B-29 Superfortress

Bockscar was the Boeing B-29 which dropped the atmic bomb on Nagasaki on 9 August 1945, effectively ending the war. It, and *Enola Gay* which had dropped the first bomb three days earlier on Hiroshima, were flown by the 509th Bomb Group, based on Tinian. The special B-29s, codenamed 'Silverplate', were painted in the markings of regular B-29 units operating from the Marianas, in this case the 444th Bomb Group

Section Two: 1945 to the Gulf War

THE COLD WAR

The dominant military feature of the half century since the end of World War II was the undeclared war of nerves known as the Cold War. Two inimical cultural and political systems, centred on the military might of the United States of America and the Union of Soviet Socialist Republics, drew a large part of the world into their respective blocs. But the key to the rivalry was in the five decades of titanic military confrontation between NATO and the Warsaw Pact, the heart of which was across the 'Iron Curtain' which divided Europe between East and West soon after the fall of Hitler.

The Iron Curtain Descends

1945-1948

Left: Douglas C-54 Skymasters from US- and European-based units participated in the Berlin Airlift. The type's high speed and 10-tonne capacity made it the workhorse of the operation, while its modern nosewheel configuration gave it excellent crosswind tolerance.

Below: A pair of Spitfire FR.Mk XIVs of No.II (AC) Squadron take-off from Wunstorf, an operational airfield also used as a crucial Airlift hub.

Three months before the defeat of Germany, Churchill, Roosevelt and Stalin met at Yalta to discuss the division of the post-War world into 'spheres of influence'. Stalin mistrusted his Western Allies, believing that they wanted to destroy the USSR. He hoped to achieve security by neutralising bordering nations and believed that Germany should be crippled to prevent German militarism from ever resurfacing. The Yalta Treaty became the basis of the peace with Germany, and the USSR was promised 55 per cent of German reparations and a sphere of influence which encompassed all of Eastern Europe. Germany surrendered in May 1945 and was divided into four zones administered by the victorious Allies, including France.

GERMAN REHABILITATION

Soon after the war the USA and Britain came to the view that Germany should be rehabilitated to play a full part in the economic recovery of Europe. The Anglo-American zones were merged, soon joined by the French. The combined Western zone established a federal government, but in the east the USSR continued to act independently. Berlin, split into four zones and controlled jointly by all four 'Allied' powers, was 160 km (100 miles) inside the Soviet zone, and Stalin felt the four-power presence to be anomalous after the unilateral creation of a virtually independent Germany by the West. Consequently, he began placing stringent controls on surface travel to Berlin from the West. On 31 March 1948 the Soviets announced that road traffic into Berlin would be subject to inspection. The West refused to abide by this unilateral decision and cancelled all surface transportation except food and freight trains. At midnight on 18 June the Soviets formally banned all passenger traffic and followed this on 24 June by stopping food trains.

AIR SUPPLY

The Western powers decided to keep West Berlin supplied by air, at least while negotiations proceeded. It was calculated that 2000 tonnes of food and essential supplies would be needed each day to maintain the 2.5 million inhabitants, and a full-scale Airlift was mounted to defeat the blockade.

Since the war Allied transport fleets had been run down, but what remained mobilised immediately for the Airlift. By 29 June the whole of RAF Transport Command's 64 aircraft Dakota fleet was based in RAF Germany, reinforced by aircrews from Australia, New Zealand and South Africa. By 1 July the Dakotas had been joined by the RAF's Yorks and Hastings and two Coastal Command Sunderland squadrons. The RAF's entire home-based transport fleet was committed to Operation 'Plainfare', supplemented by British civil aircraft, including Haltons, Lancastrians and converted Halifax, Lancaster and Liberator bombers. Under Operation 'Vittles', the USAF provided 102 C-47s and began mobilising a fleet of C-54 Skymasters, most of them based in the USA. It was very soon realised that the load estimate was far too low, and that at least 4000 tonnes of coal, food and other essentials would be needed daily in order to stockpile supplies before winter, which would inevitably disrupt air traffic. It was soon apparent that the force committed was too small to meet the requirement.

The early achievements of the RAF and USAF were impressive, with over 2000 tonnes flown into Berlin daily in July, and average daily figures of 3839 tonnes and 4600 tonnes in September and October. Meanwhile, the USAF Military Air Transport Service provided eight squadrons of C-54s, which could carry 10 tonnes of freight and weren't as maintenance-intensive as the smaller Dakotas.

REORGANISATION

The deployment of the Skymasters coincided with the arrival of a new commander, Major-General William H. Tunner, who set about organising the Airlift more efficiently, getting maximum utilisation from his most-effective resources, using a smaller number of the larger aircraft. On 15 October the RAF and USAF operations were merged officially into a Combined Airlift Task

Left: An RAF Wunstorf Air Traffic Controller signals to a taxiing Dakota with an Aldis Lamp, at the height of the Airlift.

Below: P-80s of the 62nd Fighter Squadron, 56th Fighter Group, lined up at an RAF airfield, en route to Germany during the Berlin crisis.

Post-war air power

While civilians at home still regarded Stalin as 'Uncle Joe', the West's valiant Ally against Hitler, Allied forces at the front line soon realised that the USSR's hostility and suspicion of the West could result in another war. The USSR had an entirely different approach in its zone of occupation, and Europe soon coalesced into two hostile blocks. By 1947, Churchill could declare at Fulton, Ohio, that an 'Iron Curtain' divided the continent.

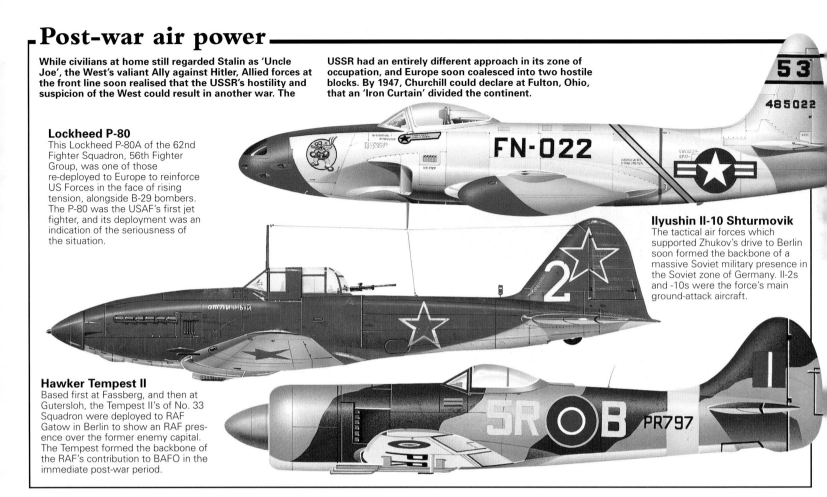

Lockheed P-80
This Lockheed P-80A of the 62nd Fighter Squadron, 56th Fighter Group, was one of those re-deployed to Europe to reinforce US Forces in the face of rising tension, alongside B-29 bombers. The P-80 was the USAF's first jet fighter, and its deployment was an indication of the seriousness of the situation.

Ilyushin Il-10 Shturmovik
The tactical air forces which supported Zhukov's drive to Berlin soon formed the backbone of a massive Soviet military presence in the Soviet zone of Germany. Il-2s and -10s were the force's main ground-attack aircraft.

Hawker Tempest II
Based first at Fassberg, and then at Gutersloh, the Tempest II's of No. 33 Squadron were deployed to RAF Gatow in Berlin to show an RAF presence over the former enemy capital. The Tempest formed the backbone of the RAF's contribution to BAFO in the immediate post-war period.

Above: Avro Yorks of RAF Transport Command were the unsung heroes of the Airlift, with an 8/9-tonne payload which could include extremely bulky loads, unlike the 10-tonne capacity C-54 or the lightweight 3-tonne capacity C-47.

Force (Provisional). The USAF C-47s were soon replaced by 300 C-54s, gathered from various sources. The importance of the RAF's contribution declined steadily, the Dakotas and Yorks completely

vacating Celle and Fassberg, moving farther from Berlin to make way for the C-54s. The four-hour cycle on which the Airlift was based placed the RAF's aircraft at a disadvantage, as they often missed their 'slot' in the next cycle because they were used to transport bulky cargo, passengers and exported manufactured goods, which required longer to load and unload.

The Soviet 16th Air Army had 3,000 combat aircraft, including Yak-3 and La-5FN fighters. When these began buzzing the heavily-laden transport aircraft, the USAF reacted by deploying two groups of B-29 Superfortresses to British bases

and a wing of P-80 jet fighters to Furstenfeldbruck. This Allied commitment increased tension, but demonstrated that intimidation would gain nothing.

At the peak of the Airlift aircraft took off and landed at Gatow and Tempelhof airports every 90 seconds, and aircraft remained on the ground at Berlin for an average of only 30 minutes. The Airlift brought in almost one tonne of supplies per Berliner, and had continued around the clock, seven days a week, except briefly during November 1948. Altogether 1586530 tonnes of coal, 92282 tonnes of fuel and 538016 tonnes of

Greek Civil War 1944-1949

During World War II Greece had been occupied by the Nazis after a very brief campaign, which ended with a humiliating British defeat at Crete. In Greece, as in other occupied countries, there had been a small but active resistance movement, dominated by the Communists. At the end of the war Greece was placed in the UK's sphere of influence, and the British immediately re-established the Greek monarchy and re-equipped and revitalised the nation's armed forces. The Royal Hellenic air force received large numbers of war surplus aircraft from the RAF, mostly drawn from the Desert Air Force. They included Oxfords, Ansons, Austers, Dakotas (which were used as bombers), Harvards, Beaufighters, Spitfires and

Wellingtons. The Communist guerrillas were unwilling to exchange Nazi oppression for reactionary monarchist rule, and rose against the new government. The Civil War was won eventually by the monarchists, who had begun to receive substantial military aid from the USA. This included aircraft to supplement those supplied by the UK and comprised C-47s, T-6 Texans and L-5 Grasshoppers.

To his credit, Stalin made no attempt to gain control of any territory not allocated at Yalta, even stopping his troops at the Greek border during the revolutionary struggle, when intervention could easily have drawn Greece into the Communist orbit. In similar compliance with the Yalta conference, Stalin withdrew his forces

from those areas of Berlin which were to be occupied by the Western Allies, just as the UK and the USA withdrew from Czechoslovakia and the east of Germany.

Royal Air Force Dakotas drop paratroopers near Athens at the end of World War II. British and American support ensured the Greek monarchists would win the civil war with the communists.

food, a total of 2325809 tonnes of supplies, had been airlifted in. The USSR realised that it could not starve Berlin into submission and the blockade was lifted at one minute past midnight on 12 May 1949. Despite this the Airlift continued until September, building up stocks in case surface links were cut again. Germany came to be seen as a valuable Ally in the fight against Soviet aggression and the Federal Republic of Germany was formally established on 21 September 1949, marking the division of Europe.

Above: A No. 201 Squadron Sunderland unloads supplies on Berlin's Lake Havel. Two RAF Coastal Command Sunderland squadrons participated, easing the strain on West Berlin's crowded airfields by flying from Hamburg's Finkenwarder to Lake Havel.

West Germany was accepted into NATO and her armed forces armed with American equipment to bring it up to operational readiness standards against the Soviet block and to take its part in the Cold War which was just beginning.

OPERATING ROUTES OF THE BERLIN AIRLIFT

(Map)

BRITISH ZONE
RUSSIAN ZONE
AMERICAN ZONE

Schleswigland
Lubeck
Fuhlsbuttel
Finkenwarder
Fassberg
Celle
Wunstorf
Buckeburg
Lake Havel
Tegel
Gatow
Tempelhof
Rhein Main
Wiesbaden

▲ BEACON
● COMBINED RAF/USAF BASES
● RAF BASES
○ USAF BASE
→ TRACKS TO BERLIN
→ TRACKS FROM BERLIN

Left: Douglas C-54 Skymasters and C-47 Skytrains formed the backbone of the USAF's transport effort during the Berlin Airlift. The C-54s were fast and efficient, but could not carry the bulkier, more awkward loads, which went by C-47, Dakota or by Avro York.

Above: The complexity of the operation to keep Berlin supplied by air was further complicated by the different speeds of the participating aircraft. The slow Yorks and C-47s often needed longer to fly to and from Berlin, and to load and unload than the four-hour blocks allocated.

Berlin Airlift transports

The Berlin Airlift transported 2325809 tonnes of cargo into the city, including 1586530 tonnes of coal, and 538016 tonnes of food. Liquid fuels (primarily oil) made up another 92282 tonnes, all of this being carried by British civil aircraft. The RAF carried 17 per cent of the total tonnage, while British civil carriers accounted for another 6.3 per cent. The USAF accounted for the lion's share, however.

Douglas C-54 Skymaster
The C-54 provided the backbone of the Berlin Airlift (with a peak total of 200 aircraft committed) and the system of time blocks for participating aircraft was optimised around the C-54's performance characteristics, even though this led to other, slower types sometimes missing their slots.

Handley Page HP.70 Halton I
The Halton I was essentially a civilianised transport derivative of the wartime Halifax bomber. BOAC's Haltons (and civilianised Halifax bombers operated by other companies) were pressed into service on the Airlift.

Avro Lancaster III
Hastily civilianised Lancasters were pressed into service on the Airlift. There were accidents, some caused by the intensive operations in what were often poor conditions. This aircraft was written-off in 1948.

Strategic Air Command

1946-1955

Boeing B-47 Stratojets provided SAC with its first truly modern jet bomber. Some 2,102 were delivered, equipping 43 bomb wings of the 2nd, 8th and 15th Air Forces. The aircraft was also used in the strategic reconnaissance, electronic warfare and weather reconnaissance roles, and served until late-1965 in its primary role. Here, six B-47Es stage a flypast.

The philosophy of deterring aggression by a world power with the threat of immediate and devastating retaliation became a reality the moment the two opposing world political blocs acquired nuclear weapons. For over 40 years, the mainstay of the Western world's airborne nuclear deterrent was the USAF's Strategic Air Command (SAC), a force of long-range bombers constantly deployed between bases throughout the world.

Long after SAC was founded under General George C. Kenney on 21 March 1946, US Air Force officers coined the motto 'peace is our profession'. In fact, once SAC got underway with a mere six com-

Above left: Strategic Air Command's badge of a mailed fist holding lightning bolts and an olive branch graphically summed up the underlying philosophy of 'peace through strength'.

bat groups of B-29 Superfortresses – and a handful of Mk III bombs similar to the plutonium weapon that had razed Nagasaki – no one was thinking of peace. For men and machines, the daily regimen consisted of rehearsal for war.

In the newly unfolding Cold War, atomic bombs were seen simply as a new kind of weapon. The US tested them repeatedly. (On 1 July 1946, a B-29 dropped a Nagasaki-type bomb on 73 ships lying off Bikini atoll in the western

Pacific.) The knowledge that the increasingly belligerent Soviet Union was also developing nuclear weapons – the first was detonated in 1949 – gave impetus to the rapid expansion and modernisation of SAC. East-West tensions also prompted the USAF to treat SAC's members as an elite fighting force. General Curtis E. LeMay, who followed Kenney and shaped the SAC

Above: The monstrous B-36 was designed during World War II as an intercontinental bomber able to hit targets in Germany or Japan from US bases. It went on to become the mainstay of SAC's long-range nuclear bomber force during the service's formative years.

of the 1950s, hyped the special duties of his men with everything from colourful scarves to spot promotions for top performers.

Left: The Boeing B-50 was an interim replacement for the B-29. It was originally designated B-29D, and redesignated in order to win funding at a time when B-29s were delivered straight to storage. These are B-50Ds of the 15th AF (identified by the circle tail marking).

Above: The USAF's new Strategic Air Command initially controlled only six B-29-equipped bomb wings. The type had a relatively brief life in SAC service, although converted KB-29s served as tankers after the basic model had been phased out by bomb squadrons.

B-36 Peacemaker: SAC's 'Big Stick'

The first B-36As were delivered to the USAF in the summer of 1948, and by the end of the year the aircraft was able to fly an unrefuelled dummy attack from Carswell AFB in Texas to Pearl Harbor on Hawaii, dropping an inert 4536-kg (10,000-lb) bomb in the sea. The 13036-km (8,100-mile) raid went undetected by local defences. The type equipped 10 bomb wings and served to 1959.

Convair B-36A
Left: The first B-36s equipped two heavy bomb groups (the 7th and 11th) of the Eighth Air Force at Carswell AFB. Most wore three-digit 'Buzz numbers', with a BM prefix.

Convair B-36J
Right: A host of improvements were fitted to the B-36 during its production life. Underwing pods with four J47 turbojets were introduced with the B-36D, along with snap-action bomb-doors. The B-36H introduced a new bomb sight, and from 1954, B-36s were lightened to improve speed and altitude performance.

The concept of airborne nuclear deterrent was evolved between 1947 and 1950, and spurred the development of newer, bigger strategic bombers for the expected nuclear war with the Soviet Union.

The B-29, which had proven so effective against Japan during World War II, was downgraded from 'very heavy' to 'heavy' to 'medium' bomber status as it was replaced by the B-50, the B-47 Stratojet and the thundering B-36 Peacemaker.

Below: During the Korean War B-29s were tasked with precision attacks against bridges. One of the weapons tested was the annular-finned, radio-controlled Tarzon. However, it proved unsuccessful in service and only three were ever dropped.

Although its development had begun even before the US entry into World War II, the giant Convair B-36 was just right for the early Cold War era – a powerful, six-engined behemoth with a 70.10-m (230-ft) wing span, a bomb bay large enough to hold a Nash Rambler automobile, and no fewer than 16 20-mm cannons arrayed from nose to tail on the silvery cigar of its fuselage. When four wingtip jet engines were added, the B-36 became the biggest, farthest-reaching nuclear bomber in the sky. Crews routinely flew 12-hour missions. Flying in the RB-36 reconnaissance versions, they were aloft for up to 22 hours.

HYDROGEN WEAPONS
Strategic Air Command also filled its expanding bomber groups with the B-50, a much-improved bomber based on the B-29 with greatly enhanced crew comforts. When hydrogen bombs were added to the arsenals of both sides in the 1950s, 'mediums' like the B-50 had difficulty handling new and enormous nuclear bombs like the Mk 15 Zombie. The B-50 sol-

diered on heroically but its contribution as a front-line bomber was limited to a span of a few years.

The veteran B-29 was the only big bomber recalled to action for the 1950-53 Korean War. The sad truth was that the Pentagon assigned a lower priority to Korea than to the expected nuclear war with Moscow. Thus, stateside SAC bases operated B-50 bombers, C-124 Globemaster II transports (used to haul nuclear weapons), and

Above: SAC was responsible for conducting strategic reconnaissance, as well as for bombing. RB-29s, RB-50s (as seen here), RB-47s and RB-36s were among the strategic bombers converted for this vital role. Numerous overflights of the Soviet Union were conducted by these types during the early days Cold War.

Convair B-36D Peacemaker
This B-36D of the 326th Bomb Squadron (Heavy), seen dropping a Mk 17 bomb, was built as a B-36B. It was converted to B-36D configuration by the addition of underwing jet engine pods, and other improvements.

Hydrogen bomb
The B-36's primary mission was intercontinental nuclear strike against targets deep within the Soviet Union for which it carried the monster Mk 17 hydrogen thermonuclear bomb. This weighed a massive 21 tonnes and measured 7.3 m (24 feet) in length.

Above: Operation 'Longstride' in August 1953 saw the deployment of 31st FEW F-84Gs to Morocco in a demonstration of long-range escort capability. The aircraft flew directly from Turner AFB, Georgia, refuelling in flight from SAC KB-29s, and supported by a C-74.

Above: Republic F-84F Thunderstreak fighter-bombers were assigned to SAC for long-range escort fighter duties, replacing straight-winged F-84Ds, Es and Gs. SAC's first escort fighter was the F-82 Twin Mustang.

the B-47 jet bomber, while all of these aircraft were withheld from the Korean commitment.

At any given time, SAC never had more than 205 of the giant B-36s (of 383 built). To build a US strategic force in the kind of numbers that would guarantee victory over the Soviet Union, LeMay and the Pentagon relied heavily on the B-47, a radical bomber different in almost every respect from every bomber before it. The B-47 was fighter-like in its appearance and configuration, with swept-back wings and podded turbojet power.

Although difficult to fly and almost impossible to bail out of, the B-47 was the most potent bomber of the early-1950s and was seen as such a threat to the USSR that Stalin ordered countermeasures. At the height of SAC's strength, nearly 2,000 B-47s formed the vanguard of the strategic bombing force – gradually, B-29s and later B-36s and B-50s were phased out as the 1960s approached – and the nuclear arsenal to equip them grew to tens of thousands of warheads. The 21-tonne Mk 17 hydrogen bomb became the American giant of nuclear bombs, and SAC crews carried them on airborne alert.

In the 1940s and 1950s, SAC operated fighter escort squadrons, beginning with the twin-boom F-82 Twin Mustang and culminating with the swept-wing F-84F Thunderstreak. LeMay was furious when his 27th Fighter Escort Group (with straightwing F-84D/E Thunderjets) was commandeered to participate in Korean fighting: he demanded his fighters back, got them, and bolstered them with improved, straightwing F-84Gs.

SAC's dedicated fighter pilots faced the grim prospect of a one-way journey into horror if nuclear war actually came. Their courage was beyond question, but the

Above: The North American RB-45 Tornado was a successful stop-gap in the strategic recce role. A handful of USAF RB-45s were used for radar mapping of IP-to-target runs inside Russia, flown by RAF crews.

Right: The FICON mix of GRB-36F and RF-84K entered service briefly with the 99th SRW and 91st SRS in 1955. The RF-84K parasite was intended to extend the combination's reconnaissance range.

SAC support

Strategic Air Command was a self-contained autonomous strategic air force, whose bomb wings were augmented by tanker, recce and even fighter escort units. At its post-war peak strength (reached in 1956), the Command fielded 3,188 aircraft, of which 1,640 were front-line B-36, B-47 and B-52 bombers. There were 844 air-refuelling tankers.

Boeing KC-97G
A massive total of 592 KC-97Gs was built before production switched to the jet-engined KC-135 in 1956. There were 60 earlier KC-97Es and 159 KC-97Fs, following three KC-97As temporarily converted to tanker configuration for evaluation and trials.

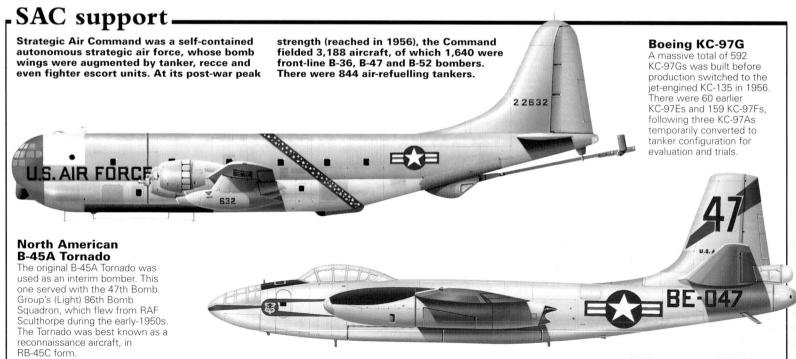

North American B-45A Tornado
The original B-45A Tornado was used as an interim bomber. This one served with the 47th Bomb Group's (Light) 86th Bomb Squadron, which flew from RAF Sculthorpe during the early-1950s. The Tornado was best known as a reconnaissance aircraft, in RB-45C form.

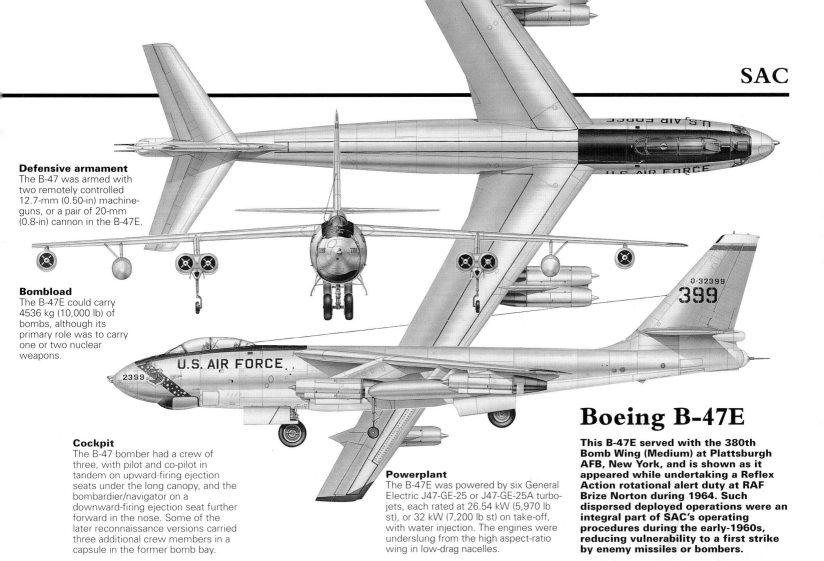

Defensive armament
The B-47 was armed with two remotely controlled 12.7-mm (0.50-in) machine-guns, or a pair of 20-mm (0.8-in) cannon in the B-47E.

Bombload
The B-47E could carry 4536 kg (10,000 lb) of bombs, although its primary role was to carry one or two nuclear weapons.

Cockpit
The B-47 bomber had a crew of three, with pilot and co-pilot in tandem on upward-firing ejection seats under the long canopy, and the bombardier/navigator on a downward-firing ejection seat further forward in the nose. Some of the later reconnaissance versions carried three additional crew members in a capsule in the former bomb bay.

Powerplant
The B-47E was powered by six General Electric J47-GE-25 or J47-GE-25A turbojets, each rated at 26.54 kW (5,970 lb st), or 32 kW (7,200 lb st) on take-off, with water injection. The engines were underslung from the high aspect-ratio wing in low-drag nacelles.

Boeing B-47E

This B-47E served with the 380th Bomb Wing (Medium) at Plattsburgh AFB, New York, and is shown as it appeared while undertaking a Reflex Action rotational alert duty at RAF Brize Norton during 1964. Such dispersed deployed operations were an integral part of SAC's operating procedures during the early-1960s, reducing vulnerability to a first strike by enemy missiles or bombers.

fighter jocks never won the heart of their leader. When swept-wing RF-84K Thunderflash reconnaissance aircraft went aloft as 'parasites' operating from the bays of B-36 bombers, LeMay was sceptical. The general told everybody within earshot that "fighters are fun but bombers are important." In the late-1950s, LeMay was unwilling to invest in newer, faster fighters – SAC operated the F-101A Voodoo only briefly – and the fighter escort force was abandoned.

TANKER SUPPORT

In one way, the most important SAC aircraft of the era was the inflight-refuelling tanker: the prop-driven KC-97 Stratofreighter and the epoch-making, jet-propelled KC-135 Stratotanker gave the

bombers worldwide reach. Tankers literally revolutionised air warfare, and the world has not been the same since.

Under the aegis of General Curtis LeMay, SAC reached the peak of its strength in 1956 when its aircraft inventory totalled 3,188 (247 B/RB-36, 97 B-52, 254 RB-47, 1,306 B-47, 16 RB-57, 51 C-124, 750 KC-97, 74 KB-29, 366 F-84, 57 RF-84F/K). SAC was never to see such numbers again. But the challenge persisted. Introduction of the B-52 Stratofortress – armed with thermonuclear weapons of unprecedented power – on 29 June 1955, followed by the image of Nikita Khruschev pounding his shoe on the table during a United Nations debate, augered a new era in the Cold War.

Above: Carrying a Bell GAM-63 Rascal missile under the starboard wingroot, the YDB-47E Stratojet refuels from a KC-97 tanker. The Rascal represented an early attempt to provide SAC's bombers with a stand-off missile capability.

Below: SAC refined and honed its capability with exercises and competitions. Here, B-47s are lined up on the ramp at Barksdale AFB waiting to participate in SAC's sixth annual bombing and navigation competition, in August 1954.

Birth of NATO and the Warsaw Pact

1948–1956

Europe's division into two armed camps began soon after VE-Day. Retaining only the minimum of troops necessary to police their sectors of defeated Germany, the Western Allies ran down their forces with all possible speed, from five million to one million within 12 months. The Soviet Union, still establishing communism in the territories from which it had ejected the Nazis, made no such reduction.

Suspicious of the West's 'delay' in launching D-Day, fearful of a Western/German alliance against him, and wary of an ideological 'Trojan horse' in the generous American offers of reconstruction aid to Europe, Josef Stalin kept the Red Army at some five million troops. As countries that were once Western oriented were forced into the Soviet bloc and Berlin was almost lost to a communist siege, the West drew its own conclusions

from the Soviet refusal to demobilise. Its first steps towards a defence against Stalin's armies were taken in March 1948 with formation of the Western Union (the UK, France, Belgium, the Netherlands and Luxembourg).

THE WESTERN UNION

The new alliance had hardly been organised before talks began on extension of the Western Union with US and Canadian elements. This followed a US Senate resolution of 11 June 1948 which allowed the country to associate itself in peacetime with 'such regional and other collective arrangements as are based on continuous and effective self-help and mutual aid, and as affect its national security'. Like God, the USA was advertising its willingness to help those who help themselves.

By the time the North Atlantic Treaty was signed in Washington

on 4 April 1949, Denmark, Iceland, Italy, Norway and Portugal had joined the seven founder nations. Later were to come Greece and Turkey (both in 1952), West Germany (in 1955) and Spain (in 1982). All endorsed a broad declaration of peaceful co-operation and willingness to solve disputes without re course to arms, but it was the fifth of the Treaty's 14 component articles which contained the most vital assertion: 'The Parties agree that an armed attack against one or more of them in Europe or North America shall be considered an attack against them all . . .' No aggressor could say that he had not been warned.

NATO TAKES SHAPE

Not until the start of the Korean War in June 1950 did NATO begin to take the form by which it is now recognised. On 2 April 1951 (two years after the North Atlantic

Above: Lockheed's F-80 Shooting Star entered service in the last months of World War II, though it saw no combat. Although outclassed by later designs, it was the US Air Force's primary air combat fighter on the establishment of NATO in March 1948.

Treaty had been signed), Allied Command Europe became operational under the former liberator of Western Europe, General Dwight Eisenhower. Simultaneously Allied Air Forces Central Europe was established with Lieutenant General Lauris Norstad as its first commander-in-chief. It was only now that NATO began to rearm with US jet aircraft through the Mutual Defense Assistance Program, starting with a handful of Republic F-84E Thunderjets. By 1952, the F-84G model was arriving in Europe in its hundreds, and the air forces of Belgium, Denmark, France Italy, the Netherlands, Norway and

Below: Built in huge numbers, the Ilyushin Il-10 was the main Soviet ground attack aircraft in the early post-war years. Rugged and hard-hitting, it was also to equip the Czechoslovak and many other Warsaw Pact air forces.

Right: Britain's Gloster Meteor was one of the world's first operational jet fighters, and was a standard NATO fighter in the early years. Belgium acquired more than 240 of the type, building many aircraft under licence at Avions Fairey.

Early Cold War jets

The first combat jets had entered service in 1944, and marked a great leap forwards in capability. Many of the wartime designs were to serve with distinction into the 1960s, but within five years they were to be outclassed by a new generation of fighting machines, incorporating advanced aerodynamics and with vastly superior performance.

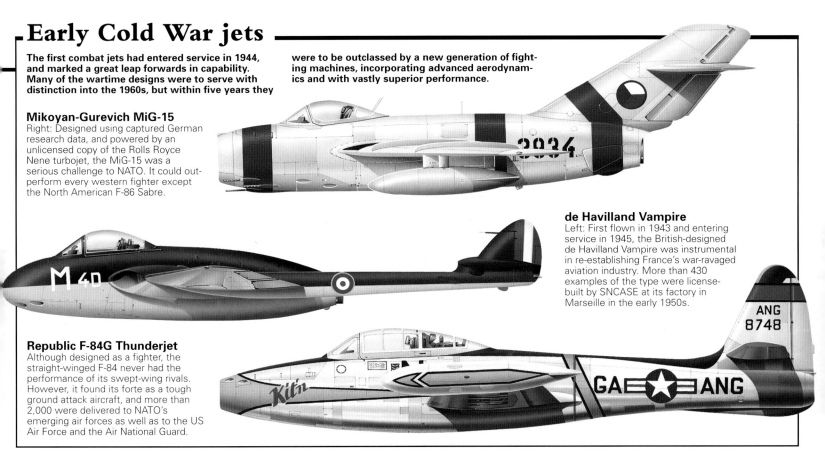

Mikoyan-Gurevich MiG-15
Right: Designed using captured German research data, and powered by an unlicensed copy of the Rolls Royce Nene turbojet, the MiG-15 was a serious challenge to NATO. It could outperform every western fighter except the North American F-86 Sabre.

de Havilland Vampire
Left: First flown in 1943 and entering service in 1945, the British-designed de Havilland Vampire was instrumental in re-establishing France's war-ravaged aviation industry. More than 430 examples of the type were license-built by SNCASE at its factory in Marseille in the early 1950s.

Republic F-84G Thunderjet
Although designed as a fighter, the straight-winged F-84 never had the performance of its swept-wing rivals. However, it found its forte as a tough ground attack aircraft, and more than 2,000 were delivered to NATO's emerging air forces as well as to the US Air Force and the Air National Guard.

Portugal were soon transformed. Later, Greece and Turkey qualified for receipt of the ubiquitous Thunderjet, and more went to southern Europe as the swept-wing F-84F Thunderstreak and its reconnaissance configured RF-84F Thunderflash variant were supplied to the central area. The F-86 Sabre was a rare sight in Europe during the Korean War, though Canadian-built examples served with RCAF units and the RAF before they were redistributed to Italy, Greece, Turkey and West Germany. In May 1953, Fiat of Italy obtained a licence to produce the limited all-weather F-86K interceptor for European use by the local air force as well as by France, the Netherlands, Norway and West Germany.

Behind what was already coming to be known as the 'Iron Curtain', the Soviet Union viewed with continued misgivings the movement towards the reunification of Germany, and then with growing alarm the plans for its rearmament by the Western powers.

Though Stalin had died in 1953, his policies were maintained in large measure by the leaders who followed, and one of their greatest priorities was to prevent West Germany from rearming. Attempts were made by the new administration in Moscow to secure the broader ideal of a demilitarised Europe — apart, that is, from the

EUROPE'S GREAT DIVIDE

Any trust the victorious Allies might have felt after the end of the war in Europe soon changed to suspicion as two mutually antagonistic power blocs were established. In Winston Churchill's inimitable words, an Iron Curtain had descended across the centre of Europe. On one side, the war-weary but free democratic states of Western Europe were backed by the military, political and industrial muscle of the United States of America. On the other side, Eastern Europe fell under the heavy hand of the Soviet Union, which exercised control by installing puppet governments backed by the ever-present threat of military intervention. The Red Army's victory in the Great Patriotic War had not been followed by an appreciable stand-down of Soviet forces, and it was to counter this huge military potential that NATO was set up.

Left: F-84Gs of the Netherlands air force fly in formation. Not a great performer, the Thunderjet was nevertheless of great value to NATO through the 1950s, being tough, easy to maintain, reliable and available in numbers.

Above: Germany became a full NATO member in 1955, and soon become a major force on the Central Front. A key item in the Luftwaffe's inventory was the Republic F-84F, 450 of which served between 1956 and 1969.

Left: Lavochkin La-5FN fighters of the 1st Czechoslovak Fighter Regiment are seen in Germany at the end of World War II. Units like this which fought alongside the Soviets were to form the core of post-war East European air forces, armed almost exclusively with Soviet equipment.

territories occupied by Soviet forces in 1945. This one-sided disarmament did not appeal to NATO, and so plans for German membership went ahead. In a remarkable attempt to render the North Atlantic Treaty impotent, the USSR suggested on 31 March 1954 that it might be prepared to join NATO, a proposal which was firmly rejected by the UK, France and the USA a month later. West

Germany became a member of NATO on 5 May 1955, and with its efforts thwarted, the USSR organised the signing of a counter declaration in Warsaw just nine days later.

THE WARSAW PACT
This Treaty of Friendship, Mutual Assistance and Co-operation (known for short as the Warsaw Pact) between Moscow and its

client states of Albania, Bulgaria, Czechoslovakia, East Germany, Hungary, Poland and Romania was dedicated only to the defence of European territory, and thus excluded the central and eastern Soviet Union. Though NATO loosely refers to the Warsaw Pact as its counterpart, the Eastern alliance merely formalised bilateral treaties already in being and later modified by status-of-forces agreements with

Poland, East Germany, Romania and Hungary in 1956-7 and with Czechoslovakia in 1968.

The Warsaw Pact had some propaganda value – it was formed after NATO and could declared as a 'response to capitalist aggression.' In all practical terms, however, it made no difference to the strategic situation, save that between 5 and 14 May 1955 the last hope for a reversal of the European arms build-up was lost. The Soviet Union continued to dictate the pace of rearmament in its territories, and if any of its signatories briefly took heart from the Warsaw Pact's declaration of 'non-interference in their internal affairs', illusions were dispelled by the Soviet invasion of Hungary only 18 months later.

From May 1955, the two sides in the Cold War were neatly defined as NATO versus the Warsaw Pact, and those whose task it is to make the man in the street understand strategic matters were able to draw different-sized ranks of blue soldiers and red soldiers to depict the balance of forces. At the time, though, the head-counting exercise had temporarily lost its point, for the era of the nuclear bomber and intercontinental missile was at hand.

Laft: One of the classic fighters of all time, the MiG-15 was designated 'Fagot' under the new NATO reporting system, and was standard Warsaw Pact equipment through the 1950s and 1960s. Built in huge numbers in the Soviet Union, it was also manufactured in Poland and Czechoslovakia. These Polish LIM-2s are versions of the more powerful MiG-15bis, which first flew in 1949.

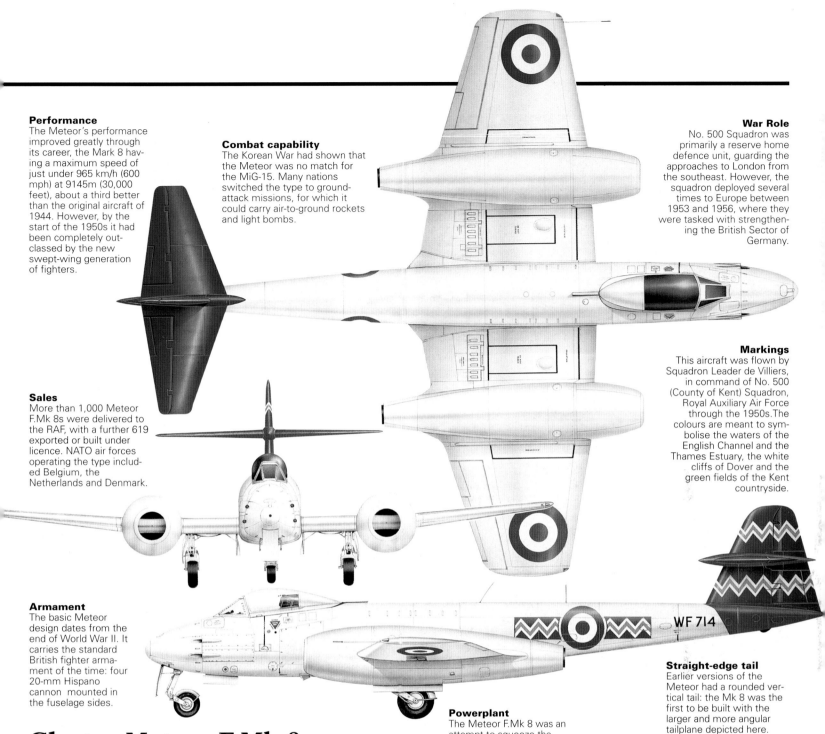

Performance
The Meteor's performance improved greatly through its career, the Mark 8 having a maximum speed of just under 965 km/h (600 mph) at 9145m (30,000 feet), about a third better than the original aircraft of 1944. However, by the start of the 1950s it had been completely outclassed by the new swept-wing generation of fighters.

Combat capability
The Korean War had shown that the Meteor was no match for the MiG-15. Many nations switched the type to ground-attack missions, for which it could carry air-to-ground rockets and light bombs.

War Role
No. 500 Squadron was primarily a reserve home defence unit, guarding the approaches to London from the southeast. However, the squadron deployed several times to Europe between 1953 and 1956, where they were tasked with strengthening the British Sector of Germany.

Sales
More than 1,000 Meteor F.Mk 8s were delivered to the RAF, with a further 619 exported or built under licence. NATO air forces operating the type included Belgium, the Netherlands and Denmark.

Markings
This aircraft was flown by Squadron Leader de Villiers, in command of No. 500 (County of Kent) Squadron, Royal Auxiliary Air Force through the 1950s.The colours are meant to symbolise the waters of the English Channel and the Thames Estuary, the white cliffs of Dover and the green fields of the Kent countryside.

Armament
The basic Meteor design dates from the end of World War II. It carries the standard British fighter armament of the time: four 20-mm Hispano cannon mounted in the fuselage sides.

Powerplant
The Meteor F.Mk 8 was an attempt to squeeze the maximum performance out of the airframe without major modification: it was powered by uprated Rolls-Royce Derwent 8 turbojets each delivering 15.57 kN (3,500 lb st).

Straight-edge tail
Earlier versions of the Meteor had a rounded vertical tail: the Mk 8 was the first to be built with the larger and more angular tailplane depicted here. Designed to decrease high-speed buffeting, the redesign was only marginally successful.

Gloster Meteor F.Mk 8
The world's first operational jet fighter (beating the Messerschmitt 262 into regular squadron service by a matter of days), the Gloster Meteor was the mainstay of the Britain's fighter force in the postwar years, and continued to serve with reserve units through the 1950s. It was sold to more than a dozen nations.

WF 714

Above: Apart from uniform and insignia, Warsaw Pact air forces were indistinguishable from those of the Soviet Union. These Polish pilots flew Soviet tactics in Soviet aircraft, and in time of war would have been under Soviet command.

Right: By 1956 the Cold War lines in Europe had been drawn, and the World War II-era equipment which had equipped both sides had been replaced by advanced new designs. These are Ilyushin Il-28 'Beagle' bombers of the Soviet air force.

Cold War over the Ocean

1945-1970

The end of World War II left both the USA and Britain with the massive navies with which they had undertaken the convoy war in the Atlantic, and the island-hopping drive to Japan. Aircraft-carriers had played a major role, but now had little to do. Large numbers of ex-Royal Navy and ex-US Navy carriers were retired: some were placed in mothballs, and others were sold or given to friendly nations to allow them to develop their own naval air arms.

Before carrier aviation could wither entirely, the Korean War broke out, and both British and American aircraft carriers played a major part in the campaign, primarily in the ground-attack role. The war allowed carrier aviation to be properly funded, and prompted renewed effort in research, development and operational analyses.

NEW TENSIONS

The world was a very different place at the end of the Korean War, with the Cold War suddenly very real. The chances of additional conflicts (perhaps proxy struggles like Korea) seemed very real. The need to keep open the sealanes to Europe and Japan became apparent

Above: Britain's RAF Coastal Command (absorbed by Strike Command from 1968) fielded a fleet of Avro Shackletons for maritime patrol and anti-submarine operations. This one is a tricycle undercarriage-equipped MR.Mk 3, and served with No. 206 Squadron.

Below: Soviet maritime patrol forces retained flying-boats for longer than most Western nations. The Beriev Be-12 'Mail' seen here did not enter service until the mid-1960s (replacing the piston-powered Be-6) and remains in service in small numbers to this day.

as the USSR raced to build a blue water navy, laying emphasis on creating a powerful submarine fleet.

The US Navy commissioned a new class of modern aircraft-carriers, laying the keel of the 60000 tonne USS *Forrestal* in July 1952. These ships were truly modern aircraft carriers, incorporating the British-developed angled flight deck and steam catapult from the start, and capable of carrying giant air wings. Moreover, the very

role of the carrier was expanded. Wartime carriers had been little more than floating fighter airfields, providing escort and air-defence fighters and light-attack aircraft, sometimes with a rudimentary anti-submarine capability. The new carriers were designed from the start to project power, with complements which would include powerful long-range attack and strike aircraft, as well as fighters and fighter-bombers. With the introduction of nuclear-armed Douglas A-3 Skywarriors (and later, briefly, A-5 Vigilantes), aircraft-carriers took on a semi-strategic role, and were integrated into SIOP.

GROWING THREAT

Their new importance made the carriers inviting targets for Russia's expanding submarine fleet, and older aircraft-carriers were hastily modified and modernised to serve as dedicated ASW carriers, equipped with ASW helicopters and aircraft. These were then deployed to screen attack carrier groups against the growing Soviet submarine threat. This threat was probably over-estimated initially, with expectations that the USSR would deploy cloned Type XXI U-boats in massive numbers for a 'Battle of the Atlantic'-type war against Allied shipping. In fact, post-war Soviet submarine development was less ambitious. Although lessons were learned from captured U-boat technology, early post-war submarines were evolved from wartime boats, with relatively minor improvements and built in relatively small numbers.

The growth of the Soviet navy

Above: The Canadair Argus was designed as an indigenous replacement for the Avro Lancaster in the ASW role. It used the wing and empennage of the Bristol Britannia, mated to a new ASW equipment-packed fuselage and four Wright R-3350 piston engines.

Left: The backbone of the US Navy's ASW force for the early years of the Cold War was the Lockheed P2V (later designated P-2) Neptune. It was gradually superseded by the P-3 Orion from the early-1960s.

Worldwide ASW

Even before submarines took over the strategic nuclear strike role, they posed a great risk to naval surface ships and to the convoys on which each superpower would have relied in the event of war. When submarines became the means by which nuclear war could have been fought, their detection (and protection from enemy submarines) brought ASW aircraft a new importance.

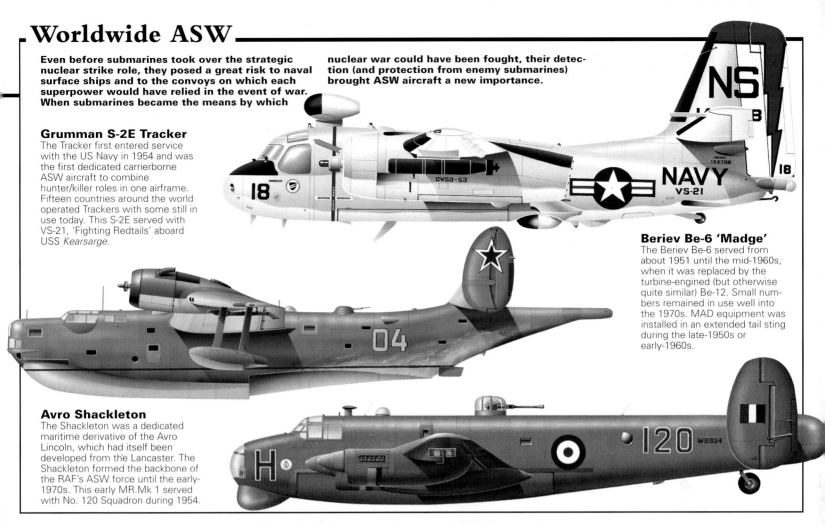

Grumman S-2E Tracker
The Tracker first entered service with the US Navy in 1954 and was the first dedicated carrierborne ASW aircraft to combine hunter/killer roles in one airframe. Fifteen countries around the world operated Trackers with some still in use today. This S-2E served with VS-21, 'Fighting Redtails' aboard USS *Kearsarge*.

Beriev Be-6 'Madge'
The Beriev Be-6 served from about 1951 until the mid-1960s, when it was replaced by the turbine-engined (but otherwise quite similar) Be-12. Small numbers remained in use well into the 1970s. MAD equipment was installed in an extended tail sting during the late-1950s or early-1960s.

Avro Shackleton
The Shackleton was a dedicated maritime derivative of the Avro Lincoln, which had itself been developed from the Lancaster. The Shackleton formed the backbone of the RAF's ASW force until the early-1970s. This early MR.Mk 1 served with No. 120 Squadron during 1954.

Left: It was impossible to cover the world using only land-based ASW aircraft, and several nations made extensive use of carrierborne ASW aircraft to cover mid-ocean gaps and to provide ASW coverage for groups of warships. Britain's carriers embarked the Fairey Gannet.

(and fear of its growth) necessitated more constant coverage of the entire oceans than could be achieved using a handful of isolated aircraft-carrier groups, and at the same time that carrier aviation was revolutionised America was developing a new generation of land-based long-range patrol aircraft. They were intended to be able to operate in both the maritime patrol role, keeping tabs on Soviet surface vessels, and also in the ASW role, monitoring the movement of Soviet submarines and engaging them if it ever became necessary. In retrospect, aircraft like the Martin Marlin flying-boat can be seen to have represented a dead-end in patrol/ASW aircraft development, although they were effective enough by the standards of the time. More important were developments in ASW radar and in

Right: Westland Wessex HAS Mk 1 was one of the first dedicated ASW helicopters. It was fitted with dipping sonar and could carry torpedoes or depth charges and operated from Royal Navy Destroyers and anti-submarine cruisers. This Wessex HAS Mk 1 is from No. 737 Squadron, Portland, Dorset.

active and passive sonar, as well as in the deployment of new systems, most notably MAD (Magnetic Anomaly Detectors) which could detect changes to the earth's magnetic field caused by the presence of a large steel submarine. Such equipment was fitted to versions of the Lockheed P-2 Neptune, the Avro Shackleton and Canadair Argus.

The introduction of nuclear submarines with teardrop hulls, capable of sustaining high underwater speeds, presented a challenge to ASW forces, which also had to react to reductions in noise levels and advances in tactics and countermeasures. In the late-1950s, the first ballistic missile-carrying submarines were deployed, and the number of submarines and submarine-launched missiles grew exponentially, driving progressive improvements in ASW aircraft and equipment.

ELINT, Spies and Ferrets

1948–1960

Left: The lead taken by the West in jet propulsion allowed aircraft such as the North American RB-45 Tornado to undertake limited cross-border incursions. However, it was not long before the Soviet defences developed the ability to ward off these unwelcome flights.

Below: At the end of World War II the principal US long-range reconnaissance aircraft was the Boeing F-13, a camera-equipped modification of the standard B-29 bomber. Redesignated as the RB-29 after the war, the aircraft continued in the role for many years, providing sterling service during the Korean War. The aircraft also began to acquire a Sigint (signals intelligence) mission, which was passed on successively to the similar RB-50, the RB-47 and then finally the RC-135 converted transport.

There was one highly secret aspect of the Cold War which merits being called a war in its own right, a struggle taking place at sea, on the ground, in the air, and even in space. There has been a large cast of supporting countries – the UK, West Germany, Libya, Syria and others – but for half a century it was primarily a superpower rivalry. It cost at least 170 lives, but its proponents claimed to have prevented conflicts of far greater magnitude, perhaps even the ultimate conflagration. It is the secret war of

Below: Early attempts to take photographs behind the Iron Curtain were undertaken by a specialist unit, the 91st SRS. It used US RB-45C aircraft, crewed by RAF personnel and repainted in RAF national insignia. Here four are seen at RAF Sculthorpe.

Right: From its earliest days, the Canberra was in great demand for risky high-altitude reconnaissance missions. Some time in 1953 or 1954, a PR.Mk 3 similar to this aircraft is believed to have photographed the Soviet missile test site at Kapustin Yar at the request of the USAF.

electromagnetic reconnaissance.

As the Cold War arrived in the late 1940s, the West (and particularly the Americans) felt an urgent need to update their information on possible targets behind the Iron Curtain. There was virtually no up-to-date intelligence on such

matters: early SAC target lists were almost exclusively based on German wartime intelligence and operational reports. But the bombers needed more accurate en-route navigational information to get them to the targets. Therefore, photo-reconnaissance Boeing RB-

US ferrets

As the iron Curtain descended across Europe, reconnaissance aircraft from both sides began a long vigil across the borders and around the peripheries of NATO and the Warsaw Pact. The vast majority of missions involved converted maritime patrol aircraft, transports and bombers being used for electronic intelligence gathering missions. Several US aircraft were shot down.

Lockheed P2V Neptune
The Neptune was the US Navy's standard maritime patrol platform, but was also used for electronic surveillance missions.

Boeing RB-29 Superfortress
The RB-29 was principally a camera platform, but was also used for Sigint flights. The RAF also used the type (known as the Washington) for Sigint work around the WarPac borders.

29 Superfortresses equipped with rudimentary World War II-era radar receiving and jamming equipment set out from the UK on lengthy radar reconnaissance missions around and occasionally over Communist territory.

By the end of the Korean War, the B-50 upgrade of the Superfortress had supplanted the RB-29 in Strategic Air Command's line-up. Over 40 RB-50E/F/G models served with the 55th Strategic Reconnaissance Wing, which went on to claim an almost unbroken post-war lineage of 'ferret' operations.

JET RECONNAISSANCE
The B-29 and B-50 were followed closely into the UK by RB-45Cs, a dedicated reconnaissance version of the the North American Tornado four-jet bomber. This performed photo-reconnaissance missions which often penetrated far behind Iron Curtain borders despite the aircraft's vulnerability to interception by the MiG-15 then coming into service. However, the Tornado's ceiling could be pushed to 13716m (45,000 ft), and its range was extended by very large wingtip tanks and by the routine 'top-ups' it received from accompanying KB-29 tanker aircraft before it entered hostile territory. In this way the RB-45C stood a chance of outrunning the opposition, and there are no recorded instances of an RB-45

coming to grief over Eastern Europe.

The same is true of the B-36, Convair's monster six-engined intercontinental bomber. This had found a reconnaissance application as the RB-36, with two of its four large bomb bays converted to carry 14 cameras. Late-model aircraft with four auxiliary turbojets could reach the same altitude as the RB-45, but they were very slow cruisers. Twelve of the massive aircraft were converted to become motherships for the Republic RF-84K Thunderstreak jet in the extraordinary FICON (FIghter CONveyor) programme: the single-seat reconnaissance fighter was carried aloft in a semi-recessed position inside the B-36 bomb bay until the target area was reached, when it was released for a low-level photographic penetration before climbing back up to the mothership for a free ride home.

Below: A pair of Republic RF-84F Thunderflashes refuel from a KB-29 tanker. Tactical aircraft such as the Thunderflash were on occasion used for short cross-border penetration missions to gather vital photographic intelligence.

Above: Designed as a patrol aircraft in competition with the Lockheed Neptune, the Martin Mercator saw most service in its P4M-1Q form. This was widely used on electronic intelligence missions, serving with the US Navy's main Sigint units, VQ-1 and 2.

The advent of the RB-45 should have decreased the vulnerability of Elint aircraft, but they too were no match for the faster MiG-15, and were forced into night time operations that were distinctly unsuccessful. Tactical reconnaissance aircraft such as the Douglas RB-26 and Lockheed RF-80 had similar problems in Korea.

More often than not, it was the Elint aircraft rather than the photographic types which proved vulnerable to interception, despite their shallower incursions into Iron Curtain territory. They were gen-

erally based on larger and slower patrol and bomber types, the only aircraft capable of lifting the heavy weight and bulk of the early intercept receivers. But the nature of the mission also made them uniquely vulnerable: in order to gain meaningful intelligence they had to stimulate the opposition into turning on their radars. This entailed dangerous 'cat and mouse' games as the ferret aircraft endeavoured to get itself 'painted' by search and tracking radars. Subsequently, they hoped to monitor any communications between ground-station controllers and the fighters scrambled to intercept – while avoiding those same fighters. Furthermore, the rudimentary nature of early Elint equipment meant that missions often had to be repeated to improve or amplify the data originally returned to the ground for analysis.

Even before the formation of NATO in 1949, the UK was developing close links with the USA in the field of airborne reconnaissance. A formal intelligence-sharing agreement was signed in 1948, the same year that SAC B-29s were first deployed to the UK (during the Berlin crisis). The British had much to offer: they had pioneered airborne Elint and ECM during

World War II, and had retained a nucleus of such experience in the Central Signals Establishment at Watton. Their front-line photo reconnaissance platform in the early post war years was the de Havilland Mosquito, which had a 5794-km (3,600-mile) range and a 11125m (36,500-ft) ceiling, characteristics which led to their employment over eastern Europe until the MiG threat became too great.

CANBERRA PENETRATIONS

The Mosquito was succeeded by the English Electric Canberra, one of the world's first jet bombers. The Canberra was fast enough and could fly high enough to make it difficult for the MiG-15s to make an intercept, and was used for a number of missions deep into the Soviet Union – missions which remain classified more than 40 years later.

In 1951 No. 192 Squadron was re-formed with modified Avro Lincoln B.Mk 2 aircraft to concentrate on the gathering of Elint. When the USA loaned the RAF a fleet of B-29 bombers (renamed the Washington by the British), a few went to this squadron to supplement the unpressurized Lincolns. The British were the first to confirm that the Soviets had developed AI (airborne intercept) radar when they brought back a 20-second recording of the 'Scan Odd' system. Later, British airborne and land-based radars first discovered the existence of Soviet ECM and LORAN systems.

In return, the UK gained access to US photo-reconnaissance operations. American RB-45Cs based at Sculthorpe in the UK acquired British roundels and some British flight crews, although they were

never officially on RAF strength. Later, British pilots trained on the Lockheed U-2 which subsequently appeared at Watton.

Meanwhile, the US services had steadily expanded their airborne surveillance fleets, concentrating increasingly on peripheral ferret missions. That such flights made some deliberate incursions into hostile territory seems obvious now, but at the time they were routinely denied. If the Soviets managed to bring down a ferret and chose to publicize the event, the incursion was put down to 'navigational error'. By the end of 1959, at least 12 US spy flights had been shot down, and not all of them were 'over international waters', to use the time-honoured phrase.

NAVY LOSSES

US naval aircraft had featured in six of the 12 losses. Four of them were Lockheed P2V Neptunes flying from Japanese or Alaskan bases. The long range of this anti-submarine aircraft was particularly well suited to the routine eavesdropping mission. However, the Navy had specialized snoopers as well and at

first used the Consolidated PB4Y Privateer, based on the wartime B-24 bomber.

On 8 April 1950, one of these aircraft became the first casualty in the undeclared reconnaissance 'war' when it was shot down by four fighters 'in the Baltic Sea' according to the US authorities, or '23 kilometres [14 miles] inland over Latvia' in the Soviet version. It had taken off from Wiesbaden in West Germany and was due to land at Copenhagen in Denmark. The dictates of geography have made the Baltic a key and continuing area of interest for the peripheral reconnaissance mission.

The Privateer gave way to the Martin P4M Mercator, a twin-piston and twin-jet aircraft designed for maritime patrol. Only 21 were built, but between 1950 and 1960 these found useful employment as 'ferrets'. One Mercator was shot down by Chinese fighters off Wenchow in August 1956. It was operated by Navy squadron VQ-1, which had been set up in the previous year as the US Navy's first dedicated ECM unit.

In the late 1950s the US Navy

Above: Relatively large numbers of the RB-47E were produced, this being a photo-reconnaissance version of the Stratojet bomber. Its primary purpose was to map the approaches to Soviet targets to aid planning nuclear bombing raids.

Below: This Consolidated PB4Y Privateer served with VP-26, a long-established intelligence gathering unit of the US Navy. This squadron was the first to lose an aircraft to Soviet fighters when a Privateer was shot down in April 1950.

ferret mission went to sea when the carrier-capable Douglas A-3 Skywarrior came into service. The five-seat RA-3B photo-reconnaissance aircraft was followed closely by the seven-seat EA-3B for Elint work, in which role several examples served until 1991 with VQ-1 and its sister squadron in the Atlantic Fleet, VQ-2. It was the heaviest-ever carrier aircraft, and latterly concentrated on interception of signals and radar emissions from Soviet naval vessels.

In SAC, the reconnaissance trio of RB-36, RB-45 and RB-50 began to give way in 1954 to the Boeing RB-47, and no fewer than five wings of dedicated reconnaissance Stratojets were established to

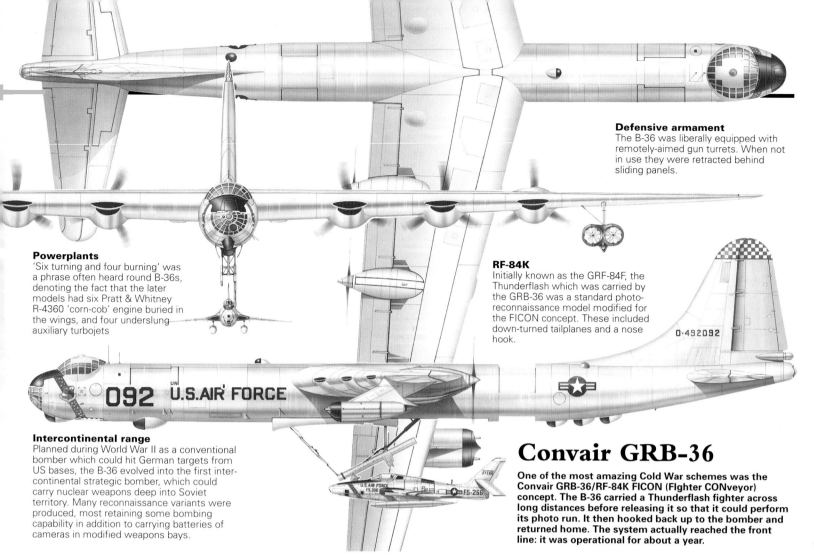

Defensive armament
The B-36 was liberally equipped with remotely-aimed gun turrets. When not in use they were retracted behind sliding panels.

Powerplants
'Six turning and four burning' was a phrase often heard round B-36s, denoting the fact that the later models had six Pratt & Whitney R-4360 'corn-cob' engine buried in the wings, and four underslung auxiliary turbojets

RF-84K
Initially known as the GRF-84F, the Thunderflash which was carried by the GRB-36 was a standard photo-reconnaissance model modified for the FICON concept. These included down-turned tailplanes and a nose hook.

Intercontinental range
Planned during World War II as a conventional bomber which could hit German targets from US bases, the B-36 evolved into the first intercontinental strategic bomber, which could carry nuclear weapons deep into Soviet territory. Many reconnaissance variants were produced, most retaining some bombing capability in addition to carrying batteries of cameras in modified weapons bays.

Convair GRB-36

One of the most amazing Cold War schemes was the Convair GRB-36/RF-84K FICON (FIghter CONveyor) concept. The B-36 carried a Thunderflash fighter across long distances before releasing it so that it could perform its photo run. It then hooked back up to the bomber and returned home. The system actually reached the front line: it was operational for about a year.

operate the 250-strong fleet. The majority of them were RB-47E camera-ships with a new suite of 11 cameras and improved photoflash bombs, but there was also a renewed emphasis on radar photography to provide accurate data for the penetrating bomber fleet. A smaller number of RB-47H and ERB-47H models served with the 55th SRW. The latter carried the Melpar ALD-4 Elint system which was originally planned to be underslung on the Convair B-58. The equipment and its three operators were housed in an enormous pod.

One of these aircraft, flying out of Brize Norton, England, was shot down by two Soviet MiGs in the remote northern waters of the Barents Sea on 1 July 1960. Two of the six-man crew survived and were taken prisoner.

The nearby Kola and Kanin peninsulas housed the Soviet navy's main northern bases as well as numerous IRBM sites and bomber airfields. The area had been scheduled for attention two months earlier on 1 May by a U-2 overflight from Pakistan that would subsequently land in Norway. But the U-2 never reached its northern objective, since it was shot down by an SA-2 missile near Sverdlovsk .

The U-2 and RB-47 incidents in 1960 marked a turning point in the reconnaissance Cold War, and not only because President Kennedy had to promise to cease overflights of the Soviet Union in order to get the two SAC crewmen back (U-2 pilot Francis Gary Powers was released a year later in exchange for a Soviet spy held in the USA).

This was a period when technological advances made a significant impact on the science of electronic intelligence gathering. 1960 was also the year when the USA achieved its first success with reconnaissance satellites, an event matched by the Soviets three years later. And the secret war expanded still further, since the Soviet Union was now adapting its long-range bombers to the stage where it felt able to send them out on increasingly wide-ranging reconnaissance missions.

Left: In its own right the B-36 was a very capable reconnaissance craft. It could reach altitudes unattainable by the early MiGs, and carried a huge sensor payload. Specially stripped 'featherweight' versions were produced for extreme altitude performance.

Below: The workhorse of the Sigint fleet for much of the Cold War was the Boeing RB-47H (and similar ERB-47H). Their many dangerous missions included flying directly at Soviet defences in an attempt to make them power up, only turning away at the last moment.

SAC: The B-52 Years

1956-1970

Left: Boeing's B-52 Stratofortress first flew on 15 April 1952, and entered service with Strategic Air Command in June 1955. In a stunning demonstration of the type's unmatched strategic capability, these three B-52Bs took off from Castle AFB in California on 16 January 1957, returning 45 hours and 19 minutes later after flying non-stop around the world.

Below: The medium-range Convair B-58 Hustler was the B-52's supersonic counterpart. Entering service in 1960, it had phenomenal performance, but it was a complex, costly machine. After a ten-year career the B-58 was retired, mainly for economic reasons

From the time the B-52 Stratofortress arrived in the mid-1950s, Strategic Air Command (SAC) was immersed in a new phase of the Cold War. SAC, quite naturally, was controlled by men who had flown B-17s and B-29s in World War II, who had shaped strategic air power, and who saw the long-range bomber as salvation for the West in the face of the Soviet nuclear threat. But by the 1960s the 'bomber generals' dominated the entire US Air Force.

Former SAC boss Curtis E. LeMay served as USAF chief of staff between 1961 and 1965. LeMay was the force behind the manned bomber as the linchpin of American policy. He swaggered and smoked his trademark cigar, insisting that aircraft on the flight line could not catch fire from it because "They wouldn't dare". LeMay often said the Air Force needed three things, "the bomber, the bomber, and the bomber". Less visible was Gen. Bernard A. Schriever, who quietly led a revolution to win the Air

Force over to the coming ICBM (intercontinental ballistic missile). But the B-52, not the ICBM, symbolised everything SAC was doing.

American policy went under different names. The strategy of containment (1947-52) aimed to prevent any encroachment across any border by the Soviets or their allies. Containment was replaced in the Eisenhower years (1953-61) by a policy of massive retaliation. This meant, as a White House aide put it, that "if the Soviets stick their head up anywhere, they're going to get sledgehammered." The slightest act of aggression would be met with a nuclear response, aimed not at Soviet bases but at cities.

SAC no longer had as many people or aircraft as in the previous decade, but in 1963 it still boasted 271,672 men and 2,424 warplanes including 32 heavy bomb wings and three aerospace wings equipped with the B-52. Apart from reconnaissance assets and two medium bomb wings with the B-58

Hustler, SAC also possessed 41 air refuelling squadrons, nearly all equipped with the KC-135 Stratotanker.

On 16 October 1963, a B-58 of the 305th Bomb Wing at Bunker Hill AFB, Indiana dashed from Tokyo to London in an elapsed time of eight hours 35 minutes (plus a few seconds), averaging 1,510 km/h (938 mph), a record for the

12,920-km (8,030-mile) journey. However, by the end of the 1960s, the B-58 was on its way out of inventory, but the manned bomber was not. With the B-52 out of production and expected to need replacement by the end of the 1960s, the USAF invested $5 billion into the Mach 3 B-70 Valkyrie – only to cancel the B-70 programme after flight testing was well

Above: Signs that the bomber could become vulnerable to enemy defences had SAC looking at a number of unmanned nuclear delivery systems. The Northrop SM-62 Snark was a bomber-sized cruise missile with a 10000-km (6,215 mile) range which pioneered many of the advanced avionics and guidance techniques used today. It was operational from 1957 to 1961.

Left: The reason that early cruise missiles were abandoned was that ballistic missiles offered so much more. Atlas was the West's first true ICBM, becoming operational in 1960 with SAC's 564th Strategic Missile Squadron at Warren AFB, Wyoming. Atlas could deliver a 3-megaton warhead over a range of more than 16000 km (10,000 miles).

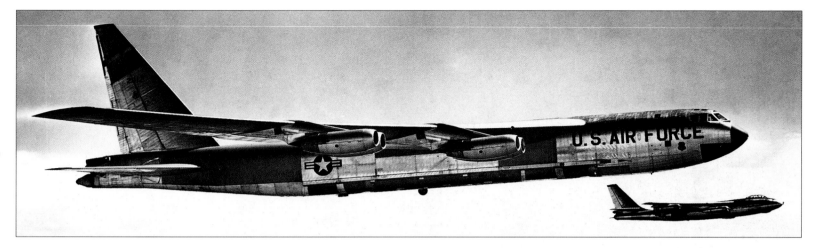

Above: A total of 744 B-52s were built between 1952 and 1961. Few could have foreseen that the last of these titanic machines would still be flying nearly half a century after the first, or that they would outlast Strategic Air Command itself.

advanced. Plans to retire the B-52 proceeded anyway.

MISSILE DOMINANCE

On 21 April 1964, SAC passed a milestone: the number of ICBMs on alert surpassed the number of bombers on ground alert. Titan II and Minuteman ICBMs were increasing in number, and most of the massive force of six-jet B-47s had been retired.

Belatedly, Secretary of Defense Robert S. McNamara replaced the policy of assured destruction with a policy of flexible response, which included the previously unthinkable concept of limited nuclear war. If

the Soviets obliterated Chicago, the United States would flatten Magnitogorsk – but the response would be proportionate and might not lead to an all-out exchange.

In 1965, the US launched a build-up in Vietnam and B-52s began flying conventional bomb mission against the Viet Cong. But much of SAC's focus stayed on the number of nuclear weapons in the world, which now exceeded 50,000. The majority, about 30,000 were American. The Soviets had 20,000 warheads, and a handful were kept elsewhere by Britain and France. Nuclear war between the two superpowers was still being taken more seriously than limited war in Asia – even by an administration which had flexible response at the root of its doctrine.

At the height of the Cold War, bombers stood alert not merely on runways but in the air. B-52s were aloft 24 hours a day, with live

hydrogen bombs in their bays. Only elite crews flew these 'Chrome Dome' missions. It was taken for granted that it was safe to fly around with 'The Bomb' on board. Even as the United States began its relentless descent into the Vietnamese quagmire, airborne alert missions pressed on.

NUCLEAR ACCIDENTS

In January 1966, a B-52 collided with a KC-135 during a refuelling and both crashed near Palomares, Spain. There were four survivors and seven fatalities. Radioactive material was released when the TNT triggers of two of the four weapons aboard the B-52 exploded on impact. All but one of the hydrogen bombs was recovered immediately. The search for the lost weapon took two months and was concluded at a water depth of 870m (2,850 feet) in the Mediterranean World attention was glued on

Palomares until 7 April when the missing weapon was recovered, using an experimental submersible.

Oddly the Palomares incident did not bring an end to aircraft flying with nuclear weapons on board during peacetime – but a second nuclear mishap, where bombs were lost in a Greenland B-52 crash, did. 'Chrome Dome' missions ended. Bombers still stood nuclear alerts, armed and ready to launch at short notice, but on the ground.

McNamara planned to retire a major part of the SAC bomber force by 1971, but plans were changed when control of the White House shifted in January 1969. Richard Nixon's advisers kept the B-52 alive and invested in the FB-111 'Aardvark' as an interim part of the SAC arsenal, but the dominance of the bomber was becoming past tense, as ICBMs and submarine-launched missiles became more important.

SAC in the 60s

Although numbers of aircraft deployed had fallen from their peak in the early 1950s, Strategic Air Command was still the world's most powerful strike force in the 1960s. SAC operated 17 B-52 wings divided between the 8th Air Force headquartered in Louisiana and the 15th Air Force with headquarters in California. To this they could add two wings of B-58s and over 700 KC-135 tankers.

Convair B-58A
Right: Powered by four General Electric J-79 afterburning turbojets exch delivering a maximum of 69.4 kN (15,600 lb st), the B-58 could reach a speed of 2128 km/h (1,322 mph). It had a range of 8248 km (5,125 miles) and could carry over eight tonnes of nuclear bombs.

Boeing B-52C
Below: Shown in the colours of the 7th Bomb Wing at Carswell AFB in Texas, the B-52C had an unrefuelled range of more than 9650 km (6,000 miles) and could carry around ten tonnes of nuclear weaponry. The similar B-52D was modified to carry conventional weapons, up to a maximum wieght of nearly 40 tonnes.

Britain's V-Force

1951-1975

Although not normally privy to the secrets of the American wartime atomic bomb, the UK, by the participation of its scientists in the production of the weapon in the USA, was favourably equipped to undertake the development of its own atomic bomb after the war. Although an aircraft such as the Lincoln would have been capable of carrying a 'tailored' atomic bomb (but over much shorter distances than the American B-29), the British Air Staff decided to embark on a programme aimed at equipping Bomber Command with large jet-powered bombers, and issued a number of very advanced requirements shortly after the end of the war. Fortunately, the world has been spared any demonstration of the true

Above: A Vulcan B.Mk 1 leads Mk 1 versions of the other two V-Bombers: Valiant off its port wing and Victor off the starboard side. All three were conceived as strategic nuclear bombers, relying on speed and high-altitude performance to evade interception.

Right: A Vulcan crew scramble to their waiting aircraft. The V-Force trained intensively to be able to be airborne and en route to their targets before hostile bombers or missiles could wipe out their bases. It was an Armageddon scenario.

credibility of these aircraft in their role of nuclear-armed deterrents.

In 1947 the Chiefs of Staff declared their belief that the possession of "weapons of mass destruction ...would be the most effective deterrent to war itself." The die was cast for the issue of Operational Requirement OR.229. This was

Below: This early Vulcan B.Mk 1 of the Waddington wing is still in the overall silver finish applied to the very earliest V-Bombers. That was soon replaced by a high-gloss white intended to reflect the 'flash' of an atomic explosion.

Right: Third of the V-Bombers was the Handley Page Victor, ordered into production as an insurance policy against failure of the revolutionary Vulcan. It proved faster than the Vulcan, and carried a larger bombload, but few were purchased.

From high-level to stand-off

During its long life, the V-Force dramatically changed its procedures and tactics, embracing quick-reaction alerts, operations from dispersed sites, and a switch to low-level operations. Perhaps most crucially, it adopted a stand-off weapon, allowing aircraft to attack targets without having to penetrate the heaviest defences. Blue Steel was to have been replaced by the US Skybolt, but this was cancelled.

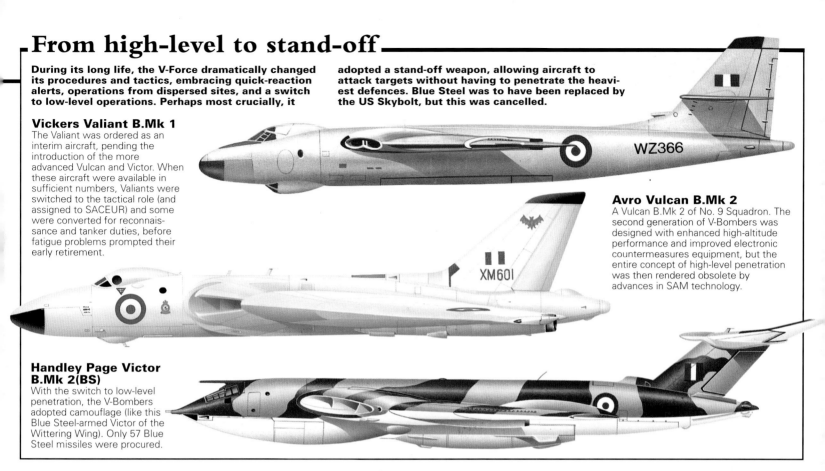

Vickers Valiant B.Mk 1
The Valiant was ordered as an interim aircraft, pending the introduction of the more advanced Vulcan and Victor. When these aircraft were available in sufficient numbers, Valiants were switched to the tactical role (and assigned to SACEUR) and some were converted for reconnaissance and tanker duties, before fatigue problems prompted their early retirement.

Avro Vulcan B.Mk 2
A Vulcan B.Mk 2 of No. 9 Squadron. The second generation of V-Bombers was designed with enhanced high-altitude performance and improved electronic countermeasures equipment, but the entire concept of high-level penetration was then rendered obsolete by advances in SAM technology.

Handley Page Victor B.Mk 2(BS)
With the switch to low-level penetration, the V-Bombers adopted camouflage (like this Blue Steel-armed Victor of the Wittering Wing). Only 57 Blue Steel missiles were procured.

for a four-jet Lincoln replacement capable of delivering a 4536-kg (10,000-lb) nuclear device, while flying at 500 kt and 13716 m (45,000 ft), with a still air range of 5633 km (3,500 miles). The performance figures were later adjusted to require a still air range of 8047 km (5,000 miles), and an over-target ceiling of 15420 m (50,000 ft). These figures, it was emphasised, were minimums, and it was hoped that they would be handsomely exceeded. The resulting specification B.35/46 also called for a high degree of manoeuvrability, and blind-bombing capability using H2S. First of the new bomber specifications, B.14/46, which brought forth the Short Sperrin, proved abortive largely through overestimated bomb dimensions hopelessly compromising the design. Shortly afterwards a follow-up requirement,

Above: A Valiant of No. 214 Squadron is towed past Bristol Bloodhound SAMs at RAF Marham. No. 214 Squadron adopted the inflight-refuelling tanker role in 1962, but continued to maintain a tactical bombing commitment.

Right: The requirement for the V-Bombers was issued in 1946, and called for a jet bomber which would have the speed and altitude performance of the Canberra (which was too small to carry contemporary nuclear weapons, until the development of small tactical devices during the 1950s), yet which would exceed the range of the piston-engined Lincoln. The V-Bombers were designed around the dimensions of Britain's first indigenous bomb, the Blue Danube, a plutonium-based weapon first tested in October 1952. This weapon was replaced by the megaton-yield Yellow Sun from 1958. Even in their initial form, the V-Bombers had a long enough radius of action to attack targets well east of Moscow, or to reach Moscow via circuitous routes which kept them clear of the heaviest defences. V-Bombers could have attacked Moscow and then recovered to bases in the Mediterranean, and the options increased when inflight refuelling was introduced. The adoption of Blue Steel added little to maximum range, but Skybolt's greater reach would have made a significant difference.

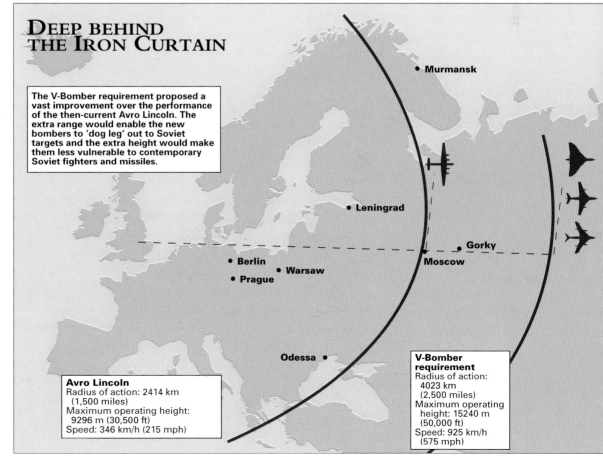

DEEP BEHIND THE IRON CURTAIN

The V-Bomber requirement proposed a vast improvement over the performance of the then-current Avro Lincoln. The extra range would enable the new bombers to 'dog leg' out to Soviet targets and the extra height would make them less vulnerable to contemporary Soviet fighters and missiles.

Murmansk

Leningrad

Gorky

Berlin

Moscow

Warsaw

Prague

Odessa

Avro Lincoln
Radius of action: 2414 km (1,500 miles)
Maximum operating height: 9296 m (30,500 ft)
Speed: 346 km/h (215 mph)

V-Bomber requirement
Radius of action: 4023 km (2,500 miles)
Maximum operating height: 15240 m (50,000 ft)
Speed: 925 km/h (575 mph)

Left: The V-Force maintained its QRA aircraft at four-minute readiness, 24 hours a day, cutting reaction time to two minutes with the introduction of runway-edge ORPs and simultaneous engine starting.

Above: This Valiant wears the low-level camouflage adopted by the V-Force during the mid-1960s with the switch to low-level ops. They proved fatal to the Valiant, causing unexpected fatigue.

B.35/46, proved more promising and, with a new specification issued in 1947, provided the basis on which the UK's nuclear bombing force was to be founded: B.35/46 was updated in 1948 by B.9/48.

The first of the new generation of V-Bombers, the Vickers Valiant, was flown on 18 May 1951 and entered service with No. 138 Squadron in February 1955. Meanwhile, the UK had detonated its first nuclear device in the Monte Bello Islands off the northwestern coast of Australia. On 11 October 1956 Valiants of No. 49 Squadron took part in trials at Maralinga, Australia, when an aircraft captained by Squadron Leader E. J. G. Flavell dropped the first British atomic bomb; on 15 May the following year, in Operation 'Grapple', another No. 49 Squadron Valiant dropped the first British hydrogen bomb over Christmas Island in the Pacific.

V-BOMBERS AT SUEZ

In the meantime, Valiants of Nos 138, 148, 207 and 214 Squadrons had been deployed to Luqa, Malta, for operations against Egypt during the Suez campaign, the first V-Bombers to drop 'conventional' bombs in anger. In 1965 Valiants were found to be suffering from metal fatigue in the main wing spars and were withdrawn from service. Their last duties with Bomber Command included those operated as inflight-refuelling tankers, all members of the V-Force being

Left: At the height of its capability, in late-1962, the V-Force's strategic nuclear deterrent numbered 15 squadrons, with two wings of three Vulcan B.Mk 2 squadrons (Nos 9, 12 and 35) at Coningsby, and Scampton (Nos 27, 83 and 617), and a three-squadron wing of B.Mk 1As (Nos 44, 50 and 101) at Waddington. Cottesmore had two squadrons of Victor B.Mk 1s (Nos 10 and 15), Honington two Victor B.Mk 1A squadrons (Nos 55 and 57), and Wittering two Victor B.Mk 2 squadrons (Nos 100 and 139). These were augmented by three SACEUR-assigned Valiant tactical strike/bomber squadrons (Nos 49, 148 and 207) at Marham, and four more Valiant tanker, ECM and recce units (Nos 90, 214, 18 and 543), based at Marham, Honington, Finningley and Wyton. V-Bomber OCUs were based at Finningley and Gaydon. The strike Valiants carried US weapons, which also equipped four Canberra squadrons based in Germany. A similar 'dual-key' nuclear force consisted of 60 Thor missiles, each with a 2414-km (1,500-mile) range and a 1-megaton warhead.

BRITAIN'S V-BOMBER BASES

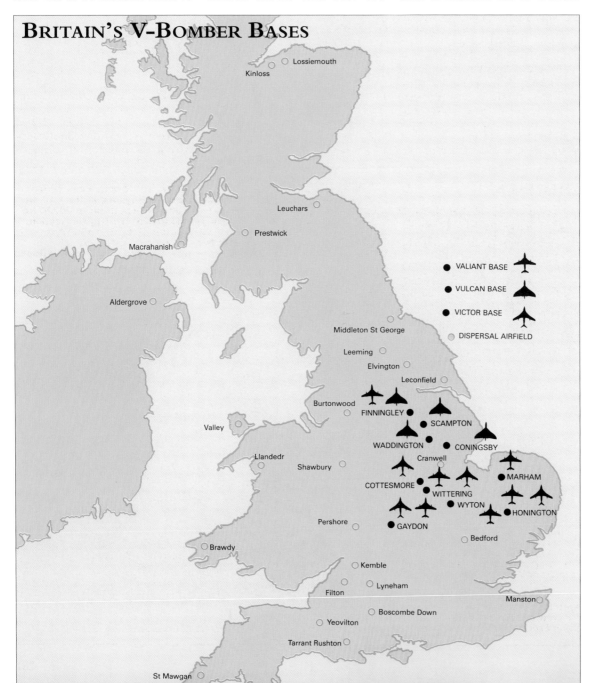
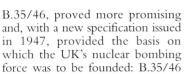

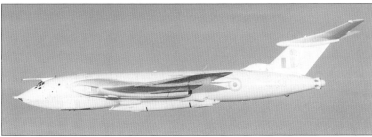

Above: In addition to anti-flash white paint, the V-Bombers also had national insignia toned down to pastel shades to avoid them becoming 'hot spots' on the skin. This is a Victor B.Mk 2(BS).

given inflight-refuelling facility.

Next of the V-Force trio to fly was the Avro Vulcan, on 30 August 1952. This, the most impressive of all the bombers, was a large delta-wing aircraft originally powered by Avon and then Sapphire turbojets, but in production by two-spool

Olympus engines which eventually produced about 88.97-kN (20,000-lb) thrust. Production of the Vulcan was very modest, only 45 Mk 1s and 68 Mk 2s (with bigger wings and elevons) being built.

LONG-LIVED VULCAN

By means of a number of life-extension expedients, however, this force remained in a service for almost 30 years, serving in turn as high- and low-level bombers, stand-off bombers, reconnaissance aircraft

and ultimately as tankers. During that period they equipped nine RAF squadrons at Coningsby, Cottesmore, Finningley, Honington, Scampton and Waddington in

the UK, and at Akrotiri in Cyprus between 1969 and 1975. Most of the Vulcan B.Mk 2s were adapted to carry the Avro Blue Steel stand-off nuclear missile, but plans to

QRA: 24-hour readiness

Ten Class One airfields were developed for the V-Force, each with a minimum 2745-m (9,000-ft) runway, hardstandings for at least 16 aircraft, and the ability to withstand aircraft weights of up to 90720 kg (200,000 lb). They were Coningsby, Cottesmore, Finningley, Gaydon, Honington, Marham, Scampton, Waddington, Wittering and Wyton. Another 27 were later upgraded to handle dispersed flights of V-Bombers, with runway ORPs, crew quarters and refuelling facilities.

Above: Operational Readiness Platforms (ORPs) were built at the V-Bomber bases, and at other airfields nominated as potential homes for dispersed flights of Vulcans or Victors in time of war.

Right: Even the reconnaissance specialists practiced QRA. Here, the crew of a No. 543 Squadron Valiant scramble for a QRA take-off.

Above: Scampton-based Vulcans make a stream take-off after scrambling from their runway-edge ORP. Four Vulcans could be airborne and en route to their targets within two minutes of the order to scramble.

V-Force weapons of war

Above: The Vulcan and Victor could perform conventional bombing duties with clips of seven 454-kg (1,000-lb) bombs. The Vulcan could drop three clips, while the Victor bomb bay accommodated five.

Below: Seventy-two Vulcans (each with two Skybolt missiles) were to have replaced 144 V-Bombers each carrying a single Blue Steel or free-fall bomb. Skybolt was selected in place of the Blue Steel Mk 2.

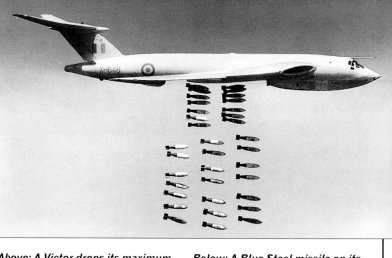

Above: A Victor drops its maximum bombload of 35 454-kg (1,000-lb) GP bombs. The Avro Vulcan, by comparison, could carry only 21 of these weapons. A normal V-Force load was a single huge nuclear weapon.

Below: A Blue Steel missile on its AEC Mandator waits to be lowered onto the trolley which will take it forward under the belly of the waiting Vulcan B.Mk 2. Blue Steel entered service in 1962.

The first nuclear weapon for the V-Force was the Blue Danube, a 7.3-m (24-ft) long, 1.5-m (5-ft) diameter monster weighing about 4990 kg (11,000 lb). In 1958, Finningley and Scampton received 12 interim Violet Clubs, essentially Green Grass hydrogen bomb warheads in the Blue Danube case. The Green Grass warhead was subsequently fitted in a new casing to create the Yellow Sun Mk 1. From 1958 the Waddington Vulcans, the Honington Victors and the Marham Valiants received US-made Mk 5 weapons under Project E; the Waddington wing later gained Yellow Sun. Yellow Sun Mk 2 used a Red Snow Mk 2 warhead similar to that of the Blue Steel missile.

equip the aircraft with the American Skybolt missile were aborted by cancellation of that programme, and the nuclear deterrent passed to the Polaris submarine force. Despite its great bulk the Vulcan was classed as a medium bomber, capable of carrying up to 21 454-kg (1,000-lb) iron bombs or a 4536-kg (10,000-lb) Blue Steel. Although employed out of context as a global nuclear deterrent, the Vulcan's last operation was the most spectacular when two aircraft were deployed to attack the Falkland Islands in 1982 during the illegal occupation by Argentine forces; in

successive sorties from Ascension Island, these aircraft attacked Port Stanley airfield with 454-kg (1,000-lb) bombs and a radar installation with anti-radiation missiles.

VICTOR

Third of the V-Bombers was the Handley Page Victor with crescent wing, an aircraft that took so long to develop that by the time it entered service in 1958 it was already obsolescent in a world of surface-to-air missiles and Mach 2+ interceptors. Fifty-five Mk 1s and Mk 1As were produced, as well as 34 Mk 2s, so small a quantity that

their unit cost was considered inordinately high. As with the Vulcan, their vulnerability at altitude resulted in a change of role to low-level bombing, equipped with Blue Steel missiles, while the last eight aircraft were completed as strategic reconnaissance aircraft for service with No. 543 Squadron at Wyton. Although capable of carrying 35 454-kg (1,000-lb) iron bombs (14 more than the Vulcan), the true value of the Victor was to be as a tanker for the other aircraft of the V-Force, Nos 55 and 57 Squadrons at Marham (as well as No. 543 Squadron) being the last surviving

operational units in existence. Victor bombers served with nine RAF squadrons.

Whether or not a force of V-Bombers, of which fewer than 50 were ever combat-capable simultaneously, constituted a credible deterrent (to which the independent French Force de Frappe might in certain circumstances be added) will for ever remain unknown. Yet while these forces have been combined with the might of American land-, sea- and air-based nuclear deterrent, nuclear war has remained a spectre... and no more.

From bomber to tanker

The premature grounding of the Valiant fleet left the RAF without tankers. Plans for the conversion of redundant Victor B.Mk 1s to tanker configuration were already in hand, with a prototype Victor tanker having flown early in 1964. The programme was expedited in order to provide a replacement for the Valiant tankers, and six

bombers were hastily fitted out as two-point tankers as Victor B(K).Mk 1As. The first of 24 three-point tanker K.Mk 1s (with new tanks in the former bomb bay) followed in November 1965. The Victor K.Mk 1s were limited by their lack of thrust, and were eventually replaced by tanker conversions of the B.Mk 2.

Victor K.Mk 2

The contract to convert Victor B.Mk 2s was awarded to Hawker Siddeley in 1970, a slap in the face which 'finished off' the ailing Handley Page.

Radar

The main H2S Mk 9A radar was augmented from July 1965, when the RAF ordered 165 General Dynamics TFRs, whose radome was housed in a small pimple on the tip of the nose, below the inflight-refuelling probe. This worked in conjunction with the altimeters to generate simple 'up' and 'down' commands in the cockpit.

Vulcan colours

Anti-flash white was adopted during 1958, and toned-down national markings followed in the early-1960s. The switch to low-level operations brought about the introduction of disruptive pattern camouflaged top surfaces. Radomes were overpainted and undersurfaces turned light-grey during the mid-1970s, and from 1977 some aircraft received a wraparound camouflage, extending over the undersides, for participation in US exercises.

Wing

The original Vulcan design had a simple delta planform, but a kinked, drooped outerwing leading edge – the so-called Phase 2 wing – was soon added to reduce buffet at high Mach numbers. This was further refined to become the Phase 2C wing with a more pronounced kink and rounder tips, used on the B.Mk 2.

Powerplant

The Avro Vulcan B.Mk 2 was powered by a quartet of Bristol Siddeley Olympus turbofans. The Scampton Wing standardised on aircraft with the BO 16 Olympus 201, while Waddington used the later machines, fitted with BO 121 Olympus 301s. The Olympus 201 provided 75.65 kN (17,000 lb st) of thrust while the 301 was rated at 89 kN (20,000 lb st). Forty-five Vulcan B.Mk 2s were powered by the original engine.

Avro Vulcan B.Mk 2

XM600 was one of the aircraft assigned to No. 617 Squadron at RAF Scampton during the mid-1970s. The squadron then used WE177B free-fall laydown nuclear weapons in its primary tactical strike role for SACEUR, but also had a secondary conventional bombing role, and a secondary maritime radar reconnaissance commitment.

Crew

The RAF's V-Bombers were crewed by a captain and co-pilot sitting forward, and by an air electronics officer and two navigators sitting side by side behind them, facing aft. Only the two pilots had ejection seats, resulting in many rear crew deaths when aircraft got into difficulties.

Left: Four Victors operated alongside No. 543 Squadron's Valiants from 1958, operating in the radar recce role. Seven B.Mk 2s were subsequently converted for reconnaissance duties to replace No. 543's Valiants from early-1966.

Right: Vulcan B.Mk 2s at RAF Akrotiri, where Nos 9 and 35 Squadrons formed a tactical strike wing from January 1969 until January 1975, operating primarily in support of CENTO. They were equipped with conventional and WE 177B nuclear bombs.

Cold War Air Defences

1950–1960

Left: The Northrop F-89 Scorpion guarded the farthest reaches of the North American continent in the 1950s. Not particularly fast, it was distinguished by long range, a powerful airborne intercept radar and a sophisticated (for the time) fire-control system. It was also the first fighter to carry nuclear-tipped air-to-air weapons.

Below: The Gloster Javelin was the first twin-engined, delta wing jet to enter service. It was also the first British warplane designed from the outset as an all-weather interceptor, integrating airframe, radar and missiles as a single weapons system. Although offering much greater capability than the Meteors it replaced, the Javelin was difficult to keep serviced .

To most military personnel, the Cold War was a time of endless training for a war which never came. But there was one group of airmen who went head-to-head with their potential enemies for real. Day in, day out, air defence and interceptor pilots both East and West took to the air against intruders, weapons live and ready to shoot if called upon.

NATO in its early days had one vital raison d'être: to counter the forcible conversion of Western Europe to communism by the might of the Soviet Union.

World War II had shown that control of the air was vital to any land campaign, and any move by the thousands of Soviet and Warsaw Pact tanks on the Central Front would have been preceded by an all-out air assault, with the main aim of knocking out NATO air defences. Europe may be small as continents go, but at the height of the Cold War it presented a very wide variety of problems when it came to air defence.

Germany was on the Iron Curtain front line. Major Soviet air bases were only a few minutes flying time from the country's industrial heartland, and the defence of Germany was a key pillar of NATO strategy. German interceptors served alongside aircraft from Belgium, the Netherlands, Denmark, the United Kingdom, France, the USA and Canada. They were kept on a high state of alert, ready to launch against intruding bombers at a moment's notice.

Britain, on the other hand, was the linchpin of NATO's plans for reinforcement across the Atlantic, and her fighters were charged with intercepting bombers far out over the ocean. Soviet long-range maritime aircraft probed the defences regularly, and fighters on quick-reaction alert went up to investigate contacts daily. Subsonic Javelins in the 1950s gave way in RAF service to supersonic Lightnings and Phantoms in the 1960s.

Other NATO countries, particularly those on NATO's flanks bordering directly with the Soviet Union had problems peculiar to their own geographical locations. The wastes of northern Norway commanded the Arctic while Turkey bottled up the Soviet Black Sea Fleet. Both were key Soviet targets and had to be defended.

And for the first time, the United States itself was under threat. Although politically worlds apart, the USA and the Soviet Union were very close geographically. It does not look that way in an atlas, but a polar projection shows that North America is not too far from Eurasia across the Arctic Ocean.

In the 1950s, the American military regarded an attack by Soviet nuclear-armed bombers as a real and imminent prospect. In the Pentagon and in the Canadian Defence Ministry, these officers

Left: Entering service only five years after the Javelin, the English Electric Lightning offered a whole new order of performance. Capable of more than two and a half times the speed of sound, it was one of the fastest-climbing interceptors ever built.

Lightning Interceptor

Britain's postwar lead in jet aircraft design did not last long: it had been overhauled by both the USA and the USSR by the early 1950s. But the gap was closed to some extent with the entry into service of the English Electric Lightning, the fastest British fighter ever. Although the Lightning's radar was primitive by modern standards, and its cockpit an ergonomic nightmare, in 1960 a missile-armed, radar-equipped single-seater with an early computerised fire control system was state of the art.

Lightning F.Mk 1A

Right: Seen in the colours of No.56 Squadron RAF, which in 1960 was the second squadron to equip with the type, the F.Mk 1A differed from the original fighter in that it had provision for inflight refuelling. This gave the short-legged Lightning the ability to deploy long distances non-stop.

faced a challenge without precedent – a likely onslaught by air that might wreak such ghastly destruction, even the recently-won World War II would seem a footnote by comparison. In 1951, intelligence analysts estimated that Moscow would soon be able to "deliver a sufficient number of atomic bombs to cause over one hundred detonations in the United States". This estimate was premature but within a decade it became real and multiplied. At the height of the Cold War, the number of nuclear warheads in the Soviet arsenal was measured not in the hundreds but in the tens of thousands.

AIR DEFENSE COMMAND

The primary defender of the USA was the fledgling Air Defense Command, or ADC, which had been founded on 21 March 1946. In 1947, the year the US Air Force broke off from the Army to become an independent service, Winston Churchill warned of an 'Iron Curtain' falling over the communist nations. By 1949, the Soviets had exploded their first atomic device and ADC grew from a 'paper' command to being the operator of a few twin-engine Northrop F-61C Black Widow night fighters. Expansion with Lockheed F-80 Shooting Stars followed, but by 1951 these relatively slow straight-winged machines

POLAR WATCH

Although the USA and the USSR might have seemed a long way apart to the transatlantic traveller of the time, in fact the two superpowers were close neighbours – as long as you were flying over the North Pole. The prospect of hordes of nuclear bombers attacking across the virtually unpopulated Arctic waste was one of the great fears of the Cold War warriors, and the United States and Canada expended a great deal of money and resources on developing a system which would give adequate warning of a surprise Soviet attack. The tripwire initially consisted of chains of radar stations stretching across the continent, to which was added the BMEWS ballistic missile early warning system as the threat changed from aircraft bombs to missile-borne warheads.

Right: The Lockheed F-94 was one of the first radar-equipped jet interceptors. Based on the T-33 trainer, the F-94 equipped more than 24 squadrons of the US Air Defense Command. Aircraft were maintained on three-minute alert, ready to intercept hostile bombers.

were being superseded by the swept-wing, state-of the art North American F-86 Sabre.

But single-seat day fighters could only do part of the job. A number of new all-weather fighters were developed to equip ADC's growing fighter-interceptor squadrons. All-weather was the new term for radar-equipped interceptors that could function by day or by night and in adverse conditions (though

NORTH AMERICAN RADAR NETS

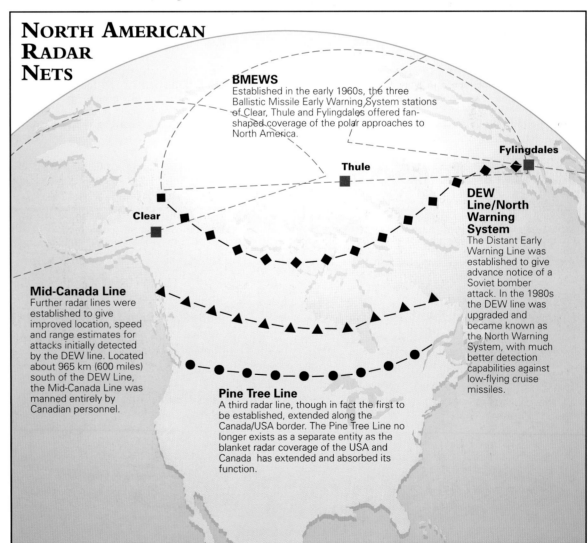

BMEWS
Established in the early 1960s, the three Ballistic Missile Early Warning System stations of Clear, Thule and Fylingdales offered fan-shaped coverage of the polar approaches to North America.

Fylingdales

Thule

Clear

DEW Line/North Warning System
The Distant Early Warning Line was established to give advance notice of a Soviet bomber attack. In the 1980s the DEW line was upgraded and became known as the North Warning System, with much better detection capabilities against low-flying cruise missiles.

Mid-Canada Line
Further radar lines were established to give improved location, speed and range estimates for attacks initially detected by the DEW line. Located about 965 km (600 miles) south of the DEW Line, the Mid-Canada Line was manned entirely by Canadian personnel.

Pine Tree Line
A third radar line, though in fact the first to be established, extended along the Canada/USA border. The Pine Tree Line no longer exists as a separate entity as the blanket radar coverage of the USA and Canada has extended and absorbed its function.

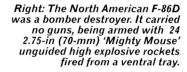

Left: A McDonnell F-101B Voodoo fires an AIR-2 Genie rocket. Designed to disrupt large bomber formations, the unguided Genie had a 1.5 kiloton nuclear warhead with a 500m (1,640 ft) lethal blast radius and could seriously damage targets at up to 1000m (3,300 ft). The missile had a range of only 10 km (6.2 miles), so the launch aircraft had to pull a very tight turn after launch to escape the blast.

the term was misleading; they could fly in some adverse weather but not all). In the USAF, the squadrons which flew them were called Fighter Interceptor Squadrons, or FISs, pronounced 'fizzes'.

The North American F-86D Sabre, Northrop F-89 Scorpion, and Lockheed F-94 (nicknamed Starfire in its F-94C variant only) were a trio of 'interim' warplanes

Right: The North American F-86D was a bomber destroyer. It carried no guns, being armed with 24 2.75-in (70-mm) 'Mighty Mouse' unguided high explosive rockets fired from a ventral tray.

tailored to carry airborne radar, guns, and rocket projectiles. Crews were trained to scramble against incoming bombers and to intercept them as far as possible from their targets – at best, north of the Arctic circle and far from vulnerable cities.

With the 1957 establishment of the joint US/Canadian North American Air Defense Command (NORAD), the Canadian Avro CF-100 Canuck joined the fighter-

Below: The 1950s saw the Soviet bomber threat made manifest with the massive Tupolev Tu-95 'Bear', a long-range heavy bomber with awesome range. US fighters based on Iceland regularly intercepted 'Bears' over the Atlantic.

interceptor forces arrayed towards the north. They practised radar-guided Ground Control Intercept (GCI) missions throughout the 1950s while planners in Washington and Ottawa searched for more advanced interceptors. Their work was characterised in a booklet of the era in which ADC attempted to coin the acronym DIID (Detect, Identify, Intercept, and Destroy) but this jargon for the air defence mission never caught on.

WEAPONS SYSTEMS

By 1954 the USAF had begun to develop an interceptor using an integrated 'weapons system' approach that would produce the aircraft and its military capability simultaneously. The result was the

Convair F-102 Delta Dagger (the nickname was not applied until more than a decade after the type was in service), which overcame early developmental problems to become an effective interceptor. It was joined in ADC squadrons – as well as Air National Guard squadrons, dedicated to the ADC mission – by the McDonnell F-101B Voodoo, a huge, powerful aircraft which was difficult to fly but which, when used properly, could bring enormous firepower into an engagement with bombers.

In Canada in mid-1950s, work progressed on the Avro CF-105 Arrow, a giant, delta-winged interceptor which offered bright hopes for the future of the Canadian aircraft industry and would give

North American defenders

NORAD, the North American Aerospace Defense Command, controls air and ground elements drawn from the air forces of the US and Canada. One of the more enduring examples of Canadian/US military collaboration, NORAD is 40 years old. It was

created in 1957 at a time when the threat posed by Soviet long-range bombers was perceived as being on the increase, with the possibility of a devastating surprise attack over the Pole.

Convair F-102A Delta Dagger

Right: Developed as one component in an all-embracing air defense system, the delta-winged F-102 entered service with the US Air Force in 1956. It was the first 'all-missile' fighter, with an armament of AIM-4 and AIM-26 Falcon missiles but no guns.

McDonnell CF-101B Voodoo

Left: Developed as a long-range interceptor, the Voodoo had a range of more than 2500 km (1,550 miles). Canada's Air Defence Group, which shared responsibility for guarding the polar approaches with the US Air Defense Command, took delivery of 66 Voodoos and operated them into the late 1980s.

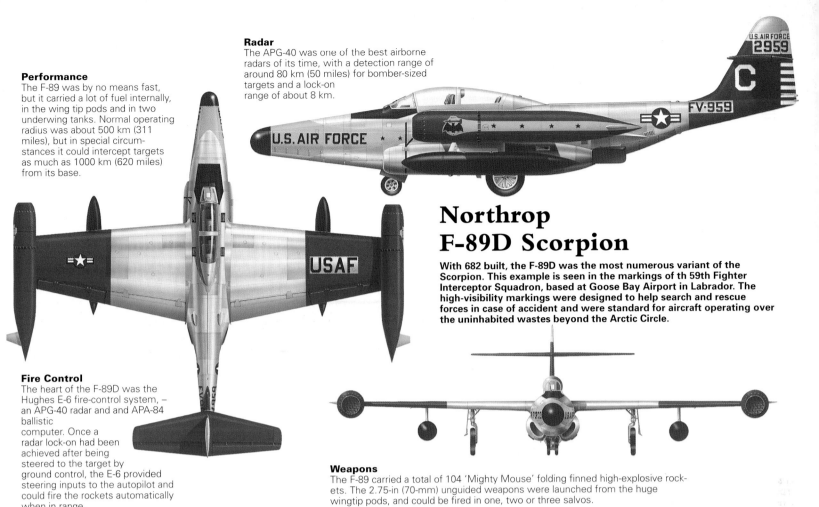

Performance
The F-89 was by no means fast, but it carried a lot of fuel internally, in the wing tip pods and in two underwing tanks. Normal operating radius was about 500 km (311 miles), but in special circumstances it could intercept targets as much as 1000 km (620 miles) from its base.

Radar
The APG-40 was one of the best airborne radars of its time, with a detection range of around 80 km (50 miles) for bomber-sized targets and a lock-on range of about 8 km.

Northrop F-89D Scorpion

With 682 built, the F-89D was the most numerous variant of the Scorpion. This example is seen in the markings of th 59th Fighter Interceptor Squadron, based at Goose Bay Airport in Labrador. The high-visibility markings were designed to help search and rescue forces in case of accident and were standard for aircraft operating over the uninhabited wastes beyond the Arctic Circle.

Fire Control
The heart of the F-89D was the Hughes E-6 fire-control system, – an APG-40 radar and and APA-84 ballistic computer. Once a radar lock-on had been achieved after being steered to the target by ground control, the E-6 provided steering inputs to the autopilot and could fire the rockets automatically when in range.

Weapons
The F-89 carried a total of 104 'Mighty Mouse' folding finned high-explosive rockets. The 2.75-in (70-mm) unguided weapons were launched from the huge wingtip pods, and could be fired in one, two or three salvos.

NORAD the capability to meet Soviet bombers as far away as the North Pole. Five Arrows underwent a flight test programme launched in 1958, but the huge white aircraft was doomed to political and technical woes. It never entered production, and Canada eventually acquired American-built CF-101B Voodoos instead.

The ultimate interceptor was the Convair F-106 Delta Dart, which eventually reached 14 ADC squadrons and was described by one pilot as "the pure thoroughbred of fighter airplanes".

To help the Cold War era's expanding fighter-interceptor force in its grim job of parrying a bomber strike, NORAD developed a DEW (Distant Early Warning) Line of ground radar stations running from Greenland to Alaska, all pointed north. Approaching bombers

would be detected by ground-based radar, then ground controllers would track the bombers and direct fighters to the intercept. The fighter pilot would receive short, voice instructions ("Your target is at 30 degrees, altitude 20, speed 430") intended to get him within range to use his own radar. Voice-directed Ground Controlled Intercepts (GCI) were replaced in the late 1950s with the SAGE (Semi-Automatic Ground Environment) System which 'flew' an interceptor to its target via automatic pilot, the pilot taking over only when it was time to fire. SAGE was used until the late 1970s when improved, secure communication made it possible again to use voice transmissions to vector an interceptor toward its target.

When NORAD came into being during the summer of 1957,

Above: Scattered across thousands of kilometres of some of the most inhospitable terrain on the planet, the DEW Line radar stations were vital components in the detection of aircraft penetrating North American air space from the north.

Below: An F-102 pilot's view of a Soviet 'Bear'. This is a peacetime scene: in combat, the fighter would never have come within range of the bomber's guns, but would have engaged from a distance with AIM-4 Falcon missiles.

Left: The Yakovlev Yak-25 was the Soviet equivalent to the American F-89, although it appeared somewhat later. Given the NATO reporting name of 'Flashlight', it was a two-seat, twin-jet all-weather interceptor which first flew in 1953. Around 1,000 were produced before production ended in 1959.

Below: Although a number of dedicated radar-equipped all-weather fighters were produced by the Soviet Union, by far the bulk of the air defence force was provided by day fighters. Some, like the MiG-19PM seen here, were modified with an all-missile armament and radar in the intake fairing.

the USA and Canada had more than 1,000 aircraft dedicated to air defence, a force level which was maintained until well into the 1960s, when it was acknowledged that the manned bomber had been supplanted by the ICBM as the vehicle most likely to be employed as a nuclear weapon delivery system in future.

Thereafter the respective interceptor fleets entered a period of decline, which had a devastating effect on overall force strength. Some idea of the impact of this contraction can be gleaned from the fact that by the mid-1970s the ADC had fallen to just six squadrons (all equipped with the Convair F-106A Delta Dart) ably supported by a rather larger number of second-line Air National Guard units flying the McDonnell F-101B Voodoo and F-102A Delta Dagger as well as some F-106s.

ADC had been renamed Aerospace Defense Command in January 1968, but continued to serve as the combat arm of NORAD. On 1 October 1979, its

Below: The MiG-25 'Foxbat' is the world's fastest fighter. Developed in the 1960s to intercept the abortive B-70 Valkyrie, production continued even after the American bomber's cancellation. It is capable of sustained speeds of Mach 2.8, with Mach 3 (3200 km/h/2,000 mph) available for short periods.

resources were transferred to Tactical Air Command which took over most of its functions, and, on 31 March 1980, ADC was disbanded.

The interceptor force remained at the ready, however. In the 1980s, years of neglect were reversed, prompted in part by Soviet deployment of cruise missile-armed bombers, and the old fighter types were replaced by modern F-15s, F-16s and CF-18s, well able to deal with any threat.

VIEW FROM THE EAST

The world looked very different to the fighter pilots on the other side of the Iron Curtain. Russia has always been paranoid about invaders — with some justification, as a cursory glimpse of history shows. From the Mongols of the 13th century to the Germans of the 20th, the country has repeatedly been ravaged by intruding powers, most of whom have had to be thrown back at fearful cost to the Russian people.

To prevent the recurrence of the German invasion of 1941, the Voyska Protivo-Vozdushnoy Oborony (V-PVO, or Air Defence Troops) was established. Directly responsible to the minister of defence, V-PVO handled all ground and air-based defensive systems and at its peak had a strength

Right: The Tupolev Tu-28 'Fiddler' entered service in the 1960s. This huge fighter had a range of more than 3000 km (1,865 miles) and was designed for patrolling the vast expanses of the northern Soviet Union. It carried four AA-5 'Ash' medium-range missiles which came in both semi-active radar and infra-red homing versions.

Right: The transonic Yak-28P 'Firebar' entered service in the mid-1960s. It bore a resemblance to the preceding Yak-25, but had better radar and was considerably faster.

of more than 500,000 personnel.

As air defence needs changed, so too did the Air Defence Troops, adding the Zenith Rocket Troops (Zenityye Raketnyye Voyska) with

their 10,000 surface-to-air missile (SAM) launchers; Radio-Technical Corps (Radiotekhnicheskiye Voyska) to operate the vast and comprehensive detection and communications network with its 5,000 radars; Anti-Space Defence (Protivokosmicheskaya Oborona); and Anti-Rocket Defence (Protivoraketnaya Oborona) to defend against ballistic missile attack.

Manned interceptors were flown by a further section of the Voyska PVO, designated Aviation of Air Defence (Aviatsiya PVO). For much of its existence, Air Defence Aviation was autonomous on a national scale, and was organised into several air defence zones with-

Soviet Interceptors

The Soviet air defence force was vastly larger than its American equivalent all through the Cold War. The bulk of the numbers was made up with standard tactical fighters, but many hundreds of specialised all-weather interceptors were also deployed, making up in numbers what they may have lacked in sophisticated avionics when compared to the best of the West.

Yakovlev Yak-25
Left: The Yak-25 'Flashlight' was very much a product of the 1950s, with a speed of around 1100 km/h (685 mph) and a range of around 2700 km (1,675 miles).

Sukhoi Su-15 'Flagon'
Right: Standard Soviet single-seat interceptor from the 1960s through to the 1980s, the Su-15 was blisteringly fast though relatively short-ranged. It was an Su-15 which shot down Korean Air Lines' Flight 007 in 1983.

Tupolev Tu 128 'Fiddler'
Below: As big as a medium bomber, the Tu-128 provided the Soviet Union with long-range interception capability from the 1960s until it was replaced by the Sukhoi Su-27 'Flanker' and the MiG-31 'Foxhound' in the late 1980s.

in each of the Soviets' 20 Military Districts.

Soviet jets were always on alert during the Cold War, ready to scramble to intercept NATO spy flights at a moment's notice. Pilots stood on alert at bases across two continents, from the Kola peninsula on the Norwegian border to Cape Dezhnev just across from Alaska.

WILLINGNESS TO SHOOT

Unlike Western intercepts, which generally picked up intruding bombers far out to sea and were content with shepherding the intruders away from forbidden air space, Soviet fighters were much more ready to shoot. In several dozen incidents, NATO spyplanes – or aircraft suspected of being spyplanes – were shot down. More disturbingly, the Soviets also showed their willingness to shoot down civil airliners straying into forbidden airspace – culminating in the destruction of a Korean Air Lines Boeing 747 with the loss of more than 300 passengers.

In the early days of the Cold War, the V-PVO depended upon large numbers of the standard day fighters of the time such as the

MiG-15 and MiG-17. As with the USA's Air Defense Command, however, it began to receive specialised aircraft more suited to its requirements. Some, like the radar-equipped MiG-19PM, were modifications of existing tactical aircraft. But these, while they had the performance to catch hostile bombers, lacked range, and range is a prerequisite in dealing with the vast expanses of the Soviet Union.

The Soviet Union's sheer size presents unique challenges to those tasked with the defence of her borders. Fighters designed to operate across the immense distances involved need good long-range performance, and the ability to carry and deliver air-to-air weaponry at beyond visual range.

The first radar-equipped all-weather jet fighter was the Yak-25, a twin-engined machine which appeared in the 1950s. It was succeeded by the transonic Yak-28. Serving alongside the Yaks were a series of delta-winged Sukhoi machines, starting with the Su-9 and Su-11. These evolved into the

very fast Su-15 'Flagon', which served into the 1990s.

For very long-range intercepts, standard equipment through the 1960s and 1970s was the massive Tu-128 'Fiddler' – as big as a medium bomber. The amazing Mach 3-capable Mikoyan MiG-25 'Foxbat' was developed in the 1960s as a counter to the threat of the USAF's abortive B-70 Valkyrie bomber. Short on range, the MiG-25 was developed into the very long-range MiG-31 'Foxhound' currently in service with the Russian air force.

Right: Rocket-assisted Su-15 'Flagons' streak skywards on an air defence exercise. The Soviet air defence system was not there for show: dozens of aircraft were shot down for intruding into Soviet air space by accident or design.

Aerial intelligence: the U-2 years

1956-1965

Left: All of the overflights performed by the U-2 were undertaken by CIA aircraft with CIA or RAF pilots. The USAF also received the aircraft, using them for high-altitude sampling missions to catch nuclear fall-out from Soviet bomb tests.

Below: The early-generation U-2s were steadily modified to encompass the electronic intelligence mission, which assumed massive importance after the Powers shootdown. This is a U-2C, fitted with an uprated J75 engine for improved performance, dorsal spine housing extra equipment and 'sugar-scoop' jetpipe to deter heat-seeking missiles.

L ockheed's U-2, the most famous of all spyplanes, was created out of a growing American realisation that the USA was simply not going to get enough Soviet intelligence from conventional means. The controlled world of communist society was not going to yield up its secrets to infiltrated agents, and the growing size and capability of Soviet air defences would shield all except their border areas from intelligence-gathering aerial intruders. Unless, that is, they could fly

Below: While its ceiling of more than 24385m (80,000 ft) kept the high-flying U-2 out of range of hostile MiGs, it was just possible that new SAMs might reach that height. The CIA had realised this at least two years before the Powers incident, and had already instigated the follow-on SR-71 programme.

above the reach of those defences

Balloons had been tried from 1953 onwards, taking advantage of the prevailing eastward-flowing jet-streams in the upper atmosphere to traverse the Soviet Union with underslung cameras: clearing Soviet Asia, such balloons received radio commands from Japan to eject their photographic payloads. However, the system was distinctly unreliable: not only was the exact course of flight at the mercy of the elements, but the balloon's internal pressure had to be controlled in order to maintain the desired flight level. This often failed to happen and the the Soviets retrieved a number of the balloons and cameras.

'OPEN SKIES'

In July 1955 at the Geneva summit conference President Eisenhower proposed an 'Open Skies' policy, in order to reduce the growing tension and arms race between the superpowers. The proposal (for mutual and agreed aerial reconnaissance) appears rather naive today, but it has been in de facto operation since the mid-1960s as a result of the use of reconnaissance satellites by both countries. In the 1950s, however, it was rejected by the Soviet Union.

Three days before that rejection, on 1 August 1955, the top-secret Lockheed U-2 spyplane, built for and operated by the Central Intelligence Agency, had taken to the air for the first time. A year

later, the type had embarked on an overflight programme which would take it deep into the Soviet heartland to photograph airfields and missile sites, and listen to radar defences and missile telemetry.

The U-2 could cruise at an unassailable 21335 to 24385m (70,000-80,000 ft) thanks to its incredible glider-type wing and its unique weight-saving design. Early flights were mounted from West Germany, and covered northern and western areas of the Soviet Union, and almost immediately discovered that Soviet bomber development and production was nowhere near as advanced as had been thought.

ICBM WATCH

In 1957 attention switched to the south as the Soviets began to test medium- and intercontinental-range ballistic missiles from Kapustin Yar near Volgograd and from the new cosmodrome misleadingly named Baikonur by the Soviets, (it is actually situated 320 km (200 miles) south of that city). The first pictures of Kapustin Yar had been brought back in 1953 by a photo-reconnaissance Canberra of the RAF, though the aircraft had been badly shot up by the Soviet defences, and since that time there had been no new information. But since the U-2 flew well above the service ceiling of the defending MiGs it could be used to find out what was happening.

A detachment moved to Turkey and conducted more overflights, as well as a much larger number of peripheral missions, cruising across Turkey and Iran, using their great height to monitor the cosmodromes visually and electronically to detect signs of impending rocket launches. Another U-2 detachment was based in Japan, to cover the growing military developments in Soviet Asia.

The whole policy of overflights and intelligence gathering missions changed dramatically in 1960. An electronics-packed Boeing RB-47, flying out of Brize Norton, England, was shot down by two Soviet MiGs in the remote northern waters of the Barents Sea on 1 July 1960. Two of the six-man crew survived and were taken prisoner.

The nearby Kola and Kanin peninsulas house the Soviet navy's main northern bases, as well as IRBM sites and bomber airfields. The area had been scheduled for attention two months earlier on 1 May by a U-2 overflight from Pakistan that would take in several sites across the Soviet Union, with the intention to land in Norway. But the U-2, flown by Francis Gary Powers, never reached its northern

Right: Dominating the instrument panel of the U-2 was the circular driftsight. This was connected to a periscope on the underside of the nose so that the pilot could see the world below.

objective, since it was shot down by an SA-2 missile near Sverdlovsk.

Nikita Khrushchev was able to turn the U-2 incident of 1 May 1960 into a powerful propaganda weapon. The Soviet leader stage managed a walk-out from the Paris summit meeting only a fortnight after the aircraft was brought down. Perhaps he was exacting revenge for the four-year U-2 operation, during which a surprisingly small number of direct overflights had assured US policy makers that Khruschev's oft-repeated boasts about Soviet strategic missile and aircraft superiority were groundless.

PHOTO-ANALYSIS

For instance, a classic example of the photo-interpreters' art had occurred in the previous year with a U-2 mission over the Tyuratam cosmodrome. From the large size of the aperture seen in photos of the base of the launch pad, analysts were able to deduce that the Soviets were still using auxiliary rockets to boost their intercontinental-range

missile - which was hardly an advance on existing US missiles then nearing operational status, and was almost certainly not a deployable, operational system.

The U-2 and RB-47 incidents marked a turning point in the reconnaissance Cold War, and not only because President Kennedy had to promise to cease overflights of the Soviet Union in order to get

the two SAC crewmen back (U-2 pilot Francis Gary Powers was released a year later in exchange for a Soviet spy held in the USA).

1960 was also the year when the USA achieved its first success with reconnaissance satellites, to be followed by the Soviets three years later. Advances in missile technology meant that flying at very high altitude was no longer a guarantee

US spyplanes

Naturally it was the United States which led the way in developing new aircraft for intelligence gathering. Most were conversions of existing aircraft, using transports or bombers for the Sigint

mission, which required the carriage of heavy equipment and numerous operators. In addition to the U-2, the high-altitude Sigint/photography mission was also undertaken by the RB-57 Canberra.

Lockheed RB-69A
Below left: A little-known variant of the US Navy's P-2 Neptune, the B-69 was used for secret missions around the fringes of Soviet and WarPac territory in the late 1950s and early 1960s. Its primary function was the collection of SIGINT and ELINT about Soviet radar systems and air defence networks.

Lockheed U-2A
Above right: Aircraft 56-6701 is typical of the U-2 fleet, having been recorded in at least 11 different colour schemes and equipment configurations since its early days with the CIA. It is seen here as it appeared soon after transfer to the US Air Force at Edwards AFB Later it was modified as a U-2B and then a U-2C, with a long dorsal 'canoe' and many special sensor fits.

General Dynamics B-57F
Left: Standard Canberras and Martin RB-57Ds (with extended wings) were widely used for high-altitude reconnaissance, but neither could match the extraordinary RB-57F, which had new outsize wings and auxiliary turbojets.

Boeing RB-47H
Right: The Sigint-dedicated Stratojet was covered in antennas to serve its onboard systems. Four 'Crows' (electronic warfare officers) were crammed into the swollen converted bomb bay to operate the equipment.

The U-2 Incident

The National Air and Space Administration's press release of May 5 1960 began prosaically enough. "One of our U-2 research planes, in use since 1956 in a continuing program to study high-altitude meteorological conditions, has been missing since 9 o'clock Sunday morning when its pilot reported that he was having oxygen difficulties over Lake Van, Turkey."

NASA went on say, amongst other things, that the aircraft was based at Incirlik in Turkey, that it carried air sampling equipment, that the pilot was a civilian employee of NASA, and that if he had blacked out, the automatic pilot would have kept the plane on a northeasterly course.

The story was almost completely fabricated. A U-2 had in fact been lost, but far from being over the Lake Van area of Turkey, it had been close to the town of Sverdlovsk, deep inside the Soviet Union. This was indeed to the northeast of the position reported by NASA, but the aircraft had been nowhere near Turkey. Neither had it been anything to do with NASA.

At 0626 on the morning of 1 May 1960, Francis Gary Powers took off from Peshawar in Pakistan. The U-2 he was flying belonged to the Central Intelligence Agency, and his mission was to photograph Soviet missile facilities at Tyuratam, going on to spy on what was believed to be a new long-range missile site at Plesetsk. From there he would recover to the Norwegian base at Bodo, having completed the first spy flight clear across the USSR.

The flight had not gone well: Powers was experiencing difficulties with the autopilot, the weather was not favourable, and he was drifting off course.

Through his drift sight, Powers had seen numerous Soviet fighters trying to intercept, and later evidence showed that many missiles had been fired to no effect. But three hours and 27 minutes into the flight, Powers felt an explosion which ripped the tail from his aircraft. He has been hit by an SA-2 'Guideline' missile, apparently at a height of 20000m (nearly 68,000 feet). There is some debate about this figure – the Soviets agreed with Powers' estimate, but evidence has been collected that for at least part of the flight the U-2 was several thousand feet lower.

Whatever the truth of the matter, there were two incontrovertible facts. Powers had not been able to trigger the destruct mechanism. The Soviets salvaged the wreckage, including its intelligence gathering equipment and now had hard evidence that the American spyflights were real. Perhaps more importantly, the flight showed that modern surface-to-air missiles meant that altitude was no longer a guarantee of safety, prompting a complete change in the way all air forces looked at war in the air.

Above: Powers' flight would have been the first complete crossing of the Soviet Union by a spy plane, but the route chosen would have left the U-2 with no fuel reserve at the end of the flight.

Left: Francis Gary Powers was tried by a Soviet court and convicted of spying. He spent two years in jail before being exchanged on 10 February 1962 for the KGB agent Rudolf Abel.

of safety. The headlong pace of electronic development was making a significant impact on the science of electronic intelligence-gathering

Radar advances in the 1950s led to the early side-looking airborne radar (SLAR) type, which had obvious application to stand-off, over-the-border reconnaissance. The first airborne reconnaissance craft to use a SLAR may have been the mysterious and little-known Lockheed/US Air Force RB-69A. This was a conversion of seven US Navy P2V Neptunes carried out in 1954. A podded SLAR was carried on each side of the rear fuselage, and the aircraft also had a number of other radomes and Elint sensors. They were deployed to Europe and Japan for a time before being reconfigured as standard US Navy Neptunes.

Their replacement was the Martin RB-57D, a big-wing development of the US version of the English Electric Canberra. This aircraft had been a rival to the U-2 for the CIA contract: although losing, it did receive a limited production order from the US Air Force. It was flown by the same SAC reconnaissance wing that operated a number of U-2As for secondary high-altitude duties – although not for the most sensitive missions, which were the province of the CIA. Some of the RB-57Ds had camera systems, but others had a SLAR faired neatly into the underside of the wing root. They too were flown from Europe and Japan, but suffered wing fatigue problems and were withdrawn from front-line reconnaissance use in 1960.

However, three years later some of them were further modified by General Dynamics with even bigger wings and turbofan engines to make the RB-57F, which was now virtually unrecognisable from the original Canberra. A US-based squadron of the aircraft had sampling of the upper atmosphere as its primary role, taking over from SAC U-2s. It should not be forgotten that minute particles of fall-out from Soviet and Chinese nuclear tests, captured on filter paper by such flights, could subsequently be analysed in laboratories to provide valuable clues to the nuclear capabilities of those countries.

LOOKING OVER THE FENCE

But other RB-57Fs went abroad, to Rhein Main, Germany and Yokota, Japan, to resume border surveillance duties. One of the German-based aircraft was shot down over the Black Sea in 1965 by a Soviet SAM. Two RB-57Fs were supplied to the Pakistan air force under CIA auspices - their Peshawar base was convenient for monitoring test sites in Soviet Kazakhstan. In the 1965 Indo-Pakistan war, one of them was nearly shot down by an example of the first SA-2 SAMs supplied to India: it was an Elint flight, trying to determine the frequency and precise location of Amritsar radar.

Left: Seen flying in company with a standard RB-57A Canberra is a Martin RB-57D. This was the first stretched-wing model and it performed useful peripheral Sigint work in Europe. It was also used by the CIA for intelligence flights over mainland China.

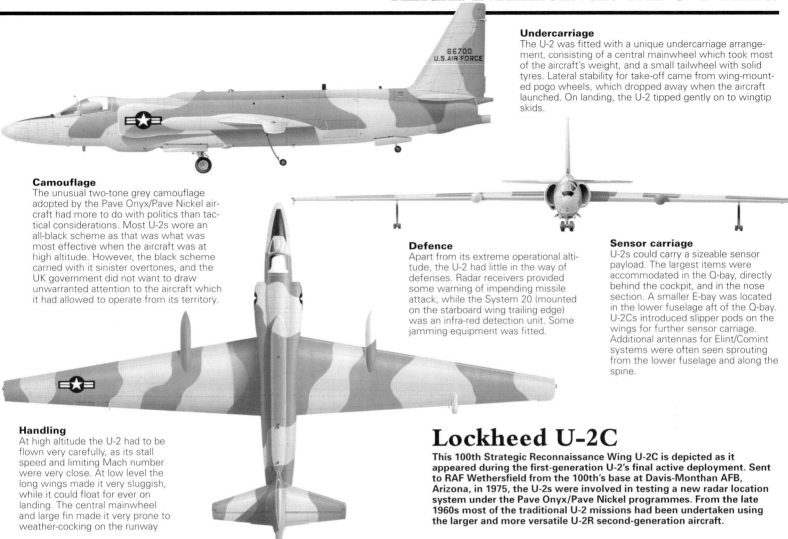

Undercarriage
The U-2 was fitted with a unique undercarriage arrangement, consisting of a central mainwheel which took most of the aircraft's weight, and a small tailwheel with solid tyres. Lateral stability for take-off came from wing-mounted pogo wheels, which dropped away when the aircraft launched. On landing, the U-2 tipped gently on to wingtip skids.

Camouflage
The unusual two-tone grey camouflage adopted by the Pave Onyx/Pave Nickel aircraft had more to do with politics than tactical considerations. Most U-2s wore an all-black scheme as that was what was most effective when the aircraft was at high altitude. However, the black scheme carried with it sinister overtones, and the UK government did not want to draw unwarranted attention to the aircraft which it had allowed to operate from its territory.

Defence
Apart from its extreme operational altitude, the U-2 had little in the way of defenses. Radar receivers provided some warning of impending missile attack, while the System 20 (mounted on the starboard wing trailing edge) was an infra-red detection unit. Some jamming equipment was fitted.

Sensor carriage
U-2s could carry a sizeable sensor payload. The largest items were accommodated in the Q-bay, directly behind the cockpit, and in the nose section. A smaller E-bay was located in the lower fuselage aft of the Q-bay. U-2Cs introduced slipper pods on the wings for further sensor carriage. Additional antennas for Elint/Comint systems were often seen sprouting from the lower fuselage and along the spine.

Handling
At high altitude the U-2 had to be flown very carefully, as its stall speed and limiting Mach number were very close. At low level the long wings made it very sluggish, while it could float for ever on landing. The central mainwheel and large fin made it very prone to weather-cocking on the runway

Lockheed U-2C

This 100th Strategic Reconnaissance Wing U-2C is depicted as it appeared during the first-generation U-2's final active deployment. Sent to RAF Wethersfield from the 100th's base at Davis-Monthan AFB, Arizona, in 1975, the U-2s were involved in testing a new radar location system under the Pave Onyx/Pave Nickel programmes. From the late 1960s most of the traditional U-2 missions had been undertaken using the larger and more versatile U-2R second-generation aircraft.

The RB-57F could sustain 22250 m (73,000 ft) in a lightly-loaded condition. The ceiling of British Canberras in the reconnaissance role was much lower, ranging from 15240 m (50,000 ft) for the 1953-vintage PR.Mk 3 model to about 18288 m (60,000 ft) for the PR.Mk 9 in 1959, which had a modified wing root. In between were the PR.Mk 7 and a few long-radome B.Mk 6s for Elint work.

Electronic intelligence was growing in importance, but even though the equipment now being introduced was generally fitted with advanced new filters, the ever-increasing amount of data being returned was beginning to swamp the analysis labs. The move from analog to digital systems promised greater discrimination and automation but was only part of the solution, the other being to perform more of the analysis in real-time by flying greater numbers of Elint system operators.

ELINT AIRLINERS

This called for the use of roomier transport-type aircraft. The British took the lead in 1957 when three de Havilland Comet C.Mk 2 jets were allocated to No. 192 Squadron. The RAF's premier Elint squad ron was renumbered No. 51 in the following year, and continued to fly the Comets into the early 1970s, when they were replaced by three specially-modified Nimrods. In the interim, the squadron moved from Watton to Wyton, where it joined the RAF's other long-range reconnaissance outfit, No. 543 Squadron. This unit flew the Vickers Valiant B(PR).Mk 1 followed by the Handley Page Victor SR.Mk 2. The converted V bombers housed large cameras in the bomb bay, but were primarily engaged on radar reconnaissance of the potential approaches to enemy territory for the V-bomber force.

The US Air Force put 13 Elint specialists plus equipment into the Lockheed Hercules and the Soviets promptly shot one of them down when it intruded into Armenia. Some reports claimed that the Soviets had 'lured' the Hercules over the border by altering the power or beam configurations of their two nearby radio beacons to resemble two beacons on the Turkish side.

The US Navy put an even greater number of operators aboard its Lockheed EC-121M Elint aircraft: 31 were on board the example that was shot down by the North Koreans in 1969. These lumbering old Super Constellation conversions were replaced by 1975 with the EP-3E variant of the Lockheed Orion patrol plane, which also had a large crew complement: 15 for the mission, plus reliefs, plus flight crew.

Left: Much of Britain's contribution to the NATO reconnaissance effort was handled by the Canberra. No. 192/51 Sqn flew Sigint 'specials' while several squadrons used high-altitude photo-platforms like the PR.Mk 7 seen here.

CUBAN MISSILE CRISIS

1962

I t seemed inevitable that the tension between the superpowers would lead to a crisis, with the world on the brink of nuclear war. But the crisis, when it came, did not involve Berlin as many had expected. Instead, it erupted in America's back yard.

The corrupt Batista regime had been in power in Cuba, less than 145 km (90 miles) from the coast of Florida, since 1952. Resistance to Batista centred on the revolutionary movement led by exiled Fidel Castro, who landed at Las Coloradas in Oriente with 81 men. Castro's guerrillas had popular support, and by the end of the 1958

Below: Shot on 4 November, this picture shows the Mariel port facility, complete with four missile transporters (top left), four fuel trailers (bottom left) and a series of oxidiser trailers (right). This kind of photography came courtesy of RF-8s or RF-101s working at low level.

Batista had fled, leaving the liberators to form a new government in Havana. It aligned itself firmly with the Soviet Union, and many of Castro's opponents fled to Florida.

By the time John F. Kennedy took office, a CIA-sponsored plan to overthrow Castro was under way. Supported by various transport aircraft and ex-USAF B-26 bombers painted in false Cuban markings, with communications handled by an old PBY Catalina, more than 1,400 Cuban exiles landed at at Bahia de Cochinos (Bay of Pigs) at 0530 on 17 April 1961. After some small success, the invaders were thrown back ignominiously, leaving 120 exiles dead and 1,200 taken. A few evaded capture and trickled back to the USA.

It was against a background of humiliation over the Bay of Pigs incident and tensions over the building of the Berlin Wall that

Above: US Navy patrol aircraft kept up a vigil over the waters around Cuba to monitor all vessels and enforce a US-imposed embargo. Here the Soviet ship Anosov is seen leaving Cuba with eight missile transporters on board at the end of the crisis. The date was 7 November 1962.

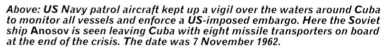

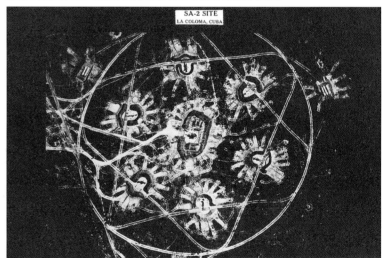

Above: The characteristic pattern is that of an SA-2 surface-to-air missile site, first seen on Cuba by the camera of a high-flying U-2. The placement of SAM defences was the first sign that something worth defending was to arrive in Cuba imminently, sparking the Missile Crisis.

Kennedy faced his toughest trial. Cuba had requested more arms from the USSR to protect herself against the continuing threat of US interference. By August 1962 the CIA was aware of significant arms shipments, and on 22 August Director John McCone advised the president of the presence of large missiles on the island.

MORE RECONNAISSANCE

Agency Lockheed U-2 flights over Cuba were stepped up, and USN and USAF patrol and reconnaissance aircraft paid special attention to Soviet shipping. A U-2 flight from McCoy AFB on 29 August photographed two SA-2 sites on Cuba, with six more under construction. Photo interpreters became anxious when it was realised that the layout was similar

to that of surface-to-air missile (SAM) sites associated with the protection of strategic missile bases in the Soviet Union. On 4 September Kennedy warned Khrushchev that the USA would not tolerate the siting of offensive weapons on Cuba; Khrushchev replied by saying that the Soviet Union had no need to place such weapons in the Caribbean. But just four days later a Lockheed P-2 Neptune of VP-44 photographed the freighter *Omsk* heading for Havana with large oblong canisters on the decks. U-2

flights were again stepped up.

Reconnaissance flights showed more construction work, and on 10 October the USAF 4080th SRW formally assumed responsibility for overflights from the CIA, using Agency U-2E variants equipped with electronic countermeasures equipment. The overt reason for the transfer to the USAF was the threat from SA-2 missiles, but in fact the CIA was not in good odour with the authorities after the Bay of Pigs fiasco and numerous intelligence errors over Berlin.

On 14 October Major Steve Heyser flew a U-2 over Cuba for just six minutes, during which time he took 928 pictures of two sites at San Cristobal and Sagua la Grande. Processed on the following day the photographs were rushed to President Kennedy on 16 October. They clearly showed SS-4 'Sandal' medium-range ballistic missile (MRBM) sites in an advanced state of preparation. Low-level reconnaissance flights by McDonnell RF-101Cs of the 29th TRS

revealed more missile sites at Guanajay and Remedios.

The Soviet Union was applying pressure to gain concessions over Berlin and possibly the removal of 45 Jupiter and 60 Thor IRBMs from Italy, Turkey and England. On 22 October a 'quarantine' (blockade) of Cuba was announced. Strategic Air Command was put on full alert and its bombers dispersed to civilian airports whilst naval vessels raced to the Caribbean to enforce the blockade. Air Defense and Tactical Air Commands moved units south to Florida. The US base

at Guantanamo Bay on Cuba was reinforced with a garrison of 8,000 US Marines and sailors and Task Force 135 was established to defend the base; ships in the force included the carriers USS *Enterprise* (CVN-65) and USS *Independence* (CVA-62). The quarantine was enforced by units of Task Force 136, which comprised 180 vessels including the carrier USS *Essex* (CVS-9) with two units of Grumman S2F-1 Trackers.

SOVIETS BACK DOWN

Khrushchev wrote to Kennedy on 26 October accepting the American terms for the removal of offensive weapons, which by now included 44 Ilyushin Il-28 bombers being assembled at San Julian, but only in exchange for American removal of the Jupiter missiles, which in fact Kennedy had previously ordered.

On 27 October the tension increased as Major Anderson was shot down by an SA-2 and killed on an overflight of naval installations at Banes. Early the following

Above: Workhorse of the low-level mission over Cuba was the McDonnell RF-101 Voodoo. Relying on speed and surprise for its defence, it was very successful in maintaining a steady flow of photographs to the US command.

day Soviet intercontinental ballistic missiles (ICBMs) came to full alert as another U-2 inadvertently but embarrassingly overflew the Chukostkiy Peninsula at the eastern tip of Siberia.

At 1000 on 28 October the crisis ended as the Soviets agreed to dismantle the missiles under inspection. But the Il-28s were still being assembled and the quarantine was not lifted until 20 November, by which time the Soviets had agreed to their removal. The first aircraft departed Cuba in crates on 15 December aboard the freighter *Kasimov*.

During the period from 14 October to 6 December the USAF flew 102 U-2 sorties over Cuba, but low-flying aircraft were able to supervise the operation with a versatility unmatched by more remote observation. The following year the superpowers agreed to instal the 'hot-line' telephone link, and as further evidence of the thaw in relations a nuclear test-ban agreement was signed in August.

Left: The US Navy's contribution to the tactical reconnaissance effort was handled by the Vought RF-8As of VFP-62, although they flew from bases in Florida rather than carrier decks. Marine squadron VMCJ-2 also flew photo-Crusaders on missions over Cuba.

Cuba's ageing air force

The Communist state of Cuba was only three years old when the Missile Crisis loomed, and it had not yet received fighters from the Soviet Union. The air force relied on a handful of aircraft which were left over from the days of the Batista

regime. Later the island state was the recipient of MiG-17s and MiG-21s from the Soviet Union, posing a further threat to the US dominance over the Caribbean region.

Douglas A-26 Invader

Right: The most potent attack aircraft available to the Cubans in 1962 was the Invader. Several had been operated prior to the revolution, and more had been seized when left behind after the Bay of Pigs fiasco. This post-revolution A-26 wears the FAR (Fuerza Aérea Revolucionara) markings carried post-1959.

Hawker Sea Fury

Left: Cuba had no military jet equipment, and its best defence rested on the Sea Fury. While this type was adequate for fighting against fighters of similar vintage which abounded in the region even in the early 1960s, it was clearly no match for US types.

Central Front Confrontation

1965–1990

For four decades, the world stood poised on the brink of nuclear destruction as the competing world views of the United States and the Soviet Union brought them into Cold War conflict. The most obvious manifestation of superpower rivalry came in the heartland of Europe, where the two titanic military alliances they headed faced each other with the most powerful concentration of military force the world has ever seen.

Fortunately for the human race, Europe's Central Front never exploded into battle, but the Cold War rivalry between NATO and the armies of the Warsaw Pact was still the dominant influence on military technology in the second half of the 20th Century. Weapons development, which had boomed through the 1950s, advanced with even more dizzying speed through

the 1960s and 1970s. And while one side in the conflict decided to apply the new technology to an older type of war, the other began to grope to whole new concept of battle.

Whilst the West devoted considerable effort towards divining the minute details of Soviet intentions and capabilities, intelligence analysts were fully aware of the basic plan of any future assault on the Free World. Not only were the broad tactics known, but also the precise date of their origin: 22 June 1941.

It was on this day more than half a century ago that Hitler invaded his former ally, the Soviet Union. The Luftwaffe established massive air superiority above the advancing German army and shattered its counterpart in the air and on the airfields. These tactics almost annihilated the air and land forces of the Soviet Union and left no doubt in

Above: The opening rounds of any war on the Central Front would have involved mass attacks on airfields. Although NATO had a technological superiority, the Warsaw Pact had numbers on its side. Low-level fighter-bombers such as the MiG-27 were available in abundance.

Below: Soviet attackers like this Sukhoi Su-7 'Fitter' were crude by comparison with their Western counterparts, but might well have been devastatingly effective, since they could have overwhelmed NATO defences by sheer weight of numbers.

Below: Warsaw Pact forces were well-versed in the art of airborne assault, and large numbers of Mil Mi-8s were available. Unlike NATO's assault helicopters, Soviet Mi-8s carried heavy armament to put down suppressive fire.

Right: Although it was the nuclear threat which held sway over the Central Front, the menace of chemical and biological warfare was never far away. Here a MiG-21 is seen spraying water during a chemical warfare trial.

Threat from the East

Forward-based in the Warsaw Pact countries, the Soviet Union possessed a mighty armada of attack aircraft, ranging from close support types to nuclear bombers. NATO could not hope to defend itself against an all-out attack, and so a pre-emptive tactical nuclear strike against WarPac airfields was the only practical means of defence.

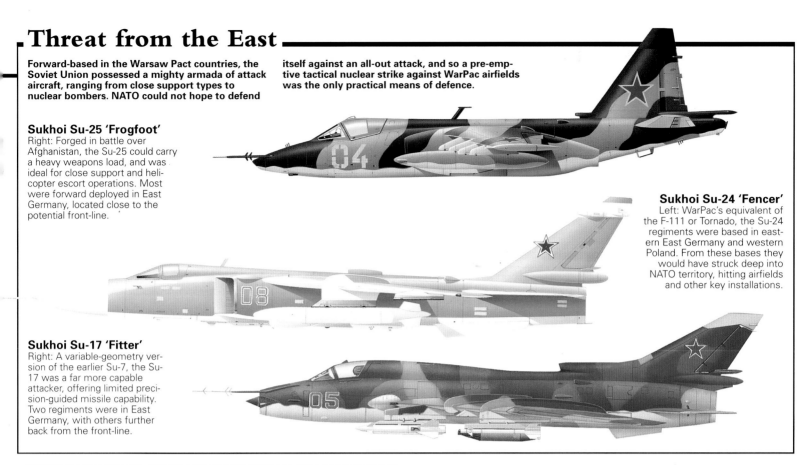

Sukhoi Su-25 'Frogfoot'
Right: Forged in battle over Afghanistan, the Su-25 could carry a heavy weapons load, and was ideal for close support and helicopter escort operations. Most were forward deployed in East Germany, located close to the potential front-line.

Sukhoi Su-24 'Fencer'
Left: WarPac's equivalent of the F-111 or Tornado, the Su-24 regiments were based in eastern East Germany and western Poland. From these bases they would have struck deep into NATO territory, hitting airfields and other key installations.

Sukhoi Su-17 'Fitter'
Right: A variable-geometry version of the earlier Su-7, the Su-17 was a far more capable attacker, offering limited precision-guided missile capability. Two regiments were in East Germany, with others further back from the front-line.

Above: The Su-25 was the Soviet answer to the A-10, but it was considerably faster (although not as capable), rendering it less vulnerable over the Central Front battlefield. Most Soviet attack aircraft had rough-field capability.

the minds of post-war Soviet planners that Blitzkrieg was by far the most effective form of assault.

Should the Warsaw Pact have marched against Western Europe in a war of conventional or limited NBC (Nuclear, Biological and Chemical) weaponry, it would have had the aggressor's privilege of choosing the time of attack. Again, there was no secret about timing: it would have been on, or shortly before a weekend or holiday, unless the build-up of diplomatic tension had lasted long enough to allow NATO forces to be placed on full alert. The Soviet Union also vowed publicly that no battles were be fought on its own territory, meaning that conflict would have taken place on Western European ground or that of its Warsaw Pact allies.

According to Soviet doctrine: 'the offensive is the basic form of combat action. Only by a resolute attack conducted at great tempo and in great depth is the destruction of the enemy achieved.'

As the Soviet armies moved forward, the main role for air power would have been the elimination of threats before they could materialise, or countering them before they are able to press home an attack. Strike bombers like the Sukhoi Su-24 'Flanker' were tasked with penetrating enemy defences to destroy key military targets such as command and control centres, airfields and runways. Other tactical aircraft – in the early days MiG-15s, 17s and Sukhoi-7s, succeeded by much more advanced types such as MiG-27s and Su-22s – would have ranged the rear areas, destroying enemy reserves, cutting lines of communication and supply and blocking reinforcements.

Provision of the air assets for these operations was the responsibility of Frontal Aviation (Frontovaya Aviatsiya) a component of the Soviet air forces, whose aircraft were assigned to Frontal Air Armies under the control of the local army group commander. Originally intended to provide a defensive umbrella over the troops advancing beneath, by the late 1960s Frontal Aviation's role was changing.

QUALITY AND QUANTITY
Having usefully employed the 1970s period of 'detente' with the West to build up Frontal Aviation, the Soviet Union by the 1980s had a powerful tactical air arm at its disposal. Optimised for support of an advancing army and with the additional capability to attack targets well behind the battle line, Frontovaya Aviatsiya was by its size and composition an overtly offensive force optimised to emulate the spectacular success of the Blitzkrieg form of attack.

By the early 1980s, Frontal Aviation operated some 5,000 fixed-wing aircraft and 3,250 helicopters, up to 70 per cent of which were based in Eastern Europe (including the westernmost military districts of the Soviet Union).

The Soviets were great believers in confusing the enemy, and parachute attacks played a big part in their plans. Airborne troops were tasked with causing confusion behind the lines as well as with seizing port facilities and key airfields, where they could be reinforced by sea or by air.

Although air units could inflict considerable damage on the enemy, their main purpose in a combined arms offensive was to prepare for the main attack of fast-moving armoured forces supported by ground-attack aircraft and heavy artillery.

Right: One of the most feared weapons in the land war was the Mil Mi-24 'Hind' armed assault helicopter. Its heavy weapon load, including anti-tank missiles, made it a powerful gunship, while its internal cabin could be used to carry up to eight troops. 'Hinds' were based throughout East Germany, flying alongside Mi-8s in assault regiments.

Left: *Mass procurement of US types by the European NATO nations went some way to redressing the imbalance of numbers. The Republic F-84F was the standard ground attack platform for many years, able to carry tactical nuclear weapons.*

Above: *Reforger exercises demonstrated the speed with which US forces could be deployed to Europe in time of tension. However, the deployment was mainly by sea, and would not have been quick enough to help in the face of a full-scale surprise attack.*

These assaults would have been pressed in army strength or larger along several axes. Speed was considered to be of the essence, so while the main punch of the assault was provided by armoured forces, paratroopers and heliborne assault troops supported by gunship helicopters and close-support aircraft would have provided the mobile element in the attack.

Meanwhile, fast-moving flanking forces were intended to go round the main enemy force, either to attack from the side or the rear, or to cut the enemy's lines of communication. The deployment of large numbers of assault helicopters and helicopter gunships in the 1970s meant that such attacks could then have been pressed home much faster than with land- or vehicle-based troops.

Soviet planning expected that all elements of an attack would work very closely together. The main assault troops were supported by large numbers of artillery pieces. Once they were engaged, however, their most flexible and responsive weapon was close air support, provided by the ground-attack fighters of Frontal Aviation and by the army's own helicopter gunships.

SKILL AND TECHNOLOGY

Hopelessly outnumbered by Warsaw Pact forces in the tank equation, the NATO allies relied on skill and technology to redress the balance. Highly trained aircrew and state-of-the-art aircraft, electronics and weapons produced very impressive displays of anti-tank firepower, but they were themselves vulnerable. The big question for western planners was 'will enough of our weapons platforms survive WarPac's initial strikes and the massive Soviet battlefield air defence system to be able to stop an endless torrent of enemy tanks?'

And it could really have been a torrent. In the early 1980s there were some 25,000 main battle tanks stationed in Central Europe, of which 18,000 were east of the Iron Curtain. Outnumbered 2.5 to 1, NATO's 7,000 battle tanks also faced 10,200 helicopter- or vehicle-mounted anti-tank guided weapon systems.

European strategy on the central front took several forms. Germany played a key role, in spite of some initial French reservations. Despite some indifference from its people West Germany's government set about forming fighting services in the mid-1950s. Re-born in September 1956, the Luftwaffe was the subject of such a large build-up that a mere four years later it included 62,000 personnel, 375 Republic F-84F Thunderstreaks in five wings, 108 RF-84F Thunderflashes in two wings and 225 North American F-86 Sabres in three wings, plus training, transport and support units. An early priority was to obtain more modern

equipment. Lockheed offered a multi-role version of the Starfighter, and with new avionics and a sizzling Mach 2 capability, the F-104G Super Starfighter was adopted for fighter-bomber, nuclear strike and reconnaissance duties as well as in its original role. F-104s also armed Belgium, Canada, Denmark, Greece, Italy, the Netherlands, Norway and Turkey.

The second major plank in NATO's defences was the commitment of large American forces to European defence. The North American F-100 Super Sabres, McDonnell F-101 Voodoos and Douglas B-66 Destroyers of the late 1950s gave way to McDonnell Douglas F-4 Phantoms, General Dynamics F-111s and General Dynamics F-16 Fighting Falcons.

Regular deployment exercises were also held for US-based units. The most impressive of these was the 'Reforger' (REinforcement of FOrces in GERmany) series which included a massive airlift of units over the Atlantic, although it must be remembered that, Lockheed C-141 StarLifters and C-5 Galaxies notwithstanding, the major resupply in wartime would be by sea.

CANADIAN CONTRIBUTION

Canada, too, with its particular affiliations to the UK and France, was represented in Europe. Most of the 200 CF-104 Starfighters obtained for what was then the Royal Canadian Air Force replaced European-based Canadair/North

Left: *Following the F-84F as NATO's principal strike platform was the Lockheed F-104 Starfighter, which also undertook the fighter and reconnaissance missions. West Germany was the largest user, with four wings dedicated to nuclear strike, two for reconnaissance, two for maritime strike and two for interception.*

Left: In the face of huge numbers, NATO could respond only by increasing capability. The F-4 Phantom was an advanced interceptor, but those purchased by West Germany were hampered by the political decision to carry only short-range Sidewinder missiles.

Below: France's Dassault Mirage IIIC was a potent interceptor which was later evolved into the multi-role Mirage IIIE.

American F-86 Sabres and Canadair CF-100 Canucks from 1962 onwards, and were themselves replaced by McDonnell Douglas CF-18 Hornets.

France was a major component of NATO at the start of the super-sonic era and contributed tactical fighters to the 4th Allied Tactical Air Force as well as discharging its obligations under the four-power air traffic agreement covering access to Berlin. French pioneering in high-speed flight found its reward

Above: Canada maintained a strong presence in the 4ATAF area with CF-104 Starfighters. The Canadian aircraft were optimised for nuclear strike, carrying a single US-owned B57 weapon which was held under a dual-key arrangement.

in the Mirage III, which entered service in 1962 as a Mach 2 fighter bomber and interceptor. Forming the backbone of French tactical and air defence commands, the Mirage III found a ready export market (mostly outside NATO) and was

joined in 1964 by a scaled-up, twin engine bomber version, designated Mirage IVA.

By 1966, France had a nuclear deterrent (popularly termed the

Force de Frappe) which restored what was seen to be its status in the world. In March 1966, President de Gaulle announced that France was leaving NATO. The country main-

USAF in Europe

The cornerstone of NATO's defence in Central Europe were the United States Air Forces in Europe (USAFE). Fighters, fighter-bombers and reconnaissance platforms were based in sizeable numbers in West Germany and France (until 1964) as part of the 4th ATAF, backed up by longer-range nuclear bombers in the United Kingdom, which never really lost its tag of being the Americans' permanent aircraft-carrier off the coast of Europe. Additional USAFE assets guarded the Southern Flank, being based in Spain and Italy.

Left: Qualitatively superior to their Soviet counterparts, USAFE tactical aircraft were flown by well-trained and highly-motivated crews. European-based aircraft were regularly bolstered by transatlantic deployments. This quartet of F-100Cs is seen over a German city.

Below left: The F-4E Phantom became the backbone of USAFE during the 1970s. It could fly the fighter and strike roles with equal ease. This machine is from the Ramstein-based 86th TFW.

Below: Two wings of General Dynamics F-111s were stationed in England. These were central to NATO's Follow-on Forces Attack concept of deep (nuclear) interdiction.

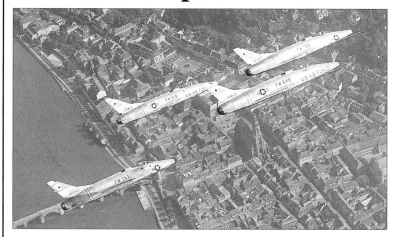

Nato Anti-tank helicopters

Above: For the British the Westland Lynx AH.Mk 1 was available for anti-armour missions, armed with eight TOW missiles. It also had a capacious cabin, allowing it to reposition Milan anti-tank teams.

Below: King of the anti-armour helicopters was the Bell AH-1 Cobra, armed with eight TOWs. The type had originated as a pure gunship for close support, but matured as an anti-tank weapon.

Above: Demonstrating its ability to hide in the vegetation (made safer by its shrouded fenestron tail rotor) this Aérospatiale SA 342 Gazelle is armed with four HOT anti-tank missile tubes.

Below: West Germany's Heeresflieger adopted the MBB BO105 as its PAH-1 anti-armour helicopter. Six HOT missiles could be carried and the type was also a useful scout.

Faced with a huge disparity in tank numbers, NATO rapidly seized on the specialist anti-armour helicopter as a means of restoring some parity. Naturally the US Army led the way, deploying large numbers of Bell AH-1 Cobras (augmented by AH-64 Apaches in the final years of the Cold War). The employment of anti-armour helicopters was intended to bottle up the Warsaw Pact armoured thrusts in key chokepoints, enabling other weapon systems to be brought to bear on the halted columns. After the Cold War, most Western military officers privately questioned whether anything short of a massive, preemptive tactical nuclear strike could have halted the Red Army.

tained a residual presence on the North Atlantic Council, but did not participate in the Defence Planning Committee.

On the other side of the English Channel, the UK did at least appear to be adding forces to NATO, although this was only a reassignment of units already in being. The UK was vital to NATO as the rear depot for assembling forces and holding reserves in the event of a European war. Having special responsibilities outside Europe, the UK retained certain elements under national control, but assigned RAF Strike Command in its entirety to

NATO in April 1975. As such, the remainder of the UK's combat aircraft joined those of RAF Germany under NATO stewardship. RAFG, equipped with Hunters and Canberras at the start of the 1960s, progressively re-equipped with V/STOL Harriers, Jaguars, F-4 Phantoms and Tornadoes.

BENELUX CO-OPERATION

Smaller nations of NATO continued to assign the bulk of their armed forces to mutual defence. This was particularly true of the central area represented by Belgium, Luxembourg and the

Netherlands. The Belgium and the Netherlands even had a joint pilot-training programme until they selected different Republic F/RF-84 replacements in the late 1960s: Dassault Mirage 5s and Canadair/Northrop NF-5As respectively. Both then elected to license produce F-16 Fighting Falcons as a Starfighter follow-on.

Denmark and Norway, too, were Fighting Falcon customers, but instead of adding depth to the Central Front, they were on the exposed Northern Flank. Their armed forces were small, for which reason they were likely to have

been one of the main deployment areas for NATO's Allied Command Europe Mobile Force (AMF).

Approved by the NATO Council in September 1961, the AMF was established as a multinational, variable-content force ready to be sent at short notice to any threatened area. It was seen to have the deterrent effect of stressing the unity of NATO and the central theme that 'an armed attack against one [is] an attack against all'. Often termed the 'NATO Fire Brigade', the AMF regular mounted training exercises involving the armed services of all members.

Britain's 'Jump-jet'

The fact that airfields would be high on the list for attack on Day One of any central European war vexed military commanders on both sides of the Iron Curtain. While WarPac invested heavily in dispersed-base operations, with all key infrastructure being

mobile and with highway strips ready prepared, NATO toyed with vertical take-off as a means of continuing the war when there were no airfields left. The Harrier was the only practical outcome of this line of thinking.

Hawker Siddeley Harrier

Right: Developed with the Central Front in mind, the Harrier was designed to operate from woods, supermarket car parks or literally anywhere it could find cover and a flat place to land and take off. Three squadrons (including No. 20, illustrated) were deployed to West Germany, based close to the front-line

Fairchild A-10A

Although officially christened the Thunderbolt II, the A-10 was known universally as the 'Warthog'. Its mission was primarily anti-armour, and a six-squadron wing was established in the UK, each squadron having a forward operating location in West Germany. A-10 pilots regularly flew from the FOLs, becoming familiar with the landmarks that they would encounter if they ever had to go to war.

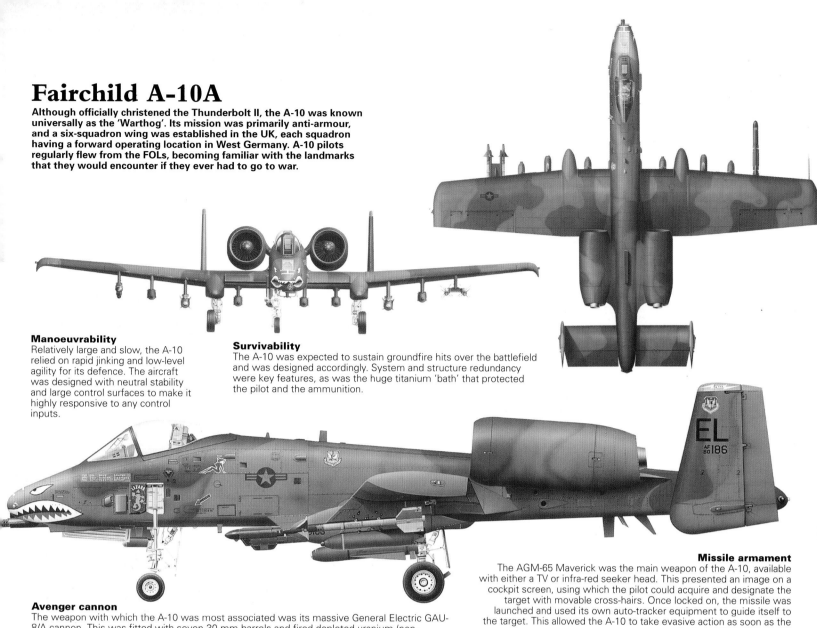

Manoeuvrability
Relatively large and slow, the A-10 relied on rapid jinking and low-level agility for its defence. The aircraft was designed with neutral stability and large control surfaces to make it highly responsive to any control inputs.

Survivability
The A-10 was expected to sustain groundfire hits over the battlefield and was designed accordingly. System and structure redundancy were key features, as was the huge titanium 'bath' that protected the pilot and the ammunition.

Missile armament
The AGM-65 Maverick was the main weapon of the A-10, available with either a TV or infra-red seeker head. This presented an image on a cockpit screen, using which the pilot could acquire and designate the target with movable cross-hairs. Once locked on, the missile was launched and used its own auto-tracker equipment to guide itself to the target. This allowed the A-10 to take evasive action as soon as the missile had been launched.

Avenger cannon
The weapon with which the A-10 was most associated was its massive General Electric GAU-8/A cannon. This was fitted with seven 30-mm barrels and fired depleted uranium (non-radioactive) rounds of great density, interspersed with high explosive. The gun itself was mounted slightly offset to port, so that the firing barrel was on the aircraft's centreline. Firing at up to 4,200 rounds per minute, the gun could easily decelerate the aircraft alarmingly if used for too long a burst.

Above and left: NATO forces evaluated and occasionally ran exercises in dispersed operations, using autobahns as runways, but never embraced the concept the way WarPac units did. Even runway lighting at Soviet bases was truck-mounted so that it could move to a nearby highway strip at a moment's notice.

Right: The business end of an A-10 is dominated by the GAU-8/A cannon. This powerful weapon could out-range light AAA guns, but in most cases 'Hog' pilots preferred to tackle targets with the longer-ranged Maverick missile.

Spies in the skies

1965–1992

Left: Many might have thought the U-2's career had come to an abrupt end in 1960 when Francis Gary Powers was shot down over Sverdlovsk, but the type continues to be vital to US intelligence-gathering capability. In the mid-1960s the U-2R was developed, essentially a new, much larger design utilising only the engine and general layout of its predecessor. Seeing action in Vietnam, the Middle East and during the Gulf War, the U-2R is still highly prized for its ability to produce Comint, Elint and radar imagery from high-altitude.

Below: Illustrating the type of reach the U-2R's sensors can provide is this image of San Francisco Bay taken by a NASA-operated ER-2 (a derivative of the U-2R).

Modern reconnaissance has split into two main areas of activity. Strategic reconnaissance is designed to help create the 'big picture' for high commands and national authorities, while tactical reconnaissance is dedicated to providing operational and tactical information for ground forces.

Intelligence comes in three varieties. Humint (human intelligence) is the stuff of spy novels with agents in target countries gathering a wide variety of information, but which has little to do with spy aircraft.

Imagery involves obtaining photographic, infra-red, or radar images of particular areas. Aircraft and satellites are the major means of obtaining such information. Lastly, the vast field of Sigint (signals intelligence) covers communications intelligence, electronic intelligence and telemetry intelligence, among others.

SHEDDING LIGHT

In peace or war, good intelligence is vital. Without it you are like a man searching for a black cat in a darkened room: you know it is there, somewhere, but finding it will be down to blind chance.

Reconnaissance is the light which enables you to do the job.

The basic and oldest-established form of reconnaissance involves making images of a target area. In the old ballooning days it involved a man with a pencil and paper making sketches of enemy fortifications, but soon aircraft were carrying cameras into the skies. Today, the camera shooting black-and-white film is still an important reconnaissance tool, although it is a far cry from the ones you would use to take your holiday snaps. Long focal lengths, high-technology optics and superfine film mean that a satellite in orbit can take a pictures with a

High Flyers

Apart from the two SR-71As which were returned to service in 1996, the USAF's U-2 is the only high-altitude reconnaissance platform in service today. The modular payload carriage, illustrated by this U-2EPX (a cancelled US Navy maritime patrol variant), provides the U-2 with great versatility. Imaging sensors include the ASARS-2 radar and SYERS camera, either of which can be carried in the nose. The former produces picture-quality radar images, and now includes a moving-target function for spotting vehicles on the move. The SYERS is a very long focal length optical sensor recording data electronically rather than on film. A wideband Comint and Elint system is usually carried to provide synergistic multi-sensor coverage across long distances. Data can be downlinked to ground stations for real-time analysis, or uplinked via the Senior Span equipment (carried in a dorsal fairing) to satellites for global relay. In the 1990s the fleet was re-engined, raising the designation to U-2S.

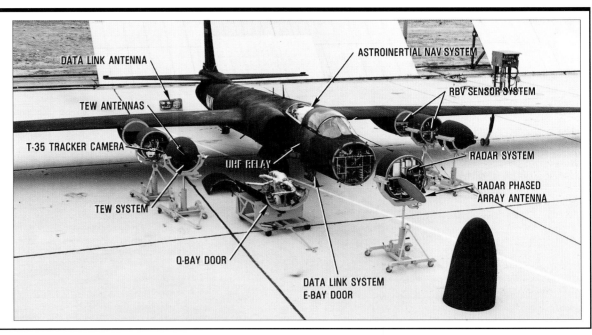

DATA LINK ANTENNA
ASTROINERTIAL NAV SYSTEM
TEW ANTENNAS
RBV SENSOR SYSTEM
T-35 TRACKER CAMERA
UHF RELAY
RADAR SYSTEM
TEW SYSTEM
RADAR PHASED ARRAY ANTENNA
Q-BAY DOOR
DATA LINK SYSTEM E-BAY DOOR

Right: When designing the U-2R, Lockheed engineers made the aircraft easier to land than its predecessors, although it still takes a skilled pilot. Visible in this view is the rear-view mirror for checking if the aircraft is pulling a contrail, and the underfuselage glass dome for the driftsight optics.

resolution of 7.6 cm (3 in) from ranges of 240 km (150 miles). It's not quite reading someone's newspaper from orbit, but you can probably read the headlines.

Other sensors used to produce imagery include infra-red and video cameras, and radar systems. Modern synthetic aperture radars can produce images of almost photographic quality, and can do so through thick cloud or in the dead of night. Television cameras are also used to transmit information via satellite to ground stations, where intelligence officers can watch the scene below in real time, as it happens.

ELECTRONIC SPYING

Sigint (signals intelligence) is a vast and ever-growing area of reconnaissance, covering the gathering of information across the whole of the electromagnetic spectrum. It splits into a variety of different forms, dealing with deliberate and accidental transmissions. Comint, or communications intelligence, is quite simply eavesdropping on a

potential opponent's radio traffic. Many countries have specialised Comint aircraft, sucking up information across all wavebands, and recording them for later analysis.

Of course, much of the information gathered is in code, so the Comint community works closely with the code-breakers. Telint (telemetry intelligence) is a specialised form of Comint, involving the interception of guidance data transmitted between missiles and ground control during tests.

Right: First seeing service in 1968 over Vietnam, the Lockheed SR-71 is the world's fastest air-breathing aircraft, combining this performance with an even greater operational altitude than that of the U-2. The type has been used in all of the world's hot-spots.

Analysis of the data can give precise details of the missile's performance, which is useful information to have when you are negotiating arms treaties.

The primary purpose of a strategic reconnaissance system is to enable national command authorities to assess the military capacity of a target nation during peacetime, and to continue such a task if war breaks out. This kind of operation, carried out continuously over long

periods of time, is more properly known as surveillance. Strategic reconnaissance platforms need to gather information about as wide an area as possible in a single pass, so they have in the past tended to be high-altitude craft such as the Lockheed U-2 and the amazing Lockheed SR-71.

Conceived of in 1959 as a U-2 successor, the SR-71 flies faster than Mach 3 at over 30000 m (nearly 100,000 ft), and is in many

Above: Both U-2 (illustrated) and SR-71 aircrew wear David Clark pressure suits to protect them in the event of cockpit depressurisation at altitude. The suits are fully sealed, with an orange-coloured outer covering to protect them.

Right: The Lockheed Skunk Works was responsible for both the U-2 and SR-71. Here the ASARS-2 radar development U-2R flies in a rare formation with the resident Palmdale test SR-71A. Both types serve operationally with the 9th Reconnaissance Wing at Beale AFB, California.

respects still ahead of its time. Its first employment was probably by the CIA over China in its pre-series A-12 guise. In the early 1960s the 'Bamboo Curtain' was even more tightly closed than the 'Iron Curtain' and the USA especially wanted to extend its knowledge of what was going on at the Chinese nuclear weapons test sites in deepest Inner Mongolia. The A-12 first flew in 1962, and a few subsequently operated from Okinawa until replaced by SR-71s in 1968. Overflights of China ceased in 1971 when the Sino-American rapprochement began. By this time, control of such reconnaissance assets had passed from the CIA to Strategic Air Command.

In spite of the fact that the 'Blackbird' was not seriously threatened by interception from either aircraft or missiles, it was not used to penetrate Soviet airspace like its predecessor, instead flying its missions along the Soviet border and probing deep with its long-range sensors.

WATCH ON CUBA

The U-2 remains an important platform. CIA U-2s had continued to monitor Cuba and China after being withdrawn from Soviet overflights in 1960, playing a major part in the Cuban missile crisis. U-2 operations over China were mounted from Taiwan using a mix of American and Nationalist Chinese pilots, six of whom were lost to communist air defences, despite the provision of ever-more sophisticated ECM devices on the fragile bird.

The Chinese also bagged a number of US Air Force reconnaissance

drones starting in 1964, when a squadron from the SAC U-2 wing moved to the Far East for the first operational deployment of such craft. The 'Lightning Bug' was a development of the Ryan Firebee drone, and had been initiated by the Pentagon as an alternative U-2 replacement. Launched from the modified DC-130 Hercules, the drone flew high altitude photo-runs over southern and eastern China, to be recovered (in theory) by helicopters over friendly territory. Despite their successes, the drones had to fight a US Air Force bureaucracy which heavily favoured manned systems.

SCALED-UP DRAGON

The U-2R was an improved and scaled-up version of the original aircraft, introduced in 1968. It eventually took over the Elint monitoring task out of Osan and also played its part in Vietnam. One was sent to Akrotiri in 1970 to monitor an Israel-Egypt ceasefire, returning after the 1973 Yom Kippur War to perform similar duties on a semi-permanent basis.

Nowadays the bulk of the intelligence used in strategic planning comes from satellites. These look for a wide range of signs of military expansion, from major troop movements or the setting-up of new missile batteries to militarily significant economic changes, such as factories producing ammunition going on to a three-shift, 24-hour production schedule.

The boundary between strategic and tactical reconnaissance is a little blurred. In general, tactical reconnaissance is carried out on behalf of the battlefield commander, and is

Above: During the Vietnam War the 100th SRW made widespread use of Ryan AQM-34 drones to gain photographs and Elint data over North Vietnam. The drones were launched from Hercules and recovered by Sikorsky CH-3 helicopters. This aircraft was the high-time drone with 68 missions.

Below: The Yakovlev Yak-25RD 'Mandrake' was the Soviet equivalent of the Martin RB-57D. It was a long-winged version of the Yak-25 fighter, and was used on some high-altitude missions in the Middle East. The aircraft could not match the U-2 for altitude or range capability.

usually provided by variants of current high-performance aircraft. But strategic systems can also be used for tactical purposes. The TR-1 was a version of the U-2 put back into production in the 1980s to provide battlefield commanders with information, though it has since reverted to the U-2 designation. And SR-71s have made Mach 3 high-altitude reconnaissance flights to check out hostile defences before US military actions in the 1980s, in places

like Grenada, Libya and Panama.

The first Soviet airframe which was entirely dedicated to reconnaissance in this period was the Yakovlev design known to NATO as 'Mandrake'. Probably designated Yak-26, this 20500-m (67,255-ft) altitude aircraft utilised a Yak-25 fuselage married to a long, high-aspect ratio wing (as on the U-2). It was in service by 1963 and was reported over the Mediterranean and West Asia. It was replaced by

Elint platforms

While high-flying U-2s and SR-71s captured the public's imagination, it was the Sigint aircraft which were the intelligence workhorses of the Cold War, flying daily missions around the Soviet Union and its allies recording and analysing electronic signals. The 55th Strategic Reconnaissance Wing was the

premier USAF Sigint unit, exchanging its Boeing RB-47Hs for Boeing RC-135s in the 1960s. These veterans are still very much in service today, their onboard equipment having been continuously updated in response to developments in air defence systems and communications networks.

Boeing RC-135V Rivet Joint

The large internal capacity and excellent range/load performance made the C-135 tanker/transport an obvious choice for a Sigint platform. Eight RC-135Vs and six similar RC-135Ws are currently in service, augmented by a pair of RC-135Us used for more specialist work.

The Sigint suite of the RC-135 is served by large aerials under the fuselage and by batteries of side-facing antennae arranged in cheek fairings. In addition to the flight crew, the RC-135 carries about 17 equipment operators and inflight maintenance technicians.

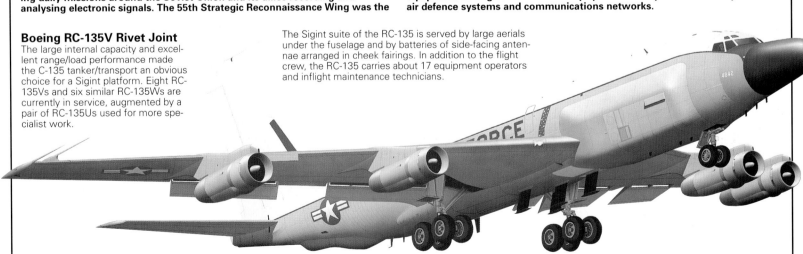

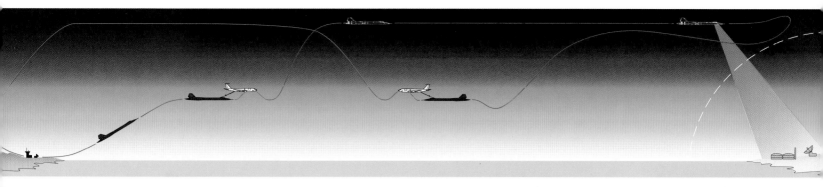

Blackbird mission

Even now, long after most of the fleet has retired, the targets, tactics and results of SR-71 missions remain highly classified. However, the US Air Force allowed its fliers to talk about other areas of their job. Major Duane Noll (pilot) and Major Tom Veltri (Reconnaissance Systems Officer) were one such crew.

"You'll always hear pilots talk about having to look in two or three places at one time," Major Noll said, "but here we have about six or seven things at one time and you're continually scanning the cockpit. In addition to the standard jet instruments we have an inlet system which incorporates another six or eight dials.

"When Tom gets in the sensitive area, he really goes to work. He not only has the cameras, but also the other sensors, the ECM gear and the repeater flight instruments. It's Tom's airplane in the sensitive area. I take off, I get the gas and get him to the target. From that point it's his mission."

Operating so close to unfriendly territory requires precise navigation to avoid embarrassing and potentially dangerous penetrations of hostile airspace. The main unit was the Northrop astro-inertial navigation system, which has a star-tracker peering through a small window behind the cockpit. Major Veltri explained the main problem:

"Because we can only hold 35° of bank, the airplane turns very slowly at supersonic speeds. We're talking about 200 miles to do a 360° turn. Quick turns are out of the question at Mach 3, so you have to keep a close check that everything is running to plan."

Even though the SR-71 was largely unassailable at its operating height and speed, it undoubtedly carried counter-measures, though details on ECM gear were classified. It was chased many times, but was never caught. Nevertheless, on paper it could have been intercepted by a well-placed MiG-25 'Foxbat' or by some of the large Soviet SAMs. As a result, it did not fly over hostile airspace, but used its great altitude and advanced equipment to peer deep into a target area from beyond any national borders.

The US Air Force would not discuss the SR-71's sensors, except for saying that they 'could survey 100,000 square miles [nearly 260000 km²] in one hour'. But it is probably accurate to propose that

they fell into three main areas: radar, optical and electronic.

The optical and radar sensors tend to be of the long range oblique type, directed sideways. Black and white photography is still a favourite medium, and the cameras carried by the SR-71 had large magnifications and ultra high resolution for the best possible interpretation. Side-looking radars were particularly good at spotting military installations and armoured formations.

Sigint (signals intelligence) gathering was the third discipline performed by the SR-71, and is considered one of great importance in today's electronic battlefield. Sigint sensors are even more classified than the radars and cameras, and can perform many tasks. The most common is the identification, location and 'fingerprinting' of hostile radars.

Above: A typical SR-71 mission shows the aircraft refuelling soon after take-off to top off its tanks before 'going hot' for its sensor pass on the target area. The aircraft then has to descend for another refuelling to enable it to reach its base safely. The aircraft usually stays outside hostile airspace, using its altitude to peer many miles inside the target territory. During overflights, the great speed keeps it safe from SAMs

Performance
The SR-71 is restricted in normal operations to Mach 3.2, but the aircraft can go faster. Its predecessor, the single-seat A-12 'Cygnus', was lighter and marginally faster, being clocked at Mach 3.56 although it was restricted in operations to Mach 3.3. The A-12 could also sustain an altitude of 27430m (90,000 ft) with ease.

Stealth features
The shape of the SR-71 was tailored to reduce its radar cross-section, while the structure incorporated large wedges of radar-attenuating material.

Powerplant
Power came from two Pratt & Whintey J58 bleed-bypass turbojets. These featured huge moveable inlet spikes.

Lockheed SR-71A

A total of 32 SR-71s was built, of which three were twin-stick trainers. Of these usually only six to ten were ever in active service at one time, based at Beale in the USA, Mildenhall in England and Kadena on Okinawa. Among the most notable missions were those launched from Kadena to photograph Iran.

Sensor carriage
Sensors were mounted in interchangeable nose sections (ASARS-1 radar or panoramic cameras) or in a series of bays along the fuselage bays (close-look Technical Objective cameras). Elint equipment could also be carried.

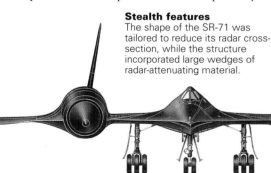

BLACKBIRD AREAS OF OPERATION

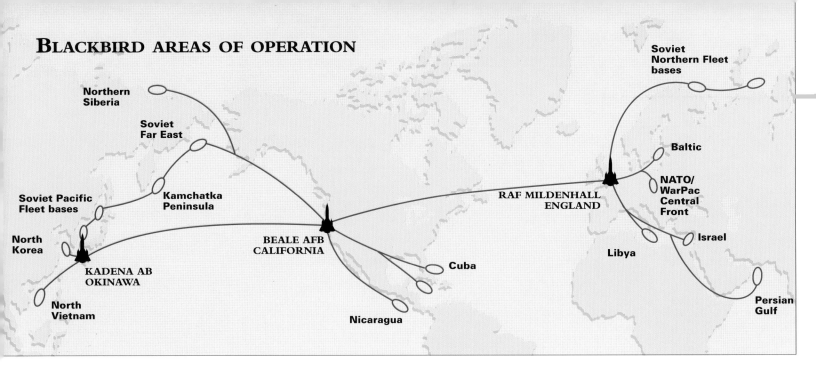

Northern Siberia · Soviet Far East · Soviet Pacific Fleet bases · Kamchatka Peninsula · North Korea · KADENA AB OKINAWA · North Vietnam · BEALE AFB CALIFORNIA · Cuba · Nicaragua · RAF MILDENHALL ENGLAND · Soviet Northern Fleet bases · Baltic · NATO/WarPac Central Front · Israel · Libya · Persian Gulf

Above: From its three bases world-wide, the SR-71 could easily reach all of the normal trouble spots, and with planning could be expected to visit anywhere else. At Beale the aircraft launched regularly on 'Clipper' sorties around Cuba, and was also used briefly over Nicaragua. From Mildenhall the SR-71 regularly covered the German border, Baltic Sea and North Cape, and ventured into the Mediterranean when required. The Kadena-based 'Habus' plied their trade along the Pacific Rim, targeting Vietnam, China, North Korea and the Soviet Far East. The longest missions were those flown from Kadena to the Persian Gulf, and by aircraft launching from the eastern US seaboard to the Suez canal zone. The latter provided intelligence to the Israelis during the Yom Kippur war, and had to be flown from the US as the UK denied the use of its bases.

Below: This Sigint-gatherer is an RC-135D, originally used by the 6th Strategic Wing in Alaska on missions aimed against the Soviet Far East. These aircraft were occasionally deployed to Kadena to augment the Vietnam War effort which was mostly flown by RC-135Ms.

Above: The Soviets developed the MiG-25R 'Foxbat-B' as a high- and fast-flying camera ship. Capable of Mach 3.2 for a short burst, the type flew missions over Israel from Egyptian bases. Later SLAR- and Elint- equipped versions were developed.

the Mikoyan Gurevich MiG-25R 'Foxbat', which is considered to be an excellent reconnaissance aircraft by Western analysts, even if its interceptor version was downgraded in esteem after one was flown to Japan by a defecting pilot in 1976. The 'Foxbat' first appeared in Egypt during 1970, and it proceeded to defeat Israeli attempts at interception during supersonic, high-altitude runs down the Suez Canal and off the Israeli coast. It also flew unopposed over Iran. The 'Foxbat-B' carries cameras and a small SLAR: the 'Foxbat-D' sacrifices the cameras for a larger SLAR. Top altitude for both models is in the order of 26800 m (87,925 ft) – only the SR-71 routinely flies higher.

Elint (electronic intelligence) is a specialised and very important form of Sigint. Elint aircraft are equipped with highly sensitive receivers tuned to the frequencies of the radar defences of a potential enemy. Their task is the recording and analysis of enemy signals in order to work out the best ways to jam or evade the radar net. Most of the time they stay well clear of the enemy borders, but occasionally they will press in close to set the enemy defences in motion. This provides a wealth of intelligence, on subjects like the sensitivity and range of the defence network and the speed of reaction of its interceptors.

ELECTRONIC C-135

A few US Air Force Boeing KC-135 tankers were modified with a SLAR system in 1962, but in 1965 the custom-built RC-135 version of the Model 707 transport was introduced. This aircraft has been the major platform for SAC's Elint collection activities ever since, and has been progressively modified with ever more sophisticated sensors and signal processing equipment. Eleven Elint specialists were carried, and the flight crew was augmented by a relief pilot and a second navigator, essential for the long-endurance, along-the-border flying in remote areas undertaken by these aircraft

At the height of the Cold War the RC-135s operated by the 55th Strategic Reconnaissance Wing flew from their home base at Offutt, and from detachments at Mildenhall in England, Athens in Greece and Kadena in Okinawa. In addition, Eielson AB Alaska and Shemya in the Aleutians have housed a few other exotic Elint conversions of the KC-135.

NAVAL EW PLATFORMS

US Navy shore-based Elint duties are performed by a dedicated variant of the Lockheed P-3 Orion, while carrier-borne duties were performed in succession by variants of the Douglas Skyknight, the Douglas Skywarrior, and most recently by the Lockheed Viking. Britain replaced its electronic warfare Comets in the 1970s with three British Aerospace Nimrod R.Mk 1s, which were supplemented by reconnaissance-dedicated variants of the Handley-Page Victor and the Avro Vulcan. Sweden, France, and Germany also used converted airliners, bombers, or long-range maritime patrol aircraft as electronic listening platforms.

By contrast, the Soviet Union did not follow the trend towards the utilisation of transport airframes as Elint platforms until the mid-1970s, when versions of the Antonov An-12 and Ilyushin Il-18 were first noted. They were also about ten years behind the West in embarking upon routine, long-range reconnaissance bomber probes of opposing defences. In high-altitude supersonic reconnaissance they were also some years in arrears. These delays were largely the result of deficiencies in the Soviets' airframe and electronics technology – never admitted, sometimes uncovered by reconnaissance, and yet still often only realised in the West by hindsight.

Of course, this time-lag was not so crucial when one considers that the equivalent of much of the intelligence that the West was painstakingly ferreting out from behind the Iron Curtain was available to the Soviets for the price of an unclassified electronics handbook or a good road map. Their own atlases deliberately displaced cities and other prominent features in order to confuse the West.

BOMBER CONVERSIONS

The trio of long-range bombers which the Soviets developed in the 1950s began to make their first appearances in international airspace towards the end of that decade. They were the Myasishchev M-4, Tupolev Tu-16 and Tupolev Tu-95, otherwise known to NATO as the 'Bison', 'Badger' and 'Bear'.

'Badger-D' models with enlarged nose radar and three additional ventral areas began flying

Above: Blessed with enormous range capability, the Tupolev Tu-95RT 'Bear-D' snooped around Western navies, fingerprinting the radar fits of NATO vessels. The aircraft also had an over-the-horizon missile targeting role.

Right: Tu-16 'Badgers' in various configurations were widely used on Sigint and general reconnaissance flights. But most of their attentions were for maritime targets, although they regularly probed NATO air defence systems.

Elint missions against US radars in the Pacific. The 'Badger-E' with large cameras in the bomb bay and nose made its first appearance in 1963, followed closely by the 'Badger-F' with pylon-mounted Elint pods under each wing.

The workhorse type was undoubtedly the 'Bear', which first entered service in 1956 and was still in production 35 years later. Its very long unrefuelled radius enabled it to be employed on flights of over 20 hours duration. The 'Bear-E' was a photographic platform, but the

major Elint version was the 'Bear-D' which was mainly flown by the Soviet naval air force. First seen in 1967, this version has flown non-stop from the Murmansk area via the Iceland-UK gap to Cuba or Conakry in the West African state of Guinea. Alternatively, it has flown down the eastern side of the UK inviting interception from RAF fighters before turning back

north, or perhaps east and into the Baltic. Another regular run was from Ukrainian airfields, across the Black Sea and through the Bosphorus for a Mediterranean patrol, perhaps continuing southwards to land in Aden or Somalia. They also probed US defences from Alaska to Pearl Harbor, often operating from the US-built facility at Cam Ranh Bay in Vietnam.

Soviet intelligence gatherers

Unlike the West, the Soviet Union did not have a string of bases surrounding its potential enemy, and relied mainly on long-range roving patrols over international waters and non-aircraft means

to gather its intelligence. A handful of bases (notably in Angola, Guinea, Cuba, Vietnam and Yemen) provide the long-range 'Bears' with some global destinations to head for.

Ilyushin Il-20 'Coot'
Left: This conversion of the Il-18 airliner performed a Sigint/radar reconnaissance role. It carried a large side-looking radar under the fuselage, and optical sensors in the fuselage side fairings. An extensive Elint suite onboard allowed sophisticated radar fingerprinting.

Tupolev Tu-95RT
Below: Equipped with a massive search radar under its belly, the Tu-95RT was used to find and track Western warships. It also had electronic listening equipment for identification and analysis of maritime air defence and other systems.

Anti Submarine Warfare

1970 – 1996

The Tupolev 'Bear' had phenomenal range, and was used by the Soviet navy for maritime patrols worldwide. But closer to home it was also tasked with hunting down Western hunter-killer submarines.

If World War III had ever broken out, it is most likely that the opening shots would have been fired in the icy waters of the North Atlantic, the Norwegian Sea and the Arctic Ocean.

Soviet naval forces had a major problem. If they were to interfere with NATO's transatlantic lifeline in time of war, they had to get out into the Atlantic. But to do that, they had to get from their bases in the Baltic, the Black Sea and the far north of the Soviet Union through geographical 'choke points', where NATO would be waiting.

The primary route was via the 'GIUK Gap': the 300 km

Right: Britain's Lynx is one of the fastest and most capable light naval helicopters currently in service. It is carried by many NATO destroyers and frigates as their principal ASW weapon.

(185 mile)-wide Denmark Strait between Greenland and Iceland, and the 800 km (500 miles) of sea between Iceland, the Faroe Islands and Britain.

Even in peacetime, maritime aircraft patrolled the GIUK Gap constantly, and the movement of every Soviet vessel passing into or out of the Atlantic was carefully monitored and plotted. ASW crews were among the few NATO personnel

Anti-sub Helicopters

The development of the helicopter has changed many aspects of warfare, and nowhere is that more true than at sea. ASW helicopters armed with dipping sonar, sonobuoys, depth charges and lightweight homing torpedoes have extended both the sensor and weapons range of surface combatants from the visual horizon out to 100 km (60 miles) and more.

Sikorsky SH-60 Sea Hawk
Right: Developed from the US Army's UH-60 Blackhawk utility helicopter, the Sea Hawk is used aboard vessels from frigate size right up to the largest US Navy supercarrier. It can be used for transport, rescue, and for light anti-shipping strikes with air-to-surface missiles as well as for ASW. It is used by Japan and Australia in addition to the US Navy

Westland Sea King
Seen here in its earlier days with the Royal Navy, the British-built variant of the long-serving Sikorsky Sea King is a sophisticated submarine hunter. It is equipped with a sea-search radar, advanced electronic systems, sonobuoys and a dipping sonar capable of being deployed more than 200 m (655 feet) beneath the surface of the ocean.

High-tech Hunters

The ocean is a big place, and a submerged submarine is not easy to find. Successful maritime reconnaissance and anti-submarine aircraft need to be able to cover vast distances in their patrols, combining incredibly long endurance with the ability to use very advanced sensors and avionics and to deliver a wide range of weaponry.

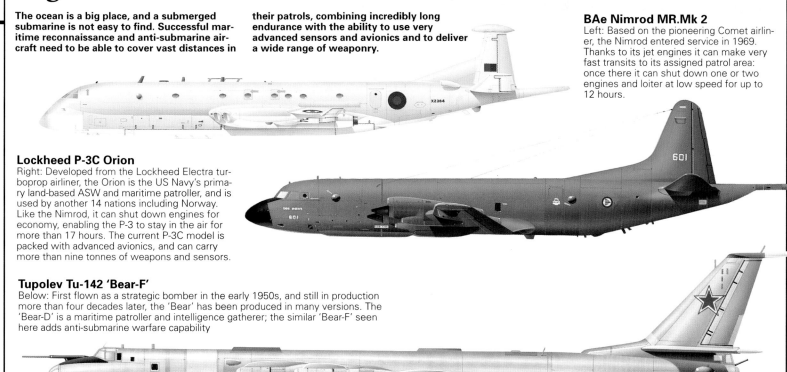

BAe Nimrod MR.Mk 2
Left: Based on the pioneering Comet airliner, the Nimrod entered service in 1969. Thanks to its jet engines it can make very fast transits to its assigned patrol area: once there it can shut down one or two engines and loiter at low speed for up to 12 hours.

Lockheed P-3C Orion
Right: Developed from the Lockheed Electra turboprop airliner, the Orion is the US Navy's primary land-based ASW and maritime patroller, and is used by another 14 nations including Norway. Like the Nimrod, it can shut down engines for economy, enabling the P-3 to stay in the air for more than 17 hours. The current P-3C model is packed with advanced avionics, and can carry more than nine tonnes of weapons and sensors.

Tupolev Tu-142 'Bear-F'
Below: First flown as a strategic bomber in the early 1950s, and still in production more than four decades later, the 'Bear' has been produced in many versions. The 'Bear-D' is a maritime patroller and intelligence gatherer; the similar 'Bear-F' seen here adds anti-submarine warfare capability

who carried out their war roles for real, with live weapons.

The Soviet threat was multi-layered. Missile-armed aircraft like the long-range Tupolev 'Bear' bomber were one part of the web, along with missile cruisers and destroyers on the surface. But the major threat came from the huge Soviet submarine force. Primitive, noisy and short-ranged in the early post-war years, by the 1980s the Red Fleet was fielding some of the largest, fastest and most sophisticated boats ever built.

A surfaced submarine is an easy target for any aircraft, but once it has slipped beneath the waves it presents a uniquely challenging problem. In every other military field you can rely on visual, radar or infra-red techniques to detect and home-in on targets, but under the sea, except for some special cases, you have to rely on sound. But it is impossible for an aircraft flying through the air to detect sound directly through the barrier of the ocean's surface. It cannot dip a hydrophone into the water like a helicopter, a surface ship or a submarine. Without some kind of sound-sensing device, it has to rely on MAD Magnetic Anomaly Detection) gear, or radar.

DETECTION BY SOUND
The solution to the problem is the sonobuoy. Sonobuoys are expendable acoustic systems, ejected from the aircraft as it flies over the surface of the ocean. These send data via radio to the aircraft overhead, which can then use homing torpedoes or nuclear depth charges to attack any target revealed.

Orions of the Royal Norwegian Air Force based at Andøya were the first to react to any movement of Soviet submarines from their bases on the Kola Peninsula. First warning would probably have come from the SOSUS line of underwater sensors stretching from Norway to Spitzbergen.

Iceland was the hinge upon which NATO'S efforts to 'bottle up' the Soviet fleet depended. US Navy P-3s based at Keflavik flew missions over the Denmark Strait and over the gap between Iceland and the Faroes. Even in peacetime, America kept an Orion squadron active on the island, with smaller detachments at bases in Britain and Norway.

Britain's Nimrod maritime patrol aircraft flew out of bases in the north of Scotland and in the far south-west of England. The Scottish-based aircraft were part of the NATO ASW force assigned to closing the GIUK Gap.

Typically, Nimrods would mount search patrols up to 1600 km (1,000 miles) from home, at which range they could stay on station for more than six hours. With aerial refuelling the aircraft could stay on patrol for as long as 18 hours, crew fatigue being a limiting factor on the length of missions.

Above: Modern ASW aircraft like the P-3 can be datalinked to specialised ASW vessels like the FFG-7-class frigate, creating an ASW team of great efficiency. Both platforms are in service with the USA, Spain and Australia.

Right: The Atlantique 2 is the latest variant of the Franco-German Atlantic. Currently in service with France's Aeronavale, the Atlantique 2 carries state-of-the-art avionics and ASW weapons.

SAC's Last Years

1970-1992

Left: The evergreen Boeing B-52 has soldiered on long beyond the wildest dreams of its designers. Even though the development of advanced Soviet defences made its survival as a penetration bomber problematical, it found a strategic role in the 1980s as a stand-off attacker armed with air-launched cruise missiles.

As the Cold War continued relentlessly into the 1970s and 1980s, the surest way for a Strategic Air Command (SAC) officer to be proven wrong was to develop a schedule to put the B-52 out to pasture. At various times, planners drew up itineraries which would fly the last Stratofortress to the boneyard in 1968, or 1975, or 1984. None of the target dates was reached. It never happened, even while exploring new technologies and looking at future bombers

Just as the B-52 refused to go away, the second candidate named as its replacement also refused to disappear. A decade after the failed XB-70, the Rockwell B-1A was developed to replace the Stratofortress. The XB-70 Valkyrie of the early 1960s was doomed when the advent of the surface-to-air missile forced bombers from high to low altitude. Modifications enabled the B-52 to adjust to this change in the conduct of warfare, but the XB-70 was intended to fly at great heights and was not amenable to being modified.

The second attempt to groom an replacement for the B-52 began with a request to American industry dated 3 November 1969. Rockwell received the nod with a 5 June 1970 contract to build five (later reduced to four) Rockwell B-1A Advanced Manned Strategic Aircraft (AMSAs). The first all-white B-1A flew at Palmdale, California on 23 December 1974.

STOP-START PROGRAM

On 30 June 1977, President Jimmy Carter cancelled B-1A development. In part because of the difficulty of developing a heavy bomber to replace the B-52, SAC began to operate two combat wings of General Dynamics FB-111A swing-wing strike aircraft, based on the F-111 used by tactical units. The FB-111A remained in service until the early 1990s.

Carter's hope to reduce the Cold War arms race did not outlast his term in office. In October 1981, President Ronald Reagan revived plans for the Rockwell bomber – in effect, rendering Carter's decision void. The US Air Force demanded significant changes in the original design, and announced in September 1981 that it would order 100 B-1Bs with improved avionics, structure, and engine inlets, now designated B-1B. A new flight program began on 23 March 1983.

In the free-spending 1980s when Ronald Reagan routinely referred to the Soviet Union as the 'Evil Empire', enormous amounts were spent on incredibly ambitious projects including an improved Intercontinental Ballistic Missile (ICBM) and the Strategic Defense Initiative: the 'Star Wars' missile defence. Many Pentagon officers regarded the prospect of nuclear war with Moscow as real, imminent, and more important than smaller conflicts around the globe – just as their predecessors had done three decades earlier. The top brass in the 1980s did not have the means to make SAC as large as it had been in the 1950s, but they did have a way to put the Strategic Air Command on the cutting edge of technology. Their shining hope was the stealthy Advanced Technology Bomber, which emerged from years of secrecy as the Northrop B-2 Spirit flying wing. The B-2's main mission was to attack 'mobile, relocatable targets' not easy to engage with ICBMs – that is, rail-

Left: The MGM-118A Peacekeeper, previously known as the MX missile, was the ultimate SAC ICBM. It carried up to 10 independently targeted manoeuvring re-entry vehicles, each accurate to within 120 m (130 yards) after a flight of 11000 km (6,835 miles).

Below: The General Dynamics FB-111 was a long-range version of the swing-wing tactical bomber. Armed with AGM-69 SRAM nuclear missiles, it was designed to race in ahead of the main bomber force to destroy key nodes in the Soviet air defence network.

Left: An evolution of the original Mach 2 B-1A, the B-1B is a highly sophisticated low-level penetrator able to carry massive weapons loads at transonic speeds.

way-based ICBMs – with nuclear bombs and stand-off weapons.

HIGH-TECH FUTURE

To those who knew, the B-2 was the future of SAC. The Air Force would procure 132 of them to equip a dozen squadrons in five combat wings, scattered among SAC's many air bases. The very public and highly publicised Rockwell B-1B was, in the view of these men, merely an 'interim'

weapon until the B-2 arrived.

One strong argument for the B-2 is its flexibility. Unlike an ICBM, the B-2 can be 'flushed' – that is, deployed in an airborne alert pattern or even started towards its target, but it is still possible for the aircraft to be recalled. And unlike a submarine-launched ballistic missile, it is extremely accurate against mobile targets, including rail-mounted ICBMs.

While the USAF publicly pro-

moted the B-1B and secretly developed the B-2, the first B-1B was ceremoniously delivered to SAC at Offutt AFB, Nebraska on 27 July 1985. The first operational B-1Bs went to the 96th Bomb Wing at Dyess AFB, Texas. One hundred B-1Bs were manufactured. Today, the USAF is upgrading them and shifting their duties so that most can now carry out conventional bombing missions.

The 1990s were a time of global change. In 1991, the world was treated to the sight of the ageless B-52 Stratofortress bombing Saddam Hussein's Republican Guards during the Gulf War. Among these were missions with C-ALCMs (Conventional warhead Air-Launched Cruise Missiles).

With the Berlin Wall being torn down, the Soviet Union fragmenting, and US attention shifting to trouble spots in the Persian Gulf, Somalia and Bosnia, the stealthy B-2 was suddenly very visible. One officer said it stood out like a sore thumb – not only because of its amazing cost but also for having capabilities which were inappropri-

ate and unnecessary for the times.

In a dramatic move reflecting the changing world order, President George Bush ordered a stand-down of all US nuclear alert forces on 28 September 1991. For the first time in nearly half a century, bombers no longer waited at the ready with thermonuclear weapons in their bays.

Striving toward a strength of 40 combat wings in the free-spending 1980s, the USAF went into the 1990s expecting to operate with only 17 combat wings. The B-2 stealth bomber, which in many ways seemed the epitome of everything SAC represented, was never to serve in SAC at all.

THE END OF AN ERA

Reflecting a new world without a Soviet Union, a world in which the 'hot' war of the 1990s had been Operation Desert Storm, Strategic Air Command went out of business on 1 June 1992. On that date, SAC's bomber wings were merged with stateside tactical air units to create a new Air Combat Command (ACC) headquartered at Langley AFB, Virginia. Since then, the tankers formerly operated by SAC have been reassigned to Air Mobility Command (AMC) at Scott AFB, Illinois.

Above: Designed for Strategic Air Command, but entering service after the reorganisation of the US Air Force which saw its dissolution, The Northrop B-2 'stealth' bomber is the most advanced and most expensive warplane ever built.

Right: As newer bombers have come on line to take up the strategic mission, the 70-odd surviving B-52H aircraft have been freed for more conventional roles. These include very long-range maritime operations.

Cruise carrier

Universally known throughout the B-52 community as the 'Cadillac', the 'H' model introduced significant enhancement of the veteran bomber's load/range performance, crew comfort and weapons delivery

capability. The 70 or so remaining aircraft, most being much older than the crews which fly them, are set to remain in service well into the 21st century, giving the B-52 over half a century of front line use.

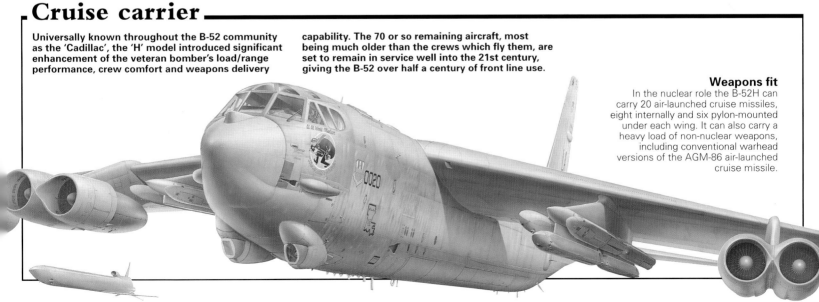

Weapons fit

In the nuclear role the B-52H can carry 20 air-launched cruise missiles, eight internally and six pylon-mounted under each wing. It can also carry a heavy load of non-nuclear weapons, including conventional warhead versions of the AGM-86 air-launched cruise missile.

Last Cold War Defenders

1980-1993

Left: To this day the F-15 Eagle rules the roost as the arguably the world's best fighter. USAF aircraft are deployed to Europe, Alaska and the Far East as the spearhead of the Western air defences. F-15s from CONUS bases regularly practise deployments to regions such as the Middle East.

Above: Elderly fighters such as the F-4 Phantom have kept apace with modern fighter development with update programmes. While little can be done with the airframes other than life extension, radar and weapon system capability can be dramatically enhanced. This is a Luftwaffe F-4F.

B y the end of the 1980s, the nature of the Cold War had altered. Perestroika and Glasnost had dramatically changed the structure and outlook of the Soviet Union, bringing the possibility of some kind of rapprochement with the West. Even so, fighter interceptors remained on the alert all over the world. From the Far East and Siberia to the North Sea and Alaska, over Scandinavia and Alaska, pilots sat ready to take off at a moment's notice. Their mission was to locate, deter, and if necessary destroy hostile aircraft penetrating defended airspace.

The quickest reactions were required along the boundary between East and West, most importantly the Central Front in Germany.

Intercepts fell into a number of categories. The primary threat was seen as aircraft from East Germany or Czechoslovakia detected by radar approaching or crossing the border. A rapid reaction was required to counter such a threat, for there was always the chance that these might have been the advance echelons of a pre-emptive strike against the West. However, navigational errors are much more likely causes of unintentional border crossings, and it was essential that the fighter pilot, whether flying and American F-15 Eagle, a Dutch F-16 or a German F-4 should divine the intentions of any intruder.

Obviously a weapon-carrying strike aircraft which showed no signs of turning back would have required swift action on the part of the fighter. All air defence interceptors carried live weapons for use in the last resort. However, the analysis of intent is of prime importance during this phase of the mission: the destruction of an aircraft that accidentally violated West German airspace would have had serious diplomatic and military repercussions. An inadvertent border crossing in peacetime requires a different reaction, and the hope was that the presence of the NATO fighter would be enough to make it turn back, though warning shots might have been required.

FACING WARPAC

By far the majority of scrambles were to the aid of Western aircraft that strayed near the border. Warsaw Pact defences were just as ready for action as those in the West, but they were far more likely to shoot than their NATO counterparts. Once the aircraft under investigation had been declared safe, or shepherded away from danger, the fighters were free to return to base.

Yet though it was never exer-

Left: In the interceptor role the F-15 uses its quick-start capability and enormous power to react rapidly to any potential threat. In Europe the F-15 stood 'Zulu' alert at Bitburg, covering the 4 ATAF region which encompassed the southern half of West Germany.

Below: The General Dynamics F-16A was a new breed of fighter: supremely agile in a dogfight, but just as capable in the attack role. The purchase of F-16s by Belgium, Denmark, the Netherlands and Norway dramatically enhanced European air defences.

NATO Interceptors

In northern Europe NATO directly faced the cream of the Warsaw Pact air forces, and deployed large numbers of interceptors to meet the expected threat from the East. USAF F-15s and RAF Phantoms stood alert in Germany, while the RAF also patrolled the northern waters from where a bomber attack was most likely to have come.

McDonnell Douglas F-15
USAF Europe was an early recipient of the F-15, and at the peak of the force had a three-squadron wing at Bitburg in West Germany, augmented by the 32nd TFS (illustrated) based at Soesterberg (Camp New Amsterdam) in the Netherlands.

Panavia Tornado ADV
The dedicated fighter version of the Tornado was an RAF-specific design with a primary mission of maritime air defence. It was expected to loiter a long way from land and then destroy bombers as they approached Europe from the Arctic Ocean. This aircraft is an F.Mk 2 from 229 OCU, the training unit.

cised, their reason for being was to counter the strike from the east. The constant nagging thought that the next alert warning might have sounded for a force of 'Fencers' or 'Backfires' instead of a lost light plane ensured that everyone in the air defence community applied 100 per cent effort and concentration. As 'games' go, none was more serious than that played by the men on air defence alert.

MARITIME AIR DEFENCE
Further away from the potential front line, fighters faced very different problems, even if the mission to intercept, identify and if necessary destroy intruders was basically the same. Island nations like Britain and Japan would have had more warning of attack, and aimed to mount their intercepts far out to sea. Norwegian and British fighters together with US interceptors on Iceland were tasked with preventing Soviet bombers from getting

Below: In the 1980s the RAF introduced the Mixed Fighter Force concept, which envisaged the use of Tornado F.Mk 3s as a 'mini-AWACS'. The Tornado's long-range Foxhunter radar enabled its navigator to vector radarless but Sidewinder-armed Hawk trainers on to hostile targets.

out into the Atlantic, while the defence of the United States and Canada was aimed at stopping attacks over the pole and across Alaska.

Britain was typical of the air defence regions which NATO established. It was a prime Warsaw Pact target during the Cold War, being NATO's vital rear depot and collecting point for men and supplies, as well as being the base for a third of the Alliance's combat aircraft. As a result, the RAF's responsibility was both to protect the citizens of the United Kingdom and to keep NATO's supply lines open.

The UK Air Defence Region covers nearly 10 million km² (4 million sq miles) around Britain's coasts, from the English Channel and the North Sea round via the Shetlands and Faeroes out into the Atlantic almost as far as Iceland. Such a huge area requires continual vigilance to patrol.

But vigilance is not enough in the modern world of fast, cruise missile-armed, low-flying bombers. In the 1980s British defences were upgraded to cope with the new threat. It was a far-reaching programme, involving the introduction of the Tornado F.Mk 3 interceptor, the Boeing Sentry

AWACS airborne early warning system, new mobile ground radars, new command and control centres hardened against nuclear attack, expanded missile defences, increased weapons stocks, increasing the number of interceptors available by arming Hawk trainers with AIM-9 Sidewinders, and developing a

Above: Although the major confrontation between East and West was in Europe, it was a world-wide phenomenon. This Alaskan-based F-15 has intercepted a Soviet 'Bear' over the North Pacific.

Below: To further its ability to detect airborne intruders from the East NATO turned to the Boeing E-3 AWACS, which in addition to the USAF was purchased by the RAF, France and a joint NATO force.

highly computerised nationwide command and communications network to improve battle management.

Literally hundreds of Soviet reconnaissance flights were intercepted in the last years of the Cold War, from the North Sea to the North Slope of Alaska. The crews of Soviet 'Bears' and 'Badgers' became accustomed to seeing a Phantom, Tornado, Tomcat or Eagle appear on their wing to escort them out of sensitive areas or to keep them clear of NATO exercises.

But the increase in capability was not confined to NATO. In many ways, the Soviet Union had an even more impressive defensive network, and it was a network which it was not afraid to use in anger. Over the years, more than 20 American aircraft – ranging from U-2 spyplanes to transports straying off course – were shot down over or around the Soviet Union. However, this readiness to open fire has led to tragedy, most notably in the 1983 destruction of an off-course Korean Air Lines Boeing 747, destroyed over Sakhalin island

in 1983, which cost the lives of all 269 passengers and crew.

In the 1980s a profound upgrading programme transformed Soviet air defence forces, the V-PVO, in part because of failings revealed in the KAL shoot down. Responsible for all ground- and air-based defensive systems, the V-PVO was reorganised in its last Soviet years. It was divided into three huge air defence zones, comprising Urals-Western Siberia; Eastern Siberia-Transbaikal; and South Urals-Volga. Only the Moscow Air Defence district survived from before.

V-PVO FORCE

In the late 1980s the V-PVO had a strength of over 1,250 aircraft These included around 500 Sukhoi Su-15 'Flagons', MiG-25 'Foxbats' and Yakovlev Yak-28 'Firebars'

from earlier generations of fighters. Competent enough to intercept high-level intruders, they (or more accurately, their radars) were much less capable against low-level threats.

However, the introduction into service of long-range interceptors like the Mikoyan MiG-31 'Foxhound' and the Sukhoi Su-27 'Flanker' gave the Soviets a new generation of fighters whose superb performance was matched by advanced new radars and some of the best air-to-air weaponry in the world.

In addition to the dedicated air defence aircraft, the Soviets could call on around 2,000 tactical interceptors from Frontal Aviation. Fighters like the swing-wing MiG-23 'Flogger' were perfectly adequate for some kinds of air defence,

Above: The Su-27 'Flanker' represented a major advance in Soviet fighter capability, and its ability to escort bombers from their home bases all the way to targets as far west as the UK posed NATO real problems.

Right: In the final years of the Cold War NATO would have found itself facing the very manoeuvrable MiG-29 over the German battlefield. By the time of the reunification of Germany, the type was the most numerous in the 16th Air Army.

Soviet Interceptors

Traditionally tied wholly to cumbersome ground controlled intercept systems and procedures, Soviet interceptors were slowly freed from these shackles during the 1980s as weapon systems became more capable. A greater accent was placed on manoeuvrability and performance, allowing a well-flown MiG-29 or Su-27 to match the West's F-15 and F-16. Weapons development also proceeded apace, capitalising in the Soviet Union's acknowledged lead in many areas of missile technology. At the same time, force numbers remained high compared to NATO.

Sukhoi Su-15 'Flagon'
Right: Representative of the 'old school' of Soviet interceptors, the Su-15 had exceptional speed and altitude performance, long-range missiles and a crude yet powerful radar. Interceptor operations were virtually always flown under tight ground control.

Sukhoi Su-27 'Flanker'
Left: One of NATO's most unpleasant surprises of the 1980s was the appearance of the phenomenally agile and fast-climbing Su-27, attended by a subtle change to more autonomous operations. Able to fly escort or intercept missions at very long range, the Su-27 also carried up to 10 missiles, including both radar- and IR-guided versions of the capable R-27/AA-10 'Alamo'.

The destruction of KAL 007

At 0326 (local time) on the morning of 1 September 1983, Major Vassily Kasmin, an experienced Soviet fighter pilot, launched two deadly AA-3 'Anab' missiles from the underwing pylons of his Sukhoi Su-15 'Flagon-F' interceptor. His target was a Boeing 747 of Korean Airlines, with 29 crew and 240 passengers aboard.

"I am closing in on the target, am in lock-on. Distance to the target 8 [hundred metres]."

With these words, Major Kasmin, on the instructions of ground control, pronounced the death sentence on 269 people.

"I have executed the launch." Two seconds later he added, "The target is destroyed. I am breaking off the attack"

The shoot down of flight KE 007, on the last leg of a scheduled passenger service from New York to Seoul, has been the subject of violent controversy in the years since the tragedy.

One of the few undoubted facts is that the airliner was more than 400 km (250 miles) north of of its planned route, taking it from the safety of international airspace into the highly dangerous skies over some of the most sensitive military installations in the Soviet Union.

Flown by an experienced crew under Captain Chun Byung In, KE 007 took off from Alaska at 1250 GMT, about 30 minutes late. It began to deviate from its planned track almost immediately. The 747 was 19 km (12 miles) north of its assigned route by the time it reached Bethel, the first waypoint.

About one hour later a small blue light would have illuminated on the instrument panel, indicating that the big Boeing was being observed on radar. Chun may have

believed that he was being tracked by an American radar based in the Aleutians, but the truth was more sinister. The monolithic Soviet air defence organisation was already treating the 747 as a potential hostile, initially referring to the radar blip as an RC-135 spyplane, and later simply as 'the target'.

At 1600 another KAL aircraft relayed a message that KE007 was passing the Neeva waypoint. In fact the straying Jumbo was 240 km (150 miles) further north, about to enter Soviet airspace, and heading straight for the Kamchatka Peninsula 645 km (400 miles) ahead. Moments later a USAF RC-135 electronic intelligence-gathering aircraft crossed in front of the Korean aircraft, leading to later claims by the Soviets that there had been a deliberate rendezvous.

As the Boeing flew over the

Kamchatka Peninsula six Soviet MiG-23 'Flogger' fighters were apparently scrambled, but not until the last moment, and they failed to intercept the airliner. As they crossed the west coast the co-pilot made a radio call, reporting that they were passing waypoint Nippi. By this time they were actually 250 miles further north. Less than an hour ahead lay the island of Sakhalin, where Soviet fighters were already being prepared to intercept the intruder.

At 1742 GMT, the Soviet fighter controllers scrambled a Sukhoi Su-15TM 'Flagon-F', flown by Major Kasmin, followed by three MiG-23 'Floggers'.

According to Major Kasmin, he flew several close passes by the 747, and fired four bursts of tracer shells past the nose all without response before making his final, fatal attack.

Nobody knows why the big airliner was so far off course. It is very unlikely to have been a spy flight. It could have been an instrument error, although with three sophisticated inertial navigation systems it seems unlikely. Pilot error is possible, even with such an experienced flight crew, especially if erroneous data had been fed into the navigation system. It could have been a simple case of mistaken identity by a rigid, inflexible Soviet air defence system which only saw an American spyplane intruding into highly restricted military airspace.

But whatever the cause, the destruction of KE 007 was a tragic illustration of the Cold War threat implicit in the words printed onto every air chart of the region:

"WARNING: aircraft infringing on Non-Free Flying Territory may be fired on without warning."

After reportedly firing warning cannon shots across the bow of the KAL 747, the Su-15TM of Major Kasmin positioned behind the airliner to fire the two K-8 missiles which destroyed the aircraft. The tragedy illustrated just how rigid the Soviet air defence system was, and how closely controlled from the ground Soviet interceptors were.

---

but with the introduction of tactical 'Flankers' and superb dogfighters like the MiG-29 'Fulcrum' battlefield intercept capability also increased dramatically.

To this should be added the potent missile net. SAM production in the mid-1980s peaked at about 50,000 missiles per year, providing for replacement of the obsolete SA-1 and augmentation of the ageing SA-2 and SA-3s. Giant SA-5s provide long-range defence (up to 300 km/185 miles) and the SA-10 and SA-12 were brought into service.

The former, a Mach 6 weapon, was claimed to be effective against the cruise missiles which formed one pillar of the West's deterrence, whilst the SA-12 will engage a target at any height from 30 to 30500 m (100 to 100,000 ft) up to 100 km (62 miles) from its launcher.

Right: Until recently elderly interceptors like this Su-15 played an important part in the defence of the Soviet Union/CIS. Although not able to deal with modern low-level attackers, they were deployed in areas where they would only be likely to face NATO's bombers.

Post-Soviet Conflicts

1991–1996

The collapse of the Soviet Union and the Communist Party after the failure of the hardline coup of August 1991 set in train a series of destructive conflicts on the fringes of the old Soviet empire. The successor states in the Caucasus have used the vast arsenals left behind by withdrawing Red Army troops to fight a series of vicious wars. These conflicts have yet to run their course.

ARMENIA AND AZERBAIJAN

The first Caucasus conflict of the post-Soviet era actually slightly pre-dated the end of the Soviet Union. Since 1989 tension had been high between Armenia and Azerbaijan over the disputed enclave of Nagorny-Karabakh, which was inside the borders of Muslim Azerbaijan but had a largely Christian Armenian population. The two newly independent states inherited much of the Soviet military materiel on their territory and

Below: The end of the Warsaw Pact has seen the huge Soviet military machine formerly in place in Easern Europe pulled back to Russia. Many like this Mil Mi-24 'Hind' have exchanged the Cold War for a bitter struggle in the breakaway republic of Chechnya.

set about forming national armies and air forces. Ex-Soviet MiG-21s, Sukhoi Su-25s, Mil Mi-8s and Mil Mi-26s were used by both sides as they struggled to gain control of the enclave. Until they were able to drive a land corridor through to Nagorny-Karabakh, the Armenians relied on a fleet of ex-Aeroflot Mi-8s to ferry supplies into their garrison and bring out refugees.

GEORGIA

Next to fall victim to war was the Republic of Georgia on the Black Sea Coast. Like its southern neighbours, Georgia was riven by political and ethnic disputes. The centre of opposition to the Georgian government was the region of Abkhazia, which had long wanted independence. With covert Russian backing the Abkhazians rose in revolt during September 1993 and besieged the Georgian garrison in the region's capital, Sukhumi. Georgian Air Force Su-25 jets intervened to rocket Abkhazian troops to little effect. The Georgians then tried to resupply their troops by air but the Abkhazians shot down several airliners using SA-7 Strela missiles. This forced the Georgians to retreat

Above: Helicopters have played a major part in the wars which have raged through the Caucasus since the collapse of the Soviet Union. The newly independent states all have access to former Soviet aircraft left on their territory, and most of the fighting men have some heliborne training from their days as Soviet conscripts.

Below: More advanced weaponry is a little more problematical, as the smaller states do not have the infrastructure to maintain and support the former Soviet fast jets left in their possession on the withdrawal of the Soviet Army. Even so, MiG-21s have seen combat in the fighting between Armenia and Azerbaijan.

from the region and call for a halt to the fighting. A Russian and UN peacekeeping mission then moved to monitor the ensuing ceasefire.

CHECHNYA

Russian forces withdrew from the Chechen capital Grozny in late 1991, leaving behind a whole division's worth of arms and equipment, including a large contingent of Aero L.39 Albatross training jets. The region's citizens then set about killing each other in a series of blood feuds.

In December 1994 the Russians decided to re-establish their control of the breakaway region. Russian air force Sukhoi Su-24s and Su-25s spearheaded the assault destroying the L-39s and a number of Mi-8s at Grozny airport. The bombers used laser-guided weapons and older 'iron' bombs to destroy their targets at the airport before reaching out to hit 'strategic' locations throughout the Chechen Republic. Television footage of the raids indicates that the Russian air strikes were far from accurate and as a result many civilians were killed and injured.

With air supremacy assured, Russian army aviation Mil Mi-24 assault helicopters and armed Mi-8s then swept ahead of tank columns entering Chechnya, hitting bridges, arms dumps and other targets with AT-6 Shturm guided missiles and unguided rockets. Western journalists reported that the Russians concentrated on hitting civilian cars, which were designated 'terrorist' supply vehicles.

At least two more squadrons of Mi-24s and two squadrons of Mi-8s, plus a flight of Mil Mi-26 heavy-lift helicopters, were drafted into the Caucasus region to support the Russian ground forces attempting to seize Grozny. The Chechens put up fanatical resistance to the Russian invaders who were thus unable to take the Chechen capital until mid-January.

Russian helicopter gunships were involved in every aspect of the operation, in spite of bad weather that forced them to fly under ceilings of less than 100 m (330 feet) and in visibility of under 1,000 metres (1,095 yards). In the brutal street fighting the Chechens used heavy machine guns and SA-7 missiles to target Russian helicopters, downing several. Shot down crews captured by the Chechens were shown no mercy.

Russian Mi-8s were in great demand to airlift the thousands of Russian casualties from frontline positions to field hospitals at the main Russian supply bases located just beyond the Chechen borders. The massive Mi-26s were used to airlift ammunition to artillery batteries blasting Chechen positions.

For the next 18 months the Chechens waged a determined guerrilla war against the Russians, including hijacking civilian passenger aircraft and staging a number of high-profile hostage takings, the

most notable being the seizure of hundreds of civilians at Kizlyar in January 1996. The Russians tried to free these hostages, the bungled rescue attempt involving Mi-24s strafing the village. These attacks culminated in the dramatic Chechen offensive that allowed them to retake Grozny from the Russians in July 1996.

The Russians unleashed their helicopter gunships again, but the Chechens were well dug-in among the ruins of the city. The failure of the Russian offensive to clear out the rebels from the city forced Boris Yeltsin to send former paratroop commander General Alexander Lebed as a trouble-shooting envoy, with instructions to negotiate a peaceful solution.

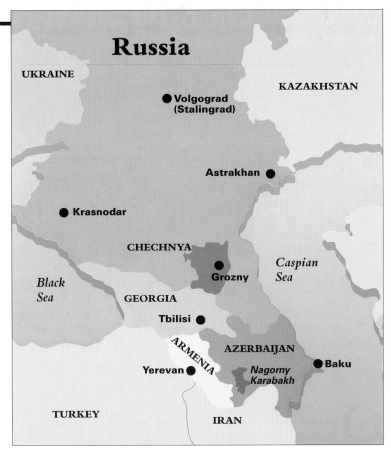

Below: The USSR's answer to the Tornado and the F-111, the Sukhoi Su-24 'Fencer' was used to deliver precision-guided weapons against Chechen targets. Results were mixed to say the least: eyewitness accounts said that Russian bombs caused many civilian casualties.

Below: Designed for a European war which never was, the Sukhoi Su-25 'Frogfoot' has been used extensively in the fighting between and within the former Soviet Republics. It was one of the main strike weapons supporting the Russian army in Chechnya.

Yugoslavia falls apart

1991–1993

Left: The shooting down of a Yugoslav Air Force Gazelle helicopter over Slovenia in June 1991 brought the simmering cauldron which was post-Tito Yugoslavia to the boil. The ensuing civil war was the most bitter to have been fought in Europe since World War II.

O n the early evening of 27 June 1991 a Federal Yugoslav air force (JRV) SA.341 Gazelle carrying a cargo of bread was trying to find a landing site in the Slovenian capital Ljubljana when a heat seeking SA-7 Strela missile zoomed up from a city street. The helicopter exploded in mid-air, showering the city with hot burning debris. This was the first aircraft to be lost in action during the bloody break up of Yugoslavia and the emergence of the new states of Slovenia, Croatia and Bosnia-Herzegovina.

SLOVENIA

Serbian strongman Slobodan Milosevic and the Federal Yugoslav military (JNA) high command reacted swiftly to the Slovenian declaration of independence with a massive military intervention. Tank columns headed into the small country, with the intention of seizing border crossing points. Federal ground attack aircraft, including SOKO J-1 Jastrebs, G-4M Super Galebs, J-22 Oraos and MiG-21s, swooped ahead of the ground troops, attacking civil aircraft at Ljubljana airport and border posts on the Austrian and Italian frontiers. But the Slovenian Territorial Defence Force (TDF) was well armed, trained and motivated. Its volunteer militiamen held their ground, cut the Federal troops' supply lines and then waited for them to surrender. Although Mil Mi-8 transport helicopters and Gazelles landed small parties of airborne troops in vain attempts seize key points, by 7 July the Federal authorities threw in the towel and agreed to an European Community peace effort. Slovenia was free.

Attention now switched to Croatia, Yugoslavia's second largest and richest republic. The JRV was in a state of crisis because of the Croat 'war of barracks' campaign, which saw thousands of federal troops besieged in their garrisons throughout Croatia. But Milosevic and his Serb nationalist supporters were not going to let the country go without a serious fight.

By the autumn the JRV had managed to pull back enough men and equipment to bases in Bosnia (Bihac, Banja Luka, Tuzla and Sarajevo) and into Serbia (Novi Sad, Vrasc and Sombor), as well as Udbina in the largely Serb-populated Krajina region of Croatia, to begin operations in earnest against the Croats.

WAR IN CROATIA

In September a state of open war existed between Croatia and Serbia along a 1600-km (1,000-mile) front, with the JRV striking at targets deep inside Croatia. MiG-21s made sweeps over the Croat capital Zagreb and on 7 October launched a precise attack on the presidential palace, using AGM-65 Maverick infra-red guided missiles. Croatian President Franjo Tudjman was only a few feet away from the impact area, but survived.

The main emphasis of the JRV offensive was in Eastern Slavonia, where Croat troops were putting up strong resistance to Serb offensives across the Danube. From August onwards, JRV jets made daily strikes against the city of Vukovar, which became known as the 'Stalingrad of the Balkans'. It held out for 100 days, until in

Above: On the face of it, the Serb-dominated federal forces had all of the advantages, controlling as they did the bulk of the former Yugoslav Air Force. Among the aircraft at its command was the Yugoslav/Romanian-designed SOKO J-22 Orao ground-attack jet.

Left: Although long past its best days as a front-line fighter, the MiG-21 'Fishbed' was still vastly more capable than anything the breakaway states of Slovenia, Croatia and Bosnia-Herzegovina could hope to offer in opposition.

Federal MiG-21

One of the classic jet fighters of the post-war years, the Soviet-built MiG-21 served in vairly large numbers with the Yugoslav air force. Over 110 aircraft equipped eight interceptor squadrons and were Yugoslavia's first line of defence until the arrival of a squadron of MiG-29s in 1987. Most survivors were used for ground-attack duties in the early stages of the Balkan war.

MiG-21bis
Right: First entering service in 1972, the MiG-21bis was an improved version of the long-serving Soviet fighter. Although fast and fairly agile at high speed, by the 1990s it was beginning to look somewhat archaic, with its poor radar, lack of long-range weaponry and almost cripplingly short range.

November the starved defenders surrendered. Serb soldiers then massacred hundreds of their prisoners.

AIRCRAFT LOSSES
Some 46 JRV aircraft and helicopters were lost in the bloody conflicts with Slovenia and Croatia. The JRV's lamentable air campaign culminated in January 1992 with the destruction over Croatia of a white painted Agusta-Bell AB.206 . The Italian helicopter was being operated on behalf of the European Community Monitoring Mission.

Newly independent Croatia found itself without an air force in the summer of 1991 after the JRV spirited away almost all its aircraft back to Bosnia and Serbia. The Croat paramilitary Special Police had a small air arm with a handful of Bell 206 and 212 helicopters, along with a couple of Mi-8s. A handful of MiG-21 pilots of Croat origin defected from the JRV with their aircraft but these were soon lost in action.

Lacking modern munitions, the new Croat air force (HRZ) had to

Below: Croatia acquired two MiG-21MFs and a MiG-21bis when their pilots defected from the Federal air force. One was lost in action, but they have since been joined by 20 more bought from Ukraine.

resort to rough and ready improvisations to take the war to the Serbs. Antonov An-2 biplanes were pressed from parachute clubs into military service, first dropping supplies to besieged Vukovar and then becoming bombers. Recycled explosives were used to fill old oil drums or gas cylinders to create Croatia's first indigenously manufactured aircraft ordnance. It is not thought that the improvised weapons killed many Serbs, but they certainly raised morale among the Croats.

The Serb-Croat war burnt itself out in the spring of 1992 and an uneasy three-year peace was maintained under the supervision of the United Nations Protection Force (UNPROFOR).

The Croats used this time to rebuild their army and air force, shopping in the international arms markets for more than 20 MiG-21s, 40 Mil Mi-8s and 15 Mil Mi-24 'Hind' attack helicopters.

In August 1995 they launched a major attack against the Serbs, seizing almost all the territory lost in the 1991 war. Croat helicopters delivered commandos behind enemy lines and HRZ MiGs flew scores of close air support and interdiction missions. Serb jets that tried to intervene suffered to Croat air defences, two aircraft being lost.

Below: As with most modern wars, much of the most important aerial work has been done by helicopters. Federal forces made some airborne assaults using Mil Mi-8 'Hips' early in the invasion of Slovenia, but they had little effect against the highly motivated and relatively well-trained Slovenian militia.

Bosnia

1992-1997

Left: NATO's initial involvement in the Balkans was primarily a watching brief. Naval forces and Boeing E-3 AWACS aircraft monitoring the skies and seas around the region in order to prevent shipments of arms to the embattled former Yugoslav republics. However, it soon became clear that a simple embargo was doing nothing to control the warring factions.

Below: The airport of the Bosnian capital of Sarajevo was the focus of an international relief effort designed to provide aid to the hundreds of thousands of refugees displaced by the war. Surrounded by mountains and within range of a variety of weaponry, it proved to be a perilous destination for United Nations relief flights.

NATO air forces first became involved in the former Yugoslavia in the summer of 1992, when the alliance decided to dispatch naval units to the Adriatic Sea. Their task was to enforce the United Nations arms embargo against the now independent republics formerly part of the Federal Socialist Republic of Yugoslavia.

The air component of this operation consisted of Boeing E-3A Sentry AWACS radar surveillance aircraft, of the multi-national NATO Airborne Early Warning Force (NAEWF) to provide top cover for alliance ships. At the same time, individual NATO countries made available tactical transport aircraft to fly humanitarian aid into the besieged capital of Bosnia-Herzegovina.

The Sarajevo airlift was run by the UN High Commissioner for Refugees (UNHCR) and continued until January 1996, flying some 12,951 sorties into the city with the loss of one Italian aircraft to an anti-aircraft missile. More than 50 aircraft were hit by ground fire while making the dangerous approach to the city's single runway airport.

In February 1993 the humanitarian airlift was expanded by the United States, France and Germany to include air drops of aid to besieged Bosnian enclaves. This operation involved some 2,828 sorties up to August 1994.

The continuing escalation of the Bosnian conflict in the autumn of 1992 forced the international community to increase its 'crisis management' efforts to contain and limit the war. In October 1992 the UN imposed a 'No Fly Zone' (NFZ) for military aircraft over Bosnia and the NAEWF extended its scope of operations to include monitoring this zone, with E-3 aircraft flying tracks over the Adriatic and Hungary. The latter move was the first time NATO air forces had operated over the territory of a former Warsaw Pact state.

USE OF FORCE APPROVED

Bosnia's warring factions showed total disregard for the NFZ and amid the Srebrenica crisis in March 1993, it was agreed by the international community that NATO airpower would be used to enforce the flight ban. American, British, Dutch, French and Turkish fighter aircraft based in Italy and on aircraft carriers in the Adriatic, under the

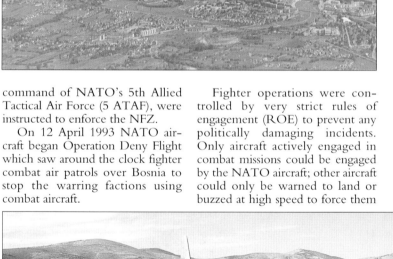

command of NATO's 5th Allied Tactical Air Force (5 ATAF), were instructed to enforce the NFZ.

On 12 April 1993 NATO aircraft began Operation Deny Flight which saw around the clock fighter combat air patrols over Bosnia to stop the warring factions using combat aircraft.

Fighter operations were controlled by very strict rules of engagement (ROE) to prevent any politically damaging incidents. Only aircraft actively engaged in combat missions could be engaged by the NATO aircraft; other aircraft could only be warned to land or buzzed at high speed to force them

Left: The primary location for NATO forces involved in maintaining the 'no fly' ban over Bosnia was the Italian base of Aviano close to the foothills of the Italian Dolomites. This is less than 70 km (44 miles) from Slovenia and the former Yugoslav border but more than 400 km (250 miles) from the Bosnian capital.

Above: The bulk of the most dangerous flying in the war zone was done by transport pilots from the USA, France, Britain and Italy among others. C-130 Hercules and C.160 Transalls flew more than 2,000 humanitarian sorties a year between 1991 and 1996, often in the face of hostile gunfire and even surface-to-air missile attack.

Peacekeeping helicopters

As it has so often shown in the last three decades, the helicopter has become an essential part of modern military operations. That is much or perhaps even more true for the assorted UN and NATO forces – involving troops from 14 NATO and as many as 18 non-NATO armies – trying to keep the peace in the former Yugoslavia as it has been in any war of the 1990s.

*Below: White painted **UNPROFOR** helicopters like this French Super Puma were often the sole means of access to the vital airport at Sarajevo when gunfire closed the runway to conventional traffic.*

*Above: A Norwegian Bell 412 'Huey' comes in to land at the Croatian port of Split in the spring of 1995. It has just flown a mission in support of embattled and besieged **UNPROFOR** observers in Bosnia.*

*Above: A Ukrainian Mil Mi-8 'Hip' makes a casualty evacuation flight. Bosnia was the region in which former Warsaw Pact troops first operated under the same command as their former **NATO** opponents.*

*Below: With the establishment of **IFOR**, **NATO** helicopters like this British Army Lynx and Royal Navy Sea King immediately adopted a more business-like attitude along with camouflage colours.*

to land. While the warring factions made great use of helicopters for resupply missions, they generally did not employ their fighter aircraft, though when Serb bombers attacked targets in central Bosnia in February 1994 USAF Lockheed Martin F-16 Fighting Falcons intercepted them and shot them down.

The next major infringements of the NFZ took place during November 1994 around Bihac, when Serb fighters based in Croatia – outside the NFZ – were making brief dashes across the border to bomb Bosnian positions in the enclave. NATO fighters could not stop the Serb aircraft because the ROE said they could not engage outside Bosnian airspace. This led

to the famous NATO airstrike on Serb held Udbina airbase in Croatia on 21 November 1994, which cratered the runway to stop the Serb air force taking off.

Further major infringements took place in the summer and autumn of 1995, when Croat and Serb air forces tried to support their armies fighting in north west Bosnia. NATO fighters protected by heavy suppression of enemy air defence (SEAD) forces made large sweeps to force the Serbs and Croats to land.

The vulnerability of UN peacekeeping troops to Serb reprisals made the issue of air strikes the subject of much political infighting in the world's capitals, with the US

Above: British light carriers in the Adriatic served as platforms both for Sea Harrier fighters and Sea King helicopters, the latter being extensively used as transports during the United Nations phase of the peacekeeping operation.

*Left: With an air wing of 85 modern combat aircraft, including three or four squadrons of the versatile F/A-18 Hornet, the **US** Navy carriers patrolling in the Adriatic provided the single most powerful and most immediately available **NATO** force in the Bosnian region.*

However, in what came to be known as the 'dual key' arrangement, they could only act if the UN Secretary General himself agreed. One month later NATO's new strike capability was used to issue an ultimatum to the Serbs to withdraw from Mount Igman overlooking Sarajevo.

During 1994 the international community agreed to make UNPROFOR's posture and ROE more robust, giving its new commander, Lt Gen Sir Michael Rose, the green light to use airpower against the warring factions' artillery sites around Sarajevo. All heavy weapons within a 32-km (20-mile) exclusion zone were to be placed under UN control or face air attack. This set the agenda for the coming year, with a series of crises developing around the Bosnian capital over the control of Serb heavy weapons. Twice General Rose called in air strikes against weapons not in control points.

In April 1994 CAS was used twice against Serb troops attacking Gorazde in eastern Bosnia after British Special Air Service troops came under fire and one was killed. A further heavy weapon exclusion zone was then established around the town to deter more Serb attacks.

Following the Udbina air strike in November 1994 and subsequent NATO attacks on Serb anti-aircraft

keen to use airpower and the Europeans more cautious. Stuck in the middle of this high level political dogfight, were the troops of the UN Protection Force (UNPRO-FOR) and the airmen of 5 ATAF.

In June 1993, the international community agreed to provide UNPROFOR with close air support (CAS) if its troops came under attack, so 5 ATAF was allowed to start flying CAS aircraft over Bosnia on a daily basis to be ready to strike if UN troops came under fire.

sites, the Serbs escalated the conflict by taking more than 300 UN troops hostage around Sarajevo. The international community backed down and refused to call the Serbs' bluff. NATO air operations were dramatically scaled down and the Serbs released their hostages.

Next spring a repeat of the hostage crisis occurred when General Rose's successor, Lt Gen Rupert Smith, ordered two NATO air strikes on a weapons dump outside Sarajevo after Serbs forcibly removed artillery from a UN collection point. Again the UN and NATO was ordered to back down by the international community in order to secure the release of the 300 UN peacekeepers held hostage by the Serbs. During this crisis USAF F-16 pilot Capt Scott O'Grady was shot down over west-

Right: Captain Scott O'Grady arrives at Frankfurt after his dramatic rescue by Marine Corps helicopters. O'Grady's F-16 had been shot down by a surface-to-air missile, but he managed to evade Serbian forces searching for him.

Targets for attack

None of the sides fighting in Bosnia showed any great respect for past agreements, but history seems to have cast the Bosnian Serbs as the most disruptive force in the region. The only way for NATO to persuade them to hold to their agreements was to use force. NATO had flown some ground attack missions earlier in the war, but it was Operation Deliberate Force in 1995 which per-

suaded them to pull back from their siege of Sarajevo. Carried out at the end of August, large scale attacks delivered more than 1,000 bombs – the majority precision-guided – against key Serb positions. The ferocity and deadly accuracy of the strikes against anti-aircraft and communications sites convinced everybody involved that NATO was through with playing games.

Left: A communications facility high in the hills between Sarajevo and the Serb stronghold of Pale lies shattered and in ruins after being subject to the surgical sledgehammer of NATO precision-guided weapon attacks.

Above: The deadly efficiency of Operation Deliberate Force persuaded the Bosnian Serbs to pull heavy artillery and surface-to-air missiles back from Sarajevo. This collection of anti-aircraft equipment was part of the withdrawal.

British Aerospace Sea Harrier FA.2

Latest incarnation of the long-serving Harrier V/STOL fighter to enter service, the Sea Harrier FA.Mk 2 made its combat debut over Bosnia in August 1994. It was flown by No. 899 Squadron, the Fleet Air Arm's Operational Evaluation Unit, from the deck of HMS *Invincible*.

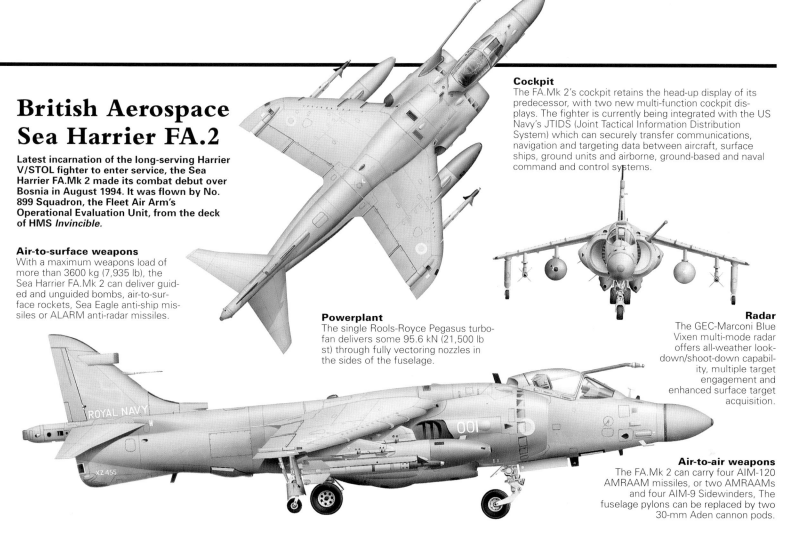

Cockpit
The FA.Mk 2's cockpit retains the head-up display of its predecessor, with two new multi-function cockpit displays. The fighter is currently being integrated with the US Navy's JTIDS (Joint Tactical Information Distribution System) which can securely transfer communications, navigation and targeting data between aircraft, surface ships, ground units and airborne, ground-based and naval command and control systems.

Air-to-surface weapons
With a maximum weapons load of more than 3600 kg (7,935 lb), the Sea Harrier FA.Mk 2 can deliver guided and unguided bombs, air-to-surface rockets, Sea Eagle anti-ship missiles or ALARM anti-radar missiles.

Powerplant
The single Rools-Royce Pegasus turbofan delivers some 95.6 kN (21,500 lb st) through fully vectoring nozzles in the sides of the fuselage.

Radar
The GEC-Marconi Blue Vixen multi-mode radar offers all-weather look-down/shoot-down capability, multiple target engagement and enhanced surface target acquisition.

Air-to-air weapons
The FA.Mk 2 can carry four AIM-120 AMRAAM missiles, or two AMRAAMs and four AIM-9 Sidewinders, The fuselage pylons can be replaced by two 30-mm Aden cannon pods.

ern Bosnia by an SA-6 SAM.

Further humiliation was heaped on the UN and NATO in July when their political masters called off air operations in support of the Dutch garrison defending the UN safe area at Srebrenica after UN troops were again taken hostage by the Serbs.

In July 1995 the UN and NATO were authorised by the London Conference to begin preparations for widespread offensive air action against the Bosnian Serbs if the safe areas came under attack again. To clear the decks and prevent further hostage taking UN troops were withdrawn from the enclaves of Gorazde and Zepa in August.

A 30 August mortar attack on Sarajevo was the trigger for 5 ATAF to launch Operation Deliberate Force. Some 300 NATO aircraft were involved, flying strike, fighter, SEAD, reconnaissance, combat search and rescue, air-to-air refuelling, transport and liaison missions over a period of two weeks.

DELIBERATE FORCE

In the course of Operation Deliberate Force NATO aircraft and UN artillery from the Rapid Reaction Force destroyed key Bosnian Serb air defence sites, command posts, communications towers, ammunition depots, bridges, surface-to-air missile batteries and artillery batteries.

Some 708 precision-guided weapons and 300 'iron' bombs were used during the air offensive, along with 13 Tomahawk cruise missiles fired from a US Navy cruiser in the Adriatic. Under the weight of this highly accurate bombardment, which was eating away at their prized military assets, the Bosnian Serbs gave in to UN demands for free access to Sarajevo and pulled back all their heavy guns from the city. Serb commanders had finally seen what NATO and the UN could do when aroused, and they did not like the result.

Barely a month later Serb, Croat and Bosnian political leaders signed the Dayton peace accords, ending the war and opening the way on 20

December 1996 for NATO to deploy its peace Implementation Force (IFOR) to take over from UNPROFOR.

IFOR troops, now in camouflage rather than UN white, were mandated to enforce vigorously the military provisions of the Dayton accords and ground commanders were free to call in air support without recourse to the cumbersome UN chain of command. 5 ATAF simply became IFOR's air component. Its aircraft continued to police the skies over Bosnia looking for prohibited military air activity; they flew CAS support for IFOR troops being threatened by former warring faction troops and conducted extensive air reconnaissance to look for activity breaching the Dayton accords.

In 1997 IFOR handed over to the new NATO military force, dubbed the Stabilisation Force (SFOR), but 5 ATAF continued going about its business in much the same way as before. NATO fighter and strike aircraft from America, Belgium, Britain, France, Germany, Holland, Italy, Spain and Turkey continue to make daily sweeps over Bosnia to support alliance ground troops.

Left: Ultimately, the major purpose of NATO's intervention in Bosnia was to allow airmen like these members of the USAF Reserve to deliver the aid so necessary to avoid a humanitarian disaster.

ASIA

Conflict in Asia since the end of World War II has been caused by a number of widely varying factors. The Cold War has been a minor contributor to many of the wars, though the first real East/West shooting confrontation fought out in Korea was a notable exception. The liberation struggles which forced the withdrawal of the old imperial powers were a much more common cause of battle, with religion being thrown in as an added irritant in the wars betwen India and Pakistan. But if there is one area which exemplifies war in Asia, it is Indochina. The region has seen more than half a century of colonial, post-colonial, tribal, capitalist and communist struggle, all fought on a foundation of more than a thousand years of local rivalry.

The Dutch East Indies & Indonesia

1945-1963

Left: The P-51D/K Mustang was the primary Dutch fighter and ground-attack aircraft at the outbreak of hostilities in the Dutch East Indies after World War II. This flight (probably from No. 120 or 122 Squadron) is seen over Medan in Sumatra in October 1948. Following the Dutch withdrawal in 1950, the Mustangs were handed over to the fledgling Indonesian air force which operated them until well into the 1970s.

Below: Dutch strike power took the form of two units with B-25D/J Mitchells; No. 18 Squadron based on Kemajoram and No. 16 Sqn at Palembang. Both were tasked with medium bombing and were used extensively between 1946 and 1950.

The Netherlands East Indies were occupied by the Japanese during World War II. On liberation the Dutch expected that power would be restored to them, though the indigenous Indonesians had been promised independence by the Japanese during the closing stages of the war. Sukharno, the nationalist leader, declared independence on 17 August 1945, three days after the Japanese surrender.

The area was under British control, and they found themselves opposed by freed Dutch POWs and internees, and by the republicans, who naturally suspected that the two European colonial nations would co-operate against their interests. Republican forces began disrupting Britain's POW repatriation operations, forcing the British into an alliance with the Dutch.

RAF aircraft (principally P-47D Thunderbolts, Mosquitoes and Spitfire Mk XIVs) began flying sorties against terrorist positions, usually after dropping warning leaflets.

Below: The heavily-armed B-26 Invader was operated by both the Indonesian air force and anti-government forces. In addition to the eight nose guns, the air force example seen here also carries four rockets and a twin 12.7-mm (0.5-in) gun pod under each wing.

Dutch forces began replacing British units, and local negotiations resulted in an informal agreement that Java and Sumatra would come under the authority of the Indonesians themselves, while the Dutch would share the task of bringing the remaining islands into a federation.

There was a ceasefire in early 1947, and agreement that Indonesia would be a federal united states, with some allegiance to the Netherlands, but the details were sketchy and ceasefire violations increased. The Dutch captured most towns, and interned the nationalist leadership, but growing international pressure and American threats to withdraw aid forced a formal ceasefire on 11 August 1949, and there was a transfer of sovereignty to a new United States of Indonesia (under the released Sukharno) on 27 December 1949.

INDONESIAN AMBITIONS

The new nation was inherently unstable, encompassing 100 million ethnically and religiously diverse people on 10,000 islands, many of whom had no wish to exchange rule from the Hague for rule from Batavia. Sukharno's ambition to expand Indonesia's territories, coupled with a tolerance of the communists, led to US hostility to his

rule, and the CIA supported his opponents when they staged an abortive rebellion in Sumatra and Celebes in February 1958. This support took the form of training, the organisation and payment of mercenaries, and an air force of ex-USAF aircraft including 15 B-26s, a C-54, various C-46s and C-47s, and, according to some sources, a B-29. These were operated from Manado on the northern tip of Celebes, and one B-26 was shot down during a raid on Ambon on 18 May 1958. An amnesty was offered in 1961, and the rebellion ended.

Sukharno claimed Dutch New Guinea from 1957, on the basis that as a Dutch colony in the Dutch East Indies, it should always have been part of Indonesia. By 1960 he was threatening to take the colony by force of arms, and in response the

Dutch deployed No.322 Squadron, with 12 Hawker Hunter F.Mk 4s and two Alouette IIs, to Biak, to augment 12 Neptunes of No.321 Squadron, a similar number of Firefly AS.Mk 4s of No.6 Squadron, and a number of C-47s. An Indonesian invasion fleet arrived on 15 January 1962, covered by F-51D Mustangs and accompanied by a paratroop drop. One landing ship was sunk by a Dutch warship, and negotiations began before the Hunters could intervene. Dutch New Guinea was handed over as West Irian in May 1963.

Below:: Indonesia's territorial claims to Dutch New Guinea in 1960 were met by a deployment of Dutch air power when 12 Hunter F. Mk 4 fighters of No. 322 Squadron were sent to Biak. The archer emblem on the fin identifies this F.4 as a Hunter of sister unit No. 323 Squadron.

Right: At the time of the Hunters' deployment, the Royal Netherlands air force already had air assets in place in the form of maritime patrol Neptunes and a unit of Firefly naval strike fighters. These flew some operational missions when a limited shooting war broke out in January 1962.

French Indochina

1945-1954

Left: Although handicapped by a lack of range, inadequate ventilation and a restricted view downwards, the F8F Bearcat proved popular and successful in Indochina, able to deliver a wide variety of ordnance and proving fast and agile enough to be a difficult target for ground fire.

Below: Ten squadrons of Bearcats were active in Indochina during the war, three of them operating in the reconnaissance role.

Left: The first US front-line aircraft type in service in Indochina was the Bell P-63C King Cobra, four squadrons of which were supplied from July 1949. These equipped Groupes des Chasse 5 and 6.

The return of French government to Indochina after the ending of Japanese occupation during World War II was followed inevitably by increasing tension created by the Viet Minh, who attempted but failed to wrest control of Hanoi and other cities from the French. However, although the French took the initiative, they never managed to crush the Vietnamese partisans, whose strength steadily increased.

As early as August 1945 the French government had ordered the embarkation of Armée de l'Air units for the Far East and, after the blocking by the USA of use of P-47 Thunderbolts in Southeast Asia, France acquired from the UK a number of Spitfire Mk IXs which arrived at Saigon to join some Spitfire Mk VIIIs (transferred after the departure of RAF No. 273 Squadron from Tan Son Nhut in January 1946) and a few Nakajima Ki-43 'Oscar' fighters seized from the Japanese after the Pacific War.

CLOSE SUPPORT

The French air forces in Indochina were employed exclusively in the ground supply and support roles as the Viet Minh possessed no combat aircraft. On the other hand, supplied increasingly and almost exclusively by Communist China in the north, the guerrillas became highly proficient in the use of light flak guns of 20-, 23- and 37-mm calibres, weapons that were to take a mounting toll of French aircraft.

The Armée de l'Air in Indochina was initially organised into two tactical groups, TFIN in Tonkin and northern Annam, and TFIS in Cochin-China and southern Annam. In 1950 these were re-deployed as three groups, GATAC North for Tonkin, GATAC Central for Annam, and GATAC South for Cochin-China. During the first half of 1947 the French flew a number of Mosquito Mk VI fighter-bombers in the theatre but, although able to reach further over guerrilla-held territory, they were plagued by poor serviceability, their wooden construction proving

Left: The Japanese surrender in Indochina was taken by Britain in the south, and by China in the north. A Vichy French administration had ruled the area until March 1945, when the Japanese proclaimed Vietnamese, independence and interning the French. British forces helped the French re-establish control (including the North, the independent Republic of Vietnam, initially recognised by France). The Viet Minh mounted a guerrilla war from across the Chinese border, and prevented the French from consolidating their position, isolating garrisons which were later over-run. The French lost 6,000 men at Cao Bang (23 walked out alive) and 2,293 dead and 9,000 PoWs at Dien Bien.

Below: The Supermarine Spitfire was France's primary combat aircraft in Indochina in the early years, because the USA blocked the use of more suitable types outside Europe.

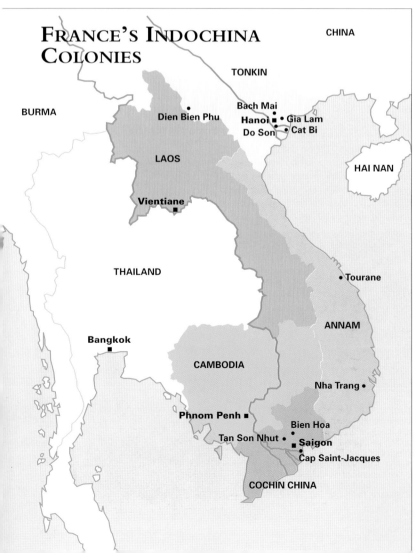

FRANCE'S INDOCHINA COLONIES

CHINA

TONKIN

BURMA

Bach Mai

Dien Bien Phu

Hanoi • Gia Lam
Do Son • Cat Bi

LAOS

HAI NAN

Vientiane

THAILAND

ANNAM

Bangkok

• Tourane

CAMBODIA

Nha Trang •

Phnom Penh ■

Bien Hoa

Tan Son Nhut • ■ Saigon

Cap Saint-Jacques

COCHIN CHINA

Borrowed and blue

The French made extensive use of single-engined fighters and attack aircraft against the Viet Minh. In the early years many of these were Spitfires borrowed and later purchased from the RAF, while the Armée de l'Air also used fighters captured from the Japanese. These were augmented by Aéronavale aircraft, operating from ship and shore bases, with American types used after an embargo was lifted in 1947.

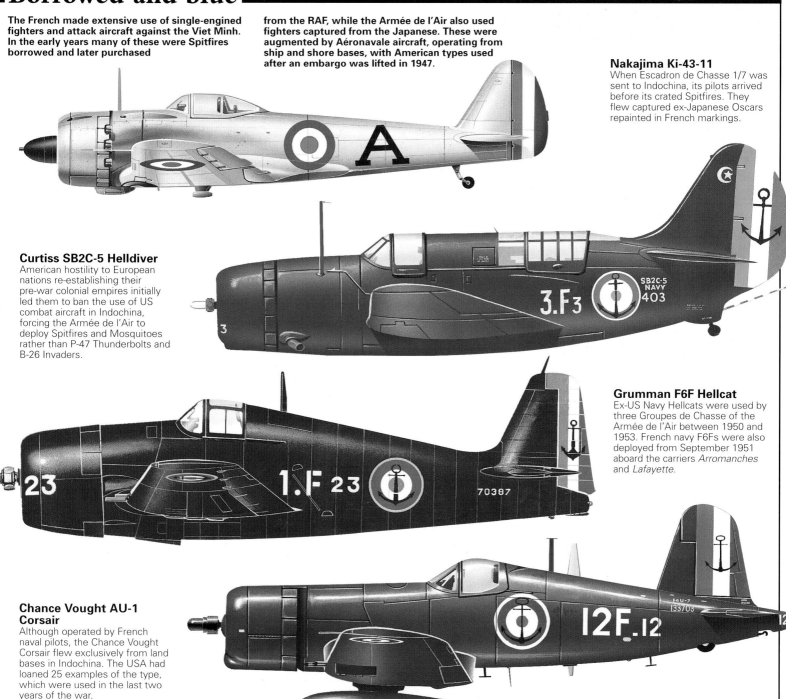

Nakajima Ki-43-II
When Escadron de Chasse 1/7 was sent to Indochina, its pilots arrived before its crated Spitfires. They flew captured ex-Japanese Oscars repainted in French markings.

Curtiss SB2C-5 Helldiver
American hostility to European nations re-establishing their pre-war colonial empires initially led them to ban the use of US combat aircraft in Indochina, forcing the Armée de l'Air to deploy Spitfires and Mosquitoes rather than P-47 Thunderbolts and B-26 Invaders.

Grumman F6F Hellcat
Ex-US Navy Hellcats were used by three Groupes de Chasse of the Armée de l'Air between 1950 and 1953. French navy F6Fs were also deployed from September 1951 aboard the carriers *Arromanches* and *Lafayette*.

Chance Vought AU-1 Corsair
Although operated by French naval pilots, the Chance Vought Corsair flew exclusively from land bases in Indochina. The USA had loaned 25 examples of the type, which were used in the last two years of the war.

unsuitable for prolonged service in the hot, humid conditions.

As the nature of the anti-guerrilla operations underwent change during 1948-49, and the Viet Minh tended to concentrate their forces closer to the distant borders with China, the French made renewed efforts to persuade the Americans to permit the use of US aircraft, at just the moment when the Communists were gaining spectacular victories over the Western-aligned Chinese nationalists. As a result of these overtures the French were able to send about 50 Bell F-63C Kingcobras to Indochina, aircraft which proved well suited to the conditions and demands of the campaign and, indeed, were superi-

Left: Despite the pressing demands of the Korean War, the USA supplied enough B-26 Invaders to equip three bomber squadrons, with another active in the reconnaissance role.

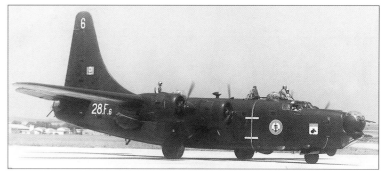

Below: The Consolidated PBY-2 Privateer saw extensive service in the long-range reconnaissance and patrol roles over Indochina. Several were lost to ground fire during the long war.

Korea, the USA supplied sufficient B-26 Invaders to equip two groups, and these aircraft undertook vital and successful bombing and reconnaissance work right up to the end of the campaign.

Air transport played a vital, albeit inconspicuous part in the French operations, the venerable World

Left: The Vietnamese Air Force was formed with French aid from June 1951, when a training centre was opened at Nha Trang. The first air observation squadrons with MS.500s was formed in July 1951.

Right: In Indochina GT 1/34 used captured German Ju 52/3ms, but other units, including GT 2/62, GT 2/63, GT 1/64 and GT 3/64 used the French-built equivalent, the Amiot AAC.1 Toucan.

or to the relatively short-range Spitfires. These two aircraft types were in turn joined and eventually replaced by Grumman F8F Bearcats which, although still possessing a disappointing radius of action, were fast and capable of delivering a wide range of ground-support weapons.

Before 1951 the French did not employ bombers as such (other than fighter-bombers with relatively modest loads), simply because the dispersal of the guerrilla forces rendered them almost immune to set-piece bombing. However, during November that year, despite pre-occupation with the war in

War II Junkers Ju 52/3m (dubbed the Toucan in the Armée de l'Air) and the C-47 later being joined by a few Bristol Type 170 Freighters and Fairchild C-119s, whose operations were limited to the small number of well-paved air bases. For the evacuation of casualties and movement of prisoners in the forward areas, the French possessed 17 Hiller UH-12 and H-23 light helicopters and 25 Westland-Sikorsky S-51 and S-55 medium helicopters.

Left: French MS.500s were used for directing air strikes and artillery barrages, as well as for liaison flying. The MS.500 was a licensed copy of the German wartime Fieseler Fi 156 Storch.

AÉRONAVALE FORCES

French naval aviation was involved in the war almost from the start. In October 1945 Flottille 8F arrived in the region with the Consolidated PBY Catalina, being joined soon afterwards by four Japanese Aichi E13A1s of Escadrille 8S. Placed at the disposal of the overall air command in Indochina, the naval air components took part in numerous operations, of which one involved the return of French forces to Tonkin in March 1946. The E13A1s were joined in August 1947 by Supermarine Sea Otters, and shortly after by two flotilles of Douglas SBD Dauntless dive-bombers.

The escalation of the war at the start of the 1950s prompted the Aéronavale to acquire Grumman F6F Hellcats, which were also being introduced by the Armée de l'Air, and Curtiss SB2C Helldivers. Flottille 3F took on charge its first Consolidated PB4Y-2 Privateer, an aircraft which eventually played a major role in the Battle of Dien Bien Phu. In March 1952 Escadrille 8S re-equipped with the Grumman JRF-5 Goose.

In September 1953, the aircraft carrier *Arromanches* arrived to reinforce the naval force with F6Fs, SB2Cs and Vought AU-1 (F4U-7) Corsairs, took part in the Battle of Dien Bien Phu.

This last chapter followed a change in French tactics by General Henri Navarrel, based on the concentration of well-supplied 'honeypot' garrisons within Viet Minh-dominated territory in the north, intended to draw the guerril-

Air transport

The thick jungles of Vietnam made communications difficult, placing a premium on air transport. The Armée de l'Air operated a massive fleet of transport aircraft to support its widespread network of garrisons. As the war in Indochina raged, transport aircraft played an increasingly active role. By the end of the war they were resupplying isolated and besieged garrisons like Dien Bien Phu.

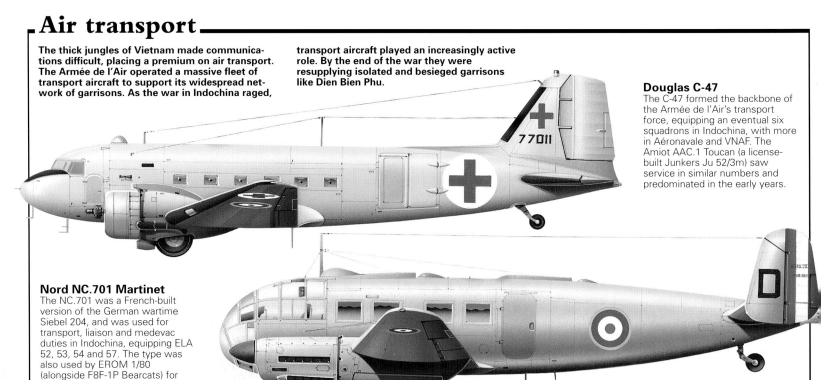

Douglas C-47
The C-47 formed the backbone of the Armée de l'Air's transport force, equipping an eventual six squadrons in Indochina, with more in Aéronavale and VNAF. The Amiot AAC.1 Toucan (a license-built Junkers Ju 52/3m) saw service in similar numbers and predominated in the early years.

Nord NC.701 Martinet
The NC.701 was a French-built version of the German wartime Siebel 204, and was used for transport, liaison and medevac duties in Indochina, equipping ELA 52, 53, 54 and 57. The type was also used by EROM 1/80 (alongside F8F-1P Bearcats) for reconnaissance duties.

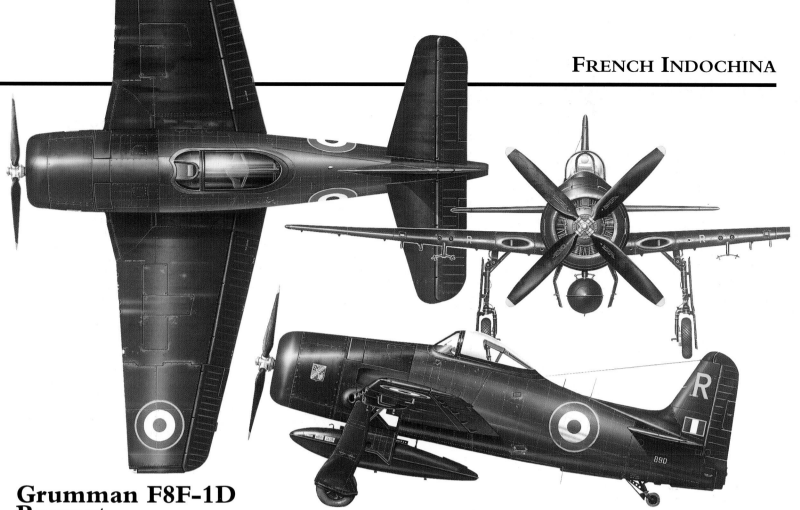

Grumman F8F-1D Bearcat

This F8F-1 wears the insignia and yellow-edged fin flash of Groupe de Chasse 9's and 2nd Escadron, GC 2/9 'Auvergne'. The unit transitioned to the F8F from the F6F-5 Hellcat, and flew mainly from Tan Son Nhut.

The Bearcat in Indochina
The F8F equipped a number of units in Indochina, including GC 1/8 (later GC 1/22), GM 2/8, GC 2/9 'Auvergne') later GC 2/22), GM 2/9 (later GC 2/21), GC 1/21 (later GC 1/22 'Saintagne').

Role
Though designed as a dedicated shipborne air-defence fighter, the F8F found its niche as a land-based fighter/bomber. Some were deployed to Dien Bien Phu, where they were destroyed on the ground.

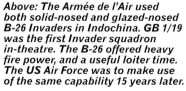

la forces into open battle. After a number of limited successes by these garrisons, the forces at Dien Bien Phu were totally surrounded by considerable Communist formations, and although constantly reinforced, supported and supplied from the air the French garrison was finally over-run in May 1954. This crushing psychological blow, coming as it did less than 10 years after France had emerged battered from World War II, lent impetus to peace negotiations which were then about to open in Geneva. A cease-fire, which in fact acknowledged defeat of the French throughout Indochina, was agreed on 20 July that year.

Above: The Armée de l'Air used both solid-nosed and glazed-nosed B-26 Invaders in Indochina. GB 1/19 was the first Invader squadron in-theatre. The B-26 offered heavy fire power, and a useful loiter time. The US Air Force was to make use of the same capability 15 years later.

Above: Bearcat pilots of GC 1/22 'Saintogne' brief before a strike mission. The Bearcat's STOL characteristics allowed it to operate from forward airstrips, which compensated for its relatively short range.

Below: Fairchild C-119s were loaned to the French in Indochina and were operated in Civil Air Transport livery, by crews supplied by Claire Chennault. A handful were lost in action.

Malaya: Operation 'Firedog'

1948-1960

There had been an anti-British guerrilla movement in Malaya before the Japanese occupation of 1942, but the British administration then supported this Chinese-led organisation as the only element able to harass and spy on the mutual enemy, Japan. Thus, at the end of the war the British found themselves with a depleted infrastructure of their own but facing a well organised and equipped guerrilla force. Under pressure, but

Above: The nuclear bombs dropped on Hiroshima and Nagasaki ended the war before the Hornet could enter service, and the jet age rendered it obsolete for home defence. The RAF's fastest piston-engined fighter found its niche as a fighter-bomber in the Far East. Here a flight of Hornets from No. 45 Squadron flies over Malaya.

otherwise reluctant to grant independence, the British attempted to shepherd the diverse sultanates and states into a federation under the British flag. The

Left: Bristol Brigands replaced ageing Beaufighters with Nos 45 and 84 Squadrons, but had a short career before they were themselves retired after an alarming spate of structural failures and accidents. Here a Brigand of No. 84 Squadron rockets a terrorist target. The Brigand gave way to the de Havilland Hornet from 1951.

Above: Australia contributed a squadron of long-range Avro Lincoln B.Mk 30 heavy bombers to the war. RAF Lincolns also took part, on temporary deployments from the UK. The Lincolns of No. 1 Squadron, RAAF, were replaced by a squadron of Canberras and two of Sabres in 1958, but by then the war was almost over.

Piston-engined warriors

The harsh climatic conditions, primitive facilities and absence of an enemy air threat allowed the RAF to make use of a number of piston-engined aircraft types in Malaya that would have been considered obsolete in Europe. The Beaufighter, Spitfire, Mosquito and Hornet finished their front-line careers in Malaya, supporting Operation 'Firedog'.

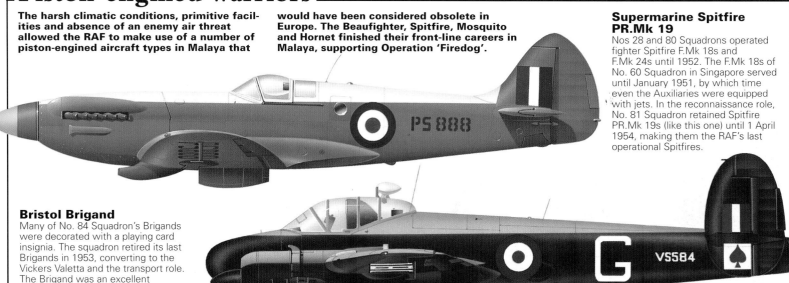

Supermarine Spitfire PR.Mk 19
Nos 28 and 80 Squadrons operated fighter Spitfire F.Mk 18s and F.Mk 24s until 1952. The F.Mk 18s of No. 60 Squadron in Singapore served until January 1951, by which time even the Auxiliaries were equipped with jets. In the reconnaissance role, No. 81 Squadron retained Spitfire PR.Mk 19s (like this one) until 1 April 1954, making them the RAF's last operational Spitfires.

Bristol Brigand
Many of No. 84 Squadron's Brigands were decorated with a playing card insignia. The squadron retired its last Brigands in 1953, converting to the Vickers Valetta and the transport role. The Brigand was an excellent weapons platform, but was plagued by problems.

guerrillas operating 'somewhere' under the triple-canopy rain forest below. Only when Lincolns were deployed from the UK to carry out area bombing did an impression begin to be made. Such deployments were sporadic, since these bombers could not be easily spared from their other duties, but the Royal Australian Air Force contributed Lincolns on a more permanent basis from 1950 onwards. The Brigands ran into serviceability and safety problems and were supplanted by de Havilland Hornets, which were very manoeuvrable and could

Below: Malaya was mainly a ground war and resupply of the troops was mostly by air as the roads were non-existent. These were mainly paradropped from Dakotas, Valettas and Hastings. Here a RAAF Dakota from No. 38 Squadron is seen returning to Changi after one such drop.

Above: The RAF Tengah wing shows its teeth, here photographed from a No. 81 Squadron Pembroke. De Havilland Venoms flank an Australian Lincoln of No. 1 Squadron. They were flown by No. 45 Squadron at Butterworth and by No. 60 Squadron, RAF, and No. 14 Squadron, RNZAF at Tengah.

Mosquitoes and these aircraft had to be quickly replaced, along with the Spitfires, the more recently deployed Tempests which could not carry sufficient stores, and the Beaufighter which was becoming obsolete.

In came the Bristol Brigand flown by No. 45 Squadron, and although they could put up impressive displays of attacks with guns, bombs and rockets, it was soon discovered that such techniques had little effect on the loose bands of

Below: During the war, Britain had equipped, organised and trained the guerrillas who had resisted the Japanese. These same groups formed the basis of the anti-British guerrilla movement after the war, resisting British attempts to organise the diverse states and sultanates of the area into a Federal Malaysia. Remarkably, the guerrillas attracted little popular support, and the British were able to isolate them in the jungle and defeat them militarily, largely using air power from an extensive network of bases.

Communist-inspired guerrillas now took on the mantle of freedom fighters and unified all independence-seeking groups behind them against the UK. So started the campaign, generally known as the Malayan Emergency, which

lasted until 1962. The military operation in Malaya was known as Operation 'Firedog'.

FORCES IN-THEATRE

When the state of emergency was declared in 1948, the RAF deployed a total of eight squadrons of Spitfires, Mosquitoes, Beaufighters and Dakotas at Changi, Seletar and Tengah on Singapore Island, and at Kuala Lumpur in the north. The tropical climate played havoc with the wooden

Below: The war against the terrorists in Malaya provided the helicopter with a unique opportunity to demonstrate its usefulness for supporting jungle warfare. Whirlwinds of No. 848 Squadron, RN, and No. 155 Squadron RAF were deployed to Malaya.

THE MALAYAN EMERGENCY

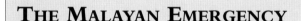

SIAM

Seletar
Tengah
Changi
Singapore
Singapore Airport

Singapore Island

Alor Star

Kota Bharu

Gong Keah

Butterworth

Kuala Trengganu

MALAYA

Ipoh

Kuantan

Kuala Lumpur

LG.

LG.
Kluang
LG.

SUMATRA

Singapore Island

Left: The Westland Dragonfly was essentially a licence-built Sikorsky S-51, though most Dragonflies also used a British Alvis Leonides engine in place of the usual Pratt & Whitney Wasp Junior. A casevac flight was sent to Malaya in 1950, and this became No. 194 Squadron on 1 February 1953.

insurgents under pressure and on the move.

Of greater importance was the transport effort. Malaya was devoid of good roads and it was a very slow business for the ground troops to make headway through the jungle and plantations. Resupply from the air was often a necessity, and Dakotas, Valettas and later Hastings paradropped essential supplies to the forces in the field while Yorks

ferried material around the peninsula. Paratrooping itself was not often employed, since the dropping zones were seldom hospitable, but Malaya saw the world's first extensive use of helicopters and these soon transformed the tactics of the security forces.

ENTER THE DRAGONFLY

Introduced in 1950, the Sikorsky S-51 Dragonfly began to take on casualty evacuation duties, which improved both efficiency and

Below: English Electric Canberras from UK-based Bomber Command squadrons deployed to Butterworth from Binbrook during 1955 and 1956 under Operation 'Mileage'. This Canberra was from No. 101 Squadron. FEAF gained its own Canberras from 1957.

attack with precision in conditions of bad weather and tricky terrain.

JET AIRCRAFT ARRIVE

By 1953, jet aircraft began to arrive in the form of Vampires and Meteors and, a little later, Venoms and Canberras. Once again, these were found to be unsuitable, with poor serviceability, range and payload, plus an inherent inability to operate slowly at low level. The tangible results of all this offensive air support was minimal, but it probably helped by keeping the

In-theatre and deployed air power

The RAF's forces in-theatre formed the Far East Air Force (FEAF) which was augmented by aircraft from a large number of home-based units. In particular FEAF relied on deployments by

home-based Lincoln and Canberra bombers, and had no organic heavy transport capability of its own. It did have its own fighter-bomber, light-bomber, reconnaissance and light-transport units.

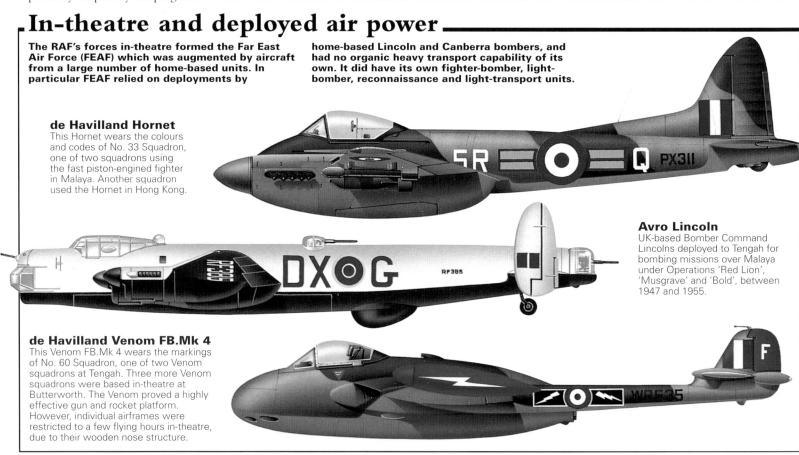

de Havilland Hornet

This Hornet wears the colours and codes of No. 33 Squadron, one of two squadrons using the fast piston-engined fighter in Malaya. Another squadron used the Hornet in Hong Kong.

Avro Lincoln

UK-based Bomber Command Lincolns deployed to Tengah for bombing missions over Malaya under Operations 'Red Lion', 'Musgrave' and 'Bold', between 1947 and 1955.

de Havilland Venom FB.Mk 4

This Venom FB.Mk 4 wears the markings of No. 60 Squadron, one of two Venom squadrons at Tengah. Three more Venom squadrons were based in-theatre at Butterworth. The Venom proved a highly effective gun and rocket platform. However, individual airframes were restricted to a few flying hours in-theatre, due to their wooden nose structure.

de Havilland Mosquito PR.MK 34
No. 81 Squadron flew the RAF's last front-line Mosquito sortie on 15 December 1955, 18 months after flying the last front-line Spitfire mission. In July 1961, the squadron flew the last front-line single-seat Meteor sortie, a month before co-located No. 60 gave up the last front-line Meteor night-fighter.

morale. By the mid-1950s, Bristol Sycamores and Westland Whirlwinds arrived to undertake assault as well as evacuation sorties. Able to insert up to nine troops into remote areas, they introduced mobility into an otherwise tough, debilitating and painfully slow-moving action. Alongside the helicopters, Auster lightplanes were

Below: The Dragonflys of No. 194 Squadron had established jungle operation techniques so by the time the Bristol Sycamores had arrived in-theatre these lessons could be put to good use. No. 194 Squadron exchanged its Dragonflys for HR.14 Sycamores in October 1954. They are seen here inserting troops into a jungle clearing.

used to support the observation posts and jungle forts essential to maintaining local security. The Auster AOP.Mk 6 and the later AOP.Mk 9 were able to land and take off in 150 metres (165 yd) and proved to be very useful. Later came the tough Scottish Aviation Pioneer, an aircraft which could carry four passengers instead of the Auster's one and could operate out of airstrips only half the length of those required by the Auster.

VITAL PHOTO RECCE
Perhaps the most essential air task of all fell to a single squadron which performed superbly throughout Operation 'Firedog'. There was

little good mapping of Malaya at the start of the operation and it was impossible to fight the war without this and other vital information. No. 81 Squadron was tasked with photographic reconnaissance of the entire peninsula. Flying a variety of aircraft (Spitfire PR.Mk 19, Mosquito PR.Mk 34, Meteor PR.Mk 10, Pembroke C(PR).Mk 1 and Canberra PR.Mk 7), the squadron unstintingly persevered in its mission and provided vital information for both air strikes and ground operations. It also incidentally flew the last operational sorties of the RAF's Spitfire and Mosquito.

The UK eventually moved towards the grant of independence, fostering the indigenous Malays as

Above: The Venom proved popular with its pilots and was extensively used in Malaya by both the RAF and Royal New Zealand Air Force. Here a line up of 14 Squadron RNZAF start up for another day's operations from Tengah in 1958.

the new ruling element. The conflict then took on a racial dimension, with the Chinese isolated against the now unified Malays and British. 'Divide and rule' succeeded and the insurgents fought a losing battle.

Operation 'Firedog' was always a war fought on the ground, but air support in the offensive, transport and reconnaissance roles played a valuable and, maybe, a vital part in the success of the operation.

Right: The RAF's last Avro York was named Ascalon II, and served with the FEAF Communications squadron at RAF Changi, Singapore, until its retirement in 1957. It served alongside Dakotas, Valettas, Devons, Pembrokes, Ansons, Harvards, Austers, Vampires, Venoms and Meteors. The aircraft was replaced by a Handley Page Hastings.

Korea: The Early Months

JUNE–OCTOBER 1950

Following some months of intermittent border 'incidents' along the 38th Parallel – the artificial boundary separating North and South Korea that had been established by the United Nations – all-out hostilities began on 25 June 1950. Eight North Korean (Communist) divisions crossed the border in an attempt to achieve a swift conquest of the Republic of Korea (ROK) and impose reunification of the whole country under a single Communist government.

Correctly assessing the almost non-existence of the ROK air force, which comprised no more than 16 unarmed trainers and observation aircraft, the North Korean Air Force (NKAF) possessed a fighter regiment of 70 Yak-9 and La-11s and a ground-attack regiment of 62 Il-10s, all Soviet aircraft of late-World War II vintage. They were

Above: Three Boeing B-29s of the Yokota-based 92nd Bomb Group fly to targets in Korea. B-29s from Guam, forward-deployed to Kadena, actually began bombing operations on 27 June 1950, one day before President Truman formally gave the OK for offensive operations.

Right: An armourer loads up the eight nose-mounted 12.7-mm (0.50-in) calibre machine-guns of a Douglas A-26 Invader of the activated AFRes 452nd Bomb Group, in September 1950. B-26s interdicted targets by day and night.

Left: The British Commonwealth maintained an aircraft-carrier on station off Korea throughout the war. The Australian contribution was provided by HMAS Sydney, one of whose Firefly fighter bombers is seen being launched after the carrier had arrived to relieve HMS Glory.

Mustangs at war

When war began, F-82 Twin Mustangs based in Japan were the only USAF fighters in the area with sufficient range to fly useful combat missions over Korea. They thus played a large role in the early fighting. Numbers of F-51D Mustangs were returned to service for use in the fighter-bomber role over Korea and some scored air-to-air victories.

F-82G Twin Mustang
This F-82G of the 68th Fighter (All Weather) Squadron, flown by Lt William 'Skeeter' Hudson and Lt Carl Hudson (radar observer), scored the first kill of the war. It occurred over Kimpo airfield, by downing a North Korean Yak-7U coded 'C6'.

F-51D Mustang
This F-51D was the personal aircraft of Major 'Moon' Mullins of the 18th Fighter Bomber Group's 67th Fighter Bomber Squadron, which scored three kills in the Mustang.

Right: When North Korea launched its attack, the South lay outside Truman's protective perimeter, and there were no USAF-based aircraft to cover the evacuation of US civilians. MacArthur solved this by ordering standing patrols by Japan-based F-82G Twin Mustangs.

Below: Grumman F9F-2 Panthers line up on the deck of the USS Leyte (CV-32). The Panther enjoyed some success against North Korean MiGs, but was primarily used in the ground-attack role.

highly effective when no air opposition existed. The North Koreans had not counted, however, on an immediate decision by the UN to resist their aggression by employing all available Western forces under the command of General Douglas MacArthur.

Few modern American combat aircraft had reached the Far East by mid-1950 and, as USAF C-54s hurriedly evacuated American citizens from Seoul, the South Korean capital, the only combat aircraft immediately available in the theatre (and then in Japan, and not Korea itself) were a small number of short-ranged F-80C Shooting Star jet fighter-bombers and some obsolescent North American F-82 Twin Mustang piston-engined fighters. On 27 June, however, the first jet fighter combat by American fighters occurred when four F-80Cs shot down four NKAF Il-10s, while elsewhere F-82Gs destroyed three Yak-9s. The inability of the ROK ground forces to defend their own territory was such that the Communists made swift progress southwards. Seoul and its airfield at Kimpo fell on 28 June as the South Korean army retreated in disarray. Realising that the immediate need was for ground support from the air, the USAF quickly moved three wings of F-51 Mustangs to the theatre, aircraft which proved excellent in the ground-attack role when armed with rockets and bombs and which equipped South African and Australian volunteer squadrons with the UN forces in Korea. At the same time, the F-80s were assigned the air combat role on occasions of interference by the NKAF.

As the UN command frantically assembled ground forces with which to stem the Communist

Below: A B-29 pilot briefs his crew for a pre-dawn take-off on 17 July 1950, when B-29s were being flung into the war in the tactical bombing role, in an attempt to halt the relentless North Korean advance on the ground. Three B-29 groups were assigned to MacArthur.

Above: Watched by an anti-aircraft gun crew, a B-29 lumbers into the air for an attack against strategic targets in North Korea. Such attacks (against harbours, railway yards, oil depots and steel factories began in August 1950, when fighter-bombers took over the tactical targets.

Right: It is unclear why this North Korean Yak trainer is taxiing with three people and a dog aboard. Presumably some heroic rescue mission was being re-enacted for the camera, but the details are lost.

THE KOREAN THEATRE OF OPERATIONS

CHINA

RUSSIA

• VLADIVOSTOK

• RASHIN

Misawa

Kwantien •

NORTH KOREA

SEA OF JAPAN

• Tatunkou
Takushan •

• HUNGNAM

K-24
K-27 • WONSAN

PYONGYANG

JAPAN

K-47

SEOUL • K-16 • K-18

INCHON   • K-46

K-13

Yokota
Johnson • • TOKYO

K-55
K-6

K-41

TAEJON • K-5

K-2 • K-3

K-8   K-37

• K-9

K-10 • K-1

K-4 • PUSAN

SOUTH KOREA

• Itazuke

K-40

• Cities

• UN air bases

• Chinese air bases

The ground situation in Korea ebbed and flowed. From the 'start line' of the 38th Parallel, the UN forces were pushed back to the Pusan pocket, around K-1. In September 1950, the 8th Army broke out of the Pusan pocket and the Marines staged a landing at Inchon, rapidly pushing on to retake Seoul. By November, the UN had advanced almost to the Chinese border. Then the Chinese intervened, and UN forces were pushed back; by 25 January they had lost Seoul, Inchon, and even Osan. By the end of the war, most territory up to the 38th Parallel was once more in UN hands.

advance, the ROK army having been all but destroyed, USAF strength in the theatre quickly increased. Japan-based B-26 light and B-29 heavy bombers joined aircraft of the US Navy in frequent raids on North Korean industrial targets as well as the key supply routes to the south. By September all but a small area around Pusan in the extreme southeast had been over-run by the invaders, and almost all operations by the UN air forces had to be launched from the US Navy's carriers at sea or from Japan. In the nick of time the advance was halted, as much by exhaustion among the Communist forces as by the relentless air attacks on their supply lines. This exercise of growing UN air superiority was to be the key to the entire war.

The UN air effort became

*Below: Armourers race to load their F4U Corsairs aboard the **Philippine Sea (CV-47)**, the second USN carrier on the scene in Korea after the **Valley Forge**. An old-fashioned straight-deck carrier, CV-47 embarked four fighter squadrons; VF-113 and VF-114 had F4Us.*

Above: Although dominated by the USA, the UN effort in Korea was a multinational one. South Africa contributed its No. 2 Squadron 'Flying Cheetahs', initially equipped with F-51Ds, subsequently replacing them with F-86F Sabres.

Below: Peasants duck as a Lockheed F-80 of the 9th FBS, 49th FBG takes off from Itazuke. In this 'bankers war', F-80 pilots lived in luxury, going to war in the morning before returning home for a leisurely round of golf, dinner and a beer in the O club.

Left: These Corsairs of the US Marine Corps' VMF-214 'Blacksheep' flew from the USS Sicily on 3 August 1950 to record the first USMC strikes of the Korean War. The squadron subsequently operated from shore bases and played a major part in the defence of the Pusan pocket.

Above: Designed for World War II but too late to see action, the Grumman F7F Tigercat made its combat debut with the Marine Corps over Korea, where it served as a night fighter.

(100 miles) up the west coast of Korea, gaining (on account of poor Communist intelligence) total surprise. Inchon itself fell that same day, and Seoul was retaken within three days of the landings, along with the vital airfield at Kimpo. Supported from the air by aircraft from the fast carriers *Philippine Sea*, *Valley Forge* and *Boxer*, the escort carriers *Bandoeng Strait* and *Sicily* and the Royal Navy's *Triumph*, the landings were co-ordinated with a break-out from the Pusan perimeter, and in a short time the invading Communist army was being systematically decimated.

AIR SUPPORT FOR MARINES

Vought F4U Corsairs, Douglas AD-4 Skyraiders and Grumman F9F-2 Panthers of the US Navy and US Marine Corps, joined by Fleet Air Arm Fireflies and Seafires, let loose a storm of gunfire, rockets and bombs in support of US Marines who went ashore at Wolmi Do. Within a couple of days, Kimpo airfield had been recaptured, and a US Marine night-fighter squadron of Grumman

F7F-2N Tigercats, together with helicopters and spotter aircraft, were operating from shore bases.

Meanwhile, US Army forces from the 8th Corps 'holed up' at Pusan broke out of the pocket, and began advancing against the North Koreans with great success.

By the end of September scarcely any organised Communist forces remained at large south of the 38th Parallel. This return to the status quo might well have brought the Korean War to an end after only

genuinely multinational on 5 September, when South Africa committed its No. 2 Squadron to the fight. America's main wartime Ally was already involved, along with another Dominion air force. Britain had already joined the fray, sending the aircraft carrier HMS *Triumph* (whose aircraft flew strikes from 3 July), while Australia committed the Japan-based No. 77 Squadron from 26 June.

On 15 September MacArthur launched a powerful amphibious assault at Inchon, 160 km

Below: Operations in Korea were hard on men and machines. Here an F-51D flown by 1st Lt David L Gray of the 16th Fighter Bomber Wing makes a wheels-up landing. His Mustang had been damaged by enemy anti-aircraft fire while on a close support mission for United Nations ground troops.

Northern combatants

When the war began, the South Korean air force consisted of 13 spotter planes and three T-6 Texans. The North Koreans were considerably better equipped, with an estimated 60 Il-2 and Il-10 Shturmoviks and more than 70 single-engined fighters, principally Yakovlev Yak-3s and Yak-7s. The NKAF also had a significant support and training element.

Ilyushin Il-10 Shturmovik

The Il-10 was an extremely effective close-support and ground-attack aircraft, although nearing obsolescence and vulnerable to jet fighters. The aircraft supported the initial Korean push and were heavily involved in attacks on Kimpo as the USA evacuated its civilians. Several Il-10s were captured by UN forces during the war, and were subsequently evaluated.

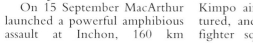

Yakovlev Yak-3

The Yak-3 was arguably the best Soviet fighter of the war, and in skilled hands was more than a match for the Mustang. Fortunately, North Korean pilots were inexperienced and poorly trained, and they expected negligible fighter opposition.

three months' fighting, together with a return to the negotiating table, had not Communist China intervened with threats of armed intervention in support of the North Koreans. Reconnaissance carried out by the Japan-based B-29s confirmed a substantial build-up of Chinese military forces immediately behind the North Korean borders with China and an increase in activity by Chinese MiG-15 jet fighters just north of the Yalu river.

Below: This Ilyushin Il-10 Shturmovik was one of three captured and later evaluated by the US Air Force. After the initial North Korean invasion, its air force played little real part in the fighting.

Right: Grumman F9F Panthers prepare to launch aboard a wooden-decked US Navy carrier. They are almost certainly aircraft from VF-51 aboard the Valley Forge, two of which scored the US Navy's first air combat kills of the Korean War.

It was at this moment that General MacArthur made clear his intention to occupy the whole of North Korea, in contrast to the UN's stated objective of simply restoring partition of the two states on the 38th Parallel. UN forces finally crossed the 38th Parallel on 1 October to begin the 'liberation' of North Korea. Wonsan fell on 10 October, and elements of the 1st US Cavalry entered Pyongyang on 19 October. Some believed

that the war would be over by Christmas, but crossing the pre-war border had made active intervention by Communist China inevitable, in turn necessitating a long struggle.

Below: Douglas AD-4 Skyraiders from VA-55 aboard Valley Forge rocket North Korean positions during September 1950. It is probably during operations in support of the Marine Corps landings at Inchon, which turned the tide of the war.

Navy and Marine Corps participation

The Marine Corps played a major role in the Korean air war, deploying to Korea and operating from Japanese bases from August 1950, in defence of the Pusan pocket. The aircraft's task for most of the war was direct support of USMC troops, but they also flew night interdiction, reconnaissance, transport, medevac and night-fighter sorties.

Grumman F7F Tigercat
VMF(N)-513 was shore-based in Japan when war broke out, equipped with a mix of night-fighter Tigercats and F4U-5N Corsairs. The squadron was immediately committed to the fighting as night intruders, transferring to a carrier in the wake of the Inchon landing. They replaced the similarly equipped and newly-arrived VMF(N)-542, which went ashore to Kimpo, then Wonsan then Yonpo.

Grumman F9F-2 Panther
This F9F of VF-51 aboard the *Valley Forge* was the aircraft used by Lt Leonard Plog to score the Navy's first kill of the Korean War, a Yak-9 on 3 July 1950. His wingman downed another during the same mission. As they steamed to Korea, the *Valley Forge* and *Philippine Sea* each carried two F9F and two F4U fighter squadrons, with AD-4 Skyraiders for attack duties.

Sikorsky HO3S-1
The US Marine Corps used the HO3S-1 for aerial resupply, medevac and light-observation duties with a number of squadrons. The US Navy's HU-1 used the type for plane guard duties, with a number of detached flights aboard US Navy carriers.

Fighting fighter-bombers

The 8th Fighter Bomber Group had re-equipped with F-80Cs just before the Korean War, and used these aircraft until they received back their old F-51Ds (still in storage on the other side of their airfield). Before they did so, the 35th and 36th Fighter Bomber Squadrons flew air-defence sorties covering the evacuation, scoring many air combat victories over the North Korean Yaks and Shturmoviks. Here, Captain Robert McKee of the 36th FBS describes a mission flown on 19 July.

"I was flying as No. 3 in a flight of four F-80s, 20 miles northeast of Taejon. We were informed by radio that four Yaks were strafing and bombing the airfield. Nos 1 and 2 started towards the action, and we moved to cover them from above and behind. At approximately 12,000 ft the No. 2 man spotted four Yak-9s in formation, headed north at about 6,000 ft. Lead still did not see them, so the No. 2 took over the No. 1 slot. We remained about 2,000 ft above them. As we got in behind the enemy and were discovered, two Yaks on our left made a sharp turn to the left and down. The two on the right turned right and up.

"At this time I noticed my lead pull straight up. Our No. 2 man hit the enemy element that had turned left and down. My element went after the other two Yaks. I used my gyro sight and closed in on the lead ship and started to fire at 15–20-degree angle off, slightly above him and at about 1,000-ft range. My hits were clustered around the engine, cockpit and left wingroot.

"Suddenly there was a fair-sized explosion around the wingroot and he began trailing grey-white smoke, with a small fire on the bottom side of the wing. I broke off the attack by breaking high and to the left, trying to spot the Nos 1 and 2 who had taken the other element.

"Completing a quick 360-degree turn, I came in on another Yak-9. As I opened fire from zero angle-off and approximately 900 ft, I observed hits on both wingroots and the rear of the cockpit."

The formation was credited with downing three of the Yak-9s, with victories being assigned to McKee, 1st Lt Charles W. Wurster and 2nd Lt Elwood A. Kees. The following day, pilots from the same squadron downed two more Yak-9s, but these were the last kills for the next 103 days.

Above: Robert Dewald of the 35th FBS was one of three squadron pilots to score a victory in a single engagement on 27 June 1950. Flight leader Captain Ray Schilleref and Dewald each claimed a single Il-10, and Lt Robert E. Wayne downed the other two.

Tip tanks
In Korea the F-80's original teardrop-shaped 625-litre (165-US gal) tank was quickly replaced by the 757-litre (200-US gal) Misawa tank, produced in Japan by adding a new cylindrical centre-section.

Armament
The F-80C had a concentrated package of six 12.7-mm (0.50-in) Colt-Browning M2/M3 machine-guns in the nose, with 300 rounds per gun. With no lead-computing gunsight, the F-80 was not an ideal dogfighter, however.

Powerplant
The prototype P-80 was powered by a British Halford turbojet, which went on to become the de Havilland Goblin, but later aircraft used the indigenous Allison J33. The initial J33-GE-9 was rated at 17.11 kN (3,850 lb st), while the 17.77-kN (4,000-lb st) GE-11 was introduced from the 30th aircraft. Later aircraft used the 23.11-kN (5,200-lb st) J33-A-21.

Lockheed F-80C

This 35th FBS F-80C was used on 17 July by Captain Francis B. Clark to score a victory over a North Korean Yak-9. This was two days before the engagement described above.

W hatever efforts might have been made by the UN to gainsay General MacArthur's hawkish ambitions, the matter was rendered academic when on 1 November 1950 an American F-80C was shot down by Chinese AA guns firing into Korean airspace from across the Yalu river. In another incident the pilots of some UN F-51s reported being fired on by MiG-15s which then made off towards Chinese territory.

PYONGYANG FALLS

By now American forces had advanced deep into North Korea, their intention (now sanctioned by the UN) being ostensibly to 'secure peace throughout the Korean peninsula'. The North Korean capital, Pyongyang, had fallen to them

Above: As UN forces advanced toward the China border, winter closed in. Rarely seen sunlight here drenches Napalm Nan, an F-51D Mustang of the 39th FBS/18th FBW carrying 454-kg (1,000-lb) bombs and 127-mm (5-in) HVAR rockets.

Right: The Lockheed F-80 Shooting Star was no match for the MiG-15 in a dogfight, but it was a lethal fighter-bomber. This aircraft is heavily laden with napalm tanks for an air-to-ground strike on intervening Chinese troops.

on 19 October, and already the USAF had begun to run down its strength in the theatre. At the moment of intervention by the Chinese jets the UN air forces in the Korean theatre comprised three F-51 wings, two of F-80Cs, two of B-26s and three of B-29s.

No further pretence at non-intervention was made by the Chinese as, on 3 November, their forces swarmed across the Yalu. An American division was forced hurriedly to retreat to protect its supply lines as the powerful US Navy Carrier Task Force 77 sailed north to launch heavy strikes against the

Below: The Douglas B-26 Invader (which had been designated A-26 during World War II) stood out as a night intruder which stalked and attacked all kinds of North Korean targets, from front-line soldiers to railway marshaling yards.

Right: A wife and kids wave Dad off on a combat mission in a picture that is posed but reflects real life for post-Occupation airmen stationed in Japan. This Korea-bound commuter is an F-82G Twin Mustang of the 68th (AW) FIS.

Ground attackers

Straight-wing victor
Right: F-84E-25-RE Thunderjet 51-493 flown by 1st Lt Jacob Kratt, Jr, of the 27th Fighter Escort Wing. Kratt was straight-wing champion of the air duels over Korea: he shot down two MiG-15s and a Yak-3.

Glessner's Yak Killer
Left: Flying this Dallas-built F-51D-30-NT Mustang (45-11736), 1st Lt James Glessner of the 12th FBS/18th FBG racked up an aerial victory over a North Korean Yakovlev Yak-9 on 2 November 1950, just as China was entering the Korean War.

MiG-killing Corsair
Right: Captain Jesse Folmar of Marine squadron VMA-312 'Checkerboards' shot down a MiG-15 on 10 September 1952 while flying this F4U-4B, but was then shot down himself and rescued.

Chinese crossing the Yalu. At first the MiG-15 pilots simply trailed their coats over Korea in efforts to tempt American aircraft into Chinese airspace, but on 8 November a section of four of the communist jets ventured too far and were boxed in by four F-80s - in the first all-jet air combat in history. Lieutenant Russell J. Brown, USAF, shot down a MiG-15 which crashed just 185 m (200 yards) inside Korean territory. On the following day a US Navy F9F Panther pilot flying off the deck of the USS *Philippine Sea* also downed a Chinese MiG. But it was not all one-way traffic: on 10 November Chinese jets shot down a B-29 heavy bomber.

By the end of the month a quarter of a million Chinese troops were in the field in Korea. The war

had certainly entered a new phase.

Forced to accept that the appearance of the modern Soviet-designed MiG-15, which with transonic performance was far superior all of the fighters then equipping the UN forces, and that the F-80 pilots could not reasonably be expected to match the new enemy fighters, the decision was quickly taken to send to Korea a wing of North American F-86A Sabres, then the latest fighters in service with the USAF. Early in December the Sabre-equipped 4th Fighter Interceptor Wing arrived at Kimpo airfield. At about the same time the 27th Fighter Escort Wing, with Republic F-84D Thunderjets, also arrived in the war theatre.

VETERAN PILOTS

Although the numbers were not

large, many of the newly-arrived American fighter pilots were World War II veterans with considerable flying and combat experience, whereas US intelligence had revealed that the Korean and Chinese pilots were much younger and lacked such experience. It was felt that the new fighters were easily enough to restore UN air

supremacy.

The first brushes with enemy jets were inconclusive, but on 22 December eight F-86s fought 15 MiG-15s and shot down six. Further combats were not immediately possible because of the advance by communist ground forces threatening Kimpo, and the Sabres were moved southwards out

Below: The MiG-15 was a devastating surprise to United Nations commanders when first spotted by Allied pilots on 1 November 1950. These MiG-15s lined up in China would have been vulnerable to attack, but for political reasons no US air strike ever came.

Right: F-86A Sabres of Lt Col John C. Meyer's 4th Fighter Group line the pierced-steel ramp surface at Kimpo. Wingtip-to-wingtip parking invites attack, but apart from nocturnal 'nuisance' raids, the North Koreans and Chinese never struck at the Sabre force.

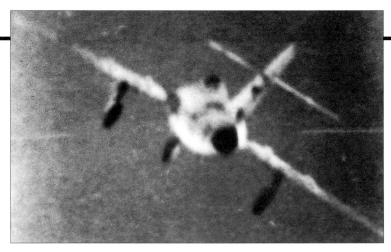

Left: F-84E Thunderjets of the 27th Fighter Escort Wing hurtle skyward carrying light ordnance. The 27th was led by Col Donald Blakeslee, the famed World War II ace. In its hands, the Thunderjet evolved into a lethal fighter-bomber.

Above: This MiG pilot lowered his gear after falling into the crosshairs of a sharpshooting Sabre pilot. At times, gun-camera film showed wheels down because US fliers strayed into the crowded air space above Manchurian airfields.

of danger. Now based far from the MiGs' patrol areas they were unable to stay long enough to enjoy long patrol sorties. By the same token, however, the communist advance southwards also moved out of range of the MiGs which remained firmly based around Antung beyond the Yalu.

It was this relative difficulty in providing air cover with jet aircraft for the UN forces that lent importance to the work of the carrier-borne strike aircraft of the US Navy and Royal Navy (the latter contributing the carriers HMS *Theseus*, *Glory* and *Ocean*, which took turns on station with HMAS *Sydney* of the Royal Australian Navy).

NAVAL AIR POWER

Task Force 77 had supported the Inchon landings early in the war with three 'Essex' class carriers, the Royal Navy's HMS *Triumph* and two escort carriers, flying aircraft which varied from jet-powered Grumman F9F Panthers through the piston-powered Douglas AD Skyraider to the World War II vet-

Left: The 'checkertails' tell us that these F-86E Sabres belong to the 51st Fighter Interceptor Wing, the second outfit to operate the Sabre in pitched duels over MiG Alley. The F-86E model introduced an 'all-flying' horizontal tail.

Left: The 'alert' pad at Kimpo where F-86A Sabre fighters belonging to 1st Lt Martin J. Bambrick (foreground) and Capt Robert J. Love of the 4th FIW are poised for action, powered-up, and ready. In the background, another Sabre rides a pillar of black exhaust smoke as it lifts off for a mission to MiG Alley. Not visible but certainly somewhere nearby are Bambrick, who later got one MiG kill flying another Sabre and Love, whose ship was named 'Bernie's Bo'. Love, who was an air racing figure in later years, was the 11th jet ace on the American side.

eran Vought F4U Corsair. The two prop-driven machines were to prove exceptionally efficient in the strike role, and the absence of hot jet exhaust meant that they could be flown from the wooden flight decks with which many of the American carriers were still equipped. Indeed a successful attack by torpedo-carrying Skyraiders against the Hwachon dam on 1 May 1951 achieved greater success

Left: The Douglas AD Skyraider was a big, versatile warplane that flew from carrier decks and land bases to challenge the Chinese onslaught. Navy and Marine 'Able Dog' pilots carried an incredible variety of bombs and rockets and delivered them accurately.

Above: The Vought F4U Corsair also flew from land and sea. At the Chosin Reservoir in November 1950, Corsair pilots braved horrendous weather and point-blank Chinese gunfire to provide direct support to Marines battling for survival on the ground.

Prop against Jet

Commander Peter Carmichael was a Royal Navy carrier pilot with World War II experience. Leading a flight of Hawker Sea Fury fighters from the light carrier HMS Ocean, he became the first pilot of a British piston-engined aircraft to shoot down a MiG-15, in an encounter on 3 April 1952.

"The first encounter my flight had with the MiGs took place at 0600 on 9 August 1952 near Chinnampo. We had been inland on a spot of rail wrecking between Manchon and Pyongyang, and were patrolling at 3,500 ft (1065 m). My No. 2, Sub-Lieutenant Carl Haines, called up 'MiGs – five o'clock, coming in!' Eight MiGs came at us out of the sun. We all turned towards the MiGs and commenced a 'scissors'.

"It soon became apparent that four MiGs were after each section of two Furies, but by continuing our break turns we presented practically impossible targets. They made no attempt to bracket us.

"One MiG came at me head on. I saw his heavy tracer shells. I fired a burst, then he flashed past me I believe Carl got some hits on him too. This aircraft then broke away and went head on to my Nos 3 and 4, Lieutenants Pete Davies and 'Smoo' Ellis. They were seen to get good hits on one who broke away with smoke coming from him .

"On another occasion a MiG pulled up in front of 'Smoo' with its airbrakes out. He gave it a long burst and noticed hits on the enemy's wings. The aircraft then proceeded northwards at reduced speed with some of the other MiGs in company. Then two more MiGs came head-on towards me, but nothing happened until I saw another down below me, going very

slowly, it seemed. I turned into him and closed to 300 yards (275 m), firing all the time.

"I lost sight of him momentarily. I turned and looked over my shoulder and saw an aircraft go into the deck and explode. For one horrible moment I thought it was one of my boys. I called up, 'Tell off' and they all came back, 'Two', 'Three', 'Four'. Over the intercom someone said, 'Wizard, you've got him!'

"The MiG looked a beautiful job – it just seemed to glide through the air, but the MiG pilots didn't observe even the most elementary rules of combat tactics. They didn't even stick

together in pairs. Two more got hit before they broke off the engagement. Though I have been credited with shooting down the first MiG, I feel that it was more of a flight effort than an individual one, because the one that crashed had been fired at by all of my flight.

"After our encounter, our boys, who had been somewhat apprehensive of the MiGs, went out looking for trouble. Though the piston-engined Sea Fury is about 200 mph (320 km/h) slower, it can cope as long as the MiG can be seen in time. If the MiG comes in and fights we are confident of the result."

THE HELO COMES OF AGE

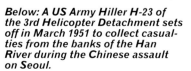

Above: The US Air Force Sikorsky H-5 rescued many downed and wounded men and whisked them to safety using an external casualty litter, shown here.

Below: A US Army Bell H-13 helicopter arrives to carry wounded infantrymen to a MASH, or Mobile Army Surgical Hospital. The Army H-13 also used an external litter.

Above: Always to the fore in exploiting rotary wing technology, the US Marine Corps introduced the Sikorsky HRS-2 nearly three years before the US Army's equivalent H-19 reached Korea.

Below: A US Army Hiller H-23 of the 3rd Helicopter Detachment sets off in March 1951 to collect casualties from the banks of the Han River during the Chinese assault on Seoul.

Korea became the crucible which forged the helicopter. In previous wars, cameo appearances were made by these bizarre machines with their spinning metal blades. Rotary-wing aviation, it was called, and American, British and German forces had flown helicopters by 1945. But in Korea, the helicopter reached maturity and supplanted the fixed wing aircraft in search and rescue duty. The first battlefield rescue in 1950 by a battered, short-ranged Sikorsky H-5 led to training, tactics, and equipment that employed vertical take-off and landing more effectively. By war's end, all military branches were using bigger, better machines like the Sikorsky H-19 (the Marine Corps' HRS).

than previous raids by B-29 heavy bombers (and a commando-style attack by US Rangers), so depriving the Communists of the ability to adjust river levels to suit their own troop movements during their build-up for their spring offensive.

The preparation for this offensive included considerable strengthening of the Communist air forces, principally with the established Yak-9s, La-lls, Il-10s and Tu-2s from the Soviet Union, but also with a few MiG-9 fighters. Meanwhile the 4th Wing's Sabres which had been temporarily moved to Japan while the winter rains flooded their Korean airfields, returned to Korea, now to be based at Suwon. They were not, however, on hand to prevent an attack on 1 March by nine MiG-15s whose pilots made a single firing pass against a formation of 18 B-29s, three of which crashlanded at Taegu.

The tables were turned on 12 April when some 60 MiGs attacked 48 B-29s, escorted by 36 F-84s and 18 F-86s. Three bombers were shot down, but the Americans destroyed 13 of the enemy jets. Notwithstanding this success, it was already becoming clear that the F-84 was no match for the MiG-15, which itself was superior in some performance aspects to the early F-86A Sabre. Only the quality of the American pilots was able to redress the balance.

Bomber 'Ace'

The Boeing B-29 Superfortress bombed North Korean industry and faced the MiG-15 near the Yalu. Some B-29s scored aerial victories. Gunners aboard 'Command Decision,' seen here, were credited with five kills, making the bomber an 'ace.' For the most part, however, the B-29 was vulnerable to the MiG. After MiGs destroyed or damaged a dozen B-29s in October 1951, most daylight raids were ended and the Superfortress – black belly and all – became a creature of the night.

'Command Decision'
Right: The 28th Bomb Squadron, part of the 19th Bomb Group, flew this B-29.

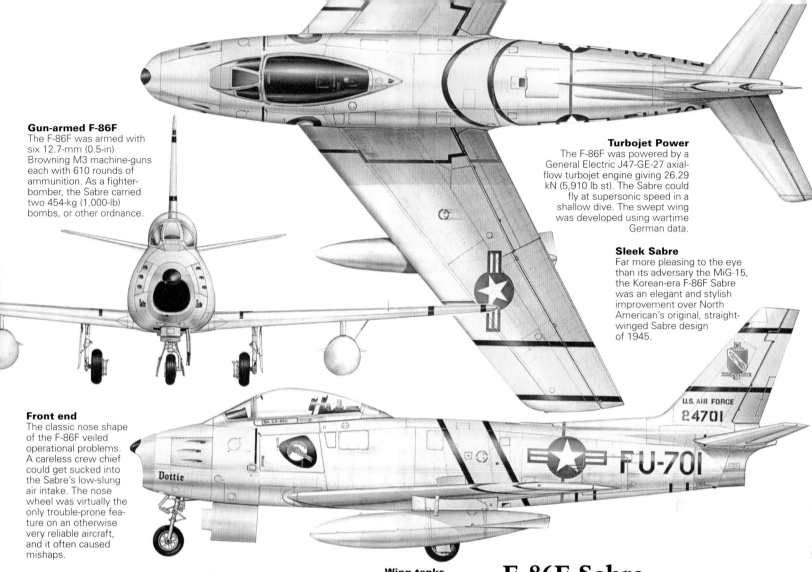

Gun-armed F-86F
The F-86F was armed with six 12.7-mm (0.5-in) Browning M3 machine-guns each with 610 rounds of ammunition. As a fighter-bomber, the Sabre carried two 454-kg (1,000-lb) bombs, or other ordnance.

Turbojet Power
The F-86F was powered by a General Electric J47-GE-27 axial-flow turbojet engine giving 26.29 kN (5,910 lb st). The Sabre could fly at supersonic speed in a shallow dive. The swept wing was developed using wartime German data.

Sleek Sabre
Far more pleasing to the eye than its adversary the MiG-15, the Korean-era F-86F Sabre was an elegant and stylish improvement over North American's original, straight-winged Sabre design of 1945.

Front end
The classic nose shape of the F-86F veiled operational problems. A careless crew chief could get sucked into the Sabre's low-slung air intake. The nose wheel was virtually the only trouble-prone feature on an otherwise very reliable aircraft, and it often caused mishaps.

Famous fighter
More than 9,000 Sabres were built, when naval variants and foreign-built aircraft are included in the total. This made the Sabre the best-known, most popular, and most numerous fighter in the West in the post-World War II era. Many were still in service as late as the early 1980s.

Wing tanks
Standard issue for a patrol to MiG Alley was a pair of finned 200 US gal (757-litre/166.5 Imp gal) fuel tanks beneath the wing. Pilots jettisoned these when combat was imminent, producing an 'aluminum rain'.

F-86F Sabre
'Dottie,' an F-86F-30-NA piloted by Capt. D. R. Hall of the 336th FIS/4th FIW at Kimpo in 1953 was an example of the final wartime version of the Sabre. With its leading-edge slats replaced by a 'hard' leading edge, the late F-86F finally became superior to the MiG-15 in every aspect of flying performance. Compared with the first Sabres, the F model had more power, longer range, and better manoeuvrability.

Left: 'Liza Gal/El Diablo' was an F-86E-10-NA (51-2800) flown by Capt Charles P. Owens of the 4th FIW who narrowly missed 'ace' status by racking up four and one-half aerial victories. Seen at Kimpo in 1953, this fighter was also flown by other Sabre pilots.

Below: Kimpo Air Base, also known as K-14, was a few miles west of Seoul near the Han River. It survives today as South Korea's principal civil airport, located just a few minutes' flying time from the frontier with North Korea.

flown P-38s in World War II, master-minding the raid that killed Japan's Admiral Yamamoto. In Korea, he bagged two MiG-15s.

The communist spring offensive of 1951 failed in its objective to overrun South Korea and had all but petered out by the end of May, but nevertheless the Chinese intervention had forced the UN to abandon its original aim of unification of North and South. As both sides now attempted to wring the last ounce of propaganda from the military situation, peace talks aimed at securing a truce opened at Kaesong on 10 July 1951, and dragged on for two years.

The hawkish MacArthur was replaced by a slightly more conciliatory General Matthew Ridgeway, but one of the last operations planned before the change of command was an all-out air offensive against the communists' supply lines which, owing to the vulnerability of the railways, depended almost exclusively on the road network. Launched after the failure of the communist offensive, it was given the code name Operation Strangle.

ALL-OUT GROUND ATTACK

All manner of aircraft, from B-26 and B-29 bombers to single-seat F-80s and F-84s – never really a match for the MiG-15 in air-to-air combat, and now being used primarily as fighter-bombers – were used. Alongside aircraft of the US Navy, US Marine Corps, the Royal Navy, the Royal Australian Air Force and the South African Air Force, they started a prolonged offensive against roads, bridges, supply depots and ports, and quickly provoked reaction from the communist MiGs, which remained based in safety beyond the Yalu but which were afforded fairly efficient

radar warning of the approach of UN aircraft.

Sabre-versus-MiG combats now became commonplace and the communists quickly became aware that the 4th Fighter Wing was operating out of Suwon, and this prompted a series of nuisance night raids by antiquated Po-2 biplanes against the base. Extremely difficult to counter, these pinprick attacks, with 11-kg (25-lb) fragmentation bombs, caused little damage but their nuisance value was disproportionately high.

The UN bombing offensive, however, did not come up to expectations because of the communist ability to repair damage using huge numbers of impressed labourers. Photo reconnaissance

Above: This Republic F-84E Thunderjet at Taegu shows off its firepower and armament, including 454-kg (1,000-lb) HE bombs, 5-inch High Velocity Aircraft Rockets, and 12.7-mm (0.5-in) Browning M3 machine-guns.

Below: A Lockheed F-80C-10-LO Shooting Star of the 51st FIW carries two 454-kg (1,000-lb) bombs and is ready for a mission while, in the background, two 4th FIW North American F-86 Sabres head aloft toward MiG Alley.

disclosed that the Chinese movement of troops and supplies was almost undiminished. Furthermore, set piece bombing attacks on North Korean cities and major ports met with intense AA fire and the raids were severely restricted by orders to the crews not to overfly neighbouring Chinese territory. Casualties among the big B-29s were fairly high in a force that never exceeded 99 aircraft.

Meanwhile development of an improved version of the Sabre, the F-86E, had gone on apace in the USA, and September brought deliveries of this aircraft to the 4th Wing, by now operating from Kimpo. The communists had also increased their force of MiG-15s by activating a second regiment equipped with the improved MiG-15bis. At once the tempo of air combat increased, and formations of 80 enemy jets were frequently sighted. One of the war's biggest

Above: A 452nd Bomb Group Douglas B-26 Invader fires rockets against targets in snowbound North Korea in February 1951. Invaders flew the first and last combat missions of the 37-month Korean War. These sorties were risky and casualties were high.

Below: US forces captured several Ilyushin Il-10 attack aircraft and shipped two of them to Cornell Aero Lab in Ithaca, New York, for study by intelligence experts. This former North Korean Il-10 was returned to flying condition and tested at Wright Field in Ohio.

Above: This photo of a B-29 strike on North Korean supply routes was released in 1951 with a caption that began, 'War is brought home to the communist hordes...' But it was mostly North Korea's manufacturing and transportation industries rather than troops that felt the impact of B-29 raids.

Below: The United Nations brass offered $100,000 to any pilot who would deliver a MiG-15. But when a North Korean flier eventually defected south with this MiG in September 1953 – three months after hostilities had been suspended – he claimed he had 'never heard' of the cash offer.

USAF FIGHTER AND FIGHTER-BOMBER OPERATIONS IN KOREA

Aircraft type	F-86	F-80	F-84	F-51	F-94	F-82
Total sorties	87,177	98,515	86,408	62,607	4,694	1,868
Average theatre inventory	184	270	247	167	56	16
AMERICAN LOSSES						
Air-to-air	78	14	18	10	1	-
Ground fire	19	113	122	172	-	4
Unknown	13	16	13	12	-	-
Total to enemy action	**110**	**143**	**153**	**194**	**1**	**4**
Non-enemy causes	61	96	63	74	6	4
Missing	13	38	33	32	2	3
Non-operational accidents	34	47	56	22	3	6
Non-operational non-committed units	6	49	30	29	16	7
Total losses	**224**	**373**	**335**	**351**	**28**	**24**
Bombs dropped (tons)	7,508	33,266	50,427	12,909	1,222	122
Napalm dropped (tons)	148	8,327	5,560	15,221	-	-
Rockets fired	270	80,935	22,154	183,034	-	1,892
Pilots killed	47	160	98	131	6	23
Pilots missing	65	164	121	133	6	13
Pilots wounded	6	38	11	41	-	1
ENEMY LOSSES						
MiGs destroyed in air	792	6	8	-	1	-
Other enemy aircraft destroyed	18	31	1	9	3	4
Enemy aircraft destroyed on the ground	4	21	-	28	-	-
Total enemy aircraft destroyed	**814**	**58**	**9**	**37**	**4**	**4**
Enemy aircraft probably destroyed	119	37	13	11	-	2
Enemy aircraft damaged	818	57	83	27	2	-

(Taken from USAF Statistical Digest , Fiscal Year 1953.)

Left: The US Air Force assembled these statistics as the war ended to reflect its performance against Chinese and North Korean forces. Later studies indicate that the overall kill ratio may have been somewhat lower, though the F-86 Sabre still established almost total dominance over the communist MiG-15 force.

single combats was fought on 22 October 1951 as eight B-29s, escorted by 55 F-84s and 34 F-86s, were bombing Namsi: suddenly 100 MiGs appeared and boxed-in the escort as 50 others made for the bombers, shooting down three and severely damaging four others. Six MiGs were shot down for the loss of an F-84.

Concerned at the large number of MiGs available to the communists, the USAF now began to withdraw some of the old F-80C Shooting Stars, replacing them with F-84Es, and a second F-84 wing, the 116th, was sent to Korea. The night-fighter F-82s of the 347th All Weather Group were also showing their age (and were of course no match for the MiG-15), and 15 Lockheed F-94 Starfires, a two-seat radar-equipped derivative of the F-80, were despatched to the war. The Starfire proved a disappointment as it lacked an adequate anti-icing system.

Left: Sabres prowl the skies above the Yalu River in the final days of the Korean conflict. By then, the MiG force on the other side of the river had been 'plucked and shorn', as one pilot said. In June and July 1953, USAF Sabre pilots downed about 50 MiGs.

Below: In spite of the starring role of jets, most of the warplanes that slugged it out in Korean skies were propeller-driven veterans of an earlier era, like this Sea Fury. Speed was less important than the ability to get bombs and rockets on target accurately and consistently.

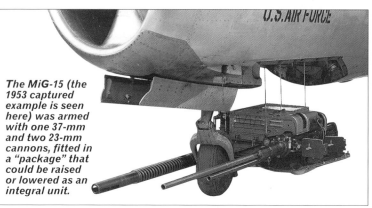

The MiG-15 (the 1953 captured example is seen here) was armed with one 37-mm and two 23-mm cannons, fitted in a "package" that could be raised or lowered as an integral unit.

New F-86 Wing

By the end of 1951 F-86Es were replacing F-80Cs with the 51st Fighter-Interceptor Wing, and the number of MiGs being destroyed rapidly started to rise. At that time the 4th Wing's combat record showed a total of 144 MiG-15s destroyed for the loss in combat of 14 Sabres. The MiG pilots themselves were becoming more aggressive – some indeed were being flown by experienced Soviet pilots,

The US Air Force's Lockheed F-94B (above) and the US Navy's Douglas F3D Skyknight (above right) replaced the North American F-82 in the night-fighting role.

Right: North Korea's Po-2 and Yak-18 biplanes were major targets for these F-82 Twin Mustangs. Often dismissed as 'nuisance' raiders, they nevertheless could inflict serious damage and had to be stopped. Allied night fighters fought them during the nocturnal hours with some success.

Night fighters

The nocturnal hours were often the province of 'Bedcheck Charlie', the irritating North Korean biplanes that kept everybody awake and dished out more real military damage than they were usually credited with. The US Air Force's response was the Lockheed F-94B, often erroneously called the Starfire (the name used for the later F-94C). Navy F4U Corsairs and F3D Skyknights also joined in the chase with some success.

Nocturnal F-94B

Right: Capt Ben L. Fithian and Lt Sam R. Lyons of the 319th FIS scored the first aerial victory for the F-94B on 30 January 1953. The two-seat, tandem F-94B was armed with four 12.7-mm (0.5-in) machine-guns and carried an early air-intercept (AI) radar set. Never intended for air-to-air dogfighting, the F-94 was developed from the F-80 to defend North America from bomber attack.

Ace's Corsair

Left: This F4U-5N Corsair (BuNo. 24453) nicknamed 'Annie Mow' was flown to glory by Lt Guy 'Lucky Pierre' Bordelon, the only American ace in Korea who did not fly the F-86 Sabre. Bordelon shot down four Yakovlev fighters and one Lavochkin in 1953 night actions.

Skyknight Victory

This F3D-2 Skyknight was the mount of Major William Stratton (pilot) and M/Sgt Hans Haglind (radar operator) of squadron VMF(N)-513 'Flying Nightmares'. The Marine duo racked up history's first jet-versus-jet night kill when they downed what was apparently a Yakovlev Yak-15 on 2 November 1952. The Skyknight scored more aerial victories in Korea than any other Navy jet.

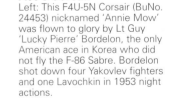

and the improved performance of both fighters resulted in numerous combats taking place above 12190 m (40,000 ft). In March 1952 39 enemy jets were destroyed; the following month the tally rose to 44.

Combat information from Korea had long since filtered through to the Sabre's designers and in June and July 1952 a further-improved Sabre, the F-86F, began to be deployed to the 51st Wing. The F-86F was the first Sabre variant which was superior in all respects to the MiG-15bis, although it was used as much in ground attacks as it was in air combat. By the spring of 1953 there were four wings of F-86s in Korea, and during the last six months of the war these fighters wholly dominated the skies. In May their pilots destroyed 56 enemy jets, and in June no fewer than 77, losing 11 and 23 respectively of their own number.

The death of the Soviet leader, Josef Stalin, on 5 March 1953 instigated a profound change of attitude in the Chinese delegation at the peace talks and, after reversing their previously intransigent demands on such matters as prisoner repatria-

Right: Douglas C-47 Skytrains, C-54 Skymasters and Fairchild C-119 Flying Boxcars of the 315th Air Division (Combat Cargo) flew troops and supplies to United Nations Forces in Korea. The 'Air Bridge' is often forgotten but in many ways was just as important as the combat jets in Korea.

tion, finally agreed to a ceasefire on 27 July 1953.

From an air combat viewpoint the Korean War was interesting in that it was the first major conflict in which large numbers of opposing jet fighters engaged each other and, while it is true that there were a number of high-scoring American Sabre pilots – 31-year-old Joseph McConnell of the 51st Wing heading the list with 16 MiG-15s to his credit – the fleeting nature of those all jet combats graphically demonstrated that the age of gun-only armament was rapidly approaching its conclusion. The era of the air-to-air missile was about to dawn.

Right: MiG killer Capt. Ralph Parr of the 334th FIS is seen at the controls of this F-86F – which was not his usual assigned aircraft, presumably down for maintenance. The 'F' was the first Sabre which could outfly the MiG-15 in all conditions.

Sabre Aces

US Far East Air Forces (FEAF) never had more than two fighter wings (4th and 51st FIW) committed to the air campaign along the Yalu River in the trouble zone known as MiG Alley. At times as few as 40

Sabres were combat-ready in all of Korea. Even though they were faced by up to 800 MiG-15s, some flown by seasoned Russian aces, the F-86 prevailed in one of the toughest air campaigns of all time.

MiG-battling 'Butch'
Right: 'Beautious Butch II' was one of several Sabres piloted by Capt Joseph M. McConnell of the 39th FIS/51st FIW at Suwon, Korea. McConnell's MiG kills appear beneath his cockpit as aircraft silhouettes rather than the usual red stars. McConnell scored 16 victories, was shot down and rescued, and went home only to lose his life in a mishap while flying the postwar F-86H Sabre.

Jabara's jet
Left: This F-86A-5-NA Sabre (48-259) was flown by Capt James Jabara during the first of his two Korean combat tours, with the 334th FIS/4th FIW at Kimpo. Jabara became the first US jet ace when he claimed his fifth and sixth MiGs on 20 May 1951. Jabara eventually achieved 15 aerial victories, the second highest score of the Korean War on the US side.

Wing commander
Right: Col Francis S. Gabreski was an ace in two wars, having flown P-47 Thunderbolts in World War II. In Korea, he commanded the 51st FIW and piloted this F-86E-10-NA (51-2740) named 'Gabby'. Like many of the aces, Gabreski flew several aircraft in Korea, and scored some of his 6.5 jet victories in another Sabre nicknamed 'Lady Frances'.

MiG vs. Sabre

Lieutenant Douglas Evans flew F-86 Sabres with the 336th FIS, 4th Fighter Interceptor Wing over Korea. He describes what it was like to fight against MiG-15s, as the dawning jet age took aerial combat into a whole new dimension of speed and performance.

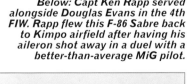

Early in the Korean War, the 4th FIW's Sabres wore black and white identity stripes. These were replaced by a yellow band in late 1951. Powered by a General Electric J47-GE-9 turbojet engine, the early F-86A model depicted here had some deficiencies compared to the MiG-15 but thanks to superior pilot skill it usually prevailed in battle.

"I was really hopped up for the afternoon mission, my 39th in combat in Korea. Charlie Mitson and I took off as numbers Three and Four in Red Flight, the lead flight in the squadron.

"No sooner had we got north of Sinanju and across the Chongchon than we saw gaggles of contrails approaching. I counted 22 MiGs in a squadron formation going by, off to our right, and 16 more further behind, but while my attention was fixed on them Al Simmons, who was Red Flight Leader and who must really have had his eyeballs extended, called eight MiGs right down on the deck. He told off the rest of the squadron to cover us and continue the patrol, and then called 'Red Flight, let's go!'

"Our attack must have come as a complete surprise. When Al fired on them, the MiGs just made a startled break without any discipline to it. I racked around to the left after the nearest two, settled on the leftmost one, and ignored everything else that was going on around me.

"Before I could fire I saw cannon shells come streaking over my right wing. Since I was already in a steep bank, I went over on my back to extend my view a little and saw this second MiG, who had just fired at me, pull up into the clouds. I snapped my attention forward again, just in time to see the first MiG duck into the clouds too. The next moment I was in the clouds myself.

"I didn't have any attention to spare for the instruments; I was too busy staring through the windscreen, trying to get a glimpse of them. There was a moment of darkness, and then the sunlight suddenly hit me in the face. It was about 3,000 ft [915 m], and there were those two MiGs, right under my nose again.

"I horsed the aircraft over and down in a roll that put me right on their tails, steadied the gunsight on the lead MiG, and pressed the trigger. My whole ship shuddered as I let go a blast.

"I wanted a MiG and this guy was it, so on over into the top of a sloppy loop we went, me still hosing him down with tracer and him still shedding pieces of his aircraft and showing more flame.

"After all the pounding and roaring my guns had been doing, I really thought something definite ought to happen. It did. As we headed down toward the cloud again in the backside of the loop, the canopy popped off the MiG and – ha! – out came the pilot like a hopping frog. I let go of the trigger then, and rolled around upright. 'That's what it's like when you have to give up,' I thought to myself."

Above: A sequence of five grainy gun-camera photos taken over the Yalu River shows a MiG-15 succumbing to a Sabre's gunfire. The MiG is hit, the pilot jettisons his canopy, and then he ejects. The Sabre's relatively light machine-gun armament meant that it often took many hits to bring down a MiG.

Left: 1st Lt Douglas Evans of the 4th FIW sits in the cockpit of his F-86A Sabre after a flight to MiG Alley. The V-shaped windscreen was a feature of the F-86A and early F-86E models.

Below: Capt Ken Rapp served alongside Douglas Evans in the 4th FIW. Rapp flew this F-86 Sabre back to Kimpo airfield after having his aileron shot away in a duel with a better-than-average MiG pilot.

China and Taiwan

1945-1996

There were two main power bases in China at the end of World War II. The Soviet Union had liberated Manchuria, and equipped the forces of communist leader, Mao Zedong, which became the People's Liberation Army. Led by Chiang Kai-Shek, the Nationalists were armed and supported by the USA, and they took the surrender of the Japanese forces in the north and in key cities and ports. Talks between the rival Chinese forces broke down as US forces departed in 1946, and the civil war which had been interrupted by Japan's invasion broke out again.

After early successes, by 1947 the Nationalists began to lose their advantage. They lost Peking and Tientsin in January 1949. The People's Republic was founded on 1 October 1949, and the Nationalist forces withdrew to the island of Formosa, establishing a rival Republic of China, now usually known as Taiwan. This has never declared its independence, and each of the rivals officially espouses an eventual reunification under its own leadership.

The outbreak of the Korean War in 1950 played an important part in the development of the Chinese People's Armed Forces Air Force (CPAFAF). In 1950 the CPAFAF had about 150 aircraft including F-51Ds, B-25Cs, C-46s, C-47s, La-11s and Yak-9s. In February the Soviets agreed to deliver the new MiG-15 fighter, and the first deliveries were made in March. The aircraft were first used in Korea in November 1950.

USA SUPPORTS TAIWAN

From 1951, the Nationalists received US support. They were seen as a useful bastion against expansion by (or even the influence of) communist 'Red' China. Taiwan also became a useful strategic base. By 1954 the CNAF operated two wings of Republic F-84Gs, two wings of F-47Ds and one of F-51s; bomber wings still operated the B-24 and B-25. The USA recognized and protected Nationalist China and in return used Taiwan: President Truman sent the US 7th Fleet to the Taiwan Straits at the start of the Korean War, and many secret missions into the mainland operated from Taiwan.

Another, less formal American involvement was with the airline Civil Air Transport, or CAT.

Right: By 1954, the Chinese Nationalist air force still had three wings of World War II era F-47s and F-51s together with some B-24 and B-25 bombers. But the most powerful element in the inventory were the two wings of Republic F-84G Thunderjets.

Founded by General Claire Chennault at the end of World War II, CAT was bought by the CIA in 1950. Used for covert intervention all over East and Southeast Asia, CAT was based on Formosa. CAT supplied the French in Indo-China and spawned further CIA covers including Air America, Southern Air Transport, Air Asia and Asiatic Aeronautical Company. Agents were dropped, but not without risk: between 1951 and 1954, 106 US citizens were killed and 124 captured on covert missions. Many aircraft were lost, including several Boeing B-17s, the last of which flew in 1958.

The Nationalists had retained forces on four offshore islands, Quemoy and Matsu, and the Tachen and Nanchi groups farther north. Mainland pressure on the latter led to withdrawal in January 1954. The US 7th Fleet, covered by F-86Fs of the USAF's 18th FBW, evacuated 17,000 civilians and 25,000 troops. The PLA also turned its attention to Quemoy. .

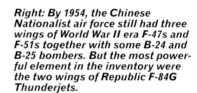

A massive artillery bombardment from the communist naval base at Amoy began on 3 September 1954, and was countered by Nationalist shelling and air raids. Shelling continued intermittently and in August 1958 CNAF RF-84Fs noted a build-up of MiG-17s on bases at Chenghai and Liencheng, followed by a new wave of shelling from 18 August.

On 29 August Peking announced an impending invasion of Quemoy and the liberation of Taiwan. At least four air divisions had moved to bases around Foochow (Nantai, Kaochi, Swatow and Chuhsein) and farther afield at Chienou Tien-ho and Nan Hai.

The CNAF in 1958 comprised 350 aircraft including three wings of F-84Gs, two wings of F-86Fs and one RF-84F squadron. In addi-

Above: The American Volunteer Group had flown C-46s in China during World War II, and many were left in the country after 1945. Both sides in the Chinese civil war made use of the capacious transport, with nationalist examples like this flying to Formosa after the communist victory in 1949.

Left: When Chiang Kai-Shek's Nationalists retreated to Formosa and the offshore islands in 1949, they took more than 200 aircraft with them. Included in that number were over 110 North American F-51D Mustangs, which provided the bulk of Taiwan's fighter strength for the next three years.

Across the Formosa Strait

At their closest, Nationalist and Comminist China are within artillery range of each other. Major clashes over Quemoy island occurred in 1954 and 1958, and the government in Taipei claimed that

nearly 400 intruder missions were mounted from the mainland in the eight years between 1963 and 1969.

Nanchang Q-5

Left: Based on the MiG-19 air-frame, the Q-5 has been in series production since 1969, and is China's primary ground attack fighter. More than 900 have been delivered to the PLA air force.

McDonnell RF-101C Voodoo

Right: Eight RF-101As were delivered to Taiwan after the 1958 Quemoy fighting. They were used on reconnaissance missions over the mainland: Peking claimed to have shot down two of them in the 1960s.

Right: From 1954 the Nationalist Chinese began exchanging their Republic F-47Ds for Sidewinder-capable North American F-86Fs. By 1958 the two Sabre wings were crucial in maintaining Taiwan's integrity when the People's Republic threatened to invade.

tion the USAF rotated a wing of F-86F Sabres as part of defence commitments agreed in March 1955.

1958 QUEMOY CRISIS

On patrols over the Taiwan Straits Sidewinder-equipped F-86s engaged increasing numbers of MiG-15s and MiG-17s until on 24 September, 10 MiGs were claimed destroyed by a force of 14 Sabres of the 3rd Wing, including four by Sidewinders, the first time that air-to-air guided missiles had been used in combat. Some 31 MiGs were claimed between 14 August and 24 September, for the loss of just two F-86s.

In October the USA increased its commitment to Taiwan with two squadrons of F-100Ds, two of F-104As, one F-101C squadron, one RF-101C squadron, two squadrons of C-130s and one squadron each of B-57s and KB-50s. In addition the US 7th Fleet moved on station: its four aircraft-carriers carried 300 aircraft. In the event there was no major confrontation, although shelling continued, and there was further air fighting when on 5 July 1959 five MiG-17s were destroyed in a 10-minute battle with CNAF Sabres.

A state of cold war continued and the Nationalists claimed to have suffered from 399 mainland raids between 1963 and 1969. The F-104A had made a significant impression on both sides during the Quemoy crisis, but US dissatisfaction during its initial service was reflected by the release of 24 F-104As to Taiwan. These were augmented by further deliveries through MAP to help counter further aggressive Chinese tactics over

Right: Three-toned green MiG-17s line up on an airfield in Shenyang province. Entering service with the PLA in 1955 and licence-produced as the J-5, it was China's main fighter into the early 1970s.

the disputed Quemoy islands. In 1967, CNAF F-104Gs proved their combat prowess when they shot down two PLAAF MiG-19s from a formation of 12 over Quemoy.

The CNAF also operated U-2 spyplanes for the CIA. Many over-flights of the mainland were made between 1959 and 1974, primarily to monitor the development of China's nuclear weapons pro-gramme at Lop Nor and Chiuchuan. Eight aircraft were lost over China. Further clashes have taken place since then, with F-5As and F-5Es predominating.

As relations between Peking and Washington improved Taiwan felt the effect, with restrictions being imposed on delivery of the latest weapons. The thaw in Sino-American relations after the end of the Cultural Revolution became more permanent, and the position of the island republic became more

tenuous. The US withdrew its forces from Taiwan in stages from 1974, and began scaling down its military assistance. In 1979, the USA broke off diplomatic relations with Taiwan.

This marked the low point in Taiwan's relations with the USA. Then the Tianenman square mas-sacre focused attention on China's human rights record, and prompted improved relations with the USA,

Right: Although the Powers inci-dent was the most famous U-2 shoot-down, it was not the only one. The CNAF operated U-2s for the CIA between 1959 and 1974, and eight aircraft were lost over China.

which most recently dispatched warships (including aircraft carriers) when China seemed to be threaten-ing invasion during Taiwan's 1996 presidential elections.

Vietnam: Early American Involvement

1960 – 1964

The US Air Force's 'Farm Gate' deployment brought the North American T-28 to Vietnam as a low-budget, all-purpose fighter-bomber for Saigon's pilots.

In 1957 the United States, in its role of bastion against what it saw as the insidious, creeping advance of world communism, took over from France the task of training and strengthening the armed forces of South Vietnam. The Vietnamese air force (VNAF) was poorly equipped and trained, despite the fact that the American Military Assistance and Advisory Group (MAAG) had been at work in the country since 1950. The aim of the USA, in line with the 1954 Geneva Protocols, was to achieve unification with North Vietnam by means of democratic elections, but this was compromised from the outset by the uncrossable divide between the communist North and the old Catholic land-owning class which dominated the South. The position was exacerbated by the presence of the Viet

Below: The Viet Cong brought their insurgency to the cities. By bombing installations associated with the South Vietnamese government and its US advisers, they unwittingly encouraged Presidents Kennedy and Johnson to send more help to Saigon.

Cong, revolutionary insurgents in South Vietnam who were backed by Hanoi.

By the end of the 1950s American advisers in South Vietnam numbered nearly 700, and updating the VNAF accelerated when its F8F Bearcats were replaced by AD-6 Skyraiders. In 1961 the Viet Cong guerrillas staged a show of strength when, supported by increased infiltration from the North, they attacked and cut many of the principal north-south trunk roads.

SPECIAL FORCES

The newly elected Kennedy administration, though unwilling to involve American forces in formally-declared warfare, redoubled its efforts to train the South Vietnamese in the skills of counter-insurgency. The first US Special Forces units entered the country, ostensibly to provide more training but increasingly being involved in leading active missions against the Viet Cong, and occasionally mounting covert intelligence or sabotage missions against the North.

As the USA supported the South, so the Northern commu-nists were the recipients of large quantities of war materiel from China and the Soviet Union. Some of these supplies were used to bol-ster the Viet Cong, moving down supply routes through Laos and Cambodia on what became known as the Ho Chi Minh Trail.

The USA responded by supply-ing US Army Piasecki H-21 heli-copters to the South, together with

Above: A South Vietnamese soldier emerges from as US Army Piasecki H-21C helicopter. In the early 1960s, Americans were supposed to be advising, not fighting, but they often joined in.

pilots to fly them. American per-sonnel were not supposed to engage in combat missions, though many did. They generally flew with at least one Vietnamese crew mem-ber who was ostensibly in com-mand, conveniently creating the fiction that no American units were actually fighting.

SUPPLY SHIP SUNK

On 2 May 1964 the American air-craft supply ship *Card* was sunk in Saigon harbour by a Viet Cong underwater demolition team while off-loading helicopters. Elsewhere Fairchild C-123 Providers of the USAF were engaged in Operation 'Ranch Hand', stripping large areas of South Vietnamese jungle of foliage by spraying chemicals and thereby depriving enemy infiltrators of their natural camouflage and cover.

On 2 August the same year the American destroyer Maddox was attacked in international waters in the Gulf of Tonkin by Soviet-built torpedo boats, and five nights later

it was claimed that the destroyer *Turner Joy* had been similarly attacked. In Washington, President Johnson announced, a 'measured response' to these unprovoked attacks, and US Navy A-1 and A-4 strike aircraft from the carriers *Ticonderoga* and *Constellation* carried out a number of attacks on North Vietnamese bases at Hon Gai and Loc Chao, losing one A-1 and one A-4 to ground fire.

UNDECLARED WAR

This progressive drift to open conflict was not accompanied by a formal declaration of war, but simply escalated by a series of local incidents of growing scale, followed by righteous indignation and retaliation. A guerrilla attack during Christmas Eve 1964 on a hotel used by US officers in Saigon was followed by a mortar attack on Pleiku Air Base which killed eight American personnel. The US Navy again retaliated, this time with

Operation Flaming Dart, sending strike aircraft from the carriers *Ranger*, *Hancock* and *Coral Sea* of Task Force 77 against North Vietnamese military targets at Dong Hoi and Vit Thuu. Further Viet Cong mortar attacks on American bases, resulting in numerous casualties, were followed by Flaming Dart II, this time involving USAF as well as US Navy aircraft in strikes against Chanh Hoa and elsewhere.

TROOPS COMMITTED

Open war, involving American ground forces, began on 7 March 1965 when 3,500 US Marines were sent to Da Nang, ostensibly to protect US facilities. Very soon, however, they were in action against the Viet Cong. Within four months the number of American combat troops in Vietnam had grown to 75,000 men; during the next three years this figure was expand enormously to reach over half a million.

Indeed, the nature of the entire

war – the absence of a 'front line', the use of guerrilla tactics on a large scale and the underlying ideologies of the combatants – all combined to stretch the endurance of the American fighting men.

Worse, these factors were misunderstood by an ill-informed but powerful pacifist lobby back home in the United States.

Above: The Fairchild C-123 Provider flew 'in-country' airlift and sprayed defoliants, including the infamous Agent Orange.

Below: The Douglas B-26 Invader suffered from wing spar fatigue, but was a superb weapon for jungle and counter-insurgecy fighting. Farm Gate's Air Commandos flew hundreds of low-level missions in the B-26.

Watching the Viet Cong

The first American combat aircraft in Vietnam were McDonnell RF-101C Voodoos of the 15th Tactical Reconnaissance Squadron from Kadena. A detachment of four, code-named 'Pipe Stem', arrived at Tan Son Nhut on 18 October 1961.

It happened to be the day the Mekong River overflowed its banks and flooded hundreds of square miles of the countryside. The four RF-101Cs began photographing both the floods and the Viet Cong on 20 October. Another detachment, known as 'Able Mable', flew missions over Laos from Don Muang, Thailand. Captain A. Robert Gould recalled:

"We lived in the Caravelle Hotel, drove our Jeeps to Tan Son Nhut for our 0800 take-off and were back at the hotel by 1500 or 1600 hours. We looked at airfields, bridges, and all the other normal military-type targets. We used French maps over Laos – there were no US maps of sufficient detail."

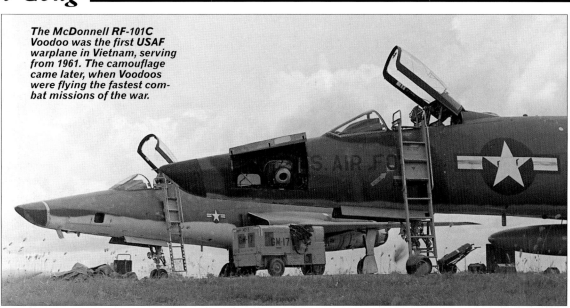

The McDonnell RF-101C Voodoo was the first USAF warplane in Vietnam, serving from 1961. The camouflage came later, when Voodoos were flying the fastest combat missions of the war.

Confrontation in Borneo

1962–1966

Left: The Hawker Hunter FGA.Mk 9s of No. 20 Squadron based at Tengah in Singapore were the RAF's only in-theatre fighter-bombers. The aircraft were used in the suppression of the initial revolts in Sarawak and Brunei, then against Indonesian armed infiltration and incursion.

Squadron. Also in Malaya were RAF Canberra PR.Mk 7s, Shackleton MR.Mk 2s and a variety of transport aircraft. At the RAAF base at Butterworth were two CAC Sabre squadrons and No. 2 Squadron RAAF with Canberras, and a Canberra squadron (No. 75) of the RNZAF, also at Tengah. In addition it had become standard RAF training practice to send small detachments of conventionally-armed V-bombers to the Far East for short periods.

Immediately after news of the rebellions in Brunei and Sarawak was received on 8 December 1962, Hastings, Beverleys and Valetta transports began delivering troops to Brunei town, its airfield having been secured from the rebels by

Possibly the least known of all post-war RAF operational deployments was that of 1962-64 in Borneo, where neighbouring Indonesia held territorial ambitions following the transfer of independence to North Borneo. The campaign in some respects had much in common with that in Malaya which had only just ended, not least in the similarity of terrain: Borneo, like the Malayan peninsula, is covered with dense jungle with few landmarks of use to navigation. Accurate maps were scarce and, on account of frequent and fairly regular tropical rainstorms, flying was impossible except for about six hours daily between mid-morning and mid-afternoon.

In very broad terms the campaign may be divided into three overlapping phases, namely the suppressing of Indonesian-inspired rebellions in Brunei and Sarawak, the subsequent deployment of units of the Far East Air Force (FEAF) to Borneo to counter

Right: The Gloster Javelins of Nos 60 and 64 Squadrons at RAF Tengah played their part during the confrontation, maintaining a permanent detachment at Kuching and another at Labuan. Great care was taken to describe the conflict as a 'confrontation' and not a war, and there have been suggestions that kills went unclaimed to avoid inflaming the situation.

Indonesian-trained terrorist infiltrators crossing the 1610-km (1,000-mile) border with Kalimantan, and wider-ranging operations to counter Indonesian air sorties across the border and the despatch of Indonesian raiding parties to Malaya itself.

RAF FORCES ON HAND

The FEAF had undergone considerable modernisation since the signing of the SEAC Defence Treaty of 1954. The RAF component comprised a squadron (No. 20) of Hunter FGA.Mk 9s at Tengah, Singapore, together with Javelin FAW.Mk 9s of No. 60 Squadron and Canberra B.Mk 2s of No. 45

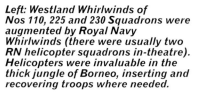

Left: Westland Whirlwinds of Nos 110, 225 and 230 Squadrons were augmented by Royal Navy Whirlwinds (there were usually two RN helicopter squadrons in-theatre). Helicopters were invaluable in the thick jungle of Borneo, inserting and recovering troops where needed.

Above: Whereas the Whirlwind could carry eight passengers, the Belvedere could carry 18, and could also lift much heavier underslung loads. Two squadrons of Belvederes served in Borneo, and proved invaluable.

Confrontation in the air

Indonesia had a well-equipped modern air force, but tended to use older, piston-engined types for incursions into Sarawak, Sabah (North Borneo) and Brunei. They proved difficult to intercept, and air activity was generally limited to ground attack, transport and patrol missions. Some helicopters and light aircraft were downed by ground fire.

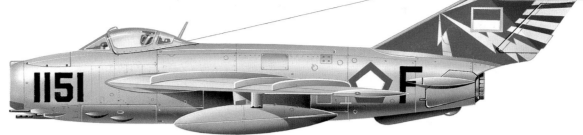

Mikoyan-Gurevich MiG-17
Indonesia's MiG-17 and MiG-21 fighters were not committed to action, to the disappointment of the RAF's Hunter and Javelin pilots. Piston-engined Mustangs flew some sorties over Borneo, but avoided interception. This aircraft wears the markings of No. 11 Squadron, then based at Iswahjudi.

Hawker Hunter FGA.Mk 9
The Hunter FGA.Mk 9 was a dedicated fighter-bomber, optimised for use in hot-and-high conditions. The Hunters of No. 20 Squadron flew numerous attacks against Indonesian infiltrators, mainly using their four 30-mm (1.2-in) cannon and underwing rockets.

Tupolev Tu-16
The Tu-16s of Indonesia's Nos 41 and 42 Squadrons at Kemajoram and Iswahjudi flew a number of provocative feints towards Singapore, being intercepted and escorted away by based Javelins. The Indonesian Tu-16s were missile-carrying 'Badger-Bs'.

Gurkha troops who were landed first. A single Britannia flew troops to the nearby island of Labuan. Within a fortnight, 3,200 troops had been delivered, together with 113 vehicles and supporting weapons and stores, and the rebellion in Sarawak put down. Joining the airlift had been an RAAF C-130A Hercules and an RNZAF Bristol Freighter, as well as RAF Shackletons of No. 205 Squadron. On arrival in Borneo the troops were moved forward by Beverleys and Pioneers and by Sycamore helicopters; also employed were the big twin-rotor Bristol Belvedere helicopters of No. 66 Squadron.

The rebellion in Brunei was being sustained by neighbouring Indonesia, and to restore the situation in the area British forces were tasked with isolating and mopping up the rebel bands, a task which involved airlifting troops to the oilfield at Seria and the airstrip at Anduki, the former being successfully undertaken by the short-field Twin Pioneers of No. 209 Squadron and the latter by a single Beverley (which was fired on by the rebels but suffered only negligible damage).

The rebellions having failed,

Above: Nos 845, 846 and 848 Squadrons aboard the HMS Albion and HMS Bulwark operated a mix of Whirlwind HAS.Mk 7s, Wessex HAS.Mk 1s and Wessex HU Mk 5s, like the aircraft illustrated. These helicopters augmented RAF Whirlwinds and Belvederes in the troop transport role. The British and allied forces in Borneo used helicopters extensively, which allowed the rapid reinforcement of remote outposts, and the insertion of troops to exactly where they were required. Light Army Air Corps helicopters were also deployed.

Left: Labuan became the RAF's operational hub in Borneo, its flight lines accommodating a wide variety of aircraft types. Visible in this photo are Beverley and Twin Pioneer transports, as well as Javelin interceptors and Canberra bombers. Labuan was an offshore island, and was thus easy to protect against infiltration, offering the RAF a secure base for its aircraft.

Left: No. 14 Squadron operated MiG-21Fs from Kemajoram. They were the most sophisticated aircraft in the AURI inventory. These fighters were not involved in the operations over Borneo, but were held back for the defence of Indonesia itself.

Below: No. 1 Squadron used a mix of P-51 Mustangs, B-25 Mitchells and B-26 Invaders, while No. 21 Squadron used B-25s and B-26s. Both units were based at Pontianak, from where they flew occasional low-level incursions over Sarawak and North Borneo.

Indonesia began infiltrating guerrilla forces across the border, to counter which the security forces established a number of strongpoints near to the known crossing points. These tiny garrisons were to be sustained wholly from the air, a task which caused a number of new squadrons to be deployed to Borneo, in particular Nos 103, 110 and 230 with the new Westland Whirlwind Mk 10 helicopter.

In a general widening of the conflict Indonesia greatly increased its cross-border incursions, even starting to send F-51 Mustangs into Borneo airspace, aircraft that were particularly difficult to counter as they were able to outmanoeuvre the big Javelins and were virtually immune from the RAF's heat-seeking missiles on account of their piston engines. The RAF V-bomber force supplied a detachment to the theatre, known as 'Matterhorn', initially with Victors

Left: Indonesia's Lockheed C-130 Hercules and Antonov An-12 transports served with No. 31 Squadron at Halim, and they dropped men and supplies in Sarawak and in East and West Malaysia. Some sources suggest that at least one C-130 was lost to a Javelin.

Jungle resupply

The RAF made extensive use of helicopters and STOL transport aircraft in Borneo. They frequently came under hostile ground fire and some were lost. Others fell victim to accidents at the often primitive landing strips from which they operated. The combination of aircraft and experienced Gurkha jungle fighters proved devastatingly effective.

Bristol Belvedere
The Belvedere was Britain's last truly indigenous military helicopter, and Borneo provided its swansong. It proved to be equally adept at transporting troops and bulky underslung loads. In Borneo the Belvedere equipped No. 66 Squadron, which was joined by No. 26 Squadron following the withdrawal from Aden.

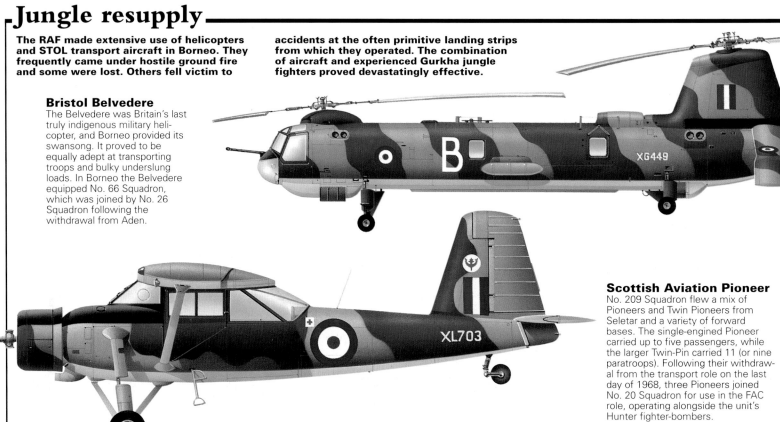

Scottish Aviation Pioneer
No. 209 Squadron flew a mix of Pioneers and Twin Pioneers from Seletar and a variety of forward bases. The single-engined Pioneer carried up to five passengers, while the larger Twin-Pin carried 11 (or nine paratroops). Following their withdrawal from the transport role on the last day of 1968, three Pioneers joined No. 20 Squadron for use in the FAC role, operating alongside the unit's Hunter fighter-bombers.

Left: With gaps in the land-based radar chain, carrierborne Gannet AEW.Mk 3s from the Hermes, Ark Royal, Victorious, Centaur and Eagle provided an invaluable addition to Britain's air-defence network in the area.

Below: A Handley Page Victor B.Mk 1A of No. 57 Sqn flies over a Malayan rubber plantation during 1965. The 'Matterhorn' V-bomber detachment saw no action, but did much to deter any thoughts of escalation by the Indonesians.

but from October 1964 consisted of Vulcan B.Mk 2s. Although for a time Victors were bombed up ready to go, the 'Matterhorn' bombers were not used in combat. In February 1964 an air-defence identification zone (ADIZ) was established, after which the Hunters and Javelins, based at Labuan and Kuching, maintained a 24-hour all-weather alert system, their pilots being authorised to engage and destroy any Indonesian aircraft entering the ADIZ.

INDONESIAN LANDINGS

In August of that year 100 regular Indonesian troops went ashore at

Left: Auster AOP.Mk 9s were deployed to Borneo with a number of units, including Nos 7 and 16 Recce Flights, and Nos 11 and 14 Liaison Flights. The aircraft was also deployed with the 4th Royal Tank Regiment's AOP Troop, and with the AOP Troop of the 1st Queen's Dragoon Guards. The AAC also deployed DHC Beavers and Scout and Sioux helicopters.

three points on the west coast of the Malayan peninsula, and two weeks later an Indonesian C-130 Hercules dropped paratroops in central Johore. Although these forces had been rounded up by mid-October, there were 40 other landings and it was against these

that the Hunters and Canberras of the RAF, RAAF and RNZAF were now deployed, and airborne early warning Gannets from Royal Navy carriers and shore bases were employed to patrol Malayan coastal airspace. However, the most effective counter to these cross-border raids was the rapid airlifting of troops by helicopter into the area.

Operations in Borneo waned during 1965, and by the middle of 1966 the 'confrontation' was fully over allowing the helicopters to return home from their forward-deployed bases in the jungle.

Above: Royal Australian Air Force Commonwealth Sabre 32s were deployed to Labuan for air-defence duties, taking over from RAF Javelins as the confrontation came to an end with the 11 August 1966 signature of a peace treaty. The Australian Sabre used a Rolls-Royce Avon engine and was armed with a pair of 30-mm (1.2-in) cannon.

Right: Troops approach a No. 5 Squadron, RAAF Bell UH-1B Iroquois. The unit was active in the confrontation from June 1964, flying from Butterworth. The white cabin top was designed to reflect heat, keeping the occupants cool. The Borneo interior had few tracks, and rivers were the primary transport routes.

Vietnam: In-Country War

1964 – 1973

The air war in south Vietnam was unlike any other. It saw the full might of the world's greatest military and economic power pitted against an elusive but highly motivated enemy, indistinguishable most of the time from the civilian population. The enemy was equipped only with small arms, but an intimate knowledge of the terrain meant that he was no easy target.

There were many different aspects to the air war, involving aircraft ranging from World War II piston-powered bombers to Mach 2 supersonic fighters, but among the most important were the support of troops in contact with the enemy, the destruction of key Viet Cong strongholds, the defence of American and South Vietnamese bases, and the interdiction of the communist supply effort both by land and by water.

AIR SUPPORT

The war against the Viet Cong was very much a short-range struggle. In a conventional war missions can be flown 'by the book'. But the Viet Cong were reading from a different script, and a whole new way of war had to be evolved. Fighters in the South were known as 'mud movers', for the simple reason that they fought down on the deck, duelling almost eye-to-eye with the insurgents on the ground.

In some cases, notably the support of American forces in close combat with the Viet Cong, it called for very great accuracy in the delivery of weaponry, occasionally to within metres of friendly troops. As a result, attacks were often pressed home at very low level.

This could be very dangerous: even though the communist insurgents lacked advanced weapons like guided missiles, they did have a lot of small arms, and low-level attacks brought the American fighters well

Above: The North American F-100 Super Sabre flew more combat sorties than any other warplane in Vietnam. Most were short hops to drop ordnance – like the napalm here tumbling from a low-flying 'Hun' of the 352nd TFS/35th TFW based at Phan Rang.

Right: The rotary bomb bay designed by Martin in the 1950s was finally combat-tested when the B-57 began operations in Vietnam in 1965. A license-built version of the British Canberra, the B-57 was the last USAF light bomber to fly combat sorties.

within their range. Small arms and light anti-aircraft fire accounted for the vast majority of American aircraft losses over South Vietnam.

In a war without front lines, firebases became the key to control of territory. Strongpoints equipped with artillery, they served as bases from which patrols moved out into the country. However, they were also magnets to Viet Cong attack, and on several occasions were subjected to major assaults. In the most serious cases these required calls for air support.

Once the decision had been made to expand the war, the original adviser-flown, piston-engined machines were replaced by a full range of modern aircraft which were brought to bear

against the Viet Cong. But for a fast-moving jet small targets moving beneath the jungle canopy are difficult to find, let alone attack, so forward air controllers flying low and slow in light planes were used to direct the fast jets.

Flying low and slow over the battlefield, the primary task of the forward air controller or FAC was to detect the enemy, mark his location in some way, and pass that information on to the fighters coming in to the area to provide aerial

Left: A USAF F-4 Phantom unleashes a barrage of 70-mm (2.75-in) rockets. The Phantom had set speed and altitude records before going to Vietnam and was recognized as a superb warplane, but air-to-ground work was difficult for a jet-powered 'fast mover'.

Above: The USAF deployed a new fighter, the Northrop F-5, to Vietnam during Operation Skoshi Tiger in 1965. The lightweight F-5 went on to become a major US export to developing nations, and was the backbone of South Vietnam's fighter force.

Busy Bird Dog
Left: This Cessna O-1A Bird Dog (51-12605) of the South Vietnamese army is typical of the more than 1,000 forward air control (FAC) aircraft that flew low and slow to spot targets for bigger, faster warplanes. Bird Dog pilots inevitably flew more combat missions than anyone else: When the fighting was heavy, it was not uncommon for a FAC to fly two or three sorties per day.

The Cessna O-1 Bird Dog evolved into the ground commander's best friend and a major irritant to the enemy. The weathered paint on this aircraft reflects the intensity of low-level combat in harsh tropical conditions

Men who flew as forward air controllers were a special breed. A FAC had to be courageous and, perhaps, lucky. Not everybody could strap into an O-1 or O-2, pinpoint enemy troops with smoke rockets, and loiter overhead while the Viet Cong shot back. FACs often brought home aircraft ventilated with small-caliber bullet holes. Some died. But starting with the heroic performance of USAF Major William 'Mac the FAC' McAllister, in 1964, they made a contribution to the war that was almost too important to measure.

Right: It was called a 'war among the treetops' by one FAC, who flew 230 missions without ever getting high enough to don an oxygen mask. Fortunately, the O-1 was nimble and responsive – as it had to be to survive

Below: The twin-boomed O-2 was an 'off the shelf' Cessna 337 Skymaster. With twin push/pull engines it was more difficult to fly than the Bird Dog but had greater speed, range and endurance and could carry light ordnance.

Hard-fighting 'Hun'
Caught up in a slugging match at treetop altitude with a lot of metal flying around, the F-100 was no longer the glamorous superstar that had set world air-speed records a decade earlier. But the Super Sabre's 75.4 kN (16,950 lb st) Pratt & Whitney J57-P-21A turbojet still gave the F-100 the ability to perform valiantly.

North American F-100 Super Sabre

'Huns' were employed mainly for in-country missions where they did not need to face Hanoi's MiG fighters, although Super Sabres flew sorties over Laos and North Vietnam in the early phases of American participation in the war in Southeast Asia. In 1968, regular Air Force F-100 units were joined by four Air National Guard squadrons. Carrying two 340-kg (750-lb) bombs and two external fuel tanks, This F-100D-75-NA (56-3184) belongs to the 416th TFS/37th TFW at Phu Cat airfield in South Vietnam.

Armament
The F-100D Super Sabre was a potent ground attacker, with its four 20-mm Pontiac M39E cannon each with 1,200 rounds and underwing pylons for up to 3193 kg (7,040 lb) of bombs, rockets, or missiles. However, some of its weapons were less than effective: early versions of the AGM-12A/B Bullpup missile bounced harmlessly off any hard target they struck and often failed to detonate.

Below: Nothing was louder or more frightening than the sound of a B-52 blasting out a pathway in the jungle. With as many as 108 bombs from a single aircraft raining down on Viet Cong targets, the result was devastating, and could be felt as an earth tremor many miles away.

Above: This black-bellied Boeing B-52F Stratofortress is sending a message to Viet Cong insurgents in South Vietnam. Crews flew from Guam on exhausting, marathon missions that could last up to 18 hours with air refuelling.

Below: A Lockheed C-130A Hercules makes its own kind of delivery, dropping supplies to a friendly outpost. 'In-country' airlift was vital when ground access was difficult and roads often blocked by the enemy.

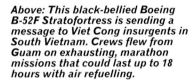

support and firepower. The 'slow movers' in their fragile prop-driven Cessnas played a vital part in finding the enemy, as well as identifying and marking targets.

INTO THE BREACH

The Cessnas carried white phosphorous or smoke rockets. Forward air controllers – FACs – often flew solo, demanding the ability to control their aircraft while simultaneously hunting for the enemy and marking targets.

The FAC pilot was expected to expose himself to enemy gunfire, primarily to learn more about the target and to determine the best way of attacking.

Nobody expected the FAC to hit the target with his rockets, but he could use the smoke to give accurate instructions to fighter pilots – 'about 200 mikes [metres]

uphill from the smoke,' would be a typical direction.

With bases the length of the country, American troops could rely on rapid air support: tactical aircraft could be armed and into the air within minutes of receiving any call for help.

Technology was also thrown at the problem, particularly in the night battle against the supply routes. The use of night vision and thermal sensors became widespread, along with seismic and even chemical sensors, and possible targets were engaged with pinpoint accuracy with the latest weapons.

One notable exception was the B-52 effort, where the massive Boeing bombers dropped huge tonnages of high explosive onto suspected Viet Cong positions and strongholds from high altitude. Results of these strikes, code named

Counter Insurgency

'Real' flying, some pilots insisted, was possible only in one of the light, nimble aircraft designed to keep the war very 'up close and personal'. The OV-10 Bronco had been developed with much fanfare as a

'COIN' (counter insurgency) warplane. The A-37 Dragonfly was an outgrowth of the USAF's standard primary trainer but was heavier, more powerful, and could carry a useful load of bombs and rockets.

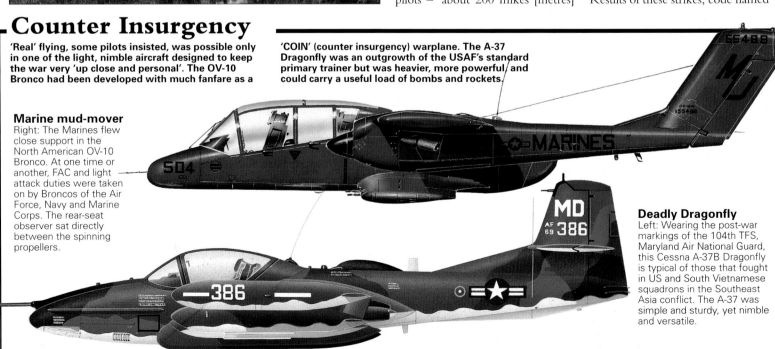

Marine mud-mover
Right: The Marines flew close support in the North American OV-10 Bronco. At one time or another, FAC and light attack duties were taken on by Broncos of the Air Force, Navy and Marine Corps. The rear-seat observer sat directly between the spinning propellers.

Deadly Dragonfly
Left: Wearing the post-war markings of the 104th TFS, Maryland Air National Guard, this Cessna A-37B Dragonfly is typical of those that fought in US and South Vietnamese squadrons in the Southeast Asia conflict. The A-37 was simple and sturdy, yet nimble and versatile.

COMBAT RESCUE

Hard-hitting 'Cowboy'

Capt Richard S. Drury of the 602nd SOS/56th SOW fires a salvo of 20-mm (2.75-in) rockets while diving his Douglas A-1H Skyraider, 'Midnight Cowboy' (BuNo. 134257) to protect a combat rescue attempt. The heavily-armed Skyraider, which could carry some 4535 kg (10,000 lb) of bombs, was the ideal escort for rescue helicopters and a welcome friend to every downed airman.

Among the most daring of the supporting roles in Vietnam was that of rescuing downed airmen from the midst of enemy-held terrain. Heavily-armed and armoured Sikorsky HH-3 and HH-53 helicopters were used to make the actual pickups, but they did so under the protection of aging Douglas A-1 Skyraiders operating under the widely-known call-sign of 'Sandy'. The old prop-driven fighter bombers were a better performance match with the helicopters than more modern jets, and their ability both to loiter for long periods over the battlefield and to deliver a wide range of munitions made them ideal rescue escorts. To do their job effectively, 'Sandy' pilots flew some of the most dangerous missions of the conflict, often in the face of concentrated and accurate anti-aircraft fire. Their

job involved making contact with the downed aircrew, drawing fire from and then destroying enemy guns and troops, laying smoke screens and supplying suppressive fire while the helicopters moved in to rescue the airmen. 'Sandy' pilots collected more than their share of gallantry medals and Purple Hearts, and many invaluable combat pilots and other aircrew owe their lives to this fearless group of men.

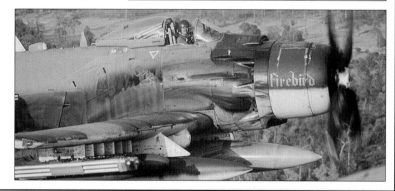

Right: This Sikorsky CH-3 is fitted with a winch above its cabin door. The better-known HH-3E 'Jolly Green Giant', was similar, but also had an in-flight refuelling probe. It was was used to rescue airmen shot down behind enemy lines.

Right: 'Firebird' is an A-1H Skyraider flying from Nakhon Phanom, Thailand. An A-1H pilot, using the radio call-sign 'Sandy', often found himself as the mission commander at a rescue site, charged to orchestrate efforts by all involved in a pick-up attempt.

Arc Light, were debatable: when they hit the target the effect was devastating, but all too often they were bombing empty jungle.

Except for the occasional major battle such as that in the A-Shau valley or at Khe Sanh, the bulk of attacks on American positions was by troops armed with rifles, machine-guns, rockets and mortars. At Khe Sanh, however, ground-attack aircraft were faced with an enemy attacking in divisional strength, with artillery and armour. In many ways this was easier to deal with, since it provided ideal target material for massive aerial attacks by a wide variety of fighters and bombers.

The main strike effort of the US forces was augmented by many supporting missions such as aerial

tanking, recovery of ditched aircraft, airborne early warning supplied by Lockheed EC-121 Warning Stars and massive airlift and ferrying involving Lockheed's C-5, C-141 and C-130, the de Havilland Canada C-7 Caribou, Douglas C-47, Boeing C-135 and numerous smaller types.

The US Navy's carriers sailing at 'Dixie Station' off the Mekong delta flew many strikes into the delta, and used these missions to work up to full strength before moving north to 'Yankee Station' in the Gulf of Tonkin, where the action was much more fierce.

Right: A McDonnell F-4B Phantom lightly armed for an air defence mission launches from the angled deck of USS Ranger (CVA-62). No serious effort was made to attack US carriers at sea near Vietnam.

Vietnam: Rolling Thunder

1965-1968

The Repubic F-105 Thunderchief was the most important strike aircraft in the early years of the war against North Vietnam, and took most losses. Known as the 'Thud', it was the biggest, fastest and loudest single-seat, single-engined bomber of its time.

Above: Packed with advanced electronics, Douglas EB-66s led radar-bombing missions by Thuds and Phantoms near Hanoi. The USAF lost six EB-66s in combat, a heavy toll for a craft that served in small numbers.

Below: The F-4 Phantom flew beside the F-105 from the start, and took on more of the burden as the Rolling Thunder campaign progressed. Air Force, Marine, and Navy fliers all 'went north' in the F-4 from bases on land and sea.

The initial Flaming Dart retaliation raids of 1964 were seen by the Johnson administration as the first steps in a gradual escalation of pressures on North Vietnam until the North Vietnamese decided that a Viet Cong victory was not worth the price. The policy of attacking North Vietnam only on a retaliatory basis was abandoned and Flaming Dart gave way to the sustained air campaign known as Rolling Thunder.

The air war against North Vietnam as consisting of four distinct phases – the Rolling Thunder campaign from 1965 to 1968, the bombing halt which lasted until 1972, the Linebacker campaign between May and October of that year, and the final intensive bomb-ing of the North known as Linebacker II, which lasted for 11 days in December 1972.

Rolling Thunder, as conceived and begun, had three objectives: to reduce infiltration, to boost South Vietnamese morale and to make it clear to Hanoi that continuation of the insurgency in the South would become increasingly expensive.

In Hanoi, however, Rolling Thunder was simply seen as one more obstacle to overcome in a long struggle to remove foreign influence and unify a divided Vietnam under Vietnamese rule. No official in the North Vietnamese leadership ever saw the American air strikes as evidence that it was time to succumb.

The first USAF Rolling Thunder missions were flown on 2 March 1965, using Martin B-57s, North American F-100Ds, and Republic F-105Ds. Of the 150 aircraft available at Thai bases, 25 F-105Ds from the 12th and 67th Tactical Fighter Squadrons (both part of the 18th Tactical Fighter Wing) accompanied B-57s to an ammunition depot at Xom Bong, about 56 km (35 miles) above the DMZ (demilitarized zone) and inflicted heavy damage.

On this first raid, no fewer than five aircraft – two F-100D Super Sabres and three F-105Ds – were lost to ground fire and the first USAF pilot, Captain Hayden J. Lockhart, was taken prisoner. Already, it was clear that the idea of bombing which would quickly subdue North Vietnam required further examination.

MUDDLED STRATEGY

From the beginning, critics of the sustained campaign against North Vietnam would argue that Rolling Thunder did not really roll and was not particularly thunderous. The planning of air strikes was a complex and unwieldy business, beginning in the Situation Room at the White House where President Johnson retained firm control over what could and could not be attacked. Decisions as routine as the choice of ordnance for a particular sortie were made at this level, thousands of miles from the fighting.

Johnson's decisions were relayed to Secretary of Defense Robert McNamara, who in turn informed the Pentagon. Directives were then passed down to CINCPAC (Commander-in-Chief, Pacific forces, in Hawaii) which then fragmented or 'fragged' the various targets among USAF, USN and – on rare occasions – South Vietnamese aircraft. The USAF headquarters in Saigon, the 2nd Air Division, made recommendations but could not choose targets.

Lt Gen Joseph Moore, who commanded 2nd Air Division, was an accomplished old fighter hand who kept making suggestions for a more effective campaign against the North Vietnamese road and rail transportation network, only to find targets approved on what seemed a random basis. The obvious targets around Hanoi and Haiphong, especially North Vietnam's air bases, were off-limits to the US forces at the time.

The most important aircraft in the early years of the war against the

North was the redoubtable Republic F-105 Thunderchief, known to most of its pilots as the 'Thud', which could lift eight 340-kg (750-lb) iron bombs and auxiliary fuel tanks. These F-105s usually attacked their targets from medium level, often on the command of a lead aircraft which was usually a Douglas EB-66 Destroyer, equipped with full electronic countermeasures (ECM) and navigation aids. Inflight refuelling was often necessary to enable the 'Thuds' to reach their targets.

ANTI-AIRCRAFT THREAT

A complicating factor was the expansion of the North Vietnamese air defences. Such losses that had been suffered in the early days were due to Soviet-supplied anti-aircraft artillery – AAA or Triple-A – which had been quickly and substantially reinforced early in 1965. Radar-directed anti-aircraft guns were a serious enough challenge to the US strike aircraft but they would soon be joined by MiGs and by guided SAMs. Northern pilots flying aged MiG-15bis fighters tended to keep well away from the US Navy Skyhawks and the USAF's F-100s. It was now that large numbers of Chinese-built MiG-17s started arriving in the North. Although not as fast as their American opponents, the MiGs were very agile, and they were to cause the Americans considerable problems in air combat. F-105s could protect themselves to some

extent, and victories were scored over MiG fighters with both Sidewinder missiles and the internal 20-mm gun, but losses began to mount.

The arrival in South East Asia of the McDonnell F-4 Phantom heralded a new era as the greater range, load and speed of the aircraft enabled many more targets to be attacked. At first the F-4s were used in the bombing role, with much the same tactics as employed by the F-105s, but increasingly effective communist defences dictated a change.

The 8th Tactical Fighter Wing, known as the 'Wolf Pack' under the command of combat veteran

Route Packages

North Vietnam was divided by American mission planners into six target areas, known as Route Packages or 'Packs'.

The most heavily defended areas were those around the capital, Hanoi, and the country's major port, Haiphong. These were in Route Package Six, which because of its importance and the large numbers of targets it contained was subdivided into Pack 6A and Pack 6B.

Although there were no hard and fast divisions of responsibility, and aircraft from any service could attack any target, the Air Force generally dealt with inland targets and the Navy attacked those on the coast. Marine Corps aircraft operating out of I Corps in the north of South Vietnam were also occasionally used against North Vietnamese targets, generally in Pack 1.

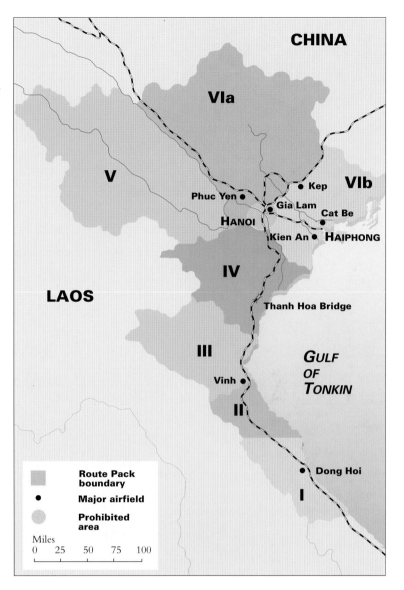

CHINA

VIa

V

Phuc Yen • • Kep   VIb

• Gia Lam   Cat Be •

HANOI   Kien An • HAIPHONG

IV

LAOS

Thanh Hoa Bridge

III

GULF OF TONKIN

Vinh •

II

• Dong Hoi

I

■ Route Pack boundary

● Major airfield

● Prohibited area

Miles
0   25   50   75   100

The Fighters

Americans saw air-to-air action as secondary to their bombing effort. To the North Vietnamese, every dogfight was a defence of home turf. Both sides flew state-of-the-art fighters. Hanoi relied on MiGs that were short-legged but nimble and deadly. Americans flew costlier, more complex jets with longer range that were less manoeuvrable in close quarters but, being missile-armed, lethal from afar.

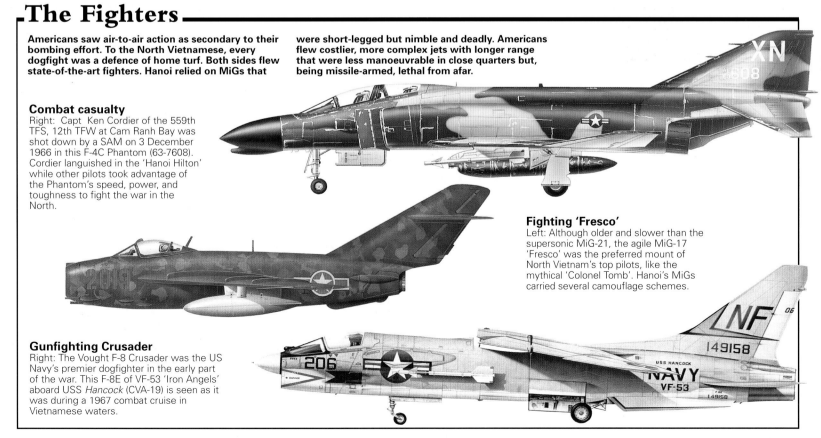

Combat casualty
Right: Capt Ken Cordier of the 559th TFS, 12th TFW at Cam Ranh Bay was shot down by a SAM on 3 December 1966 in this F-4C Phantom (63-7608). Cordier languished in the 'Hanoi Hilton' while other pilots took advantage of the Phantom's speed, power, and toughness to fight the war in the North.

Fighting 'Fresco'
Left: Although older and slower than the supersonic MiG-21, the agile MiG-17 'Fresco' was the preferred mount of North Vietnam's top pilots, like the mythical 'Colonel Tomb'. Hanoi's MiGs carried several camouflage schemes.

Gunfighting Crusader
Right: The Vought F-8 Crusader was the US Navy's premier dogfighter in the early part of the war. This F-8E of VF-53 'Iron Angels' aboard USS *Hancock* (CVA-19) is seen as it was during a 1967 combat cruise in Vietnamese waters.

Operation 'Bolo'

Life expectancy for American pilots over North Vietnam was falling fast. By 1967, growing North Vietnamese fighter and missile strength was reaping a costly harvest from the American fighter bombers. And the USAF could not strike back at the enemy airfields, forbidden by restrictive rules of engagement dictated in Washington.

Clearly something had to be done, and Colonel Robin Olds was the man to do it. World War II ace Olds commanded the 8th Tactical Fighter Wing, the 'Wolf Pack', flying F-4C Phantoms out of Ubon in Thailand. Olds was a tough, seat-of-the pants flyer of the old school. But he was a fine tactician and a superb leader.

If the 'Wolf Pack' could convince the North Vietnamese that they were bombers rather than fighters, then the MiGs might be lured into combat before they could realise their mistake. On the morning of 2 January 1967, Olds led 14 flights of Phantoms, six flights of 'Wild Weasel' defence suppression F-105s, and four flights of F-104 Starfighters, a total of nearly 100 aircraft. At least the same number of aircraft flew in supporting roles. These included EC-121 airborne radar planes, EB-66 electronic warfare platforms, more F-4Cs making diversionary sweeps, and A-1 Skyraiders, F-100s and helicopters on alert for possible rescue missions.

The Phantoms headed north along Route Package Six, the heavily defended approaches to Hanoi. The Phantoms flew at speeds and heights typical of a large-scale F-105 raid. Each of the F-4Cs was equipped with an ECM pod usually carried by Thunderchiefs, so on the North Vietnamese radar they would look like a bomber.

The first wave – three flights of four Phantoms, characteristically led from the front by Robin Olds – wheeled past Phuc Yen, an air base and major petroleum depot southwest of Hanoi. As they headed for the North Vietnamese capital, an EC-121 radar plane over the Gulf of Tonkin warned that MiGs were taking off and others were converging on the area. It looked as though the bait had been taken.

MISSILE FIGHT

The MiGs bored in unsuspectingly, and Olds' flight manoeuvred to engage. Olds himself fired two Sparrows and a Sidewinder at a silver MiG, but all three missiles missed. However, Lieutenant Ralph Wettrehahn and Captain Walt Radeker, flying Olds 2 and 4 respectively, were more successful, each destroying an enemy.

It was about this time that the North Vietnamese realised what was happening, and immediately began to manoeuvre defensively. However, by now the 'Wolf Pack' was roaring. Olds barrel-rolled around another MiG before shooting it down with a Sidewinder. At the same time Captain Everett T. Raspberry was downing another.

The second Phantom flight, code-named Rambler, now arrived. Diving down on a pair of MiGs Captain John B. Stone in Rambler 1 fired two Sparrows. As one missile hit the target, Stone was attacked from behind by more MiGs. Breaking left and down with Rambler 2, Lt Lawrence Glynn, Stone brought the MiGs into the sights of Major Philip P. Combies in Rambler 4, who shot one of the enemy down. Lieutenant Glynn in Rambler 2

now turned inside the MiGs, loosed off a pair of Sparrows and destroyed a seventh North Vietnamese jet.

The MiGs broke off before any more of the 'Wolf Pack' could arrive on the scene, so there were to be no more successes that day. Olds and his men headed homewards, satisfied in the knowledge that they had downed seven of North Vietnam's best aircraft without loss to themselves. Colonel Olds had shown the way to beat the MiGs. In the following 12 months, USAF Phantoms were to shoot down another 36 North Vietnamese fighters, with the 'Wolf Pack' accounting for 23 of them. But thanks to a politically-motivated bombing halt which lasted until 1972, it was to be another four years before the US Air Force achieved similar success.

Colonel Robin Olds, laid a trap for the MiGs. Nearly 100 fighters followed exactly the same pattern as that regularly used by bombing F-105s and F-4s, but these aircraft carried only air-to-air missiles. The MiGs, under the control of excellent ground radar, soon intercepted the force and in the ensuing battle seven were destroyed without loss to the Americans, Olds himself bagging two.

Following this action, which was

to remain one of the the largest aerial fights of the war, the North Vietnamese were considerably more cautious with their interceptions, especially as the Americans introduced MIGCAP fighter cover flights equipped with F-4s carrying Sidewinder and Sparrow missiles

At the same time as the MiGs were being tamed, the SAMs became an ever increasing problem as supplies of the Soviet SA-2 'Guideline' established themselves. To combat the SAMs, the USAF deployed 'Wild Weasel' F-100s and F-105s. These carried extra electronics and Shrike anti-radiation missiles (ARMs) which homed-in on the radar emissions of the 'Fan Song' guidance system of the SA-2. Under the codename Iron Hand, the 'Wild Weasels' and their naval equivalents streaked in ahead of the main attacking force to try to suppress the SAM forces before the main strike. Though partially successful, the war against the SAMs

Above: To 'sucker' Hanoi's MiG pilots, Col. Robin Olds used intelligence photos snapped by the RF-101C Voodoo. Olds later ordered that no Voodoo pilot pay for a drink at his fighter wing's bar in Ubon, Thailand.

Right: MiG-17s sheltered at an airfield in North Vietnam. For much of the war, US fliers were forbidden to bomb airfields like Kep, so their only resort was air-to-air action. It was an expensive way to fight MiGs.

F-105 Thunderchief

The Republic F-105 Thunderchief had been designed as a supersonic nuclear bomber carrying its weapons internally. In Vietnam, it was a subsonic striker, carrying ordnance externally and extra fuel in the bay. A big, powerful aircraft, the 'Thud' required excessive runway length when operating with heavy bombloads in the high ambient temperature of Southeast Asia and often required aerial refuelling to complete its missions.

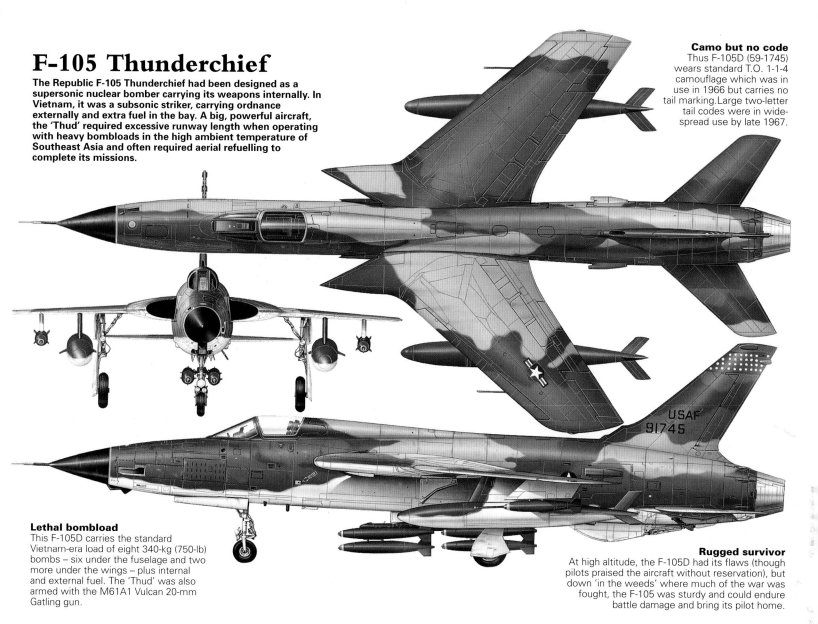

Camo but no code
Thus F-105D (59-1745) wears standard T.O. 1-1-4 camouflage which was in use in 1966 but carries no tail marking.Large two-letter tail codes were in widespread use by late 1967.

Lethal bombload
This F-105D carries the standard Vietnam-era load of eight 340-kg (750-lb) bombs – six under the fuselage and two more under the wings – plus internal and external fuel. The 'Thud' was also armed with the M61A1 Vulcan 20-mm Gatling gun.

Rugged survivor
At high altitude, the F-105D had its flaws (though pilots praised the aircraft without reservation), but down 'in the weeds' where much of the war was fought, the F-105 was sturdy and could endure battle damage and bring its pilot home.

continued throughout the conflict, the Americans continuing to lose aircraft to this often unseen threat.

The first electronic countermeasures (ECM) capability to be mounted in the conflict was employed on 29 March 1965, when three RF-101C Voodoos, each carrying QRC-160 pods, flew ECM support missions accompanying a Rolling Thunder strike force to target. The QRC-160 proved unsatisfactory and was quickly withdrawn from combat, but steps were under way to develop some means of jamming or deceiving the enemy's radar defences.

Several of the low-level, small-scale strikes were controlled from a 'fast-mover FAC', an adviser sitting in the back-seat of a two-seat F-100, A-4 or TF-9 Cougar. These aircraft were able to survive the defensive fire by agility and speed, whereas more typical FAC aircraft were too slow for this hostile environment.

Overall control of the battle zone was entrusted to ships sailing in the Gulf of Tonkin and to Lockheed EC-121 Warning Star airborne early-warning aircraft circling over the sea or Thailand. Under the codename College Eye, these veteran machines used their powerful radars to co-ordinate

strikes and to warn of the approach of hostile MiGs.

Many Air Force, Navy and Marines officers and pilots, who felt that their hands were tied behind their backs, considered the long air campaign to be a violation of the basic principle of combat: when you fight, you must fight to win. Men in 'Thuds' and Crusaders, Skyhawks and Phantoms believed that they had been sent against formidable defences, to attack questionable targets, under too many restrictions, with no realistic chance of waging the war in a manner that would make it possible to win.

DAMAGE TO THE NORTH

Despite all the restrictions, the on-again, off-again mood of the campaign, and the general confusion, these pilots had, in fact, done more damage to North Vietnam than is generally recognized. In the years since the conflict, a few North Vietnamese have acknowledged that at times in 1967 and 1968 the bombing was hurting badly. The diversion of resources to repair,

Right: The Douglas EB-66 served as a new kind of pathfinder, using its onboard electronic suite to carve out a route for fighter-bombers. On radar-directed raids, the EB-66 crew called 'Bombs away' for all.

maintain and expand bridges, roads and railways – to say nothing of infiltration routes – was a drain on an already overburdened society.

When Rolling Thunder came to an end with the bombing halt of 30 October 1968, preliminary peace talks were taking shape in Paris, though they had hardly progressed beyond such issues as the shape of the table to be used at meetings.

With the benefit of hindsight, it is clear that Rolling Thunder could have been successful only if the

civilian leaders in Washington had made a policy decision to use military power effectively. Most professional airmen believed then, and still believe now, that North Vietnam could have been taken out of the war in a matter of weeks with the men and machines already located in Southeast Asia, and with no additional resources. What they felt was missing was a plan, a policy, and a coherent decision to use airmen and aircraft as they were intended to be used.

Vietnam: The Helicopter War

1961 - 1975

Left: South Vietnamese troops pour from a Bell UH-1D/H Iroquois helicopter – the ubiquitous Huey – at a landing zone (LZ) in a rice paddy. Helicopter pilots had to scout out and 'secure' the LZ before landing and disgorging infantrymen.

Below: An US Navy Huey gunship flies as escort to riverine patrol boats in the Mekong Delta. Helicopters and light naval forces were the only way of moving troops and firepower around the myriad of waterways of the Delta, a hotbed of Viet Cong activity.

Helicopters had seen action in Korea, Malaya and Algeria, but it was Vietnam which was to become the first true helicopter war. Helicopters flying into 'hot' landing zones became one of the most enduring images of the war, and that was certainly the helicopter's most outstanding role, but most missions were very different. Helicopters did everything. They delivered mail and new personnel, flying men on leave and returning men full of the pleasures of Hong Kong, Tokyo or Australia. They served as taxis for the brass and television crews, and as trucks, replenishing ammunition and stores at isolated fire support bases. Other tasks included heavy lift of outsize objects, gunship fire support, combat rescue, observation, liaison and psychological warfare.

So important was the helicopter that by the end of the Vietnam War the US Army, the major user of rotary-winged machines, had become the world's third largest air force after that of the Soviet Union

and the USAF. But large numbers in battle meant large numbers of casualties: in a decade of conflict, the United States lost 4,869 helicopters, of which 2,382 were destroyed by enemy action.

Helicopters were in right from the start. The first complete US Army units in action in Vietnam were the 8th and 57th Transportation Companies, which in December 1961 landed 32 twin-rotor Piasecki H-21s from the USS *Card*. Less than two weeks later they were in action, airlifting 1,000 Vietnamese paratroopers in a surprise attack on a suspected Viet Cong headquarters. The successful mission was notable as the first major use of US combat power in Vietnam, and as the beginning of a new era in air mobility.

Early in 1962 the H-21s were joined in-country by Marine Corps HUS-1 Seahorses which operated in the Mekong Delta. But the most notable arrival of the year was the US Army's 57th Medical Detachment. Its medical evacuation mission, soon to be nicknamed

'Dust Off', introduced one of the great icons of the war, the Bell UH-1 Iroquois. Known universally as the Huey, the UH-1 also equipped the Utility Tactical Transport Helicopter Company (UTTHC) based at Tan Son Nhut.

As a result of assessment of experience gained by the UTTHC, which included fitting guns and rockets, the US Army quickly

adapted to the jungle conditions in Vietnam and numerous helicopter units were activated in the USA for deployment to the theatre. When American ground troops were committed to action in 1965, they came with large numbers of helicopters.

Prominent among the units which arrived in 1965 was the Air Cavalry. Since the late 1950s, the

Left: The Piasecki H-21 served in Vietnam between 1962 and 1964 and was the first US helicopter to carry a door gunner as a matter of course, usually armed with a 7.62-mm (0.3-in) M60 machine-gun.

Below: US Marine Corps Sikorsky UH-34Ds (known as HUS-1s until late 1962) were the backbone of Operation Shy Fly, the first major effort to provide helicopter 'lift' to South Vietnamese troops.

The Ubiquitous 'Huey'

Among the most recognised flying machines in the history of aviation, the turboshaft-powered Huey revolutionised the support of combat units in the field. Transport Hueys flew men, equipment, and supplies, while gunships flew escort missions and served as a kind of flying artillery in support of troops on the ground. Hueys were used as aerial ambulances, lifting wounded soldiers from the heart of a firefight directly to medical help – in the process reducing the battlefield fatality rate in Vietnam to the lowest level in the history of warfare. The sight and distinctive sound of this great aircraft, seen on virtually every American television news broadcast of the period, became one of the great icons of the Vietnam experience.

'B model' Huey
Left: This UH-1B (64-13912) flew with 'A' Company, 1st Aviation Battalion, 1st Infantry Division and wears the Division's 'Big Red One' emblem on its tail. Early Hueys had short bodies – note the differences between this and the longer UH-1H medevac Huey seen below.

'DustOff' samaritan
Right: the UH-1D/H model, seen here with medical evacuation Red Cross markings, had a 14.63-m (48-ft) rotor and a much bigger fuselage, enabling it to carry 12 troops. On a medevac mission (universally known as 'DustOff' from the callsign of one of its early practicioners) the bigger 'D' and 'H' Hueys accommodated the pilot plus six stretchers and a medic, or up to 1814 kg (4,000 lb) of freight.

Armed to the teeth
Left: There were three essential Army Hueys – 'Slicks' (troop carriers), 'Dustoffs' (medevac machines), and heavily-armed 'Guns' or 'Hogs'. A UH-1B gunship like this 1st Air Cavalry Division example could carry 70-mm (2.75-in) rocket pods, 7.62-mm (0.3-in) multi-barrel Miniguns, 40-mm grenade launchers, and a host of other weapons.

Above: UH-1 pilots planted troops in landing zones, 'hot' with enemy action nearby or 'cold' without, and spent no more time on the ground than necessary. It took about a minute to unload troops.

Right: With a smoke grenade serving as a marker and his M16A1 rifle held aloft, this soldier is guiding a Bell UH-1 Iroquois to touchdown in an area obviously free of Viet Cong opposition.

US Army had been experimenting in using helicopters to give large units unprecedented battlefield mobility. Using large numbers of helicopters, a division-sized force could make an extremely rapid assault, seizing control of a large area of territory in a very short space of time.

The 11th Air Assault Division (Test) at Fort Benning proved the new air mobile concept to be feasible. It was seen as being ideal for Vietnam operations, so the 11th, renamed 1st Cavalry Division (Airmobile), became the first complete US Army division to be deployed to Southeast Asia. In spite of the vulnerability of the helicopter to ground fire, the Air Cav proved itself to be one of the most effective combat formations to serve in Vietnam.

A typical assault mission involving, say, about 100 troops, would require some 16-18 helicopters of which one UH-1 would be equipped as a communications command aircraft carrying the force commander and an air liaison officer whose task would be to call up any USAF support required; another UH-1 would deliver the landing zone (LZ) control party which

Air Assault

In 1965, at the height of their strength, North Vietnam's elite regulars faced inexperienced Americans of the 1st Air Cavalry Division, but thanks to helicopter assault pioneer General Hamilton Howze, the Americans brought along a new way to fight. The helicopter gave the American 'skytroopers' an unprecedented mobility: transported by large numbers of Hueys, the Cav defeated Hanoi's finest in the First and Second Battles of la Drang Valley. The helicopter had changed the very nature of warfare, probably forever.

Door gunner
Above: The crew chief (always a flight crew member in the US Army) often doubled as a door gunner, although climbing completely out of the Huey in mid-air was a little unusual. Scattered fire from a hand-held M60 machine-gun was unlikely to hit any Viet Cong, but it was designed not so much to hit the enemy as to force him to keep his head down, increasing the UH-1's chance of getting into and out of an LZ unscathed.

Air Cavalry
Above: Air mobility advocates viewed the helicopter not as an odd kind of flying machine but as a substitute for the Jeep, the 4x4 truck, and the armoured personnel carrier. When the 1st and 101st Air Cavalry Divisions took air mobility ideas with them to South Vietnam, they were committed to seizing the advantage every time a helicopter could help them do it. One way of doing so was in tight formation flying, which could deliver the maximum number of troops on a landing zone in the minimum possible time.

Observation
Right: With its superb visibility and ability to fly slowly or even hover, the helicopter is an unrivalled observation platform. The US Army in Vietnam used the agile Hughes OH-6A Cayuse as its standard rotary-wing spotter . The 'Loach' drew its unofficial nickname from the acronym LOH, or Light Observation Helicopter.

would land first and guide the assault force in.

Agile light observation helicopters like the Hughes OH-6A Cayuse, known as the Loach, would be used to seek out enemy forces. Support weapons too large for carriage by the assault heli-copters, which included artillery up to the size of 105-mm howitzers, could be delivered as slung loads by medium- and heavy-lift helicopters.

Not unnaturally, the development of new assault weapons was accelerated, and more and more sophisticated equipment was fitted in the helicopters to bring increased firepower the US Army's airmobile companies in the field. The AH-1 HueyCobra, a potent gunship which mounted an armament mix selected from Miniguns, 20-mm cannon, automatic grenade-launchers and high-explosive rockets first, entered service in Vietnam in 1967; later, integrated television and infra-red sensors were introduced. By 1968 about 50 assault helicopter companies, equipped with between 600 and 700 HueyCobras, were based at such locations as Ban Me Thuot, Phuoc Vinh, Pleiku, Bien Hoa, Nha Trang and Tuy Hoa.

Apart from the constant and massive use of assault helicopters by the US Army, other large heli-copters were also widely used for numerous heavy-lift tasks, not least of which was the recovery of downed aircraft from otherwise inaccessible locations. It has been stated that during the course of the entire Vietnam war the Boeing Vertol CH-47 Chinook alone recovered thousands of downed air-craft, worth a reputed $2.9 billion. The big twin-rotor Chinook, more than 680 examples of which had been produced by the end of the war, could carry up to 44 troops, light armoured vehicles, artillery or ten tonnes of stores on external load hooks. The bigger Sikorsky CH-54 Tarhe crane helicopter was also used and was capable of carrying items like bulldozers as slung loads.

The most powerful helicopters used in Vietnam were the variants of the Sikorsky Sea Stallion. Used as a heavy-lift troop and cargo trans-port by the Marines, it was selected by the US Air Force to equip the 37th Aerospace Rescue and

Left: It was inevitable that bigger helicopters would join the fray as soon as they could be built. The Boeing CH-47 Chinook, also dubbed the 'Sh--thook' by crew members, gave new size and versa-tility to Army rotary-wing units.

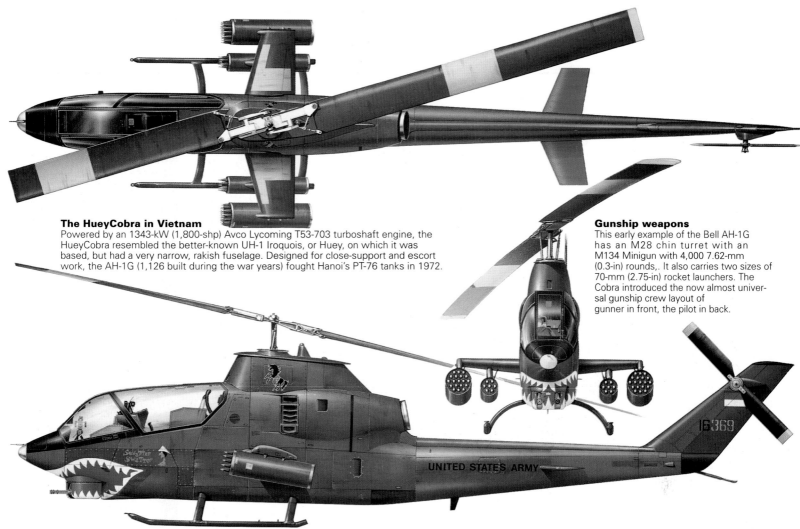

The HueyCobra in Vietnam
Powered by an 1343-kW (1,800-shp) Avco Lycoming T53-703 turboshaft engine, the HueyCobra resembled the better-known UH-1 Iroquois, or Huey, on which it was based, but had a very narrow, rakish fuselage. Designed for close-support and escort work, the AH-1G (1,126 built during the war years) fought Hanoi's PT-76 tanks in 1972.

Gunship weapons
This early example of the Bell AH-1G has an M28 chin turret with an M134 Minigun with 4,000 7.62-mm (0.3-in) rounds,. It also carries two sizes of 70-mm (2.75-in) rocket launchers. The Cobra introduced the now almost universal gunship crew layout of gunner in front, the pilot in back.

Bell AH-1 HueyCobra

The HueyCobra was developed quickly to meet urgent war needs, but the design was a superb one. While other gunship helicopters failed to reach production, the Cobra remained the standard US helicopter gunship for 18 years.

Battlefield response
The armament of the HueyCobra might have been its most obvious and important feature, but this first true battlefield helicopter was also equipped with VHF and UHF radios and associated electronics gear to enhance communication between helicopters, and between the air and the ground.

Recovery Squadron at Phu Cat later in the war. The HH-53 was heavily armed and armoured for the perilous mission of rescuing downed aircrew from hostile territory, often under intense enemy fire.

By the early 1970s, as America began to disengage from Vietnam, the process of Vietnamization saw a large number of UH-1 and CH-47 helicopters supplied to the VNAF – indeed, the number of Hueys left behind and struck off US Army charge exceeded the helicopter strength of any West European air force. The aim was to make the Vietnamese self-sufficient by the time the Americans left.

However, American financial aid did not match the massive inventory of equipment left behind, and by the time North Vietnam overran the south in 1975, most of the once powerful force was grounded and in storage for lack of operating funds.

But the helicopter still had one major role to play, being there for the end of America's Vietnam War as it had been for the beginning. As the North Vietnamese army finally took the capital in April 1975, American and Vietnamese helicopters lifted thousands of refugees to safety in the last days of Operation Frequent Wind.

Above: Sailors push a South Vietnamese UH-1H Huey over the side of USS Midway (CVA-41) during Operation Frequent Wind, the hectic April 1975 evacuation of Saigon. Dozens of aircraft were dumped.

Right: Attired for the climate, a ground crew member directs a USAF Sikorsky HH-53B/C 'Super Jolly'. The HH-53 was the largest helicopter employed for combat rescue, often penetrating deep into North Vietnamese territory..

Vietnam: War against the Trail

1963 – 1973

Left: Pilot Lt Victor Seavers and back seater Lt Tom Noonan flew out of Ubon, Thailand with the 497th TFS/8th TFW, part of the famous 'Wolf Pack'. Known as the 'Night Owls', the 497th pioneered night bombing work in McDonnell Douglas F-4C Phantoms, flying ultra low-level missions in pitch darkness against the Ho Chi Minh Trail and other targets.

Below: Early examples of the Martin B-57 Canberra generally attacked the trail by day, but like all warplanes in Southeast Asia they were fuelled and armed during the nocturnal hours by hard-working ground crews. B-57s gave way to fighter-bombers like the F-100 and F-4 in air-to-ground action against the Viet Cong.

Nakhon Phanom Air Base in Thailand was the centre of a major operation which was to assume ever increasing importance as the war dragged on. The North Vietnamese supplied the Viet Cong guerrillas operating in the South via the Ho Chi Minh Trail, a series of winding mud tracks running the length of Laos and Cambodia so bypassing the heavily defended area in the middle of Vietnam. The American forces went to great lengths to cut off the supply of materiel to the South by using all manner of air-

Below: Withdrawn in 1963, the Douglas B-26 Invader returned in 1967 in its B-26K variant. 56th SOS Invaders used the call-sign 'Nimrod' and harried North Vietnamese supply routes from their base at Nakhon Phanom, ('NKP' for short) in Thailand.

borne strike-power, from area bombing by B-52s to attacks by converted light aircraft such as the Cessna O-2.

As a result of their low-speed manoeuvrability, the two most successful types in the early years were the elderly Douglas A-1 Skyraider and the same company's even older B-26 Invader, both capable of carrying considerable loads and able to deliver them extremely accurately on to the truck targets hidden beneath the jungle. These were controlled by forward air controllers (FACs) which located the targets from light aircraft circling above the canopy. Favourite weapons of the attackers were unguided rockets and napalm.

A novel use of transport aircraft in Vietnam was as 'gunships', in which guns of all calibres were mounted to fire from the side while the aircraft circled an area suspected of occupation by an enemy force. After proving the concept with Douglas AC-47s, the USAF converted a number of Fairchild C-119s and Lockheed C-130s as AC-119s and AC-130 Spectres. The AC-130 was the definitive gunship, acquiring advanced night sensors to direct devastating gun batteries with deadly precision. Weapons included 7.62-mm (0.3-in) Miniguns, 20-

mm Vulcan cannon, 40-mm Bofors guns and, ultimately a 105-mm (4.13-in) howitzer.

As the trail war grew, the US command invested more time and money in it and new types such as the General Dynamics F-111 were employed, this type operating with considerable success thanks to its unprecedented accuracy under blind first-pass conditions.

MOTION SENSORS

In order to monitor the traffic along the trail the Igloo White programme saw seismic sensors scattered across the trail by F-4s, C-130s and specially adapted Lockheed P-2 Neptunes of the US Navy. Tens of thousands of small devices remained inert on the ground or suspended from trees until activated by the nearby movements of a human being or vehicle; the sensor would then transmit a coded signal denoting the nature of the disturbance, its signals being received by relay drones or aircraft flying in the vicinity. The signals were processed by EC-121s and automatically relayed to the Infiltration Surveillance Center at Nakhon Phanom Air Base in neighbouring Thailand, from where target information could be

Above: This is a contemporary photo and map showing intense activity in th Mu Gia Pass, which led from North Vietnam into Laos. US warplanes bombed the pass relentlessly.

passed to forces alerted for a possible air or ground strike.

The US Navy also played its part against the infiltrators. Apart from operations against the trail itself, with Douglas RA-3s using camouflage detection film and real-time video cameras to find the trucks hidden beneath the triple-canopy forest, naval aircraft were also heavily involved in monitoring and intercepting junk and sampan traffic carrying war materiel.

WATCHING THE WATER

Under the name Market Time, Lockheed P-2 Neptunes and Martin P-5 Marlins plied the coasts around Vietnam, keeping watch on all movements, including Soviet supply vessels entering Haiphong harbour. These elderly aircraft were supplemented by the Lockheed P-3 Orion in the late 1960s and the maritime patrols lasted throughout the war.

Another facet of the US Navy's work was the 'brown water navy', which plied the endless creeks of the Mekong delta, policing the waterways and searching for Viet Cong guerrillas. The surface vessels were supported in the air by Bell UH-1s and OV-10 Broncos.

HO CHI MINH TRAIL

[Map showing Vientiane, Mu Gia Pass, Nakhon Phanom, Khe Sanh, Quang Tri, Hue, Da Nang, Thailand, Laos, Ubon, Kontum, Pleiku, Cambodia, Cam Ranh, Phnom Penh, An Loc, Saigon, Mekong Delta]

Although the Viet Cong had roots in the south and grabbed up some of their weapons from defeated South Vietnamese troops, they relied heavily on the flow of supplies from the north to keep their war alive.

The Ho Chi Minh Trail was not really a trail but a web of supply lines. It was named not by the Ho's followers but by the Americans, who needed a simple concept to explain a complex infiltration effort. In the end, it was a perplexing target for air power, and one that air strikes could never fully take out of action.

Below: Tracer arcs down out of the night as an AC-47 gunship engages a supply column moving down the trail.

However, despite all the effort thrown in to the anti-infiltration war, the Viet Cong continued to be supplied and reinforced along the mass of seemingly impassable, almost undetectable tracks, and this was to seal the fate of South Vietnam as much as any other factor.

Right: An OP-2E Neptune of VO-67 dispenses electronic sensing devices on the Ho Chi Minh Trail, one of dozens of measures taken to inhibit Hanoi's well-orchestrated infiltration effort.

High-tech hunters

The finest science the American taxpayer could pay for was used in a spectacular response to the Viet Cong's night infiltration campaign. The C-130 'trash hauler' became an instrument-packed, nocturnal gunship. The Neptune patrol craft took on missions where infra-red sensors, and acoustic devices were principal weapons. But despite some success US air interdiction was never totally effective, and Hanoi continued to run a 'low-tech' supply effort through Laos and Cambodia.

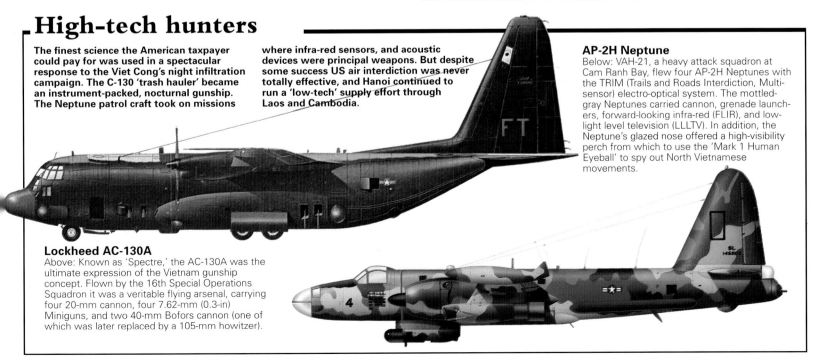

Lockheed AC-130A
Above: Known as 'Spectre,' the AC-130A was the ultimate expression of the Vietnam gunship concept. Flown by the 16th Special Operations Squadron it was a veritable flying arsenal, carrying four 20-mm cannon, four 7.62-mm (0.3-in) Miniguns, and two 40-mm Bofors cannon (one of which was later replaced by a 105-mm howitzer).

AP-2H Neptune
Below: VAH-21, a heavy attack squadron at Cam Ranh Bay, flew four AP-2H Neptunes with the TRIM (Trails and Roads Interdiction, Multisensor) electro-optical system. The mottled-gray Neptunes carried cannon, grenade launchers, forward-looking infra-red (FLIR), and low-light level television (LLLTV). In addition, the Neptune's glazed nose offered a high-visibility perch from which to use the 'Mark 1 Human Eyeball' to spy out North Vietnamese movements.

Vietnam: On Yankee Station

1964 - 1975

Following the Tonkin Gulf incident of 1964, the US Navy launched retaliatory strikes from the decks of the carriers *Ticonderoga* and *Constellation*. It was to be the start of the US Navy's intense involvement in combat in Southeast Asia, during which the Navy flew 52 percent of all American sorties over North Vietnam, as against 43 percent by the USAF and five percent by the Marine Corps.

Naval aviation was under the command of the 7th Fleet's Attack Carrier Striking Force, or Task Force 77. TF 77 executed raids on North Vietnam from a position known as 'Yankee Station', at the mouth of the Gulf of Tonkin, less than 320 km (200 miles) from Hanoi and Haiphong. Early in the

war, however, carriers also operated from 'Dixie Station' about 160 km (100 miles) south east of Cam Ranh Bay. From there they were used to provide air support over South Vietnam until the Air Force could take on that responsibility. From that time carriers used the southern operating area primarily to work up before heading north. Between 1965 and 1973 the Navy always had four or five carriers deployed for operations in Southeast Asia. Intensive use meant that deployed carriers actually spent about 75 percent of their time at sea.

LARGE AND SMALL

Attack carriers or CVAs fell loosely into two categories. The large-deck carriers which could operate 80 or 90 aircraft included the 'Midway',

'Forrestal' and 'Kitty Hawk' classes as well as the nuclear-powered USS *Enterprise*. Smaller types, which had air wings of up to 60 aircraft, included the modified survivors of the wartime 'Essex', 'Ticonderoga' and 'Oriskany' classes'

The strike power of each carrier air wing was invested in a mix of fighter and attack squadrons (nominally 12 aircraft per squadron). Early in the war, small-deck types usually operated two squadrons of Vought F-8 Crusader fighters, and three attack squadrons equipped with Douglas A-4 Skyhawks and Douglas A-1 Skyraiders. Large-deck wings included two McDonnell F-4 Phantom II fighter squadrons and four A-4 attack squadrons as well as heavy attack aircraft like the Douglas A-3

Above: Douglas A-1 Skyraiders make their contribution to the noise and fury on a carrier deck. These aging but effective propeller-driven warplanes were replaced in carrier air wings by the end of 1968, but continued to serve with the US and Vietnamese air forces ashore.

Skywarrior and North American A-5 Vigilante. These last two types were soon converted to support or reconnaissance roles.

Gradually the A-1, A-4 and F-8 squadrons were phased out of service aboard the larger carriers such as *Constellation*, *Forrestal*, *Kitty Hawk* and *Midway*. However, they continued to serve on the smaller carriers such as *Bon Homme Richard*, *Hancock*, *Intrepid*, *Oriskany* and *Ticonderoga*. Aboard the big-deck vessels they were replaced by newer, vastly more capable types

Below: The McDonnell F-4 Phantom was the most important carrier-based warplane of the war. Designed as a fleet interceptor, it was used to counter North Vietnamese MiGs, but it also went into action heavily laden with air-to-surface bombs and missiles.

Right: The Douglas A-4 Skyhawk was in the fight from the beginning, and a few were still around when US involvement in the war ended. The bantamweight Skyhawk was so small it did not need folding wings on the carrier, yet it carried a heavy bombload.

Left: Although the modified World War II-vintage 'Essex' class carriers were too small to berth the F-4 Phantom, they took on a major part of the air war with lighter jet- and prop-driven warplanes.

Below: Though it had a reputation as a gunfighter, the Vought F-8 Crusader achieved all but one of its 20 aerial victories with Sidewinder missiles like the one visible during this carrier launch.

Carrier Air Wing

Life was fast and hectic on a carrier deck. A CVW (Carrier Air Wing) had two squadrons each of fighters and attack craft, plus detachments of helicopters and electronic warfare and reconnaissance ships. This 'mix' required skillful juggling during a busy flying schedule.

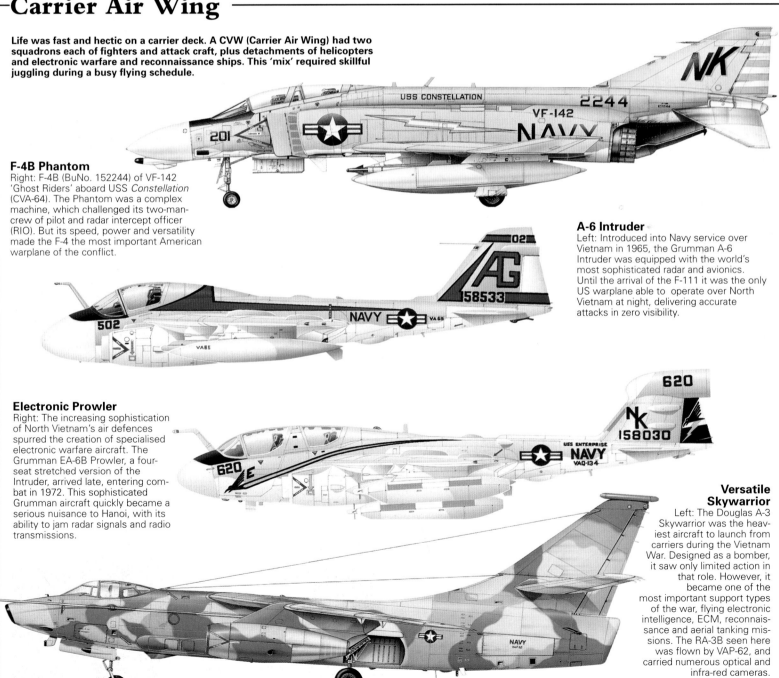

F-4B Phantom
Right: F-4B (BuNo. 152244) of VF-142 'Ghost Riders' aboard USS *Constellation* (CVA-64). The Phantom was a complex machine, which challenged its two-man-crew of pilot and radar intercept officer (RIO). But its speed, power and versatility made the F-4 the most important American warplane of the conflict.

A-6 Intruder
Left: Introduced into Navy service over Vietnam in 1965, the Grumman A-6 Intruder was equipped with the world's most sophisticated radar and avionics. Until the arrival of the F-111 it was the only US warplane able to operate over North Vietnam at night, delivering accurate attacks in zero visibility.

Electronic Prowler
Right: The increasing sophistication of North Vietnam's air defences spurred the creation of specialised electronic warfare aircraft. The Grumman EA-6B Prowler, a four-seat stretched version of the Intruder, arrived late, entering combat in 1972. This sophisticated Grumman aircraft quickly became a serious nuisance to Hanoi, with its ability to jam radar signals and radio transmissions.

Versatile Skywarrior
Left: The Douglas A-3 Skywarrior was the heaviest aircraft to launch from carriers during the Vietnam War. Designed as a bomber, it saw only limited action in that role. However, it became one of the most important support types of the war, flying electronic intelligence, ECM, reconnaissance and aerial tanking missions. The RA-3B seen here was flown by VAP-62, and carried numerous optical and infra-red cameras.

THE FIRST VIETNAM ACES: CUNNINGHAM AND DRISCOLL

10 May 1972 saw some of the biggest air battles of the Vietnam War, during which the US Navy produced the first American aces of the conflict.

The F-4J Phantom team of Randall 'Duke' Cunningham and William 'Irish' Driscoll, flew with VF-96 from the USS *Constellation*. Both men had benefited from the new Top Gun tactical training which was revolutionising the efficiency of the US Navy's combat pilots. Although neither had been to Top Gun, both Cunningham and Driscoll had been taught by its instructors. Cunningham was at Miramar when Top Gun was just starting there, and Driscoll had been taught by Top Gun instructors in their fleet adversary role.

The resumption of missions against North Vietnam had already seen the pilot/RIO combination run up two victo-ries against MiGs before they set off on a 10 May strike mission. VF-96 aircraft were given the callsign 'Showtime', and the aircraft flown by Cunningham and Driscoll on this mission, nominally the squadron commander's machine, was known as 'Showtime 100'.

Showtime 100 had already scored twice in the big battle southeast of Hanoi, bringing the team's victory total up to four. They were heading home-wards when they encountered a superbly-flown MiG-17 – thought later to have been piloted by top North Vietnamese ace 'Colonel Tomb' though his existence has never been confirmed.

In a tightly-fought battle, neither air-craft could gain the upper hand, the Phantom having the advantage in power and speed, the MiG in agility. The two aircraft were climbing vertically, almost cockpit to cockpit, when Cunningham realised they were in a situation he had encountered several times in training with Top Gun instructors.

Chopping power suddenly and extend-ing airbrakes, he allowed the MiG to race ahead for the first time. As both aircraft nosed down, Cunningham found himself behind the MiG. Pouring on the power, he closed to firing range and fired a Sidewinder, making his third kill of the day, and his fifth of the war. The Top Gun-trained team of Cunningham and Driscoll had just become America's first Vietnam aces.

Minutes later, Showtime 100 was hit by a surface-to-air missile. Cunningham managed to wrestle the stricken aircraft safely out to sea before the two men ejected. They were quickly picked up by helicopter and returned safely to the *Constellation*.

*Left: **SHOWTIME** 100 was the call-sign of Cunningham's F-4J, which bagged three MiGs before being downed by a SAM missile.*

Above: Following the victories that made them aces on 10 May 1972, Cunningham (right) and Driscoll celebrate aboard Constellation.

like the Grumman A-6 Intruder, Grumman E-2 Hawkeye, and Vought A-7 Corsair II. A typical late-war big-deck air wing included two F-4 squadrons, two A-7 attack squadrons and one A-6 all-weather attack squadron.

All these aircraft were flown on strikes against the North with Skyraiders, Skyhawks, Intruders and Corsairs providing the teeth, with Phantoms and Crusaders pro-viding protective combat air patrols known as MIGCAPs. F-4s were also on ground attack missions as well as flying fleet defence missions known as BARCAPs. Specially adapted A-3s and A-6s were equipped for the inflight-refuelling and ECM roles.

Initial success against the North Vietnamese MiGs was elusive, but once the Navy instituted a realistic air combat training scheme, the famous Top Gun school, the num-ber of combat kills rose dramatical-ly, and in 1972 the team of Randy Cunningham and Willie Driscoll flying from the *Constellation* became the first American aces of the war. However, the gun-armed A-4 and A-7 also made occasional MiG kills, and, on one historic occasion, two elderly A-1s downed a MiG-17 between them.

VERSATILE 'SPAD'

The Skyraider had started the war as the US Navy's main attack air-craft. It was already 20 years old, and it continued in fleet service until 1968 – a few surviving in the electronic warfare role beyond this date. The 'Spad' could lift phenom-enal loads and absorb massive battle damage and flew many RESCAP missions in support of search-and-rescue Kaman SH-2 and Sikorsky SH-3 helicopters, in much the same way as the USAF 'Spads' supported combat rescues on land.

The A-4 Skyhawk was another brilliant Douglas design which served on the attack squadrons throughout the war, its agility enabling it to perform attacks on the most heavily defended targets. Its place was being taken by the A-7 towards the end of the conflict, an aircraft capable of carrying out the same role but with much heavier warloads. Both the A-4s and A-7s could deliver Shrike anti-radar mis-siles in the 'Iron Hand' defence suppression role.

Perhaps the greatest addition to the air wings was the A-6 Intruder, which at the time had the most advanced weapons delivery and navigation system in the world. It was able to deliver low-level first-pass strikes with extraordinary accu-racy in weather that often prevent-ed other aircraft from flying, let alone perform combat missions.

Reconnaissance and battle dam-age assessment for the fleet was pro-vided by the RA-5 Vigilante and the RF-8 Crusader. These were often escorted by F-4s and F-8s over North Vietnam as they carried no defensive armament; additional-ly, though very fast, the big Vigilante was not particularly manoeuvrable.

The US Marine Corps flew large numbers of aircraft in Vietnam, mainly on short-range attacks from

Experiment with Camouflage

In 1965, the US Navy experimented with several versions of a green camouflage paint scheme on carrier aircraft. It helped little in combat, however, and created confusion on the carrier deck at night.

Green machine
Right: This F-4G Phantom wears one version of the camou-flage paint scheme and carries a typical bombload for a mis-sion 'up North'.

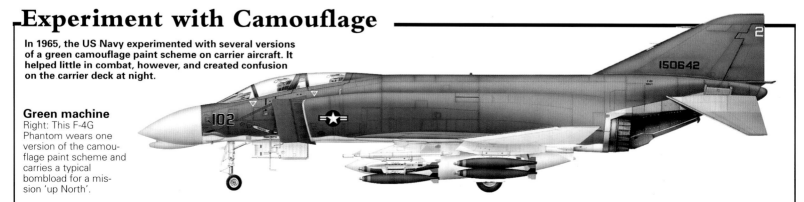

F-4J Phantom II 'Showtime 100'

Slammed into the air by a steam catapult that could handle the weight of a railroad box car, Cunningham and Driscoll went into North Vietnam flying a heavy, complex, costly, and powerful aircraft that was regarded as the finest in the world. Their F-4J Phantom II (BuNo. 155800) of squadron VF-96 'Fighting Falcons' was bigger than many World War II bombers and faster than a pistol bullet.

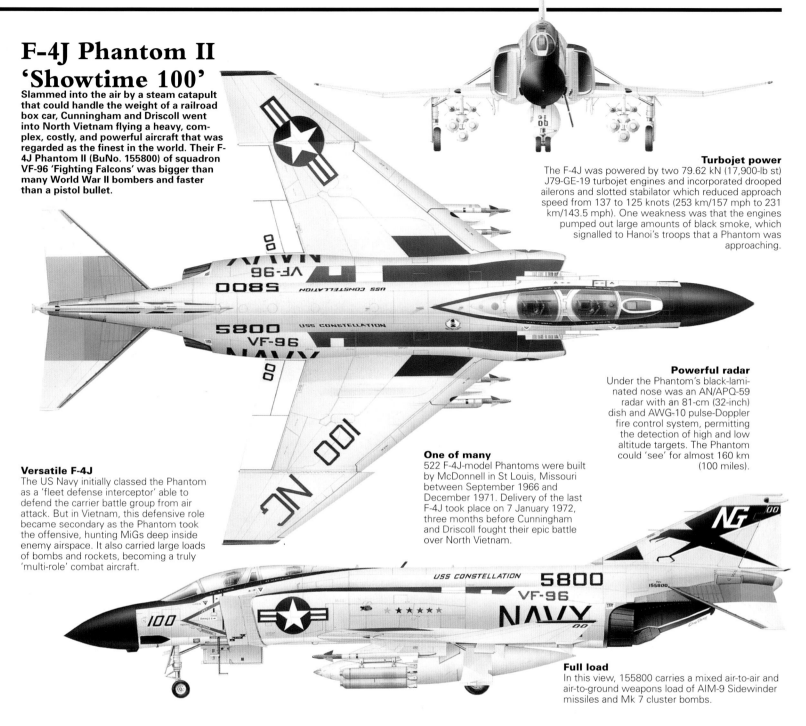

Turbojet power
The F-4J was powered by two 79.62 kN (17,900-lb st) J79-GE-19 turbojet engines and incorporated drooped ailerons and slotted stabilator which reduced approach speed from 137 to 125 knots (253 km/157 mph to 231 km/143.5 mph). One weakness was that the engines pumped out large amounts of black smoke, which signalled to Hanoi's troops that a Phantom was approaching.

Powerful radar
Under the Phantom's black-laminated nose was an AN/APQ-59 radar with an 81-cm (32-inch) dish and AWG-10 pulse-Doppler fire control system, permitting the detection of high and low altitude targets. The Phantom could 'see' for almost 160 km (100 miles).

Versatile F-4J
The US Navy initially classed the Phantom as a 'fleet defense interceptor' able to defend the carrier battle group from air attack. But in Vietnam, this defensive role became secondary as the Phantom took the offensive, hunting MiGs deep inside enemy airspace. It also carried large loads of bombs and rockets, becoming a truly 'multi-role' combat aircraft.

One of many
522 F-4J-model Phantoms were built by McDonnell in St Louis, Missouri between September 1966 and December 1971. Delivery of the last F-4J took place on 7 January 1972, three months before Cunningham and Driscoll fought their epic battle over North Vietnam.

Full load
In this view, 155800 carries a mixed air-to-air and air-to-ground weapons load of AIM-9 Sidewinder missiles and Mk 7 cluster bombs.

their bases at Chu Lai and Da Nang. Aircraft types involved were the A-4 Skyhawk, A-6 Intruder, F-4 Phantom and F-8 Crusader, used almost exclusively as ground attack 'mud-movers'.

These were controlled by 'Fast FAC' aircraft such as TA-4s and Grumman TF-9 Cougars, and an element of ECM was provided by the Douglas EF-10 Skyknight, a modified version of a Korean War-vintage jet night fighter. Rockwell OV-10s were later procured to perform light strike and FAC duties.

Following the peace talks in 1973, the last act of the US Navy in the American phase of the war was to clear Haiphong harbour under Operation End Sweep, using minesweeping Sikorsky RH-53 helicopters.

In 1975 the carriers *Enterprise*, *Midway* and *Coral Sea* provided air cover for the evacuation of Saigon, an operation notable for being the first combat deployment of the Grumman F-14 Tomcat. In the final few panic-stricken hours, helicopters were being pushed over the side as soon as they had unloaded to create landing room for further aircraft on the already overcrowded flight decks.

Right: As part of the settlement that ended the shooting, the US Navy provided Sikorsky RH-53D Sea Stallion helicopters to 'clean up' the mines in Haiphong harbor. This RH-53D tows a sled which detects mines.

Vietnam: Linebacker I and II

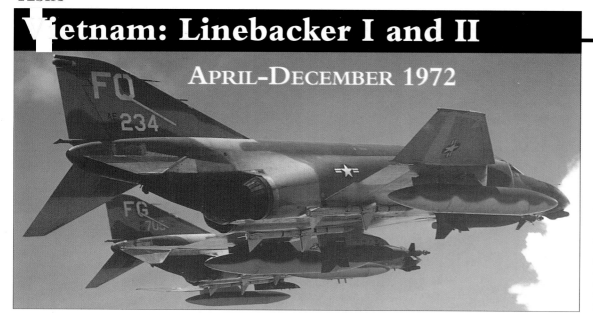

APRIL-DECEMBER 1972

Left: F-4D Phantoms of the 435th TFS/8th TFW head north from Ubon, Thailand. The Phantom became the backbone of the 1972 Linebacker campaign, which saw the first widespread use of precision-guided munitions (PGMs). Most of these 'smart' bombs were carried and delivered by Air Force Phantoms.

Below: Navy jets were essential to Linebacker, and Navy-Air Force cooperation was far better than in 1965-68. Here, a Shrike-armed A-4F Skyhawk prepares to take the war to Hanoi's air defences. Homing-in on the enemy's radar emitters, the Shrike and the larger Standard anti-radar missiles were vital to allow bombers to successfully penetrate Hanoi's defences.

A false calm had fallen over North Vietnam. While politicians wrangled in Paris, US prisoners in Hanoi heard no friendly warplanes overhead for more than three years. But in 1972, talk gave way to action, political speeches to a new air campaign. From land bases and from carrier decks, the jets flew north again – in the final campaign against targets north of the 17th Parallel.

In the spring of 1972 the communists unleashed a full scale military offensive against South Vietnam. American ground troops had been withdrawn from the combat zone, so it fell to air power to support the South Vietnamese fight for survival.

Allied air power had fallen dramatically from the peak years of 1968-1969. USAF assets in Vietnam, Thailand and on Guam totalled 83 B-52s, 203 F-4s, 16 F-105s, 23 A-37s, 10 B-57s, 15 A-1s and a gunship force of 15 AC-119s and 13 AC-130s. Additionally the VNAF deployed around 150 A-1s and a squadron of Northrop F-5s.

At the beginning of April, the B-52 force was put on standby for a massive operation to stem the NVA offensive. On the 6th the first break in the weather allowed fighter-bombers to go into action, initially aimed at NVA units engaged below the DMZ. The forward deployment of communist SA-2 missiles gave US aircraft their first taste of a high-threat environment within South Vietnam.

By 6 April air power started to take its toll - in one instance two cells of three B-52s destroyed an entire NVA tank battalion. In all, some 285 NVA tanks were destroyed by allied aircraft in I Corps alone during the four and a half months following the communist assault.

'BUFFS' MOVE NORTH

B-52 operations against the southern portion of North Vietnam began on 9 April, with strikes as far north as Vinh. Operations expand-

Left: The USAF brought the A-7D to Korat, Thailand in 1972. Never officially given the Corsair II name assigned to its US Navy counterpart, the A-7D replaced the prop-driven A-1 Skyraider in the 'Sandy' mission, escorting rescue helicopters behind the lines.

ed over the next week to include most major target complexes from Thanh Hoa south. By 16 April the areas immediately surrounding Hanoi and Haiphong had been added to the B-52 target list.

At the outbreak of the invasion the USN had two carriers on station, the *Coral Sea* and the *Hancock*. The *Kitty Hawk* was dispatched from the Philippines, arriving on 3 April, and *Constellation* was recalled from Hong Kong. Sailing orders were also given to the *Midway* in the eastern Pacific and the *Saratoga* of the Atlantic Fleet.

Marine Air Group 15's three F-4 squadrons arrived early in May to join an A-6 squadron aboard the *Coral Sea*. Two A-4 squadrons arrived soon after, followed by another A-6 squadron and two further Phantom squadrons.

By the beginning of May there were six carriers on line at Yankee Station. They cheerfully received the news that on 8 May President Nixon had authorised the mining of Haiphong, Cam Pha, Vinh, Quang Khe, Dong Hoi, Thanh Hoa, Hon Gai, and the Red River delta. This was done, with the minimum of trouble, by 15 May.

The United States, too late in the war, was finally getting serious about hitting the North Vietnamese supply line where it hurt. The mining operation effectively cut the main overseas supply route into North Vietnam. The only way that cargo could reach Haiphong was for a ship to stop outside the mined area and offload into small boats – a process requiring up to a month for even a 5,000-ton freighter.

INTENSIFIED COMBAT

In the days following the mining effort, naval air operations in the Hanoi and Haiphong areas grew in intensity. North Vietnamese MiG opposition provided Lt Randy 'Duke' Cunningham and his backseater Lt Willie 'Irish' Driscoll of the *Constellation* a record three kills in one day and an overall score of five, to make them the first US ace of the war.

By 23 May, the USAF had added a further 10 fighter squadrons, an electronic warfare squadron and a couple of C-130 squadrons to Thailand, and tripled

Phantom Gunfighter

The F-4E was the first version of the Phantom armed with what pilots really wanted – an internal 20-mm cannon. Unfortunately, it arrived in the combat zone only weeks after the 'bombing halt' of October 1968. Thus, pilots had to wait until the 1972 Linebacker actions more than three years

later before they got a shot at a MiG. Ironically, better radar and more reliable missiles as well as improved tactics proved more important in combat than the internal gun. Even so, the F-4E became the definitive land-based Phantom.

Fighting Phantom
This F-4E (67-0288) of the 469th TFS/388th TFW carries bombs with extended 'daisy cutter' fuses. These were designed to detonate the bombs before they dug themselves into the earth, maximising the blast effect. The shark's teeth, painted on the plane by Capt Steve Stephen with support from squadron commander Lt Col Edward Hillding, were very much non-regulation. Eventually, they were removed.

the size of the B-52 force. These reinforcements included 180 F-4s (many being improved 'E' models), 12 F-105Gs, 8 EB-66s, 32 C-130s, 124 B-52s. Also in theatre were the first Air Force examples of the Vought A-7 attack jet.

Having started bombing the north after a pause of four years, President Nixon authorised and expanded air offensive known as Linebacker. The aims of the campaign incorporated the isolation of North Vietnam from outside supply, destruction of stockpiles of materiel in the north, and interdiction of NVA supplies going south.

By mid-May, missions in the

southern route packages succeeded in knocking out the pumping facilities for the Ho Chi Minh Trail pipeline which supported tank and truck operations in the South. In line with the port mining operations in May, raids against the rail lines to China reduced these supply routes to a small fraction of their former capacity.

Aircraft taking part in the renewed air offensive against North Vietnam were equipped with new weapons which had not been available during Rolling Thunder. Precision-guided weapons were used in large numbers for the first time. Two- and three-thousand pound laser-guided bombs (LGBs) and electro-optical guided bombs (EOGBs) were delivered by the Phantoms of the 8th Tactical Fighter Wing. In a three-month period the 8th TFW dropped 106 bridges all over North Vietnam, including the notorious Thanh Hoa and Paul Doumer bridges, which had shrugged off repeated and very costly conventional attacks (and even a commando raid by US Army Rangers).

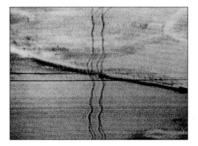

Clockwise from above: The destruction of the Ninh Binh road and rail bridge, located 50 km (32 miles) north of Thanh Hoa, during the later stages of the Linebacker campaign. The first three photos are from the guidance camera of a US Navy Walleye glide bomb, and show the accuracy with which the new precision-guided weapons could strike. The larger photo records the highly effective result.

Below: A 'tall-tailed' B-52D of the kind that made up the bulk of the Linebacker II bombing force. The big bombers usually flew further apart in the danger zone.

TAIL GUNNER'S WAR
During the December 1972 bombing of North Vietnam, B-52 tail gunners claimed credit for shooting down five MiG-21 interceptors. USAF officials reviewed the claims and endorsed two of them. B-52Ds and Gs had four 12.7-mm (0.5-in) machineguns in a manned tail turret.

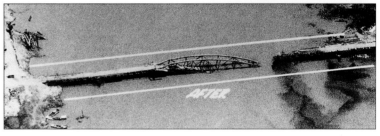

B-52G MISSION
This 'short-tailed' B-52G (compare its fin shape with that of the B-52D in the photo above) typifies those that joined the fighting when Operation Linebacker II, alias the 'Eleven Day War' was unleashed on Hanoi.

HEAVY BOMBER
Until 1972, the giant B-52 Stratofotress had been employed solely against targets in the south, while fighter-bombers handled missions against military installations and industrial facilities in the north. The decision to send B-52s into North Vietnam was a major escalation of the conflict and is widely credited with persuading Hanoi's leaders to negotiate a truce.

Below: The standard B-52 formation was a 'cell' of three aircraft, in
close formation in the south but
more widely separated in the
north. This was cited by critics as
one of many tactics that made the
bombers vulnerable over Hanoi in
the first days of Linebacker II.

North Vietnamese air bases were back on the target list, with Phuc Yen and several other fields being virtually knocked out in September along with 14 MiGs destroyed or damaged on the ground.

On 24 October, President Nixon acknowledged Hanoi's apparently genuine desire to nego-tiate in good faith by halting all bombing north of the 20th Parallel. Linebacker and the port mining had reduced North Vietnam's supplies to 20 percent of the levels they had enjoyed at the start.

It did not last. The North Vietnamese negotiators quickly

Above: During the height of the Linebacker II effort, the B-52 force had 12,000 men and women at Andersen Air Force Base, Guam, alias 'And,' or 'The Rock', located some 4675 km (2,905 miles) from their principal target, Hanoi.

returned to their former intransi-gence and by December, Nixon had had enough. He ordered a renewed bombing offensive with all the stops pulled out.

Linebacker II was conceived as a knock-out blow to the very heart of North Vietnam, namely Hanoi and Haiphong. It finally saw US air power let loose in the sort of role for which it was intended. Striking

military targets within the Hanoi/Haiphong region between 18 and 29 December 1972, the heavy bombing was carried out by Boeing B-52s from U-Tapao in Thailand and Andersen AFB, Guam. A supporting cast of Navy

and Air Force fighters, 'Iron Hand' and 'Wild Weasel' aircraft and ECM jamming platforms softened-up targets and hit others.

In the whole 'eleven-day war' there was only one night clear enough for good visual bombing,

Above: North Vietnamese troopers aim a Soviet-built SA-2 'Guideline' surface-to-air missile, or SAM. In December 1972, 884 SAM launches were counted by B-52 crews, and they downed 15 bombers.

Right: The anti-aircraft artillery, or Triple-A, in the region around Hanoi consisted of guns of all sizes and calibres, including many that were located adjacent to residences and office buildings.

'BUFFS' against Hanoi

The Boeing B-52 Stratofortress was active in Southeast Asia from 1965 on, but not until the Linebacker campaigns was it used against North Vietnam. The '11-day war' of Linebacker II in December 1972 was this classic bomber's finest

hour: in eleven days, B-52Ds and B-52Gs flew 729 sorties against 34 targets in North Vietnam above the 20th Parallel. US assessments showed that this unfettered bombing campaign came close to oblit-erating Hanoi's ability to wage war.

B-52G
Above: The B-52G model of the 'Big Ugly Fat Fellow' is easy to iden-tify from its short, broad tail fin. It had integral fuel tanks in the wing giving much greater range than earlier models, but being principally a nuclear bomber lacked the heavy conventional weapons carrying capability of the B-52D.

B-52D
Below: Although older than the B-52G, the tall-tailed B-52D used in Vietnam had received a modification known as 'Big Belly', designed to increase conventional weapon capacity. A fully laden B-52D could carry 108 'iron' bombs, each nominally of 340-kg (750-lb) but actually weighing 374 kg (825 lb), for a total warload of 40392 kg (89,100 lb)

Through Hanoi's ring of steel

The high point of the Linebacker campaign came on day eight, 26 December, when 120 B-52s unloaded their bombs over the targets in the space of just 15 minutes. Colonel James R. McArthy commanded the 43rd Strategic Wing, and was also the airborne commander of the entire mission on that 'special night'.

"The flak started coming up when we made our first landfall. We were most vividly aware of the heavy, black, ugly explosions of 100-mm (3.94-in) shells, visible even at night. Since we were at a lower altitude than we'd flown before, our wave was more vulnerable to the AAA than on previous missions, and the closer we got to the initial point, the more intense it got.

"Then the SAMs really started coming. The missiles that had been tracking us lifted off and headed for the aircraft. Now that the whole force was committed and we were on the bomb run, for the moment I had nothing to do, so I decided to count the SAMs launched against us. After 26 I quit counting. They were coming up too fast to keep an accurate tally. From the cockpit, it looked like they were barraging SAMs in order to make the lead element of the wave turn from its intended course. Some were close; some were too close for comfort.

"About one hundred seconds prior to bombs away, the cockpit lit up like it was daylight. The light came from the rocket exhaust of a SAM that had come up right under our nose. The electronic warfare officer had reported an extremely strong signal, and he'd been right. That one looked like it missed us by less than 15 metres (50 feet).

"At bombs away, it looked like we were right in the middle of a fireworks factory that was in the process of blowing up. The radio was completely saturated with SAM calls and MiG fighter warnings. As the bomb doors closed, several SAMs exploded nearby. Others could be seen arcing over and starting a descent, then detonating. If the proximity fuse didn't find a target, SA-2s were set to self-destruct at the end of a predetermined time interval."

but the B-52s operated regardless ot the weather. In all, 15 B-52s were lost from a total of 729 sorties, mostly in the first days of the campaign. By the end of the period, tactics had been refined to the point where 113 B-52s were all over the target area within the space of 15 minutes and suffered no losses.

LINEBACKER RESULTS

The B-52 raids were immensely destructive. According to Hanoi, they killed 1,400 civilians, but even if this figure is accurate that is an astonishingly low total given the huge tonnage of bombs dropped onto targets in the middle of densely populated urban areas. The bombers were credited with destroying a quarter of Vietnam's petroleum reserves and 80 percent of the country's electricity generating capacity, as well as smashing armaments factories, military barracks, railways, roads, bridges and communications centres.

Vietnam's entire stock of several thousand surface-to-air missiles had been fired off, and since Haiphong and other major harbours had been closed off by mines, there was no prospect of resupply. Hanoi's war-making capability was at an end, smashed by US air power.

The offensive brought the North Vietnamese back to the peace talks, genuinely ready to make a deal. Linebacker II allowed America to withdraw from the Vietnam morass, recovering most of the POWs held in Northern camps. But for South Vietnam, it only put a temporary check on communist plans, and within three years, without the benefit of American air support, Saigon would finally fall.

Right: The Hanoi Thermal Power Plant was a key B-52 target. Bombs put the entire facility temporarily out of business: only the end of the 11-day war prevented the plant from being completely flattened.

Below: American prisoners or war, or POWs, prepare go home. The release of the POWs was a key point in US demands, and was completed within three months after the bombing campaign.

Below: The US estimate was 372 pieces of rolling stock damaged or destroyed, a monstrous toll on North Vietnam's railway infrastructure. This scene is typical of the bombing results.

HANOI THERMAL POWER PLANT
AFTER

Indo-Pakistan Wars

1965–1971

THE INDIAN NAVY AT WAR
The Sea Hawks of No. 300 Squadron played a part in both 1965 and 1971, operating from shore-bases at Jamnagar and Santa Cruz in 1965 and from the **INS** *Vikrant* in 1971.

Following the end of the British Raj in 1947, the Indian sub-continent was bloodily partitioned into the independent states of Moslem Pakistan and predominantly Hindu India. The British had held together a fragmented indigenous administration and a host of traditional hereditary rulers, while reconciling divided religious interests and suppressing tribal revolts. These problems now re-emerged, and on

these were superimposed rival ambitions for certain disputed areas. The most important of these was the state of Jammu and Kashmir, whose ruler was a Hindu Maharajah, but whose population was overwhelmingly Moslem. The Maharajah wanted independence and refused to accede to integration with Pakistan, which funded and armed the Azad Kashmiris to carry out an insurrection. At the same time, Pathans staged an

invasion. The Maharajah asked India for help, which sent troops after the state's accession. The Azad Kashmiris were supported by

Pakistani artillery, across the border, and Pakistani AAA defended some Azad targets against the IAF. There was direct conflict between

Below: Both Pakistan and India inherited Douglas C-47 Dakotas from the RAF and RIAF, and these were used in the confusion of partition, and in the various small-scale conflicts which followed, in Kashmir and on the North West Frontier. Small numbers remained in use even as late as 1971.

Right: Many of Pakistan's victory claims were denied by India, and were later found to be unsubstantiated. Squadron Leader Mohammed Alam was credited with downing five Indian Hunters in a single engagement over Sargodha during the 1965 war, but the IAF lost only three Hunters on that day, two of them to enemy action. Two of the 'Hunter pilots' named by the PAF as victims actually flew Mystères on another strike.

Early conflicts

The partition of the former British Raj into independent Moslem Pakistan and predominantly Hindu India left a legacy of bitterness and rivalry, with both sides disputing certain key border areas including Jammu and Kashmir, which was predominantly Muslim but ruled by a Hindu Maharajah. In 1947 Kashmir was invaded by Pathan tribesmen and Azad 'Free Kashmiris' carried

out an insurrection. These were put down by the Indian army, with air support from Spitfires and Tempests. Meanwhile Pakistani Hawker Tempests (and later Furies) were kept busy policing the troubled North West Frontier where the tribes were in open revolt.

Hawker Fury
The Pakistan air force was allocated 35 Hawker Tempests from IAF stocks when it formed, though it only received 12 of these aircraft initially. Eighty Tempest IIs and Furies were eventually taken on charge, equipping Nos 5, 9 and 14 Squadrons. This aircraft flew with No. 9 Squadron during offensive support operations on the North West Frontier.

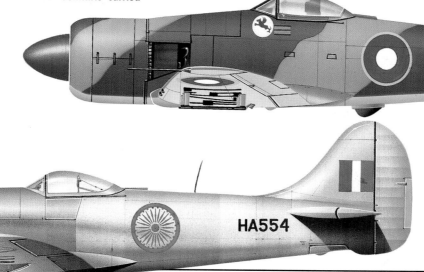

Hawker Tempest II
This Hawker Tempest II of No. 3 Squadron, based at Kolar, wears the original IAF insignia, soon replaced by a simple green, white and orange roundel. No. 3 Squadron was heavily involved in the fighting in Kashmir between 1947 and 1949 operating in the ground-attack role. The Tempest II and Spitfire XIV formed the backbone of the Indian Air Force at the end of the war.

Fighters at war, 1965

The Indo-Pakistani war of 1965 is often presented as a 'David and Goliath' struggle, though in fact, the two sides were remarkably evenly matched, since India had to keep many of its best units in the East, to guard against Chinese intervention, and these played no part in the fighting. Clever post-war propaganda by the PAF created the illusion that the war had been something of a Turkey shoot for the PAF, but while the Pakistanis enjoyed a 26:12 kill:loss ratio in air combat, they were unable to prevent offensive operations by India's bombers and fighter bombers.

NA F-86F Sabre
Pakistan claimed a kill:loss ratio of about 4:1 in the 1965 air war, crediting most victories to the Sabre, with a handful of credits for the then-new F-104 Starfighter. One individual Sabre pilot was credited with a total of nine kills (with two more probables), including five in one mission. On that sortie his real tally was two!

Hawker Hunter
At least 25 per cent of PAF Sabres were equipped to fire the AIM-9 Sidewinder AAM, whereas Indian Hunters had to rely on their four 30-mm cannon alone. The Hunter's heavy punch and high thrust made it a formidable adversary, and the type was responsible for most IAF kills. This one served with No. 7 Squadron.

India and Pakistan further north, in the Karakoram mountains, and a PAF Dakota was damaged by IAF Tempests. A UN ceasefire came into force on 31 January 1949.

Pakistan conducted its own war against insurrection on the North West Frontier, this tying down a fighter squadron from 1947 until 1960. Initially the air forces of both India and Pakistan were equipped with ex-RAF and ex-RIAF aircraft. India used Spitfires, Tempests, Liberators and Dakotas. The fledgling Pakistani air force had similar equipment, but lacked Liberators. The UK continued to supply aircraft to Pakistan (Furies,

Attackers, Halifax bombers and Bristol 170 freighters) and to India (Vampires, Canberras and Hunters) although both nations also started looking for arms elsewhere. Pakistan acquired 100 F-86Fs, 12 F-104s and 24 B-57s as military aid from the USA from 1955, while India obtained Ouragan and Mystère IVA fighters from France and Il-14 and An-12 transports, Mi-4 helicopters and MiG-21 fighters from the USSR.

In 1957 Kashmir was integrated into the Indian Union despite Pakistani protests, and UN sponsored talks broke down in 1963. In February 1965 Indian troops took

over a Pakistani police post in the disputed Rann of Kutch, an uninhabitable border area under water for much of the year. The post was recaptured in April, but air activity was limited. One IAF Ouregan was shot down when it strayed over the Pakistan border.

WAR IN THE KASHMIR
In May 1965 Pakistan armed and trained irregulars to infiltrate Kashmir, hoping to ferment a revolution which would then topple the state into Pakistan. The insurgents were backed by Pakistani artillery, and the Pakistan army then launched a major offensive against

Indian forces in the Chhamb salient. The IAF lost four obsolete Vampires to PAF Sabres in the battle, on 1 September. This led to the immediate withdrawal of the Vampire and the Ouregan from front-line use.

All-out war erupted between India and Pakistan, and during the vicious 17-day conflict the PAF flew defensive CAPs over its own bases, offensive counter-air missions against Indian airfields, and close-support and interdiction sorties, to which the Indians responded in kind. India retained much of its air force in the East, against the possibility of Chinese intervention, and as a result the air forces were

THE WARZONE – 1965
The 1965 war began with an attack against Kashmir by Pakistani-trained infiltrators, supported by Pakistani artillery. The Pakistanis then launched a full-scale pre-emptive assault near Jammu. Fighting was concentrated along the northern part of the Indo-Pakistani border, with only a brief outbreak of fighting in the East, when IAF and PAF fighter bombers mounted a short burst of airfield attacks against one another. India was forced to maintain large standing forces in the East, however, against the very real possibility that China might intervene. The fighting had little effect – at post-war peace talks both sides recognised the pre-war border in Kashmir.

Chaklala
Srinagar
Peshawar
Jammu
Mianwali
Pathankot
Sargodha
Adampur
Amritsar
Rafiqi
Malwara
Chandigarh
Ambala
Palam

PAKISTAN
CHINA
NEPAL
Jodhpur
Bagdogra
BHUTAN
Masroor
Gauhat
INDIA
EAST PAKISTAN
Tezgoan/Dhaka
Agartala
Calcutta
Chittagong
Kalaikunda
Jessore
Barrackpore
Jamnagar
Dum Dum
Cox's Bazar
Arabian Sea

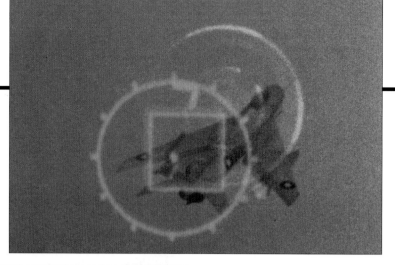

Below: The Lockheed F-104 Starfighter played a part in the 1965 war, proving particularly successful in intercepting IAF Canberras at night. Three such aircraft were claimed as shot down by the F-104s.

quite evenly balanced in the West. The PAF used skillful tactics to maintain an edge in the air, and were initially able to keep the IAF from excessive interference with Pakistan army operations, although after 6 September, little attempt was made by either side to stop fighter-bomber raids by the enemy. From this point on, the Indians flew more sorties, while the PAF tried to conserve its strength. Unfortunately, the IAF never mounted missions in strength against its key targets, sending out its aircraft in what were little better than penny packets.

Indian ground forces launched a counter-offensive which drove the Pakistanis back across their own border in places, but generally the war became a bloody stalemate, and with 2,763 Indian dead and 6,917 Pakistani dead (and with 375 and 350 tanks destroyed, respectively) a ceasefire was declared. The pre-war borders of Kashmir were confirmed by the subsequent peace talks.

The PAF lost some 25 aircraft (11 in air combat), while the Indians lost 60 (25 in air combat). This was an impressive result, but it was simply not good enough.

Pakistan ended the war having depleted 17 per cent of its front-line strength, while India's losses amounted to less than 10 per cent. Moreover, the loss rate had begun to even out, and it has been estimated that another three week's fighting would have seen the Pakistani losses rising to 33 per cent and India's losses totalling 15 per cent. Air superiority was not achieved, and were unable to prevent IAF fighter-bombers and recce Canberras from flying daylight missions over Pakistan. Thus 1965 was an expensive victory for the PAF, and one which was tainted by ridiculously exaggerated propaganda, which claimed a 4:1 or 5:1 kill:loss ratio.

LEARNING THE LESSONS

India realised that its air force had been something of a glorified flying club for its pilots before 1965, and that serious effort needed to be made to improve operational

Right: The survivors of Pakistan's original US-supplied F-86F Sabres were augmented post-war by 90 Canadair-built Sabres procured from West Germany, with Iran acting as a middleman. Five squadrons were still in service in 1971 when war broke out again.

readiness and training, and to provide even the most basic essentials, like camouflage netting (and even camouflage paint for some of its front-line types!). By contrast, the PAF began to believe their own propaganda, that the kill:loss ratio had been about 4:1, rather than the actual 2:1, still an impressive achievement, but simply not good enough in a war against India. They were completely unable to perceive that whatever had happened in the air, the war had ended in a draw. They also failed to realise that despite a slightly higher kill tally, the smaller size of their force meant that they could not win a war of attrition with India. Had the war lasted a little longer, the weight of Indian numbers alone might have defeated the PAF, even though India had retained more than half of its forces in the East, against the

Fighter-bombers at war, 1965

The Hawker Hunter bore the brunt of the fighting in both 1965 and 1971, and was augmented in both wars by the Mystère IV and Gnat. In 1965, small numbers of Ouregans and Vampires were also serving in the fighter-bomber role, but by 1971 the older types had been retired and the Hunters, Mystères and Gnats were augmented by indigenous HAL HF-24 Maruts and

Sukhoi Su-7 'Fitters'. In both wars, the short-range fighter-bombers were also augmented by Canberras operating in the interdiction role. Although the pace of operations was relatively leisurely, Indian ground-attack aircraft played their part in blunting the Pakistani ground offensive, and in contributing to Pakistan's loss of 16 per cent of its aircraft.

Dassault Mystère IVA

Inspired by the success of the Ouregan (known as Toofani in IAF service), the Indian Air Force acquired 110 Mystère IVAs between 1956 and 1958, and these equipped five squadrons, serving until 1973, latterly with a reconnaissance capability. The Mystère IVAs were heavily committed in 1965, while the older Ouregans remained on standby in the East, playing no part in the fighting.

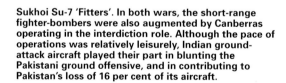

Folland Gnat

Affectionately dubbed 'Sabre Slayer' in PAF service, the Gnat proved popular and successful in IAF service, operating in the fighter and fighter-bomber roles with equal facility. Some 23 Folland-built Gnats were followed by 20 built by HAL from Folland-supplied assemblies, and 193 built under licence by HAL. Some 89 improved Ajeets were also built.

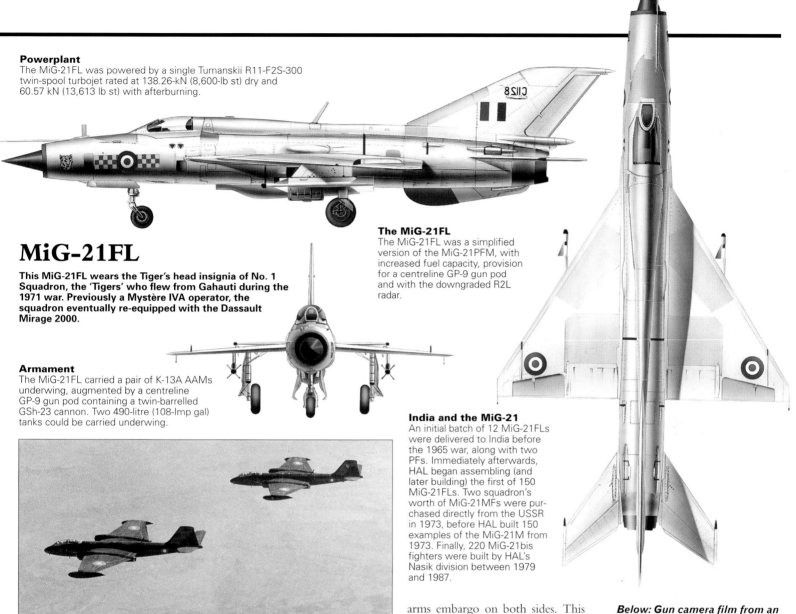

Powerplant
The MiG-21FL was powered by a single Tumanskii R11-F2S-300 twin-spool turbojet rated at 138.26-kN (8,600-lb st) dry and 60.57 kN (13,613 lb st) with afterburning.

The MiG-21FL
The MiG-21FL was a simplified version of the MiG-21PFM, with increased fuel capacity, provision for a centreline GP-9 gun pod and with the downgraded R2L radar.

MiG-21FL

This MiG-21FL wears the Tiger's head insignia of No. 1 Squadron, the 'Tigers' who flew from Gahauti during the 1971 war. Previously a Mystère IVA operator, the squadron eventually re-equipped with the Dassault Mirage 2000.

Armament
The MiG-21FL carried a pair of K-13A AAMs underwing, augmented by a centreline GP-9 gun pod containing a twin-barrelled GSh-23 cannon. Two 490-litre (108-Imp gal) tanks could be carried underwing.

India and the MiG-21
An initial batch of 12 MiG-21FLs were delivered to India before the 1965 war, along with two PFs. Immediately afterwards, HAL began assembling (and later building) the first of 150 MiG-21FLs. Two squadron's worth of MiG-21MFs were purchased directly from the USSR in 1973, before HAL built 150 examples of the MiG-21M from 1973. Finally, 220 MiG-21bis fighters were built by HAL's Nasik division between 1979 and 1987.

Above: While the Indian Air Force used the English Electric Canberra in the bomber and reconnaissance roles, Pakistan used its US-built derivative, the Martin B-57. Both types saw service in 1965 and 1971.

arms embargo on both sides. This had no effect on India, which had always looked to Britain, France and even Russia for arms, but was disastrous for Pakistan, which was forced to acquire 90 obsolete second-hand Sabres via Iran, a mere 28 Mirage IIIs from France, and 74 maintenance-intensive Shenyang F-6s. It was quite unable to replace losses among its (already weak) force of B-57s, or to acquire a modern interceptor in realistic numbers. Moreover, re-equipment and strengthening was not accorded a high priority, and the PAF was ill-prepared for war in 1971.

The 1971 war was rooted in the growing resentment in East Pakistan to rule from Islamabad, and the subsequent civil war, in

Below: Gun camera film from an Indian Hunter taken during a cannon attack against a Pakistani military train. Indian Hawker Hunters performed valiantly in both 1965 and 1971, and the type remained in IAF service in 1996.

threat of Chinese intervention. Had India committed its entire strength the war might have been very different. Alternatively, had India been prepared to allow the war to continue for longer, then its superior numbers would inevitably have proved telling. Finally the Pakistanis failed to take account of the extent to which they had relied on two factors which the IAF could not take for granted – complete ground-based defensive radar coverage and an adequate supply of air-to-air missiles. Much effort was

expended in India to remedy these deficiencies before 1971.

With Soviet aid, India established a modern early-warning radar system, including the recently introduced 'Fansong-E' low-level radar, linked with SA-2 'Guideline' surface-to-air missiles and a large number of AA guns. By December 1971 the IAF comprised a total of 36 combat squadrons (of which 10 were deployed in the Bengal sector) with some 650 combat aircraft.

Moreover, the 1965 war resulted in the USA imposing a 10-year

Right: The Mil Mi-8 augmented and eventually replaced the battle-hardened and popular Mi-4 in IAF service. The Mi-8 joined the Indian Air Force in December 1971, just too late to play a part in the fighting.

PAF Fighters, 1971

When war broke out in 1971 Pakistan still relied heavily on the F-86 Sabre, with five operational squadrons. These were backed by three squadrons of F-6s and a single Mirage III squadron, together with one light bomber squadron operating the Martin B-57. This force was outnumbered by the IAF, which arguably enjoyed a qualitative edge, too.

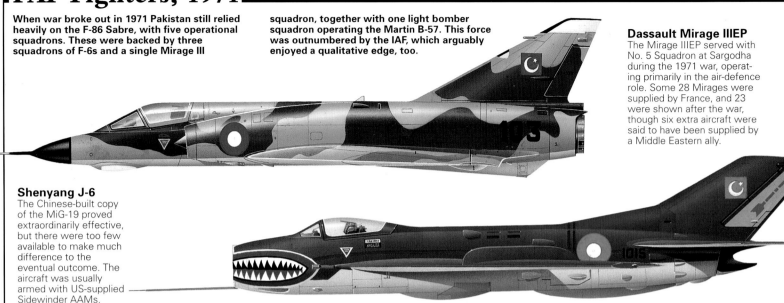

Dassault Mirage IIIEP
The Mirage IIIEP served with No. 5 Squadron at Sargodha during the 1971 war, operating primarily in the air-defence role. Some 28 Mirages were supplied by France, and 23 were shown after the war, though six extra aircraft were said to have been supplied by a Middle Eastern ally.

Shenyang J-6
The Chinese-built copy of the MiG-19 proved extraordinarily effective, but there were too few available to make much difference to the eventual outcome. The aircraft was usually armed with US-supplied Sidewinder AAMs.

which the popular Mukhti Bahini independence movement received much aid from India. Pakistani forces were airlifted in when Bangladesh declared its independence, and when these started massacring the educated classes, India felt it had to intervene, and limited operations began in late-October. In late-November two PAF Sabres strafing Indian troops were downed by Ajeets, marking the first air combat between the two sides since 1965. On 3 December Pakistan launched what was intended to be a decisive pre-emptive strike against Indian airfields, but managed only 28 sorties, spread thinly and with insufficient accuracy to cause serious damage. The IAF hit back with retaliatory strikes which proved more successful, and at sea, the Indian Navy sank a Pakistani submarine (actually leased from the US Navy, and the only Pakistani vessel with enough range to threaten India's fleet), leaving the Bay of Bengal clear for operations by the carrier *Vikrant*. From then on Pakistan was forced on the defensive by numerically superior Indian forces.

The PAF's handful of Sabres at Tezgaon near Dacca in East Pakistan put up a useful resistance against all-out attacks by Indian fighters from 4 December. Between four and 11 of the attackers were claimed as shot down in air combat, with 17 more lost to ground fire. Five Sabres were shot down in air combat. On 6 December, an IAF attack cratered the runways at both Tezgaon and Kurmitola, effectively putting them out of action for the rest of the campaign. Apart from the IAF squadrons deployed in East Bengal, India's sole aircraft-carrier, INS *Vikrant* (with its Sea Hawk fighter-bombers and Breguet Alizé ASW aircraft) mounted attacks against the civil airport at Cox's Bazaar and Chittagong harbour. The embryo Bangladesh air force, with three DHC Otters (fitted with machine-guns) of the Mukhti Bahini Air Wing made an appearance on 7 December. Indian airborne troops,

in battalion strength, made an assault on Dacca on 11 December using An-12s and Fairchild C-119Gs. This was preceded on 7 December by a heliborne infantry assault by two companies, in some nine Mil Mi-4s and Mi-8s, escorted by 'gunship' Alouettes.

ATTACKS ON PAKISTAN
While India's grip on what had been East Pakistan tightened, the IAF continued to press home attacks against Pakistan itself. The campaign settled down to a series of daylight anti-airfield, anti-radar and close-support attacks by fighters, with night attacks against airfields and strategic targets by B-57s and C-130s (Pakistan), and Canberras and An-12s (India). The PAF's F-6s were employed mainly on defensive combat air patrols over their own bases, but without air superiority the PAF was unable to conduct effective offensive operations,

and its attacks were largely ineffective. During the IAF's airfield attacks one US and one UN aircraft were damaged in Dacca, while a Canadian Air Force Caribou was destroyed at Islamabad, along with US military liaison chief Brigadier General Chuck Yeager's USAF Beech U-8 light twin.

Sporadic raids by the IAF continued against Pakistan's forward air bases in the West until the end of the war, and large-scale interdiction and close-support operations were maintained. The PAF played a more limited part in the operations, and was reinforced by F-104s from Jordan, Mirages from an unidentified Middle Eastern ally (probably

Below: Bombs explode on Cox's Bazaar airfield on 4 December 1971 during an attack by No. 300 Squadron's Sea Hawks. A low-flying Sea Hawk is just visible on the original print, by the small bend in the river at the left of the picture.

Right: A hastily-camouflaged Su-7 lands at Pathankot after a bombing attack over Pakistan, on 11 December 1971. The 'Fitter' was handicapped by its lack of payload/range capability, but proved fast at low level, and remarkably resilient.

Left: Sea Hawks of No. 300 Squadron (the 'White Tigers') ranged on the deck of the INS Vikrant during a lull in the 1971 fighting. The aircraft are armed with underwing rockets, in addition to their internal 20-mm (0.7-in) cannon. The 227-kg (500-lb) bomb was also used.

Above: Indian Navy Breguet Alizés attacked and sank this ferry near the Bangladeshi port of Khulna when it attempted to run the Indian Navy's blockade. One INAS Alizé was shot down by an F-104 during the 1971 war, but overall the type gave sterling service.

Libya) and by F-86s from Saudi Arabia. Their arrival helped camouflage the extent of Pakistan's losses. Libyan F-5s were reportedly deployed to Sargodha, perhaps as a potential training unit to prepare Pakistani pilots for an influx of more F-5s from Saudi Arabia.

Hostilities officially ended at 14.30 GMT on 17 December, after the fall of Dacca on 15 December.

India claimed large gains of territory in West Pakistan (although pre-war boundaries were recognised after the war), though the independence of Pakistan's east wing, as Bangladesh, was confirmed. India flew 1,978 sorties in the East and about 4,000 in the West, while the PAF flew about 30 and 2,840. More than 80 per cent of the IAF's sorties were close support and inter-diction, and about 65 IAF aircraft were lost (54 losses were admitted), perhaps as many as 27 of them in air combat. Pakistan lost about 72 air-craft (51 of them combat types, but admitting only 25 to enemy action). At least 16 of the Pakistani losses,

and probably 24 fell in air combat (although only 10 air combat losses were admitted, not including any F-6s, Mirage IIIs, or the six Jordanian F-104s which failed to return to their donors). But the imbalance in air losses was explained by the IAF's considerably higher sortie rate, and its emphasis on ground-attack missions. On the ground Pakistan suffered most, with 8,000 killed and 25,000 wounded while India lost 3,000 dead and 12,000 wounded. The losses of armoured vehicles were similarly unbalanced. This represented a major defeat for Pakistan.

India and Pakistan have not gone to war again, but the two

Above: Two Canberra B(I).Mk 58s attacking harbour installations at Karachi at low level, December 1971. India placed a heavy emphasis on interdiction during the 1971 war, and this proved a successful tactic.

nations retain their emnity, and have conducted small-scale military operations high in the Karakoram Mountains.

Below: The Alizés of No. 310 Squadron (The 'Cobras') operated from the carrier Vikrant and from Bombay, flying maritime patrol, ASW, minelaying and attack sor-ties. The Indian Navy's Sea Hawk fighter-bombers were even more heavily committed, flying some 160 sorties, mainly against airfields and harbour installations.

IAF fighter-bombers, 1971

By 1971 the IAF had several squadrons of supersonic fighter bombers (HAL Maruts and Sukhoi Su-7s), but these proved little more effective than the remaining Hawker Hunters and Canberras, though the Maruts, operating at high level, suffered no casualties and were even responsible for downing a single Sabre.

HAL HF-24 Marut Mk 1
The HF-24 Marut entered service with No. 10 Squadron in April 1967, and with No. 220 Squadron in April 1969. Escorted by MiG-21s the Maruts attacked targets 322 km (200 miles) inside Pakistan with 454-kg (1,000-lb) bombs.

D-1224

Sukhoi Su-7BMK
The Su-7 was acquired due to delays to the Marut programme. The aircraft entered service in 1968, and six squadrons were operational by 1971. These oper-ated in the low-level interdiction and tactical reconnaissance roles. One shot down a PAF Su-7. Losses were heavy.

The southern Far East region, encompassing Southeast Asia and the island states, represents a fascinating mix of nations with widely contrasting economic backgrounds and political ideologies. The idealogical battle between communism and capitalism which replaced the old colonial struggles has exploded into warfare on numerous occasions, not only between nations but also within those nations. Above all, the shadow of China lies over the region, a shadow which can only grow as the most populous nation on Earth begins to flex its industrial and military muscle.

VIETNAM

The end of the Vietnam war saw the Republic of Vietnam fielding the most powerful military forces in the region.

In 1978 Vietnam invaded Cambodia. The Vietnamese air force, equipped with large numbers of former South Vietnamese aircraft, had little opposition. Military air activity in Cambodia had virtually ceased after the Khmer Rouge ousted the US-supported government in 1975 and began its genoci-

dal reconstruction of the country. The Khmer Rouge's ally China supplied a few J-6 (MiG-19) fighter-bombers, but they offered little resistance.

The Northrop F-5s, Cessna A-37s and Bell UH-1s were replaced by Soviet-supplied aircraft over the next 11 years, with Mil Mi-24 'Hind' gunships seeing action against the Khmer Rouge.

Soon after the invasion, Vietnam found itself at war with a much more serious opponent. In spite of a traditional enmity dating back a thousand years or more, China had supported North Vietnam during the war with the Americans. But

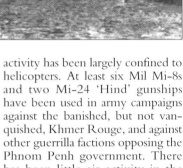

with the war over the unnatural alliance ceased. China invaded Vietnam on 17 February 1979 – largely in response to Vietnam's own invasion of China's ally, Kampuchea (formerly Cambodia).

85,000 troops of the People's Liberation Army (with 200,000 more in reserve) crossed the border, taking and razing the cities of Lao Cai, Cao Bang and Lang Son. The Chinese were beaten back by the Vietnamese before they could reach Hanoi. The PLA lost 62,500 troops killed or wounded, and 280 tanks. Poor weather limited air activity to a few ground attack sorties (mainly by Nanchang A-5s) and there were few clashes with the better organised, better equipped and vastly more experienced VNAF.

CAMBODIA/KAMPUCHEA

No attempt to re-organise the Kampuchean air force took place until 1984, when the government sent some pilots to the Soviet Union for training. Since then,

activity has been largely confined to helicopters. At least six Mil Mi-8s and two Mi-24 'Hind' gunships have been used in army campaigns against the banished, but not vanquished, Khmer Rouge, and against other guerrilla factions opposing the Phnom Penh government. There has been little air activity in the struggle for control of the country which broke out in 1997.

THAILAND

Thailand was a major base for US combat operations in Southeast Asia. Following the US withdrawal from Thailand at the end of the Vietnam War, and the communist takeover of neighbouring Kampuchea, Thailand adopted a nominally neutral political stance. All US military aid to Thailand ended in 1978, although limited purchases of US equipment continued under the Foreign Military Sales programme.

Additional emergency aid was provided by the US State Department when Vietnamese occupation troops crossed the Thai border from Cambodia in June 1980. Arms deliveries were accelerated in April 1983 after the Vietnamese continued to pursue Cambodian Khmer Rouge anti-

government guerrillas into Thai territory. Guerrilla activity within Thailand has been reduced considerably, but continued unrest across the border means that Thai forces must remain alert.

MYANMAR (BURMA)

Ever since independence in 1948, the government in Rangoon has struggled to exert control over the far-flung forested uplands to the north and east known as the 'Golden Triangle'. For almost all of that time, military or military-controlled regimes have fought periodic campaigns against entrenched warlords, communist guerrillas and ethnic groups. These include the Karen and Shan, which seek independence, and in the meantime finance their insurgency by cultivating and selling opium.

Aircraft used in the long counter-insurgency war have ranged from Spitfires in the 1950s

Below: Although the SIAI-Marchetti SF.260 was designed as a basic trainer, its ability to deliver light weapons with accuracy in a counter-insurgency context has seen the type enter service with Myanmar, the Philippines (seen here), Singapore, and Thailand.

Right: Although the repressive military regime has been unable to acquire modern combat aircraft from the major exporting nations, Myanmar took delivery of six SOKO G-4 Super Galeb light attack-capable advanced trainers from Yugoslavia in 1990, just before that nation began to break apart.

to Bell 205s, SF.260s, Pilatus PC-7s, SOKO Super Galebs and Nanchang A-5s in the 1970s and 1980s. A number of these aircraft have been lost to small-arms fire.

Burma was renamed Myanmar in 1989, and continues to profess strict non-alignment. It has therefore received little military aid from the major power blocs, and the repressive nature of the current government makes the provision of such aid unlikely.

PHILIPPINES

Following the end of the Huk insurrection in the mid 1950s, there was relative peace in the Philippines until 1964. It was then that ethnically Malay, religiously Muslim separatists, feeling themselves under threat from new Christian settlers, formed the Moro National Liberation Front (MNLF) and began a long guerrilla war.

Ferdinand Marcos was elected

President in 1965. In 1968, a second threat to Manilla emerged with the formation of the PKP, the Philippine communist party. This formed a military wing (the New People's Army, or NPA) and began its own campaign of terrorism, initially favouring the sabotage of civilian airliners. In 1972, using the insurrections at least in part as an excuse, Marcos declared martial law, and began 14 years of dictatorial rule.

Air force units have supported the Philippine army in the long counter-insurgency war ever since, with T-28s and F-5s being augmented by AC-47 gunships, and gunship helicopters. The ageing T-28s have been replaced by SF.260s and Rockwell Broncos.

The MNLF eventually took de facto control over the Sulu archipelago and Cotabato province. Although limited regional autonomy was granted in 1977, continual wrangling has seen few of the terms of the agreement being met, and there has been a resurgence of violence in the southern portion of the Philippines in the mid 1990s.

Violence has continued, despite of the replacement of the corrupt Marcos regime by that of Cory Aquino (widow of an assassinated opposition leader) in 1986. Mrs. Aquino survived at least six coup

attempts before passing power on to defence minister Ramos.

The withdrawal of US forces from Clark Air Force Base and Subic Bay has since thrown the Phillipines much more onto its own resources since 1991.

INDONESIA

The 1974 coup in Portugal resulted in a rapid withdrawal from the country's overseas possessions, one of which was East Timor. Three factions vied for control: one favoured a continuing association with Portugal, another wanted full independence, while a third wanted an association with Indonesia, which already included neighbouring West Timor. The pro-independence Fretilin took control and declared a republic on 28 November, provoking an Indonesian invasion by Marines and 1,000 paratroops (dropped by C-130Bs and C-47s), covered by F-51D Mustangs. Although the Fretilin took to the hills, they enjoy great popular support. East Timor has not been pacified, despite great repression and violence by Indonesian forces. These have fought a fierce, decades-long counter-insurgency war, supported by a wide variety of aircraft types, including OV-10 Broncos and British Aerospace Hawks.

Fighters and COIN

Although warfare has been endemic through Southeast Asia over the last 25 years, it has generally been of low intensity. With a couple of exceptions there has been little aerial conflict, though there has been plenty of COIN action and helicopters have become vital to the movement

of troops. As a result, regional air forces have operated with a bewildering mix of combat aircraft, from former front line fighters cast off as obsolete by the major powers through armed trainers to dedicated counter-insurgency designs.

Vought F-8 Crusader
Left: Although its glory days with the US Navy were over by the end of the 1960s, the Crusader served the Philippine air force for many years after the end of the Vietnam War. The aircraft were not really suitable for the kind of action prevalent in the region, however, and were placed in storage at the end of the 1980s.

Rockwell OV-10F Bronco
Right: Designed to a US Marine Corps requirement for a counter-insurgency aircraft, the Bronco has seen extensive combat in Southeast Asia. Indonesia acquired 16 aircraft, which have been used to counter the long-running rebellion in East Timor.

Soviet and Russian interest in Afghanistan dates back many years. In the middle of the last century, this rugged, mountainous country was the scene of much tension and manoeuvring between the expanding empire of the tsars (who wanted a warm-water open-ocean port) and the Imperial might of Great Britain, determined to defend its interests in India. Soviet interest in the area intensified after World War II, hoping to see the subcontinent and Southwest Asia fall into its sphere of influence. Afghanistan and neighbouring Iran both have long, common borders with the USSR and represented useful buffers against hostile forces. Russian support for the then-Royal Afghan air force began in 1925, and Russian equipment began to predominate during the 1950s.

In 1973 the Afghan monarchy was overthrown, and a republican government under General Mohammad Daud remained on friendly terms with Moscow. The armed forces acquired large amounts of new Soviet equipment, especially the air force which by the end of the 1970s had a strength of over 180 combat aircraft, including MiG-17, MiG-19 and MiG-21 fighters, Su-7BM close-support aircraft and Il-28 bombers.

In April 1978 the army and air force led a coup which saw Daud dead and power placed in the hands of the People's Democratic Party of Afghanistan (PDPA) under Mohammad Nur Taraki. He was replaced by Hafizullah Amin, who was distrusted by the USSR because of his American education. Inflamed by a hastily enacted Marxist land-reform programme, there was a popular rebellion, to which several army elements deserted in divisional and regimental strength. March 1979 saw the rebels strong enough to seize the western city of Herat, where they massacred hundreds of government soldiers and about 50 Soviet advisers and their families.

INVASION PREPARATIONS

With over 1,000 Soviet advisers at risk in Afghanistan, the USSR began planning to invade and restabilise the country, alarmed at the apparent resurgence of Muslim fundamentalism and keen to send warning signals to Iran and Pakistan. Army General Yepishev arranged to bolster the regime with an agreement to supply 100 T-62

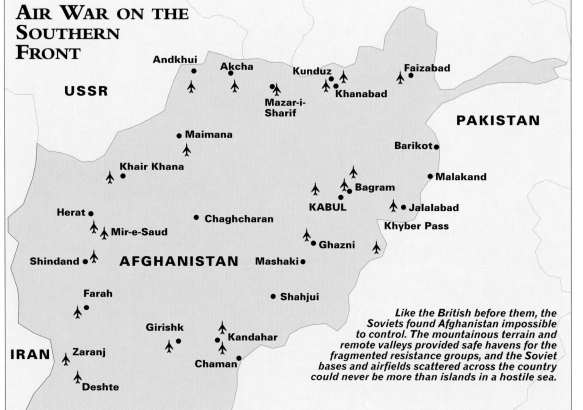

AIR WAR ON THE SOUTHERN FRONT

Like the British before them, the Soviets found Afghanistan impossible to control. The mountainous terrain and remote valleys provided safe havens for the fragmented resistance groups, and the Soviet bases and airfields scattered across the country could never be more than islands in a hostile sea.

Airlift into Kabul

With roads impassable, except to heavily escorted convoys, the Soviet and government forces in Afghanistan were forced to rely heavily on air transport both to bring men and material into Afghanistan, and to move it around in-country. Even the initial Soviet invasion was airborne, with 6,000 troops flown into Kabul in 300 aircraft movements.

Antonov An-26 'Curl'

The Afghan air force's own small transport element used a variety of aircraft types, of which the An-26 was the most modern. With an auxiliary turbojet in one nacelle, the An-26 enjoyed a remarkably good hot-and-high performance, and proved a useful light transport.

Ilyushin Il-76 'Candid'

By the time the USSR intervened in Afghanistan, the VTA had largely replaced its turbo-prop-powered An-12 'Cubs' with fan-engined Il-76 'Candids'. These performed the bulk of transport operations into and inside Afghanistan.

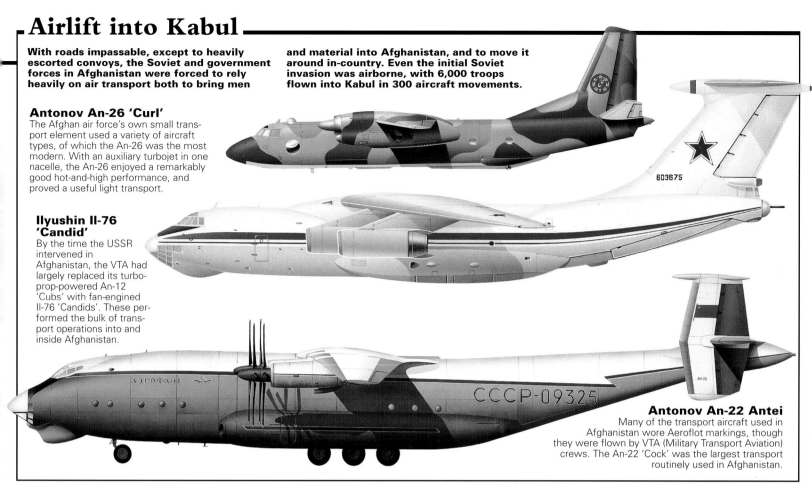

Antonov An-22 Antei
Many of the transport aircraft used in Afghanistan wore Aeroflot markings, though they were flown by VTA (Military Transport Aviation) crews. The An-22 'Cock' was the largest transport routinely used in Afghanistan.

Left: The original Mi-24 'Hind-A' saw extensive service in Afghanistan, and small numbers survived long after the introduction of later variants. The big glasshouse cockpit proved vulnerable to ground fire, while the single forward-firing gun was inadequate.

Below: The Afghan air force included a large number of MiG-17s, and these were used extensively in the ground-attack role, despite their age, poor payload and lack of advanced avionics and defensive systems. Attrition was high, however.

tanks and 18 Mi-24 'Hind' assault helicopters. Another 18 'Hinds' were supplied, including some potent 'Hind-D' gunships following further guerrilla attacks.

Left: This Afghan Mujahideen soldier fires an American-supplied Stinger ground-to-air missile at Soviet or Afghan air force aircraft. The Mujahideen were very successful in downing aircraft with both the Stinger and the Shorts Blowpipe missiles, especially helicopters.

A Soviet-Afghan friendship treaty was signed in December 1978 and registered with the UN in September 1989. Specifically allowing either party to intervene if the security of either was threatened.

After prepositioning troops a few weeks before at the air base granted to them at Bagram and Shindand, the initial Soviet mass airlift of 6,000 combat soldiers in 300 transport aircraft movements took place over the period 24-26 December 1979, when the entire Christian world was politically and militarily impotent. The Russians attacked the Kabul regime on 27 December, installing exiled former Deputy PM, Babrak Karmal, who had 'requested the Soviet assistance' then being fraternally given.

Simultaneously, up to 15,000 troops advanced from the Soviet border with armour and air support from MiG-21 fighter-bombers and Mi-24 'Hind' gunship helicopters.

The fiercely independent Afghans put up strong resistance in the country areas, declaring a Jihad, or holy war against the invaders. The USA responded by covertly arming the resistance (initially with Soviet weaponry from Egypt).

The Soviet occupation soon developed into a stalemate, in which periodic operations were mounted to clear rebel forces from specific areas, into which they generally returned as soon as the Soviets themselves withdrew. The USSR made extensive use of helicopters and air support by both in-country fighter-bombers and longer range bombers operating from Soviet bases. Tactics were

Left: The Mi-24D could pack a heavy punch, with its four-barrelled turret-mounted 12.7-mm (0.5-in) machine-gun. The under-wing weapons pylons were most often used for the carriage of podded 57-mm (2.2-in) unguided rocket projectiles. This one wears Afghan markings.

Below left: Mujahideen fighters pose on the wreck of a downed 'Hip'. The success of the Mujahideen in downing helicopters led to improved armour, better infra-red screening of engine exhausts, and the provision of IR decoy flares.

evolved using mobile ground forces as 'hammers' to drive guerrillas onto heli-landed 'anvils'.

GUNSHIPS IN ACTION

During the months following the invasion, the 'Hind-A' and the more heavily armed 'Hind-D' helicopters were augmented by Mi-8 'Hips' (some of them from the nominally civilian airline, Aeroflot). In order to relieve government forces under siege at Ishkashin, a paratroop force of 5,000 men was deployed.

The Afghan air force remained loyal to the pro-Moscow puppet government in Kabul, so there was no air-to-air combat over Afghanistan. Instead, Soviet and Afghan units provided close-air support for

The helicopter war

The helicopter allowed Soviet forces to respond quickly to hit-and-run attacks by Mujahideen guerrillas, and were used to mount offensive sweeps, undertake defensive patrols, and escort convoys. They became flying tanks and APCs, moving swiftly over even difficult terrain. They were immediately a priority target for the Afghan resistance.

Mil Mi-4
The Afghan air force began the war with a significant number of ageing Mi-4 'Hounds' on charge. The Mi-4 was soon replaced by the larger and more versatile Mi-8 'Hip' which offered twin-engined reliability and survivability, as well as a larger cabin and higher performance.

Mil Mi-24 'Hind-A'
The original Mi-24 saw extensive service in Afghanistan, especially during the early years of the conflict. 'Hind-As' operated in both Afghan and Soviet markings, and performed rocket attacks and troop transport missions with equal facility.

Mil Mi-24D 'Hind-D'
An Afghan air force Mi-24D. The Mi-24D entered service in 1977, but was rapidly blooded in Afghanistan. Large numbers were transferred to the Afghan air force, especially after the introduction of the further improved Mi-24V 'Hind-E'.

Soviet 'Floggers' over Afghanistan

Afghanistan provided a useful proving ground for a variety of Soviet aircraft types. Among the most successful was the MiG-23ML/MLD ('Flogger-G' and 'Flogger-K'), which was a fighter but was also used in the ground-attack role in Afghanistan. The MiG-27 saw less service in Afghanistan, where the Su-25 and Su-17 were the most numerous fighter-bombers.

MiG-27D "Flogger-D"

The MiG-27 was optimised for the kind of low-level strike operations that were anticipated in Western Europe, and proved unnecessarily sophisticated for the war in Afghanistan, where robust, reliable and simple aircraft enjoyed an edge.

MiG-23ML 'Flogger-G'

Apart from occasional interference by Pakistani F-16s when Soviet fighter-bombers struck Mujahideen camps in Pakistan, the Soviet air forces in Afghanistan had no air threat to deal with. MiG-23s deployed to Afghanistan thus found themselves pressed into service as fighter-bombers.

Left: Tu-22M-3 'Backfire-C' bombers were deployed to support the Soviet withdrawal between October 1988 and January 1989. It was common practice to fire flares to distract any heat-seeking missiles fired by the Mujahideen.

Below: The supersonic MiG-21 performed surprisingly well as a fighter-bomber over Afghanistan, armed with unguided bombs and rockets. The Afghan air force lost several to ground fire, however, and at least one defected to Pakistan.

army attacks against guerrilla strongholds, often with helicopters as the prime air weapon. High-performance combat aircraft also played a limited part, though pitting a Mach 2 Su-24 'Fencer' against ragged hill tribesmen proved ineffective and costly.

Early 1980 set the pattern for subsequent years as Soviet troops conducted a major spring offensive, amid unsubstantiated claims from the USA that they were using chemical and biological weapons against the Mujahideen guerrillas. During May, Mi-24s were first seen

Below: Equipped with intake filters and exhaust gas mixers, a Mil Mi-24V 'Hind-E' taxis at a forward airfield. The Mi-24 won its spurs in Afghanistan, and its crews won every possible award for gallantry in the face of the enemy.

with rearward-facing machine-guns fitted in response to the guerrilla tactic of allowing helicopters to overfly their concealed positions before opening fire.

SOVIET LOSSES

The guerrillas gained a major propaganda victory when they shot down an An-12 as it was approaching Kabul airport. At first their main anti-aircraft weapon had been the twin-barrelled 20-mm cannon, but further armament was quickly made available through Pakistan from sources as diverse as Saudi Arabia, China, Iran and particularly Egypt. The successes of the SA-7 man-portable SAM were varied, and many Soviet aircraft dispensed flares while operating close to the ground to decoy the heat-seeking missile. British Blowpipes and US Stinger

SAMs were delivered later in the war, and proved harder to decoy.

By 1982, the Soviet forces were destroying crops and villages in the areas they cleared, denying their use to returning Mujahideen fighters, but further alienating the populace from the Kabul regime. Lack of co-operation between different resistance groups prevented them from exploiting Soviet weaknesses, and besieged Soviet outposts were

generally able to hold out, or sometimes to break out and destroy their attackers.

Despite the growing military success of their offensives, the

Below: Despite lacking the glamour of the heavily armed Mi-24 gunships, the Mi-8 and Mi-17 'Hip' were probably more useful and versatile. Although they carried a heavier rocket load than the 'Hind', they served primarily as assault transport and support helicopters.

Soviet and Afghan strike power

The Soviets and the Afghan air force relied heavily on MiGs during the war. Both MiG-17s and -21s were used mainly in the ground-attack role. The Soviets also made use of more conventional bomber types for high-level bombing missions, including Su-24 'Fencers', Tu-16 'Badgers', Tu-22M 'Backfires' and even ancient Il-28 'Beagles'.

Mikoyan MiG-17
The Afghan air force used the MiG-17 'Fresco' to good effect in the ground-attack role, including a devastating attack in 1985 on the refugee camps in Pakistan.

Mikoyan MiG-21
The MiG-21 was one of the most common types of aircraft used by both the Russian and Afghan air forces in the ground-attack and army-support roles.

Soviets were unable to destroy the resistance movement, and in 1987 moved politically by replacing Karmal with Mohammed Najibullah, former head of the Secret Police. The new President brought some fresh allies into the fold, drawn from among disillusioned tribal chiefs.

The war against the Mujahideen intensified, especially against the forces of Ahmad Shah Massoud, an ethnic Tadjik who had achieved considerable success against the Soviets from his Panjshir Valley power base in the northeast of the country.

At the same time President Gorbachev announced a limited Soviet withdrawal, which began in October. It was soon decided that a complete withdrawal was possible, and Kabul's forces were given a massive influx of new weaponry.

Fifty per cent of Soviet forces had been pulled back into the USSR by August 1988, and the withdrawal of all Soviet forces was completed in February 1989. Russia's Vietnam was over.

The withdrawal of Soviet forces from Afghanistan did little to halt the fighting, which almost immediately degenerated into a three or more sided struggle between former factions of the resistance and the Kabul regime, which amazingly still held on to power for three years. This was in part due to the former communists sharing power with the most powerful of the Mujahideen factions.

President Najibullah was finally overthrown in April 1992, and the installation of an Islamic regime in April 1992, the new President Rabbani's forces, led by Massoud who had been appointed defence minister, went to war with the forces of the Pathan Hezb-E-Islami leader and former Prime Minister Gulbeddin Hekhmatyar.

Hekhmatyar's attempt to seize power was opposed by an alliance between Massoud and General Abdul Rashid Dostam, a former communist commander and warlord of the region around Mazar-i-Sharif in the north of the country.

The air force of the Democratic Republic of Afghanistan was Islamicised and purged. Different bases went over to different forces, with Kabul and Bagram becoming the de facto air force of Massoud, Shindand and Jalalabad going to Hekmatyar and Mazar-e-Sharif to Dostam. To further complicate the situation, tribal rivalries underly the situation, and these have often exploded into armed conflict.

Hekhmatyar's power base had been in the Afghan refugee camps in Pakistan, and it was from those camps that a far more potent force was to emerge in 1994.

RISE OF THE TALIBAN

The Taliban Islamic militia was composed primarily of religious students following the fundamentalist teaching of Mullah Mohammad Umar. Capitalizing on the unpopularity of the various warring factions, the Taliban quickly gained popular support and made rapid gains as they swept through the south of the country.

Fierce fighting continued until 28 September 1996, when Taliban forces finally seized Kabul, and it appeared that it would only be a matter of time before the north of the country followed.

But the Taleban have alienated many of their former supporters by their insistence on the world's most rigorous interpretation of Islamic law. Ahmad Shah Massoud has bounced back, leading resurgent former Mujahideen forces against a common enemy, pushing the Taleban back on Kabul.

Air force units have not been maintained to any great degree by any of the warring factions, but occasional flights (mainly by transport aircraft and helicopters) are made, and several Afghan air force fighters and at least three Mujahideen Su-20s were shot down during 1995, one by an Afghan AF MiG. The Taliban militia lost several helicopters.

It would be an incurable optimist who dared to predict the end of the long war in the troubled nation of Afghanistan.

Below: Painted in standard Soviet land forces European-style camouflage and heavily shrouded by tarpaulins, an Afghan air force 'Hind-A' gunship sits in front of a 'Hind-D' at Kabul.

The Il-76 'Candid' never fully replaced the older An-12 'Cub', which saw extensive service in Afghanistan, including participation in large-scale paratroop operations. Seen in 1988 at Kabul airport, this An-12 is participating in the withdrawal of among the last Soviet troops from Afghanistan.

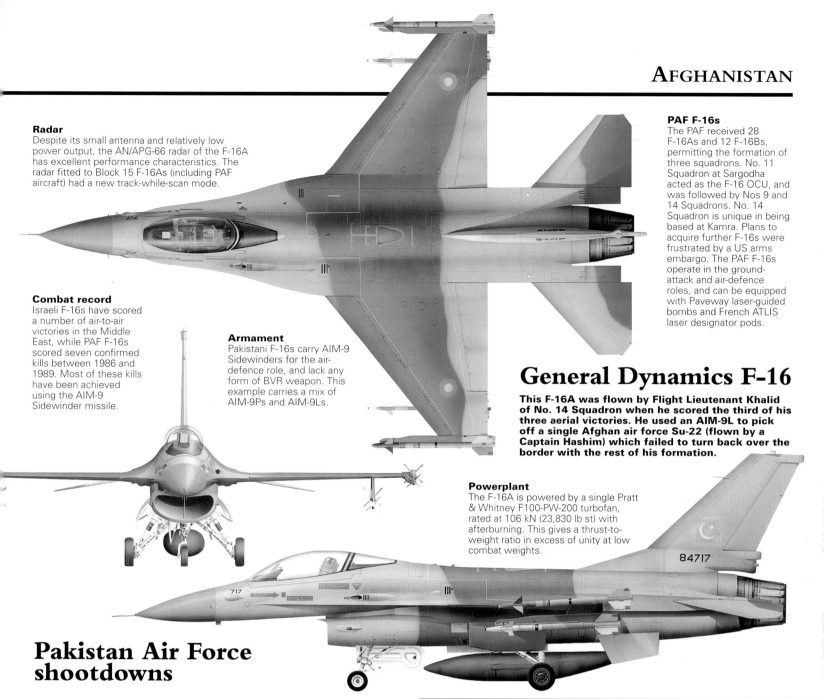

Radar
Despite its small antenna and relatively low power output, the AN/APG-66 radar of the F-16A has excellent performance characteristics. The radar fitted to Block 15 F-16As (including PAF aircraft) had a new track-while-scan mode.

PAF F-16s
The PAF received 28 F-16As and 12 F-16Bs, permitting the formation of three squadrons. No. 11 Squadron at Sargodha acted as the F-16 OCU, and was followed by Nos 9 and 14 Squadrons. No. 14 Squadron is unique in being based at Kamra. Plans to acquire further F-16s were frustrated by a US arms embargo. The PAF F-16s operate in the ground-attack and air-defence roles, and can be equipped with Paveway laser-guided bombs and French ATLIS laser designator pods.

Combat record
Israeli F-16s have scored a number of air-to-air victories in the Middle East, while PAF F-16s scored seven confirmed kills between 1986 and 1989. Most of these kills have been achieved using the AIM-9 Sidewinder missile.

Armament
Pakistani F-16s carry AIM-9 Sidewinders for the air-defence role, and lack any form of BVR weapon. This example carries a mix of AIM-9Ps and AIM-9Ls.

General Dynamics F-16

This F-16A was flown by Flight Lieutenant Khalid of No. 14 Squadron when he scored the third of his three aerial victories. He used an AIM-9L to pick off a single Afghan air force Su-22 (flown by a Captain Hashim) which failed to turn back over the border with the rest of his formation.

Powerplant
The F-16A is powered by a single Pratt & Whitney F100-PW-200 turbofan, rated at 106 kN (23,830 lb st) with afterburning. This gives a thrust-to-weight ratio in excess of unity at low combat weights.

84717

Pakistan Air Force shootdowns

Only rarely did the Soviet presence in Afghanistan cause problems in neighbouring countries, except in Pakistan, where the effect was immediate and far-reaching. Thousands of refugees fled across the border into Pakistan, and among them were Mujahideen fighters, who established bases from which they launched attacks against Soviet forces in Afghanistan itself. With an ill-defined border between the two countries, and with the Soviets and their Afghan allies eager to hit back, border violations were inevitable, sometimes accidental and sometimes deliberate. This posed a major problem to Pakistan, which could not ignore cross-border attacks on its territory, yet which did not wish to be drawn into a war with Afghanistan or its powerful supporter.

It was soon decided that the PAF would respond to border violations, and the squadrons at Peshawar (only 24 km/15 miles from the border) and Kamra maintained an alert status in order to be able to respond. Stringent rules of engagement were enforced, including a requirement that only fighters or bombers could be attacked, and that any wreckage would have to fall inside Pakistan. Although they were scrambled many times from 1980, PAF fighters were unable to engage an intruder until May 1986.

Between then and November 1988, PAF F-16s from Nos 9 and 14 Squadrons shot down eight intruding aircraft (one classified as a probable). In the first engagement one Su-22 was downed by an AIM-9 fired by Sqn Ldr Qadri of No. 9 Squadron, while another escaped, on fire, damaged by gunfire, and classed as a probable. On 30 March 1987 Wg Cdr Razzaq (also from No. 9 Squadron) downed an An-26. On 16 April 1987 Sqn Ldr Badar of No. 14 Squadron shot down another Su-22. Things went less well on 29 April, when an F-16 was shot down while engaging six Afghan air force aircraft. The F-16 probably fell victim to his own flight lead (who claimed a kill), and the Afghan formation escaped unscathed. On 4 August 1988 No. 14 Squadron's Sqn Ldr Bokhari downed a Soviet Su-25 (flown by Alexander Rutskoi, later Russia's Prime Minister), and on 12 September Flt Lt Mahmood of No. 14 Squadron opened his score by downing two MiG-23s. The same pilot shot down an Su-22 on 3 November and on 31 January 1989 was able to watch with glee as an An-24 he was intercepting crashed while attempting to land. This was the second An-24/26 loss that winter, another having been

Above: A pair of No. 9 Squadron F-16As patrols. PAF F-16s shot down seven enemy aircraft using AIM-9 Sidewinders, claimed another probable using the F-16's internal gun, and forced another manoeuvre kill. The total number of aircraft destroyed by the PAF may even be higher.

shot down (unclaimed by the PAF) on the night of 20/21 November 1988. Soviet sources suggest that a small number of PAF fighters fell victim to Soviet fighters (a MiG-23MLD accounting for one F-16), but this cannot be confirmed.

Ceylon and Sri Lanka

1958-1997

Above: Sri Lanka received six PT6-engined Harbin Y-12 transports in 1986. Illustrating the air force's pressing need for armed aircraft, all six were subsequently modified as makeshift bombers, each carrying a payload of 454 kg (1,000 lb).

Left: Weapons at the ready, Indian para-commandos disembark from an IAF Mil Mi-8 'Hip' in Sri Lanka. With its capacious cabin and excellent payload, the Mi-8 played a major part in Indian operations in Sri Lanka. The 'Hip' could be quickly transformed from a transport into a heavily-armed assault helicopter and was used to mount rocket attacks against LTTE strongholds in the jungles of northeast Sri Lanka.

Ceylon became independent in 1948 as the British withdrew from south Asia after World War II. The new country found itself with a potentially serious ethnic problem, in the shape of a significant Tamil minority which was mainly concentrated in the north of the island state. Small-scale Tamil riots took place in 1958, but but the first major conflict came in March 1971, when the deteriorating economic situation prompted a Sinhalese group to begin a campaign of terrorist insurgency, attacking police stations and other government targets.

The Royal Ceylon Air Force initially played a minor part in the suppression of the revolt, with the Bell JetRanger helicopters of No.4 Squadron and the de Havilland Dove and Heron transports of Nos

2 and 3 Squadrons flying resupply, reconnaissance and casevac sorties. British-supplied Jet Provosts were in storage, but were reactivated to form a new No.6 Squadron, which was immediately thrown into counter-insurgency action.

SOVIET ASSISTANCE

Ceylon appealed for aid on 12 April, and a number of countries responded. Eight Alouette III helicopters were supplied by Pakistan and India (which also supplied six Bell 47s, these being shipped to Ceylon aboard RAF Argosies). More controversially, the Soviet Union supplied two Ka-26s and six MiGs: five MiG-17 fighters and one MiG-15UTI trainer. The latter joined No.6 Squadron's Jet Provosts, while the helicopters went to No.2. The rebellion was crushed in May 1971. The MiGs

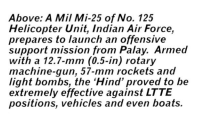

may have flown a few combat sorties in the hands of Soviet pilots.

Ceylon became a republic in 1972, when it became Sri Lanka. A state of emergency, aimed at containing further Sinhalese violence continued until 1977, but was by then aimed at the wrong target. The Hindu Tamil minority had suffered discrimination at the hands of the predominantly Buddhist Sinhalese since independence, and started demanding a separate state from May 1972, encouraged by the change to the *status quo* demonstrat-

Left: Known as Sutlej in Indian Air Force service, the rugged and dependable Antonov An-32 'Clines' of No.32 Squadron provided the Indian Peace-Keeping Force with most of its supplies and reinforcements. On 4 June 1987, five An-32s took off from Bangalore and carried out a relief mission over selected zones on the Jaffna peninsula, airdropping 24 tonnes of supplies.

Above: A Mil Mi-25 of No. 125 Helicopter Unit, Indian Air Force, prepares to launch an offensive support mission from Palay. Armed with a 12.7-mm (0.5-in) rotary machine-gun, 57-mm rockets and light bombs, the 'Hind' proved to be extremely effective against LTTE positions, vehicles and even boats.

ed by the founding of the republic.

The Tamil United Liberation Front spawned a militant wing, the Liberation Tigers of Tamil Eelam or LTTE. The organisation was banned in May 1978, following attacks on police stations, but the Tamil Tigers' activities increased as anti-Tamil rioting by the majority Sinhalese intensified. The Tigers blew up an Air Ceylon HS.748 in September, and in June 1981 a new state of emergency was declared.

The Sri Lanka air force began an ambitious re-equipment programme in 1985, ordering SIAI-Marchetti SF.260s and Bell 206 and

CEYLON/SRI LANKA

Left: Four Mirage 2000s operating from the mainland, provided fighter support for the An-32s' relief operations of 4 June 1987. This early Indian air action proved to be the precursor to a massive intervention, involving up to 100,000 troops.

Below: Sri Lankan helicopters have been used extensively in the continuing conflict with LTTE separatist guerrillas. These are the three major types in operation with No. 4 Helicopter Unit at Katunayake: the Bell 206 JetRanger, Bell 212 and Bell 412. Four 212s and nine 412s are dedicated gunships. At least one gunship has been lost during operations.

Above: Sri Lanka's response to the deteriorating situation in the Jaffna peninsula was to procure combat aircraft. Six SF.260TPs were quickly in action in the COIN role against LTTE guerillas. Two losses were made good by two attrition replacements, and by 12 further SF.260s in 1990.

212 helicopters, and these were soon in action, flying strikes against Tamil Tiger targets. The Tamil Tigers stepped up their own campaign of terrorism in response.

With the situation worsening, the government appealed to Pakistan for help in preventing arms flights to the Tamils, but in the event help was to come from a surprising quarter. India, traditionally sympathetic to the Hindu Tamils, had tried to apply pressure on the Sri Lankan government to halt its offensive against the Tamils in Jaffna, and had mounted An-32 relief-dropping flights (escorted by Mirage 2000s) from 4 June 1987.

On 29 July India and Sri Lanka signed an agreement aimed at restoring peace and 'normalcy'. India provided a massive peace-keeping force as Operation Pawan from 29 July 1987. The IPKF (Indian Peace-Keeping Force) initially consisted of 6,000 men, but numbers soon grew to 25,000 and then to 50,322 by May 1988, and eventually to over 100,000, with four full infantry divisions and their support arms.

These included two Mi-8 'Hip' and one Mi-25 'Hind' assault helicopter squadrons, and two Chetak/Cheetah-equipped light helicopter units. Although there was some surrender of arms by the Tamils, the Indians soon found themselves having to disarm the Tamils by force, capturing Jaffna and hunting the Tamil Tigers in their jungle hideouts. Extensive use was made of the Indian helicopters deployed, with Mi-8s and Mi-25s carrying out rocket and bomb attacks on the Tigers.

INDIA WITHDRAWS

India's presence helped ensure fair provincial council, presidential and parliamentary elections in 1989 and 1990, and prompted direct talks between the Tigers and the government. The IPKF began to withdraw on 28 July 1989, the withdrawal being completed in March 1990. Indian air power had played a major role in the IPKF's operations, and made a major contribution to their success. During 32 months of operations, IAF aircraft had flown over 70,000 sorties and had suffered not a single loss nor accident.

Unfortunately, the conflict has remained unresolved, and the war continues. Sri Lanka's own air force has expanded its operational arm steadily. In particular, the fixed-wing combat aircraft element has been significantly upgraded with the replacement of the 18 SF.260 and SF.260TP COIN aircraft by FMA IA-58 Pucarás, and a squadron of supersonic Chengdu F-7s, Guizhou FT-7s and Shenyang FT-5s, and most recently IAI Kfirs.

Indian helicopter support

Having committed over 100,000 troops, India's massive intervention on the Jaffna peninsula was supported by three combat helicopter squadrons, comprising the 'Hind' gunships of No. 125 Helicopter Unit and 'Hip' assault transports of Nos. 109 and 119 HUs. Indian Army Chetak and Cheetah light helicopters were backed up by the Chetaks from No. 321 Squadron, Indian Navy, which also committed a squadron of Alizé maritime patrol aircraft.

HAL Chetak
Right: Chetaks (licence-built versions of the Aérospatiale SA.316A Alouette III) of No.664 AOP Squadron, Indian Army, were used for casualty evacuation and as airborne observation posts for Mi-25 gunships. They served alongside Cheetahs, HAL versions of the Aérospatiale SA.315 Lama. The squadron was split into three operating units: Nos 10, 26 and 31 Flights.

MIDDLE EAST

The Middle East has been scarred by warfare since the dawn of recorded history, but the years since the end of World War II have seen a particularly ferocious series of conflicts. Central to the seemingly never-ending struggle has been the state of Israel, whose battles for survival against far more numerous Arab neighbours have seen this tiny country develop into a regional superpower, with one of the best trained and most efficient air forces in the world. But Arab-Israeli tension is just one of a whole series of historic ethnic and religious rivalries and hatreds, often dating back hundreds of years, which have erupted in battle since 1945.

Israel's Birth Pangs

1948-1949

Left: Avia S.199s of No. 101 Squadron (Israel's first fighter unit) taxi out for a combat patrol. Many of Israel's pilots were Jews who had fought with the USAF or RAF during the war, gaining much experience. Others were simply mercenaries or adventurers.

Below: Israel's B-17s enjoyed no more success than Egypt's hastily converted Stirling transports, though the ability to mount bombing missions was a morale booster for the Israelis.

Following the termination on 15 May 1948 of the UK's mandate in Palestine, it was almost inevitable that open strife would erupt between Jew and Arab, a situation that had been aggravated by Jewish opposition to an international (UN-approved) plan for the partition of the country into Arab and Jewish states. Neighbouring Arab states were forced to support ever-growing numbers of Palestinian refugees displaced from their lands by uncontrolled Jewish immigration.

Faced with the threat of military action by neighbouring Egypt, Iraq and Jordan, the Zionists had in November 1947 started to assemble an air arm (Shin Aleph) of the Jewish 'underground' army, the Haganah. This small force, with its collection of light aircraft, was initially confined to ground support during the civil war between the Palestinian Arabs and the Jewish immigrants.

On 15 May the state of Israel came into being, and the remaining RAF units were given orders to start dispersing to Habbaniyah in Iraq or to the Suez Canal Zone. The Royal Egyptian Air Force (REAF) possessed an expeditionary force based at El Arish in Sinai to support the Palestinians, a force that comprised a squadron of Spitfire Mk 9s, five C-47s (adapted as bombers) and a flight of Westland Lysanders. The moment the state of Israel was proclaimed it became the aim of the REAF to prevent the creation of an effective Israeli air force.

MORE ISRAELI AIRCRAFT

Israel was making frantic efforts in Europe to obtain more effective combat aircraft. The first such aircraft, Avia S.199s (a Junkers Jumo-powered development of the Messerschmitt Bf 109G), arrived from Czechoslovakia on 20 May and were first in action nine days later. On 31 May the Israeli air force (Heyl Ha'Avir) was officially established. On 3 June the S.199s forced down two Egyptian C-47s.

While the Israelis gained minor successes in the south, they suffered setbacks in the north and east where Syrian and Iraqi forces, supported by their tiny air forces, attacked Jenin, Degania and Semakh.

In the second phase of fighting, which persisted from 9 July until 18 July, Israel took the initiative, with reinforcements obtained during the ceasefire, bombing Lydda and Ramleh on the first day. On 14 July three Israeli B-17 Fortresses bombed Cairo in retaliation for an alleged attack on Old Jerusalem.

The second truce, which remained intact until 15 October, enabled Israel to greatly strengthen its air force, so that when fighting resumed it possessed five Beaufighters, three B-17s, five C-47s, six C-46s, 20 S.199s, four F-51 Mustangs, six Norsemans, three Constellations, two Hudsons, one Mosquito and nearly 50 ex-Czech

Left: Egyptian C-47s served in the transport role, but were hastily pressed into service as makeshift bombers. They operated from El Arish with No. 4 Squadron.

air force Spitfire LF.Mk 9Es and Mk 16s.

The Syrian and Iraqi governments began to voice their reluctance to continue involvement in the war, enabling Israel to bring the great majority of its forces to bear on the Egyptian front. By December, despite being reinforced by a second Spitfire squadron at El Arish, the strength of the REAF's force in eastern Sinai had dropped so that it faced odds of almost four to one. To the north a force of 5,000 Egyptian troops was cut off at Faluja, and only sustained by air-dropped supplies. Four Egyptian Stirlings, intended as transports, were pressed into use as bombers, and made daylight attacks on an Israeli force threatening El Arish from the south; this vital forward Egyptian base fell on 29 December.

In little more than six months the neo-nationalist state of Israel had become a powerful force with which to be reckoned.

Spitfire versus Spitfire

Both Israel and Egypt used Supermarine Spitfires during the war of independence, in the ground-attack and fighter roles. As if this were not confusing enough, RAF squadrons (which moved from Palestine to the Canal Zone) were also Spitfire-equipped. Spitfires of the three air arms clashed on some occasions, and each lost Spitfires in air combat.

Spitfire Mk IX

Spitfires equipped a number of Egyptian air force units, including No. 2 Squadron at El Arish, and No. 6 Squadron at the same base, which included a number of older Spitfire Vs. Egyptian Spitfires played a major part in the Egyptian offensive against Israel, primarily as fighter-bombers, but reportedly scoring some air-to-air victories.

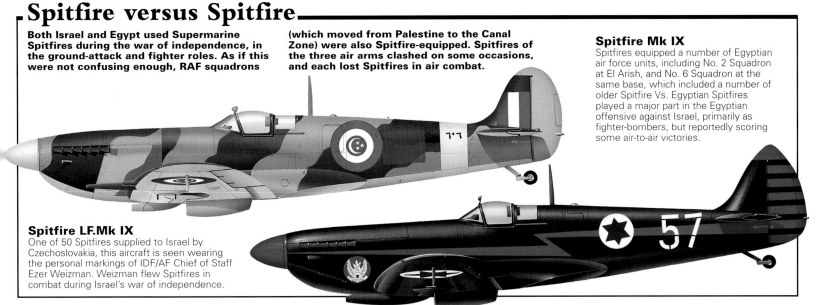

Spitfire LF.Mk IX

One of 50 Spitfires supplied to Israel by Czechoslovakia, this aircraft is seen wearing the personal markings of IDF/AF Chief of Staff Ezer Weizman. Weizman flew Spitfires in combat during Israel's war of independence.

Suez Crisis

NOVEMBER 1956

FLEET AIR ARM GROUND ATTACK
Three Royal Navy aircraft-carriers participated in
Operation 'Musketeer'. Here Sea Hawks from No. 804
Squadron, operating from HMS *Bulwark*, attack
Egyptian ground targets. Sea Venoms and Wyverns
performed similar duties.

I n 1952 Egypt's ruler King Farouk was toppled in a military coup and replaced by Colonel Gamal Abdel Nasser. Determined to end the British military presence in his country, he forced their withdrawal by 1956. That same year he nationalised the Anglo-French Suez Canal Company, seizing control of that vital waterway and thus threatening French and British trade interests with their colonies in the Middle and Far East. Britain and France decided on a military solution and gathered their forces to launch Operation 'Musketeer' in early-November 1956. The conflict ended in the humbling of the two powers that had hitherto been dominant in the Middle East.

A military plan was drawn up by Britain and France in August 1956 to seize control of the Canal. It was delayed and modified to accommodate an Israeli paratroop raid against the western end of the Mitla Pass in Sinai as retaliation for Palestinian

guerrilla attacks from the Gaza Strip. On 24 October the Sèvres Agreement was signed by the UK, France and Israel, with 29 October as the planned date for the Israeli 'raid' to trigger an Anglo-French 'ultimatum'.

EGYPTIAN DEFENDERS

At the start of hostilities, the Egyptian air force had nearly 70 front-line combat aircraft. The most potent arm was provided by Soviet equipment in the form of two squadrons of MiG-15 fighters and a squadron of Il-28 bombers. Though being phased out, one squadron of Vampires and another of Meteors (both at Fayid) were still operational, with forward strips in Sinai. Supporting them were three transport squadrons (60 aircraft at Almaza and Deversoir). Six other units (84 assorted piston- and jet-engined aircraft) were non-operational, being in the process of conversion or disbandment. The Egyptian army had also withdrawn

Above: The Republic RF-84F Thunderflashes of Escadron de Reconnaissance 4/33 flew tactical reconnaissance missions from Akrotiri. Four squadrons of F-84F fighters were also involved.

half its normal strength from Sinai to the Delta to face a British and French build-up in Malta and Cyprus. Much of the air force was also 'facing north' rather than east towards Israel.

ANGLO-FRENCH FORCES

France had four fighter-bomber wings (100 aircraft), three transport wings and two carriers, *Arromanches* and *La Fayette*, with F4U-7 Corsair fighters. On 23 October three French squadrons arrived in Israel. Their Mystères would defend Tel Aviv, helped by F-84s which would afterwards support the Israeli army in Sinai. The Noratlases would supply Israel's paratroops in Mitla and central Sinai. Aircraft operating over Egyptian territory were given Israeli markings. Thus, the Israeli air force's 69 jet- and 45 piston-engined fighters could be committed to Sinai, plus its B-17s and assorted transports. Mystères provided top

cover, while Meteors, Ouragans, P-51s and Mosquitoes operated for ground attack, and B-17s carried out night bombing raids.

By far the most modern forces deployed were those of Britain, whose Royal Air Force moved four Valiant heavy bomber and six Canberra medium bomber squadrons to Luqa on Malta. The heaviest concentration of air power was based on Cyprus, with another 10 Canberra squadrons, four Hunter and Meteor units for air defence, four Venom squadrons for ground-attack, and six transport squadrons with Hastings and Valetta aircraft. The Fleet Air Arm deployed three aircraft-carriers – *Albion*, *Bulwark* and *Eagle* – to the Mediterranean.

Above: Fighter cover for the RAF's bombers was provided by the Sapphire-engined Hunter F.Mk 5s of Nos 1 and 34 Squadrons, which usually formed the Tangmere Hunter wing.

Right: A Canberra B.Mk 6 of No. 109 Squadron takes off from RAF Luqa, Malta, for a bombing mission. The RAF's Canberra B.Mk 2s, with their shorter range, operated from Nicosia on the island of Cyprus.

Anglo-French air power

The British and French assembled a massive tactical air armada for the assault on Egypt, with fighter-bombers and medium bombers, together with fighter and reconnaissance support. They were based on Malta and Cyprus, and aboard five aircraft-carriers and a commando carrier. Ground forces included airborne and seaborne troops with tanks; they would have seized the entire Canal Zone if the ceasefire had not been agreed.

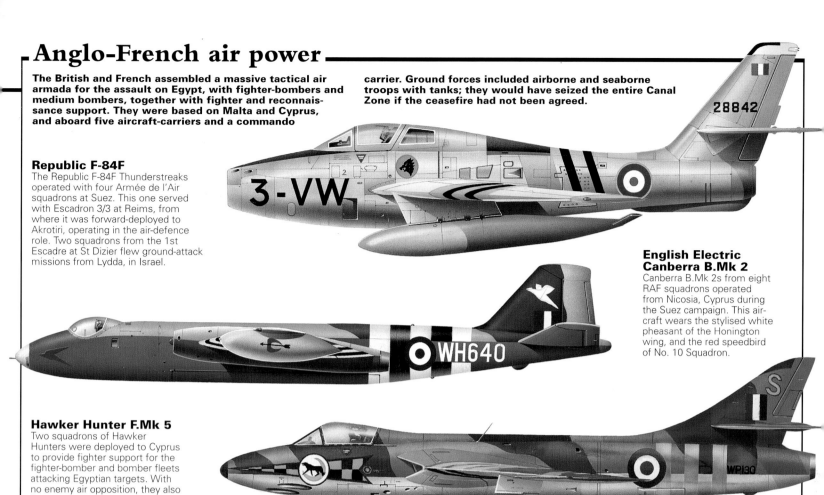

Republic F-84F
The Republic F-84F Thunderstreaks operated with four Armée de l'Air squadrons at Suez. This one served with Escadron 3/3 at Reims, from where it was forward-deployed to Akrotiri, operating in the air-defence role. Two squadrons from the 1st Escadre at St Dizier flew ground-attack missions from Lydda, in Israel.

English Electric Canberra B.Mk 2
Canberra B.Mk 2s from eight RAF squadrons operated from Nicosia, Cyprus during the Suez campaign. This aircraft wears the stylised white pheasant of the Honington wing, and the red speedbird of No. 10 Squadron.

Hawker Hunter F.Mk 5
Two squadrons of Hawker Hunters were deployed to Cyprus to provide fighter support for the fighter-bomber and bomber fleets attacking Egyptian targets. With no enemy air opposition, they also flew close-support missions.

LIGHTNING STRIKES

The Anglo-French intervention in Suez followed the nationalisation of the Canal by Nasser. This justification was undermined by inclusion of a third partner in the venture – Israel, Egypt's long-standing enemy. The Suez operation began with heliborne and paratroop landings, which were covered by fighter-bomber support.

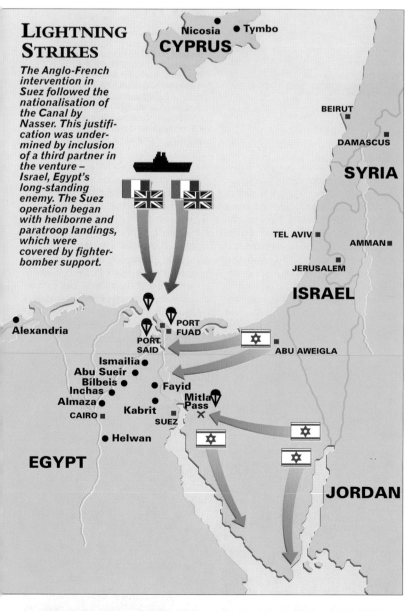

They contributed 11 squadrons of Wyvern, Sea Venom and Sea Hawk combat aircraft.

The Suez war began late on the afternoon of 29 October when Israeli forces entered Sinai at two points. Approximately 1,600 paratroopers were then dropped from C-47s near the eastern end of the Mitla Pass while IAF Mystères patrolled central Sinai to watch for EAF reaction. By 20.00 that evening, Egyptian troops were heading across the Suez Canal towards the Mitla Pass. An hour later six French transports dropped heavy equipment to the Israeli paratroops.

At dawn on 30 October four RAF Canberras attempted a reconnaissance of Egyptian reaction in

Above: Vickers Valiants from Nos 138, 148, 207 and 214 Squadrons flew conventional bombing missions from Luqa on the island of Malta.

the Canal Zone. All were intercepted by MiG-15s, one being damaged. Early that same morning the Egyptian destroyer *Ibrahim al Awwal* tried to bombard Haifa harbour but was so damaged by IAF Ouragans that it had to surrender to Israeli destroyers. At almost the same moment a flight of four EAF Vampires made a reconnaissance of Israeli forces at Mitla and El

Below: The Avro Shackletons of No. 37 Squadron at Luqa flew maritime and anti-submarine patrols to protect allied shipping in the Mediterranean, but also found time to fly air transport missions in support of the British task force.

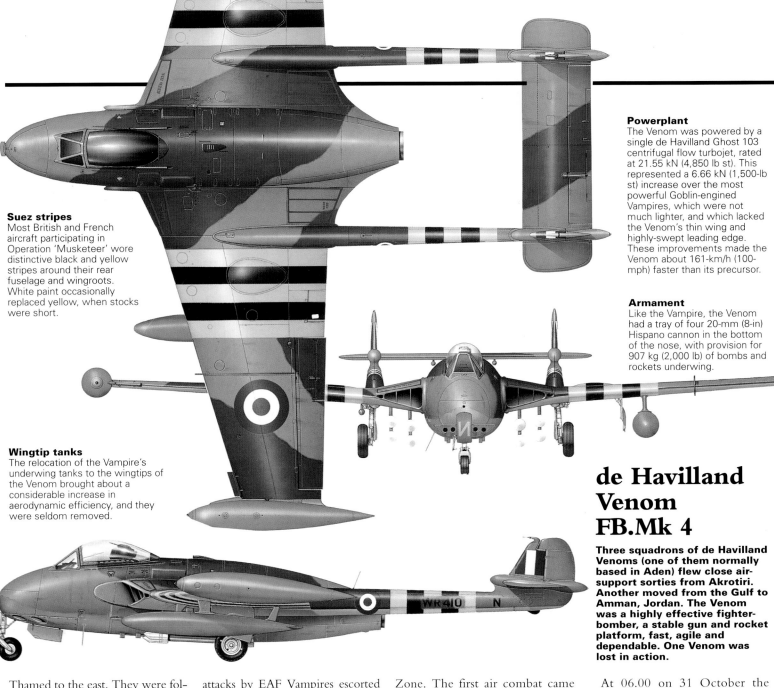

Suez stripes
Most British and French aircraft participating in Operation 'Musketeer' wore distinctive black and yellow stripes around their rear fuselage and wingroots. White paint occasionally replaced yellow, when stocks were short.

Wingtip tanks
The relocation of the Vampire's underwing tanks to the wingtips of the Venom brought about a considerable increase in aerodynamic efficiency, and they were seldom removed.

Powerplant
The Venom was powered by a single de Havilland Ghost 103 centrifugal flow turbojet, rated at 21.55 kN (4,850 lb st). This represented a 6.66 kN (1,500-lb st) increase over the most powerful Goblin-engined Vampires, which were not much lighter, and which lacked the Venom's thin wing and highly-swept leading edge. These improvements made the Venom about 161-km/h (100-mph) faster than its precursor.

Armament
Like the Vampire, the Venom had a tray of four 20-mm (8-in) Hispano cannon in the bottom of the nose, with provision for 907 kg (2,000 lb) of bombs and rockets underwing.

de Havilland Venom FB.Mk 4

Three squadrons of de Havilland Venoms (one of them normally based in Aden) flew close air-support sorties from Akrotiri. Another moved from the Gulf to Amman, Jordan. The Venom was a highly effective fighter-bomber, a stable gun and rocket platform, fast, agile and dependable. One Venom was lost in action.

Thamed to the east. They were followed two hours later by MiG-15s, which destroyed six vehicles and a Piper Cub on the ground. Further

Two Egyptian MiG-15s on a combat air patrol. The EAF performed well initially, but when the Anglo-French air attacks began it played little part since aircraft were either destroyed or fled south.

Right: Egypt's Ilyushin Il-28 bombers fled south to Luxor, out of range of the allied aircraft on Cyprus. They were eventually found and destroyed by French F-84Fs operating from bases in Israel.

attacks by EAF Vampires escorted by MiGs destroyed more vehicles. A standing patrol of IAF Mystères was therefore set up over the Canal

Zone. The first air combat came late in the afternoon, when six MiGs held off the six Mystères of this patrol while two EAF Meteors caused further heavy loss to the paras east of Mitla. The air battle rapidly drew in more aircraft and ended with two MiGs being destroyed for a Mystère seriously damaged.

The EAF had been caught by surprise by the Israeli invasion but nevertheless managed almost 50 sorties on 30 October. The IAF flew over 100 sorties, the most effective being against Egyptian troops entering the western end of the Mitla Pass. These lost almost all their vehicles but were able to take up strong defensive positions overlooking the pass along the Heitan Defile.

Zone. The first air combat came late in the afternoon, when six MiGs held off the six Mystères of this patrol while two EAF Meteors caused further heavy loss to the paras east of Mitla. The air battle rapidly drew in more aircraft and ended with two MiGs being destroyed for a Mystère seriously damaged.

At 06.00 on 31 October the British and French issued their ultimatums, demanding that both sides withdraw from the Canal Zone – which the Israelis had not reached at all. As predicted, the Egyptians refused. At dawn, four EAF Vampires attempted to attack Israeli positions at Mitla before the IAF standing patrol arrived, and were caught by six Mystères as they began their bombing runs. By pressing on the Vampires again caused serious damage but two were downed. An attempt by a solitary Il-28 to hit Lod air base failed and the aircraft dropped its bombs near Ramat Rachel.

To the east, two IAF Ouragans were sent against an isolated flight of EAF aircraft at Bir Gifgafa but were jumped by the MiG-15 top cover for EAF Meteors which had in turn just halted a column of Israeli light tanks near Bir Hasan. Both Ouragans were damaged, one subsequently force-landing in the desert, before IAF Mystères intervened. IAF aircraft then attacked Egyptian armour, which was moving south towards Bir Gifgafa, but

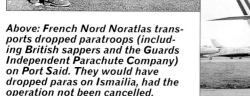

Above: French Nord Noratlas transports dropped paratroops (including British sappers and the Guards Independent Parachute Company) on Port Said. They would have dropped paras on Ismailia, had the operation not been cancelled.

Left: Dassault Mystère IVAs from Escadre de Chasse 2 at Dijon flew air-defence missions from Haifa, freeing Israeli fighter-bombers for offensive operations. Many of the French aircraft operating within Israel wore Israeli national insignia.

were themselves intercepted by EAF Meteors, one of which was shot down. The IAF continued to strafe this Egyptian column but failed to stop it, while the EAF was similarly engaged against Israelis advancing on Bir Hama.

To the north, on 31 October the Israeli army suffered its only real defeat of the campaign, when a series of attacks on Abu Ageila was driven off with serious loss. So great were the demands now being put on the IAF that French aircraft based in Israel had to intervene against another Egyptian column advancing on Abu Ageila from the Canal Zone.

Egyptian air defences were put on full alert in the Nile Delta and Canal Zone, expecting air attack in the early hours of 31 October after the expiry of the Anglo-French ultimatum. Twenty Il-28s and 20 MiG-15s destined for the Syrian air force had already been flown to Syria via Saudi Arabia by Russian and Czech pilots. They were escorted by 20 non-operational

EAF MiGs. Meanwhile, the EAF's operational and non-operational Il-28s went south to Luxor, where it was hoped they would be safe.

Until the last moment the Egyptians thought the British and French were bluffing, so there was neither black-out nor dispersal when the first bombers attacked Almaza shortly after dark.

Tasked with the destruction of the Egyptian air force, the RAF mounted a series of bombing raids later that evening. Three waves of Canberra and Valiant bombers came in from Cyprus and Malta to hit Almaza, Inchas, Abu Sueir,

Kabrit and Cairo International before midnight. Bombing from 12190 m (40,000 ft), they destroyed or damaged only 14 aircraft. The EAF made only two interception attempts and only once did a Meteor NF.Mk 13 fire on a Valiant.

A pair of reconnaissance Canberras was intercepted by MiGs early on 1 November, one Canberra being damaged. They reported the limited effect of the night assault and so by day the tactics were changed. Anglo-French land- and carrier-based aircraft attacked every EAF airfield west of Sinai. The MiGs were hurriedly

dispersed throughout the Delta but found it hard even to take off as each strip was under almost constant surveillance. On 2 and 3 November Bilbeis Air Academy and the Helwan repair depot were attacked, and on 6 November railway communications, barracks and anti-aircraft sites were added.

On 2 November the French carrier *Arromanches* launched its Corsairs against Alexandria harbour but was in turn attacked by the Egyptian destroyers *El Nasr* and

Below: English Electric Canberra B.Mk 6s of No. 12 Squadron lined up at RAF Luqa for operations over Egypt. Canberras performed the bulk of the bombing missions, even marking targets for the larger, more modern Valiants.

Israeli and Egyptian air power

Many on the British side were uncomfortable about operating with the Israelis, not wishing to offend Arab allies. Operation 'Cordage' was prepared for the bombing of Israeli airfields, and would have been set in motion had Israel attacked Jordan or Iraq. France and Britain had ostensibly intervened to separate Israeli and Egyptian forces and protect the Canal.

Dassault Ouragan
Israeli fighter-bombers, like this Ouragan of No. 113 Squadron, wore black and yellow Suez stripes. The sharkmouth was a unit marking.

Douglas C-47
Israel was desperately short of transport aircraft, and was forced to impress civil airliners and to rely on French Nord Noratlases to fill the gap. IDF/AF and impressed C-47s and DC-3s were used to drop Israeli paratroops.

Armstrong Whitworth Meteor NF.Mk 13
Egypt's armed forces still included a great deal of British equipment, supplied when Britain and Egypt were allies. The air force included Meteor day and night fighters.

Fleet Air Arm fighter-bombers

In the absence of enemy air opposition, most of the aircraft aboard the carriers *Albion, Bulwark* and *Eagle* actually operated in the fighter-bomber and close-support roles. The FAA was heavily committed to supporting British paratroops after their landing at Port Said on 5 November. Two Sea Hawks and a Wyvern were lost in action.

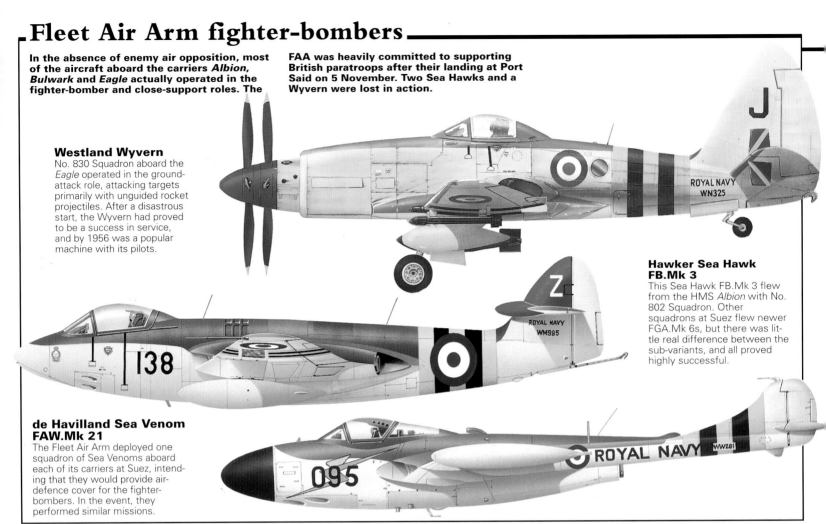

Westland Wyvern
No. 830 Squadron aboard the *Eagle* operated in the ground-attack role, attacking targets primarily with unguided rocket projectiles. After a disastrous start, the Wyvern had proved to be a success in service, and by 1956 was a popular machine with its pilots.

Hawker Sea Hawk FB.Mk 3
This Sea Hawk FB.Mk 3 flew from the HMS *Albion* with No. 802 Squadron. Other squadrons at Suez flew newer FGA.Mk 6s, but there was little real difference between the sub-variants, and all proved highly successful.

de Havilland Sea Venom FAW.Mk 21
The Fleet Air Arm deployed one squadron of Sea Venoms aboard each of its carriers at Suez, intending that they would provide air-defence cover for the fighter-bombers. In the event, they performed similar missions.

Tarek. These ships were forced to retire beneath a smoke-screen when the aircraft turned on them. The attacks continued on 4 and 5 November as British carrier-based aircraft hit airfields outside Alexandria in a further attempt to divert Egyptian attention away from the intended invasion of Port Said and Port Fuad. Another Canberra was damaged by a MiG near Luxor on 3 November, but Egyptian ground defences put up a more effective resistance, bringing down a Wyvern over Port Said, and a Hellcat and a Mystère over Cairo on 3 November.

The British and French air offensive against the EAF enabled the Israelis to unleash a full-scale armoured assault. It also led the Egyptians to withdraw from Sinai;

they had crossed the Canal on 2 November.

Although there was only rear-guard skirmishing on the ground, the IAF and surviving units fought a bitter fight above it. Vampires from El Arish withdrew to Bir Gifgafa and Bir Rod Salim. They attacked Israeli paratroops at Mitla later in the morning of 1 November, losing one aircraft to IAF interception. Despite British and French air raids three Meteor NF.Mk 13s with an escort of MiGs appeared over Sinai in the afternoon. One MiG was downed by two IAF Mystères.

Down at Sharm el Sheikh a major battle developed from 2 November. Paratroops and their heavy equipment were dropped at El Tor on the western shore of the peninsula while other units advanced down the eastern side. The IAF, meanwhile, bombed the British frigate HMS *Crane* which, blockading Sharm, was mistaken

Above: French carrier Arromanches included a detachment of TBM-3S and TBM-3W Avengers, operating in the ASW and AEW roles. The two French carriers at Suez were smaller than the British ships, with smaller, older air groups.

for an Egyptian ship. On 3 November Mustangs and B-17s destroyed two of the heavy guns overlooking the Straits of Tiran at Ras Nasrani. The rest were destroyed on the night of 3/4 November by their gunners, who then retired into Sharm el Sheikh which, with its harbour and airstrip, could hope to hold out longer. Israeli troops reached Sharm from Ras Nasrani at 14.00 on 4 November. A night attack failed but a second assault backed up by Mustangs dropping napalm broke the Egyptian perimeter. Upon the arrival of Israeli paras from El Tor the garrison surrendered at 09.30 on 5 November.

Left: A Sea Venom launches from the crowded deck of HMS Albion, the catapult strop falling away into the sea. Sea Venoms provided fighter cover for the first wave of RAF bombers, Cyprus-based Hunters lacking the range.

By now the British and French assaults had begun. At dawn on 5 November, carrier-based aircraft attacked Egyptian defensive positions and at 08.20 British paratroops hit Gamil airfield on the outskirts of Port Said. Fifteen minutes later the French dropped just south of Port Fuad. A planned British helicopter-borne raid against Canal bridges was abandoned, but further para drops reinforced the invaders. At dawn the next day, seaborne landings supported by naval bombardment and close air-support seized the waterfront. Two Sea Hawks and a Venom were lost to ground fire, and in the subsequent street fighting air supremacy meant little. It was, however, able to cover a dash down the Suez Canal in the small hours of 7 November. This reached El Kap before the ceasefire which the British and French governments had finally accepted under both domestic and international pressure. This was exerted chiefly by the US government, which had underestimated Soviet influence throughout the Middle East.

The British and French claimed to have destroyed or damaged 260 aircraft, including 207 combat jets. The EAF, however, claimed that only eight MiG-15s, seven Il-28s, nine Harvards, six C-46s, four C-47s, three civil Dakotas and a grounded Avro Lancaster were destroyed, with another 62 aircraft damaged. The Ilyushins were among those in the supposed haven of Luxor which were hit by French F-84Fs fitted with extra tanks and based in southern Israel. About 10 MiG-15s and MiG-15UTIs of the Syrian training mission were also destroyed at Abu Sueir.

LOSSES

In Sinai the EAF lost four MiGs, four Vampires, a Meteor and the Mraz Sokol. The IAF admitted the loss of one Mystère, two Ouragans, 10 Mustangs (some of which were later repaired) and two Piper Cubs. Another five damaged aircraft are

Above: France's carrier-based fighter/fighter-bomber squadrons still used the veteran F4U-7 Corsair. Flottille 14F was deployed aboard the Arromanches, while 15F flew from the La Fayette.

believed to have crashed on their way home. The French lost only one aircraft (one of the Lydda-based F-84s), and the British four (a Canberra which crashed on landing, two Sea Hawks, a Wyvern) plus a Canberra PR.Mk 7 shot down over the Syrian-Lebanese border.

Both politically and militarily the entire Suez operation was a fruitless venture. The disarray created in the Western Bloc merely served to commit Egypt (and therefore Arab influence in the Middle East) more firmly than ever to the Soviet Union, and effectively destroyed all Western credibility in the Middle East for two decades.

Above: This Sea Venom of No. 893 Squadron made a successful wheels-up landing aboard the Eagle after being damaged by flak. The aircraft was soon repaired and flying operational missions.

Right: Sea Hawk FGA.Mk 6s are re-armed and refuelled aboard the Albion. The furthest aircraft has part-finished Suez stripes, while the nearer machine still has no recognition stripes at all.

AEW for the Task Force

The British carriers *Eagle* and *Albion*, and the two French carriers, embarked dedicated AEW aircraft. With the Egyptian air force hardly showing itself, the possibility of attacks on the carriers became increasingly remote, and the British Skyraiders and French Avengers found themselves with little to do.

Douglas Skyraider AEW.Mk 1
No. 849 Squadron deployed its 'A' Flight aboard the *Eagle*, with 'C' Flight aboard the *Albion*. These flights operated the Skyraider AEW.Mk 1, the Royal Navy designation for the AD-4W, then the US Navy's front-line AEW platform.

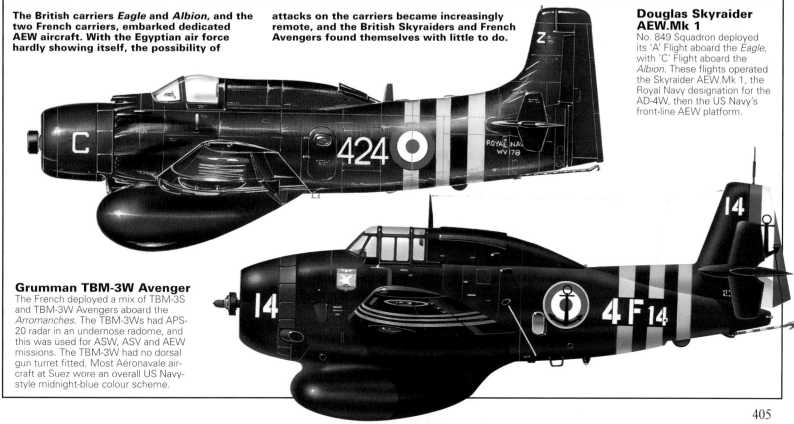

Grumman TBM-3W Avenger
The French deployed a mix of TBM-3S and TBM-3W Avengers aboard the *Arromanches*. The TBM-3Ws had APS-20 radar in an undernose radome, and this was used for ASW, ASV and AEW missions. The TBM-3W had no dorsal gun turret fitted. Most Aéronavale aircraft at Suez wore an overall US Navy-style midnight-blue colour scheme.

Britain in the Middle East

1945–1975

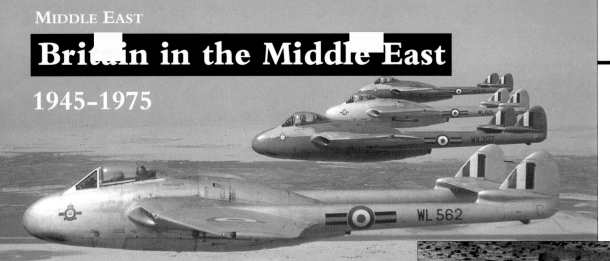

Left: De Havilland Vampires of No. 213 Squadron on patrol over the Canal Zone, where the squadron was based until its disbandment in September 1954. Britain started to withdraw from Egypt in 1952, in the face of growing hostility.

Below: The Avro Shackletons of No. 37 Squadron flew patrols from Luqa, Malta and then, from 1957, from Khormaksar, Aden.

Left: These Royal Marine Commandos are ready to start a patrol after deplaning from a Royal Navy Wessex HAS.Mk 3. The type was hastily pressed into service as a transport helicopter during operations in the Radfan.

During World War II the RAF's Desert Air Force played a crucial role in the defeat of Rommel's Afrika Korps, and then supported the Eighth Army in its drive through Italy. After the war, RAF units returned to the area and resumed the kind of colonial policing roles they had undertaken between the wars.

The first problem faced by the British in the Middle East, following the end of the war, was the deteriorating situation in Palestine, which Britain had administered under a League of Nations Mandate since the 1920s. Massive illegal immigration by displaced Jews, along with terrorism by Jewish extremists, had to be countered until the end of the Mandate in May 1948, when Britain withdrew and the Jews and Arabs went to war, each unhappy with the partition which divided Palestine into separate Jewish and Arab states. The RAF (with massive forces stationed in the Canal Zone in neighbouring Egypt) became involved in this war by accident, when four unarmed Spitfires flying a tactical reconnaissance mission along Egypt's ill-defined border were shot down by Israeli Spitfires and ground fire. The following day a Tempest involved in the search-and-rescue operation was

Jet-powered colonial policing

During the British withdrawal from their Empire, extensive use was made of air power for demonstrating a British presence, for controlling insurgent and resistance groups, and for retaliating against attacks. Fighter-bombers, from Tempests and Hornets through Vampires, Venoms and Hunters, provided cost-effective firepower for such missions.

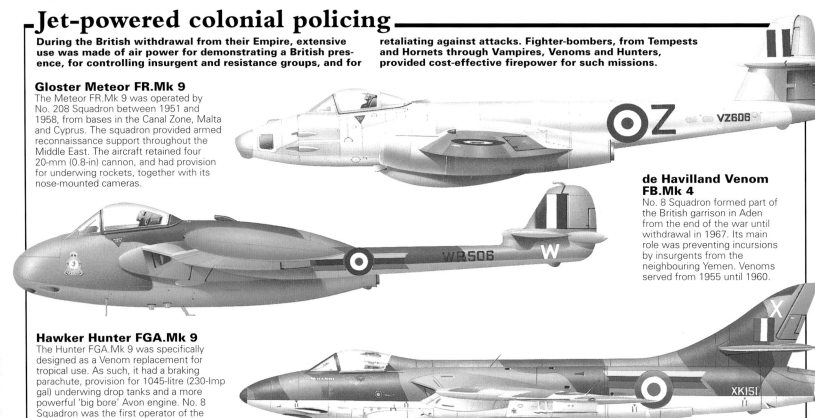

Gloster Meteor FR.Mk 9
The Meteor FR.Mk 9 was operated by No. 208 Squadron between 1951 and 1958, from bases in the Canal Zone, Malta and Cyprus. The squadron provided armed reconnaissance support throughout the Middle East. The aircraft retained four 20-mm (0.8-in) cannon, and had provision for underwing rockets, together with its nose-mounted cameras.

de Havilland Venom FB.Mk 4
No. 8 Squadron formed part of the British garrison in Aden from the end of the war until withdrawal in 1967. Its main role was preventing incursions by insurgents from the neighbouring Yemen. Venoms served from 1955 until 1960.

Hawker Hunter FGA.Mk 9
The Hunter FGA.Mk 9 was specifically designed as a Venom replacement for tropical use. As such, it had a braking parachute, provision for 1045-litre (230-Imp gal) underwing drop tanks and a more powerful 'big bore' Avon engine. No. 8 Squadron was the first operator of the FGA.Mk 9, using the aircraft on operations against Yemeni insurgents in Aden.

Transport support

RAF operations in what Britain referred to as the Near and Middle East required massive logistic support, and transport aircraft were permanently based in-theatre. They were frequently augmented by UK-based transport aircraft for specific operations, including the Anglo-French Suez operation in 1956 and the Kuwait operation of 1961. NEAF and MEAF transport bases provided useful stopovers for RAF aircraft en route to the Far East.

Vickers Valetta
Green spinners and cheatline identify this Vickers Valetta as belonging to No. 114 Squadron, which operated the type between 1949 and 1957 from Kabrit in Egypt and then from Nicosia, Cyprus. The Valetta proved to be an excellent replacement for the Douglas Dakota.

Armstrong Whitworth Argosy
The Argosy was developed as a Valetta replacement, and the first examples went to No. 114 Squadron (by then based at Benson) in March 1962, before re-equipping squadrons in Aden, Cyprus and Singapore. The massive rear loading ramps allowed easy para-dropping.

Above: The Scottish Aviation Twin Pioneer was a dedicated STOL transport, which needed a landing strip only 275-m (900-ft) long. Users included one squadron in Aden and two in Bahrain.

also shot down. Fortunately, only one pilot was killed.

LONG-STANDING LINKS
Britain already had links with the Sultanate of Oman going back more than 150 years, when it signed a new friendship treaty in December 1951. Oman called for help in late-1952, when a group of Saudis occupied an important strategic village at an oasis on the Omani-Abu Dhabi border. The RAF flew intimidatory low-level sorties over the area, then policed a blockade of routes to the oasis, eventually supporting Omani troops who moved in to expel the Saudis in July 1954. Although this problem was solved without a shot being fired, the Saudi-supported Omani Liberation Army (formed by the Imam Ghalib from rebellious

Right: Blackburn Beverleys from No. 84 Sqn from Khormaksar and from squadrons based in England flew men into Kuwait in 1961 to deter an attack by Iraq. The Beverley enjoyed superb STOL performance.

tribesmen) proved a tougher nut to crack. The Imam was captured when British troops attacked his stronghold at Nizwa, but his brother Talib escaped and continued the rebellion. In 1957 rebel strongholds were attacked by Venoms from Nos 8 and 249 Squadrons (after Shackletons had dropped warning leaflets) and in January 1959 supported an SAS assault on the Jebel Akhdar. Unfortunately, Talib escaped, but the rebellion was over.

The Canal Zone initially provided a safe home for British reserves which could be deployed elsewhere in the area as required, but, as opposition to the British presence intensified, the position of the Canal Zone bases became steadily more untenable. Units moved to bases in Cyprus, Jordan and Iraq. MEAF reformed in Cyprus in December 1954, and the last flying unit left Egypt in October 1955. The Arab nationalism which prompted this withdrawal was later to force withdrawals from Iraq and Jordan, and eventually resulted in the Anglo-French invasion in 1956 – the Suez crisis.

PROBLEMS IN CYPRUS
Although Cyprus replaced the Canal Zone as Britain's main base in the area, it proved just as troublesome. A Crown Colony since 1925, Cyprus had a Greek majority who wished for union with Greece (Enosis), against the wishes of the substantial Turkish minority. From April 1955 to February 1959, Britain was forced to fight a vigorous anti-terrorist campaign against EOKA terrorists using Shackletons to prevent arms shipments from the mainland, Austers, Pioneers and Chipmunks for reconnaissance, and helicopters (principally Sycamores) in search-and-destroy missions.

Growing opposition to the British presence in Iraq led to a 1955 agreement to withdraw and hand over the RAF stations at Habbaniyah and Shaibah, retaining facilities at the former as a staging post. Withdrawal of based aircraft was completed in April 1956, but when RAF aircraft were prevented from using Habbaniyah following

Below: No. 26 Squadron in Aden used the Bristol Belvedere from 1963 to 1965, operating in support of Army operations in the Radfan.

Above: The Bristol Sycamore was the first British-designed helicopter in service. No. 284 Sqn's Sycamores played a major role in the war against EOKA terrorists in Cyprus.

Right: An Army Bell Sioux hovers behind a Saladin armoured car. The co-operative use of aircraft and armoured cars was pioneered in the Middle East by the RAF from 1918.

Above: De Havilland Vampire F.Mk 3s of No. 601 ('County of London') Squadron, a Royal Auxiliary Air Force squadron, are seen at an annual armament practice camp at Hal Far, Malta.

Right: A pair of English Electric Lightnings of No. 56 Squadron takes off from its Akrotiri base. Lightnings took over the fighter defence of NEAF in 1967, and finally withdrew in 1976, with the withdrawal of British forces.

the July 1958 coup and assasination of the pro-British king, remaining personnel were withdrawn.

A similar situation arose in Jordan, where the ill-considered Suez operation forced the king to rescind the 1948 treaty with Britain. The single fighter-bomber squadron at Amman withdrew to Cyprus in January 1957. The breakdown in relations with Jordan was short-lived and British forces returned briefly in July 1958, when growing instability in neighbouring Lebanon threatened the stability of the Hashemite kingdom itself.

Relations with Iraq remained strained. In 1961 matters worsened, when Iraq appeared to challenge the independence of Kuwait, with whom Britain had a longstanding (since 1899) treaty relationship. Britain (by now a major customer for Kuwaiti oil) renewed its pledge to defend the country's independence in June 1961, prompting an angry Iraq to move troops to the Kuwaiti border. Kuwait formally requested British assistance on 30 June, and Britain flew No. 45 Commando, Royal Marines, and the Hunters of Nos 8 and 208 Squadrons into Kuwait, where they were later reinforced by a parachute battalion and by Canberras from Cyprus and Germany. An Iraqi invasion was deterred, and Britain was able to withdraw its forces.

REORGANISATION

With the changing centre of gravity of British forces in the area, the former Middle East Command was renamed Near East Command in March 1961, with its air element becoming the Near East Air Force instead of the Middle East Air Force. Both were headquartered in Cyprus, which steadily gained in importance as forces elsewhere withdrew (most notably in Aden and the Persian Gulf).

A coup and change of regime in the Yemen led to an increase in the campaign of propaganda and incursion mounted against the British in Aden, which had gained in impor-

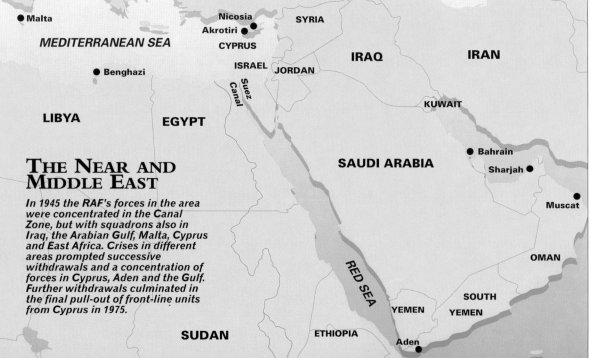

THE NEAR AND MIDDLE EAST

In 1945 the RAF's forces in the area were concentrated in the Canal Zone, but with squadrons also in Iraq, the Arabian Gulf, Malta, Cyprus and East Africa. Crises in different areas prompted successive withdrawals and a concentration of forces in Cyprus, Aden and the Gulf. Further withdrawals culminated in the final pull-out of front-line units from Cyprus in 1975.

Malta • Nicosia SYRIA
Akrotiri
MEDITERRANEAN SEA CYPRUS
ISRAEL JORDAN IRAQ IRAN
• Benghazi
KUWAIT
LIBYA EGYPT
• Bahrain
SAUDI ARABIA Sharjah •
Muscat •
RED SEA OMAN
SOUTH
YEMEN YEMEN
SUDAN ETHIOPIA Aden •

British air power on Cyprus

Cyprus fulfilled vital functions for the RAF, serving as a base for aircraft and units operating on NATO's vulnerable southern flank (usually assigned to CENTO), frustrating Russian ambitions and operations in the region. Units and aircraft in Cyprus also operated in support of British forces in the Middle East and the Gulf, supporting national interests as Britain withdrew from its Empire.

English Electric Canberra B.Mk 2
Four squadrons of English Electric Canberras formed the Akrotiri Strike Wing from 1957, replacing de Havilland Venoms. This B.Mk 2 served with No. 249 Squadron. B.Mk 2s gave way to B.Mk 6s in 1959, then B.Mk 15s and 16s from 1962. The Canberras were replaced by Vulcans in 1969.

Westland Scout AH.Mk 1
The Army Air Corps served throughout the Middle East from its formation in September 1957, with fixed-wing Austers and a variety of helicopters, including the Saro Skeeter, the Bell Sioux, and the Sud Alouette II. This Scout wears United Nations markings, signifying use by a squadron assigned to UN support duties in Cyprus.

Left: Carrier-based air power played a crucial role in augmenting RAF aircraft based in-theatre, and in reinforcing local-based forces during operations. Here Vickers Supermarine Scimitars, de Havilland Sea Venoms and Skyraiders are ranged on the deck of the HMS Victorious.

Right: Following Turkey's invasion of northern Cyprus, No. 84 Squadron's Westland Whirlwinds supported UN forces stationed between the Greek and Turkish front lines. The unit re-equipped with Wessexes in 1981.

States able to take over the burden of their own defence (having been trained to do so by the British) the RAF was able to withdraw its two Hunter squadrons from Muharraq, and its Andovers and Wessexes from Sharjah during 1971. The two airfields closed as RAF bases in December.

The Turkish invasion of northern Cyprus brought based aircraft to a high state of readiness, but Turkish fighters and fighter-bombers avoided threatening the British Sovereign Base areas and the RAF remained on the sidelines. The invasion made training difficult for based units, and a government decision to end the declaration of forces to CENTO led to a mass withdrawal of the remaining units. NEAF was disbanded and replaced by an AHQ Cyprus within RAF Strike Command.

Mid-1976 saw only a single RAF squadron permanently based in the area, No. 84 Sqn, whose Whirlwinds performed search and rescue and UN support missions in Cyprus. An Army Air Corps flight with Alouette IIs also flew similar missions after the main withdrawal.

Closer to home, the RAF withdrew from its other Mediterranean base, RAF Luqa on the island of Malta. No. 203 Squadron disbanded in December 1977, its Nimrods returning to UK-based squadrons. No. 13 Squadron brought its Canberra PR.Mk 7s to RAF Wyton the following year, and the RAF withdrawal was completed in 1979. On Cyprus the RAF maintained its massive base at Akrotiri, which was used regularly as a destination for training flights and for armament practice camps by front-line fighter squadrons.

tance as the home for a strategic reserve covering East Africa, the Horn of Africa and the western part of Arabia, but from which Britain had announced its intention to withdraw by 1968. The Yemeni campaign against Aden was two-pronged, with support for subversion and terrorism in Aden itself, and with similar support for dissident tribesmen who undertook their traditional activities of raiding caravans in the north of Aden, the Radfan. Successive operations (commencing in January 1964, with 'Nutcracker') by fighter-bombers and heliborne troops, and artillery eventually resulted in the capture of the last rebel point, the Jebel Huriyah, on 10 June 1964.

It was less easy to solve the problem of terrorism in the city of Aden, and difficult even to contain it. Helicopters were used to transport troops rapidly to deal with incidents, while Twin Pioneers performed reconnaissance and leaflet dropping missions. With little reason to remain, and in the face of worsening opposition, the British pulled out in late-1967, with some units relocating to the Gulf.

WITHDRAWAL
After the ignominious withdrawal from Aden, the departure of RAF units from the Gulf was altogether more dignified. With the Gulf

Right: Avro Vulcan B.Mk 2s of Nos 9 and 35 Squadrons replaced four Canberra bomber squadrons as NEAF's strike-attack element in 1969, serving until 1975. Two more Vulcan squadrons were declared to CENTO, but remained at UK bases.

The Six-Day War

JUNE 1967

Antagonism in the Middle East region had blazed into full-scale war in the late-1940s and in 1956. Tension had been rising since early-April 1967 with clashes over Syria's Golan Heights. It was heightened further by the UN's decision to withdraw its peacekeeping forces from the Egypt/Israel border on 17 May 1967. This encouraged Egypt to close the Gulf of Aqaba to Israeli shipping.

At the end of May a renewed Egyptian-Syrian-Jordanian defence agreement was signed and led to the formation of the United Arab Republic Air Force. This was equipped with the latest Soviet combat aircraft – MiG-19 and -21 fighters, Su-7 ground-attack aircraft, and Il-28 and Tu-16 bombers. The main problems suffered by the Arab air force were the poor serviceability of its aircraft (20 per cent were non-operational), and the chronic shortage of qualified aircrew. Only 125 of its approximately 500 pilots could fly MiG-21s or MiG-19s, and there was no reserve pool of pilots.

PRE-EMPTIVE STRIKE

Egyptian Air Marshal Sidki and his military staff feared a pre-emptive Israeli attack in early June, and ordered an advanced state of alert. President Nasser, however, was convinced that there would be no war. He over-ruled them, and the Arab forces relaxed their posture.

Shortly after dawn on 5 June, 40 Israeli Mirage IIICJs and Super Mystères flew west, followed by two more waves, 120 in all. As usual, the Israeli aircraft dipped below the search height of Egyptian radars. Since they had been doing this regularly on training exercises, no action was taken and the Egyptian dawn fighter patrols were stood down. However, this time, the Israeli fighters turned south to cross the Egyptian coast, undetected.

At 08.45 (Cairo time), when UARAF dawn patrols had landed and most senior officers were between home and office, the airfields at El Arish, Bir Gifgafa, Cairo West, Jebel Libni, Bir Thamada, Abu Sueir, Kabrit, Beni Sueif, Inchas and, a minute or so later, Fayid, were all struck. Ten flights, each of four aircraft, made one bombing and several strafing passes, followed at 10-minute intervals by the second and third waves. An exceptionally efficient turnaround time back in Israel meant that eight waves attacked for 80 minutes. A 10-minute lull was then followed by a further 80-minute blitz. Only 12 IAF aircraft were held back to defend Israeli skies during this assault. Sixty Magister trainers, converted for ground attack, were meanwhile committed to support the Israeli army and took no part in these raids.

During this three-hour assault over 300 UARAF aircraft were destroyed or damaged, mostly on the ground. The big Tu-16

Above: A Mirage IIICJ of No. 119 Squadron gets airborne from its base at Egron. The unit's distinctive battle insignia and red tail chevron were subsequently worn by F-4E Phantoms.

Left: Israel's strikes were claimed as being pre-emptive, but, although the Arabs were engaging in brinkmanship, they had no plans for military operations against Israel. Egyptian President Nasser was confident that his closure of the Gulf of Aqaba to Israeli shipping would not be sufficient to provoke Israeli military action. This was a major misjudgement, and provided Israel with an excuse to launch its offensive, following a carefully worked-out plan which must have taken years to perfect. Israel's first act was to destroy the Egyptian air force on the ground, turning on Jordan and Syria later the same day. Only when Israeli aircraft attacked Iraqi airfields did they encounter serious resistance.

Below: A formation of Mirage IIICJs of No. 101 Squadron wears the unit's traditional red and white candy-striped rudder decoration, first applied to Spitfires and S.199s.

SURPRISE ATTACKS

MEDITERRANEAN SEA

SYRIA
Damascus

IRAQ

ISRAEL
Jerusalem • Amman

JORDAN

Cairo

SAUDI ARABIA

EGYPT

RED SEA

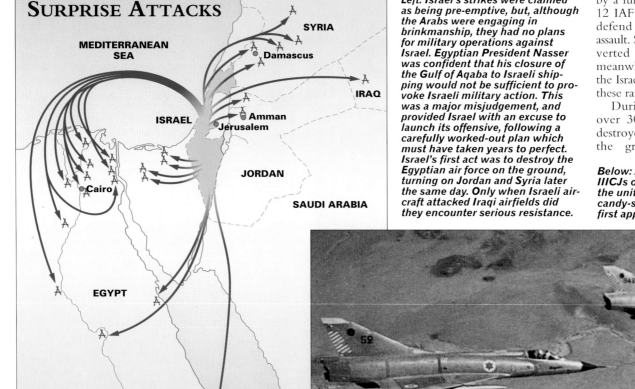

bombers were considered vital targets by the IAF, because of their ability to fire large stand-off air-to-ground missiles capable of reaching Israeli towns and cities. The entire force of two squadrons of Tu-16s was destroyed. Israeli losses for these raids were 19 aircraft.

In the air, the UARAF lost four unarmed trainers near Imbaba – the first casualties of the war – and one MiG-21 as it took off from Abu Sueir. Another MiG-21 was destroyed as it attempted to land on the cratered runway after driving off four IAF Super Mystères. Three surviving MiG-21s lifted off from Inchas at 08.56 in the minutes between Israeli assaults. Ground control had collapsed, but over Cairo West they shot down an Ouragan which crashed, perhaps intentionally, into a parked Tu-16. At Abu Sueir another MiG-21 managed to take off at 10.01 and

Below: A bombed-up Dassault Mystère IVA awaits its pilot before the first wave of attacks on Egyptian airfields. Three Mystère IVA squadrons, and one Super Mystère unit, flew the vital attack missions.

Right: Israel received 72 Mirage IIICJs and five two-seat IIIBJs, which formed the backbone of the IDF/AFs fighter force in 1967, equipping five or six squadrons. They had simplified avionics.

brought down a Mystère just beyond the airfield perimeter. The last two serviceable MiG-21s were then destroyed as they tried to get into the air minutes later, both hit by the same Mirage III.

The MiG-19s and -21s at Herghada flew north to help, but were jumped by 16 Mirages as they tried to land at Abu Sueir at 10.30. Four went down at once but in the dogfight that followed neither side scored additional victories. Nevertheless, all the MiGs were destroyed, either in wheels-up landings alongside shattered runways or when they ran out of fuel. The only airfield whose runways were not damaged was El Arish. Here the IAF relied on cannon-fire and a guided bomb similar to the American Bullpup to pick off parked aircraft. Only one Egyptian aircraft now remained in the air: the Ilyushin Il-14 transport carrying Air Marshal

Sidki and most of the Egyptian high command had been flying over the battle zone since before the attack began. By keeping the enemy's top brass in this 'limbo', alive but out of action, the Israelis virtually paralysed Egypt's capacity to respond.

THE EASTERN FRONT

Within hours, Israel's other Arab neighbours had entered the fray in response to the attack on Egypt. Jordanian long-range artillery cratered at least one runway at Ramat David during the morning. The Israelis had, however, already moved against Jerusalem by the time the Royal Jordanian Air Force (RJAF) made its first move, an airstrike on Natanya and Kfar Sirkin by 16 Hunters.

At 14.30 (Tel Aviv time) the IAF turned its attention from the UARAF to the RJAF, attacking Mafraq and Amman air-bases and a strategic radar site at Ajlun. All but

one of Jordan's 18 Hunter fighters were destroyed on the ground for the loss of one Israeli aircraft. The remaining Hunter was also damaged and two aircrew were killed, so King Hussein told his surviving Hunter pilots to place themselves under IrAF command at the Iraqi air base of H-3. Other Jordanian targets attacked by the IAF on this first day of the war included Iraqi and Palestinian units moving westwards from Mafraq, defensive positions around Jerusalem, the Jordanian HQ at Jericho, a relief column east of the Mount of Olives and the royal palace in Amman.

The SAF was also on the IAF's target list for 5 June. At 11.45 (Tel Aviv time) 12 SAF MiG-21s bombed the Haifa oil refinery and strafed Mahanayim airfield. Just over an hour later came the IAF's massive response, with strikes on the SAF bases at Damascus followed by others on Marj Rial, Dumayr

Israel strikes first

The Israeli first wave consisted of only 40 aircraft: 10 sections of four Mirages or Super Mystères which flew out over the Mediterranean, as if undertaking normal training, before swinging south to attack

their targets. Once the element of surprise was lost the IDF/AF mounted an all-out offensive, rapidly turning around its attack aircraft to shuttle them back and forth to their targets.

Dassault Super Mystère
The Super Mystère was probably Israel's most effective fighter-bomber. Twenty-four were in service, augmenting a larger number of ageing Mystère IVAs and Ouregans. They equipped a single squadron, and maintained a secondary air defence commitment. Super Mystères were heavily committed to the first wave of Israeli warplanes, which mounted the devastating surprise attacks on Egyptian air bases. Four of the aircraft were lost in action during the war.

Dassault Mirage IIICJ
A Mirage IIICJ of No. 117 Squadron. The Mirage IIICJ was used for air-defence and ground-attack duties, and proved devastatingly successful in both roles. Armed largely with cannon and ordinary iron bombs, the aircraft was popular with its pilots. The Mirages did not get things entirely their own way, however, at least three being among the nine aircraft downed by Hawker Hunters during the attack on Iraq's H-3 aerodrome.

Arab MiGs

The Arab air forces mainly used aircraft of Soviet origin, although the Jordanian and Lebanese air forces used only Western equipment, and Iraq's strength included three squadrons of British Hawker Hunters. Few

Arab fighters survived the Israeli airfield attacks, and the handful which ventured into the air never seriously challenged Israeli air superiority.

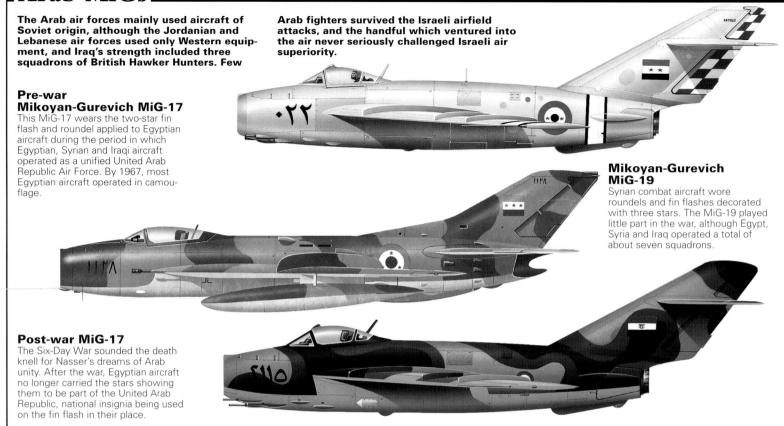

Pre-war Mikoyan-Gurevich MiG-17
This MiG-17 wears the two-star fin flash and roundel applied to Egyptian aircraft during the period in which Egyptian, Syrian and Iraqi aircraft operated as a unified United Arab Republic Air Force. By 1967, most Egyptian aircraft operated in camouflage.

Mikoyan-Gurevich MiG-19
Syrian combat aircraft wore roundels and fin flashes decorated with three stars. The MiG-19 played little part in the war, although Egypt, Syria and Iraq operated a total of about seven squadrons.

Post-war MiG-17
The Six-Day War sounded the death knell for Nasser's dreams of Arab unity. After the war, Egyptian aircraft no longer carried the stars showing them to be part of the United Arab Republic, national insignia being used on the fin flash in their place.

Left: Egypt's Il-28 light bombers played little part in the conflict. Twenty-seven were destroyed in their revetments, and the rest remained on the ground for most of the brief conflict.

and Seikal. The more distant airfield at T-4 was not struck until mid-afternoon, shortly after three Israeli aircraft had also attacked the Iraqi base at H-3. Although the SAF was not as badly damaged as the UARAF or RJAF, it did lose two-thirds of its front-line strength.

During the afternoon the IAF returned to Egypt, ranging farther afield to hit Mansura, Cairo International, Helwan, Al Minya, Bilbeis, Herghada, Luxor and Ras Banas airfields in the deep south and 23 radar sites.

DAYS TWO AND THREE

The second day, 6 June, saw the IAF put most of its effort into supporting the Israeli army in Sinai and on the West Bank. A strike against artillery positions west of Rafah had already enabled the Israelis to successfully break through the main Egyptian defences. That night, a helicopter-borne commando attack using S-58s was made behind Jordanian lines east of Jerusalem. Another helicopter-borne attack preceded the fall of Egypt's vital

Abu Agheila position near the Sinai border. Close-support attacks were made at Gaza and Bir Lahfan on 6 June, but by early morning the entire Egyptian army was already withdrawing from Sinai.

Seeing the Egyptians in full retreat, the Israelis sent a rapid force through the crumbling enemy lines to seize the Mitla and Giddi Passes. This manoeuvre succeeded and trapped a large part of the Egyptian army east of the mountains. Here it was ruthlessly bombed by the IAF, which destroyed thousands of vehi-cles in front of the Mitla Pass alone.

The UARAF then threw what strength it had left into a desperate attempt to break the Israeli hold on the passes. During the night of 5/6 June the UARAF managed to put together a scratch force of 50 aircraft by repairing damaged aircraft and hurriedly assembling crated equipment. The biggest blow had been to the pilot pool, over 70 of whom had been killed, with a further 200 wounded. The first sign that the UARAF still existed came at 05.36 on 6 June, when two MiG-21s were sent against an Israeli column near Bir Lahfan. Both were shot down. The same fate befell a pair of Su-7s which ran the IAF gauntlet as far as El Arish at 06.00. Egyptian Su-7s and MiG-21s twice tried to shoot down IAF

helicopters. These attacks were pin-pricks compared with the pounding that the Egyptian army was receiving from the IAF.

During the night of 5/6 June the Iraqis and Jordanians had joined forces to reinforce the defences of H-3. At dawn on 6 June, an IrAF Tu-16 bombed the Natanya industrial complex in Israel but was brought down by ground fire. Not long afterwards the IAF struck again at H-3. This time it met fierce resistance from defending fighters flown by both Iraqis and Jordanians. Nine Israeli aircraft were claimed, while the IAF admitted the loss of two. The Israelis also brought down one of a pair of Lebanese reconnaissance Hunters over Galilee. Throughout 6 and 7 June the IAF blasted Jordanian positions across

Below: Jordan's Hunters were destroyed on the ground, but their pilots were then absorbed by the Iraqi Hunter wing, where several gained their revenge: one almost became an ace in a single mission.

Right: Although Egypt operated Tu-16 'Badgers', Soviet Tu-16s were also active in the Mediterranean during the 1960s and 1970s. After the Six-Day War uncamouflaged examples were based in Egypt and Syria, wearing Arab markings but retaining Soviet crews.

the West Bank. Israel also reported eight air battles on the eastern front between 6 and 9 June, mostly over H-3, where, by the end of the war, one Royal Jordanian air force Hunter pilot, Captain Ihsan Shurdom, had claimed one Mirage, two Mystères and a Sud-Ouest Vautour.

The UARAF kept up small-scale but increasingly effective strikes for the rest of the war in Sinai, although it could not alter the outcome. At dawn on 7 June four MiG-19s hit an Israeli column on the Mediterranean coastal road, though three aircraft soon went down to an IAF standing patrol. Additional United Arab Republic Air Force and Egyptian naval attacks in this sector certainly slowed the Israeli advance. The Israeli air force shot down a solitary

Right: This ex-Iraqi MiG-21F defected to Israel in August 1966, allowing the IDF/AF to comprehensively evaluate what would be its most potent foe in the Six-Day War.

Il-28 and a MiG at El Arish. Flights of MiG-17s sent against the Mitla Pass and southern Sinai suffered severe losses, but were sometimes able to hit back. A Super Mystère fell to MiG-17s east of Ismailia.

THE FINAL DAYS

By 8 June Algerian volunteers were reportedly flying alongside the Egyptians, who were also now joined by men from UARAF units in Yemen. Despite this upsurge of Egyptian air activity, IAF combat successes declined, only nine UARAF aircraft being claimed on 8 June. Late in that evening the

Israelis severely damaged the USS *Liberty,* an American intelligence-gathering ship, in a still unexplained air and sea attack. The war in Sinai was, however, virtually over and Egypt accepted a UN ceasefire at 04.35 on 9 June.

Now the IAF geared itself up for another campaign, this time against Syria. Following frequent IAF attacks on the Golan defences, and finding itself alone since Egypt and Jordan had been defeated, Syria accepted a UN ceasefire on the evening of 8 June. Israel, however, did not. At 11.30 on 9 June an all-

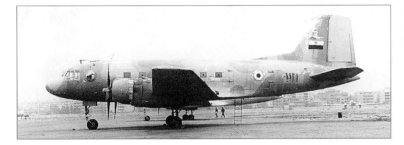

Left: Egyptian Ilyushin Il-14 light transports were based at Almaza. About half a dozen of the 20 or so in service were destroyed on the ground, but survivors continued in use until after the Yom Kippur War.

Below: From the very first shot, the Arab air forces were at a disadvantage: an Israeli pilot's eye view of an Egyptian airbase just outside Cairo shows the carnage inflicted by the initial surprise attacks.

Israel consolidates

With Arab air power neutralised, Israel was able to operate over the battlefield with virtual impunity. Israel threw everything it had into the operation against its Arab neighbours, and this commitment, allied with a superb tactical plan and an element of good fortune, brought forth great success. Israel's initial airfield attacks were followed by an armoured push into the Sinai, which was itself supported by air power.

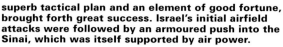

Sud Vautour
About 25 Vautours were committed to Israel's air strikes, initially operating in the medium bomber role. One was shot down by an Egyptian MiG on the first day. The aircraft were subsequently used in close-support operations, attacking Egyptian troops trapped by Israel's rapid advance. Five Vautour losses were admitted at the war's end.

Fouga Magister
Two squadrons of Fouga Magister trainers were soon thrown into the fighting, operating mainly in the close air-support and ground-attack roles. In the almost total absence of enemy air opposition, the Magisters undertook their missions virtually unmolested.

Sikorsky S-58
For the first time, the IDF/AF was able to make extensive use of helicopters to infiltrate commandos and airborne troops ahead of advancing Israeli armoured forces. Sikorsky S-58s and S-55s augmented smaller French-built Alouettes. Helicopters were also used for Casevac and SAR operations, and repeatedly proved their worth.

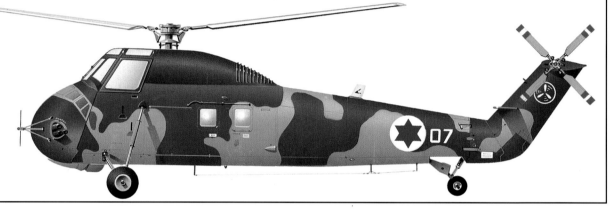

out attack was launched against the Golan Heights. Fighting was at first bitter but, after protesting vehemently to the UN, the Syrian government withdrew its forces to defend its capital. Air combat was minimal, although SAF and UARAF units brought down a Mystère and possibly a Vautour near Damascus. Other Israeli aircraft were hit by anti-aircraft fire. The IAF, although claiming 12 SAF aircraft in air combat during the

Above: Boeing Stratocruisers provided the IDF/AF with its only heavy transport capability. Smaller DC-3s and Noratlases formed the tactical transport force, and were used more intensively.

Six-Day War, was more concerned to support its army and to seize the Golan Heights and the town of Qunaytra before the final UN ceasefire at 06.30 on 10 June.

The so-called Six-Day War was over, and Israel had won a resounding victory. The Israeli Air Force had destroyed about 286 UARAF aircraft (approximately 60 in air combat), 22 Royal Jordanian Air Force aircraft, 54 Syrian Air Force aircraft, 15 to 20 IrAF aircraft and one Lebanese machine. This had been achieved for the loss of at least 45 aircraft and probably more, about 12 of them in air combat, plus 20 pilots killed and 13

Left: The Sikorsky S-58 was the largest and most capable helicopter available to the IDF/AF in 1967. It played a vital role in the operations which resulted in the capture of the West Bank from Jordan.

Above: An Israeli Bell UH-1 lifts off after dropping a stick of soldiers. Troop transport was one of many roles undertaken by Israeli helicopters, which played a decisive part in the brief but bloody war.

captured.

A lasting peace had failed to be imposed in the region, however. There was to be no short-term reconciliation between Arab and Jew; both sides simply set about rebuilding their forces before embarking on the next — inevitable — confrontation.

Armament
Although Israel's Mirage IIICJs were supplied with MATRA 530 AAMs (and later carried AIM-9 Sidewinders), all IDF/AF air-to-air victories in the Six-Day War were scored using cannon alone.

Dassault Mirage IIICJ

This Mirage IIICJ wears the camouflage colours introduced during the 1970s. The Mirage IIICJ played a major role in the War of Attrition, and continued to form the backbone of Israel's air defence until the introduction of the F-4 Phantom. This aircraft wears an impressive tally of victory claims from the Six-Day War.

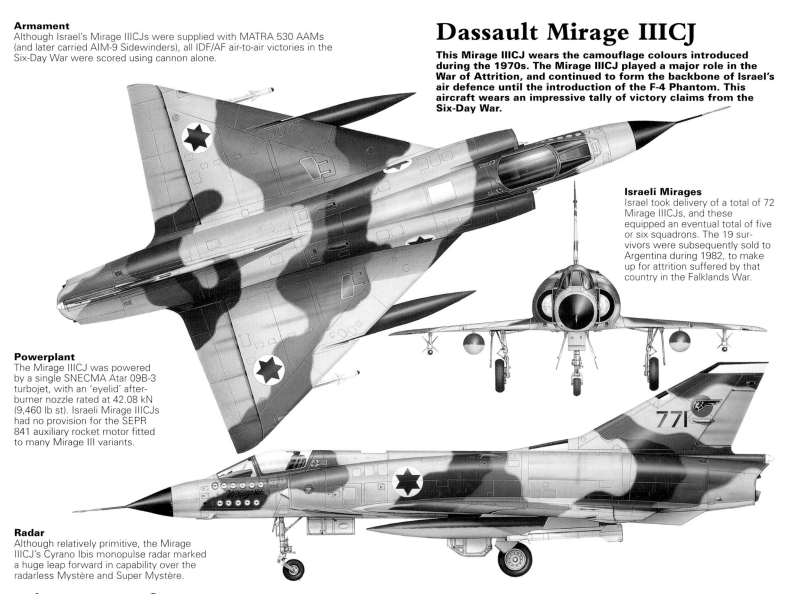

Israeli Mirages
Israel took delivery of a total of 72 Mirage IIICJs, and these equipped an eventual total of five or six squadrons. The 19 survivors were subsequently sold to Argentina during 1982, to make up for attrition suffered by that country in the Falklands War.

Powerplant
The Mirage IIICJ was powered by a single SNECMA Atar 09B-3 turbojet, with an 'eyelid' afterburner nozzle rated at 42.08 kN (9,460 lb st). Israeli Mirage IIICJs had no provision for the SEPR 841 auxiliary rocket motor fitted to many Mirage III variants.

Radar
Although relatively primitive, the Mirage IIICJ's Cyrano Ibis monopulse radar marked a huge leap forward in capability over the radarless Mystère and Super Mystère.

The War of Attrition 1969–1970

The ceasefire at the end of the Six-Day War brought about only a brief respite in the fighting between Israel and its neighbours. Just as the war of 1967 had been preceded by periodic artillery attacks, airspace intrusions (often dealt with by simply shooting down the intruder) and commando raids, so such actions continued to take place after the war. On 1 July 1967, for instance, Egyptian troops ambushed an Israeli patrol on the Eastern side of the Suez Canal, and 10 days later there were artillery duels across the canal. This prompted aerial intervention, with Israel claiming four Egyptian MiG-17s, three MiG-21s

in July and four Syrian MiG-19s in October.

The French embargo on the delivery of 50 Mirage 5J fighters ordered before the war forced Israel to look elsewhere for aircraft to make good its losses and strengthen its order of battle. Fifty F-4Es and six RF-4Es were ordered from the USA, together with 25 ex-US Navy A-4Es to augment 48 A-4Hs (and two TA-4Hs) ordered before the war. The IDF/AF also took delivery of 20 Bell UH-1s in 1968.

September 1968 saw a resumption of cross-Canal shelling and, in October, Israel mounted a number of commando raids far behind Egyptian lines. Nasser announced a war of attrition in March 1969, as Israel finished its fortified Bar Lev line on the East bank of the Suez Canal. Israel responded to Egyptian artillery barrages with shelling and massive airstrikes, shooting down 21 enemy aircraft for the loss of three of its own by the end of May. By November, the IDF/AF could claim 34 enemy aircraft in air combat (of 51 EAF aircraft downed).

Massive raids on 'military' targets around Cairo in January 1970 prompted the deployment of five squadrons of Soviet MiG-21s and their 'volunteer' pilots, and these proved better able to counter the IDF/AF raiders (who dropped 8000 tonnes of bombs by the end of April). From April, Egyptian fighter bombers began mounting hit-and-run raids across the Canal. Israel took a hammering in the air as well, losing five F-4Es to Soviet MiG-21s in July alone. A ceasefire was finally declared on 8 August 1970.

Right: A dramatic gun camera sequence records the destruction of an Arab MiG-21 by gunfire. Israel's fighter pilots enjoy a reputation second to none, the result of superb training and combat experience.

The Yom Kippur War

OCTOBER 1973

Left: Egyptian MiG-21s played a vital role in the air war, and downed a number of Israeli aircraft. Israeli losses in air combat were almost certainly higher than admitted, and most fell to the MiG-21.

Above: The IDF/AF was forced into a costly war against the Egyptian SAM system. Here an F-4E launches an AGM-45 Shrike anti-radar missile.

I n 1967, the resounding victory by Israel during the Six-Day War over its historically hostile Arab neighbours had bred a dangerous complacency. Israel was a nation of 2.5 million surrounded by 100 million potential enemies. Egyptian and Syrian leaders were vowing to restore Arab pride by planning a campaign which would catch Israel completely off guard. The brutal War of Attrition had seen the gradual wearing down of Israel's air force. As the countdown to further conflict began, Israel could muster 375 combat aircraft, against 730 for Egypt and Syria. Jordan, though too weak to participate in another war, could tie down Israeli troops merely by the act of ordering mobilisation, and friendly Arab states further afield would be willing to send token forces. By October 1973, all was ready for a war which would have a profound effect on the theory and practice of air combat.

Earlier victories had confirmed Israeli opinions that the Arabs were disorganised and incapable of effective military action, despite their large, Soviet-supplied armouries. Egypt's leader, Anwar Sadat, adopted a plan in which the Arabs could win the war without winning the battlefield. A surprise two-front

attack in the north (by Syria) and south (by Egypt) would be the opening move. As the Syrians retook the Golan Heights and advanced into Israeli territory, Egypt would initiate a set-piece battle across the Suez Canal.

SUCCESSFUL ASSAULT

Brought forward under the cover of training exercises, the Arab forces launched their onslaught at 14:00 on 6 October 1973. In Israel, vigilance was at its lowest for the Yom Kippur (Day of Atonement) religious holiday, as wave upon

Right: Sukhoi Su-7s supported Egyptian and Syrian ground forces, and attacked Israeli airfields and other interdiction targets. They proved highly effective, if lacking in range and endurance.

wave of Egyptian aircraft streaked over the Suez Canal to attack Israeli airfields, SAM batteries, radar sites and numerous other military positions in Sinai. In addition to 222 fighter-bombers, Egypt used 25 AS-5 'Kelt' stand-off missiles launched from Tu-16 bombers, and a number of FROG tactical SSMs.

In the north, Syrian aircraft supported a thrust forward over the Golan plateau. Low-level attack missions were flown by MiG-17s and Su-7s with top cover provided by MiG-21s. Assault troops travelled by Mi-8 'Hip' helicopter to

seize key objectives, either in Sinai or on the Golan Heights.

The first Israeli aircraft to react were in the air within 30 minutes, although it was to be two hours before the IDF/AF appeared in strength. In the attack role was the A-4 Skyhawk, supported by its more capable stable-mate, the F-4 Phantom. The Mirage IIICJ, aided by the first few IAI Nesher copies built in Israel, was employed against ground targets, though both it and the F-4 were also useful in air defence. Even a dozen or so ageing Super Mystère B2s were brought in

Right: An Egyptian MiG-17 flies past an exploding tank at ultra-low level over the battlefield. The MiG-17's agility and robustness gave it an edge over more modern fighter bombers.

Right: The Egyptian push over the Suez canal was spearheaded by the dropping of heliborne commandos. The robust Mil Mi-8s performed admirably, but suffered heavy losses to Israeli ground fire.

for attack. Supporting helicopters included Super Frelons and smaller UH-1s.

Though the Sinai desert acted as a buffer zone, there was no such luxury for Israel in the north. Thus, the war against Egypt was put on 'hold' and first priority given to defeating the Syrian armies only a few miles from Israeli towns and villages. The IDF just managed to hold out until reserves could be assembled and brought to bear. After three days of fighting, including a fierce tank battle, the Syrians were too weak to exploit their dearly-won gains and were forced to withdraw. At the same time (9 October) the IDF/AF replied to a FROG missile attack by bombing its opponent's HQ in Damascus and an oil refinery at Homs.

IRAQ JOINS THE FRAY

Iraq had added a squadron of Hunters to Syrian air forces on 7 October, and a unit of MiG-21s soon after this. Jordan's contribution to the air war was restricted to firing SAMs at IDF/AF aircraft coming within range of its territory. With Syrian units now falling back, air defence assumed crucial importance as the IDF/AF ranged almost

as far as the Turkish border in its campaign of strategic bombing. By 12 October, the air defence network was in such disarray, with many MiG-21s destroyed or damaged, that the outclassed MiG-17 had to be diverted to interception.

Meanwhile, on the Egyptian front the situation was bleak for Israel. Within two days of the first attack, the east bank of the Suez Canal was firmly in Egyptian hands, despite no less than 23 Israeli counterattacks. IDF/AF aircraft managed to disrupt further Mi-8 commando-insertion operations and shoot down 10 helicopters on 7 October, yet the SAM screen was proving devastatingly effective, as were the anti-tank missiles defending the Egyptian-occupied strip on the ground.

IDF/AF loss returns tell almost the whole story. During the first four days, Israel lost 81 aircraft. This was two-thirds of the total it was to suffer during 19 days of conflict. In 1967, the IDF/AF had contemptuously evaded the SA-2 'Guideline' SAM, and now it suffered for its over-confidence. Stretching the whole length of the Canal on the Egyptian side were additional new

Egyptian first strikes

Egypt and Israel agreed to invade Israel simultaneously on two fronts, aiming to recover territory lost in 1967, when Israel had been the aggressor. They chose to strike on 6 October, the Jewish Day of Atonement, or Yom Kippur. Egypt's initial strikes were well planned and skillfully executed. Egyptian aircraft struck against airfields in the Sinai, as well as HAWK SAM sites and radar installations.

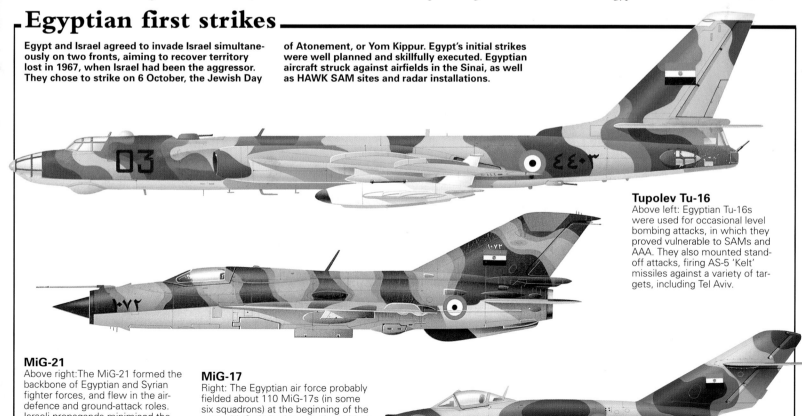

Tupolev Tu-16
Above left: Egyptian Tu-16s were used for occasional level bombing attacks, in which they proved vulnerable to SAMs and AAA. They also mounted stand-off attacks, firing AS-5 'Kelt' missiles against a variety of targets, including Tel Aviv.

MiG-21
Above right: The MiG-21 formed the backbone of Egyptian and Syrian fighter forces, and flew in the air-defence and ground-attack roles. Israeli propaganda minimised the danger presented by the MiG-21, though it now seems that the type proved an unpleasant surprise.

MiG-17
Right: The Egyptian air force probably fielded about 110 MiG-17s (in some six squadrons) at the beginning of the war, with Syria having a further 100 aircraft. These were thrown into the thick of the fighting, and proved particularly effective at strafing Israeli convoys.

Above: An Israeli A-4 Skyhawk flashes over the top of an armoured column. With an increasing use of sophisticated SAMs and AAA by both sides, the casualty rate among the fighter bombers was high.

Below: Israel's fighter pilots were the world's best, amassing the highest victory tallies of the jet age, but their achievements in the Yom Kippur War were undermined by unrealistic propaganda.

Above: Heavy losses prompted massive airlifts of new supplies by the USA (to Israel) and the USSR (to its Arab clients). Here USAF C-141 Starlifters and C-5 Galaxies unload and turnaround at an Israeli base.

SAMs: the SA-3 'Goa', SA-6 'Gainful', SA-9 'Gaskin' and shoulder-launched SA-7 'Grail' or Strela. The SA-6 was an unknown quantity in the West, and no countermeasures were known for its combined radar and electro-optical guidance system, or for the associated 'Straight Flush' target-acquisition radar.

The SAMs were set up in the classic Soviet concept of layered air defences, so that tactics to evade one known type of missile brought the IDF/AF fighters into the engagement zones of others. The SA-6, however, also proved a mixed blessing, allegedly shooting down 40 Egyptian and four Iraqi aircraft. Before the war was over, at least six SA-6 fire units had been captured and flown to the USA, where their secrets were probed and appropriate countermeasures devised.

ARAB BRETHREN

A squadron of Algerian Su-7s joined Egyptian forces on 8 October, when both sides continued the bombing of their opponent's airfields. In stark contrast with 1967, when the Arab air forces had been annihilated on the ground in the first hours of combat, not one Egyptian machine was lost in this way, though the Israelis' attempts cost them dear. Syria was less fortunate, losing a dozen in raids on three airfields during 8 October, for example. Libya committed a squadron of Mirage III/5s to the battles from 14 October, these reportedly flying 400 sorties in the hands of mercenary pilots, including Pakistanis.

It was now time for both sides to be resupplied with fresh arms from their respective superpower backers. Both the USA and USSR had begun airlifting weapons on 9 October, some American aid being flown straight into Sinai airfields. Syria received about 15000 tonnes in 934 transport sorties. USAF C-141 StarLifters and C-5 Galaxies made 566 sorties with 22395 tonnes of equipment (including dismantled CH-53D helicopters) up to 15 November. El Al Boeing 707s and 747s brought a further 5500 tonnes, and there was also a sizeable seaborne effort.

Aircraft losses were restored, with the supply of 100 Soviet fighters each to Egypt and Syria, in whose air forces they entered service between 14 and 20 October. Israel had made the exaggerated claim that only four days of war supplies were left by 13 October, and this resulted in the acceleration of the previously low-key US reinforcement effort. Phantoms and Skyhawks were commandeered

Arabian follow-up

While the Egyptians hammered Israeli targets from the south and west, her allies were busy mounting attacks in the north and west. Israel's aggression in 1967 was remembered with anger and bitterness, and allowed the formation of a powerful coalition, whose main partners were Egypt, Syria, Iraq and Jordan, but which also drew support from further afield, including Algeria and even Pakistan.

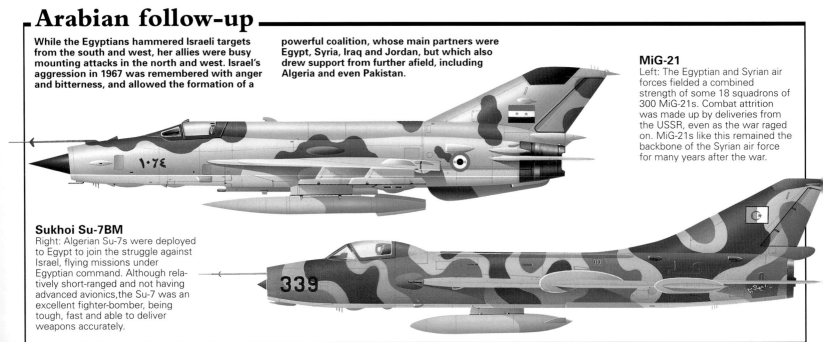

MiG-21
Left: The Egyptian and Syrian air forces fielded a combined strength of some 18 squadrons of 300 MiG-21s. Combat attrition was made up by deliveries from the USSR, even as the war raged on. MiG-21s like this remained the backbone of the Syrian air force for many years after the war.

Sukhoi Su-7BM
Right: Algerian Su-7s were deployed to Egypt to join the struggle against Israel, flying missions under Egyptian command. Although relatively short-ranged and not having advanced avionics, the Su-7 was an excellent fighter-bomber, being tough, fast and able to deliver weapons accurately.

F-4E Phantom

This F-4E wears the markings of No. 119 Squadron, based at Tel Nov during the Yom Kippur War. The squadrons flying F-4Es in 1973 were Nos 69, 107, 119 and 201. One more F-4E squadron formed after the war.

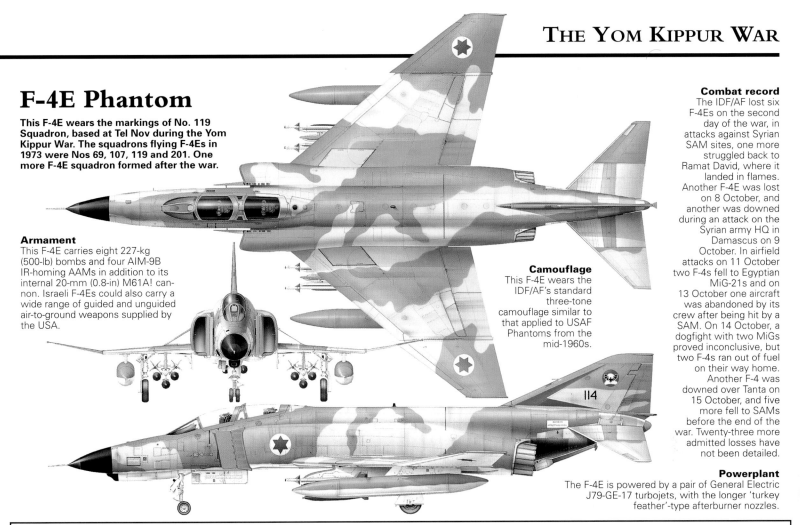

Armament
This F-4E carries eight 227-kg (500-lb) bombs and four AIM-9B IR-homing AAMs in addition to its internal 20-mm (0.8-in) M61A1 cannon. Israeli F-4Es could also carry a wide range of guided and unguided air-to-ground weapons supplied by the USA.

Combat record
The IDF/AF lost six F-4Es on the second day of the war, in attacks against Syrian SAM sites, one more struggled back to Ramat David, where it landed in flames. Another F-4E was lost on 8 October, and another was downed during an attack on the Syrian army HQ in Damascus on 9 October. In airfield attacks on 11 October two F-4s fell to Egyptian MiG-21s and on 13 October one aircraft was abandoned by its crew after being hit by a SAM. On 14 October, a dogfight with two MiGs proved inconclusive, but two F-4s ran out of fuel on their way home. Another F-4 was downed over Tanta on 15 October, and five more fell to SAMs before the end of the war. Twenty-three more admitted losses have not been detailed.

Camouflage
This F-4E wears the IDF/AF's standard three-tone camouflage similar to that applied to USAF Phantoms from the mid-1960s.

Powerplant
The F-4E is powered by a pair of General Electric J79-GE-17 turbojets, with the longer 'turkey feather'-type afterburner nozzles.

Phantom at war

In the opening Egyptian attack on Ophir AB on 6 October 1973 by 28 MiG-17s and MiG-21s, a pair of IDF/AF Phantoms on QRA (Quick Reaction Alert) were able to scramble and claimed seven enemy aircraft. Elsewhere, F-4s intercepted Mi-8 'Hip' helicopters attempting to land commandos at key points in the Sinai. Five were claimed of some 40 encountered.

The next day opened with hastily planned operations against Syrian SAM sites, but these cost six Phantoms, with two aircrew killed and nine captured. At least one more F-4E was able to land back at Ramat David, in flames! Attacks against Egyptian airfields were less costly. On 8 October, the Phantoms attacked Syrian airfields and Egyptian pontoon bridges across the Sinai and mounted CAPs in various areas. Four MiG-17s were downed when they tried to attack Om Khasiba. On the debit side a single F-4E on an undisclosed mission was lost, probably shot down by a Syrian MiG-21.

On 9 October, 16 Phantoms were launched in an attack against the Syrian army HQ in Damascus. Only eight were able to attack, due to the weather, but they scored some hits. One aircraft was lost (the pilot was killed and the navigator

taken prisoner) and another crawled home with several 57-mm cannon hits. Another F-4 was lost, together with its crew, during attacks on power stations and Egyptian airfields. The following day the Phantoms attacked various Egyptian and Syrian air bases suffering no losses, but in similar operations on 11 October two F-4Es fell to Egyptian MiG-21s over Banbah airfield. No losses occurred on 12 October, but the next day an F-4 was badly damaged by AAA during an attack on El Mazza airfield near Damascus. The campaign against Syrian airfields ended on 14 October, while attacks on Egypt continued. During an attack on Mansurah, two MiG-21s were claimed (but only as probables), but the MiG's resistance was sufficient that two F-4Es ran out of fuel on their way home, forcing them to land at primitive strips at Baluza and Refidim.

SAM KILLER
On 15 October, 12 Phantoms attacked Tanta airfield and downed a MiG-21, but one F-4 and its navigator was lost (the pilot becoming a PoW) and another suffered severe damage but managed to limp home without an aileron. SAM positions at Port Said were attacked on 16 October, and more SAM sites were

attacked during the following two days. Unfortunately, three Phantoms were shot down and a fourth was badly damaged. Four Syrian MiG-17s were intercepted and claimed destroyed near Kuneitra on 18 October – at least one using the new indigenous Rafael Shafrir AAM. On 20 October, two more Phantoms were shot down by Egyptian SAMs.

During 11,233 IDF/AF combat sorties (by all types), 37 Phantoms were lost (including those described above) and six more were so badly damaged that they had to be written off. This attrition rate was second only to that suffered by the A-4 Skyhawk, and was a result of the difficult anti-airfield and anti-SAM missions flown by the aircraft. The losses were largely made good

by the transfer of 36 USAF F-4E Phantoms during Operation 'Nickel Grass' (mainly from the 4th and 401st TFWs). These aircraft flew 200 combat missions, sometimes in USAF camouflage and with only national insignia and USAFE tailcodes overpainted. During the fighting, the four Phantom units, usually described as Nos 69, 107, 119 and 201 Squadrons, had claimed a large number (115) of enemy aircraft destroyed and had carried out devastating attacks on key enemy command centres, airfields and SAM sites.

Below: Some 43 Israeli Phantoms were destroyed during the Yom Kippur War, but these losses were largely made good with the delivery of 36 USAFE F-4Es. Israeli Phantom pilots claimed 115 aerial victories.

Israel fights back

The 1973 war was very different from that of six years previously, and the Israeli air force did not find it nearly as easy as in 1967. Fighter and fighter-bomber pilots needed all of their legendary skills to come out victorious, but other aviators also came to the fore, notably the helicopter crews whose work was becoming of increasing importance.

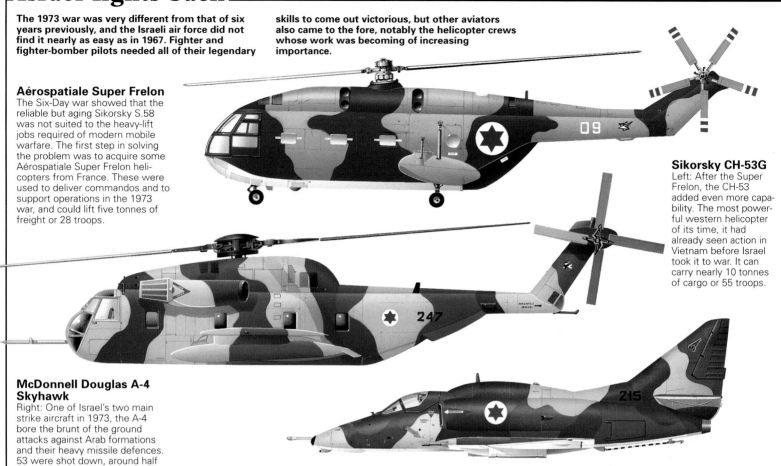

Aérospatiale Super Frelon
The Six-Day war showed that the reliable but aging Sikorsky S.58 was not suited to the heavy-lift jobs required of modern mobile warfare. The first step in solving the problem was to acquire some Aérospatiale Super Frelon helicopters from France. These were used to deliver commandos and to support operations in the 1973 war, and could lift five tonnes of freight or 28 troops.

Sikorsky CH-53G
Left: After the Super Frelon, the CH-53 added even more capability. The most powerful western helicopter of its time, it had already seen action in Vietnam before Israel took it to war. It can carry nearly 10 tonnes of cargo or 55 troops.

McDonnell Douglas A-4 Skyhawk
Right: One of Israel's two main strike aircraft in 1973, the A-4 bore the brunt of the ground attacks against Arab formations and their heavy missile defences. 53 were shot down, around half of all Israeli combat losses.

from US Air Force and Navy squadrons and flown out to the Middle East at short notice. The first 28 were available for combat by 17 October, followed by a further 50 on 22 October.

It was not the extra fighters which won the war for Israel, however, but the transports. Inside the USAF transports came new technology: airborne ECM kits to confuse the SA-2s and SA-3s, Walleye and HOBOS 'smart'

bombs, AGM-45 Shrike air-launched anti-radar missiles, AGM-65 Maverick TV-guided missiles, Rockeye cluster bombs and TOW anti-tank missiles for the army. There were also fresh supplies of HAWK SAMs as well as AIM-9 and AIM-7 AAMs.

TURNING THE TIDE
Reinvigorated by these new weapons, Israel was well poised to exploit Egypt's tactical error of

14 October. Egyptian forces abandoned their original plan and advanced outside their extended SAM umbrella. The battle now became the fluid fight at which Israel excels, and the result was predictable. On the night of 15/16 October, as Israeli naval units, supported by helicopters, were attacking the Egyptian coast far to the west, a rift in the Egyptian

front line was exploited for the insertion of Israeli troops on the opposite bank.

Air operations intensified to the extent that the northern front was sufficiently denuded of cover to allow the Syrians a rare chance to use Mi-17s and Su-7s against Israeli bases and an oil refinery. Egypt threw its Aero L-29 jet trainers into the fray, using them

Below: While Israel's pilots were feted as heroes, the achievements of the groundcrews were no less spectacular and proved just as decisive. Turnaround times were slashed, allowing the IDF/AF to maintain a high sortie rate.

Right: Yom Kippur marked the dawn of a new era of air warfare, and Egypt's sophisticated air-defence network almost carried the day. The ageing but potent SA-2 'Guideline' missile provided high-level cover to Egyptian troops.

Above: A formation of A-4 Skyhawks release a tumbling mass of napalm tanks during a low-level attack. The Israeli Skyhawks performed the bulk of the ground-attack missions, and large numbers were lost, including an estimated 30 in the first week alone.

Right: An Israeli F-4E falls in flames. The achievement of Israel's pilots in defeating a well-trained, well-equipped and capable foe has sometimes been hidden behind inflated claims and an unwillingness to acknowledge the extent of air combat losses.

(as expected, with little success) in the ground-attack role. Even more remarkably, Mil-8 helicopters turned bomber on 19 October in a futile attempt to disrupt Israeli Canal crossings with napalm pushed out of the hold at low level. As Israel 'rolled up' the strips of SAM sites, capturing 12 of the 40 or so installed along the Canal, the precious defensive umbrella disintegrated, leaving Egyptian air force aircraft at the mercy of the IDF/AF, not to mention the army's HAWK SAMs.

CEASEFIRE

As the Israeli bridgehead on the western bank of the Suez Canal was consolidated, it became clear that it was going to be Egypt which lost territory, not Israel. Now was the time for the Arabs to bring in their ultimate weapon: on 20 October, Saudi Arabia suspended oil shipments to the West. Egypt simultaneously requested a ceasefire. Under superpower pressure, this was agreed as coming into effect at 18.52 on 22 October. Israel had other ideas, though, and continued its southern drive towards Suez to encircle the Egyptian 3rd Army until the USA forced it to halt on 24 October. There was jockeying for final positions in the north, too, as Syrian and Israeli helicopters reinforced mountain-top posts under the cover of their own fighter aircraft. Helicopters and parachute troops assisted in taking the observation post atop Mt

Hermon in one of Israel's final acts of the conflict.

To this day, each side disputes the other's aircraft loss admissions. What is beyond doubt is that they were staggering. Egypt and Syria suffered the destruction of some 220 machines each, to which must be added 21 Iraqi Hunters and MiG-21s, plus 30 Algerian and Libyan fighters. Israel appears to have lost 120, including at least 33 Phantoms, 52 Skyhawks and 11 Mirages or Neshers. Helicopters are excluded from the above and account for a further 42 Egyptian, 13 Syrian and six Israeli losses.

Left: The Yom Kippur War saw the first appearance of the IAI Nesher, an unlicensed copy of the Mirage 5 produced after the Mirage 5Js built for Israel were embargoed by the French.

Some 40 and 31 IDF/AF aircraft fell to SAMs and ground fire respectively, mainly in the opening days, whilst combined Arab losses to these causes were just 17 and 19. Air-to-air, where there were around 400 combats, only 21 IDF losses were admitted, compared with a claimed 335 (two-thirds by cannon, and the rest by AIM-9 Sidewinders or the similar IAI Shafrir AAM at close range) of the Arab air forces. 'Own goals' were Israel two, and the Arabs 58.

After the war, analysts looked for the lessons of Yom Kippur. New respect was afforded to Soviet SAM systems, and the importance of ECM equipment in increasing the likelihood of mission success was better appreciated. 'Smart' ordnance, which had already been used with success in Vietnam gained wider acceptance in view of the demonstrable effect it had upon IDF/AF attack accuracy in the latter half of the fighting. Drones and RPVs, used for data-gathering and decoy work by Israel, became an important item of equipment for any modern army.

Left: A sharkmouthed F-4E lands after a combat sortie. Several aircraft were painted in this fashion as a disinformation exercise, intended to show that No. 113 Squadron was Phantom-equipped.

Long-distance Israeli raids

1976-1985

I n four major middle-east wars, Israel proved it had the world's best fighting air force. But in 1976 it showed for the first time that it also had the means of projecting power over long distances.

On 27 June 1976, Air France Flight 139 took off from Athens en route to Paris. Aboard the Airbus A300 were 258 passengers and crew. Among that number were four hijackers, who had transferred from a Bahrain flight at Athens. Just eight minutes after take off, the hijackers produced pistols and grenades and seized control of the aircraft. Flying first to Benghazi, it then went on to Uganda where President Idi Amin provided refuge.

The hijackers, an unholy mix of Baader-Meinhof and PLO terrorists, demanded the release of 53 'freedom fighters' from prisons in several countries. Some passengers were released, but numerous Jewish passengers were held hostage. The French crew of the aircraft elected to remain with the hostages.

Israel had long been a target for terrorist action, and immediately began planning a rescue. However, the move to Entebbe put the hijackers beyond the range of most Israeli aircraft. Nevertheless, a daring mission was put into effect with breakneck speed. It was given the codename Operation Thunderbolt

On Saturday 3 July, three heavily laden C-130s took off from Ophir, at the tip of occupied Sinai and Israel's southernmost airfield. Along with a Boeing 707 which provided airborne control and communications for the mission, the force flew over Ethiopia and Kenya. Bypassing Nairobi, where a second 707 – a hospital aircraft – had already landed, the flight approached Uganda's airport at Entebbe. Israeli agents had already infiltrated the airport and reported that the hijacked plane was parked next to the old terminal, where the hostages were being held.

The three C-130s landed just after midnight. The first moved openly to the terminal building and disgorged a black Mercedes (identical to Amin's, even down to the numberplate). It was escorted by Land Rovers driven by men in

Above: The entry into service of advanced new fighters like the General Dynamics F-16A Fighting Falcon gave the Israeli air force of the early 1980s the ability to strike hard over very long distances.

Palestinian clothing and carrying AK-47 rifles. The Ugandan guards saluted what they thought was their president, before being shot down by the disguised Israeli commandos.

More commandos rushed from the other aircraft entering the terminal building shouting, 'We're Israelis, get down.' Another unit assaulted the control tower and destroyed its radios, but not before Lt Colonel Yehonatan Netanyahu, the strike force commander, had been killed by a sniper. Others destroyed eleven MiG fighters – almost the entire combat-worthy Ugandan air force – to forestall any aerial pursuit

Within minutes, the terrorists had been shot and the hostages were being rushed to a fourth, empty C-130 which had just landed. Unfortunately, three hostages were killed in the crossfire.

The C-130s took off, leaving the dead hijackers, as well as 20 dead and over 100 wounded Ugandan soldiers. Landing in Kenya, they refuelled, the wounded were transferred to the waiting hospital plane, and the formation continued on to Israel and a triumphant recepton at Tel Aviv's Ben Gurion airport.

OSIRAK

Five years later, Israel made another long-range strike, but of a very different nature.

Iraq had long been suspected of having a secret nuclear weapons programme, for which the Osirak nuclear plant was the key. It was being built with French and Italian assistance in the desert some 19 km (12 miles) southeast of Baghdad.

Israeli intelligence had reported that the power station would be in operation by September of 1981, and that enriched uranium and weapons grade plutonium would

Rescue at Entebbe

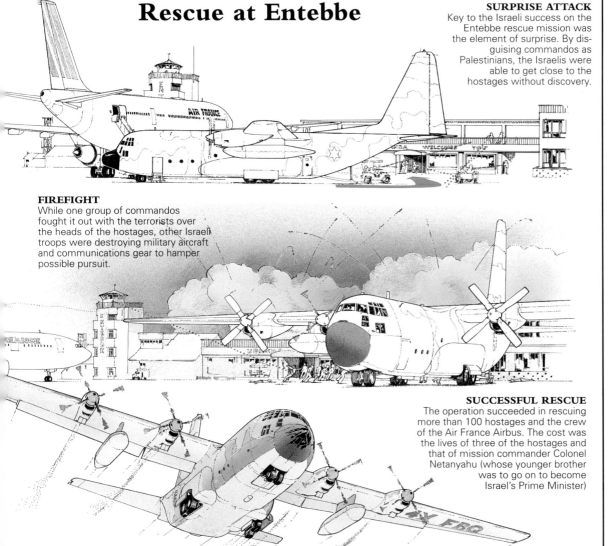

SURPRISE ATTACK
Key to the Israeli success on the Entebbe rescue mission was the element of surprise. By disguising commandos as Palestinians, the Israelis were able to get close to the hostages without discovery.

FIREFIGHT
While one group of commandos fought it out with the terrorists over the heads of the hostages, other Israeli troops were destroying military aircraft and communications gear to hamper possible pursuit.

SUCCESSFUL RESCUE
The operation succeeded in rescuing more than 100 hostages and the crew of the Air France Airbus. The cost was the lives of three of the hostages and that of mission commander Colonel Netanyahu (whose younger brother was to go on to become Israel's Prime Minister)

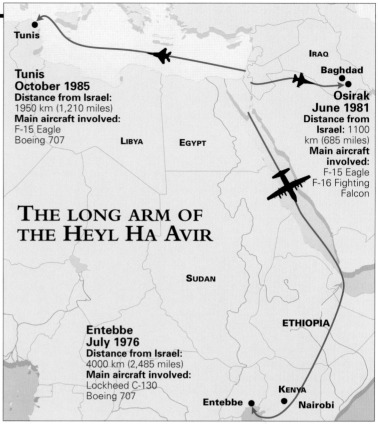

THE LONG ARM OF THE HEYL HA AVIR

Tunis
October 1985
Distance from Israel:
1950 km (1,210 miles)
Main aircraft involved:
F-15 Eagle
Boeing 707

Osirak
June 1981
Distance from Israel: 1100 km (685 miles)
Main aircraft involved:
F-15 Eagle
F-16 Fighting Falcon

Entebbe
July 1976
Distance from Israel:
4000 km (2,485 miles)
Main aircraft involved:
Lockheed C-130
Boeing 707

be produced soon after. This was looked on with misgivings by all of Iraq's neighbours. But it was Israel which would have been the prime target, and it was Israel's decision to attack the reactor from the air.

It would not be easy. Baghdad is more than 1100 km (685 miles) from Israel. However, Israel had recently acquired American-built F-15 and F-16 fighters, which could carry out such a long mission.

After meticulous preparation, which included Israel's best pilots flying rehearsals against full-scale mock-ups of the target, the mission was given the go-ahead. The pilots were briefed by General Rafael Eitan, the IDF's chief of staff, who stated that it was vital for them to succeed since, "the alternative is our destruction".

On Sunday 6 June 1981, six F-15 Eagles, which were to provide fighter cover, and eight F-16 Fighting Falcons, each armed with two 1000-kg (2,205-lb) bombs, took off from Etzion air base.

Flying a low-level course across deserted portions of Jordan and Saudi Arabia, the Falcons reached their target some 80 minutes later. Popping up from their low level flight, the F-16s quickly acquired the distinctive dome shape of the reactor and made their attacks. It is believed that all 16 bombs hit the target, although one failed to go off.

Above: Israel uses the F-15 in the air defence role, but it was the big fighter's long range which decided its use in the long overwater raid on the PLO headquarters in Tunis.

Iraqi air defences woke up, but it was too late. Even as the anti-aircraft guns opened fire, the Israeli jets were heading homewards.

The attack aroused great public anger in the Arab world (and possibly some secret satisfaction at Iraq's set back) but it also demonstrated that the Israelis had both the ability and the will to strike hard and far in what they saw as their own interest.

That was again made plain in 1985.

Entebbe had been a rescue. Osirak had been a strategic strike. But the raid on the PLO headquarters was a classic example of Israel's firm belief that terrorist acts should not go unpunished.

RAID ON TUNIS

On 25 September 1985, three Israelis were brutally murdered aboard a yacht at Larnaca in Cyprus. The perpetrators werre identified as Force 17, a terrorist organization linked with the PLO.

Israel decided to retaliate by striking at the PLO's headquarters in Tunis. The challenge was the distance: almost 2000 km (nearly 1250 miles) there and back called for the longest strike mission in

Israeli history. Planners decided to use McDonnell Douglas F-15 Eagles for the mission, refuelling from a Boeing 707 tanker en route.

The target was the PLO complex at Hamam-al-Shatt, which included Yasser Arafat's office and those of his senior advisers, as well as PLO operations, communications and public relations centres. The complex was also reported to house Force 17.

The raid was launched on 1 October, and the air-to-air refuelling went without a hitch. The only worry was the weather: the Gulf of Tunis was covered in cloud. However, as the fighters approached the coast the weather cleared, and the F-15 pilots were

Israel's air force, the Heyl Ha'Avir, has always had fast reactions, since nowhere in the tiny country is more than a few minutes flying time from the border. But the missions to Entebbe, Baghdad and Tunis called for very different skills, involving long-distance navigation and the ability to find a target after long hours in the cockpit.

able to identify and fix their targets, attacking with complete surprise and with deadly effect. All targets were damaged or destroyed. Arafat's headquarters took a direct hit, as did the Force 17 barracks.

Israel had once again shown that she would retaliate for any actions against her or her people – no matter what the cost politically or in world opinion.

Israel's aerial spearhead

The superb skills and training of Israel's pilots have given them a considerable advantage in their long struggle with hostile neighbours. But for the last 18 years, they have had the further advantage of being equipped with better aircraft than their opponents – particularly in the shape of the

supremely agile Fighting Falcon and Eagle. Israel was one of the the first export customers for both of these types, taking them into service soon after the US Air Force, and giving both types their baptisms of fire.

General Dynamics F-16A Fighting Falcon

Left: The first of an initial order for 75 single-seat F-16As and two-seat F-16Bs were delivered to Israel in July 1980. Known as *Netz* or Hawk in Heyl Ha'Avir service, they have since been joined by large numbers of improved F-16Cs and Ds, which are called *Barak* or Lightning by the Israelis.

McDonnell Douglas F-15A Eagle

Right: The Eagle has been the world's best fighter for more than two decades. It has been used primarily as an air superiority fighter by the Heyl Ha'avir, in whose hands the type has shot down more than 60 enemy aircraft without loss since its first victory in 1979.

The First Gulf War

1980-1989

An American military official famously concluded his briefing on the early days of the Iran/Iraq War by saying, "It's a pity they can't both lose." America's public antipathy and hostility towards Iran was provoked by the fact that its new Islamic government had overthrown a loyal US ally, seized American hostages in the US embassy in Teheran and roundly denounced the USA as 'the Great Satan'. At the same time, the USA had no more time for Iran's enemy, Iraq, whose Marxist regime enjoyed close links with the USSR and which had threatened US allies including Israel, Saudi Arabia and Kuwait, as well as threatening the political stability of the conservative part of the Arab world. Behind the scenes, the USA was later forced to offer some support to Iran, providing arms in return for the release of its hostages, following the failure of the USA's ambitious hostage rescue plan, Operation 'Eagle Claw'.

War between Iran and Iraq became inevitable following the Islamic revolution in Iran. The Mullahs loudly declared their intent to export their fundamentalist revolution to neighbouring nations which had turned away from Islam. Iraq also feared that the new regime would renounce the 1975 agreement which placed the border of the two nations along the Shatt al Arab, and feared for the future of the tiny strip of land which gave it access to the Persian Gulf.

Political pressure on Iran to withdraw from a number of islands

Above: Iraqi pilots have a last-minute briefing behind their Mirage F1EQ fighter-bombers. There have been reports that some of the F1s were flown by mercenaries, and even that the aircraft operated from Dhahran in Saudi Arabia.

Above: Iran's Boeing 747Fs were capable of refuelling in flight from the IRIAF's fleet of 14 Boeing 707-3J9C tankers. Iran's fleet of US-supplied aircraft was handicapped by the shortages of spares caused by sanctions.

Right: Iran managed to keep a high proportion of its F-4D and F-4E Phantom fleet serviceable with Israeli assistance, and with covert CIA assistance supplied in return for the release of hostages.

The American Embassy hostage rescue attempt

The US forces participating in Operation 'Eagle Claw' primarily consisted of the air wings of the carriers *Nimitz* and *Kitty Hawk*, with a force of Special Operations Hercules operating from Masirah in Oman, and a squadron of converted RH-53Ds to insert and recover the rescue teams and the hostages. All fixed-wing aircraft wore broad black-edged red bands on their wings. The mission was aborted due to helicopter unserviceability, and ended in tragedy as one of the RH-53Ds collided with its EC-130H tanker on the ground at Desert One, killing eight aircrew.

Left: The RH-53D was selected for the hostage rescue mission primarily because it did not look out of place on the deck of a carrier.

Above: F-14s, A-6s, A-7s (seen here) and USMC F-4s, supported by EA-3B Skywarriors and E-2C Hawkeyes, would have provided top cover and fighter-bomber support for the hostage rescue mission.

Iranian air power

Under the Shah, Iran was one of the best customers for American weapons and systems; he was determined to build himself a truly modern air force and was able to pay in cash. When the Shah was toppled, the revolutionary Islamic regime which took over had to operate a host of American weapons systems without US support, and in the face of strict sanctions.

Lockheed P-3F Orion
The IRIAF used its fleet of P-3F Orions for maritime patrol duties, but also pressed the aircraft into service as AWACS and battle management platforms. The five survivors served with a squadron based at Bandar Abbas.

McDonnell Douglas F-4D Phantom
Iran was able to keep more of its US-supplied aircraft operational than was supposed at the time, thanks in no small measure to Israel (which was happy to help any opponent of Iraq), and to the CIA, which mounted a covert if unwilling assistance programme.

Northrop F-5E
Before the fall of the Shah, Iran fielded seven F-5 squadrons, most of which were kept operational with assistance from Vietnam and Israel, and (after the Arms for Hostages deal) the CIA. An estimated 50 F-5s were lost in action during the early years of the war.

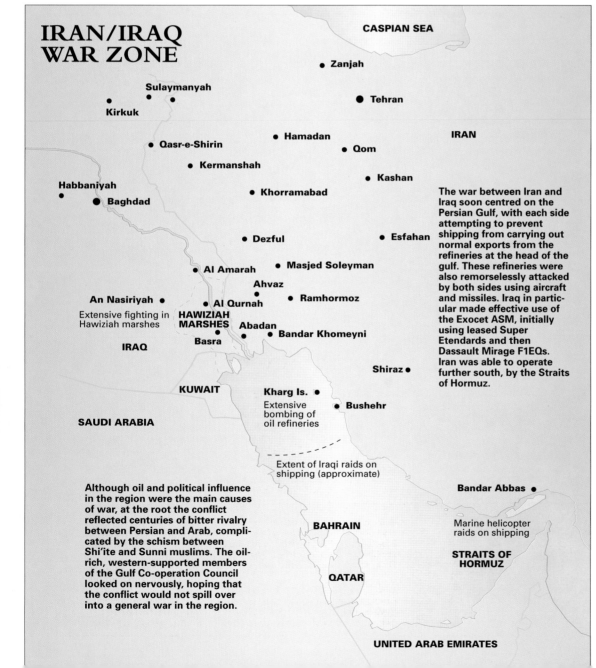

IRAN/IRAQ WAR ZONE

The war between Iran and Iraq soon centred on the Persian Gulf, with each side attempting to prevent shipping from carrying out normal exports from the refineries at the head of the gulf. These refineries were also remorselessly attacked by both sides using aircraft and missiles. Iraq in particular made effective use of the Exocet ASM, initially using leased Super Etendards and then Dassault Mirage F1EQs. Iran was able to operate further south, by the Straits of Hormuz.

Kharg Is.
Extensive bombing of oil refineries

Marine helicopter raids on shipping

Extent of Iraqi raids on shipping (approximate)

An Nasiriyah
Extensive fighting in Hawiziah marshes

Although oil and political influence in the region were the main causes of war, at the root the conflict reflected centuries of bitter rivalry between Persian and Arab, complicated by the schism between Shi'ite and Sunni muslims. The oil-rich, western-supported members of the Gulf Co-operation Council looked on nervously, hoping that the conflict would not spill over into a general war in the region.

in the Shatt drew little response, apart from some desultory artillery shelling of frontier positions on 4 September 1980. Iraq pre-empted further action by launching an attack on Iran. On 22 September Iraqi aircraft ineffectively attacked 10 Iranian airfields, and on the next day Iraqi troops invaded on several fronts. Iraqi aircraft mounted additional raids, and Iranian F-4 Phantoms and F-5E Tiger IIs attacked Baghdad, Kirkuk and a number of airfields. Eight of Iraq's Tu-22 'Blinders' bombed Teheran on 28 September, flying on to sanctuary in Riyadh. Both sides had large air forces but air activity was limited, although inflated kill claims suggested otherwise. Iraq claimed 140 enemy aircraft, and Iran 68.

NATURE OF THE WAR
Iraq hoped that its attack would prompt a new revolution in Iran, expecting that the Iranian armed forces would have little loyalty to the new regime. When they met fierce resistance, it became clear that the war would become a grinding battle of attrition. For its part, Iran bombed targets in Kurdestan, hoping to provoke a Kurdish uprising against the Baath party regime in Baghdad.

After the initial weeks of the war, further sporadic air activity was largely restricted to the battle zone by a mutual undeclared agreement, with attacks on enemy troops and oil installations by aircraft and surface-to-surface missiles, with some strategic raids against power stations and command facilities.

There was intermittent air activity in support of the regular offen-

Iraqi air power

Iraq's air force was primarily built around Soviet-built aircraft types, augmented by some new French-built combat aircraft and helicopters, plus a handful of surviving aircraft from the 1950s and early-1960s when the country enjoyed closer links with Britain. Attrition during the war was made up from the USSR, France and China, which supplied aircraft and weapons to both sides.

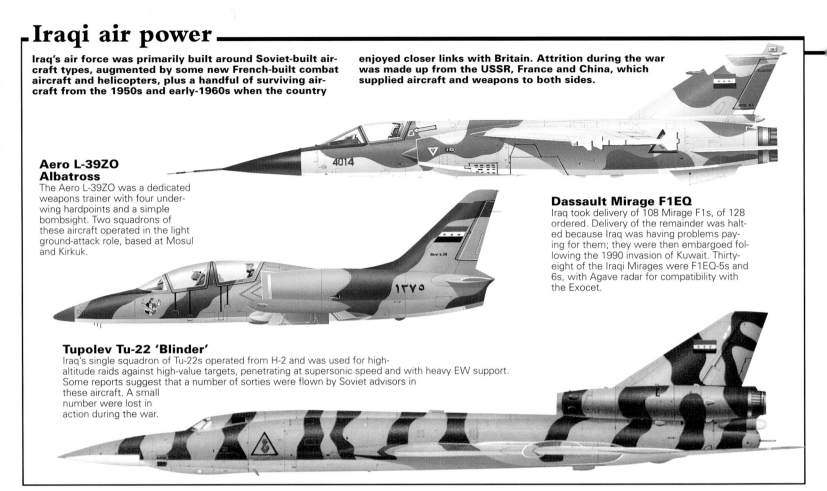

Aero L-39ZO Albatross
The Aero L-39ZO was a dedicated weapons trainer with four under-wing hardpoints and a simple bombsight. Two squadrons of these aircraft operated in the light ground-attack role, based at Mosul and Kirkuk.

Dassault Mirage F1EQ
Iraq took delivery of 108 Mirage F1s, of 128 ordered. Delivery of the remainder was halted because Iraq was having problems paying for them; they were then embargoed following the 1990 invasion of Kuwait. Thirty-eight of the Iraqi Mirages were F1EQ-5s and 6s, with Agave radar for compatibility with the Exocet.

Tupolev Tu-22 'Blinder'
Iraq's single squadron of Tu-22s operated from H-2 and was used for high-altitude raids against high-value targets, penetrating at supersonic speed and with heavy EW support. Some reports suggest that a number of sorties were flown by Soviet advisors in these aircraft. A small number were lost in action during the war.

sives and counter-offensives. Helicopter gunships were used more often than fixed-wing close-support aircraft, even when Iran mounted a major armoured counter-attack at Susangerd in January 1981.

Right: An AM39 Exocet anti-ship missile is loaded under an Iraqi Dassault Mirage F1EQ. Many of the Mirage F1s capable of delivering the missiles were delivered with dark-grey topsides to suit them to over-water operation.

FIGHTER COMBAT
Some fighter combat occurred in early-1981 in the fighting around Qasr-e-Shirin – in which Iraqi MiG-21s scored some kills with French Magic AAMs and Iranian F-14s saw combat as they countered Iraqi raids – but this was exceptional. Ground-attack aircraft occasionally flew intensive close-support operations, with the Iraqi air force generating 400-500 sorties per day at peak times. In mid-1983 Iraq admitted to the loss of 85 aircraft (including about 35 MiG-19s and MiG-21s, and six

Mirage F1s) since the beginning of hostilities, two years earlier.

Bombing raids on cities (notably by high-flying Tu-22 'Blinders') had been restricted to 'nuisance raids' by one or two pairs of aircraft.

The war soon assumed a predictable pattern. Iran used its Revolutionary Guards (or Pasdaran) to launch impressive (but ultimately futile) human wave assaults on Iraq's defensive positions, often in a massive spring offensive intended finally to finish the war. In March 1982 the push was from Dezful, and in February 1983 across the marshes

towards Al Amarah. In May 1982 the Iranians recaptured Khorramshahr, but a massive offensive in July was unable to take Basra. In March 1984, Iran pushed across the Hawizah marsh, intending to drive a wedge between the defenders of Al Amarah and Basra.

IRANIAN OFFENSIVES
In February 1986 Iran successfully captured Al Faw after crossing the Shatt. Encouraged by this success it launched another major offensive against Sulamaniyah. Tanks massing at Dezful were prevented from launching a third push only by a massive Iraqi fighter-bomber operation, involving more than 50 MiG-

Left: Iraq replaced its ageing Mi-4s with Mil Mi-8 'Hip' helicopters and operated these on transport, assault and anti-tank duties. The Mi-8s proved robust and reliable. Large numbers were acquired, and losses were heavy.

23BNs alone. The January 1987 Karbala 5 offensive against Basra (with a second front against Sumar) threatened to break Iraq, and both Jordan and Saudi Arabia offered to send F-5s and pilots to help stem the Iranian push, which was halted for the loss of at least 50 Iraqi aircraft. Further offensives were launched against Kurdestan in March, and Basra in April.

There was no Iranian offensive in 1988, with Iraq attacking and retaking the Faw peninsula, pushing on until both sides were left where they had been in 1980. There was little more fighting on the ground.

From late-1983 it had become clear that Iraq enjoyed a measure of superiority in the air, but could not make a serious impact on the ground. Merely halting Iranian attacks required extreme measures, and Iraq began using napalm and chemical weapons. On the other side, the Iranian air force was ham-

Below: The Iranian army acquired 68 Italian-built Elicotteri Meridionali (Boeing Vertol) CH-47C Chinooks, and used these intensively during the long war with Iraq. Serviceability proved good.

Right: The Bell 214A 16-seat utility helicopter was developed specifically to meet an Imperial Iranian Army requirement, and was named Isfahan in Iranian service. Iraq used gunship-configured 214STs.

pered by the poor serviceability of its aircraft and a lack of experienced pilots. Serviceability improved as Israel began covert support, but the release of imprisoned aircrew to fight had mixed effects, many taking the opportunity to defect in their F-4s to Turkey and Saudi Arabia. With stalemate at the front, both sides looked to continue the

war elsewhere, launching strategic attacks on each other's cities and also against oil targets and shipping in the gulf.

The Iraqi air force began attacking Iranian population centres during late-1983, in an effort to undermine civilian morale and perhaps provoke revolt. Iran responded with similar attacks on Iraqi cities.

The offensive petered out, but was resumed in December 1986, when Iran launched 'Scuds' against Baghdad, with Iraq retaliating with air strikes. Iraq mounted 200 sorties against Iranian cities from January 1987, losing two Tu-16s in the process. In February 1988 there was another round of city attacks, with Iraq firing 40 SS-12s at Teheran and

the holy city of Qom.

TANKER WAR

The oil industry was of such vital economic importance to both nations that it was always a key strategic target. Iraq attacked the oil production plant at Abadan within a month of the war starting, while Iran attacked Kuwaiti oil facilities

Grumman F-14A Tomcat

Iran took delivery of 79 of the 80 F-14As it purchased, the final aircraft being embargoed before delivery. After experiencing some difficulties in keeping the Tomcats serviceable, a significant number of F-14s were maintained in service. They were used in mixed fighter force tactics, often acting as mini-AWACS platforms. The F-14 scored some victories but it was not invulnerable; at least one fell to an Iraqi Mirage F1.

Radar
Imperial Iran was one of a tiny handful of nations considered safe enough to receive AN/AWG-9 technology, which remains impressive even by today's standards. F-14A can track 24 targets, and can engage six of them simultaneously.

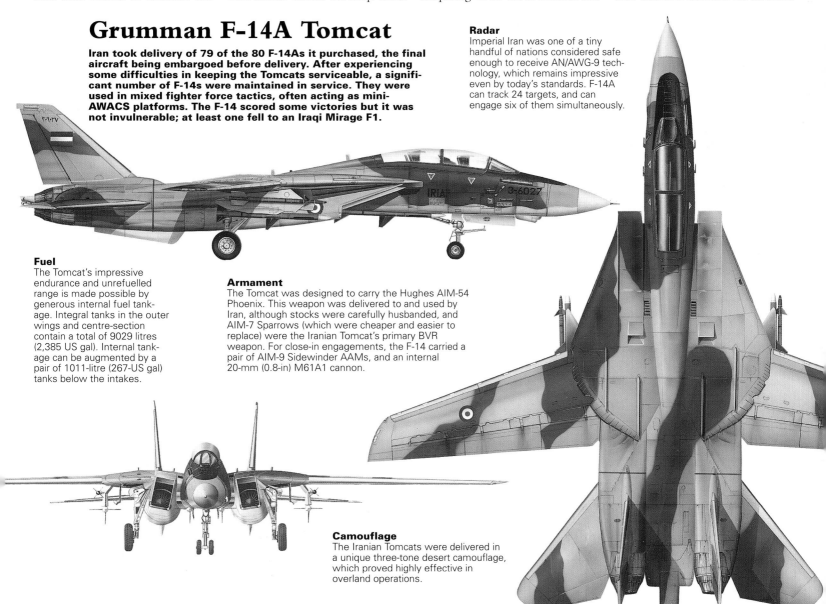

Fuel
The Tomcat's impressive endurance and unrefuelled range is made possible by generous internal fuel tankage. Integral tanks in the outer wings and centre-section contain a total of 9029 litres (2,385 US gal). Internal tankage can be augmented by a pair of 1011-litre (267-US gal) tanks below the intakes.

Armament
The Tomcat was designed to carry the Hughes AIM-54 Phoenix. This weapon was delivered to and used by Iran, although stocks were carefully husbanded, and AIM-7 Sparrows (which were cheaper and easier to replace) were the Iranian Tomcat's primary BVR weapon. For close-in engagements, the F-14 carried a pair of AIM-9 Sidewinder AAMs, and an internal 20-mm (0.8-in) M61A1 cannon.

Camouflage
The Iranian Tomcats were delivered in a unique three-tone desert camouflage, which proved highly effective in overland operations.

Above: Both sides made heavy use of helicopter gunships. Iran took delivery of 202 Bell AH-1J Cobras, many of which were equipped with nose-mounted *TOW* missile sights. All featured the more powerful engine of the AH-1T, which gave much improved hot-and-high capability.

Above: An Iraqi Mi-24 'Hind' gunship flies over the battlefield. The heavily-armed Mi-24 was Iraq's most capable combat helicopter, and played a decisive part in supporting Iraqi army offensives.

Right: Iraq's helicopter inventory at the start of the war included 11 Aérospatiale Super Frelons. They were used for anti-shipping, transport and *SAR* operations, and suffered some losses.

Iran's weapon of choice for its tanker attacks. Two F-4Es were shot down by Saudi F-15s on 5 June, but the pace of attacks increased steadily.

KHARG ISLAND TARGET

In 1985 Iraq concentrated on attacking the main terminal at Kharg Island, while Iran began mounting attacks on tankers in the lower gulf, using missile-armed AB 212 helicopters operating from a floating platform. Iraqi attacks were so effective that the use of Kharg Island virtually halted, and super-tankers instead unloaded at Sirri, further down the gulf, where the oil was transferred to lower-value ships which shuttled to Kharg and to Larak.

Both Sirri and Larak had been outside the range of Iraqi strike aircraft, but the introduction of An-12 tankers (and the alleged use of Dhahran in Saudi Arabia) allowed Mirage F1EQs to attack both targets in 1986.

(on the basis that they were handling Iraqi oil) during 1981. Iraqi aircraft using Exocet missiles attacked Iran's main oil terminal at Kharg Island from 1983, sinking a Greek tanker there on 22 November 1983, and a British tanker in February 1984. Iran began to retaliate by attacking tankers leaving Kuwaiti and Saudi ports, since they were believed to be exporting Iraqi oil. F-4Es firing AGM-65 Maverick missiles were

Opposing helicopters

Iran's reliance on 'human wave' tactics – throwing into battle thousands of young men, all intent on becoming martyrs – threatened to overwhelm Iraq's professional army, and great reliance had to be placed on high-technology weapons to counter Iran's numerical superiority in men. Attack helicopters proved an effective way of countering Iranian offensives.

Aérospatiale Gazelle
Iraq took delivery of 40 Aérospatiale SA 342M Gazelles, armed with Euromissile HOT anti-tank missiles and equipped with a roof-mounted sight. They augmented the larger Russian-built Mi-24s and proved devastatingly effective against Iranian armour.

Bell 214A Isfahan
The Iranian army also made considerable use of helicopters, with more than 400 Bell 214s and Bell AH-1s on charge when the war began. The Bell 214 had been developed specifically to meet Iranian requirements.

Above: A crude-oil tanker lists and burns fiercely after being fatally struck by an Exocet missile. Some reports suggest that mercenary pilots flew the long-range Mirage F1/Exocet sorties. A total of 37 tankers were hit and sunk by both Iran and Iraq during the conflict, while a further 23 were badly damaged.

1987 saw the tanker war intensify further, with Iranian Revolutionary Guard speedboats planting mines and machine-gunning ships, and with the stationing of HY-2 'Silkworm' anti-ship missiles at Bandar Abbas. Iraqi Mirages continued to attack tankers near Iranian oil terminals, and the terminals themselves, but generally avoided attacking neutral shipping. It damaged the US frigate Stark on 17 May, but Iraq quickly apologised for the damage and the 37 deaths.

It was also the year in which the tanker war widened to draw in new combatants. Kuwait reflagged some of its tankers (re-registering them as Soviet or American ships) and called on the US Navy for protection. From July the US Navy began escorting convoys of reflagged tankers up and down the gulf and deployed mine-clearing helicopters to the region. Britain and France also deployed warships (carrying helicopters) to the gulf, Britain increasing a presence which dated from 1980. From late 1987, the US began attacking Iranian vessels, using USMC AH-1 Cobras and US Army OH-58Ds. On 3 July 1988 the USS Vincennes engaged what it thought was a hostile Iranian F-14 with two standard SAMs, then found it had shot down an unarmed Iran Air A300

Right: As an interim solution to acquiring its own fixed-wing maritime strike capability, Iraq leased five Dassault Super Étendards, along with a large number of AM39 Exocet missiles, pending the delivery of its own Exocet-capable Mirage F1EQs.

Airbus. Although the shootdown was a mistake, it was also a potent declaration of intent.

On 19 July 1988 two Iranian F-14As were shot down over the gulf by Iraqi fighters (possibly the newly delivered MiG-29s). In an unconnected move on the same day, Iran accepted UN Resolution 598 calling for a ceasefire. The war was over.

Above: As the tanker war intensified, Western nations were forced to intervene, clearing mines and escorting neutral ships in the Persian Gulf. Although the bulk of the protection force was provided by the US Navy, Britain also had traditional interest in the region. As a result, a succession of Royal Navy warships, each with Lynx or Sea King helicopters, was deployed to the region for what was known as the 'Armilla Patrol'.

Above: Operation 'Prime Chance' saw US Army OH-58Ds operating against Iranian patrol boats attacking tankers transitting the Persian Gulf. They could carry Stinger and Hellfire missiles, as well as gun and rocket pods.

Left: As the oil war intensified, Saudi Arabia and Kuwait began to be drawn into the conflict, and with them came western allies. The US Navy together with Britain and France deployed warships to protect the tankers and oil platforms. Here, a rig used as a base by Iranian Revolutionary Guard speedboats burns after an attack by US Navy SEALs, backed by US Army Special Forces helicopters and naval gunfire.

Air War over the Beka'a

JUNE 1982

Following the realignment by Egypt with the West after the historic Camp David agreement in 1978, Israel's principal Arab antagonist automatically became Syria. This Arab country had for many years championed the cause of the Palestinians in their continuing efforts to secure their own formally recognised state. Opposition to the peace pact between Israel and Egypt came in the form of cross-border attacks by Palestine Liberation Organisation (PLO) guerrillas operating from bases in southern Lebanon. In retaliation, PLO bases had been bombed by strike aircraft of the Israeli Defence Force/Air Force (IDF/AF).

SYRIAN FORCES

Syria had moved its troops into neighbouring Lebanon in what was ostensibly a gesture to halt the Lebanese civil war. The Syrian force was not to be seen as one of occupation, so it left its air cover and large SAM units behind. Many of the latter were stationed in the border regions where they could counter any Israeli aircraft seeking

Above: Israel's F-16s were in action from soon after their delivery in July 1980. From the start, the F-16s were used as fighter-bombers and as air superiority fighters, escorting bombladen F-4Es or conducting sweeps or CAPs. Israeli F-16s claimed 44 kills over the Beka'a.

Above: This bombladen IAI Kfir-C7 is from No. 144 Squadron. Used primarily in the fighter-bomber role, the Kfir also enjoyed some success as an air-to-air fighter. In the 1982 fighting, the IDF/AF's Kfirs were used primarily for attacking Syrian SAM and radar sites.

to attack Damascus.

Parallel with the border, running southwards from Rayak to the Israeli-occupied Golan Heights, is the Beka'a valley. Israel mounted an intense reconnaissance effort to gain intelligence on these Syrian positions and lost several Firebee RPVs (Remotely Piloted Vehicles) to Syrian ground fire.

IDF/AF clashes with the Syrian air force between 1979 and June 1982 led to the loss of at least 12

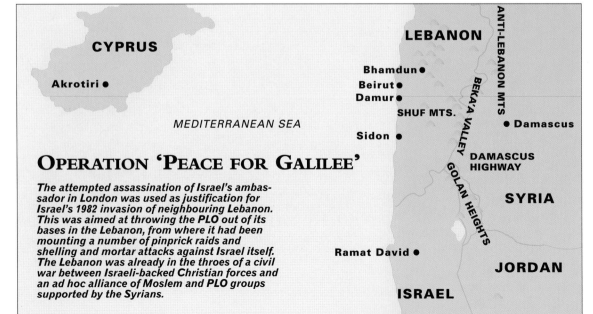

Above: A flight of F-15s overflies the fortress at Masada. The F-15 has been Israel's primary air-defence fighter since 1976, opening its tally in June 1977 with four Syrian MiG-21s. In 1982, they despatched many of the IDF/AF's claimed 92 victories.

Syrian MiGs, including two MiG-25s shot down while attacking RF-4E reconnaissance aircraft.

By mid-1982, Israel had been planning for some time an armoured thrust into Lebanon to remove the threat posed by the PLO. In order to lessen international reprobation, the onslaught was to be presented initially as revenge for a PLO atrocity and thus the *casus belli* became the attempted assassination of the Israeli ambassador in London on 3 June.

At 15.15 on the following

OPERATION 'PEACE FOR GALILEE'

The attempted assassination of Israel's ambassador in London was used as justification for Israel's 1982 invasion of neighbouring Lebanon. This was aimed at throwing the PLO out of its bases in the Lebanon, from where it had been mounting a number of pinprick raids and shelling and mortar attacks against Israel itself. The Lebanon was already in the throes of a civil war between Israeli-backed Christian forces and an ad hoc alliance of Moslem and PLO groups supported by the Syrians.

CYPRUS

Akrotiri ●

MEDITERRANEAN SEA

LEBANON

Bhamdun ●
Beirut ●
Damur ●

SHUF MTS.

Sidon ●

ANTI-LEBANON MTS

BEKA'A VALLEY

● Damascus

DAMASCUS HIGHWAY

GOLAN HEIGHTS

SYRIA

Ramat David ●

JORDAN

ISRAEL

Tel Aviv ●

Syria's defenders

Syria invaded the Lebanon on the last day of May 1976 in an effort to enforce a peace between the warring factions. Israeli forces themselves occupied part of southern Lebanon (up to the Litani river) in March and April 1978. The IDF/AF periodically attacked targets inside the Lebanon thereafter, often drawing a response from Syrian air forces.

MiG-25

Despite its breathtaking performance, the MiG-25 proved to be ineffective as a fighter, hampered by poor agility and above all by its undue reliance on GCI control. Nevertheless, Arab sources suggest that the type achieved some success.

MiG-23MLD

Cold War propaganda and a lack of hard information wrote off the MiG-23 as a typically crude, primitive and ineffective fighter. When Israelis evaluated a MiG-23MLD which defected from Syria, they judged it to be a better aircraft than expected. It is likely that some of the IDF/AF aircraft officially lost to SAMs actually fell to 'Floggers'.

Left: Israeli Hughes 500MDs operated principally in the anti-tank role, using their TOW missiles to devastating effect. The Israeli gunship helicopters (operating alongside AH-1 Cobras) had their day on 10 June, going into action when Syrian armour attempted to stop an Israeli armoured column.

afternoon, seven waves of A-4s, F-4s and F-16s of the Israel Defence Force/Air Force streaked over Beirut, the Lebanese capital, attacking the Palestinian refugee camps. During the next morning, Beirut, the coast road and a PLO stronghold were hit from the air; a Skyhawk fell to an SA-7 as the IDF/AF's first casualty.

FULL-SCALE INVASION

Not until 6 June was the full scale of Israel's plans apparent. Ground forces, with helicopter support, began a northward thrust through the coastal area which was eventually to lead almost to the gates of Beirut. The claimed objective of the full-scale invasion was to establish a demilitarised buffer zone in front of Israel. PLO resistance was swept aside, obliging Syria, as an ally, to provide assistance. The SAF first appeared on 7 June in a limited attempt to intercept F-16s over Beirut and Damur, losing two MiGs as a result. To protect its flanks, Israel used CH-53 heavy helicopters to airlift a strong force

into the Shouf mountains (southeast of Beirut) on the following day. This threatened to outflank the Syrian positions in the Beka'a valley and cut communications between Beirut and Damascus, so Syria reacted with an attack by Gazelle helicopter gunships. Syrian strike aircraft penetrated farther into Lebanese airspace to attack Israeli armour near the port of Sidon.

By now, it was clear to the Israelis that the Syrians would have to be prevented from interfering with the anti-PLO operations being undertaken on the coastal plain. IDF/AF freedom of action was being hampered by the Beka'a valley SAM sites, and, since more missiles were reportedly being installed, early action was advisable.

At this time there were 19 SAM sites in the Beka'a valley, and in

Right: The McDonnell Douglas F-4E was arguably the most important IDF/AF type engaged in Operation 'Peace for Galilee'. They flew close-support, interdiction, and anti-SAM sorties, as well as CAPs and reconnaissance flights.

four closely-spaced raids on 9 June at least 17 of the sites were put out of action by 90 aircraft. First, soon after 14.00, a force of 26 F-4s launched AGM-65 Maverick air-to-surface missiles and AGM-45 and AGM-78 Standard anti-radar missiles against both the SAM bases and their control posts. This was supported by Ze'ev short-range SSMs fired by the Israeli ground forces, and resulted in 10 sites being rendered inoperative in the first 10 minutes. Almost completely blinded, the Syrian air-defence organisation was delivered a body-blow by 40 F-4s, A-4s and Kfirs which went

for the weapons themselves, using more TV-guided Mavericks, together with cluster bombs and GBU-15 guided bombs to rip apart the missile positions. This second phase was completed at 14.35, and was followed by a back-up wave which in the third phase attacked other Syrian positions on the front, plus any SAM sites which had escaped.

Higher above, the top-cover component of IDF/AF F-16s and F-15 Eagles was involved in large-scale clashes with Syrian fighters. Forces of MiG-21s and MiG-23s were severely mauled, resulting in IDF/AF claims of 22 shot down plus seven damaged, for no loss. Syria admitted 16, but claimed 26: the majority of these were probably RPVs.

THE END OF THE SAMs

On 10 June, the remaining two SAM sites were destroyed, leaving the SAF as the only weapon which could challenge Israel in the air. In more fierce fighting, Israel claimed 28 aircraft including three helicopters shot down. The latter resulted from Syrian attempts to

Israel's strike force

Israeli fighter-bombers operated in huge waves during Operation 'Peace for Galilee' (30 to 90 aircraft per wave), closely escorted by F-16s and F-15s. Phantoms armed with AGM-78 Standard ARMs and AGM-45 Shrikes took out Syrian SAM and GCI radar sites, while Kfirs attacked using free-fall and cluster bombs. Syrian air defences were effectively blinded within a day.

IAI Kfir C2
The indigenous Kfir served with IDF/AF five squadrons during Operation 'Peace for Galilee', and outnumbered the older A-4 Skyhawk. Only the F-4E Phantom was available in similar numbers. During the operation, the Kfir was mainly used for strike missions.

McDonnell Douglas F-4E Phantom II
Although operating mainly as a fighter-bomber, one of the Israeli kills over the Beka'a was scored by an F-4E using an indigenous Rafael Python missile. This brought the Israeli F-4's kill tally to a claimed 116, and made its pilot an ace. It was to be the F-4's last aerial victory.

Left: Laden with a centreline tank and six 454-kg (1,000-lb) bombs, an F-4E of No. 105 Squadron sets out on a mission. The F-4E has continued to be involved in raids on targets in Lebanon since the end of Operation 'Peace for Galilee'.

halt an Israeli column penetrating the Beka'a valley, while Israel responded with its own force of AH-1 Cobra and Hughes 500MD Defender gunships. On the next day (11 June) similar battles took place when Syria attacked a force which appeared to be intent on cutting the road from the Beka'a valley to Beirut. This cost the SAF 18 more aircraft, according to Israeli accounts, before an intermittent ceasefire was arranged. It was, in effect, the end of the air war, although more strikes were made by the IDF/AF. Israeli helicopters were kept busy in the days and months afterwards supporting the Israeli forces occupying the southern part of Lebanon.

AIR SUPREMACY
Israeli supremacy over the SAF was absolute and owed much to the support elements. The key element was Israel's multi-faceted Air Battle Management System, one of whose major components was the newly acquired E-2C Hawkeye airborne early warning aircraft. During operations, two of the four available E-2s were kept on station off the coast. Syria later admitted that all its aircraft were detected almost as soon as they left base, robbing them of any possibility of the surprise attack. The E-2s were backed up by a number of Westinghouse low-altitude surveillance radar systems (essentially an AN/TPS-63 tactical radar slung beneath a tethered balloon). Tactical reconnaissance was provided by RF-4E Phantoms. One was lost to ground fire and, because of the sensitive nature of its avionics and sensors (some of which were of Israeli origin), the IDF/AF mounted a raid to destroy the wreckage. This raid arrived in time to catch a group of 11 Soviet personnel in the act of removing some of the 'black boxes', but was pressed home regardless. Remotely piloted vehicles (RPVs) were widely used throughout the Beka'a fighting, both for decoy and reconnaissance work. The Israeli forces used Firebee drones backed up by propeller-driven IAI Scouts. The latter were equipped with both TV and wide-angle film cameras and provided immediate post-attack intelligence.

When attacking the SAM sites, the IDF/AF planned its moves carefully. The first wave kept well clear of the opposition (about 35

Israeli tank killers

Although Israel decisively defeated Egyptian and Syrian tanks during the 1973 Yom Kippur War, the conflict illustrated the shortcomings of fixed-wing fast-jet fighter-bombers as tank killers, and set Israel on the path of acquiring dedicated anti-tank helicopters. The latter first saw service in Operation 'Peace for Galilee', and largely justified the faith which had been placed in them.

Bell AH-1S Cobra
This Israeli Cobra is in up-gunned AH-1S or AH-1E configuration. The universal under-nose turret contains an M197 triple-barrelled 20-mm (0.8-in) cannon, a lightweight derivative of the tried and tested M61 Vulcan cannon used in a large number of fixed-wing aircraft installations.

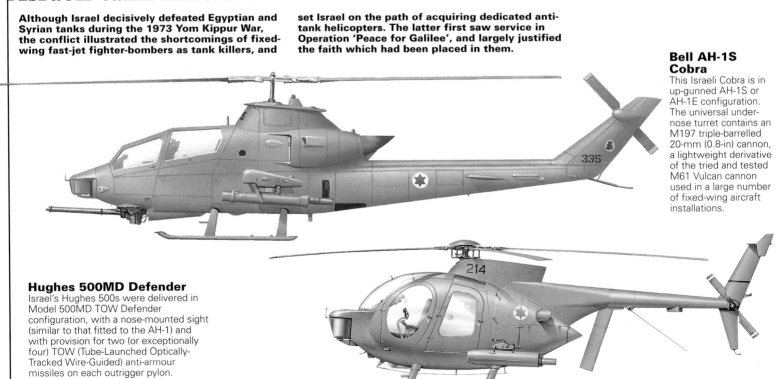

Hughes 500MD Defender
Israel's Hughes 500s were delivered in Model 500MD TOW Defender configuration, with a nose-mounted sight (similar to that fitted to the AH-1) and with provision for two (or exceptionally four) TOW (Tube-Launched Optically-Tracked Wire-Guided) anti-armour missiles on each outrigger pylon.

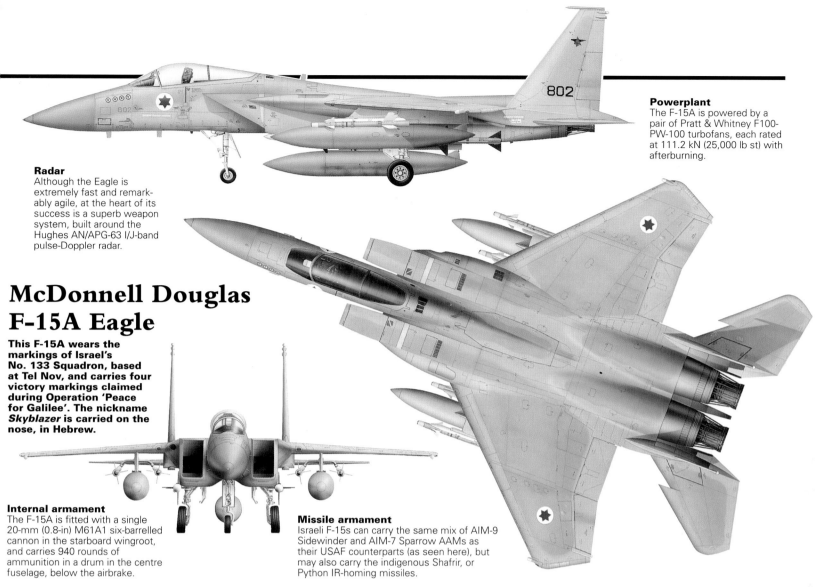

Radar
Although the Eagle is extremely fast and remarkably agile, at the heart of its success is a superb weapon system, built around the Hughes AN/APG-63 I/J-band pulse-Doppler radar.

Powerplant
The F-15A is powered by a pair of Pratt & Whitney F100-PW-100 turbofans, each rated at 111.2 kN (25,000 lb st) with afterburning.

McDonnell Douglas F-15A Eagle

This F-15A wears the markings of Israel's No. 133 Squadron, based at Tel Nov, and carries four victory markings claimed during Operation 'Peace for Galilee'. The nickname *Skyblazer* is carried on the nose, in Hebrew.

Internal armament
The F-15A is fitted with a single 20-mm (0.8-in) M61A1 six-barrelled cannon in the starboard wingroot, and carries 940 rounds of ammunition in a drum in the centre fuselage, below the airbrake.

Missile armament
Israeli F-15s can carry the same mix of AIM-9 Sidewinder and AIM-7 Sparrow AAMs as their USAF counterparts (as seen here), but may also carry the indigenous Shafrir, or Python IR-homing missiles.

km/22 miles) as it launched its missiles. They were intended for pinpoint attack against the nerve-centres of the SAM network, and so comprised TV-guided Mavericks as well as AGM-45 Shrike and AGM-78 Standard anti-radar weapons. With their nerve centres inoperative, the SAM sites could be attacked from closer quarters and torn apart with cluster bombs and high explosive. Phantoms undertook much of this work.

Also active before and during the attacks were the IDF/AF's Boeing 707s, much modified versions of the airliner. Fitted with side-looking radar for surveillance, they also undertook stand-off jamming of the SAM radar, as well as jamming the SAF's fighter control and navigation aid networks.

In all, 40 SAF aircraft, equally divided between MiG-21s and MiG-23s, were claimed by the 37 F-15 Eagles then in IDF/AF service (bringing that aircraft's air-fighting score to 58 for no losses). The McDonnell Douglas stable was credited with an additional victory by an F-4E. The remaining 44 SAF losses claimed by Israel went to the 72 F-16s, and again comprised MiG-21s and MiG-23s in about equal numbers.

Syria admitted the loss of 60 aircraft and 'less than 30' SAM sites. Israel claimed 92 aircraft including five Gazelle helicopters, of which 85 were fighters shot down in air-to-air combat. After initially high estimates Syria settled for a claim of 19 Israeli

aircraft, of which just three were conceded: a Skyhawk and two helicopters. True IDF/AF losses seem to be two Skyhawks, a Phantom, a probable F-16, seven other aircraft (which may have been technical write-offs after returning home), and two shootdowns by the PLO (an AH-1 Cobra and a Bell 212).

ISRAELI AERIAL VICTORY
The inevitable wrangle over shootdowns must not be allowed to obscure the fact that Israel won a resounding victory in fighter-versus-fighter combat over the Beka'a valley. Even the Syrian loss figures do not seek to deny that truth, questioning only the margin of Israel's superiority.

Above: An IDF/AF F-4E Phantom dispenses IR-decoy flares in a low-level attack. By 1982, Israeli Phantoms were equipped with comprehensive defensive systems, and had warning systems and countermeasures adequate for the modern battlefield.

Right: F-16 claimed almost half of Israel's 92 claimed victories over the Beka'a. At least one contributed to 13 admitted IDF losses. Israel maintained that all its losses were to SAMs; Syrian fighters claimed at least 21 air-to-air victories and admitted to 40 air combat losses.

Peacekeepers in Lebanon

DECEMBER 1983

FRENCH RETALIATION
A Super Etendard rockets Syrian positions on 17 November, in retaliation for a suicide bomb attack on its soldiers. The aircraft operated from the carrier Clémenceau, *with top cover provided by F-8E(FN) Crusaders.*

In 1983 the USA moved to shore up the beleaguered Lebanese government by stationing Marines in Beirut and keeping the Sixth Fleet on alert nearby. Lebanon's fragile ethnic and religious balance had been torn asunder by the Israeli invasion and partial occupation, by Syrian partial occupation, and by the stirrings of an indigenous home-grown revolution. The US effort at peacekeeping was opposed on all sides.

The American presence was first challenged by two bombings of the US embassy in Beirut. On 24 October the US Marines compound in Beirut was struck by a suicide truck-bomb which killed 242 men. Syrian and Druze artillery positions took regular pot-shots at American ships offshore.

By September 1983, with the USS *Dwight D. Eisenhower*

Below: US Marines are delivered to Beirut by a Sikorsky CH-53E Super Stallion. The Marine positions around the airport were vulnerable to artillery fire from the nearby Chouf mountains, but suicide truck bombers proved to be a far more devastating threat.

(CVN-69) off Lebanon, naval aviators were regularly evading gunfire while carrying out reconnaissance missions, but the *Eisenhower* was replaced before her pilots could have retribution. By October USS *John F. Kennedy* (CV-67) was the carrier on 'Bagel Station', and was soon joined by USS *Independence* (CV-62), which reached the Mediterranean after a detour to Grenada.

On 3 December the Syrians directed no fewer than 10 SAMs at a pair of TARPS-equipped VF-32 Tomcats. This was sufficient provocation for both carriers to launch an Alpha Strike of 12 A-7E Corsairs and 16 A-6E Intruders, with two F-14s providing MiGCAP above them. The A-6Es attacked Syrian gun positions and munitions sites at Falouga and Hammana, some 16-km (10-miles) north of the highway linking Beirut and Damascus. One A-6E was shot down while rolling in on a SAM radar site at Hammana. The pilot died soon after ejecting, but his bombardier-navigator ejected, and was captured.

The Corsairs, laden with cluster bombs, struck at Jabal al Knaisse and Mghite 31-km (19-miles) east of Beirut. After hitting his target, *Independence*'s carrier air wing commander (CAG) Commander Edward T. Andrews, led a SAR effort to recover the downed A-6E crew. He was shot down, but ejected safely. His parachute was carried out to sea, where he was quickly picked up by a US Navy helicopter. The two losses were perhaps

Above: RAF Boeing Vertol Chinooks were used to resupply British peacekeepers on the ground in Beirut, and then to evacuate the troops when their mission became completely impossible.

inevitable, after the decision was made to send the strike aircraft into battle without organic ECM support, failing to make use of the electronic warfare capabilities of the carrier's EA-6Bs and E-2s.

The 4 December 1983 mission failed to reinforce the US presence in Lebanon, and actually intensified hostility to that presence, and even to US influence. The Marines were soon withdrawn, leaving only a residual US presence which thereafter fell prey to hostage-taking and hijacking.

EUROPEAN PEACEKEEPERS

As foreign peacekeepers assumed the perilous and thankless task of attempting to separate warring factions in West Beirut, they brought with them their own air support. France had begun the practice of rooftop 'showing the flag' when *Foch* arrived in Lebanese waters on 6 September. Included in the air group were three Flotilles of Super Etendards, plus reconnaissance-tasked Etendard IVPs.

Farther to the rear, at the British sovereign base of Akrotiri, the RAF deployed three Chinooks and six Buccaneer S.Mk 2Bs between 7 and 9 September. These helicopters were tasked with re-supply flights to Beirut. The Buccaneers' were retasked from maritime strike to overland attack and were maintained on alert at all times, loaded with 454-kg (1,000-lb) bombs. They announced their arrival on 11 September with a low-level beat-up of Beirut, but thereafter kept a discreet distance. Six Aeritalia F-104S Starfighters of the Italian air force were also deployed to Akrotiri, and were similarly circumspect.

HUNTERS IN ACTION

On 16 September the Lebanese Air Force (LAF) undertook its first combat action for a decade. Operating from a motorway airstrip 30-km (19-miles) north of Beirut, five Hunters struck at Druze militia positions in the Chouf mountains. One was badly hit by 23-mm AAA fire, forcing the pilot to eject into the sea, from where he was rescued by a USN helicopter. One more Hunter suffered damage and two more diverted to Akrotiri. On

19 September, a Bulldog trainer used as an observation aircraft was shot down by ground fire.

In response to an attack on its troops, France launched a reprisal raid on 22 September, sending four Aéronavale Super Etendards to bomb four Druze gun batteries, some 20-km (12-miles) east of Beirut. F-8E(FN) Crusaders provided top cover, and Etendard IVMs undertook pre- and post-raid reconnaissance. The air group transferred to *Foch*'s newly-arrived sister ship *Clémenceau* early in October. In a further attack on 17 November (mounted in retaliation for a suicide 'lorry bomb'

which killed 58 French soldiers) 14 Super Etendards made two largely unsuccessful raids against Shia militia barracks close to the Syrian border. Also active was the IDF/AF, which had raided targets near Baalbek on 16 November. It returned to strike Palestinian guerrilla bases in three Lebanese towns on 20 November, losing a Kfir to a Syrian missile near Bhamdoun. Another Israeli mission on 3 December coincided with the US Navy Alpha Strike.

WITHDRAWAL

The other would-be peacekeepers had fared no better than the United States. France, Italy and the UK all withdrew their troops

US carrier aircraft were used to strike at Lebanese artillery threatening the Marine positions in Beirut. One A-6 and one A-7 were lost to SAMs.

during March and April 1984 when it became apparent that their task was impossible. Royal Navy Sea King HC.M 4s were used to extract the British contingent from Lebanon. On 14 February, the LAF was back in action when two Hunters fired rockets at Druze militia. Four sorties failed to prevent the Druze linking up with the Shia forces then controlling south and west Beirut, and supporting US naval gunfire was equally unsuccessful. Israel returned to the fray on 19 February, launching its fighter-bombers against the southern port of Damour and the towns of Aley and Bhamdoun southeast of Beirut.

As the multi-national peacekeeping force completed its withdrawal, Israel and Syria were left alone to resume their strategy of playing off the rival Lebanese factions against each other, backed by the periodic IDF/AF air raids against alleged Palestinian guerrilla targets. Israel long ago learned that keeping its hostile neighbours fighting amongst themselves can be an effective means of deterring direct attacks.

Left: A detachment of six Blackburn Buccaneers of Nos 12 and 208 Squadron flew low-level flag-waving sorties over Beirut and stood ready to mount retaliatory air strikes. Fortunately, the order to attack never came.

Ageing warriors

Peacekeeping operations over the Lebanon provided an opportunity for a number of elderly aircraft types to prove their mettle. The French carrier air groups included Etendard IVP reconnaissance aircraft and Crusader fighters, while the RAF deployed Buccaneers to its base on the island of Cyprus. Lebanon's own air force used its ancient Hawker Hunters.

Hawker Hunter F.Mk 70
Left: While Lebanon's Mach 2 Mirage fighters remained in storage, a flight of Hawker Hunters was thrown into the fighting, attacking militia targets with accuracy and daring. One of the Hunters was shot down, but the credibility of the Lebanese armed forces was enhanced.

LTV F-8E(FN) Crusader
Right: Both the *Foch* and the *Clémenceau* deployed F-8E(FN) Crusaders from Flotille 12F for air-defence duties. These flew CAP and escort missions, but were not called upon to engage hostile aircraft.

US-Libyan confrontations

1981-1989

During the 1980s, the USA found itself clashing with Colonel Khadaffi's Libya on a number of occasions, a war of words boiling over into military action several times. Both the USA and Britain maintained bases in Libya until 1967, when growing nationalism prompted the Libyan government to ask for the two foreign nations to withdraw. In 1969 the government (and King Idris) were overthrown by the young Colonel Khadaffi, a revolutionary nationalist and devout Muslim who was implacably opposed to Imperialism. Within two years of seizing power, Khadaffi had established links and military aid agreements with the USSR, and in 1972 nationalised British oil interests in the country.

In October 1973 Libya unilaterally expanded its territorial waters to latitude 32°30' N, enclosing the Gulf of Sidra (also known as the Gulf of Sirte). A USAF Hercules flying in the general area was inconclusively attacked by Libyan fighters shortly afterwards.

As he consolidated power,

Khadaffi became more active internationally, lending support to forces fighting against what he saw as Imperialism, from the PLO to the IRA (most of the rest of the world seeing this support as being tantamount to the state sponsorship of terrorism). As a convinced Pan Arab he was bitterly opposed to Egypt's rapprochement with Israel, and instigated a brief border war with Egypt in 1977 aiming to discourage peace initiatives. In 1980 Libyan-backed rebels operating from within Libya attacked neighbouring Tunisia. But Khadaffi was willing to confront the USA directly, and not just its client states.

Left: An A-6E Intruder of VMA-533 'Hawks' launches from the USS Saratoga, passing a parked VMAQ-2 'Playboys' EA-6B. Each of the three carriers involved in Operation 'El Dorado Canyon' carried a single squadron of A-6s, with a detachment of EA-6Bs.

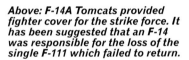

Above: F-14A Tomcats provided fighter cover for the strike force. It has been suggested that an F-14 was responsible for the loss of the single F-111 which failed to return.

The USA had never recognised Libya's unilateral extension of its territorial waters, and units from the Mediterranean-based Sixth Fleet regularly exercised in the Gulf of Sidra, ostensibly undertaking 'Freedom of Navigation' exercises, but also demonstrating America's military power and Libya's inability to prevent such manoeuvres. US Navy aircraft participating in such exercises frequently found themselves intercepting or being intercepted by a mix of Libyan fighters, from French-supplied Mirage F1s to Mikoyan MiG-25s. Rules of engagement were strict, and initially neither side fired upon the other.

FIRST KILLS

All that changed on 19 August 1981, when two F-14 Tomcats of

Below: Final preparations are made to an A-7E Corsair of VA-81 aboard the USS Saratoga. The aircraft carries a single fuel tank, two Rockeye cluster bombs and a single HARM missile, with two AIM-9s.

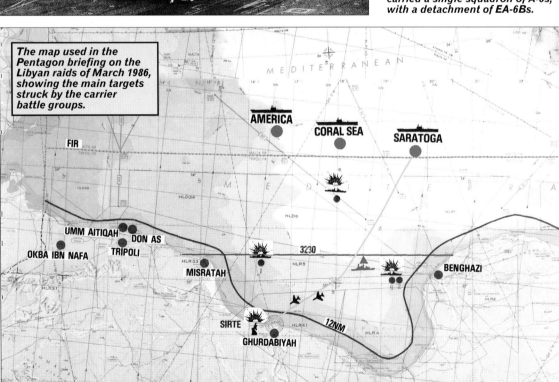

The map used in the Pentagon briefing on the Libyan raids of March 1986, showing the main targets struck by the carrier battle groups.

MEDITERRANEAN

FIR

AMERICA
CORAL SEA
SARATOGA

UMM AITIQAH
DON AS
OKBA IBN NAFA
TRIPOLI
MISRATAH
3230
BENGHAZI

SIRTE
12NM
GHURDABIYAH

The USAF in El Dorado Canyon

Many US military operations in the 1980s were planned to involve as many of the four armed services as possible, since none wanted to be left out and all wanted a share in the glory. This proved fatal in Operation 'Eagle Claw', when helicopter pilots were selected to involve the USMC, rather than for their suitability. El Dorado Canyon could have been undertaken solely by carrier-based aircraft, but the USAF ensured that it was not left out.

McDonnell Douglas KC-10A
Left: The flight of 24 F-111Fs (including six back-up aircraft which turned back after one inflight refuelling) and six EF-111As (one of which turned back) from Britain to Libya required massive tanker support. KC-10As from three units were involved.

Grumman/General Dynamics EF-111A Raven
Right: Six EF-111As from the 42nd Electronic Combat Squadron took off from RAF Upper Heyford fin England or Operation 'El Dorado Canyon'. Two were spares, one of which turned back after the first refuelling, while the other went all the way to the target. The EF-111As provided electronic warfare support for the F-111Fs, jamming Libyan air defence and SAM guidance radars.

General Dynamics F-111F
Left: Some 24 F-111Fs took off from Lakenheath for El Dorado Canyon, the six air spares dropping out as planned after the first refuelling over the Bay of Biscay. Unfortunately, five of the remaining 18 strike aircraft aborted before reaching their targets. Eight attacked Khadaffi's HQ at Al Aziziyah, and the barracks at Sidi Bilal, while the other five attacked Tripoli airport's military ramps.

VF-41, based aboard the USS *Nimitz*, were intercepted by a pair of Sukhoi Su-22 'Fitter-Js'. These non-radar fighter-bombers were occasionally used as fighters by the Libyans, and had been encountered carrying AA-2 'Atoll' IR-homing missiles, so did represent a threat, of sorts. As he manoeuvred to try to get on the tails of the Sukhois, one of the F-14 pilots thought he saw a missile being fired at him (perhaps a missile which failed to track, perhaps only an external fuel tank being jettisoned), and under the Rules of Engagement, this allowed him to fire back. Both of the Libyan fighters were despatched in short order, one pilot bailing out successfully.

PRAIRIE FIRE

Increasing Libyan support for terrorism (and especially for the PLO) prompted a 1985 Washington dec-

Left: A bombladen A-6E Intruder taxies forward onto the catapult. The A-6Es were capable of precision strikes, using their Norden AN/APQ-148 radars and AN/AAS-33 TRAM packages of EO sensors and laser designators.

laration that terrorist actions would meet with a strong military reaction, and it was made clear that Libya itself might be targeted. Khadaffi responded by declaring a 'Line of Death' across the Gulf of Sidra. This was an open invitation for the Sixth Fleet to conduct more 'Freedom of Navigation' exercises, and the carriers *Saratoga* and *America* (with *Coral Sea*) entered the Gulf of Sidra. This marked the start of Operation 'Prairie Fire', which was specifically aimed at drawing a Libyan reaction that would itself justify US military action. On 24 March 1986 Libya responded to the provocation by launching SA-5 SAMs at USN aircraft, and this in turn drew a response, with A-7Es from VA-83 attacking the SAM site with HARM missiles. When Libyan navy vessels threatened US Navy ships they were attacked, with a Combattante II patrol boat being

sunk by a pair of VA-34 Intruders, and with another patrol boat and a Nanuchka II Corvette falling victim

to more A-6Es that evening and the next day. Another patrol boat was sunk by the USS *Yorktown*.

A terrorist attack on a Berlin disco on 5 April 1986 killed a US soldier, and was thought to have had Libyan backing, and the USA decided to react more strongly, justifying its actions by its 'inherent right of self defence, recognised in Article 51 of the UN Charter'. Plans were made for a massive co-ordinated air attack by the USAF and the USN on Libya, aimed at Libyan military targets

Below: Lakenheath's F-111Fs attacked their targets with GBU-10 Paveway 907-kg (2,000-lb) laser-guided bombs. Each carried four of these weapons, designating targets with its underfuselage AN/AVQ-26 Pave Tack pod. The F-111s achieved superb accuracy, but there was heavy collateral damage.

Above: Il-76s at Tripoli airport seen through the AN/AVQ-26 Pave Tack laser designator of one of the attacking F-111Fs. Six Il-76s, a Boeing 737 and a G.222 were destroyed in the attack.

(including Khadaffi himself), and terrorist training facilities. Ironically, while the USA was launching what it liked to describe as a decisive blow against terrorism, it was itself conducting an arms-for-hostages deal with another sponsor of terrorism, Iran.

PREPARATIONS UNDERWAY

Boeing RC-135s based in Greece, augmented by Rota-based EA-3Bs and EP-3Es flew intensive Elint missions against Libya, while Cyprus-based TR-1As and SR-71s from RAF Mildenhall flew photo-reconnaissance missions over possible targets.

France and Spain were not prepared to allow aircraft involved in an attack on Libya to overfly their territory, but the participation of USAF F-111s based in Britain was felt to be essential, and a 8047-km (5,000-mile) round trip around France and Spain then through the Straits of Gibraltar and along the north-African coast by these aircraft was accepted willingly. This necessitated the provision of massive tanker support, and 32 KC-10A Extenders and 34 KC-135 Stratotankers were deployed to British bases!

On 15 April 1986, Operation 'El Dorado Canyon' was launched.

Above: Cluster bombs are wheeled out to waiting F/A-18A Hornets aboard the USS Coral Sea. CVW-13 embarked four instead of the usual two Hornet attack squadrons, including two Marines Corps units.

The 18 F-111Fs (plus six air-spares) of the 48th TFW took off from Lakenheath at about 18.30 BST (20:30 in Libya), at about the same time as three EF-111As (plus two air-spares) took off from Upper Heyford. With all of the designated attack aircraft fully-serviceable, the six spare F-111Fs, and one of the spare EF-111As, turned back after the first refuelling, over the Bay of Biscay. A small fleet of support aircraft, protected by a HVACAP of US Navy F-14s arrived on station at about 00:30 (local). These included an EC-135E from the 7th ACCS,

Above: F/A-18s from the Coral Sea used AGM-88A HARM missiles for defence suppression, and cluster bombs to attack vulnerable radar arrays. CVW-13's Hornet units were backed up by a medium attack-squadron with eight A-6E Intruders.

an E-3A of the 960th AWCS, E-2Cs from VAW-123 and VAW-127 and EA-3Bs from VQ-2.

Several of the USAF F-111s had started to experience problems, and by the time they reached Libya, five had been forced to abort. This left a group of eight aircraft (instead of the planned 12) to attack Khadaffi's headquarters at Al Aziziyah barracks, and the Sidi Bilal training camp. The remaining five (instead of the planned six) attacked the military area of Tripoli airport, destroying six Il-76s, a Boeing 737 and a G.222 on the ground. The F-111s attacked at high speed (400 kts +) and low level (61 m/200 ft), using their AN/AVQ-26 Pave Tack equipment to designate for their GBU-10 907-kg (2,000-lb) Paveway laser-guided bombs. One

Below: Pylons empty, an F-111F approaches a tanker on its long journey home. Poor serviceability detracted from the F-111Fs success, with five aircraft failing to attack their targets.

F-111F crashed into the sea on its egress, possibly shot down by a SAM or groudfire, or even by a US Navy F-14.

While the USAF attacked targets in the west of Libya, around Tripoli, the Navy took targets in the east, around Benghazi. Eight A-6Es from VA-196 (with a single EA-6B) aboard the USS *Coral Sea* attacked Benina airfield, supported by six F/A-18s from VFA-132 and

MCDONNELL DOUGLAS F/A-18A HORNET

USS *Coral Sea* (CV-43) arrived on station with the Sixth Fleet carrying an experimental Air Wing with no less than 48 F/A-18s in four squadrons. The F/A-18 was still very new, and the cruise was the aircraft's first. While a US carrier force gathered off Libya, Hornets flew Combat Air Patrols to protect their battle group from threat. Libyan interceptors came out to pry around and the F/A-18A pilots found themselves intercepting, challenging and escorting MiG-25s, Su-22s and Mirages. The Hornet proved versatile and dependable during subsequent combat operations and began what was to be a highly successful US Navy career.

Defence suppression mission
The Hornet made its combat debut carrying out the SEAD (Suppression of Enemy Air Defences) role, using its comprehensive onboard RHAWS equipment and AGM-88A HARM defence suppression weapons. F/A-18s participating in Operation 'Prairie Fire' used HARMs to knock out SA-5 SAM sites at Sirte. One month later, HARMs were used once again with devastating effect against Libyan air defence radars around Benina airfield during 'El Dorado Canyon'.

Markings
For operations aboard the *Coral Sea*, VMFA-314's normal 'VW' tailcode was replaced by the 'AK' tailcode normally allocated to CVW-13.

Hornet deployment
The two Navy Hornet squadrons, VFA-131 'Wildcats' and VFA-132 'Privateers' were augmented by two Marine Corps units; VMF(A)-314 'Black Knights' and VMFA-232 'Death Ratters' for combat operations over Libya. Although USMC F/A-18 squadrons are regularly deployed today aboard Navy carriers, in 1986 such deployments were rare.

The Tomcat draws blood

The USA has made extensive use of carrier-based aircraft to challenge and intimidate Libya when it has attempted to extend its territorial waters. Libyan and US Navy fighters have met over the Gulf of Sidra regularly, and on two separate occasions, in 1981 and 1989, pairs of Libyan fighters have been shot down by US Navy F-14 Tomcats. In both instances all participants were flying 'swing-wing' fighters: F-14s, Su-22s and MiG-23s.

Grumman F-14A Tomcat
Left: This F-14A of VF-41 (callsign 'Fast Eagle 107') was flown by Cdr Hank Kleeman in the 19 August 1981 engagement which resulted in the downing of two Libyan Su-22 'Fitters'. Kleeman himself downed one of the enemy aircraft, the other falling to an AIM-9 Sidewinder fired by his wingman, Lt Harry ('Music') Muczynski.

Mikoyan MiG-23MF 'Flogger-B'
Right: Two Libyan MiG-23s were shot down on 4 January 1989, after making what the US Navy claimed was a threatening approach. Images from the Tomcats' Television Camera System were released purporting to show that the aircraft were 'Flogger-Bs' armed with R-23 (AA-7 'Apex') semi-active radar-homing AAMs, whereas others maintained that they were 'Flogger-Es' with only close-in R-60 (AA-8 'Aphid') IR-homing AAMs.

Grumman F-14A Tomcat
Left: On 4 January 1989 two Libyan MiG-23s kept turning in towards two F-14s from VF-32 'Swordsmen' as the latter manoeuvred to get on the MiGs' tails. This was construed as hostile and Cdr. Joseph B.Connolly, flying the lead F-14, fired two AIM-7s and an AIM-9 to down the two enemy aircraft. The MiG pilots ejected, but were reportedly not rescued by Libyan SAR forces.

VMFA-323 and by six VA-46 and VA-72 A-7Es from the USS *America*, armed with HARM and Shrike missiles. Four MiG-23s, two Mi-8s and two F27s were destroyed at Benina, and many more aircraft were damaged. Six A-6Es from VA-34, and a single EA-6B from VAQ-135 aboard the *America* attacked Al Jamahiriyak Barracks. The A-6Es dropped conventional 227- and 340-kg (500- and 750-lb) dumb bombs.

MORE KILLS FOR THE F-14

The 1986 airstrikes did not resolve the situation between the USA and Libya. On 4 January 1989 two F-14s of VF-32, operating from the *John F. Kennedy*, (carrying out Freedom of Navigation operations in the Gulf of Sidra), felt threatened by a pair of Libyan MiG-23s. Rules of Engagement did not require the F-14s to be fired upon, and the Libyan fighters were shot down. By 1988, the USA was more concerned with Iran (attempting to deny the Persian Gulf to shipping), and the 1990 invasion of Kuwait elevated Saddam Hussein's Iraq to the status of 'Public Enemy No. 1', while the peace deal between Israel and the

Palestinians has dramatically reduced the impact of terrorism against US interests. But it would be premature to believe that the tension between Libya and the USA is over.

Below: Other Libyan aircraft regularly intercepted by US Navy fighters during the 1980s were MiG-25P 'Foxbat-As' and MiG-25PD 'Foxbat-Es'. Some were rumoured to have been flown by Soviet pilots.

Above: Libyan Su-20 and Su-22 'Fitters' are used for air-defence duties, as well as fulfilling their intended ground-attack role. Two were shot down by US Navy F-14As on 19 August 1981.

Right: One of 16 radar-equipped Mirage F1EDs delivered to Libya from January 1978, alongside 16 Mirage F1AD fighter bombers and six F1BD two-seat trainers. All are based at Okba ibn Nafa.

Gulf War: Desert Shield

AUGUST 1990-JANUARY 1991

The F-15C Eagles of the USAF's 1st Tactical Fighter Wing were the first warplanes to deploy to the Gulf, making a 17-hour flight with numerous air refuellings.

The Iraqi invasion of Kuwait in August 1990 was the culmination of a long dispute between two neighbouring but very different Arab states. Both were oil producers, but Iraq was a brutal dictatorship fielding the fourth-largest army in the world, while Kuwait was a more benign totalitarian state whose native population was outnumbered by resident Palestinians and guest workers drawn from all over the Arab and Muslim world.

After the conclusion of his war with Iran, Saddam Hussein turned his attention towards Kuwait. The ruler of Iraq accused the Kuwaitis of 'slant-drilling' oil wells from their own territory to steal oil from the Iraqi fields around Basra. This,

together with the allegation that Kuwait and the Saudis had kept oil prices low in order to hurt Iraq, provided the pretext for invasion. An unspoken, but probably very important, reason for military action was Iraq's lack of an unrestricted port on the Gulf, without which its trade would always be at the mercy of the Iranians or the members of the Gulf Co-operation Council.

Iraq began massing troops on the Kuwaiti border. April Glaspie, the American ambassador to Iraq, in a meeting two weeks before the invasion of Kuwait, informed Saddam Hussein that the USA had no interest in internal affairs of the Gulf region. Saddam took this to mean that there would be no oppo-

sition to his annexation of Kuwait.

On 2 August 1990, overwhelming Iraqi forces overran Kuwait. At a stroke, Saddam Hussein had seized control of the world's second-largest oil reserves, and threatened the world's largest, just over the border in Saudi Arabia. His troops immediately began a reign of terror, seizing anything valuable and shipping their ill-gotten gains back to Baghdad.

WORLD REACTION

The world community, led by the United States, immediately took action in response to this threat to vital oil resources. Large American air and naval forces together with elements of the 82nd Airborne Division were deployed to the Gulf in an operation called Desert

Shield, with the intention of defending the Saudi oil fields.

First into the breach, in a powerful display of the strategic mobility of air power, were 48 F-15C/D Eagles of the USAF's 1st Tactical Fighter Wing. Deploying from Langley Air Force Base on 7 August, less than a day after King Fahd of Saudi Arabia requested assistance, they flew armed and ready to fight their way in on the possibility that Saddam had not stopped at Kuwait. They were on the Kuwaiti border 16 hours later.

At the same time the USS *Dwight D. Eisenhower* entered the Red Sea, the first element of the most powerful carrier force ever deployed, which would include six carrier air wings by the time war broke out. B-52 bombers were

Left: A Tornado under guard. Given Saddam Hussein's 'grab' of Kuwait, an Iraqi march onward to Saudi oilfields and air bases looked imminent. The first members of the Coalition to arrive had little real security but protected their aircraft as well as they could.

Below: Kuwait's principal combat aircraft in 1990 was the Douglas A-4KU Skyhawk. Some of these, with their pilots, escaped the takeover of their country by Iraqi forces. Exiled, they became part of the forces of 'Free Kuwait', in the growing anti-Saddam coalition.

deployed to Diego Garcia in the Indian Ocean, and forces from other nations began to arrive in the region. These included a squadron of air defence Tornados from Britain's Royal Air Force deployed alongside similar Saudi machines, a Jaguar squadron in Oman, and the initial elements of France's rapid reaction force. By the end of August large numbers of US Marine F/A-18 Hornets and AV-8B Harriers were in-theatre. And for the first time, the Lockheed F-117 Nighthawk – the 'stealth fighter' – was openly committed to battle, the first 22 examples of the type arriving on 21st August.

American diplomatic pressure nudged the United Nations into action with unprecedented speed, resolutions being passed which demanded immediate Iraqi withdrawal and implementing economic sanctions against the aggressor.

In November, US President George Bush decided to double the size of American forces deployed to the Gulf. Along with contributions from other nations, including the United Kingdom, France, Egypt,

Syria and the Gulf states, the anti-Saddam Coalition now had more than enough power to defend Saudi Arabia from any threat. In fact, Coalition forces were now strong enough to undertake the expulsion of the Iraqis from Kuwait if necessary. Further United Nations resolutions gave Saddam Hussein until 15 January to get out of Kuwait; should he not do so, the Coalition was authorised to go to war.

IRAQ INTENDS TO STAY

Far from withdrawing, the Iraqis moved massive reinforcements into Kuwait, and began digging a formidable series of fortifications along the Kuwaiti/Saudi border. Media pundits talked knowledgeably about the Iraqi 'berms', or sand-walls, backed by anti-tank ditches and minefields, which with entrenched troops and large quantities of dug-in armour and artillery would make any frontal assault ruinously expensive in terms of human lives. But the war did not start on the ground, and the extensive Iraqi fortifications did them no good at all.

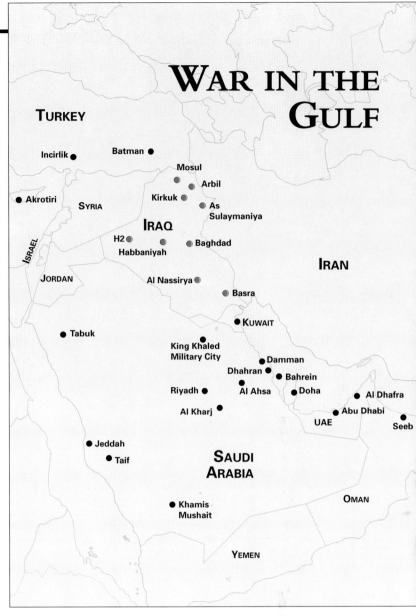

WAR IN THE GULF

Left: American troops poured into Saudi Arabia and the Gulf states. First on the scene was the US 82nd Airborne Division, which always keeps at least one battalion ready for instant rapid deployment. Soon, more troops with heavier equipment bulwarked the Coalition as war grew more likely.

Above: Oil-rich Kuwait was a tempting prize for Iraq's Saddam Hussein, who apparently expected to seize a neighbour's turf and get away with it. The Coalition allies' first task was to mount a defence of Saudi Arabia, and then to get the Iraqis out of Kuwait, by force if necessary.

Oil defenders

A US Air Force pilot stepped out of his F-15 Eagle in Dhahran after the 17-hour trip, looked around, and was relieved to see the airfield still in friendly hands. For tense days and weeks beginning in

August 1990, no one knew how long that situation would prevail, and F-15C Eagle and Tornado F.Mk 3 ADV (Air Defence Variant) interceptors flew patrols to keep Iraqi warplanes from crossing the line.

Victorious 'Spirit'
Left: 'Gulf Spirit' was the F-15C Eagle piloted by 33rd TFW wing commander Col Rick Parsons, who claimed two aerial victories when the buildup became a conflict. Crew chief on this Eagle was Staff Sergeant Craig Sniff.

Saudi ADV
Right: Saudi Arabia integrated its 24 Tornado F.Mk 3 ADV interceptors into the Coalition air defence network, which also included British ADVs. These aircraft scored no combat 'kills' once the shooting started, but a Saudi pilot in one of that country's F-15C Eagles got two victories on one mission.

Gulf War: Desert Storm

JANUARY 1991

On the night of 16/17 January, the skies of Baghdad lit up as Iraqi gunners blasted at targets they could not see. Explosions ripped through the night, as American F-117A 'stealth fighters' and BGM-109 Tomahawk cruise missiles hit with pinpoint accuracy at Iraqi command and communications targets. Operation Desert Shield had now become Operation Desert Storm.

The F-117 had not covered itself in glory on its first combat outing, over Panama in 1989, but any doubts about its utility were resolved in the Gulf, where the stealth fighter proved to be an outstanding success. Its unique facetted construction scattered radar energy away from enemy transmitters, making it next to impossible for defenders to get a radar 'fix'.

Its low observability meant that the F-117 could orbit in the general area of a target, giving its pilot plenty of time to locate targets with forward-looking and downward-looking infra-red sensors. With much less time pressure than in conventional aircraft, the pilot could also concentrate more on the delivery of its weapons. Over Baghdad the 'Black Jet' showed phenomenal accuracy, being able to deliver 907-kg (2,000-lb) GBU-24 laser guided bombs through doorways and down ventilation holes to destroy underground bunker.

In parallel with the knock-out blow against Saddam Hussein's ability to command his armies, the Coalition air forces also made a determined effort to obliterate Iraq's air defences, in order to deny the enemy the skies. American defence suppression aircraft, which included McDonnell Douglas F-4G 'Wild Weasels', F/A-18 Hornets, General Dynamics/Grumman EF-111 'Sparkvaarks', Grumman A-6 Intruders and EA-6 Prowlers, targetted Iraqi air defence radars and missile sites with powerful electronic jamming systems and HARM anti-radiation missiles.

Iraq's air facilities came under particularly heavy attack. Strike aircraft like the Anglo-French Jaguar, the F-16 Fighting Falcon and the F/A-18 Hornet mounted heavy raids with conventional bombs and cluster munitions against the major airfield complexes. British and Saudi Tornados used their JP233 runway-denial munitions against runways and taxiways, though thanks to their low-level tactics British losses were relatively high. However the real knock-out blows came when the allies attacked the Iraqis in their hangars.

Iraq made extensive use of the hardened aircraft shelter or HAS, based on those used in Europe at the end of the Cold War. Each

Above: It was the first war which started live on worldwide television. In Baghdad, journalists hunkered down in their hotel rooms and continued broadcasting while Iraqi anti-aircraft fire lit up the night skies. Some of the shooting was aimed at American F-117s and cruise missiles, but much of it was fired blind, and had no affect on the attackers.

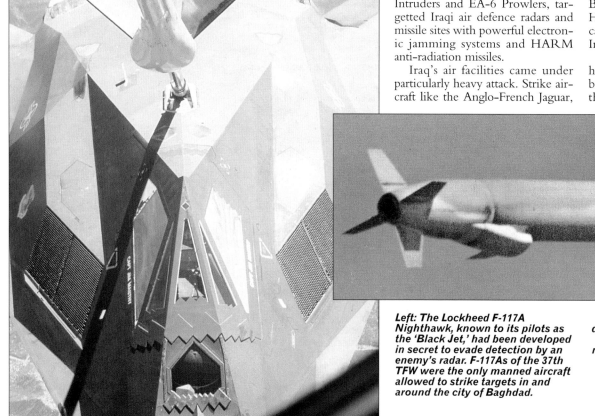

Left: The Lockheed F-117A Nighthawk, known to its pilots as the 'Black Jet,' had been developed in secret to evade detection by an enemy's radar. F-117As of the 37th TFW were the only manned aircraft allowed to strike targets in and around the city of Baghdad.

Above: Making its combat debut during Operation Desert Storm, the BGM-109 Tomahawk, originally a nuclear weapon, proved stunningly accurate with conventional warheads. Tomahawks were launched from warships, submarines and B-52 bombers.

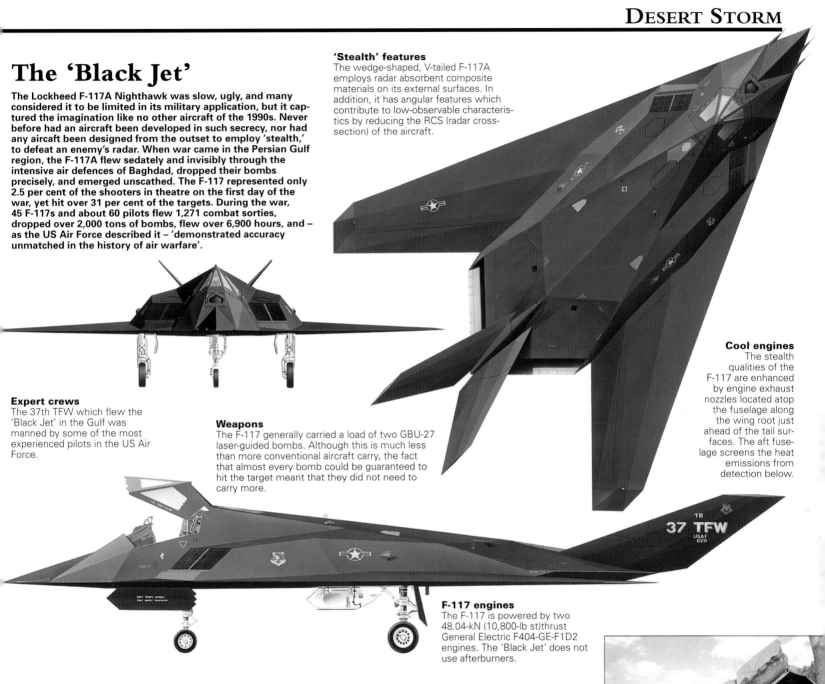

The 'Black Jet'

The Lockheed F-117A Nighthawk was slow, ugly, and many considered it to be limited in its military application, but it captured the imagination like no other aircraft of the 1990s. Never before had an aircraft been developed in such secrecy, nor had any aircaft been designed from the outset to employ 'stealth,' to defeat an enemy's radar. When war came in the Persian Gulf region, the F-117A flew sedately and invisibly through the intensive air defences of Baghdad, dropped their bombs precisely, and emerged unscathed. The F-117 represented only 2.5 per cent of the shooters in theatre on the first day of the war, yet hit over 31 per cent of the targets. During the war, 45 F-117s and about 60 pilots flew 1,271 combat sorties, dropped over 2,000 tons of bombs, flew over 6,900 hours, and – as the US Air Force described it – 'demonstrated accuracy unmatched in the history of air warfare'.

'Stealth' features
The wedge-shaped, V-tailed F-117A employs radar absorbent composite materials on its external surfaces. In addition, it has angular features which contribute to low-observable characteristics by reducing the RCS (radar cross-section) of the aircraft.

Cool engines
The stealth qualities of the F-117 are enhanced by engine exhaust nozzles located atop the fuselage along the wing root just ahead of the tail surfaces. The aft fuselage screens the heat emissions from detection below.

Expert crews
The 37th TFW which flew the 'Black Jet' in the Gulf was manned by some of the most experienced pilots in the US Air Force.

Weapons
The F-117 generally carried a load of two GBU-27 laser-guided bombs. Although this is much less than more conventional aircraft carry, the fact that almost every bomb could be guaranteed to hit the target meant that they did not need to carry more.

F-117 engines
The F-117 is powered by two 48.04-kN (10,800-lb st)thrust General Electric F404-GE-F1D2 engines. The 'Black Jet' does not use afterburners.

HAS was a strong concrete structure often covered with a thick layer of earth, and was intended to withstand almost any strike in less than nuclear strength.

But the safety they provided was illusory. No matter how tough a building is, it still needs large doors to allow aircraft in and out, and doors are a weakness. Coalition precision-guided weapons like the French AS.30L laser-guided missile were accurate enough to attack the doors directly. And the supposedly bomb-proof construction was also less effective in reality.

Coalition aircraft like the McDonnell Douglas F-15E and the F-111 dropped large numbers of laser-guided bombs onto Iraqi airfields. The 2,000-pound high-explosive GBU-24 was dropped onto taxiways and hard stands, to prevent Iraqi aircraft from being moved around. And the steel-cased GBU-27 was solid enough to penetrate the thick concrete of the

Right: Iraq's airfield hangars were heavily reinforced, but were nearly all above ground. Standard 907-kg (2,000-lb) bombs were more than capable of destroying most of these structures, but as the war progressed, the Coalition developed even more potent weapons to deal with high-value targets buried deep underground.

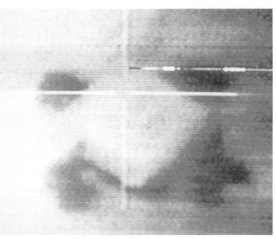

Right: The accuracy of precision-guided weapons is demonstrated in this strike on a building that hits exactly on the mark. A coalition spokesman said, with little exaggeration, that allied warplanes were able to 'put a bomb down an elevator shaft'.

Iraq's MiG threat

Iraq began the desert war with the world's fourth largest army and a formidable air arm that included Mirage F1s, MiG-23 'Floggers' and a small number of the spectacular, Soviet-built MiG-29 'Flanker' fighters (below) that were among the most agile and lethal warplanes in the world. But in spite of their great potential, the MiGs were never to prove a real threat. Iraq's command structure, communications system and air defence network were smashed by Coalition air power on the first night of the war, and the training and committment of the Iraqi air force's pilots proved inadequate when they mattered most, in combat.

Iraqi MiG-29
Above: The MiG-29 failed to up to its promise. At least four were shot down by F-15C Eagles and not one 'Fulcrum' pilot was able to seriously threaten a Coalition aircraft, let alone turn the tables and achieve an aerial victory.

hangar roofs before exploding within, destroying any aircraft inside.

Starting from the first night of the war, raids were repeated every night for weeks. The effect was obvious: in spite of a sortie rate of more than 2,000 missions per day, Coalition air losses were under one-tenth of one per cent.

But no aerial campaign against ground targets is ever completely effective, and the Iraqis still had fighters available. At the start of the war, the Iraqi air force had about 200 modern combat aircraft. These included two squadrons of Soviet-supplied MiG-29 'Fulcrums', one of the most agile fighters ever built. The Coalition could field 350 air superiority fighters, including McDonnell Douglas F-15C Eagles, Grumman F-14 Tomcats, Panavia Tornado ADVs and Dassault Mirage 2000s. On top of that there were also more than 500 dual-purpose fighter-bombers available, including General Dynamics F-16 Fighting Falcons and McDonnell Douglas F/A-18 Hornets.

The allies were superior to the Iraqis in numbers, control, quality and training. Thanks to the sophisticated, long-range radar and advanced command and control capabilities of the Boeing E-3 AWACS, Coalition pilots knew exactly what was going on in the skies over the war zone, which was much more than their opponents knew. When Iraqi pilots tried to make a fight of it, they were knocked out of the sky, primarily by the F-15 Eagles of the US Air Force.

At least 120 USAF Eagles partic-ipated in the Gulf War, together with four Saudi squadrons. Eagles scored 35 out of a total of 41 Coalition aerial victories in the Gulf, including the only two non-American kills – by an Eagle of the Royal Saudi Air Force's No.13 Squadron. The most successful unit was the 58th Tactical Fighter Squadron of the 33rd Tactical Fighter Wing, normally based at Eglin AFB in Florida, but operating out of Tabuk.

Eagles carry a variety of weaponry, including a Vulcan can-non and up to four AIM-9 Sidewinders. However, in spite of its long-standing reputation for unreliability, the majority of enemy aircraft destroyed in combat were brought down by AIM-7 Sparrow radar-guided missiles.

The result of all the attention by Coalition assets both on the ground and in the air meant that the Iraqi air force played very little part in the battle, and indeed a large proportion of its most modern aircraft was flown to internment in Iran to escape destruction.

Above: US Navy carrier air wings relied on the Grumman F-14 Tomcat for the air-to-air mission, and for defence of the fleet. They had no chance to test themselves against Iraqi fighters: unlike the Air Force's Eagles, the Tomcats were tied down on the escort mission and could not go hunting MiGs. One F-14 was shot down. Its back-seater, Lt Lawrence Slade of VF-103 became the only downed airman to be rescued from enemy territory during the war.

Left: Four French Dassault Mirage 2000C air defence fighters were among the first allied combat aircraft to reach the Gulf. They were on station at Al Ahsa, 370 km (230 miles) south of Kuwait, three months before the war started.

Eagles Triumphant

The F-15's domination of the Gulf air war is recalled by Captain Anthony Schiavi of the 58th TFS, USAF. On 26 January 1991 he was on the wing of Captain Rhory Draeger on patrol over western Iraq. After failing to intercept four Iraqi jets – they were too far away – they were warned by fighter controllers aloft in an AWACS radar plane of three more enemy fighters closer to hand

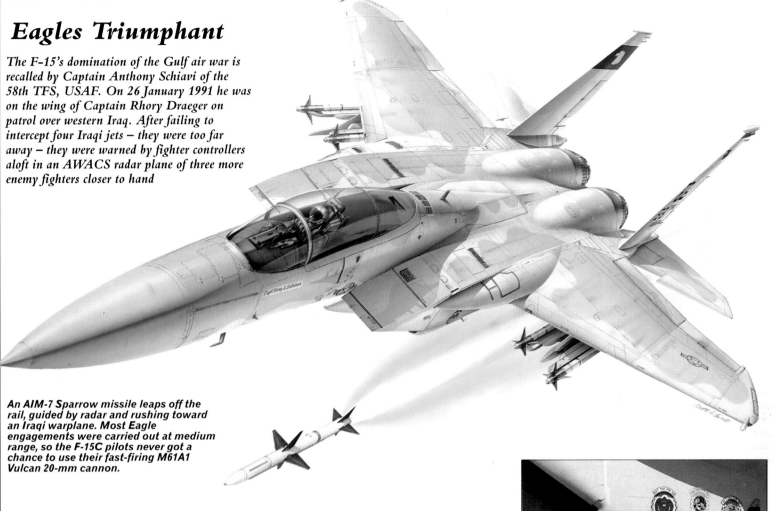

An AIM-7 Sparrow missile leaps off the rail, guided by radar and rushing toward an Iraqi warplane. Most Eagle engagements were carried out at medium range, so the F-15C pilots never got a chance to use their fast-firing M61A1 Vulcan 20-mm cannon.

"We'd been up on CAP for about an hour and a half, and had just gone down to a tanker to refuel. As we were coming off the tanker, AWACS called and said 'Hey, we've got Bandits taking off from H2, a whole group of them heading northeast.'"

The Eagles turned northeast to intercept. H2 was an airfield in the desert of western Iraq, not far from the borders with Jordan and Syria. It was too far from Iran for the Iraqis to be fleeing there for safety, so they were probably just moving from airfield to airfield, as they had been doing for several days in an attempt to avoid destruction. But they were more than 100 miles away, heading on the same course as the Eagles, and as the old saying goes, 'a tail chase is a long chase'.

"I'm thinking, 'There's no way we're going to catch these guys. We're starting to cut them off, but it's going to take a lot of a time and more gas than we've got.'"

The Eagles had closed the gap to about 130 km (80 miles), but were fast approaching the point where low fuel meant that they would have to turn back. Then four more Iraqi jets took off from H2, and this time the F-15s were ideally placed to bounce them. But Schiavi was worried. Could it be an Iraqi trap? There was only one way to find out.

To increase their manoeuvrability, the F-15s dropped their wing tanks, keeping only the centreline tank. Diving down from 7620 m (25,000 feet) they accelerated through the speed of sound. The American pilots could not see the ground or their targets through the overcast, so once they fired their missiles the best they could expect would have been a glow as they hit.

Captain Draeger locked on to the enemy leader. He knew that the other Iraqis were probably concentrating on keeping formation, not bothering much about navigation, and he was working on the well-tried tactic of 'kill the leader, and the rest will panic'. Schiavi took the fighter trailing to the northwest, leaving the remaining enemy to the other two Eagles. Schiavi's AIM-7 Sparrow missiles soon locked on, and he was ready to fire.

"We're now well inside 20 miles [32 km]. I see Captain Draeger's missile come off then I see it guiding. I shoot next, just a couple of seconds later. Because Bruce and Rico [Captain Bruce Till and Captain Cesar Rodriguez, flying the other two F-15s] are offset from us they have to wait a little longer."

As the Sparrows accelerated rapidly away, a big hole opened up in the weather. The Eagles dived through, and immediately sighted the enemy, three MiG-23 'Floggers' running fast and low across the desert.

"Captain Draeger's missile hits his man, which is so low that you can see dust kick up around it. He calls 'Splash'. Then he looks again: the airplane has flown right through the fireball and out the other side! He had been hit and is burning, but is not knocked out. Draeger goes to a heater [prepares to fire a heat-seeking Sidewinder missile], but before he can shoot the fire reaches the wingroot of the target and it suddenly explodes in a huge fireball. I'm so busy watching this guy blow up that I've almost forgotten my own missile.

Above: Capt Tony Schiavi of the 33rd TFW leans on the radome of an AIM-7 Sparrow medium-range radar-guided missile. The F-15C carrying the weapon is marked with the emblems of the wing's combat squadrons.

"After the first guy blows up, the other two do a hard right hand turn, right into us. Whether they've picked up a visual on us, I don't know, but what they are doing is too late. Right about then, my missile hits my guy. I call a second 'Splash' and there's another big fireball. Number four's missiles are maybe two seconds late, so number three – Captain Rodriguez – gets the third kill.

"There was a road right underneath them; I think they were navigating along it. The first guy blows up on one side, and the other two go down the other side, three fireballs in a row!"

This was to be a scene repeated every time Iraqi and American pilots met in battle. The combination of good pilots and a superb aeroplane proved to be a winner. There might be faster jets, there might be more manoeuvrable machines, but when it comes to the combat crunch, a well-handled F-15 is still the world's best fighter.

Gulf War: Strategic Campaign

JANUARY–FEBRUARY 1991

A heavily-laden Boeing B-52G Stratofortress lifts off the wintery runway of RAF Fairford in England, en route to contribute to the round-the-clock punishment being inflicted on Iraq's Republican Guard. B-52s also flew the longest combat missions in the history of warfare, when aircraft from Barksdale AFB, Louisiana were used to launch cruise missile attacks on key targets in Iraq and occupied Kuwait.

Air superiority makes it much simpler to win a ground offensive. Having smashed the Iraqi air defences on the ground and in the air, taking out the radar network and airfields with precision-guided munitions and airfield denial weapons, the Coalition could move on to other matters.

Iraq's ability to reinforce and resupply its troops became the target of a concentrated bombing campaign involving tactical fighters, all-weather strike fighters, fighter-bombers and giant B-52 bombers operating from bases as far apart as Lousiana, the United Kingdom and the island of Diego Garcia in the Indian Ocean. Power stations, command centres, communications systems and government buildings were struck on the first night of the war. Other important targets included nuclear and chemical

Below: Precision-guided munitions like these Paveway bombs aboard an F-111 dramatically enhanced the effectiveness of air-to-ground attacks. Although ten times more expensive than conventional bombs, they were far more than ten times as effective.

Right: The Boeing E-3 Sentry AWACS kept watch on activity by aircraft on both sides. Most air-to-air victories were made possible when alert AWACS crews told Coalition fighter pilots where the enemy was, where he was going, and how best to make an intercept.

Aardvark in action

Colonel Tom Lennon commanded the 66 F-111Fs of the 48th Tactical Fighter Wing deployed to Saudi Arabia for the Gulf War. With its range, speed, bombload, advanced night-flying capability and above all its highly effective Pave Tack target acquisition and designation system, the veteran F-111F proved to be one of the most important combat aircraft of the conflict.

"Initially we were tasked against the strategic targets, because of the size of the threat. This was the fourth largest army in the world. Airfields, command and control centers, chemical storage sites all had to be kept under control. We worked the strategic targets for the first 30 days of the war and then shifted over to softening up the battlefield, going against tanks and artillery.

"For me it was the first time I'd got to lead a large F-111 strike package. On the first night we had 54 aircraft leaving Taif, with six EF-111s as EW support. The target I selected was a large airfield north of Baghdad. To save fuel I'd planned to go about half way to Baghdad at medium altitude before dropping down, but about 30 miles [48 km] inside Iraq we started getting a lot of indications that people were looking at us and locking onto us, so we were forced to descend a lot earlier than planned. Going across the Euphrates you could see all the lights on, and the blink-blink of people shooting at us. About abeam of Baghdad we saw an aircraft, but it looked like he couldn't do a conversion on us. We were running at about 650 kt [1200 km/750 mph] on the TF (Terrain Following radar) at 200 ft [60 m], and we just accelerated on out. We swung north around Baghdad, heading west for our target area. I've never seen any defenses like it. The sky was red with triple-A.

"I was the first one in, aiming to drop a GBU-15 on a hangar. We came to release point, hit the pickle button and for some reason the bomb didn't come off. We went into our turn and came back but the triple-A, even though it was an unaimed barrage for the most part, tended to follow me - they were using the sound of the jet. We had three missiles launched at us just as we released the second weapon, which had to be negated.

"We ended up dropping back down to 200 ft on the TF, rolling out, hitting a tanker and coming back to our field, only to find it just like the UK, socked-in with fog! Tankers were scrambled and we stayed around until the sun opened up a little hole and we could start landing. Out of 53 aircraft launching that night, 26 of them got into Taif, the others having to divert to other bases for fuel. We got them home and still launched 40 aircraft that night.

"Two other missions stand out for me. One was where we had absolutely no defenses against us, and we took a five-ship in with four bombs each. We took out 20 aircraft shelters that night. The other one was when I was involved in the concept validation of dropping PGMs against tanks and armored vehicles, which we did the last 12 days of the war and at which we ended up being very, very successful - something like 920 tanks and armored vehicles.

"We used 500-lb (227-kg) GBU-12 laser-guided munitions against the tanks, but for other targets it was mostly 2,000-lb (907-kg) munitions. We also dropped a lot of mines, sub-munitions from CBU-89 dispensers, to keep people out of areas at, for instance, chemical storage areas or airfields. We did a little bit of 'Scud' hunting and were partially successful. It was very difficult to find the mobile launchers: the F-111F and Pave Tack is much better against fixed targets. If we could preplan our mission we'd have very high success rates: if it was a catch-can, we were not as successful."

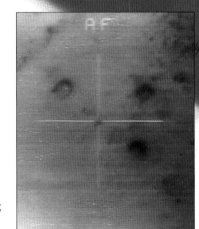

Above: Although primarily an interdiction platform, the F-111 proved to be a successful tank killer, picking up enemy armoured formations on its Pave Tack system and destroying vehicles with small laser-guided bombs.

weapons facilities, ammunition stores, military barracks, military manufacturing centres, weapons dumps, as well as railways, roads, and bridges. Command and control of the air offensive was provided by American and Saudi E-3 AWACS aircraft, while the new and still experimental J-STARS battlefield control system, mounted in Boeing E-8s, kept a close watch on enemy ground movements.

GUIDED MUNITIONS

One of the abiding images of the war is that of American guided bombs entering doorways and plunging down air shafts of strategic targets in Iraq. The accuracy demonstrated in those early attacks was confirmed in the campaign to destroy Iraq's communications network, when the majority of the road and rail bridges across the Tigris and Euphrates rivers were dropped in precision attacks. Weapons in use included Paveway laser-guided bombs, designed to home in on the reflected 'sparkle' of a laser beam held on the target by an airborne or ground-based Special Forces designator, and electro-optical bombs and missiles. These have infra-red TV sensors in their noses and can be computer-guided onto targets, whatever the light or weather.

The General Dynamics F-111F was among the most successful of all

Right: Two F-111F Aardvarks of Col Tom Lennon's 48th TFW in flight over the Middle East just before the Gulf War. The combat performance of the F-111F – probably the best of the war – was largely overlooked by the press.

Left: F-15E Strike Eagles and F-16C Fighting Falcons celebrate the end of the war with a joint sortie over oil field fires in newly liberated Kuwait.

Above: Iraq claimed that allied bombs were falling on schools, hospitals, even a children's milk factory. Only certain selected journalists were shown the rubble.

Coalition warplanes, although at the time its performance was overshadowed by other, more glamorous machines. Flown by the 48th Tactical Fighter Wing out of the Saudi base at Taif, the 'Aardvarks' went everywhere – even to the outskirts of Baghdad, which was otherwise reserved for F-117s and cruise missiles. F-111s destroyed bridges, airfields, radio transmitters, tanks, artillery, pumping stations and 'anything that would hold still long enough for us to put a bomb on it!'

In 2,500 sorties, the 66 F-111s deployed to the Gulf destroyed 2,203 targets, all claims being backed up by videotaped proof taken from the Pave Tack sensor carried by each of the big fighter-bombers. These including 252 artillery pieces, 245 hardened aircraft shelters, 13 runways and 12 bridges (with another 52 seriously damaged. More than 8,000 precision-guided munitions were dropped by the USAF during the war: F-111s accounted for 4,660 of them.

'SCUD' ATTACKS

On 18 January the Iraqis dramatically widened the scope of the war when they started firing extended-range 'Scud' surface-to-surface missiles at Israel and Saudi Arabia. Although of little consequence militarily, politically they were highly dangerous. Should Israel retaliate, the Arab members of the anti-Iraqi coalition might withdraw. Allied air forces were diverted into an all-out

Left: The two Boeing E-8A Joint STARS prototypes were rushed into use during Operation Desert Storm to direct fighter-bombers in attacks on Iraqi tanks and troop formations pinpointed by the E-8A's sophisticated belly-mounted radar system. Like the E-3 Sentry AWACS aircraft which directs aerial action, the ground-monitoring E-8A is based on the Boeing 707-320B airliner.

Panavia Tornado GR.Mk 1

'MiG Eater' was one of the most heavily used of the RAF's Tornado bombers. Based at Tabuk, in northwestern Saudi Arabia, it flew some 40 missions into hostile territory. The Tabuk force was led by No. 16 Squadron, but included elements of Nos 2, 9, 13, 14, 20 and 617 Squadrons.

Below: 'Sky Pirates' Buccaneer S.Mk 2Bs joined the fighting on 2 February 1991 and enhanced the accuracy of the Tornado strike force by designating targets for 'smart' bombs.

Sky Shadow
The ARI 23246/1 Sky Shadow electronic countermeasures system is an autonomous ECM pod which incorporates both active and passive electronic warfare systems, using an integral transmitter/receiver and a powerful signal processor.

Weapons
With all wing pylons occupied by pods or fuel tanks, the Tornado's offensive weaponry was carried almost exclusively under the fuselage. Weapons carried included bombs, JP233 airfield denial weapons, and ALARM missiles.

Performance
The Tornado's small, variable-geometry wing gives its two-man crew a very comfortable ride in most flight regimes, especially during the high-speed, low-level mission for which it was designed. The RB.199 engines are also optimised for low-level work: so much so, in fact, that when Tornados switched to medium-level bombing in the Gulf they had problems reaching altitude with a full load of bombs and tanks.

Radar warning
The tip of the Tornado's large tail houses a VHF communications aerial, with a pair of GEC-Marconi passive radar-warning receivers projecting fore and aft beneath.

Self-defence
Tornados, in common with most allied aircraft, were fitted with AIM-9L Sidewinders for self-defence against Iraqi air attack. Two missiles were carried, one on the inside of each inner wing pylon.

Guided munitions
This Tornado is depicted with a pair of British 454-kg (1,000-lb) bombs to which have been fitted Paveway II laser-guidance systems.

Radar
The Tornado's multi-mode, terrain-following, ground-mapping radar is its primary attack/navigation system. A chin-mounted sensor contains the windows for a Ferranti laser-range finder/marked target seeker, which enables the Tornado to drop LGBs onto designated targets.

Right: Saudi Arabia's Panavia Tornado IDS (Interdictor/Strike) aircraft flew alongside the RAF's similar GR.Mk 1 Tornados in low-level strikes on airfields and other strategic targets deep inside Iraq.

Carrier Strikers

The first aircraft carrier on the scene following Iraq's 1990 invasion of Kuwait was USS *Independence* (CV-62), followed by the USS *Dwight D. Eisenhower* (CVN-69). Both had been nearing the end of their cruises when Iraq invaded Kuwait, and both had been relieved by the time Desert Shield had become Desert Storm. Ultimately, the US Navy had six carrier battle groups in the war zone: The USS *Saratoga* (CV-60), *America* (CV-66), *John F. Kennedy* (CV-67) and *Theodore Roosevelt* (CVN-71) in the Red Sea, and the USS *Ranger* (CV-61) and *Midway* (CV-41) in the Persian Gulf itself. Navy carriers maintained continuous air operations on both sides of the Arabian peninsula. Although Iraq launched some attacks on Coalition vessels, none came near the carriers.

Above: Carrier air wings have their own tankers, but these proved too limited to handle the intense scale of operations in the Gulf, and Navy jets relied heavily on land-based tankers like this USAF KC-135.

Left: 'Ike' was within range of Iraqi missiles when it passed through the Suez Canal during the Desert Shield build-up, but its passage proved uneventful. The ability to position forces quickly in the region was the key to the allies' success when fighting began.

search for the missile-launchers.

Special Forces patrols were inserted deep into hostile territory by helicopter, to locate and occasionally destroy transporter-erector-launchers (although more often they would designate targets for allied strike aircraft. Reconnaissance aircraft like the RAF's infra-red-equipped Tornado GR.Mk 1A, quartered vast areas of desert looking for the elusive 'Scuds'. J-STARS aircraft looked for missile launchers on the move, while AWACs radar planes located the missiles after launch. Target data was passed to Coalition strike air-

craft, though one of the few systems capable of responding fast enough to trap a mobile launcher before it could move was the brand new F-15E Eagle. Receiving target information via datalink while on patrol over Iraq, the Eagle could be delivering weaponry on target within minutes.

CONTINUING THREAT

However, in spite of destroying a number of missile sites, the Coalition was never able to eliminate the 'Scud' threat completely. Defence against incoming 'Scuds' was the responsibility of the US

Army's Patriot missile batteries. Designed to take out aircraft, the Patriot's radars and computer software had been upgraded in an attempt to deal with tactical ballistic missiles. Never more than a temporary stop-gap, the Patriot system destroyed some incoming missiles in flight, but had nothing like the success claimed at the time.

At sea, aircraft from six of the US Navy's carrier battle groups played their part in the air war. In addition to conventional gun, bomb and rocket attacks, Grumman A-6 intruders made the first combat firings of the SLAM

missile. This is a variant of the Harpoon anti-ship weapon equipped with an imaging infra-red seeker head, designed to attack land targets in all weathers.

The threat offered by the Iraqi navy to the hundred-strong allied fleet in the Gulf was limited. Already in a poor state after the Iran-Iraq war, the Iraqis were in no position to challenge the carrier battle groups, battleships, cruisers, destroyers and frigates of the coalition navies. Nevertheless, on some occasions they did come out of port, led by TNC 45 fast patrol craft captured from Kuwait.

Multi-mission Hornet

With a position for a back-seater who provided an extra pair of eyes and ears, the McDonnell F/A-18D Hornet suddenly took on new missions, including battlefield surveillance and forward air control (FAC) duty. Two-seat Hornets do not operate from shipboard, but land-based F/A-18Ds flown by Marine pilots and observers

became, in effect, tools of the ground commander, who used them to keep tabs on Iraqi movements and to guide strike aircraft, artillery, and ground movements.

Versatile F/A-18D
This F/A-18D Hornet of VMFA(AW)-121 'Moonlighters' carries external fuel tanks and rocket pods, the latter being the ideal weapon in 'Fast FAC' work.

Defeating Saddam's Navy

The upper reaches of Persian Gulf was deemed too confining for aircraft carriers, but other Coalition ships plied the waterway despite an ever-present threat. Iraq's modest-sized navy included some missile-armed fast attack craft as well as several craft seized from Kuwait, that could have challenged the Coalition's frigates and destroyers.

However, Iraq had nothing to compare to the American Sikorsky

SH-60B Sea Hawk, the British Lynx HAS Mk 3, and other aircraft and helicopters. These gave extended range and versatility to the Coalition's warships, and destroyed or damaged most of Iraq's fleet.

Below: The ten Lynx helicopters that flew from HMS Gloucester and six other vessels in the Gulf used Sea Skua surface-skimming anti-ship missiles to engage fast-moving Iraqi patrol craft.

Above: An Exocet-armed TNC-45 fast attack craft. Iraq captured several of these missile boats when it occupied Kuwait, but never made effective use of them.

Below: An Iraqi patrol boat burns after being disabled by a hit from a Lynx-launched Sea Skua missile. This kind of hit left a vessel dead in the water even if it never sank.

The Iraqis did not do very well. Some were sunk by Royal Navy Lynx helicopters firing Sea Skua missiles. Others were destroyed by rockets, cluster munitions and gunfire from aircraft like the US Navy's A-6 Intruder and the Anglo-French Jaguar.

When they had had enough, many vessels tried to flee from Basra to Iran, but few managed to complete the trip. The only Iraqi success was the damaging of the assault ship USS *Tripoli* and the 'Aegis' class cruiser *Princeton* by mines, but coalition mine-countermeasures, which included US Navy MH-53 heli-

copters in adition to more conventional minesweepers and minehunters, managed to clear enough of the Gulf to allow the fleet to operate without further damage.

NEW WEAPONS

Modern weaponry was a vital ingredient in Coalition success with many advanced systems making their combat debuts from Day 1 of the conflict. The list includes Panavia Tornados with JP233 runway-cratering munitions, F-15E strike fighters, and the improved AV-8B Harrier II. Another missile making its combat debut was the

Tomahawk. The US Navy lifted the usual veil of secrecy that it keeps over submarine operations to announce that USS *Louisville* had successfully made a submerged launch of a Tomahawk against Iraqi targets from a position in the Red Sea. Less widely publicised was the fact that B-52s from Barksdale AFB in Louisiana attacked Iraqi targets with conventional warhead air-launched cruise missiles, in the process making by far the longest bombing raids in history.

Other weapons which had seen brief or unsuccessful outings in previous conflicts were used much

more extensively and with considerable success in the Gulf. These included McDonnell Douglas F/A-18 Hornets with HARM missiles, British Aerospace Sea Skua light anti-ship missiles, AH-64 Apache helicopters, A-10A Thunderbolt II tank-busters, and, above all, the US Air Force's F-117A 'stealth' fighter.

Below: The Grumman EA-6B Prowler was the nemesis of Iraqi air defense system. In 332 combat sorties, some 30 Navy and Marine Prowlers jammed, confused and confounded enemy radar transmitters, and attacked SAM sites with HARM missiles.

Gulf War: Winning the Ground War

FEBRUARY–MARCH 1991

The commander of Coalition forces, General Norman Schwartzkopf, called it "Preparing the battle-field". He knew that neither intense diplomatic efforts nor the condemnation of the United Nations were likely to persuade Iraq to leave Kuwait voluntarily. The problem would be decided by military action, and ultimately by battles on the ground.

The Coalition could call on some of the toughest and best-trained troops in the world, but the Iraqis promised to be a hard nut to crack. Possessed of the fourth largest army in the world, and equipped with large numbers of modern tanks and artillery, they needed to be softened up.

This is where air power was brought into play with such devastating effect. From the start of the shooting in January 1991, Iraq's invasion forces were subject to incessant attack. And by the end of

Above: The hard-fighting Fairchild A-10 Thunderbolt II, the 'Warthog' to its pilots, had a key role as the Coalition launched its ground offensive. The A-10 supported friendly troops, hunted 'Scud' sites, and stalked Iraqi vehicles on the 'Highway of Death'.

the month, as the interdiction campaign progressively smashed Iraq's air power, command and control networks, communications and industry, more and more Coalition air assets were free to be turned against Iraq's troops, artillery positions, rear supply centres, and lines of communication, destroying their effectiveness for the land battles to come.

CONSTANT ATTACK

Ground-attack fighters were in action day and night, pounding Iraqi troops, artillery positions, rear base areas and supply centres. Giant B-52 bombers unloaded thousands of tons of explosive on Iraq's best troops, the Republican Guard,

which was being held back as a mobile reserve. The army's communications with Baghdad were also primary targets, and coalition aircraft using laser- and TV-guided missiles destroyed many of which

Above: With 251 examples in the war zone, the F-16 Fighting Falcon was the most numerous 'shooter' in the Coalition's air arm. Dust, sand, and haze fouled the infra-red sensor pods employed by some F-16s, but their overall performance was good.

'Wild Weasel'

The F-4G Advanced Wild Weasel was the ultimate weapon against Iraqi SAM sites. The USAF deployed 35 of these modified Phantoms to the Gulf, flying hundreds of sorties with the loss of only one aircraft. The two-man crew of pilot and electronic warfare officer used the AN/APR-47 system to detect and seek out hostile radars. Part of the system was located in the nose, part in the rounded 'football' atop the fin. Using its 'black boxes', the F-4G found SAM sites, shut them down with HARM missile shots, enabling other warplanes to get through to their targets safely.

AGM-88 HARM

Developed by Texas Instruments, the AGM-88A HARM (High-speed Anti-Radiation Missile) had a 66-kg (146-lb) warhead designed to explode into 25,000 pre-formed fragments. The 360-kg (800-lb) missile 'locked on' to emissions from an Iraqi radar unit and homed in on it. At times, forcing the enemy to shut down his radar was as effective as achieving a 'kill' of a radar site.

Fighting F-4G
This F-4G Phantom II (69-7244) belongs to the 52nd TFW, Spangdahlem Air Base, Germany. The 52nd deployed aircraft like this to the Gulf where they became part of the 35th TFW (Provisional). They were painted in standard USAF tactical grey and carried 'mission markers' astride the engine air intakes.

Right: France's role in the Coalition was considerable, but one of the the Armée de l'Air's main combat aircraft could not play as active a part as its pilots might have liked. Dassault Mirage F.1 fighters were flown by the Iraqi air force as well as the French, and considerable effort had to be spent to keep the Allies from mistaking one for the other. Here, a Mirage F.1CR of Escadre de Reconnaissance 33 flies with a Sepecat Jaguar. The reconnaissance Mirages served as 'pathfinders' for the Jaguars, by virtue of their more comprehensive navigation equipment.

had survived the strategic campaign.

In spite of the pounding being received by his country, Saddam Hussein showed no signs of withdrawing from Kuwait. Allied air forces were destroying his armies, and artillery duels were being fought across the Saudi/ Kuwaiti frontier. The Multiple Launch Rocket System operated by the US and British armies was striking hard at Iraqi positions up to 30 km (18.5 miles) across the border. Specialist tank-killers like the AH-1 Cobra and AH-64 Apache helicopters, and the AV-8B Harrier, A-10 'Warthog' and SEPECAT Jaguar close support aircraft were hammering enemy front-line positions.

Clearly, the Coalition ground offensive was coming, but without aerial reconnaissance the Iraqis could not know when or where. And when the offensive steamroller did get into action, the survival of the Iraqi army in the face of overwhelming armour, artillery and tactical air superiority was to be measured in hours and days.

Before the allies moved into the ground war, the commanders wanted the Iraqi army to be at least half-destroyed. Armed with cluster bombs, rocket pods and laser or TV-guided missiles, the attack air-

Right: These Vought A-7E Corsair IIs of squadrons VA-46 'Clansmen' and VA-72 'Blue Tail Flies' aboard USS John F. Kennedy (CV-67) were fighting their final war. The Corsair made its combat debut in Vietnam, and was finally withdrawn from service on 23 May 1991, only weeks after the end of the Gulf War.

Above: Continuing a tradition from World War II, Coalition aircrew painted bomb silhouettes on their aircraft to 'count' successful combat missions. This B-52G Stratofortress has completed 24 missions, and has picked up a piece of non-regulation nose art in the process.

Right: The AV-8B Harrier II 'jump jet' operated from bases close to the front line, providing quick-reaction support to Marines on the ground. But with its jet pipes near the centre of the fuselage, it proved a little vulnerable to heat-seeking missiles, and four were lost to Iraqi SAMs.

craft were guided onto the target by forward air controllers in scout helicopters, or observers on the ground with laser designators. Apache helicopters also joined the attack.

The priority targets were the Republican Guard, the elite of the Iraqi army. Roving at will over the battlefield in the absence of Iraqi air opposition, the ground-attack aircraft hammered home their attacks on enemy troops already demoralised by weeks of round-the-clock bombing.

IRAQIS HELPLESS

The Iraqi forces could do little to interrupt the constant bombardment, as their battlefield air defence system had been reduced to limited numbers of missiles and obsolete gun systems. Although a small number of allied aircraft were shot down or damaged, the devastation of Iraq's army was complete.

When the Coalition moved, it moved fast. The assault burst upon the Iraqi army on 24 March. US Marine, US Army, Saudi, Kuwaiti, Egyptian, Syrian and other Arab forces poured into Kuwait through engineer-blasted gaps in the Iraqi

defences. Far to the west, American airborne and air assault troops in company with a French light armoured division were racing north through the Iraqi desert, heading for the Euphrates, with the aim of cutting off all Iraqi forces in the Kuwaiti theatre of operations.

In the centre came the main punch. The US Army's VII Corps, a heavily-armoured five-division force including the British 1st Armoured Division, drove along the Kuwait/Iraq border outflanking the main defence lines and engaged the Republican Guard. Iraqi troops, already demoralised by weeks of bombing, gave themselves up by the thousand.

Close support aircraft were one of the starring features of the land war. McDonnell Douglas AH-64 Apaches were involved in battle from the start of the war when they eliminated an air defence centre to allow tactical aircraft to launch their strikes into Iraq. In the quickening tempo of operations before the land war was launched, Apaches even managed to capture Iraqi ground troops, holding them under guns and missiles until larger helicopters

could come and transport the prisoners to the rear. The Apache's Hellfire missile system proved lethal to enemy tanks in the last days of the war.

Helicopters were everywhere in the Gulf. Apache and Cobra gunships tore out the heart of Iraqi armoured forces and proved dab hands at taking out bunkers.

Above: The Sikorsky UH-60 Black Hawk was the US Army's standard utility helicopter and greatly aided the mobility of Coalition ground forces. The Black Hawk was powered by two 1,261-kW (1,690 shp) General Electric T700-GE-700/701 turboshaft engines. Heat, sand and bad weather were a challenge to the UH-60, as they were to other aircraft, but it proved itself a tough and reliable combatant.

Ground attack

There was little glory or glamour in it, but pilots who flew air-to-ground missions had the riskiest job of the Desert Storm war. Even after the air campaign had weakened it, the Iraqi army was able to 'throw up a tremendous amount of flying metal,' as one pilot described the shells, bullets, and missiles that swirled upward from the ground. Even so, remarkably few ground attack aircraft were lost to ground fire.

Desert Jaguar
Right: SEPECAT Jaguar GR.Mk 1A (XZ364/Q) 'Sandman' was one of two RAF Jaguars that flew 47 missions during the Gulf War. Note the AIM-9L Sidewinder missiles on overwing pylons, carried for self-defense early in the fighting.

Marine Machine
Left: AV-8B Harrier II (Bu.no. 163668) of VMA-311 'Tomcats.' The squadron was home-ported at MCAS Yuma, Arizona but took up station during the conflict at King Abdul Aziz air base, later moving closer to the Kuwaiti border. Harriers in the Gulf carried a variety of weapons, including the 12 bombs and two Sidewinders shown.

Warrior 'Warthog'
Right: This Fairchild A-10 Thunderbolt II (80-0186), 'Tiger 1,' belonged to the wing commander of the 23rd TFW and was deployed to Saudi Arabia from England AFB, Louisiana. Under its inboard pylons, this 'Warthog' carries a pair of Hughes AGM-65A/B Maverick missiles. Note also the two bombs, ECM pod, and twin AIM-9 Sidewinder air-to-air missiles.

Apache Rampage

Colonel William Bryan commanded the AH-64s of the US Army's 2nd Battalion, 229th Aviation Regiment, attached to the 101st Airborne Division in the Gulf. The Apaches were a key feature in the initial Coalition attacks.

"The sector we were in was far to the west of the main Iraqi troop concentrations. It was lightly defended and lightly populated. We reached the Euphrates, about 50 km [31 miles] north of the division's forward base, that first day of the ground offensive.

"The Iraqis we did see realised that they were about to be bypassed, and they tried to run north. Once they saw the armed helicopters appear they would get out of their vehicles and take cover. We destroyed the vehicles.

"When we came across a convoy, one company would attack, one was about 30 km [18.5 miles] back in a holding area, and one 50 km [31 miles] back at the FARP [Forward Area Refueling Point] at the division's forward operating base. Each company would attack in turn, ensuring the enemy was being engaged continuously. If you really want to pile them all in, you can, but then there's going to be a break in the action when everybody goes back to re-arm and refuel.

"Companies normally operate in two teams. The light team of two Apaches will usually be the first to engage, then the heavy team of three or four helicopters-swill take up the fight.

"In Europe we were taught to mask, to use the terrain as cover from behind which we launch attacks. In the desert, you can't hide. It should have been extremely dangerous, since some of their anti-aircraft missile systems outranged us, but the Iraqis showed little or no desire to fight.

"Had the Iraqis been an armoured force we would have made stand-off attacks, but in this case we shot them with 30-mm cannon fire to get them stopped and the people dismounted. Then we fired three Hellfires, which took out the three lead vehicles. From that point we were able to finish them off with 30-mm and 2.75-inch [70-mm] high-explosive rockets.

Above: AH-64 Apache helicopters at a Forward Air Refueling Point, or FARP. As the 101st Airborne Division drove ahead, the Apaches stayed with the main ground force. One group of Iraqi soldiers actually surrendered to an AH-64.

"Our greatest concerns were the Iraqi shoulder-fired air-defense weapons. We could get around the long-range systems by flying low and letting the ground clutter mask our signature. But with the man-pack SAMs one person in a hole in the ground can take you out. We also knew that the enemy had over 5,000 armored vehicles, each with a heavy anti-aircraft machine-gun, and he had large numbers of 23-mm and 57-mm cannon. But as long as we stayed more than 3 km [just under 2 miles] away we were generally out of range. In any case we were usually flying at a height of 10 metres [33 feet] or less.

McDonnell Douglas AH-64A Apache

Developed as a 'state-of-the-art' anti-tank weapon during the Cold War, where it was intended to counter the threat of a massive Soviet armoured attack on Western Europe, the Apache is an immensely tough helicopter. Equipped with powerful weapons and advanced all-weather sensors, it devastated Iraqi vehicles and troops during the final phases of Operation Desert Storm. It proved surprisingly reliable for such a complex machine, in spite of the harsh desert operating conditions.

High-power helicopter
The Apache's two 1285-kW (1,723-shp) General Electric T700-GE-701 turboshaft engines drive a four-blade rotor with a diameter of 14.63-m (48 ft). The engine exhaust is via McDonnell Douglas's 'Black Hole' infra-red suppression system, consisting of nozzles which reduce the temperature of exhaust gases, reducing vulnerability to heat-seeking missiles.

Gun
The AH-64's fixed armament consists of one 30-mm M230E-1 Chain Gun automatic cannon. It is mounted in a hydraulically-operated turret which traverses 110 degrees either side of the centerline, with 11 degrees of elevation and 60 degrees of depression.

Missiles
Seen firing two 19-round pods of 70-mm (2.75-inc) Folding-Fin Aircraft Rockets or FFAR, this Apache also carries eight Hellfire laser-guided heavy anti-tank missiles.

Battlefield survival
The Apache was designed to withstand fire from weapons of up to 23-mm. Its structure is stressed to absorb and to withstand a vertical impact of 12.80-m (42 ft) per second.

General-purpose battlefield helicopters in use included Sikorsky UH-60 Black Hawks, Bell UH-1 'Hueys', British Lynxes, and French-built Gazelles. Heavy lift was provided by Boeing Helicopters CH-47 Chinooks, Sikorsky CH-53 Super Stallions, and Anglo-French Pumas and Super Pumas.

CLOSE SUPPORT

Fixed-wing close support was provided in the main by Air Force F-16s, A-10s and Marine Corps AV-8Bs. The A-10's huge gun and powerful weapons load ripped through Iraqi artillery and armour with ease: two A-10s established a record at the end of the war by destroying 35 tanks in a day. Other aircraft used for close support included British and French Jaguars, US Navy Hornets and Free Kuwaiti A-4 Skyhawks. Curiously, one of the most successful tank killers of the war was the long-range F-111, which had been heavily engaged on strategic missions in the early part of the battle. The big swing-wing bombers used small laser-guided bombs to 'plink' tanks to deadly effect.

Normally, one would expect

Left: US Marine Corps commanders are great believers in helicopter mobility. Four squadrons of Marine UH-1N Huey helicopters (foreground) were used to support troops in the field, while CH-53D/E Sea Stallion heavy lifters from six squadrons provided heavy logistics support from land bases and from amphibious vessels offshore.

Below: A Kuwaiti SA.342 Gazelle helicopter herds surrendered Iraqi soldiers into captivity. Once feared for their numbers and their supposed fighting prowess, the Iraqis wilted under relentless pounding by Coalition air power and quickly folded once the hard-hitting ground campaign began.

that with so much complicated machinery being used en masse under combat conditions for the first time, there would have been teething troubles. The astonishing thing about the war was the fact that most things worked as advertised, or even better than expected.

IRAQI FAILURE

On the other side, there was little to cheer about. The Iraqi air force hardly took to the skies, and its best aircraft fled ignominiously to internment in Iran well before the end of the war. The army's artillery included some of the best equipment in the world, but without air cover it proved a sitting duck to allied air power. Iraqi armour was present in huge numbers, and while most of its tanks were inferior to Coalition vehicles, they could have proved a major threat had they been used effectively. After all, the Germans beat the French in 1940 with smaller numbers of less well-protected and armed tanks than those of the French army. Unfortunately for Saddam Hussein his generals had no real grasp of modern mobile

Right: The business end of an open-jawed, angry-eyed Fairchild A-10 Thunderbolt II was a sight that repeatedly confronted Iraqi tanks, vehicles, and troops as the Coalition pressed ahead with the ground war.

warfare, and the armour proved no more effective in the face of overwhelming Coalition air power than had the Iraqi air force or navy.

Those who stood and fought were no match for the state-of-the-art armour fielded by the powerful Coalition forces. The final impetus to surrender came when the close support aircraft brought the battle to a close by annihilating the massive Iraqi column fleeing from Kuwait along the Basra road. In under 100 hours, the half-million strong Iraqi force in Kuwait and southern Iraq was finished, and Kuwait could be liberated.

Right: US Secretary of Defense Richard Cheney was stating the obvious when he pointed out that the collapsing Iraqi army was performing the 'mother of all retreats'. The moving target imagery from a J-STARS aircraft shows the routes followed by Saddam Hussein's forces as they withdrew from Kuwait – routes that were to become a killing ground.

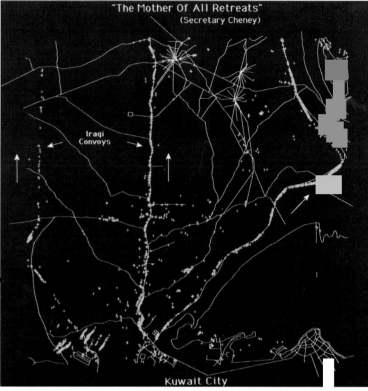

"The Mother Of All Retreats"
(Secretary Cheney)

Iraqi Convoys

Kuwait City

After the Storm

In large measure, the end of the Persian Gulf war signalled a new era for military affairs and for air warfare. There was now a 'New World Order', said US President George Bush in 1991.

Western nations would increasingly find themselves in smaller, shorter wars, with more elusive enemies – not merely Third World tyrants but rebels, renegades, and terrorists. Special operations forces might become more important than strategic bombers. Instead of practising the delivery of nuclear warheads, air forces would rehearse unconventional fighting deep into potentially hostile territory. Typical of the new kind of military endeavour was Operation Provide Comfort, begun in April 1991 and continued by the USA, Britain and other allies until December 1996. A Combined Task Force was assembled to enforce the 'no-fly' zone in northern Iraq (above the 36th Parallel) and to support Coalition humanitarian relief operations in the region, in particular providing protection, foods and medicine to the Kurdish settlements that had been a focus of repression by the Iraqi regime.

The air effort to police the Desert Storm truce included helicopter missions hauling food to the Kurds, reconnaissance and surveillance flights, and combat air patrols. Almost immediately, it became clear that Iraq might challenge the results of the hard-fought war. For example, the first 'postwar' aerial victory came on 20 March 1991 when an Iraqi Sukhoi Su-22 'Fitter' was shot down by 36th TFW F-15C Eagle pilot Captain Thomas N. Dietz. Two days later, another F-15C downed an Su-22. An accompanying Iraqi Pilatus PC-7 prop-driven trainer was taken under attack but its pilot bailed out before a shot was fired, creating a weaponless 'kill.'

OPERATION SOUTHERN WATCH

A similar 'no-fly' zone was established in August 1992, south of the 32nd Parallel. Operation Southern Watch was set up to monitor UN Security Council Resolution 688, calling for Saddam Husssein to cease air and ground attacks on insurgents in south east Iraq.

The Iraqis began challenging the zone late in 1992, and a US F-16 shot down an intruding MiG-23. In January 1993, Southern Watch aircraft attacked Iraqi air defence sites, and US Navy missiles destroyed the Zaafaraniyah nuclear fabrication facility.

Above: The Union Jack emblazoned on its tail, an RAF Chinook HC.Mk 1 helicopter puts in heavy lifting duty during humanitarian relief operations in the northern part of Iraq, where Kurdish opposition groups suffered under Saddam Hussein's tyranny.

In October 1994, Operation Vigilant Warrior saw coalition troops deploy to Kuwait and the Gulf States in response to aggressive Iraqi troop movements in southern Iraq. Operation Vigilant Sentinel a year later followed the same pattern. Meanwhile, as Operation Desert Storm receded, other conflicts around the world demonstrated that times had indeed changed, that air power would now face a new era, and that training, tactics, and technology would become more important than ever.

AFRICA

As with many of the wars in Asia, much of the conflict in Africa since 1945 has been associated with the withdrawal of the European imperial powers from their colonies. But the liberation struggles of the 1950s and 1960s did not bring the rewards of peace so many had hoped for, with the first generation of African leaders often proving to be despots of the worst order. Bloody internal struggles – often driven by religious or tribal rivalries – have continued all over the continent into the 1990s. The relatively peaceful transition to majority rule in South Africa, where diplomacy has replaced active-military intervention in neighbouring states, is a sign of hope, however. But there is still a long way to go.

Kenya

1951-1955

Left: Avro Lincoln heavy bombers were used extensively against the Mau Mau. The Lincolns operated from November 1953 to July 1955, bombing Mau Mau concentrations in the Aberdare mountains and around Mount Kenya.

Below: A detachment of Vampire FB.Mk 9 ground attack jets was deployed from Aden to Kenya in April 1954. The aircraft supported Operation Anvil, a major sweep in and around Nairobi which led to the detention of more than 16,000 suspected Mau Mau supporters.

At the end of World War II more than 85 per cent of Africa was distributed between the empires of the UK, France, Belgium and Portugal, or about to be administered by these nations under United Nations trusteeship. Within 30 years the entire continent, comprising almost 50 states, had divested itself of the trappings of colonial rule and was to a great extent independent of its traditional imperial parents. A more insidious style of imperial domination emerged, based on the strategic interests and embracing the world ambitions of the superpowers, the Soviet Union, the United States and communist China. But in varying degrees (depending on the relations that existed at the time of independence) many emergent states opted to retain defence agreements with their former colonial parents in exchange for economic and cultural aid.

In Kenya, a British crown colony since 1920, Jomo Kenyatta, British-educated president of the Kenya African Union and a long-standing nationalist, was arrested on charges of inciting an uprising in the Kikuyu tribal area in 1952. His removal did not end the rebellion and the British authorities declared an emergency, detained suspected leaders, organised Kikuyu loyalists and isolated the rebels in the forests. Between 1952 and 1955 11,000 casualties were inflicted for the loss of 95 white lives. Initial involvement by air forces began in April 1953 when 12 North American Harvard trainers were flown up from Rhodesia to operate as light ground-attack aircraft; within a year these had flown 2,000 sorties, fired 750,000 rounds of 7.7-mm (0.303-in) ammunition and dropped 15,000 8.6-kg (19-lb) fragmentation bombs. In November 1953 Avro Lincoln heavy bombers of No. 49 (Bomber) Squadron arrived at Eastleigh on a three-month detachment from the UK, being relieved in turn by Lincolns of Nos 110 and 214 Squadrons during 1954. Middle East Air Force sent a small number of de Havilland Vampires and photo-reconnaissance Gloster Meteors, while support of the ground forces was undertaken by Vickers Valettas, Hunting Pembrokes, Auster AOPs and Bristol Sycamore helicopters. The use of aircraft proved decisive in quelling the rebellion, which ended in 1955, but the uprising by the Mau Mau (the Kikuyu secret society involved) demonstrated the inadequacy of colonial political structures, and Kenya was to become independent within the British Commonwealth eight years later, and a republic in 1965.

Above: The Mau Mau was a secret Kikuyu rebel group, poorly armed and equipped. But they knew the country, and it was hard for ground troops to catch them. The use of air power was something the rebels could not deal with, however.

Right: It was difficult for the authorities to gather information about Mau Mau movements or to gauge the effect of air strikes. To help in the process, a detachment of photo-reconnaissance Meteors was sent to Kenya in August 1954.

Anti-Mau Mau Lincoln strike

Foreshadowing America's use of B-52s in Vietnam more than a decade later, the Royal Air Force's Lincoln bombers were used to mount pattern bombing attacks on suspected Mau Mau hideouts in the heavily-forested highlands of Kenya. A typical Lincoln load consisted of five 454-kg (1,000-lb) bombs and up to nine 227-kg (500-lb) bombs or 159-kg (350-lb) cluster bombs, with attacks often flown at low level because of low tropical clouds.

Avro Lincoln B.Mk II

Left: A long-range evolution of the classic World War II Lancaster, the Lincoln was swiftly rendered obsolete by the rapid postwar development of jet bombers. Powered by four Rolls-Royce Merlin piston engines, the Lincoln could carry a six-tonne bomb load over a combat radius of 2500 km (1,500 miles) at a maximum speed of 475 km/h (295 mph).

Algeria
1954–1962

North American T-6Gs played an important light-attack role during France's involvement in Algeria. Some 700 were delivered to the escadrilles d'aviation légère d'appui (light-attack squadrons) in Algeria. They equipped 38 squadrons, with a peak total of 21 squadrons active within Groupe d'Aviation Légère d'Appui 72. They were armed with two 7.5-mm (0.3-in) gun pods, napalm, 10-kg (22-lb) bombs or rockets.

Above: The vulnerability of the T-6G to ground fire led to the introduction of the North American T-28 Trojan and the Douglas AD-4N Skyraider. The Skyraiders equipped the three squadrons of Escadre de Chasse 20, and were redeployed to French Somalia (now Djibouti) and Madagascar after the withdrawal.

Below: Escadre de Chasse 6 used the Sud Est Mistral (the Nene-engined French-built Vampire) until the unit withdrew from Algeria in December 1960. Several other units in Algeria also used the Mistral, operating primarily in the air-defence and ground-attack roles.

oming within months of the humiliating defeat in Indochina, the rebellion in Algeria – a state that was closer to being a *département* of metropolitan France than a colony – carried profound portents. Only the authoritarian grasp of President Charles de Gaulle, to whom that nation turned for leadership in 1958, prevented the horror of open revolution at home from becoming a reality.

As in Indochina, the armed Algerian nationalists – the Front de Libération Nationale – possessed no air arm but, having intimate familiarity with the local terrain, preferred to conduct guerrilla

Below: The Douglas B-26 Invader equipped four bomber escadrilles (one a dedicated night-attack unit) in Algeria, with a fourth unit operating in the recce role. The bombers served until 1962, and the recce aircraft left in December 1963.

War against the FLN

Algeria was actually part of metropolitan France, and the French government had to contend with both Muslim separatists (who wanted independence), and a significant European population who were prepared to fight for the status quo, and who mounted an abortive coup and a campaign of terrorism when de Gaulle 'sold out'.

de Havilland Mosquito
Among the aircraft stationed in North Africa at the end of the war were the Mosquitoes of GC 19 'Gascogne', but they were transferred to Indochina in 1949 before the troubles in Algeria became serious.

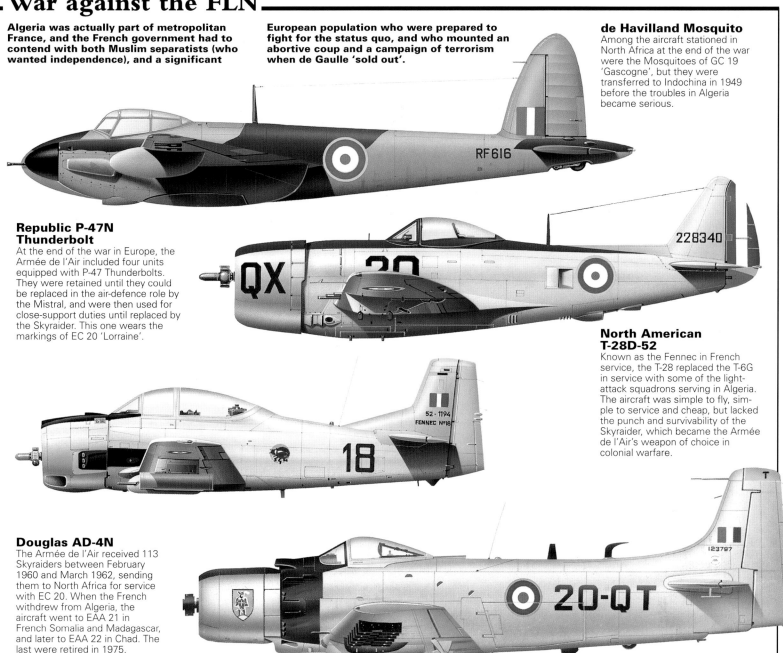

Republic P-47N Thunderbolt
At the end of the war in Europe, the Armée de l'Air included four units equipped with P-47 Thunderbolts. They were retained until they could be replaced in the air-defence role by the Mistral, and were then used for close-support duties until replaced by the Skyraider. This one wears the markings of EC 20 'Lorraine'.

North American T-28D-52
Known as the Fennec in French service, the T-28 replaced the T-6G in service with some of the light-attack squadrons serving in Algeria. The aircraft was simple to fly, simple to service and cheap, but lacked the punch and survivability of the Skyraider, which became the Armée de l'Air's weapon of choice in colonial warfare.

Douglas AD-4N
The Armée de l'Air received 113 Skyraiders between February 1960 and March 1962, sending them to North Africa for service with EC 20. When the French withdrew from Algeria, the aircraft went to EAA 21 in French Somalia and Madagascar, and later to EAA 22 in Chad. The last were retired in 1975.

warfare. Despite the commitment of almost one million troops against them, they proved not only highly proficient but eventually persuaded France that, once again, no military solution was attainable. And in 1962, despite everything that sophisticated weaponry could achieve, Algeria won its independence

Below: The SIPA 111A was a French-built Arado 396, and was known as the S.10, S.11, S.111 or S.12 in French service. Three squadrons saw service in Algeria during the mid-1950s.

under the erstwhile nationalist leader Ahmed Ben Bella.

At the beginning of the war in November 1954 the French air force in Algeria comprised a squadron of S.E.535 Mistral jet interceptors (licence-built Vampires) and a training squadron flying aged F-47 Thunderbolts, as well as a hotch-potch of obsolete second-line aircraft and trainers. None of these aircraft was in any way suitable for operations in the desert against fleet, mobile guerrilla forces whose tactics were based on

lightning strikes and instant dispersal.

SMALL COINs

As a matter of expediency, therefore, the local French commanders ordered a host of light aircraft and trainers into operational use, hurriedly modified with machine-guns and light bomb racks. Quite fortuitously, they had hit upon an ideal counter-insurgency weapon and one that was to sire a whole new

Above: The Dassault Flamant was a common sight in Algeria, for not only was it the Armée de l'Air's standard light transport and liaison aircraft, but some served in the bomber and navigation training roles. This aircraft was a six-seat MD312 transport.

operational philosophy employing dedicated COIN aircraft. Such aircraft as the North American T-6 Texan became synonymous with the world's mounting problem of anti-guerrilla operations.

Observation and recce

The Armée de l'Air has used a variety of aircraft types in the observation and light reconnaissance roles. Such aircraft played a vital role in Algeria, helping ground forces to react quickly to incursions and terrorist incidents, and helping to patrol Algeria's least populated areas. With an absence of enemy air opposition, such aircraft could also fulfil a limited close-support role.

Morane MS.500

The French aviation industry was reduced to little more than a branch of the German industry during the long years of occupation of World War II, producing sub-assemblies and even whole aircraft of German design. The Fieseler Storch was built for the Luftwaffe, and remained in production after the war as the Morane-Saulnier MS.500 and 502 Criquet (with a Salmson radial engine). Substantial numbers were supplied to the Armée de l'Air and some served in Algeria.

Thus, in 1955, as the regular squadrons of conventional fighters retained their normal air defence tasks, the first escadrilles d'aviation légère d'appui (EALA, or light support squadrons) equipped with Morane-Saulnier MS.500s and 733s became operational. The following year they were joined by a groupe, GALA 72, of four escadrilles with T-6 Texans, and three of SIPA S.111s and 112s (the latter distributed between Tunisia, Morocco and Algeria).

More significant was the introduction of the Max Holste Broussard, the first aircraft formally customised for the counter-insurgency role and capable of lifting small numbers of troops to remote areas of local trouble. Following de Gaulle's resumption of command of the state in 1958, General Maurice Challe was given the task of crushing the Algerian rebellion and undertook a complete overhaul and reorganisation of the air force. One of his first priorities was to replace the excellent but

Above: Between 1959 and 1961 EC 1/3 operated its F-100Ds on bombing raids over Algeria, though the aircraft operated from their Rheims base, refuelling at Istres in the south of France on their return journeys. The F-100's primary role was one of nuclear strike.

Above: A white cabin top and upper centre section were added to Broussards in Algeria to reduce cabin and fuel-tank temperatures. The type performed liaison and observation duties in Algeria, supplanting aircraft like the MS.500.

aged T-6s which had hitherto flown the majority of operations against the rebel forces. An adaptation of the T-28 Trojan, itself a modern derivative of the T-6, was selected (being named the Fennec in French service).

CROSSHEAD PLEASE

Major weapon in the counter-insurgency arsenal was the heli-copter, the Armée de l'Air having formed its first light helicopter squadron in Algeria in 1955 with Bell 47Gs and Sikorsky H-19s (S-55s). Pioneer operations by this escadrille had quickly demonstrated the flexibility of the helicopter, as much for casualty evacuation as delivery of troops into combat, and by the end of 1956 the 12-man Sikorsky H-34 was in service in the assault role. Within a year the French forces in Algeria possessed a total of 250 helicopters, of which the army flew 139, the Armée de l'Air 90 and the Aéronavale 18. In due course the French gave some of their helicopters a 'ground-attack' capability by mounting guns of 7.5-mm (0.3-in), 12.7-mm (0.5-in) and 20-mm (0.8-in) calibre, as well as

rockets. Among the army helicopters were such troop-carrying aircraft as the Vertol-Piasecki H-21.

INCREASED COMMITMENT

As the war dragged on, and the rebel forces (far from acknowledging defeat) stepped up their operations, so the French brought greater pressure to bear in Algeria, not least in the air. Two medium-attack bomber groups with B-26 Invaders were deployed in Algeria, together with a growing number of ex-US Navy AD-4 Skyraiders (of which France had ordered 113 from the USA in 1956).

The latter proved to be a highly-effective COIN aircraft, capable of delivering a very heavy punch in the ground-attack role and suppressing ground opposition during helicopter assaults.

Effective as Challe's 'steamroller' campaign was — forcing the rebels to revert to isolated guerrilla tactics by the end of 1960 — the mounting

Left: Probably the most important transport aircraft flying resupply missions to French forces in Algeria was the Nord 2501 Noratlas. Some 426 were built, in France and Germany, and the type was widely exported. It equipped two escadres des transports, with three escadrons being based in North Africa.

Below: T-28 Trojans, called Fennec in French service, replaced T-6Gs in the close air support and COIN roles, but were themselves soon replaced by AD-4N Skyraiders.

Right: France received 135 Sikorsky H-34s built in the United States, and 130 built by Sud Aviation. The type served with GMH 57 in Algeria, and with six Algeria-based escadrilles of EH 22 and EH 23 and their forerunners. The H-34 proved to be the most successful of the French helicopters deployed in Algeria.

Below: Piasecki (Vertol) H-21s were used by both the Aéronavale and the Aviation Légère de l'Armée de Terre in Algeria. This H-21C wears the markings of GH 2, which was based at Sétif during early-1962.

Below: Probably the most effective of all the ground-attack aircraft that were used by the French air force was the ex-United States Navy Douglas AD-4N Skyraider. Large numbers served with the escadrons de chasse (fighter squadrons).

cost of the war and the depradations imposed on French society by increasing terrorist activities in metropolitan France combined to sap the enthusiasm for an apparently fruitless continuation of the war. In 1962 de Gaulle was forced to accept terms for Algerian independence.

Militarily, whatever else the war in Algeria demonstrated, it illustrated the impotence of a conventional air force, equipped and organised for air defence, when it tried to operate in an environment of concerted guerrilla warfare. The lessons were there for the US to digest when, just two years later, it faced a similar threat in Vietnam. Ironically, it took 10 years for the United States to arrive at no less a humiliating political defeat than the French had suffered in Algeria.

Helicopters in support

The war in Algeria probably cost one million lives, including 17,456 French servicemen. It also provoked massive political unrest in France, and damaged France's reputation overseas. But, at the same time, the war provided an excellent training ground for the French armed forces, which operated with great flexibility and with a high degree of inter-service co-operation. Nowhere was this more apparent than in the use of helicopters, aircraft from all three services being jointly tasked to perform troop transport, assault, observation and liaison duties.

Sikorsky S-55
The Sikorsky S-55 (sometimes referred to by the US military designation H-19) was used by all three services in Algeria, giving way to the H-34 in Armée de l'Air service, and to the HSS-1 in Aéronavale squadrons. ALAT H-19s remained active until the end of the war in Algeria.

Piasecki (Vertol) H-21C
The H-21C saw service with the ALAT's GH 2, and also with the Aéronavale's Flottille 31F. The aircraft's ungainly appearance belied its effectiveness, the aircraft proving able to transport 20 fully-armed troops.

Central Africa

1960-1997

Left: To see Swedish warplanes in action outside Swedish airspace is an extremely rare occurrence, but the Congo emergency of the 1960s saw Saab J29 fighters flying support missions for UN troops on the ground.

Below: Also forming part of the United Nations force, the Indian contingent was centred on a detachment of English Electric Canberra bombers, which often flew missions alongside the Swedish fighters.

Bottom: Flygflottij 22 was a volunteer unit, flying both fighter bomber and reconnaissance versions of the barrel-like J29. The photo-ships wore camouflage, while the standard combat aircraft were overall natural metal.

Belgium had for many years adopted a much more exploitative attitude than the other European colonial powers in Africa. When native peoples in British and French territories started campaigning for self-determination, Belgium hoped to prevent such demands spreading to the Congo. It quickly became obvious that such hopes would prove vain, and Belgium reversed its policy overnight and offered immediate political independence in 1960. Civil war of a tribalist nature broke out almost immediately and continued intermittently for seven years. During this period, numerous acts of atrocity were carried out against Belgian nationals who had chosen to remain in the former colony.

The immediate threat to peaceful transition to independence was posed when Moise Tshombe led a movement for the separation of the Katanga region from Kinshasa, and when the United Nations charter was invoked to provide a peacekeeping force there were immediate difficulties in selecting forces from member nations that had no colonialist connotations and were thus acceptable in an area seething with violently anti-imperialist hatred.

In due course Sweden, Canada, India and Ethiopia contributed air force elements, of which Sweden's Flygflottij 22 Voluntary Air Component with Saab J29s provided the most significant part, together with a number of de Havilland Canada Otters and de Havilland Canada Beavers; ground crews were also provided by Norway and Denmark. A particularly remarkable aspect of F22's contribution was the fact that the Swedish air force was not equipped, organised or trained for prolonged operation overseas, yet served with ONUC (Organisation Nations-Unies au Congo) from 1961 until 1963; moreover when called on to fly operations the unit maintained a consistent 90 per cent serviceability rate.

SWEDISH J29s IN ACTION

Based in turn at Luluabourg and Kamina, the nine J29Bs and two J29C reconnaissance versions undertook numerous gun and

India's Peacekeeper

The establishment of an armed United Nations presence in the Congo called for forces from non-aligned countries, calculated to be seen as less likely to be partisan in the vicious civil struggle. India, Ethiopia, Italy and Sweden sent combat aircraft to provide air support for UN forces, as they began to take a more active role in the ground fighting, and they soon began flying missions against the Katangan separatists.

English Electric Canberra B(I).Mk 58
India's Canberras were equivalent to the British B(I).Mk 8. They were night intruder versions of the Canberra bomber, stressed for low-level agility and able to carry a wide variety of weaponry, including a powerful belly-mounted cannon pack.

French Workhorse

Although Belgium was the major colonial power in central Africa, it is the French, whose imperial possessions tended to be further to the north, who have been most active in military rescues in the region. French forces have intervened at least 30 times since the 1960s, primarily with troops on the ground but supported by Armée de l'Air logistics squadrons. On occasion, French paratroopers have made combat drops in the course of their duties, almost invariably from the cargo compartment of Transall C.160 transports.

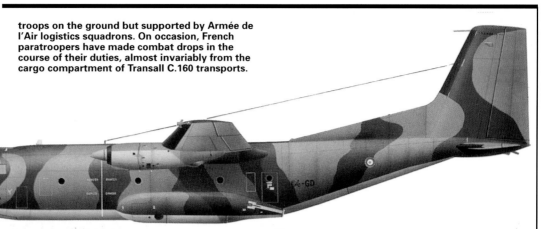

Transall C.160
Smaller than the American C-130 Hercules, the Franco-German C.160 entered service in the late 1960s, and has been one of France's main transport assets since that time. It can take a payload of up to 16 tonnes, 88 fully-equipped paratroops or more than 90 conventional troops.

Above: Paratroopers descend from a C.160 Transall as the African sun sets. Western powers have been involved in central Africa since colonial days, primarily in protecting their interests and personnel, but occasionally in the thankless peacekeeping role.

Right: Foreign Legion Paratroopers check passers-by on a road in Katanga. The 1978 crisis was distinguished by singularly brutal behaviour on the part of the rebels, and only the airborne troopers could be inserted fast enough to protect innocent foreigners.

rocket attacks and reconnaissance sorties, often in company with Indian air force English Electric Canberras. The Swedes' most significant operations were the surprise attacks of December 1962-January 1963 against the base at Kolwezi, where almost the entire Katangese air strength was eliminated by the J29s. The precision of this series of attacks had such a profound psychological effect upon the white mercenaries of the Katangese air force that many promptly defected and escaped to Angola.

KATANGA REVISITED

The Republic of Zaire, as the former Belgian Congo became, was not to have an easy existence. In March 1977 President Mobutu declared a state of emergency when foreign mercenaries invaded the southern province of Shaba with the intention of supporting the establishment of an independent state of Katanga. France and Morocco answered his appeal for military assistance and, in Operation 'Verveine', 13 Armée de l'Air Transall C-160 transports airlifted 1,500 Moroccan troops to the air base at Kolwezi. With the addition of limited military aid from the United States, and after increased efforts by Mirage IIIs and Aermacchi M.B.326s of the Force Aérienne Zaïroise, the initial invasion was repulsed. A second invasion in May 1978 was better supported by air defence weapons, however, and only after about 10 FAZ aircraft had been lost (including six M.B.326s) was this attack defeated with the help of French and Belgian paratroops.

GREAT LAKES WARS

One area which has seen more than its share of warfare in the last two decades has been around the great lakes of central Africa. Idi Amin's Uganda was a brutal dictatorship which was eventually overthrown by tribal rebels. Although Amin had received a number of MiGs from Warsaw Pact countries, they played little part in the war, which was largely fought out on the ground. Amin's successor, Milton Obote, was in turn overthrown.

Further south, Rwanda and Burundi have long been on the

Left: Zaire's MB.326 trainers should have been of some advantage in the counter-insurgency fighting that has erupted in the last two decades, but poor maintenance and poor training meant that they never played a major part in the final struggle for the country.

brink of (and some time over the edge of) bitter tribal violence between the majority Hutus and the formerly dominant Tutsis. Massacres in the 1970s and 1980s were made to seem as nothing in the 1990s as the tribal communities in each country tore each other apart. Once again, air power played little part in the fighting, although it was the death of the president of Rwanda in a plane crash in Burundi which was the spark to the worst violence. But air power was vital in getting relief supplies to the millions of people fleeing the horrors which had overwhelmed their homes.

MOBUTU'S FALL

The violence in Rwanda and Burundi spilled over into Zaire, where the ailing President Mobutu's long time grip on power was starting to slacken. Guerrilla forces under the control of Laurent Desiré Kabila advanced towards the capital, and the collapse of central government led to yet another multi-national evacuation, with European and Americans being airlifted to safety. Mobutu fled to Morrocco, where he died of cancer, while the new government renamed Zaire. It is now the Democratic Republic of Congo.

Rhodesian bush wars

1965–1979

For much of the period of African decolonisation one state sought to resist the granting of independence on terms unacceptable to its minority white administration. In 1965 Southern Rhodesia unilaterally declared itself independent from the United Kingdom. Despite efforts at mediation by the UK, international sanctions were imposed by the United Nations on Rhodesia.

The predominantly white-staffed Royal Rhodesian Air Force (RRAF) had a long and honourable tradition which stretched back to before World War II. In the post-war years the RRAF had continued to maintain a small number of squadrons, equipped with British aircraft, and by the time of the unilateral declaration of independence (UDI) this force was spearheaded by a squadron of Hawker Hunters and one of English Electric Canberras. Despite sympathies among members of the RAF, Rhodesia found herself without many allies and the UN sanctions were fairly effective in preventing a significant build-up of the RRAF.

EVADING SANCTIONS

The air force's immediate task was supporting the Rhodesian army, and consisted mainly of supply missions and limited patrol and reconnaissance duties. Ten Aermacchi AL.60-F5 transports were obtained covertly in 1967. With the 1969 proclamation of a republic, the 'Royal' prefix was dropped by the air force, which now amounted to seven squadrons of Hunters, Canberras, de Havilland Vampires, Trojans, Douglas Dakotas and other assorted transports.

Above: the essence of bush warfare is tracking down lightly-armed, mobile guerrillas in largely track-less terrain. Aircraft and helicopters provide the mobility necessary to flush targets out of the long grass.

Right: Rhodesian Alouette IIIs, known as 'G-Cars', usually carried 12.7-mm (0.5-in) door guns. Some, known as 'K-Cars', were fitted with 20-mm cannon or quadruple 'fifties' for the escort role.

Frustration by neighbouring black states at the failure of sanctions to bring down the administration under Ian Smith led to an escalation of infiltration of 'Patriotic Front' terrorists into Rhodesian territory from bases in Botswana, Mozambique and Zambia. These were the guerrillas of ZANU and ZAPU, led respectively by Joshua N'komo and Robert Mugabe.

By 1972 the role of the RhAF hardened to one of active counter-guerrilla operations, with hot-chase, airborne landings by the Rhodesian Special Air Service and commando-style units in the outlying bush country, as well as rocket and bomb attacks by Hunters and Canberras on terrorist bases.

In 1976 17 Reims Cessna F337s were obtained by covert means for counter-insurgency tasks and around 34 Aérospatiale (Sud) Alouette III helicopters were supplied by South Africa. In the transport role the aged Dakotas were joined by a dozen ex-civil Britten-Norman Islanders, and in 1978 about 20 SIAI-Marchetti SF.260W Warriors were also obtained by clandestine means.

RhAF aircraft were frequently deployed on 'externals' over Mozambique, and to a smaller extent over Zambia and Botswana, the last posing the least threat. The only air opposition encountered by the RhAF came from a Botswana Defence Force Britten-Norman Defender, flown by a British pilot, which attacked ground troops during a raid near Francistown but was itself shot down by a 'K-Car' heli-

Rhodesian attack jets

The Royal Rhodesian Air Force had a long and distinguished history stretching back to the years before World War II. At the time of Ian Smith's unilateral declaration of independence, it was one of the most powerful air forces in southern Africa, with an all-jet strike force. Not strictly suitable for a counter-insurgency bush war, the aircraft were kept flying by a variety of means, and were used on many of the longer cross-border raids against guerrilla camps in neighbouring countries.

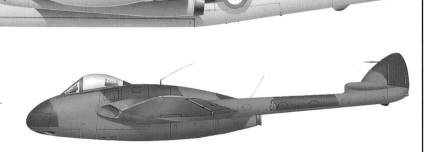

English Electric Canberra B.Mk 2
Above right: The Canberra was one of the first truly successful jet bombers. The Royal Rhodesian Air Force took delivery of 15 B.Mk 2 bombers and three T.Mk 4 trainers before UDI, and survivors continued to operate with No.5 Squadron into the 1990s. Canberras were used both for counter-insurgency work and in attacks on guerrilla camps in Angola and Mozambique, two being lost over the latter country.

de Havilland Vampire FB.Mk 9
Right: The Royal Rhodesian Air Force operated 25 Vampires when the former colony broke with Britain in 1965. Used primarily for ground attack, they served through the civil war, and some trainers were still flying with Zimbabwe in the 1980s.

Fire Force

A total of 17 Reims Cessna 337s acquired clandestinely in 1976 were quickly transformed into hard-hitting Lynxes and became among the most important RhAF combat aircraft during Rhodesia's long bush war. The Lynxes were armed with two 7.7-mm (0.303-in) machine-guns above the cabin, and typically carried two 37-mm rocket pods and 15 boosted HE rockets underwing.

The loss over Mozambique of two AL.60s to SA-7 Strela SAMs made the Rhodesian Air Force highly SAM-conscious. On the Lynx both engine exhausts were covered with heat shields to reduce their infra-red signature to missiles.

Equipped with full blind-flying instrumentation, the Lynxes also carried out night casualty evacuation and a limited amount of reconnaissance. Flare dropping was carried out over farms in isolated areas that were being attacked by terrorists.

COMBAT EQUIPMENT

The aircraft were also given comprehensive nav/com equipment, and during 'external operations', they were used frequently as an airborne communications relay stations between the ground forces, fast jets and helicopters, this task being codenamed Telstar. This system was also used extensively at night in support of external paradrops from Dakotas, Douglas DC-7s and INS-equipped Bell Model 205s.

Most Lynx sorties were mounted in support of the Fire Force, for rapid-response highly mobile anti-terrorist operations. On Fire Force missions the Lynx would usually operate with up to three 'K-Car' Alouette III gunships, and as many 'G-Cars' (troop-carrying Alouettes) or 'Cheetahs' (Bell Model 205 troop carriers) that could be gathered together. Even the troop-carrying 'choppers' were armed, with a pair of side-firing Browning 7.7-mm (0.303-in) machine-guns. A 'Para-Dak' (Douglas C-47 Dakota) with 16-20 paratroopers, and a 'Skyshout' (Cessna 185) 'Kiwit' or Britten Norman Islander could accompany the Fire Force. These 'Skyshout' psychological warfare aircraft were equipped with a powerful loudspeaker system, used to spread government propaganda to encourage the 'Terrs' or terrorists to surrender.

Another Lynx role was forward air control, generally in support of the fast jet force. A 'jet effort' was usually laid on against targets too heavily defended for Fire Force action. Using a high dive profile the Lynx would mark the target area with 37-mm smoke or phosphorus rockets, and frangible (napalm) fuel bombs. The Lynx pilot would then direct the jets, usually controlling pairs of Hunters, Vampires or Canberras.

copter (Aérospatiale Alouette IIIs configured as gunship with 20-mm cannon). Zambian MiGs were sometimes scrambled against the Rhodesian raiders but usually arrived too late.

FUEL STARVATION

One of the potential dangers always faced by the RhAF was a possible drying-up of fuel supplies following imposition of oil sanctions, and alongside the Royal Navy Britain's RAF undertook a limited patrol task with Avro Shackletons based in Madagascar to keep watch for sanction-breaking tankers from the Middle East attempting to land their cargoes on the African coast.

Despite the presence of communist-supplied SAMs to neighbouring black states, the RhAF continued to operate highly effectively both over and beyond Rhodesian

Right: The most advanced aircraft available to the Rhodesian air force at UDI were the Hawker Hunter FGA.Mk 9s of No. 1 Squadron, which with the notable exception of South Africa outclassed anything used by other air forces in the region at that time.

territory right up to the point at which an internal settlement of the country's future administration was reached in 1979. However, with Marxist support of the ZANU and ZAPU, which had by 1979 reached substantial proportions, there is no doubt that the cost of military operations by the Rhodesian security forces was biting deep into the state's economy.

Yet throughout the 14 years in which the country lay in the economic wilderness, the RhAF's adaptability and determination saw it survive as an efficient counter-insurgency force.

Below: Jets are not the best way to counter insurgents in the bush. Rhodesia managed to clandestinely acquire Cessna 337s and SIAI-Marchetti SF.260s which were much more suitable for COIN operations.

Right: The end of the civil war saw the transformation of Rhodesia into Zimbabwe. The new state was free to acquire modern aircraft, and the first BAe Hawk armed trainers were ordered in 1982.

Portugal in Africa

1959-1975

Left: Portugal was one of the biggest users of the Fiat G91, which saw extensive service in the later stages of the country's colonial wars in Africa. G91Rs were sent to Mozambique in 1969, and were also used in Angola from 1963 to 1975.

By the early 1960s, Portugal's surviving colonial possessions in Africa began to reject Portuguese authority, the first armed rebellion emerging in Portuguese Guinea. Fighting broke out in August 1959 with the PAIGC (Partido Africano de Independencia da Guiné e Capo Verde). At first only a handful of T-6 Texans of the FAP (Força Aérea Portugesa – Portuguese air force) were available to deal with the emergency, until supplemented by Republic F-84G Thunderjets in 1963. FAP presence increased to match the rebel activity and in 1967, Esq. 121 'Tigres' with eight G91R-4s was set up at Bissalau, along with additional T-6s and Do 27 liaison aircraft. The G91s flew in support of Portuguese troops and against the PAIGC's supply trails near the Senegalese and French Guinean borders. Five of the type were lost to enemy action, at least two of them shot down by SA-7 missiles.

In May 1968 General Antonio de Spinola was appointed governor, and he ordered 12 Alouette III helicopters, which were essential for operations in a country that was comprised largely of marsh and soft terrain. The Alouette IIIs were part of Esq. 121, as was a flight of Nord Noratlas transports which undertook all local supply flights.

By 1970 the campaign had taken on a much tougher approach and the FAP was using napalm and defoliants against PAIGC targets. The PAIGC received limited air support from a number of diverse sources. Conakry-based Nigerian MiG-17s were used for reconnaissance flights, while Soviet-supplied Mi-4s carried out supply flights in the east of the country. Several FAP aircraft were lost to SA-7s and AAA fire: PAIGC claimed to have shot down 21 aircraft in seven years.

The PAIGC declared an independent republic in September 1973. Seven months later, the military seized power in Portugal in a nearly bloodless coup and established a provisional military government which installed Spinola as president. As a result, independence was granted to Guinea-Bissau on 10 September 1974. The FAP undertook the withdrawal of most military and civilian personnel by 15 October.

ANGOLA

While the situation in Portuguese Guinea was worsening, trouble flared up farther south in Angola. The actions of the Marxist Movimento Popular de Libertação de Angola (MPLA) forced the stationing of FAP C-47s and PV-2 Harpoons at Luanda to support the army. Several major towns soon came under MPLA siege and the small Portuguese army element in Mozambique was stretched to breaking point. A number of civilian aircraft, such as Piper Cubs, were pressed into service as light transports to resupply outlying settlements, while DC-3s and Beech 18s were used as makeshift bombers. These and the other FAP aircraft were joined in June 1961 by F-84Gs. A substantial paratroop-dropping effort was sustained, first by the C-47s and later by Noratlases, to relieve several towns under siege. Fighting continued, mostly in the north of the country, and the Noratlas detachment made regular parachute drops with the 21st Battalion of the Regimento de Caçadores Paraquedistas to garrison towns.

Although Portugal was the subject of a US arms embargo due to its African conflicts, seven B-26 were sold to the FAP in 1965 to supplement the PV-2s. These helped to compensate for the F-84G losses, which stood at five (mostly through accident rather than action) and growing Soviet support for the MPLA. Yet another guerrilla group materialised in 1966, when a breakaway MPLA group established itself as the Uniao Naçional de Independençia Total de Angola (UNITA), under the

---

Piston veterans at war

Portugal was the first of Europe's maritime powers to establish an overseas colonial empire, but by the 1950s it was becoming more and more difficult for one of the poorest nations in Europe to maintain its position in Africa. Air power was important to the struggle with independence movements, but the aircraft used were often aging and unreliable veterans of World War II.

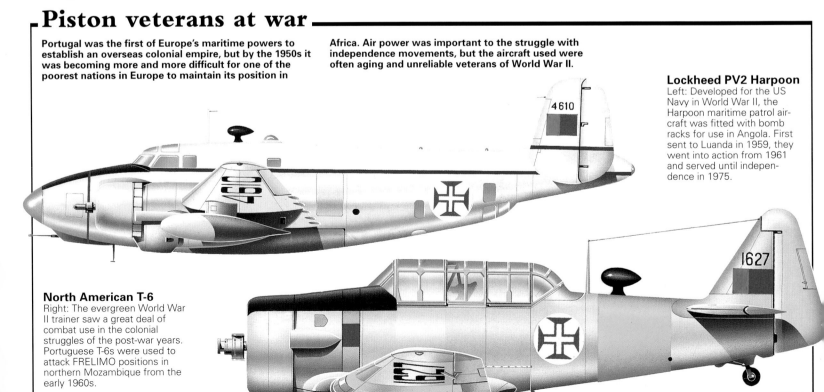

Lockheed PV2 Harpoon
Left: Developed for the US Navy in World War II, the Harpoon maritime patrol aircraft was fitted with bomb racks for use in Angola. First sent to Luanda in 1959, they went into action from 1961 and served until independence in 1975.

North American T-6
Right: The evergreen World War II trainer saw a great deal of combat use in the colonial struggles of the post-war years. Portuguese T-6s were used to attack FRELIMO positions in northern Mozambique from the early 1960s.

Portuguese air power in Angola

The war in Angola began in the early 1960s. In the beginning, Portugal had complete control of the air in its fight with the MPLA, the FNLA and Unita. However, by the end of the 1960s the guerrilla movements began to receive heavier weapons from neighbouring countries, and the first shoot down occurred in 1967, when the MPLA destroyed a Do 27. Several helicopters were shot down in 1968.

Aeritalia (Fiat) G91R-4

Right: During its African combat career, the 'Gina' proved to be a reliable and sturdy fighter-bomber and reconnaissance platform, operating mostly in adverse conditions. All active aircraft were forward deployed during operations and rearmed and refuelled as close to their operational areas as possible. In at least one instance Esq. 121 engaged MiG-17s from Guinea-Bissau, but with inconclusive results.

Aérospatiale Alouette III

Left: The essence of counter insurgency operations is the rapid deployment of troops directly into the operational area. From the middle of the 1960s, Portugal began to rely more and more heavily on its helicopter force to fill that function, initially with Alouette IIs but later with the more capacious Alouette III, which could carry up to six troops.

Right: The independence wars in Africa placed great strain on Portugal's transport capability. In 1962 the air force acquired the Nord Noratlas for parachute operations and for supplying outlying areas.

leadership of Jonas Savimbi. FAP aircraft maintained constant attacks against the MPLA, which was advancing inexorably westward towards the capital.

The arrival of G91R-4s in 1972 (some coming from FAP units stationed in neighbouring Mozambique) boosted the FAP's combat power. Helicopters also became an increasingly important part of operations. The Alouettes were used to move troops rapidly to trouble spots and by 1969 they had been joined in country by the first Pumas. F-84Gs, B-26s, T-6Gs and even armed Do 27s which kept up a constant cycle of air attacks on rebel positions.

However, the strain of fighting across Africa was proving too much

for Portugal. The coup heralded the end of Portugal's involvement in Angola, which was offered independence on 1 July 1974.

MOZAMBIQUE

The third chapter of Portugal's African wars concerned Mozambique. Following the other colonies' struggle for independence, Mozambique saw the rise of Eduardo Mondlan's Frente de Libertação de Moçambique (FRELIMO) movement in 1962. Again, only small numbers of FAP C-47s and T-6s were on hand when serious trouble broke out in 1964. In a short space of time, 16,000 troops had arrived in the country and additional T-6s, PV-2s (eight), Do 27s (12) and some Alouette IIIs were despatched to support them. FRELIMO operated from bases in Tanzania and later Zambia.

The FAP commitment to Mozambique became larger than that in either Guinea or Angola, though combat operations did not begin in earnest until 1968. A network of new air bases was set up as a result at Beira (T-6Gs, PV-2s, Auster D.5s and Noratlas transports)

and at Tete (T-6Gs, Do 27s, Auster D.5s, Alouette IIIs and G91R-4s). Additional G91s were based at Nacala. Nova Freixo was occupied by T-6s, Austers and Alouettes while C-47 transports were based Lourenço Marques.

Now under the command of Samora Machel (later to become president), FRELIMO began vigorous operations against the Portuguese from 1970. South African-registered crop-sprayers were used to spray herbicides over FRELIMO's border strongholds, in an attempt to deny them food. These aircraft departed the country prematurely, after AAA fire shot down escorting T-6s and one of the crop-sprayers.

Once again Portugal found itself fighting a losing battle with a conscript army. The G91s returned to Portugal in 1974 in anticipation of an offer of full independence. Mozambique gained independence on 25 June 1975 and took possession of several T-6s and Noratlases for its own use.

Left: Very tough and with excellent short-field ability, the Dornier Do 27 saw extensive service in Africa. Portuguese Do 27s were used for liaison, to support T-6s operating deep in the bush and, rarely, to carry and deliver weapons.

South African Bush Wars

1975–1996

The political circumstances by which South Africa slid into isolation in the 1960s and 1970s are well documented, but resulted from the desire of the minority white population to retain political power, which was achieved by the maintenance of a system of separate development – Apartheid – for the different races. This became increasingly unacceptable to the international community, especially after America had put its own house in order by abolishing segregation and discouraging discrimination.

A culture in which politicians advocated a 'total onslaught' against minority white regimes soon began to prevail in those nearby countries which had black majority governments. Initially, however, the presence of white-ruled Rhodesia and Portuguese Angola insulated South Africa itself, and provided alternative targets for potential enemies.

Above: The South African Defence Force was the major military power in sub-Saharan Africa. The Blackburn Buccaneer was seen as a key element of that power, being able to fly interdiction missions far beyond South Africa's borders.

Over a period of time, South Africa found itself becoming increasingly involved in a counter-insurgency war in the territory then known as South West Africa. This started in the early 1960s, when the South West Africa People's Organisation (SWAPO), began its infiltration of what it called Namibia.

South African forces had conquered the territory from the Germans during World War I, and South Africa had been awarded the

Right: The Aérospatiale Alouette III was the South African Air Force's first modern helicopter. Entering service in 1962 it remains in use in a number of roles, including liaison and mountain rescue.

Helicopter mismatch

The essence of counter-insurgency warfare, especially in the bush, is the rapid movement of small units at great speed. The helicopter is in many ways the ideal bush war weapon, and South Africa used helicopters extensively in Namibia and Angola. However, they are vulnerable to modern weapons, and as the war went on and more advanced Soviet weaponry began to appear, a number were lost to anti-aircraft fire and to surface-to-air missiles.

Aérospatiale Alouette III
Right: Although the basic design dates back to the 1950s, the French-built Alouette III is a highly effective light general purpose helicopter, with excellent 'hot and high' performance. South Africa had as many as 60 on strength through the period of the Bush War, in spite of supplying a number to Rhodesia. The Alouette III can carry up to five troops in addition to the pilot, and in the operational area was used as an assault transport as well as for command, liaison and search and rescue.

Mil Mi-24 'Hind'
Left: South African raids into Angola found themselves opposed by troops equipped with high-quality Soviet-built weaponry. The SADF had nothing to compare with the 'Hind' gunships. With their speed and heavy armament, the 30 delivered to the MPLA could have been a major threat, but fortunately for the SADF they were never used to their best effect.

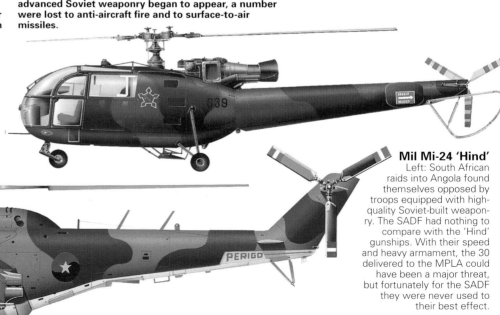

Right: France became the major supplier of military equipment to South Africa after political differences arose with Britain in the 1960s. The South African Air Force took delivery of a variety of new French weapons in the 1960s and 1970s, before mandatory United Nations sanctions made France cease trading with the Apartheid regime. First delivered in 1969, the Aérospatiale SA.330 Puma is the country's most important transport helicopter, and its 3-tonne or 16-man payload was vital to the success of SADF operations in Namibia and Angola.

League of Nations mandate to administer the area. The United Nations did not recognise the mandate, and this consequently put South Africa at odds with the international community.

CROSS-BORDER RAIDS

The first SWAPO incursion into Ovamboland in northern South West Africa took place in September 1965. South African police units retaliated by attacking a SWAPO camp at Ongulumbashe, arriving there by Alouette III helicopter. For most of the 1960s and early 1970s, the conflict in Namibia remained at a low intensity, with the Alouettes active in the counter-insurgency role.

A direct result of the 1974 Portuguese revolution and the ensuing withdrawal from Angola was SWAPO's freedom to establish bases, with backing from the de facto rulers of the former colony, the Marxist MPLA. The situation was deemed serious enough for direct military involvement by South Africa.

The resulting Bush War saw South African Defence Force units, supported by the SAAF, involved in numerous operations in southern

Right: Helicopters are vulnerable on the ground, so South African troops learned to embark and disembark in a hurry. On one occasion a Puma picked up a squad while under fire from a Cuban tank!

Above: South African Mirage IIIs gave the SAAF unmatched regional air-to-air capability in the 1960s. But by the time that South African forces became embroiled in Angola in the late 1970s and 1980s, the opposition included Cuban-piloted MiG-23s and Sukhoi Su-22s, and only superior training gave the Mirages the edge.

Right: First entering South African service in 1963, the Canberra was intended to provide bombing experience for Buccaneer crews. But the Canberra is a potent warplane in its own right, and it was used with some success in preparatory strikes against SWAPO base areas before major ground operations.

Angola between 1974 and 1987. The protracted conflict began on the 23 August 1976 when C-130Bs flew troops to South West Africa to occupy the strategic waterworks at Calueque, a few kilometres into

Angola. Eight SAAF Alouette IIIs assisted with the actual occupation. The water plant had been built with South African funding during the Portuguese administration of Angola, and provided much-need-

ed irrigation water to the farmlands in the north of South West Africa. This was the beginning of Operation Savannah, which saw South African forces, supported by SAAF helicopter, transport and reconnaissance missions, penetrate Angola right up to the outskirts of Luanda. The aim of Operation Savannah was to help the pro-Western FNLA and UNITA liberation movements against the Cuban-backed Marxist MPLA. The MPLA aimed to take over the country before the elections which would accompany Angolan independence on 11 November 1975. The South Africans were forced to withdraw when US support for the initiative failed to materialise.

Angolan support for SWAPO's Peoples Liberation Army/PLAN, South African forces found themselves involved in clashes with Angolan government (FAPLA) forces during their incursions into southern Angola.

Operation Reindeer began on 4 May 1978 and saw the SAAF attack SWAPO training bases at Cassinga and Chetequera in response to a dramatic SWAPO incursion into South West Africa. The air attack was initiated by Mirages, which were followed by Buccaneers. On completion of the raid, ground forces were evacuated using Pumas and Super Frelons. By now there were permanent detachments of Pumas and Alouette IIIs to Ondangwa, Mpacha and Rundu, with a Super Frelon detachment at Mpacha. During Operations Rekstok and Safraan, mounted during March 1979, Impala Mk IIs, Mirage IIIEZs, Bosboks and Kudus made their operational debut in the combat area, with Impala and Mirage detachments at Ondangua, and an Impala detachment at Mpacha in the Caprivi Strip. Operation Safraan was mounted against SWAPO training camps near the Caprivi strip, while Operation Rekstok consisted of air strikes and heliborne raids on

ANGOLAN BASES

With the end of Operation Savannah, the MPLA formed the new government, actively supporting SWAPO and giving it sanctuary in southern Angola. South Africa's quarrel was essentially with SWAPO, but because of the active

The Atlas Kudu is a tough utility aircraft developed from an Italian Aermacchi design. Kudus were often flown on route navigation missions and as communications relay aircraft during operations in Namibia – essential given the flat, featureless nature of the terrain .

Ground attack

South African external operations into Angola initially met with very little aerial opposition, and SAAF aircraft could concentrate on their main function, which was the support of troops on the ground. Aircraft used ranged from high-performance jets to light utility aircraft, and targets varied from individual guerrillas in the bush to large, well-protected SWAPO base camps protected by surface-to-air missiles and anti-aircraft guns.

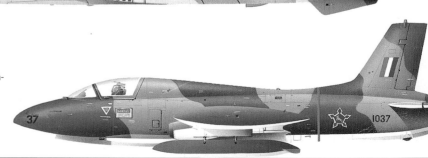

Canberra B(I).Mk 12
Above: Designed in the 1950s as a high-level night intruder/bomber, South African Canberras were switched to low-level operations in the 1970s. Normal combat radius in bush operations was 1300 km (808 miles), with a bombload of 2720 kg (6,000 lb) internally and a further 454-kg (1,000 lb) weapon under each wing.

Mirage F.1
Above right: The Mirage F.1CZ, South Africa's main interceptor in the 1980s, was the also a capable ground attacker. It served alongside the F.1AZ attack variant, which was delivered with improved navigation equipment and better air-to-surface fire-control systems.

Atlas Impala Mk.II
Right: Based on the single-seat light strike variant of the MB326 trainer, the Impala is a no-frills combat aircraft which was used with great success in the operational area. Armed with two 20-mm cannon, it can also carry 1814 kg (4,000 lb) of bombs or rockets on six underwing hard points.

Above: Lieutenant Adriano Bomba of the Mozambique air force defected to South Africa on 8 July 1981. His well-maintained MiG-17 was escorted into Hoedspruit air base by SAAF Mirage F.1AZs. South African pilots took the opportunity to make a thorough evaluation of the fighter before it was returned to its owners in November.

Right: The first real opposition to to South African fighters over Angola came from MiG-21s flown by Cuban and East German pilots. This aircraft force landed in South Africa after a defection attempt. Repaired and flown by the South African Air Force, it was thoroughly evaluated before finding a home in the SAAF museum.

SWAPO camps in southern Angola. While performing a low-level air attack on 14 March 1979, in southern Angola, the SAAF suffered its only Canberra loss, when the pilot was wounded by small arms fire and was unable to maintain control of his aircraft.

Operation Sceptic saw the largest SADF mechanised infantry assault since World War II. It was launched on 20 May 1980 against SWAPO bases and its southern headquarters. The operation commenced on 7 June with attacks by 12 Mirages and four Buccaneers on the southern HQ, and by 16 Mirages on the main SWAPO HQ at Lubango. Two of these Mirages were damaged by SA-3 missiles but returned safely, landing at Ruacana

and Rundu. Three days later two further air strikes followed. Eighteen Mirages attacked the southern HQ with eight 250-kg (551-lb) bombs each, while four Buccaneers attacked a SWAPO camp at Mulola with eight 450-kg (992-lb) bombs each.

HELICOPTER ASSAULTS

Operation Sceptic lasted for three weeks and saw the extensive use of Pumas and Alouette IIIs in support of ground forces. During this operation the SAAF suffered its first loss by an surface-to-air missile when an Alouette III was shot down. During this period, three Impala Mk II pilots were killed after being shot down in separate incidents. A month later, Alouette III gunships,

armed with side-firing 20-mm cannon, were first reported in Operation Klipklop performing an attack on the SWAPO transit point at Chitado.

During Operation Protea, which was initiated in August 1981, a

major SAAF attack was made on 23 August against Angolan air defence installations, and these were seriously damaged – although the main objective of Protea was to attack the SWAPO North Western and Northern Front headquarters at Xangongo and Ongiva. An Alouette III was shot down on 25 August. In November 1981, Operation Daisy was launched against SWAPO bases at Bambi and Cheraqurera, which were captured by ground troops following an SAAF attack. On 6 November 1981 an SAAF Mirage F1CZ flown by Major Johann Rankin, shot down an Angolan Air Force MiG-21 using its 30-mm cannon, the first SAAF dogfight kill since World War II.

Left: Mil-24 'Hind-Es' sit in front of of Mi-8 and M-17 transports. Although fitted with launch rails for anti-tank missiles, UV-32-57 rocket pods were a more common weapons load. Angolan 'Hinds' rarely carried a full weapons load, probably because of the hot climate which reduced performance.

Early in 1982 a SAAF Puma was shot down, and later in May 1982 an Impala Mk II was downed near Cuvelai. During an attack on Cassinga (Operation Mebos) a SAAF Puma was shot down, killing all 15 on board. A Bosbok was also lost in July, killing both crew. Whilst escorting a recce mission in southern Angola during December 1982, two Mirage F.1CZs were jumped by four Angolan MiG-21s. In the ensuing engagement, one of the MiGs was shot down by Major Rankin (the same pilot responsible for the first kill, again using the Mirage's 30-mm cannon). This added to six air-to-air victories scored by SAAF Impalas during the Bush War.

During Operation Askan, the SAAF mounted a major attack on Angolan air defences. During this, on 22 December 1983 an Impala Mk II was hit by a SAM which failed to explode. The warhead of a new SAM-9 was identified stuck in the rudder of the Impala. It was now clear that Angola had acquired the very latest air defence systems, and this was a source of grave concern.

Attempted peace negotiations in 1985 produced a Joint Angolan South African Monitoring Commission which aimed to oversee the withdrawal of South African forces from Angola, but SWAPO could not be persuaded to take part

and the conflict continued. An SAAF Dakota was hit in the tail by an SA-7 on 1 May 1986 but the pilot made an exceptionally skilful landing at Ondangua without further damage to the aircraft. During Operation Egret in September 1985, aimed at preventing a major SWAPO infiltration into SWA, the Angolan air force took an increasingly offensive stand, and in addition to MiG-21s the SAAF encountered MiG-23s, although engagements were inconclusive.

FINAL BATTLES

During Operation Moduler, which took place in the latter half of 1987, the SAAF was faced with what was arguably the most sophisticated air defence system of Soviet origin outside the WarPac countries, but fortunately there were no losses. Moduler was followed by Operation Hooper, the last major SADF offensive. This opened on 13 January 1988 with an attack northeast of Cuito Cuanavale. By now the South African forces were not only operating against SWAPO, but were actively supporting the pro-

Right: The MiG-23 'Flogger' has replaced the older MiG-21 in the fighter role in Angola. Surprisingly the Angolans were given the late-model MiG-23ML 'Flogger-G' by the Soviets. This was considerably more capable than the earlier variants used by some Warsaw Pact air forces of the day.

Western Angolan UNITA forces against the government's own armed forces.

The SAAF played a major part in this and follow up attacks, but was restricted by a loss of air supremacy. The Mirage F.1AZs of No. 1 Squadron flew 683 sorties, supporting ground forces, and delivering 3,068 bombs. Most of these sorties had to be flown low, under Angolan MiG-23 CAPs and avoiding FAPLA radar defences. One F.1AZ was shot down and another was lost in an landing accident at Rundu following a missile hit. The small Buccaneer contingent from No. 24 Squadron, by now reduced to five operational aircraft, delivered 701 bombs dur-

ing 99 sorties, without loss.

By this time, the politicians had succeeded in negotiating a withdrawal of Cuban forces from Angolan soil, in exchange for South African withdrawal from Angola, the granting of independence to Namibia, and the ultimate withdrawal of South African forces from Namibia itself. During August 1988, the last South African forces left Angola. Peace had finally arrived – at least in the air. In Angola itself, the civil war continued to be fought out with savage ferocity well into the 1990s. However, a shaky United Nations-brokered peace has gradually taken hold in the war-torn former Portuguese colony.

Angola's quiet air war

Left: Executive Outcomes pilots first went into action in armed PC-7 trainers. They were ideal platforms for fast-moving counter-insurgency warfare, but they were also vulnerable to ground fire.

Below: The South African pilots were very experienced. Colonel 'P' was a former Mirage and Cheetah instructor who also had more than 2,000 hours on Impalas, including combat time over Angola.

One of the more interesting sidelights on the long civil war in Angola has been the key role played by a South African firm, Executive Outcomes. South Africa had been a long-time supporter of UNITA guerrillas, one of the three main groups struggling for control of the former Portuguese colony. However, in 1993 this privately run firm, staffed by ex-South African military personnel, was contracted to train the armed forces of Angola's MPLA government – the very people who many of the South Africans concerned had been fighting (and winning) against for more than a decade – to beat UNITA.

The aerial portion of the contract saw extremely experienced former SAAF pilots flying combat missions in support of EO-trained ground troops. After quick and somewhat primitive familiarisation courses, the South Africans found themselves going into action in Angolan air force Mil Mi-17 helicopters, armed Pilatus PC-7 trainers and even MiG-23 'Floggers'.

Up until that point, the Angolans had been fighting along the rigid lines dictated by their previous Warsaw-Pact style training and had not been doing well. In 28 months, the EO advisers and a handful of pilots turned the situation around. Applying their own hard-won bush war experience, they trained the MPLA to first hold UNITA's advances, and then begin to force them back. By the time EO left Angola in 1995, UNITA had sued for peace, and, somewhat reluctantly, joined the government to forge a new fragile peace agreement.

NEW COMBAT AIRCRAFT DESIGNS

South Africa's political and military isolation began in the 1960s, as international condemnation of the racist Apartheid system grew. As a United Nations arms embargo began to bite, sources of modern weaponry began to to dry up.

At the same time South Africa felt that it was under increasing threat from a ring of neighbouring Marxist- and Communist-inspired African governments. By the early 1980s, the escalation of the bush war in Namibia and Angola had left the South African Air Force (SAAF) hard-pressed to counter the sophisticated Soviet-supplied aircraft and SAM systems deployed against it, and the search began for new and better combat aircraft.

South Africa's state-owned Atlas Aerospace already had experience in assembling the Impala Mk 1 jet trainer and Impala Mk 2 light attack aircraft (licence-built versions of the Aermacchi M.B.326M/K).

From 1975 onwards Atlas had assembled the SAAF's Mirage F1AZ fighters and also built Puma and Alouette III helicopters. It was Atlas's experience with the Mirage, and the SAAF's large but ageing fleet of Mirage IIIs, that would allow the South African firm to proceed with a series of upgrades to the French jets that would ultimately provide the SAAF with one of the most capable combat aircraft in the world.

However, South Africa could not embark on such an ambitious programme completely alone. It needed a little help from its friends – and that help came from Israel. Drawing on IAI experience with the Kfir upgrade, Atlas developed the two-seat Cheetah D attack aircraft, based on the Mirage IIIDZ, which appeared in 1986. Next came the single-seat Cheetah E fighter, but this was only a stepping stone to the

Cheetah C, the ultimate Mirage upgrade. Cheetah C boasts a new multi-mode radar and cockpit avionics, advanced ECM and self-protection systems, much expanded weapons capability and a refuelling probe. The Cheetah C was a highly secret programme , which only became known in the early 1990s. Mystery still surrounds the source of the upgraded airframes, as all of the SAAF's existing Mirage IIIs are believed to be accounted for as either crashed, withdrawn from use or converted to Cheetah E/D standard. The Cheetah D and C are now the front-line combat jets in South Africa's air force.

Bush war experience also drove the requirement for a dedicated attack helicopter, a type greatly missed by the SAAF, which had to field armed transport helicopters instead. Development of this new aircraft began in 1981 and, in 1990, the

Above: The Atlas-developed Cheetah E was a stop-gap conversion of the SAAF's single-seat Mirage IIIEZs, that closely resembled Israel's Kfir C.7

The Rooivalk helicopter is armed with a 20-mm cannon under the nose, laser-guided Atlas Swift anti-tank missiles, 68-mm rockets and Darter or Viper air-to-air missiles.

prototype of what became the Rooivalk (Red Falcon) attack helicopter was flown. Rooivalk is now in the final development stage and is on the verge of entering SAAF

squadron service. Atlas are also hoping for export sales as the new political situation in South Africa frees them to show their work to the rest of the world.

Weapons
The primary air-to-air weapon for the Cheetah is the Kentron V3C Darter all-aspect infra-red guided missile. Developed from the V3B Kukri, it can acquire targets from the pilot's helmet-mounted sight.

Atlas Cheetah C

The Cheetah C emerged in a relative blaze of publicity in 1995 when the wraps were taken off what had hitherto been South Africa's most secret aviation project. Earlier Cheetahs had been the result of a mid-life update programme for elderly Mirage IIIs. The Cheetah C is a significantly more capable aircraft, probably owing much to Israeli engineering experience with the Kfir although this has never been officially confirmed.

Refuelling probe
Mirage IIIs were not built with refuelling probes, so that was one of the first pieces of equipment Atlas added to the Cheetah. Aerial refuelling from converted Boeing 707 tankers has greatly increased the flexibility of South Africa's fighter force.

Avionics upgrade
The Cheetah's precise avionics fit remains classified, but it is almost certainly a modern low-workload 'glass' cockpit with a multi-mode radar and with all vital controls on the throttle lever and joystick.

Morocco and Chad

1976-1986

Above: In retaliation for the Ouadi Doum strike, Libyan Tu-22s mounted at least two missions against N'Djamena airport. The first, on 24 February 1986, was successful, putting the airport out of action for two days, while the Crotale SAMs sat idle, unable to engage such a high-flying target. On 7 September a Tu-22 was downed over N'Djamena by a HAWK SAM.

Left: BAP-100 anti-runway bombs dropped by Armée de l'Air Jaguar As rain down on the Libyan airfield at Ouadi Doum in illegally-occupied northern Chad. Mounted in February 1986, the strike severely damaged the runway.

Chad, which gained independence from France in 1960, was left with a minority Christian government ruling over a majority Muslim population. French forces returned to Chad in 1968 to help fight the Islamic Front de Libération Nationale de Tchad, withdrawing in 1975 after a coup installed an Islamic government.

Libyan leader Colonel Gaddafi was always enthusiastic to support other Islamic movements, and Libyan interest in Chad was further sharpened by the possibility of mineral resources in the disputed Aouzou strip in the extreme north of Chad.

Libya occupied the strip in 1973, shortly before the French withdrawal. In 1978 the new Muslim government invited French forces back to eject the Libyans, but the regime proved precarious and in 1980 civil war broke out between the factions of the men who had

previously shared power, Habré and Oueddi. Habré was ousted, retiring to the Sudanese border area, where he formed the Forces Armées du Nord (FAN). Oueddi invited Libyan forces into Chad, which attacked FAN bases in Chad and Sudan (mainly using SIAI-Marchetti SF.260WLs). By 1981, however, Habré controlled most of the east and centre of the country, including the capital, and his FAN became the Forces Armées Nationales Tchadiennes (FANT). A peacekeeping force from Nigeria, Senegal and Zaïre replaced the Libyans, and Oueddi fled north to raise the Libyan-backed Armée de Liberation Nationale (ALN).

For the next decade the FANT (with support from French and Zairean forces) fought off Libyan air attacks and ALN military action. In 1983 French forces established a red line roughly along the 15th Parallel, from Torodum to Oum Chalouba, which became the bor-

CONFRONTATION IN CHAD

Ghat
Al Khofra
LIBYA
Aouzou
Maartenes Sarra
AOUZOU STRIP (Annexed to Libya, 1973)
Aouzou
NIGER
Ouadi Doum
Faya Largeau
Fade
Koro Toro
Torodoum
Oum Chalouba
• Towns
RED LINE
Kouba Olango
• Airfields
Ziguey •
Arada
Salal
Biltine
Abeche
• Moussoro
SUDAN
• N'Djamena • Mongo
NIGERIA
CHAD
Sarh
Moundon
CENTRAL AFRICA REPUBLIC
Approximate route of Operation 'Epervier' strike aircraft from Bangui M'Poko Airport

French Jaguars in Chad and Morocco

France's defence links with her former colonies saw French combat aircraft commited to combat operations over North Africa during the 1970s and 1980s. Jaguar As of the Armée de l'Air's 11ᵉ Escadre de Chasse (three squadrons of which are assigned to the Force d'Intervention) have been responsible for most overseas interventions, supported by personnel, and sometimes aircraft, from EC 7. The first action took place in December 1977 after Jaguars had been deployed to Dakar, Senegal (Operation Lamantin) for raids on Polisario Front guerillas attacking Mauritanian territory in the former Spanish Sahara. Two Jaguars were shot down in December and another on 3 May 1978 during the fourth French air strike.

During Operation Tacaud, the Dakar detachment sent eight Jaguars to Chad in April 1978. Operating from N'djamena, the Chad flight lost a Jaguar to an SA-7 SAM on 31 May 1978 while supporting French troops. Another crashed on a recce flight on 8 August; two were lost in separate collisions in August and October. By then the guerrillas had formed a coalition government and French forces began a withdrawal completed in May 1980. France maintained regular detachments at Bangui/M'poko airport in the Central African Republic under the title of Eléments Français d'Assistance Opérationelle for assisting its former colonies and the help of these units was requested in 1983 when civil war again erupted. Operation Manta, the establishment

of a 'red line' between the warring factions in Chad, included arrivals of Jaguars at N'djamena on 21 august. Regular patrols were flown with tanker support from Boeing C-135Fs and Transall C.160NGs, but no action was seen until 25 January 1984, when one Jaguar was shot down by 23-mm cannon while attacking a rebel convoy. Another was lost in an accident on 16 May, but a stalemate allowed the French to withdraw, and the Jaguar flight, mostly of aircraft from EC 4/11, left N'djamena on 3 October. Libya built a major air base at Ouadi Doum in illegally-occupied northern Chad to support a further rebel offensive. Requested to assist, France launched eight Jaguars, supported by C-135Fs, from

Bangui on 16 February 1986, and in a five-hour round trip, they seriously damaged the runway. This mission was part of Operation Epervier during the course of which a Jaguar accidentally crashed near Bangui on 27 March 1986. The aircraft undertook regular surveillance flights punctuated by a further attack on Ouadi Doum on 7 January 1987. Launched from N'djamena, 10 Jaguars attacked radar installations with Martel ARMs. This was the Jaguars' last offensive action of Operation Epervier.

SEPECAT Jaguar A

Based at Toul/Rosières, two escadrons of EC 11, 3/11 and 4/11, were attached to the Force d'Action Eteriuere for overseas intervention and were extensively committed to operations in north Africa. Wearing a two-tone camouflage scheme of sand and chocolate brown, this Jaguar A of EC 4/11 carries the secretary bird emblem of its first escadrille, SPA158, on the port side of its fin.

11-YC

A107

Moroccan COIN air power

Morocco's annexation in November 1975 of the Western Sahara territory vacated by Spain embroiled it in a little-reported war with Algerian- and Libyan-backed Polisario guerillas.

Rockwell OV-10 Bronco
First seeing combat with US forces in Southeast Asia, the Rockwell OV-10 is one of the few aircraft currently in service which was designed from the outset as a counter-insurgency platform. The Moroccan air force received six refurbished former USMC OV-10As in 1981. Three have been lost.

Dassault-Dornier Alpha Jet E
The major Moroccan re-equipment programme of the 1980s saw the air force acquire 24 examples of the Franco-German Alpha Jet. Primarily used as an advanced trainer, it can also carry more than 2500 kg of ordnance in the light attack role.

Below: Among the Libyan air force aircraft captured in Chad were SF.260s and Mi-25 gunships. A few of these 'Hinds' were passed on to NATO air forces by France for further evaluation. The Ispanka infra-red jammer and faded camouflage are noteworthy.

der between the government and rebel forces. French forces withdrew in the Autumn of 1984, but Libyan forces remained, and built a massive base at Ouadi Doum. The ALN crossed the red line in February 1986, supported by Libyan aircraft from Ouadi Doum. French forces returned to Chad and counter-attacked, putting the airfield out of action. Libya responded with a high-level bombing raid on N'Djamena by Tu-22s. Fighting broke out again in early-1987, with intensive bombing raids by both sides. French aircraft supported an infantry attack against the

north, and Ouadi Doum was captured on 22 March. Aouzou was recaptured on 8 August, and on 5 September Chad invaded Libya, destroying 22 aircraft at Sara airfield before withdrawing. Both sides then accepted a ceasefire, though Libyan overflights have continued sporadically.

MOROCCAN WAR
Following the 1974 Spanish withdrawal from Spanish Sahara, Morocco and Mauretania agreed to partition the territory. This was opposed by the Algerian-backed and based Polisario (Popular Front for the Liberation of Saguiet el-Hamra and Rio de Oro) resistance. Fighting broke out in the spring of 1976 and Morcco received substantial help from France, including French equipment and deployments of French combat aircraft.

Moroccan air force Mirage F1s, Alpha Jets and F-5s (together with Mauretanian BN Defenders) were supported by French Jaguars and Mirage F1s deployed to Dakar. Morocco's F-5A/E force was based at Kenitra and initially bore the brunt of air operations (along with a squadron of Magisters). Mauretania agreed a ceasefire with the Polisario in 1978, following a coup, and the Polisario were then able to operate from bases in the southern part of Spanish Sahara. However, Morocco's war with the Polisario intensified, and many warplanes fell to Polisario SAMs during subsequent operations. Several F-5s were lost

Above: Moroccan F-5A/Es were heavily committed in the ground-attack role against Polisario guerillas and many were downed by SAMs and groundfire. Losses were offset by the delivery of surplus Aggressor F-5Es from the USA in 1980 and 1989 funded by Saudi Arabia

to SA-7s in 1978. Polisario surface-to-air defences were strengthened during the mid-1980s with the supply of SA-6 batteries and these claimed several Moroccan aircraft, including two F-5Es in 1985 and 1987. An uneasy peace was finally bought to to the region in 1991 when a transitional period with UN forces preparing the region for a referendum on its future.

Morocco's Mirages at war

From 1978 Morcco received 50 Mirage F1s comprising 30 F1CHs, 14 F1EHs and six F1EH-200s. These are all based in hardened air shelters at Sidi Slimane, from where detachments were made to El Aïoune for combat operations against Polisario guerillas in Western Sahara until Morocco relinquished its territorial claims in August 1988. F1EHs have undertaken attack and reconnaissance operations (using an indigenously-developed recce pod) during which several were lost to Polisario groundfire. Documented instances include two on 13 October 1981 and aother on 14 January 1985. The first pair was hit be SAMs during a rebel attack on the garrison at Gelta Zemmour, at least one of the aircraft being at 30,000 ft (9145 m) when struck. The 1985 loss was also to a SAM – apparently fired from Algerian territory – during a clash with Polisario forces which claimed to have destroyed three Moroccan aircraft of unknown type.

Below: Transall C.160 transports played a crucial role in supporting the French deployments to Morocco and Chad. In Chad the Transalls air-dropped supplies and acted as inflight-refuelling tankers for Jaguars and Mirage F1s. With French and Zairean support, the government forces in Chad were eventually able to defeat the Libyan-backed rebels, and even ejected Libya from the Aouzou strip, which had been occupied for 15 years.

Horn of Africa

1970- THE PRESENT

Political allegiances of the nations of the so-called Horn of Africa have become so blurred in the past 25 years that it has often been hard to say where civil wars ended and wars with neighbouring states began. What is clear is the fact that a quarter of a century of fighting has managed to inflict the worst horrors of war on a drought-stricken civilian population which would have had to struggle to survive at the best of times.

Soviet military influence in the area dates back to 1963 when, following the creation of independent Somalia out of the unification of British and Italian Somalilands in 1960, Russia supplied MiG-15s and MiG-17s in return for use of a number of sea and air bases in the country. The Soviet aim was to influence the southern approaches to the oil-rich Gulf states; later a modest strike potential was added by the arrival of a number of Ilyushin Il-28 bombers. In 1969 this

influence was extended to the Sudan, where a left-wing coup was followed by the arrival of Chinese and Soviet technicians to organise a squadron of MiG-17s, later supplemented by MiG-21s.

ETHIOPIA AND ERITREA

By the early 1970s the Western-backed but domestically fragile nation of Ethiopia was almost entirely surrounded by potentially hostile communist-backed states. For some years an almost mediaeval administration, headed by the veteran Emperor Haile Selassie, had been propped up by half-hearted American military and economic aid, and as the plight of Ethiopia became all too obvious a $100 million military equipment order, including Northrop F-5s and Cessna A-37 strike aircraft (to bolster previous deliveries), was negotiated with the USA. In 1974, however, the emperor was overthrown by a cabal of middle-ranking military officers known as the Derg.

After three years of internecine fighting Mengistu Haile Mariam emerged as the dominant power and began leading the country down the road to Marxism.

To complicate the situation a guerrilla war broke out between the Soviet-backed government forces and the Arab-backed Eritrean Liberation Front in northern Ethiopia, while Ethiopian royalist forces conducted a guerrilla war using bases in the Sudan, a situation which at one time threatened to erupt into open war between the two Soviet-equipped countries. The Eritrean secessionists were joined by a highly active rebel group in Tigre, while further groups were active in the south.

By the late 1980s, the country was suffering from famine and economic collapse. The government's refusal to deal with the former, together with its misappropriation of international aid, led to worldwide condemnation and provided an even greater spur to the rebels,

Above: The sight of an aircraft delivering relief supplies in the Horn of Africa has become one of the staples of news reports over the last two decades. But drought and famine are only part of the region's tragedy: continual warfare has heightened the almost unbearable misery of the people.

who continued to gain ground.

In 1990, Eritrean forces surrounded and took the government stronghold of Asmara in spite of being subject to cluster bomb attacks by MiG-23 'Floggers', and also captured the port of Masawa. A year later, Ethiopian air force personnel fled with their aircraft as rebels closed in on the capital, but not before several MiGs had been shot down by rebels armed with captured ZSU-23-4 anti-aircraft guns. Government forces were on the brink of defeat.

A ceasefire on May 27 1991 resulted in the overthrow of the Derg, and the establishment of the free and independent state of Eritrea.

SOMALIA

Power in Somalia, independent since 1960, was seized by Major General Muhammad Siyad Barre in 1969. The socialist, centralised regime established close ties with Moscow, but droughts and famine in the mid-1970s hit hard.

Barre took Somalia into war with Ethiopia in 1977, primarily in support of ethnic Somali rebels liv-

Left: Ethiopia and its air force were largely Western-influenced in the quarter of a century following World War II. But after the Marxist overthrow of Emperor Haile Selassie aircraft like this Canberra lost in combat with Somalia were replaced by Soviet-built machines.

ing in the Ogaden region. Attrition among Ethiopia's surviving Canberras and F-5As had been exceptionally high, and, both opposing air forces operated Soviet-supplied MiG-17s, MiG-21s, Il-28s, Mil helicopters and Antonov transports.

In the course of the first six months' fighting, when Cuban mercenaries were flying Ethiopian MiG-21s, as well as some newly delivered MiG-23s, Somalia suffered the loss of at least 20 MiGs.

FAMINE AND PESTILENCE

Inevitably, in an area almost entirely populated by scattered peoples seeking to scratch a meagre living in an environment scarcely capable of supporting crops and livestock, the ferocity of modern warfare and weapons left large numbers of helpless civilians starving and without water. Disease and hunger killed huge numbers of people whose plight was largely ignored in the bitterness of war.

Before long, however, the attrition among aircraft and other military equipment on both sides convinced the Moscow authorities of the futility of this conflict and, following Somalia's discontinuation of all ties with the Soviet Union in November 1977, a ceasefire was agreed in March 1978.

Armed opposition to Siyad Barre, largely inspired by clan loyalties, began to surface in 1988. By 1990 government control was slipping, and the president fled in January 1991. Fighting then broke out between rival warlords, disrupting all economic activity and when this was exacerbated by drought, within 18 months a third of all Somalis faced starvation, and more than one million had become refugees.

International relief agencies attempted to give aid, but to no avail. Military assistance was sought,

and Operation Provide Relief saw four USAF C-130s begin flying in aid to a gravel airstrip at Belet Huen, 400 km (250 miles) north of Mogadishu. These were joined by two British C-130 Hercules.

In December 1992, Operation Restore Hope got under way as a

It would be easy to blame the almost continual warfare which the Horn of Africa has suffered over the last half century on the artificial borders drawn by the old imperial powers without reference to the situation on the ground, but that is only part of the story. Rather, conflict has been the product of a devil's brew of ethnic, tribal, political and religious differences, combined with endemic famine and drought. Tensions in the area have been exacerbated further by the intervention of the superpowers playing for influence in this strategically-located region. Any alliances in the area are purely a matter of expediency, founded upon perceptions of a common enemy rather than any recognition of common causes.

WAR ZONE: HORN OF AFRICA

Left: Designed mainly to provide small, technologically backward air forces with a simple, easy-to-maintain combat jet, the Northrop F-5 equipped a number of countries in north and east Africa, including Ethiopia and the Sudan.

Below: China's burgeoning arms export business has seen its F-7 fighter – a copy of the Soviet MiG-21 'Fishbed' – enter service in many countries. The new Muslim government in Sudan has acquired the type via Iran.

United Nations peacekeeping force led by 2,000 US Marines was sent to restore order enough to allow the relief agencies to do their jobs. The food airlift into refugee camps ceased on 28 February, road convoys by then having become safe. American troops officially handed over the peacekeeping effort to the 3,500-strong UNOSOM (United Nations Operations in Somalia) force on 4 May, though the 17,700 men of the US Joint Task Force in Somalia remained on station but not under UN control.

However, failure to disarm the warring factions proved to be a critical error as the period of relative peace was used primarily to re-arm. The warlords also looted aid supplies, and extorted money from the aid agencies in order to fill their war chests. Fighting soon broke out again, and over the next two years some 50,000 people were killed in factional violence, with an estimated 300,000 dying from starvation.

SOMALI FIREFIGHTS

UN and US peacekeepers began to be drawn involuntarily into the fighting. In June 1993, a Pakistani unit engaged in collecting weapons was ambushed by Somali militiamen loyal to Mohammed Farah Aidid, the most powerful of the warlords, and 21 were killed. In August four US military policemen were killed by a mine. In September militiamen attacked Nigerian peacekeepers, and the US responded by sending a Special Forces unit known as Task Force Ranger into action, with the aim of hunting down Aidid and his Lieutenants.

During September Aidid's militia group became the target for sustained operations, with heliborne US troops supported by Marine AH-1 Cobra gunship helicopters mounting numerous operations. On 25 September one helicopter was shot down and its three crew killed, with more casualties taken in the ensuing rescue attempt.

The most notable battle took place on 3 October, when six senior militia commanders were captured in a raid. Two UH-60s were shot down during the withdrawal, and troops on the ground came under heavy attack. In the fierce fight which lasted through the night and into 4 October, at least 300 Somalis were killed, while American losses totalled 18 dead and 81 wounded. Aidid was not captured, however, and he remained a dominant figure until his death in 1996. The only result of the fighting was to convince President Clinton to pull US troops out of Somalia.

The withdrawal began in March 1994. Cobras covered a heli-borne evacuation to US Navy assault ships off shore, while C-130s, C-141s and C-5 Galaxies lifted troops and heavy equipment out of Mogadishu. The USAF also discontinued fixed-wing gunship operations: four AC-130H Spectres had been flying out of Mombasa in Kenya since 1993.

Although attempts have been made to find a negotiated peace, Somalia remains an armed camp.

OTHER CONFLICTS

Sudan gained independence from a joint Egyptian and British protec-

Above: For much of the time, fighting in Somalia made surface transportation of relief supplies nothing less than suicide. Aircraft were the only means of distributing aid, and the aircraft most often used was the Lockheed C-130 Hercules. This is an American Air National Guard example of the type delivering supplies at Mogadishu.

Below: Sudan's relations with the Soviet Union deteriorated in the 1970s, and after a ten-year gap the country acquired a number of western aircraft, including six C-130s. But the rise of Islamic fundamentalism in the 1980s and America's belief that Sudan was a terrorist sponsor meant that the rapprochement was short-lived.

Offshore support

The fighting in September and October 1993 saw the US presence at sea beefed up to cover a possible withdrawal from Somalia. The USS *Abraham Lincoln* carrier battle group joined amphibious ready groups centred on the USS *New Orleans* and *Guadalcanal*, each of which could deploy a brigade-sized Marine Expeditionary Unit. In the event, they were not required, but US troops began withdrawing from the region early in 1994.

Right: A Marine Corps CH-53E ferries supplies between the US Navy's amphibious task force in the Indian Ocean and the Marine Corps peacekeepers ashore in Somalia.

Below: In addition to their force of Marines, the US Navy's amphibious ready groups also operated Marine Corps AH-1, CH-46 and CH-53 helicopters and AV-8B STOVL attack jets.

Cockpit

Cobras have the near standard gunship layout of pilot high up in the rear cockpit with the gunner low down in front. The SuperCobra has a completely new avionics, navigation and communications fit.

Night vision

A new pilot head-up display is compatible with night vision goggles. The gunner's TOW sight now incorporates a thermal imaging systems for use in all weathers.

Missions

Marine Cobras in Somalia were used for convoy escort, fire support and armed reconnaissance missions.

Bell AH-1W SuperCobra

Used extensively by American forces in Somalia, the 'Whiskey Cobra' is the most advanced variant of the pioneering helicopter gunship. It originated as the AH-1T+, an upgrade of existing aircraft with improved weapons systems and more power. Subsequent new-build aircraft were given the AH-1W designation.

Weapons

This aircraft carries the standard USMC fit of eight BGM-71 TOW anti-tank missiles, two LAU-68 seven-round rocket pods and an M197 20-mm cannon. Hellfire laser-guided missiles can also be used.

Powerplant

The SuperCobra is powered by two General Electric T700 turboshafts, each rated at 1211 kW (1,625 shp). The exhaust jetpipes are each fitted with an infra-red suppressor.

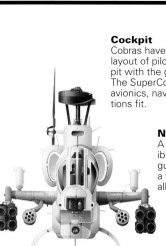

torate in 1954. This vast country saw military coups in 1958, 1969, 1985 and 1989. Since then, General Omar Hassan Ahmed al Bashir and his 15-member Revolutionary Council have transformed Sudan into a Muslim state.

However, this has exacerbated traditional religious and tribal rivalries between the Muslim north and the Christian south, and for much of the 1990s the Sudanese People's Liberation Movement has been has been fighting against the funda-

mentalist regime in Khartoum. The government has responded by attacking rebel positions with Chinese-built Chengdu F-7 fighters, apparently supplied by Iran.

Djibouti was granted independence from France in 1981. Led by Hassan Gouled, the one-party state fought a low-key guerrilla war against pro-democracy rebels, though this was brought to a negotiated settlement in 1994. France maintains a strong presence in the region, and used Djibouti as a staging post in moving aircraft, helicopters, troops and equipment into the region during the Gulf War.

YEMEN CIVIL WAR

Not part of the Horn of Africa, but separated by less than 32 km (20 miles) across the mouth of the Red Sea, the Yemen has also been infected by internecine struggles. Britain's withdrawal from Aden and the closure of the Suez Canal in 1967 brought the economy to the verge of ruin. Rivalry between the

Yemen Arab Republic to the north and the People's Democratic Republic of Yemen to the south saw the two states fight short border wars in 1972, 1978 and 1979. By 1990, however, political differences had apparently been settled, and the two countries combined at least notionally, as the Republic of Yemen.

In April 1994 fighting erupted as the Southern government refused to merge with the North. All-out war followed on 5 May, when both sides launched air attacks. The increasing pace of the war, together with a number of SS-1 'Scud' attacks by both sides saw a mass evacuation of foreigners from Aden. Aircraft used included a British Airways DC-10 and two RAF Hercules flying from Cyprus.

The advantage lay with the South, which had some 70 combat aircraft – MiG-17s, MiG-21s and Su-22s – against around 35 similar aircraft plus a few Northrop F-5s in the North. By the end of May, 30 aircraft were reported to have been shot down on both sides. In June, the South deployed the MiG-29 'Fulcrum', 12 of which had been bought from Moldova with Saudi funds. One was shot down, and six were destroyed on the ground.

Despite its aerial advantage, the South was no match for the Northern army on the ground, and by the beginning of July Northern columns were closing on Aden. The capture of the airport and the fall of the city on July 7 brought the war to an end.

Left: Originally supplied to South Yemen by the former Soviet state of Moldova, the MiG-29 'Fulcrum' fighters of the Republic of Yemen air force are the most capable combat aircraft in the region.

Right: French army Pumas land aboard the carrier Clemenceau after exercising ashore in Djibouti. France used the small African country as a staging post for its forces involved in the Gulf War.

West Africa

1966–1997

G ranted independence in 1960, Nigeria seemed set on a course of peaceful transition until 1966 when the first federation's central government collapsed followed by appalling massacres of the Ibo people in the Northern Region. Colonel Ojukwu, military ruler of the Eastern Region, declared independence for his area, homeland of the Ibo tribe. For three years a bloody civil war raged between the rebel state of Biafra and forces of the central government. The federal government obtained its first combat equipment in the form of 16 MiG-17 fighters and MiG-15UTI trainers from communist bloc countries (followed later by 28 further MiG-17s). These were later joined by five Ilyushin Il-28

bombers, flown by Egyptians and other mercenaries. About a dozen Czech Aero L-29 Delfin strike trainers were also purchased. Ojukwu's air force comprised a motley collection of ancient aircraft (some of them of World War II vintage) flown almost exclusively by white mercenaries; his cause nonetheless gained diplomatic recognition by several African states, notably Zambia and Tanzania. In the air war itself only one jet aircraft was lost in combat by the government forces. The Nigerian Civil War ended in January 1970 with the collapse of the secessionist government as Ojukwu fled to the Ivory Coast. More recently a military coup in July 1975 resulted in considerable modernisation of the Nigerian air

Above: A United Nations Sikorsky S-58 takes off from the airport at Port Harcourt, past an Ilyushin Il-28 bomber of the Federal air force. Before the war, Nigeria had no air arm to speak of: by the end it was operating jet fighters and bombers.

Below: The plight of the starving in Biafra saw the world's charities mobilised in an attempt to provide relief to the helpless and seriously wounded in the war zone. This DC-6 is a flying ambulance, chartered by the Swedish Red Cross.

Aid and Weapons

Both sides in the Biafran war had need of weaponry, supplies and armaments, and the Biafrans had the added problem of having hundreds of thousands of starving people to feed. Modern weapons arrived, and aid was flown in in large

quantities, but aid flights into Biafra were often attacked: they had to operate by night and the Federal forces could not tell which aircraft were bringing in guns and which were bringing in food, clothing and medicines.

Ilyushin Il-28 'Beagle'
Left: One of the earliest successful jet bombers, the Il-28 was sold to Soviet client states around the world. Nigeria acquired six via Egypt. Flown by Egyptian and Czech crews, the 'Beagles' mounted an indiscriminate bombing campaign against Biafran villages, killing at least 2,000 people between May and October 1968.

Boeing C-97G
Right: This ex-USAF freighter owned by Balair was one of many cargo aircraft employed by charitable organisations delivering aid to the war zone. 20 tonnes of aid was being flown into Biafra each night, but at great risk – one Red Cross flight was shot down by a MiG-17.

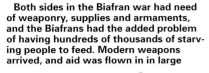

Left: A Nigerian Air Force MiG-17 stands on the tarmac at Enugu with a Dornier Do 27 in the background. The arrival of such relatively sophisticated weaponry gave the Federal forces the edge over the poorly-equipped Biafrans.

Above: Six Swedish-built MFI-9B trainers were fitted with Matra rocket pods and used by the Biafrans for light attack duties. Known as Minicons, the tiny aircraft were used primarily in attacks on the Nigerian oil industry.

force, and the East/West balance of aircraft procurement has been maintained by purchases from the UK, France, South Africa, West Germany, the USA and the Soviet Union.

Elsewhere in West Africa there has been considerable political and military turmoil, but in general air power has played only a minor part in conflicts in the region.

LIBERIA

Founded in 1847 by freed American slaves, the Republic of Liberia has suffered violent changes since 1980, when native Liberians under Samuel K. Doe overthrew the ruling American-descended oligarchy. Doe paid lip-service to democracy but kept power for the next decade.

In 1989, opposition factions under Charles Taylor and Prince Johnson rebelled, and after a year of fighting overthrew Doe – who was tortured to death. US Marines had to mount a rescue operation as the country descended into anarchy, the start of six years of bitter fighting that was to lead to more than 200,000 deaths.

There has been little air action in the fighting: apart from rescue missions the only aircraft flying have been those of the peacekeepers flown in by the Nigerian-dominated Economic Community of West Africa. Supposedly in place to unite

the warring factions, they have had little effect – indeed, as fighting reached new heights in 1996 they even took part in looting the capital Monrovia. Meanwhile, the USA airlifted more than 1,400 foreigners to safety in nearby Sierra Leone. But this was not to remain a safe haven for long.

SIERRA LEONE

Since 1991 the National Provisional Ruling Council, the military junta controlling Sierra Leone, had been fighting the Revolutionary United Front or RUF. Led by former corporal Alfred Foday Sankoh and supplied with arms by Liberian warlord Charles Taylor, the RUF had waged a terror campaign which peacekeeping troops sent from the West African Economic Community Monitoring Group (ECOMOG) in neighbouring Liberia could do little to control. By 1995 the RUF were threatening the capital, Freetown.

The government contracted Executive Outcomes, the South African company which had been so successful in Angola. EO provided high-quality tactical leadership to the government troops, and flew air support in three Mil Mi-17 'Hips' and one Mil Mi-24 'Hind' gunship.

By the beginning of 1997 EO's professional skills had made a considerable difference. A ceasefire was

holding, and a democratically elected government was in power. But in May, things went from hopeful to awful.

Middle-ranking officers, led by Major Johnny Paul Koroma but backed by the RUF, overthrew the government of President Ahmed Tejan Kabbah. US Marines evacuated hundreds of foreigners, lifting them to the assault ship USS *Kearsarge* and then on to Conakry in Guinea.

The United Nations and the

Organisation of African States condemned the coup. Nigeria went further, however, ordering its ECOMOG contingent into battle. So far, the powerful Nigerian air force has played little part in the increasingly fierce conflict, which has been fought out with small arms, mortars and artillery, though helicopters have provided most of ECOMOG's communications. But along with the Nigerian navy it is helping to enforce a tight sea and air blockade of Sierra Leone.

Above: Sierra Leone goverment troops unload mortar ammunition from an Executive Outcomes 'Hip' helicopter. The ammunition will be used in a successful assault on a RUF strongpoint 25 km (16 miles) south of Koidu.

Below: A door gunner's view as Sierra Leone's Mi-24V 'Hind' gunship flies in formation with a Mil Mi-17 transport helicopter, en route from Koidu to Kailahun. The helicopters gave the government a serious advantage over the RUF.

THE AMERICAS

Dominated by the mighty presence of the United States, the Americas have presented rather a different pattern of combat than has been common in the rest of the world since 1945. Even though the Cuban missile crisis was in many ways the zenith of the Cold War, most conflicts have been internal, although there have been a few border skirmishes, and American troops have been active in the region several times on peace-keeping duties. One notable exception was the Falklands War, which was probably the last major conflict of the European colonial era.

Latin America

1955–1995

Latin America has largely avoided the cataclysmic wars which have raged throughout the world through much of the 20th century. That is not to say that the continent has been a stranger to violence, however. There have been numerous relatively minor border clashes between neighbouring nations, but by far the majority of conflicts have been internal, and rebellions, coups and counter-insurgency campaigns have been endemic in most of the region since World War II.

ARGENTINA
After the death of Eva Peron in 1955, the right-wing dictatorship of Juan Domingo Peron lost popular support. In June a naval mutiny saw Government House bombed. In September, a more serious naval uprising saw several Meteor fighters seized and used against government troops. Strikes were also flown by such unlikely types as navy PBYs, SNJs, AT-11s and J2Fs. In response, air force Meteors attacked the naval base at Rio Santiago, damaging two destroyers but losing one aircraft to anti-aircraft fire. A Meteor is also reported to have downed a navy SNJ in combat. Air force Lincoln bombers made demonstration flights, but are not thought to have been used in action.

Many troops switched sides after the navy began shelling coastal installations, and by the end of June Peron had been forced into exile and a military junta took power.

In a two-day rising in April 1963, naval aircraft supported the rebels, while the air force supported the government. Navy F4Us, F9Fs, PBYs, SNJs were used on ground –

Above: Early Latin American wars were distinguished by the use of weaponry long discarded from the armouries of the major powers. But by the 1980s, many South American air forces were equipped with modern high-performance aircraft like these Ecuadorian Kfirs.

attack strikes against army formations; one SNJ and one F9F were shot down. Air force Meteors, MS.760s, F-86Fs, and Lincolns were used on bombing raids before the rebellion was defeated on 3 April. Two years later, in a border dispute with Chile, one F4U was lost but there was no aerial combat.

In 1975 an air force revolt saw Mirage IIIs fly a number of threatening sorties. Navy A-4 Skyhawks attacked rebels in Buenos Aires

BOLIVIA
Che Guevara instigated a 1965 revolt against right-wing dictator General Barrientos. Bolivian air force F-51s, T-28s and T-6s were used against guerrilla positions with limited success. Aircraft were also used as communications relays and H-19 helicopters moved troops in the successful hunt for Che, who was killed in October 1967.

Barrientos was killed in a helicopter accident in 1969, and the air force played a part in a series of military coups over the next decade. The most notorious incident was in 1971, when F-51 Mustangs were used to strafe protesting students

occupying the university quarter of the capital, La Paz.

CHILE
In September 1973 a military coup led by General Augusto Pinochet Ugarte overthrew democratically

Below: Argentina is one of the few nations to have used heavy bombers in anger. During a 1963 coup attempt by elements of the navy, ageing Avro Lincolns of the Fuerza Aerea Argentina mounted attacks on rebel positions.

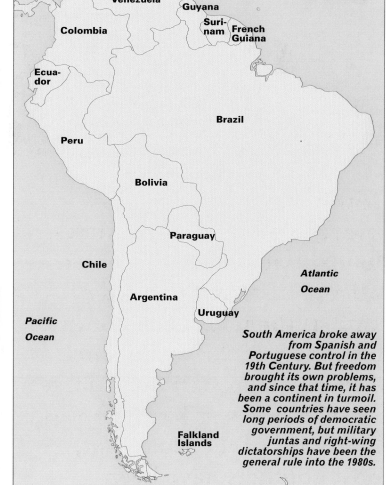

CONTINENT OF COUPS

South America broke away from Spanish and Portuguese control in the 19th Century. But freedom brought its own problems, and since that time, it has been a continent in turmoil. Some countries have seen long periods of democratic government, but military juntas and right-wing dictatorships have been the general rule into the 1980s.

Above: South American air forces have given many great aircraft their last exposure to combat, but it has not always been an honorable usage. In 1971, Bolivian Mustangs were used to strafe demonstrating students in the capital, La Paz.

Right: The Cold War saw Soviet influence in the region increase, primarily in the supply of military equipment. Here a Kalashnikov-armed Peruvian soldier fires from a Mil Mi-8 'Hip' helicopter during the 1981 border clash with Ecuador.

elected Marxist President Salvador Allende. Hawker Hunters were used to bomb the presidential palace just before Allende's surrender and subsequent death – which was claimed as suicide by the military but thought to be murder by the socialists.

COLOMBIA

A continuous civil war known as La Violencia lasted from 1948 to 1958. The air force used AT-6s and F-47Ds in COIN operations.

In the 1970s and 1980s the air force was in action in two different campaigns: in countering the flourishing cocaine trade and in operations against numerous left-wing guerrilla groups. Air force A-37s were used to strike at guerrilla strongpoints, and in 1986 air attacks drove rebels out of the town of Morales which they had captured.

ECUADOR AGAINST PERU

In 1981 a minor and inconclusive border conflict with Peru saw Cessna T-37s, Mirage F.1Es and Jaguars flying armed reconnaissance sorties.

A more serious clash occurred in the Cordillera del Condor region in

1995. Ecuadorian Mirage F.1JAs claimed to have shot down two Peruvian Sukhoi Su-22 'Fitters' on 10 February. A Cessna A-37 was shot down by an Ecuadorian Kfir on the same date. Three Peruvian Mil Mi-8 helicopters were also claimed destroyed by Ecuadorian Blowpipe SAMs or ground fire on 30 January and 7 February, while similar hits, with unknown results, were reported on two FAE Kfirs and an A-37B on 12 February.

PARAGUAY

Converted transports bombed Asuncion in a 1947 army revolt. In 1959 exiles invaded from Bolivia to attempt the overthrow of fascist dictator General Alfredo Stroessner. The air force used T-6s and C-47s fitted with bomb racks to support troops used to crush rebellion

PERU

A long-lasting counter-insurgency struggle against numerous rebel groups has been under way since the 1980s, most notably against the Maoist movement known as Sendero Luminoso, or Shining Path. Air force strikes have been used to support army operations

against the guerrillas and against Colombian cocaine cartel-backed drug traffickers, during which Mil Mi-8 and Mil Mi-24 helicopters have provided troops with the ability to make surprise assaults on revolutionary positions.

VENEZUELA

In 1958 The arrest of the army commander and his chief of staff, Colonel Leon, led to an uprising, initially by the air force followed by the navy and parts of the army. Vampires and Sabres were used to strafe the presidential palace and the defence ministry, and to bomb the National Security headquarters. They had little support from the populace, however, and the coup leaders fled or surrendered. Leon was released however, and went into exile in Colombia. In 1960, he led a further rebellion, which was put down when rebel units were bombed by loyal air force Canberras.

Canberras were used to bomb rebel troops in 1961, and again in 1962 when a Marine battalion mutinied. A month later air force Vampires strafed rebel buildings after an unsuccessful naval rebellion

at Puerto Cabello.

Reacting to violations of its air space by Ecuadorian Mirage 5s, Venezuelan troops supported by F-16 fighters and Tucano COIN aircraft were moved to the border region as a deterrent in 1987. The confrontation concerned a territorial dispute over parts of the Gulf of Venezuela.

In 1992 a failed coup by army paratroopers in February was followed in November by an uprising of parts of the air force. The government's F-16 wing remained loyal, however, and played a major part in putting the rebellion down.

CENTRAL AMERICA

For decades, most of countries in Central America have been wracked by internal strife. The civil war in El Salvador and the attempt to bring down the left-wing Sandinista revolutionary government of Nicaragua by right-wing, US-backed guerrillas were perhaps the bloodiest conflicts, but few areas escaped unscathed.

Guerrilla subversion was endemic in Guatemala from the 1960s, in a bloody war which saw the death of over 100,000 people. At the

Ecuadorian dogfighter

Ecuador originally agreed to buy ex-Israeli Kfirs in the late 1970s, but the sale was initially embargoed by the US who would not agree to the re-export of the J79 engines. After a long delay the sale was approved, and 12 aircraft were delivered

in 1982. The Kfirs featured strongly in Ecuador's border clash with Peru in 1995, where one of the type was credited with shooting down a Peruvian Cessna A-37.

IAI Kfir C2

Left: Developed by Israel Aircraft Industries from the Dassault Mirage III, the Kfir features a more powerful American-designed General Electric J79 engine than the original French Atar powerplant. Ecuadorian aircraft are nominally Kfir C2s, but feature many of the avionics upgrades fitted to the later Kfir C7. The aircraft depicted is flown by Escuadron de Combate 2113, part of Grupo 211 based at Taura.

Coup attempt in Venezuela

By comparison to other nations in the region, Venzuela has enjoyed a relatively stable government. The Fuerza Aérea Venezolana suffered from a long period of limited funding which had left a number of units in non-operational state, but in the 1980s this situation was rectified with the delivery of modern equipment such as F-16As and upgraded Mirages.

In spite of this seemingly progressive situation within the air force, a failed coup attempt was made on 4 February 1992 by the paratroopers of Grupo de Parcaidistas 'Aragua' led by Lt Col Chavaz. Athough quashed, feelings within the air force apparently remained high and at dawn on 27 November a further coup attempt was made by elements of the FAV led by Brigadier General Visconti, the air force logistic service inspector.

Under the cover of Air Force Day preparations, Visconti contrived to move forces sympathetic to Chavaz to the El Libertador Air Base, Palo Negro, Aragua. These included one NF-5B, five T-2Ds, three OV-10Es, six OV-10As and two A-27s, which, together with units stationed within the complex, gave him a very commanding situation.

Visconti seized control of the base at 0330 on the morning of 27 November. He was supported by the bulk of the

10th Special Operations Group which operates most of the FAV's helicopters and by Grupo de Caza 11.

The crews from the FAV's F-16 wing, Grupo de Caza 16, refused to join the rebellion and managed to scramble the two 'QRA' aircraft which fled to Barquisimeto. This base appears to have remained loyal to the president. The remainder of Grupo 16 were either captured or managed to retreat under fire to the administrative compound.

At the same time , other personnel took control of nearby Mariscal Sucre air base, in Boca Del Rio, Maracay, This houses the FAV's training wing, operating EMB-312 Tucano and T-34A trainers.

REBEL ATTACKS

At first light three Mirage 50EV fighters of Grupo 11 strafed army barracks in Caracas while a mixed formation of a dozen aircraft including Broncos, Tucanos and a single Buckeye attacked the presidential palace, the Presidential Guard barracks, the foreign ministry and police headquarters.

The two F-16s that had escaped to Barquisimeto returned over the city at around 0700 and chased away the rebel Broncos and Tucanos, going on to attack El Libertador with their 20-mm cannon. Meanwhile, loyal troops holding out at both Sucre and El Libertador were subjected to repeated attacks by rebel helicopters and aircraft. In the process one Bronco was downed by small arms and AAA fire.

Rebel Mirages and Broncos in turn attacked the air base at Barquisimeto to prevent further sorties being flown in support of the government, destroying three stored CF-5As. A civilian MD-80 airliner was also hit by cannon fire.

Grupo de Caza 12 managed to scramble its sole NF-5A, and one of the F-16s got airborne to shoot down two of the attacking OV-10s. The few defending fighters kept up the struggle against the rebel forces but the only other kill was an A-27 Tucano brought down by an F-16. A further Bronco was lost over Caracas when it was either hit by small arms fire or had an engine problem. Both crewmen ejected, the aircraft crashing by the La Carlota runway.

By 1300 La Carlota air base was secured against the remaining limited resistance and both El Libertador and Sucre followed shortly afterwards when tanks and paratroops entered the bases.

Above: The Venezuelan F-16 units remained loyal to the President, and played a significant part in defeating the rebels.

This followed the departure of Brigadier General Visconti and 92 officers in a Grupo 6 C-130H Hercules to Peru, where they sought asylum. Two of the four Grupo 11 Mirage 50EVs escaped to the Dutch island of Aruba and an OV-10 Bronco was flown to Curaçao. One thousand FAV officers and NCOs were reportedly arrested, which no doubt created a major setback to the FAV in its struggle to become an integrated front-line force once again.

Below: Mirage 50EVs started the air portion of the rebellion, shooting up government troops with their powerful 30-mm cannon.

Below: OV-10s taxi down the apron at El Libertador. At least four rebel Broncos were shot doen in the coup attempt, two by F-16s.

---

same time Guatemalan claims on Belize brought the country into confrontation with British troops and warplanes sent to protect the former colony. Relatively tranquil Honduras, which fought a brief but nasty little war with El Salvador in 1969, and pacifist Costa Rica, which had abolished its army 20 years earlier, were both threatened by an overspill of violence from their neighbours. Hovering in the background was Latin America's most formidable military power, Fidel Castro's Cuba.

EL SALVADOR

Although the Salvadorean army was victorious in the 10-day 'Football War' against Honduras in 1969, the Honduran air force gained control of the air from an early stage of that slightly bizarre conflict. During the following years El Salvador engaged in a concentrated build-up of its armed forces and in particular of its air force, which by the late 1970s was marginally stronger than that of

its neighbour and former enemy.

The final ratification of a peace treaty between El Salvador and Honduras in 1980 coincided with the escalation of internal violence in El Salvador into something approaching a full-scale civil war, and from 1980 onwards the attention of the Salvadorean armed forces became increasingly focused on internal security. It was a brutal war marked by the activities of death squads who seemed beyond the control of any leaders.

At this time the 1,000-man Salvadorean air force consisted of a fighter squadron equipped with 18 Dassault Ouragans purchased from Israel five years earlier, a light strike squadron equipped with nine

Right: Central America has seen more than its share of violence over the last three decades, with border tensions and territorial claims contributing in part. But much of the bloodshed has been internal, with both right and left-wing regimes countering rebels backed by Cuba or the United States respectively.

CENTRAL AMERICA

Gulf of Mexico

Cuba

Yucutan (Mexico)

Belize

Jamaica

Guatemala

Honduras

El Salvador

Caribbean Sea

Nicaragua

Pacific Ocean

Costa Rica

Panama

Colombia

The Football War

The Mustang's last air-to-air conflict was the El Salvador/Honduras 'Soccer War' (Guerra de Futbol) of July 1969. It erupted after the two nations played three bitterly contested matches in the World Cup. Behind it lay other grievances. Spurred by riots against Salvadorean immigrants (who formed one-eighth of the Honduran population) and by long-standing territorial ambitions, El Salvador opened hostilities on 14 July 1969 after alleged mistreatment of its national football team. A ceasefire took effect four days later but El Salvador continued spradic military operations until the Organisation of American States threatened sanctions on 29 July. The 'Soccer War' is listed in one encyclopedia as 'costing thousands of lives' but the actual number may be as few as a dozen; a peace treaty was not signed until 1980.

Honduras' air arm consisted mainly of Vought F4U Corsairs, while El Salvador possessed Goodyear FG-1D Corsairs and a handful of C-47 transports pressed into service as bombers, in addition to its new fleet of Mustangs. Another F-51D had been a pristine warbird owned by a local businessman and engineer, which was impressed into combat service. On a typical mission, Salvadorean C-47s and FG-1Ds carrying bombs were escorted by 'clean' F-51D Mustangs performing escort duty like that at which they had excelled during World War II mis-

sions over Europe. Ranges were short, however, and the Mustangs went into battle with minimal fuel loads, except for the occasional deep strike to Tegucigalpa. The FAS had help from some colourful mercenaries who flew a number of the Mustang sorties. Documentation is lacking, but it appears that five Mustangs were lost in action in a conflict which saw virtually all aircraft hit by friendly and hostile fire. Two Mustangs were lost in a mid-air collision, and two to fuel starvation. No Salvadorean pilot claimed an air-to-air victory while flying an F-51, but at least one FAS F-51D was shot down by a Honduran F4U Corsair – and some sources say two were. These marked the final instance of air combat between World War II fighters. The final Mustang ever to be lost in an air-to-air engagement was piloted by FAS Captain Humberto Varela and was shot down on 17 July 1969 by an F4U-5 flown Honduran Major Soto, who also downed an FG-1D.

Both sides in the Football War employed Vought Corsairs, the El Salvador version being the Goodyear-built FG-1.

Right: With very few aircraft able to perform ground attack missions, both El Salvador and Honduras pressed Douglas C-47 transports into service as make-shift bombers. Salvador lost four aircraft in the war, while Honduras lost eight, including two C-47s.

Above: British troops, helicopters and a flight of Royal Air Force Harriers were deployed to Belize as a deterrent to prevent Guatemala from invading the former British colony.

Fouga Magisters also used for advanced training, and assorted transports, trainers and helicopters. US military assistance, which had been suspended during the Carter administration, began again in 1981 with the delivery of at least 12 Bell UH-1H helicopters together with advisory help.

The air force's principal task was in flying strike missions against elusive guerrillas, redeploying infantry to points often inaccessible by land (mainly in its tired transport force of C-47s), inserting small units of special forces into areas of high guerrilla activity, and evacuating casualties.

But it was a war of attrition, with a notable guerrilla success occuring in 1982 with an immensely destructive attack on the Ilopango air base on 27 January 1982. Within weeks, however, the USA had delivered another 12 UH-1Hs, eight Cessna A-37B light strike aircraft, four Cessna O-2A forward air control aircraft and three Fairchild C-123 transports as replacements for the lost materiel.

During the closing months of 1983 the civil war acquired a new dimension with the creation of a 'strategic brigade' by the guerrillas, who engaged elements of the 1st and 3rd Brigades of the Army and the ATLACATL and ATONAL immediate-reaction battalions in conventional military operations in the north and east of the country, causing grave casualties which in turn heavily stressed the air force's casevac capabilities.

Although the Salvadorean fixed-wing aircraft continued to fly ground support and transport missions, the helicopter had (as in Vietnam) already proved to be the most useful type of aircraft in the continuing war against an elusive enemy. The helicopter arm therefore continued to enjoy a fairly spectacular growth although there was attrition through guerrilla ground fire and accidents.

The Salvadorean air force car-

Sandinista Workhorse

The Mil Mi-8 was the most important aircraft in the Nicaraguan inventory for much of the struggle with the 'Contras'. The first 10 aircraft in service were Mi-8TBKs, known to NATO as the 'Hip-F', which could carry six

UV-32-57 rocket pods. These were joined through the 1980s by at least 15 examples of the more powerful Mil Mi-17, which can carry the same six-pylon outrigger as the earlier variant.

Mil Mi-8 'Hip'

Left: One of the greatest helicopter designs in history, the rugged Mil Mi-8 'Hip' has seen combat in Africa, Asia and South America since its first flight in 1961. Twin turbine-powered, the 'Hip' can carry up to 28 troops or a heavy load of weaponry on outrigger pylons. Improved versions with uprated engines are designated Mi-17.

A rocket-armed Cessna Skywagon of the Sandinista air arm is seen on a dirt airstrip in Nicaragua with a Mil Mi-8 and an Antonov An-2 transport biplane.

ried out 227 air strikes against the guerrillas in 1983 and 158 more strikes during the first six months of 1984 (74 of them in June alone). Although plans for the transfer of a number of Douglas AC-47 gunships were shelved two of the existing C-47 transport aircraft were armed with 12.7-mm (0.5-in) machine-guns which effectively transformed them into similar weapons platforms.

Government forces now totalled approximately 40,000, with the guerrillas, who had united under Cuban and Nicaraguan auspices as the Farabundo Marti National Liberation Front, or FMLN, being less than a third as strong. Even so, they retained control of almost 30 per cent of the republic, principally in the north and northeast, and had by now raised a second 'strategic brigade' for conventional military operations against the government forces.

The election of Jose Napoleon Duarte in 1984, the first freely elected president in 50 years, sig-

nalled a change. Although the war of attrition continued, politicians were now talking about dialogue, and Alfredo Christiani, who defeated Duarte in an election in 1989, strove to come to terms with the guerrillas. The FMLN had other ideas, however, and in November of that year launched a bloody offensive which killed thousands.

At the instigation of other central American leaders, UN mediation was called for. A peace agreement was signed in 1991, with the conclusion of decades of struggle coming on 15 December 1992.

NICARAGUA

To the south, the left-wing Sandinista revolutionary government of Nicaragua had toppled the corrupt Somoza dictatorship in 1979. In 1981 the Sandinistas were seen by newly elected US President Reagan as a major threat to stability in the region, and determined American-backed efforts to overthrow it were made by CIA-trained groups of right-wing guerrillas

based in neighbouring Honduras and Costa Rica. These were composed both of emigré Nicaraguans and mercenaries colloquially as 'Contras'. They were supported by their own helicopters and by the Honduran air force.

Air power did not play much part in the Nicaraguan war, although the reported presence of a dozen Mikoyan-Gurevich MiG-21s, supposedly transferred to Nicaragua from Cuba during 1981 but never actually confirmed, loomed large in American thinking at the time.

As the Sandinistas had very few serviceable fixed-wing aircraft, the burden of ground support in the war against the guerrillas fell mainly on the helicopter arm, which suffered several casualties to 'Contra' ground fire. Three Mi-24 'Hind' gunship helicopters were delivered, to join a growing fleet which by

Helicopters played a major part in the civil war in Nicaragua. Soviet-built Mil Mi-8 and Mi-17 'Hip' transports, escorted and supported Mi-24 'Hind' gunships, proved vital in giving mobility to Sandinista troops fighting the American-backed 'Contra' guerrillas.

Above: The only air assets available to the Sandinistas after they came to power in Nicaragua were a few light attack types like this T-28 Trojan. T-28s were also used by the opposition Contras, some having been flown into exile in 1979. A T-28 based in Costa Rica attacked Managua airport in 1983, destroying one C-47 before being shot down.

1984 included a dozen Mi-8s in addition to two Alouette IIIs and a miscellaneous collection of US-built types which had survived the civil war which overthrew the Somoza dictatorship.

The majority of the military Mi-8s seemed to have been acquired from the second half of 1983 onwards and appear to be employed in the gunship configuration, photographs of them in this role having appeared in the Cuban press as early as May 1984.

Although Sandinista president Daniel Ortega won a fair popular election in 1984, the civil war and US attempts to topple the government continued until 1990, when the Sandinistas were defeated in the polls and Violeta Chamorro came to power.

Falklands Invaded

APRIL 1982

The Falklands have been a British possession since 1833, when the Royal Navy evicted newly-arrived Argentinian settlers and claimed the islands for Britain. They are bleak and inhospitable, but have served as a useful base for whaling, as a strategic naval base, and have given Britain an internationally recognised 'share' of Antarctica. The islands' inhabitants regard themselves as British, and fiercely oppose any transfer of sovereignty to Argentina, which has long claimed the islands as the Malvinas.

A military government was established in Argentina in 1976, and in 1977 a British naval task force was sent to the area after reports that an occupation of near-by South Georgia was likely. This signalled that Britain would maintain sovereignty over the islands, but doubt resurfaced when a new Conservative government came to power. It announced cuts in defence expenditure, including the planned withdrawal, without replacement, of the Antarctic survey vessel HMS *Endurance*, the area's *de facto* garrison ship.

To many this was an indication that an Argentinian invasion of the Malvinas might not be opposed militarily. Argentinian scrap metal workers landed on South Georgia on 19 March 1982, and began dismantling the disused whaling station. Such an action was almost certainly intended to gauge how Britain might react to a full-scale invasion. Britain landed observation

teams and Royal Marines from the *Endurance* on 23 and 31 March, while nuclear submarines headed south on 25 March. Had more publicity been given to these responses the Argentinians might have reconsidered their decision to proceed with an invasion, taken on 23 March. Two Argentinian Task Groups set sail on 28 March.

ARGENTINE ASSAULT

Meanwhile, on 2 April, 2,800 Argentinians landed on the Falklands. The 80-strong British garrison surrendered after brisk fighting, on the orders of the island's governor, Sir Rex Hunt. South Georgia was invaded the following day, by a third Argentinian task group. The Royal Marine defenders put up fierce resistance,

Right: The normally quiet airfield at Ascension was soon packed with RAF aircraft, including Hercules transports, Nimrod ASW aircraft and virtually the RAF's entire fleet of Victor tankers. Fourteen Victors can be seen in this view alone, along with a single Vulcan.

even downing an Argentine Puma, with a Carl Gustav anti-tank rocket and a support Allouette was damaged by machine-gun fire before the Marines surrendered and followed their comrades into captivity. Argentina installed an AN/TPS43F radar and established a control centre at Port Stanley, providing an integrated air defence for the islands.

Having failed to deter the Argentine invasion, Britain assembled a task force to retake the

Above: A Lynx hovers over the deck of HMS Invincible, having dropped an underslung load of stores. The despatch of the Task Force was a triumph of logistics, and intensive use was made of helicopters during all phases of the operation.

Left: HMS Antrim's obsolescent Wessex HAS.Mk 3 played a significant role in the war, recovering an SAS patrol from South Georgia (and the crews of the two Wessex HU.Mk 5s originally sent to do the job) and later attacking the Argentine submarine Santa Fé.

islands, under the codename Operation 'Corporate'. The surface ships committed to the operation became TF.317, while the submarines already despatched became TF.324. RAF air traffic control staff were sent to Wideawake airfield (a facility built by the USA to support a tracking station and normally run by Pan Am) on the British island of Ascension, to prepare it for its potential role as a staging post to the Falklands. Victor tankers and

Above: A Sea Skua-armed Lynx of No. 815 Squadron flies off the coast of South Georgia. Similarly-armed Lynxes were deployed aboard the 'Sheffield'-, 'Broadsword'- and 'Amazon'-class ships, and one from Brilliant torpedoed the submarine Santa Fé after it had been depth-charged by the Antrim's Wessex.

Right: Argentine ground crew load a Pucará with unguided rockets. Argentina deployed only light-weight attack aircraft to the Falklands, instead of laying a PSP runway from which Skyhawks could operate. This was probably a factor in costing Argentina the war.

Nimrod maritime patrol aircraft soon began flying operations.

The task force commander, Rear-Admiral John 'Sandy' Woodward, sailed from Gibraltar for Ascension on 2 April, aboard HMS *Glamorgan*, accompanied by four destroyers, five frigates and three support vessels assembled for exercises in the Mediterranean. The carriers *Hermes* and *Invincible*, with the assault ship *Fearless*, four support ships, two frigates and four landing ships sailed from Portsmouth on 5 and 6 April. The hastily requisitioned liner *Canberra* set sail from Southampton on 9 April, with 2,000 troops drawn from 40 and 42 Commandos and from 3 Para. These caught up with Woodward as he paused at Ascension.

On 7 April Britain declared a 322-km (200-mile) Maritime Exclusion Zone around the Falklands, to become effective on 14 April, after which shipping in the area would be liable to attack

without warning. From 21 April, a small element of the task force retook South Georgia. SAS and SBS soldiers were inserted and then recovered after the weather deteriorated before Wessex, Lynx and Wasp helicopters attacked and beached the submarine *Santa Fé* on 23 October. Troops landed to take advantage of the surprise this caused, and the Argentine garrison surrendered without a fight after a 235-shot naval bombardment.

Below: This Fuerza Aérea Argentina Boeing 707 was the aircraft which discovered the Task Force as it sailed south, confirming to the Junta that the British meant business.

Argentine garrison

Argentina's invasion of the Falklands was primarily seaborne, although a small number of helicopters did participate. However, once the British garrison surrendered, the Argentinians brought in Pucarás, T-34Cs and MB.339s for light attack duties, Short Skyvans for communications and patrol, and a mixed bag of helicopters from the army, air force and Prefectura.

Agusta A 109 Hirundo
Two A 109s were used by the Combat Aviation Battalion 601 of the Army Aviation Command in the Falklands. These were later captured by the British Forces and flown in Royal Marine markings. They still serve today as ZE411 and 412 with 7 Regiment (8 Flight) AAC in support of the SAS.

Aermacchi MB.339A
The Argentinian navy deployed six Aermacchi MB.339As to Port Stanley from their mainland base. They operated in the light-ground-attack role, and participated in attacks on British shipping, despite their inadequate armament and lack of defensive avionics.

Lockheed C-130E Hercules
The C-130Es and C-130Hs of GTA.1 were augmented by Fokker F27s and F28s on the air bridge between their base at Comodoro Rivadavia and Port Stanley. One C-130 was lost during the war, shot down by a Sea Harrier.

Falklands First Strikes

1 MAY – 20 MAY 1982

Left: Vulcan XM607 lands at Wideawake airfield, Ascension Island, after the first Black Buck bombing mission on 30 April 1982. The aircraft carried 14 454-kg (1,000-lb) bombs for this mission, but only one clipped the Port Stanley runway.

Above: The first of the Black Buck Vulcans refuels in flight from a Victor K.Mk 2 tanker during one of its three successful bombing raids against the airfield at Port Stanley. Another Vulcan flew two successful anti-radar missions, and two Vulcan missions were aborted.

As the British task force sailed south, it was reinforced by men and materiel (later including the Harrier GR.Mk 3s of No. 1 Squadron, and aircraft from a third Sea Harrier squadron) flown to Ascension and then helicoptered or flown on to the waiting ships, while other elements of the British force got into position. Canberra PR.Mk 9s and Nimrod R.Mk 1s flew reconnaissance and Elint sorties from a still undisclosed location (perhaps in Chile, or even Brazil), while maritime Nimrods and radar reconnaissance Victors operated from Ascension. Back in the UK, the MoD requisitioned the *Queen Elizabeth II* to carry 3,500 Welsh Guards, Scots Guards and Gurkhas to the Falklands.

On the Falkland Islands, the Argentine garrison prepared defensive positions, and by late-April had its own detachment of 24 Pucaras for close-support, six naval MB-339As and four T-34Cs, alongside a disparate group of army and air force helicopters. Port Stanley and Goose Green airfields were well defended by Roland SAMs and 20- and 35-mm AAA.

Above: Britain's operation to recapture the Falklands would have been impossible without its pair of carriers, Hermes (shown) and Invincible. These allowed the task force to fly south with its own organic air-defence and close air-support/ground-attack assets.

Right: An Argentine pilot's target view. The Dagger and Skyhawk pilots pressed home their attacks at very low level: so low, in fact, that their bombs frequently failed to fuse before they hit their targets.

Left: Argentina's five Dassault Super Étendards had an importance far beyond that suggested by their limited numbers. They were the launch aircraft for Argentina's five AM-39 Exocet anti-ship missiles, which destroyed two task force vessels.

Argentine attackers

While Argentina's ageing Canberras were never likely to prove too much of an embarrassment to the Sea Harrier, the British jet's superiority over the supersonic Mirage III and IAI Dagger came as a pleasant surprise to some senior officers, who had not thought that agility and the all-aspect Sidewinder would provide quite such an edge over the Argentine fighters and fighter bombers.

Dassault Super Etendard

Right: Only five Super Etendards had been delivered by the time that France imposed its embargo on Argentina. These aircraft equipped 2 Escuadrilla, 3 Escuadra Aéronaval, based at Rio Grande.

English Electric Canberra B.Mk 62

Left: The Canberras of Grupo 2 flew 54 missions, including five surveillance, three tactical reconnaissance and four long-range anti-shipping missions, together with 14 day and 22 night bomber sorties.

IAI Dagger

Right: The IAI Dagger equipped two squadrons of Grupo de Caza 6, and served in the fighter bomber and escort roles. The type was used intensively in raids against the task force, and suffered correspondingly heavy losses.

Left: Harriers and Sea Harriers cocooned on the deck of the Atlantic Conveyor. The aircraft boarded the ship at Ascension, and were transported down to the Falklands, where they were flown off before the vessel was sunk.

against the task force, damaging a handful of ships but losing two Mirage IIIs, a Dagger, and a Canberra to patrolling Sea Harriers.

On 2 May the Argentine cruiser *Belgrano* was sunk by a British submarine, and Lynxes from *Glasgow* and *Coventry* damaged a patrol craft as SAS parties were landed on the islands, while the night of 3/4 May saw the second Black Buck Vulcan raid against Port Stanley. There was also a second Sea Harrier airfield attack, one aircraft falling to a Tigercat SAM. Later on 4 May two Super Etendards struck back by attacking RN ships on picket duty, fatally damaging HMS *Sheffield* (which sank while under tow six days later) and killing 26 of its crew. One Sea Harrier was shot down by AAA during an attack on Goose Green. Air attacks by both sides were mounted as the weather permitted, with Argentine losses

The Task Force was located by an Argentine Boeing 707 on 21 April before being escorted from the scene by a Sea Harrier. On 30 April, with diplomatic moves to find a solution exhausted, Britain transformed its Maritime Exclusion Zone into a Total Exclusion Zone, while the USA formally endorsed Britain's position.

LONG-RANGE BOMBING

On 1 May a single Vulcan bombed Port Stanley, dropping a stick of bombs obliquely across the runway, and also sending a clear signal that no Argentine target could be deemed safe from potential air attack. Later that morning, the airfields at Port Stanley and Goose Green were attacked by Sea Harriers. From midday, warships began bombarding military positions in and around Port Stanley. The Fuerza Aerea Argentina (FAA) responded by launching attacks

Right: The British had a range advantage over the Falklands. The much more numerous Argentine aircraft had to fly between 700 and 950 km (435/590 miles) to reach the combat zone. Sea Harriers, on the other hand, were flying off carriers less than 160 km (100 miles) to the east of the Falklands.

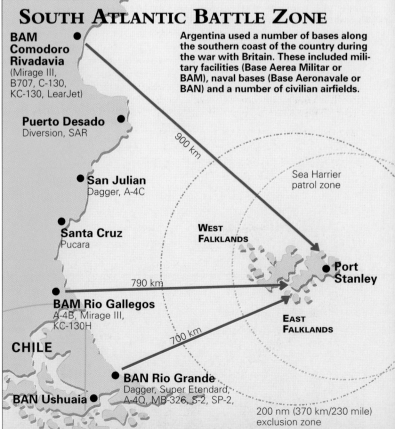

SOUTH ATLANTIC BATTLE ZONE

BAM Comodoro Rivadavia
(Mirage III, B707, C-130, KC-130, LearJet)

Argentina used a number of bases along the southern coast of the country during the war with Britain. These included military facilities (Base Aerea Militar or BAM), naval bases (Base Aeronavale or BAN) and a number of civilian airfields.

Puerto Desado
Diversion, SAR

San Julian
Dagger, A-4C

Sea Harrier patrol zone

Santa Cruz
Pucara

WEST FALKLANDS

900 km

790 km

BAM Rio Gallegos
A-4B, Mirage III, KC-130H

Port Stanley

EAST FALKLANDS

700 km

CHILE

BAN Rio Grande
Dagger, Super Etendard, A-4Q, MB-326, S-2, SP-2,

BAN Ushuaia

200 nm (370 km/230 mile) exclusion zone

Above: Bomb racks and fuel tanks nearly empty, a Skyhawk refuels as it heads homewards for Argentina, after an anti-shipping strike over the Falklands.

Below: A Harrier GR.Mk 3 from No. 1 Squadron RAF is seen at Ascension Island before setting off on the long flight to the task force in the South Atlantic.

near Punta Arenas in Chile, after an SAS insertion mission. The SAS and SBS teams inserted before the invasion spotted for naval guns.

While SAS and SBS units made diversionary attacks on Goose Green and Darwin, the full-scale British landings (Operation Sutton) began at San Carlos under cover of mist and darkness , before dawn on 21 May. The FAA made a series of spirited attacks on the invasion fleet, damaging several ships for the loss of five Daggers, two Pucaras, and five Skyhawks. The Argentine pilots won the respect of their adversaries, flying their attacks with reckless bravery and some degree of accuracy. One of the Falklands-based MB.339s even entered the fray, making an accurate if relatively ineffective attack against the *Argonaut*, which suffered minor damage. Had Argentine bombs been better fused, or had the FAA been able to sustain a higher sortie rate, many ships might have been worse damaged than they were. Nevertheless, one of the damaged ships sank the following day. The British lost a Harrier GR.Mk 3 to a Blowpipe SAM, and two Gazelles to small arms fire. But at the end of the day, the British were able to land forces ashore, and consolidated their position the following day, when bad weather prevented further attacks.

mounting steadily to the weather, Sea Harriers and SAMs. On 9 May SBS soldiers dropped from Sea Kings boarded the Argentine intelligence gatherer *Narwal* after it had been attacked by Sea Harriers. A raid by Skyhawks on 12 May against RN ships bombarding Port Stanley put the *Glasgow* out of action, though the bomb which hit the ship fortunately failed to explode. A planned third Vulcan raid was aborted due to high winds over the target on 13 May, but an

SAS raid destroyed six Pucaras, a Skyvan and four Mentors at Pebble Island on 14 May. Task force helicopter losses continued to mount to birdstrikes, and accidents, while on 17 May a Sea King was burned by its crew at Agua Fresca,

Right: The Mirage IIIEAs of Grupo de Caza 8 were mainly retained at Comodoro Rivadavia for air defence duties, though they flew a handful of long-range escort sorties over the Falklands, losing a number of aircraft to Royal Navy Sea Harriers.

The empire strikes back

The ships of the British task force were accompanied and supported by a wide range of aircraft performing a variety of roles. Sea Harriers and Harriers aboard the two carriers flew air defence, attack and reconnaissance sorties, while Nimrods, Vulcans and Victors based at at Wideawake on Ascension Island flew maritime reconnaissance, ASW, bomber, SEAD, tanker and radar reconnaissance missions. It is believed that Canberra PR.Mk 9s and Nimrod R.Mk 1s flew intelligence-gathering sorties from a South American base, possibly in Chile or even Brazil, but this has never been confirmed by the Ministry of Defence.

Lockheed C-130 Hercules
Right: Some 25 RAF Hercules were given refuelling probes to allow them to make the long journey south to the task force, where they dropped urgently-needed items to task force ships. Six aircraft were also equipped to serve as inflight-refuelling tankers, with a simple hose-and-drogue unit in the rear fuselage.

BAe Nimrod MR.Mk 2P
Left: The programme to fit inflight-refuelling probes to the RAF's Nimrods was expedited as a result of the Falklands War, this modification allowing the aircraft to operate right into the Total Exclusion Zone around the Falkland Islands. The Nimrods were augmented by Victors operating in the maritime radar reconnaissance role.

BAe Sea Harrier FRS.Mk 1
Right: Sea Harriers were embarked aboard the two carriers, HMS *Hermes* and *Invincible* and were the first aircraft to see combat against the Argentine air force. The Sea Harrier became known as 'La Muerta Negra' (The Black Death) to its Argentine opponents.

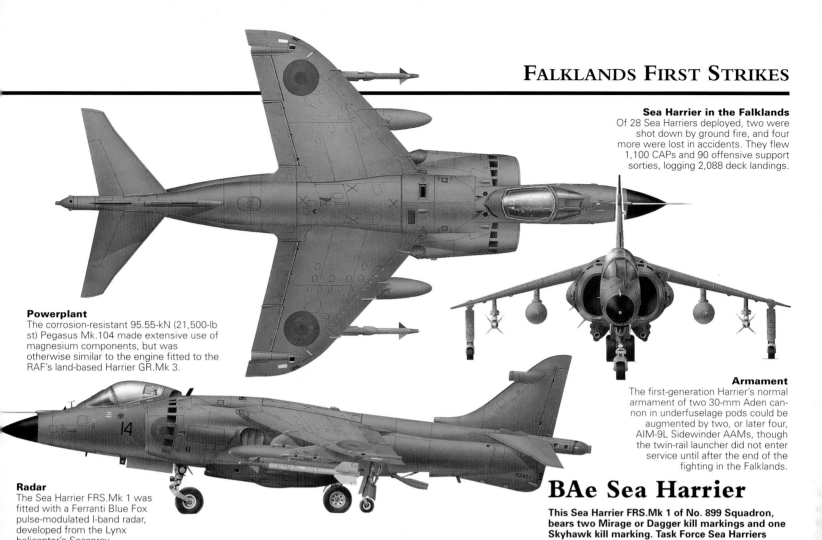

Powerplant
The corrosion-resistant 95.55-kN (21,500-lb st) Pegasus Mk.104 made extensive use of magnesium components, but was otherwise similar to the engine fitted to the RAF's land-based Harrier GR.Mk 3.

Armament
The first-generation Harrier's normal armament of two 30-mm Aden cannon in underfuselage pods could be augmented by two, or later four, AIM-9L Sidewinder AAMs, though the twin-rail launcher did not enter service until after the end of the fighting in the Falklands.

Radar
The Sea Harrier FRS.Mk 1 was fitted with a Ferranti Blue Fox pulse-modulated I-band radar, developed from the Lynx helicopter's Seaspray.

BAe Sea Harrier

This Sea Harrier FRS.Mk 1 of No. 899 Squadron, bears two Mirage or Dagger kill markings and one Skyhawk kill marking. Task Force Sea Harriers claimed large numbers of Argentine aircraft during the conflict while none were lost to enemy fighters. The aircraft's overall dark-grey colour scheme earned it the nickname 'Black Death'.

First Harrier victory

Flight Lieutenant Paul Barton, an experienced Harrier pilot seconded to the Royal Navy, was leading Lieutenant Steve Thomas in a pair of 801 Squadron Sea Harriers on patrol west of the Task Force on 1 May 1982. Port Stanley had been bombed, the Argentines were coming out in strength, and one of the warships on radar picket had detected incoming enemy fighters. Thomas was first to make radar contact.

"We were running in towards each other, head-on. I was doing about 400 kt [740 km/460 mph], Paul accelerated to about 550 kt [1020 km/635 mph] and pulled away to the right, to try and get around the back of them. I locked my radar on to their leader, then I began looking for the others – I couldn't believe that a pair of fighters would come in alone like that. Their formation was poor, what the Americans call 'welded wing', flying very close together."

The incoming aircraft were Mirage IIIs from Grupo 8, the Argentine air force's only dedicated interceptor unit. Capt Garcia Cuerva was leading the pair, with Lt Carlos Perona as wing man.

"This is the sort of thing one learns not to do on Day 1 at the Tactical Weapons Unit." Paul Barton recalled, drily. "We would never dream of flying that sort of formation, so it was mildly surprising when they did."

"My job now was to act as 'shooter', to get round behind the bogeys and attack if they proved hostile. I accelerated to maximum speed, locking my radar on to the No. 2. I dived down, visually acquiring the bogeys at about five miles [8 km]."

By now the Argentine fighters had almost reached Thomas. Hurtling toward the Mirages at a combined closing speed of over 1600 km/h (1,000 mph), he eased back on his stick to pass over the top of them, then dropped his right wing and pulled into a turn. As he did so the enemy fighters passed close underneath him. The Mirages continued in their shallow turn to port, oblivious to the presence of Paul Barton who was now moving rapidly into a firing position behind Perona's aircraft. The Sea Harrier pilot was sure he had still not been seen. Had either of the enemy pilots known where he was they would have pulled their turn far

tighter to try to shake him off.

Barton eased forward on his stick to descend a little and silhouette the Mirage against the cold background of the powder-blue sky, to give the Sidewinder the best possible chance. Then he squeezed the firing button and the missile roared off the starboard launcher leaving a trail of grey smoke as it accelerated away.

"At first I thought it had failed. It came off the rail and ducked down. I had not fired a 'winder before so its behaviour at launch was new to me. I was surprised not to see it home straight in – to see it duck down was disconcerting. I'd begun to wonder if it was a dud. It took about half a mile for it to get its trajectory sorted out, then it picked itself up and for the last half mile it just homed straight in. The missile flight time was about four seconds, then the Mirage exploded in a brilliant blue orange and red fireball."

So it was that Perona gained the dubious distinction of being the first pilot ever to be shot down by a 'jump' jet. Although at the time Barton was convinced that nobody could have survived from the blazing Mirage, in fact the Argentine pilot was able to eject to safety. Like so many of those shot down in fighter-versus-fighter combat, he never saw the aircraft that hit him.

Left: A Sea Harrier FRS.Mk 1 takes off from the ski jump, streaming spray from its undercarriage. Weather conditions in the South Atlantic were often very poor indeed, and three Sea Harriers were probably lost directly due to the poor conditions.

Falklands, Final Victory

21 MAY – 14 JUNE 1982

An FAA Skyhawk receives damage during an attack on the HMS Fearless. The FAA's Skyhawks were the most destructive aircraft fielded by Argentina, and proved a formidable foe, although they were very vulnerable to fighters and SAMs.

Above: The Argentine pilots pressed home their attacks at very low level. One of Grupo 6's Daggers is visible behind the assault ship HMS Fearless, flying past the main mast at bridge level only a few feet above the deck. The landing ships and support vessels were vulnerable to air attack, yet remarkably all survived the landings at San Carlos.

The Falklands War entered its third and final phase with the success of the British landings at San Carlos. Argentine air attacks had failed to prevent a beach-head from being established on 21 May, and bad weather prevented the FAA from intervening on 22 May, while the British continued landing men and supplies, and established rudimentary air defences for the positions on shore and for the ships in San Carlos Water. By 23 May it was too late to prevent an eventual break-out from the beach-head, which in fact took place on 27 May. Nevertheless the FAA pressed home further attacks, losing an A-4 and a Dagger, but sinking the *Antelope*, which was lost while another unexploded bomb was being made safe. Three more Daggers and an A-4 were lost the following day during attacks on shipping, and three A-4s were downed on 25 May, two of them being downed by Sea Dart SAMs fired by the *Coventry* on picket duty west of the Falklands. The ship was sunk by Skyhawks immediately after its successes.

Below: A Sidewinder-armed Sea Harrier FRS.Mk 1 lands aboard the amphibious assault ship Intrepid during the final stages of the war. The Royal Navy took the fullest possible advantage of the Sea Harrier's legendary flexibility, which included forward refuelling platforms aboard Intrepid and Fearless.

On the same day the CANA fired the third and fourth of its five Exocet missiles, one of these accounting for the *Atlantic Conveyor* and its cargo of spares, supplies, and Wessex and Chinook helicopters, only one of the latter escaping the catastrophe.

GROUNDFIRE LOSSES

On 27 May, an RAF Harrier was lost to groundfire while the Argentines resisted the British advance, losing an A-4, an MB-339 and two Pucaras in the process. The next day Pucaras made an unsuccessful attack using napalm, but fortunately this was the only occasion on which this horrific weapon was used. The fourth Vulcan raid (intended as an anti-radar sortie using Shrike missiles) was aborted when one of the Victor tankers went unserviceable. Air activity continued unabated as the British

A Sea King and a Type 21 frigate come to the assistance of HMS Plymouth, burning in San Carlos Water after being hit by bombs. The frigate survived, thanks to the faulty fusing of the Argentine weapons.

Supporting the advance

While the Royal Navy's Sea Harriers won the glory, other aircraft were more directly involved in supporting the Army's rapid advance across the Falklands. RAF Harrier GR.Mk 3s provided expert close air support, while helicopters from all four services played their part in resupply, transport and casevac missions. The sole Chinook to escape the catastrophic sinking of the *Atlantic Conveyor* was used especially intensively, though the larger number of Sea Kings available played a more important role.

BAe Harrier GR.Mk 3
Left: The RAF Harrier GR.Mk 3s of No. 1 Squadron deployed with the task force were originally intended as attrition replacements for the Sea Harriers, and were armed with AIM-9s. Losses were lower than anticipated, though, and the RAF Harriers were used almost exclusively in the ground-attack role.

Boeing Vertol Chinook HC.Mk 1
Right: Known by its twin letter code, 'Bravo November' was the sole Chinook to escape the destruction of the *Atlantic Conveyor*. The aircraft lacked spares, manuals and equipment and no-one expected it to be serviceable for long, but remarkably the helicopter remained airworthy for the rest of the war, performing a number of spectacular transport missions.

Westland Sea King HC.Mk 4
Left: British versions of the troop-carrying Commando served with No. 846 Squadron, and were augmented by stripped examples of the ASW HAS.Mk 2 and HAS.Mk 5. Three squadrons in the Falklands still used the ancient Wessex HU.Mk 5. The peacetime rulebook was thrown away by helicopter squadrons in the Falklands. Aircraft frequently flew at very high weights, and the usual servicing intervals were often stretched.

infantry pushed eastwards towards Port Stanley, with both sides suffering losses. Another Sea Harrier fell victim to an accident on 29 May, and another was shot down by a Roland SAM on 1 June. Sea Harriers shot down a C-130 Hercules on the same day. The Argentines lost a Dagger on 29 May, and two A-4s on 30 May, all to Rapier or Sea Dart SAMs. The A-4s were reportedly supporting the CANA's final Exocet attack, the fifth missile apparently having been successfully decoyed away from its target, the *Invincible*. Poor weather limited air activity until 8 June, one RAF Harrier being lost on 30 May after groundfire severed a fuel line. The pilot was forced to eject when he could not reach the *Hermes*.

The Harrier's reliance on the carriers (which had to stand off out of range of Argentine aircraft) was eased on 2 June, with the completion of 'Sid's strip', a temporary airfield at San Carlos where aircraft

Above: Wessex HU.Mk 5s flew with five flights of No. 845 Squadron, four of No. 848 Squadron and with No. 847 Squadron. These operated detachments onboard a variety of support ships, and onshore.

Right: Sea Kings were among the most useful aircraft available to task force commanders, capable of lifting heavy underslung loads.

Above: Army and Royal Marines Gazelles saw extensive service in the observation and reconnaissance, liaison, casevac and gunship roles, but proved very vulnerable to small arms fire.

could be refuelled and re-armed. The Vulcan flew an unsuccessful fifth mission on 31 May, but followed this with a third anti-radar mission on 3 June, damaging a Skyguard radar in the process. Unfortunately the aircraft was forced to divert to Rio de Janeiro after its refuelling probe broke on the journey home, and it was detained until the end of the war. During the poor weather, the FAA mounted a number of Canberra night-bombing raids, and a reconnaissance Learjet was downed by a Sea Dart SAM on 7 June.

When the weather cleared on 8 June, the Argentines were faced with plum targets as the assault ships *Fearless* and *Intrepid*, together with the landing ships *Sir Galahad* and *Sir*

Above: Napalm tanks were among the weapons used by the Argentine Pucaras during the Falklands campaign. However they were dropped on only one mission – without success – and were then dumped.

Tristram, which were busy moving troops from San Carlos to Fitzroy Cove in preparation for the final push on Port Stanley. The FAA mounted a raid by five A-4Bs and six Daggers (with four Mirages making a diversionary raid on San Carlos to draw off the Sea Harriers).

Sir Galahad and *Sir Tristram* were badly damaged, and 43 Welsh Guardsmen and seven seamen were killed. Outbound, the Daggers crippled HMS *Plymouth*, and all the FAA aircraft returned to base safely.

SEA HARRIER REVENGE

Things went less well for the second wave of Argentine attack aircraft that afternoon. Three Skyhawks were destroyed by Sea Harriers after sinking a landing craft. The temporary landing strip

was put out of action when a Harrier made a heavy landing.

12 and 13 June saw some of the heaviest fighting of the war, as the Paras fought to take Mount Longdon and Wireless Ridge, being supported by SS.11-firing Westland Scouts in the latter attack. *Glamorgan* was hit by a ground-launched Exocet that day (losing her Wessex helicopter) and soon afterwards, the Vulcan force launched its seventh and final mission, dropping airburst bombs on Port Stanley airfield. A final air attack came when a single Wessex HU.Mk 5 attacked Port Stanley Town Hall with an AS.12 missile, aiming to hit a major conference taking place there. One missile hit the neighbouring police station, and the second missed altogether.

Below: An armed Gazelle hovers over a forward position, while a Wessex flies in another load of ammunition. The effective use of support helicopters was crucial to the success of the task force.

On 13 June, Argentine Skyhawks attacked the British Brigade HQ on Mount Kent, and a Canberra was shot down in the type's final

'Black Buck'

The five Vulcans deployed to Wideawake flew seven missions under the codenames Black Buck 1 to Black Buck 7. Two primary Vulcans flew all five successful missions. Plans to disband No. 44 Squadron were put on hold, and the squadron flew a number of realistic conventional bombing exercises over Scotland before the first aircraft was deployed to Ascension Island. The Vulcans had not used inflight refuelling for some years, and a massive search had to be mounted for serviceable inflight-refuelling probes, to the extent of salvaging

probes from aircraft already retired to museums. The five aircraft selected for Black Buck were all aircraft once intended to carry Skybolt, so had attachment points for underwing pylons. These were used for the carriage of a Westinghouse AN/ALQ-101(V)-10 ECM pod under the starboard wing, with two or four Shrike ARMs for Black Bucks 4, 5 and 6. Drop tests of the 454-kg (1,000-lb) laser-guided bomb were undertaken before the deployment, using a laser designator in the bomb-aimer's undernose cupola, but this weapon was not deployed operationally. The most important result of the Vulcan raids was that they raised a real fear that the RAF could attack targets on the mainland, forcing the FAA to retain its best fighters for air defence.

Left: Bombs were loaded in clips of seven, two such clips being carried for Black Buck missions.

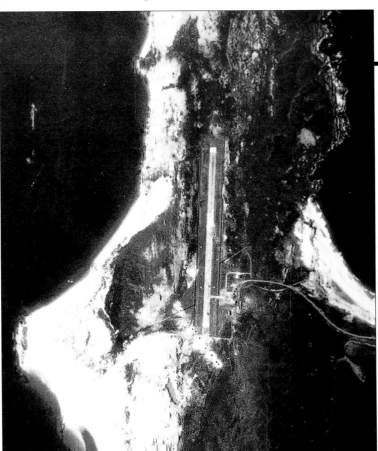

Above: Bombs damage at Port Stanley airport. Two parallel strings of craters marking Vulcan attacks can be seen, one of which comes to an end with a crater in the centre of the runway.

Left: A hastily camouflaged AGM-45 Shrike anti-radar missile under the wing of XM597 before Black Buck 4, the first abandoned Shrike mission. Black Buck 5, flown two nights later, was more successful. Before they deployed to Wideawake the Vulcans conducted trials and live firings with the AS.37 Martel as well as the AGM-45 Shrike. Six Shrikes were fired during the war.

Radar
The Mirage IIIE featured a Thomson-CSF Cyrano II operating in the I- and J-bands with a range of air-to-air and air-to-ground modes. Although designed as a multi-role fighter-bomber, the Mirage IIIRA was used by Argentina as a pure air-defence aircraft.

Powerplant
The Mirage IIIE was powered by a single SNECMA Atar 09C-3 engine, with a conventional petal-type afterburner nozzle replacing the eyelid-type nozzle fitted to the Mirage IIIC's Atar 9B-3. Provision was made for the fitting of a SEPR 844 rocket booster engine, but few customers actually specified this as an option.

Dassault Mirage IIIEA

This Mirage IIIEA was one of 17 delivered to Argentina from France during 1973. It wears the markings of I Escuadrón de Caza, Grupo 8 de Caza. The squadron had detachments at Rio Gallegos and Comodoro Rivadavia during the Falklands War, and lost two aircraft in action, both falling to Sea Harriers. The squadron remains in service today, flying from Tandil.

Armament
The Mirage IIIE carried a pair of internal 30-mm cannon, and augmented these with underwing R.550 Magic IR-homing close-range missiles. The Argentine Mirage IIIEA differed from the basic Mirage IIIE in being equipped to fire the BVR Matra R.530 AAM.

appearance over the Falklands. Although LGB attacks had begun on 10 June, designation problems had rendered them unsuccessful. On 13 June everything came right, and Harriers successfully bombed a company HQ at Tumbledown and a 105-mm (4.13-in) gun at Moody Brook.

On 14 June two Harriers took off for an LGB attack against Sapper Hill, but were recalled because white flags were already flying in Port Stanley. An Argentine

Below: Wrecked Pucaras lie beside the runway at Port Stanley after the war, as an RAF Hercules makes its final approach. Some 29 aircraft were captured at Port Stanley alone, though few were flyable.

surrender was signed at one minute before midnight.

Britain had recovered the Falklands at minimal cost, with an apparently decisive victory which did much to enhance the reputation of its armed forces. The war also brought the government much-needed popularity (despite the fact that the war had been caused by its own defence cuts and inability to foresee their consequences), and an early election was called, bringing a victory which many ascribed to the 'Falklands Factor'. The disparity in losses hid the fact that the war had been a close-run thing at several points, while it was seldom recognised that Britain's continuing defence cuts would have made the

Above: Four of the 10 RAF Harrier GR.Mk 3s deployed to the Falklands were lost in action. Modifications included the addition of AIM-9 Sidewinders, and Tracor AN/ALE-40 chaff/flare dispensers.

operation impossible to carry out only a few months later. Useful lessons were learned from the conflict, and it also led to the rapid

development and deployment of a number of key systems, perhaps the most important being the AEW Sea King, which was just too late to see front-line service in the war itself.

Argentina has not lost its ambitions to gain sovereignty over what it calls the Malvinas, but has been prevented from attempting further military adventures by a much enlarged British military presence on the Falklands, and by the construction of a major international airport, which would allow rapid reinforcement by air, and which houses a permanent detachment of Tornado fighters.

US police actions: Grenada, Panama and Haiti

1983-1995

Having been under British rule since 1763, Grenada was granted full independence in February 1974 with a democratic government being formed under Sir Eric Gairy. Five years later following a nearly bloodless coup d'etat, a People's Revolutionary Government (PRG) was organised by Maurice Bishop and his left-wing New Joint Endeavour for Welfare, Education and Liberation (JEWEL) movement.

The Cuban presence in Grenada quickly grew with the building a new airport which had potential military application in spite of its avowed commercial purpose, and became a source of concern for the US government over its potential use for Cuban military operations in Central America.

TURMOIL IN GRENADA

Then, in October 1983, Prime Minister Bishop and several members of his cabinet were arrested and subsequently executed by elements of the People's Revolutionary Army (PRA). The emerging leaders – General Hudson Austin of the PRA and the former Deputy Prime

Minister, Bernard Coard – benefitted from the support of about 50 military advisers of Cuba's Fuerzas Armadas Revolucionarias (FAR), several hundred Cuban civilian advisers and construction workers, and a small number of Soviet military personnel from the Spetsnaz.

Chaos set in, and the lives of US and other foreign nationals were thought to be endangered. Still, there was no legal ground for US intervention until 23 October ,when six eastern Caribbean nations

together with Jamaica and Barbados issued a formal request for assistance by the United States. Shortly thereafter, a letter from Governor General Sir Paul Scoon, the Queen's representative in Grenada, requested outside intervention and provided a legitimate cover for military action. Earlier US plans for a non-combat rescue evacuation of Americans from the island were discarded and preparations for full military operations were initiated. Urgent Fury was under way.

To carry out the assignment, CINCLANT – the US Navy's Commander-in-Chief, Atlantic – was given operational control over Air Force, Army and Marine units in addition to his own forces. Land operations were to be conducted by Army special forces, two Ranger battalions and the 82nd Airborne Division, Navy SEAL special

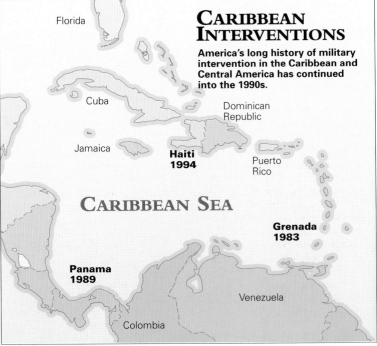

The Lockheed AC-130 Spectre gunship, much-improved and upgraded since the Vietnam war, was the ideal weapon for Grenada, a setting where the other side had little or no anti-aircraft weaponry.

forces, and Marines of the 22nd Marine Amphibious Unit. Transportation and paradrop of Army troops was to be performed by USAF C-130 Hercules, heavy-lift support coming from C-141B StarLifters and giant C-5A Galaxy aircraft. The Marines, escorted by AH-1T Cobra attack helicopters, were to be taken ashore by CH-46Es and CH-53Ds based aboard the assault ship USS *Guam* (LPH-9) and by four landing ships of Phibron (Amphibious Squadron) Four.

Air support for Joint Task Force 120, as the combined service force was called, was to be provided by

Grenada was the first big US effort since Vietnam, so it was the baptism of fire for the Sikorsky UH-60 Black Hawk, the helicopter which had replaced the ubiquitous UH-1 Huey in the US Army's inventory.

Below: A Bell AH-1T Cobra of US Marine Corps squadron HMM-261 runs up its engines as deck crews on the USS Guam (LPH-9) top off its fuel tanks for an assault on Grenada's Pearls Airport.

CARIBBEAN INTERVENTIONS

America's long history of military intervention in the Caribbean and Central America has continued into the 1990s.

Florida

Cuba

Jamaica

Dominican Republic

Haiti 1994

Puerto Rico

CARIBBEAN SEA

Grenada 1983

Panama 1989

Venezuela

Colombia

Marine Corps helicopters

The Marine Corps was always out in front in introducing helicopters to combat. In Korea in 1950, they fielded the Sikorsky HRS-1 thirty months before the US Army flew the equivalent H-19. In Vietnam in 1965, the Marines were flying the Sikorsky CH-53A Sea Stallion more than a year before other service branches introduced their own versions. Helicopters were vital to the Grenada operation, which was itself a harbinger of the post-Cold War world.

Bell AH-1T Cobra

Right: A development of the Vietnam-era AH-1J (and a predecessor of the AH-1W of the 1990s), this Marine AH-1T typifies dozens that covered the landing in Grenada. The small nose-mounted turret above the twin-barreled M197 20-mm cannon houses a stabilized sight for use with TOW wire-guided anti-tank missiles. The larger white cylinders house 70-mm (2.75-in) FFAR rockets.

Boeing-Vertol CH-46E Sea Knight

Left: The predominant aircraft type in HMM-261's inventory during the Grenada assault was the CH-46E, twelve of which were operated in the medium transport role. Much-loved, versatile, but long in the tooth, the Sea Knight is expected to remain the principal transport helicopter of the Marine Corps until the expected arrival of the V-22 Osprey early in the 21st century.

AC-130H gunships of the 1st Special Operations Wing and by three attack squadrons of Carrier Air Wing Six from the USS *Independence* (CV-62).

MAPPING GRENADA

No adequate maps were available and the Army's 63rd Engineer Company was forced to use a Grenadian Chamber of Commerce map to develop a grid system and produce the maps used by Army forces in the assault. Even less factual were the limited data on the likely strength of the enemy opposition: Intelligence estimated that the 600 PRA regular troops were supplemented by some 2,500 auxiliaries including the ill-disciplined and ineffectually-trained People's Revolutionary Militia (PRM) and the police. Cuban strength on the island was estimated at 50 military advisers and some 700 armed construction workers. Precious little was known of weapons and precise locations of this motley opposition

As finally drawn, plans called for nearly simultaneous insertions of Marines near Pearls Airport and Rangers at the Point Salines Airport, the first Marines being brought in by CH-46Es from the *Guam* and the first Rangers being para-dropped by C-130. Re-inforcements at Point Salines were to be air landed after the Rangers secured the partially completed runway, while those at Pearls were to be taken ashore by landing ships.

After the go-ahead for the intervention was given by President Reagan during the evening of 23 October, Vice Admiral Joseph Metcalf III and his JTF-120 staff

aboard the *Guam* set the operation into motion.

Two platoon-size SEAL teams went ashore the next night, where they discovered that reefs rendered the scheduled amphibious assault impractical. The location of one of the proposed helicopter landing sites also had to be moved as the SEALs found anti-aircraft defences at Pearls Airport to be heavier than expected.

GUNSHIP LEADS THE WAY

First into the fray was an AC-130H of the 16th Special Operations Squadron. It flew over the Point Salines Airport during the early hours of 25 October using its advanced sensors to scan the area for anti-aircraft weapons and runway obstructions. Attracting much AAA fire, the gunship radioed back valuable information in time for field commanders to revise plans for the initial assault.

The Marines were first inserted by Sea Stallion helicopters near Pearls Airport at 0520 on 25 October, and 16 minutes later

Left: Operation Urgent Fury was successful in part because of the Sikorsky CH-53D Sea Stallion, by far the largest helicopter used by US forces during the attack. Four of these were assigned to HMM-261, which covered the Marines' landing on the island.

Below: The only aircraft lost during the Grand Anse rescue operation was this battered Marine CH-46E Sea Knight. This helicopter was disabled by ground fire during the initial insertion of the Ranger rescue force and was then abandoned on Grand Anse beach.

Rangers began jumping from Air Force C-130s over Point Salines. The fight was on.

The principal Navy fixed-wing aircraft used during Urgent Fury were the Vought A-7E Corsair IIs and Grumman A-6E Intruders of Air Wing Six operating from the USS *Independence*. In general, the Corsair proved effective in providing air support for the ground forces, but the type was also involved in two unfortunate incidents. In the afternoon of 25

October, an A-7 caused numerous Grenadian civilian casualties when after taking AAA fire from the direction of a large building, it bombed the suspected area; unfortunately, this building turned out to be a mental hospital. Two days later, due to poor communications yet another A-7E accidentally strafed an outpost of the 82nd Airborne Division; the accident, in which one GI was killed and 15 others wounded, was blamed on poor co-ordinates having been

Airlift of troops

The biggest operator of aircraft during the Grenada invasion was the US Air Force's Military Airlift Command (MAC), which kept C-130s, C-5s, and C-141s flowing to the island. After the initial assault from the sea and parachute assault from C-130s, most long-range troop movements were handled by civil airliners flown by contract companies. MAC's main function was the movement of huge amounts of supplies and equipment, though airlifters like the C-141 also transported hundreds of soldiers and Marines to the island from bases in the USA.

Lockheed C-141B Starlifter
Left: Enlarged by a 'stretching' programme that lengthened its fuselage and increased its carrying capacity, the C-141B was the workhorse of the Grenada campaign. The rear-loading ramp and 'roll on, roll off' capability of the Starlifter enabled it to haul a variety of cargoes including many large vehicles.

Above: American military aircraft are seen alongside civil transport on the ramp at Pearls Airport, Grenada. Although the invasion received mixed reaction abroad, the general feeling on Grenada was one of satisfaction at the restoration of democracy.

given to the pilot.

As part of its reinforced complement, HMM-261 had four Bell AH-1T Cobra attack helicopters aboard the *Guam*. These four machines saw much action, and two were shot down by the PRA during the fighting for Fort Frederick on 25 October. The last two remained in the thick of the fight until the final Urgent Fury actions.

Boeing-Vertol CH-46E Sea Knights, the main Marine Corps transport helicopters, performed well from the assault against Pearls and Grenville in the early morning hours of 25 October until the last Marine operation, the taking of Carriacou Island on 1 November. One CH-46E was shot down on 26 October during the rescue of American students at the Grand Anse campus of the Medical School.

Another type making its combat debut during Urgent Fury, the Sikorsky UH-60A Black Hawk earned praises on account of its reliability and, thanks to its twin-engined configuration, its ability to be ferried over long overwater distances (ie from Barbados to

Above: The compound for the Cuban airport construction workers had a distinctly military look, with its perimeter security fencing, vehicle storage sheds and a military-style assault course.

Grenada). However, three were shot down or damaged beyond repair, one heavily damaged, and two lightly damaged. Other helicopter losses included one Hughes 500 Defender shot down on 25 October during operations against the Richmond Hill Prison and one OH-58C Kiowa receiving major damage.

CASUALTY BILL

American casualties during Urgent Fury included 19 dead and 116 wounded; Cuban casualties were 25 dead and 59 wounded, while Grenadian casualties, including civilians, were 45 dead and 350 wounded.

Although successful, Urgent Fury raised numerous political questions, both in the United States and abroad, and lent credence to doubts expressed in many quarters about the combat use of helicopters in the face of determined and well-armed opponents. On the other hand, the happy conclusion of the intervention in Grenada did much to boost the confidence of the American public in its armed forces and helped the latter to regain most of the pride which had been lost 10 years earlier in the Vietnamese quagmire, and lessons learned during the operation were put to good use in Panama and Haiti over the next decade.

Haiti: Operation Uphold Democracy

The military junta of General Raoul Cedras held on to power in Haiti in spite of elections won by Jean-Bertrand Aristide. A full-scale US invasion to restore democracy was averted when a last-minute agreement was brokered by former US President Jimmy Carter. General Cedras agreed to stand down with effect from 15 October 1994 and permit exiled President Aristide to assume power the following day.

On 19 September 2,000 US troops, most of whom were from the 10th Mountain Division (Light) at Fort Drum, NY were airlifted ashore from ships of Joint Task Force 190 located off the Haitian coast. US Army UH-60s ferried the troops to Haiti while AH-1 Cobras flew protective air cover. The helicopters operated from the aircraft carrier USS *Eisenhower* (CVN-69).

This was the first occasion in which the Adaptive Joint Force Package concept, involving the integration of various services, had been employed operationally. In excess of 50 US Army helicopters were embarked on the US Navy aircraft-carrier for the operation.

US Air Force aircraft played a supporting role, with the majority forward-deployed to the naval station at Roosevelt Roads, Puerto Rico. E-3 Sentries of the 552nd ACW from Tinker AFB, Oklahoma monitored the skies above Haiti as well as the air space around Cuba.

Twenty-four F-15Cs of the 33rd FW from Eglin AFB, Florida were stationed at Roosevelt Roads along with nine KC-135s, as a precautionary measure to perform combat air patrols if needed. In the event, the Eagles were not required when the invasion was cancelled and they returned home after only four days.

Other USAF types included three EC-130Es of the 42nd ACCS, 355th Wing from Davis-Monthan AFB, Arizona which performed airborne battlefield management. AC-130H Spectre gunships were on hand to provide firepower if necessary, while RC-135 Rivet Joint aircraft monitored communications.

The initial complement of 2,000 US Army forces was boosted to 15,000 within a week to ensure the country remained stable during the transition back to democracy.

Right: US Army helicopters use the broad flight deck of the USS Dwight D. Eisenhower as a mobile base from which to launch the Haitian peacekeeping force.

Panama: Operation Just Cause

Panama's leader, General Manuel Noriega, had been needling the United States for years. He had been indicted in an American court for drug offences, and after surviving a failed coup d'état went so far as to 'declare war' on the US on 15 December 1989. He had pushed the Americans too far and they decided to take action against him.

Hints of impending action in Panama began on 16 December when a US Marine Corps lieutenant was murdered by Panamanian soldiers at a roadblock, and a US Navy officer and his wife were detained and mistreated.

ACTION BEGINS

Operation Just Cause began in the early hours of Wednesday 20 December 1989, when US Navy SEALs attacked Paitilla Airport, where Noriega kept a possible get-away LearJet. Four SEALs were killed confronting unexpectedly heavy resistance before the aerodrome was secured and the LearJet destroyed.

AC-130H Spectre gunships of the 16th Special Operations Squadron attacked key targets, including the Panama Defense Forces fortress known as the Comandancia, as well as the Puma Battalion barracks just outside Omar Torrijos Airport. US artillery already deployed at the US Army base of Fort Amador opened up on PDF barracks nearby.

The initial assault made use of 7,000 of the 22,500 American troops eventually deployed for the operation, divided into five groups. The first wave of 77 C-141B StarLifters, 22 C-130 Hercules, and 12 C-5 Galaxies made a total of 84 air drops, followed by a second

wave of 40 C-141Bs and 13 C-5s. These airlifted troops from the 82nd Airborne Division, the 7th Infantry Division and other Army units.

Task Force Bayonet, including light tanks and infantry, assaulted and destroyed the Comandancia. Other troops were helicoptered from Howard Air Force Base to reinforce friendlies and block the PDF at Fort Amador. Bayonet included the SEAL assault at Paitilla.

Task Force Red made a parachute assault on Torrijos Airport and the Puma barracks, spearheaded by an Army Ranger battalion and 82nd Airborne troopers. A second Ranger battalion parachuted into Rio Hato where some of Noriega's most loyal units were based, seizing an armoury after fierce fighting.

Task Force Pacific brought 20 C-141B loads of additional troops, who formed a second wave parachuting into Torrijos Airport and then blocked a bridge over the Pacora River to prevent PDF forces from advancing into Panama City from the east.

Task Force Semper Fidelis, made up of US Marines and a light armoured infantry company, seized the Bridge of the Americas, the only access into Panama City from the west. Task Force Atlantic, consisting of 82nd Airborne and 7th Light Infantry troopers, took the electrical powerplant at Sierra Tigre, the Madden Dam and Gamboa Prison.

STEALTH EMERGES

In retrospect, the most noteworthy event was the first combat use of the Lockheed F-117A Nighthawk 'stealth fighter'.Flying nonstop from Nevada, with the aid of air refuelling, two F-117As from the

37th TFW dropped 907-kg (2,000-lb) LGBs in a field next to the barracks to frighten the troops and to destroy an anti-aircraft position defending the airfield.

After the first day, fighting was sporadic and scattered, though some PDF continued to resist. Noriega took refuge in the Vatican ambassador's residence, before surrendering on 3 January. He was flown on a US Army UH-60A Black Hawk to Howard, then taken aboard an MC-130E Combat Talon I to Florida to be arraigned on a drug indictment. Once Noriega was gone, resistance collapsed and by 22 January 1990 the 82nd Airborne could return to the US.

Operation Just Cause's casualties included 23 American and 200 Panamanian combatants killed, as well as 202 Panamanian civilian fatalities. A number of Panamanian

Above: Noriega sought asylum in the Vatican Embassy, which was immediately surrounded. A Special Forces Sikorsky MH-53J lands on a football pitch nearby while in the foreground an American soldier keeps watch on the Embassy.

aircraft were destroyed or damaged. Numerous US aircraft were damaged, including 11 C-130s, and US Army losses included one OH-58 and three AH-6s.

Left: The less than stellar performance of the Lockheed F-117 Nighthawk in Panama evoked some controversy. US officials had a hard time demonstrating that the high-ticket 'stealth' jet was really worth the money.

Right: Panama's Manuel Noriega, carried to the US aboard a C-130, became the United States' only prisoner of war. He was charged with and in a Florida court trial convicted of a string of narcotics offences.

Drug Wars

1970- THE PRESENT

Left: Colombian commandos, advised by agents from the US Drug Enforcement Agency (DEA), set off in a US-supplied Bell UH-1 on a raid against a jungle cocaine processing site. Helicopter mobility has been essential in the campaign by Colombian law-enforcement units against the ever-spreading tentacles of the drug barons.

In most countries, dealing with the drug trade is a job for the police, but in the United States it is a war. The drug problem on America's streets is so serious that the full weight of the government has been thrown into the struggle to terminate supplies. Apart from the Drug Enforcement Agency, the president's anti-drug task force can call on the Department of Defense, the Coast Guard, the State Department, the Department of Justice, the US Customs Service, the FBI, and the Bureau of Alcohol, Tobacco and Firearms.

The South American trade is a little different from the heroin trails of Asia. Cocaine is the big money-maker in Colombia, and the producers have established the drug business in a big way. Despite the best efforts of the Colombian government and judiciary, which have seen the virtual elimination of the Medellin cartel and the imprisonment or death of many of the leaders of the Cali cartel, they remain multi-billion dollar businesses, corrupting everyone from local judges and policemen to entire Central American and Caribbean governments.

STOPPING THE SOURCE

The war against drugs is being fought on several fronts. Drugs can be stopped at source by bringing political pressure to bear on the supplier countries. This can take the form of economic assistance, given

Right: Peru uses armed EMBRAER Tucano trainers in an aggressive programme of interdiction. Drug flights are intercepted and ordered to land: should they fail to do so then they are shot down. More than 50 drug-laden aircraft have been taken out by the Peruvian and Colombian air forces since 1994.

when the local government makes serious efforts to stop the trade, or military assistance, in the form of weapons and Special Forces training teams.

Most of the coca leaf from which cocaine is produced is actually grown in Peru and Bolivia. Hundreds of tonnes of cocaine base are shipped into Colombia where it is converted in clandestine laboratories into cocaine hydrochloride, the finished drug. From there it is exported to the target markets of the United States and Europe.

The military has a number of options in dealing with the trade at source. The first step is to destroy the coca leaves on the trees, using aircraft to spray herbicides. This is not entirely effective, as it also destroys legitimate crops and arouses hostility in the peasantry. The second option is to destroy the processing centres by direct attack. This generally involves helicopter assaults supported by ground attack aircraft. But the country is rugged, and even when one jungle factory is raided the producers can simply set up in some other valley.

If one cannot control the drugs at source, one must try to stop them in transit. Cocaine from Colombia

Left: the US Customs Service operates an airborne early warning version of the Lockheed P-3 Orion maritime patrol aircraft to monitor sea and air traffic in the Caribbean and the Gulf of Mexico.

Above: US Military airborne radar in the shape of the E-3 AWACS and E-2 Hawkeye (seen here) are also used in the war against drugs. Each aircraft can monitor thousands of square miles of the surface.

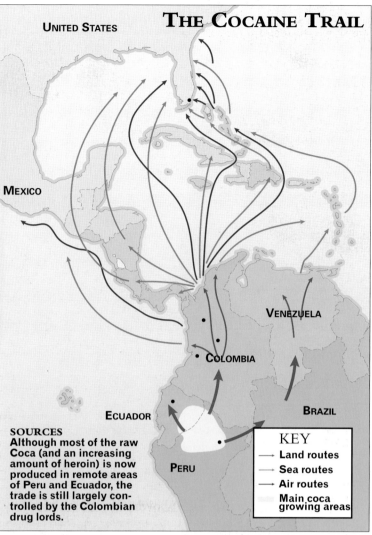

SOURCES
Although most of the raw Coca (and an increasing amount of heroin) is now produced in remote areas of Peru and Ecuador, the trade is still largely controlled by the Colombian drug lords.

KEY
→ Land routes
→ Sea routes
→ Air routes
▨ Main coca growing areas

is shipped via neighbouring Brazil, Peru, Venezuela and Ecuador, and increasingly via Mexico.

Cocaine is a high-value, low-bulk product, so a light plane can carry a valuable load quite easily. Indeed, when moving a couple of suitcases worth a million dollars or so, the $50,000 it costs to buy a second-hand plane is an incidental expense, and the plane is very definitely expendable. In the past, the drugs were flown from jungle airstrips to transhipment points, but aggressive actions on the part of the governments of Peru and Brazil, in particular, have seen a large number of drug flights shot down over the jungle, most often by armed trainers like the EMBRAER Tucano.

However, drugs still reach shipping ports, and they are still exported across the Caribbean in a variety of ways.

Stopping the trade involves cutters from the US Coast Guard, often supported by larger US Navy vessels, up to and including aircraft carriers. Navy, Air Force and US

Above: Suspicious flights are shadowed by aircraft from one of the many agencies involved. Once the suspected drugs runner has landed, customs and DEA agents use Sikorsky Black Hawk helicopters to move in, hopefully catching the criminals in possession of illicit drugs.

Customs Service airborne early warning aircraft keep track of air and surface movements by day or night, supported by tethered aerostats - unmanned airships carrying radar.

If there is a suspicion that a ship is running drugs, it can be boarded and searched. However, it is difficult to search an aircraft unless one forces it down, so suspect aircraft are shadowed. This can be done by radar, using airborne early warning planes, or it can involve physically trailing the aircraft.

INTERDICTION

High-performance military jets are not necessarily the best aircraft to follow a piston-engined plane flying low and slow, so the US Customs

Above: Aerial interdiction by key South American nations has forced a considerable change on the patterns of the traffickers. The risk of being shot down has cut the use of aircraft within South America by at least half. The drugs barons are now shipping the raw material by land for conversion to cocaine, which is then transhipped via a

Service has a number of light aircraft – often confiscated from drug-runners – fitted with extra tanks and low-light vision gear to do the job.

bewildering variety of routes through central America and the Caribbean. Anti-drug efforts resulted in the seizure of at least 250 tonnes of cocaine in 1995 – but that was only a third of the estimated production for that year, and had little effect on the amount of the drug on the streets. It is clear that there is still a long way to go.

Other aircraft which have been used for the job include the awesome AC-130 gunships of the US Air Force, whose highly sophisticated night vision devices are ideal for the purpose.

But no matter how good the sensors, it can be like looking for a needle in a haystack. A hundred or more light planes make the crossing between the Bahamas and Florida every day, and cabin cruisers and powerboats are just as common in the 85-km (53-mile) wide Florida Strait. Aircraft making directly for Miami airport will probably be honest, but those making for some point in the Everglades are probably intending to land drugs, and are worth checking out.

Drug runners might risk a direct flight into an airfield deep in the Florida swamps, particularly when confederates can make a rapid pick-up. Helicopters are the best means of dealing with these deliveries, as they are able to drop in and catch the smugglers in the act.

Joint Interagency Task Forces

As the struggle to control the drugs trade has come to resemble warfare, the US military found it necessary to establish co-ordinating bodies to make most effective use of the high-tech (and high-cost) resources available. Established in April 1994, the three Joint Interagency Task Forces are just what their titles proclaim: international, interagency bodies which coordinate the operational aspects of the drugs war.

JIATF East, based at NAS Key West, is the largest. Reporting to the Commander-in-Chief, US Atlantic Command, it has representatives from the Federal Bureau of Investigation, Defense Intelligence Agency, Drug Enforcement Agency, US Coast Guard and allied militaries. JIATF West, based at Alameda in California, is responsible for West Coast and Mexican border operations. JIATF South is the third operational unit, headquartered with US Southern Command at Howard AFB, Panama.

The control centre at JIATF-E monitors the primary sea- and airborne approaches to the USA across the Caribbean and the Gulf of Mexico.

INDEX

All aircraft are listed under their manufacturer. Shorter headings are also given under the name or designation of the aircraft, unless they can be identified from the designation, e.g. "Do" for Dornier, "Tu" for Tupolev. The names of ships are in italics.

Page numbers in italics refer to illustrations; those in bold type refer to panels or articles separate from the main text.

506

INDEX